Handbook of Neuroevolution Through Erlang

Gene I. Sher

Handbook of Neuroevolution
Through Erlang

Springer

Gene I. Sher
Department of Electrical Engineering and Computer Science
University of Central Florida
Orlando, FL, USA

ISBN 978-1-4939-4588-7   ISBN 978-1-4614-4463-3 (eBook)
DOI 10.1007/978-1-4614-4463-3
Springer New York Heidelberg Dordrecht London

Printed on acid-free paper

Springer is part of Springer Science+Business Media (www.springer.com)

Foreword

by Joe Armstrong

I was delighted to be asked to write a foreword to Gene Sher's book on Neuroevolution.

To be honest I didn't have a clue what Neuroevolution was before I started reading his manuscript, but the more I read the more I became engaged in the content.

Gene addresses what is a fascinating problem: How can we simulate a biological system in a computer. Can we make a system that learns from its mistakes?

Gene chose to program his system in Erlang, which is where I come in. Erlang was designed over twenty five years ago to solve a completely different problem. What we were trying to do at the time and we are still trying, is to make a language for programming extremely large systems that never stop.

Our application was telephony. We wanted to write the control software for a set of large telephone exchanges. This software should in principle run forever. The telephone networks span the planet, and the control systems for these networks were running before the invention of the computer.

Any system like this must be able to tolerate both software and hardware failures, and thus we built a programming language where failures were not a problem. Our approach was to say, "well if something crashes, some other part of the system will detect the error, fix the problem and the system as a whole will not fail."

We also thought that such a system should evolve and change with time. It would never be the case that the software in the system would be correct, right from the start, instead we would have to change the software many times during the life of the product. And we would also have to make these changes without stopping the system.

The view of the world that Erlang presents the programmer is intrinsically distributed, intrinsically changing and capable of self-repair. Neuroevolution was far from our thoughts.

Twenty years later Gene comes along and discovers Erlang - to him, Erlang processes are neurons. Well of course Erlang processes are not neurons, but they can easily be programmed to behave like neurons.

Erlang was designed to scale. So today we can run a few million processes per node, and a few dozen nodes per chip. Computer architectures have changed from the single core Von-Neumann machine, to the multicore processor, and the architectures will change again. Nobody actually knows how they are going to change, but my bet is that the change will be towards network-on-chip architectures.

We're already talking about putting a few hundred to a thousand cores on a single chip, but for this to happen we have to move to network on chip architectures. We can imagine large regular matrices of CPUs connected into a regular switching infrastructure. So we'll soon end up with thousands of cores, each capable of running millions of Erlang processes.

What will we do with such a monster computer and how are we going to program it? Well I suspect Gene has an answer to this question; he'll want to build a brain.

This book will tell you how. Will it work in the near future or will this take hundreds of years? Nobody knows, but the journey will be interesting and we might build some other useful things on the way.

Joe Armstrong
Stockholm

Dedication

To my father Ilya Aleksandrovich Sher
To my mother Zinaida Lvovna Sher

Preface

We biological organisms are fragile things. We are machines whose only armor is skin, a thin layer composed of lipids and proteins, easily damageable. The cells that make us up require constant nourishment, this nourishment is supplied by our blood, which itself easily and rapidly begins to leak when our thin shield is penetrated. We can only exist in a very limited range of temperatures. 36.7 degrees Celsius is our standard, a few degrees above that and we are uncomfortable, a bit higher and our cells begin to die and our flesh suffers permanent damage. When our temperature drops below 36.7 by a few degrees Celsius, we too can begin to suffer permanent damage unless the temperature is raised again. We burn easily. Our sensory organs are limited, we see electromagnetic radiation in only a very narrow spectrum, between 400 and 800 THz. The same for pressure waves, sound, which we only perceive between 12 and 20000 Hz. Our actuators, how and where we can move are, once again, extremely limited. The maximum speed we can achieve on land, without mechanical assistance, is 44.72km/h (record by Usain Bolt), and only for a limited amount of time, in water 2.29 m/s (record by Tom Jager). We require a constant supply of energy, food and fluid, if we do not consume fluids for just a few days we die, we survive only a bit longer when left without food. We are mortal, decaying, with only a few decades of being functional, and that only if everything else goes perfectly right.

We can study as much as we want, but at the end of the day we will still be limited by our biological nature. Within our brains the signals propagate from neuron to neuron at a maximum speed of 120m/s, this cannot be improved much further. The best of our kind, Feynman, Newton, Gauss, Einstein... They are at the limit of what our specie can achieve, and yet even they are limited by time and what they can do with it. Because there is no longer an evolutionary push towards greater level of intelligence, evolution will not save us, we will not give birth to another biological specie with greater minds, and natural evolution is too slow in either case. Plus, let us be perfectly honest, the evolutionary pressure in our modern society is actually against intelligence, the Feynmans, Newtons and Einsteins of our world have less children on average than anyone else.

But we have Science on our side, and through the application of the Scientific method we are hill climbing towards deeper knowledge and understanding of what we are, how we work, and most importantly, how to improve upon our condition.

Make no mistake, there is absolutely nothing mystical about the human brain. It is but a vast graph of interconnected simple biological signal integrators. But though our brain is limited, the non biological based intelligence does not have to be so. Unlike a biological computer, the non biological one, its speed, the vastness and the complexity it can achieve, can all be improved and increased at the speed of technological evolution, which would be under its own control. The brain is complex, and we are actively trying to reverse engineer it [1]... so we are on our way. But even if we somehow won't be able to reverse engineer our own brains, there is another approach to the creation of intelligence, by creating a new one using the basic elements that we know work, neurons, and through a process that we know works, evolution. We know that this method works, we are the proof of it. We are the proof that evolution works, that simple spatio-temporal signal processors evolved to be connected in vast topologies can produce intelligent systems. If we can supply the elements flexible enough, the environment complex enough, the evolutionary process dynamic enough, and enough computational power to simulate trillions of organisms... it will only be a matter of time... once again, we are the proof of that.

[1] The Blue Brain Project EPFL, http://bluebrain.epfl.ch

-Gene I. Sher

Acknowledgments

I would like to thank my father for always showing by example, for his love of knowledge and erudition and instilling the same in me, for his creativity and dedication, for his support of my work and research, for teaching me to always pursue the highest possible standard within all my work, and to never waste a moment. I would also like to thank Joe Armstrong for his Foreword, and his numerous contributions to Erlang, and for Erlang itself, a language which I believe is the future of computational intelligence. And finally, I would like to thank my editors, for making the publication of this volume such a pleasant experience.

Contents

PART V
APPLICATIONS

PART VI
PROMISES KEPT

Chapter 1 Introduction: Applications & Motivations

Abstract This chapter discusses the numerous reasons for why one might wish to study the subject of neuroevolution. I cover a number of different applications of such a system, giving examples and scenarios of a neuroevolutionary system being applied within a variety of different fields. A discussion then follows on where all of this research is heading, and what the next step within this field might be. Finally, a whirlwind introduction of the book is given, with a short summary of what is covered in every chapter.

One of the most ambitious and long standing goals within the field of Computational Intelligence (CI), is the creation of thinking and self aware machines of human and greater than human intelligence. An intelligent system that once seeded, can learn, improve on itself, and then cut its own evolutionary path upwards. We have come a long way, we have made progress. Starting with symbol manipulation based "good old fashioned AI" systems of the 1950s, we have advanced to artificial neurocomputation. Today, these intelligent systems can analyze images, control the walking gait of a robot, navigate an Unmanned Aerial Vehicle (UAV) through the sky, and even act as brains for artificial organisms inhabiting artificial worlds [1,2,3]. We have advanced a lot in the past few decades. Like the history of flying machines, most believed that flight could either not be achieved, or if achieved could only be done so through machines that would flap their wings or were lighter than air... Yet today, we have made super flying machines. Our technological flying machines can do what the biological flying machines would not even dream off, leave and go beyond this planet. I have no doubt that the same story will repeat itself with regards to intelligent machines.

Today's most advanced approaches to computational intelligence are through neuroevolution [4,5,6], a combination of artificial neural networks and evolutionary computation. The discipline of Neuroscience has progressed rapidly, and we've learned quite a bit about the biological neural circuits, and the process of cognition. We've also had a lot of time to experiment with Evolutionary Biology, and know very well of its power when it comes to problem solving. After all, we are one of its solutions. Neuroevolution is based on the extrapolation of the concepts we've learned in neuroscience and evolutionary biology, and the application of those concepts to machine intelligence.

Both, evolution and neurocomputation, are highly distributed and concurrent problem solving approaches. Evolution is the process of change in the inherited traits within populations due to the constant competition of the organisms within it. As the billions of organisms fight for resources, some survive and create offspring, while others die out. Those that survive and create offspring pass on their

G.I. Sher, *Handbook of Neuroevolution Through Erlang*,
DOI 10.1007/978-1-4614-4463-3_1, © Springer Science+Business Media New York 2013

traits to their offspring; and those organisms that create less offspring than others are slowly expunged from the environment. Thus evolutionary computation occurs on the entire surface of the planet, billions of organisms solving the problem of survival in a harsh environment, all in parallel. On the other hand, the carbon based cognitive computer we call our brain, is composed of over a hundred billion neurons, each neuron processing information in parallel with other neurons, each being affected to some degree by the signals it processes. The emergent property of this neurocomputation is self awareness, the mind, and the ability to learn and act upon the world.

If we are to map biological neurocomputational systems and evolutionary processes to software, we need to use a tool that makes this mapping as direct and as true as possible. Beyond the direct mapping of these processes from biological representations to their software representations, we also need to take into account their robustness, the fault tolerance of these biological processes. There is one particular programming language that has all these features, the language that was developed from the very start for highly distributed and fault tolerant systems, that language is Erlang, and it will be our primary tool in this book.

****A note from the author****
References: I have added references to a number of books and papers that I came across over the years, and which I had the chance to read. Though I have included a reference section in a number of chapters, the referenced material is neither needed, nor is it essential, for the understanding of this volume, but it is there if you'd like to take a look.
Species/Specie: The word species is both plural and singular. But when programming and having to go between different species and single species and Ids of species, and species in populations, and agents which belong to multiple species and single species... things become confusing. Thus at times I had to use the incorrect term: Specie. Nevertheless, I do believe that the use of the word Specie allowed for some discussions to be much clearer.
****

1.1 Motivations

I will start this book by answering the *why* & *what-for of* neuroevolution. You want to know why you should study this subject, why should you be interested in it, and *what* you would gain from being able to build such computational intelligence systems. The answer to the later stands with the fact that traditional neural networks, and thus by extension even more so with regards to neuroevolutionary systems, have already proven themselves in numerous problem domains, the following of which is but a brief list:

1. Optimization: You have a problem to solve, you know what you want but you don't exactly know how to achieve that result, thus you need an intelligent agent to figure out the patterns of this problem for you and come up with an efficient solution. [7,8,9]
2. Neurocontroller: You have a complex task that needs to be performed, the task itself changes and thus you need an intelligent agent to learn how to perform this task through experience, learn how to use the tools necessary to perform the task, and perform that task efficiently and without tiring. [10,11,12,13,14,15]
3. Invention: You have a rough idea or a database of already existing inventions and you want to create a system that will improve on the designs, creating new patents. Or you wish to explore new designs in previously unexplored fields. For this you need an intelligent agent that can extrapolate ideas from existing designs, or come up with and explore new ideas within various fields. [16,17,18]

Neuroevolutionary systems are force multipliers. Even if you yourself don't know how to program a controller that uses the robot's cameras and servomotors to move around on a rough terrain while panning & tilting its solar array to collect energy, *you can* evolve a brain that will perform these tasks efficiently. If you know just a little bit about financial markets, about stock market or foreign exchange market (forex/FX), you can still create a system that learns on its own how to buy and sell profitably (but it is not easy, and thus far the profits from such systems have not been staggering, nevertheless we will build such a system). The set of problem domains to which such systems are applied is growing, and as we continue to advance these systems, making them more powerful and adaptable, the rewards gained from using these NN based intelligent agents will only continue to grow. Application domains like financial market analysis, robotics, art, and entertainment, are but the tip of the iceberg.

With regards to the *why* of neuroevolution, the answer stands with the fact that neuroevolutionary systems, particularly the Topology and Weight Evolving Artificial Neural Networks (TWEANNS), are the most advanced forms of computational intelligence creation. These systems are our best bet at creating intelligence that rivals our own, achieving what some call, a technological singularity. TWEANN systems use evolutionary processes to evolve complex systems with neural elements acting as the main building blocks. We already have proof that intelligence through neural networks can be evolved, that proof is you and I. That which makes you who you are, that part which allows you to think, adapt, learn, is a result of billions of years of evolution. The problem domain was that of survival in a hostile and volatile environment, and the solution was a carbon based parallel computational machine, a learning system which could deal with such complex environments. These neurocomputational machines which we call brains, have been evolving for a long time, starting with a simple cell that could sense the presence of some chemical percept... over the billions of years these simple systems became more advanced, these cells became more specialized for signal processing and began to resemble something we today call neurons. Evolution generated various interconnected networks of these cells, various topologies, because different groups of neurons could more effectively deal with complex signals than a single neuron could... and after trillions of permutations of neural types and topologies in which they are joined, eventually a stable solution emerged... A few billions of years of building on top of that stable solution, evolving new features and neural circuits through random mutation and perturbation, and the result is a vast parallel neurocomputational system which resides within our skulls. This is the process of neuroevolution.

Why *Erlang*? Though a more detailed answer will be given in Chapter-5, the quick version is that Erlang's architecture perfectly matches that of evolutionary and neurocomputational systems. Everything is concurrent and distributed, each neuron is an independent and concurrent element which processes its information along with over a hundred billion other neurons. When it comes to evolution, each organism in a population exists in parallel with all other organisms. All of these features can be easily mapped to Erlang's architecture through its process based and message passing approach to computing. And because there is such a direct match, we will not have to worry as much about how to first map these distributed and complex systems into a form that some programming language uses. Thus, because our systems will be much more concise and because our programs will so naturally represent these concurrent systems, it will be easier for us to further expand them, to add new features, features that would otherwise have proven too difficult to add or even consider due to the way in which some programming language represents its programs.

By the time you finish this book, you will have created a system which can generate a population of intelligent agents which are able to interact with the real world, and simulated worlds called scapes. These intelligent agents will be powered by complex neural networks (NNs), evolved synthetic brains whose topologies can expand and learn as they interact with their environment. When we get to the Artificial Life chapter of this book, these intelligent agents will be embodied through simulated robots, existing and moving around in a Flatland, interacting with each other, fighting each other, and collaborating with each other... These NN based intelligent agents will have morphologies, sensors and actuators through which the NNs will be able to learn how to interact with simulated environments and other programs... These agents will live, die, create offspring, form new species... they can be uploaded into UAVs and other mechanical bodies, embodying those machines with the ability to learn and to survive... Though some of this may sound like science fiction, it is not the case, for by the end of this book you and I will have built neurocomputational systems capable of all these things.

1.2 Applications

In this section I will provide examples and scenarios of the various problem domains to which NN based intelligent agents can be applied to. Where possible, I will cite already existing projects in that field, and the results of said projects.

When reading through the examples, you will notice that all the scenarios follow the basic evolutionary loop shown in Fig-1.1a. Also, when I mention neural network based intelligent agents, I simply refer to programs that use NNs to process their sensory signals and use their actuators when interacting with the world, as shown in Fig-1.1b.

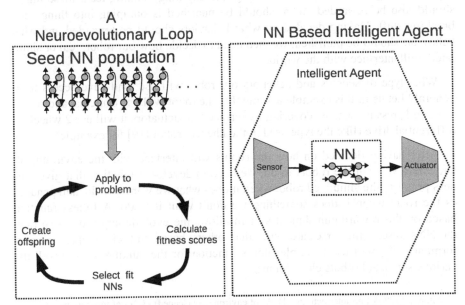

Fig. 1.1 a. The standard evolutionary/neuroevolutionary loop. and b. A NN based agent.

1.2.1 Robotics

When discussing computational intelligence the first thing that comes to mind is robotics and cybernetics. How to make all the parts of a robot act intelligently and in a cohesive manner such that the robot can move around, either on wheels or legs, accomplish useful tasks, and learn from its experience. Or for example how to evolve a controller for a teleoperated robot, where the robot mimics the actions of the human agent. All of these applications can be accomplished using a neuroevolutionary system.

Example 1: Evolving the neurocomputational brain of a robot.

To evolve a NN based intelligent agent for this particular task, we first decide on what the robot should do, and whether we want to evolve the neurocontroller (the brain of the robot) in the real world, or in a simulated world and then have it transferred into a real world robot. Whichever of the two approaches we take, we then need to agree on what types of behavioral patterns we wish to evolve, and what behavioral patterns we wish our evolved neurocontroller to avoid. For example, the longer the robot lasts without losing all of its power the better, if the robot can, when low on energy, go to an outlet and recharge itself, that type of behavior needs to be rewarded. If we wish to create a robot that services the house by cleaning it, moving around and not bumping into anything, making tea... these things should also be rewarded. What should be punished is bumping into things and breaking stuff. Having decided on what behaviors should be rewarded and what behaviors should be punished, we then need to decide how our robot, real or simulated, will interface with the world.

What type of sensors and actuators our robot will use, and have access to in general? Let us in this example assume that the robot will use cameras, audio sensors, and pressure sensors covering its surface. For actuators it will use 2 wheels, a differential drive (like the type used in the khepera robot [19] for example).

After having decided on how the robots will interface with the environment, and what we want the robots to do, we need to develop a function that gives fitness points to the simulated robot when it does what we want it to do, and penalizes the robot when it does something we don't want it to do. A fitness function based on this reward/punishment system allows the evolutionary process to rank the NNs to see which ones are better than others, based on their comparative performance. We will use a simple fitness function for the ranking of how well the various simulated robots clean rooms:

$$\text{Fitness} = A*(\text{\# of minutes active}) + B*(\text{\% of environment cleaned}) - C*(\text{\# of furniture bumps})$$

Where A, B, and C are weight variables set by the researcher, and depend on which of these qualities the researcher finds most important. If we have decided to evolve a simulated robot in a simulated world before transferring the resulting NN into a real robot in a real world, we need to create a simulation of the environment as close to the real world as possible, an environment that should also be able to keep track of the robot's behavior. Since the simulated world has knowledge of where all the things within it are located, it can keep track of furniture collisions through collision detection. Such a simulated world should very easily be able to track the robot's fitness. After the robot runs out of energy, or after it has lived for some predetermined amount of time, the fitness tracking virtual world will score the NN that controlled the robot. In this document, we will call such self contained simulated worlds: *scapes*, or *scape* for singular.

Having now agreed on the fitness function, and having decided to simulate the robot and the virtual world using one of the more popular of such simulators,

Player/Stage/Gazebo [20,21] for example, we can now run the neuroevolutionary system. The system generates an initial population of random NN based intelligent agents, each controlling its own simulated robot within a scape. After some time the neuroevolutionary system scores each NN, removes the bottom 50% of the population, and then creates mutant offspring from the surviving fit 50% (the ratio of fit to unfit agents can of course be set to a different value) of the genotypes. After the mutants have been created to replace the removed 50% of the NNs, the neuroevolutionary platform applies the NNs to the simulations again. This process goes on and on, every new generation comes with new mutants, each of which has a chance of outperforming its parent, though in most cases it will not... Given long enough time (in hours, rather than billions of years) and a flexible & powerful enough neuroevolutionary system/algorithm with a detailed enough scape, eventually NN based intelligent agents will be evolved that are adapted to their chosen environment. The neuroevolutionary process will evolve NNs that can make tea, clean all the rooms, and not bump into furniture. Once highly fit NNs become present in the population, we simply extract them and import them into real robot bodies (Fig. 1.2).

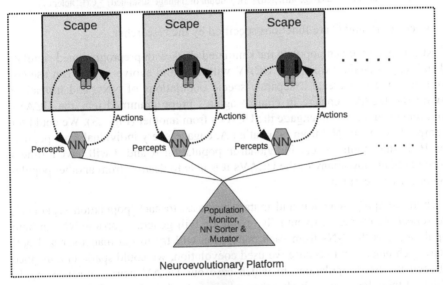

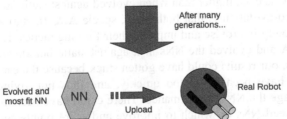

Fig. 1.2 Evolving fit simulated robots, and then uploading the evolved NN based controllers from a simulation into a real robot body.

The reason that we need to make our simulations of environments and robots as detailed as possible is because real sensors, actuators, environments, motors... are flawed, and there is always noise in the data which needs to be taken into account when evolving intelligent agents, so that they are ready for this noise when uploaded to real bodies. The more detailed the simulations, the greater the chance that a NN evolved to control a simulated robot, will be able to just as effectively control a real robot.

Example 2: Evolving aerial dogfighting abilities

In another scenario, we might want a killing robot rather than a cleaning one. Lets say we want to evolve a neurocontroller for an Unmanned Combat Aerial Vehicle (UCAV), we want to evolve a neural network which will enable the UCAV to engage other fighter jets in combat. The approach will be the same as before, first we create a detailed simulation of the UCAV and the simulation environment/scape. Then we develop a fitness function through which we can guide evolution in the right direction:

Fitness = A(Amount of damage inflicted) – B(Amount of damage sustained) + C(Efficiency)

Where A, B, and C are functions specified by the researcher.

At this point we can populate the simulated skies with preprogrammed simulated fighter jets against which the UCAV will fight and evolve, or, we can use coevolution. We can create 2 separate specie populations of NNs, and instead of having the UCAVs engage in combat against preprogrammed jets, the UCAVs from one population will engage the UCAVs from another (Fig-1.3). We could for example have every NN from population A, engage every individual from population B, in this manner every individual in population A and B will have a fitness score based on how many of the UCAVs it is able to destroy from another population in a 1 on 1 combat.

Then we apply selection and mutation phases to each population separately, and repeat the process... Eventually, evolution will generate capable NNs in both populations, as the NNs from each population will try to out maneuver and outsmart each other. And because we used coevolution, we could spark an arms race between the two populations in which case our UCAV neurocontrollers might achieve fitness levels even higher than when evolved against static strategies. Another benefit of co-evolution is that both sides, specie A & B, start as incompetents, and then slowly improvise and improve their fighting tactics. If we had just used population A and evolved the NNs in it against static but already advanced air combat tactics, our results could have gotten stuck because the early incompetent NNs would have been killed too quickly, and thus not giving the scape enough time to gage the NN's performance. There could have been no evolutionary path for the seed NNs by which to improve and score points against the already existing, preprogrammed and deadly UCAVs. Coevolution allows the two species to build their own fitness landscape which provides for a smooth evolutionary path upwards as both species try to improve from seed, to competent level.

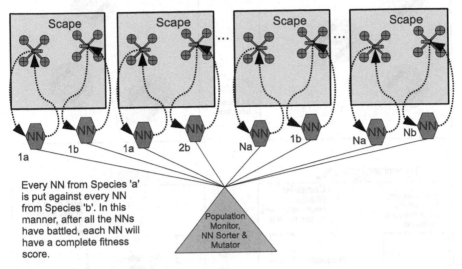

Fig. 1.3 Coevolution of UCAV Neurocontrollers.

With regards to using real robot systems in the evolution of NN based controllers: To evolve the neurocontrollers directly inside the real robots, we will either: 1. Need to somehow create a supervisor program within the robot itself which would tell it when it bumps into stuff, or when the robot does not clean the room properly, or 2. We could have the NN's fitness based on how the owner responds to the robot, whether the owner for example yells at the robot (fitness point is subtracted) or thanks the robot (fitness point is added)... When using real robots, the evolution is slower since it has to occur in real time, and on top of that, we will not have access to all the information from which to calculate the fitness of the neurocontroller. For example, how do we establish the percentage of the house cleaned by the robot, who keeps track of this information, and how? Another problem is that real robots cost money, so it could be much more expensive as well. Do we buy a large number of robots to establish an evolutionary robotics system? Or do we buy just one robot and then try out all the different NNs in the population using that same robot, giving them access to this robot one at a time (Fig-1.4)... In all cases we follow a similar pattern, except that when using a scape, the scape has all the data about the robot's performance and environment, and when using real robots, we need to find another way to make those fitness value calculations.

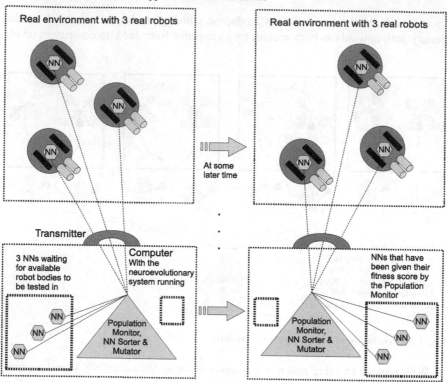

Fig. 1.4 Evolutionary robotics experiment with 3 real robots, but a population of 6 NNs. Since only 3 robots exist, 3 NNs are uploaded into real robot bodies and have their fitness gaged, while the other 3 wait for the first 3 to finish.

There is an advantage to using real robots though. When evolving neurocontrollers inside real robots, when a solution finally is evolved, we can be sure that it will behave exactly the same during application as it did during training because the real robot's fitness scores were based on its real world performance.

1.2.2 Financial Markets

Financial analysis is another area where NN based systems can be successfully applied. Because NNs are universal function approximators, if the market does have an exploitable pattern, NN based systems are our best bet at finding it. With this in mind, we can try evolving a NN based algorithmic trader.

Example 1: Automated currency trader

Unlike the stock market, Forex (FX) market deals with trading currencies and is up ~ 24/7. FX market had a turnover of roughly $4 trillion in 2011, and a huge trading volume leading to its high liquidity. It is thus reasonable to think that with a flexible enough system and a well chosen training set, we could teach a NN to buy and sell currencies automatically.

To evolve a NN based currency trader we first need to decide on how and what to present to the NN's sensors. The most direct approach would be to implement a type of sliding window protocol with regards to the traded currency's historical data. In this approach we feed the NN the historical data from X number of ticks (A tick is a calculated opening or closing price taken every K number of seconds) until the current time T, and ask it to make a decision of whether to buy, hold, or sell this currency at time T+1, as shown in Fig. 1.5. We could for example inform the NN that yesterday Euro traded against the Dollar at a ratio of 1.4324, and then ask the NN to output its decision on whether we should buy, sell, or hold our Euros today.

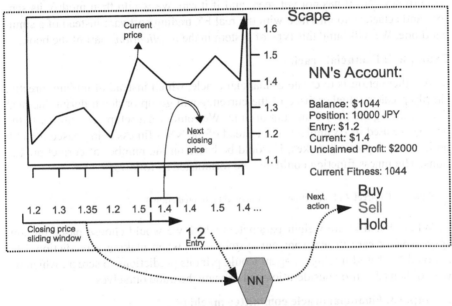

Fig. 1.5 A currency trading NN that uses a sliding window protocol.

Let's set up a system where we wish to trade Dollars against JPY (Japanese Yen). In this scenario our scape will be a simulated FX market using real historical data. Our NN based intelligent agent will interface with the scape using sensors which read some amount and some particular combination of historical data, and then immediately output a trinary signal, -1, 0, or 1. The output will be fed into an actuator which will, based on this signal, make a decision of whether to buy, sell, or hold (if there is anything to hold) a certain amount of JPY. As soon as the trade request is made, the scape will move the sliding window 1 tick forward, and feed our NN the new set of historical data. This can be done for a 1000 ticks for example, after which the scape will calculate the fitness of the NN, which in this case can be the actual profit after those 1000 ticks. We can set up the fitness function to be as follows:

Fitness = 300 + P

Where 300 is the amount of money the NN initially started with, and P is a positive or negative number that represents the amount of profit generated during 1000 ticks.

Again we would use evolution to evolve a population of this type of currency traders, choosing those that were more profitable over those that were not, letting them create mutant offspring with yet higher profit generating potential. Once our neuroevolutionary system has finally generated a profitable NN, we would test it on new currency data to make sure that the trading NN can generalize and be used on currency data it has not yet seen, and if it can, we would then modify its sensors and actuators to interface with the real FX trading software instead of a simulated one. We will build this type of system in the *Applications* part of the book.

Example 2: Financial oracle

Another option is to create a financial oracle, which instead of trading directly, simply predicts whether price of the currency will go up or down during the next tick, or during the next T amount of time. We could use a setup very similar to the one we've used in Example-1, but instead of the NN's fitness being based directly on how much profit it makes, it would be based on the number of correct predictions. The fitness function could then be formulated as follows:

Fitness = P(correct # of predictions) + N(incorrect # of predictions)

Where P and N are weight parameters which we would choose based on how aggressive or careful we want our system to be when making a prediction. The evolved NN based intelligent agent would print its predictions to screen, which we would then take into consideration and execute the trade ourselves.

Example 3: Financial oracle committee machine

Finally, because our evolutionary approach will produce many NNs, and because we can have multiple neuroevolutionary systems running at the same time, we could form NN oracle committees. Some of the champion (high fitness) NNs will have very different internal structure from other champions, we could form groups of these high fitness NNs, ask them all the same question (input signal), then weigh their votes (output signal), and base the final suggestion of the committee on the weighted average of these votes.

A committee machine is simply a group of trained agents, where the final action is based on this committee as opposed to being based on any single agent. Furthermore, one can setup a committee in different ways. We could form the committee from champion NNs which were evolved on all historical information indiscriminately, and then simply ask the group of these champion NNs the same question and weigh their votes. This type of committee is called a *homogeneous committee*. Or we could create 7 different populations, and then evolve each of the 7 populations on a different training set. We could evolve the first population on the financial historical data of every Monday in the dataset, the second population on the financial historical data of every Tuesday, and so on. We would do this because the market's behavior has patterns, and those patterns are specific to certain months and certain hours of day due to the market's dependency on seasons (when certain crops become available for example) and on active trading hours of certain countries (when USA's brokers sleep, Japan's brokers are actively trading, and vice versa). These patterns might require different trading strategies, and each population would concentrate on that particular trading strategy. After each of these populations has evolved a set of high fitness NNs, we would extract the champions from them and put them into groups within the committee. The committee would then filter the input signals, routing the signals to the cluster of NN champions which specializes in that particular data set (Monday data, or second half of the day data...). These types of committees are called *filtered or specialized committees*. These two different types of committees are shown in Fig. 1.6.

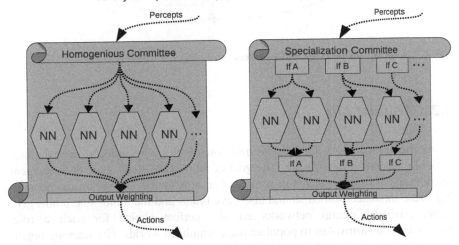

Fig. 1.6 The architectures of the homogenious and specialized committee machines.

Basing our trading decision on a large population of highly diverse champion NNs could yield a safer trading signal (Fig-1.7), since for our whole committee's final action to be wrong, it would require for the majority of the champion NNs to all be wrong at the same time. We could further try to tune our committee system by specifying that at least X% of NNs in the committee have to agree on the trading signal before the committee executes the trade... Though this might decrease the number of trades our committee machine executes in total, it could further improve the chance that when the trade is executed, it is a lucrative one.

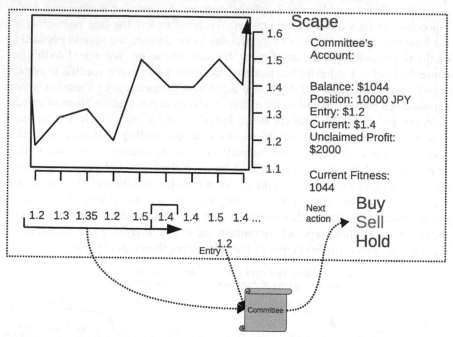

Fig. 1.7. A committee machine of NN traders.

1.2.3 Artificial Life

Artificial life, or ALife, imitates traditional biology by trying to recreate biological phenomena in software. The goal of ALife is to study logic and emergent phenomena of living systems in simulated environments. The organisms populating these simulated worlds should also have brains and the minds that brains generate. Artificial neural networks are the perfect choice for such a role. Neuroevolution allows us to populate these simulated worlds with learning organisms. Through neuroevolution the simulated environments allow the behavior of these artificial organisms to evolve over time, changing as the organisms interact with the environment and compete against each other.

If the software based sensors and actuators are themselves implemented as nodes, similar to how neurons are implemented, then through mutation operators they too can be added and removed to and from the NN during evolution. Through such an implementation we can then allow a neuroevolutionary system to evolve not merely the brain of the artificial organism, but also its morphology. Using this approach, the evolutionary processes will allow for the created mutant offspring to expand and try out different combinations of sensors and actuators, and thus potentially different types of bodily morphologies.

Example 1: Predator vs. Prey

We could populate a simulated 3d world with two populations of artificial organisms. Those artificial organisms could be in the form of small tanks controlled by NNs. The *prey* tank population would have wheel based propulsion, and no gun turret. The *predator* tank population would start with track based propulsion, and a small gun turret which it could use to fire. Furthermore, each organism would start with range based sensors. Each tank would have a certain amount of energy, and a maximum lifespan of 20 simulated hours. In this simulated world, the prey organisms can only gain energy for propulsion by drinking it from the randomly scattered and self replenishing energy pools. The predator organisms can only gain energy by killing the prey, thus consuming their energy. We will actually implement and use our neuroevolutionary platform in a similar, though slightly simpler, ALife simulation in Chapter-18.

In the scenario above the prey start with the following list of sensors: [Range_Sensor], and the following list of actuators: [Differential_WheelDrive]. While the predators start with [Range_Sensor] sensors, and [Differential_TracksDrive,Gun_Turret] actuators. Each sensor and actuator name is a tag, a name of a program that we need to develop. These programs either act as simulated sensors/actuators (if the robot itself is simulated for example), or interface with a hardware driver of the real sensors/actuators. Furthermore, each sensor and actuator will need to have some visual and physical representation if implemented in a virtual environment. The NNs should be able to poll the sensor programs for signals, and output signals to the actuator programs, which themselves can then further post-process and act upon those signals.

In this particular example, the offspring are simply mutated versions of their fit parents. In the real world, not only the neural structures but also the organism morphologies evolve. Morphological evolution can be integrated as a sort of side effect of neuroevolution. We can accomplish this by extending the list of mutation operators used by our neuroevolutionary system. One of these possible additional mutational operators could be an *Add_Random_Sensor,* or *Add_Random_Actuator.* Using the sensor and actuator based mutation operators, we could generate offspring which will have a chance of integrating a new sensor or actuator into their simulated bodies. Through new sensor and actuator incorporation the organism's morphology, visual representation, and physical properties would change, and thus allow evolution from simple organisms, to the more complex ones with regards to both, morphology and neurocognitive ability (structural morphology and neural network based brains).

To use Add_Random_Sensor and Add_Random_Actuator mutation operators, we also need to build the extended sensor and actuator lists, so that the neuroevolutionary system will actually have some new sensors and actuators to randomly choose from when using these mutation operators. For the prey we could provide the following sensor list: [Range_Sensor,Color_Sensor], from which the Add_Random_Sensor operator could choose its sensors. And the following list of actuators: [Differential_WheelDrive,Drop_Smokebomb,Extended_Fueltank, Change_Color,Range_Sensor_PanTilter,Color_Sensor_PanTilter]. For the predators we could provide the same sensor list as for the prey, and the following actuator list: [Differential_TracksDrive,Rockets,Afterburner,Change_Color, Range_Sensor_PanTilter,Color_Sensor_PanTilter].

There is a problem though, in such ALife simulations we cannot use the "generational" evolutionary approach, where we wait for all organisms to finish their evaluation on the problem (In this case, surviving in the environment) and then calculate which ones are more fit. Instead we need to maintain a constant or semi-constant population size within the environment, we need to set up a *steady state evolutionary loop*. One of the ways in which to set up such a system is as follows: When a NN dies, a tuple composed of its genotype and its achieved fitness score is entered into a Dead_Pool list of some finite size. Immediately afterwards, a new offspring is generated of the same specie, with the parent of the offspring chosen from the NN genotypes stored in the Dead_Pool. The probability with which a parent genotype is chosen from the Dead_Pool is based on that genotype's fitness. In this manner the populations are constantly replenished, as soon as an organism dies, another one of the same specie is spawned.

Thus the hypothetical sequence of events in such an ALife system could go as follows: The two initial species of NNs controlling predator and prey tanks are created. Each NN has its own random minimalistic initial NN topology and set of sensors and actuators, the sensors and actuators the NN is using are reflected by the morphology and physical properties of the tank the NN is controlling in the virtual world. The NN controlled organisms/tanks interact with the environment and each other. When an organism dies, another organism is generated by selecting a parent NN from the dead pool of that specie with the probability dependent on that NN's fitness. The offspring is a mutated version of the parent. Through statistics alone, one of the offspring undergoes a mutation of the form: Add_Random_Sensor, which adds a Color_Sensor. Though perhaps this particular organism will not have the NN capable of making any effective use of the new sensory data, and thus will die out or be just as fit as other NNs not using color data, eventually, after a few thousand of such occurrences, one of the mutant NNs will have the topology capable of using the Color_Sensor at least to some degree. If the predator and prey tanks are of different colors, then the color sensing NN mutant will have an advantage over other organisms since it will be able to tell the difference between prey and predators, and know which ones to avoid. If the color sensing mutant offspring is a predator NN (NN controlling a predator tank), then it too will have an advantage over its fellow predator NNs, since it will now be able to discern the prey from the predators, and thus be able to choose its targets more effectively.

Over time, evolution will produce predators that use better weaponry (new actuators) and larger NNs capable of more complex reasoning and the ability to take control of these newly integrated actuators. At the same time, only those prey will survive that can better evade such predatory tanks... and only those predators will survive which can hunt these smarter prey... In this manner, evolution will produce smarter and more complex versions of predator and prey, with better strategies, more sensory modules, and greater offensive and defensive capabilities (Fig. 1.8). Evolution will fit together through trial and error, fitter NNs and morphologies of the organisms inhabiting the scape. Evolution will create these fit NNs (and their tank representations in the ALife simulation) by trying the different variations and permutations of neurons, sensors, and actuators.

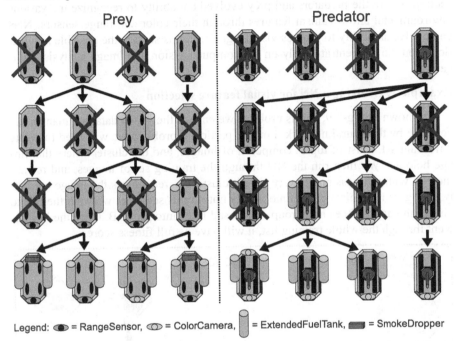

Fig. 1.8 A possible evolutionary path of the predator and prey tanks. Evolving morphology and the NNs.

This scenario should remind you a bit of the robotics application, they are related. Although in ALife the goal is to simply observe the evolved behaviors and the emergent properties, rather than to upload the evolved NNs to real robots, the transference to hardware is also possible. If these simulated sensor and actuator modules have real world counterparts, in which case this evolutionary approach will not only evolve the brains of these autonomous hunting and evading tanks, but also their morphologies by putting together a good combination of offensive and defensive modules on some standardized chassis, being controlled by the fit NN which can effectively use these modules, then the utilization of the evolved

NNs based agents in actual robot systems would follow the same steps as in the robotics application example.

The scenario in this section is actually very easy to implement, and we will have a chance to develop a similar 2d version of this ALife simulation.

1.2.4 Image Analysis & Computer Vision

Image data is just like any other type of data, and thus we can evolve NNs to analyze and pick out certain features within the image. As alluded to in a previous section, where the predators and prey evolved the ability to recognize the various environmental and organism features through their color and range sensors, NNs can evolve an ability to process visual signals. In this section the possible application scenario concentrates only on the computer vision and image analysis applications.

Example 1: Evolving a NN for visual feature selection

As shown in Fig-1.9, in this problem we encode the visual data in a manner acceptable by the neural network. For this particular problem we will need to create a training set, a list of tuples composed of images, and the cluster where that image belongs. We then run the NN through the training set of images, and reward the NN with a fitness point every time it clusters or recognizes the image correctly, and give it 0 points every time it does not. In this scenario, we want the NN to cluster the happy faces into group A, and sad faces into group B. Once the NN has went through the whole training list, it will have its full fitness score.

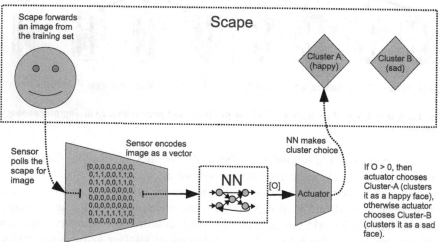

Fig. 1.9 The image is first encoded as a vector (a bitmap for example), and then fed into a NN which decides whether the image belongs to cluster A or B.

We generate a population of NNs, each NN goes through the training set and at the end once all the NNs are scored, we again choose the most fit networks and let them generate mutant offspring. Some of these offspring will recognize or cluster the images better than others, and through this selection-mutation-application loop, eventually the neuroevolutionary process will generate highly fit NNs. Once a particular/goal fitness score is reached, or the population no longer generates organisms of greater fitness, we choose the most fit NN within the population, and count it as the solution generated by our neuroevolutionary system. This champion NN can now be applied to the real world image analysis problem for which it was evolved.

Example-2: Facial stress signal analysis

To create the necessary training set for this type of problem, we would have to manually generate images of faces that show stress and those that do not, and then flag these training images with *stress|no_stress* tags. With this type of training set, a neuroevolutionary system can properly score the NN's performance and fitness. In a more complex version, the images do not have to be static, they could be fluid images coming directly from a camera.

Thus performing the same type of training as in Example-1, we would evolve a stress recognizing NN, which could then be used in various applications. This type of NN system can be connected to a camera at an ATM machine for example, and then used to signal duress, which might further imply that the withdrawal is being made under pressure, and that the person might require help. There are numerous other possible, and useful applications for such a NN system.

1.2.5 Data Compression

Even data compression can be done through NNs. The next example demonstrates two simple approaches to give an idea of how to tackle this type of problem.

Example 1: Transmitting compressed signals.

Shown in Fig-1.10 is a feed forward neural network composed of 3 layers. The first layer has 10 neurons, the second 5, and the third 10 neurons again. Assume we have a dataset A composed of 100 values. We divide these 100 values into sets of 10, and then evolve the weights of the NN such that it can output the same signal as its input. So that for example if the input of the NN is the vector: [0,0,0,1,0,1,0,1,1,1], then its output would be the same vector: [0,0,0,1,0,1,0,1,1,1].

Once the NN is able to output the same signals as its input, we break the NN into two parts. The first is the compressor/transmitter part composed of the first two layers, and the second is the decompresser/receiver network composed of the last, 3rd layer, as shown in Fig-1.10. When you pass the signal of length 10 to the transmitter NN, it outputs a compressed signal of length 5. This signal can then be stored or passed to another machine over the net, where the receiver NN is waiting. This receiver NN would accept the compressed signal of length 5 and convert it back to the original signal of length 10. This is so because the combination of the Transmitter-NN and Receiver-NN, form the original NN system which accepts and outputs the same signal of length 10.

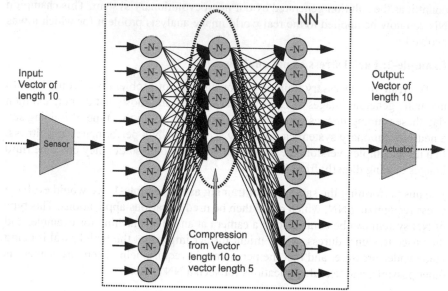

Fig. 1.10 A simple Feed Forward NN composed of 3 layers with a topology of: [10,5,10].

Though simple, this data compression NN can produce a half sized compressed signal, which can later be decompressed by the receiver NN. This approach could be further extended. It is not known ahead of time whether the compression of this magnitude is possible (or perhaps whether it is possible to compress the signal at all), and whether it is possible with a neural network of the topology we originally chose as a guess (the [10,5,10] feed forward NN).

A better approach to this problem would be to use neuroevolution and evolve the topology of the compression NN. In such a scenario we would constrain the NN to use the sensor (input channel) which can read signals of length 10, an actuator (output channel) which outputs a signal of length 10, and one hidden layer whose length is initially set to 1. Then through neuroevolution we would evolve various topologies of the hidden layers. In this manner, a compression solution can be evolved for any unknown data. Evolution will strive to produce a fit compressor, though perhaps not optimal, it will be evolved for that particular type of data, rather than any general dataset.

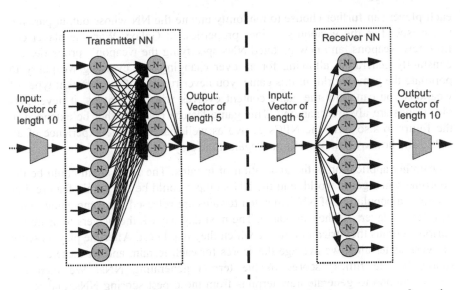

Fig. 1.11 The Feed Forward NN broken into its transmitter/compressor and receiver/decompressor parts.

1.2.6 Games & Entertainment

It would be great to see Non-Player Characters (NPCs) in a computer game evolve and advance over time as you play. Wouldn't it be great if the NPCs inside a game learned from their experience, and interacted with you in new and exciting ways, with you never knowing what they would come up with next? It would keep the game challenging, the game would be a world of its own, and you interacting with that living and breathing system. Because the NPCs already have morphologies and the game usually has goals (gathering gold coins, fragging other players, driving better than others within the race...), it would be very easy to extract a fitness function for NPCs, and then use neuroevolution to evolve new NPCs as time went on. This would be similar to the Artificial Life example, here the artificial organisms are the NPCs, the game world is their scape, and their fitness functions would be based on the game's goal. Not much would have to be changed from the examples given in the ALife section, except that now you get to interact with them through your own avatar within their scape. Games would become ALife simulations, with you a traveler through the simulated world.

Another approach to improving games is by using a neuroevolutionary system to generate new game features, as for example is done in the Galaxy War [23] game. In Galaxy War, the neural networks determine the various properties of the player's ship weapons, such as the shape of the laser beams, the shot's trajectory, the color of the laser and plasma blasts, the speed of the projectiles... In that game, each player can further choose to randomly mutate the NN whose output parameterizes/specifies the weapon's various properties. In Galaxy War, the player can find new weapons, and new mutated NNs specifying the weapon's properties are constantly generated, allowing for an ever changing and evolving weaponry to populate the game world. In this game, you never run out of the different types of weapons you can find, the game content evolves with the players, it never gets old, things are always changing. This game feature could further be extended in the future to also have the NPCs evolve as well, based on the experience of all NPCs and how well they performed against the players...

Another application is the generation of terrains. The NN's input could be the coordinate in a game world, and the NN's output could be the terrain feature. For example a population of NN generated terrains are released for some game to the beta tester players of the said game. The next day we ask the players to score the various terrains they tried out, to see which they liked best. After the players score the various terrains, we average the scores for each terrain, and let these average scores be the fitness scores of the terrain generating NNs. We then use neuroevolution to generate new terrains from these best scoring NNs, and repeat the process. After a few months, the beta testers themselves would have guided the evolution of the terrains in their game, terrains that they find most appealing.

Although this and the previous application requires a human in the loop, the result is an exploration of possibilities, possibilities that would not have been considered without the help of the evolutionary process and the NN's generating the features of the said applications. And because neural networks are universal function approximators, neuroevolution provides the flexibility and the variety of the results that would have been more difficult, or perhaps even impossible to create with other methods.

1.2.7 Cyber Warfare

If you have been reading these listed application scenarios/examples in order, then you're already familiar with the pattern of applying a neuroevolutionary system to a problem. The pattern is:

1. Create a virtual environment (scape) for the problem, where if the goal is to simply train the NN on some training set (rather than interact with some simulation), then that virtual environment should interface with the NN's sensors and actuators, present to it the training set, and gage the NN's performance.
2. Let all the NNs in the population solve the problem, or be trained on some training set until the terminating condition is reached, at which point the scape scores each NN's performance.
3. Sort the NNs in the population based on their performance.

4. Choose some percentage of the top performing NNs, and use their genotypes to generate mutant offspring by mutating the parent NN's topology and/or weights.
5. Apply the new population composed of the top performing NNs and their mutant offspring to the problem again.
6. Finally, repeat steps 2-5 until some terminating condition is reached, where such a condition could be an emergence of a NN in the population with some fitness/performance level that you are seeking, or when the population is no longer generating better performing NNs, when evolution has stagnated.

In the scenario covered here, the neuroevolutionary system is used to evolve NN based computer system attackers and defenders, cyberwarfare agents.

Example-1: Cyber warfare, evolving offensive cyberwarfare agents.

The way we apply a neuroevolutionary system to a cyber warfare or network security application is similar to the way we dealt with robotics and artificial life, as shown in Fig-1.12. In this particular scenario the simulated environment is not a 2d or 3d world, but a computer network, with various simulated hosts. Instead of having the evolving NNs control simulated tanks or UCAVs, they control offensive and defensive software packages, like metasploit [24] for example. In the figure, these NN based cyberwarfare agents are represented with a red lightning bolt. The sensors are used to gather signals coming from the network to the local host on which the NN and the attack package is running, and the actuators use the output of the NN to interface with a software package that can execute attacks, a parametrized metasploit suit would work in this scenario as such an attack package. Metasploit can be looked at as a large library of prepared attacks/exploits, the way to select the various attacks, methods of running those attacks and options to execute them with, can be parameterized, and the NN's output can then be used to make these various choices.

Let's say the NN sends to an actuator a vector of length 20, this particular actuator uses the values in this vector to decide: 1. Which particular attack vector to select from the metasploit or another custom tailored network penetration package. 2. What options to use with this attack. 3. To what (IP, port...) target should this attack be applied to. The scape where we would evolve these cyber warfare agents is a simulated computer network, built using a network simulator like ns3 [25], or DETER [26] perhaps. The simulated computer networks would have simulated hosts with some intrusion detection capabilities. The scape which has access to the entire network simulation could then see whether any of the targets have been compromised, and whether the attacker was traced, and thus gage how well a NN is attacking the simulated targets, and how well it is concealing itself from detection, if at all. As before, we use an entire population of such NNs, each interacting with its own scape. After some time, when they are all scored based on their performance, we again sort them, select the best, and create a new population composed of these champion NNs and their mutant offspring. This is effectively an ALife simulation, the primary difference is the avatars controlled by the NNs, and the environment being not a 2d or 3d system, but a simulated computer network. As before, the NNs are simply evolving to exploit the environment they inhabit.

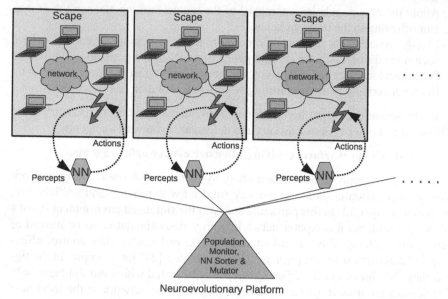

Fig. 1.12 Evolving a population of NN controlled network attackers. The offensive network program, like metasploit for example, is controlled by a NN and is represented as a red lightning bolt in the figure. The other simulated hosts on the network are represented as laptop computers.

As with ALife, eventually the neuroevolutionary process will produce NNs that are capable of properly using their parametrized defensive and offensive software packages. Evolution will produce NNs able to "see" and properly react to the signals intersecting its host's ports, and NNs able to select based on the situation, the proper offensive or defensive programs to protect its host, and attack others.

Example-2: Coevolution of NN controlled cyber attackers and defenders

Again, as in the ALife example, we can evolve all the NNs in the same scape, interacting with, and attacking/defending against each other rather than the simulated static hosts as in Example-1. We could evolve two species, one composed of cyber attackers, and another composed of cyber defenders (just like the scenario where we evolved predator and prey tanks), all populating the same simulated computer network, as shown in Fig-1.13. The goal of the cyber attackers, their fitness, is based on how well they can attack other hosts on the network. The fitness of the cyber defenders on the other hand can be based on how well they defend the host machine they are located on. The cyber defenders could be NNs whose sensors gather the signals which intersect their host, and their actuators would control the ports, either allowing those signals through, or blocking and tagging those signals as offensive. The defensive NNs could simply be evolved for the purpose of effectively controlling an intrusion detection program.

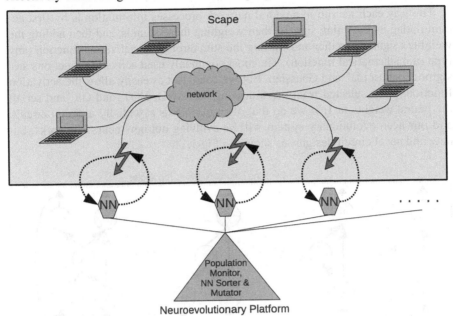

Fig. 1.13 Co-evolving cyberwarfare agents. Attackers and defenders populating the same network scape.

At the same time there should be a number of untouchable simulated hosts which send out normal, non aggressive signals to the various hosts on the network, thus simulating normal network traffic. Because the simulated network, and the operating attackers and defenders are all within the same scape, the scape will know which of the signals are non offensive (coming from the untouchable normal hosts), which are offensive (coming from the cyber attackers), and thus the scape will be able to properly distribute fitness scores to the NN based systems interfacing with it. The fitness functions for the cyber attackers and defenders respectively could be of the following form:

Attacker_Fitness = A(# cyber defenders compromised) − B(# times detected)
Defender_Fitness = A(# attacks blocked) + B(# normal signals passed) − C(# compromised)

In this manner we can co-evolve these two species, we hope that this co-evolution will spark an arms race between them. Since at the very start both of the species would be composed of random and incompetent NNs, both of these species can start on equal footing. Both of these species, attackers and defenders, can then slowly climb upwards as they try to out-compete each other in their environment.

1.2.8 Circuit Creation & Optimization

The way each neuron in a neural network processes information is by first accumulating its incoming signals, then weighing those signals, and then adding the weighted signals together and passing the sum through an activation function (any type of mathematical function). The most commonly used activation functions are: sigmoid, sinusoidal, and Gaussian. But we could just as easily allow the activation functions to be selected from the following list: AND, NOT, and OR, and set all the neural weights to 1. If we do that, then our NN is essentially a digital circuit, and our neuroevolutionary system will be evolving not new neural networks, but new and novel circuit designs, as shown in Fig-1.14.

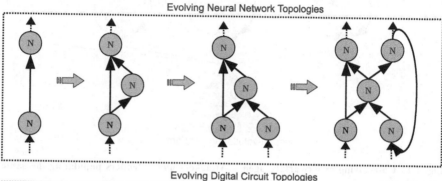

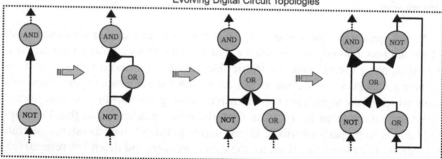

Fig. 1.14 Similarities between evolving NNs and evolving digital circuits.

The neuroevolutionary platform we will be developing in this book will be very flexible, and every feature fully decoupled from the rest. We will allow the researcher to specify the list of activation functions from which the neuroevolutionary platform should be choosing its activation functions during the offspring creation and mutation phase, and so switching from evolving neural networks to evolving digital circuits will be as easy as specifying whether the platform should use list A, composed of [tanh, sin, Gaussian...] or list B, composed of [AND, NOT, OR...] activation functions.

Example-1: Evolving a circuit.

Because we evolve our circuits with a particular behavior and feature set in mind, we can easily come up with a fitness function for it. The first thing we do is build a training set, a list composed of training tuples: [{X1,Y1}, {X2,Y2}...{Xi,Yi}], because we know that for every input Xi, we want our circuit to produce an output Yi. We want to evolve not only a correct circuit, that has the logic based on the training set, but also an efficient circuit. Our fitness function should take into account the transistor cost of every gate. To take both, the correctness and the efficiency of the circuit into account, our fitness function should be as follows:

Fitness = A(% of correct outputs) - B(# of AND gates) - C(# of OR gates) - D(# of NOT gates)

Where A, B, C, and D would be set up by the researcher, and be dependent on how important each of the said features is. The parameters (or even potentially functions) B, C, and D ensure that the evolved circuits which have the lowest number of gates but the same correctness as their less efficient cousins, will have a higher fitness.

Having now set up the training set, the activation function (AF) list our evolving network will take its AFs from, and the fitness function our neuroevolutonary system will use, we can start evolving the circuits. As before, we start by creating a random population of minimalistic digital circuits (NNs). We let each of the networks go through the training set, and using the fitness function we let the scape calculate the circuit's fitness. Once every circuit in the population has finished, we sort the circuits based on their fitness, choose the most top performing of the networks, and create their offspring. We generate the circuit offspring in the same way we did with NNs: first the parent is cloned, and then we mutate the clone's topology and parameters. The parametric mutation operators could include one which mutates one activation function into another. For example the parametric mutation operator could take any logic gate in the circuit, and then change it to one of the other gates in the gate list available (OR, NOT, AND). On the other hand the topological mutation operator could add a new gate in series or in parallel with another randomly chosen gate already in the network.

Once all of the mutant offspring have been created, we apply the new population composed of the fit parents and their mutant offspring to the training set again, repeating the whole process. In this manner we evolve a circuit through a complexification process. Let's go through a possible flow of events in evolving a XOR operation from the AND, NOT, and OR gates as shown in Fig-1.15. In that figure the initial population at generation-1, is composed of 4 minimalistic random circuits: A, B, C and D. We apply each circuit to the training set composed of the input: {[1,1],[-1,-1],[-1,1],[1,-1]}, to which a XOR operation is expected to produce an output: {-1,-1,1,1}.

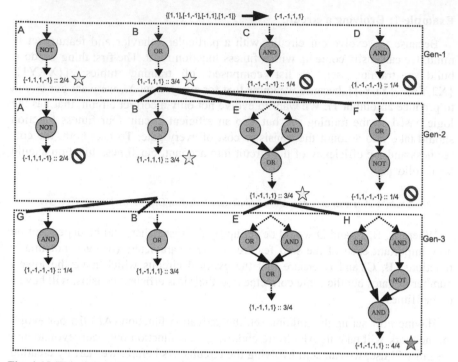

Fig. 1.15 This figure shows a possible flow of events in evolving a XOR operation from AND, NOT, and OR gates.

Let's say that in this simple example, the fitness function is: Fitness = (% of correct outputs). Each circuit in the population is fed the input signals, and the circuits output is checked against the expected output for each input (Note that the NOT circuit (A) can only accept the first value of each input vector in the input vector set, and does not care about the value of the second value). Once all the circuits have produced their outputs to the given inputs, using the fitness function we calculated that circuits A and B belong to the top 50% of the population, with scores 0.5 and 0.75 respectively. To maintain a constant population of 4, we remove the bottom 50% of the population (circuits C and D), and create two offspring from the fit circuits. Though both circuits A and B survive to the second generation, because circuit B scored higher than A, we allow it to create both of the new offspring.

Circuit B creates 2 mutant offspring called: E and F. Offspring E is created by applying two random topological mutation operators to B's clone. The first operator adds a random gate before OR, in this case that random gate is AND, and the second operator adds the OR gate in parallel to the new AND gate. The resulting circuit is *((p OR q) or (p AND q))*. Offspring F is created by applying one mutation operator to B's clone. This randomly chosen mutation operator adds a NOT gate after the existing OR gate. The resulting circuit is: NOT(p OR q). Finally, the two fit parents themselves, A and B, also both survive to the next generation.

Once all the circuits of the second generation have been created, we again feed them the Input vectors, and compare their outputs to the *Expected Outputs*. During the second generation, circuits B and E are the best performing, both with an equal score of 0.75. Thus both B and E survive to the next generation, and each creates a single offspring.

The third generation is composed of the circuits G, B, E, and H, with G and H being the new mutant offspring. We again test each of the circuits against the Input and the Expected Output. During this evaluation, Circuit H gets a perfect score of 4/4, which means that it has evolved the XOR behavior and is the evolved solution to the problem.

Though the flow of events could have went differently, sooner or later, even if it would have taken a few hundred generations and thousands of mutation operators, a XOR circuit would have been evolved.

Example-2: Optimizing an existing circuit

If we already have an existing circuit, we could try to optimize it by attempting to decrease the number of gates used, or by creating a version of the circuit whose topology is more concise. Neuroevolution can use any mutation operators that its designer wishes to implement. Usually it works by mutating various parameters, and by adding elements to, and/or deleting elements from, the NN. Complexification is the neuroevolutionary process of starting from a minimalistic network and slowly making it more complex by adding various features and structures, as the evolutionary process tries to create a fitter organism. The process of *pruning* on the other hand starts from a complex topology, and then slowly chips away the unnecessary elements of the network, while trying to maintain the same functionality and fitness. A complete neuroevolutionary system could use a combination of both, thus it is possible to start with an existing complex network, and re-factor it into a more concise version if that's what the fitness function dictates of evolution.

This type of problem would be tackled by initially creating a population composed of the circuit we wish to optimize and a few of its mutant offspring. We then apply this initial population to the training set. As would be expected, the actual circuit we wish to optimize will get the perfect score with regards to functionality, but if any of its offspring possess the same level of functionality but with a more concise topology, they will have the higher total fitness. We could use the same fitness function as in Example-1 to accomplish this:

Fitness = A(% of correct outputs) - B(# of AND gates) - C(# of OR gates) - D(# of NOT gates)

Here we would make sure that A has the greatest amount of weight, so that the circuit does not lose any of its functionality during its topological optimization.

The B, C, and D of the fitness function will ensure that if through evolution one of the mutants is a more concise version of the original network, yet it still retains the same functionality, its fitness score will be higher than that of the original circuit.

The possible mutation operators that we'd want our neuroevolutionary platform to have for this type of problem are:

1. *Desplice*: This mutation operator deletes a randomly chosen gate in the circuit, and directly connects the wires that originally lead to and from this chosen gate respectively.
2. *Perturb_Gate*: This mutation operator chooses a random gate and then changes it from one type to another (from OR to AND or NOT for example).
3. *Hard_Delete*: This mutation operator removes one of the gates and the wires leading to and from it, potentially even breaking the circuit.

To produce offspring, we would apply a random number of these mutation operators to each clone. Thus by performing the same steps as in the previous example, then if it is possible, a more efficient digital circuit will eventually evolve. One of the possible open source circuits to which this could be applied is the OpenSPARC [27] CPU. It is a very large and complex circuit, perhaps applying a pruning method to some parts of this circuit would work. In the same way, one could try to evolve OpenSPARC beyond what it currently is through complexification. Finally, we could also evolve new modules for OpenSPARC, advancing the CPU even further. With a clever enough graph-evolving algorithm, this is possible, and advanced and highly effective NN branch predictors have been evolved [34] for CPUs in this manner. Perhaps soon it will be easier to evolve the next generation of CPUs and all other advanced circuits, rather than further engineer them.

1.2.9 Optimizing Shapes and Structures

Even the optimization of multidimensional shapes and structures can be accomplished through neuroevolution. Let's say that you're trying to create some aerodynamic 3d shape, you also need to make sure that this particular structure adheres to certain constraints, perhaps some specific mass and volume constraints. How would you present this problem in such a way that you could use a neuroevolutionary system to solve it?

One way to solve this problem is by using the NN to paint the shape on a multidimensional *substrate* (Fig-1.16). A substrate is a hypercube with each of its coordinate axis ranging from *-1 to 1*. The range for each axis is then divided into K parts, effectively determining the resolution of that axis. For example if we have a hypercube with 2 dimensions: X and Y, and we decided that each dimension will have a resolution of 3, then we divide X and Y ranges into 3 sections each. The X axis' sections will range from: *-1 to -0.33, -0.33 to 0.33, and 0.33 to 1.* The Y axis' sections will range from: *-1 to -0.33, -0.33 to 0.33, 0.33 to 1*. We then give a coordinate to each section, placing that coordinate at its section's center. The section coordinates for X and Y will be at points: *-0.66, 0, and 0.66*. What this accomplishes is that we now have created a plane whose resolution is 3 by 3, and each "pixel" on this plane has its own [X,Y] coordinate. For example as shown in Figure-1.16b, the pixel in the very center is 0.66 by 0.66 units of length on each side, and has a coordinate of [0,0]. The units of length used, if any, is determined by the researcher, and is chosen to be specific to the particular problem this methodology is applied, and scaled accordingly.

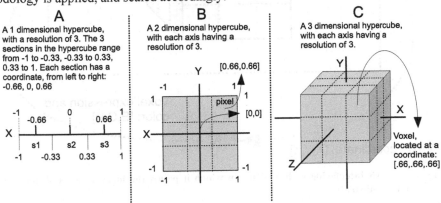

Fig. 1.16 Examples of multidimensional substrates, with a single dimension in (A), two dimensions in (B), and 3 dimensions in (C).

Instead of a 2d substrate, we could use the same approach to create a 3d substrate on the X, Y, and Z axis. Once we've decided on the resolution of each axis in a new 3d substrate we wish to create, the way we can make the NN "paint" or form the 3d shapes in this hypercube is by feeding it the coordinates [X,Y,Z] of each *voxel*, and use the NN's output to determine whether that voxel is expressed or not, whether it is filled or whether it's empty, and even what color it should be given. For example if we have a NN that accepts an input vector of length 3, and outputs a vector of length 1, then we can feed the coordinates (vector: [X,Y,Z]), and use the output vector (vector: [O]) to determine whether that voxel is filled in or is empty. If $O >= 0$, then the voxel is filled in, and if $O < 0$, then the voxel is empty.

This method could be extended even further, for example our NN could output a vector of length 3: [E, C, P], where E would determine whether the voxel is expressed, C would determine the voxel's color, and P could determine the physical properties of that voxel. A NN used to shape and determine the properties of a substrate is shown in Fig-1.17. In this figure a 3d substrate with a resolution of 3x3x3 is simulated in a scape. The NN interfaces with the scape, and requests a coordinate of each voxel in the substrate, and outputting a vector: [E,C,P], which specifies whether that voxel is expressed, its color, and from what material the voxel is made.

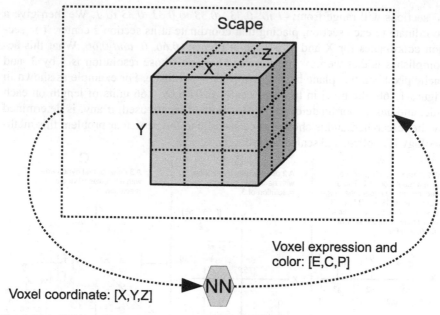

Fig. 1.17 A NN interfacing with a scape, in which it paints the form, color, and material used on a 3d substrate.

There are a number of Neural Network systems that are used for this approach, popularized by HyperNEAT [28], painting shapes on the 2d and 3d substrates. For example, a 2d version of such system is the Pic Breeder [29], and a 3d version is the Endless Forms project [30].

In the next example we will examine a possible scenario of evolving an optimized shape for a gas tank using a neuroevolutionary system.

Example-1: Evolving the shape for a gas tank.

We first decide on the number of dimensions. Because a gas tank is a three dimensional object, we want to use a 3d substrate to evolve its shape. Because the substrate's axis are each *-1 to 1*, and what we're evolving is a physical object, we will need to decide what -1 to 1 represents in real physical units of length, that is, how this range scales. We could decide that -1 to 1 on a substrate is equivalent to -0.5m to 0.5m in real space. Thus our substrate, when converted to physical units, is a 1 cubic meter slab of material, on which we will carve out (evolve) the shape of the gas tank. We also want to use high resolution for each axis, high enough that the NN has a smooth enough 3d slab of "clay" to shape, but we don't want the resolution to be too high, since we will need to pass each voxel's coordinate through the NN. If for example the resolution of each axis is 1000000, then there are a total of 1000000*1000000*1000000 coordinate triplets that will need to be passed to the NN, which might make the evaluation of the physical properties of each evolved shape too slow. For this example, let's say that the resolution for each axis is chosen to be 100. Once the shape has been evolved/optimized, we can always smooth it out through averaging methods, before creating the metal replica. In summary, we're using a 3d substrate, every point [X,Y,Z] in the substrate specifies a voxel with sides of length 1cm, and we're using the NN to evolve a 3d form by painting with 1 cubic cm voxels.

Having now agreed on the substrate's properties, we need to decide on the interpretation of the NN's output. Let's assume that we only wish to evolve the shape of the gas tank, rather than have the NN to also play around with different materials from which this gas tank can be shaped. Then, our NNs for this problem should output a vector of length 1: [E], where E specifies whether the voxel is filled in or left empty. For every 3d coordinate of a voxel in the substrate sent to the NN, the network outputs an E, where if E >= 0 then the voxel is filled in, and if E < 0, then the voxel is empty.

Finally, we now need to come up with a fitness function by which we would gage how good the evolved gas tank shapes are. Because the physical shape of the gas tank needs to be made up to some specification, our fitness function should take various physical constraints into account. If for example we need for the gas tank to hold at least 1 litre, be no larger than 0.5 meters on each side, and also that it must be aerodynamic (perhaps this is a miniature plane wing that also holds fuel), then these constraints need to be somehow represented in the fitness function, for example as follows:

Fitness = A(% fuel hold constraint) – B(% overstep on dimensional constraint) + C(aerodynamic properties).

The more fuel the evolved shape can hold, while not overstepping the length, width, and height, and being as aerodynamic as possible, the more fit is the NN. By setting A, B, and C, the researcher weighs the importance of each constraint of the design.

Having now set everything, we can begin the neuroevolutionary process like we did in other examples. We start a population of minimalistic NNs, and analyze the shapes they generate in the substrate. Each NN's crafted 3d shape is scored based on how well it fulfills the constraints, the NN's are then sorted based on their fitness, and the best of the population are allowed to create offspring. Once the new population composed of the offspring and their fit parents is created, the process repeats. Neuroevolution continues until a stopping condition is reached (a NN with a fitness level we find high enough is reached, or after the neuroevolutionary process has ran for a long enough time). Once the shape is generated, we can create a physical version of it, perhaps using a 3d printer.

Example-2: Two and three dimensional shape exploration.

It is also possible to "optimize" and explore multidimensional shapes with a researcher being part of the neuroevolutionary process. In this scenario a population of NNs describe two or three dimensional shapes, and we use the following steps:

1. The shapes are presented to a researcher.
2. The researcher decides which of the shapes he finds most interesting.
3. The NN which generated that shape is then chosen to create mutant offspring, which are the mutated versions of the interesting shapes, with variations of those shapes and images (if 2d).
4. Then the shape produced by the chosen NN and its offspring are again presented to the researcher...

In a sense, this is selective breeding of art and structure, and an approach based on Richard Dawkin's Biomorphs [31]. There are a number of such implementations available to play around with online. As mentioned, an example of a neuroevolutionary system that works with 2d substrates, exploring 2d images, is the Pic Breeder [29]. Another one that explores 3d structures is Endless Forms [30].

1.2.10 Computational Intelligence & Towards Singularity

Perhaps you have picked up this book because you are as immensely interested in computational intelligence as I am. Because you wish to contribute to the field, advance it further, and get us that much closer to what some call, the technological singularity. There is no reason why human or greater than human intelligence cannot be reached through neuroevolution. After all, it has been done before, and we are the proof of that, we are the product of that. Our very own brains, carbon based neurocomputers, have been evolved over billions of years. We already know the end goal, the approach, the basic building blocks that we should use, so perhaps we could do the same thing faster in silicone, or some other substrate. To that end, the field of Neural Networks, and a related and more general field of Universal Learning Networks (to some degree, this book is in a sense the presentation of Topology and Parameter Evolving Universal Learning Networks, rather than simply Neural Networks, since our nodes will be much more general than neurons) can take you towards that goal. And I'm hoping that this book will help you on your way of creating such a system, a system capable of evolving something of that level of complexity, and intelligence.

1.3 A Whirlwind Overview

This book covers the theory and methodology behind a neuroevolutionary system. The aim of the book is to present new algorithms, new concepts, and to provide a detailed tutorial on how to develop a state of the art Topology and Weight Evolving Artificial Neural Networks (TWEANN) platform using Erlang. This text will guide you step by step, from simulating a single neuron, to building up a complete and fully general evolutionary platform able to evolve neural network systems for any application. Source code for everything covered in this book will be provided and explained within the text, and also be available online as supplementary material [33].

Chapter-1 covers the goals this book seeks to achieve, and the various motivations for the creation and application of neuroevolutionary systems. In Chapter-2 we begin exploring the morphological and information processing properties of a single biological neuron, followed by a brief introduction to the properties of biological neural networks. We then extrapolate the important parts of neural networks, and see how an artificial neuron can mirror these signal processing features. In Chapters 3 and 4 we discuss evolution, how it optimizes organisms over time, and how the evolutionary process can be used to optimize and evolve neural networks. With these basics covered, in Chapter-5 I will make my claims with regards to Erlang, and why I think that it is perfect for computational intelligence research and development, and why I consider it the quintessential neural network programming language.

In Chapter-6 we will take our first step in developing a concurrent neural network based system. We will implement a single artificial neuron, represented by a process. Then we will combine multiple such neurons into a simple feed forward neural network (NN), with each neuron an independent process and thus the whole neural network being fully concurrent. Having implemented a simple static feed forward NN, we will develop a genotype encoding for the representation of our neural network, and a mapping function from this genotype to its phenotype, which is the actual neural system.

In Chapter-7 we will implement an augmented version of the stochastic hill-climbing (SHC) optimization algorithm, and add it to the simple NN system we have created. Having created a proper optimization algorithm and a decoupled method of applying our NN system to problems through something we call a Scape, we will conclude the chapter with us benchmarking the developed optimizable NN system on the XOR emulation problem.

In Chapter-8 we take our first step towards neuroevolution. Having developed a NN system capable of having its synaptic weights optimized, we will combine it with an evolutionary algorithm. We will create a population_monitor, a process that spawns a population of NN systems, monitors their performance, applies a selection algorithm to the NNs in the population, and generates the mutant offspring from the fit NNs, while removing the unfit. We add topological mutation operators to our neuroevolutionary system, which will allow the population_monitor to evolve the NNs by adding new neural elements to their topologies. With these features added to our neuroevolutionary system, the chapter concludes with us now having developed a simple yet fully distributed and powerful Topology and Weight Evolving Artificial Neural Network (TWEANN) platform.

In Chapter-9 we test the various mutation operators, observing the types of topologies the operator produces when applied to a simple default seed NN. This chapter concentrates on debugging, testing, and analyzing our neuroevolutionary system. Because we have implemented quiet a number of mutation operators, we test how they work, and debug the problem hiding within.

Before moving forward with further expanding and improving our TWEANN platform, we take Chapter-10 to discuss a TWEANN case study. In this chapter I present a case study of a memetic algorithm based TWEANN system called DXNN which I developed through Erlang. In this chapter we discuss the various details and implementation choices made while building it. We also discuss the various features that it has, and which we will need to add to the system we're building in this book, which itself has a much cleaner and decoupled implementation, and which by the time we're done will supersede DXNN. After exploring the ideas contained in the DXNN case study, we continue with advancing our own platform in the following chapters.

In Chapter-11 we modify the implementation of our TWEANN system, making all its parts decoupled from one another. By doing so, the plasticity functions, the activation functions, the evolutionary loops, the mutation operators... become independent, called and referenced through their own modules and function names, and thus allowing for our system to be crowdsourced, letting anyone else modify and add new activation functions, mutation operators, and other features, without having to modify or augment any other part of the TWEANN system. This effectively makes our system more scalable, and easier to augment and improve in the future.

In Chapter-12 we extend the population_monitor process to keep track of the evolved population, building up a trace of its performance, and keeping track of the various evolutionary parameters of the evolving species by calculating performance statistics every X number of evaluations, where X is set by the researcher.

In Chapter-13 we add the benchmarker process which can sequentially spawn population_monitors and apply them to some specified problem. We also extend the database to include the *experiment* record, which the benchmarker uses to deposit the traces of the population's evolutionary statistics, and to recover from crashes to continue with the specified experiment. The benchmarker can compose experiments by performing multiple evolutionary runs, and then produce statistical data and *gnuplot* ready files of the various statistics calculated from the experiment.

In Chapter-14 we create two new benchmarking problems. To be able to test a neuroevolutionary system after having made some modification requires problems more complex than the simple XOR mimicking problem. Thus in this chapter we create the pole balancing benchmark (single and double pole, with and without damping), and the T-Maze benchmarking problem.

In Chapter-15 we add plasticity to our direct encoded NN system. We implement numerous plasticity encoding approaches, and develop numerous plasticity learning rules, amongst which are variations of the Hebbian Learning Rule, Oja's Rule, and Neural Modulation.

In Chapter-16 we add substrate encoding to our neuroevolutionary platform. Substrate encoding, popularized by HyperNEAT, is a powerful encoding method which uses the NN to paint the synaptic weights and connectivity patterns on a multidimensional substrate with embedded neurodes within. A Substrate Encoded NN system (SENN) offers superior geometrical regularity exploitation abilities to the NN based agent, when such geometrical regularity is present within the problem domain.

In Chapter-17 we add substrate based plasticity. We implement the ABC and the Iterative plasticity rules.

At this point we will have one of the most advanced, fully distributed, and an incredibly general TWEANN platforms to date (as you will see, this is not an overstatement). Thus we begin the applications part of the book, and apply our developed systems to two very different and interesting areas: Artificial Life, and autonomous currency trading.

In Chapter-18 we develop *Flatland*, a 2d artificial life simulator. We create new morphological specifications, sensors, and actuators, which can then be used by our NN based system to spawn an avatar within the flatland simulated 2d world. Through the avatar the NN will be able to interact with the environment, and other avatars inhabiting it. Afterwards, we run a number of experiments applying our system to the ALife simulation, and then plot the results produced by the benchmarker process for each such experiment.

In Chapter-19 we create a Forex simulator, a private scape with which our neuroevolutionary system can interface, and evolve to autonomously trade currency pairs. We perform numerous experiments, and develop a system that analyzes not merely the sliding window based input signals, but the actual graphical charts, and through substrate encoding is able to extract the geometrical patterns within those charts.

With the entire platform now developed, Chapter-20 will conclude this book with a concluding discussion on neuroevolution, the new and improved version of the DXNN platform that we've developed here, the role such systems will play in evolving general computational intelligence based systems in the future, and the movement towards singularity.

1.4 Endgame

Make no mistake, there is absolutely nothing mystical about the human brain, it is nothing more than a carbon based neurocomputational machine, a vast directed graph structure composed of biological signal processing elements we call neurons. A vast parallel computing system carved out in flesh by billions of years of evolution. The goal of creating a non-biological substrate based Computational Intelligence(CI) system of similar and greater potential is not a matter of if, but of when. The projects like "The Blue Brain Project" [32] in which large cortical columns are simulated on a super computer, demonstrate that the silicone based systems perform just like their biological counterparts. We already know that it is possible for machines to think, you and I are the very proof of that, our brains are organic computers, chemical based computing machines and nothing more. It does not matter what performs the computation, a wet slimy cell, or an immaculate silicone based processing unit... as long as both elements can accept the same input and produce the same response, they will generate the same minds. It makes no difference whether this vast Neural Network system called the brain is carved on a biological substrate, or etched in a non-biological one. And unlike the superstitious and backwards humans, the universe itself simply does not care whether the computations are conducted in flesh, or in machine, as long as they are the same computations...

But before all these grand goals are realized though, we still need to create the tools to build systems with such potential, we still need to build the substrate, the hardware fast enough to support such a CI system, and finally we need a programming language capable of representing such dynamic, fault tolerant, and fully distributed Neural Networks and the ideas behind them. The necessary hardware is improving at a steady pace, moving in the right direction of ever increasing number of cores and per-core computational power with every year, and so it is only the programming language which could offer the scalability, extendibility, and robustness to the neurocomputational system that is still lacking. I believe that I found this neural network programming language in Erlang, and I will demonstrate that fact in this book.

1.5 References

[1] Bedau M (2003) Artificial Life: Organization, Adaptation and Complexity From the Bottom Up. Trends in Cognitive Sciences 7, 505-512.
[2] Edition S (2005) Artificial Life Models in Software A. Adamatzky and M. Komosinski, eds. (Springer).
[3] Johnston J (2008) The Allure of Machinic Life: Cybernetics, Artificial Life, and The New AI. (MIT Press).
[4] Gauci J, Stanley K (2007) Generating Large-Scale Neural Networks Through Discovering Geometric Regularities. Proceedings of the 9th annual conference on Genetic and evolutionary computation GECCO 07, 997.
[5] Siebel NT, Sommer G (2007) Evolutionary Reinforcement Learning of Artificial Neural Networks. International Journal of Hybrid Intelligent Systems 4, 171-183.
[6] Gomez F, Schmidhuber J, Miikkulainen R (2008) Accelerated Neural Evolution through Cooperatively Coevolved Synapses. Journal of Machine Learning Research 9, 937-965.
[7] Back T, Schwefel HP (1993) An Overview of Evolutionary Algorithms for Parameter Optimization. Evolutionary Computation 1, 1-23.

[8] Fonseca CM, Fleming PJ (1995) An Overview of Evolutionary Algorithms in Multiobjective Optimization. Evolutionary Computation 3, 1-16.

[9] Alfredo AM, Carlos AC, Efren MM (2011) Evolutionary Algorithms Applied to Multi-Objective Aerodynamic Shape Optimization. Studies in Computational Intelligence.

[10] Alon K (2004) Analyzing Evolved Fault-Tolerant Neurocontrollers. In Proceedings of the Ninth International Conference on the Simulation and Synthesis of Living Systems. (ALIFE9).

[11] Floreano D, Mondada F (1998) Evolutionary Neurocontrollers For Autonomous Mobile Robots. Neural Networks 11, 1461-1478.

[12] Engel Y, Szabo P, Volkinshtein D (2006) Learning to Control an Octopus Arm with Gaussian Process Temporal Difference Methods. Advances in Neural Information Processing Systems 18 c, 347-354.

[13] Kaelbling LP, Littman ML, Moore AW (1996) Reinforcement Learning: A Survey. Journal of Artificial Intelligence Research 4, 237-285.

[14] Braun H, Weisbrod J (1993) Evolving Feedforward Neural Networks. In Proceedings of ANNGA93, International Conference on Artificial Neural Networks and Genetic Algorithms. Inns-bruck: Springer-Verlag

[15] Floreano D, Urzelai J (2000) Evolutionary Robots With On-Line Self-Organization and Behavioral Fitness. Neural Networks 13, 431-443.

[16] Boden MA (1994) Dimensions of creativity M. A. Boden, ed. (MIT Press).

[17] Bringsjord S, Ferrucci DA (2000) Artificial Intelligence and Literary Creativity: Inside the Mind of BRUTUS, a Storytelling Machine. Computational Linguistics 26, 642-647.

[18] Bentley, P., and Corne, D. (2002). Creative Evolutionary Systems P. Bentley and D. Corne, eds. (Morgan Kaufmann Pub).

[19] Khepera robot: http://www.k-team.com/

[20] The Player Project: http://playerstage.sourceforge.net/

[21] Gazebo, a modern open source 3d robot simulator: http://gazebosim.org/

[22] Sher GI (2010) DXNN Platform: The Shedding of Biological Inefficiencies. Neuron, 1-36. Available at: http://arxiv.org/abs/1011.6022.

[23] Hastings EJ, Guha RK, Stanley KO (2009) Automatic Content Generation in the Galactic Arms Race Video Game. IEEE Transactions on Computational Intelligence and AI in Games 1, 1-19.

[24] Penetration Testing Software, Metasploit: http://www.metasploit.com/

[25] A discrete-event network simulator for Internet systems, ns-3: http://www.nsnam.org/

[26] DETER Network Security Testbed: http://isi.deterlab.net/

[27] OpenSPARC, an open source 64bit CMT Microprocessor: http://www.opensparc.net/

[28] Gauci J, Stanley K (2007) Generating Large-Scale Neural Networks Through Discovering Geometric Regularities. Proceedings of the 9th annual conference on Genetic and evolutionary computation GECCO 07, 997.

[29] Picbreeder, a collaborative evolutionary art project: http://picbreeder.org/

[30] Collaborative art, evolving 3d shapes: http://endlessforms.com/

[31] Dawkins R (1986) The Blind Watchmaker. (Norton), ISBN 0393315703.

[32] The Blue Brain Project: http://bluebrain.epfl.ch/

[33] All source code developed in this book is also available at: https://github.com/CorticalComputer/Book_NeuroevolutionThroughErlang

[34] Vintan LN, Iridon M (2002) Towards a High Performance Neural Branch Predictor. In IJCNN99 International Joint Conference on Neural Networks Proceedings (IEEE Service Center), p. 868-873.

Part I

FOUNDATIONS

In this first part we will cover the necessary foundations for this text. We will first discuss what neural networks are and how they function, both the biological and the artificial kind. Afterwards we will briefly cover evolutionary computation, its history, and how the various flavors (genetic algorithms, genetic programming, evolutionary programming, evolutionary strategies) are related to each other. Having now covered the two main parts separately, neural networks and evolution, we will delve into how the combination of the two works, and thus start our discussion on Neuroevolution. We will talk about a few different approaches to neuroevolution, and the accomplishments such systems have made thus far. We will note how related they are to genetic programming, and how indeed neuroevolutionary systems can be simply considered as a variation on genetic programming systems. Finally, we will discuss why Erlang is such an important programming language for this field. What benefit we will gain by using it, and why I have chosen it as the language of choice for this text, and this research in general.

Chapter 2 Introduction to Neural Networks

Abstract In this chapter we discuss how the biological neurons process information, the difference between the spatiotemporal processing of frequency encoded information conducted by a biological neuron and the amplitude and frequency encoded signals processed by the artificial neural networks. We discuss the various types of artificial neural networks that exist, their architectures and topologies, and how to allow such neural networks to possess plasticity, which allows the neurons to adapt and change as they process presynaptic signals.

Our brains are biological parallel computers, composed of roughly 100,000,000,000 (one hundred billion) signal processing elements called Neurons. Like a vast graph, these neurons are connected with each other in complex topological patterns. Each neuron in this vast processing graph accepts signals from thousands of other neurons, processes those signals, and then outputs a frequency encoded signal and passes it onwards to thousands of other neurons. Though each neuron on its own is relatively easy to understand, when you connect together a few billion of them, it becomes incredibly difficult to predict the outcome given some specific input. If you are careful and connect these biological signal processing elements in some particular pattern, the final output of this vast graph might even be something useful, an intelligent system for example. An output signal can for example control muscle tissue in your legs, so that they move in synchrony and give you the ability to walk and run. Or this vast neural network's output can be a solution to some problem which was fed into it as an image from its sensory organs, like cameras or eyes for example. We don't yet completely know how and which neurons, and in what patterns we need to connect them to allow us to produce useful results, but we're getting there, we're reverse engineering the brain [1].

Evolution used billions of years to try out trillions upon trillions of various permutations of chemical setups for each neuron and connections between them... we and other inhabitants of this planet are the result of this vast stochastic optimization, an optimization for a more fit replicator (a gene). We are, as Richard Dawkins noted, that replicator's tools of survival, we are its survival machines [2,3].

In biological organisms born of evolution, there was only one goal, to create a copy (usually mutated due to environmental factors), to create an offspring. Billions and billions of permutations of atoms and simple molecules and environments on this planet eventually resulted in a molecule which was able to copy itself if there was enough of the right material around it to do so. Of course as soon as such a molecule appears in the environment, it quickly consumes all the raw material its able to use to create copies of itself... but due to radiation and the simple fact that biology is not perfect, there are variations of this molecule. Some of

G.I. Sher, *Handbook of Neuroevolution Through Erlang*,
DOI 10.1007/978-1-4614-4463-3_2, © Springer Science+Business Media New York 2013

these mutant clones of the molecule were smaller and unable to replicate, others were able to do so more efficiently when using raw materials, yet others were even able to break apart surrounding compounds to make the missing necessary raw materials... though it's still just chemistry at this point, in essence this is already competition and predation. The replicating molecules are competing against each other, not by choice, but simply because that's what naturally happens when something can make copies of itself. Anything that does not make a copy, does not take over the environment, and is either expunged from the environment, or used as raw material by replicators.

The molecules split and vary/mutate, new features are added, so that for example some new molecule is able to break apart another molecule, or merge with it. If some complex molecule does not replicate in some manner or another, it has no future... because it will not create an offspring molecule to carry its behavior forward in time.

These mutations, variations, collisions between molecules and atoms, all giving a chance for a more fit replicator to emerge, this was occurring on the entire surface of the planet, and below it. The entire planet was like a computational system, where every inch of the surface gave space for the calculations of the mutations and permutations of molecules to take place... And after billions of years, trillions upon trillions of these replications and mutations, more and more fit systems emerged. Sure, most of the mutations were harmful and produced mostly unfit offspring that could not replicate at all, or were able to replicate but at a slower pace or lower efficiency level... But when you have trillions of opportunities for improvement to work with... no matter how small the probability, eventually, every once in a while... a better combination of molecules results in a better replicator, able to take advantage of some niche within the environment... *That is evolution.*

Through these trillions of permutations, offspring and molecules combined into better replicators, some of which could defend themselves against other replicators, some of which could attack other kinds of replicators so that they could create more of their own kind... To know whom to attack, to know who is composed of the resources that you need to create an offspring, you need a system that is able to tell the difference between the different kinds "stuff" out there, you need some kind of sensory setup... These adaptations continued on and on, and the competition still rages on to this day, from molecules to groups of molecules, cells, the "Survival Machines", tools evolved by the replicators to defend themselves, tools growing more and more complex to deal with other rival replicators and their Survival Machines... a vast biological arms race.

Eventually, through evolution, a new information storage methods was discovered, RNA evolved[9]... the result of all this turmoil is what we see around us today. We are still banding together, we are still competing for limited resources, we are the "Survival Machines" as Dawkins pointed out, machines used by these replicators, by genes, to wage war on each other and make as many copies of themselves as possible. Their newest invention, a feature that evolved to deal with the ever changing and dangerous world, is an interconnected graph of cells that can control these Survival Machines more precisely, deal with much more complex Survival Machines, store information about the world, and keep the genes safe long enough to create more copies of them, with their own survival machine to control. One of the most significant features that arisen in biological organisms, is the parallel biological computer, the vast neural network system, the brain. Over the billions of years of evolution the brain too has been changed, evolution has trended toward more complex brains. Evolution has been slowly exploring the various neural network topologies.

This text is dedicated to the study of evolutionary methods as applied to simulated neural networks. Instead of using atoms and molecules as the building blocks for our evolutionary algorithms, we will use neurons. These neurons, when grouped in particular patterns and topologies, form brains. Biological computers evolved the ability to invent, imagine, scheme, and most importantly, these parallel computers evolved self awareness. Thus we know that such things are possible to evolve, it already happened, nature has proven it possible, we are the proof. In this book we will develop non biological neural networks, and we will apply evolutionary principles to evolve neural systems capable of solving complex problems, adapting to artificial environments, and build a platform that perhaps, some day, could too evolve self aware NN based agents.

In the following section I will discuss in more detail the Biological Neural Networks, how they work, how each neuron processes data, how the neuron encodes data, and how it connects to other neurons in the vast neural network we call our brain.

2.1 Biological Neural Network

Our brain is a vast graph of interconnected neurons, a vast biological neural network. A neuron is just a cell that can accept signals, and based on its chemical and geometrical properties, produce an output. There are roughly 100 billion neurons in the human brain, with trillions of connections between them. Though it might seem surprising that they can work so coherently, the result of which is us, our consciousness and intelligence, it is not surprising at all when we take into account that it took evolution billions of years and trillions of permutations to fine tune this system to get the result that we see today.

A typical neuron, as shown in Fig-2.1, is a cell composed of three main parts, the soma (cell body), the dendrites, and the axon. The soma is a compact body containing the nucleus, and other standard cell internals, and the dendrites and axon are filaments that extrude from it. A single neuron usually has a large number of dendrites, all of which branch profusely but usually retain their filament thickness. Unlike the case with the dendrites, a neuron has only a single axon, originating from a base of the neuron called the "axon hillock". The axon is usually a long filament which can branch and thus connect to multiple other neurons, with the axonal filament itself usually getting thinner the further it extends and the more it branches. *"Synaptic signals from other neurons are received by the soma and dendrites; signals to other neurons are transmitted by the axon. A typical synapse, then, is a contact between the axon of one neuron and a dendrite or soma of another. Synaptic signals may be excitatory or inhibitory. If the net excitation received by a neuron over a short period of time is large enough, the neuron generates a brief pulse called an action potential, which originates at the soma and propagates rapidly along the axon, activating synapses onto other neurons as it goes."* [22].

A multipolar neuron (Ex. spinal motor neuron)

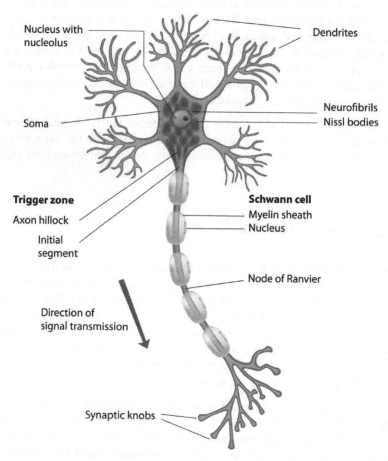

Fig. 2.1 A typical biological neuron.

It would be difficult to describe the biological neuron and its operation any more clearly than is done in the following quote [22] from the ever growing compendium of human knowledge, Wikipedia: *"Neurons are highly specialized for the processing and transmission of cellular signals. Given the diversity of functions performed by neurons in different parts of the nervous system, there is, as expected, a wide variety in the shape, size, and electrochemical properties of neurons. For instance, the soma of a neuron can vary from 4 to 100 micrometers in diameter.*

- *The soma is the central part of the neuron. It contains the nucleus of the cell, and therefore is where most protein synthesis occurs. The nucleus ranges from 3 to 18 micrometers in diameter.*
- *The dendrites of a neuron are cellular extensions with many branches, and metaphorically this overall shape and structure is referred to as a dendritic tree. This is where the majority of input to the neuron occurs.*
- *The axon is a finer, cable-like projection that can extend tens, hundreds, or even tens of thousands of times the diameter of the soma in length. The axon carries nerve signals away from the soma (and also carries some types of information back to it). Many neurons have only one axon, but this axon may— and usually will—undergo extensive branching, enabling communication with many target cells. The part of the axon where it emerges from the soma is called the axon hillock. Besides being an anatomical structure, the axon hillock is also the part of the neuron that has the greatest density of voltage-dependent sodium channels. This makes it the most easily-excited part of the neuron and the spike initiation zone for the axon: in electrophysiological terms it has the most negative action potential threshold. While the axon and axon hillock are generally involved in information outflow, this region can also receive input from other neurons.*
- *The axon terminal contains synapses, specialized structures where neurotransmitter chemicals are released to communicate with target neurons."*

The neuron to neuron signaling is a three step electrochemical process, as shown in Fig-2.2. First an ion based electrical signal is propagated down the axon, and towards every branch of that axon down to the axonal terminals. At the synaptic cleft of those axonal terminals, where the axon is in very close proximity to the cell bodies and dendrites of other neurons, the electrical signal is converted into a chemical one. The neurotransmitters, chemical signals, pass the distance between the axon terminal of the presynaptic neuron, and the dendrite (or soma, and sometimes even axons) of the post-synaptic neuron. How excited the post-synaptic neuron gets, the strength of the signal that the dendrites perceive from these neurotransmitters, all depend on the number of receptors that are present on the surface where the neurotransmitters contact the postsynaptic neuron. Thus, it is the number of, and type of receptors found on the soma and dendrites that weigh the incoming chemical signal, and decide whether it is excitatory when combined with other signals, or inhibitory. The receptors convert the chemical signals they perceive, back into electrical impulses. This train of signals continues its journey down the dendrites and towards the soma. Thus, as we can see, the complete signal is an electrical one, converted into a chemical one, and then converted back into an electrical one.

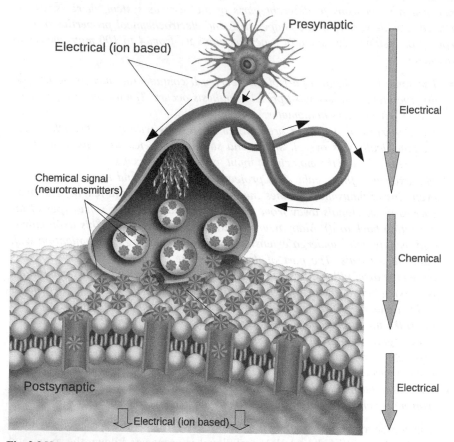

Fig. 2.2 Neuron to neuron signaling, a three step electrochemical process.

Furthermore, the way the signals are perceived is not based on a single spike, a single electrical impulse that some neuron A sends to neuron B, but the signal's frequency. The message is encoded not in the amplitude, but in the frequency. Evolutionary this makes perfect sense, in biological systems it would be difficult to regulate a perfect amplitude as it passes down the wires, but frequency is much simpler to manage using the imperfect biological wetware.

A neuron B could have hundreds to thousands of axons connecting to its soma and dendrites. The way a neuron calculates whether it should produce an output signal, also called action potential or simply spike, at any given time, depends on the intensity of the electrical signal at the axon hillock at that time, as shown in Fig-2.3. Since the intensity of the signal experienced by the axon hillock (trigger zone) depends on how many spikes at that moment excite that region at the same time, the signal is based not only on how many spikes there are, but also on the shape of the neuron and the timing of the signals. The neuron performs a spatio-temporal integration of the incoming signals. If the excitation level at a given time surpasses its threshold, an action potential is generated and passed down the axon. Furthermore, the output signal's amplitude is independent of signals arriving at the axon hillock, it is an all-or-none type of system. The neuron either produces an action potential (if there is enough excitation at the trigger zone), or it does not. Rather than encoding the message in the action potential's amplitude, it is encoded in the frequency, and the frequency depends on the spatiotemporal signal integration and processing that occur within the soma and at the axon hillock.

The signal is based on the spatial properties of the incoming spikes, because if the axon hillock is located in a strange position, or its properties are distributed in space within the neuron differently, it will perceive the incoming signals in a different way. For example, thinking purely mathematically, if the trigger zone is somehow spread thinly over a great area, then to trigger it we would need to send electrical signals that intersect on this wide area, the distribution of the incoming action potentials would have to cover this wide area, all the different places of the axon hillock that sense the electrical signals. On the other hand, if the axon hillock is concentrated at a single point, then to produce the same output we would need to send just a few of the signals towards that point.

On the other hand, the neuron's signal processing is temporal based processing because, if for example 10 spikes come across the axon hillock, each at a rate of 1ms after the other, the axon hillock feels an excitation of only 1 spike every 1ms, which might not be enough excitation beyond the threshold to trigger an output action potential. On the other hand, if 10 spikes come from different sides, and all come across the axon hillock at the same time, the intensity now is 10 spikes rather than one, during the same single ms, which will overcome the biological threshold and the neuron will send an action potential down the axon.

Thus, the output signal, an electrical spike encoded signal produced by the neuron, is based on the spatial and temporal properties of its input signals. Something similar is shown in Fig-2.3, where I loosely defined the timings of when the spikes will arrive at the trigger zone using t which defines the arrival at the trigger zone, t-1 which defines arrival at the trigger zone in 1 delta, t-2 which defines the arrival at the trigger zone in 2 deltas, and so on. At *t-1* we see that there will be 4 spikes, at *t-2* only 2. If it requires 3 spikes to overcome the threshold (which itself is defined by the shape and chemical properties at the axon hillock) and to set off an action potential down the axon, then the signals arriving at *t-2*, when they do finally arrive at the hillock in 2 deltas (time units), will not trigger an action potential, while the signals currently at *t-1* will generate a spike when they finally arrive at the trigger zone.

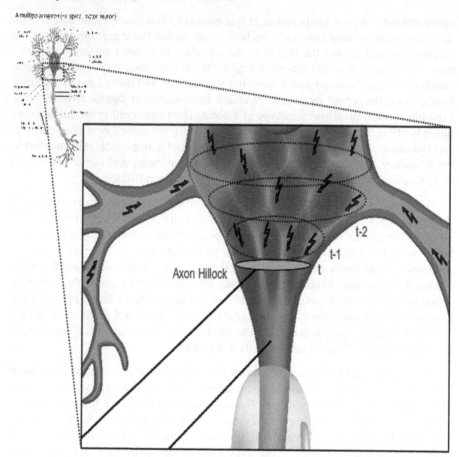

Fig. 2.3 Spatiotemporal signal integration.

Furthermore, the neurons don't just accept incoming signals and produce outgoing signals, the neurons also change over time based on the signals they process. This change in the way neurons respond to signals by adding more receptors to the dendrites, or subtracting receptors from the dendrites, or modifying the way their receptors work, is one of the processes by which a neural network learns and changes its excitability towards certain signals, it is how we accumulate experience and form memories. Other ways by which a neural network learns is through the axons branching and making new connections, or breaking old connections. And finally the NN changes in the way it processes signals through having the very fluid in which the neurons are bathed changed and chemically modified, through drugs or other means for example.

The most important part to take away from this chapter is that the biological neurons output frequency encoded signals, and that they process the incoming frequency encoded signals through spatiotemporal integration of those signals. And that the neurons can change over time based on the signals they process, the neurons change biologically, they change their information processing strategies, and they can form new connections to other neurons, and break old ones. This process is called *neuronal plasticity*, or just plasticity. In the next section we will discuss artificial neural networks, how they function, and how they can differ from their biological counterparts.

2.2 Artificial Neural Network

Artificial neural networks (NN), as shown in Fig-2.4, are simulated biological neural networks to different levels of precision. In this section we will cover the typical artificial neural network, which are not perfect simulations. A typical artificial neuron, aka neurode, *does not* simulate a biological neuron at the atomic, or even molecular level. Artificial neurons are abstractions of biological neurons, they represent the essentials of biological neurons, their nonlinear signal integration, plasticity, and concurrency.

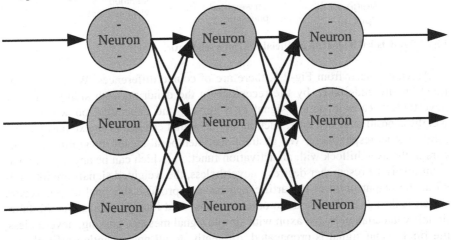

Fig. 2.4 An artificial neural network.

As shown in Fig-2.5, like a biological neuron, an artificial one accepts signals through its artificial dendrites, processes those signals in its artificial soma, and outputs the processed signals to other neurons it is connected with. It is a concise representation of what a biological neuron does. A biological neuron simply accepts signals, weighs each signal, where the weight depends on the receptors on the dendrites on which the axons from other neurons intercepted, then based on its internal structure and chemical composition, produces the final frequency encoded output and passes that output onwards to other neurons. In the same way, an artificial neuron accepts signals, weighs each signal using its weight parameters, integrates all the weighted signals through its activation function which simulates the biological neuron's spatiotemporal processing at the axon hillock, and then propagates the final output signal to other neurons it is connected to.

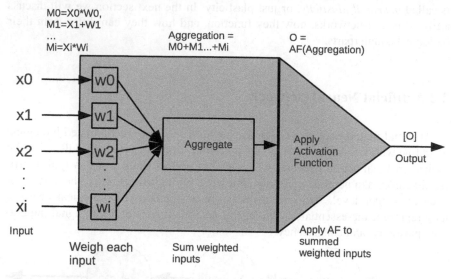

Fig. 2.5 A detailed look at an artificial neuron's schematic.

As can be seen from Fig-2.5, there are of course differences. We abstract the functionality undertaken by the receptors on the dendrites with simple weights, nevertheless, each incoming signal is weighted, and depending on whether the weight is positive or negative, each incoming signal can act as an excitatory or inhibitory one, respectively. We abstract spatiotemporal signal integration that occurs at the axon hillock with an activation function (which can be anything, and as complex as the researcher desires), nevertheless, the weighted signals are integrated at the output point of the artificial neuron to produce the final output vector, which is then passed onwards to other neurons. And finally, we abstract the functionality undertaken by the axon with simple signal message passing, nevertheless, the final output signal is propagated, diligently, to all postsynaptic artificial neurons.

The biological neural network is a vast graph of parallel processing simple biological signal integrators, and the artificial neural network too is a vast graph of parallel processing simple signal integrators. The neurons in a biological neural network can adapt, and change its functionality over time, which too can be done in artificial neural network through simulated neural plasticity, as we will discuss in later sections, and eventually implement in the NN systems we will build ourselves.

There is one thing though that differs significantly in the typical artificial neural networks, and the biological neural networks. The neurons in a biological NN frequency encode their signals, whereas in the artificial NNs, the neurons amplitude encode their signals. What has more flexibility? Frequency encoded NN systems or the amplitude encoded ones? It is difficult to say, but we do know that both, biological and artificial neural networks are Turing complete [4], which means that both possess the same amount of flexibility. The implications of the fact that both systems are universal Turing machines is that even if a single artificial neuron does not do as much, or perform as a complex computation as a single biological neuron, we could put a few artificial neurons together into an artificial neural circuit, and this artificial neural circuit will have the same processing power and flexibility as a biological neuron. On the other hand, note that frequency encoding signals takes more time, because it will at least take the amount of time between multiple spikes in the spike train of the signal for the message to be forwarded (since it is the frequency, the time between the spikes that is important), whereas in an amplitude encoded message, the single spike, its amplitude, carries all the information needed.

How much of the biology and chemistry of the biological neuron is actually needed? After all, the biological neuron is the way it is now due to the fact that it was the first *randomly found solution*, the easiest solution found by evolution. Wetware has no choice but to use ions instead of electrons for electrical signal propagation. Wetware has no choice but to use frequency encoding, instead of amplitude encoding, because wetware is so much more unreliable than hardware (but the biological neural network as a whole, due to a high level of interconnections, is highly fault tolerant, reliable, and precise). The human neuron is not a perfect processing element, it is simply the processing element that was found through evolution, by chance, the easiest one to evolve over time, that's all. Thus, perhaps a typical plasticity incorporating artificial neuron has all the right features already. We have after all evolved ALife organisms with just a few dozen neurons that exhibited interesting and evolutionary appropriate behaviors with regards to food foraging and hunting [5,6,7]. We do know one thing though, the limits of speed, signal propagation, neural plasticity, life span of the neuron, integration of new neural systems over the organism's lifetime, are all limited in wetware by biology. *None of these limitations are present in hardware*, the only speed limit of signal propagation is that of light in a hardware based neural computing system. The non biological neural computer can add new neural circuits to itself over lifetime, and that lifetime span is unlimited, given that hardware upkeep is possible.

I think that amplitude encoded signaling is just as powerful, and the activation functions of the artificial neurons, the integration of the weighted signals, is also as flexible, or can be as flexible as the spatiotemporal signal integration performed by a biological neuron. An artificial neuron can simulate different kinds of receptor densities on the dendrites by different values for weights. An artificial neuron can simulate different kinds of neuron types through the use of different kinds of activation functions. Even plasticity is easy to add to an artificial neuron. And of course, there are also artificial spiking neural network systems [23,24,25], which use frequency encoding like a biological neural network does. There is absolutely no reason why artificial neural networks cannot achieve the same level of performance, robustness, and intelligence, as biological neural networks have.

2.2.1 The Neurode in Detail

In this section we will do a more detailed analysis of the architecture of an artificial neuron, how it processes an incoming signal, and how such an artificial neuron could be represented in software. In Fig-2.6 we use the schematic of an artificial neuron in a simple example where the neuron receives two incoming signals. Each of the signals is a vector. The third signal is not from any other neuron, but is simply a bias value, which modifies the neuron's processing. The neuron processes the signal based on its internals, and then forwards its output, in a vector form, to postsynaptic neurons. In the figure, the "axon" of the neuron branches into 3 strands.

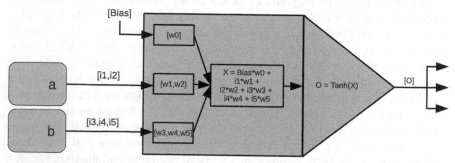

Fig. 2.6 An artificial neuron in action, receiving signals from two other elements, a and b.

Artificial neurons accept vector input signals, and output a vector signal of length 1. Each input signal is weighted; each element in the input vector is multiplied by a weight in a weight list associated with that input vector, and that particular element in the input vector. Thus, the integration of the incoming signals is done by calculating a dot product of the incoming vectors and the weight vectors associated with those input vectors. In the above figure, there are two incoming signals from other elements, and a bias signal (which we'll talk about next). The incoming signal from element 'a' is a vector signal of length 2, the signal from element 'b', is a vector of length 3, and the bias signal is a vector of length 1. The neuron has a weight list for each incoming signal. The weight lists weigh the importance of each input vector. The way we integrate the input signal is by calculating a dot product of the weights and the input signals. Once the dot product is calculated, we compute the output of the neuron, Output = F(X), where F is the activation function, and X = Dot_Product + Bias. The neuron then packages this result into a vector of length 1, like so: [Output], and then fans out this output vector to the elements that it is connected to. A sigmoid function, or hyperbolic tangent, is the typically used activation function in artificial neurons. A multi-layered feed forward neural circuit composed of neurons using sigmoid activation functions can act as a universal function approximator [8], which means that a neural network composed of such neural circuits can do anything.

Now regarding the bias input, it is simply an input vector which is used to increase the flexibility of the neuron by giving it an extra weight that it can use to skew the dot product of the input signals. Not every neuron needs to have a bias input, it's optional, and if the weight for the bias input is 0, then that is equivalent to a neuron that does not have a bias input at all. The neuron can use the bias to modify the point at which the weighted dot product produces a positive output when passed through the activation function, in which case the bias acts as a threshold. If the bias is a large positive number, then no matter what the input will be, the neuron has a much greater chance of outputting a positive value. If the bias is a negative number, then the incoming signals will have to be high enough to overcome this bias for the neuron to output a positive value. In essence, the bias controls how excitable in general the neuron is, whereas the weights of the non bias inputs control how significant those inputs are, and whether the neuron considers them excitatory or inhibitory. In future figures we will use a much simpler neuron schematic than the one we used in Fig-2.6. Having now demonstrated the inner workings of a neuron, in the future when diagramming a neuron we will use a circle, with multiple inputs, and an output link that fans out the neuron's output signal.

When we connect a few of these neurons together in the right topology and set their weights to the right values, forming a small neural network like the one in Fig-2.7, such a neural network could perform useful tasks. In Fig-2.7 for example, the neural circuit composed of 3 neurons calculates the XOR of the inputs. We can demonstrate that this neural circuit does indeed calculate the XOR of its inputs by feeding it the signals from a XOR truth table, and comparing its output to the proper output of the XOR logical operator. The input signals, in this case a single vector of length 2, is fed from the truth table to the neurons A and B, each neuron calculates an output signal based on its weights, and then forwards that signal to neuron C. Then neuron C calculates an output based on the inputs it receives from neuron A and B, and then forwards that output onwards. It is this final output, the output of the neuron C, that is the output of the neural circuit. And it is this output that we will compare to the proper output that a XOR logical operator would produce

Table 1. The XOR truth table, and the vector form which can be used as input/output signals of a NN. In this table, 1 == true, -1 == false.

Pattern	[X1, X2, Y]	Input: [X1, X2]	Output: [Y]
1	[-1,-1,-1]	[-1,-1]	[-1]
2	[-1, 1, 1]	[-1, 1]	[1]
3	[1,-1, 1]	[1,-1]	[1]
4	[1, 1,-1]	[1, 1]	[-1]

when fed the same input signals as the neural circuit at hand. The XOR truth table is shown in the following table, where X1 and X2 are the inputs to the XOR logical operator, and Y is the XOR operator's output.

We will now walk through the neural circuit, neuron by neuron, step by step, and calculate its output for every input in the XOR truth table. As shown in Fig-2.7, the neural circuit has 3 neurons, A, B, and C. Neuron A has the following weight vector: [2.1081,2.2440,2.2533], where: W1=2.1081, W2=2.2440, and Bias=2.2533. Neuron B has the following weight vector: [3.4963,-2.7463,3.5200], where W1=3.4963, W2=-2.7463, and Bias = 3.5200. Finally, Neuron C has the following weight vector: [-2.5983,2.7354,2.7255], where W1=-2.5983, W2=2.7354, and Bias=2.7255. With this information we can now calculate the output of the neural circuit for every input vector, as shown in Fig-2.7.

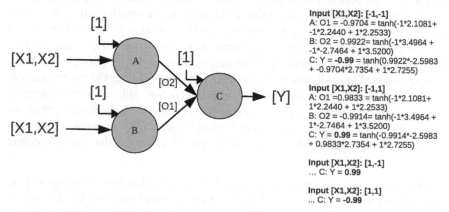

Fig. 2.7 Calculating the output of the XOR neural circuit.

As can be seen in the above figure, the neural circuit simulates a XOR. In this manner we could even build a universal Turing machine, by combining such XOR neural circuits. Another network of neurons with another set of activation functions and neural weights would yield something different...

The main question though is, how do we figure out the synaptic weights and the NN topologies needed to solve some problem, how for example did we figure out the weights for each of these 3 neurons to get this neural circuit to act as a XOR operator? The answer is, a learning algorithm, an automated algorithm that sets up the weights. There are many types of algorithms that can be used to setup the synaptic weights within a NN. Some require that we have some kind of training sample first, a set of inputs and outputs, which a mathematical function can then use to set up the weights of a neural network. Other algorithms do not require such prior knowledge, all that is needed is for each NN to be gaged on how well it performed and how its performance on some problem compares to those of other NNs. We will discuss the various learning algorithms in section 2.4, but before we move on to that section, we will first cover the standard Neural Network terminology when it comes to NN topological structures, and discuss the two types of basic NN topologies, feedforward and recurrent, in the next section.

2.3 Neural Networks and Neural Network Based Systems

A neuron by itself is a simple processing element. It is when we interconnect these neurons together, in parallel and in series, when we form a neural network (NN), that true computational power emerges. A NN is usually composed of multiple layers, as the example shows in Fig. 2.8. The depth of a NN is the number of layers that compose it.

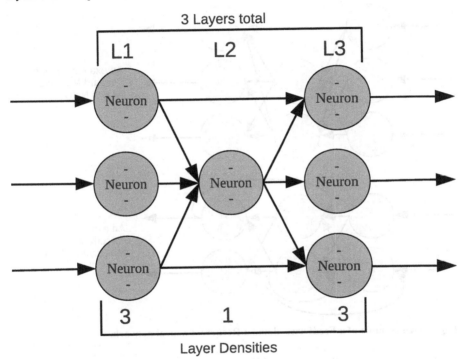

Fig. 2.8 A multi-layered NN, with a NN composed of 3 layers. The first layer has 3 neurons, the second layer has 1 neuron, and the third layer has 3 neurons.

Using layers when discussing and developing NN topologies gives us an ability to see the depth of a NN, it gives us the ability to calculate the minimum number of neurons the input has to be processed by in series, before a NN produces an output. The depth tells us the minimum amount of non parallel processing that has to be done by a distributed NN. Finally, assigning each neuron a layer allows us to see whether the connections from one neuron to another are feed forward, meaning some neuron A sends signals to a neuron B which is in front of neuron A, or whether the connection is recurrent, meaning some neuron A sends a signal to neuron B which itself is behind A, and whose original output signal is either fed directly to neuron A, or was forwarded to other neurons and then eventually got to neuron A before it itself produced its output signal (the recurrent signal that it sent back to neuron B). Indeed in recurrent NNs, one can have feedforward and feed-back loop based neural circuits, and a neuron B could have sent a signal to neuron A, which then processed it and sent its output back to neuron B... When a neural network is composed of neurons whose output signals go only in the forward facing direction, such a network is called a feedforward NN. If the NN also includes some recurrent connections, then it is a recurrent NN. An example of a feedforward and a recurrent neural network is shown in Fig-2.9.

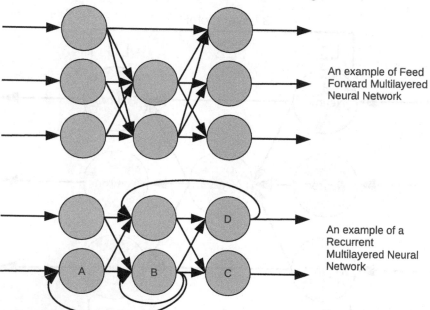

An example of Feed Forward Multilayered Neural Network

An example of a Recurrent Multilayered Neural Network

Fig. 2.9 An example of a Feedforward and a Recurrent neural network.

As can be seen in the recurrent NN example, neuron A receives a signal from somewhere, processes it, sends a signal to neuron B, which processes the signals sent to it and then sends an output signal to neuron C, D, but also a recurrent signal back to A and itself.

2.3.1 Recurrent Neural Networks and Memory Loops

What is significant about recurrent neural networks is that they can form memory circuits. For example, the Fig-2.10 shows four examples of a recurrent NN. Note that in 2.10A, the neuron sends a signal back to itself. This means that at every moment, it is aware of its previous output, and that output is taken into account when producing a new output. The neuron has memory of its previous action, and depending on the weight for that recurrent connection, its previous signal at time step T can play a large or a small part in its output at a time step T+1. In 2.10C neuron *1* has a recurrent connection to neuron *2*, which outputs a signal back to neuron *1*. This neural circuit too forms a memory system, because this circuit does not simply process signals, but takes into account the information from time step T-2, when making a decision with regards to the output at time step T. Why T-2?, because at T-2 neuron *1* outputs a signal to *2* rather than itself, it is

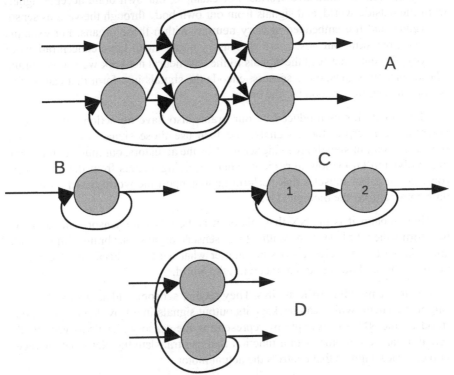

Fig. 2.10 An example of recurrent NNs that could potentially represent memory loops. A is a general, 3 layer recurrent neural network, with 3 recurrent connections. B is a self recurrent neuron, which thus has a trailing memory of its previous output, depending on its weight with its own recurrent connection. C is a two layer recurrent NN, with neuron-2 receiving a signal from neuron-1, which processes the signal that came from neuron-2 in the first place, thus neuron-2 receives a signal that it itself produced T-2 steps before, processed by neuron-1. Finally, D is a one layer recurrent NN, which has the topology of a flip flop circuit.

then at T-1 that *2* outputs a signal to *1*, and it is only at time T that *1* outputs a signal after processing an input from some other element, and a signal it output at T-2, which was processed by *2* before coming back to *1* again. Thus this memory loop is deeper, and more involved. Even more complex systems can of course be easily evolved, or engineered by hand.

2.3.2 A Neural Network Based System

We have discussed neural networks, and in all figures I've shown the NNs as having input signals sent to them from the outside, but from where? In real implementations the NNs have to interact with the real or simulated world, and the signals they produce need to be somehow used to accomplish useful tasks and act upon those real or simulated worlds. For example, our own brain accepts signals from the outside world, and signals from our own body through the various sensory organs, and the embedded sensory neurons within those organs. For example our eyes, our skin, our nose... are all sensory organs with large concentrations of sensory elements that feed the signals to the vast neural network we call our brain. These sensory organs, these sensors, encode the signals in a form that can be forwarded to, and understood by, the brain.

The output signals produced by our brains also have no action without some actuators to interpret those signals, and then use those signals to act upon the world. The output signals are made sense of by the actuators, our muscles for example evolved to know how to respond when receiving signals from the motor neurons, and it is our muscles that perform actions upon the world based on the signals coming from the biological NN.

Thus, though it is the NN that thinks, it is the NN with sensors and actuators that forms the whole system. Without our sensory organs, our brain is in the dark, and without our muscles, it does not matter what we think, because we can have no affect on, and no way to interact with, the world.

It is the same with artificial NNs. They require sensors, and actuators. A sensor can be a camera, which can package its output signals in a way that can be understood by the NN, for example by representing the sensory signals as vectors. An actuator can be a motor, with a function that can translate the NN's output vector into electrical signals that controls the actual motor.

Thus it is the whole thing, the sensors connected to and sending the sensory signals to the NN, and the NN connected to and sending its output signals to the actuators, that forms the full system, as shown in Fig-2.11. In this book we will refer to such a complete and self contained system, the Sensors connected to the Neural Network, which itself is connected to Actuators, as the NN based system, or NN based agent. It is only when we are discussing the NN in isolation, the to-pology of a NN for example, that I will use the term NN on its own. When it's clear from the discussion though, the two terms will sometimes be used inter-changeably.

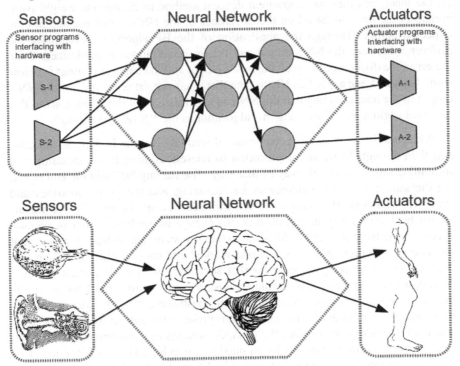

Fig. 2.11 The Biological and the Artificial Neural Network Systems compared.

Having now discussed the basics of NNs, the different types of topologies, and what a complete NN system is, and what parts form a NN system, we now move forward and briefly cover how the classical, typical NNs learn and get trained. In the following sections we will discuss the typical algorithms used to modify the weights of the neurons belonging to some NN applied to a problem, and the dif-ference between the term learning and training.

2.4 Learning Vs. Training

Though most of the time you will hear the terms *learning* and *training* used in-terchangeably when people discuss the processes and algorithms that modify the weights and the topology of a NN such that it is more fit, such that it is able to solve some problem it is applied to, in this book we will discriminate between the two. Take for example the Back Propagation (BP) Learning algorithm we will discuss in the next section. In that algorithm we have a list of tuples of inputs and expected outputs. The inputs are the vectors we would feed to a NN system, and the outputs are the expected outputs we'd like the NN system to produce. The way the BP learning algorithm works is by letting a neural network output a vector based on the input, and then use a gradient descent method to change the weight parameters of the neurons based on the difference of the NN's actual output, and the expected output. Through the application of the BP algorithm, eventually the difference between the NN's output and the expected output, is minimized. Once the error, the difference between the NN's output and the expected output is below some threshold, we apply this NN to data that it has not yet seen, and use the NN's output as the result, hoping that the NN can generalize from the training set to this new real world data. When using this algorithm, is the NN really learning?

When we think of learning, we think of studying, of one looking at the data, and then through logic, and explanation to oneself, coming to a conclusion that something should work this way or that way. The starting NN, and the end result, are the same NN, and the change to the reasoning, and thus to the topology and synaptic weights is self initiated and self inflicted. We are the same before and after we learn something, in a sense that this change in our logic in our perception was not done from the outside by some external system, but instead, it was us that has done the change, it was us that had worked and came to the conclusion that another way of thinking is better, or that something works this particular way... That is learning. In the BP algorithm we just discussed above, the NNs are static, they are not learning. We simply bring into existence a NN, see whether how it behaves now is appropriate and whether it represents the answer to some question, and then we change its weights, the synaptic weights of the neurons are modified and optimized from the outside, by an outside supervisor. The NN is trained. This is something that is referred to in the standard Neural Network literature as Supervised Learning, where the NN has a supervisor that tells it whether its answers are right or wrong, and it is the supervisor (an external algorithm) that modifies the NN so that the next time it will hopefully produce a better answer.

In true learning, the NNs are able to change on their own through experience. The NN only lives ones, and during that lifetime it is modified through experience. And what experience it is exposed to is to a great degree guided by the NN itself. In the way that what we choose to expose ourselves to, influences what we learn, and how our perspectives, how we think, and what we know, changes. The phenomenon of the neural networks changing and adapting through experience, is due to neural plasticity. Neural plasticity is the ability of the neuron to change due to experience. Thus for example if we create a large NN system composed of plastic (those possessing plasticity) neurons, and then release it into a virtual environment and it improves on its behavior, it learns how to survive in the environment through experience... that is what I would refer to as learning. This is called Unsupervised Learning, and indeed that is completely possible to do in artificial neural networks, by for example giving each neurode the functionality which allows it to change its information processing strategy based on the signals it processes.

Thus the main idea to be taken from this section with regards to the difference between what I call training and learning, is this: The process of training a neural network is accomplished by changing its weights and topology from the outside, by some algorithm external to the NN based system. On the other hand, a neural network is learning if it is adjusting and improving itself of its own volition, through its exposure to experience and the change of its NN topology and neural parameters. Thus it would be possible to bootstrap a NN system, by first training some static system, then adding plasticity to the NN, and then releasing this boot-strapped NN system into some environment, where based on the bootstrapped part it is able to survive, and as it survives it is being exposed to the environment, at which point its plastic neural system changes and adapts, and the NN learns. We will explore this further in later chapters, after we've built a neuroevolutionary system that can evolve NN systems, and where the NN systems are then released into some simulated environment. We will evolve NN systems which have plastic-ity, we will evolve them so that they can use that plasticity to *learn* new things on their own.

In the following two sections we will discuss the typical supervised and unsu-pervised training and learning algorithms respectively.

2.5 Neural Network Supervised "Learning" Algorithms

Supervised learning is a machine learning approach to inferring a target func-tion from a training data set composed of a set of training examples. Each training example is composed of an input vector, and a desired or expected output vector. The desired output vector is also referred to as the supervisory signal. When ap-plied to neural networks, supervised learning, or training, is an approach to the modification and automation of weight setting of a neural network through the use of a supervisor, or external system, that compares the NN's output to a correct, pre-calculated output, and thus expected output, and then based on the difference between the NN's output and the expected output, modifies the weights of the neurons in the NN based on some optimization algorithm. A supervised "learning" algorithm can only be applied to problems where you already know the answers, where you can build a *training set*. A training set is a list of tuples, where every tuple is composed of the input vector, and the expected output vector: [{Input, ExpectedOutput}...]. Thus we need to know the outputs ahead of time, so that we can train the neural network before we can use it with input signals it has not yet seen. Note, this is not always possible. For example, let's say we wish to create a neurocontroller for a robot, to survive in some environment. There is no training set for such a problem, there is no list of tuples where for every camera input that act as robots eyes there is an expected and correct move that the robot must make.

That is usually never the case, in fact, we do not know what the right move is, if we knew that, we would not need to create the neurocontroller. Another example is the creation of a neurocontroller that can make a robotic arm reach for some point in space. Again, if we knew what the right combination of moves that the motors needed to make, we would not need for the NN to figure that out.

The most widely used of such supervised algorithms, is the Error Backpropagation algorithm [10]. The backpropagation algorithm uses gradient descent to look for the minimum error function between the NN's output, and the expected output. The most typical NN topology that this algorithm is applied to, is a standard feedforward neural network (though there is a BP algorithm for a recurrent NN topology too). As we discussed, a supervised learning algorithm trains a NN to approximate some function implicitly, by training the NN on a set of inputs and expected outputs. The error that must be minimized is the error between the NN's output, and the expected output.

Because we will concentrate on neuroevolution, we will not cover this algorithm in great detail. But an extensive coverage of this supervised learning algorithm can be found in: [11,12]. In summary, the training of the NN through the backprop algorithm works as follows:

1. Create a multi-layered feed forward neural network, where each neuron has a random set of weights. Set the neurons in the first/input layer to have X number of weights, plus bias, where X is the vector length of the input vectors. Set the last/output layer to have Y number of neurons, where Y is the length of the expected output vector.
2. **For every tuple(i) in the training list, DO:**
   3. Feedforward Phase:

      1.   Forward Input(i) vector to the neurons in the first layer of NN.
      2.   Gather the output signals from the neurons in the last layer of NN.
      3.   Combine the gathered signals into an Output(i) vector.

   4. Backprop Phase:

      1.   Calculate the error between the NN's Output(i) and ExpectedOutput(i)
      2.   Propagate the errors back to the neurons, and update the weights of the neurons based on their contribution to that error. The weights are updated through gradient descent such that the error is decreased.
      3.   The errors are propagated recurrently from the last neural layer to the first.

5. **EndDO**
6. Repeat steps 2-5 until the average total error between the NN's outputs and the expected outputs is less than some chosen value e.

Schematically, the feedforward phase and the error backprop phase, is demonstrated in Fig. 2.12.

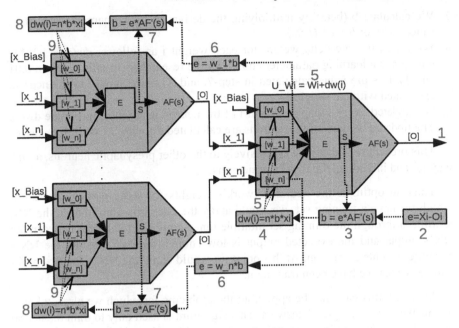

Fig. 2.12 The schematic of the backprop learning algorithm.

The steps of recursively updating the synaptic weights of all the neurons in the feedforward NN based on the error between the NN's output and the expected output is demonstrated by the figure through the step numbers. Starting with step *1*, the NN's output is O, and the expected output is X. If there were more than one output neurons, then each neuron *i* would produce an output Oi, and for each Oi there would be an expected output Xi. The meaning of the steps is elaborated on in the following list:

1. The neuron in the output layer of the feedforward NN produces an output O.
2. The error of the neuron's output as compared to the expected output is e, calculated as: $e = Xi\text{-}Oi$ where Xi and Oi are the output of neuron i, and expected output i, respectively, if there are i number of output neurons in the NN.
3. We calculate b (beta) by multiplying the derivative of the activation function by e: $b = e*AF'(S)$, where S is the dot product of the neuron's input signals and synaptic weights for those input signals.
4. We then calculate the delta (change in) weight for each weight i as follows: $dw(i) = n*b*Xi$, where n is a learning parameter chosen by the researcher (usually between 0.01 and 1), b is the value calculated in step-3, and Xi is the input i to the neuron, associated with the weight i.
5. We updated every synaptic weight i of the neuron using the appropriate $dw(i)$ for each Wi. The updated weight is produced through: $U\_Wi = Wi+dw(i)$.
6. The next e *(error)* is recursively calculated for every presynaptic neuron using the equation: $e=Wi*b$, where Wi is the synaptic weight associated with the neuron whose output was Xi.

7. We calculate b (beta) by multiplying the derivative of the neuron's activation function by e: $b = e*AF'(s)$.
8. We then calculate delta weight for each weight i as follows: $dw(i) = n*b*Xi$ where n is a learning parameter chosen by the researcher (usually between 0.01 and 1), b is the value calculated in step-7, and Xi is the input i to the neuron, associated with the weight i.
9. We updated every synaptic weight i of the neuron using the appropriate dw(i). The updated weights of the neurons are calculated through: $U\_Wi = Wi+dw(i)$.

This procedure is continued recursively to the other presynaptic neurons, all the way to, and including, the first layer neurons.

Thus, to optimize the neural network's weights for some particular task for which we have a training set, we would apply the backprop algorithm to the NN, running it through the training set multiple times, until the total error between the NN's output and the expected output is low enough that we consider the NN's synaptic weights a solution. At this point we would apply the NN to the real problem for which we have been training it.

As noted, this can only be applied to the problems for which we already know the answers, or a sample of answers. This algorithm is used only to train the neural network, once it is trained, its weights will remain static, and the neural circuit is used as a program, unchanging for the remainder of its life. There are numerous extensions and improvements to this basic algorithm, covered in the referenced texts. But no matter the improvements, at the end of the day it is still a supervised approach, and the resulting NN is static. In the next section we will briefly discuss unsupervised learning algorithms, the addition of plasticity to the neurons of a NN, and other methods which allow the NN to self organize, and adapt and change through the interaction with the environment, and/or data it comes across.

2.6 Neural Network Unsupervised Learning Algorithms

Unsupervised learning refers to the problem of trying to determine structure in incoming, unlabeled data. In such a learning algorithm, because the input is unlabeled, unlike the case with the training data set discussed in section 2.5, here there is no error or reward signals which can be used to guide the modification process of neural weights based on the difference between the output and the expected output. Instead, the NN self modifies its parameters based on the inputs and its own outputs through some algorithm. There are two general kinds of such learning algorithms; a learning algorithm can either be a system that has a global view of the NN, and which uses this global view to modify neural weights (kohonen, competitive...), or a learning algorithm can be a local on, embedded in each neuron and letting it modify its own synaptic weights based on its inputs and outputs (hebbian, modulated...).

Our brains do not have an external supervisor, our brain, the biological neurons that compose it, use different types of unsupervised learning, in a sense that they have plasticity and they change based on their experience. There is evidence that the hippocampus plays a very important role [13] in the formation of new memories, which means that a neural circuit like the hippocampus can modulate, or affect the topology and neural weights located in other parts of the brain, other neural networks. Thus, in a sense there is also modulation of learning algorithms at a more global scale of the neural network, and not just at the level of single neurons. Our brains of course have evolved the different features, the different rates of neural learning through experience, and the different neural circuits within our brain which affect and modulate other parts of our brain...

Though we could include a form of hebbian learning in neurons (discussed next), and create a large homogeneous hebbian or kohonen neural network... it will still be nothing more than a clustering network, there will be no self awareness within it. To create a truly intelligent neurocomputing system, we need to combine static neurons, neurons with plasticity, and different forms of unsupervised learning algorithms... all into a vast neural network. And combine it in a way that all these different parts work together perfectly, and allow for the whole emergent NN system to truly learn, which is the case with evolved biological neural networks.

In this section we cover the unsupervised learning approaches, how to make neurons plastic, how to allow neurons to change their own weights through experience... The actual method of putting all these various systems together into a vast network that can have the potential of true learning, will be the subject of the rest of this book, with the method taken to accomplish this goal, being evolution. For the sake of exposure, and because we will use these particular unsupervised forms of NN learning once we've developed our basic neuroevolutionary platform and began expanding it beyond the current state of the art, we will briefly cover 4 particular unsupervised learning algorithms next.

2.6.1 Hebbian Learning

In 1949 Donald Hebb proposed a computational algorithm to explain memory and the computational adaptation process within the brain, he proposed a rule we now refer to as the Hebbian learning. The Hebbian learning is a neural learning algorithm that emulates plasticity exhibited by neurons, and which has been confirmed to a great extent to exist in the visual cortex [14].

As Hebb noted [26], "The general idea is an old one, that any two cells or systems of cells that are repeatedly active at the same time will tend to become 'associated', so that activity in one facilitates activity in the other.", or more concisely: "neurons that fire together, wire together".

The basic Hebbian rule for associative learning can be written as follows: For every weight w(i) in a neuron B, we add to the weight w(i) the value dw(i) where *dw(i) = x(i)*O.* This equation simply states that if we have a neuron B, which is connected from a number of other elements, and which produces an output *O* after processing the presynaptic *x(i)* input signals, and has a weight *w(i)* for every input signal x(i), then the change in the weight w(i) is x(i)*O. We can see that if both x(i) and O have the same sign, then the change in synaptic weight is positive and the weight will increase, whereas if x(i) and O are of opposite signs, then the weight will decrease for the synaptic connection between neuron B and the pre-synaptic element which sent it the signal x(i). So then for example, imagine that we have a NN with 2 neurons, in which neuron A is connected to neuron B. If neuron A sends a positive signal to neuron B, and this makes neuron B output a positive signal, then B's synaptic weight for the connection coming from A increases. On the other hand, if A's signal to B makes B produce a negative signal, then B's synaptic weight associated with A's signals is lowered. In this manner the two neurons synchronize. Fig-2.13 demonstrates this scenario and shows the hebbian rule in action.

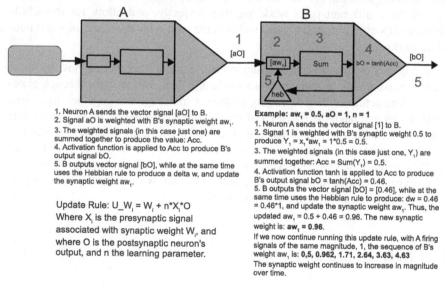

1. Neuron A sends the vector signal [aO] to B.
2. Signal aO is weighted with B's synaptic weight aw_1.
3. The weighted signals (in this case just one) are summed together to produce the value: Acc.
4. Activation function is applied to Acc to produce B's output signal bO.
5. B outputs vector signal [bO], while at the same time uses the Hebbian rule to produce a delta w, and update the synaptic weight aw_1.

Update Rule: $U\_W_i = W_i + n*X_i*O$
Where X_i is the presynaptic signal associated with synaptic weight W_i, and where O is the postsynaptic neuron's output, and n the learning parameter.

Example: $aw_1 = 0.5$, $aO = 1$, $n = 1$
1. Neuron A sends the vector signal [1] to B.
2. Signal 1 is weighted with B's synaptic weight 0.5 to produce $Y_1 = x_1*aw_1 = 1*0.5 = 0.5$.
3. The weighted signals (in this case just one, Y_1) are summed together: Acc = Sum(Y_1) = 0.5.
4. Activation function tanh is applied to Acc to produce B's output signal bO = tanh(Acc) = 0.46.
5. B outputs the vector signal [bO] = [0.46], while at the same time uses the Hebbian rule to produce: dw = 0.46 = 0.46*1, and update the synaptic weight aw_1. Thus, the updated $aw_1 = 0.5 + 0.46 = 0.96$. The new synaptic weight is: $aw_1 = 0.96$.
If we now continue running this update rule, with A firing signals of the same magnitude, 1, the sequence of B's weight aw_1 is: **0,5, 0.962, 1.71, 2.64, 3.63, 4.63**
The synaptic weight continues to increase in magnitude over time.

Fig. 2.13 Neuroplasticity through Hebbian learning.

In the above figure, we can see that just from one signal coming from Neuron *A*, a signal that was positive and thus producing a positive delta weight with regards to the positive synaptic weight of B, B's neural weight nearly doubled for the connection with *A*. A few more signals from *A*, and the weight aw1 would have grown significantly larger, and eventually drowned out any other weights to other links. Thus the problem with the original and very simple Hebbian learning rule is that it is computationally unstable. For example, as noted, the weights do not saturate, they can continue growing indefinitely. If that does occur, then the weights that grow fastest will eventually drown out all other signals, and the output of the neuron, being a sigmoid of tanh, will always be 1. Thus eventually the neuron will stop truly discerning between signals, since its weights will be so large that no matter the input, 1 will always be the neuron's output. Another problem is that, unlike in a biological neuron, there is no weight decay in the original Hebb's rule, there is no way for the synaptic weights for the incoming signals to become weaker.

New learning algorithms that fix computational instabilities of the original Hebbian rule have been created. For example, three versions of such rules are the Oja's rule [15], the Generalized Hebbian Algorithm (GHA) aka Sanger's rule [16], and the BCM rule [17]. The Oja's and BCM rules in particular, incorporate weight decay, and are more biologically faithful. In Fig. 2.14 I demonstrate how a neuron using the Oja's learning algorithm updates its synaptic weights after having processed its input vector.

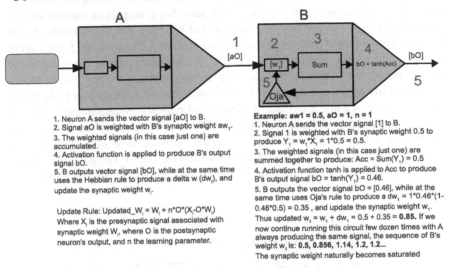

1. Neuron A sends the vector signal [aO] to B.
2. Signal aO is weighted with B's synaptic weight aw_i.
3. The weighted signals (in this case just one) are accumulated.
4. Activation function is applied to produce B's output signal bO.
5. B outputs vector signal [bO], while at the same time uses the Hebbian rule to produce a delta w (dw_i), and update the synaptic weight w_i.

Update Rule: Updated_W_i = W_i + n*O*(X_i-O*W_i)
Where X_i is the presynaptic signal associated with synaptic weight W_i, where O is the postsynaptic neuron's output, and n the learning parameter.

Example: $aw1 = 0.5$, $aO = 1$, $n = 1$
1. Neuron A sends the vector signal [1] to B.
2. Signal 1 is weighted with B's synaptic weight 0.5 to produce $Y_1 = w_1 * X_1 = 1*0.5 = 0.5$.
3. The weighted signals (in this case just one) are summed together to produce: Acc = Sum(Y_1) = 0.5
4. Activation function tanh is applied to Acc to produce B's output signal bO = tanh(Y_1) = 0.46.
5. B outputs the vector signal bO = [0.46], while at the same time uses Oja's rule to produce a $dw_1 = 1*0.46*(1-0.46*0.5) = 0.35$, and update the synaptic weight w_1.
Thus updated w_1 = w_1 + dw_1 = 0.5 + 0.35 = **0.85**. If we now continue running this circuit few dozen times with A always producing the same signal, the sequence of B's weight w_1 is: **0.5, 0.856, 1.14, 1.2, 1.2...**
The synaptic weight naturally becomes saturated

Fig. 2.14 Neuroplasticity through Oja's rule.

As can be seen in Fig-2.14, unlike the original Hebbian rule, Oja's rule produces a smaller weight increase, but more importantly, if we process a few more signals, then we would notice that the weight does not grow indefinitely. This computational system is stable, the weight eventually saturates at some viable value, and if that particular synapse, and thus the synaptic weight associated with it, is not stimulated any further by incoming signals (the incoming signals are not as high in magnitude), the weight begins to decay, memory slowly deteriorates.

The only problem is that, if there were to have been more than one synaptic weights (w1, w2...wi), they would all still follow the same type of rule, the same learning rate 'n'. To make that rule even more flexible, we can employ neuromodulation, which allows for every synaptic weight to update differently from every other, making the plasticity of the neuron even more flexible and realistic. This form of unsupervised learning is discussed next.

2.6.2 Neuromodulation

In biological neural networks, neuromodulation refers to the process of the re-lease of several classes of neurotransmitters into the cerebrospinal fluid, which then modulate a varied class of neurons within reach of the released neurotrans-mitters. In this manner, a neural circuit that releases the neurotransmitters into the cerebrospinal fluid, can affect some area of neural tissue, augmenting its behavior by making it more easily exited or inhibited for example. Neuromodulation can al-so be direct, when one neuron is connected to another, and depending on this modulatory neuron's signals, the behavior of the modulated neuron, the way it processes information, is modified.

In artificial neural networks, the same can be accomplished. We can allow a neuron or a neural circuit to use its output to modulate, or control the plasticity type and the adaptation pace (learning parameter for example) of another neuron or neural circuit. Thus for example assume that we have 2 neural circuits, A and B, which form a neural network based system. Circuit A is connected from a set of sensors, and to a set of actuators. Circuit B is also connected to the same set of sensors, but its output signals, instead of going to the actuators, are used to modu-late and dictate how the weights of the neurons in circuit A change and adapt over time, as shown in Fig-2.15. Thus, in this neural network system circuit B modu-lates circuit A, and controls that circuit's ability to learn, pace of learning, and the learning algorithm in general. Since a neural network is a universal function approximator, this type of learning algorithm can be highly versatile and robust, and the modulatory signals produced by the neural circuits can be of any form.

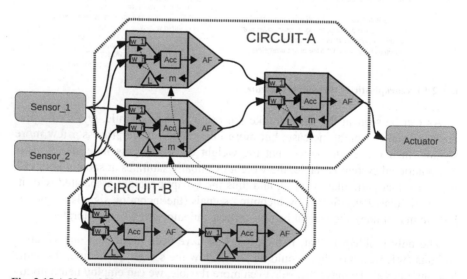

Fig. 2.15 A Neural Network based system with plasticity through neuromodulation. In this figure, Circuit-B modulates Circuit-A's learning algorithm.

The equation used to add plasticity to a neuron through neuromodulation is: $DWij = L = f*N(A*Oi*Oj + B*Oi + C*Oj)$. DWij is the delta weight, change in the synaptic weight of neuron j for the link coming from neuron i. N is the learning rate, which dictates the general magnitude of weight change after the neuron processes a signal. A, B, and C are parameters weighting the contribution of the output signal coming from the presynaptic element i and the output signal produced by the postsynaptic neuron j, and together forming the non linear plasticity factor. Finally, the value **f** is a further modulatory signal which dictates how rapidly, and in what direction the weight will change based on the learning rule **L.** In standard neuromodulation, the value f is produced by the modulating neuron or neural circuit, and the parameters N, A, B, and C are set by the researcher, or evolved and optimized through a neuroevolutionary process. But the parameters N, A, B, and C can also be produced by the modulatory neural circuit B in vector form for each neuron in circuit A, to modulate and give those neurons even more dynamic neuroplasticity.

In a sense, we can think of Circuit-B as being the biological part of circuit A, that part which produces plasticity. We can recreate the neural network shown in Fig-2.15 to be composed not of two separate neural circuits, one which does the actual processing (A) and one which does neuromodulation (B), but instead composed of one neural network, where every neuron has an embedded circuit B, which gives it plasticity. This type of neural architecture is shown in Fig-2.16.

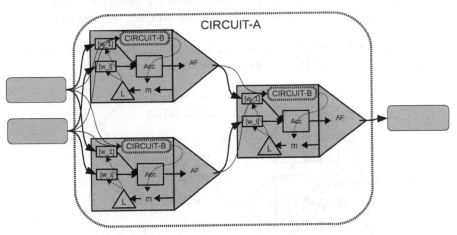

Fig. 2.16 Another type of neuromodulatory architecture.

From the above figure, we can see that each neuron now has the functionality of Circuit-B embedded inside of it. Also, there is a small change in how this new Circuit-A functions. The embedded Circuit-B does not use as input the signals coming from the two sensors, but instead uses as its input the same input as the neuron to which it adds plasticity. In this manner the modulatory circuit sees the input signals of the neuron which it modulates, making the modulation signal specific to the data of the neuron in which it is embedded.

An actual example of the steps taken in processing signals by a neural network with plasticity shown in Fig-2.15 is presented in Fig-2.17. The sequence of events in such a NN is demonstrated by the numbers given for the various steps, and is further elaborated in the following list:

1. The two sensors produce signals, and forward them to the neurons in the first layers of Circuit-A and Circuit-B.
2. The two neurons of Circuit-A process the signals from the two sensors, and produce outputs. The neuron of Circuit-B also at the same time processes the signals from the two sensors, producing the output and forwarding it to the neuron in the next neural layer of Circuit-B.
3. The second neuron in the Circuit-B processes the signal coming from the presynaptic neuron.
4. Circuit-B produces the modulatory signal, sending it to all neurons of Circuit-A. Since the first two neurons in Circuit-A have already processed their input signals, they use this modulatory signal and then do both, update their synaptic weights based on this modulatory signal, and update their learning rule parameters, where the used learning rule might be: General Hebbian, Oja's Rule, or some other.
5. The neuron in the second layer of Circuit-A produces an output after processing the signals sent to it by the two presynaptic neurons in the first layer of Circuit-A.
6. The neuron in the second layer of Circuit-A uses the modulatory signal sent to it by Circuit-B in step-4 to update its synaptic weights, and learning rule parameters.
7. The sensors produce another set of signals and forward those signals to the neurons they are connected to. The loop repeats itself.

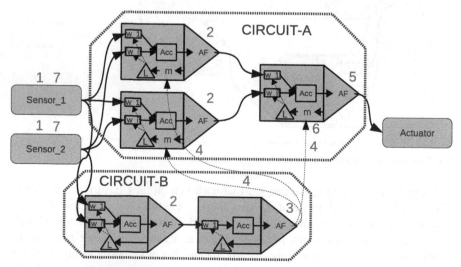

Fig. 2.17 Neuromodulation in action.

At this point you are probably asking yourself the following question: *Sure, now we can allow for some neuron to learn and adapt, to possess plasticity... but plasticity is controlled by another type of neural network, so how do we set up that other neural network's synaptic weights and parameters so that it can actually produce the modulatory signals that are useful in the first place?* That is a valid question, in fact, for example in the figure above where we modulate two neurons, instead of having to set up those neuron's synaptic weights, we have to set up the weights of the neurons in Circuit-B, each possessing 2 weights. We can do this through evolution. Evolution can optimize the synaptic weights and the various parameters needed by the modulatory neural circuits, which would then modulate effectively the other neural circuits of the complete neural network.

Unlike the static simple neurons, the neurons shown in the above figure are complex, plastic, but highly robust and adaptive elements. A neural network of such elements, evolved to work coherently as biological neural networks do, would have quite a significant amount of learning ability. We will build such systems and variants of it in later chapters, we will embed such adaptive and plastic neural networks in artificial organisms when we'll apply our neuroevolutionary system to ALife simulations, and as you will see, such systems do indeed have high potency, and might be exactly the building blocks needed when the goal is to evolve an intelligent neurocognitive system.

2.6.3 Competitive Learning

Competitive Learning [18] is another form of unsupervised learning, but unlike the Hebbian and the neuromodulation methods which add plasticity to each neuron, this one requires some system/process that has a global view of all the neurons forming the neural network undergoing competitive learning. In competitive learning we have a set of neurons, each of which is connected to a given list of sensors, and where each neuron competes with the others for the right to respond to a subset of sensory signals. Over time, competitive learning increases the specialization of each neuron for some particular set of signals, and thus allows the NN to act and spontaneously form a clustering/classification network.

A NN which uses competitive learning (CL) is realized through the implementation of the following set of steps:

1. Choose *j* number of sensors whose signals you wish to cluster or classify.
2. Create *i* number of neurons, each connected to all j sensors, and each neuron using a random set of synaptic weights.
3. **DO:**
    1. Propagate the signals from sensors to the neurons.
    2. Each neuron processes the sensory signals and produces an output signal.
    3. An external CL process chooses the neuron with the highest output signal magnitude.

4. The CL updates the synaptic weights of that neuron by applying to it a form of Hebbian learning (by using the Oja's rule for example).

4. **UNTIL:** The network begins to cluster signals, and a pattern begins to emerge.

This is a simple learning rule that can be used to see if there is a pattern in the data, and if those signals can be clustered. Fig-2.18 shows a diagram of a NN system utilizing the competitive learning algorithm.

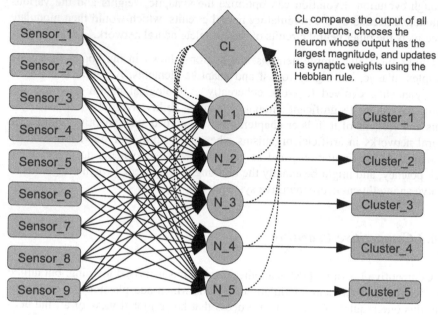

Fig. 2.18 A neural network employing competitive learning.

2.6.4 Kohonen/Self Organizing Map

A Kohonen map [19], also known as a self organizing map (SOM), is a type of neural network that in a sense represents a hypercube or a multidimensional grid of local functions, and through the use of a form of competitive learning the SOM performs a mapping of data from a high dimensional space into a lower dimensional one, while preserving that data's topology. These types of neural networks originated in the 80s and are loosely based on associative memory and adaptive learning models of the brain. Like the competitive learning neural network, a SOM system requires a process that has a global view of the NN, so that learning can be achieved. An example of a 2d SOM system is shown in Fig-2.19.

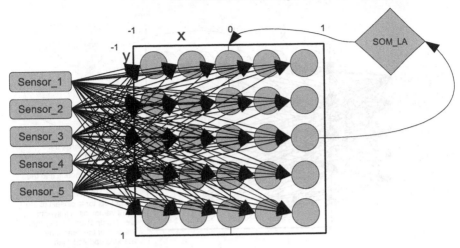

Fig. 2.19 A self organizing map, where the SOM_LA process performs SOM based Learning Algorithm computations, and synaptic weight updates.

To set up a Kohonen map we create a hypercube based substrate with embedded neurons within, where each neuron has a set of weights and a coordinate within the substrate. Each axis of the hypercube ranges from -1 to 1, and the neurons are embedded regularly within the substrate (this is somewhat similar to the hypercube representation we discussed in Chapter 1.2.10, which is used by the HyperNEAT system). The actual density, the number of neurons forming the SOM, is set by the researcher. Finally, each neuron in this hypercube is connected to the same list of sensors.

The learning algorithm used by a SOM is somewhat similar to one utilized by the competitive learning we discussed in the previous section. When the sensors propagate their vectors to the neurons, we check which of the neurons within the hypercube has a weight vector which is closest to the input vector based on a Cartesian distance to it. The neuron whose weight vector is the closest to the input vector is called the best matching unit, or BMU. Once this neuron is found we apply the weight update rule: $Wv(t + 1) = Wv(t) + \Theta(d)*\alpha(t)*(I(t) - Wv(t))$, to all neurons in the hypercube, where $\mathbf{Wv}(t+1)$ is the updated weight vector, $\mathbf{Wv}(t)$ is the neuron's weight vector before the update, $\alpha(t)$ is a monotonically decreasing learning coefficient similar to the one used in simulated annealing [20,12], $\mathbf{I}(t)$ is the input vector, and $\Theta(d)$ is usually the Gaussian or the Mexican-Hat function of the distance between the BMU and the neuron in question (thus it is greatest for the BMU neuron, and decreases the further you move away from the BMU). Once the new weight vector is calculated for every neuron in the hypercube, the sensors once again fanout their sensory vectors to the neurons. We continue with this process for some maximum X number of iterations, or until $\alpha(t)$ reaches a low enough value. Once this occurs, the SOM's output can be used for data mapping. A trip through a single iteration of the SOM learning algorithm is shown in Fig-2.20.

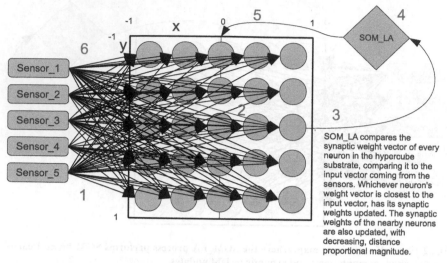

Fig. 2.20 Self Organizing Map in action.

The following list elaborates on each of the algorithm steps in the above figure:

1. The sensors forward their signals to all the neurons in the substrate (each neuron has its own coordinate).
2. Each neuron in the substrate processes the incoming signals, and produces an output.
3. A process by the name SOM_LA which has a global view of all the neurons in the substrate, compares the neural weights to the input vectors for every neuron.
4. SOM_LA finds the neuron whose synaptic weight vector is closest to the input vector coming from the sensors.
5. SOM_LA updates that neuron's synaptic weights, and updates the synaptic weights of the neurons around it, with the synaptic weight update decreasing in magnitude proportionally to the distance of those other neurons to the winning/chosen neuron.
6. The sensors forward their signals to all the neurons in the substrate... The loop repeats itself.

There are numerous variations on the original Kohonen map, for example the General Topographic Map (GTM) and the Growing Self Organizing Map (GSOM), are two of such advanced self organizing maps.

2.6.5 Putting it All Together

In this chapter we have discussed 4 different types of unsupervised learning algorithms. There are of course many others, like the Hopfield memory network that models associative memory, and the Attenuated Resonance Theory (ART) NN that models a scalable memory system. We can see that such unsupervised learning algorithms add plasticity to the neurons, and the neural networks in general. But, these types of learning algorithms themselves have parameters that need to be set up before the system can function. And what about the general topology of the NNs which possess plasticity? After all, we can't simply add some unsupervised learning algorithm to a random NN structure, and then expect it to immediately possess intelligence. The way neurons are connected to one another in the NN, the topology itself, is just as important, if not more so, than the synaptic weights of the neurons. A neurocognitive system possessing intelligence will certainly have to utilize many of these types of NNs and the different plasticity types they possess. This possible future neurocognitive system will integrate all these learning neural circuits into a single, cohesive, synchronized, vast neural network system, possessing the topology and architecture similar to an example shown in Fig-2.21.

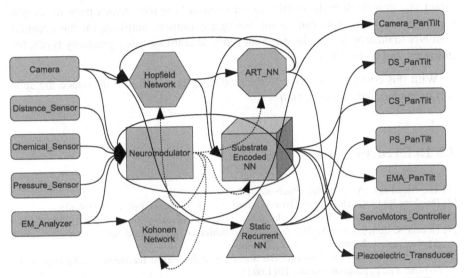

Fig. 2.21 A possible vast NN composed of neurons with and without plasticity, and different interconnected neural circuit modules. The flexibility of an evolved NN based system which draws upon and uses all the available learning algorithms, encodings, neuron types... could potentially be immense.

How can we figure out how to put these modules together, how to connect the neurons in the right manner, how to bootstrap a NN system so that it can take over from there, and so that its own intelligence and ability to learn can continue the work from that point onwards? That problem has already been solved once before, we are the result; the solution is evolution.

2.7 Summary

In this section we have discussed how biological neurons process information, their ability to integrate spatiotemporal input signals, and change their signal processing strategy, a process called *plasticity*. We then discussed how artificial neural networks process signals, and that the most common such neural networks deal with amplitude encoded signals, rather than frequency encoded signals as is the case with biological neural networks. Although as noted, there are artificial neural networks called spiking neural networks, which like biological NNs deal with frequency encoded signals.

We then discussed the various topologies, architectures and NN plasticity rules. We discussed how a recurrent NN exhibits memory, and how the Hebbian, Oja's, and neuromodulation learning rules allow for NNs to adapt and change as they interact and process signals. Finally, we discussed how the various parameters and topologies of these NNs can be set, through evolution, allowing for the eventual vast NN to incorporate all the different types of learning rules, plasticity types, topologies, and architectures.

With this covered, we move to the next chapter which will introduce the subject of evolutionary computation.

2.8 References

[1] The Blue Brain Project: http://bluebrain.epfl.ch/
[2] Dawkins R (1976) The Selfish Gene. (Oxford University Press), ISBN 0192860925.
[3] Dawkins R (1982) The Extended Phenotype. (Oxford University Press), ISBN 0192880519.
[4] Hornik K, Stinchcombe M, White H (1989) Multilayer Feedforward Networks are Universal Approximators. Neural Networks 2, 359-366.
[5] Sher GI (2010) DXNN Platform: The Shedding of Biological Inefficiencies. Neuron, 1-36. Available at: http://arxiv.org/abs/1011.6022.
[6] Parisi D, Cecconi F, Nolfi S (1990) Econets: Neural Networks That Learn in an Environment. Network Computation in Neural Systems 1, 149-168.
[7] Predators and Prey in simulated 2d environment, Flatland: http://www.youtube.com/watch?v=HzsDZt8EO70&list=UUdBTNtB1C3Jt90X1I26Vmhg&index=2&feature=plcp
[8] Hassoun MH (1995) Fundamentals of Artificial Neural Networks. (The MIT Press).
[9] Lynch M (2007) The Origins of Genome Architecture S. Associates, ed. (Sinauer Associates Inc).
[10] Haykin S (1999) Neural Networks: A Comprehensive Foundation J. Griffin, ed. (Prentice Hall).
[11] Rojas R (1996) Neural Networks: A Systematic Introduction. (Springer).
[12] Gupta MM, Jin L, Homma N (2003) Static and Dynamic Neural Networks From Fundamentals to Advanced Theory. (John Wiley & Sons).
[13] Di GG, Grammaldo LG, Quarato PP, Esposito V, Mascia A, Sparano A, Meldolesi GN, Picardi A (2006) Severe Amnesia Following Bilateral Medial Temporal Lobe Damage Occurring On Two Distinct Occasions. Neurological sciences official journal of the Italian Neurological Society and of the Italian Society of Clinical Neurophysiology 27, 129-133.

[14] Kirkwood A, Rioult MG, Bear MF (1996) Experience-Dependent Modification of Synaptic Plasticity in Visual Cortex. Nature 381, 526-528.

[15] Oja E (1982) A Simplified Neuron as a Principal Component Analyzer. Journal of Mathematical Biology 15, 267-273.

[16] Sanger T (1989) Optimal Unsupervised Learning in a Single-Layer Linear Feedforward Neural Network. Neural Networks 2, 459-473.

[17] Bienenstock EL, Cooper LN, Munro PW (1982) Theory For The Development of Neuron Selectivity: Orientation Specificity and Binocular Interaction in Visual Cortex. Journal of Neuroscience 2, 32-48.

[18] Rumelhart DE, McClelland JL (1986) Parallel Distributed Processing M.I.T. Press, ed. (MIT Press).

[19] Kohonen T (1982) Self-Organized Formation of Topologically Correct Feature Maps. Biological Cybernetics 43, 59-69.

[20] Kirkpatrick S, Gelatt CD, Vecchi MP (1983) Optimization by Simulated Annealing. Science 220, 671-680.

[21] Cerny V (1985) Thermodynamical Approach to The Traveling Salesman Problem: An Efficient Simulation Algorithm. Journal of Optimization Theory and Applications 45, 41-51.

[22] An excellent discussion of neuron and synapse: http://en.wikipedia.org/wiki/Neuron

[23] Gerstner W (1998) Spiking Neurons. In Pulsed Neural Networks, W. Maass and C. M. Bishop, eds. (MIT-Press), pp. 3-53.

[24] Ang CH, Jin C, Leong PHW, Schaik AV (2011) Spiking Neural Network-Based Auto-Associative Memory Using FPGA Interconnect Delays. 2011 International Conference on FieldProgrammable Technology, 1-4.

[25] Qingxiang W, T MM, Liam PM, Rongtai C, Meigui C (2011) Simulation of Visual Attention Using Hierarchical Spiking Neural Networks. ICIC: 26-31

[26] Hebb DO (1949) The organization of behavior. Wiley, eds. (Wiley)

Chapter 3 Introduction to Evolutionary Computation

Abstract In this chapter we discuss biological evolution, and the way it has evolved the organisms and structures that we see around us today. We then extract the essentials of this natural stochastic search method, and discuss how one could implement the same, or an even more efficient version, in software. Once the standard evolutionary algorithm methods are introduced (genetic algorithms, genetic programming, evolutionary strategies, and evolutionary programming), we also discuss the slightly lesser known memetic algorithm approaches (hybrid algorithms), and how it compares to the already discussed methods. Finally, we discuss the equivalency between all these methods, and the fact that all of them are just different sides of the same coin.

Evolutionary computation algorithms are population based optimization algorithms inspired and derived from the Darwinian principles of biological evolution. Instead of simply listing the general steps of an evolutionary algorithm, let us discuss evolution in general, and then extract the essence of it, and see how such principles can be implemented in software, and used to evolve solutions to any problem.

As has been mentioned to some degree in the first and second chapter, evolution is the driving force, the phenomenon that has birthed us. What are the principles of evolution, how does it work? Let us again discuss the history of life on earth, the path it took, and the evolutionary principles that shaped it.

3.1 Evolution

At its core, replication, creating copies, is really the main thing [1,2,3]. There can really be no other way for life to emerge, without it all starting with a replicator. After all, whatever does not replicate, does not make copies, and thus will eventually be drowned out by a system that uses up all the available resources and makes copies of itself. But how do we get to a replicator, even the most simplest of ones? It is for this reason why it took billions of years, once you have a replicator things get easy. A simple replicator is just a molecule that through chemical reactions can make a copy of itself, given that there are resources around it that can be used. Through physical principles alone, such a molecule simply makes copies of itself [4,5], a physical chain reaction. But how do we get to such a molecule in the first place is of course the question.

G.I. Sher, *Handbook of Neuroevolution Through Erlang*,
DOI 10.1007/978-1-4614-4463-3_3, © Springer Science+Business Media New York 2013

If such a molecule is small and simple enough, then, given enough time (billions of years), if you randomly bang atoms against each other, in different environments, under different circumstances, trillions upon trillions of times per second, eventually you'll hit the right combination and such a molecule will arise. Now there are trillions of stars in our universe, multiple planets for each star, each planet with a different environment. If simple molecules and atoms are banging against each other, and normal chemical reactions take place on those planets, and they do, then given a few billion years, by statistics alone, there is 100% chance that at one point or another, the right combination of simple inorganic molecules and atoms will combine just right to create such a simple replicator. And then it starts...

There's no avoiding it, probability itself demands it. If there is a chance that through standard physical properties a particular combination of molecules and atoms can come together to form a replicator, then given enough permutations and chances, that combination of atoms will occur. It might be so rare though, that we might even be the first ones, but we won't be the last. Given enough time, sooner or later another planet will have the right conditions, and be at the right place at the right time, that after a few billion years on its surface too, the right combination will occur through probability and chance alone. And that is the spark, that is the start, after that, there is no choice but for evolution to start carving out a path toward complexity.

When making copies, sooner or later, there will always be an error. At some point or another, either due to the environment the replicator is in, or due to a high energy photon slamming into the replicator, there will be an error, the copy will be slightly different. Certainly, majority, almost all the errors will end up in the mutated copy being damaged in one way or another. But every once in a while, the mutant copy will be an even better replicator. It might perhaps be a bit more robust, and not affected by errors as much (thus being able to produce more surviving offspring), or it might be more efficient. Whatever the minuscule advantage, if there is one, then it and its kind will make more copies of itself than its parent replicator, in the long run. Of course at this point there is now not a homogeneous pool of replicators using up all the available resources, but different kinds, variations of each other. We now have competition, even if the replicators themselves don't know this. After all, the replicator wants to make a copy of itself, and its fitness is defined by how many copies it makes... If another replicator is using up the same resources, or space, then this is competition.

At this point the replicators could have spread out through the entire planet, slowly using up the resources, converting the resources into copies of themselves. And again, due to probability alone, due to stochastics alone, one of the errors during replication will end up generating a clone offspring that has the ability to break apart other replicators around, through its chemical properties alone. This would be a great evolutionary discovery, this would be the discovery of predation. At the same time, this would spark a new type of drive towards complexity, because now replicators can affect each other, they are more unstable too, because they can break each other apart. There is also now a direct competition, if you can be broken apart by another replicator merely because you are proximal to it, you will not create any offspring. Any error, where the error is simply a mutation in the created offspring, that leads to the offspring ability to not be absorbed, or be able to somehow chemically sense the aggressive replicator, will be of great benefit. Sooner or later, that combination of mutations will occur.

When such a mutant offspring is birthed, it will be able to create many more offspring than its parent. Which also means that the amount of replicators that can be broken up by the aggressive replicators will dwindle... Another mutation that results in the aggressive replicator having the ability to break apart these new resistant replicators, will certainly be useful. Though of course, it would again take trillions of mutations that lead no where... but sooner or later, the right mutation combination, if such a combination of mutations is possible, will occur. This will lead to a more and more complex type of replicators. It is an arms race between replicating molecules. It is evolution.

Now remember, all of this is guided simply by the fact that replicators replicate. There is no thinking, it's simply what they do, create copies. This is a completely natural process; there is no other way for evolution to be. It has to be replication, and replication has to be at its core. This is what the natural world is based on. As soon as a replicator is introduced to the environment through stochastic processes, there is no other path that can be taken than a path towards an arms race and evolution towards complexity as the replicators make copies of themselves, make errors during the creation of those copies, and unknowingly compete for limited resources as each replicator makes a copy.

At some point a mutation might lead to a replicator to form a sort of molecular boundary around itself. This will give it an advantage against predation. Again complexity will have to rise. Stochastic processes will try out different combinations of morphologies. Different combinations of attacking and defending... The older parents, the first ones, do not necessarily have to be wiped out. But some will, and some will remain.

We are now at a level of an organism, a replicator with a shell, a replicator with some kind of protective boundary. Its complexity is increased, this is at the level of single celled organisms. From there, multi celled organisms are just a few million years, a few trillions of combinations and mutation attempts away.

With every new species, with every new biological invention through evolution, the organisms are not just interacting with each other, they are interacting with the environment itself. If we start off with a completely flat and boring environment, and all the organisms are adept at existing in that simple environment, and then suddenly one of the organisms evolves an ability to modify it, by for example digging holes... then that takes everyone to a whole new level of complexity. On the one hand, the organism that can dig holes, does not only make the environment more complex, but also creates its own niche, and therefore could become more fit and create more offspring. If that organism eventually becomes dominant through replication, then evolution will drive other organisms towards species that can deal with this more complex environment... which would require some kind of chemical or other type of sensory ability. As new organisms arise that can deal with the new environmental complexity, and have abilities to attack or defend themselves from environment modifying organisms... new evolved inventions will follow.

The organisms modify the environment, and the environment grows more complex, requiring the organisms to evolve new methods of dealing with it, of sensing it, of traversing and surviving in it. The organisms change the entire planet through their interaction with it. This is a never ending drive towards complexity, and as you can see, there is really no other way for it to happen. This is what competition and replication leads to.

The stochastic processes of mutation, and the never ending replication and the resulting competition for resources to replicate continues for billions of years, trillions upon trillions of failed attempts at improvement, and a few successful ones... until finally you see in front of you what you see today. The replicators have evolved through arms race a new type of boundary around themselves for protection against each other.... that eventual end result, through the slow path of time and mutation, through evolution, that protective boundary and that invention is you and I, or as Richard Dawkins put it: one of the ultimate survivor machines [6] that the replicators had evolved.

Now before we begin extracting the algorithm from this biological phenomenon of evolution, and see how we can do the same thing with software, let us tackle the final question, which will also be useful for our understanding of the evolutionary process. The question is, why are there broken links in the organisms we see today? Why don't we see a smooth spectrum, all the way from the first replicator, to the complex organisms like mammals?

There are many reasons for this phenomenon, we will cover two of the simplest. The first way in which such breakages in the phylogenetic tree can occur is through extinction. Some organism might just be very good at consuming a particular species. If that organism consumes some other species at a fast enough rate, that other species will become extinct. If the environment continues to change as the new, and younger species interact with it, the older species from eons past, might not be fit for it, and they will become extinct. For example, as plankton and other oxygen releasing organisms covered earth, more and more oxygen was released, and higher and higher concentration of it were present everywhere. Any species to which oxygen was toxic, for some reason due to its chemical makeup for example, that species would become extinct if it did not evolve fast enough into an oxygen tolerant species, and evolution is just stochastics, so not every species would have the chance to evolve. Any species that needed a high carbon dioxide content in the atmosphere, would become extinct as the concentration of oxygen increased at the expense of carbon dioxide...

The second reason for the breakages in the phylogenetic tree is due to the evolution of the species as a whole through interbreeding. For example, let's say there is some ape that creates an offspring. That offspring has had just the right mutations which gave it a slightly larger brain. Its genetics are different, we have just witnessed the birth of a new type of ape. Now that ape is still close enough genetically to its parents, and so it can breed with the apes in that species. His genetic mutation is advantageous. This new ape will breed, and some of his offspring will inherit this genetic pattern that gives them a larger brain. Eventually that new mutation will spread through the population, over the next hundreds of generations. Thus, this whole population, the community of apes, will integrate this new complementary mutation, and the whole population evolves together. The old population, the old species, changes into a new one as it integrates new genetic patterns. Through such mutations we can go from species A to species B smoothly, over thousands of generations, without even leaving a trace of there ever being an A, because through slow change the population has become B. Then today, we would only see a species B.

With regards to reason 2, you might then pose a question, what about the fact that we do sometimes see species A and B? That also can occur, as another example, let's say we have a population, and as it explores the environment and spreads through it, it separates into a few different groups. The mutation is rare, and it will occur in one of the groups, in one of those subpopulations. If those subpopulations, if those groups do not interbreed, because for example they have become separated by a large distance, geographically, then when one of these populations A begins to evolve towards B, the other groups will still stay as A. At some later time, after thousands of generations, we have a population that has evolved from A to B, and another that might have not acquired any new mutations, or have went into another evolutionary direction. And so we would have A, B, and perhaps some population that evolved in another direction, C for example. Then we would have 3 species, the original A, and the mutated but sufficiently different species B and C that can no longer breed with A or each other.

We have now covered the biological properties, how evolution occurs and the path it takes. In the next section, we will figure out and extract the most essential parts of evolution, and then see how to create the same form of optimization in non biological systems.

3.2 Extracting the Essentials of Biological Evolution

The evolutionary process discussed in the previous section needs the following elements to work: We have to have a population of organisms/agents, and some way of representing their genome. We need a way to represent their genome because the process of evolution requires variation, it requires for a process of creating offspring that have a chance of being different from their parents. The way we create mutated offspring is by applying mutation operators to the genomes of their parents, by for example first cloning the parent genome and then mutating that cloned genome. Another element that is required is the process of selection. In biological evolution, the most fit organisms are the ones that create the most offspring, indeed the ability to create offspring (which requires the organism to have enough resources, and be able to successfully compete against other organisms) is that which defines the organism's fitness.

But when we evolve programs, they are not always applied to the problem where they have control over their replication processes. Neither do we want to add any more complexity to the agents, the complexity which would be needed for their ability to decide on when and how to replicate. Finally, each agent will not know his own fitness with relation to the rest, thus each agent will not know how many offspring it should create if any, and we would not want to leave such decisions in that agent's "hands" in the first place, since we want to be able to guide the evolution ourselves. Thus, the selection process is a method of choosing those agents, or those genomes, that are more fit than others.

If you think about the genotype being in a search space, and the phenotype being in the solution space, with the evolutionary algorithm trying out genotypes in the search space, and mapping each genotype to a phenotype in the solution space, to see whether it is, or how close it is, to the right solution, then an evolutionary algorithm is simply an advanced search algorithm. It is an optimization algorithm, where the term optimization simply means, searching for the best. The algorithm conducts a search for solutions, trying out different genotypes, and checking if they represent better solutions or not, as shown in Fig-3.1.

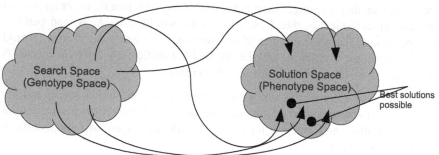

Fig. 3.1 Evolution as a search algorithm, from search space to solution space.

Thus, to sum it up, an evolutionary process requires a population of agents and a way to represent their genotypes in the search space. It requires reproduction, a way for parents to create offspring by creating new variations of their own genotypes. It requires a mapping system, to convert the genotype (in the case of biological organisms, DNA & RNA) in the search space, to phenotypes (the actual organism, its morphology, and its behavior) in the solution space. Finally, it requires a selection method, a way to choose the fit agents, a way to discern the fit from the unfit. Thus, evolution is a directed parallel search, directed by the principle of survival of the fittest, however that fitness is defined.

In the biological evolution, there was a point before the first replicator emerged, when various atoms and molecules simply collided with each other randomly... until one of those combinations was a replicator. But in artificial evolution, we do not need to have that moment, we can create the initial population of simple organisms, and decide how their genotypes are represented, so that they can be mutated, mapped to their phenotypic forms, and evaluated for fitness. Based on all these essentials, the evolutionary process can be represented with the following set of steps:

1. Create a seed population of simple organisms. The organisms must have both, genotypic and phenotypic representations, and a function capable of mapping between the two. The genotype must have a form such that mutation operators can be applied to it, thus allowing the population of organisms to evolve.
2. Create a fitness function, a function that can give each agent in the population a fitness score, such that the agents can be compared against one another, to see which is more fit.
3. **DO:**
    1. Evaluate each organism's fitness in the population. Give each organism a fitness score using the fitness function, based on that organism's performance.
    2. Choose the fit organisms within the population.
    3. Remove the unfit organisms from the population.
    4. Create offspring from the fit agent genotypes. The offspring are variations on the genotype of their fit parents. The offspring can be created through the process of cross over, mutation, or both. For example an offspring can be created by first creating a clone of a fit parent, and then applying various mutation operators to the clone, and thus generating a mutant of the fit parent.
    5. Compose the new population from the offspring and their parents (this method is called an elitist selection, because the fit organisms of each generation always survive to the next generation).
4. **UNTIL:** Termination condition is reached. Where that condition can be some goal fitness score, or some maximum amount of computational power or time expanded on the problem to which the evolutionary algorithm is being applied.

Now when I say evaluate each organism's fitness, I of course refer to the phenotype of the organism. The genotype is the representation, it is that to which we apply mutation operators, it is that string or program from which the actual phenotype of the organism can be derived. The genotype is a mutatable encoding of the organism, a point in the search space of all possible genotypes. The phenotype is the actual characteristics of the organism, its behavior and morphological properties, a point on the solution space, of all possible solutions.

For example, in the case of biological organisms, our DNA is our genotype. Evolution occurs through the mutation of our genotype. We, you and I, are phenotypes mapped from our genotypes. A genotype is converted to the phenotype by using some type of mapping function. In the case of biological organisms, it is the biological process of translating from genes to proteins, and the composition of those proteins into a cohesive and synchronized organism. It is the phenotype whose fitness is judged, it is the phenotype that interacts directly with the environment it inhabits. And if it is fit enough to survive, and thus to create offspring, it passes on its genome, sometimes in a mutated form so as to explore other points in the search space, and thus giving its offspring a chance to perhaps find a better position in the solution space and achieve an even greater fitness than its parent.

*********Note*********

Evolution is the process undertaken by a population of agents. What is evolving is the population rather than an individual. It is the population as a whole that is changing, through the generation of new mutant individuals within the population, some of which have the traits more fit for the environment in which they exist. In a sense, an individual within the population represents the current state that the population achieved through evolution at that point in its evolutionary history. When it is clear from the content, I will at times state "as the agent evolves...", because we can look at any given agent and concentrate only **on that agent's evolutionary path** by back-tracing it through its ancestors, or its earlier forms. Or if we concentrate only on a genotype's future offspring which are more fit than it is, and thus trace forward the path of the genotype through its surviving offspring, the term "as the agent evolves..." also applies.

****

Though we now know the essentials of evolution, and even the evolutionary algorithm and the necessary parts that allow it to create variation, and explore genotypic variations in search for a more fit one, there are still the following two linked questions we need to answer before we can put this knowledge to use: How do we represent these genotypes and phenotypes in software? and how do we formulate the problem we're working on, in evolutionary terms?

In the next section we will discuss the task of problem formulation, and genotype/phenotype representation.

3.3 Formulating a Given Problem in Evolutionary Terms

Let us first set out in concrete terms the problem and solution that biological evolution solves in the real world.

- **Problem:** If you are a replicator, how do you create as many copies of yourself as possible in a dynamic and hazardous environment?
- **Solution:** Put the replicator inside a survival machine, an adaptable system able to create copies of the replicator with its own similar copy of a survival machine that can deal with the hardships the environment produces. The replicator is the gene, as noted by Richard Dawkins.

The way biological evolution solved the problem is by creating trillions of solutions, and then evaluating how good those solutions were. The way to evaluate the solution is to simply let it interact with the hazardous environment, those solutions that are able to replicate, have a high fitness (dependent on how many copies it was able to make). The replicator offspring will differ slightly from the parent, and in this way new solutions are explored again and again, in a hill climbing fashion. Hill climbing in the sense that if an inferior solution to the current one is found, it usually does not do well when compared (when it competes) to the current solutions, and so it does not survive. There are millions of possible solutions, ranging from single celled survival machines without any type of adaptive capabilities, to multicellular survival machines that have some embedded information about the environment, a predisposition of learning certain essential patterns within the environment, and an organ that can remember and adapt to new challenges within the environment.

Thus, the way the problem is solved is: Take the problem, and let it evaluate the fitness of the different solutions. Create multiple solutions, and let the problem decide which are good and which are bad. Then take the good ones, create new variations of those good solutions, and then repeat this cycle.

We see that the answer depends heavily on the problem to which we wish to evolve a solution. Let us now take a non biological problem, and formulate it in such a way that we can apply an evolutionary algorithm to it, and evolve a solution. For example, let's say that we have the following problem: We are given some unknown graph, as shown in Fig-3.2, and we want to find a mathematical function that represents this graph. How can this problem be formulated in evolutionary terms?

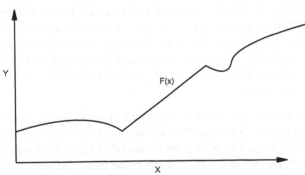

Fig. 3.2 A graph, the problem to which a solution, a function which describes it, needs to be evolved.

An organism in this problem is some function f(x). The function f(x) is the genotype of the individual organism. The solution space for this problem is one of all possible graphs, where we are searching for the graph shown in the figure above. Thus we map the genotype f(x), to its phenotype, the actual graph of that function. Finally, the fitness is decided by the solution space, and is based on how close the graph represented by the organism is to the one in the above figure.

Thus, to evolve a solution to the problem, we would first need to create a seed population of very simple agents, where each agent is simply a function. We then compare the graph of each of the functions to the above graph, calculating the Cartesian distance between each point on the given graph, and the coordinate on the graph the agent function represents. The fitness is then 1/Cartesian_Distance. The smaller the total Cartesian distance, the greater the fitness of the agent, and the more offspring it should be allowed to create. The offspring are mutated versions of the parent equation; we compose them by taking the fit function, and then adding, subtracting, multiplying, and dividing it by other primitive functions and constants. Once the low fitness agents are removed and replaced by offspring agents, we re-evaluate the whole population again, as per the evolutionary algorithm discussed in the previous section. Eventually, by chance, there will be offspring agents, offspring functions, which represent graphs that are closer to the given graph than their parents. Thus, through evolution, eventually we will find better and better approximation to the given graph. Eventually, we will evolve a solution, a function whose phenotype, the graph, is very close to, or even exactly as, the above given graph.

The above sounds like it should work, and indeed it does work, it is using an evolutionary approach. We have simply replaced the biological organism's DNA by a string f(x) representing the function, and the organism's phenotype by the function's graph. Each organism can have a higher or lower fitness, and that fitness is evaluated based on its performance in the environment, how close the graph produced by f(x) is to the given graph. Although in this case, unlike in the biological system, the creation of offspring is done not by the organism/agent itself, but by the researcher, or some other outside system created by the researcher. Nevertheless, the offspring creation process is still dependent on the fitness of the organism, and thus the main features of evolution are retained. Finally, as mentioned, the environment in this problem is not a three dimensional world, but instead is a *scape*. The environment is the given graph in a sense, and the way to survive in this environment is to possess a graph that is as close to the given graph as possible. The only thing we have not yet decided on is how to represent the genotypes of these agents.

We need to create a genotype to represent these agents such that it makes it easy for us to apply mutation operators to them, such that it makes it easy for us to create mutant offspring. The phenotype on the other hand is what is getting evaluated. The phenotype can be the same thing as the genotype, and depending on the problem, that might even be optimal. For example, the problem might be such that the goal is to create a particular genotype, in which case we could then evaluate the fitness of the genotype directly by comparing it to the provided goal genotype. In this problem though, the phenotype is the actual graph that the function paints, and we do not know what the genotype of the goal phenotype is. Thus, our agent's genotype is the function f(x), and the phenotype of our agent is the graph that f(x) represents, a graph which can be compared to the goal graph.

One of the representations for a computer program, or a function, which yields easily to mutation and variation, is through the use of trees, as shown in Fig-3.3. This is the representation used in Genetic Programming popularized by John Koza [7,8,9,10].

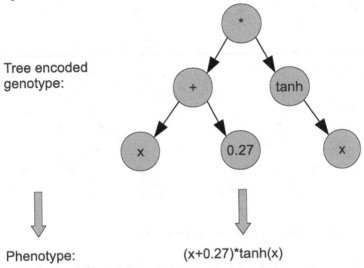

Fig. 3.3 **Function as a tree structure, the genetic programming way.**

In such a representation, the non-leaf nodes represent mathematical operators, and the leaf nodes represent inputs, whether those inputs be variables or constants. We can then evaluate this tree structure by following the paths from the leafs to the root, executing the mathematical operators on the input values.

The leaf nodes can be elements like: 0, 1, Pi, X(i) input. The non leaf nodes are the mathematical functions, and other types of programs. When the problem posed is mathematical in nature, we can use the following nodes: tanh, +,-, %, /, *, sin, cos, tan... basically any standard mathematical operators, and trigonometric functions that can be used to form various functions.

This representation makes it very easy to create mutant offspring. For example we can mutate agents by simply adding new nodes to the tree, in random locations of that tree. Or we can take two or more trees and swap branches between them,

thus creating an offspring not through mutation but through crossover. The following figure shows the agents with tree like genotypes, the functions that those genotypes evaluate to, and the mutated genotypes produced through the application of
mutation operators and cross-over.

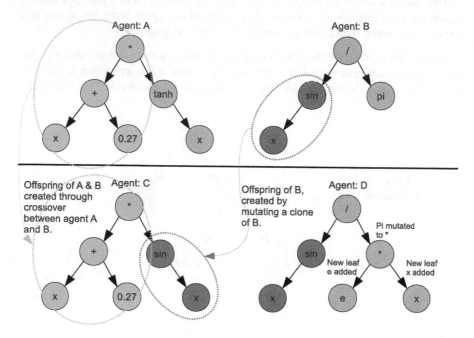

Fig. 3.4 Evaluating and mutating tree encoded genotypes.

Thus, having now decided on the genotype representation, on the phenotype
representation, and on the fitness function (graph similarity through Cartesian distance between the agent graph and the goal graph), we can employ the evolutionary process to evolve a solution to this problem. We would start with a seed population of very simple functions, whose genotypes are represented as trees. We
would then map each of the genotypes to their phenotypes, the graphs they represent in two dimensional space. For each graph, we would see how close it is to the
wanted graph, and using the fitness function give each of the individuals its fitness
score. Based on these fitness scores we could then choose the top 50% of the population, the most fit of the population, and discard the bottom 50%. We then allow
each of these fit individuals to create a single offspring. The offspring can be mutated clones of their parents, or some crossover between the fittest agents in the
population. Once the offspring are created, we form a new population composed
of the fit parents and their offspring, this new population represents the next generation. The new population is then once again evaluated for fitness... The evolutionary loop continues.

This could continue on and on, and through evolution, through the search conducted in the solution space, more and more fit individuals would arise, those whose graphs, whose phenotypes, are closer to the wanted graph.

Using these same set of steps we could apply the evolutionary algorithms to other problems. For example we could create a genotype encoding for antennas, where the fitness of those antennas is their performance, signal clarity of their reception. In this way we could then evolve new antennas, better at catching some particular signal. Or we could create an encoding for circuits, after all, circuits are simply graphs, and graphs are trees with more than one root, as shown in Fig-3.5.

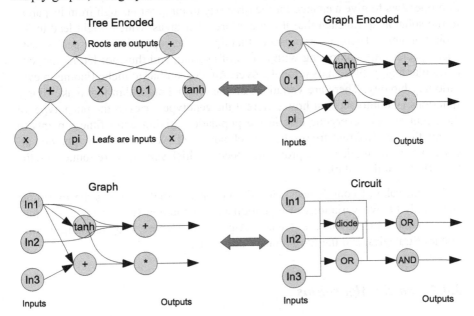

Fig. 3.5 Multi-rooted trees as graphs, and graphs as circuits.

The fitness function could then be the lowest number of logic gates or transistors, while maintaining the same functionality as the original circuit. Then, through evolution, we could evolve more efficient circuits, more efficient CPUs...

We are then only limited by our imagination, and coming up with how to encode the genotypes of something we wish to evolve. There are numerous variations and "sub categories" of evolutionary algorithms. In the next section we will briefly discuss them, and how they differ from one another.

3.4 The Different Flavors of Evolutionary Algorithms

You already know how to apply evolutionary computation to various problems. You need only create a genotype encoding with a mapping to phenotype, a fitness function, a selection algorithm, and the mutation operators you wish to apply during the reproduction/offspring-creation phase to create variation in the offspring. The evolutionary process takes care of the rest. Indeed it is so robust, that even a poorly formulated approach will still usually lead to a good enough solution.

Granted, some approaches do get stuck in local optima. Being deceived by the environment, by the solution space, and lead to local optimal solutions, never being able to jump out of that area using the given mutation operators. Thus there are all kinds of extensions, and advancements made to the simple formulation we've covered. The increasing number of phases during evolution, the specialized mutation operators to give a chance for the offspring to jump far enough from its parent in the solution space such that it can explore other areas, which might lead to the global optima... There are approaches that divide the population into species, with each species only competing with others of its kind, and thus not letting any one particular highly fit organism to take over. An idea similar to niche finding in evolutionary biology. There are variations on the original algorithm that make fitness functions take into account how different the genotype, or even the phenotype, of the agent is from everyone else in the population, giving extra fitness points to agents that are different from others. Such advanced evolutionary computation algorithms can dramatically improve the speed at which solutions are found, and the final fitness of the solution.

For the sake of completeness, in this section we briefly discuss the four most commonly known variations of evolutionary computation (EC) flavors. The four most common EC flavors are: Genetic Algorithms, Genetic Programming, Evolutionary Strategies, and the Evolutionary Algorithms.

3.4.1 Genetic Algorithms

Genetic algorithms (GA) is one of the most well known approaches to evolutionary computation. Although computer simulation of evolution was being explored as early as 1954, they became popularized in early 1970s, due to John Holland's book *Adaptation in Natural and Artificial Systems* [11]. In his attempt to discuss natural evolutionary processes, and emulate the same in artificial systems, his algorithm implements the standard features of evolution, selection, crossover, mutation, and survival of the fittest.

The algorithm primarily relies on crossover. Putting the fit individuals into a "matting pool" from which two random fit parents are then drawn, and their genotype is then used to create an offspring. The offspring is created by taking the genotype of individual A, choosing a random sequence slice of it (if represented as a string), of random length, then doing the same with individual B, and then finally creating a new offspring C by putting the two sequence slices from A and B together. Mutation is also used for the purpose of creating offspring, but is usually only used lightly, and only for the purpose of maintaining some minimal level of diversity within the population.

A simple example of evolving individuals through crossover, where the genotype is represented as a binary string, and the phenotype as simply the translation of the bits 0 and 1 to colors green and white respectively, is shown in Fig-3.6.

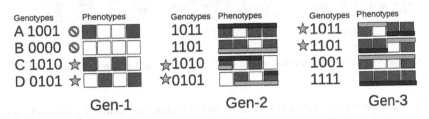

The fitness is determined by how well an individual is able to blend in with a green background. The more green an individual, the better it is able to blend in. In this scenario a population contains 4 individuals, and each new generation is composed out of 2 individuals from the old generation, and two new offspring created from the fit parents, by splicing their genomes together.

Fig. 3.6 Evolving an individual that can blend in with a green background, with offspring creation through crossover.

In the figure above we use GA to evolve an individual capable of blending into its background, which we have decided to be green. This is somewhat similar to the story of light and dark moths [12]. The dark moths had an advantage over their lighter variants due to the background on which the moths would sit being dark, letting the darker moths blend into their background more effectively than their lighter cousins. Eventually most of the moths in the location in question became dark, as the lighter ones stood out in their environment, got eaten by predators, and thus on average produced less offspring. In this simple setup, the genotype is represented as a binary string. The phenotype is created by mapping 0 to white, and 1 to green. If the fitness function is then based on how well an individual is able to blend into a green background, we would then assume that green individuals are more fit in such environments, than white individuals which would stand out. In this example we use crossover. The population is composed of 4 individuals, and each generation we choose 2 of the 4 individuals that are most fit, and use those fit individuals to create 2 offspring for the next generation. The offspring are created by taking parent A and cutting its genotype in two, then taking B and cutting its genotype in two, finally, we create the two offspring by connecting the random half from A to a half from B, creating the two new offspring. As can be seen from the example, eventually, when generation 3 is reached, one of the offspring is completely green. At this point we would have reached the termination condition, having achieved the maximum fitness level within the green environment.

Genetic algorithm systems also use mutations, and indeed this same problem can be just as easily solved through mutation alone, as shown in the next figure.

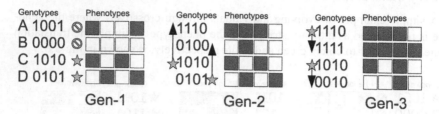

Fig. 3.7 Evolving an individual that can blend into a green background, through mutation alone.

The main drawback with old GA approaches is that they primarily utilized static sized genotypes. The genotypes could not grow or shrink, if you had started with a genotype string of size 4, that is all you would have to work with. Later on this problem was eliminated by simply adding a few extra mutation operators that could add and subtract sequences from the string encoded genotype, resulting in a dynamically sized genotype.

3.4.2 Genetic Programming

Genetic programming (GP) is a specialized type of GA that deals with not string encoded genotypes or chromosomes, but tree based programs. GP evolves programs represented as trees, similar to the types we developed in Section-3.2 when evolving a solution for the graph problem. GP also comes with a specialized set of mutation operators, like branch swapping between two individuals to create an offspring through crossover. Node mutation, node addition, and other types of mutation operators that the researcher decides to implement. Also, unlike the original GA, the genotypes in GP are of variable length, GP can expand and grow programs/trees of any size. Of course this can also be done by modifying the GA approach as we discussed, by adding mutation operators to grow and shrink the string encoded genomes.

GP was originally introduced by Cramer [13], but popularized by Koza [1992]. John Koza has also further modified the genotypes and specialized GP to be applied in evolution of new materials, antennas, and other structures [14,15]. Having access to a large cluster of machines, a cluster which he dubbed the "*Invention Machine*" [16], John Koza is able to run parallel GP algorithms with large populations, evolving new programs, and applying the approach to the evolution of patentable materials and hardware. This invention machine has produced numerous artifacts for which patents were granted. Thus when used to its full potential, evolution is easily able to generate results rivaling, or on par and competitive with, the innovations produced by human inventors.

3.4.3 Evolutionary Strategies

Thus far we spoke of mutation operators, and said that there is a certain chance that so and so mutation is applied, or so and so number of offspring are created from a fit parent... In actual evolutionary systems, we have to specify these probabilities. For example, let us say we have a GP system which creates offspring purely through the application of mutation operators. For such a system, we can specify the following evolutionary parameters:

- Only the top X% of the population gets to create offspring, where X = 50.
- Each fit individual creates Y number of offspring, where Y is proportional to the individual's fitness in comparison to others, and the available amount of free space in the population, based on the number of individuals removed due to being unfit, where: *FreeSpace% = 100% - X%*, and thus the number of offspring that can be created during the generation to fill up the provided free space: *TotalNumberOfNewOffspring = (FreeSpace%)*PopulationSizeLimit*.
- Offspring are created by first cloning the fit parent, and then applying K randomly chosen mutation operators from the following list: *[Add_New_Node, Remove_Node, Swap_Node]*. Where each mutation operator has a probability *M(i)* of being chosen.
- The program representing the non leaf node is chosen randomly from the following list: *[*, /, %, +, -, sin, cos, tan, tanh]*, each being chosen with a probability of *N(k)*.
- The program representing the leaf node is chosen randomly from the following list: *[Input(n), 1, 0, Pi]*, each being chosen with a probability of *L(l)*.

As you can see, there are lots of different parameters that need to be set up before we can run the evolutionary algorithm. The parameters specify the mutation probabilities, selection probabilities... Evolutionary Strategies (ES), is another variation on the simple GA approach, which evolves not only the genotype, but also these evolutionary parameters, the evolutionary strategy itself. Thus, as each organism evolves, the probabilities with which mutation operators are applied, and various other evolutionary strategy parameters, are also mutated and evolved. The evolutionary algorithm itself, can change over time for every agent. Thus, we end up not just with a population of genetically different individuals, but genetically different individuals which also evolve at different rates, and use different probabilities for choosing various mutation operators during their reproduction/offspring-creation phase.

Evolutionary strategies [17,18,19] were originally proposed and introduced by Schwefel, and then continued being researched by Rechenberg a decade later. There are advantages to this approach. The evolutionary process itself evolves as well, which is a phenomenon that exists in biological evolution. After all, we are all susceptible to mutation rates at different levels. Our DNA differs in robustness from one another, though to a low degree. So there are certainly features in the biological world where evolutionary strategy changes, if not due to the way DNA itself is structured, then at least due to the fact that different environments on this planet have different levels of exposure to mutagens, radiation... Which means that organisms living in different environments, will have different number of mutation operators applied to their genotype, and at different intensities. The intensities can be based on the level of exposure and presence of mutagens in the particular environmental niches that the organisms inhabit.

3.4.4 Evolutionary Programming

Evolutionary Programming (EP) is a search algorithm closely related to ES, but developed earlier, independently, and specialized to the evolution of state transition tables for finite state machines (FSM). Developed by Lawerence Fogel [20] in the 1960s during the rise of Artificial Intelligence popularity, and developed for the purpose of evolving Finite State Machines (FSM) with ability to predict next actions and environmental states, this particular search algorithm eventually became less and less used, until it finally fell into obscurity. In the 1980s though, it again gained popularity as it was further advanced and reintroduced to the computational intelligence community by David Fogel.

This is another variation and specialization of evolutionary algorithms. Like genetic programming and genetic algorithms, this approach simply specializes in evolving a different type of genotype. Instead of applying the evolutionary algorithm to the evolution of strings, or tree structure encoded programs, it is instead used to evolve FSM based systems, with an inclusion of the self adaptability used by evolutionary strategies.

3.5 A Few Words on Memetic Computing

Memetic Algorithms (MA) sometimes also referred to as Hybrid Algorithms (HA), are evolutionary algorithms that separate the evolutionary process into two phases, global search and local search. The global search part of the evolutionary algorithm might be the type that produces offspring that are spread far and wide within the solution space by creating those offspring through the use of powerful and high impact mutation operators. The local search would then allow each such individual in the population to self optimize, to tune in further and explore its local space/optima and find the best position on it. These types of algorithms have been found to be extremely efficient, more so than the standard, single phase algorithms [21,22].

Let us consider an example where we wish to find/evolve a single small trigonometric function as shown in Fig-3.8, using a memetic algorithm. Unlike the problem discussed in Section-3.3 though, this one is a very simple function, and we will use a very short, static string based genotype encoding. This simple genotype encoding will be as follows: $A+B*F(X*C+D)^E$, where A, B, C, D, and E are variables, and F is a function. The variables span the entire number line, whereas F is a function that can be chosen from the following trigonometric function list: *[Sin, Cos, Tan, Tanh].*

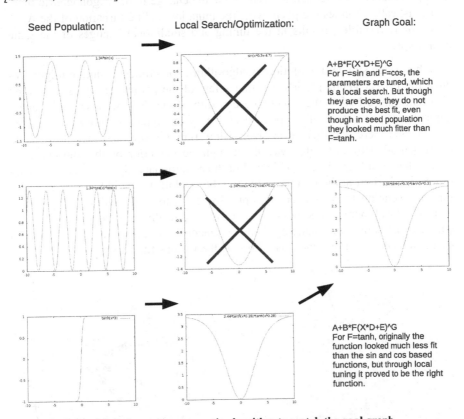

Fig. 3.8 Evolving a function using a memetic algorithm to match the goal graph.

Since the evolution is separated into two phases in memetic algorithms, we will also have two different classes of mutation operators, one for global search, and one for local search. The global search would then search through all the types of trigonometric functions. The list composing the mutation operators (in this case just a single one) for the global search, is as follows: *[ChangeF]*. The global search mutation operator list is composed of a single mutation operator that changes the individual's trigonometric function from the one it is currently using to a new one in the trigonometric function list. Each trigonometric function is very different from every other in its nature, and thus the agents/graphs produced from the different trigonometric functions will be very different from one another. The local search is composed of the following mutation operator: [Perterb_Value]. Where the mutation operator is applied to one of the values in the genotype: *[A, B, C, D, E]*, adding a random value to one of these variables to see if the new phenotype, the graph, is a better match to the goal graph. The local search, the exploration of the local solution space by tuning in the values of the function, allows us to explore each local space of the trigonometric function used, before deciding on its final fitness score. As can be seen, while the change in the trigonometric function drastically changes the phenotype, the mutation and perturbation of the A, B, C, D, or E variables, results in the tuning and small/local changes of the same phenotype.

When using standard evolutionary algorithms, sometimes evolution might produce the perfect genotype, it's just that a few of the parameters need to take on different values before the phenotype can truly shine. But because evolutionary algorithm is just a "one-off" type of deal, if this genotype does not have the right values right there and then, it is given a low fitness score, and then most likely discarded off. Think of it this way, there might be a position on the solution space where there is a high fitness position, but the evolutionary algorithm created a solution that is right at the bottom of the this fitness hill. It would be more effective for each solution to search locally, optimize itself, to truly achieve the potential that its global parameters possess. This is graphically represented in Fig-3.8, which again shows the mapping from the genotype/search space to the solution space, with the solution space also showing the various fitness scores.

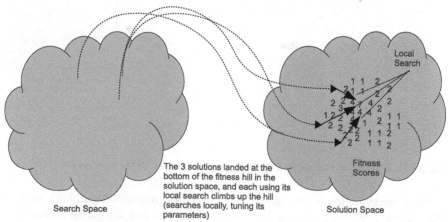

Fig. 3.9 A global search, and a local search. Moving up the fitness hill.

For example, walking only on two legs requires a significant amount of balance, it leaves our hands free to use tools. What if a genotype specifying a pair of legs came into existence, but the part of the brain that deals with balance was still solving a problem for a quadrupedal system? The phenotype would be unable to balance, it would thus be given a poor fitness score, and would disappear from the population. For the bipedal system to work, it would have to be reinvented by evolution with the right balancing neurocontroller at the same time, before it would be given its true fitness. Solving two problems at the same time, like rolling two dice to try and hit the same number at the same time, has a much lower probability than rolling a single die, and then re-rolling the second die until the same number is hit again. The probability of evolving the right set of parameters in the genotype to yield a balancing neurocontroller for a bipedal form might be very low. The probability of evolving bipedal morphology might also be very low. Thus, evolving both at the same time, to be just right to work together, might have an especially low probability of occurring. On the other hand, if we have came across the genotype for bipedal morphology, and then tune in the various parameters to achieve the best performance with this morphology and thus produce a neurocontroller to make this morphology achieve its full potential, is much easier (has a higher probability of being achieved through pure stochastic processes). That is the pattern of operation when it comes to memetic algorithms, separating the global and local searches, however they are defined for a particular genome encoding.

In a sense, a memetic algorithm gives each individual's genotype in the population a chance to demonstrate its best possible fitness. It allows each individual to show what is possible using its general genotypical properties, given that we can tune its "local" parameters to work best with its more globally affecting genotypic structures.

The final example I'll give for memetic computing, and this is us jumping slightly ahead to the subject that will be discussed in detail in the next chapter, is one of evolving neural network systems. In neural networks in particular, as we saw in Chapter 2, we can make a clear distinction between the neural network topologies, the manner in which the neurons are interconnected, and the synaptic weights those neurons possess. The global search part could then be done through the mutation operators which modify the NN's topology itself. While the local search can then be accomplished through the tuning of synaptic weights. This would provide us with scenarios where we could, through mutation, add and connect a few new neurons to an existing NN. But of course simply connecting new neurons to a NN, each with its own randomly selected activation function and synaptic weights, will disrupt that NN system, and most likely make it less fit. So if we then take the time during a separate phase to see if we can tune the synaptic weights of these new neurons, we can try to make these newly added neurons work complementary with the already existing and fit NN system.

Through this approach, we give each NN topology a chance to show its true fitness. We give it time to adjust the synaptic weights, and are then able to judge the actual topological structure, rather than judging how a random topology works with a random set of synaptic weights. This two phase memetic approach has proven to work exceptionally well, and is the method being popularized by the topology and weight evolving systems like DXNN [23] and EANT [24,25].

Are all these systems different: GA, GP, ES, EP, MA? Or are they simply different sides of the same coin? The concluding section of this chapter discusses just that, before we take our first step and dive into neuroevolution.

3.6 The Different Sides of the Same Coin

Today there are advanced versions of GA, GP, ES, EP, and MA. The lines between these flavors of evolutionary computation are blurred to the point where it's difficult to pinpoint where one system ends and another begins. Indeed, they are all technically the same. After all, GP is just GA that operates on a tree algorithm. And if we add the ability to also mutate evolutionary strategy parameters, then we've just went from GA to ES. EP is just GA specialized for finite state machines, and Memetic Computing (MC) is simply a variation on the standard evolutionary computing, which splits the local and global search into separate phases...

How we represent the genotype and phenotype, and how we map from genotype to phenotype, is entirely up to us. Whether we also wish to include the mutation of the evolutionary strategy, the mutation operator probabilities and the particular list of mutation operators; all of this is up to the researcher to choose. Thus, all of this is simply evolutionary computation.

For example, there are GP approaches that evolve not trees but strings, and these strings encode operations taken by a computer, a program in linear form. This type of approach is called linear genetic programming. On the other hand, if instead of a tree we use a graph, the approach is called Cartesian GP. A Cartesian GP can use any type of function or program for the nodes. If we decide that each of the nodes should first sum up the incoming signals and then apply the tanh function to the sum, our Cartesian GP system becomes a neuroevolutionary system. Yet in a neuroevolutionary system, the neurons can also use tanh, sin, cos, or really any other function as well. Learning networks which use different kinds of activation functions, not just tanh, are referred to as *Universal Learning Networks* rather than *Neural Networks*...

We can use GA to evolve building architectures, by for example encoding in the string the position of the various elements of the building, and then evolving a population of such genotypes for some particular fitness, for some particular size and aerodynamic properties for example. We could also represent the genotype of the building as a tree, or as a graph, to make it easier for the GA to apply certain mutation operators... We could also split the single phase of reproduction where offspring are created through mutation, into two phases. In one phase the offspring are created through the application of large scale, high intensity mutations. Then during another phase the offspring could use something like hill climbing, a local search algorithm, to tune in the various parameters of their phenotype, looking around in close proximity to their position on the solution space. At this point our GA would be called MA...

As you can see, everything is pretty much blurred together, a few modifications to your algorithm, modifications that simply make it easier to encode the genotype for some particular project you are working on, and there will be those who will start calling your evolutionary algorithm approach by a new name. These different names simply make it a bit easier to describe quickly some of the features of your evolutionary approach. But in reality, when you continue to advance any evolutionary algorithm, trying to make it more agile, more robust, applicable to more problems... you will continue adding more and more features, including graph encoding, linear encoding, multi phase evolution, evolutionary parameter adaptation, the ability to use functions like tanh, logical operators like XOR, AND... and programs like IF, While... for the nodes within the genotype... An advanced evolutionary system, one that can be applied to any problem and self adapt to it, seeing on its own which features, which encoding, and which evolutionary strategy is best for it, will most likely need to have all of these features.

In conclusion, you can encode the genotype of a system using any type of data structure you want, as long as you can also create the mutation operators to operate on that data structure, and a mapper that can map the genotype from that data structure to its phenotype. It does not matter what that data structure is, or what set of mutation operators you're using, whether you're also using crossover or not, and whether your evolutionary parameters themselves adapt or not. It's all the same evolutionary system, tailored to your problem, by you.

The next chapter introduces neuroevolution, the evolutionary process applied to the evolution of neural networks.

3.7 References

[1] Cracraft J, Donoghue MJ (2004) Assembling the Tree of Life J. Cracraft and M. J. Donoghue, eds. (Oxford University Press), ISBN 0195172345.

[2] Lewontin RC (1970) The Units of Selection. Annual Review of Ecology and Systematics 1, 1-18.

[3] Kimura M (1991) The Neutral Theory of Molecular Evolution: A Review of Recent Evidence. Japan Journal of Genetics 66, 367-386.

[4] Tjivikua T, Ballester P, Rebek J (1990) Self-Replicating System. Journal of the American Chemical Society 112, 1249-1250.

[5] Graur D, Li WH (2000) Fundamentals of Molecular Evolution D. Graur and W.-H. Li, eds. (Sinauer Associates), ISBN 0878932666.

[6] Dawkins R (1976) The Selfish Gene. (Oxford University Press), ISBN 0192860925.

[7] Luke S, Hohn C, Farris J, Jackson G, Hendler J (1997) Co-evolving Soccer Softbot Team Coordination with Genetic Programming. Proceedings of the First International Workshop on RoboCup at the International Joint Conference on Artificial Intelligence 1395: 398-411.

[8] Koza JR (1992) Genetic Programming: On the Programming of Computers by Means of Natural Selection. (MIT Press), ISBN 0262111705.

[9] Koza JR (1994) Genetic Programming II: Automatic Discovery of Reusable Programs. (MIT Press), ISBN 0262111896.

[10] Koza JR et al. (1998) Genetic Programming. Morgan Kaufmann Publishers. ISBN 1558605487.

[11] Holland JH (1975) Adaptation in Natural and Artificial Systems J. H. Holland, ed. (University of Michigan Press).

[12] Mike M (1998) Melanism: Evolution In Action. (Oxford University Press).

[13] Cramer NL (1985) A Representation for the Adaptive Generation of Simple Sequential Programs. In Proceedings of an International Conference on Genetic Algorithms and the Applications, J. J. Grefenstette, ed. (Lawrence Erlbaum Associates), pp. 183-187.

[14] Koza JR, Bennett FH, Andre D, Keane MA (1999) Genetic Programming III: Darwinian Invention and Problem Solving (Morgan Kaufmann), Springer. ISBN 1558605436.

[15] Koza JR, Keane MA, Streeter MJ, Mydlowec W, Yu J, Lanza G (2003) Genetic Programming: Routine Human-Competitive Machine Intelligence. (Kluwer Academic Publishers), Springer. ISBN 1402074468.

[16] Koza JR, Keane MA, Yu J, Bennett FH, Mydlowec W (2000) Automatic Creation of Human-Competitive Programs and Controllers by Means of Genetic Programming. Genetic Programming and Evolvable Machines 1, 121-164.

[17] Hans S. (1974) Numerische Optimerung von Computer-Modellen. (PhD thesis).

[18] Back T, Hoffmeister F, Schwefel HP (1991) A Survey of Evolution Strategies. In Proceedings of the Fourth International Conference on Genetic Algorithms, L. B. Belew and R. K. Booker, eds. (Morgan Kaufmann), pp. 2-9.

[19] Auger A, Hansen N (2011) Theory of Evolution Strategies: a New Perspective. In Theory of Randomized Search Heuristics Foundations and Recent Developments, A. Auger and B. Doerr, eds. (World Scientific Publishing), pp. 289-325.

[20] Fogel LJ, Owens AJ, Walsh MJ (1966) Artificial Intelligence through Simulated Evolution L. J. Fogel, A. J. Owens, and M. J. Walsh, eds. (John Wiley & Sons).

[21] Moscato P (1989) On Evolution, Search, Optimization, Genetic Algorithms and Martial Arts: Towards memetic Algorithms. citeseerx.ist.psu.edu/viewdoc/summary?doi=10.1.1.27.9474 Accessed March 20 2012

[22] Krasnogor, N. (1999). Coevolution of Genes and Memes in Memetic Algorithms. Proceedings of the 1999 Genetic And Evolutionary Computation Conference Workshop Program, 1999-1999.

[23] Sher GI (2010) DXNN Platform: The Shedding of Biological Inefficiencies. Neuron, 1-36. Available at: http://arxiv.org/abs/1011.6022.

[24] Kassahun Y, Sommer G (2005) Efficient Reinforcement Learning Through Evolutionary Acquisition of Neural Topologies. In Proceedings of the 13th European Symposium on Artificial Neural Networks ESANN 2005 (ACM Press), pp. 259-266.

[25] Siebel NT, Sommer G (2007) Evolutionary Reinforcement Learning of Artificial Neural Networks. International Journal of Hybrid Intelligent Systems 4, 171-183.

Chapter 4 Introduction to Neuroevolutionary Methods

Abstract Neuroevolution is the machine learning approach through neural networks and evolutionary computation. Before a neural network can do something useful, before it can learn, or be applied to some problem, its topology and the synaptic weights and other parameters of every neuron in the neural network must be set to just the right values to produce the final functional system. Both, the topology and the synaptic weights can be set using the evolutionary process. In this chapter we discuss what Neuroevolution is, what Topology and Weight Evolving Artificial Neural Network (TWEANN) systems are, and how they function. We also discuss how this highly advanced approach to computational intelligence can be implemented, and what some of the problems that the evolved neural network based agents can be applied to.

We have talked about how the genotype encoding, the mapping from genotype to phenotype, and the phenotypic representation of that genotype, is all completely up to us. We can apply the evolutionary process to any problem, just as long as we can come up with a good genotype encoding and a set of mutation operators that we can use to generate offspring from the fit individuals in the population.

In Chapter 2 we discussed neural networks, ways to optimize and train them (through back propagation for example), and how to imbue them with plasticity, such that they can truly learn and self organize, and adapt on their own, as biological neural systems do. Still though, the self organizing maps, and the Hebbian learning rule based plasticity imbued neurons, are not general. Self organizing maps (SOM) can only be applied to some specific problems, and when we are creating a SOM, we don't really know what map density we should use, what parameters we should use with the map, and what set of inputs to feed it with. The same goes for competitive neural networks. Finally, with regards to plasticity imbued neurons, though each neuron can adapt and learn, it is the neural network as a whole, all its various parameters, and the NN's topology that determines what the cognitive system does. Each neuron might have plasticity, but it only learns if everything is synchronized in the neurocognitive computer, only if the parameters the neurons are using and the topology of the NN as a whole, all have the right settings to do something useful.

Thus, we still need a way to set up all these various parameters in the NN, and to be able to grow and interconnect vast neural networks composed of neurons which have plasticity. For complex problems, supervised learning like the back-propagation will not work, plus we need something to set the right topology and NN parameters, not just the synaptic weights of the neurons...

G.I. Sher, *Handbook of Neuroevolution Through Erlang*,
DOI 10.1007/978-1-4614-4463-3_4, © Springer Science+Business Media New York 2013

There is one optimization algorithm that can do all of this, that can optimize and grow neural network (NN) systems. That algorithm is of course, the evolutionary algorithm. In this chapter we discuss how we can combine neural networks and evolutionary computing into a single system: a neuroevolutionary system.

4.1 Neural Network Encoding Approaches and Mutation Operators

As we discussed, an evolutionary approach can be used with anything, as long as we can come up with its genotype representation, genotype encoding, and a set of mutation operators (programs that can change the genotype). Neural networks are graphs, which themselves are simply multi rooted trees. All that is necessary is for us to come up with how to represent the genotype, how to encode it, and a set of mutation operators that is flexible enough for the evolutionary process to be able to evolve any genotype A into a genotype B, given the chance to apply some set of these mutation operators in some order.

4.1.1 Neural Network Mutation Operators

What would be a good set of mutation operators for the evolution of neural network systems? Well, we know that we need a way to tune the weights of the neurons, thus we need some kind of mutation operator that can modify a synaptic weight. We also need the NN to be able to expand, grow, and have new neurons added to it. Thus, we need a mutation operator that adds new neurons. There are different ways of adding a new neuron: for example we can select an existing layer in the NN and then add a new neuron to that layer and connect it randomly from some randomly chosen neuron and to some randomly chosen neuron in the NN. Or, we can grab two neurons that are already connected, and then disconnect them and reconnect them through a newly created neuron. Finally, another mutation operator that could be of use is one that adds new synaptic connections. For this new synaptic connection establishing mutation operator, we choose a random neuron in the NN, and then connect it to another randomly selected neuron in the NN. These types of mutation operators are referred to as: "complexifying", they add to the existing NN and make it more complex, they grow the NN. A few examples of these types of mutation operators being applied to a simple NN, are shown in Fig-4.1.

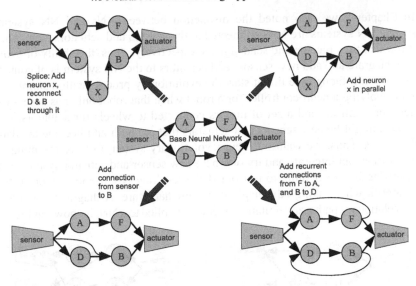

Fig. 4.1 Complexifying mutation operators.

Sometimes it is also a good idea to be able to prune, or remove connections and neurons from a NN. After all, environments change, and a phenotypic feature that might have been useful at one point, might no longer be useful in the new environment. A way to simplify a NN, or a graph in general, can be useful in evolutionary computation and allow it to get from any type of graph A to a graph B, where graph B is a subgraph of A. Thus, a neuroevolutionary system should also have access to mutation operators that can randomly select and delete neurons in the NN, and randomly select and delete connections between neurons and other elements in the NNs, as shown in Fig-4.2.

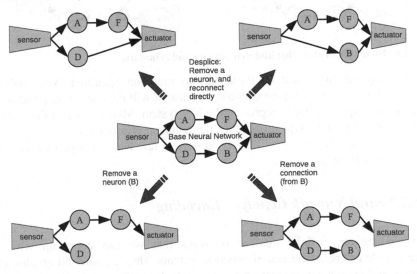

Fig. 4.2 Deleterious mutation operators.

In Chapter-2 we also noted the distinction between NNs and NN systems, where the NN systems are NNs connected to the sensors and actuators from which and to which they receive and send signals respectively. Thus, the ability of evolution to integrate and add new sensors and actuators to the NN system is of course a must. After all, though we might start the evolutionary process with a simple NN system, evolving a neurocontroller for a robot when that robot only has access to a camera for a sensor, and a set of motors connected to wheels for actuators, over time there might be new sensors and actuators that are built and become available to that robot. Thus, we want our neuroevolutionary system to have the mutation operators that can integrate and try out these new sensor and actuator systems with the evolving NN over time, to test out if the resulting NN becomes more robust and more fit when taking advantage of its new hardware. A diagram example of such evolutionary paths, and mutation operators applied to a NN, is shown in Fig-4.3.

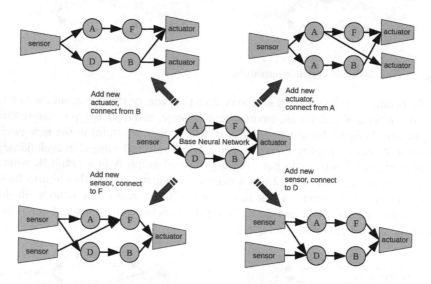

Fig. 4.3 Mutation operators that add new sensors and actuators.

The way we implement all these various mutation operators (MO) will of course depend on the genotype encoding we use, it will depend on how and what kind of data types we use to represent the NN system. MOs are a set of programs that operate on the genotype, to produce the mutation effects we've just discussed. In the following section we will briefly discuss a few ways in which we can encode the NN genotypes.

4.1.2 Neural Network Genotype Encoding

There are any infinite number of ways that we can come up with to store/encode and represent neural network systems. They are after all graphs, and so we could choose any standard manner in which graphs are usually stored. We could encode our NN systems using a string format, strings composed of tuples that contain the input and output node ids, and synaptic weights. A string encoding method is for example the method used in a neuroevolutionary system called NEAT [1]. An example of this genotype encoding method, and the small NN it maps to, is shown in Fig-4.4.

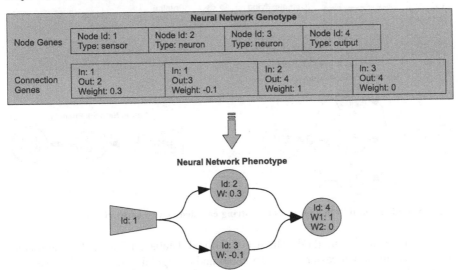

Fig. 4.4 A string encoded neural network.

You can note that just by reading the string, it is not so easy to immediately form the image of what the phenotype, what the actual NN looks like based on its genome. The genotype is composed of two parts, a string of tuples that specify the node ids and node types, and a string of tuples that dictate the connections and synaptic weights between the neurons.

The mutation operators we would need to implement to work with this type of genome encoding would need to be able to add and delete such tuples. For example a mutation operator that adds a new connection between two nodes would first randomly choose the ids of two nodes from the node string, and then compose a tuple that specifies the link between these two nodes, and a random synaptic weight for the postsynaptic neuron of this connection. A synaptic link deleting mutation operator would simply remove any one of the tuples in the connection string. A mutation operator that adds a new node and connects it randomly to other nodes in the NN, would first simply create a new tuple in the node string, with its own unique id, and then add two tuples to the connection string. One tuple would specify the connection from some existing presynaptic node to the new node, and the other tuple would specify a synaptic connection from the new node to some other random postsynaptic existing node in the neural network. Two examples of mutation operators being applied to this form of genotype encoding, and the resulting phenotypes, are shown in Fig-4.5.

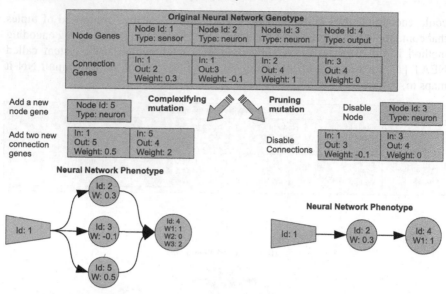

Fig. 4.5 Applying mutation operators to a string encoded neural network.

Another encoding method, which is relational database friendly, human reada-ble, and is thus much easier to reason about and change/mutate, is the one used by DXNN [2] neuroevolutionary system. The encoding simply specifies all the details of each neuron in its own tuple, where the simplified version of this type of tuple has the following format: {Id, Input_IdPs,Output_Ids}, where Input_IdPs is a list of tuples of the form: [{Input_Id,SynapticWeights}....], and where Output_Ids is a list of ids: [OutputId1,OutputId2...]. Each tuple is self contained, possessing all the information needed to define a processing element it represents, whether it be a neuron, a sensor, or an actuator. Each node representing tuple keeps track of the the Ids of the presynaptic elements and the synaptic weights associated with them, and a list of postsynaptic Ids. This genotype encoding makes it very easy for a human to read it, allowing the person to comfortably see which elements are con-nected together, and what the general topology of the NN system is. Finally, be-cause each node representing tuple has its own Id, this encoding also has the per-fect form for being stored in a relational database. An example of a neural network genotype encoded using this method, and the neural network system it maps to, is shown in Fig-4.6.

You will notice in the following figure that in the case of the sensor and actua-tor, their ids are respectively as follows: {sensor_function_name,1} and {actua-tor_function_name,5}. The ids include not only unique identifiers (1 and 5), but also sensor and actuator function names. Like neurons, the sensor and actuator nodes can be represented as processes, and these nodes could then execute the sensor or actuator functions through the function names. If we are talking about a sensor node, then when it executes the function *sensor_function_name*, it would produce sensory signals that it would then forward, by message passing, to the neurons it is connected to. If we are talking about an actuator, then the actuator would accumulate the incoming signals from the presynaptic neurons, and then use this composed vector as a parameter when executing the *actuator_function_name* function. It is a much more dynamic and flexible approach than the above demonstrated string encoding. The few extra bytes of space this tuple encoding method takes, is well paid for by the utility, flexibility, readability, scalability, and usability it provides. Today, even a laptop can easily hold over 16Gb of ram. Why make a system less understandable, and thus much more difficult to work on, expand, and advance, by using a poorly formed encoding that lacks the agility, and does not provide an easy way to think about it? The simpler and more architecturally direct the encoding, the easier it is for the researcher to improve it, work with it, and use and apply it to new areas.

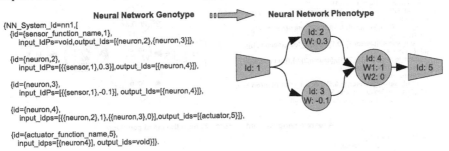

Fig. 4.6 A tuple based neural network genotype encoding.

This tuple encoded genotype makes no attempt at emulating a biological genome. It takes full advantage of the much greater flexibility that software provides. Since the genotype is very similar to how graphs are usually represented, the mutation operators are also very easy to develop and apply. For example, to create a synaptic connection between two neurons, the program simply chooses two random neurons A and B from the NN, and adds a synaptic link from neuron A to B by adding the id of B to A's output_ids list, and by adding the id and a new synaptic weight for A to neuron B's input_idps list. To add a new neuron to the genotype, the *mutator* program simply generates a new neuron tuple, with a new unique id C, and sets up a link between C and some randomly chosen presynaptic neuron A, and to some randomly chosen postsynaptic neuron B. These mutation operators are just graph operators. A few examples of mutation operators being applied to a tuple encoded NN, and the resulting phenotypes, are shown in Fig-4.7.

In Fig-4.7a I show the genotype of the initial NN system, and its phenotype. I then apply a mutation operator where I add a new neuron with id *{neuron,6}* to the initial NN system, the added parts of the genotype are presented in bold in Fig-4.7b, with the phenotype shown on the right side of the updated genotype. Finally, in Fig-4.7c I apply to the initial genotype a mutation operator that removes a random

neuron from the NN, in this case this neuron's Id is *{neuron,3}*. The updated genotype and the phenotype is then shown, with the removed parts of the genotype
highlighted with red (looks as bold font in the black & white printed version).

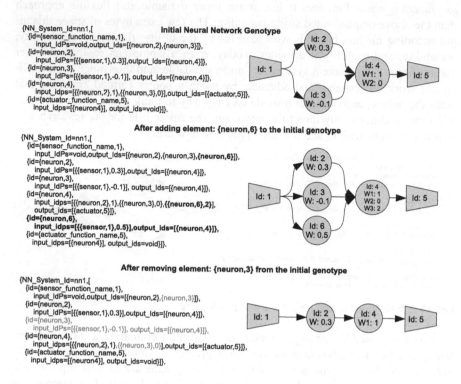

Fig. 4.7 Mutation operators applied to a tuple encoded NN genotype, and the resulting phenotypes.

Undoubtedly there are many other ways to encode neural network systems.
Back in the day when storage space and ram was limited, there were a number of
encoding approaches that tried to minimize the amount of space used by such encodings. But today, storage space and ram are no longer the limiting factors. Our
current computational intelligence systems are only limited by our ability to reason about them, expand them, and improve them. Thus, we should strive to represent the genotypes in manners that are not most space conservative, but in ways
which makes them most easily accessible to being reasoned about. We should create the genotypes and phenotypes in a way that makes it easy to work with, to
think about, to expand, and to improve.

When it comes to neural networks, tuple encoding is one such genotype encoding method, and as we will find out in the next chapter, Erlang gives us the ability to create a phenotypic representation that is just as easy to reason about and work with as its genotype, if not more so. But more importantly, the phenotype implementation in Erlang is a direct mapping of the NN representation, making it unprecedentedly easy to work with, scale, and improve. Neural networks are vast graphs, and so we use an encoding approach that is prevalent in graph representations [3], and one that yields to graph operations most easily. We can go through the genotype and quickly see what type of phenotype, what type of neural network structure that it represents. And because it is so easy to see it, to visualize it, it is easier for us to modify it, it is easier for us to, in the future, expand this encoding method, and to add to it as our knowledge of neuroevolutionary systems and computational intelligence increases.

The ability to easily visualize the system, gives us the ability to think about it more clearly and without us having to constantly map the NNs in our mind back and forth between the way which makes it easy to reason about, and the way in which they are actually implemented in some programming language that does not have the same architecture as the NN systems.

4.1.3 The Neural Network Phenotype

The phenotype is the actual, functional representation of the neural network. It is the system that can process the input signals, and based on those input signals produce output signals from the neurons in the output layer (those neurons which are connected to the actuators). The actual input signals that the NN acquires as input is based on the sensors that it uses to sense the environment, and the actions the NN system takes within the world is done through its actuators, which act upon the world using the control signals coming from the presynaptic neurons. In biological organisms, our DNA is our genotype, and our nervous system is part of our complete phenotype.

The mapping from genotype to phenotype can be direct, where the genotype specifies every part of the phenotype directly, or indirect [4], where the genotype has to go through some kind of developmental cycle, or use some other external information to construct the actual phenotype. We have seen the direct encoded neural networks in the previous subsection. The genotype directly represented the phenotype, every synaptic weight, every connection, and every neuron, was specified within the tuple encoded and string encoded genotypes discussed. Thus, next we will briefly discuss what the indirect encoded NNs are.

In indirect encoding the resulting phenotype is not directly based on the genotype, but is merely controlled or guided by it as it *develops*. The development process is the mapping of genotype to phenotype, sometimes through multiple stages, and where the phenotype can also be affected or produced by incorporating multiple features generated by stochastic processes and through the system's initial interaction with the environment in which it is developing, as shown in Fig-4.8. In this manner, the phenotypes might also be somewhat environment specific, since their development can be influenced by the environmental features during the mapping process.

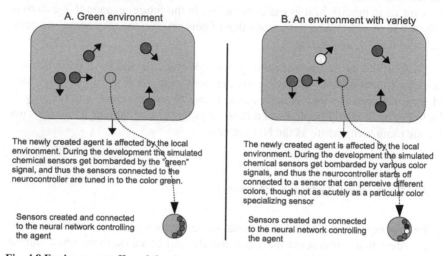

A. Green environment

B. An environment with variety

The newly created agent is affected by the local environment. During the development the simulated chemical sensors get bombarded by the "green" signal, and thus the sensors connected to the neurocontroller are tuned in to the color green.

The newly created agent is affected by the local environment. During the development the simulated chemical sensors get bombarded by various color signals, and thus the neurocontroller starts off connected to a sensor that can perceive different colors, though not as acutely as a particular color specializing sensor

Sensors created and connected to the neural network controlling the agent

Sensors created and connected to the neural network controlling the agent

Fig. 4.8 Environment affected development of a neural network.

The above figure shows two scenarios; in Fig-4.8a a NN is controlling an agent in an ALife environment where most of the agents around it are green, thus the NN created has all 5 of its sensors be green color sensing, such that the agent can better discern the various elements within its environment, and have a higher ability to extract features in a world where most of the things are green. In Fig-4.8b, a neurocontroller is created in an area where there are agents and features in the environment of all kinds of colors, and so the same neurocontroller as in Fig-4.8a now has a different set of sensors, each concentrating on a different color, and thus allowing the agent to have the ability to discern between all the different colored agents within the environment. If we are to create an agent with an ability to see multiple colors in a green environment, its *green resolution* is too low, and it would not compete well in that niche where its color sensing abilities are not needed. If we are to create the green color specializing agent in an environment composed of agents of different colors, it would be blind to anyone that is not green, and thus not be able to compete with color discerning agents. But because the phenotype is not directly specified by the genotype, and because as the genotype is developing/being-mapped to a phenotype, it is being affected by the chemistry of the environment, the phenotype is specialized for the environment in which it is born. If these organisms were biological, and there were two environments, an underground tunnel environment, and a color filled jungle environment, it would be advantageous for the organism born in the tunnel environment to start off with sonar sensors, but color sensors when born in the jungle environment.

Another type of indirect encoding is shown in Fig-4.9. Here it is the particular mapping and the NN implementation that defines what the resulting phenotype is, and how it behaves. The genotype shown is a composition of a tuple encoded NN system shown in the previous subsection, with an extra third and fourth element in the NN. The third element is a list: *[3,5,2]*, and the fourth element is the tuple: *{SensorList,ActuatorList}*. What is interesting here is that it is the third list, [3,5,2] that defines the actual sensory signal processing, and actuator signal producing, NN. The [3,5,2] list defines a neural substrate composed of 3 layers, with 3 neurodes in the first, 5 in the second, and 2 in the third. Furthermore, it is implicit that this neural substrate is two dimensional, and each neurode in this substrate is given a Cartesian coordinate based on its position in the layer, and its layer's position in the substrate. The program that constructs the phenotype, spaces out these layers equidistantly from each other, with the first layer of density 3 positioned at Y = -1, the second at Y =0, and the last at Y = 1 end.

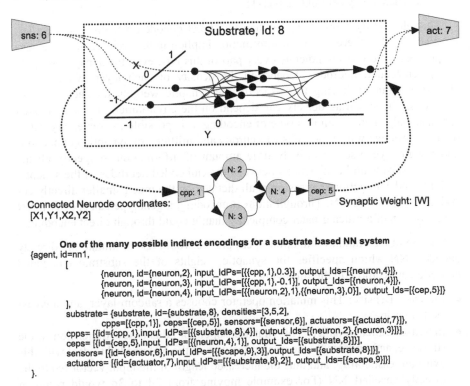

One of the many possible indirect encodings for a substrate based NN system
{agent, id=nn1,
        [
                {neuron, id={neuron,2}, input_IdPs=[{{cpp,1},0.3}], output_Ids=[{neuron,4}]},
                {neuron, id={neuron,3}, input_IdPs=[{{cpp,1},-0.1}], output_Ids=[{neuron,4}]},
                {neuron, id={neuron,4}, input_IdPs=[{{neuron,2},1},{{neuron,3},0}], output_Ids=[{cep,5}]}
        ],
        substrate= {substrate, id={substrate,8}, densities=[3,5,2],
                cpps=[{cpp,1}], ceps=[{cep,5}], sensors=[{sensor,6}], actuators=[{actuator,7}]},
        cpps= [{id={cpp,1},input_IdPs=[{{substrate,8},4}], output_Ids=[{neuron,2},{neuron,3}]}],
        ceps= [{id={cep,5},input_IdPs=[{{neuron,4},1}], output_Ids=[{substrate,8}]}],
        sensors= [{id={sensor,6},input_IdPs=[{{scape,9},3}],output_Ids=[{substrate,8}]}],
        actuators= [{id={actuator,7},input_IdPs=[{{substrate,8},2}], output_Ids=[{scape,9}]}]
}.

Fig. 4.9 Substrate encoded neural network system.

It is further implicit that the first layer of density 3 defines the sensory signal outports, rather than neurons, and that all neurodes in each layer are equally spaced from each other, and thus each neurode has its own coordinate [X,Y]. It is also this first neurode layer that specifies the sensory resolution, but is independent of the neural network, and thus can be specified through development based on the environment (after all, higher resolution requires more processing power, and some environments might not require high resolution...). Finally, the implementation is such, that the directly encoded NN is fed the coordinates of these substrate embedded neurodes (and sensory outports), and the output signal produced by the direct encoded NN is the synaptic weight between the connected neurodes in the substrate. Thus the synaptic weights of the neurodes are defined by this secondary NN.

At the end we end up with a substrate where each embedded neurode has the synaptic weight for its presynaptic connection. The first layer at Y = -1 represents the sensory outports, with the sensors specified in the SensorList (in this case just a single sensor), and the output layer at Y = 1 is connected to the actuators specified in the ActuatorList (in this case a single actuator which can accept a signal of vector length 2). This is in essence a very simplified version of substrate encoding popularized by the HyperNEAT system [17]. We will create a much more advanced substrate encoded system in Chapter-16.

Though slightly more complex than the direct encoded NN discussed earlier, we also note that there is a lot of information implicit in the architecture. The genotype does not on its own dictate every part of this NN, even the synaptic weights of the embedded neurodes depend on the density of each layer, which might change without us having to re-specify the synaptic weights for each of these neurodes. The substrate density can depend on the environment, or be generated stochastically. Thus, with this type of encoding, it is possible to create very dense neural substrates with thousands of neurons and millions of synaptic connections and weights, yet use a relatively little amount of information to specify all the synaptic weights and connections between the embedded neurodes, if the synaptic weights and connection expression is all dictated by the much smaller directly encoded and specified NN. Through indirect encoding, a genotype can specify a NN based system of a much greater complexity than it could through direct encoding.

On top of the standard mutation operators we would use to mutate the directly encoded NN which specifies the synaptic weights of the substrate embedded neurodes, we could add the following:

- Increase_Density: This mutation operator chooses a random layer, and increases its density.
- Increase_Dimensionality: This mutation operator adds a new dimension to the substrate, and updates the necessary features of the NN needed to deal with this extra dimensionality, and thus the increased length of the input vector fed to the directly encoded NN (For example moving from 2d to 3d would result in switching from feeding the NN [X1,Y1,X2,Y2] to [X1,Y1,Z1,X2,Y2,Z2]).

- Decrease_Density: This mutation operator chooses a random layer, and decreases its density.
- Decrease_Dimensionality: Same as the "Increase_Dimensionality" function, but in reverse.
- Add_Coordinate_Preprocessor: The directly encoded NN is fed the coordinates of the two connected neurodes, but we can also first preprocess those coordinates, changing them from Cartesian to polar, or spherical... or instead of feeding the coordinates, we can feed a vector composed of the distances between the Cartesian points where the neurodes are located... This mutation operator performs a task analogous to the Add_Sensor and Add_Actuator, but adds preprocessors used by the NN.
- And of course we could add many other mutation operators, problem specific or general in nature.

For example, you and I are not a direct representation of our DNA, instead, we are based on our DNA, the development process, the chemical environment of the womb, and the nutrition we've been provided with at an early stage of our development. All of this influenced our various phenotypic features, body size and type, and even intelligence. For example, given the same DNA, a fetus in a womb of a mother who consumes alcohol and methamphetamines, will certainly be born with different features than if the mother did not consume these drugs during pregnancy. Thus the mapping from DNA to the actual organism is an indirect process, it is not one-to-one. There are a number of systems that use indirect encoding to produce the resulting neural networks, by simulating chemical diffusion [5,6,7], by using multiple development phases and phase timing [8,9], and many other approaches. And we too will discuss and develop an indirect encoding approach in this book, though in a much later chapter.

In general, the phenotype, the way the neural network system is represented, is at the discretion of the researcher. We can implement the phenotype in hardware [10,11,12,13], on FPGAs for example, in software, or even in wetware using the technology that allows us to grow and connect biological neurons on a substrate [14,15,16]. When implementing in software, we can decide whether the phenotype is fully distributed, like a biological neural network system, or whether it will actually be all processed in series, on a single core. Whatever the choice, as long as the information is processed in the same way, as long as the plasticity and the weights are the same, as long as the events occur at the same time and at the same rate in all these implementations, it does not matter whether the phenotype is hardware, software, or wetware based. The results will be the same; at the end, it's all just information processing.

The mapping from genotype to phenotype itself is done by a program that can read the genotype and then produce the phenotype based on that data. The mapper for the direct or indirect encoded NN system can also be a program implemented in many different ways, and the implementation is of course dependent on the genotype and the phenotype chosen. If for example the genotype is tuple encoded, stored in the Mnesia database, and the phenotype is a process based neural network system, and all of it is written in Erlang, then the mapper simply reads every tuple representing the neurons, sensors, and actuators from the mnesia database, and creates a process for each such node with the properties specified within the tuples. Each process then knows the Ids of the elements it is connected from and from which it should be expecting signals, and the elements to which it is connected to and to which it should be sending its output signals. Had the genotype been string encoded, and the actual neural network represented on an FPGA, then the mapping would have to be completely different.

********Note********
In a biological organism, a ribosome reads the information in RNA and produces proteins making up and used by our bodies. Thus a ribosome, and all the machinery needed for it to work, is a part of the biological mapper program.
****

4.2 Neuroevolution Through Genetic Algorithms

In this section we discuss how a standard, single phased, genetic algorithm based neuroevolutionary approach works. We've seen in the previous section two different ways to encode a NN genotype, and the possible mutation operators needed to evolve populations composed of NNs encoded using such methods. Given this, how do we solve problems through neuroevolution?

To demonstrate how neuroevolution works, we will apply it to the following three example problems: 1. Creating a neural network system that functions as a XOR gate, 2. Creating a neural network system that balances a pole on a moving cart, and 3. Evolving a NN based intelligent system, with all the perks of neural plasticity, the ability to learn, and even the ability to modify its own neural structure, its own brain.

4.2.1 Example 1: Evolving a XOR Logical Operator

As we have seen in Section 2.2.1, if we connect 3 neurons in just the right manner, and set their synaptic weights to the right values, the neural circuit will behave as a XOR operator. But how do we figure out what the right neural network topology is, what is the most optimal topology, and what the right synaptic weights for each neuron in that topology should be set to?

For each problem, we need only to create and set up a set of sensors and actuators that the NN system will use to interface with the environment/scape of that problem. We need only one sensor for this problem, one that can read from the XOR truth table a value, then feed it to the NN in a vector form, and then move to the next row in the truth table. We also need only a single actuator, one to which the NN passes its signal, and where the actuator then simply prints that value to console. The environment or scape in this case, is not some kind of 3d simulation, but instead is the truth table itself, a small database that contains the inputs and the expected outputs, and a small program that monitors the NN system's output, calculates how close it is to the correct output, and then gives the NN a fitness score based on the total error. The system setup is diagrammed in Fig-4.10.

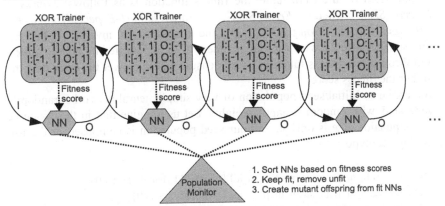

Fig. 4.10 A neuroevolutionary system setup to evolve a XOR logic operator.

What set of steps will a neuroevolutionary system follow to evolve a solution? The set of events would go something like this:

1. We develop a general neuroevolutionary system, which uses a tuple based genotype encoding, and which uses a fully distributed, process based, NN system implementation. The mapping from tuple encoded genotype to phenotype is performed by reading the tuples from the database, and converting each tuple to a process. Each such process expects signals coming from some set of ids, and after it has processed all the expected signals, it outputs a signal to the ids in its output_ids list, or it executes some function (if it is an actuator for example), and then begins the wait for the input signals anew.

2. We develop a set of general mutation operators, whose names and functionality are as follows:

   - add_Neuron
     Generates a new neuron, and connects it from some randomly chosen neuron in the NN, and to some randomly chosen neuron in the NN.
   - add_SynapticConnection
     Selects a random neuron, which then randomly selects and adds either an input or output synaptic link to another randomly selected element in the NN system (neuron, sensor, or actuator).
   - splice
     Chooses a random neuron, then a random element that the neuron is connected to, disconnects the two, and then reconnects them through a newly created neuron.
   - add_Bias
     Chooses a random neuron without a bias, and adds a bias to its weights list.

3. We set up a fitness function for this problem. In this case, since we wish to minimize the general error between the NN system's output and the correct output based on the truth table, the fitness function is as follows: *Fitness = 1/Error_Sum*, where: *Error_Sum = sqrt((Output1-ExpectedOutput1)^2 +(Output2-ExpectedOoutput2)^2 ...)*. The fitness is an inverse of the Error_Sum because we wish for higher fitness to be represented by higher values, and through this fitness function we can ensure that the lower the error then the higher the fitness score.

4. We create an initial/seed population of very simple neural networks, randomly generated, with random synaptic weights. Let us imagine that in this example the population size is only 4, and our seed population is composed of the following genotypes:

```
NN_1: [{s_id1,[n_id1]},{a_id1,[n_id1]},{n_id1,[{s_id1,0.3},{bias,0.2}],[a_id1]}]
NN_2: [{s_id2,[n_id2]},{a_id2,[n_id2]},{n_id2,[{s_id2,0.5}],[a_id2]}]
NN_3: [{s_id3,[n_id3]},{a_id3,[n_id3]},{n_id3,[{s_id3,-1}],[a_id3]}]
NN_4: [{s_id4,[n_id4]},{a_id4,[n_id4]},{n_id4,[{s_id4,-0.2}],[a_id4]}]
```

Genotype encoding is tuple based: *[{sensor_id, fanout_ids}, {actuator_id, fanin_ids}, {neuron_id, input_idps, output_ids} ...]*. The possible initial population might be composed of the above genotypes, where each genotype is just a single neuron NN connected from a sensor and to an actuator, and where the single neuron in NN_1 starts off with a bias value in its weights list.

5. We convert each genotype in the population to its phenotype, and then calculate the fitness of each individual/phenotype by going through each input vector in the truth table and having the NN produce an output, which is then compared to the correct output of the truth table. The fitness of the phenotype is based on the general error of the 4 outputs the NN system provides for the 4 inputs it senses from the truth table. The fitness is calculated using the equation in step 3.

6. We choose 50% of the most fit individuals in the population for the next step, and remove the remaining least fit 50% of the population. Because the population size in this example is 4, this translates into choosing the two most fit agents within the population, and removing the 2 least fit agents.

7. We then use the genotype of these two individuals to create two offspring. To do so, we first clone both genotypes, and then apply X number of mutation operators to each of the clones to produce the mutant clones which are then designated as offspring of the fit NNs. For each clone, the value X is chosen randomly to be between 1 and the square root of total number of neurons the NN is composed of. Thus, the larger the NN, the greater the range from which we choose X (we might apply just 1 mutation operator, or as many as sqrt(Tot_Neurons) to create the offspring). This method gives the mutant clones a chance to both, be genetically close to their parents if only a few mutation operators are applied, and be far out on the search and solution space if a large number of mutation operators is applied.

8. We compose the new population from the two parents, and the two mutant offspring. This new population is the new generation, and is again of size 4.

9. Go to step 5, until one of the NN systems achieves a fitness of at least 1000 (An error of less than 0.001).

In evolution it's all about exploring new genotypes and phenotypes, and the more permutations and combinations of synaptic weights and NN system topologies that is tried out, the greater the chance that an offspring superior to its parent is evolved. The greater the population size, the more varied the mutation operators, and the more varied the number of said mutation operators applied to the clone to produce an offspring, which results in greater NN population diversity. In an actual neuroevolutionary system, we would use a population size greater than 4. Though of course, each individual in the population requires computational time to think, and so the larger the population, the more computational time required to evaluate it... Whether it is better to have a larger population or a smaller one, whether it is best to choose the top 90%, top 50%, or only top 10% of the population to produce offspring from... are all dependent on the system and the mutation operators used. And even all of these features can be dynamic and evolvable, as is the case with the previously briefly discussed approach called "evolutionary strategies".

By going through steps 1-9, we would eventually evolve a neural circuit that acts as a XOR logic operator. Assuming that the available activation functions to the neurons in this hypothetical neuroevolutionary system are the functions composing: [tanh,cos,sin,abs,gaussian,sgn], one of the possible evolutionary paths towards a solution is shown in the following figure.

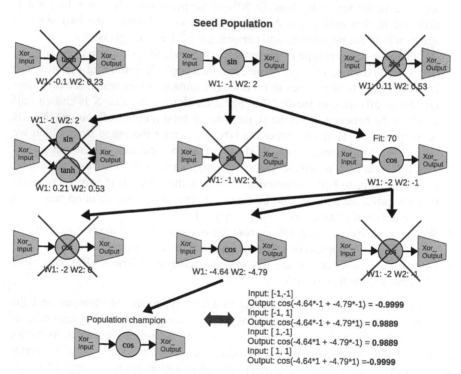

Fig. 4.11 A possible evolutionary path towards a XOR logic operator.

4.2.2 Example 2: Evolving a pole balancing neurocontroller

The problem: Let us say that we have been given a problem of having to develop a way to balance two poles on a cart, where the cart itself is positioned on a 2 meter track, as shown in Fig-4.12. Our only ability to affect the environment is by pushing the cart with a force we choose, either back or forth on the track, every 0.02 seconds. Furthermore, every 0.02 seconds we are allowed to measure the angle that the two poles make with the vertical, and the cart's position on the track. Finally, the solution must satisfy the following constraints: The cart must always remain on the track, the poles must never be more than 35 degrees from the vertical, the poles must be balanced for at least 30 minutes, and we can only interact with the track/cart/poles system by pushing the cart back and forth on the track. What we are seeking is to create a neurocontroller that can produce the force values with which to push the cart to balance these poles, how can this be done through neuroevolution?

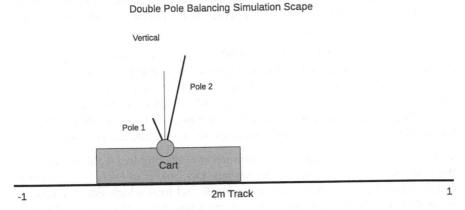

Fig. 4.12 The double pole balancing problem.

Let us do the same thing we did in the previous section. For this problem we will decide on what needs to be set up, before evolution can take its toll and evolve a neural network system that solves the given problem by sensing the system state, and outputting force values to control the cart.

The Problem representation: If we are given the actual hardware, the physical track, cart, and the poles attached to it, we would not really be able to apply an evolutionary process to it to create a neurocontroller that can push and pull the cart to balance the poles, since it would require us to create physical pushers and pullers, each controlled with its own neurocontroller... It would be a mess. Not to mention, since we have to at least balance the pole for 30 minutes, and everything is done in real time, it would take us an enormous amount of effort, real hardware, and time to do this. Every evaluation of a NN's performance would take from a few seconds to 30 minutes, and it could take thousands of evaluations in total (thousands of offspring tested) before one of high enough fitness is found. Finally, we would also need the same number of cart/track/poles systems as the number of NNs in the population, if we wish to perform the said tasks in parallel. Otherwise we would need to perform the evaluations of the NNs one after the other, and thus further decrease the speed at which we would evolve a fit NN.

What we could do instead is create a simulation of the whole thing. Since the cart has to stay on the track, and the pole is attached with a hinge to the cart, it is constrained to two dimensions. The physical simulation would be rather simple, and require just a few equations to implement. Also, because we can use a simulation of the whole thing, we do not have to run it in real time, we can run the simulation as fast as our computer allows. So then, the way we can represent this problem and evolve a neurocontroller to solve it, is through a simulation of the track-cart-poles system, with the ability for the cart to be pushed back and forth on the track. The next question is, how do we represent the neural network genotype encoding?

The Genotype: We can use the same NN genotype encoding as in the previous problem, it is general enough to be used almost for anything, easy to read, easy to operate on, and easy to store in databases. In fact, the NN genotype encoding is independent of the problems we apply the NN based controllers to. Using the same NN genotype encoding, we need only to figure out how our NN would interface with the track-cart-pole simulation scape so that the NN can push the cart.

The Interface: We've created the simulation of the problem we'd like to solve. We know how to encode our NN genotypes. Our goal is to evolve a NN system that decides when to push the cart on the track, and from which side. So then, we know that our NN can have access to the cart's position on the track, and the angles between the poles and the vertical every 0.02 seconds of the simulation. We need to create a way for our NN to interface with the simulation, and that is where sensors and actuators come into play. It is the sensors and actuators that, in a sense, define what the NN is applied to and what it does. Our brain might be a highly adaptive system, capable of learning and processing very complex data inputs, but without our body, without our arms, legs, muscles, without our eyes, ears, and nose, we cannot interface with the world, and there would be no way of telling what any of those output neural signals mean if they were not connected to our biological actuators.

For the NN to be able to interface with the simulation of the track-cart-poles system, we create a sensor that can gather a vector signal from the simulation every 0.02 seconds and feed it to its NN, which then processes that signal and sends its output to the actuator. The actuator of the NN needs to be able to use this signal to then push the cart back or forth. Thus, the actuator interfaces with the simulation, and tells the physical simulation from which side of the cart the force should be applied to push it. Furthermore, the sensor will forward to the NN a sensory signal encoded as a vector of length 3: [CartPos,Pole1Ang,Pole2Ang], where CartPos is cart position value, Pole1Ang is the first pole's angle to the vertical, and Pole2Ang is the second pole's angle to the vertical. The actuator will accept a connection from a single neuron in the NN, because it only needs one value, between -1 and 1, which dictates which way to push the cart, and with what force. Thus the NN will forward to the actuator a vector of length 1: [F], where F is force. The only remaining thing to consider is how to set it all up into a neuroevolutionary process.

The setup: Having decided on all the parts, the NN encoding, the problem formulation (A simulation) so that we can solve it through evolution, and the way in which the NN systems will interface with the simulation so that we can assess their phenotypic fitness, we can now put it all together to evolve a solution to the given problem. A diagram of the setup of how a NN system would interface with the pole balancing simulation through its sensors and actuators, is shown in Fig-4.13.

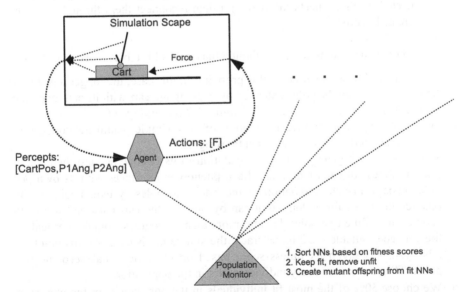

Fig. 4.13 This figure shows a neural network system interfacing with the pole balancing simulation. The NN based agent can sense the position of the cart, and the pole_1 & pole_2 angles with respect to the vertical, and push the cart on the track using its sensors and actuators respectively, to interface with the pole balancing simulation scape.

Our neuroevolutionary approach would take the following set of steps to produce a solution:

1. We develop a general neuroevolutionary system, which uses a tuple based genotype encoding, and which uses a fully distributed, process based, NN system implementation. The mapping from tuple encoded genotype to phenotype is performed by reading the tuples from the database, and converting each tuple to a process. Each such process expects signals coming from some set of ids, and after it has processed all the expected signals, it outputs a signal to the ids in its output_ids list, or it executes some function (if it is an actuator for example), and then begins the wait for the input signals anew.

2. We develop a set of general mutation operators, whose names and functionalities are as follows:

   – add_Neuron
     Generates a new neuron, and connects it to a random postsynaptic neuron in the NN, and a random presynaptic neuron in the NN.
   – add_SynapticConnection
     Selects a random neuron, which then randomly selects and adds either an input or output synaptic link to another randomly selected element (neuron, sensor, or actuator) in the NN system.
   – splice
     Chooses a random neuron, then a random element that the neuron is connected to, disconnects the two, and then reconnect them through a newly created neuron.
   – add_Bias
     Chooses a random neuron without a bias, and adds a bias to its weights list.

3. We set up a fitness function for this problem. In this case, the longer a NN system is able to keep the poles balanced by pushing the cart with its actuators, the higher its fitness. Thus : *Fitness = Simulated_Time_Balanced*.

4. We create an initial or seed population of very simple neural networks, randomly generated, with random synaptic weights.

5. We convert each genotype in the population to its phenotype, and then calculate the fitness of each individual. Each phenotype interfaces with its own private scape, a private simulation of the track-cart-poles system. Each tries to balance the poles for as long as it can by pushing the cart back and forth. As soon as any of the two poles deviates more than 35 degrees from the vertical, or the cart goes outside the 2 meter track, the simulation is over. At this point the NN system is given its fitness score based on the time it balanced the two poles. This is done for every individual/NN in the population.

6. We choose 50% of the most fit individuals in the population for the next step, and remove the least fit in the population by deleting their genotypes from the database.

7. We then use the genotype of these fit individuals to create offspring. We clone the fit genotypes, and then apply X number of mutation operators to each of the clones to produce the mutant clones which we designate as the offspring. For each clone, X is chosen randomly to be between 1 and the square root of total number of neurons making up the clone's NN. Thus, the larger the NN, the greater the range from which we choose X (we might apply just 1 mutation operator, or as many as sqrt(Tot_Neurons) to produce a mutant-clone/offspring).
8. We compose the new population from the fit parents, and their offspring. This new population is the new generation.
9. *Go to step 5, until one of the NN systems achieves a fitness of at least 30 simulated minutes balanced. This resulting NN system is the sought after neurocontroller.*

Once such a NN system is generated, we extract it from the population, and embed the phenotype into the hardware that supplies the sensors and actuators. The NN system is then connected and embedded in this robot system, the actual piece of hardware that interfaces with the physical track-cart-poles system. The robot's sensors then feed the NN with the signals it gathers from the track-cart-poles system (like our eyes that gather the visual information, propagating it to our brain), and the NN's output controls the robot's actuator, which then based on those signals (like our muscles based on the nerve signals coming from our brain) pushes the physical cart on the track.

Thus we have taken this problem all the way from formulating it in neuroevolutionary terms, to evolving the solution, and then using the evolved solution to solve the actual problem. In the next section we try to see how we would use the same principles to solve a slightly more complex problem.

4.2.3 Example 3: End Game; Evolving Intelligence

What if the goal is to evolve intelligence? There is no better approach than the one through neuroevolution. Biological evolution had to evolve both: The morphology of the organism, and the neurocognitive computer to control it. It did this protein by protein, taking billions of years and trillions of permutations, but we can cut a few corners. And where the biologically evolved intelligence was simply a side effect of evolving a survival machine which can replicate in a hostile and uncertain world, where learning and adapting to the ever capricious environment is a must, for our problem we can ensure that adaptability and intelligence are directly tied in with the fitness function.

As we previously discussed though, there is a certain problem with the granularity of simulation, and the dynamic and complexifying environment, as well as the organisms. For there to be a smooth evolutionary path from a simple organism to an intelligent and complex one, not only the organisms must smoothly increase in complexity as they evolve, but they must also be able to affect the environment, and the environment must have a granularity fine enough that it too can slowly become complex, such that the complexifying organisms and the environment compose a positive feedback loop, slowly ratcheting their mutual complexity upwards.

For the environment to provide enough flexibility for the organisms to interact with, it must be simulated at a very high level of granularity, perhaps even atomic. The population size must also be vast, after all, it took billions of years of evolution with the population of various species and organisms inhabiting and spread out across the entire planet. All of this will require an enormous amount of computational power.

The place where we can cut corners and speed things up is in the actual genotype representation, morphology, and neural network systems. With regards to genome, we do not need for the evolutionary process to discover RNA and evolve it into DNA, we can start off with systems which already have this genome encoding mechanism. We also don't need for the evolutionary process to discover from scratch how to create a biological information-processing element, the neuron. We can start off using agents which can already use neurons from the very start. We also can cut a few corners with regards to evolving viable morphologies. We could provide the NN with the various sensors and actuators that it can integrate into itself through evolution. The sensors and actuators would in effect represent the morphology of the organism, and so we could allow the evolution, through this approach, to evolve agents from the morphological form which uses a simple flagella to move, to an agent with a sophisticated neurocognitive computer and bipedal morphology. We need not rediscover bipedal organisms, legs, fins... and we do not need to rediscover the various chemical pathways to use energy, or supportive structures like bones... thus our evolutionary system just needs to primarily concentrate on the evolution of the neurocognitive computer, the rest is taken care of by science and engineering, rather than chance.

What about the fitness function? We could of course create organisms which are capable of producing offspring once they have gathered enough energy from the artificial environment, thus letting them control their own reproductive cycles. Or we could create an outside system that chooses the genotypes from which to create the offspring. It is interesting to consider what would be the difference in evolutionary paths taken by such two disparate approaches. The organisms capable of initiating their own reproductive cycle need no fitness function because only those will survive whom can create offspring, since only they will be able to pass their genetic material to the next generation, and their offspring too will try to create offspring of their own, mutating and evolving over time. The ability of an agent to control its reproductive cycle, and having to compete for resources, will drive the system towards complexity. But since we start the seed population with random and very simple NN systems, initially no one would be able to create their own offspring, or have capabilities to effectively gather the needed resources to do so. So we would actually have to bootstrap the system until it has achieved a steady-state. To do so, we would run the simulation, restarting populations and generating new offspring, until finally one of the individuals in the population acquires the ability to reproduce, at which point the agents will take over when it comes to creating their offspring. This is similar to how it took a few billion years of random collisions and molecular permutations on our planet, before by chance alone, one of the combinations of those molecules formed a chemical replicator.

If we were to not allow self initiated reproduction, and instead used a program which chose whom of the individuals had the most fit and diverse genotype, and whom should be chosen as the base for offspring creation, then we would have to think which of the traits and accomplishments of the organism during its lifetime that we should reward? Where to place the new offspring in the physical environment? In the case of self initiated reproduction, the offspring can be placed right next to the parent, which might also evolve the behavior of teaching, after all, those offspring that have the neural plasticity to learn, and a parent that can teach it the already learned tricks of survival, would have a much greater chance of surviving, and thus passing onwards its genotype which encoded for teaching its offspring in the first place... To solve this problem we could set up spawning pools, certain designated areas where we would put offspring. Or we could randomly position them somewhere in the environment. Or perhaps we could randomly choose an organism in the environment that most closely resembles the genome of the new offspring, and place that offspring next to that currently living individual. All of these are viable approaches, but for this example, we will choose the bootstrapping self initiated reproduction approach.

Let us then think how, if computational power was limitless, and high precision physics simulations at the level of atomic particles was also available, would we then set up a neuroevolutionary system to evolve intelligence? We will follow the same steps and approaches we did in the previous section, we will define the problem, the possible genotype encoding, the interface, and the setup.

The Problem: Evolve a population of organisms capable of intelligence, learning, adaptation, and inhabiting/controlling a body similar to the form of a sapient organism.

The Genotype Encoding: The NN system genotype encoding is the same as in the previous two sections. But because we need for there to be a whole different set of morphologies, all the way from a bacteria to that of a bipedal robot, we need to somehow include the evolution of morphology, integrated with the evolution of the NN, all in a single system. We can do this through the use of sensors, actuators, and modular robotics, as shown in Fig-4.14.

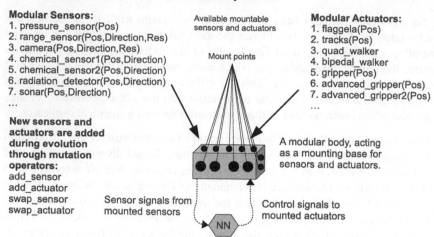

Modular Sensors:
1. pressure_sensor(Pos)
2. range_sensor(Pos,Direction,Res)
3. camera(Pos,Direction,Res)
4. chemical_sensor1(Pos,Direction)
5. chemical_sensor2(Pos,Direction)
6. radiation_detector(Pos,Direction)
7. sonar(Pos,Direction)
...

New sensors and actuators are added during evolution through mutation operators:
add_sensor
add_actuator
swap_sensor
swap_actuator

Available mountable sensors and actuators

Mount points

Modular Actuators:
1. flaggela(Pos)
2. tracks(Pos)
3. quad_walker
4. bipedal_walker
5. gripper(Pos)
6. advanced_gripper(Pos)
7. advanced_gripper2(Pos)
...

A modular body, acting as a mounting base for sensors and actuators.

Sensor signals from mounted sensors

Control signals to mounted actuators

NN

Fig. 4.14 Evolving morphology through sensor and actuator modules of the NN system.

The above figure demonstrates how to encode morphological properties and integrate them into the same encoding as the NN, and thus evolve morphology fluently and in synchrony with the neural network. A sensor is a program used by the NN to gather data from the scape it interfaces with. A sensor can be anything, and a sensor program can also define, when simulated in some physical environment, a shape, or morphological property, location on a body... An actuator is a program that the NN uses to act upon the world. There can be many different kinds of actuators, each possessing some particular morphological property, look, and defining some particular body part. But also, just like the case with the sensor which might read sensory signals coming from inside the NN, the actuator might be a system that affects the agent's own NN topology. Again, a sensor and an actuator is anything we can come up with to feed the NN signals, and used by the NN to perform some function, respectively.

We can further tie-in the sensor and actuator combinations with particular body structures when simulated inside environments. For example there could be a flagella actuator, and if some NN uses a chemical receptor sensor, and has a flagella actuator, meaning the NN gathers data from the environment through its chemical receptor, and can only move through the environment using its flagella, then the physical simulation can represent this individual as a bacteria, with the appropriate physical properties and size. The sensor and the actuator both have a particular way they look, and their own physical properties. When for example the noted sensors and actuators occur together in the NN, the scape would set the morphology of the NN's avatar to a bacterium, representing the actuator as the flagella, and the sensor as a small attachment capable of sensing the chemical properties of the avatar's immediate surroundings.

Thus, on top of the tuple encoded NN genotype, we also want to have a very large list of sensors and actuators that the NN systems can integrate over time into themselves through the application of the add_sensor, add_actuator, and swap_sensor/swap_actuator mutation operators. The swap_sensor and swap_actuator mutation operators choose an already integrated sensor or actuator, and swap it with a new randomly chosen sensor or actuator respectively. The different sensors could be as follows: [chemo_sensor, photo_sensor, pressure_sensor, monoscopic_camera, telescopic_camera...]. The different actuators could be as follows: [flagella, differential_drive_wheels, 3_degfree_leg, 4_degfree_leg, 5_degfree_leg, 3_degfree_arm, 4_degfree_arm, 5_degfree_arm, 3_fingeredhand, 4_fingeredhand, 5_fingeredhand, 6_fingeredhand, pivot_tilt_sensor_mount, 3part_torso, 4part_torso...]. The sensor and actuator tags are names of functions, which when integrated into a NN existing in a simulation, also have simulated physical representations. The sensors and actuators do not need to be evolved from atomic or molecular building blocks, the NN needs only to learn how to control these mountable interfaces.

Furthermore, the type of actuators used and integrated could define the general body type, and we could set it up such that the increase in size of the neural network automatically increases the general size of the body and energy drain. Or we could use a finer level of granularity when adding new sensors and actuators, and simply add one joint at a time, thus building up the gripper and other types of actuators. This could then possibly make the add_sensor and add_actuator mutations more flexible, allow them to randomly also specify the position where to attach the simple new morphological pieces (joints, connectors...), but at the same time this would provide a few orders of magnitude more permutations resulting in unusable, unstable, and unfit morphologies.

Finally, we could also add a sensor list as follows: [read_self_genotype, read_other_genotype] and actuator list as follows: [modify_node, next_node, swap_node, move_node...]. These functions would allow the organisms to evolve capabilities to self augment, and to have the ability to read the genotypes belonging to others, which would perhaps require the simulation environment to set up certain rules, like having the other organism be willing, or be subdued or killed first, before its genotype can be examined.

These are all possibilities, and there is really no reason why abilities to use these types of skills should not be possible to evolve. As long as the environment and the mutation operators available are flexible and robust enough, there will be an evolutionary path to integrate these capabilities. In this book, when we begin discussing applications, we will actually build a small 2d ALife system, where prey organisms could evolve "teeth", and learn how to attack other prey. In fact I have implemented such a system, and indeed simple prey and predators did evolve to hunt and evade each other, to use plants (simulated food elements) as bait, and even evolve from prey to predator by evolving (through the use of add_sensor and add_actuator mutation operators) new morphological parts, integrating them, and becoming more effective at hunting, evading, and navigating.

The Interface: Somewhat of a continuation of the above, the interface of the NN to the physical simulated environment is done through the sensors and actuators. The NN receives through the sensors all the information that its avatar senses, and whatever signals it sends to the actuators, the avatar performs. When the avatar dies, the NN dies, at which point the phenotype's, and therefore the NN system's performance in the environment, is given a fitness score depending on the organism's achievements during its lifetime. The achievements could be the following: the amount of food gathered during lifetime, the number of inventions made, the amount of world explored, or simply the number of offspring created if the system is a bootstrapped one where agents can replicate of their own accord.

The Setup: In this hypothetical example we will choose to use a bootstrapped approach, bootstrapping the initial seed population of organisms, until one emerges that can effectively use the *create_offspring* actuator to produce an offspring when it has enough energy to do so. The environment, the world, is a simulated 3d environment. It is simulated all the way at the atomic level, since we assume that we have access to unlimited computational power, and thus the processing power required to simulate an entire planet at an atomic level is not an issue. Each NN interfaces with the simulated world through its avatar, a simulated body whose sensors feed sensory signals to the NN, and whose actuators are controlled by the NN. We could even go as far as simulate the actual NN topology in physical form, and position that NN physical representation inside the avatar.

The physical form the organism takes is determined by the sensors and actuators that belong to the NN, the sensors and actuators that the NN evolved over time. The size and shape of the avatar is further dependent on the size of the NN system, and the energy requirements, the amount of energy the organism burns per simulated second, also depends on the sensors, actuators, the NN size, and the organism's size. Each organism will also start with a create_offspring actuator, which requires a certain amount of energy and time to be used, after which there is a delay time during which an offspring is created. The offspring is created in the same fashion as in the previous section, it is a mutated clone of the organism, and the number of mutation operators applied to produce it depends, with random intensity, on the complexity of the parent's NN. Unlike in the previous problem, each NN system does not interface with their own *private scape*, but instead all the NN systems (the avatars/agents), inhabit the same large simulated world, the same *public scape*. Because each organism creates its own offspring based on the energy it has gathered by eating other organisms in the environment, we do not need to set up a fitness function. Instead only the create_offspring function needs to be set up in such a way that it has a cost to the organism, and that perhaps during the first few simulated years of the offspring, the offspring does not function at full capacity, and neither does it function at full capacity when it is in its more advanced age. Its power output, efficiency, speed, could follow a Gaussian curve proportional to its age. Finally, the organisms are set to die when they get eaten, or when reaching some specific age, which might itself be based on the total number of sense-think-act cycles the NN has performed. This could have an interesting effect, since larger NNs will not react as quickly as smaller ones, due to it taking a longer time to process a signal with 100 billion neurons than it does with a single neuron. This will mean that more complex organisms, though slower, will live longer (same number of sense-think-act cycles, but longer period of time), and be able to do much more complex computations per cycle than simpler organisms. So age could also be based on the neural network complexity of the organism. With this in mind, the evolutionary system might follow the following steps:

1. We develop a general neuroevolutionary system, which uses a tuple based genotype encoding, and which uses a fully distributed, process based, NN system implementation. The mapping from tuple encoded genotype to phenotype is performed by reading the tuples from the database, and converting each tuple to a process. Each such process expects signals coming from some set of ids, and after it has processed all the expected signals, it outputs a signal to the ids in its output_ids list, or it executes some function (if it is an actuator for example), and then begins the wait for the input signals anew.

2. We develop a set of general mutation operators, whose names and functionalities are as follows:

   - add_Neuron
     Generates a new neuron, and connects it to a random postsynaptic neuron in the NN, and a random presynaptic neuron in the NN.
   - add_SynapticConnection
     Selects a random neuron, which then randomly selects and adds either an input or output synaptic link to another randomly selected element (neuron, sensor, or actuator) in the NN system.
   - splice
     Chooses a random neuron, then a random element that the neuron is connected to, disconnects the two, and then reconnect them through a newly created neuron.
   - add_Bias
     Chooses a random neuron without a bias, and adds a bias to its weights list.
   - add_sensor
     This mutation operator chooses a random sensor from the available list of sensors, and connects it to a randomly chosen neuron in the NN.
   - swap_sensor
     This mutation operator randomly chooses a currently used sensor, and swaps it for another available sensor.
   - add_actuator
     This mutation operator chooses a random actuator from the available list of actuators, and connects to it a random neuron in the NN.

– swap_actuator
This mutation operator randomly chooses a currently used actuator, and swaps it for another available actuator.

3. We set up the physical simulation of the environment, and all non biological properties to be ran by the simulation. We also set up the metabolism simulation within the environment, such that agents are drained of energy proportional to the size of their avatars, and NN size.

4. We create an initial/seed population of very simple neural network systems, each with its own set of sensors and actuators that defines the morphological properties of their avatars.

5. We convert each genotype in the population to its phenotype, and then let the organisms live out their lives. Some will starve to death, some will flourish.

6. If all organisms die, and non are able to create an offspring, we supplement the population by creating offspring from the genotypes that were most fit, exhibited most intelligence, survived the longest... (this is the population bootstrapping part, used until one of the generated agents can control its *create_offspring* actuator, and is able to create an offspring that can continue the cycle).

7. Once the organisms begin to emerge which know how to use create_offspring actuators, and the population stabilizes and begins to grow, the bootstrapping and population supplementation stops. Whereas until this point we in a sense simulated the stochastic collisions and interactions and the creation of various invalid replicators, after this point a replicator has been generated through random processes, and evolution takes over where stochastic search left off. At this point the properties of the simulated world and evolution take over.

8. Due to the flexibility and fine granularity of the environment, it is morphed and shaped by the evolving organisms, which are morphed and shaped by co-evolution, arms race, competition, and the environment that they shape and morph.

9. As organisms compete with each other in an environment that is growing ever more complex, different species will begin to emerge as various agents find niches in the environment to exploit, separating from others to occupy and specialize in those niches. Different sized NNs and avatars will begin to emerge...

10. The simulation is allowed to run indefinitely, so that the increasing complexity of the environment and agent interaction ratchets the increase in complexity of the system... setting up a positive feedback loop. If at any moment complexity stops increasing, if it stabilizes, or evolution takes the wrong turn somewhere, and becomes unable through mutation to jump out of a local intelligence optima, the researcher can then modify the environment to try to set up scenarios that require an increase in intelligence. This can be done by for example setting up famine scenarios, increasing the difficulty of reaching certain foods, adding new elements to the environment that require cleverness to be exploited, or making the environment more fine grained, more realistic.

As you can see, the setup is pretty much the same as in the previous examples. As long as we can formulate the problem in evolutionary terms, and any problem can be, we can then evolve a solution for it. In the next section we will briefly explore a variation on the standard evolutionary algorithm based approach. In the next section we will discuss a memetic algorithm based neuroevolution.

4.3 Neuroevolution Through Memetic Algorithms

A memetic algorithm subdivides the search algorithm into two phases, global search and local search. In neural networks, this separation into two phases might mean the separation of the topological mutation operators from the synaptic weight mutation operators. When we mutate the topology of the neural network, we are exploring NN systems that differ from each other significantly. On the other hand, when we tune and perturb synaptic weights, we are exploring the local solution space of the NN system of a particular topology, tuning the synaptic weights and guiding them towards the local optima that the topology can achieve. The following figure shows and compares the steps of the genetic and memetic algorithm based neuroevolutionary systems.

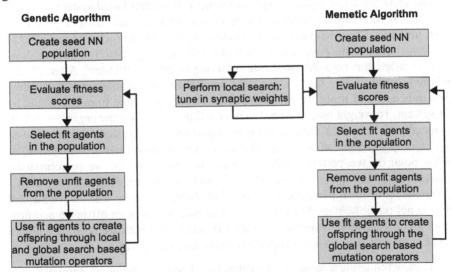

Fig. 4.15 The comparison of genetic and memetic algorithm based neuroevolution.

There are both, advantages and at times disadvantages when using memetic computing instead of genetic computing. One of the main advantages is that when we evolve a new topology for an organism, we do not immediately discard it if it does not function better than its parent. Instead we give it time to tune in the synaptic weights for its neural topology, giving it time to reach its full potential (given a reasonable amount of computational time), and only then judge it. In a genetic algorithm type system, we would randomly mutate a fit topology, giving the new features random synaptic weights, and then expect it to outperform its parent. That is of course highly unlikely, after all, when we perturb a functional topology with random features which can technically be considered garbage DNA until proven otherwise, there is very little chance that the new synaptic weights will be in tune with the whole system and make it superior to its parent. At the same time, when we mutate a topology, there are usually only a few new weights added (when adding a new neuron, making new synaptic connections, or adding a bias...), and so it would not be difficult or costly, to try out a few different weight setups before discarding the topological innovation. Thus, where memetic algorithm keeps topology as a constant while searching through the synaptic weights that make this new topology functional (before trying out a new topology), the genetic algorithm system hopes to hit the perfect combination with regards to the NN topology and its synaptic weights in one throw. But getting both at the same time, from the sea of such combinations, is not likely to occur, and it is for this reason why evolution takes so much time.

But there are a few disadvantages to memetic algorithm based systems as well, particularly in ALife simulations where organisms can create offspring by their own initiative. For example, how do we do weight tuning in such a scenario? If to perform weight tuning we use a stochastic hill-climbing (SHC) algorithm, how can we allow the organism to create offspring during its lifetime? After all, the whole point of SCH is that we see if the new locally found solution is better than previous one, and if not we destroy it and recreate a new one from the originally fit system. To weight tune, we need to have a fitness score for the organism, which is usually given once it dies. In a genetic algorithm based system, an organism or agent simply creates an offspring. But in a memetic algorithm driven system, at what point do we perform global search? At what point do we perform local search? Also, during the local search we would try one organism at a time with a different set of local parameters, to see if it's better or worse than its parent, but that is not possible in an ALife scenario. The parent creates an offspring and now both are alive, and we won't know which is better until both are dead. If both are dead, what will create a new offspring to continue local search?...

Thus, when using a memetic algorithm based neuroevolutionary approach, it is no longer as trivial as giving an organism an actuator that allows it to create an offspring. Thus if we are willing to have a program external to the ALife simulation create the offspring of the agents within the scape, then memetic algorithm based neuroevolution can also be used in ALife. To do this, we remove the ability of each organism to control its own reproduction, and use an external program that calculates each organism's fitness during its lifetime. When some agent within the environment dies, this program creates an offspring based on some already dead but fit genotype. Finally, this selection algorithm program then randomly positions this newly created offspring in some kind of spawning pool in the ALife environment.

ALife Simulation/Scape

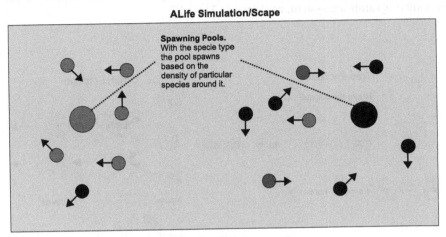

Fig. 4.16 Using spawning pools in ALife for offspring creation.

A spawning pool is basically a designated location where the offspring will be spawned. We might set up as many spawning pools as there are different species in the population, and position the spawning pools in the area which has the highest density of its species around. Then, when an offspring is created, it is not created near the parent, but in the species communal spawning pool. To perform synaptic weight tuning in ALife when using the memetic algorithm approach, we would then wait for the parent to die, and then respawn it with a new set of synaptic weights. The organism would be spawned in the spawning pool location. We would do this multiple times, as appropriate for a memetic algorithm. Once we've given enough processing time to tune the synaptic weights of some given genotype, we would give that agent's genotype its final fitness score. At this point, when a new offspring is created from some set of fit genotypes, that list of fit genotypes (to which I also refer to as dead_pool at times) has the newly scored genotype added to it, with its true fitness score.

4.4 Neural Networks as Graph Based Genetic Programming Systems

We discussed in Chapter-3 four flavors of evolutionary computation: genetic algorithms, genetic programming, evolutionary algorithms, and evolutionary programming. We also noted that they are all virtually the same thing, just with a slightly different encoding method. Neuroevolution can be added to this list as just another side of the coin, and which is basically a specialization of a graph based genetic programming system, as shown in Fig-4.17.

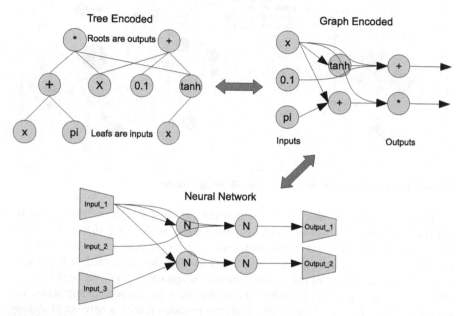

Fig. 4.17 Tree encoding to graph encoding to neural networks.

Where in Chapter-3 we saw how genetic programming can be used to evolve circuits, here instead of letting each node be a logic gate, it is a function that weighs incoming signals with synaptic weights, sums up the weighted signals in some fashion, and then applies some activation function to this sum to produce the final output. A neuron is just a particular set of functions, it can be considered as a program, and thus a genetic programming approach, whether it be tree encoded (single output) or graph encoded (multi-input and multi-output), is effectively a neural network.

Just as you may create a genetic programming framework, and provide a number of different programs to be used as nodes in your system, so may you create a neuroevolutionary framework, and provide a number of different activation functions to be used by the neurons. The more advanced these two types of frameworks become, the more the same they become. If we are to take the position of stating that neuroevolution is a specialized form of genetic programming which concentrates on using smooth functions in its nodes, we have to admit that a neural circuit whose neurons use tanh as activation functions, is a universal function approximator... and since a neural network is a graph of interconnected neural circuits, then a neural network is a graph of any type of functions as well, as shown in Fig-4.18.

Various functions created through neural circuits, which are universal function approximators

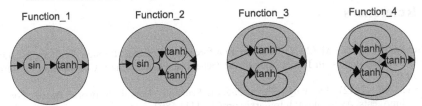

The following Neural Network is composed from the above neural circuits. Since any function can be created by a neural circuit, the NNs are just as flexible as a genetic programming based system.

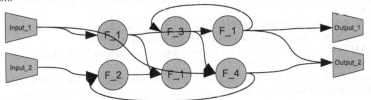

Fig. 4.18 Neural network as a graph of neural circuits using tanh activation functions.

Thus, an advanced enough neuroevolutionary system, and an advanced enough genetic programming system, would be equivalent. Whatever nodes a genetic programming framework would have access to, a neuroevolutionary system could also have access to. Sure, it would feel less like a neural network if we were to start using activation functions: *"while"* and *"if"* from the very start inside the neurons... But why? After all, a threshold neuron is basically an *if*, and a recurrent connection is in some sense a *while* loop. Why not allow access to these programs directly, rather than having to re-evolve them through combinations of activation functions and particular topologies, neuron by neuron? In the same way, a Hopfield network circuit, or a small self organizing map, can be evolved through genetic programming by letting the programs be neurons...

Though I know I've already made a comment to the effect that all these systems, genetic algorithms, genetic programming, evolutionary strategies, evolutionary programming, neural networks, universal networks... are all the same, it is important that this is seen. A genetic algorithm works on string based genotypes, genetic programming is just a genetic algorithm that is applied to tree based encoding, and a graph encoded genetic programming system is a standard genetic programming algorithm applied to multi-rooted trees. Evolutionary strategies is just a standard genetic algorithm which also allows for the parameters dictating the various evolutionary features to mutate, and evolutionary programming is just genetic programming applied to finite state machines instead of tree, or graph encoded systems... Nevertheless, as per the standard, in this book we will view a graph as a neural network if the majority of the nodes are biologically inspired.

4.5 References

[1] Stanley KO, Risto M (2002) Efficient Reinforcement Learning through Evolving Neural Network Topologies. In Proceedings of the Genetic and Evolutionary Computation Conference.

[2] Sher GI (2012) Evolving Chart Pattern Sensitive Neural Network Based Forex TradingAgents. Available at: http://arxiv.org/abs/1111.5892.

[3] Cormen TH, Leiserson CE, Rivest RL, Stein C (2001) Introduction to Algorithms T. H. Cormen, C. E. Leiserson, R. L. Rivest, and C. Stein, eds. (MIT Press).

[4] Stanley KO, Miikkulainen R (2003) A Taxonomy for Artificial Embryogeny. Artificial Life 9, 93-130.

[5] Cangelosi A, Parisi D, Nolfi S (1994) Cell Division and Migration in a "Genotype" for Neural Networks. Network Computation in Neural Systems 5, 497-515.

[6] Turing AM (1952) The Chemical Basis of Morphogenesis. Philosophical Transactions of the Royal Society B Biological Sciences 237, 37-72.

[7] Fleischer K, Barr AH (1993) A Simulation Testbed for The Study of Multicellular Development: The Multiple Mechanisms of Morphogenesis. In C. G. Langton (Ed.), Artificial life III, 389-416.

[8] De M, Suzuki R, Arita T (2007) Heterochrony and Evolvability in Neural Network Development. Artificial Life and Robotics 11, 175-182.

[9] Matos A, Suzuki R, Arita T (2009) Heterochrony and Artificial Embryogeny: a Method for Analyzing Artificial Embryogenies Based on Developmental Dynamics. Artificial Life 15, 131-160.

[10] Thiran P, Peiris V, Heim P, Hochet B (1994) Quantization Effects in Digitally Behaving Circuit Implementations of Kohonen Networks. IEEE Transactions on Neural Networks 5, 450-458.

[11] Glesner M, Pochmuller W, (1994) An Overview of Neural Networks in VLSI. Chapman & Hall, London.

[12] Schwartz TJ (1990) A Neural Chips Survey. AI Expert 5, 34-38.

[13] Heemskerk JNH (1995) Overview of Neural Hardware. Neurocomputers for BrainStyle Processing Design Implementation and Application, 1-23.

[14] Matsuzawa M, Potember RS, Stenger DA, et al (1993) GABA-Activated Whole-Cell Currents in Containment and Growth of Neuroblastoma Cells on Chemically Patterned Substrates. J. Neurosci. Meth. 50, 253-260.

[15] Matsuzawa M, Kobayashi K, Sugioka K, Knoll W (1998) A Biocompatible Interface for The Geometrical Guidance of Central Neurons in Vitro. Journal of Colloid and Interface Science 202, 213-221.

[16] Matsuzawa M, Krauthamer V, Richard S (1999) Fabrication of Biological Neuronal Networks for the Study of Physiological Information Processing. Johns Hopkins APL Tech. Dig. 20(3), 262-270

Chapter 5 The Unintentional Neural Network Programming Language

Abstract The programming language Erlang has a perfect 1:1 mapping to the problem domain of developing neural network computational intelligence based systems. Erlang was created to develop distributed, process based, message passing paradigm oriented, robust, fault tolerant, concurrent systems. All of these features are exactly what a programming language created specifically for developing neural network based systems would have. In this chapter I make claims to why Erlang is such a perfect choice for the development of distributed computational intelligence systems, and how the features of this programming language map perfectly to the features needed by a neural network programming language. In this chapter I briefly discuss my reasons for considering Erlang to be, though unintentionally so, the quintessential neural network programming language.

We have discussed what neural networks are, how they process data, and one of the goals in computational intelligence, the creation of one that rivals our own. I think that neural networks are really the best way to achieve singularity, and to create general computational intelligence, a truly intelligent neurocognitive system. But there is a problem, the way neural networks function, their architecture, the way they process information, the amount of processing they require, the concurrency the NN system needs, and how such neural networks need to be distributed among available computing systems, is not easily mapped-to by the standard programming language architectures like C/C++/C#/Java/Lisp...

If you're wondering "Why should it matter?", here is the thing: If you wanted to build a neural network system in C++, and there have been a number of such systems built, you have to think in C++ and its architecture, and translate those ideas into the NN architecture. Though it does not sound like it should matter, it does, and it has to do with linguistic determinism [1], which roughly states that it is difficult to think in, and create new ideas in, languages which have not been designed for, or have the elements required for, such ideas. For example, if your natural language does not support the concept of mathematics, thinking about mathematics would be very difficult, it would require a revolution within the language, making it support such concepts. When you are programming in C++, you are thinking about systems in C++, instead of thinking and visualizing neural network systems, which is the real goal of your project. You are thinking about C++ and worrying about how you can represent NNs through it. Neural Networks are very different in their architecture from the programming languages used today. To develop robust NN systems, to advance them, to be able to concentrate just on computational intelligence (CI) without having to worry about the programming language, and to have to the tools which can concisely map to the NN based CI architecture is important. It not only makes things easier, it makes it possible to consider such things, and thus it makes it possible to create and develop such things. This is what Erlang [4,5,6] offers.

5.1 The Necessary Features

If you had the chance to make a programming language from scratch, with any features you wanted, and you wanted to create a language with the architecture that maps perfectly to neural networks, and for the development of true computational intelligence, what features would it need?

We would of course first want the programming language to make it architecturally mirror neural networks, so that all ideas and inventions in the field of neural computation could exactly and directly be represented by this new programming language. This means that this programming language must have structures similar to neural networks. To do this, the programming language would need the following:

1. Neural networks are composed of independent, concurrent, distributed processing units called neurons. Thus the programming language architecture would need to support having such elements, having independently acting processes which can all function in parallel, and which can be easily distributed throughout the modern parallel hardware.
2. The neurons in NNs communicate with each other through signals. Thus the programming language architecture needs to allow the processes to communicate with each other through messages or signals too.

Having the programming language's architecture that mirrors the architecture of neural networks is not enough. Our brains are robust, we usually don't encounter situations where we get a "bug", and suddenly we crash. In other words, our brains, our neural systems, our biological makeup is robust, fault tolerant, and self recovering/healing. For the language architecture to support the creation of a true computational intelligence, it needs to allow for a similar level of robustness. To accommodate this it needs the following features:

1. Allow for an easy way to recover from errors.
2. If one of the elements of the computational intelligence system crashes or goes down, the CI system must have features that can recover and restart the crashed elements automatically. There must be multiple levels of security, such that the processes are able to watch each other's performance, monitoring for crashes and assisting in recovering the crashed elements.

But simply being able to recover from crashes is not enough, simply being robust is not enough. Though the neural network itself takes care of the learning part, performs the incorporation of new ideas, the growth and experience gaining, there is one thing that biological organisms do not have the ability to do with regards to their intelligence. Biological organisms do not have the ability to modify their our own neural structures, we do not have the ability to rewrite our neural networks at will, the ability to update the very manner in which our biological neural networks process information... but that is the limitation of biological systems only, and non biological systems need not have such limitations. Thus a programming language architecture must also provide the following features:

1. The programming language must allow for code hot-swapping. For the ability for the CI system to rewrite the code that defines its own structure, its own neural network, or fix errors and then update itself, its own source code without taking anything offline.
2. The programming language architecture must allow for the CI system to be able to run forever, crashes should be local in nature, which should be fixable by the CI itself.

Finally, taking into account that the neural network based CI systems should be able to interface and control robotic systems, be used in Unmanned Ariel Vehicles (UAVs), or in humanoid robots, the programming language should from the start make it easy to develop and allow for control of a lot of different types of hardware. It should allow: for an easy ability to develop different and numerous hardware drivers.

In short, the programming language architecture that we are looking for must process information through the use of independent concurrent and distributed processes. It should allow for code hot-swapping. It should allow for fault tolerance, and error fixing, and self healing and recovery. And finally, it should be made with ability to interface with large number of hardware parts, it should allow for an easy way to develop hardware drivers, so that not only the software part of the CI be allowed to grow and self modify and update, but it should also be able to incorporate and add new hardware parts, whatever those new parts may be.

A list of features that a neural network based computational intelligence system needs, as quoted from the list made by Bjarne Dacker [2], is as follows:

1. *The system must be able to handle very large numbers of concurrent activities.*
2. *Actions must be performed at a certain point in time or within a certain time.*
3. *Systems may be distributed over several computers.*
4. *The system is used to control hardware.*
5. *The software systems are very large.*
6. *The system exhibits complex functionality such as, feature interaction.*
7. *The systems should be in continuous operation for many years.*
8. *Software maintenance (reconfiguration, etc) should be performed without stopping the system.*
9. *There are stringent quality, and reliability requirements.*
10. *Fault tolerance*

Surprisingly enough, Dacker was not talking about neural network based general computational intelligence systems when he made this list, he was talking about telecom switching systems.

5.2 Erlang: From Telecommunications Networks To Neural Networks

Erlang is a concurrency oriented (CO) programming language. It was developed at Ericsson, a project lead by Dr. Joe Armstrong. Erlang was created for the purpose of developing telecom switching systems. Telecom switching systems have a number of demanding requirements, such systems are required to be highly reliable, fault tolerant, they should be able to operate forever, and act reasonably in the presence of hardware and software errors. And these features are so close to those needed by NN based systems, that the resulting language's features are exactly those of a neural network programming language. Quoting these necessary features of the programming language from [3]:

1. *"Encapsulation primitives — there must be a number of mechanisms for limiting the consequences of an error. It should be possible to isolate processes so that they cannot damage each other.*
2. *Concurrency — the language must support a lightweight mechanism to create parallel process, and to send messages between the processes. Context switching between process, and message passing, should be efficient. Concurrent processes must also time-share the CPU in some reasonable manner, so that CPU bound processes do not monopolize the CPU, and prevent progress of other processes which are "ready to run."*
3. *Fault detection primitives — which allow one process to observe another process, and to detect if the observed process has terminated for any reason.*
4. *Location transparency — If we know the PId of a process then we should be able to send a message to the process.*
5. *Dynamic code upgrade — It should be possible to dynamically change code in a running system. Note that since many processes will be running the same code, we need a mechanism to allow existing processes to run "old" code, and for "new" processes to run the modified code at the same time.*

With a set of libraries to provide:

6. *Stable storage — this is storage which survives a crash.*
7. *Device drivers — these must provide a mechanism for communication with the outside world.*
8. *Code upgrade — this allows us to upgrade code in a running system.*
9. *Infrastructure — for starting, and stopping the system, logging errors , etc. "*

It is this that Erlang provides, and it is for this reason why we use it for the development of neural network based systems in this book. I have found this language to be so perfect for the task, that I must admit to be unable to see myself using anything else in future research within this field.

Whereas before I would need to first create the NN algorithms, topologies, and architectures separately, and then try to figure out how to map the programming language like C++ to the task, or even worse, think in C++, and thus create a subpar and compromised NN based system, or still worse think in C++ and not be able to see the forest for the trees when it comes to CI and NN... With Erlang, the ideas, the algorithms and NN structures are mapped to Erlang perfectly, and vice versa. The ideas that would otherwise be impossible to implement, or even consider when one thinks in one of the more commonly used languages, are easily and clearly mapped to Erlang. You do not need to switch from thinking about neural network systems, algorithms, and architecture of a NN based CI when developing in Erlang. The conciseness of the language, the clarity of the code and the programming language's architecture... make even the most complex problems which would otherwise not be possible to solve, *effortless*.

5.3 The Conceptual Mapping of a NN to Erlang's Architecture

In Erlang, concurrency is achieved through processes. Processes are self contained, independent, concurrently running micro server/clients, only able to interact with each other through message passing. Already you can visualize that these processes are basically neurons, independent, distributed, concurrent... only able to communicate with each other by sending signals, action potentials.

Once again taking a quote from Armstrong's thesis, where he notes the importance of there being a one to one mapping between the problem and the program, the architecture of the programming language and that which is being developed with it: *"It is extremely important that the mapping is exactly 1:1. The reason for this is that it minimizes the conceptual gap between the problem and the solution. If this mapping is not 1:1 the program will quickly degenerate, and become difficult to understand. This degeneration is often observed when non-CO languages are used to solve concurrent problems. Often the only way to get the program to work is to force several independent activities to be controlled by the same language thread or process. This leads to an inevitable loss of clarity, and makes the programs subject to complex and irreproducible interference errors. "* We see that the mapping from Erlang's architecture to neural networks is 1:1, as shown in Fig-5.1.

From the figure it becomes obvious that indeed, there is a perfect correlation between the architecture of this programming language, and the NN problem domain. In the figure each neuron is directly mapped to a process, each connection between the neurons is a connection between processes. Every signal, simulated action potential that is sent from one neuron to another is a signal, a message in vector/list or tuple form, from one process to another. We could not have hoped for a better mapping.

Erlang was also created with an eye towards scaling to millions of processes working in parallel, so even here we are in great luck, for the future in this field will require vast neural network based systems, with millions or even billions of neurons on every computing node. Also, because robotics is such a close field to computational intelligence, the evolved NN based systems will need to be able to interface with the sensors and actuators, with the hardware in which the CI is embedded and which it inhabits; again Erlang is perfect for this, it was made for this, it was created to interface and interact with varied types of hardware, and it was created such that developing drivers is easy.

Erlang was created to be not just concurrent, but distributed, over the web or any other medium. Thus again, the CI system that needs to be distributed over a number of machines, or over Internet, is achievable through Erlang, in fact it is a natural quality when being written in Erlang.

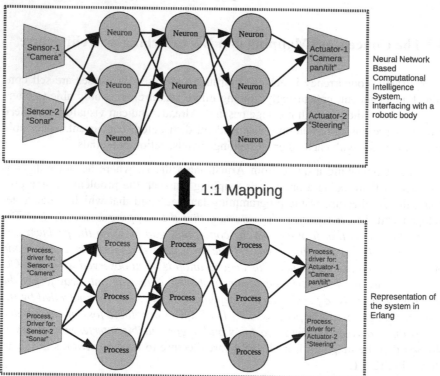

Fig. 5.1 The mapping from Erlang's architecture to the domain of neural network based CI.

But of course there are other important features, beyond that of scaling and the perfect mapping from the problem to the solution domain. There is also the issue of fault tolerance, the issue of robustness...

5.4 Robustness and Fault Tolerance in Computational Intelligence

It would be rather comical if it were possible for an advanced CI system to be brought down by a single bug. Here again Erlang saves us. This programming language was designed to develop systems that must run forever, that can not be taken offline, even when there is a bug, and even when it absolutely must be fixed. Through supervision trees Erlang allows for processes to monitor each other, and to restore each other. Thus if any element of the neural network crashes, another part, an *exoself* of the CI system can restore it to the previously functional form. But not only can it restore the CI to a previously functional form in the case of emergency, but it can also allow for the bug to be fixed, and the new updated source to be ran without going offline. It allows for the system to fix itself, to self heal, to recover, to upgrade and evolve. What other programming language offers such features so easily and so effortlessly?

5.5 I've Done This Once Before; And We Are On Our Way

In the following chapters we will develop a neural network based computational intelligence system. All these features that are offered by Erlang will make it easy for you and I to create it. If you think that the thus far described type of NN based CI system is unreachable, or impossible... you will be surprised, because we will build it by the end of this book. We will create ALife simulations, we will allow the NN systems to control the simulated organisms, evolving ability to hunt in a virtual 2d environment, to find food, to trick and bait prey... We will create a system that can evolve NNs which recognize visual patterns in financial data, analyzing the actual charts and plots, rather than simply lists of prices. We will create a universal learning network, a system that can be used to evolve and optimize digital circuits. And all of this will be easily achieved, to a great extent thanks to Erlang.

It is incredible that a single individual can create a system of such complexity, or more precisely, create a system that can evolve intelligent systems of such complexity, all by himself. And you will be that individual, by the end of this volume you will have created such a system, and you will know exactly how to develop a neuroevolutionary platform that can evolve general neural networks, evolved for intelligence, for pattern recognition, for anything you can imagine and apply them to.

There are no requirements for this book, you need only have the most basic experience with Erlang. Everything about neural networks and neuroevolution I'll show you. We'll build this first NN CI system together, I've built one before and so I can guide you. By the time we're done, we'll have built one of the most advanced neuroevolutionary systems currently available in the world. Afterwards, you'll continue your travels on your own, and you'll use what you've learned here to build something that even I can't foretell. So common, what are you waiting for, let's go!

5.6 References

[1] Everett DL (2005). Cultural Constraints on Grammar and Cognition in Piraha Another Look at the Design Features of Human Language. Current Anthropology 46, 621-646.

[2] Dacker B (2000) Concurrent Functional Programming for Telecommunications: A Case Study of Technology Introduction. Masters thesis KTH Royal Institute of Technology Stockholm.

[3] Joe Armstrong (2003) Making Reliable Distributed Systems in The Presence of Software Errors. The Royal Institute of Technology Stockholm, Sweden, (PhD thesis).

[4] Armstrong, J. (2007). Programming Erlang Software for a Concurrent World. Pragmatic Bookshelf. ISBN 9781934356005.

[5] Thompson SJ; Cesarini F (2009) Erlang Programming: A Concurrent Approach to Software Development. Sebastopol, California: O'Reilly Media, Inc. ISBN 978059651818.

[6] Logan M, Merritt E, Carlsson R (2010) Erlang and OTP in Action. Greenwich, CT: Manning Publications. ISBN 9781933988788.

Part II

NEUROEVOLUTION: TAKING THE FIRST STEP

In this part of the book we will develop a simple yet powerful Topology and Weight Evolving Artificial Neural Network (TWEANN) platform. We will develop it in Erlang, and I will present all the source code within the chapters. Most functions that we will develop will require some function by function explanation and elaboration, and I will add the description and elaboration of the functions developed through the use of comments within the presented source code. In this manner, you will be able to read the source code and the comments in the same flow. It is important to read the comments, as they make up part of the text, and will assist in the explanation of how the particular functions work, and what it is that they do.

In Chapter-6 we will develop the genotype encoding, the phenotype representation, and the mapping between the two for our NN system. In Chapter-7 we will add a local search algorithm, the stochastic hill climber, and the random restart stochastic hill climbing optimization algorithm, and test our simple optimizable NN on the XOR problem. In Chapter-8 we will expand our system further, develop the population_monitor and the genome_mutator, thus transforming our system into a simple, yet already very powerful TWEANN. Finally, in Chapter-9 we will analyze our system, and find a few difficult to notice bugs. This chapter will show how to look for errors in a system such as this, and how easy it is to miss small logical based errors. The evolutionary algorithm tends to route around such small errors, allowing the system to still function and find solutions even in the presence of such errors, and thus hiding them and making them difficult to spot.

All the code developed in the following chapters is available at: https://github.com/CorticalComputer/Book_NeuroevolutionThroughErlang. This provides the folders containing the source code for each chapter, so that you can follow along and perform the testing, code exploration, and try out examples if you wish so. Or if you wish, you can just look over the code within the text as you read, without performing the demonstrated tests in the console yourself.

Chapter 6 Developing a Feed Forward Neural Network

Abstract In this chapter we discuss how a single artificial neuron processes signals, and how to simulate it. We then develop a single artificial neuron and test its functionality. Having discussed and developed a single neuron, we decide on the NN architecture we will implement, and then develop a genotype constructor, and a mapper from genotype to phenotype. Finally, we then ensure that that our simple NN system works by using a simple sensor and actuator attached to the NN to test its sense-think-act ability.

As we discussed in an earlier chapter, Neural Networks (NN) are directed graphs composed of simple processing elements as shown in Figure-6.1. Every vertex in such a directed graph is a Neuron, every edge is an outgoing axon and a path along which the neuron sends information to other Neurons. A NN has an input layer which is a set of neurons that receive signals from sensors, and an output layer which is a set of neurons that connect to actuators. In a general NN system the sensors can be anything, from cameras, to programs that read from a database and pass that data to the neurons. The Actuators too can range from functions which control motors, to simple programs which print the output signals to the screen. Every neuron processes its incoming signals, produces an output signal, and passes it on to other neurons.

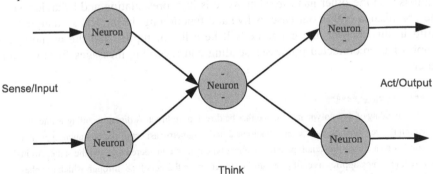

Fig. 6.1 A simple Neural Network.

Whether the NN does something intelligent or useful is based on its topology and parameters. The method of modifying the NN topology and parameters to make it do something useful, is the task of its learning algorithm. A learning algorithm can be supervised, like in the case of the error back propagation learning algorithm, or it can be unsupervised like in the evolutionary or reinforcement learning algorithms. In a supervised learning algorithm the outputs of the NN need to be known in advance, such that corrections can be given to the NN based on the differences in its produced outputs and the correct outputs. Once we have minimized the differences between the answers we want and the answers the NN gives, we apply the NN to a new set of data, to another problem in the same field but one which the NN has not encountered during its training. In the case of unsupervised learning, it is only important to be able to tell whether one NN system performs better than another. There is no need to know exactly how the problem should be solved, the NNs will try to figure that out for themselves; the researcher only needs to choose the neural networks that produce better results over those that do not. We will develop these types of systems in future sections.

In this chapter we will learn how to program a static neural network system whose topological and parametric properties are specified during its creation, and are not changed during training. We will develop a genotype encoding for a simple monolithic Neural Network, and then we'll create a mapper program which converts the NN genotype to its phenotypic representation. The process of modifying these weights, parameters, and the NN topology is the job of a learning algorithm, the subject that we will cover in the chapters that follow.

In the following sections when we discuss genotypes and phenotypes, we mean their standard definitions: a genotype is the organism's full hereditary information, which is passed to offspring in mutated or unchanged form, and the phenotype is the organism's actual observed properties, its morphology and behavior. The process of mapping a genotypical representation of the organism to the phenotypical one is done through a process called development, to which we also will refer to as: mapping. A genotype of the organism is the form in which we store it in our database, on the other hand its phenotype is its representation and behavior when the organism, a NN in our case, is live and functioning. In the NN system that we build in this chapter, the genotype will be a list of tuples, and the phenotype a graph of interconnected processes sending and receiving messages from one another.

********Note********

The encoding of a genotype itself can either be direct, or indirect. A direct encoding is one in which the genotype encodes every topological and parametric aspect of the NN phenotype in a one to one manner, the genotype and the phenotype can be considered one and the same. An indirect encoding applies a set of programs, or functions to the genotype, through which the phenotype is developed. This development process can be highly complex and stochastic in nature which takes into consideration the environmental factors during the time of development, and producing a one too many mapping from a genotype to the phenotype. An example of a direct encoding is that of a bit string which maps to a colored strip in which the 0s are directly converted to white sections and 1s to black. An example of an indirect encoding is the case of DNA, where the development from the genotype to a phenotype is a multi-stage process, with complex interactions between the developing organism and the environment it is in.
****

We will now slowly build up a NN system, from a single neuron, to a fully functional feed forward neural network. In the next section we take our first step and develop an artificial neuron using Erlang.

6.1 Simulating A Neuron

Let us again briefly review the representation and functionality of a single artificial neuron, as shown in Figure-6.2. A neuron is but a simple processing element which accepts input signals, weighs the importance of each signal by multiplying it by a weight associated with it, adds a bias to the result, applies an activation function to this sum, and then forwards the result to other elements it is connected to. As an example, assume we have a list of input signals to the neuron: [I1,I2,I3,I4], this input is represented as a vector composed of 4 elements. The neuron then must have a list of weights, one weight for every incoming signal: [W1,W2,W3,W4]. We weigh each signal with its weight by taking a dot product of the input vector and the weight vector as follows: Dot_Product = I1*W1 + I2*W2 + I3*W3 + I4*W4. If the neuron also has a threshold value or bias, we simply add this bias value to the Dot_Product. Finally, we apply the activation

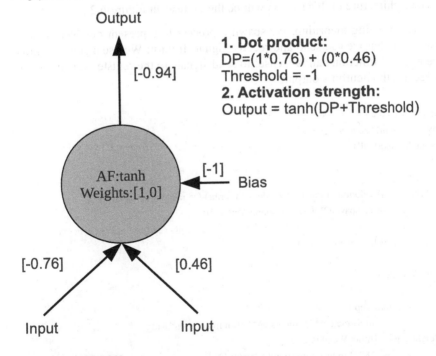

Fig. 6.2 An artificial Neuron.

function to the dot product to produce the final output of the neuron: Output = Activation_Function(Dot_Product), and for a neuron that also has a bias: Output = Activation_Function(Dot_Product + Bias). A bias is an extra floating point parameter not associated with any particular incoming signal, and it adds a level of tunable asymmetry to the activation function.

Mathematically, the neuron that uses a set of weights and a bias is equivalent to a neuron that accepts an "extended input vector" and uses an "extended weight vector" to weigh the signals. An extended input vector has "1" appended to the input vector and an extended weight vector has the bias appended to the weight vector. Using the extended vectors, we then take a single dot product as follows: [I1,I2,I3,I4,1]dot[W1,W2,W3,W4,Bias]= (I1*W1) +(I2*W2) +(I3*W3) +(I4*W4) +(1*Bias), which is equal to the dot product of the input and weight vector, plus the bias as before. Neurons that do not use a bias would simply not append the extension to the input, and thus produce the dot product without a bias value.

Lets simulate and test a very simple neuron, which we will represent using a process. The neuron will have a predetermined number of weights, 2, and it will include a bias. With 2 wights, this neuron can process input vectors of length 2. The activation function will be the standard sigmoid function, in our neuron it's approximated by the hyperbolic tangent (tanh) function included in the math module. The architecture of this neuron will be the same as in Figure-6.2.

In the following algorithm, we spawn a process to represent our Neuron, and register it so that we can send and receive signals from it. We use a simple remote procedure call function called 'sense' to send signals to the registered neuron, and then receive the neuron's output.

```
simple_neuron.erl
-module(simple_neuron).
-compile(export_all).

create()->
    Weights = [random:uniform()-0.5,random:uniform()-0.5,random:uniform()-0.5],
    register(neuron, spawn(?MODULE,loop,[Weights])).
%The create function spawns a single neuron, where the weights and the bias are generated
randomly to be between -0.5 and 0.5.

loop(Weights) ->
    receive
        {From, Input} ->
            io:format("****Processing****~n Input:~p~n Using
Weights:~p~n",[Input,Weights]),
            Dot_Product = dot(Input,Weights,0),
            Output = [math:tanh(Dot_Product)],
```

```
                From ! {result,Output},
                loop(Weights)
    end.
```

%The spawned neuron process accepts an input vector, prints it and the weight vector to the
screen, calculates the output, and then sends the output to the contacting process. The output is
also a vector of length one.

```
    dot([I|Input],[W|Weights],Acc) ->
            dot(Input,Weights,I*W+Acc);
    dot([],[Bias],Acc)->
            Acc + Bias.
```

%The dot product function that we use works on the assumption that the bias is incorporated into the weight list as the last value in that list. After calculating the dot product, the input list will
empty out while the weight list will still have the single bias value remaining, which we then
add to the accumulator.

```
sense(Signal)->
    case is_list(Signal) and (length(Signal) == 2) of
            true->
                    neuron ! {self(),Signal},
                    receive
                            {result,Output}->
                            io:format(" Output: ~p~n",[Output])
                    end;
            false->
                    io:format("The Signal must be a list of length 2~n")
    end.
```

%We use the sense function to contact the neuron and send it an input vector. The sense function ensures that the signal we are sending is a vector of length 2.

Now let's compile and test our module:

```
1> c(simple_neuron).
{ok,simple_neuron}
2> simple_neuron:create().
true.
3> simple_neuron:sense([1,2]).
****Processing****
Input:[1,2]
Using Weights:[0.44581636451986995,0.0014907142064750634, -0.18867324519560702]
Output: [0.25441202264242263]
```

It works! We can expand this neuron further by letting it accept signals only from certain predetermined list of PIds, and then output the result not back to those same processes, but instead to another set of PIds. With such modifications this neuron could then be used as a fully functional processing element in a NN. In the next section we will build a single neuron neural network that uses such processing element.

6.2 A One Neuron Neural Network

Next we will create the simplest possible NN. Our NN topology will be composed of a single Neuron which receives a signal from a Sensor, calculates an output based on its weights and activation function, and then passes that output signal to the Actuator. This topology and architecture is shown in Figure-6.3. You will also notice that there is a 4th element called Cortex. This element is used to trigger the sensor to start producing sensory data, and it also contains the PIds of all the processes in the system so that it can be used to shut down the NN when we are done with it. Finally, this type of element can also be used as a supervisor of the NN, and play a role in the NN's synchronization with the learning algorithm. These features will become important when we start developing the more complex NN systems in the chapters that follow.

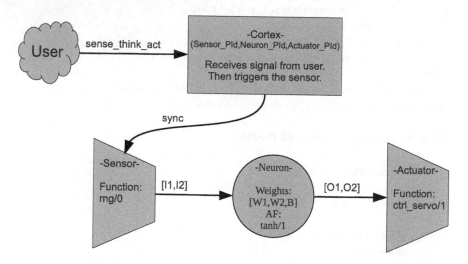

Fig. 6.3 One Neuron Neural Network.

To create this system, we will need to significantly modify the functions in our simple_neuron module, and add new features as shown in the following source code:

```erlang
simplest_nn.erl
-module(simplest_nn).
-compile(export_all).

create() ->
    Weights = [random:uniform()-0.5,random:uniform()-0.5,random:uniform()-0.5],
    N_PId = spawn(?MODULE,neuron,[Weights,undefined,undefined]),
    S_PId = spawn(?MODULE,sensor,[N_PId]),
    A_PId = spawn(?MODULE,actuator,[N_PId]),
    N_PId ! {init,S_PId,A_PId},
    register(cortex,spawn(?MODULE,cortex,[S_PId,N_PId,A_PId])).
%The create function first generates 3 weights, with the 3rd weight being the Bias. The Neuron
is spawned first, and is then sent the PIds of the Sensor and Actuator that it's connected with.
Then the Cortex element is registered and provided with the PIds of all the elements in the NN
system.

neuron(Weights,S_PId,A_PId) ->
    receive
        {S_PId, forward, Input} ->
            io:format("****Thinking****~n Input:~p~n with
Weights:~p~n",[Input,Weights]),
            Dot_Product = dot(Input,Weights,0),
            Output = [math:tanh(Dot_Product)],
            A_PId ! {self(), forward, Output},
            neuron(Weights,S_PId,A_PId);
        {init, New_SPId, New_APId} ->
            neuron(Weights,New_SPId,New_APId);
        terminate ->
            ok
    end.
%After the neuron finishes setting its SPId and APId to that of the Sensor and Actuator respec-
tively, it starts waiting for the incoming signals. The neuron expects a vector of length 2 as in-
put, and as soon as the input arrives, the neuron processes the signal and passes the output vec-
tor to the outgoing APId.

dot([I|Input],[W|Weights],Acc) ->
    dot(Input,Weights,I*W+Acc);
dot([],[],Acc)->
```

```
        Acc;
    dot([],[Bias],Acc)->
        Acc + Bias.
```

%The dot function takes a dot product of two vectors, it can operate on a weight vector with and without a bias. When there is no bias in the weight list, both the Input vector and the Weight vector are of the same length. When Bias is present, then when the Input list empties out, the Weights list still has 1 value remaining, its Bias.

```
sensor(N_PId) ->
  receive
      sync ->
              Sensory_Signal = [random:uniform(),random:uniform()],
              io:format("****Sensing****:~n Signal from the environment
~p~n",[Sensory_Signal]),
              N_PId ! {self(),forward,Sensory_Signal},
              sensor(N_PId);
          terminate ->
              ok
  end.
```

%The Sensor function waits to be triggered by the Cortex element, and then produces a random vector of length 2, which it passes to the connected neuron. In a proper system the sensory signal would not be a random vector but instead would be produced by a function associated with the sensor, a function that for example reads and vector-encodes a signal coming from a GPS attached to a robot.

```
actuator(N_PId) ->
  receive
      {N_PId,forward,Control_Signal}->
              pts(Control_Signal),
              actuator(N_PId);
          terminate ->
              ok
  end.

  pts(Control_Signal)->
          io:format("****Acting****:~n Using:~p to act on environ-
ment.~n",[Control_Signal]).
```

%The Actuator function waits for a control signal coming from a Neuron. As soon as the signal arrives, the actuator executes its function, pts/1, which prints the value to the screen.

```
cortex(Sensor_PId,Neuron_PId,Actuator_PId)->
    receive
            sense_think_act ->
                    Sensor_PId ! sync,
                    cortex(Sensor_PId,Neuron_PId,Actuator_PId);
            terminate ->
                    Sensor_PId ! terminate,
                    Neuron_PId ! terminate,
                    Actuator_PId ! terminate,
                    ok
    end.
%The Cortex function triggers the sensor to action when commanded by the user. This process
also has all the PIds of the elements in the NN system, so that it can terminate the whole system
when requested.
```

Lets compile and try out this system:

```
1>c(simplest_nn).
{ok,simplest_nn}
2>simplest_nn:create().
true
3> cortex ! sense_think_act.
****Sensing****:
 Signal from the environment [0.09230089279334841,0.4435846174457203]
sense_think_act
****Thinking****
Input:[0.09230089279334841,0.4435846174457203]
 with Weights:[-0.4076991072066516,-0.05641538255427969,0.2230402056221108]
****Acting****:
Using:[0.15902302907693572] to act on environment.
```

It works! But though this system does embody many important features of a real NN, it is still rather useless since it's composed of a single neuron, the sensor produces random data, and the NN has no learning algorithm so we can not teach it to do something useful. In the following sections we are going to design a NN system for which we can specify different starting topologies, for which we can specify sensors and actuators, and which will have the ability to learn to accomplish useful tasks.

6.3 Planning Our Neural Network System's Architecture

A standard Neural Network (NN) is a graph of interconnected Neurons, where every neuron can send and receive signals from other neurons and/or sensors and actuators. The simplest of NN architectures is that of a monolithic feed forward neural network (FFNN), as shown in Figure-6.4. In a FFNN, the signals only propagate in the forward direction, from sensors, through the neural layers, and finally reaching the actuators which use the output signals to act on the environment. In such a NN system there are no recursive or cyclical connections. After the Actuators have acted upon the environment, the sensors once again produce and send sensory signals to the neurons in the first layer, and the "Sense-Think-Act" cycle repeats.

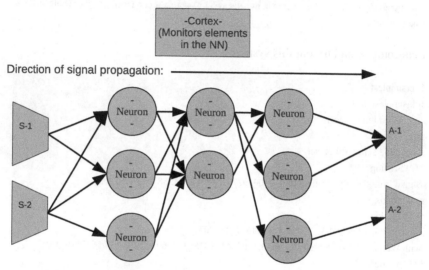

Fig. 6.4 A Feed Forward Neural Network.

Every neuron must be able to accept a vector input of length 1+, and produce a vector output of length 1. Since all neural inputs and outputs are in vector form, and the sensory signals sent from the sensors are also in vector form, the neurons neither need to know nor care whether the incoming signals are coming from other neurons or sensors. Let's take a closer look at the two types of connections that occur in a NN, the [neuron|sensor]-to-neuron and the neuron-to-actuator connection as shown in Figure-6.5.

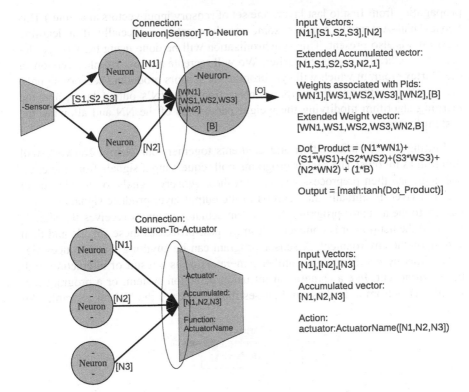

Connection:
[Neuron|Sensor]-To-Neuron

Input Vectors:
[N1],[S1,S2,S3],[N2]

Extended Accumulated vector:
[N1,S1,S2,S3,N2,1]

Weights associated with PIds:
[WN1],[WS1,WS2,WS3],[WN2],[B]

Extended Weight vector:
[WN1,WS1,WS2,WS3,WN2,B]

Dot_Product = (N1*WN1)+
(S1*WS1)+(S2*WS2)+(S3*WS3)+
(N2*WN2) + (1*B)

Output = [math:tanh(Dot_Product)]

Connection:
Neuron-To-Actuator

Input Vectors:
[N1],[N2],[N3]

Accumulated vector:
[N1,N2,N3]

Action:
actuator:ActuatorName([N1,N2,N3])

Fig. 6.5 Neuron/Sensor-To-Neuron & Neuron-To-Actuator connections.

Every input signal to a neuron is a list of values [I1...In], a vector of length 1 or greater. The neuron's output signal is also a vector, a list of length 1, [O]. Because each Neuron outputs a vector of length 1, the actuators accumulate the signals coming from the Neurons into properly ordered vectors of length 1+. The order of values in the vector is the same as the order of PIds in its fanin pid list. Once the actuator has finished gathering the signals coming from all the neurons connected to it, it uses the accumulated vector as a parameter to its actuation function.

Once all the neurons in the output layer have produced and forwarded their signals to actuators, the NN can start accepting new sensory inputs again (*Note* It is possible for a NN to process multiple sensory input vectors, one after the other, rather than one at a time and waiting until an output vector is produced before accepting a new wave of sensory vectors. This would be somewhat similar to the way a multi-stage pipeline in a CPU works, with every neural layer in the NN processing signals at the same time, as opposed to the processing of sensory vectors propagating from first to last layer, one set of sensory input vectors at a time.) This Sense-Think-Act cycle requires some synchronization, especially if a learning algorithm is also present. This synchronization will be done using the Cortex element we've briefly discussed earlier. We will recreate a more complex version of the Cortex program which will synchronize the sensors producing sensory signals, the actuators gathering the output vectors from the NN's output layer, and the learning algorithm modifying the weight parameters of the NN and allowing the system to learn.

Putting all this information and elements together, our Neural Network will function as follows: The sensor programs poll/request input signals from the environment, and then preprocess and fan out these sensory signals to the neurons in the first layer. Eventually the neurons in the output layer produce signals that are passed to the actuator program(s). Once an actuator program receives the signals from all the neurons it is connected from, it post-processes these signals and then acts upon the environment. A sensor program can be anything that produces signals, either by itself (random number generator) or as a result of interacting with the environment, like a camera, an intrusion detection system, or a program that simply reads from a database and passes those values to the NN for example. An

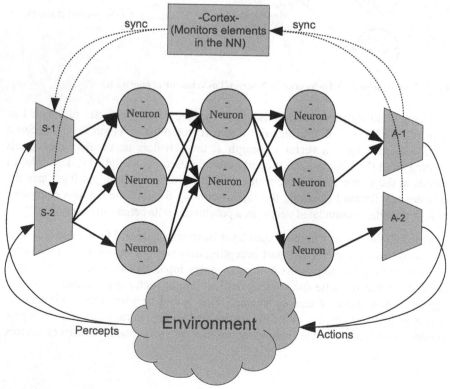

Fig. 6.6 All the elements of a NN system.

actuator program is any program that accepts signals and then acts upon the environment based on those signals. For example, a robot actuator steering program can accept a single floating point value, post process the value so that its range is from -1 to 1, and then execute the motor driver using this value as the parameter, where the sign and magnitude of the parameter designates which way to steer and how hard. Another example actuator is one that accepts signals from the NN, and then buys or sells a stock based on that signal, with a complementary sensor which reads the earlier price values of the same stock. This type of NN system architecture is visually represented in Figure-6.6.

A sensor, actuator, neuron, and the cortex are just 4 different types of processes that accept signals, process them, and execute some kind of element specific function. Lets discuss every one of these processes in detail, to see what information we might need to create them in their genotypic and phenotypic form.

Sensor: A sensor is any process that produces a vector signal that the NN then processes. This signal can be produced from the sensor interacting with the environment, for example the data coming from a camera, or from the sensor somehow generating the signal internally.

Actuator: An actuator is a process that accepts signals from the Neurons in the output layer, orders them into a vector, and then uses this vector to control some function that acts on the environment or even the NN itself. An actuator might have incoming connections from 3 Neurons, in which case it would then have to wait until all 3 of the neurons have sent it their output signals, accumulate these signals into a vector, and then use this vector as a parameter to its actuation function. The function could for example dictate the voltage signal to be sent to a servo that controls a robot's gripper.

Neuron: The neuron is a signal processing element. It accepts signals, accumulates them into an ordered vector, then processes this input vector to produce an output, and finally passes the output to other elements it is connected to. The Neuron never interacts with the environment directly, and even when it does receive signals and produces output signals, it does not know whether these input signals are coming from sensors or neurons, or whether it is sending its output signals to other neurons or actuators. All the neuron does is have a list of input PIds from which it expects to receive signals, a list of output PIds to which the neuron sends its output, a weight list correlated with the input PIds, and an activation function it applies to the dot product of the input vector and its weight vector. The neuron waits until it receives all the input signals, processes those signals, and then passes the output onwards.

Cortex: The cortex is a NN synchronizing element. It needs to know the PId of every sensor and actuator, so that it will know when all the actuators have received their control inputs, and that it's time for the sensors to again gather and fanout sensory data to the neurons in the input layer. At the same time, the Cortex element can also act as a supervisor of all the Neuron, Sensor, and Actuator elements in the NN system.

Now that we know how these elements should work and process signals, we need to come up with an encoding which can be used to store any type of NN topology in a database, or a flat file. This stored representation of the NN is its genotype. We should be able to specify the topology and the parameters of the NN within the genotype, and then generate from it a process based NN system, the phenotype. Using a genotype also allows us to train a NN to do something useful, and then save the updated and trained NN to a file for later use. Finally, once we decide to use an evolutionary learning algorithm, the NN genotypes are what the mutation operators will be applied to, and from what the mutated offspring will be generated.

In the next section we will develop a simple, human readable, and tuple based genotype encoding for our NN system. This type of encoding will be easy to understand, work with, and easy to encode and operate on using standard directional graph based functions. The use of such a direct way to store the genotype will also make it easy to think about it, and thus to advance, scale, and utilize it in the more advanced systems we'll develop in the future.

6.4 Developing a Genotype Representation

There are a number of ways to encode the genotype of a monolithic Neural Network (NN). Since NNs are directed graphs, we could simply use Erlang's digraph module. The digraph module in particular has functions with which to create Nodes/Neurons, Edges/Connections between the nodes, and even sub graphs, thus easily allowing us to develop modular topologies. Another simple way to encode the genotype is by representing the NN as a list of tuples, where every tuple is a record representing either a Neuron, Sensor, Actuator, or the Cortex element. Finally, we could also use a hash table, ets for example, instead of a simple list to store the tuples.

In every one of these cases, every element in the genotype is encoded as a human readable tuple. Our records will directly reflect the information that would be included and needed by every process in the phenotype. The 4 elements can be represented using the following records:

Sensor: -record(sensor, {id, cx_id, name, vl, fanout_ids}).

The sensor id has the following format: *{sensor, UniqueVal}*. *cx_id* is the Id of the Cortex element. 'name' is the name of the function the sensor executes to generate or acquire the sensory data, and *vl* is the vector length of the produced sensory signal. Finally, *fanout_ids* is a list of neuron ids to which the sensory data will be fanned out.

Actuator: **-record(actuator, {id, cx_id, name, vl, fanin_ids}).**

The actuator id has the following format: *{actuator, UniqueVal}*. *cx_id* is the the Id of the Cortex element. '*name*' is the name of the function the actuator executes to act upon the environment, with the function parameter being the vector it accumulates from the incoming neural signals. '*vl*' is the vector length of the accumulated actuation vector. Finally, the *fanin_ids* is a list of neuron ids which are connected to the actuator.

Neuron: **-record(neuron, {id, cx_id, af, input_idps, output_ids}).**

A neuron id uses the following format: *{neuron,{LayerIndex, UniqueVal}}*. *cx_id* is the the Id of the Cortex element. The activation function, *af*, is the name of the function the neuron uses on the extended dot product (dot product plus bias). The activation function that we will use in the simple NN we design in this chapter will be 'tanh', later we will extend the list of available activation functions our NNs can use. '*input_idps*' stands for Input Ids "Plus", which is a list of tuples as follows: *[{Id1,Weights1} ... {IdN,WeightsN},{bias,Val}]*. Each tuple is composed of the Id of the element that is connected to the neuron, and weights correlated with the input vector coming from the neuron with the listed Id. The last tuple in the input_idps is {bias,Val}, which is not associated with any incoming signal, and represents the Bias value. Finally, *output_ids* is a list of Ids to which the neuron will fanout its output signal.

Cortex: **-record(cortex, {id, sensor_ids, actuator_ids, nids}).**

The cortex Id has the following format: *{cortex, UniqueVal}*. '*sensor_ids*' is a list of sensor ids that produce and pass the sensory signals to the neurons in the input layer. '*actuator_ids*' is a list of actuator ids that the neural output layer is connected to. When the actuator is done affecting the environment, it sends the cortex a synchronization signal. After the cortex receives the sync signal from all the ids in its actuator_ids list, it triggers all the sensors in the sensor_ids list. Finally, *nids* is the list of all neuron ids in the NN.

Figure-6.7 shows the correlation between the tuples/records and the process based phenotypic representations to which they map. Using this record representation in our genotype allows us to easily and safely store all the information of our NN. We need only decide whether to use a digraph, a hash table, or a simple list to store the Genotype of a NN. Because we will be building a very simple Feed Forward Neural Network in this chapter, let us start by using a simple list. For the more advanced evolutionary NN systems that we'll build in the later chapters, we will switch to an ETS or a Digraph representation.

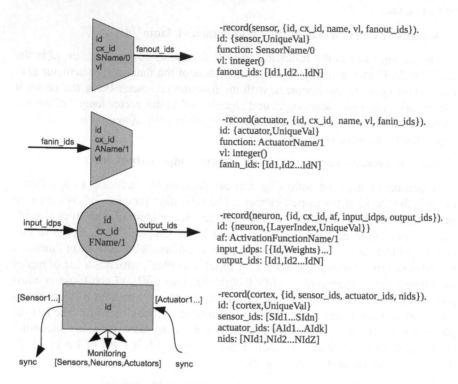

Fig. 6.7 Record to process correlation.

In the next section we will develop a program which accepts high level specification parameters of the NN genotype we wish to construct, and which outputs the genotype represented as a list of tuples. We will then develop a mapping function which will use our NN genotype to create a process based phenotype, which is the actual NN system that senses, thinks, and takes action based on its sensory signals and neural processing.

6.5 Programming the Genotype Constructor

Now that we've decided on the necessary elements and their genotypic representation in our NN system, we need to create a program that accepts as input the high level NN specification parameters, and produces the genotype as output.

When creating a NN, we need to be able to specify the sensors it will use, the actuators it will use, and the general NN topology. The NN topology specification should state how many layers and how many neurons per layer the feed forward NN will have. Because we wish to keep this particular NN system very simple, we will only require that the genotype constructor is able to generate NNs with a single sensor and actuator. For the number of layers and layer densities of the NN, all the information can be contained in a single LayerDensities list as shown in Figure-6.8. Thus, our genotype constructor should be able to construct everything from a parameter list composed of a sensor name, an actuator name, and a LayerDensities list. The LayerDensities parameter will actually only specify the hidden layer densities, where the hidden LayerDensities are all the non output layer densities. The output layer density will be calculated from the vector length of the actuator. An empty HiddenLayerDensities list implies that the NN will only have a single neural layer, whose density is equal to the actuator's vector length.

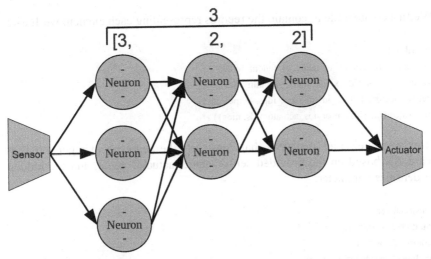

Fig. 6.8 A NN composed of 3 layers, with a [3, 2, 2] layer density pattern.

For example, a genotype creating program which accepts (SensorName,ActuatorName,[1,3]) as input, where the sensor vector length is 3 and the actuator vector length is 1, should produce a NN with 3 layers, whose output layer has 1 neuron, as shown in Figure-6.9. The input layer will have a single neuron which has 3 weights and a bias, so that the neurons in the first layer can process input vectors of length 3 coming from the sensor. The output layer has a single neuron, due to actuator's vl equaling 1.

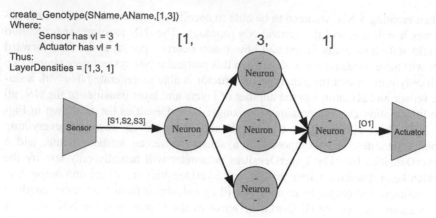

```
create_Genotype(SName,AName,[1,3])
Where:
        Sensor has vl = 3
        Actuator has vl = 1
Thus:
LayerDensities = [1,3, 1]
```

Fig. 6.9 Genotype with: LayerDensities == [1,3,1], and HiddenLayerDensities == [1,3].

We first create a file to contain the records representing each element we'll use:

```
records.hrl
-record(sensor, {id, cx_id, name, vl, fanout_ids}).
-record(actuator,{id, cx_id, name, vl, fanin_ids}).
-record(neuron, {id, cx_id, af, input_idps, output_ids}).
-record(cortex, {id, sensor_ids, actuator_ids, nids}).
```

Now we develop an algorithm that constructs the genotype of a general feed forward NN based on the provided sensor name, actuator name, and the hidden layer densities parameter:

```
constructor.erl
-module(constructor).
-compile(export_all).
-include("records.hrl").

construct_Genotype(SensorName,ActuatorName,HiddenLayerDensities)->
    construct_Genotype(ffnn,SensorName,ActuatorName,HiddenLayerDensities).
construct_Genotype(FileName,SensorName,ActuatorName,HiddenLayerDensities)->
    S = create_Sensor(SensorName),
    A = create_Actuator(ActuatorName),
    Output_VL = A#actuator.vl,
    LayerDensities = lists:append(HiddenLayerDensities,[Output_VL]),
    Cx_Id = {cortex,generate_id()},

    Neurons = create_NeuroLayers(Cx_Id,S,A,LayerDensities),
    [Input_Layer|_] = Neurons,
    [Output_Layer|_] = lists:reverse(Neurons),
    FL_NIds = [N#neuron.id || N <- Input_Layer],
```

```
LL_NIds = [N#neuron.id || N <- Output_Layer],
NIds = [N#neuron.id || N <- lists:flatten(Neurons)],
Sensor = S#sensor{cx_id = Cx_Id, fanout_ids = FL_NIds},
Actuator = A#actuator{cx_id=Cx_Id,fanin_ids = LL_NIds},
Cortex = create_Cortex(Cx_Id,[S#sensor.id],[A#actuator.id],NIds),
Genotype = lists:flatten([Cortex,Sensor,Actuator|Neurons]),
{ok, File} = file:open(FileName, write),
lists:foreach(fun(X) -> io:format(File, "~p.~n",[X]) end, Genotype),
file:close(File).
```
%The construct_Genotype function accepts the name of the file to which we'll save the genotype, sensor name, actuator name, and the hidden layer density parameters. We have to generate unique Ids for every sensor and actuator. The sensor and actuator names are used as input to the create_Sensor and create_Actuator functions, which in turn generate the actual Sensor and Actuator representing tuples. We create unique Ids for sensors and actuators so that when in the future a NN uses 2 or more sensors or actuators of the same type, we will be able to differentiate between them using their Ids. After the Sensor and Actuator tuples are generated, we extract the NN's input and output vector lengths from the sensor and actuator used by the system. The Input_VL is then used to specify how many weights the neurons in the input layer will need, and the Output_VL specifies how many neurons are in the output layer of the NN. After appending the HiddenLayerDensites to the now known number of neurons in the last layer to generate the full LayerDensities list, we use the create_NeuroLayers function to generate the Neuron representing tuples. We then update the Sensor and Actuator records with proper fanin and fanout ids from the freshly created Neuron tuples, compose the Cortex, and write the genotype to file.

```
create_Sensor(SensorName) ->
        case SensorName of
                rng ->
                        #sensor{id={sensor,generate_id()},name=rng,vl=2};
                _ ->
                        exit("System does not yet support a sensor by the
name:~p.",[SensorName])
        end.


create_Actuator(ActuatorName) ->
        case ActuatorName of
                pts ->
                        #actuator{id={actuator,generate_id()},name=pts,vl=1};
                _ ->
                        exit("System does not yet support an actuator by the
name:~p.",[ActuatorName])
        end.
```
%Every sensor and actuator uses some kind of function associated with it, a function that either polls the environment for sensory signals (in the case of a sensor) or acts upon the environment (in the case of an actuator). It is the function that we need to define and program before it is

used, and the name of the function is the same as the name of the sensor or actuator itself. For example, the create_Sensor/1 has specified only the rng sensor, because that is the only sensor function we've finished developing. The rng function has its own vl specification, which will determine the number of weights that a neuron will need to allocate if it is to accept this sensor's output vector. The same principles apply to the create_Actuator function. Both, create_Sensor and create_Actuator function, given the name of the sensor or actuator, will return a record with all the specifications of that element, each with its own unique Id.

```
create_NeuroLayers(Cx_Id,Sensor,Actuator,LayerDensities) ->
        Input_IdPs = [{Sensor#sensor.id,Sensor#sensor.vl}],
        Tot_Layers = length(LayerDensities),
        [FL_Neurons|Next_LDs] = LayerDensities,
        NIds = [{neuron,{1,Id}}|| Id <- generate_ids(FL_Neurons,[])],
        cre-
ate_NeuroLayers(Cx_Id,Actuator#actuator.id,1,Tot_Layers,Input_IdPs,NIds,Next_LDs,[]).
```
%The function create_NeuroLayers/3 prepares the initial step before starting the recursive create_NeuroLayers/7 function which will create all the Neuron records. We first generate the place holder Input Ids "Plus"(Input_IdPs), which are tuples composed of Ids and the vector lengths of the incoming signals associated with them. The proper input_idps will have a weight list in the tuple instead of the vector length. Because we are only building NNs each with only a single Sensor and Actuator, the IdP to the first layer is composed of the single Sensor Id with the vector length of its sensory signal, likewise in the case of the Actuator. We then generate unique ids for the neurons in the first layer, and drop into the recursive create_NeuroLayers/7 function.

```
    cre-
ate_NeuroLayers(Cx_Id,Actuator_Id,LayerIndex,Tot_Layers,Input_IdPs,NIds,[Next_LD|LDs],
Acc) ->
        Output_NIds = [{neuron,{LayerIndex+1,Id}} || Id <- generate_ids(Next_LD,[])],
        Layer_Neurons = create_NeuroLayer(Cx_Id,Input_IdPs,NIds,Output_NIds,[]),
        Next_InputIdPs = [{NId,1}|| NId <- NIds],
        cre-
ate_NeuroLayers(Cx_Id,Actuator_Id,LayerIndex+1,Tot_Layers,Next_InputIdPs,Output_NIds,
LDs,[Layer_Neurons|Acc]);
    create_NeuroLayers(Cx_Id,Actuator_Id,Tot_Layers,Tot_Layers,Input_IdPs,NIds,[],Acc) ->
        Output_Ids = [Actuator_Id],
        Layer_Neurons = create_NeuroLayer(Cx_Id,Input_IdPs,NIds,Output_Ids,[]),
        lists:reverse([Layer_Neurons|Acc]).
```
%During the first iteration, the first layer neuron ids constructed in create_NeuroLayers/3 are held in the NIds variable. In create_NeuroLayers/7, with every iteration we generate the Output_NIds, which are the Ids of the neurons in the next layer. The last layer is a special case which occurs when LayerIndex == Tot_Layers. Having the Input_IdPs, and the Output_NIds, we are able to construct a neuron record for every Id in NIds using the function create_layer/4. The Ids of the constructed Output_NIds will become the NIds variable of the next iteration, and the Ids of the neurons in the current layer will be extended and become Next_InputIdPs. We

then drop into the next iteration with the newly prepared Next_InputIdPs and Output_NIds. Finally, when we reach the last layer, the Output_Ids is the list containing a single Id of the Actuator element. We use the same function, create_NeuroLayer/4, to construct the last layer and return the result.

```
create_NeuroLayer(Cx_Id,Input_IdPs,[Id|NIds],Output_Ids,Acc) ->
        Neuron = create_Neuron(Input_IdPs,Id,Cx_Id,Output_Ids),
        create_NeuroLayer(Cx_Id,Input_IdPs,NIds,Output_Ids,[Neuron|Acc]);
create_NeuroLayer(_Cx_Id,_Input_IdPs,[],_Output_Ids,Acc) ->
        Acc.
```
%To create neurons from the same layer, all that is needed are the Ids for those neurons, a list of Input_IdPs for every neuron so that we can create the proper number of weights, and a list of Output_Ids. Since in our simple feed forward neural network all neurons are fully connected to the neurons in the next layer, the Input_IdPs and Output_Ids are the same for every neuron belonging to the same layer.

```
create_Neuron(Input_IdPs,Id,Cx_Id,Output_Ids)->
        Proper_InputIdPS = create_NeuralInput(Input_IdPs,[]),
        #neuron{id=Id,cx_id =
Cx_Id,af=tanh,input_idps=Proper_InputIdPS,output_ids=Output_Ids}.

create_NeuralInput([{Input_Id,Input_VL}|Input_IdPs],Acc) ->
        Weights = create_NeuralWeights(Input_VL,[]),
        create_NeuralInput(Input_IdPs,[{Input_Id,Weights}|Acc]);
create_NeuralInput([],Acc)->
        lists:reverse([{bias,random:uniform()-0.5}|Acc]).

create_NeuralWeights(0,Acc) ->
        Acc;
create_NeuralWeights(Index,Acc) ->
        W = random:uniform()-0.5,
        create_NeuralWeights(Index-1,[W|Acc]).
```
%Each neuron record is composed by the create_Neuron/3 function. The create_Neuron/3 function creates the Input list from the tuples [{Id,Weights}...] using the vector lengths specified in the place holder Input_IdPs. The create_NeuralInput/2 function uses create_NeuralWeights/2 to generate the random weights in the range of -0.5 to 0.5, adding the bias to the end of the list.

```
generate_ids(0,Acc) ->
        Acc;
generate_ids(Index,Acc)->
        Id = generate_id(),
        generate_ids(Index-1,[Id|Acc]).

generate_id() ->
        {MegaSeconds,Seconds,MicroSeconds} = now(),
```

```
                    1/(MegaSeconds*1000000 + Seconds + MicroSeconds/1000000).
%The generate_id/0 creates a unique Id using current time, the Id is a floating point value. The
generate_ids/2 function creates a list of unique Ids.


create_Cortex(Cx_Id,S_Ids,A_Ids,NIds) ->
        #cortex{id = Cx_Id, sensor_ids=S_Ids, actuator_ids=A_Ids, nids = NIds}.
%The create_Cortex/4 function generates the record encoded genotypical representation of the
cortex element. The Cortex element needs to know the Id of every Neuron, Sensor, and Actua-
tor in the NN.
```

Note that the constructor can only create sensor and actuator records that are specified in the create_Sensor/1 and create_Actuator/1 functions, and it can only create the genotype if it knows the Sensor and Actuator **vl** parameters. Let us now compile and test our genotype constructing algorithm:

```
1>c(constructor).
{ok,constructor}.
2>constructor:construct_Genotype(ffnn,rng,pts,[1,3]).
ok
```

It works! Make sure to open the file to which the Genotype was written (ffnn in the above example), and peruse the generated list of tuples to ensure that all the elements are properly interconnected by looking at their fanin/fanout and input/output ids. This list is a genotype of the NN which is composed of 3 feed forward neural layers, with 1 neuron in the first layer, 3 in the second, and 1 in the third. The created NN genotype uses the **rng** sensor and **pts** actuator. In the next section we will create a genotype to phenotype mapper which will convert inert genotypes of this form, into live phenotypes which can process sensory signals and act on the world using their actuators.

6.6 Developing the Genotype to Phenotype Mapping Module

We've invented a tuple based genotype representation for our Neural Network, and we have developed an algorithm which creates the NN genotypes when provided with 3 high level parameters, SensorName, ActuatorName, and HiddenLayerDensities. But our genotypical representation of the NN is only used as a method of storing it in a database or some file. We now need to create a function that converts the NN genotype, to an active phenotype.

In the previous chapter we have discussed how Erlang, unlike any other language, is perfect for developing fault tolerant and concurrent NN systems. The NN topology and functionality maps perfectly to Erlang's process based architecture. We now need to design an algorithm that creates a process for every tuple encoded element (Cortex, Neurons, Actuator, Sensor) stored in the genotype, and then interconnects those processes to produce the proper NN topology. This mapping is an example of direct encoding, where every tuple becomes a process, and every connection is explicitly specified in the genotype. The mapping is shown in Figure-6.10.

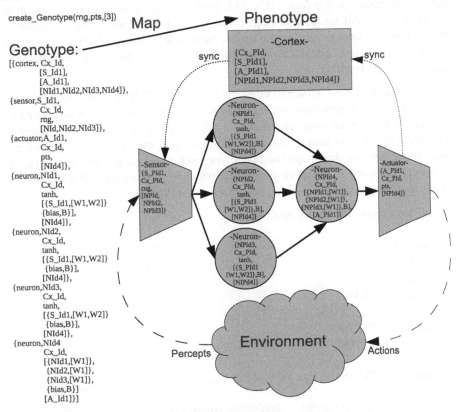

Fig. 6.10 A direct genotype to phenotype mapping.

In our genotype to phenotype direct mapping, we first spawn every element to create a correlation from Ids to their respective process PIds, and then initialize every process's state using the information in its correlated record. But to get these processes to communicate, we still need to standardize the messages they will exchange between each other.

Because we want our neurons to be ambivalent to whether the signal is coming from another neuron or a sensor, all signal vector messages must be of the same form. We can let the messages passed from sensors and neurons to other neurons and actuators use the following form: {Sender_PId, forward, Signal_Vector}. The Sender_PId will allow the Neurons to match the Signal_Vector with its appropriate weight vector.

Once the actuator has accumulated all the incoming neural signals, it should be able to notify the cortex element of this, so that the cortex can trigger the sensor processes to poll for new sensory data. The actuators will use the following messages for this task: {Actuator_PId,sync}. Once the cortex has received the sync messages from all the actuators connected to its NN, it will trigger all the sensors using a messages of the form: {Cx_PId,sync}. Finally, every element other than the cortex will also accept a message of the form: {Cx_PId,terminate}. The cortex itself should be able to receive the simple 'terminate' message. In this manner we can request that the cortex terminates all the elements in the NN it oversees, and then terminates itself.

Now that we know what messages the processes will be exchanging, and how the phenotype is represented, we can start developing the cortex, sensor, actuator, neuron, and the phenotype constructor module we'll call exoself. The 'exoself' module will not only contain the algorithm that maps the genotype to phenotype, but also a function that maps the phenotype back to genotype. The phenotype to genotype mapping is a backup procedure, which will allow us to backup phenotypes that have learned something new, back to the database.

We now create the cortex module:

```
cortex.erl
-module(cortex).
-compile(export_all).
-include("records.hrl").

gen(ExoSelf_PId,Node)->
    spawn(Node,?MODULE,loop,[ExoSelf_PId]).

loop(ExoSelf_PId) ->
    receive
            {ExoSelf_PId,{Id,SPIds,APIds,NPIds},TotSteps} ->
                [SPId ! {self(),sync} || SPId <- SPIds],
                loop(Id,ExoSelf_PId,SPIds,{APIds,APIds},NPIds,TotSteps)
    end.
%The gen/2 function spawns the cortex element, which immediately starts to wait for a the
state message from the same process that spawned it, exoself. The initial state message contains
the sensor, actuator, and neuron PId lists. The message also specifies how many total Sense-
Think-Act cycles the Cortex should execute before terminating the NN system. Once we im-
plement the learning algorithm, the termination criteria will depend on the fitness of the NN, or
some other useful property

loop(Id,ExoSelf_PId,SPIds,{_APIds,MAPIds},NPIds,0) ->
    io:format("Cortex:~p is backing up and terminating.~n",[Id]),
    Neuron_IdsNWeights = get_backup(NPIds,[]),
    ExoSelf_PId ! {self(),backup,Neuron_IdsNWeights},
```

```
    [PId ! {self(),terminate} || PId <- SPIds],
    [PId ! {self(),terminate} || PId <- MAPIds],
    [PId ! {self(),termiante} || PId <- NPIds];
loop(Id,ExoSelf_PId,SPIds,{[APId|APIds],MAPIds},NPIds,Step) ->
    receive
        {APId,sync} ->
                loop(Id,ExoSelf_PId,SPIds,{APIds,MAPIds},NPIds,Step);
        terminate ->
                io:format("Cortex:~p is terminating.~n",[Id]),
                [PId ! {self(),terminate} || PId <- SPIds],
                [PId ! {self(),terminate} || PId <- MAPIds],
                [PId ! {self(),termiante} || PId <- NPIds]
    end;
loop(Id,ExoSelf_PId,SPIds,{[],MAPIds},NPIds,Step)->
    [PId ! {self(),sync} || PId <- SPIds],
    loop(Id,ExoSelf_PId,SPIds,{MAPIds,MAPIds},NPIds,Step-1).
```
%The cortex's goal is to synchronize the NN system such that when the actuators have received all their control signals, the sensors are once again triggered to gather new sensory information. Thus the cortex waits for the sync messages from the actuator PIds in its system, and once it has received all the sync messages, it triggers the sensors and then drops back to waiting for a new set of sync messages. The cortex stores 2 copies of the actuator PIds: the APIds, and the MemoryAPIds (MAPIds). Once all the actuators have sent it the sync messages, it can restore the APIds list from the MAPIds. Finally, there is also the Step variable which decrements every time a full cycle of Sense-Think-Act completes, once this reaches 0, the NN system begins its termination and backup process.

```
    get_backup([NPId|NPIds],Acc)->
            NPId ! {self(),get_backup},
            receive
                {NPId,NId,WeightTuples}->
                        get_backup(NPIds,[{NId,WeightTuples}|Acc])
            end;
    get_backup([],Acc)->
            Acc.
```
%During backup, cortex contacts all the neurons in its NN and requests for the neuron's Ids and their Input_IdPs. Once the updated Input_IdPs from all the neurons have been accumulated, the list is sent to exoself for the actual backup and storage.

Now the sensor module:

```
sensor.erl
-module(sensor).
-compile(export_all).
-include("records.hrl").
```

```erlang
gen(ExoSelf_PId,Node)->
    spawn(Node,?MODULE,loop,[ExoSelf_PId]).


loop(ExoSelf_PId) ->
    receive
            {ExoSelf_PId,{Id,Cx_PId,SensorName,VL,Fanout_PIds}} ->
                    loop(Id,Cx_PId,SensorName,VL,Fanout_PIds)
    end.
```
%When gen/2 is executed it spawns the sensor element and immediately begins to wait for its initial state message.

```erlang
loop(Id,Cx_PId,SensorName,VL,Fanout_PIds)->
    receive
            {Cx_PId,sync}->
                    SensoryVector = sensor:SensorName(VL),
                    [Pid ! {self(),forward,SensoryVector} || Pid <- Fanout_PIds],
                    loop(Id,Cx_PId,SensorName,VL,Fanout_PIds);
            {Cx_PId,terminate} ->
                    ok
    end.
```
%The sensor process accepts only 2 types of messages, both from the cortex. The sensor can either be triggered to begin gathering sensory data based on its sensory role, or terminate if the cortex requests so.

```erlang
rng(VL)->
    rng(VL,[]).
rng(0,Acc)->
    Acc;
rng(VL,Acc)->
    rng(VL-1,[random:uniform()|Acc]).
```

%'rng' is a simple random number generator that produces a vector of random values, each between 0 and 1. The length of the vector is defined by the VL, which itself is specified within the sensor record.

The actuator module:

```erlang
actuator.erl
-module(actuator).
-compile(export_all).
-include("records.hrl").


gen(ExoSelf_PId,Node)->
    spawn(Node,?MODULE,loop,[ExoSelf_PId]).
```

```
loop(ExoSelf_PId) ->
    receive
            {ExoSelf_PId,{Id,Cx_PId,ActuatorName,Fanin_PIds}} ->
                    loop(Id,Cx_PId,ActuatorName,{Fanin_PIds,Fanin_PIds},[])
    end.
%When gen/2 is executed it spawns the actuator element and immediately begins to wait for its
initial state message.

loop(Id,Cx_PId,AName,{[From_PId|Fanin_PIds],MFanin_PIds},Acc) ->
    receive
            {From_PId,forward,Input} ->
                    loop(Id,Cx_PId,AName,{Fanin_PIds,MFanin_PIds},lists:append(Input,Acc));
            {Cx_PId,terminate} ->
                    ok
    end;
loop(Id,Cx_PId,AName,{[],MFanin_PIds},Acc)->
    actuator:AName(lists:reverse(Acc)),
    Cx_PId ! {self(),sync},
    loop(Id,Cx_PId,AName,{MFanin_PIds,MFanin_PIds},[]).
%The actuator process gathers the control signals from the neurons, appending them to the ac-
cumulator. The order in which the signals are accumulated into a vector is in the same order as
the neuron ids are stored within NIds. Once all the signals have been gathered, the actuator
sends cortex the sync signal, executes its function, and then again begins to wait for the neural
signals from the output layer by reseting the Fanin_PIds from the second copy of the list.


pts(Result)->
    io:format("actuator:pts(Result): ~p~n",[Result]).
%The pts actuation function simply prints to screen the vector passed to it.
```

And finally the neuron module:

```
neuron.erl
-module(neuron).
-compile(export_all).
-include("records.hrl").

gen(ExoSelf_PId,Node)->
    spawn(Node,?MODULE,loop,[ExoSelf_PId]).

loop(ExoSelf_PId) ->
    receive
            {ExoSelf_PId,{Id,Cx_PId,AF,Input_PIdPs,Output_PIds}} ->
                    loop(Id,Cx_PId,AF,{Input_PIdPs,Input_PIdPs},Output_PIds,0)
    end.
```

%When gen/2 is executed it spawns the neuron element and immediately begins to wait for its
initial state message.

```
loop(Id,Cx_PId,AF,{[{Input_PId,Weights}|Input_PIdPs],MInput_PIdPs},Output_PIds,Acc)->
    receive
        {Input_PId,forward,Input}->
            Result = dot(Input,Weights,0),
            loop(Id,Cx_PId,AF,{Input_PIdPs,MInput_PIdPs},Output_PIds,Result+Acc);
        {Cx_PId,get_backup}->
            Cx_PId ! {self(),Id,MInput_PIdPs},

    loop(Id,Cx_PId,AF,{[{Input_PId,Weights}|Input_PIdPs],MInput_PIdPs},Output_PIds,Acc);
        {Cx_PId,terminate}->
            ok
    end;
loop(Id,Cx_PId,AF,{[Bias],MInput_PIdPs},Output_PIds,Acc)->
    Output = neuron:AF(Acc+Bias),
    [Output_PId ! {self(),forward,[Output]} || Output_PId <- Output_PIds],
    loop(Id,Cx_PId,AF,{MInput_PIdPs,MInput_PIdPs},Output_PIds,0);
loop(Id,Cx_PId,AF,{[],MInput_PIdPs},Output_PIds,Acc)->
    Output = neuron:AF(Acc),
    [Output_PId ! {self(),forward,[Output]} || Output_PId <- Output_PIds],
    loop(Id,Cx_PId,AF,{MInput_PIdPs,MInput_PIdPs},Output_PIds,0).

    dot([I|Input],[W|Weights],Acc) ->
        dot(Input,Weights,I*W+Acc);
    dot([],[],Acc)->
        Acc.
```
%The neuron process waits for vector signals from all the processes that it's connected from,
taking the dot product of the input and weight vectors, and then adding it to the accumulator.
Once all the signals from Input_PIds are received, the accumulator contains the dot product to
which the neuron then adds the bias and executes the activation function on. After fanning out
the output signal, the neuron again returns to waiting for incoming signals. When the neuron receives the {Cx_PId,get_backup} message, it forwards to the cortex its full MInput_PIdPs list,
and its Id. Once the training/learning algorithm is added to the system, the MInput_PIdPs
would contain a full set of the most recent and updated version of the weights.

```
    tanh(Val)->
        math:tanh(Val).
```
%Though in this current implementation the neuron has only the tanh/1 function available to it,
we will later extend the system to allow different neurons to use different activation functions.

Now we create the exoself module, which will map the genotype to phenotype,
spawning all the appropriate processes. The exoself module will also provide the
algorithm for the Cortex element to update the genotype with the newly trained

weights from the phenotype, and in this manner saving the trained and learned NNs for future use.

```erlang
exoself.erl
-module(exoself).
-compile(export_all).
-include("records.hrl").

map()->
    map(ffnn).
map(FileName)->
    {ok,Genotype} = file:consult(FileName),
    spawn(exoself,map,[FileName,Genotype]).
map(FileName,Genotype)->
    IdsNPIds = ets:new(idsNpids,[set,private]),
    [Cx|CerebralUnits] = Genotype,
    Sensor_Ids = Cx#cortex.sensor_ids,
    Actuator_Ids = Cx#cortex.actuator_ids,
    NIds = Cx#cortex.nids,
    spawn_CerebralUnits(IdsNPIds,cortex,[Cx#cortex.id]),
    spawn_CerebralUnits(IdsNPIds,sensor,Sensor_Ids),
    spawn_CerebralUnits(IdsNPIds,actuator,Actuator_Ids),
    spawn_CerebralUnits(IdsNPIds,neuron,NIds),
    link_CerebralUnits(CerebralUnits,IdsNPIds),
    link_Cortex(Cx,IdsNPIds),
    Cx_PId = ets:lookup_element(IdsNPIds,Cx#cortex.id,2),
    receive
            {Cx_PId,backup,Neuron_IdsNWeights}->
                    U_Genotype = update_genotype(IdsNPIds,Genotype,Neuron_IdsNWeights),
                    {ok, File} = file:open(FileName, write),
                    lists:foreach(fun(X) -> io:format(File, "~p.~n",[X]) end, U_Genotype),
                    file:close(File),
                    io:format("Finished updating to file:~p~n",[FileName])
    end.
```

%The map/1 function maps the tuple encoded genotype into a process based phenotype. The map function expects for the Cx record to be the leading tuple in the tuple list it reads from the FileName. We create an ets table to map Ids to PIds and back again. Since the Cortex element contains all the Sensor, Actuator, and Neuron Ids, we are able to spawn each neuron using its own gen function, and in the process construct a map from Ids to PIds. We then use link_CerebralUnits to link all non Cortex elements to each other by sending each spawned process the information contained in its record, but with Ids converted to Pids where appropriate. Finally, we provide the Cortex process with all the PIds in the NN system by executing the link_Cortex/2 function. Once the NN is up and running, exoself starts its wait until the NN has finished its job and is ready to backup. When the cortex initiates the backup process it sends exoself the updated Input_PIdPs from its neurons. Exoself uses the update_genotype/3 function to update the old genotype with new weights, and then stores the updated version back to its file.

```
spawn_CerebralUnits(IdsNPIds,CerebralUnitType,[Id|Ids])->
      PId = CerebralUnitType:gen(self(),node()),
      ets:insert(IdsNPIds,{Id,PId}),
      ets:insert(IdsNPIds,{PId,Id}),
      spawn_CerebralUnits(IdsNPIds,CerebralUnitType,Ids);
spawn_CerebralUnits(_IdsNPIds,_CerebralUnitType,[])->
      true.
```

%We spawn the process for each element based on its type: CerebralUnitType, and the gen function that belongs to the CerebralUnitType module. We then enter the {Id,PId} tuple into our ETS table for later use.

```
link_CerebralUnits([R|Records],IdsNPIds) when is_record(R,sensor) ->
      SId = R#sensor.id,
      SPId = ets:lookup_element(IdsNPIds,SId,2),
      Cx_PId = ets:lookup_element(IdsNPIds,R#sensor.cx_id,2),
      SName = R#sensor.name,
      Fanout_Ids = R#sensor.fanout_ids,
      Fanout_PIds = [ets:lookup_element(IdsNPIds,Id,2) || Id <- Fanout_Ids],
      SPId ! {self(),{SId,Cx_PId,SName,R#sensor.vl,Fanout_PIds}},
      link_CerebralUnits(Records,IdsNPIds);
link_CerebralUnits([R|Records],IdsNPIds) when is_record(R,actuator) ->
      AId = R#actuator.id,
      APId = ets:lookup_element(IdsNPIds,AId,2),
      Cx_PId = ets:lookup_element(IdsNPIds,R#actuator.cx_id,2),
      AName = R#actuator.name,
      Fanin_Ids = R#actuator.fanin_ids,
      Fanin_PIds = [ets:lookup_element(IdsNPIds,Id,2) || Id <- Fanin_Ids],
      APId ! {self(),{AId,Cx_PId,AName,Fanin_PIds}},
      link_CerebralUnits(Records,IdsNPIds);
link_CerebralUnits([R|Records],IdsNPIds) when is_record(R,neuron) ->
      NId = R#neuron.id,
      NPId = ets:lookup_element(IdsNPIds,NId,2),
      Cx_PId = ets:lookup_element(IdsNPIds,R#neuron.cx_id,2),
      AFName = R#neuron.af,
      Input_IdPs = R#neuron.input_idps,
      Output_Ids = R#neuron.output_ids,
      Input_PIdPs = convert_IdPs2PIdPs(IdsNPIds,Input_IdPs,[]),
      Output_PIds = [ets:lookup_element(IdsNPIds,Id,2) || Id <- Output_Ids],
      NPId ! {self(),{NId,Cx_PId,AFName,Input_PIdPs,Output_PIds}},
      link_CerebralUnits(Records,IdsNPIds);
link_CerebralUnits([],_IdsNPIds)->
      ok.
```

```
        convert_IdPs2PIdPs(_IdsNPIds,[{bias,Bias}],Acc)->
            lists:reverse([Bias|Acc]);
        convert_IdPs2PIdPs(IdsNPIds,[{Id,Weights}|Fanin_IdPs],Acc)->
            convert_IdPs2PIdPs(IdsNPIds,Fanin_IdPs,
[{ets:lookup_element(IdsNPIds,Id,2),Weights}|Acc]).
```
%The link_CerebralUnits/2 converts the Ids to PIds using the created IdsNPids ETS table. At this point all the elements are spawned, and the processes are waiting for their initial states. convert_IdPs2PIdPs/3 converts the IdPs tuples into tuples that use PIds instead of Ids, such that the Neuron will know which weights are to be associated with which incoming vector signals. The last element is the bias, which is added to the list in a non tuple form. Afterwards, the list is reversed to take its proper order.

```
  link_Cortex(Cx,IdsNPIds) ->
        Cx_Id = Cx#cortex.id,
        Cx_PId = ets:lookup_element(IdsNPIds,Cx_Id,2),
        SIds = Cx#cortex.sensor_ids,
        AIds = Cx#cortex.actuator_ids,
        NIds = Cx#cortex.nids,
        SPIds = [ets:lookup_element(IdsNPIds,SId,2) || SId <- SIds],
        APIds = [ets:lookup_element(IdsNPIds,AId,2) || AId <- AIds],
        NPIds = [ets:lookup_element(IdsNPIds,NId,2) || NId <- NIds],
        Cx_PId ! {self(),{Cx_Id,SPIds,APIds,NPIds},1000}.
```
%The cortex is initialized to its proper state just as other elements. Because we have not yet implemented a learning algorithm for our NN system, we need to specify when the NN should shutdown. We do this by specifying the total number of cycles the NN should execute before terminating, which is 1000 in this case.

```
update_genotype(IdsNPIds,Genotype,[{N_Id,PIdPs}|WeightPs])->
    N = lists:keyfind(N_Id, 2, Genotype),
    io:format("PIdPs:~p~n",[PIdPs]),
    Updated_InputIdPs = convert_PIdPs2IdPs(IdsNPIds,PIdPs,[]),
    U_N = N#neuron{input_idps = Updated_InputIdPs},
    U_Genotype = lists:keyreplace(N_Id, 2, Genotype, U_N),
    io:format("N:~p~n U_N:~p~n Genotype:~p~n
U_Genotype:~p~n",[N,U_N,Genotype,U_Genotype]),
    update_genotype(IdsNPIds,U_Genotype,WeightPs);
update_genotype(_IdsNPIds,Genotype,[])->
    Genotype.

  convert_PIdPs2IdPs(IdsNPIds,[{PId,Weights}|Input_PIdPs],Acc)->
        con-
vert_PIdPs2IdPs(IdsNPIds,Input_PIdPs,[{ets:lookup_element(IdsNPIds,PId,2),Weights}|Acc]);
    convert_PIdPs2IdPs(_IdsNPIds,[Bias],Acc)->
        lists:reverse([{bias,Bias}|Acc]).
```

```
%For every {N_Id,PIdPs} tuple the update_genotype/3 function extracts the neuron with the id:
N_Id, and updates its weights. The convert_PIdPs2IdPs/3 performs the conversion from PIds to
Ids of every {PId,Weights} tuple in the Input_PIdPs list. The updated Genotype is then returned
back to the caller.
```

Now lets compile the cortex, neuron, sensor, actuator, and the exoself module, and test the NN system:

```
1> c(cortex).
ok
...
```

We now create a new NN genotype which uses the rng sensor, a pts actuator, and employs a [1,2] hidden density list. Then we map it to its phenotype by using the exoself module.

```
1> constructor:construct_Genotype(ffnn,rng,pts,[1,2]).
ok
2> exoself:map(ffnn).
...
```

It works! Our NN system has sensed, thought, and acted using its sensor, neurons, and the actuator, while being synchronized through the cortex process. Yet still this system does nothing but process random vectors using neural processes which themselves use random weights. We now need to develop a learning algorithm, and then devise a problem on which to test how well the NN can learn and solve problems using its learning method. In the next chapter we will develop an augmented version one of the most commonly used unsupervised learning algorithms: the Stochastic Hill-Climber.

6.7 Summary

We have started with just a discussion of how a single artificial neuron processes an incoming signal, which is vector encoded. We then developed a simple sensor and actuator, so that the neuron has something to acquire sensory signals with, and so that it can use its output signal to act upon the world, in this case simply printing that output signal to screen. We then began designing the architecture of the NN system we wish to develop, and the genotype encoding we wanted to store that NN system in. After we had agreed on the architecture and the encoding, we created the genotype constructor which built the NN genotype, and then a mapper function which converted the genotype to its phenotype form. With this, we had now developed a system that can create NN genotypes, and convert them to phenotypes, We tested the ability of the NN to sense using its sensors, thinking about the signals it acquired through its sensors, and then act upon the world by using its actuators; the system worked. Though our NN system does not yet have a way to learn, or be optimized for any particular task, we have developed a complete encoding method, a genotypical and phenotypical representation of a fully concurrent NN system, in just a few pages. With Erlang, a neuron is a process, an action potential is a message, there is a 1:1 mapping, which made developing this system so easy.

Chapter 7 Adding the "Stochastic Hill-Climber" Learning Algorithm

Abstract In this chapter we discuss the functionality of an optimization method called the *Stochastic Hill Climber*, and the *Stochastic Hill Climber With Random Restarts*. We then implement this optimization algorithm, allowing the exoself process to train and optimize the neural network it is overlooking. Afterwards, we implement a new problem interfacing method through the use of public and private *scapes*, which are simulated environments, not necessarily physical. We apply the new system to the XOR emulation problem, testing its performance on it. Finally, looking to the future and the need for us to be able to test and benchmark our neuroevolutionary system as we add new features to it, we create the *benchmarker* process, which summons the trainer and the NN it trains, applying it to some specified problem X number of times. Once the benchmarker has applied the trainer to the problem X number of times and accumulated the resulting statistics, it calculates the averages and the associated standard deviations for the important performance parameters of the benchmark.

Though we have now created a functional NN system, synchronized by the cortex element and able to use sensors and actuators to interact with the world, it still lacks the functionality to learn or be trained to solve a given problem or perform some given task. What our system needs now is a learning algorithm, a method by which we can train the NN to do something useful. Beside the learning algorithm itself, we will also need some external system that can automatically train and apply this learning algorithm to the NN, and a system that can monitor the NN for any unexpected crashes or errors, restoring it to a functional state when necessary. Finally, though we have implemented sensors and actuators which the NN can use to interact with the world and other programs, we have not yet developed a way to present to the NN the problems we wish it to solve, or tasks that we wish to train it to perform. It is these extensions that we will concern ourselves with in this chapter.

Here we will continue extending the NN system we've developed in the previous chapter. In the following sections we will discuss and add these new algorithms and features, and develop the necessary modules and module extensions to incorporate the new functionality.

7.1 The Learning Method

An evolutionary algorithm (EA) is a population based optimization algorithm which works by utilizing biologically analogous operators: Selection, Mutation, and Crossover. We will begin developing a population based approach in the next chapter, at this point though, we will still use a single NN based system. In such a case, there is one particular optimization algorithm that is commonly compared to an EA due to some similarities, that algorithm is the Stochastic Hill-Climber (SHC), and is the one we will be implementing.

In an evolutionary algorithm we use a population of organisms/agents, all of whom we apply to the same problem in parallel. Afterwards, based on the fitness each agent demonstrated, we use a selection algorithm to pick the fit from the un-fit, and then create offspring from these chosen fit agents. The offspring are created by taking the fit agents and perturbing/mutating them, or by crossing two or more fit agents together to create a new one. The new population is then composed from some combination of the original fit agents and their offspring (their mutated forms, and/or their crossover based combinations). In this manner, through selection and mutation, with every new generation we produce organisms of greater and greater fitness.

In the Stochastic Hill-Climbing algorithm that we will apply to a single agent, we do something similar. We apply a single NN to a problem, gage its performance on the problem, save its genotype and fitness, and then mutate/perturb its genome in some manner and then re-apply the resulting mutant to the problem again. If the mutated agent performs better, then we save its genotype and fitness, and mutate it again. If the mutated agent performs worse, then we simply reset the agent's genotype to its previous state, and mutate it again to see if the new mutant will perform better. In this manner we slowly climb upwards on the fitness landscape, taking a step back if the new mutant performs worse, and retrying in a different direction until we generate a mutant that performs better. If at some point it is noticed that no new mutants of this agent (in our case the agent is a NN based system) seem to be increasing in fitness, we then consider our agent to have reached a local optimum, at which point we could save its genotype and fitness score, and then apply this fit NN to the problem it was optimized for. Or we could try to restart the whole thing again, generate a completely new random genotype and try to hill-climb it to greater fitness. By generating a completely new NN genotype we hope that its initial weight (or topology and weight) combination will spawn it in a new and perhaps better location of the fitness landscape, from which a higher local optimum is reachable. In this manner the random restart stochastic hill-climber optimization algorithm can reach local and even global optimum.

The following steps represent the Stochastic Hill-Climbing (SHC) algorithm:

1. Repeat:
    2. Apply the NN to some problem.

3. Save the NN's genotype and its fitness.
4. Perturb the NN's synaptic weights, and re-apply the NN to the same problem.
5. If the fitness of the *perturbed* NN is higher, discard *original* NN and keep the new. If the fitness of the *original* NN is higher, discard the *perturbed* NN and keep the old.
6. **Until**: Acceptable solution is found, or some stopping condition is reached.
7. **Return**: The genotype with the fittest combination of weights.

The algorithm is further extended by generating completely new random genotypes when the NN currently being trained ceases to make progress. The following steps extend the SHC to the Random-Restart SHC version:

8. **Repeat:**
    9. Generate a completely new genotype, and perform steps *1-7* again.
    10. If the new genotype reaches a higher fitness, overwrite the old genotype with the new one. If the new genotype reaches a lower fitness, discard the new genotype.
11. **Until**: Acceptable solution is found, or some stopping condition is reached.
12. **Return**: The final resulting genotype with its fitness score.

Steps 8-11 are necessary in the case that the original/seed combination of NN topology and weights could not be optimized (hill climbed) to the level that would solve the problem. Generating a new genotype, either of the same topology but with different random weights, or of a different topology and weights, could land this new genotype in a place of the fitness landscape from which a much higher fitness can be reached. We will create a process which can apply steps *8-12* to a NN system, and we'll call this process: **trainer**.

We will not use the most basic version of the SHC. Instead we will modify it to be a bit more flexible and dynamic. Rather than perturbing the NN's weights some predefined K number of times before giving up, we will make K dynamic and based on a *Max_Attempts* value, which itself can be defined by the researcher or based on some feature of the NN that is being optimized. If for example we have perturbed the NN's weights $K==Max\_Attempts$ number of times, and none of them improved the NN's fitness, this implies that based on where it was originally created on the fitness landscape, the particular genotype has reached a good combination of weights, and that the NN is roughly the best that its topology allows it to be. But if on $K =< Max\_Attempts$ the NN's fitness improves, we reset K back to 0. Since the NN has just improved its fitness, it might have just escaped from some local optimum on the fitness landscape, and thus deserves another full set of attempts to try and improve its weights further. Thus, before the NN is considered to be at the top of its reachable potential, it has to fail to improve its fitness **Max_Attempts** number of times *in a row*. Max_Attempts can be set up by the researcher, the larger the Max_Attempts value, the more processing we're willing to spend on tunning the NN's synaptic weights. This method will ensure that if the NN can jump to a fitter place from the location on the fitness landscape that it's currently on, it will be given that chance. Using this augmented SHC algorithm we will tune the NN's synaptic weights, allowing the particular NN topology to reach its potential, before considering that this NN and its topology is at its limits.

The number of times the trainer process should create a new genotype (same topology but with a new set of random weights), will also be based on a similar approach. The trainer process will use *Trainer_MaxAttempts* variable for this. And it is only after Trainer_MaxAttempts number of genotypes in a row fail to produce higher fitness, will the training phase be considered complete. Once training is complete, the trainer process will return the best found genotype, and store it in the file with the name "best". This augmented SHC is diagrammed in Fig-7.1.

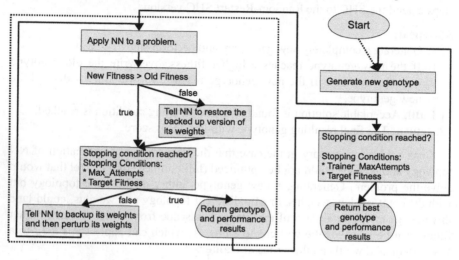

Fig. 7.1 Augmented Stochastic Hill Climber algorithm.

Further deviation from the standard algorithm will be with regards to the intensity of the weight perturbations we'll apply, and which weights and neurons we will apply those perturbations to:

1. Each neuron in the trained NN will be chosen for perturbation with a probability of 1/sqrt(NN_Size), where NN_Size is the total number of neurons in the NN.
2. Within the chosen neuron, the weights which will be perturbed will be chosen with the probability of 1/sqrt(Tot_Weights), where Tot_Weights is the total number of synaptic weights in the weights list.
3. The intensity of the synaptic weight perturbation will be randomly chosen with uniform distribution between -Pi and Pi.
4. Max_Attempts variable will be proportional to sqrt(NN_Size).

Features 1, 2 & 3 allow our system to have a chance of producing very high intensity mutations, where perturbations are large and applied to many neurons and many synaptic weights within those neurons, all at once. At the same time there is a chance that the general perturbation intensity will be small, and applied only to a few neurons and a few of their synaptic weights. Thus this approach allows our system to use highly variable mutation/perturbation intensities. Small intensity mutations can fine tune the weights of the NN, while large intensity mutations give our NN a chance to jump out of local synaptic weight optima. Feature 4 will ensure that larger NNs will have a greater amount of processing resources allocated to the tuning of their synaptic weights, because the larger the NN the greater the chance that a larger combination of weights needs to be set to just the right values all at once for the NN to become fitter, which requires a larger number of attempts to do so.

7.1.1 Comparing EA to Random Restart SHC

Note how similar the random-restart stochastic hill-climber (RR-SHC) and the standard evolutionary algorithm (EA) are. The RR-SHC is almost like a sequential version of the EA. The following list is a comparison of that:

1.

   - **EA**: In generational EA we start by creating a population of NNs, each with the same topology and thus belonging to the same species. Though each individual will have the same NN topology, each one will have a different combination of synaptic weights.
   - **RR-SHC**: In RR-SHC we create a particular genotype, a NN topology. We then try out different combinations of weights. Each new combination of weights represents an individual belonging to the same species. We are thus trying out the different individuals belonging to the same specie sequentially, one at a time, instead of all in parallel.
   But unlike in EA, these different individuals belonging to the same species are not generated randomly, and are not tried in a random order. Instead we generate one individual by perturbing its "ancestor". Each new individual in the specie is based on the previous version of itself, which is used as a stepping stone in an attempt to create a fitter version.

2.

   - **EA**: After all the organisms have been given their fitness, we create the next generation from the subset of the fit organisms. The next generation might contain new NN topologies and new species, generated from the old species through mutation and crossover. Again, each NN species will contain multiple members whose only difference is in their synaptic weights.
   But here the new species are generated as an attempt at improvement (hill climbing), with the parent individuals acting as the stepping stone for the next topological and parametric innovation.

- **RR-SHC**: After trying out the different permutations of synaptic weights for the original topology, we generate a new one (either the same or a new topology). We then again try out the different synaptic weight combinations for the genotype that starts from a different spot on the fitness landscape.

  But here we are trying out the same topology. Although of course the algorithm can be augmented, and during this step we could generate a new genotype, not simply having a different set of starting weights but one having a topology that is a perturbation of the previous version, or even completely new and random.

The EA will eventually have a population composed of numerous species, each with multiple members, and thus EA explores the solution space far and wide. If one species or a particular combination of weights in a species leads to a dead end on the fitness landscape, there will be plenty of others working in parallel which will, if there is a path, find a way to higher fitness by another route.

On the other hand the RR-SHC, during its generation of a new genotype or perturbation of weights, can only select that 1 option, the first combination that leads to a greater fitness is the path selected. If that particular selection is on the path to a dead end, it will not be known until it's too late and the system begins to fail to produce individuals of greater fitness. A dead-end that is reached when perturbing weights is not so bad because our system also generates and tries out new genotypes. But if we start generating new topologies based on the old ones in this sequential hill climbing manner, then the topological dead end reached at this point could be much more dire, since we will not know when the first step towards the dead end was taken, and we will not have multiple other species exploring paths around the topological dead end in parallel... Fig-7.2 shows the similarities and differences in the evolutionary paths taken by organisms optimized using these two methods.

In the following figure, the red colored NNs represent the most fit NNs within the particular specie they belong to. For the evolutionary computation, the flow of time is from top to bottom, whereas for the RR-SHC it is from top to bottom for a species, but the NNs and species are tried one after the other, so it is also from left to right. Evolutionary process for both, the evolutionary computation algorithm and the RR-SHC algorithm, is outlined by the step numbers, discussed next.

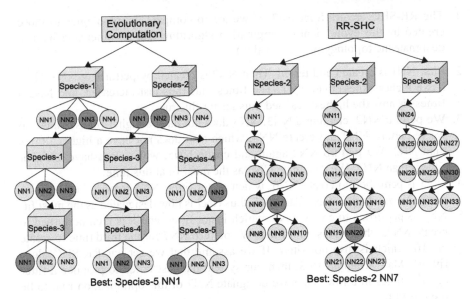

Fig. 7.2 Similarities and Differences in the evolutionary paths taken by organisms evolved through EA and RR-SHC.

Let us first go through the evolutionary path taken by the *Evolutionary Computation* algorithm, by following the specified steps:

1. Species-1 and Species-2 are created, each with 4 NNs, thus the population is composed of 8 NNs in total, separated into 2 species.
2. In Species-1, NN2 and NN3 are the most fit. NN2 creates 3 offspring, which all belong to Species-1. NN3 creates offspring which belong to Species-4. In Species-2, NN1 and NN2 are the most fit. The NN1 of Species-2 creates offspring which make up Species-3, while NN2 creates offspring which go into Species-4. In this scenario, the parents do not survive when creating an offspring, and thus Species-2 does not make it to the next generation.
3. During the second generation, the population is composed of Species-1, Species-4, and Species-3, and 9 NNs in total. In this population, the most fit NNs are NN2 and NN3 of Species-1, and NN3 of Species-4. NN2 of Species-1 creates 3 offspring, all of which have the topology of Species-3. NN3 creates 3 offspring, all of which have the topology of Species-4. Finally, NN3 of Species-4 creates 3 offspring, all of which have a new topology, and are thus designated as Species-5.
4. The third generation, composed of Species-3, Species-4, and Species-5, make up the population of size 9. The most fit of this population is the NN1 of Species-3, NN2 of Species-4, and NN1 of Species-5. The most fit of the three NNs, is NN1 of Species-5, which is designated as Champion.

Similarly, let us go through the steps taken by the RR-SHC algorithm:

1. The RR-SHC creates Species-2 (if we are to compare the topologies to those created by the evolutionary computation algorithm that is, otherwise we can designate the topology with any value).

2. First NN1 is created and tested. Then NN2 is created by perturbing NN1. NN2 has a higher fitness than NN1. The fitness has thus just increased, and NN2's fitness is now the highest reached thus far for this run.

3. We perturb NN2, creating a NN3. NN3 does not have a higher fitness value, so we re-perturb NN2 and create NN4, which also does not have a higher fitness than NN2. We perturb NN2 again and create NN5, which does have a higher fitness than NN2. We designate NN5 as the most fit at this time.

4. NN5 is perturbed to create NN6, which is not fitter. NN5 is perturbed again to create NN7, which is fitter than NN5, thus NN7 is now designated as the most fit.

5. NN7 is perturbed to create NN8, which is not fitter, and it is then perturbed to create NN9, which is also not fitter. We perturb NN7 for the third time to create NN10, which is also not fitter. If we assume that we set our RR-SHC algorithm's Max_Attempts to 3, then our system has just failed to produce a fitter agent 3 times in a row. Thus we designate NN7 of this optimization run, to be the most fit.

6. NN7 is saved as the best NN achieved during this stochastic hill climbing run.

7. The RR-SHC creates a new random NN11, whose topology designates it to be of Species-3.

8. The NN11 is perturbed to create NN12, which is not fitter than NN11. It is perturbed again to create NN13, which is fitter than NN11, and is thus designated as the fittest thus far achieved in this particular optimization run.

9. This continues until termination condition is reached for this hill climbing run as well. At which point we see that NN20 is the most fit.

10. A new random NN21 is generated. It is optimized through the same process. Until finally NN30 is designated to be the most fit of this hill climbing run.

11. Amongst the three most fit NNs, [NN7, NN20, NN30], produced from 3 random restarts of the hill climbing optimization algorithm, NN7 is the most fit. Thus, NN7 is designated as the champion produced by the RR-SHC algorithm.

We will return to these issues again in later chapters. And eventually build a hybrid composed of these two approaches, in an attempt to take advantage of the greedy and effective manner in which SHC can find good combinations of synaptic weights, and the excellent global optima searching abilities of the population based evolutionary approach.

7.2 The Trainer

The trainer will be a very simple program that first generates a NN genotype under the name "experimental", and then applies it to the problem. After the exoself (discussed in the next section) finishes performing synaptic weight tuning of its NN, it sends the trainer process a message with the NN's highest achieved fitness score and total number of evaluations it took to reach it (the number of times NN's total fitness had been evaluated). The trainer will then compare this NN's fitness to the fitness of the genotype under the name "best" (which will be 0 if there is no genotype under such name yet). If the fitness of "experimental" is higher than that of "best", the trainer will rename experimental to best, thus over-writing and removing it. If the fitness of "best" is higher than that of "experi-mental", the trainer will not overwrite the old genotype. In either case, the trainer then generates a new genotype under the name "experimental", and repeats the process.

As noted in section 7.1, the trainer will use *Trainer_MaxAttempts* variable to determine how many times to generate a new genotype. Only once the Trainer fails to generate a fitter genotype *Trainer_MaxAttempts* number of times in a row, will it be finished, at which point the trainer process will have stored the fittest genotype in the file "best".

7.3 The Exoself

We now need to create an external process to the NN system which tunes the NN's weights through the use of augmented SHC algorithm. A modified version of the *Exoself* process we created in the previous chapter is an excellent contender for this role. We cannot use the *cortex* element for this new functionality because it is part of the NN system itself. The cortex is the synchronizer, and also the ele-ment that can perform duties that require global view of the neural topology. For example in something like competitive learning where the neural response intensi-ties to some signal need to be compared to one another for the entire network, an element like cortex can be used. But if for example it is necessary to shut down the entire NN system, or to add new sensors and actuators or new neurons while the NN itself is live and running, or update the system's source code, or recover a previous state of the NN system, that duty could be better performed by an exter-nal process like the *exoself*.

Imagine an advanced ALife scenario where a simulated organism is controlled by a NN. In this simulation the organism is already able to modify its own neural topology and add new sensors and actuators to itself. To survive in the environ-ment, it learned to experiment with its own sensors, actuators, and neural architec-ture so as to give itself an advantage. During one of its experimentations, some-thing goes terribly wrong: synchronization becomes broken and the whole NN system stops functioning. For example the NN based agent (an *infomorph*) is ex-perimenting with its own neural topology, and by mistake deletes a large chunk of itself. The system would become too broken to fix itself after such a thing, and thus the problem would have to be fixed from the outside of the NN system, by some process that is monitoring it and can revert it back to its previous functional state. For such, and more common events, we need a process which would act as a constant *monitor of the self, while being external to the self.* This process is the *Exoself.*

The exoself is a process that will function in a cooperative manner with the self (NN). It will perform jobs like backing up the NN's genotype to file, reverting to earlier versions of the NN, adding new neurons in live systems when asked by the NN itself... In slightly less advanced scenarios, the exoself will be used to optimize the weights of the NN it is monitoring. Since the exoself is outside the NN, it could keep track of which combination of weights in the NN produced a fitter individual, and then tell the NN when to perturb its neural weights, and when to revert to the previous combination of the weights if that yielded a fitter form. The architecture of such a system is presented in Fig-7.3.

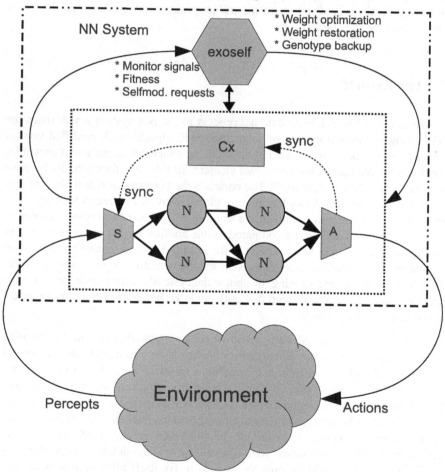

Fig. 7.3 The architecture of a NN system with an exoself process.

Having now covered the trainer and the exoself, which act as the appliers of the augmented RR-SHC optimization algorithm to the NN system, we now need to come up with a way to apply the NN to the problems, or present tasks to the NN that we wish it to learn how to perform. The simulations, tasks, and problems that we wish to apply our NN to, will be abstracted into *scape* packages, which we discuss in the next section.

7.4 The Scape

Scapes are composed of two parts, a simulation of an environment or a problem we are applying the NN to, and a function that can keep track of the NN's performance. Scapes run outside the NN systems, as independent processes with which the NNs interact using their sensors and actuators. There are 2 types of scapes. One type of scapes, private, is spawned for each NN during the NN's creation, and destroyed when that NN is taken offline. Another type of scapes, public, is persistent, they exist regardless of the NNs, and allow multiple NNs to interact with them at the same time, and thus they can allow those NNs to interact with each other too. The following are examples of these two types of scapes:

1. For example, let's assume we wish to use a NN to control a simulated robot in a simulated environment where other simulated robots exist. The fitness in this environment is based on how many simulated plants the robot eats before running out of energy. The robot's energy decreases at some constant rate. First we generate the NN with appropriate Sensors and Actuators with which it can interface with the scape. The sensors could be cameras, and the actuators could control the speed and direction of the robot's navigation through the environment, as shown in Fig-7.4. This scape exists outside the NN system, and for the scape to be able to judge how well the NN is able to control the simulated robot, it needs a way to give the NN fitness points. Furthermore, the scape can either give the NN a fitness point every time the robot eats a plant (event based), or it can keep track of the number of plants eaten throughout the robot's lifetime, until the robot runs out of energy, at which point the scape would use some function to give the NN its total fitness (life based) by processing the total number of plants eaten using that function. The simulated environment could have many robots in it, interacting with the simulated environment and each other. When one of the simulated robots within the scape runs out of energy, or dies, it is removed from the scape, while the remaining organisms in the scape persist. The scape continues to exist independently of the NNs interacting with it, it is a *public scape*.

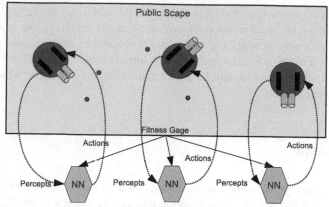

Fig. 7.4 Public simulation, with multiple organisms being controlled by NNs.

2. We want to create a NN that is able to balance a pole on a cart which can be pushed back and forth on a 2 meter track, as shown in Fig-7.5. We could create a scape with the physics simulation of the pole and the cart, which can be inter-acted with through the NN's sensors and actuators. The job of the NN would be to push the cart back and forth, thus balancing the pole on it. The NN's sensors would gather information like the velocity and the position of the cart, and the angular velocity and the position of the pole. The NN's actuators would push the cart back and forth on the track. The scape, having access to the whole sim-ulation, could then distribute fitness points to the NN based on how well and how long it balances the pole. When the NN is done with its pole balancing training and is deactivated, the scape is deactivated with it. If there are 3 differ-ent NNs, each will have its own pole balancing simulation scape created, and those simulations will only exist for as long as the NNs exist. Some problems or simulations are created specifically, and only, for that NN which needs it. This is an example of a *private scape*.

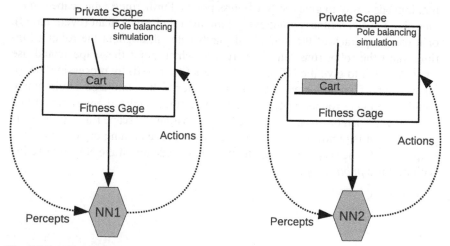

Fig. 7.5 Private simulation, with multiple NN based agents, each with its own private scape.

Though both of these problems (Artificial life and pole balancing) are represented as scapes, they have an important difference. The first scape is a 3d environment where multiple robots can exist, the scape's existence is fully independent of the NNs interacting with it, it is a public scape. The scape exists on its own, whether there are organisms interacting with it or not. It has to be spawned independently and before the NNs can start interacting with it. The second scape example on the other hand is created specifically for each NN when that neural network goes online, it is an example of a private scape. A private scape is in a sense summoned by the NN itself for the purpose of practicing something, or training to perform some task in isolation, a scape to which other organisms should not have access. It's like a privately spawned universe which is extinguished when the NN terminates.

We will present the problems we wish our NNs to learn to solve through these scape environments. Furthermore, we will specify within the sensors and actuators which scapes the NN should spawn (if the scape is private), or interface with (if the scape is public). Sensors and actuators are created to interact with things, thus they provide a perfect place where we can specify what scapes, if any, they should spawn or interface with. The next important design decision is: how do we want the scapes to notify the NNs of their fitness scores. A problem we solve in the next section.

7.5 Scapes, Sensors, Actuators, Morphologies, and Fitness

Now that we've agreed on the definition of a scape, (a simulation of an environment, not necessarily physical or 3 dimensional, that can also gage fitness and which can be interfaced with, through sensors and actuators), we will need to devise a way by which the Scape can contact the NN and give it its fitness score.

The NN uses the sensors and actuators to interface with the scape, and since a scape exists as a separate process, the sensors and actuators will interact with it by sending it messages. When the cortex sends a particular sensor the {Cx_PId, sync} message, that sensor is awoken to action and if it is the type of sensor that interfaces with a scape, it will send the scape a message and tell it what kind of sensory data it needs. We will make the message from sensor to scape have the following format: {Sensor_PId, sensor_name}, and the scape will then send the Sensor_PId the sensory signals based on the sensor_name. If the sensor is a camera, it will tell the scape that it needs camera based data associated with that sensor. If the sensor is a sonar scanner, then it would request sonar data. The scape then sends some *sensor-specific* data as a reply to the sensor's message. Finally, the sensor could then preprocess this data, package it, and forward the vector to the neurons and neural structures it's connected to.

After the NN has processed the sensory data, the actuator will have received the output signals from all the neurons connecting to it. The actuator could then postprocess the accumulated vector and, if it is the type of actuator that interfaces with a scape, it will then send this scape the {Actuator_PId, actuator_name, Action} message. At this point the actuator could be finished, and then inform the cortex of it by sending it the {self(), sync} message. But we could also, instead of making our actuator immediately send the cortex a sync message, take this opportunity to make the actuator wait for the scape to send it some message. For example at this point, based on the actuator's action, the scape could send back to it a fitness score message. Or it could send the NN a message telling it that the simulated robot had just exploded. If the scape uses this opportunity to send some fitness based information back to the actuator, the actuator could then, instead of simply sending the {self(), sync} message to the cortex, send a message containing the fitness points it was rewarded with by the scape, and whether the scape has notified it that the simulation or some training session has just ended. For example, in the case where the simulated organism dies within the simulated environment, or in the case where the NN has solved or won the game... there needs to be a way for the scape to notify the NN that something significant had just happened. This approach could be a way to do just that.

What makes the actuator a perfect process to which the scape should send this information, is: 1. Because each separate actuator belonging to the same NN could be interfacing with a different scape and so different scapes could each send to the cortex a message through its own interfacing actuator, and 2. Because the cortex synchronizes the sensors based on the signals it receives from actuators. This is important because if at any point one of the actuators sends it a halt message, the cortex has the chance to stop or pause the whole thing by simply not triggering the sensors to action. Thus if any of the actuators propagates the "end of the simulation/training message" from the scape to the cortex, the cortex will then know that the simulation is over, that it should not trigger the sensors to action, and that it should await new instructions from the exoself. If we were to allow the scape to contact the cortex directly, for example by sending it a message containing the gaged performance of the NN, and send it information of whether the training session is over or not, then there would be a chance that all the actuators had already contacted it, and that the cortex has already triggered its sensors to action. Using the actuators for this purpose ensures that we can stop the NN at the end of its training session and sense-think-act cycle.

Once the cortex receives some kind of halting message from the actuators, it could inform the exoself that it's done, and pass to it the accumulated fitness points as the NN's final fitness score. The exoself could then decide what to do next, whether to perturb the NN's weights, or revert the weights back to their previous state... the cortex will sit and wait until the exoself decides on its next action.

We will implement the above described interface between the sensor/actuator/cortex and scape programs. Figure-7.6 shows the signal exchange steps. After exoself spawns the NN, the cortex immediately calls the sensors to action by sending them the: {CxPId,sync} messages (1). When a sensor receives the sync message from the cortex, it contacts the scape (if any) that it interfaces with, by sending it the: {SPId,ControlMsg} message (2). When the scape receives a message from a sensor, it executes the function associated with the ControlMsg, and then returns the sensory signal back to the calling sensor process. The sensory signal is sent to the sensor through the message: {ScPId,percept,SensoryVector} (3). After the sensor preprocesses (if at all) the sensory signal, it fans out the sensory vector to the neurons it is connected to (4). Then the actual neural net processes the sensory signal, (5), this is the thinking part of the NN system's sense-think-act loop. Once the neural net has processed the signal, the actuator gathers the processed signals from the output layer neurons (6). At this point the actuator does some postprocessing (if at all) of the output vector, and then executes the actuator function. The actuator function, like the sensory function, could be an action in itself, or an action message sent to some scape. In the case where the actuator is interfacing with a scape, it sends the scape a message of the form: {APid,ControlMsg,Output} (7). The scape executes the particular function associated with the ControlMsg atom, with the Output as the parameter. The executed function *IS* the action that the NN system takes within the virtual environment of the scape. After the scape executes the function that was requested by the actuator, it sends that same actuator a message: {SCPId,Fitness,HaltFlag}. This message contains the NN's complete or partial gage of fitness, and a notification if the simulation has ended, or if the avatar that the NN system controls within the scape has perished... or anything else one might wish to use the HaltFlag for (8). Finally, the actuator passes the message to the cortex in the form of a message: {APId,sync,Fitness,HaltFlag}, (9).

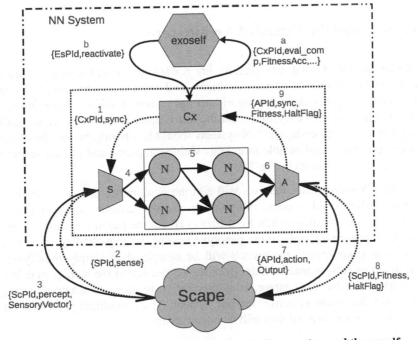

Fig. 7.6 The signal flow between the scape, sensors, actuators, cortex, and the exoself.

The cortex accumulates all the messages from the actuators, adding together the fitness scores, and seeing if any of the scapes have triggered the HaltFlag, which is set to 1 when triggered. If none of the HaltFlags were set to 1, then the cortex process syncs up the sensors, calling them to action, and the steps 1-9 repeat again. If any of the scapes set the HaltFlag to 1, then the cortex process takes a different course of action. At this point we could make the cortex decide whether to restart the scape, whether to start off some particular set of functions, or do any other useful task. In the version of the NN we are building in this chapter though, the XOR simulation scape will activate the HaltFlag when the training has ended, when the simulation has ran to completion. At this point the cortex simply pauses and informs the exoself process that it has finished and that the NN has been evaluated, by sending exoself the message: {CxPId, evaluation_complete, FitnessAcc, CycleAcc, TimeAcc} (a). Once again, the actions that the exoself takes are based on operational mode we chose for the system, and in the version of the system we're building in this chapter, it will apply the SHC optimization algorithm to the NN, and then reactivate the NN system by sending cortex the following message: {ExoselfPId, reactivate} (b). After receiving the reactivation message from the exoself, the cortex's process again loops through the steps 1-9. Note that these 9 steps represent the standard *Sense-Think-Act* cycle, where *Sense* is steps 1-4, *Think* is step 5, and *Act* is steps 6-9.

In the next section we extend the previous chapter's architecture by developing and adding the new features we've discussed here.

7.6 Developing the Extended Architecture

Having discussed what new features are needed to extend the architecture so that it can be applied to various problems and simulations presented through scapes, and having decided what algorithms our system should use to optimize its neural weights, we are ready to extend the last chapter's system. After we finish modifying the source code, our NN systems should be optimizable by the exoself & trainer processes, and be able to interact with both, public and private scapes in various manners as shown in Fig-7.7.

In the following subsections we will add the new trainer and scape modules, and modify the exoself, cortex, morphology, sensor, actuator, and neuron modules. Finally, we will also switch from *lists* to *ets* for the purpose of storing genotypes. And because we isolated the genotype reading, writing, loading, and saving functions in genotype.erl, the switch will be composed of simply modifying 4 functions to use ets instead of lists. Because we decoupled the storage and interface methods in the last chapter, it is easy for us to move to whatever storage method we find most effective for our system. Thus, modifying the genotype module to use ets instead of lists will be our first step.

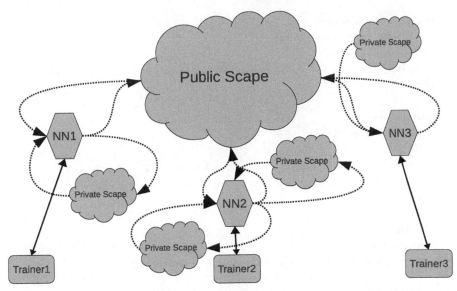

Fig. 7.7 Possible combinations of NN systems and their public/private scape interaction.

7.6.1 Modifying the genotype Module

Ets tables provide us with an efficient way to store and retrieve terms. Particularly if we need to access random terms within the table, it is better done using ets. The quick modification applied to the genotype.erl to switch from lists to ets is shown in the following listing.

Listing-7.1 Changing the genotype storage method from the simple list and file to the ets table.

```
save_genotype(FileName,Genotype)->
    TId = ets:new(FileName, [public,set,{keypos,2}]),
    [ets:insert(TId,Element) || Element <- Genotype],
    ets:tab2file(TId,FileName).
%The save_genotype/2 function expects that the Genotype is a list composed of the neuron,
sensor, actuator, cortex, and exoself elements. The function creates a new ets table, writes all
the element representing tuples from the Genotype list to the ets table, and then writes the ets
table to file.

save_to_file(Genotype,FileName)->
    ets:tab2file(Genotype,FileName).
%The save_to_file/2 function saves the ets table by the name Genotype to the file by the name
FileName.
```

```
load_from_file(FileName)->
    {ok,TId} = ets:file2tab(FileName),
    TId.
%The load_from_file/1 loads an ets representing file by the name FileName, returning the ets
table id to the caller.

read(TId,Key)->
    [R] = ets:lookup(TId,Key),
    R.
%The read/2 function reads a record associated with Key from the ets table with the id TId, re-
turning the record R to the caller. It expects that only a single record exists with the specified
Key.

write(TId,R)->
    ets:insert(TId,R).
%The function write/2 writes the record R to the ets table with the id TId.

print(FileName)->
    Genotype = load_from_file(FileName),
    Cx = read(Genotype,cortex),
    SIds = Cx#cortex.sensor_ids,
    NIds = Cx#cortex.nids,
    AIds = Cx#cortex.actuator_ids,
    io:format("~p~n",[Cx]),
    [io:format("~p~n",[read(Genotype,Id)]) || Id <- SIds],
    [io:format("~p~n",[read(Genotype,Id)]) || Id <- NIds],
    [io:format("~p~n",[read(Genotype,Id)]) || Id <- Aids].
%The function print/1 reads a stored Genotype from the file FileName, and then prints to con-
sole all the elements making up the NN's genotype.
```

The function print/1 is a new addition. It is a simple and easy way to dump the tuple encoded genotype to terminal. It is useful when you wish to see what the topology looks like, and when you need to analyze the genotype when debugging the system.

7.6.2 Modifying the morphology Module

As we discussed earlier, we want to specify the scape and its type in the sensors and actuators belonging to some particular morphology. We thus modify the records.hrl file and extend the sensor and actuator records to also contain the scape element. The new sensor and actuator records will be represented as:

```
-record(sensor,{id,name,cx_id,scape,vl,fanout_ids}).
-record(actuator,{id,name,cx_id,scape,vl,fanin_ids}).
```

In the previous chapter, we only had one type of morphology called: *test*, we now modify the morphology module by removing "test", and adding *xor_mimic*. Both, the sensor and the actuator of the xor_mimic morphology, interact with a private scape called *xor_sim*. Because the same private scape is specified for both the sensor and the actuator, only one private scape by the name xor_sim will be spawned, and they (the sensor and the actuator) will both connect to it, rather than each separately spawning its own separate xor_sim scape. The following listing shows the new xor_mimic morphology with its lists of sensors and actuators.

```
Listing-7.2: The new morphological type and specification added to morphology.erl

xor_mimic(sensors)->
    [
        #sensor{id={sensor,generate_id()}, name=xor_GetInput, scape={private,xor_sim},
vl=2}
    ];
xor_mimic(actuators)->
    [
        #actuator{id={actuator,generate_id()}, name=xor_SendOutput,
scape={private,xor_sim}, vl=1}
    ].
```

Having now modified the genotype to use ets tables, and having extended the records of our sensors and actuators, we are ready to start adding new features to our system.

7.6.3 Developing the trainer Module

When training a NN we should be able to specify all the stopping conditions, the NN based agent's morphology, and the neural network's topology. Thus the trainer process should perform the following steps:

1. **Repeat:**
    2. Create a NN of specified topology with random weights.
    3. Wait for the trained NN's final fitness
    4. Compare the trained NN's fitness to an already stored NN's fitness, if any.
    5. If the new NN is better, overwrite the old one with it.
6. **Until:** One of the stopping conditions is reached
7. **Return:** Best genotype and its fitness score.

We will implement all 3 types of stopping conditions:

1. A fitness score that we wish to reach,
2. The Max_Attempts that we're willing to perform before giving up.
3. The maximum number of evaluations we're willing to perform before giving up.

If any one of these conditions is triggered, the training ends. For default, we set maximum number of evaluations (EVAL_LIMIT) and the minimum required fitness (FITNESS_TARGET) to inf, which means that these conditions will never be reached since in Erlang an atom is considered greater than a number. Thus when starting the trainer by executing go/2, the process will default to simply using MAX_ATTEMPTS, which is set to 5. The complete source code for trainer.erl is shown in the following listing.

Listing-7.3 The implementation of the trainer module.

```
-module(trainer).
-compile(export_all).
-include("records.hrl").
-define(MAX_ATTEMPTS,5).
-define(EVAL_LIMIT,inf).
-define(FITNESS_TARGET,inf).

go(Morphology,HiddenLayerDensities)->
    go(Morphology,HiddenLayerDensities,?MAX_ATTEMPTS,?EVAL_LIMIT,
?FITNESS_TARGET).
go(Morphology,HiddenLayerDensities,MaxAttempts,EvalLimit,FitnessTarget)->
    PId = spawn(trainer,loop,[Morphology,HiddenLayerDensities,FitnessTarget,
{1,MaxAttempts},{0,EvalLimit},{0,best},experimental]),
    register(trainer,PId).
%The function go/2 is executed to start the training process based on the Morphology and
HiddenLayerDensities specified. The go/2 function uses a default values for the Max_Attempts,
Eval_Limit, and Fitness_Target parameters, which makes the training based purely on the
Max_Attempts value. Function go/5 allows for all the stopping conditions to be specified.

loop(Morphology,_HLD,FT,{AttemptAcc,MA},{EvalAcc,EL},{BestFitness,BestG},_ExpG,
CAcc,TAcc) when (AttemptAcc>=MA) or (EvalAcc>=EL) or (BestFitness>=FT)->
    genotype:print(BestG),
    io:format(" Morphology:~p Best Fitness:~p EvalAcc:~p~n", [Morphology, BestFitness,
EvalAcc]);
loop(Morphology,HLD,FT,{AttemptAcc,MA},{EvalAcc,EvalLimit},{BestFitness,BestG},
ExpG,CAcc,TAcc)->
    genotype:construct(ExpG,Morphology,HLD),
    Agent_PId=exoself:map(ExpG),
```

```
receive
        {Agent_PId,Fitness,Evals,Cycles,Time}->
                U_EvalAcc = EvalAcc+Evals,
                U_CAcc = CAcc+Cycles,
                U_TAcc = TAcc+Time,
                case Fitness > BestFitness of
                        true ->
                                file:rename(ExpG,BestG),
                                ?MODULE:loop(Morphology,HLD,FT,{1,MA}, {U_EvalAcc,
EvalLimit}, {Fitness,BestG},ExpG,U_CAcc,U_TAcc);
                        false ->
                                ?MODULE:loop(Morphology,HLD,FT,{AttemptAcc+1,MA},
{U_EvalAcc,EvalLimit}, {BestFitness,BestG}, ExpG,U_CAcc,U_TAcc)
                        end;
                terminate ->
                        io:format("Trainer Terminated:~n"),
                        genotype:print(BestG),
                        io:format(" Morphology:~p Best Fitness:~p EvalAcc:~p~n", [Morphology,
BestFitness,EvalAcc])
        end.
%loop/7 generates new NNs and trains them until a stopping condition is reached. Once any
one of the stopping conditions is reached, the trainer prints to screen the genotype, the morpho-
logical name of the organism being trained, the best fitness score achieved, and the number of
evaluations taken to find this fitness score.
```

7.6.4 Modifying the exoself Module

The Exoself's purpose is to train and monitor the NN system. Though at this point we will only implement the NN activation, training, and termination. But the way we will design the exoself process, and its general position in the NN based agent's architecture, will allow it to be modified (and we eventually will modify it) to support the NN's fault tolerance and self repair functionality. In the following listing we add to the exoself module the necessary source code it needs to train the NN system using the augmented SHC algorithm we covered in section 7.1.

```
Listing-7.4: Modifications added to the exoself.erl

prep(FileName,Genotype)->
    {V1,V2,V3} = now(),
    random:seed(V1,V2,V3),
    IdsNPIds = ets:new(idsNpids,[set,private]),
    Cx = genotype:read(Genotype,cortex),
    Sensor_Ids = Cx#cortex.sensor_ids,
```

```
    Actuator_Ids = Cx#cortex.actuator_ids,
    NIds = Cx#cortex.nids,
    ScapePIds=spawn_Scapes(IdsNPIds,Genotype,Sensor_Ids,Actuator_Ids),
    spawn_CerebralUnits(IdsNPIds,cortex,[Cx#cortex.id]),
    spawn_CerebralUnits(IdsNPIds,sensor,Sensor_Ids),
    spawn_CerebralUnits(IdsNPIds,actuator,Actuator_Ids),
    spawn_CerebralUnits(IdsNPIds,neuron,NIds),
    link_Sensors(Genotype,Sensor_Ids,IdsNPIds),
    link_Actuators(Genotype,Actuator_Ids,IdsNPIds),
    link_Neurons(Genotype,NIds,IdsNPIds),
    {SPIds,NPIds,APIds}=link_Cortex(Cx,IdsNPIds),
    Cx_PId = ets:lookup_element(IdsNPIds,Cx#cortex.id,2),
    loop(FileName,Genotype,IdsNPIds,Cx_PId,SPIds,NPIds,APIds,ScapePIds,0,0,0,0,1).
```

%Once the FileName and the Genotype are dropped into the prep/2 function, the function uses the current time to create a new random seed. Then the cortex is extracted from the genotype and the Sensor, Actuator, and Neural Ids are extracted from it. The sensors and actuators are dropped into the spawn_Scapes/4, which extracts the scapes that need to be spawned, and then spawns them. Afterwards, the sensor, actuator, neuron, and the cortex elements are spawned. Then the exoself process sends these spawned elements the PIds of the elements they are connected to, thus linking all the elements together into a proper interconnected structure. The cortex element is the last one to be linked, because once it receives the message from the exoself with all the data, it immediately starts synchronizing the NN by prompting the sensors to action. Afterwards, prep/2 drops into the exoself's main process loop.

```
loop(FileName,Genotype,IdsNPIds,Cx_PId,SPIds,NPIds,APIds,ScapePIds,HighestFitness,
EvalAcc,CycleAcc,TimeAcc,Attempt)->
    receive
        {Cx_PId,evaluation_completed,Fitness,Cycles,Time}->
            {U_HighestFitness,U_Attempt}=case Fitness > HighestFitness of
                true ->
                        [NPId ! {self(),weight_backup} || NPId <- NPIds],
                        {Fitness,0};
                false ->
                        Perturbed_NPIds=get(perturbed),
                        [NPId ! {self(),weight_restore} || NPId <- Perturbed_NPIds],
                        {HighestFitness,Attempt+1}
            end,
            case U_Attempt >= ?MAX_ATTEMPTS of
                true ->%End training
                        U_CycleAcc = CycleAcc+Cycles,
                        U_TimeAcc = TimeAcc+Time,
                        backup_genotype(FileName,IdsNPIds,Genotype,NPIds),
                        terminate_phenotype(Cx_PId,SPIds,NPIds,APIds,ScapePIds),
                        io:format("Cortex:~p finished training. Genotype has been
```

```
backed up.~n Fitness:~p~n TotEvaluations:~p~n TotCycles:~p~n TimeAcc:~p~n", [Cx_PId,
U_HighestFitness, EvalAcc, U_CycleAcc, U_TimeAcc]),
                    case whereis(trainer) of
                        undefined ->
                            ok;
                        PId ->
                                    PId!{self(),U_HighestFitness, EvalAcc,
U_CycleAcc, U_TimeAcc}
                    end;
                false -> %Continue training
                    Tot_Neurons = length(NPIds),
                    MP = 1/math:sqrt(Tot_Neurons),
                    Perturb_NPIds=[NPId || NPId <- NPIds,random:uniform()<MP],
                    put(perturbed,Perturb_NPIds),
                    [NPId ! {self(),weight_perturb} || NPId <- Perturb_NPIds],
                    Cx_PId ! {self(),reactivate},
                    loop(FileName,Genotype, IdsNPIds,Cx_PId,SPIds, NPIds,APIds,
ScapePIds,U_HighestFitness, EvalAcc,  EvalAcc+1, CycleAcc+Cycles, TimeAcc+Time, U_Attempt)
            end
    end.
```

%The main process loop waits for the NN to complete the task, receive its fitness score, and send Exoself the: {Cx_PId,evaluation_completed,Fitness,Cycles,Time} message. The message contains all the information about that particular evaluation, the acquired fitness score, the number of total Sense-Think-Act cycles executed, and the time it took to complete the evaluation. The exoself then compares the Fitness to the one it has on record (if any), and based on that decides whether to revert the previously perturbed neurons back to their original state or not. If the new Fitness is lower, then the perturbed neurons are contacted and their weights are reverted. If the new Fitness is greater than the one stored on record, then the NN is backed up to file, and the variable EvalAcc is reset to 0. Finally, depending on whether the NN has failed to improve its fitness Max_Attempts number of times, the exoself decides whether another NN perturbation attempt is warranted. If it is warranted, then the exoself chooses which neurons to mutate by randomly choosing each neuron with the probability of $1/sqrt(Tot\_Neurons)$, where Tot_Neurons is the total number of neurons in the neural network. The exoself saves the PIds of those chosen neurons to process dictionary, and then sends those neurons a signal that they should perturb their weights. Finally it tells cortex to reactivate and start syncing the sensors and actuators again. But if the NN has failed to improve its fitness for Max_Attempts number of times, if EvalAcc > Max_Attempts, then the exoself terminates all the elements in the NN, and if there is a registered process by the name 'trainer', the exoself sends it the HighestFitness score that its NN achieved and the number of total evaluations it took to achieve it.

```
spawn_Scapes(IdsNPIds,Genotype,Sensor_Ids,Actuator_Ids)->
    Sensor_Scapes = [(genotype:read(Genotype,Id))#sensor.scape || Id<-Sensor_Ids],
    Actuator_Scapes = [(genotype:read(Genotype,Id))#actuator.scape || Id<-
```

```
Actuator_Ids],
        Unique_Scapes = Sensor_Scapes++(Actuator_Scapes--Sensor_Scapes),
        SN_Tuples=[{scape:gen(self(),node()),ScapeName} || {private,ScapeName}<-
Unique_Scapes],
        [ets:insert(IdsNPIds,{ScapeName,PId}) || {PId,ScapeName} <- SN_Tuples],
        [ets:insert(IdsNPIds,{PId,ScapeName}) || {PId,ScapeName} <-SN_Tuples],
        [PId ! {self(),ScapeName} || {PId,ScapeName} <- SN_Tuples],
        [PId || {PId,_ScapeName} <-SN_Tuples].
```
%spawn_Scapes/4 first extracts all the scape names from sensors and actuators, then builds a list of unique scapes, and then finally extracts and spawns the private scapes. The public scapes are not spawned since they are independent of the NN, and should already be running. The reason for extracting the list of unique scapes is because if both, a sensor and an actuator are pointing to the same scape, then that means that they will interface with the same scape, and it does not mean that each one should spawn its own scape of the same name. Afterwards we use the IdsNPids ETS table to create a map from scape PId to scape name, and from scape name to scape PId for later use. The function then sends each spawned scape a message composed of the exoself's PId, and the scape's name: {self(),ScapeName}. Finally, a spawned scape PId list is composed and returned to the caller.

We also modify the *terminate_Phenotype* function to also accept the ScapePIds parameter, and terminate all the scapes before terminating the Cortex process. Thus the following line is added to the function:

```
[PId ! {self(),terminate} || PId <- ScapePIds]
```

Having created the function which extracts the names of the scapes from the sensors and actuators of the NN system, we now develop our first scape and the very first problem on which we'll test our learning algorithm on.

7.6.5 Developing the scape Module

Looking ahead, we will certainly apply our Neuroevolutionary system to many different problems. Our system should be able to deal with ALife problems as easily as with pole balancing, financial trading, circuit design & optimization, image analysis, or any other of the infinite problems that exist. It is for this reason that we've made the sensors/actuators/scape a separate part from the NN itself, all specified through the morphology module. This way, for every problem we wish to apply our neuroevolutionary system to, we can keep the NN specific modules the same, and simply create a new morphology/scape packages.

Because there will be many scapes, a new scape for almost every problem that we'll want to solve or apply our neuroevolutionary system to, we will use the same scape.erl module and specify the different scapes within it by function name. Because the first and standard problem to apply a NN to is the XOR (Exclusive-OR) problem, our first scape will be a scape called xor_sim. The xor problem is the "hello world" of NN problems. The goal is to teach a NN to act like a XOR operation. The truth table of the 2 input XOR operation is presented in the following listing.

Listing-7.5: Truth table of the XOR operation.

X1	X2	X1 XOR X2
false	true	true
false	false	false
true	false	true
true	true	false

Because the range of tanh, the activation function of our neuron, is between -1 and 1, we will represent false as -1, and true as 1 (a bipolar encoding), rather than 0 and 1 (a unipolar encoding). This way we can use the full output range of our neurons. The following listing shows the complete source code of the scape module, which at this point contains only the single scape named xor_sim.

Listing-7.6: The complete scape module.

```
-module(scape).
-compile(export_all).
-include("records.hrl").

gen(ExoSelf_PId,Node)->
    spawn(Node,?MODULE,prep,[ExoSelf_PId]).

prep(ExoSelf_PId) ->
    receive
            {ExoSelf_PId,Name} ->
                    scape:Name(ExoSelf_PId)
    end.
```

%gen/2 is executed by the exoself. The function spawns prep/1 process, and awaits the name of the scape from the exoself. Each scape is a separate and independent process, a self contained system that was developed to interface with the sensors and actuators from which its name was extracted. The name of the scape is the name of its main process loop.

```erlang
xor_sim(ExoSelf_PId)->
    XOR = [{[-1,-1],[-1]},{[1,-1],[1]},{[-1,1],[1]},{[1,1],[-1]}],
    xor_sim(ExoSelf_PId,{XOR,XOR},0).


xor_sim(ExoSelf_PId,{[{Input,CorrectOutput}|XOR],MXOR},ErrAcc) ->
    receive
        {From,sense} ->
                From ! {self(),percept,Input},
                xor_sim(ExoSelf_PId,{[{Input,CorrectOutput}|XOR],MXOR},ErrAcc);
        {From,action,Output}->
                Error = list_compare(Output,CorrectOutput,0),
                case XOR of
                    [] ->
                            MSE = math:sqrt(ErrAcc+Error),
                            Fitness = 1/(MSE+0.00001),
                            From ! {self(),Fitness,1},
                            xor_sim(ExoSelf_PId,{MXOR,MXOR},0);
                    _ ->
                            From ! {self(),0,0},
                            xor_sim(ExoSelf_PId,{XOR,MXOR},ErrAcc+Error)
                end;
        {ExoSelf_PId,terminate}->
                ok
    end.

list_compare([X|List1],[Y|List2],ErrorAcc)->
        list_compare(List1,List2,ErrorAcc+math:pow(X-Y,2));
list_compare([],[],ErrorAcc)->
        math:sqrt(ErrorAcc).
```

%xor_sim/3 is a scape that simulates the XOR operation, interacts with the NN, and gages the NN's performance. xor_sim expects two types of messages from the NN, one message from the sensor and one from the actuator. The message: {From,sense} prompts the scape to send the NN the percept, which is a vector of length 2 and contains the XOR input. The second expected message from the NN is the message from the actuator, which is expected to be an output of the NN and packaged into the form: {From,action,Output}. At this point xor_sim/3 compares the Output with the expected output that is associated with the sensory message that should have been gathered by the sensors, and then sends back to the actuator process a message composed of the scape's PId, Fitness, and a HaltFlag which specifies whether the simulation has ended for the NN. The scape keeps track of the Mean Squared Error between the NN's output and the correct output. Once the NN has processed all 4 signals for the XOR, the scape computes the total MSE, converts it to fitness, and finally forwards this fitness and the HaltFlag=1 to the NN. This particular scape uses the lifetime based fitness, rather than step-based fitness. During all the other steps the scape sends the actuator the signal: {Scape_PId,0,0}, while it accumulates the errors, and only at the very end does it calculate the total fitness, which is the inverse of the error with a small extra added value to avoid the divide by 0 errors. Afterwards, xor_sim resets back to its initial state and awaits anew for signals from the NN.

7.6.6 Modifying the cortex Module

As in the previous chapter, the cortex element still acts as the synchronizer of the sensors and actuators. But now, it will also keep track of the accumulated fitness score, propagated to it by the actuators. The cortex will also keep track of whether the *HaltFlag==1* was sent to it by any of the actuators, which would signify that the cortex element should halt, notify its exoself of the achieved fitness score, and then await for further instructions from it. Finally, the cortex will also keep track of the number of sense-think-act cycles performed during its lifetime. The augmented cortex module is shown in the following listing.

```
Listing-7.7 The updated cortex module.

-module(cortex).
-compile(export_all).
-include("records.hrl").
-record(state,{id,exoself_pid,spids,npids,apids,cycle_acc=0,fitness_acc=0,endflag=0,status}).

gen(ExoSelf_PId,Node)->
    spawn(Node,?MODULE,prep,[ExoSelf_PId]).

prep(ExoSelf_PId) ->
    {V1,V2,V3} = now(),
    random:seed(V1,V2,V3),
    receive
            {ExoSelf_PId,Id,SPIds,NPIds,APIds} ->
                    put(start_time,now()),
                    [SPId ! {self(),sync} || SPId <- SPIds],
                    loop(Id,ExoSelf_PId,SPIds,{APIds,APIds},NPIds,1,0,0,active)
    end.
%The gen/2 function spawns the cortex element, which immediately starts to wait for its initial
state message from the same process that spawned it, exoself. The initial state message contains
the sensor, actuator, and neuron PId lists. Before dropping into the main loop, CycleAcc,
FitnessAcc, and HFAcc (HaltFlag Acc), are all set to 0, and the status of the cortex is set to ac-
tive, prompting it to begin the synchronization process and call the sensors to action.

loop(Id, ExoSelf_PId, SPIds, {[APId|APIds], MAPIds}, NPIds, CycleAcc, FitnessAcc, HFAcc,
active) ->
    receive
            {APId,sync,Fitness,HaltFlag} ->
                    loop(Id,ExoSelf_PId,SPIds,{APIds,MAPIds},NPIds,CycleAcc,FitnessAcc+
Fitness, HFAcc+HaltFlag,active);
            terminate ->
                    io:format("Cortex:~p is terminating.~n",[Id]),
                    [PId ! {self(),terminate} || PId <- SPIds],
```

```
                [PId ! {self(),terminate} || PId <- MAPIds],
                [PId ! {self(),termiante} || PId <- NPIds]
    end;
loop(Id,ExoSelf_PId,SPIds,{[],MAPIds},NPIds,CycleAcc,FitnessAcc,HFAcc,active)->
    case EFAcc > 0 of
        true ->%Organism finished evaluation
            TimeDif=timer:now_diff(now(),get(start_time)),
            ExoSelf_PId ! {self(),evaluation_completed,FitnessAcc,CycleAcc,TimeDif},
                loop(Id,ExoSelf_PId,SPIds,{MAPIds,MAPIds},NPIds,CycleAcc,FitnessAcc,
HFAcc, inactive);
        false ->
            [PId ! {self(),sync} || PId <- SPIds],

    loop(Id,ExoSelf_PId,SPIds,{MAPIds,MAPIds},NPIds,CycleAcc+1,FitnessAcc,
HFAcc,active)
    end;
loop(Id, ExoSelf_PId, SPIds, {MAPIds,MAPIds}, NPIds, _CycleAcc, _FitnessAcc, _HFAcc,
inactive)->
    receive
        {ExoSelf_PId,reactivate}->
                put(start_time,now()),
                [SPId ! {self(),sync} || SPId <- SPIds],
                loop(Id,ExoSelf_PId,SPIds,{MAPIds,MAPIds},NPIds,1,0,0,active);
        {ExoSelf_PId,terminate}->
                ok
    end.
```

%The cortex's goal is to synchronize the NN system's sensors and actuators. When the actuators have received all their control signals, they forward the sync messages, the Fitness, and the HaltFlag messages to the cortex. The cortex accumulates these Fitness and HaltFlag signals, and if any of the HaltFlag signals have been set to 1, HFAcc will be greater than 0, signifying that the cortex should halt. When EFAcc > 0, the cortex calculates the total amount of time it has ran (TimeDiff), and forwards to exoself the values: FitnessAcc, CycleAcc, and TimeDiff. Afterwards, the cortex enters the inactive mode and awaits further instructions from the exoself. If none of the HaltFlags were set to 0, then the value HFAcc == 0, and the cortex triggers off another Sense-Think-Act cycle. The reason the cortex process stores 2 copies of the actuator PIds: the APIds, and the MemoryAPIds (MAPIds), is so that once all the actuators have sent it the sync messages, it can restore the APIds list from the MAPIds.

7.6.7 Modifying the neuron Module

To allow the exoself process to optimize the weights of the NN through the SHC algorithm, we will need to give our neurons the ability to have their weights perturbed when requested to do so by the exoself, and have their weights reverted when/if requested by the same. We will also specify the range of these weight perturbations in this module, and the weight saturation values, the maximum and minimum values that the weights can take. It is usually not a good idea to let the weights reach very large positive or negative values, as that would allow any single weight to completely overwhelm other synaptic weights of the same neuron. For example if a neuron has 100 weights in total, and one of the weights has a value of 1000000, no other weight can compete with it unless it too is raised to such a high value. This results in a single weight controlling the information processing ability of the entire neuron. It is important that no weight can overwhelm all others (which prevents the neuron from performing coherent processing of signals), for this reason we will set the saturation limit to 2*Pi, and the perturbation intensity to half that. The perturbation intensity is half the value of weight saturation point so that there will always be a chance that the weight could flip from a positive to a negative value. The range of the weight perturbation intensity is specified by the DELTA_MULTIPLIER macro as: -define(DELTA_MULTIPLIER,math:pi()*2), since we will multiply it by (random:uniform()-0.5), the actual range will be between -Pi and Pi.

The complete neuron module is shown in the following listing.

```
Listing-7.8 The neuron module.

-module(neuron).
-compile(export_all).
-include("records.hrl").
-define(DELTA_MULTIPLIER,math:pi()*2).
-define(SAT_LIMIT,math:pi()*2).

gen(ExoSelf_PId,Node)->
    spawn(Node,?MODULE,prep,[ExoSelf_PId]).


prep(ExoSelf_PId) ->
    {V1,V2,V3} = now(),
    random:seed(V1,V2,V3),
    receive
            {ExoSelf_PId,{Id,Cx_PId,AF,Input_PIdPs,Output_PIds}} ->
                    loop(Id,ExoSelf_PId,Cx_PId,AF,{Input_PIdPs,Input_PIdPs},Output_PIds,0)
    end.
```
%When gen/2 is executed it spawns the neuron element, which seeds the pseudo random number generator, and immediately begins to wait for its initial state message. It is essential that we seed the random number generator to make sure that every NN will have a different set of mutation probabilities and different combination of perturbation intensities. Once the initial state signal from the exoself is received, the neuron drops into its main loop.

```erlang
loop(Id,ExoSelf_PId,Cx_PId,AF,{[[{Input_PId,Weights}|Input_PIdPs],MInput_PIdPs},Output_
PIds,Acc)->
    receive
            {Input_PId,forward,Input}->
                    Result = dot(Input,Weights,0),

    loop(Id,ExoSelf_PId,Cx_PId,AF,{Input_PIdPs,MInput_PIdPs},Output_PIds,Result+Acc);
            {ExoSelf_PId,weight_backup}->
                    put(weights,MInput_PIdPs),

    loop(Id,ExoSelf_PId,Cx_PId,AF,{[[{Input_PId,Weights}|Input_PIdPs],MInput_PIdPs},Outp
ut_PIds,Acc);
            {ExoSelf_PId,weight_restore}->
                    RInput_PIdPs = get(weights),

    loop(Id,ExoSelf_PId,Cx_PId,AF,{RInput_PIdPs,RInput_PIdPs},Output_PIds,Acc);
            {ExoSelf_PId,weight_perturb}->
                    PInput_PIdPs=perturb_IPIdPs(MInput_PIdPs),

    loop(Id,ExoSelf_PId,Cx_PId,AF,{PInput_PIdPs,PInput_PIdPs},Output_PIds,Acc);
            {ExoSelf_PId,get_backup}->
                    ExoSelf_PId ! {self(),Id,MInput_PIdPs},

    loop(Id,ExoSelf_PId,Cx_PId,AF,{[[{Input_PId,Weights}|Input_PIdPs],MInput_PIdPs},Outp
ut_PIds,Acc);
            {ExoSelf_PId,terminate}->
                    ok
    end;
loop(Id,ExoSelf_PId,Cx_PId,AF,{[Bias],MInput_PIdPs},Output_PIds,Acc)->
    Output = neuron:AF(Acc+Bias),
    [Output_PId ! {self(),forward,[Output]} || Output_PId <- Output_PIds],
    loop(Id,ExoSelf_PId,Cx_PId,AF,{MInput_PIdPs,MInput_PIdPs},Output_PIds,0);
loop(Id,ExoSelf_PId,Cx_PId,AF,{[],MInput_PIdPs},Output_PIds,Acc)->
    Output = neuron:AF(Acc),
    [Output_PId ! {self(),forward,[Output]} || Output_PId <- Output_PIds],
    loop(Id,ExoSelf_PId,Cx_PId,AF,{MInput_PIdPs,MInput_PIdPs},Output_PIds,0).

    dot([I|Input],[W|Weights],Acc) ->
            dot(Input,Weights,I*W+Acc);
    dot([],[],Acc)->
            Acc.
```

%The neuron process waits for vector signals from all the processes that it's connected from. As the presynaptic signals fanin, the neuron takes the dot product of the input and their associated weight vectors, and then adds it to the accumulator. Once all the signals from Input_PIds are received, the accumulator contains the dot product to which the neuron then adds the bias (if it exists) and executes the activation function. After fanning out the output signal, the neuron again returns to waiting for incoming signals. When the neuron receives the {ExoSelf_PId, get_backup} message, it forwards to the exoself its full MInput_PIdPs list, and its Id. The MInput_PIdPs contains the current version of the neural weights. When the neuron receives the {ExoSelf_PId,weight_perturb} message, it executes the perturb_IPIdPs/1, after which the neuron drops back into the loop but with MInput_PIdPs replaced by the new PInput_PIdPs. It is important to note that the neuron expects to be synchronized, and expects that it has at this point not received any signals from the other elements it is connected from, because if it has and it then changes out the Input_PIdPs with PInput_PIdPs, it might start waiting for signals from the elements from which it has already received the signals. When the neuron receives the {ExoSelf_PId,weight_backup}, it stores its weights in its process dictionary. When the neuron receives the {ExoSelf,weight_restore}, it restores its weights to the state they were before being perturbed by restoring the saved synaptic weights from its process dictionary.

```
    tanh(Val)->
          math:tanh(Val).
%The activation function is a sigmoid function, tanh.

perturb_IPIdPs(Input_PIdPs)->
    Tot_Weights=lists:sum([length(Weights) || {_Input_PId,Weights}<-Input_PIdPs]),
    MP = 1/math:sqrt(Tot_Weights),
    perturb_IPIdPs(MP,Input_PIdPs,[]).
perturb_IPIdPs(MP,[{Input_PId,Weights}|Input_PIdPs],Acc)->
    U_Weights = perturb_weights(MP,Weights,[]),
    perturb_IPIdPs(MP,Input_PIdPs,[{Input_PId,U_Weights}|Acc]);
perturb_IPIdPs(MP,[Bias],Acc)->
    U_Bias = case random:uniform() < MP of
          true-> sat((random:uniform()-0.5)*?DELTA_MULTIPLIER+Bias,-
?SAT_LIMIT,?SAT_LIMIT);
          false -> Bias
    end,
    lists:reverse([U_Bias|Acc]);
perturb_IPIdPs(_MP,[],Acc)->
    lists:reverse(Acc).
```

%perturb_IPIdPs/1 first calculates the probability that a weight will be perturbed, the probability being the inverse square root of the total number of weights in the neuron. The function then drops into perturb_IPIdPs/3, which executes perturb_weights/3 for every set of weights associated with a particular Input_PId in the Input_PIdPs list. If bias is present in the weights list, it is reached last and perturbed just as any other weight, based on the probability. Afterwards, the perturbed and inverted version of the Input_PIdPs is reversed back to the proper order and returned to the calling function.

```erlang
perturb_weights(MP,[W|Weights],Acc)->
        U_W = case random:uniform() < MP of
                true->
                        sat((random:uniform()-0.5)*?DELTA_MULTIPLIER+W,-?SAT_LIMIT,?SAT_LIMIT);
                false ->
                        W
        end,
        perturb_weights(MP,Weights,[U_W|Acc]);
perturb_weights(_MP,[],Acc)->
        lists:reverse(Acc).

sat(Val,Min,Max)->
        if
                Val < Min -> Min;
                Val > Max -> Max;
                true -> Val
        end.
```

%perturb_weights/3 accepts a probability value, a list of weights, and an empty list to act as an accumulator. The function then goes through the weight list perturbing each weight with a probability of MP. The weights are constrained to be within the range of -?SAT_LIMIT and SAT_LIMIT through the use of the sat/3 function.

7.6.8 Modifying the sensor Module

We have already created the xor_sim scape which expects a particular set of messages from the sensors and actuators interfacing with it. The scape expects the message: {Sensor_PId,sense} from the sensor, to which it responds with the sensory data sent in the: {Scape_PId,percept,SensoryVector} format. We now add to the sensor module a new function which can send and receive such messages. As we decided in the morphology module, the name of the new sensor will be xor_GetInput. The new function is shown in the following listing.

Listing-7.9 The implementation of the xor_GetInput sensor.

```erlang
xor_GetInput(VL,Scape)->
    Scape ! {self(),sense},
    receive
            {Scape,percept,SensoryVector}->
                    case length(SensoryVector)==VL of
```

```
        true ->
            SensoryVector;
        false ->
            io:format("Error in sensor:xor_sim/2, VL:~p
SensoryVector:~p~n", [VL,SensoryVector]),
            lists:duplicate(VL,0)
    end
end.
```
%xor_GetInput/2 contacts the XOR simulator and requests the sensory vector, which in this case should be a vector of length 2. The sensor checks that the incoming sensory signal, the percept, is indeed of length 2. If the vector length differs, then this is printed to the console and a dummy vector of appropriate length is constructed and used. This prevents unnecessary crashes in the case of errors, and gives the researcher a chance to fix the error and hotswap the code.

7.6.9 Modifying the actuator Module

The scape expects the message: {Actuator_PId,action,Output} from the actuator, to which it responds with the: {Scape_PId,FItness,EndFlag} message. We decided in the morphology module to call the actuator that will interface with the xor_sim scape: xor_SendOutput. The following listing shows this newly added function to the actuator module.

Listing-7.10 The implementation of the xor_SendOutput actuator.

```
xor_SendOutput(Output,Scape)->
    Scape ! {self(),action,Output},
    receive
        {Scape,Fitness,HaltFlag}->
            {Fitness,HaltFlag}
    end.
```
%xor_SendOutput/2 function simply forwards the Output vector to the XOR simulator, and then waits for the resulting Fitness and HaltFlag message from the scape.

7.7 Compiling Modules & Simulating the XOR Operation

We have now added all the new features, functions, and elements we needed to implement the learning algorithm with our NN system. When modifying our system to give it the ability to learn through the use of the augmented stochastic hill-climbing, we also implemented the xor_sim scape and the associated morphology with its sensors and actuators. We now compile all the modules we've created and modified to see if they work, and then test if our system can indeed learn. To compile everything in one step, make sure you're in the folder where all the modules are stored, and then execute the following command:

```
1>make:all([load]).
...
up_to_date
```

Now that everything is compiled, we can test to see if our NN can learn to simulate the XOR operation. The XOR operation cannot be performed by a single neuron. To solve this problem by a strictly feed forward neural network, the minimum required topology to perform this task is: [2,1], 2 neurons in the first layer and 1 in the output layer. We can specify the morphology, the NN topology, and the stopping condition, right from the trainer. The morphology, xor_mimic, specifies the problem we wish to apply the NN to, and the sensors and actuators that will interface with the xor_sim scape which will simulate the XOR operation and gage the NN's ability to simulate it. For the stopping condition we will choose to use fitness. We'll decide on the minimum fitness we wish our NN to achieve by calculating the total error in the NN's approximation of XOR that we're willing to accept. For example, a maximum error of 0.001 translates into a minimum fitness of 1/(0.01+ 0.00001), or: 99.9. Since we do not wish to use other stopping conditions, we'll set them to inf. Thus each training session will run until the NN can approximate XOR with an error no greater than 0.001 (a fitness no less than 99.9).

```
1>trainer:go(xor_mimic,[2],inf,inf,99.9).
Finished updating genotype to file:experimental
Cortex:<0.104.0> finished training. Genotype has been backed up.
Fitness:188.94639182995695
TotEvaluations:224
TotCycles:896
{cortex,cortex,
    [{sensor,7.617035388076853e-10}],
    [{actuator,7.617035388076819e-10}],
    [{neuron,{1,7.61703538807679e-10}},
    {neuron,{1,7.617035388076778e-10}},
    {neuron,{2,7.617035388076755e-10}}]}
{sensor,{sensor,7.617035388076853e-10},
    xor_GetInput,cortex,undefined,
    {private,xor_sim},
    2,
    [{neuron,{1,7.61703538807679e-10}},{neuron,{1,7.617035388076778e-10}}],
    undefined,[],[]}
{neuron,{neuron,{1,7.61703538807679e-10}},
    cortex,tanh,
    [{{sensor,7.617035388076853e-10},
```

```
      [-6.283185307179586,6.283185307179586]},
      {bias,-6.283185307179586}],
      [{neuron,{2,7.617035388076755e-10}}]]}
{neuron,{neuron,{1,7.617035388076778e-10}},
      cortex,tanh,
      [{{sensor,7.617035388076853e-10},
      [-5.663623085487123,6.283185307179586]},
      {bias,6.283185307179586}],
      [{neuron,{2,7.617035388076755e-10}}]]}
{neuron,{neuron,{2,7.617035388076755e-10}},
      cortex,tanh,
      [{{neuron,{1,7.617035388076778e-10}},[-6.283185307179586]},
      {{neuron,{1,7.61703538807679e-10}},[6.283185307179586]},
      {bias,6.283185307179586}],
      [{actuator,7.617035388076819e-10}]]}
{actuator,{actuator,7.617035388076819e-10},
      xor_SendOutput,cortex,undefined,
      {private,xor_sim},
      1,
      [{neuron,{2,7.617035388076755e-10}}]],
      undefined,[],[]}
Morphology:xor_mimic Best Fitness:188.94639182995695 EvalAcc:224
```

It works!. The trainer used the specified morphology to generate genotypes with the particular set of sensors and actuators to interface with the scape, and eventually produced a trained NN. In this particular case, the best fitness was 188.9, and it took only 224 evaluations to reach it. The trainer also used the genotype:print/1 function to print the genotype topology to screen when it was done, which allows us to now analyze the genotype and double check it for accuracy.

Since the learning algorithm is stochastic, the number of evaluations it takes will differ from one attempt to another, some will go as high as a few thousand, other will stay in the hundreds. But if you've attempted this exercise, you might have also noted that you got roughly the same fitness, and this requires an explanation.

We're using tanh as the activation function. This activation function has *1* and *-1* as its limit, and because we're using the weight saturation limit set to *2*PI*, the neuron's output can only get so close to -1 and 1 through the tanh function, and hence the final error in the XOR operation approximation. Thus the fitness we can achieve is limited by *how close tanh(PI*2) can get to 1, and tanh(-PI*2) can get to -1*. Since you and I are using the same SAT_LIMIT parameters, we can achieve the same maximum fitness scores, which is what we saw in the above result: (188.9), when using the SAT_LIMIT = 2*PI. If we for example modify the SAT_LIMIT in our neuron module as follows:

```
From: -define(SAT_LIMIT,math:pi()*2)
To: -define(SAT_LIMIT,math:pi()*20)
```

Then recompile and apply the NN to the problem again, then the best fitness will come out to be *99999.99*. Nevertheless, the SAT_LIMIT equaling to *math:pi()*2* is high enough for most situations, and as noted, when we allow the weights to take a value of any magnitude, we run the risk of any one synaptic weight to overwhelm the whole neuron and make it essentially useless. Also, returning the neural weight that has ran afoul and exploded in magnitude back to an appropriate value would be difficult with small perturbations... Throughout the years I've found that having the SAT_LIMIT set to *math:pi()* or *math:pi()*2* is the most effective choice.

We've now created a completely functional, static feed forward neural network system that can be applied to a lot of different problem types through the use of the system's *scape*, *sensors*, and *actuators* packages. It's an excellent start, and because our learning algorithm is unsupervised, we can even use our NNs as controllers in ALife. But there is also a problem, our NN system is only feedforward and so it does not possess memory, achievable through recursive connections. Also, our system only uses the *tanh* activation function, which might make problems like fourier analysis, fourier synthesis, and many other problems difficult to tackle. Our system can achieve an even greater flexibility if it can use other activation functions, and just like randomly choosing synaptic weights during neuron creation, it should be able to randomly choose activation functions from some predetermined list of said functions. Another problem we've noticed even when solving the XOR problem is that we had to know the minimal topology beforehand. If in the previous problem we would have chosen a *topology of: [1] or [2]*, our NN would not have been able to solve that problem. Thus our NN has a flaw, the flaw is that we need to know the proper topology, or the minimal topology which can solve the problem we're applying our NN to. We need to devise a plan to overcome this problem, by letting our NN evolve topology as well. Another problem is that even though our NN "learns", it actually does not. It is, in reality, just being optimized by an external process, the exoself. What is missing is neural plasticity, the ability of the neurons to self modify based on sensory signals, and past experience... that would be true learning, learning as self modification based on interaction with the environment within the lifetime of the organism. Finally, even though our system does have all the necessary features for us to start implementing supervision trees and process monitoring, we will first implement and develop the neuroevolutionary functionality, before transforming our system into a truly fault tolerant distributed CI system.

Before we continue on to the next chapter where we will start adding some of these mentioned features, and finally move to a population based approach and topological evolution, we first need to create a small benchmarking function. For example, we've used the trainer to solve the XOR problem and we noted that it took K number of evaluations to solve it. When you've solved it with a trainer on your computer, you probably have gotten another value... we need to create a function that automates the process of applying the trainer to some problem many times, and then calculates the average performance of the system. We need a benchmarking method because it will allow us to calculate dependable average performance of our system and allow us to compare it to other machine learning approaches. It will also allow us to test new features and get a good idea of what affect they have on our system's performance across the spectrum of problems we might have in our benchmark suit. Thus, in the next section we will develop a small benchmarking function.

7.8 Adding the benchmarker Module

In this section we want to create a small system that performs benchmarking of the NN system we've developed, on some problem or problem set. This benchmarking system should be able to summon the trainer process X number of times, applying it to some problem of our choosing. After the *benchmarker* process has spawned the trainer, it should wait for it to finish optimizing the NN system. At some point the trainer will reach its stopping condition, and then send the benchmarking process the various performance statistics of the optimization run. For example the trainer could send to the benchmarker the number of evaluations it took to train the NN to solve some problem, the amount of time it took it, and the NN size required to solve it. The benchmarker should accumulate a list of these values, and once it has applied the trainer to the chosen problem X number of times, it should calculate the averages and standard deviations of these various performance statistics. Finally, our benchmarking system should print these performance results to console. At this point the researcher could use this performance data to for example compare his system to other state of the art machine learning algorithms, or the researcher could vary some parameter or add some new features to his system and benchmark it again, and in this manner see if the new features make the system more or less effective. Thus our *benchmarker* should perform the following steps:

1. **Repeat:**
    2. Apply the trainer to some experiment or problem.
    3. Receive from the trainer the resulting data (total evaluations, total cycles, NN size...).
    4. Add this data to the statistics accumulator.
5. **Until**: The trainer has been applied to the given problem, X number of times.
6. **Return**: Calculate averages and standard deviations of the various features in the accumulator.

The following listing shows the implementation of the benchmarker module.

```
Listing-7.11: The implementation of the benchmarker module.

-module(benchmarker).
-compile(export_all).
-include("records.hrl").
-define(MAX_ATTEMPTS,5).
-define(EVAL_LIMIT,inf).
-define(FITNESS_TARGET,inf).
-define(TOT_RUNS,100).
-define(MORPHOLOGY,xor_mimic).

go(Morphology,HiddenLayerDensities)->
    go(Morphology,HiddenLayerDensities,?TOT_RUNS).
go(Morphology,HiddenLayerDensities,TotRuns)->
    go(Morphology,HiddenLayerDensities,?MAX_ATTEMPTS,?EVAL_LIMIT,
?FITNESS_TARGET,TotRuns).
go(Morphology,HiddenLayerDensities,MaxAttempts,EvalLimit,FitnessTarget,TotRuns)->
    PId = spawn(benchmarker,loop,[Morphology,HiddenLayerDensities,MaxAttempts,
EvalLimit,FitnessTarget,TotRuns,[],[],[],[]]),
    register(benchmarker,PId).
```
% The benchmarker is started through the go/2, go/3, or go/6 function. The parameters the benchmark uses can be specified through the macros, and then used by executing go/2 or go/3 for which the researcher simply specifies the Morphology (the problem on which the NN will be benchmarked) and the HiddenLayerDensities (NN topology). The go/2 and go/3 functions execute go/6 function with default parameters. The benchmarker can also be started through go/6, using which the researcher can manually specify all the parameters: morphology, NN topology, Max Attempts, Max Evaluations, target fitness, and the total number of times to run the trainer. Before dropping into the main loop, go/6 registers the benchmarker process so that the trainer can send it the performance stats when it finishes.

```
loop(Morphology,_HiddenLayerDensities,_MA,_EL,_FT,0,FitnessAcc,EvalsAcc,CyclesAcc,
TimeAcc)->
    io:format("Benchmark results for:~p~n",[Morphology]),
    io:format("Fitness::~n Max:~p~n Min:~p~n Avg:~p~n Std:~p~n",
        [lists:max(FitnessAcc),lists:min(FitnessAcc),avg(FitnessAcc),std(FitnessAcc)]),
    io:format("Evals::~n Max:~p~n Min:~p~n Avg:~p~n Std:~p~n",
        [lists:max(EvalsAcc),lists:min(EvalsAcc),avg(EvalsAcc),std(EvalsAcc)]),
    io:format("Cycles::~n Max:~p~n Min:~p~n Avg:~p~n Std:~p~n",
        [lists:max(CyclesAcc),lists:min(CyclesAcc),avg(CyclesAcc),std(CyclesAcc)]),
    io:format("Time::~n Max:~p~n Min:~p~n Avg:~p~n Std:~p~n",
        [lists:max(TimeAcc),lists:min(TimeAcc),avg(TimeAcc),std(TimeAcc)]);
```

```
loop(Morphology,HiddenLayerDensities,MA,EL,FT,BenchmarkIndex,FitnessAcc,EvalsAcc,
CyclesAcc,TimeAcc)->
    Trainer_PId = trainer:go(Morphology,HiddenLayerDensities,MA,EL,FT),
    receive
            {Trainer_PId,Fitness,Evals,Cycles,Time}->
                    loop(Morphology,HiddenLayerDensities,MA,EL,FT,BenchmarkIndex-1,
[Fitness|FitnessAcc],[Evals|EvalsAcc],[Cycles|CyclesAcc],[Time|TimeAcc]);
            terminate ->
                    loop(Morphology,HiddenLayerDensities,MA,EL,FT,0,FitnessAcc,EvalsAcc,
CyclesAcc,TimeAcc)
    end.
% Once the benchmarker is started, it drops into its main loop. The main loop spawns the train-
er and waits for it to finish optimizing the NN system, after which it sends to the benchmarker
the performance based statistics. The benchmarker accumulates these performance statistics in
lists, rerunning the trainer TotRuns number of times. Once the benchmarker has ran the trainer
TotRuns number of times, indicated to be so when BenchmarkIndex reaches 0, it calculates the
Max, Min, Average, and Standard Deviation values for every statistic list it accumulated.

avg(List)->
    lists:sum(List)/length(List).
avg_std(List)->
    Avg = avg(List),
    std(List,Avg,[]).

    std([Val|List],Avg,Acc)->
            std(List,Avg,[math:pow(Avg-Val,2)|Acc]);
    std([],_,Avg,Acc)->
            Variance = lists:sum(Acc)/length(Acc),
            math:sqrt(Variance).
%avg/1 and std/1 functions calculate the average and the standard deviation values of the lists
passed to them.
```

To make the whole system functional, we also have to slightly modify the trainer module so that when the stopping condition is reached, the trainer prints the genotype to console, unregisters itself, checks if a process by the name *benchmarker* exists, and if it does, sends it the performance stats of the optimization session. To make this modification, we add the following lines of code to our trainer module:

```
unregister(trainer),
case whereis(benchmarker) of
    undefined ->
            ok;
    PId ->
            PId ! {self(),BestFitness,EvalAcc,CAcc,TAcc}
end;
```

We now compile and recompile the benchmarker and the trainer modules respectively, and then test our new benchmarker system. To test it, we apply it to the XOR problem, executing it with the following parameters:

- Morphology: xor_mimic
- HiddenLayerDensities: [2]
- MaxAttempts: inf
- EvalLimit: inf
- FitnessTarget: 100
- TotRuns: 100

Based on these parameters, each trainer will generate genotypes until one of them solves the problem with a fitness of at least 100. Thus, the benchmarker will calculate the resulting performance statistics from 100 experiments. To start the benchmarker, execute the following command:

```
1>benchmarker:go(xor_mimic,[2],inf,inf,100,100).
...
Benchmark results for:xor_mimic
Fitness::
 Max:99999.99999999999
 Min:796.7693071321515
 Avg:96674.025859051
 Std:16508.11828048093
Evals::
 Max:2222
 Min:258
 Avg:807.1
 Std:415.8308670601546
...
```

It works! The benchmarker ran 100 training sessions and calculated averages, standard deviations, maxs, and mins for the accumulated Fitness, Evaluations, Cycles, and Time lists. Our system now has all the basic features of a solid machine learning platform.

7.9 Summary

In this chapter we added the augmented stochastic hill-climber optimization algorithm to our system, and extended the exoself process so that it can use it to tune its NN's synaptic weights. We also developed a trainer, a system which further extends the SHC optimization algorithm by restarting genotypes when the exoself had tuned the NN's synaptic weights and reached its stopping condition. This effectively allows the trainer process to use the Random Restart Stochastic

Hill Climbing optimization algorithm to train NNs. Finally, we created the *benchmarker* program, a system that can apply the trainer process to some problem, X number of times, and then average the performance statistics and print the results to console.

Our NN system now has all the features necessary to solve and be applied to various problems and simulations. The learning algorithm our system implements is the simple yet very powerful augmented version of the random-restart stochastic hill-climber. We also now have a standardized method of presenting simulations, training scenarios, and problems to our NN system, all through the decoupled scape packages and morphologies.

In the next chapter we will take this system even further, combining it with population based evolutionary computation and topological mutation, thus creating a simple topology and weight evolving artificial neural network system.

Chapter 8 Developing a Simple Neuroevolutionary Platform

Abstract In this chapter, we take our first step towards neuroevolution. Having developed a NN system capable of having its synaptic weights optimized, we will combine it with an evolutionary algorithm. We will create a population_monitor, a process that spawns a population of NN systems, monitors their performance, applies a selection algorithm to the NNs in the population, and generates the mutant offspring from the fit NNs, while removing the unfit. In this chapter we also add topological mutation operators to our neuroevolutionary system, which will allow the population_monitor to evolve the NNs by adding new neural elements to their topologies. By the end of this chapter, our system becomes a fully-fledged Topology and Weight Evolving Artificial Neural Network.

In this book, we develop an entire neuroevolutionary platform, from a simple neuron, to an advanced topology and weight evolving artificial neural network platform. The final platform will be able to evolve fully distributed NNs, substrate encoded NNs, circuits, and NNs capable of learning within their lifetime through neural plasticity. Thus far we've developed a tuple based genotype encoder, a mapper from the genotype to the phenotype, a process based phenotype representation, and an exoself program which runs outside the NN it's coupled to, capable of performing various assistive functions (though at this point exoself's only function is the ability to tune the NN's weights, map between the genotype and phenotype, and backup the NN's genotype to database). Finally, we also created a *trainer* program that generates and applies the NN systems to a problem specified by the researcher. The NNs generated by the *trainer* are all of the same topology, and the NNs are generated and applied to a problem in series, so that at any one time only a single NN is active. We now make our first leap towards neuroevolution.

Evolution is "the change over time of one or more inherited traits of individuals found in a population." When it comes to neuroevolution, the individuals of the population are neural network based systems. As we discussed in Chapter-4, a neuroevolutionary system performs the following steps:

1. Seed initial population of simple NNs.
2. **Repeat:**
   3. Apply each NN in the population to some problem.
   4. Calculate fitness score of each NN.
   5. Using a selection algorithm, choose the most fit NNs of the population.
   6. Let the fit NNs create offspring, where the offspring's genotype is generated through any of the following approaches:

G.I. Sher, *Handbook of Neuroevolution Through Erlang*,
DOI 10.1007/978-1-4614-4463-3_8, © Springer Science+Business Media New York 2013

    –   Mutation: by mutating the parent's genotype.
    –   Crossover: by somehow combining the genotypes of two or more fit parents.
    –   Using a combination of mutation and crossover.
    7. Create a new population composed of the fit parents and their offspring.
8. **Until:** A stopping condition (if any) is reached.

If we have been evolving the NNs for some particular problem or application, then once the stopping condition is reached, we can pick out the best performing NNs within the population, and count these NNs as solutions.

In the previous chapter, we have created a standardized method of training and applying NNs to problems through the use of scapes, which can gage the fitness of the NNs interfacing with them. Thus, we have the solution for step 3 (if we are to use more than one NN based system in parallel at any one time) and 4 of this loop. Step 5 requires us to develop a selection algorithm, a function which can pick out the most fit NNs in the population, and use them as the base from which to create the offspring for the next generation. This also means that since we will now deal with populations of NNs instead of a single NN, we will need to create some kind of database which can store these populations of genotypes. Step 6 requires that we create a function which can generate offspring that are based on, but genetically differ from, their parents. This is done through mutation and crossover, and we will need to create modules that can perform these types of operations on the genotypes of fit NNs. For step 7 we will compose the new population by simply replacing the unfit NNs in the population by the newly created offspring. For step 8, we can use the same approach to stopping conditions as we used in the *trainer* program. The evolutionary process will stop either when one of the NNs in the population has reached a level of fitness that we find high enough, or when there is innovation stagnation in the population. Meaning, the evolutionary process has stopped generating fitter organisms for a long enough time that makes us believe that a local or global optimum has been reached.

Whereas before the *trainer* program trained and dealt with a single NN at a time, we now need something that can monitor and supervise an entire population of NNs. Thus, we will remove the *trainer* program and develop a *population_monitor* program that can synchronize the evolutionary processes of a population of NN based intelligent agents. The population_monitor system shall be the one that will synchronize all these noted steps and functions, an independent process that constantly monitors the agents, and decides when and who creates offspring... but because it is dependent on all these other parts, we will create and discuss in detail the population_monitor last.

********Note********
Due to the source code heaviness of this chapter, it is essential that the comments within the presented source code be read. It is the comments that elaborate on, and explain how the presented functions work, what they do, and how they do it.
****

8.1 The New Architecture

Before we begin putting together the neuroevolutionary platform, we will first create a diagram of the whole architecture, to try and visualize what new data structures we might need, as shown in Fig-8.1.

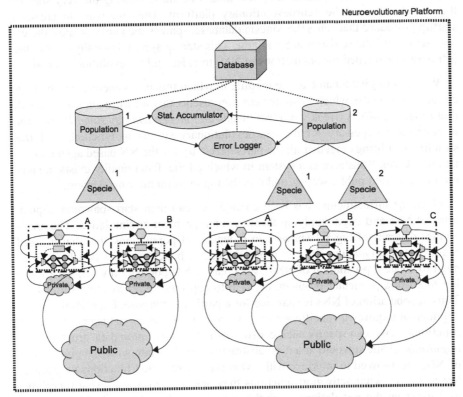

Fig. 8.1 The architecture of a complete neuroevolutionary platform.

Figure 8.1 shows the diagram of the entire neuroevolutionary platform, and the manner in which the various modules are linked and related to each other. We are already familiar with NNs, private and public scapes, but the new elements of this architecture: database, population, species, Stat. Accumulator, and Error Logger, still need to be further explained.

We are now dealing with populations of NNs; we need a safe and secure way to store a large number of genotypes. This is done by using a stable and robust database, Mnesia. The database though does not start itself, so we need some kind of startup procedure for the whole neuroevolutionary platform so that when we start it, it starts mnesia and sets up all other types of global parameters and processes that might be necessary. In addition, as we discussed in the previous chapter, there are public and private scapes. The private scapes are summoned by each NN independently, but the public scapes should already be running. These public scapes can be initiated and started during this initial startup procedure, indeed, these public scapes can belong, and be monitored by, some initial startup process. Also error logging, and the gathering of, and accumulation of, statistics and system performance data, are all independent of the NNs and the evolutionary process, thus if we are to use these systems, they too should be started during the very start of the initialization of the neuroevolutionary platform. Thus we want to create a startup procedure that starts the Mnesia database, spawns the public scapes, the error logger, and the statistics accumulator. This startup system basically creates the infrastructure needed for populations of NNs to exist, and for evolution to occur.

We need to give a name to the module in which this infrastructure will be coded, and the process which in some sense represents this infrastructure. Let us call that module: *polis,* a Greek word that means *an independent city state. Polis* is the infrastructure necessary for the neuroevolutionary system to function, an infrastructure that brings together all the parts necessary for the NN based agents to exist and evolve. Polis acts as a system in which all this functionality exists, it summons the needed public scapes, and it is the top most monitoring element.

Once the infrastructure has been created, we can then start spawning populations of NNs and begin applying them to some problem or simulation. The architecture diagram of Fig-8.1 shows two independent populations, and that in itself requires an explanation. What is a population? A better question is, when do we need to create a population of NNs? We create a NN population when we are trying to solve a particular problem, or wish to apply our NNs to some simulation. Thus, a population of NNs is spawned for a particular purpose. Each simulation or application requires a specific set of morphologies (sensors, actuators, activation functions...), we can specify such constraints in the *population* data structure. The *population* element would at a high abstraction level dictate what the given group of NNs are allowed to interface with, what type of selection functions they are allowed to use, what activation functions they are allowed to use, what morphologies make up the population... For this reason we should have multiple populations, because we will be running multiple simulations and experiments using the same system, and we want to safely store these populations in the same database. If we allow the polis to have different populations, where each population is keeping track of its own NNs and the types of morphologies those NNs have access to, then we can run different experiments and simulations in parallel.

Furthermore, each population is composed of many evolving NNs. When NNs evolve, their genotypes change. When the difference of two genotypes is greater than some threshold X, then those genotypes belong to two different species. It would be useful for us to track speciation of NNs, and how these new species are formed, because speciation implies innovation. Thus we should also be able to group the NNs into different species through the use of a specie data structure. Each population should be broken down into species, where the number of species and the size of each species, should be completely dynamic and depend on the NNs composing the population.

Finally, the Stat. Accumulator and Error Logger should be explained. We are now creating a rather large system, we need a way to keep track of errors, and a way to keep track of various statistics of the experiments we are running. For example we should keep track of how quickly the fitness is increasing on average, or how many evaluations it took to solve some problem, or how many generations, or what were the most and least fit NNs and when during evolution they came into existence... or the running average fitness of some species... Keeping track of this will be the job of the Stat. Accumulator. Finally, the Error Logger is another process that should always be running, keeping track and catching any errors or alerts that occur during the time that the polis is online.

> ********Note********
> Technically an error logger already exists within the Erlang system itself. Thus we have a choice of taking advantage of this already existing and robust system, or creating our own. Also the Stat. Accumulator can be implemented in many different ways, not all requiring it to be a completely separate process. For example the population_monitor will already have access to all the NNs belonging to a particular population. It will already have access to their sizes, fitness scores... and all other features, since it will be the one mutating them. Thus, the population_monitor can easily also perform the function of performance statistics accumulation and tracking.
> ********************

Having now agreed on the new architecture of our system, we can start devising the necessary data structures for our platform.

8.2 The New Data Structures

A population is a group of agents, in a neuroevolutionary system those agents are NN based systems. The genotypes of our NNs are represented as lists of records. Currently in our system, each NN genome is composed of a single cortex, one or more sensors, one or more actuators, and one or more neurons. Each element of the NN system knows what other elements it is connected to through element ids. But that is not the whole story, there is also meta-information that each NN should keep track off. For example, the NN topology that we specify during the genotype creation, such as: *[1,2,3]*, which specifies a NN with 1 neuron in the first layer, 2 neurons in the second, and 3 in the third, is an important piece of information which can specify what specie this NN belongs to. Besides the NN topology, the following other features should be tracked by each NN:

1. **id**: The unique Id of the NN based agent by which the population_monitor can identify it, and contact it if necessary.

2. **population_id**: The Id of the population the NN belongs to.
3. **specie_id**: The Id of the specie the NN belongs to.
4. **cx_id**: The Id of the cortex of the NN, the cortex element which has the Ids of all the neurons, sensors and actuators of the NN.
5. **fingerprint**: The NN's particular "fingerprint", a tuple composed of the NN's topological structure, and the types of sensors and actuators it is using. Fingerprints can be used to calculate how much one NN system differs from another.
6. **constraint**: Constraint will define the NN's morphological type, what types of sensors, actuators, activation functions, and other features that the NN has access to during its evolution. Different species will have different constraints, and different constraints will define what different elements the NN and its offspring can integrate during evolution. In essence, *constraint* keeps track of the available parameters, mutation operators, activation functions, morphologies, and various other parameters available to the NN as it evolves. It ensures that the NN using a particular *constraint* tuple produces offspring related to it in a particular manner, in a manner that ensures that the offspring too can be applied to the same problem, or stay within certain specification constraints.
7. **evo_hist**: The evolutionary history of the NN, a list of mutation operators that were used on the seed NN system to evolve the current NN based system. It is the NN's evolutionary path from the simple topology it started with, to its current state. This way we can keep track of how the particular NN topology was reached, what path it took, and perhaps extract the why behind it all.
8. **fitness**: The NN's current fitness.
9. **innovation_factor**: The number of generations that have passed since the NN last increased in fitness.
10. **pattern**: The NN's topology.
11. **generation**: The generation to which this NN system belongs. The seed NN system has a generation of 0. When an offspring is created, its generation is that of its parent +*1*.

Since the cortex already performs a specific function in the NN system, which is synchronizing the sensors, actuators, and neurons into a cohesive neurocomputational system, we should not overburden it with also having to track this new data. Instead what we will do is create a wrapper, another element to be added to the NN system's genotype. This new element will be part of the genotype and store this useful information. We will call this new element: *agent*, and it will store in itself these 11 noted features. Each NN based system will now also have its own id, the id of the agent element, an id by which it can be uniquely identified within a population. Finally, the reason why we name this new element agent, is because that is in essence what our NN based adaptive systems are, intelligent adaptive agents.

As we noted, each NN will belong to its own *species*, which is dependent on that NN's particular fingerprint. We thus also need to create a species data structure. The species abstraction should keep track of the following information:

1. **id**: The species' unique Id.
2. **fingerprint**: The particular rough identification of the species, any NN with the same fingerprint belongs to this species.
3. **agent_ids**: The list of agent Ids which belong to this species.
4. **champion_ids**: A list of Ids of the best performing agents within the species, the species' champions.
5. **avg_fitness**: The average fitness of this species.
6. **innovation_factor**: Innovation factor is based on how long ago the average fitness of this species increased.
7. **population_id**: The Id of the population that this species belongs to.
8. **constraint**: Constraint specifies the list of sensors, actuators, activation functions... that the agents belonging to this species have access to. And the name of the morphology of this species.

During one of our simulations we might want to start the experiment with many different species. Since the NNs depend on their morphologies, we can create a population with two different species, each with its own morphology. Then, when the NNs are created in those species, they would naturally start off with different sets of sensors and actuators, and the sensor and actuator sets available to them and belonging to the particular species they were seeded in. For example, this would be the case in the ALife simulation where we want to start the experiment with two separate species, predator and prey, each having its own different morphology, and access to its own set of different sensors and actuators.

An even higher level of abstraction is that of the *population*. A population contains all the NN based agents associated with some particular experiment or simulation. Thus if we wish to run multiple experiments, we don't want these NNs to intermingle; they belong to different worlds or simulation runs and experiments. To keep track of our populations, we will need to create a population abstraction. Through populations, we can for example stop an experiment at any time, at which point the NNs will be reverted back to their genotypes and stored in the database. We can then start another experiment with another population, which will have its own id. At some other point we might want to continue with our original simulation or experiment, and so all we would have to do is summon that original population, which would in return spawn all the NNs belonging to it, and the original simulation would continue from where it was left off. The population abstraction should contain the following information:

1. **id**: A unique population Id or the id/name of the experiment.
2. **specie_ids**: The list of the species Ids that belong to this population.
3. **avg_fitness**: The average fitness of this population.
4. **innovation_factor**: Innovation factor is based on how long ago the average fitness of this population increased.
5. **morphologies**: List of available morphologies for this population. The list of morphologies defines the list of sensors and actuators available to the NNs in this population. Since the morphology defines the sensors and actuators of the

NN system, this list effectively defines the problem or simulation to which the evolving population of NN systems will be applied, and for what purpose the agents will be evolved.

Having now discussed what new data structures we need, it is time to begin developing our neuroevolutionary platform. In the next section we will add the needed records to our records.hrl to accommodate these new data structures, and develop the polis module.

8.3 Developing the polis Module

The polis module should contain the functions that perform general, global tasks, and deal with initializing, starting, stopping and deleting the mnesia database used by the neuroevolutionary platform. Furthermore, it should also have the functions to initialize and start or spawn public scapes specified through their parameters. Because there should be only one mnesia database per node, there needs to be only a single polis per node, representing a single neuroevolutionary platform. The following list summarizes the types of functions we want to be able to execute through the polis module:

1. Initialize new mnesia database.
2. Reset the mnesia database.
3. Start all the neuroevolutionary platform supporting processes (scapes, any error logging and statistics tracking programs...), so that the population_monitor systems will have all the necessary infrastructure they need to apply evolutionary processes to their populations.
4. Stop and shut down the neuroevolutionary platform.

The following listing shows the polis module:

```
Listing-8.1: The polis module.

-module(polis).
%% API
-export([start/1,start/0,stop/0,init/2,create/0,reset/0,sync/0]).
%% gen_server callbacks
-export([init/1, handle_call/3, handle_cast/2, handle_info/2,terminate/2, code_change/3]).
-behaviour(gen_server).
-include("records.hrl").
%%==================================== Polis Configuration Options
-record(state,{active_mods=[],active_scapes=[]}).
-record(scape_summary,{address,type,parameters=[]}).
-define(MODS,[]).
-define(PUBLIC_SCAPES,[ ]).
```

%The MODS list contains the names of the processes, functions, or other databases that also need to be executed and started when we start our neuroevolutionary platform. In the same manner, when we have created a new public scape, we can add a scape_summary tuple with this scape's information to the PUBLIC_SCAPES list, so that it is initialized and started with the system. The state record for the polis has all the elements needed to track the currently active mods and public scapes, which are either started during the startup of the neuroevolutionary platform, or spawned later, while the polis is already online.

```erlang
%%%============================================ API
sync()->
    make:all([load]).
% A sync/1 function can compile and reload all the modules pertaining to the project within the
% folder.

start() ->
    case whereis(polis) of
        undefined ->
            gen_server:start(?MODULE, {?MODS,?PUBLIC_SCAPES}, []);
        Polis_PId ->
            io:format("Polis:~p is already running on this node.~n",[Polis_PId])
    end.

start(Start_Parameters) ->
    gen_server:start(?MODULE, Start_Parameters, []).
init(Pid,InitState)->
    gen_server:cast(Pid,{init,InitState}).
%The start/0 function first checks whether a polis process has already been spawned, by checking if one is registered. If it's not, then the start/1 function starts up the neuroevolutionary platform.

stop()->
    case whereis(polis) of
        undefined ->
            io:format("Polis cannot be stopped, it is not online~n");
        Polis_PId ->
            gen_server:cast(Polis_PId,{stop,normal})
    end.
%The stop/0 function first checks whether a polis process is online. If there is an online polis process running on the node, then the stop function sends a signal to it requesting it to stop.

%%%============================================ gen_server callbacks
init({Mods,PublicScapes}) ->
    {A,B,C} = now(),
    random:seed(A,B,C),
    process_flag(trap_exit,true),
```

```
    register(polis,self()),
    io:format("Parameters:~p~n",[{Mods,PublicScapes}]),
    mnesia:start(),
    start_supmods(Mods),
    Active_PublicScapes = start_scapes(PublicScapes,[]),
    io:format("******** Polis: ##MATHEMA## is now online.~n"),
    InitState = #state{active_mods=Mods,active_scapes=Active_PublicScapes},
    {ok, InitState}.
```

%The init/1 function first seeds random with a new seed, in the case a random number generator will be needed. The polis process is then registered, the mnesia database is started, and the supporting modules, if any, are then started through the start_supmods/1 function. Then all the specified public scapes, if any, are activated. Having called our neuroevolutionary platform polis, we give this polis a name "MATHEMA", which is a Greek word for knowledge, and learning. Finally we create the initial state, which contains the PIds of the currently active public scapes, and the names of the activated mods. Finally, the function then drops into the main gen_server loop.

```
handle_call({get_scape,Type},{Cx_PId,_Ref},S)->
    Active_PublicScapes = S#state.active_scapes,
    Scape_PId = case lists:keyfind(Type,3,Active_PublicScapes) of
            false ->
                    undefined;
            PS ->
                    PS#scape_summary.address
    end,
    {reply,Scape_PId,S};
handle_call({stop,normal},_From, State)->
    {stop, normal, State};
handle_call({stop,shutdown},_From,State)->
    {stop, shutdown, State}.
```

%At this point the polis only accepts a get_scape call, to which it replies with the PId or undefined message, and the two standard {stop,normal} and {stop,shutdown} calls.

```
handle_cast({init,InitState},_State)->
    {noreply,InitState};
handle_cast({stop,normal},State)->
    {stop, normal,State};
handle_cast({stop,shutdown},State)->
    {stop, shutdown, State}.
```

%At this point the polis allows only for 3 standard casts: {init,InitState}, {stop,normal}, and {stop,shutdown}.

```
handle_info(_Info, State) ->
    {noreply, State}.
```

%The handle_info/2 function is unused by the polis process at this time.

```
terminate(Reason, S) ->
    Active_Mods = S#state.active_mods,
    stop_supmods(Active_Mods),
    stop_scapes(S#state.active_scapes),
    io:format("******** Polis: ##MATHEMA## is now offline, terminated with rea-
son:~p~n",[Reason]),
    ok.

code_change(_OldVsn, State, _Extra) ->
    {ok, State}.
```
%When polis is terminated, it first shuts down all the supporting mods by calling the stop_supmods/1 function, and then it shuts down all the public scapes by calling the stop_scapes/1 function.

```
%%-------------------------------------------------------------------
%%% Internal functions
%%-------------------------------------------------------------------
create()->
    mnesia:create_schema([node()]),
    mnesia:start(),
    mnesia:create_table(agent,[{disc_copies, [node()]},{type,set},{attributes, rec-
ord_info(fields,agent)}]),
    mnesia:create_table(cortex,[{disc_copies, [node()]},{type,set},{attributes, rec-
ord_info(fields,cortex)}]),
    mnesia:create_table(neuron,[{disc_copies, [node()]},{type,set},{attributes, rec-
ord_info(fields,neuron)}]),
    mnesia:create_table(sensor,[{disc_copies, [node()]},{type,set},{attributes, rec-
ord_info(fields,sensor)}]),
    mnesia:create_table(actuator,[{disc_copies, [node()]},{type,set},{attributes, rec-
ord_info(fields,actuator)}]),
    mnesia:create_table(population,[{disc_copies, [node()]},{type,set},{attributes, rec-
ord_info(fields,population)}]),
    mnesia:create_table(specie.[{disc_copies, [node()]},{type,set},{attributes, rec-
ord_info(fields,specie)}]).
```
%The create/0 function sets up new mnesia database composed of the agent, cortex, neuron, sensor, actuator, polis, population, and specie tables.

```
reset()->
    mnesia:stop(),
    ok = mnesia:delete_schema([node()]),
    polis:create().
```
%The reset/0 function deletes the schema, and recreates a fresh database from scratch.

%Start/Stop environmental modules: DBs, Environments. Network Access systems, and tools...

```
start_supmods([ModName|ActiveMods])->
   ModName:start(),
   start_supmods(ActiveMods);
start_supmods([])->
   done.
```
%The start_supmods/1 function expects a list of module names of the mods that are to be started with the startup of the neuroevolutionary platform. Each module must have a start/0 function that starts-up the supporting mod process.

```
stop_supmods([ModName|ActiveMods])->
   ModName:stop(),
   stop_supmods(ActiveMods);
stop_supmods([])->
   done.
```
%The stop_supmods/1 expects a list of supporting mod names, the mod's name must be the name of its module, and that module must have a stop/0 function that stops the module. stop_supmods/1 goes through the list of the mods, and executes the stop() function for each one.

```
start_scapes([S|Scapes],Acc)->
   Type = S#scape_summary.type,
   Parameters = S#scape_summary.parameters,
   {ok,PId} = scape:start_link({self(),Type,Parameters}),
   start_scapes(Scapes,[S#scape_summary{address=PId}|Acc]);
start_scapes([],Acc)->
   lists:reverse(Acc).
```
%The start_scapes/2 function accepts a list of scape_summary records, which specify the names of the public scapes and any parameters with which those scapes should be started. What specifies the scape which is going to be created by the scape module is the Type that is dropped into the function. Of course the scape module should already be able to create the Type of scape that is dropped into the start_link function. Once the scape is started, we record its PId in its scape_summary's record. Once all the public scapes have been started, the function returns a list of updated scape_summary records.

```
stop_scapes([S|Scapes])->
   PId = S#scape_summary.address,
   gen_server:cast(PId,{self(),stop,normal}),
   stop_scapes(Scapes);
stop_scapes([])->
   ok.
```
%The stop_scapes/1 function accepts a list of scape_summary records, and then stops all the scapes in the list. The function extracts a PId from every scape_summary in the list, and then requests the specified scapes to terminate themselves.

The polis process represents an interfacing point with the neuroevolutionary platform infrastructure. Through the polis module we can start and initialize the mnesia database that will support the evolutionary processes and store the genotype of the NN based systems. Polis is the infrastructure and the system within which the database, the NN based agents, and the scapes they interface with, exist. It is for this reason that I gave this module the name polis, an independent and self governing city state of intelligent agents. Perhaps at some future time when multiple such systems are running on different nodes, each polis itself will have its own id, and each polis will concentrate on some particular goal towards which the neuroevolutionary system is aimed. It is only fitting to give this polis the name: "MATHEMA", which stands for knowledge and learning.

We saw in the previous listing that the create/0 function creates a new mnesia database composed of the following list of tables: sensor, actuator, neuron, cortex, agent, specie, and population. Our original records.hrl is still missing the following records to accommodate the listed tables: agent, specie, population, and polis. The updated records.hrl is shown in the following listing.

```
Listing-8.2: Updated contents of records.hrl

-record(sensor,{id,name,cx_id,scape,vl,fanout_ids=[]}).
-record(actuator,{id,name,cx_id,scape,vl,fanin_ids=[]}).
-record(neuron, {id, generation, cx_id, af, input_idps=[], output_ids=[], ro_ids=[]}).
-record(cortex, {id, agent_id, sensor_ids=[], actuator_ids=[]}).
-record(agent,{id, generation, population_id, specie_id, cx_id,fingerprint, constraint,
evo_hist=[], fitness, innovation_factor, pattern=[]}).
-record(specie,{id,population_id, fingerprint, constraint, agent_ids=[], champion_ids=[],
avg_fitness, innovation_factor}).
-record(population,{id,polis_id,specie_ids=[],morphologies=[],innovation_factor}).
```

As you've noted from the updated records.hrl file, we've also added the elements: *generation* and *ro_ids*, to the neuron record. The generation element will track the number of generations that had passed since the last time the neuron was either mutated, or affected directly by some mutation which affects the NN's topology. In this way we can keep track of which parts of the NN system were most recently added to the network. The ro_ids (recurrent output ids) element keeps track of the recurrent output connections, and is a subset of the output_ids list. Thus, if a neuron A sends an output to a neuron B, and neuron B is located in the layer whose index is lower than A's layer, then B's id is entered not only into the output_ids list, but also into the ro_ids list. We need the ro_ids element because we need a way to track recurrent connections. Recurrent connections have to be treated differently than standard synaptic connections in a NN, as we will see and discuss in the following sections.

Before moving forward though, let's test the polis module and create a mnesia database. To do so, we first create the mnesia database by executing the function *polis:create()*, and then test the polis starting and stopping functions by executing *polis:start()* and *polis:stop()*:

```
1> polis:create().
{atomic,ok}
2> polis:start().
Parameters:{[],[]}
******** Polis: ##MATHEMA## is now online.
{ok,<0.133.0>}
3> polis:stop().
ok
******** Polis: ##MATHEMA## is now offline, terminated with reason:normal
```

It works!. With the *polis:create()* function we created the necessary mnesia database tables, which we will need when we start testing other modules as we update and create them. The start function took the polis online successfully, and the stop function took the polis offline successfully. With this done, we can now move forward and begin updating the genotype module.

8.4 Updating the genotype Module

The genotype module encapsulates the NN based system creation and NN genotype access and storage. The move from ETS to Mnesia requires us to update the genotype access and storage functions. The addition of the *agent* record as part of the NN based system requires us to modify the NN system creation module. The new ability to add recursive connections to neurons will require us to rethink the way we represent the NN's topology, and the element's id structure.

Unlike in static NN based systems, topology and weight evolving artificial neural network systems (TWEANNs) can modify the very topology and structure of a NN. We do not need to figure out what NN topology we should give to our NN system, because it will evolve the topology most optimal for the problem we give it. Plus, we never really know ahead of time what the most optimal NN topology needed to solve some particular problem anyway. The seed NN genotype should be the simplest possible, given the particular morphology of the agent, we let the neuroevolutionary process to complexify the topology of the NN system over time. Finally, because we will now use different kinds of activation functions, not only tanh but also sin, abs, sgn... we might wish for some species in the population to be started with a particular subset of these activation functions, and other species with another subset, to perhaps observe how and which evolutionary paths they take due to these different constraints. For this reason, we will also implement a *constraint* record which the population_monitor can use when constructing agents. The constraint record specifies which morphology and which set of activation functions the seed agent and its offspring should have access to during evolution. In the following subsections we discuss in more detail each of these factors, and then update our genotype module's source code.

8.4.1 Moving from ETS to Mnesia

Again, because we wrapped the retrieval and storage functions of the NN system elements inside their own functions within the genotype, the move from ETS to Mnesia will only necessitate the update of those specific functions. The main functions, read/2 and write/2, will need to be updated so that they use mnesia. The functions save_genotype/2, save_to_file/2, load_from_file/2, are no longer needed. Whereas the original save_genotype/2 function expected the genotype to be dropped in as a list, which it then entered into a table one record at a time, our new genotype will save each element as soon as it's created, instead of first forming a list of all the tuples and then saving them all at once. The save_to_file/2 and load_from_file/2 functions are ETS specific. Since mnesia is started and stopped by the polis, these two functions no longer have a role to play in our neuroevolutionary platform.

8.4.2 A NN Based Adaptive Agent

Our NN based adaptive system has been increasing in the number of elements, functions, and processes that it is composed of, and which define it. We now add another element to the genotype, the *agent* element. The agent element will store all the supporting information that the NN based system needs to keep track of the evolutionary history and other supplementary information not kept track of by the other elements. Neurons, Sensors, Actuators, and the Cortex elements keep track of only the data needed for their own specific functionality, whereas the *agent* element will maintain all the global NN data (general topology of the NN, constraints, specie id...). Thus, the complete NN based system genotype will now be composed of: one or more neuron records, one or more sensor records, one or more actuator records, a cortex record, and an agent record. Mirroring the genotype, the phenotype of our NN based system is composed of: one or more neuron processes, one or more sensor processes, one or more actuator processes, the NN synchronizing cortex process, and the exoself process. In a way, the exoself process embodies the agent record of the genotype. The exoself process performs assistive services that might be needed by the NN system, it is the process that is external to the NN, but is part of the whole NN based system, and it also has a PId that is unique to the agent, since an agent can have multiple sensors and actuators, but only a single exoself. It contains information about the entire NN based system; information that might be needed to restore and recover a NN, and perform other numerous supportive tasks. This type of NN based system can also be referred to as an adaptive agent, and thus for the remainder of the book, I will use the terms: "NN based system", "adaptive agent", and "agent", interchangeably.

8.4.3 A New Neuron Id Structure; Adding Recursive Connections

Neuroevolution allows for any neuron to make a connection to any other neuron, and that includes recursive connections. Our current neuron Id structure is a tuple containing the atom neuron (to identify the id as that which belongs to a neuron element), an integer based layer index (to specify where in the NN the neuron is located), and a unique Id (to ensure that every neuron id is unique): {{LayerIndex, Unique_Id}, neuron}. Using this neuron id structure, we can encode both, feed forward, and recursive NNs... but there is a problem.

As shown in Fig-8.2, imagine we have a NN which contains a neuron A in layer N and a neuron B in layer M. If we now apply a mutation to this NN, establishing a connection from neuron A to neuron B, and M > N, then the resulting NN is simply a feed forward connection, and everything works. If you we start with the same simple initial NN, and this time the mutation produces a connection from B to A, because M > N, the connection is recursive... everything still works ok. But what if during the mutation a new neural layer is added, right in the middle of layer N and M?

This scenario occurs when for example a new neuron is added to the NN, and it is not added to an existing layer, but instead it is added as an element of a new layer (thus increasing the depth of the NN), in the middle of two other existing neural layers. One of the possible mutation operators that produces this effect is the splice mutation operator. For example the splice mutation chooses a random neuron A in the NN, it then chooses a random output Id of neuron A to neuron B, disconnects neuron A from B, and then reconnects them through a newly created neuron C, placed in between them.

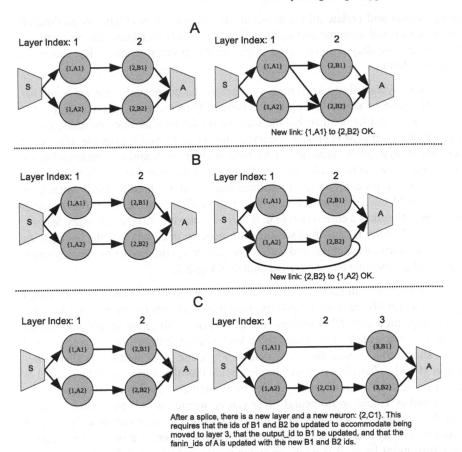

After a splice, there is a new layer and a new neuron: {2,C1}. This requires that the ids of B1 and B2 be updated to accommodate being moved to layer 3, that the output_id to B1 be updated, and that the fanin_ids of A is updated with the new B1 and B2 ids.

Fig. 8.2 Three types of mutations, showing the NN topologies before and after those mutations are applied. In A, a new link is created from neuron {1,A1} in layer 1, to neuron {2,B2} in layer 2. In B, a new recursive link is created from neuron {2,B2} in layer 2, to neuron {1,A2} in layer 1. In C, a splice is done, neurons {1,A2} and {2,B2} are unlinked/disconnected, and then relinked/connected through a new neuron, which is placed in a new layer between the two neurons. Due to a new layer, the Ids of B1 and B2 have to be adjusted, since the B1 and B2 neurons are moved from layer 2 to layer 3.

The problem is that when a mutation adds a new layer, it changes the topology, the layer indecies change for all the layers that come after the newly inserted layer. Since the layer index is a part of the neuron's id which is needed to keep track of whether the synaptic connections are feed forward or recursive, after such a mutation we must go in and update the ids of every neuron contained in the layers located after the newly inserted layer, and we need to update all the output id lists of the neurons which connect to these affected neurons. Since we don't know which neurons are affected and which neurons are connected to which ahead of time, after every such mutation, we have to access the NN genotype, go through every neuron and update all the affected Ids. Then we would have to go through every sensor and actuator and update their fanout_ids and fanin_ids respectively as well, in case they are connected to any of the affected neurons. But there is a simpler solution.

We use layers only to keep track of whether the connections that are made between the neurons are feed forward, or recurrent. Thus the most important part of the layer index is not its number, but the location on the number line, the order, meaning, whether a layer M is greater or smaller than layer N. So for example, if we have neurons in layer M=3 connected to neurons in layer N=4, and a mutation adds another layer between M and N, we can give this new layer an index of K = (N+M)/2, which is 3.5 in this case. Its value indicates that it is in the middle, thus if any neuron from layer M makes a connection to it, it will be feed forward. And if any neuron from layer N makes a connection to it, it will be recursive. All the necessary features are retained, using this method we can still properly track whether the connections are feedforward or recursive, and we do not have to update any of the already existing ids when inserting a new layer, as shown in Fig-8.3.

Eventually we will update our neuroevolutionary system to allow the NN based systems to modify their own topology, read their own NN topology using sensors, and change their own NN topology using actuators... Since the inputs and outputs of the NNs are usually normalized to be vectors containing values between *-1* and *1*, we should think ahead and use a system where the layer indices are also all between -1 and 1. This is easy, we simply decide that the sensors will be located at the -1 point, and so no neural layer can be located at -1. And we let the actuators be located at 1, and so no neural layer can be located at 1. Thus, when creating seed NN topologies, as discussed in the next section, we create them with that first initial neural layer at index 0, as shown in Fig-8.4. Then, if a new layer is added after this initial layer, it is given an index at *(0+1)/2*, if a new layer is added before, then its index is set to *(0+(-1))/2*. Once a new layer has been added after layer 0, we will now have the layers [0,0.5] composing the NN. If we need to add another layer after layer index 0.5, we follow the same pattern: (0.5 + 1)/2, thus the new layer index after 0.5, is 0.75. If on the other hand we need to add a new layer between 0.5 and 0, we give that layer an index of (0+0.5)/2, or 0.25. In this manner we can have infinitely many layers, and when adding or removing layers, none of the already existing neuron ids need to be modified or updated.

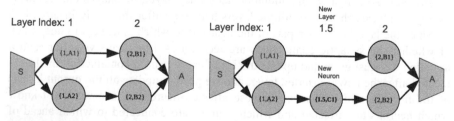

Fig. 8.3 A new way to designate neural layer indices, and the resulting ability to easily add and remove new layers without disrupting or having to update existing neural Ids.

8.4.4 Seed Computational Intelligence

We can neither predict nor derive ahead of time, not how large the NN should be nor what the topology of that NN should be, to optimally adapt to some environment, or solve some problem. The job of devising the proper topology, architecture, functionality... everything, is that of evolution. Evolution alone decides what is fit to survive, and what is not. Evolution complexifies systems overtime, adding new features, elements, topological structures. Retaining what is useful, discarding what is not. Thus, we need only seed the minimal NN topologies, start with the simplest NN topologies and let evolution convert them into the more complex structures over time.

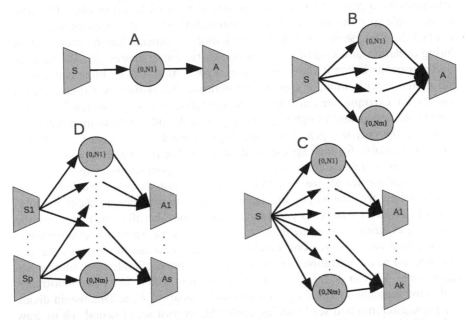

Fig. 8.4 Four types of minimalistic seed NN topologies are shown. Type A starts with a single Sensor and a single Actuator with an input vector length of 1, resulting in a NN with 1 neuron in layer 0 (the preferred seed topology). Type B starts with 1 sensor and 1 actuator whose input vl > 1. Type C starts with a single sensor and multiple actuators. And type D starts with multiple sensors and actuators.

The simplest seed NNs are composed of a single layer of neurons, connected from sensors, and connected to actuators, as shown in Fig-8.4. The minimal starting topology depends on the total number of Sensors and Actuators the researcher decides to seed the population with. If the NN is set to start with P number of Sensors and one Actuator, where the actuator's input vector length is 1, then the seed NN starts with a single neuron connected from all the sensors and connected to a single actuator. If on the other hand the NN is initiated with P number of Sensors and K number of actuators, the seed NNs will contain 1 layer of neurons, where each neuron is connected to a random subset of P Sensors, and to exactly 1 actuator. This neural layer will contain $A_1+...A_k$ total Neurons, where A_i is the size of the vector that is destined for each $Actuator_i$. It is customary for the seed NNs to be initialized with a single Sensor and a single Actuator, letting the NN systems discover any other existing Sensors and Actuators through neuroevolution.

8.4.5 Constraints

The constraints should do just that, specify the set of general evolutionary guidelines for a particular organism, or neural network based system. The *constraints* tuple specifies the morphology, and therefore the set of sensors and actuators that the NN system can draw its new sensor and actuator based elements from during evolution, and a set of neural activation functions: *neural_afs*. The idea behind constraints is that it allows us to start a population with multiple constraints, and therefore with multiple species and multiple fitness functions (one for each specie). For example, we can start a new population of size 100 with a list of two constraints, one whose morphology is *prey*, and the other whose morphology is *predator*. The prey and predator morphologies have different sets of sensors and actuators available for their species to draw from. The population monitor, seeing that there are two constraints, could then create the population composed of two species, each species of size 50, and each species using its own constraints. Since the constraints are inherited by the agent systems, the offspring an agent produces would be created based on its constraints. Constraints also allow us to perform the following experiment: Assume that we would like to see whether neural networks that use *tanh* and *sin* activation functions, or whether a neural networks that use *sin*, *abs*, and *gauss* activation functions, evolve a more profitable stock trading NN based agent. We can do this by starting a population with a list of two constraints which use the same morphology, but different *neural_afs* lists. This would divide the population into two seed species, each with its own set of neural_afs to draw from. We could even create two species of the same type/morphology, and release them into a public scape, where the only difference between the two species is their constraints with regards to neural_afs available to the evolving agents. This would allow us to see what set of neural_afs is better suited to evolve intelligent/adaptive systems faster and more effectively in the provided environment. It would even allow us to let the two species of the same type/morphology compete and fight each other, demonstrating which set of activation functions is more fit in that way. Finally, the *constraint* record also simply allows us to specify the morphology and neural_afs that we'd like to use during any particular simulation or experiment, the list of sensors, actuators, and activation functions that we would like our evolving NN based systems to incorporate their elements from, as they try to solve some particular problem. The *constraint* record we will add to our records.hrl file will use the following format:

```
-record(constraint,{morphology=[], neural_afs=[]}).
```

During the seed population creation, the function constructing the genotypes of the NN based systems would then be passed the specie id that the agents will belong to, the id that the created agent should use, and the constraint record, set within the *population_monitor* beforehand.

8.4.6 The Updated genotype Module

Having now covered all the new features and properties of the genotype module, we can put these parts together: The *construct_Agent* function accepts as its parameters the *specie_Id, agent_Id*, and the *constraint* tuple. It then uses these parameters to construct a seed population. The NNs in this seed population use minimalistic topologies, connected to and from one of the sensors and actuators belonging to the morphology specified within the constraints. Each neuron is created with a random set of weights but without a bias/threshold value, which can be later incorporated through a mutation if needed. Finally, the activation function for the neuron is randomly chosen from the *neural_afs* list specified within the *constraint* record.

Beyond these additions, we add to the genotype module three new functions: *delete_Agent/1, clone_Agent/2, mutate/1*, and *test/0*. The first three will be necessary when we begin deleting unfit NNs, and creating offspring based on the fit NNs. One of the ways to create an offspring based on a fit genotype in the population is by first cloning that genotype, and then mutating it, which is the approach we take for offspring creation in our neuroevolutionary platform. All mutation operator functions will be kept in one module, while the *mutate* function wrapper is kept in the genotype module. This will allow us to keep the genome mutator module indifferent to where and how the genotype is stored, since the genotype module will keep track of that. In this manner, it will be mostly the *genotype* module which will need to deal with mnesia transactions, and be aware of how the genome is stored. The fourth function we create will be test/0, we will use this function to test whether our module can create a new agent, then clone it, then print the genotypes of the two agents (original and its clone) to console, and then finally delete them both.

The following listing shows the source code for the updated genotype module:

Listing-8.3 The updated genotype module.

```
-module(genotype).
-compile(export_all).
-include("records.hrl").
```

```
construct_Agent(Specie_Id,Agent_Id,SpecCon)->
    random:seed(now()),
    Generation = 0,
    {Cx_Id,Pattern} = construct_Cortex(Agent_Id,Generation,SpecCon),
    Fingerprint = create_fingerprint(Agent_Id),
    Agent = #agent{
            id = Agent_Id,
            cx_id = Cx_Id,
            specie_id = Specie_Id,
            fingerprint = Fingerprint,
            constraint = SpecCon,
            generation = Generation,
            pattern = Pattern,
            evo_hist = []
    },
    write(Agent).
```

%The population monitor should have all the information with regards to the morphologies and species constraints under which the agent's genotype should be created. Thus the construct_Agent/3 is ran with the parameter Specie_Id to which this NN based system will belong, the Agent_Id that this NN based intelligent agent will have, and the SpecCon (specie constraint) that will define the list of activation functions and other parameters from which the seed agent can choose its parameters. In this function, first the generation is set to 0, since the agent is just created, then the construct_Cortex/3 is ran, which creates the NN and returns its Cx_Id. Once the NN is created and the cortex's id is returned, we can fill out the information needed by the agent record, and then finally write it to the mnesia database

```
construct_Cortex(Agent_Id,Generation,SpecCon)->
    Cx_Id = {{origin,generate_UniqueId()},cortex},
    Morphology = SpecCon#constraint.morphology,
    Sensors = [S#sensor{id={{-1,generate_UniqueId()},sensor},cx_id=Cx_Id}|| S <-
morphology:get_InitSensors(Morphology)],
    Actuators = [A#actuator{id={{1,generate_UniqueId()},actuator},cx_id=Cx_Id}||A<-
morphology:get_InitActuators(Morphology)],
    N_Ids=construct_InitialNeuroLayer(Cx_Id,Generation,SpecCon,Sensors,Actuators,[],[]),
    S_Ids = [S#sensor.id || S<-Sensors],
    A_Ids = [A#actuator.id || A<-Actuators],
    Cortex = #cortex{
            id = Cx_Id,
            agent_id = Agent_Id,
            neuron_ids = N_Ids,
            sensor_ids = S_Ids,
            actuator_ids = A_Ids
    },
    write(Cortex),
    {Cx_Id,[{0,N_Ids}]}.
```

%construct_Cortex/3 generates a new Cx_Id, extracts the morphology from the constraint record passed to it in SpecCon, and then extracts the initial sensors and actuators for that morphology. After the sensors and actuators are extracted, the function calls construct_InitialNeuroLayer/7, which creates a single layer of neurons connected from the specified sensors and to the specified actuators, and then returns the ids of the created neurons. Finally, the sensor and actuator ids are extracted from the sensors and actuators, and the cortex record is composed and written to the database.

```
    construct_InitialNeuroLayer(Cx_Id,Generation,SpecCon,Sensors,[A|Actuators],
AAcc,NIdAcc)->
        N_Ids = [{{0,Unique_Id},neuron}|| Unique_Id<-generate_ids(A#actuator.vl,[])],
        U_Sensors=construct_InitialNeurons(Cx_Id,Generation,SpecCon,N_Ids,Sensors,A),
        U_A = A#actuator{fanin_ids=N_Ids},
        construct_InitialNeuroLayer(Cx_Id,Generation,SpecCon,U_Sensors,Actuators,
[U_A|AAcc],lists:append(N_Ids,NIdAcc));
    construct_InitialNeuroLayer(_Cx_Id,_Generation,_SpecCon,Sensors,[],AAcc,NIdAcc)->
        [write(S) || S <- Sensors],
        [write(A) || A <- AAcc],
        NIdAcc.
```
%construct_InitialNeuroLayer/7 creates a set of neurons for each Actuator in the actuator list. The neurons are initialized in the construct_InitialNeurons/6, where they are connected to the actuator, and from a random subset of the sensors passed to the function. The construct_InitialNeurons/6 function returns the updated sensors, some of which have now an updated set of fanout_ids which includes the new neuron ids they were connected to. The actuator's fanin_ids is then updated to include the neuron ids that were connected to it. Once all the actuators have been connected to, the sensors and the actuators are written to the database, and the set of neuron ids created within the function is returned to the caller.

```
    construct_InitialNeurons(Cx_Id,Generation,SpecCon,[N_Id|N_Ids], Sensors,Actuator)->
        case random:uniform() >= 0.5 of
            true ->
                S = lists:nth(random:uniform(length(Sensors)),Sensors),
                U_Sensors = lists:keyreplace(S#sensor.id, 2, Sensors,
S#sensor{fanout_ids=[N_Id|S#sensor.fanout_ids]}),
                Input_Specs = [{S#sensor.id,S#sensor.vl}];
            false ->
                U_Sensors = [S#sensor{fanout_ids=[N_Id|S#sensor.fanout_ids]} || S <-
Sensors],
                Input_Specs=[{S#sensor.id,S#sensor.vl}||S<-Sensors]
        end,
        construct_Neuron(Cx_Id,Generation,SpecCon,N_Id,Input_Specs, [Actuator#actuator.id]),
        construct_InitialNeurons(Cx_Id,Generation,SpecCon,N_Ids, U_Sensors,Actuator);
    construct_InitialNeurons(_Cx_Id,_Generation,_SpecCon,[],Sensors,_Actuator)->
        Sensors.
```

%construct_InitialNeurons/6 accepts the list of sensors and a single actuator, connects each neuron to the actuator, and randomly chooses whether to connect it from all the sensors or a subset of the given sensors. Once all the neurons have been connected to the actuator and from the sensors, the updated sensors whose fanout_ids have been updated with the ids of the neurons, are returned to the caller.

```
construct_Neuron(Cx_Id,Generation,SpecCon,N_Id,Input_Specs,Output_Ids)->
        Input_IdPs = create_InputIdPs(Input_Specs,[]),
        Neuron=#neuron{
            id=N_Id,
            cx_id = Cx_Id,
            generation=Generation,
            af=generate_NeuronAF(SpecCon#constraint.neural_afs),
            input_idps=Input_IdPs,
            output_ids=Output_Ids,
            ro_ids = calculate_ROIds(N_Id,Output_Ids,[])
        },
        write(Neuron).

create_InputIdPs([{Input_Id,Input_VL}|Input_IdPs],Acc) ->
        Weights = create_NeuralWeights(Input_VL,[]),
        create_InputIdPs(Input_IdPs,[{Input_Id,Weights}|Acc]);
create_InputIdPs([],Acc)->
        Acc.

create_NeuralWeights(0,Acc) ->
        Acc;
create_NeuralWeights(Index,Acc) ->
        W = random:uniform()-0.5,
        create_NeuralWeights(Index-1,[W|Acc]).
```
%Each neuron record is composed by the construct_Neuron/6 function. The construct_Neuron/6 creates the Input list from the tuples [{Id,Weights}...] using the vector lengths specified in the Input_Specs list. The create_InputIdPs/3 function uses create_NeuralWeights/2 to generate the random weights in the range of -0.5 to 0.5. The activation function that the neuron uses is chosen randomly from the neural_afs list within the constraint record passed to the construct_Neuron/6 function. construct_Neuron uses calculate_ROIds/3 to extract the list of recursive connection ids from the Output_Ids passed to it. Once the neuron record is filled in, it is saved to database.

```
generate_NeuronAF(Activation_Functions)->
        case Activation_Functions of
            [] ->
                    tanh;
            Other ->
                    lists:nth(random:uniform(length(Other)),Other)
```

```
                end.
%The generate_NeuronAF/1 accepts a list of activation function tags, and returns a randomly
chosen one. If an empty list was passed as the parameter, the function returns the standard tanh
tag.

            calculate_ROIds(Self_Id,[Output_Id|Ids],Acc)->
                case Output_Id of
                    {_,actuator} ->
                        calculate_ROIds(Self_Id,Ids,Acc);
                    Output_Id ->
                        {{TLI,_},_NodeType} = Self_Id,
                        {{LI,_},_} = Output_Id,
                        case LI =< TLI of
                            true ->
                                calculate_ROIds(Self_Id,Ids,[Output_Id|Acc]);
                            false ->
                                calculate_ROIds(Self_Id,Ids,Acc)
                        end
                end;
            calculate_ROIds(_Self_Id,[],Acc)->
                lists:reverse(Acc).
%The function calculate_ROIds/3 accepts as input the Self_Id of the neuron, and the Out-
put_Ids of the elements the neuron connects to. Since each element specifies its type and, in the
case of neurons, the layer index it belongs to, the function checks if the Output_Id's layer index
is lower than the Self_Id's layer index. If it is, the output connection is recursive and the Out-
put_Id is added to the recursive output list. Once the recursive connection ids have been ex-
tracted from the Output_Ids, the extracted id list is returned to the caller.

                generate_ids(0,Acc) ->
                    Acc;
                generate_ids(Index,Acc)->
                    Id = generate_UniqueId(),
                    generate_ids(Index-1,[Id|Acc]).

                generate_UniqueId()->
                    {MegaSeconds,Seconds,MicroSeconds} = now(),
                    1/(MegaSeconds*1000000 + Seconds + MicroSeconds/1000000).
%The generate_UniqueId/0 creates a unique Id using current time, the Id is a floating point val-
ue. The generate_ids/2 function creates a list of unique Ids.

create_fingerprint(Agent_Id)->
    A = read({agent,Agent_Id}),
    Cx = read({cortex,A#agent.cx_id}),
    GeneralizedSensors = [(read({sensor,S_Id}))#sensor{id=undefined,cx_id=undefined} ||
S_Id<-Cx#cortex.sensor_ids],
```

```
    GeneralizedActuators = [(read({sensor,A_Id}))#actuator{id=undefined,cx_id=undefined} ||
A_Id<-Cx#cortex.actuator_ids],
    GeneralizedPattern = [{LayerIndex,length(LNIds)}||{LayerIndex,LNIds}<-A#agent.pattern],
    GeneralizedEvoHist = generalize_EvoHist(A#agent.evo_hist,[]),
    {GeneralizedPattern,GeneralizedEvoHist,GeneralizedSensors,GeneralizedActuators}.
```

%create_fingerprint/1 calculates the fingerprint of the agent, where the fingerprint is just a tuple of the various general features of the NN based system, a list of features that play some role in distinguishing its genotype's general properties from those of other NN systems. Here, the fingerprint is composed of the generalized pattern (pattern minus the unique ids), generalized evolutionary history (evolutionary history minus the unique ids of the elements), a generalized sensor set, and a generalized actuator set of the agent in question.

```
generalize_EvoHist([{MO,{{ALI,_AUId},AType},{{BLI,_BUId},BType}, {{CLI,_CUId},
CType}}|EvoHist],Acc)->
    generalize_EvoHist(EvoHist,[{MO,{ALI,AType},{BLI,BType}, {CLI,CType}}|Acc]);
generalize_EvoHist([{MO,{{ALI,_AUId},AType},{{BLI,_BUId},BType}}|EvoHist],Acc)->
    generalize_EvoHist(EvoHist,[{MO,{ALI,AType},{BLI,BType}}|Acc]);
generalize_EvoHist([{MO,{{ALI,_AUId},AType}}|EvoHist],Acc)->
    generalize_EvoHist(EvoHist,[{MO,{ALI,AType}}|Acc]);
generalize_EvoHist([],Acc)->
    lists:reverse(Acc).
```

%generalize_EvoHist/2 generalizes the evolutionary history tuples by removing the unique element ids. Two neurons which are using exactly the same activation function, located in exactly the same layer, and using exactly the same synaptic weights, will still have different unique ids. Thus, these ids must be removed to produce a more general set of tuples. There are 3 types of tuples in evo_hist list, with 3, 2 and 1 element ids. Once the evolutionary history list is generalized, it is returned to the caller.

```
read(TnK)->
    case mnesia:read(TnK) of
        [] ->
                undefined;
        [R] ->
                R
    end.
```

%read/1 accepts the tuple composed of a table name and a key: {TableName,Key}, which it then uses to read from the mnesia database and return the record or the atom: undefined, to the caller.

```
write(R)->
    mnesia:write(R).
```

% write/1 accepts a record and writes it to the database

```
delete(TnK)->
    mnesia:delete(TnK).
```

% delete/1 accepts the parameter tuple: {TableName,Key}, and deletes the associated record
from the table.

```
print(Agent_Id)->
  A = read({agent,Agent_Id}),
  Cx = read({cortex,A#agent.cx_id}),
  io:format("~p~n",[A]),
  io:format("~p~n",[Cx]),
  [io:format("~p~n",[read({sensor,Id})]) || Id <- Cx#cortex.sensor_ids],
  [io:format("~p~n",[read({neuron,Id})]) || Id <- Cx#cortex.neuron_ids],
  [io:format("~p~n",[read({actuator,Id})]) || Id <- Cx#cortex.actuator_ids].
```
%print/1 accepts an agent's id, finds all the elements composing the agent in question, and
prints out the complete genotype of the agent.

```
delete_Agent(Agent_Id)->
  A = read({agent,Agent_Id}),
  Cx = read({cortex,A#agent.cx_id}),
  [delete({neuron,Id}) || Id <- Cx#cortex.neuron_ids],
  [delete({sensor,Id}) || Id <- Cx#cortex.sensor_ids],
  [delete({actuator,Id}) || Id <- Cx#cortex.actuator_ids],
  delete({cortex,A#agent.cx_id}),
  delete({agent,Agent_Id}).
```
%delete_Agent/1 accepts the id of an agent, and then deletes that agent's genotype. This func-
tion assumes that the id of the agent will be removed from the specie's agent_ids list, and any
other needed clean up procedure will be performed by the calling function.

```
delete_Agent(Agent_Id,safe)->
  F = fun()->
        A = genotype:read({agent,Agent_Id}),
        S = genotype:read({specie,A#agent.specie_id}),
        Agent_Ids = S#specie.agent_ids,
        write(S#specie{agent_ids = lists:delete(Agent_Id,Agent_Ids)}),
        delete_Agent(Agent_Id)
  end,
  Result=mnesia:transaction(F),
  io:format("delete_agent(Agent_Id,safe):~p Result:~p~n",[Agent_Id,Result]).
```
%delete_Agent/2 accepts the id of an agent, and then deletes that agent's genotype, but ensures
that the species to which the agent belongs, has its agent_ids element updated. Unlike de-
lete_Agent/1, this function updates the species' record.

```
clone_Agent(Agent_Id,CloneAgent_Id)->
  F = fun()->
        A = read({agent,Agent_Id}),
        Cx = read({cortex,A#agent.cx_id}),
        IdsNCloneIds = ets:new(idsNcloneids,[set,private]),
```

```
            ets:insert(IdsNCloneIds,{threshold,threshold}),
            ets:insert(IdsNCloneIds,{Agent_Id,CloneAgent_Id}),
            [CloneCx_Id] = map_ids(IdsNCloneIds,[A#agent.cx_id],[]),
            CloneN_Ids = map_ids(IdsNCloneIds,Cx#cortex.neuron_ids,[]),
            CloneS_Ids = map_ids(IdsNCloneIds,Cx#cortex.sensor_ids,[]),
            CloneA_Ids = map_ids(IdsNCloneIds,Cx#cortex.actuator_ids,[]),
            clone_neurons(IdsNCloneIds,Cx#cortex.neuron_ids),
            clone_sensors(IdsNCloneIds,Cx#cortex.sensor_ids),
            clone_actuators(IdsNCloneIds,Cx#cortex.actuator_ids),

            write(Cx#cortex{
                    id = CloneCx_Id,
                    agent_id = CloneAgent_Id,
                    sensor_ids = CloneS_Ids,
                    actuator_ids = CloneA_Ids,
                    neuron_ids = CloneN_Ids
            }),
            write(A#agent{
                    id = CloneAgent_Id ,
                    cx_id = CloneCx_Id
            }),
            ets:delete(IdsNCloneIds)
    end,
    mnesia:transaction(F).
```
%clone_Agent/2 accepts Agent_Id and CloneAgent_Id as parameters, and then clones the agent, giving the clone the CloneAgent_Id. The function first creates an ETS table to which it writes the ids of all the elements of the genotype and their correspondingly generated clone ids. Once all ids and clone ids have been generated, the function begins to clone the actual elements. clone_Agent/2 first clones the neurons using clone_neurons/2, then the sensors using clone_sensors/2, and finally the actuators using clone_actuators. Once these elements are cloned, the function writes to database the clone versions of the cortex and the agent records, by writing to database the original records with updated clone ids.

```
    map_ids(TableName,[Id|Ids],Acc)->
        CloneId=case Id of
                {{LayerIndex,_NumId},Type}->%maps neuron and cortex ids.
                    {{LayerIndex,generate_UniqueId()},Type};
                {_NumId,Type}->%maps sensor and actuator ids.
                    {generate_UniqueId(),Type}
        end,
        ets:insert(TableName,{Id,CloneId}),
        map_ids(TableName,Ids,[CloneId|Acc]);
    map_ids(_TableName,[],Acc)->
        Acc.
```

%map_ids/3 accepts the name of the ets table, and a list of ids as parameters. It then goes through every id and creates a clone version of the id by generating a new unique id. The function is able to generate new id structures for neuron, cortex, sensor, and actuator id types.

```
clone_sensors(TableName,[S_Id|S_Ids])->
        S = read({sensor,S_Id}),
        CloneS_Id = ets:lookup_element(TableName,S_Id,2),
        CloneCx_Id = ets:lookup_element(TableName,S#sensor.cx_id,2),
        CloneFanout_Ids =[ets:lookup_element(TableName,Fanout_Id,2)|| Fanout_Id <-
S#sensor.fanout_ids],
        write(S#sensor{
                id = CloneS_Id,
                cx_id = CloneCx_Id,
                fanout_ids = CloneFanout_Ids
        }),
        clone_sensors(TableName,S_Ids);
  clone_sensors(_TableName,[])->
        done.
```

%clone_sensors/2 accepts as input the name of the ets table and the list of sensor ids. It then goes through every sensor id, reads the sensor from the database, and updates all its ids (id, cx_id, and fanout_ids) from their original values to their clone version values stored in the ets table. Afterwards, the new version of the sensor is written to database, effectively cloning the original sensor.

```
clone_actuators(TableName,[A_Id|A_Ids])->
        A = read({actuator,A_Id}),
        CloneA_Id = ets:lookup_element(TableName,A_Id,2),
        CloneCx_Id = ets:lookup_element(TableName,A#actuator.cx_id,2),
        CloneFanin_Ids =[ets:lookup_element(TableName,Fanin_Id,2)|| Fanin_Id <-
A#actuator.fanin_ids],
        write(A#actuator{
                id = CloneA_Id,
                cx_id = CloneCx_Id,
                fanin_ids = CloneFanin_Ids
        }),
        clone_actuators(TableName,A_Ids);
  clone_actuators(_TableName,[])->
        done.
```

%clone_actuators/2 accepts as input the name of the ets table and the list of actuator ids. It then goes through every actuator id, reads the actuator from the database, and updates all its ids (id, cx_id, and fanin_ids) from their original values to their clone version values stored in the ets table. Afterwards, the new version of the actuator is written to database, effectively cloning the original actuator.

```
clone_neurons(TableName,[N_Id|N_Ids])->
```

```
            N = read({neuron,N_Id}),
            CloneN_Id = ets:lookup_element(TableName,N_Id,2),
            CloneCx_Id = ets:lookup_element(TableName,N#neuron.cx_id,2),
            CloneInput_IdPs = [{ets:lookup_element(TableName,I_Id,2),Weights}||
{I_Id,Weights} <- N#neuron.input_idps],
            CloneOutput_Ids = [ets:lookup_element(TableName,O_Id,2)|| O_Id <-
N#neuron.output_ids],
            CloneRO_Ids =[ets:lookup_element(TableName,RO_Id,2)|| RO_Id <-
N#neuron.ro_ids],
         write(N#neuron{
                id = CloneN_Id,
                cx_id = CloneCx_Id,
                input_idps = CloneInput_IdPs,
                output_ids = CloneOutput_Ids,
                ro_ids = CloneRO_Ids
         }),
         clone_neurons(TableName,N_Ids);
    clone_neurons(_TableName,[])->
         done.
```

%clone_neuron/2 accepts as input the name of the ets table and the list of neuron ids. It then goes through every neuron id, reads the neuron from the database, and updates all its ids (id, cx_id, output_ids, ro_ids, and input_idps) from their original values to their clone version values stored in the ets table. Once everything is updated, the new (clone) version of the neuron is written to database.

```
test()->
    Specie_Id = test,
    Agent_Id = test,
    CloneAgent_Id = test_clone,
    SpecCon = #constraint{},
    F = fun()->
            construct_Agent(Specie_Id,Agent_Id,SpecCon),
            clone_Agent(Specie_Id,CloneAgent_Id),
            print(Agent_Id),
            print(CloneAgent_Id),
            delete_Agent(Agent_Id) ,
            delete_Agent(CloneAgent_Id)
    end,
    mnesia:transaction(F).
```

%test/0 performs a test of the standard functions of the genotype module, by first creating a new agent, then cloning that agent, then printing the genotype of the original agent and its clone, and then finally deleting both of these agents.

```
create_test()->
    Specie_Id = test,
```

```
    Agent_Id = test,
    SpecCon = #constraint{},
    F = fun()->
            case genotype:read({agent,test}) of
                    undefined ->
                            construct_Agent(Specie_Id,Agent_Id,SpecCon),
                            print(Agent_Id);
                    _ ->
                            delete_Agent(Agent_Id),
                            construct_Agent(Specie_Id,Agent_Id,SpecCon),
                            print(Agent_Id)
            end
    end,
    mnesia:transaction(F).
%create_test/0 creates a simple NN based agent using the default constraint record. The func-
tion first checks if an agent with the id 'test' already exists, if it does, the function deletes that
agent and creates a new one. Otherwise, the function just creates a brand new agent with the id
'test'.
```

Having now updated the genotype, let us compile and test it using the test/0 and create_test/0 functions. Since we already compiled and tested polis in the previous section, at this point we already have a mnesia database (if you have not yet compiled polis and ran polis:create(), do so before testing the genotype module). To test the genotype module, we first take the polis online, then run the genotype:test() function, and then take the polis offline, as is shown next:

```
1> polis:start().
Parameters:{[],[]}
******** Polis: ##MATHEMA## is now online.
{ok,<0.34.0>}
2> genotype:test().
{agent,test,0,undefined,test,
    {{origin,7.522621162363539e-10},cortex},
    {[{0,1}],
    [],
    [{sensor,undefined,xor_GetInput,undefined,
            {private,xor_sim},
            2,
            [{{0,7.522621162361355e-10},neuron}],
            undefined}],
    [{actuator,undefined,xor_SendOutput,undefined,
            {private,xor_sim},
            1,
            [{{0,7.522621162361355e-10},neuron}],
            undefined}]},
```

        {constraint,xor_mimic,[tanh,cos,gauss,abs]},
        [],undefined,0,
        [{0,[{{0,7.522621162361355e-10},neuron}]}]]}
{cortex,{{origin,7.522621162363539e-10},cortex},
        test,
        [{{0,7.522621162361355e-10},neuron}],
        [{{-1,7.522621162361434e-10},sensor}],
        [{{1,7.522621162361411e-10},actuator}]}
{sensor,{{-1,7.522621162361434e-10},sensor},
        xor_GetInput,
        {{origin,7.522621162363539e-10},cortex},
        {private,xor_sim},
        2,
        [{{0,7.522621162361355e-10},neuron}],
        undefined}
{neuron,{{0,7.522621162361355e-10},neuron},
        0,
        {{origin,7.522621162363539e-10},cortex},
        tanh,
        [{{{-1,7.522621162361434e-10},sensor},
          [-0.20275596630526205,0.14421756025063392]}],
        [{{1,7.522621162361411e-10},actuator}],
        []}
{actuator,{{1,7.522621162361411e-10},actuator},
        xor_SendOutput,
        {{origin,7.522621162363539e-10},cortex},
        {private,xor_sim},
        1,
        [{{0,7.522621162361355e-10},neuron}],
        undefined}
{agent,test_clone,0,undefined,test,
        {{origin,7.522621162358474e-10},cortex},
        {[{0,1}],
        [],
        [{sensor,undefined,xor_GetInput,undefined,
              {private,xor_sim},
              2,
              [{{0,7.522621162361355e-10},neuron}],
              undefined}],
        [{actuator,undefined,xor_SendOutput,undefined,
              {private,xor_sim},
              1,
              [{{0,7.522621162361355e-10},neuron}],
              undefined}]},
        {constraint,xor_mimic,[tanh,cos,gauss,abs]},

```
[],undefined,0,
    [{0,[{{0,7.522621162361355e-10},neuron}]}]]}

...

{atomic,ok}
3> polis:stop().
ok
******** Polis: ##MATHEMA## is now offline, terminated with reason:normal
```

It works! Though for the sake of brevity, the above console printout does not show the whole genotype of the *test_clone agent* (shown in boldface), we can still see that there were no errors, and that this test function created, cloned, printed, and then deleted both of the agents.

At some point in the future we might wish to test mutation operators on simple NN system genotypes, for this reason our genotype module also includes the *create_test/0 function*. This function, unlike the test/0 function, creates a default agent genotype with an id: *test*, using the default constraint stored in the records.hrl file. Furthermore, the function first checks whether such a test agent already exists, and if it does, the function deletes the test agent, and creates a brand new one. This function will become very handy when testing and experimenting with mutation operators, since it will allow us to create a simple NN topology, apply mutation operators to it as a test of some functionality, then print the mutated topology for manual analysis, and then recreate the test agent and apply a different set of mutation operators if needed... Being able to create individual NNs to test mutation operators on, and being able to map the test genotype to a phenotype and test the functionality of the same, is essential when developing and advancing a complex system like this. We now test the create_test/0 function by starting the polis, executing the create_test/0 function twice, and then stopping the polis:

```
1> polis:start().
Parameters:{[],[]}
******** Polis: ##MATHEMA## is now online.
{ok,<0.34.0>}
2> genotype:create_test().
{agent,test,0,undefined,test,
    {{origin,7.588472966671075e-10},cortex},
    undefined,
    {constraint,xor_mimic,[tanh,sin,abs]},
    [],undefined,undefined,
    [{0,[{{0,7.588472966664959e-10},neuron}]}]]}
...
{atomic,{atomic,[ok]}}
3> genotype:create_test().
{agent,test,0,undefined,test,
    {{origin,7.588472880658339e-10},cortex},
```

```
undefined,
{constraint,xor_mimic,[tanh,sin,abs]},
[],undefined,undefined,
[{0,[{{0,7.588472880658257e-10},neuron}]}]}
...
4> polis:stop().
******** Polis: ##MATHEMA## is now offline, terminated with reason:normal
ok
```

It works! The create_test/0 created a brand new test agent, and then when the create_test/0 was executed again, it deleted the old test agent, and created a new one. As before, for the sake of brevity, not the whole genotypes that were printed to console are shown, as they are very similar to the one shown in the test/0 function earlier.

Having now developed a genotype module with all the necessary features to support a neuroevolutionary platform, we can move forward and begin working on the genotype mutator module.

8.5 Developing the genotype_mutator

We already have a mechanism used by the exoself to mutate/perturb the synaptic weights during the NN tuning phase. But for a NN to grow, become more complex, and for a population to evolve, we need mutation operators that modify the topologies and architectures of the NN systems belonging to a population. The mutation operators should be able to add new neurons to the NN system, add new sensors, new actuators, and be able to modify other features of the NN based system. By having the ability to modify NN topologies, the evolutionary process can take hold and generate new species (topologically different organisms) within the population, and just as in the biological case, produce ever more complex NN based agents, more adept to their environment, and more fit with regards to the problem they are evolving to solve.

We need to have a set of mutation operators which are flexible enough so that any NN topology A can be turned into a NN topology B, by applying the available mutation operators to the NN system in some sequence. It is only then that our neuroevolutionary system will have the necessary tools and flexibility to evolve any type of NN based system given enough time and the appropriate fitness function.

In this section we will concentrate on developing such a flexible and general set of mutation operators (MOs). The following set of MOs are required by evolution such that it has the ability to do both, complexify and/or prune one NN topology into any other by applying the below listed MOs in some order:

1. **add_bias**:
   Choose a random neuron *A*, check if it has a bias in its weights list, if it does not, add the bias value. If the neuron already has a bias value, do nothing.

2. **remove_bias**:
   Choose a random neuron *A*, check if it has a bias in its weights list, if it does, remove it. If the neuron does not have a bias value, do nothing.

3. **mutate_weights**:
   Choose a random neuron *A*, and perturb each weight in its weight list with a probability of *1/sqrt(length(weights))*, with the perturbation intensity randomly chosen between *-Pi/2* and *Pi/2*.

4. **reset_weights**:
   Choose a random neuron *A*, and reset all its synaptic weights to random values ranging between *-Pi/2* and *Pi/2*.

5. **mutate_af**:
   Choose a random neuron A, and change its activation function to a new random activation function chosen from the *af_list* in the constraint record belonging to the NN.

6. **add_inlink**:
   Choose a random *neuron A*, and an *element B*, and then add a connection from element B (possibly an existing sensor) to neuron A.

7. **add_outlink**:
   Choose a random *neuron A*, and an *element B*, and then add a connection from neuron A to element B (possibly an existing actuator). The difference between this mutation operator and the add_inlink mutation operator, is that in one we choose a random neuron and then choose a random *element from which* we make a connection to the chosen neuron. While in the other we choose a random neuron, and then choose a random *element to which* the neuron makes a connection. The first (add_inlink) is capable of making links to sensors, while the second (add_outlink) is capable of potentially making links to actuators.

8. **add_neuron**:
   Create a new neuron A, giving it a unique id and positioning it in a randomly selected layer of the NN. Then give the neuron A a randomly chosen activation function. Then choose a random neuron B in the NN and connect neuron A's inport to the neuron B's outport. Then choose a random neuron C in the NN and connect neuron A's outport to the neuron C's inport.

9. splice: There are 2 versions of this mutation operator, outsplice, and insplice:

   – **outsplice**: Create a new neuron A with a random activation function. Then choose a random neuron B in the NN. Randomly select neuron B's outport leading to some element C's (neuron or actuator) inport. Then disconnect neuron B from element C, and reconnect them through the newly created neuron A.

   – **insplice**: Create a new neuron A with a random activation function. Then choose a random neuron B in the NN. Randomly select neuron B's inport from some element C's (neuron or sensor) outport. Then disconnect neuron B from element C, and reconnect them through the newly created neuron A. The reason for having an outsplice and an insplice, is that the outsplice can insert a new neuron between some random element and an actuator, while the insplice can insert a new neuron between an element and a sensor.

10. **add_sensorlink**:

Compared to the number of neurons, there are very few sensors, and so the probability of the add_inlink connecting a neuron to a sensor is very low. To increase the probability that the NN connects to a sensor, we can create the add_sensorlink mutation operator. This mutation operator first chooses a random existing sensor A, it then chooses a random neuron B to which A is not yet connected, and then connects A to B.

11. **add_actuatorlink**:

As in add_sensorlink, when compared to the number of neurons, there are very few actuators, and so the probability of the add_outlink connecting a neuron to an actuator is very low. Thus, we can implement the add_actuatorlink to increase the probability of connecting a neuron to an actuator. In this mutation operator, first a random actuator A is chosen which is connected to less neurons than its *vl* element dictates (an incompletely connected actuator). Then a random neuron B is chosen to which the actuator is not yet connected. Then A is connected from B.

12. **remove_sensorlink**:

First a random sensor A is chosen. From the sensor's fanout_ids list, a random neuron id is chosen, and then the sensor is disconnected from the corresponding neuron.

13. **remove_actuatorlink**:

First a random actuator A is chosen. From the actuator's fanin_ids list, a random neuron id is chosen, and then the actuator is disconnected from the corresponding neuron.

14. **add_sensor**:

Choose a random sensor from the sensor list belonging to the NN's morphology, but which is not yet used. Then connect the sensor to a random neuron A in the NN, thus adding a new sensory organ to the NN system.

15. **add_actuator**:

Choose a random actuator from the actuator list belonging to the NN's morphology, but which is not yet used. Then connect a random neuron A in the NN to this actuator, thus adding a new morphological feature to the NN that can be used to interact with the world.

16. **remove_inlink**:

Choose a random neuron A, and disconnect it from a randomly chosen element in its input_idps list.

17. **remove_outlink**:

Choose a random neuron A, and disconnect it from a randomly chosen element in its output_ids list.

18. **remove_neuron**:
Choose a random neuron A in the NN, and remove it from the topology. Then fix the presynaptic neuron B's and postsynaptic neuron C's outports and inports respectively to accommodate the removal of the connection with neuron A.

19. desplice: There are 2 versions of this operator, deoutspolice, and deinsplice:

- **deoutsplice**: Choose a random neuron B in the NN, such that B's outport is connected to an element (neuron or actuator) C through some neuron A. Then delete neuron A and reconnect neuron B and element C directly.
- **deinsplice**: Choose a random neuron B in the NN, such that B's inport is connected to by an element (neuron or sensor) C through some neuron A. Then delete neuron A and connect neuron B and element C directly.

20. **remove_sensor**:
If a NN has more than one sensor, choose a random sensor belonging to the NN, and remove it by first disconnecting it from the neurons it is connected to, and then removing the tuple representing it from the genotype altogether.

21. **remove_actuator**:
If a NN has more than one actuator, choose a random actuator belonging the NN, and remove it by first disconnecting it from the neurons it is connected from, and then removing the tuple representing it from the genotype altogether.

Note that when choosing random neurons to connect to, we do not specify whether that neuron should be in the next layer, or whether that neuron should be in the previous layer. These mutations allow for both, feedforward, and recurrent connections to be formed.

Technically, we do not need every one of these mutation operators, the following list will be enough for a highly versatile complexifying topology and weight evolving artificial neural network (TWEANN) system: mutate_weights, add_bias, remove_bias, mutate_af, add_neuron, splice (just one of them), add_inlink, add_outlink, add_sensorlink, add_actuatorlink, add_sensor, and add_actuator. Note that this combination of MOs can convert any NN topology A into a NN topology B, given that A is contained (smaller, and simpler in a sense) within B. The add_inlink, add_outlink, add_sensorlink, add_actuatorlink mutation operators allow for neurons to form new connections to neurons, sensors and actuators. The add_sensor and add_actuator, can add/integrate the new sensor and actuator programs into the NN system. The add_neuron will add new neurons in parallel with other neurons in a layer, while outsplice will create new layers, increasing the depth of the NN system, and form new connections in series. The weight perturbations will be performed by the exoself, in a separate phase from the topological mutation phase, which will effectively make our system a memetic algorithm based TWEANN. On the other hand, if we also add mutate_weights operator to the mutation phase, and remove the exoself's weight tuning/perturbing ability in its separate phase, then our system will become a standard genetic algorithm based TWEANN.

In this section we will only create these 12 mutation operators. The deletory (except for the remove_bias, which does not delete or simplify a NN, but modifies the processing functionality of the neuron, by biasing and unbiasing its activation function) operators can be added later, because they share very similar logic to their complexifying mutator counterparts. Due to the exoself, we can easily switch between genetic and memetic TWEANN approaches by simply turning the exoself's tuning ability on or off. We can easily implement both, the genetic and the memetic approaches in our system. We will be able to turn the tuning on and off, and see the difference in the TWEANN's efficiency and robustness when using the two different methods.

In the following subsections we will discuss each mutation operator, and develop that operator's source code. Once all the operators have been discussed, and their algorithms implemented, we will put it all together into a single genotype_mutator module.

8.5.1 The Precursor Connection Making and Breaking Functions

Almost every mutation operator that is discussed next, relies on elements being connected and disconnected. For this purpose we create dedicated functions that can link and unlink any two elements. When connecting two elements, there are three possible connection types: a sensor-to-neuron, a neuron-to-neuron, and a neuron-to-actuator. The same for when we are disconnecting one element from another, we can disconnect: a sensor-from-neuron, a neuron-from-neuron, and a neuron-from-actuator.

When we establish a connection from element A to element B, we first use the ids of the connecting elements to deduce which type of connection is going to be made, and then dependent on that, establish the link between the two elements. If element A is a neuron and element B is a neuron, we perform the following set of steps to create a link from the presynaptic Neuron A to the postsynaptic Neuron B:

1. Read neuron A from the database.
2. Add neuron B's id to neuron A's output_ids list, if a connection is recursive, add neuron B's id to the ro_ids list as well.
3. Write the updated neuron A to database.
4. Read neuron B from the database.
5. Append to neuron B's input_idps list a new tuple with neuron A's id, and a new randomly generated weight: {NeuronA_Id,[Weight]}.
6. Write the updated neuron B to database.

If element A is a sensor, and the element B is a neuron, then to create a link from the presynaptic Sensor A to postsynaptic Neuron B, we perform the following set of steps:

1. Read sensor A from the database.
2. Add neuron B's id to sensor A's fanout_ids list.
3. Write the updated sensor A to database.
4. Read neuron B from the database.
5. Append to neuron B's input_idps list a new tuple with sensor A's id, and a weights list of length vl, where vl is the output vector length of sensor A.
6. Write the updated neuron B to database.

Finally, if element A is a neuron, and element B is an actuator, then to create the link From Neuron A to Actuator B, we perform the following steps:

1. Read neuron A from database.
2. Add actuator B's id to neuron A's output_ids list.
3. Write the updated neuron A to database.
4. Read actuator B from database.
5. If the number of neurons connected to the actuator is less than the actuator's vl, then add neuron A's id to actuator B's fanin_ids list. Otherwise exit with error to stop the mutation. This is done to prevent unnecessary connections, since if the actuator can only use a *vl* number of signals as parameters for executing its action function, there is no need to add any more connections to the actuator than that. The calling function can choose an actuator that still has space for connections, or even create a completely new actuator.
6. Write the updated actuator B to database.

The source code for the function that establishes the connection from element A to element B, is shown in the following listing.

Listing 8.4: The implementation of the link_FromElementToElement(Agent_Id, FromElement_Id, ToElement_Id) function.

```
link_FromElementToElement(Agent_Id,From_ElementId,To_ElementId)->
    case {From_ElementId,To_ElementId} of
        {{_FromSId,neuron},{_ToSId,neuron}} ->
            link_FromNeuronToNeuron(Agent_Id,From_ElementId,To_ElementId);
        {{_FromSId,sensor},{_ToSId,neuron}} ->
            link_FromSensorToNeuron(Agent_Id,From_ElementId,To_ElementId);
        {{_FromNId,neuron},{_ToAId,actuator}} ->
            link_FromNeuronToActuator(Agent_Id,From_ElementId,To_ElementId)
    end.
%The function link_FromElementToElement/3 first calculates what type of link is going to be
established (neuron to neuron, sensor to neuron, or neuron to actuator), and then calls the spe-
cific linking function based on that.

link_FromNeuronToNeuron(Agent_Id,From_NeuronId,To_NeuronId)->
    A = genotype:read({agent,Agent_Id}),
    Generation = A#agent.generation,
```

```
%From Part
   FromN = genotype:read({neuron,From_NeuronId}),
   U_FromN = link_FromNeuron(FromN,To_NeuronId,Generation),
   genotype:write(U_FromN),
%To Part
   ToN = genotype:read({neuron,To_NeuronId}),%We read it afterwards, in the case that it's
the same Element. Thus we do not overwrite the earlier changes.
   FromOVL = 1,
   U_ToN = link_ToNeuron(From_NeuronId,FromOVL,ToN,Generation),
   genotype:write(U_ToN).
```

%link_FromNeuronToNeuron/3 establishes a link from neuron with id = From_NeuronId, to a
neuron with an id = To_NeuronId. The function then calls link_FromNeuron/4, which establishes the link on the From_NeuronId's side. The updated neuron associated with the
From_NeuronId is then written to database. To decide how long the weight list that is going to
be added to the To_NeuronId's input_idps should be, the function calculates From_NeuronId's
output vector length. Since the connection is from a neuron, FromOVL is set to 1.
link_ToNeuron/4 is then called, and the link is established on the To_NeuronId's side. Finally,
the updated neuron associated with the To_NeuronId is written to database. The order of reading the FromN and ToN neuron records from the database is important. It is essential that ToN
is read after the U_FromN is written to database, in the case that From_NeuronId and
To_NeuronId refer to the same neuron (a recurrent connection from the neuron to itself). If both
neurons are read at the same time, for example before the links are established, then the link established in the U_FromN will be overwritten when the U_ToN is written to file. Thus, order is
important in this function.

```
   link_FromNeuron(FromN,ToId,Generation)->
          {{FromLI,_},_} = FromN#neuron.id,
          {{ToLI,_},_} = To_NeuronId,
          FromOutput_Ids = FromN#neuron.output_ids,
          FromRO_Ids = FromN#neuron.ro_ids,
          case lists:member(ToId, FromOutput_Ids) of
                 true ->
                         exit("******** ERROR:add_NeuronO[cannot add O_Id to Neuron]: ~p
already a member of ~p~n",[ToId,FromN#neuron.id]);
                 false ->
                         {U_FromOutput_Ids,U_FromRO_Ids} = case FromLI >= ToLI of
                             true ->
                                     {[ToId|FromOutput_Ids],[ToId|FromRO_Ids]};
                             false ->
                                     {[ToId|FromOutput_Ids],FromRO_Ids}
                         end,
                         FromN#neuron{
                             output_ids = U_FromOutput_Ids,
                             ro_ids = U_FromRO_Ids,
                             generation = Generation
```

```
                    }
        end.
```
%link_FromNeuron/4 updates the record of the neuron from which the link is being created. FromN is the record of the neuron from which the link/connection emanates, and ToId is the id of the element to which the link is headed towards. The function extracts the layer index of the neuron FromN, and the layer index of the element with the id ToId. Then the two layer indexes are compared, and the ToId is either added only to the FromN's output_ids list, or if the connection is recursive, when ToLayerIndex =< FromLayerIndex, it is added to output_ids and ro_ids lists. The FromN's generation is updated to the value Generation, which is the current, most recent generation, since this neuron has just been modified. Finally, the updated neuron record is returned to the caller. If ToId, which is the id of the element to which the connection is being established, is already a member of the FromN's output_ids list, then the function exits with error.

```
    link_ToNeuron(FromId,FromOVL,ToN,Generation)->
            ToInput_IdPs = ToN#neuron.input_idps,
            case lists:keymember(FromId, 1, ToInput_IdPs) of
                true ->
                        exit("ERROR:add_NeuronI::[cannot add I_Id]: ~p already a member of
~p~n",[FromId,ToN#neuron.id]);
                false ->
                        U_ToInput_IdPs = [{FromId, geno-
type:create_NeuralWeights(FromOVL,[])}|ToInput_IdPs],
                        ToN#neuron{
                                input_idps = U_ToInput_IdPs,
                                generation = Generation
                        }
        end.
```
%link_ToNeuron/4 updates the record of ToN, so that it is prepared to receive a connection from the element FromId. The link emanates from element with the id FromId, whose output vector length is FromOVL, and the connection is made to the neuron ToN, the record which is updated in this function. The ToN's input_idps is updated with the tuple {FromId, [W_1... W_FromOVL]}, then the neuron's generation is updated to Generation (the current, most recent generation), and the updated ToN's record is returned to the caller. If FromId is already part of the ToN's input_idps list, which means that the link already exists between the neuron ToN, and element FromId, then the function exits with an error.

```
link_FromSensorToNeuron(Agent_Id,From_SensorId,To_NeuronId)->
    A = genotype:read({agent,Agent_Id}),
    Generation = A#agent.generation,
%From Part
    FromS = genotype:read({sensor,From_SensorId}),
    U_FromS = link_FromSensor(FromS,To_NeuronId),
    genotype:write(U_FromS),
%To Part
```

```
ToN = genotype:read({neuron,To_NeuronId}),
FromOVL = FromS#sensor.vl,
U_ToN = link_ToNeuron(From_SensorId,FromOVL,ToN,Generation),
genotype:write(U_ToN).
```

%The function link_FromSensorToNeuron/3 establishes a connection from the sensor with id From_SensorId, to the neuron with id To_NeuronId. First the sensor record is updated with the connection details using the function link_FromSensor, and the updated sensor record is written to database. Then the record of the neuron to which the link is being established is updated using the function link_ToNeuron/4, after which the updated neuron is written to database.

```
link_FromSensor(FromS,ToId)->
        FromFanout_Ids = FromS#sensor.fanout_ids,
        case lists:member(ToId, FromFanout_Ids) of
                true ->
                        exit("******** ERROR:link_FromSensor[cannot add ToId to Sensor]:
~p already a member of ~p~n",[ToId,FromS#sensor.id]);
                false ->
                        FromS#sensor{fanout_ids = [ToId|FromFanout_Ids]}
        end.
```

%The function link_FromSensor/2 updates the record of the sensor FromS, from whom the link emanates towards the element with id ToId. First the function ensures that there is no connection that is already established between FromS and ToId, if a connection between these two elements already exists, then the function exits with error. If there is no connection between the two elements, then ToId is added to the sensor's fanout_ids list, and the updated record of the sensor is returned to the caller.

```
link_FromNeuronToActuator(Agent_Id,From_NeuronId,To_ActuatorId)->
    A = genotype:read({agent,Agent_Id}),
    Generation = A#agent.generation,
%From Part
    FromN = genotype:read({neuron,From_NeuronId}),
    U_FromN = link_FromNeuron(FromN,To_ActuatorId,Generation),
    genotype:write(U_FromN),
%To Part
    ToA = genotype:read({actuator,To_ActuatorId}),
    Fanin_Ids = ToA#actuator.fanin_ids,
    case length(Fanin_Ids) >= ToA#actuator.vl of
            true ->
                    exit("******** ERROR:link_FromNeuronToActuator:: Actuator already fully
connected");
            false ->
                    U_Fanin_Ids = [From_NeuronId|Fanin_Ids],
                    genotype:write(ToA#actuator{fanin_ids = U_Fanin_Ids})
    end.
```

%The function Link_FromNeuronToActuator/4 establishes a link emanating from the neuron with an id From_NeuronId, to an actuator with the id To_ActuatorId. First the From_NeuronId's record is updated using the function link_FromNeuron/3, after which the updated neuron record is written to database. Then the function checks whether the actuator to which the neuron is establishing the link, still has space for that link (length(Fanin_Ids) is less than the actuator's vector length, vl). If there is no more room, then the function exits with error, if there is room, then the actuator's fanin_ids list is updated by appending to it the id of the neuron's id. Finally, then the updated actuator is written to database.

Though at this point our neuroevolutionary system will only perform mutations that add to the NN system's topology, the splice mutation operator does require a function that disconnects one element from another. For this reason, we also create the functions needed to cut the links between two elements. As before, there are three types of links that exist and can be cut: 1. From Element A and To Element B, where A & B are both neurons, 2. From Element A is a sensor, and To Element B is a neuron, and finally 3. From Element A is a neuron and To Element B is an Actuator. The following listing shows the implementation of the functions that cut the link between some "From Element A" and "To Element B".

Listing 8.5: The cutlink_FromElementToElement(Agent_Id,FromElement_Id,ToElement_Id) function.

```
cutlink_FromElementToElement(Agent_Id,From_ElementId,To_ElementId)->
    case {From_ElementId,To_ElementId} of
        {{_FromId,neuron},{_ToId,neuron}} ->
            cutlink_FromNeuronToNeuron(Agent_Id,From_ElementId,To_ElementId);
        {{_FromId,sensor},{_ToId,neuron}} ->
            cutlink_FromSensorToNeuron(Agent_Id,From_ElementId,To_ElementId);
        {{_FromId,neuron},{_ToId,actuator}} ->
            cutlink_FromNeuronToActuator(Agent_Id,From_ElementId,To_ElementId)
    end.
%cutlink_FromElementToElement/3 first checks which of the three types of connections exists
between From_ElementId and To_ElementId (neuron to neuron, sensor to neuron, or neuron to
actuator), and then disconnects the two elements using one of the three specialized cutlink_...
functions.

cutlink_FromNeuronToNeuron(Agent_Id,From_NeuronId,To_NeuronId)->
    A = genotype:read({agent,Agent_Id}),
    Generation = A#agent.generation,
%From Part
    FromN = genotype:read({neuron,From_NeuronId}),
    U_FromN = cutlink_FromNeuron(FromN,To_NeuronId,Generation),
    genotype:write(U_FromN),
%To Part
    ToN = genotype:read({neuron,To_NeuronId}),
```

```
      U_ToN = cutlink_ToNeuron(From_NeuronId,ToN,Generation),
      genotype:write(U_ToN).
```
%The cutlink_FromNeuronToNeuron/3 function disconnects the connection from the From_NeuronId to the To_NeuronId. The function first disconnects the neuron associated with From_NeuronId by calling the cutlink_FromNeuron/3, and then writes to database the updated neuron record. The function then disconnects the neuron associated with the To_NeuronId from the connection using the cutlink_ToNeuron/3, and writes to database the updated ToN record. If the From_NeuronId and the To_NeuronId are ids of the same neuron, then it is important to first write U_FromN to database, before reading the ToN neuron from the database, so as not to lose the update made by the cutlink_FromNeuron/3, before reading the updated neuron from the database and calling the cutlink_ToNeuron. Thus, this order of reading and writing the neurons from the database is essential to cover the corner cases.

```
   cutlink_FromNeuron(FromN,ToId,Generation)->
      FromOutput_Ids = FromN#neuron.output_ids,
      FromRO_Ids = FromN#neuron.ro_ids,
      case lists:member(ToId, FromOutput_Ids) of
            true ->
                  U_FromOutput_Ids = FromOutput_Ids--[ToId],
                  U_FromRO_Ids = FromRO_Ids--[ToId],%Does nothing if not recursive.
                  FromN#neuron{
                        output_ids = U_FromOutput_Ids,
                        ro_ids = U_FromRO_Ids,
                        generation = Generation};
            false ->
                  exit("ERROR::cutlink_FromNeuron [cannot remove O_Id]: ~p not a
member of ~p~n",[ToId,FromN#neuron.id])
      end.
```
%cutlink_FromNeuron/3 cuts the connection on the FromNeuron (FromN) side. The function first checks if the ToId is a member of the output_ids list. If it's not, then the function exits with an error. If the ToId is a member of the output_ids list, then the function removes the ToId from the FromOutput_Ids list and from the FromRO_Ids list. Even if the ToId is not a recursive connection, we still try to remove it from ro_ids list, in which case the result returns the original FromRO_Ids, and no change is made to it. Once the lists are updated, the updated neuron record of FromN is returned to the caller.

```
   cutlink_ToNeuron(FromId,ToN,Generation)->
      ToInput_IdPs = ToN#neuron.input_idps,
      case lists:keymember(FromId, 1, ToInput_IdPs) of
            true ->
                  U_ToInput_IdPs = lists:keydelete(FromId,1,ToInput_IdPs),
                  ToN#neuron{
                        input_idps = U_ToInput_IdPs,
                        generation = Generation};
            false ->
```

```
                     exit("ERROR[cannot remove I_Id]: ~p not a member of
~p~n",[FromId,ToN#neuron.id])
        end.
```
%cutlink_ToNeuron/3 cuts the connection on the ToNeuron (ToN) side. The function first checks if the FromId is a member of the ToN's input_idps list, if it's not, then the function exits with error. If FromId is a member, then that tuple is removed from the ToInput_IdPs list, and the updated ToN record is returned to the caller.

```
cutlink_FromSensorToNeuron(Agent_Id,From_SensorId,To_NeuronId)->
    A = genotype:read({agent,Agent_Id}),
    Generation = A#agent.generation,
%From Part
    FromS = genotype:read({sensor,From_SensorId}),
    U_FromS = cutlink_FromSensor(FromS,To_NeuronId,Generation),
    genotype:write(U_FromS),
%To Part
    ToN = genotype:read({neuron,To_NeuronId}),
    U_ToN = cutlink_ToNeuron(From_SensorId,ToN,Generation),
    genotype:write(U_ToN).
```
%The cutlink_FromSensorToNeuron/3 cuts the connection from the From_SensorId to To_NeuronId. The function first cuts the connection on the From_SensorId side using the cutlink_FromSensor/3 function, and writes the updated sensor to database. The function then cuts the connection on the To_NeuronId side using the cutlink_ToNeuron/3 function, and writes the updated neuron record to database.

```
    cutlink_FromSensor(FromS,ToId,Generation)->
            FromFanout_Ids = FromS#sensor.fanout_ids,
            case lists:member(ToId, FromFanout_Ids) of
                    true ->
                            U_FromFanout_Ids = FromFanout_Ids--[ToId],
                            FromS#sensor{
                                    fanout_ids = U_FromFanout_Ids,
                                    generation=Generation};
                    false ->
                            exit("ERROR::cutlink_FromSensor [cannot remove ToId]: ~p not a
member of ~p~n",[ToId,FromS#sensor.id])
            end.
```
%The cutlink_FromSensor/3 function first checks whether ToId is a member of the sensor's FromS fanout_ids list. If it is not, then the function exits with an error. If ToId is a member of FromS's fanout_ids list, then it is removed from the list, and the updated sensor record of FromS is returned to the caller.

```
cutlink_FromNeuronToActuator(Agent_Id,From_NeuronId,To_ActuatorId)->
    A = genotype:read({agent,Agent_Id}),
    Generation = A#agent.generation,
```

```
%From Part
    FromN = genotype:read({neuron,From_NeuronId}),
    U_FromN = cutlink_FromNeuron(FromN,To_ActuatorId,Generation),
    genotype:write(U_FromN),
%To Part
    ToA = genotype:read({actuator,To_ActuatorId}),
    U_ToA = cutlink_ToActuator(From_NeuronId,ToA,Generation),
    genotype:write(U_ToA).
```

%cutlink_FromNeuronToActuator/3 cuts the connection from the From_NeuronId to
To_ActuatorId. The function first cuts the connection on the From_NeuronId side using the
cutlink_FromNeuron/3 function, and writes the updated U_FromN to database. Then the connection on the To_ActuatorId is cut using the cutlink_ToActuator/3 function, after which the
updated actuator record is written to database.

```
    cutlink_ToActuator(FromId,ToA,Generation)->
        ToFanin_Ids = ToA#actuator.fanin_ids,
        case lists:member(FromId, ToFanin_Ids) of
                true ->
                        U_ToFanin_Ids = ToFanin_Ids--[FromId],
                        ToA#actuator{
                                fanin_ids = U_ToFanin_Ids,
                                generation=Generation};
                false ->
                        exit("ERROR::cutlink_ToActuator [cannot remove FromId]: ~p not a
member of ~p~n",[FromId,ToA])
        end.
```

%The cutlink_ToActuator/3 function cuts the connection on the ToActuator's side. The function first checks if the FromId is a member of the actuator ToA's fanin_ids list. If it is not, the
function exits with an error. If FromId is a member of the actuator's fanin_ids list, then the id is
removed from the list, and the updated actuator record is returned to the caller.

8.5.2 mutate_weights

This is one of the simplest mutation operators. We first access the *cx_id* from
the agent's record. After reading the cortex tuple from the database, we then
choose a random id from the neuron_ids list, and using this id, read the neuron
record from the database. Once we have the record, we access the neuron's *in-
put_idps* list. Then calculate the total number of weights belonging to the neuron
by adding the weight list lengths of each *idp*. We will have the probability of a
weight in the input_idps list being mutated, set to *1/sqrt(tot_weights)*. Once the
mutation probability has been calculated, we go through every weight in the in-
put_idps list, and mutate it with the probability of the calculated mutation probability. Thus on average, a total of *(1/sqrt(tot_weights))*tot_weights* number of

weights in the list will be perturbed/mutated, sometimes less, and sometimes more. We will also set the weight perturbation intensity to be between $-Pi$ and Pi. Once the weights have been perturbed, we write the updated neuron record back to mnesia with its updated (perturbed) input_idps. The code for this mutation operator is shown in the following listing.

Listing – 8.6: The implementation of the mutate_weights mutation operator.

```
mutate_weights(Agent_Id)->
   A = genotype:read({agent,Agent_Id}),
   Cx_Id = A#agent.cx_id,
   Cx = genotype:read({cortex,Cx_Id}),
   N_Ids = Cx#cortex.neuron_ids,

   N_Id = lists:nth(random:uniform(length(N_Ids)),N_Ids),
   N = genotype:read({neuron,N_Id}),
   Input_IdPs = N#neuron.input_idps,
   U_Input_IdPs = perturb_IdPs(Input_IdPs),
   U_N = N#neuron{input_idps = U_Input_IdPs},
   EvoHist = A#agent.evo_hist,
   U_EvoHist = [{mutate_weights,N_Id}|EvoHist],
   U_A = A#agent{evo_hist = U_EvoHist},
   genotype:write(U_N),
   genotype:write(U_A).
```

%The mutate_weights/1 function accepts the Agent_Id parameter, extracts the NN's cortex, and then chooses a random neuron belonging to the NN with a uniform distribution probability. Then the neuron's input_idps list is extracted, and the function perturb_IdPs/1 is used to perturb/mutate the weights. Once the Input_IdPs have been perturbed, the agent's evolutionary history: EvoHist, is updated to include the successfully applied mutate_weights mutation operator. Then the updated Agent and the updated neuron are written back to database.

```
   perturb_IdPs(Input_IdPs)->
        Tot_Weights=lists:sum([length(Weights) || {_Input_Id,Weights}<-Input_IdPs]),
        MP = 1/math:sqrt(Tot_Weights),
        perturb_IdPs(MP,Input_IdPs,[]).
   perturb_IdPs(MP,[{Input_Id,Weights}|Input_IdPs],Acc)->
        U_Weights = perturb_weights(MP,Weights,[]),
        perturb_IdPs(MP,Input_IdPs,[{Input_Id,U_Weights}|Acc]);
   perturb_IdPs(_MP,[],Acc)->
        lists:reverse(Acc).
```

%perturb_IdPs/1 accepts the Input_IdPs list of format: [{Id,Weights}...], calculates the total number of weights in the Input_IdPs, and then calculates the mutation probability MP, using the equation: 1/sqrt(Tot_Weights). Once the mutation probability is calculated, each weight in the Input_IdPs list has a chance of MP to be perturbed/mutated. Once all the weights in the Input_IdPs list had a chance of being perturbed, the updated Input_IdPs is returned to the caller.

```
perturb_weights(MP,[W|Weights],Acc)->
    U_W = case random:uniform() < MP of
        true->
            sat((random:uniform()-0.5)*?DELTA_MULTIPLIER+W,-
?SAT_LIMIT,?SAT_LIMIT);
        false ->
            W
    end,
    perturb_weights(MP,Weights,[U_W|Acc]);
perturb_weights(_MP,[],Acc)->
    lists:reverse(Acc).
```
%perturb_weights/3 is called with the mutation probability MP, a weights list, and an empty list
[] to be used as an accumulator. The function goes through every weight, where every weight
has a chance of MP to be mutated/perturbed. The perturbations have a random intensity between -Pi and Pi. Once all the weights in the weights list had a chance of being perturbed, the
updated weights list is reversed back to its original order, and returned back to the caller.

```
sat(Val,Min,Max)->
    if
        Val < Min -> Min;
        Val > Max -> Max;
        true -> Val
    end.
```
%The sat/3 function calculates whether Val is between Min and Max. If it is, then Val is returned as is. If Val is less than Min, then Min is returned. If Val is greater than Max, then Max
is returned.

8.5.3 add_bias & remove_bias

These mutation operators are applied to a randomly chosen neuron in a NN.
First we select a random neuron id from neuron_ids list, then read the neuron
record, and then search the input_idps to see if it already has a *bias* value. If
input_idps has a bias, we exit the mutation with an error, and try another mutation.
If the input_idps list does not yet use a bias, we append the bias tuple to the list's
end. The remove_bias mutation operator is very similar to the add_bias, but uses
the lists:keydelete/3 to remove the bias if one is present in the input_idps list of a
randomly chosen neuron. The following listing shows the implementation for
these two mutation operators.

Listing – 8.7: The implementation of the add_bias & remove_bias mutation operators.

```erlang
add_bias(Agent_Id)->
    A = genotype:read({agent,Agent_Id}),
    Cx_Id = A#agent.cx_id,
    Cx = genotype:read({cortex,Cx_Id}),
    N_Ids = Cx#cortex.neuron_ids,
    N_Id = lists:nth(random:uniform(length(N_Ids)),N_Ids),
    Generation = A#agent.generation,

    N = genotype:read({neuron,N_Id}),
    Input_IdPs = N#neuron.input_idps,
    case lists:keymember(bias, 1, Input_IdPs) of
        true ->
            exit("*********ERROR:add_bias:: This Neuron already has a bias part.");
        false ->
            U_Input_IdPs = lists:append(Input_IdPs,[{bias,[random:uniform()-0.5]}]),
            U_N = N#neuron{
                input_idps = U_Input_IdPs,
                generation = Generation},
            EvoHist = A#agent.evo_hist,
            U_EvoHist = [{add_bias,N_Id}|EvoHist],
            U_A = A#agent{evo_hist=U_EvoHist},
            genotype:write(U_N),
            genotype:write(U_A)
    end.
```

%The add_bias/1 function is called with the Agent_Id parameter. The function first extracts the neuron_ids list from the cortex element and chooses a random neuron from the id list. The neuron is then read from the database and its input_idps list is checked for the bias element. If the neuron's input_idps list already has a bias tuple, then the function is exited. If the input_idps list does not have the bias tuple, then the bias is added and the agent's evolutionary history EvoHist is updated. Finally, the updated neuron and agent are written back to mnesia.

```erlang
remove_bias(Agent_Id)->
    A = genotype:read({agent,Agent_Id}),
    Cx_Id = A#agent.cx_id,
    Cx = genotype:read({cortex,Cx_Id}),
    N_Ids = Cx#cortex.neuron_ids,
    N_Id = lists:nth(random:uniform(length(N_Ids)),N_Ids),
    Generation = A#agent.generation,

    N = genotype:read({neuron,N_Id}),
    Input_IdPs = N#neuron.input_idps,
    case lists:keymember(bias, 1, Input_IdPs) of
        false ->
```

```
                    exit("********ERROR:remove_bias:: This Neuron does not have a bias
part.");
            true ->
                    U_Input_IdPs = lists:keydelete(bias,1,Input_IdPs),
                    U_N = N#neuron{
                            input_idps = U_Input_IdPs,
                            generation = Generation},
                    EvoHist = A#agent.evo_hist,
                    U_EvoHist = [{remove_bias,N_Id}|EvoHist],
                    U_A = A#agent{evo_hist=U_EvoHist},
                    genotype:write(U_N),
                    genotype:write(U_A)
    end.
%The remove_bias/1 function is called with the Agent_Id parameter. The function first extracts
the neuron_ids list from the cortex element and chooses a random neuron id from it. The neuron
is then read from the database and its input_idps list checked for a bias element. If the neuron's
input_idps list has a bias tuple, it is removed and the agent's evolutionary history list is updated
with the tuple {remove_bias,N_Id}, and the updated neuron and agent records are then written
to database. If the input_idps list does not have the bias tuple, the function exits with an error
stating so.
```

8.5.4 mutate_af

To execute this mutation operator, we first choose a random neuron A in the NN. This neuron keeps the tag/name of the activation function it uses in an atom form, stored in its record's *af* element. We retrieve this activation function tag, and then randomly choose a new activation function tag from the list of available activation functions, which are specified within the specie's constraint tuple. To ensure that the mutate_af chooses a new activation function, the currently used activation function tag is first subtracted from the available activations list, and the new *af* tag is then chosen from the remaining tags. If the remaining activation function list is empty, then the neuron is assigned the standard tanh activation function. The implementation of the mutate_af function is shown in the following listing.

Listing 8.8: The implementation of the mutate_af mutation operator.

```
mutate_af(Agent_Id)->
    A = genotype:read({agent,Agent_Id}),
    Cx_Id = A#agent.cx_id,
    Cx = genotype:read({cortex,Cx_Id}),
```

```
N_Ids = Cx#cortex.neuron_ids,
N_Id = lists:nth(random:uniform(length(N_Ids)),N_Ids),
Generation = A#agent.generation,


N = genotype:read({neuron,N_Id}),
AF = N#neuron.af,
Activation_Functions = (A#agent.constraint)#constraint.neural_afs -- [AF],
NewAF = genotype:generate_NeuronAF(Activation_Functions),
U_N = N#neuron{af=NewAF,generation=Generation},
EvoHist = A#agent.evo_hist,
U_EvoHist = [{mutate_af,Agent_Id}|EvoHist],
U_A = A#agent{evo_hist=U_EvoHist},
  genotype:write(U_N),
  genotype:write(U_A).
%The mutate_af/1 function chooses a random neuron, and then changes its currently used acti-
vation function into another one available from the neural_afs list of the agent's constraint rec-
ord.
```

8.5.5 add_outlink

To apply the *add_outlink* mutation operator to a NN, we first choose a random neuron A. This neuron keeps track of whom it sends its signals to using its *output_ids* list. We then extract the NN's *neuron_ids* and *actuator_ids* list from the cortex record, and then subtract the neuron's output_ids list from the *neuron_ids++actuator_ids*, which gives us a list of element (neuron and actuator) ids that this neuron is not yet connected to. If this list is empty, we exit the mutation and try another one. If the list is not empty, we randomly select the id from this list, and *connect the neuron to this randomly selected element B*. There are two types of elements we could have randomly chosen, a neuron element, and an actuator element. Let's look at each possible outlink (an outgoing link) connection in turn.

If this randomly chosen element B is a neuron, we perform the following steps to form a connection from neuron A to neuron B:

1. Modify neuron A: We first add B's id to the A's output_ids list, then we check if B's layer is equal to or less than A's layer, if so we add B's id to A's ro_ids list as well. We then set A's generation to that of the agent, the current generation, and write the updated neuron record to database.
2. Modify neuron B: We first add a new input_idp of the form: {NeuronA_Id, Weights}, to the B's input_idps list, where Weights is a list composed of a single weight generated randomly between -Pi/2 and Pi/2. We then update B's generation, and write the updated neuron record to database.

On the other hand, if this randomly chosen element B is an actuator, we perform the following steps to form a connection from neuron A to actuator B:

1. We first check if actuator B's length(fanin_ids) is lower than its vl. If it is, then this actuator can accept another connection. If it's not, then we exit the mutation operator and try another one. Let us assume that the actuator can still accept new connections.
2. Modify neuron A: We add B's id to A's output_ids list. B is an actuator, so we do not need to check its layer, we know that it's the last one, with index *1*. We then update A's generation to that of the agent's, and write the updated neuron record to the database.
3. Modify actuator B: We add A's id to B's fanin_ids list. We then write the updated actuator to the database.

Having updated the elements of both, record A and B, the connection between them is formed. Having now performed a successful mutation operator, the agent's evo_hist list is updated. For this type of mutation, we form the tuple of the form: {MutationOperator,FromId,ToId}, which in this case is: {add_outlink, ElementA_Id,ElementB_Id}, and then append it the to evo_hist list. Then the updated agent record is stored to database. Finally, the add_outlink function returns control back to the caller. A few variations of how this mutation operator can modify a NN's topology is shown in Fig-8.5.

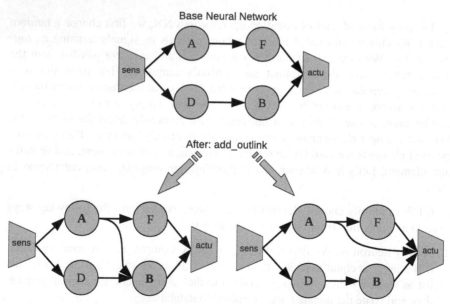

Fig. 8.5 Applying add_outlink mutation operator to a NN system.

The source code for the add_outlink, is reliant on the link_FromElementTo Element/3 function, covered earlier. The implementation of the add_outlink function, is shown in the following listing.

Listing-8.9: The implementation of the add_outlink mutation operator.

```
add_outlink(Agent_Id)->
  A = genotype:read({agent,Agent_Id}),
  Cx_Id = A#agent.cx_id,
  Cx = genotype:read({cortex,Cx_Id}),
  N_Ids = Cx#cortex.neuron_ids,
  A_Ids = Cx#cortex.actuator_ids,
  N_Id = lists:nth(random:uniform(length(N_Ids)),N_Ids),
  N = genotype:read({neuron,N_Id}),
  Output_Ids = N#neuron.output_ids,
  case lists:append(A_Ids,N_Ids) -- Output_Ids of
      [] ->
              exit("********ERROR:add_outlink:: Neuron already connected to all ids");
      Available_Ids ->
              To_Id = lists:nth(random:uniform(length(Available_Ids)),Available_Ids),
              link_FromElementToElement(Agent_Id,N_Id,To_Id),
              EvoHist = A#agent.evo_hist,
              U_EvoHist = [{add_outlink,N_Id,To_Id}|EvoHist],
              U_A = A#agent{evo_hist=U_EvoHist},
              genotype:write(U_A)
  end.
```
%The add_outlink/1 function reads the cortex record from the database based on the cortex id extracted from the agent record. The function then selects a random neuron from the neuron_ids stored in the cortex record. The function then subtracts the neuron's output_ids from the combined list of the actuator and neuron ids belonging to the neural network to get a list of ids belonging to the elements to which this neuron is not yet connected. If this list is empty, the function exits with error. If the list is not empty, it is given the name Available_Ids, from which a random id is chosen, and the neuron is then connected to it. Finally, the agent's evo_hist list is updated, and the updated agent record is written to the database.

8.5.6 add_inlink

Similarly to the mutation operator: add_outlink, when performing the mutation *add_inlink*, we first choose a random neuron A from the agent's neuron_ids list. After reading the neuron record, we extract the ids from neuron A's *input_idps* list. Once the input ids are extracted, we subtract that list from the agent's *neuron_ids++sensor_ids*, to acquire a list of elements that neuron A has not yet been connected from. If this list is empty, we exit the mutation and try another one. If the list is not empty, we randomly select the id of B from this list, *and connect from it*, to neuron A. There are two types of elements we could have randomly chosen, a neuron element, and a sensor element. Let's look at each possible inlink connection in turn.

If this randomly chosen element B is a neuron, we perform the same set of steps as we did in the add_outlink section, but with the two neuron ids reversed. Thus, we perform the following steps to form a connection from neuron B to neuron A:

1. Modify neuron B: We first add A's id to the B's output_ids list, then we check if A's layer is equal to or less than B's layer, if so we add A's id to B's ro_ids list as well. We then reset B's generation to 0, and write the updated neuron record to database.
2. Modify neuron A: We first add a new input_idp of the form: {NeuronB_Id, Weights}, to the A's input_idps list, where Weights is a list composed of a single weight generated randomly between -Pi/2 and Pi/2. We then reset A's generation to that of the agent, and write the updated neuron record to database.

If this randomly chosen element B is a sensor, we perform the following steps to form a connection from sensor B to neuron A:

1. We first check if A's id is already in sensor B's fanout_ids list. If it is, then we exit the mutation operator and try another one. Let us assume that sensor B is not yet connected to neuron A.
2. Modify sensor B: We add A's id to B's fanout_ids list. We then write the updated sensor to the database.
3. Modify neuron A: We first add a new input_idp of the form: {SensorB_Id,Weights} to the A's input_idps list, where the length of the Weights list is dependent on the sensor B's vl (output vector length). The weights list is composed of values generated randomly to be between -Pi/2 and Pi/2 each. We then reset A's generation to that of the agent, and write the updated neuron record to database.

As in the add_outlink function, having now updated the elements of both, record A and B, the connection between them is formed. And having now performed a successful mutation operator, the agent's evo_hist list is updated. For this type of mutation, we form the tuple of the form: {MutationOperator, FromId, ToId}, which in this case is: {add_inlink, ElementB_Id, ElementA_Id}, and then append it to the evo_hist list. Finally, the updated agent record is stored to database and the add_inlink function returns control back to the caller. A few variations of how this mutator can modify a NN's topology is shown in Fig-8.6.

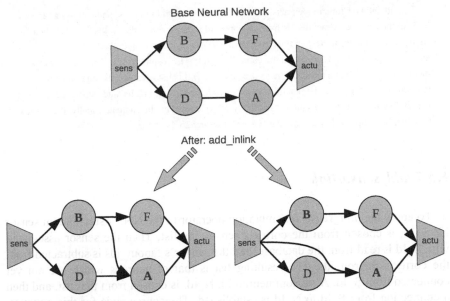

Fig. 8.6 Applying add_inlink mutation operator to a NN system.

Listing-8.10: The implementation of the add_inlink mutation operator.

```
add_inlink(Agent_Id)->
    A = genotype:read({agent,Agent_Id}),
    Cx_Id = A#agent.cx_id,
    Cx = genotype:read({cortex,Cx_Id}),
    N_Ids = Cx#cortex.neuron_ids,
    S_Ids = Cx#cortex.sensor_ids,
    N_Id = lists:nth(random:uniform(length(N_Ids)),N_Ids),
    N = genotype:read({neuron,N_Id}),
    {I_Ids,_WeightLists} = lists:unzip(N#neuron.input_idps),
    case lists:append(S_Ids,N_Ids) -- I_Ids of
        [] ->
                exit("********ERROR:add_INLink:: Neuron already connected from all
ids");
        Available_Ids ->
                From_Id = lists:nth(random:uniform(length(Available_Ids)),Available_Ids),
                link_FromElementToElement(Agent_Id,From_Id,N_Id),
                EvoHist = A#agent.evo_hist,
                U_EvoHist = [{add_inlink,From_Id,N_Id}|EvoHist],
                genotype:write(A#agent{evo_hist=U_EvoHist})
    end.
```

%The add_inlink/1 function extracts the list of neuron ids within the NN, and chooses a random id from the list. We extract the ids from the input_Idps list, forming the "I_Ids" list. We then subtract the I_Ids from the combined neuron and sensor ids belonging to the NN (neuron_ids and sensor_ids lists extracted from the cortex's record). The result is a list of presynaptic element ids from which the neuron is not yet connected. If this list is empty, the function exits with an error. Otherwise, the function chooses a random id from this list and establishes a connection between the neuron and this randomly selected presynaptic element. Finally, the agent's evo_hist list is updated, and the updated agent is written to database.

8.5.7 add_sensorlink

To apply the *add_sensorlink* mutation operator to the NN, first a random sensor id: S_Id, is chosen from the cortex's sensor_ids list. Then the sensor associated with S_Id is read from the database, and the sensor's fanout_ids is subtracted from the cortex's neuron_ids. The resulting list is that of neurons which are not yet connected from S_Id. A random neuron id: N_Id, is chosen from that list, and then a connection from S_Id to N_Id is established. The source code for this mutation operator is shown in the following listing.

Listing-8.11: The implementation of the add_sensorlink mutation operator.

```
add_sensorlink(Agent_Id)->
    A = genotype:read({agent,Agent_Id}),
    Cx_Id = A#agent.cx_id,
    Cx = genotype:read({cortex,Cx_Id}),
    N_Ids = Cx#cortex.neuron_ids,
    S_Ids = Cx#cortex.sensor_ids,
    S_Id = lists:nth(random:uniform(length(S_Ids)),S_Ids),
    S = genotype:read({sensor,S_Id}),
    case N_Ids -- S#sensor.fanout_ids of
        [] ->
            exit("********ERROR:add_sensorlink:: Sensor already connected to all
N_Ids");
        Available_Ids ->
            N_Id = lists:nth(random:uniform(length(Available_Ids)),Available_Ids),
            link_FromElementToElement(Agent_Id,S_Id,N_Id),
            EvoHist = A#agent.evo_hist,
            U_EvoHist = [{add_sensorlink,S_Id,N_Id}|EvoHist],
            genotype:write(A#agent{evo_hist=U_EvoHist})
    end.
```

%The function add_sensorlink/1 randomly selects a sensor id: S_Id, from the cortex's sen-
sor_ids list, and then establishes from that sensor a connection to a neuron still unlinked to this
sensor, randomly selected from the cortex's neuron_ids list. To perform this, the function first
selects a random sensor id S_Id from the cortex's sensor_ids list. Then a list of N_Ids to which
S_Id is not yet connected is calculated by subtracting from the N_Ids the S_Id's fanout_ids list.
If the resulting list is empty, then the function exits with an error since there are no other neurons to which the sensor can establish a new connection. If the list is not empty, then a random
neuron id, N_Id, is selected from this list, and a connection is established from S_Id to N_Id.
Finally, the agent's evo_hist is then updated and written to database.

A possible topological mutation scenario when applying the add_sensorlink mutation operator to a neural network, is shown in the following figure.

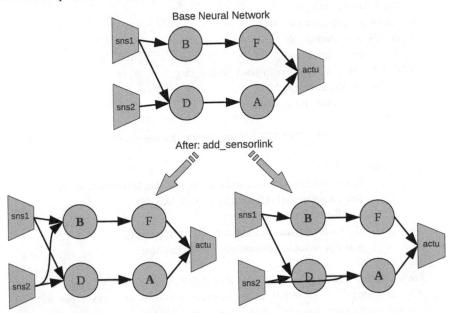

Fig. 8.7 Applying the add_sensorlink mutation operator to a neural network.

8.5.8 add_actuatorlink

To apply the *add_actuatorlink* mutation operator to a NN, first a random actuator id A_Id is chosen from the cortex's actuator_ids list. Then the actuator associated with the A_Id is read from database. Then we check whether the length of
A_Id's *fanin_ids* list is less than that of its *vl*. If it is, it would imply that it has not
yet been fully connected, and that some of the parameters for controlling its action
function are still using some default values within the actuator functions, and that
the actuator should be connected from more neurons. If on the other hand the

length of the fanin_ids is equal to vl, then the actuator does not need to be connected from any more neurons, and the mutation operator function exits with error. If the actuator can still be connected from new neurons, then its fanin_ids list is subtracted from the cortex's neuron_ids. The resulting list is that of the neurons which are not yet connected to A_Id. A random neuron id, N_Id, is selected from the list, and a connection is then established from N_Id to A_Id. The source code for this mutation operator is shown in the following listing.

Listing-8.12: The implementation of the add_actuatorlink mutation operator.

```
add_actuatorlink(Agent_Id)->
    Agent = genotype:read({agent,Agent_Id}),
    Cx_Id = Agent#agent.cx_id,
    Cx = genotype:read({cortex,Cx_Id}),
    N_Ids = Cx#cortex.neuron_ids,
    A_Ids = Cx#cortex.actuator_ids,
    A_Id = lists:nth(random:uniform(length(A_Ids)),A_Ids),
    A = genotype:read({actuator,A_Id}),
    case N_Ids -- A#actuator.fanin_ids of
        [] ->
                exit("*********ERROR:add_actuatorlink:: Neuron already connected from all
ids");
        Available_Ids ->
                N_Id = lists:nth(random:uniform(length(Available_Ids)),Available_Ids),
                link_FromElementToElement(Agent_Id,N_Id,A_Id),
                EvoHist = Agent#agent.evo_hist,
                U_EvoHist = [{add_actuatorlink,N_Id,A_Id}|EvoHist],
                genotype:write(Agent#agent{evo_hist=U_EvoHist})
    end.
%The add_actuatorlink/1 selects a random actuator id A_Id from the cortex's actuator_ids list,
and then connects to A_Id a randomly selected neuron from which A_Id is not yet connected.
To accomplish this, the function first selects a random actuator id A_Id from the cortex's actua-
tor_ids list. Then the function creates a list of neuron ids from which it is not yet connected,
done by subtracting the actuator's fanin_ids list from the cortex's neuron_ids list. If the result-
ing id pool is empty, then the function exits with error. If the resulting id pool is not empty, a
neuron id N_Id is randomly chosen from this id list, and the actuator is connected to this ran-
domly chosen neuron. Finally, the agent's evo_hist is updated, and the updated agent is written
to database.
```

A possible topological mutation scenario when applying the add_actuatorlink mutation operator to a neural network based system is shown in the following figure.

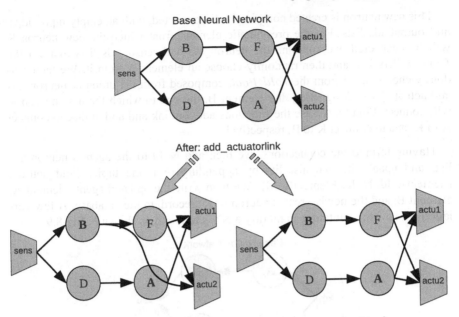

Fig. 8.8 Applying the add_actuatorlink mutation operator to a neural network.

8.5.9 add_neuron

To apply the *add_neuron* mutation operator to a NN, we first read selected agent's *pattern* list, which specifies the general topological pattern of its NN. The topological pattern list has the following structure: *[...{LayerIndex(n), LayerNeuron_Ids(n)}...]*, where the *LayerIndex* variable specifies the index, and the *LayerNeuron_Ids* is a list of the *ids* that belong to this layer. Next, we randomly (with uniform distribution) select a tuple from this list. This tuple specifies to which layer we will add the new neuron.

Having now decided on the neural layer, we then create a new neuron Id, with the layer index specified by the LayerIndex value. Next we construct a new neuron *K* using the *construct_Neuron/6* function from the genotype module, with the following parameters: construct_Neuron(Cx_Id, Generation=CurrentGen, SpecCon, N_Id, Input_Specs=[], Output_Ids=[]). The N_Id is the one just created. Cx_Id is retrieved from the agent record, and the specie constraint (SpecCon) is acquired by first getting the Specie_Id from the agent record, reading the specie record, and then retrieving its *constraint* parameter.

This new neuron is created completely disconnected, with an empty input_idps, and output_ids lists. For the presynaptic element from which the new neuron K will be connected, we combine the neuron_ids and sensor_ids lists to form the *FromId_Pool* list, and then randomly choose an element A from it. We then randomly choose an id from the *ToId_Pool*, composed from the union of neuron_ids and actuator_ids, designating that element B, the one to which the new neuron K will connect. Finally, we use the functions add_outlink and add_inlink to connect A to K, and to connect K to B, respectively.

Having formed the connections, we then add N_Id to the agent's neuron_ids list, and update its evo_hist list by appending to it the tuple: {add_neuron, ElementA_Id, N_Id, ElementB_Id}. We then write the updated agent, element A, element B, and the newly created neuron's (K) record, to the database. A few variations of how this mutator can modify a NN's topology is shown in Fig-8.9.

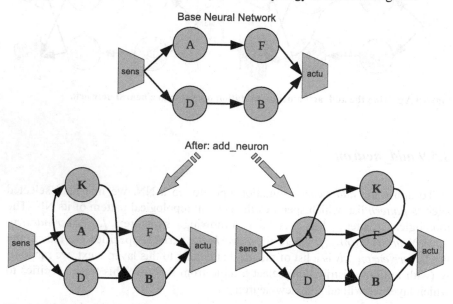

Fig. 8.9 Applying add_neuron mutation operator to a NN system.

Listing-8.13: The implementation of the add_neuron mutation operator.

```
add_neuron(Agent_Id)->
    A = genotype:read({agent,Agent_Id}),
    Generation = A#agent.generation,
    Pattern = A#agent.pattern,
    Cx_Id = A#agent.cx_id,
    Cx = genotype:read({cortex,Cx_Id}),
    N_Ids = Cx#cortex.neuron_ids,
    S_Ids = Cx#cortex.sensor_ids,
```

```
    A_Ids = Cx#cortex.actuator_ids,
    {TargetLayer,TargetNeuron_Ids} = lists:nth(random:uniform(length(Pattern)),Pattern),
    NewN_Id = {{TargetLayer,genotype:generate_UniqueId()},neuron},
    U_N_Ids = [NewN_Id|N_Ids],
    U_Pattern = lists:keyreplace(TargetLayer, 1, Pattern, {TargetLayer, [NewN_Id|
TargetNeuron_Ids]}),
    SpecCon = A#agent.constraint,
    genotype:construct_Neuron(Cx_Id,Generation,SpecCon,NewN_Id,[],[]),
    FromId_Pool = N_Ids++S_Ids,
    ToId_Pool = N_Ids ++ A_Ids,
    From_ElementId = lists:nth(random:uniform(length(FromId_Pool)), FromId_Pool),
    To_ElementId = lists:nth(random:uniform(length(ToId_Pool)),ToId_Pool),
    link_FromElementToElement(Agent_Id,From_ElementId,NewN_Id),
    link_FromElementToElement(Agent_Id,NewN_Id,To_ElementId),
    U_EvoHist = [{add_neuron,From_ElementId,NewN_Id,To_ElementId}|A#agent.evo_hist],
    genotype:write(Cx#cortex{neuron_ids = U_N_Ids}),
    genotype:write(A#agent{pattern=U_Pattern,evo_hist=U_EvoHist}).
```

%The function add_neuron/1 creates a new neuron, and connects it to a randomly selected element in the NN, and from a randomly selected element in the NN. The function first reads the agent's pattern list, selects a random layer from the pattern, and then creates a new neuron id for that layer. Then a new unconnected neuron is created with that neuron id. The function then extracts the neuron_ids and the sensor_ids lists from the cortex. A random id, From_ElementId, is then chosen from the union of the sensor_ids and neuron_ids lists. Then a random id, To_ElementId, is chosen from the union of neuron_ids and actuator_ids (can be the same id as the From_ElementId). The function then establishes a connection from the neuron to To_ElemenId, and a connection to the neuron from From_ElementId. Finally, the cortex's neuron_ids list is updated with the id of the newly created neuron, the agent's evo_hist is updated, and finally, the updated cortex and agent records are written to database.

8.5.10 outsplice

The *splice* mutation operator increases the depth of the NN system through the side effect of adding a new neural layer when adding a new neuron to the NN. This mutation operator chooses a random neuron A in the NN, then chooses a random id in its output_ids list, which we designate as the id of element B. Finally, the mutation operator creates a new neuron K, disconnects A from B, and then reconnects them through K. If element B is in the layer directly after A's layer, then a new layer must be created, into which the new neuron K is inserted. It is through this that the depth of the NN is increased. However, to create neuron K, we first have to create K's id, and to do so we perform the following steps:

1. Retrieve the agent's pattern list (the NN's topology).
2. From pattern, extract the LayerIndex that is between A and B. If there is no layer separating A and B (for example, B's layer comes right after A's), then create a new layer whose layer index is *LayerIndex_K = (LayerIdex_A + LayerIndex_B)/2*. If A is in the last neural layer, then the next layer is the one that belongs to the actuators, LayerIndex 1, and so a new layer can still be inserted: *LayerIndex_K = (LayerIdex_A + 1)/2*.
3. K's id is then: *{{LayerIndex_K,Unique_Id},neuron}*.

Once K's id is created and neuron K is constructed, we insert tuple *{LayerIndex_K, [NeuronK_Id]}* into the agent's Pattern list, unless the pattern already has LayerIndex_K, in which case we add the NeuronK_Id to the list of ids belonging to the existing LayerIndex_K. We then update the agent's evo_hist list by appending to it the tuple: *{splice, ElementA_Id, NeuronK_Id, ElementB_Id}*, and then finally write the updated agent to file. Having updated the agent record, we update the A, B, and K elements.

The first step is to cut the connection from A to B using the cutlink_From ElementToElement/3 function, and then depending on whether B is another neuron or actuator, the following one of the two possible approaches is taken:

If element B is a neuron:

1. Delete B's id from A's output_ids list.
2. Use the function link_FromElementToElement/3 to create a connection from A to K.
3. Delete A's input_idp tuple from B's input_idps list.
4. Use the function link_FromElementToElement/3 to create a connection from K to B.
5. Reset A's, B's, and K's generation values to that of the most current generation (the one of agent's).
6. Write to database the updated neurons A, B, and K.

If element B is an actuator:

1. Delete B's id from A's output_ids list.
2. Use the function link_FromElementToElement/3 to create a connection from A to K.
3. Delete A's id from B's fanin_ids list.
4. Use the function link_FromElementToElement/3 to create a connection from K to B.
5. Reset the generation parameter for neuron A, and K.
6. Write to database the updated elements A, B, and K.

We made a good choice in isolating the linking and link cutting functionality within their own respective functions. We have used these two functions, *link_FromElementToElement/3* and *cutlink_FromElementToElement/3*, in almost every mutation operator we've implemented thus far. Fig-8.10 demonstrates a few variations of how the splice mutator can modify a NN's topology.

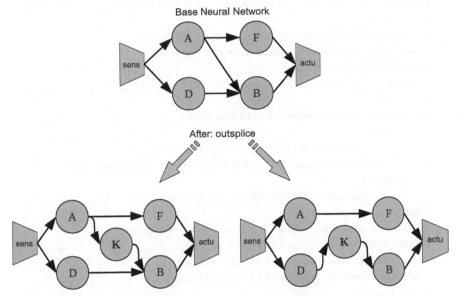

Fig. 8.10 Applying the outsplice mutation operator to a NN system.

Listing-8.14: The implmenetnation of the outsplice mutation operator.

```
outsplice(Agent_Id)->
    A = genotype:read({agent,Agent_Id}),
    Generation = A#agent.generation,
    Pattern = A#agent.pattern,
    Cx_Id = A#agent.cx_id,
    Cx = genotype:read({cortex,Cx_Id}),
    N_Ids = Cx#cortex.neuron_ids,
    N_Id = lists:nth(random:uniform(length(N_Ids)),N_Ids),
    N = genotype:read({neuron,N_Id}),
    {{LayerIndex,_UId},neuron} = N_Id,
%Compose a feedforward Id pool, to create the splice from.
    O_IdPool = case [{{TargetLayerIndex,TargetUId},TargetType} ||
{{TargetLayerIndex,TargetUId},TargetType} <- N#neuron.output_ids, TargetLayerIndex >
LayerIndex] of
            [] ->
                    exit("*********ERROR:outsplice:: O_IdPool== []");
            Ids ->
                    Ids
    end,
%Choose a random neuron in the output_ids for splicing.
```

```
    O_Id = lists:nth(random:uniform(length(O_IdPool)),O_IdPool),
    {{OutputLayerIndex,_Output_UId},_OutputType} = O_Id,
%Create a new Layer, or select an existing one between N_Id and the O_Id, and create the new
unlinked neuron.
    NewLI = get_NewLI(LayerIndex,OutputLayerIndex,next,Pattern),
    NewN_Id={{NewLI,genotype:generate_UniqueId()},neuron},
    SpecCon = A#agent.constraint,
    genotype:construct_Neuron(Cx_Id,Generation,SpecCon,NewN_Id,[],[]),
%Update pattern.
    U_Pattern=case lists:keymember(NewLI,1,Pattern) of
        true->
                {NewLI,InLayerIds}=lists:keyfind(NewLI, 1, Pattern),
                lists:keyreplace(NewLI, 1, Pattern, {NewLI,[NewN_Id|InLayerIds]});
        false ->
                lists:sort([{NewLI,[NewN_Id]}|Pattern])
    end,
%Disconnect N_Id from the O_Id, and then reconnect them through NewN_Id
    cutlink_FromElementToElement(Agent_Id,N_Id,O_Id),
    link_FromElementToElement(Agent_Id,N_Id,NewN_Id),
    link_FromElementToElement(Agent_Id,NewN_Id,O_Id),
%Updated agent
    EvoHist = A#agent.evo_hist,
    U_EvoHist = [{outsplice,N_Id,NewN_Id,O_Id}|EvoHist],
    U_Cx = Cx#cortex{neuron_ids = [NewN_Id|Cx#cortex.neuron_ids]},
    genotype:write(U_Cx),
    genotype:write(A#agent{pattern=U_Pattern,evo_hist=U_EvoHist}).
```

%The function outsplice/1 chooses a random neuron id from the cortex's neuron_ids list, disconnects it from a randomly chosen id in its output_ids list, and then reconnects it to the same element through a newly created neuron. The function first chooses a random neuron N with the neuron id N_Id from the cortex's neuron_ids list. Then the neuron N's output_ids list is extracted, and a new id list O_IdPool is created from the ids in the output_ids list which are located in the layers after the N_Id's layer (the ids of elements to whom the N_Id forms a feed forward connection). From this subset of the output_ids list, a random O_Id is chosen (if the sublist is empty, then the function exits with an error). First, N_Id is disconnected from the O_Id. The function then creates or extracts a new layer index, NewLI, located between N_Id and O_Id. If there exists a layer between N_Id and O_Id, NewLI is simply that layer. If on the other hand O_Id's layer comes immediately after N_Id's, then a new layer is created between O_Id and N_Id, whose layer index is in the middle of the two elements. A new unconnected neuron is then created in that layer, with a neuron id NewN_Id. The neuron NewN_Id is then connected to the O_Id, and from the N_Id, thus establishing a path from N_Id to O_Id through the NewN_Id. The cortex's neuron_ids is updated with the NewN_Id, and the agent's evo_hist list is updated with the new mutation operator tuple {outsplice,N_Id,Newn_Id,O_Id}. Finally, the updated cortex and agent are written to database.

```
get_NewLI(LI,LI,_Direction,_Pattern)->
```

```erlang
        exit("********* ERROR: get_NewLI FromLI == ToLI");
get_NewLI(FromLI,ToLI,Direction,Pattern)->
    NewLI = case Direction of
            next ->
                    get_NextLI(Pattern,FromLI,ToLI);
            prev ->
                    get_PrevLI(lists:reverse(Pattern),FromLI,ToLI)
    end,
    NewLI.
```

%get_NewLI/4 calculates or creates a new layer index located between FromLI and ToLI. This function calls get_NextLI/3 or get_PrevLI/3, depending on whether the direction of the connection is from sensors towards actuators (Direction = next), or from actuators towards sensors (Direction = prev), which is the case when executing an insplice/1 function, which calculates or creates a new layer between the N_Id and one of the ids in its input_idps list. If the FromLI == ToLI, the function exits with an error.

```erlang
    get_NextLI([{FromLI,_LastLayerNIds}],FromLI,ToLI)->
            (FromLI+ToLI)/2;
    get_NextLI([{LI,_LayerNIds}|Pattern],FromLI,ToLI)->
            case LI == FromLI of
                    true ->
                            [{NextLI,_NextLayerNIds}|_] = Pattern,
                            case NextLI == ToLI of
                                    true ->
                                            (FromLI + ToLI)/2;
                                    false ->
                                            NextLI
                            end;
                    false ->
                            get_NextLI(Pattern,FromLI,ToLI)
            end.
```

%get_NextLI checks whether the ToLI comes directly after FromLI, or whether there is another layer between them. If there is another layer between them, then that layer is returned, and the splice neuron is put into it. If there is no layer between FromLI and ToLI, then a new layer is created in the middle. Such a new layer index has the value of (FromLI+ToLI)/2.

```erlang
    get_PrevLI([{FromLI,_FirstLayerNIds}],FromLI,ToLI)->
            (FromLI+ToLI)/2;
    get_PrevLI([{LI,_LayerNIds}|Pattern],FromLI,ToLI)->
            case LI == FromLI of
                    true ->
                            [{PrevLI,_PrevLayerNIds}|_] = Pattern,
                            case PrevLI == ToLI of
                                    true ->
                                            (FromLI + ToLI)/2;
```

```
                          false ->
                                PrevLI
                    end;
            false ->
                    get_PrevLI(Pattern,FromLI,ToLI)
      end.
```
%get_PrevLI checks whether the layer index ToLI, comes directly before FromLI, or whether there is another layer in between them. If there is another layer, then the function returns that layer, if no such layer is found, the function creates a new layer index with value: (FromLI+ToLI)/2.

8.5.11 add_sensor

The *add_sensor* mutation operator (MO) modifies the agent's architecture, its morphology in a sense, by adding new sensory "organs" to the NN based system. If the NN system was started with just a camera sensor, but its specie morphology provides for a larger list of sensory organs, then it is through the add_sensor mutation operator that the NN system can also acquire pressure and radiation sensors (if available for that agent's morphology), for example. By acquiring new sensory organs slowly, through evolution, the NN based system has the chance to evolve connections to only the most useful sensors in the environment the agent inhabits, and work best with the agent's morphology and NN topology.

An agent can have multiple sensors of the same type, as long as they differ in at least some specification. For example, some sensors also specify parameters, which can vary between sensors of the same name. Assume that the agent controls a robot, there can be numerous sensors available to the robot that the NN based system can make use of to improve its performance within the world. But the same type of sensors, let's say camera sensor, can also be installed at different locations on the same real, or simulated robot. This installation location can be specified within the parameters, thus there can be a large list of the same *type* of sensors which simply differ in their coordinate parameters.

To apply this mutation to the NN based system, first the agent's morphology name is retrieved. Using the agent's morphology name we then access the morphology module to get the list of all the available sensors for that morphology. The function *morphology:get_sensors/1* returns the list of all such available sensors. From this list we subtract the list of sensors that the agent is already using, and thus create a *Sensor_Pool*. Finally, we select a random sensor from this list, let us call that sensor, A.

Afterwards, Sensor A's id is created and then added to the cortex's sensor_ids list. Then a random neuron B is chosen from the cortex's neuron_ids list, and using the function link_FromElementToElement, the connection from A to B is established. Agent's evo_hist list is updated by adding to it a new tuple: *{add_sensor,SensorA_Id,NeuronB_Id}*. Then the updated agent, cortex, sensor, and neuron tuples are written to the database. Fig-8.11 demonstrates a few variations of how this MO can modify a NN's topology.

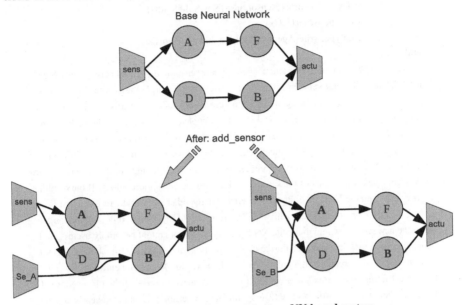

Fig. 8.11 Applying the add_sensor mutation operator to a NN based system.

Listing-8.15: The implementation of the add_sensor mutation operator.

```
add_sensor(Agent_Id)->
    Agent = genotype:read({agent,Agent_Id}),
    Cx_Id = Agent#agent.cx_id,
    Cx = genotype:read({cortex,Cx_Id}),
    S_Ids = Cx#cortex.sensor_ids,
    SpeCon = Agent#agent.constraint,
    Morphology = SpeCon#constraint.morphology,
    case morphology:get_Sensors(Morphology)--[(genotype:read({sensor, S_Id}))#sensor{
id=undefined, cx_id=undefined,fanout_ids=[]} || S_Id<-S_Ids] of
        [] ->
            exit("********ERROR:add_sensor(Agent_Id):: NN system is already using
all available sensors");
        Available_Sensors ->io:format("Available_Sensors"),
            NewS_Id = {{-1,genotype:generate_UniqueId()},sensor},
            NewSensor = (lists:nth(random:uniform(length(Available_Sensors)),
Available_Sensors))#sensor{id=NewS_Id,cx_id=Cx_Id},
            genotype:write(NewSensor),
            N_Ids = Cx#cortex.neuron_ids,
```

```
                    N_Id = lists:nth(random:uniform(length(N_Ids)),N_Ids),
                    link_FromElementToElement(Agent_Id,NewS_Id,N_Id),
                    EvoHist = Agent#agent.evo_hist,
                    U_EvoHist = [{add_sensor,NewS_Id,N_Id}|EvoHist],
                    U_Cx = Cx#cortex{sensor_ids=[NewS_Id|S_Ids]},
                    genotype:write(U_Cx),
                    genotype:write(Agent#agent{evo_hist=U_EvoHist})
        end.
```

%The add_sensor/1 function adds and connects a new sensor to the neural network, a sensor from which the NN is not yet connected. After retrieving the morphology name from the constraint record retrieved from the agent, the complete set of available sensors is retrieved using the morphology:get_Sensors/1 function. From this complete sensor list we subtract the sensor tuples used by the NN based system. But before we can do so, we first revert the sensor id and cx_id of each used sensor, back to undefined, since that is what their initial state within the sensor tuples is. With the NN's sensor ids and cx_ids reverted back to undefined, they can be subtracted from the complete set of the sensors available to the given morphology. If the resulting list is empty, then the function exits with an error. On the other hand, if the resulting list is not empty, then there are still sensors which the NN is not yet using (though it does not mean that using the new sensors would make the NN better, these sensors might be simply useless, and hence not previously incorporated during evolution). From this resulting list we then select a random sensor, and create for it a unique sensor id: NewS_Id. A random neuron id: N_Id, is then selected from the cortex's neuron_ids list, and a connection is established from NewS_Id to N_Id. The cortex's sensor_ids is updated with the new sensor's id, and the agent's evo_hist is updated with the new tuple. Finally, the updated cortex and agent records are then written to database.

8.5.12 add_actuator

Similarly to the add_sensor mutation operator, the add_actuator MO modifies the agent's architecture, by adding to it new morphological element which it can then use to interact with the world. Just as with any other new addition to the NN's topology, or architecture (when adding sensors and actuators), some NN based systems will not integrate well with the newly added element, while others will. Some will not get an advantage in the environment, while others will. Those that do successfully integrate a new element into their architecture, and those that gain benefit from that new element, will have an advantage over those that do not have such an element integrated.

The add_actuator mutator first accesses the agent's morphology name and retrieves the list of all currently available actuators through the execution of the *morphology:get_Actuators/1* function. An Actuator_Pool is then formed by subtracting from this actuator list the list of actuators already used by the NN based agent. A random actuator A is then chosen from this Actuator_Pool. From the cortex's neuron_ids list, a random id of a neuron B is retrieved. Then, using the link_FromElementToElement/3 function, a connection from B to A is established. Finally, A's id is added to the cortex's actuator_ids list, agent's evo_hist is updated by appending to it the tuple: *{add_actuator, NeuronB_Id, ActuatorA_Id}*, and the updated neuron, actuator, agent, and cortex records are written to database. Fig-8.12 demonstrates a few variations of how this mutation operator can modify a NN's topology.

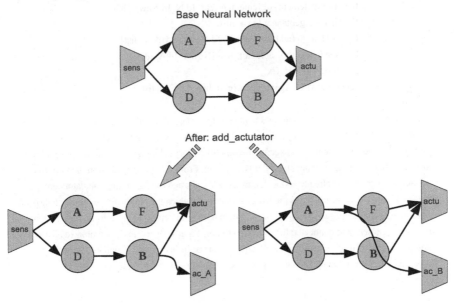

Fig. 8.12 Applying the add_actuator mutation operator to a NN system.

Listing-8.14: The implementation of the add_actuator mutation operator.

```
add_actuator(Agent_Id)->
    Agent = genotype:read({agent,Agent_Id}),
    Cx_Id = Agent#agent.cx_id,
    Cx = genotype:read({cortex,Cx_Id}),
    A_Ids = Cx#cortex.actuator_ids,%TODO: Should we fill in all the fanin_ids locations, or
just 1? and let evolution fill the rest? We can go either way, or compare the performance of one
implementation against the other. In this implementation, we take the second approach.
    SpeCon = Agent#agent.constraint,
    Morphology = SpeCon#constraint.morphology,
    case morphology:get_Actuators(Morphology)--[(genotype:read({actuator,
A_Id}))#actuator{cx_id =undefined, id=undefined,fanin_ids=[]} || A_Id<-A_Ids] of
        [] ->
                exit("********ERROR:add_actuator(Agent_Id):: NN system is already using
all available actuators");
```

```
        Available_Actuators ->
                NewA_Id = {{1,genotype:generate_UniqueId()},actuator},
                NewActuator=(lists:nth(random:uniform(length(Available_Actuators)),
     Available_Actuators))#actuator{id=NewA_Id,cx_id=Cx_Id},
                genotype:write(NewActuator),
                N_Ids = Cx#cortex.neuron_ids,
                N_Id = lists:nth(random:uniform(length(N_Ids)),N_Ids),
                link_FromElementToElement(Agent_Id,N_Id,NewA_Id),
                EvoHist = Agent#agent.evo_hist,
                U_EvoHist = [{add_actuator,N_Id,NewA_Id}|EvoHist],
                U_Cx = Cx#cortex{actuator_ids=[NewA_Id|A_Ids]},
                genotype:write(U_Cx),
                genotype:write(Agent#agent{evo_hist=U_EvoHist})
    end.
```

%The add_actuator/1 function adds and connects a new actuator to the neural network, an actuator type to which the NN is not yet connected to. After we extract the morphology name from the agent's constraint record, we execute the function: morphology:get_Actuators(Morphology) to get the list of actuators available to the NN system. From that list the function then removes the actuators the NN is already connected to, after the ids and cx_ids of those actuators are set to undefined. The resulting list is the list of actuators to which the NN is not yet connected. A random actuator is chosen from that list, and then a random neuron id N_Id from cortex's neuron_ids is chosen, and connected to the new actuator. Finally, the cortex's actuator_ids list is updated with the id of the newly created actuator, the agent's evo_hist is updated with the new tuple, and then both, the updated cortex and the agent are written to database.

8.5.13 Planning the Remaining Few Details of the Genotype Mutator Module

Having now discussed the functionality of every mutation operator, we can start creating the actual mutator module. There are three remaining issues that are in need of a resolution:

1. When creating a mutant clone from some fit genotype, how many mutation operators in sequence should be applied to this clone to produce the final mutant? And what should that number depend on?

I have came to the conclusion that the total number of Mutation Operators (MOs) that should be applied to a clone of a NN to create a mutant offspring, is a value that should in some manner depend on the size of the parent NN system. To see why, consider the following: Imagine you have a NN system composed of a single neuron. We now apply a mutation to this NN system, any mutation operator applied will result in this very simple single neuron NN to function very differently. Now assume that we have a NN system composed of one million neurons, interconnected to a great extent. If we apply a single mutation operator to this NN system, then the effect on its functionality will not be as drastic. So then, when compared to smaller NNs, the larger NN systems require a larger number of mutations to function differently.

But, sometimes drastic changes are not needed, sometimes we only wish to tune the NN system, just add a neuron here, or a single connection there... We do not know ahead of time how many mutation operators need to be applied to a NN system to produce a functional offspring that will be able to jump out of a local optima, or reach a higher fitness level. Thus, not only should the number of mutation operators applied be proportional to the size of the NN system, but it should also be chosen randomly. Thus, offspring should be created by applying a random number of mutation operators, within the range of 1 and some maximum number which is dependent on the NN's size. This will result in a system that creates offspring by at times applying a large number of mutation operators when creating an offspring, and at times a small number of mutation operators. The larger the NN, the greater the spread from which the number of MOs to be applied is chosen.

In our system, the number of mutation operators to be applied should be a random number, chosen with uniform distribution, between 1 and sqrt(Tot_Neurons), where Tot_Neurons is the variable containing the total number of neurons within the NN system. Thus, by increasing the range of the possible number of MOs applied to a cloned NN in proportion to the size of the parent NN, allows us to make the mutation intensity significant enough to allow the mutant offspring to continue producing innovations in its behavior when compared to its parent, and thus explore the fitness landscape far and wide. At the same time, some offspring will only acquire a few MOs and differ topologically only slightly, and thus have a chance to tune and explore the local topological areas on the topological fitness landscape. Let us give this approach a name, let us call it a *"Random Intensity Mutation"*, *(RIM)*. We will call this method: Random Intensity Mutation, because the intensity, which in this case is the range of the number of the MOs applied, is randomly chosen. In the same way that we chose randomly the number of weight perturbations to be applied to the NN by the exoself, which too can be considered to have been an application of RIM.

I think, and we will benchmark this later to test the theory, that RIM provides an advantage over those neuroevolutionary systems that only apply a static number of mutation operators when generating offspring. Also, note that the system we are now creating does not use recombination (the crossover of two or more genotypes to create an offspring), and so the use of RIM is an approach to getting just as much of genetical change as would the use of recombination give. But RIM allows us to do this in a controlled manner. Plus, when we are creating a new genotype by combining two different genotypes in some manner, there is very little chance that the two parts of two different genotypes whose phenotypes process information in completely different manner, or completely the same (when those genotypes are very closely or completely related), will yield a fit or an improved agent, respectively. The use of RIM allows us to slowly complexify the NN systems, to build on top of fit genotypes. Using the RIM approach, sometimes we fine tune the genotype, to see if the genotype can be made more effective. While at other times, the genotypical space is explored far and wide, as we try to free the NN system from some local optima that it is stuck in.

********Note********

Sometimes, progress can only be made when multiple mutation operators are applied in sequence, in one go and before fitness evaluation, to create a new offspring. Evolution is such that a fitness function, especially one that considers that the more concise genotypes are fitter, does not allow for certain combination of mutations to take place over multiple generations. For example consider the scenario shown in Fig-8.13. Assume that in this scenario, an agent inhabits a flatland world, it has a camera sensor, a differential drive actuator [1], and a single neuron neural network, where the neuron uses a tanh activation function. In this flatland, the organism would greatly benefit if it also had a radiation sensor that connects to a neuron that uses sin activation function, which itself is connected to neuron which uses tanh activation function. While at the same time, this world might not be a good place for agents that either have NN topologies composed of a camera sensor connected to two neurons in layer 0, where one neuron uses a tanh and the other uses a sin activation function. This world might also not be favorable to NN systems that have two sensors, a camera and a radiation sensor, both connected to a neuron using a tanh activation function, which then connects to the differential drive actuator. If our neuroevolutionary system only creates offspring by applying a single mutation operator to a parent clone, then we would only generate NNs that are unfavorable in the flatland. These offspring would not get a chance to live on to the next generation and create their own offspring, generated through the mutation resulting in a NN composed of the two neuron two sensor based topology. It is only when our neuroevolutionary system is able to apply at least two mutation operators in series, in a single go, that we have a chance of generating this favorable NN based mutant system. It is this mutant offspring composed of two neurons and two sensors, that has a chance to jump out of the local optima.

****

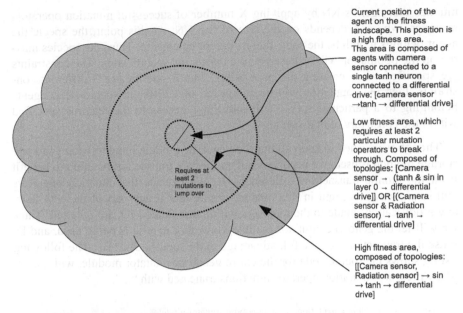

Current position of the agent on the fitness landscape. This position is a high fitness area. This area is composed of agents with camera sensor connected to a single tanh neuron connected to a differential drive: [camera sensor →tanh → differential drive]

Low fitness area, which requires at least 2 particular mutation operators to break through. Composed of topologies: [Camera sensor → (tanh & sin in layer 0 → differential drive]] OR [(Camera sensor & Radiation sensor) → tanh → differential drive]

High fitness area, composed of topologies: [[Camera sensor, Radiation sensor] → sin → tanh → differential drive]

Requires at least 2 mutations to jump over

Fig. 8.13 Climbing out of a local optima using RIM.

2. When adding a new actuator to a NN, and this new actuator has $vl = X$, should we randomly connect to it X number of neurons, or just one?

When adding a new actuator, the simplest and best approach would be to connect to it only a single neuron in the NN. We can let the mutation operators like add_outlink, add_actuatorlink, and add_neuron, be the ones to establish the remaining connections between the NN and the new actuator, over multiple generations as the agent evolves. We can create the actuator functions such that they use default values for all elements in their input vector that are not yet fed from real neurons. After all, there might be some actuators whose vl is larger than the total number of neurons in the NN at the time of being added. Yet it would still be a good idea to connect it to the NN, letting evolution slowly link the right neurons (the ones that lead to a fitter NN system) to the actuator, over multiple generations. Eventually, the NN would integrate such an actuator into itself fully, connecting to it vl number of neurons.

Having decided on these two remaining details of the mutator module, we can now implement it.

8.5.14 Implementing the genotype_mutator Module

We now construct the *genotype_mutator* module using everything we've discussed in this section. The mutate function accepts the parameter Agent_Id, and mutates that agent's NN by applying X number of successful mutation operators in series, where X depends on the size of the NN. At this point, the specie the agent belongs to will be the same that its parent belongs to. Thus, the species making up the population will be based on the *constraint* specification. The constraints are specified when creating the population, thus if one creates 3 different constraints, then the population will be composed of 3 different species. The agents belonging to a particular specie will only have access to the features specified within the *constraint* of that specie.

Though we wished to keep all but the genotype module blind to what genotype storage method is used, we need to use the mnesia's transaction function to benefit from the atomic transactions offered by it. We execute the mutation operators within a *transaction*, and in this manner ensure that if any part of the MO fails, any modifications made to the topology within that failed MO, are reverted. Thus, we will let the genotype_mutator module know that mnesia is being used, and let it use the transactions to take full advantage of the mnesia database. The following listing shows the source code for the entire genotype_mutator module, with the already presented mutation operator functions truncated with "...".

Listing-8.17: The implementation of the genotype_mutator module.

```erlang
-module(genome_mutator).
-compile(export_all).
-include("records.hrl").
-define(DELTA_MULTIPLIER,math:pi()*2).
-define(SAT_LIMIT,math:pi()*2).
-define(MUTATORS,[
    mutate_weights,
    add_bias,
    remove_bias,
    add_outlink,
%   remove_outLink,
    add_inlink,
%   remove_inlink,
    add_sensorlink,
    add_actuatorlink,
    add_neuron,
%   remove_neuron,
    outsplice,
%   insplice,
    add_sensor,
%   remove_sensor,
    add_actuator
%   remove_actuator
    ]).
```

```
-define(ACTUATORS,morphology:get_Actuators(A#agent.morphology)).
-define(SENSORS,morphology:get_Sensors(A#agent.morphology)).
%%%%%%%%%%%%%%%%%%%%%%%%%%%%%%%%%%%%%%%%%%%%%%%%%%%%%%%%%%%%%%%%%
test()->
   Result = genotype:mutate(test),
   case Result of
         {atomic,_} ->
                  io:format("******** Mutation Succesful.~n");
         _->
                  io:format("******** Mutation Failure:~p~n",[Result])
   end.
%The test/1 function simply tests the mutate/1 function using a random mutation operator, on
an agent whose id is 'test'.

test(Agent_Id,Mutator)->
   F = fun()->
         genome_mutator:Mutator(Agent_Id)
   end,
   mnesia:transaction(F).
%test/2 function tests the mutation operator "Mutator" on the agent with an id Agent_Id.

mutate(Agent_Id)->
   random:seed(now()),
   F = fun()->
         A = genotype:read({agent,Agent_Id}),
         OldGeneration = A#agent.generation,
         NewGeneration = OldGeneration+1,
         genotype:write(A#agent{generation = NewGeneration}),
         apply_Mutators(Agent_Id)
   end,
   mnesia:transaction(F).
%The mutate/1 function applies a random available mutation operator to an agent with an id:
Agent_Id.

   apply_Mutators(Agent_Id)->
         A = gcnotype:read({agent,Agent_Id}),
         Cx = genotype:read({cortex,A#agent.cx_id}),
         TotNeurons = length(Cx#cortex.neuron_ids),
         TotMutations = random:uniform(round(math:pow(TotNeurons,1/2))),
         io:format("Tot neurons:~p Performing Tot mutations:~p
on:~p~n",[TotNeurons,TotMutations,Agent_Id]),
         apply_Mutators(Agent_Id,TotMutations).
%apply_Mutators/1 chooses a random number X between 1 and math:sqrt(Tot_Neurons)),
where Tot_Neurons is the total number of neurons in the neural network, and then applies X
number of randomly chosen mutation operators to the NN. The function first calculates the
```

length of the neuron_ids list, from which it then calculates the TotMutations value by choosing the random number between 1 and sqrt of the length of neuron_ids list. Having now chosen how many mutation operators to apply to the NN based system, the function apply_Mutators/1 calls apply_Mutators/2.

```erlang
apply_Mutators(_Agent_Id,0)->
    done;
apply_Mutators(Agent_Id,MutationIndex)->
    Result = apply_NeuralMutator(Agent_Id),
    case Result of
        {atomic,_} ->
            apply_Mutators(Agent_Id,MutationIndex-1);
        Error ->
            io:format("******** Error:~p~nRetrying with new Muta-
tion...~n",[Error]),
            apply_Mutators(Agent_Id,MutationIndex)
    end.
```

%apply_Mutators/2 applies the set number of successful mutation operators to the Agent. If a mutation operator exits with an error, the function tries another mutation operator. It is only after a successful mutation operator is applied that the MutationIndex is decremented.

```erlang
apply_NeuralMutator(Agent_Id)->
    F = fun()->
        Mutators = ?MUTATORS,
        Mutator = lists:nth(random:uniform(length(Mutators)),Mutators),
        io:format("Mutation Operator:~p~n",[Mutator]),
        genome_mutator:Mutator(Agent_Id)
    end,
    mnesia:transaction(F).
```

%apply_NeuralMutator/1 applies the actual mutation operator to the NN. Because the genotype is stored in mnesia, if the mutation operator function exits with an error, the database made changes are retracted, and a new mutation operator can then be applied to the agent, as if the previous unsuccessful mutation operator was never applied. The mutation operator to be applied to the agent is chosen randomly from the mutation operator list: ?MUTATORS.

```erlang
mutate_weights(Agent_Id)->
...

add_bias(Agent_Id)->
...

remove_bias(Agent_Id)->
...

mutate_af(Agent_Id)->
```

```
...

link_FromElementToElement(Agent_Id,From_ElementId,To_ElementId)->
...

cutlink_FromElementToElement(Agent_Id,From_ElementId,To_ElementId)->
...

add_outlink(Agent_Id)->
...

add_inlink(Agent_Id)->
...

add_sensorlink(Agent_Id)->
...

add_actuatorlink(Agent_Id)->
...

add_neuron(Agent_Id)->
...

outsplice(Agent_Id)->
...

insplice(Agent_Id)->
...

add_sensor(Agent_Id)->
...

add_actuator(Agent_Id)->
...
```

Having now created the polis, genotype, and the mutator module, we have all the modules and functions necessary to perform a few simple mutation tests using the *genome_mutator*'s *test/2* function. The test/2 function will allow us to use the genotype module to create a test agent, apply specific mutation operators to it, and then check whether they executed correctly by analyzing the genotype printed to screen using the *print/1* function. Since we know that a seed NN with a single neuron is created without a threshold element, we will first test the simplest mutator, *add_threshold*, as shown below. For the sake of brevity, only the neuron record is shown when *print/1* is executed.

```
1> polis:start().
Parameters:{[],[]}
******** Polis: ##MATHEMA## is now online.
{ok,<0.34.0>}
2> genotype:create_test().
...
{neuron,{{0,7.588454795555494e-10},neuron},
    0,
    {{origin,7.588454795561199e-10},cortex},
    abs,
    [{{{-1,7.588454795555557e-10},sensor},
      [0.03387578757696197,-0.35293313204412424]}],
    [{{1,7.588454795555509e-10},actuator}],
    []}
...
{atomic,{atomic,[ok]}}
3> genome_mutator:test(test,add_bias).
{atomic,ok}
4> genotype:print(test).
...
{neuron,{{0,7.588454795555494e-10},neuron},
    0,
    {{origin,7.588454795561199e-10},cortex},
    abs,
    [{{{-1,7.588454795555557e-10},sensor},
      [0.03387578757696197,-0.35293313204412424]},
     {bias,[0.28866429973097785]}}],
    [{{1,7.588454795555509e-10},actuator}],
    []}
...
{atomic,[ok]}
```

It works! If we compare the neuron record before and after the add_bias mutation operator was applied, we can see that a bias tuple was added to the neuron's input_idps (shown in bold face in the above console printout). Let's test a mutation operator that is a bit more complex, let's test the outsplice MO. Before we execute the function, let us think of what should happen, and then test that theory. We know that the default agent is created with a single sensor, a neuron in layer 0, and a single actuator. An outsplice adds a new neuron between the neuron and one of the ids in its output_ids list. Since this *test* agent's neuron is only connected to the actuator, only the actuator's id should be in the neurons output_ids list. Thus, the outsplice function should add a new neuron in its own new layer: *0.5 = (0+1)/2*. Let us now test our prediction, and again for the sake of brevity, I will not show the agent and cortex records, because this mutation operator only affects the NN topology, the sensors, neurons, and actuators:

```
1> polis:start().
Parameters:{[],[]}
******** Polis: ##MATHEMA## is now online.
{ok,<0.34.0>}
2> genotype:create_test().
...
{sensor,{{-1,7.588451156728372e-10},sensor},
    xor_GetInput,
    {{origin,7.588451156734038e-10},cortex},
    {private,xor_sim},
    2,
    [{{0,7.588451156728286e-10},neuron}],
    undefined}
{neuron,{{0,7.588451156728286e-10},neuron},
    0,
    {{origin,7.588451156734038e-10},cortex},
    abs,
    [{{{-1,7.588451156728372e-10},sensor},
     [-0.38419731227432274,0.2612339422607457]}],
    [{{1,7.588451156728309e-10},actuator}],
    []}
{actuator,{{1,7.588451156728309e-10},actuator},
    xor_SendOutput,
    {{origin,7.588451156734038e-10},cortex},
    {private,xor_sim},
    1,
    [{{0,7.588451156728286e-10},neuron}],
    undefined}
{atomic,{atomic,[ok]}}
3> genome_mutator:test(test,outsplice).
{atomic,ok}
4> genotype:print(test).
...
{sensor,{{-1,7.588451156728372e-10},sensor},
    xor_GetInput,
    {{origin,7.588451156734038e-10},cortex},
    {private,xor_sim},
    2,
    [{{0,7.588451156728286e-10},neuron}],
    undefined}
{neuron,{{0.5,7.58845109269042e-10},neuron},
    0,
    {{origin,7.588451156734038e-10},cortex},
    sin,
    [{{{0,7.588451156728286e-10},neuron},[0.3623116220700018]}],
```

```
    [{{1,7.588451156728309e-10},actuator}],
    []}
{neuron,{{0,7.588451156728286e-10},neuron},
    0,
    {{origin,7.588451156734038e-10},cortex},
    abs,
    [{{{-1,7.588451156728372e-10},sensor},
    [-0.38419731227432274,0.2612339422607457]}}],
    [{{0.5,7.58845109269042e-10},neuron}],
    []}
{actuator,{{1,7.588451156728309e-10},actuator},
    xor_SendOutput,
    {{origin,7.588451156734038e-10},cortex},
    {private,xor_sim},
    1,
    [{{0.5,7.58845109269042e-10},neuron}],
    0}
{atomic,[ok]}
```

It works! No errors. And from the output to console we can compare the genotypes of the NN systems before and after the mutation. As we predicted, when the genotype printed at 4> is compared to one printed at 2>, we see a new neuron with id: **{{0.5,7.58845109269042e-10},neuron}** added to the system, shown in bold-face in the above console printout. The new neuron is inserted into its own layer with index 0.5, connected from the first neuron, and to the actuator. The NN pattern, which specifies the number of layers composing the NN, and the layer density, was also changed. The initial, and the final patterns, stored in the *agent* record, are as follows:

```
Initial topology: [{0,[{{0,7.588451156728286e-10},neuron}]}]
Final topology: [{0,[{{0,7.588451156728286e-10},neuron}]},
    {0.5,[{{0.5,7.58845109269042e-10},neuron}]}]
```

In this way we can continue going through each mutation operator, applying it to a test agent, and then confirming manually that the MO works as designed. Catching errors in mutation operators can be difficult, and in general catching small errors in evolutionary systems is even more so because if the error does not crash the program and only slightly affects the system, the evolved organisms will evolve around such problems. If for example the add_inlink operator constantly produces damaged links, the agents will still adapt and solve the problem they are applied to, by using the remaining MOs to compensate. It would require a manual analysis of the topology and functionality of the NN based system to finally realize that there is some minor problem with a mutation operator.

A long while back when experimenting with different ways a neuron can process incoming data, I was testing a theory which required me to filter all neuron incoming signals through a *tanh* function, before calculating a dot product of those signals with their corresponding synaptic weights, and then sent through the activation function. By mistake, I forgot to remove that modification after the tests. I continued applying the system to real world problems, and the system continued to work. It was only a few months later, when I was going over the neuron module implementation, that I realized I left it in. The system continued performing well, evolution routed around this small problem. But the point is that errors can go unnoticed because the system will continue functioning relatively well, even with a few flaws or bugs. This is even more so when it comes in developing such systems in Erlang, because it is even more difficult to crash an Erlang based system.

We have now covered all the genotype related issues of our neuroevolutionary system. In the next section we discuss and develop the new *population_monitor* module.

8.5.15 Developing the population_monitor

The *population_monitor* module is the only remaining large module we need to create before we have a functional topology and weight evolving artificial neural network system. The remaining modules (exoself, cortex, & neuron), need merely be slightly updated. The *population_monitor* process will have to perform a number of complex functions, keeping track of an entire population of agents, selecting fit, removing the unfit, creating offspring from the fit agents through cloning and mutation, and then finally reapplying the new generation of agents to the problem or simulation set by the researcher.

After the polis is started and the public scapes are spawned, we can generate a seed population from which a solution, or simply an ever more intelligent population of agents, will evolve. Towards what the neuroevolution is applied depends and is specified by the scape, which itself is a simulation of some physical or mathematical space. The goal of neuroevolution is to generate and guide the population towards higher fitness. Where, how, and when, the fitness points are distributed to the neural networks, and under what conditions, is determined by the scape itself. Once all agents have finished interacting with the scapes, or scape, we are left with a population of agents, each of whom has a fitness score. How and when the agent finishes, or dies, or terminates, is once again dependent on the scape and the problem. The agent "finishes" when for example it has gone through every element in the database, or dies of "old age" when the agent controls an avatar within some simulated environment... At this point, the population_monitor uses a selection function to select a certain percentage of the population as fit or valid, while marking the rest as unfit, or invalid. We will not implement crossover approaches for offspring generation, since the topological RIM system will create enough variation, and do so much faster and safer than any crossover algorithm can.

The offspring are created through cloning and mutation. Not all fit agents are equal, some are more equal than others, some have a higher fitness level. Though all the fit agents will survive to the next generation, the number of offspring each agent creates will depend on that agent's fitness. The population_monitor will decide how many offspring to allocate to each agent. The offspring will be created by first cloning the fit agent, and then by mutating the clone to produce a variation, a mutant, of it. The clone, with its own unique agent id, is assigned to the same specie that its parent belongs to. Once all the offspring are created, where "all" means the same number as was deleted during the selection process, the new generation of agents is then released back into the scape, or applied again to the problem. Then, the evolutionary cycle repeats.

The way we specify what to apply the neuroevolutionary system and the particular population to, is through the *constraint* record. The constraint records specify the morphologies into which the population will be subdivided, where each morphology has its own sensors and actuators from which the agent will draw its sensors and actuators from during evolution. The scapes define the problem, and the sensors and actuators specify what scapes the agent can interact with, and how it can interface with them. The constraints also specify activation functions available to the evolving adaptive agents, and thus we can further specify and try out the same morphologies but with different activation function sets. Thus, the seed population of agents that the population_monitor tracks will, from the very start, be subdivided into multiple species, where the number of species depends on the number of constraint records in the list dropped as a parameter into the population initialization function.

Based on this narrative, we can see that the population_monitor program has to do quite a few things, let us break it down into steps, and then compose the algorithm for each step:

1. Create a Seed_Species list, composed of constraint records as follows: Seed_Species=[#constraint{morphology=A,neural_afs=[...]},#constraint{ morphology=B}...]
2. Specify seed population size, and max population size. The seed population size specifies the number of seed agents to create, which will compose the seed population. The max population size specifies the maximum number of agents that the population can sustain.
3. Divide the total number of X seed agents by *length(Seed_Species)*, letting the resulting number Y specify the number each seed specie will start with. Thus, each *Seed_Specie* will have Y number of agents, and the seed population will have $X = Y*length(Seed\_Species)$ number of agents in total.
4. Spawn the agents belonging to the population by starting up their exoselfs. Each exoself is started with the Agent_Id, and PopulationMonitor_PId as

parameters. The exoself of the agent bootstraps itself, converting its genotype into its phenotype.

5. Each agent then interacts with the scape, until it dies, or finishes its session with the scape, at which point the agent's exoself notifies the population_monitor of its fitness score, and that it is done. The agent then terminates itself by terminating all the processes that it is composed of.

6. The population_monitor waits for the fitness score from every agent in the population it is monitoring. Once all the agents have finished and terminated, the population_monitor runs a selection algorithm on the agent list, to seperate the fit from the unfit.

7. The population_monitor composes a list of tuples: *[{TrueFitness, Agent_Id}...]*, where: *TrueFitness = Fitness/math:pow(TotN,?EFF,)* and where *TotN* is the total number of neurons, and *?EFF* is a researcher specified efficiency index, usually set to *0.1*. What this does is make the agent's fitness dependent on the agent's NN size. For example, if two agents have the same fitness, but one is composed of 2 neurons, and the other of 20, then we should choose the 2 neuron based agent because it is that much more efficient. How much weight is given to the NN size is specified through the ?EFF parameter, the Efficiency parameter.

8. At this point, we apply a selection algorithm, an algorithm that removes unfit agents, and allows the fit ones to produce offspring. I have developed a selection algorithm which I dubbed *competition*, and which has yielded excellent results in the past. The steps of this algorithm are as follows, and which I will explain in more detail afterwards:

    1. Calculate the average energy cost of a Neuron in the population using the following steps:
    TotEnergy = Agent(1)_Fitness + Agent(2)_Fitness...
    TotNeurons = Agent(1)_TotNeurons + Agent(2)_TotNeurons...
    NeuronEnergyCost = TotEnergy/TotNeurons

    2. Sort the Agents in the population based on TrueFitness.

    3. Remove the bottom 50% of the population.

    4. Calculate the number of allotted offspring for each Agent(i):
    AllotedNeurons = (AgentFitness/NeuronEnergyCost),
    AllotedOffsprings(i) = round(AllotedNeurons(i)/Agent(i)_TotNeurons)

    5. Calculate total number of offspring being produced for the next generation:
    TotalNewOffsprings = AllotedOffsprings(1)+...AllotedOffsprings(n).

    6. Calculate PopulationNormalizer, to keep the population within a certain limit:
    PopulationNormalizer = TotalNewOffsprings/PopulationLimit

    7. Calculate the normalized number of offspring allotted to each NN based system (Normalized Allotted Offsprin = NAO):
    NAO(i)= round(AllotedOffsprings(i)/PopulationNormalizer(i))

    8. If NAO == 1, then the agent is allowed to survive to the next generation without offspring, if NAO > 1, then the agent is allowed to produce (NAO

-1) number of mutated copies of itself, if NAO = 0, then the agent is removed from the population and deleted.

9. Then the Topological Mutation Phase is initiated, and the mutator program passes through the database creating the appropriate NAO number of mutant clones of the surviving fit agents.

9. Go to 4, until stopping condition is reached, where the following stopping conditions are available:

- The best fitness of the population is not increased some X number of times, where X is set by the researcher.
- The goal fitness level is reached by one of the agents in the population.
- The preset maximum number of generations has passed.
- The preset maximum number of evaluations has passed.

From the fitness score modification (making it dependent on the NN size as well) and the *competition* selection algorithm, it can be seen that it becomes very difficult for bloated NNs to survive when smaller systems produce better or similar results. Yet when a large NN produces significantly better results justifying its complexity and size, it can begin to compete and push out the smaller NN systems. This selection algorithm takes into account that a NN composed of 2 Neurons is double the size of a 1 Neuron NN, and thus should also have an increased fitness if it wants to produce just as many offspring. On the other hand, a NN of size 101 is only slightly larger than a NN of size 100, and thus should pay only slightly more per offspring. This selection algorithm has proven excellent when it comes to keeping neural network bloating to a minimum. At the same time, this does not mean that the system will be too greedy, after all, we allow for the top 50% to survive, as long as they show some level of competitiveness. Because of the application of RIM during the mutation phase, we can expect that if there is a path towards greater complexity and fitness, eventually one of the mutant offspring will find it.

Having now discussed all the steps and features the population_monitor needs to make and have respectively, we can begin developing the source code. The following listing shows the population_monitor module.

Listing-8.18: The implementation of the population_monitor module.

```
-module(population_monitor).
-include("records.hrl").
%% API
-export([start_link/1,start_link/0,start/1,start/0,stop/0,init/2]).
%% gen_server callbacks
-export([init/1, handle_call/3, handle_cast/2, handle_info/2, terminate/2, code_change/3, create_MutantAgentCopy/1,test/0, create_specie/3, continue/2, continue/3,init_population/1, extract_AgentIds/2,delete_population/1]).
-behaviour(gen_server).
```

```
%%%%%%%%%%%% Population Monitor Options & Parameters
-define(SELECTION_ALGORITHM,competition).
-define(EFF,0.05).
-define(INIT_CONSTRAINTS,[#constraint{morphology=Morphology,neural_afs
=Neural_AFs} || Morphology<-[xor_mimic],Neural_AFs<-[[tanh]]]).
-define(SURVIVAL_PERCENTAGE,0.5).
-define(SPECIE_SIZE_LIMIT,10).
-define(INIT_SPECIE_SIZE,10).
-define(INIT_POPULATION_ID,test).
-define(OP_MODE,gt).
-define(INIT_POLIS,mathema).
-define(GENERATION_LIMIT,100).
-define(EVALUATIONS_LIMIT,100000).
-define(DIVERSITY_COUNT_STEP,500).
-define(GEN_UID,genotype:generate_UniqueId()).
-define(CHAMPION_COUNT_STEP,500).
-define(FITNESS_GOAL,inf).
-record(state,{op_mode,population_id,activeAgent_IdPs=[],agent_ids=[],tot_agents,agents_left,
op_tag,agent_summaries=[],pop_gen=0,eval_acc=0,cycle_acc=0,time_acc=0,step_size,
next_step,goal_status,selection_algorithm}).
%%=======================================================================API
%%----------------------------------------------------------------
%% Function: start_link() -> {ok,Pid} | ignore | {error,Error}
%% Description: Starts the server
%%----------------------------------------------------------------
start_link(Start_Parameters) ->
    gen_server:start_link(?MODULE, Start_Parameters, []).

start(Start_Parameters) ->
    gen_server:start(?MODULE, Start_Parameters, []).

start_link() ->
    gen_server:start_link(?MODULE, [], []).

start() ->
    gen_server:start(?MODULE, [], []).

stop() ->
    gen_server:cast(monitor,{stop,normal}).

init(Pid,InitState)->
    gen_server:cast(Pid,{init,InitState}).

%%=======================================================gen_server callbacks
%%----------------------------------------------------------------
```

```erlang
%%% Function: init(Args) -> {ok, State} |
%%%                  {ok, State, Timeout} |
%%%                  ignore          |
%%%                  {stop, Reason}
%%% Description: Initiates the server
%%%-------------------------------------------------------------------
init(Parameters) ->
    process_flag(trap_exit,true),
    register(monitor,self()),
    io:format("******** Population monitor started with parameters:~p~n",[Parameters]),
    State = case Parameters of
            {OpMode,Population_Id,Selection_Algorithm}->
                Agent_Ids = extract_AgentIds(Population_Id,all),
                ActiveAgent_IdPs = summon_agents(OpMode,Agent_Ids),
                #state{op_mode=OpMode,
                    population_id = Population_Id,
                    activeAgent_IdPs = ActiveAgent_IdPs,
                    tot_agents = length(Agent_Ids),
                    agents_left = length(Agent_Ids),
                    op_tag = continue,
                    selection_algorithm = Selection_Algorithm}
    end,
    {ok, State}.
```

%In init/1 the population_monitor process registers itself with the node under the name monitor, and sets all the needed parameters within its #state record. The function first extracts all the Agent_Ids that belong to the population using the extract_AgentIds/2 function. Each agent is then spawned/activated, and converted from genotype to phenotype in the summon_agents/2 function. The summon_agents/2 function summons the agents and returns to the caller a list of tuples with the following format: [{Agent_Id,Agent_PId}...]. Finally, once the state record's parameters have been set, the function drops into the main gen_server loop.

```erlang
%%%-------------------------------------------------------------------
%%% Function: %%% handle_call(Request, From, State) -> {reply, Reply, State} |
%%%                  {reply, Reply, State, Timeout} |
%%%                  {noreply, State} |
%%%                  {noreply, State, Timeout} |
%%%                  {stop, Reason, Reply, State} |
%%%                  {stop, Reason, State}
%%% Description: Handling call messages
%%%-------------------------------------------------------------------
handle_call({stop,normal},_From, S)->
    ActiveAgent_IdPs = S#state.activeAgent_IdPs,
    [Agent_PId ! {self(),terminate} || {_DAgent_Id,Agent_PId}<-ActiveAgent_IdPs],
    {stop, normal, S};
handle_call({stop,shutdown},_From,State)->
```

```
    {stop, shutdown, State}.
%If the population_monitor process receives a {stop,normal} call, it checks if there are any
agents that are still active. If there are any, it terminates them, and then itself terminates.


%%----------------------------------------------------------------------
%%% Function: handle_cast(Msg, State) -> {noreply, State} |
%%%                                {noreply, State, Timeout} |
%%%                                {stop, Reason, State}
%%% Description: Handling cast messages
%%----------------------------------------------------------------------
handle_cast({Agent_Id,terminated,Fitness,AgentEvalAcc,AgentCycleAcc,AgentTimeAcc},S)
when S#state.selection_algorithm == competition ->
    Population_Id = S#state.population_id,
    OpTag = S#state.op_tag,
    AgentsLeft = S#state.agents_left,
    OpMode = S#state.op_mode,
    U_EvalAcc = S#state.eval_acc+AgentEvalAcc,
    U_CycleAcc = S#state.cycle_acc+AgentCycleAcc,
    U_TimeAcc = S#state.time_acc+AgentTimeAcc,
    case (AgentsLeft-1) =< 0 of
            true ->
                    mutate_population(Population_Id,?SPECIE_SIZE_LIMIT,
S#state.selection_algorithm),
                    U_PopGen = S#state.pop_gen+1,
                    io:format("Population Generation:~p Ended.~n~n~n",[U_PopGen]),
                    case OpTag of
                        continue ->
                            Specie_Ids = (genotype:dirty_read({population,
Population_Id}))#population.specie_ids,
                            SpecFitList=[(genotype:dirty_read({specie,
Specie_Id}))#specie.fitness || Specie_Id <- Specie_Ids],
                            BestFitness=lists:nth(1,lists:reverse(lists:sort([MaxFitness ||
{_,_,MaxFitness,_} <- SpecFitList]))),
                            case (U_PopGen >= ?GENERATION_LIMIT) or
(S#state.eval_acc >= ?EVALUATIONS_LIMIT) or (BestFitness > ?FITNESS_GOAL) of
                                true ->%termination condition reached
                                    Agent_Ids = extract_AgentIds(Population_Id,all),
                                    TotAgents=length(Agent_Ids),
                                    U_S=S#state{agent_ids=Agent_Ids, tot_agents
=TotAgents,agents_left=TotAgents,pop_gen=U_PopGen,eval_acc=U_EvalAcc, cycle_acc
=U_CycleAcc,time_acc=U_TimeAcc},
                                    {stop,normal,U_S};
                                false ->%in progress
                                    Agent_Ids = extract_AgentIds(Population_Id,all),
```

```
                                         U_ActiveAgent_IdPs =summon_agents(OpMode,
Agent_Ids),
                                         TotAgents=length(Agent_Ids),
                                         U_S=S#state{activeAgent_IdPs
=U_ActiveAgent_IdPs, tot_agents=TotAgents,agents_left=TotAgents, pop_gen=U_PopGen,
eval_acc=U_EvalAcc,cycle_acc=U_CycleAcc, time_acc=U_TimeAcc},
                                         {noreply,U_S}
                    end;
            done ->
                    io:format("Shutting down Population Monitor~n"),
                    U_S = S#state{agents_left = 0,pop_gen=U_PopGen, eval_acc
=U_EvalAcc, cycle_acc=U_CycleAcc,time_acc=U_TimeAcc},
                    {stop,normal,U_S};
            pause ->
                    io:format("Population Monitor has paused.~n"),
                    U_S = S#state{agents_left=0,pop_gen=U_PopGen, eval_acc
=U_EvalAcc, cycle_acc=U_CycleAcc,time_acc=U_TimeAcc},
                    {noreply,U_S}
        end;
    false ->
            ActiveAgent_IdPs = S#state.activeAgent_IdPs,
            U_ActiveAgent_Ids = lists:keydelete(Agent_Id,1,ActiveAgent_IdPs),
            U_S = S#state{activeAgent_IdPs = U_ActiveAgent_Ids,agents_left =
AgentsLeft-1,eval_acc=U_EvalAcc,cycle_acc=U_CycleAcc,time_acc=U_TimeAcc},
            {noreply,U_S}
    end;
```

%This clause accepts the cast signals sent by the agents which terminate after finishing with their evaluations. The clause specializes in the "competition" selection algorithm, which is a generational selection algorithm. As a generational selection algorithm, it waits until the entire population has finished being evaluated, and only then selects the fit from the unfit, and composes an updated population for the next generation. The OpTag can be set from the outside to shutdown the population_monitor by setting it to done. Once a stopping condition is reached, either through a generation limit, an evaluations limit, or fitness goal, the population_monitor exits normally. If the stopping condition is not reached, the population_monitor spawns the new generation of agents, and waits again for all the agents in the population to complete their evaluations. If the OpTag is set to pause, it does not generate a new population, and instead goes into a waiting mode, during which it waits to be either restarted or terminated.

```
handle_cast({op_tag,pause},S) when S#state.op_tag == continue ->
    U_S = S#state{op_tag = pause},
    {noreply,U_S};
```

%The population_monitor process can accept a pause command cast. When it receives it, it goes into pause mode after all the agents have completed with their evaluations. The process can only go into a pause mode if it is currently in the continue mode (its op_tag is set to continue).

```
handle_cast({op_tag,continue},S) when S#state.op_tag == pause ->
    Population_Id = S#state.population_id,
    OpMode = S#state.op_mode,
    Agent_Ids = extract_AgentIds(Population_Id,all),
    U_ActiveAgent_IdPs=summon_agents(OpMode,Agent_Ids),
    TotAgents=length(Agent_Ids),
    U_S=S#state{activeAgent_IdPs=U_ActiveAgent_IdPs,tot_agents=TotAgents,agents_left
=TotAgents,op_tag=continue},
    {noreply,U_S};
%The population_monitor process can accept a continue command if its current op_tag is set to
pause. When it receives a continue command, it summons all the agents in the population, and
continues with its neuroevolution synchronization duties.

handle_cast({init,InitState},_State)->
    {noreply,InitState};
handle_cast({stop,normal},State)->
    {stop, normal,State};
handle_cast({stop,shutdown},State)->
    {stop, shutdown, State}.
%%-------------------------------------------------------------------
%% Function: handle_info(Info, State) -> {noreply, State} |
%%                          {noreply, State, Timeout} |
%%                          {stop, Reason, State}
%% Description: Handling all non call/cast messages
%%-------------------------------------------------------------------
handle_info(_Info, State) ->
    {noreply, State}.

terminate(Reason, S) ->
    case S of
        [] ->
            io:format("******** Population_Monitor shut down with Reason:~p, with
State: []~n",[Reason]);
        _ ->
            Population_Id = S#state.population_id,
            OpTag = S#state.op_tag,
            OpMode = S#state.op_mode,
            io:format("******** Population_Monitor:~p shut down with Reason:~p
OpTag:~p, while in OpMode:~p~n",[Population_Id,Reason,OpTag,OpMode]),
            io:format("******** Tot Agents:~p Population Generation:~p Eval_Acc:~p
Cycle_Acc:~p Time_Acc:~p~n",[S#state.tot_agents,S#state.pop_gen,S#state.eval_acc,
S#state.cycle_acc,S#state.time_acc])
    end.
```

```
%When the population_monitor process terminates, it states so, notifies with what op_tag and
op_mode it terminated, all the stats gathered, and then shuts down.


%%-----------------------------------------------------------------
%% Func: code_change(OldVsn, State, Extra) -> {ok, NewState}
%% Description: Convert process state when code is changed
%%-----------------------------------------------------------------
code_change(_OldVsn, State, _Extra) ->
    {ok, State}.


%%-----------------------------------------------------------------
%% Internal functions
%%-----------------------------------------------------------------
extract_AgentIds(Population_Id,AgentType)->
    P = genotype:dirty_read({population,Population_Id}),
    Specie_Ids = P#population.specie_ids,
    case AgentType of
        champions ->
                extract_ChampionAgentIds(Specie_Ids,[]);
        all ->
                extract_AllAgentIds(Specie_Ids,[])
    end.
```

%The extract_AgentIds/2 function accepts the Population_Id and a parameter which specifies
what type of agents (all agent, or just champions) to extract from the population, after which it
extracts the ids of those agents. Depending on the AgentType parameter, the function either
calls extract_ChampionAgentIds/2 or extract_AllAgentIds/2, which return the list of agent ids
to the caller.

```
    extract_ChampionAgentIds([Specie_Id|Specie_Ids],Acc)->
        S = genotype:dirty_read({specie,Specie_Id}),
        ChampionAgent_Ids = S#specie.champion_ids,
        extract_ChampionAgentIds(Specie_Ids,lists:append(ChampionAgent_Ids,Acc));
    extract_ChampionAgentIds([],Acc)->
        Acc.
```

%extract_ChampionAgentIds/2 accumulates the ids of champion agents from every specie in
the Specie_Ids list, and then returns that list to the caller.

```
    extract_AllAgentIds([Specie_Id|Specie_Ids],Acc)->
        extract_AllAgentIds(Specie_Ids,lists:append(extract_SpecieAgentIds(Specie_Id),
Acc));
    extract_AllAgentIds([],Acc)->
        Acc.
```

%extract_AllAgentIds/2 accumulates and returns to the caller an id list of all the agents belonging to all the species in the Specie_Ids list.

```
extract_SpecieAgentIds(Specie_Id)->
    S = genotype:dirty_read({specie,Specie_Id}),
    S#specie.agent_ids.
%extract_SpecieAgentIds/1 returns a list of agent ids belonging to some particular specie, back
to the caller.


summon_agents(OpMode,Agent_Ids)->
    summon_agents(OpMode,Agent_Ids,[]).
summon_agents(OpMode,[Agent_Id|Agent_Ids],Acc)->
    Agent_PId = exoself:start(Agent_Id,self()),
    summon_agents(OpMode,Agent_Ids,[{Agent_Id,Agent_PId}|Acc]);
summon_agents(_OpMode,[],Acc)->
    Acc.
%The summon_agents/2 and summon_agents/3 functions spawns all the agents in the
Agent_ids list, and return to the caller a list of tuples of the following form:
[{Agent_Id,Agent_PId}...].


%%%%%%%%%%%%%%%%%%%%%%%%%%%%%%%%%%%%%%%%%%%%%%%%%%%%%%%%%%%%%%%%%%
test()->
    init_population({?INIT_POPULATION_ID,?INIT_CONSTRAINTS,?OP_MODE,
?SELECTION_ALGORITHM}).
%The test/0 function starts the population monitor through init_population/1 with a set of de-
fault parameters specified through the macros of this module.


init_population({Population_Id,Specie_Constraints,OpMode,Selection_Algorithm})->
    random:seed(now()),
    F = fun()->
            case genotype:read({population,Population_Id}) of
                undefined ->
                    create_Population(Population_Id,Specie_Constraints);
                _ ->
                    delete_population(Population_Id),
                    create_Population(Population_Id,Specie_Constraints)
            end
    end,
    Result = mnesia:transaction(F),
    case Result of
        {atomic,_} ->
            population_monitor:start({OpMode,Population_Id,Selection_Algorithm});
        Error ->
            io:format("******** ERROR in PopulationMonitor:~p~n",[Error])
    end.
%The function init_population/1 creates a new population with the id Population_Id, composed
of length(Specie_Constraints) species, where each specie uses the particular specie constraint
specified within the Specie_Constraints list. The function first checks if a population with the
```

noted Population_Id already exists. If a population with such an id does already exist, then the function first deletes it, and then creates a new one. Since the ids are usually generated with the genotype:create_UniqueId/0, the only way an already existing Population_Id is dropped into the function as a parameter is if it is intended by the researcher. When performing benchmarks or running other tests on the system, the Population_Id is set to test: Population_Id = test.

```
create_Population(Population_Id,Specie_Constraints)->
        SpecieSize = ?INIT_SPECIE_SIZE,
        Specie_Ids = [create_specie(Population_Id,SpecCon,origin,SpecieSize) || SpecCon <-
Specie_Constraints],
        Population = #population{
               id = Population_Id,
               specie_ids = Specie_Ids
        },
        genotype:write(Population).

    create_specie(Population_Id,SpeCon,Fingerprint)->
               Specie_Id = genotype:generate_UniqueId(),
               create_specie(Population_Id,Specie_Id,0,[],SpeCon,Fingerprint).
    create_specie(Population_Id,SpeCon,Fingerprint,SpecieSize)->
               Specie_Id = genotype:generate_UniqueId(),
               create_specie(Population_Id,Specie_Id,SpecieSize,[],SpeCon,Fingerprint).
    create_specie(Population_Id,Specie_Id,0,IdAcc,SpeCon,Fingerprint)->
               io:format("Specie_Id:~p Morphology:~p~n",[Specie_Id,
SpeCon#constraint.morphology]),
               Specie = #specie{
                      id = Specie_Id,
                      population_id = Population_Id,
                      fingerprint = Fingerprint,
                      constraint = SpeCon,
                      agent_ids = IdAcc
               },
               genotype:write(Specie),
               Specie_Id;
    create_specie(Population_Id,Specie_Id,Agent_Index,IdAcc,SpeCon,Fingerprint)->
               Agent_Id = {genotype:generate_UniqueId(),agent},
               genotype:construct_Agent(Specie_Id,Agent_Id,SpeCon),
               create_specie(Population_Id,Specie_Id,Agent_Index-1,[Agent_Id|IdAcc],
SpeCon,Fingerprint).
```
%The create_Population/3 generates length(Specie_Constraints) number of species, where each specie is composed of ?INIT_SPECIE_SIZE number of agents. The function uses the create_specie/4 to generate the species. The create_specie/3 and create_specie/4 functions are simplified versions which use default parameters to call the create_specie/6 function. The create_specie/6 function constructs the agents using the genotype:construct_Agent/3 function, accumulating the Agent_Ids in the IdAcc list. Once all the agents have been created, the func-

tion creates the specie record, fills in the required elements, writes the specie record to database, and then returns the Specie_Id to the caller.

```
continue(OpMode,Selection_Algorithm)->
    Population_Id = test,
    population_monitor:start({OpMode,Population_Id,Selection_Algorithm}).
continue(OpMode,Selection_Algorithm,Population_Id)->
    population_monitor:start({OpMode,Population_Id,Selection_Algorithm}).
```
%The function continue/2 and continue/3 are used to summon an already existing population with Population_Id, and continue with the experiment using the chosen Selection_Algorithm.

```
mutate_population(Population_Id,KeepTot,Selection_Algorithm)->
    NeuralEnergyCost = calculate_EnergyCost(Population_Id),
    F = fun()->
            P = genotype:read({population,Population_Id}),
            Specie_Ids = P#population.specie_ids,
            [mutate_Specie(Specie_Id,KeepTot,NeuralEnergyCost,Selection_Algorithm) ||
Specie_Id <- Specie_Ids]
    end,
    {atomic,_} = mnesia:transaction(F).
```
%The function mutate_population/3 mutates the agents in every specie in its specie_ids list, maintaining each specie within the size of KeepTot. The function first calculates the average cost of each neuron, and then mutates each species separately using the calculated NeuralEnergyCost and Selection_Algorithm as parameters.

```
    mutate_Specie(Specie_Id,PopulationLimit,NeuralEnergyCost,Selection_Algorithm)->
        S = genotype:dirty_read({specie,Specie_Id}),
        {AvgFitness,Std,MaxFitness,MinFitness} = calculate_SpecieFitness({specie,S}),
        Agent_Ids = S#specie.agent_ids,
        AgentSummaries = construct_AgentSummaries(Agent_Ids,[]),
        io:format("Selection Algorirthm:~p~n",[Selection_Algorithm]),
        case Selection_Algorithm of
                competition ->
                    TotSurvivors =
round(length(AgentSummaries)*?SURVIVAL_PERCENTAGE),
                    SDX=lists:reverse(lists:sort([{Fitness/math:pow(TotN,?EFF), {Fitness,
TotN,Agent_Id}}||{Fitness,TotN,Agent_Id}<-AgentSummaries])),
                    ProperlySorted_AgentSummaries = [Val || {_,Val}<-SDX],
                    Valid_AgentSummaries=lists:sublist(ProperlySorted_AgentSummaries,
TotSurvivors),
                    Invalid_AgentSummaries=AgentSummaries--Valid_AgentSummaries,
                    {_,_,Invalid_AgentIds} = lists:unzip3(Invalid_AgentSummaries),
                    [genotype:delete_Agent(Agent_Id) || Agent_Id <- Invalid_AgentIds],
                    io:format("Valid_AgentSummaries:~p~n",[Valid_AgentSummaries]),
```

```
                        io:format("Invalid_AgentSummaries:~p~n", [Inva-
lid_AgentSummaries]),
                        TopAgentSummaries = lists:sublist(Valid_AgentSummaries,3),
                        {_TopFitnessList,_TopTotNs,TopAgent_Ids} =
lists:unzip3(TopAgentSummaries),
                        io:format("NeuralEnergyCost:~p~n",[NeuralEnergyCost]),
                        NewGenAgent_Ids = competition(Valid_AgentSummaries,
PopulationLimit,NeuralEnergyCost);
                top3 ->
                        TotSurvivors = 3,
                        ProperlySorted_AgentSummaries =
lists:reverse(lists:sort(AgentSummaries)),
                        Valid_AgentSummaries= lists:sublist(ProperlySorted_AgentSummaries,
TotSurvivors),
                        Invalid_AgentSummaries=AgentSummaries--Valid_AgentSummaries,
                        {_,_,Invalid_AgentIds} = lists:unzip3(Invalid_AgentSummaries),
                        {_,_,Valid_AgentIds} = lists:unzip3(Valid_AgentSummaries),
                        [genotype:delete_Agent(Agent_Id) || Agent_Id <- Invalid_AgentIds],
                        io:format("Valid_AgentSummaries:~p~n",[Valid_AgentSummaries]),
                        io:format("Invalid_AgentSummaries:~p~n", [Inva-
lid_AgentSummaries]),
                        TopAgentSummaries = lists:sublist(Valid_AgentSummaries,3),
                        {_TopFitnessList,_TopTotNs,TopAgent_Ids} =
lists:unzip3(TopAgentSummaries),
                        io:format("NeuralEnergyCost:~p~n",[NeuralEnergyCost]),
                        NewGenAgent_Ids = top3(Valid_AgentIds,PopulationLimit-
TotSurvivors,[])
        end,
        {FList,_TNList,_AgentIds}=lists:unzip3(ProperlySorted_AgentSummaries),
        [TopFitness|_] = FList,
        U_InnovationFactor = case TopFitness > S#specie.innovation_factor of
                true ->
                        0;
                false ->
                        S#specie.innovation_factor-1
        end,
        genotype:write(S#specie{
                agent_ids = NewGenAgent_Ids,
                champion_ids = TopAgent_Ids,
                fitness = {AvgFitness,Std,MaxFitness,MinFitness},
                innovation_factor = U_InnovationFactor}).
```
%The function mutate_Specie/4 uses the selection algorithm of type Selection_Algorithm to separate the fit from the unfit agents within the same species, and then mutates the fit agents to produce the final mutant offspring, maintaining the total specie size within PopulationLimit. The function first creates a list of agent summaries, which is a list of the format: [{Fit-

ness,TotNeurons,Agent_Id}...]. The function then modifies the fitness scores to be proportional to the agent's efficiency, which is based on the number of neurons it took the agent to produce this fitness (the NN's size). The function then sorts the updated summaries, and then splits the sorted summary list into a valid (fit) and invalid (unfit) lists of agents. The invalid agents are deleted, and the valid agents are used to create offspring using the Selection_Algorithm with which the function was called. The agent ids belonging to the next generation (the valid agents and their offspring) are then produced by the selection function. Afterward, the innovation factor (the last time the specie's top fitness improved) is updated. Finally, the ids of the top 3 agents within the specie are noted (these are the champion agents, best performing agents within the specie), and the updated specie record is written to database. The above function shows two types of selection algorithms, the 'competition' selection algorithm, and the 'top3' selection algorithm.

```
    construct_AgentSummaries([Agent_Id|Agent_Ids],Acc)->
        A = genotype:dirty_read({agent,Agent_Id}),
        construct_AgentSummaries(Agent_Ids,[{A#agent.fitness,
length((genotype:dirty_read({cortex, A#agent.cx_id}))#cortex.neuron_ids),Agent_Id}|Acc]);
    construct_AgentSummaries([],Acc)->
        Acc.
```
%The construct_AgentSummaries/2 reads the agents in the Agent_Ids list, and composes a list of tuples with the following format: [{AgentFitness,AgentTotNeurons,Agent_Id}...]. This list of tuples is referred to as: AgentSummaries. Once the AgentSummaries list is created, it is returned to the caller.

```
competition(Sorted_AgentSummaries,PopulationLimit,NeuralEnergyCost)->
    {AlotmentsP,NextGenSize_Estimate} = calculate_alotments(Sorted_AgentSummaries,
NeuralEnergyCost,[],0),
    Normalizer = NextGenSize_Estimate/PopulationLimit,
    io:format("Population size normalizer:~p~n",[Normalizer]),
    gather_survivors(AlotmentsP,Normalizer,[]).
```
%The competition/3 is part of the selection algorithm called 'competition'. This function first executes calculate_alotments/4 to calculate the number of offspring allotted to each agent in the AgentSummaries list. The function then calculates the Normalizer value, which is used to normalize the allotted number of offspring for each agent, to ensure that the final species size is within PopulationLimit. The function then drops into the gather_survivors/3 function, which uses the normalized offspring allotment values to create the actual mutant offspring for each agent.

```
    calculate_alotments([{Fitness,TotNeurons,Agent_Id}|Sorted_AgentSummaries],
NeuralEnergyCost,Acc,NewPopAcc)->
        NeuralAlotment = Fitness/NeuralEnergyCost,
        MutantAlotment = NeuralAlotment/TotNeurons,
        U_NewPopAcc = NewPopAcc+MutantAlotment,
        calculate_alotments(Sorted_AgentSummaries,NeuralEnergyCost, [{MutantAlotment,
Fitness,TotNeurons,Agent_Id}|Acc],U_NewPopAcc);
```

```
calculate_alotments([],_NeuralEnergyCost,Acc,NewPopAcc)->
        io:format("NewPopAcc:~p~n",[NewPopAcc]),
        {Acc,NewPopAcc}.
```

%The calculate_alotments/4 function accepts the AgentSummaries list and for each agent, using the NeuralEnergyCost, calculates how many offspring that agent can produce by using the agent's Fitness, TotNeurons, and NeuralEnergyCost parameters. The function first calculates how many neurons the agent is allotted, based on the agent's fitness and the cost of each neuron (which itself was calculated based on the average performance of the population). From the number of neurons allotted to the agent, the function then calculates how many offspring the agent should be allotted, by dividing the number of neurons it is allotted by the agent's NN size. The function also keeps track of how many offspring will be created from all these agents in general, by adding up all the offspring allotments. The calculate_alotments/4 function does this for each tuple in the AgentSummaries, and then returns the calculated allotment list and NewPopAcc to the caller.

```
gather_survivors([{MutantAlotment,Fitness,TotNeurons,Agent_Id}|AlotmentsP],
Normalizer, Acc)->
        Normalized_MutantAlotment = round(MutantAlotment/Normalizer),
        io:format("Agent_Id:~p Normalized_MutantAlotment:~p~n", [Agent_Id,
Normalized_MutantAlotment]),
        SurvivingAgent_Ids = case Normalized_MutantAlotment >= 1 of
                true ->
                        MutantAgent_Ids = case Normalized_MutantAlotment >= 2 of
                                true ->
                                        [create_MutantAgentCopy(Agent_Id)|| _ <-
lists:seq(1,Normalized_MutantAlotment-1)];
                                false ->
                                        []
                        end,
                        [Agent_Id|MutantAgent_Ids];
                false ->
                        io:format("Deleting agent:~p~n",[Agent_Id]),
                        genotype:delete_Agent(Agent_Id),
                        []
        end,
        gather_survivors(AlotmentsP,Normalizer,lists:append(SurvivingAgent_Ids,Acc));
gather_survivors([],_Normalizer,Acc)->
        io:format("New Population:~p PopSize:~p~n",[Acc,length(Acc)]),
        Acc.
```

%The gather_survivors/3 function accepts the list composed of the allotment tuples and the population normalizer value calculated by the competition/3 function. Using these values it calculates the actual number of offspring that each agent should produce, creates the mutant offspring, and accumulates the new generation agent ids. For each Agent_Id the function first calculates the normalized offspring allotment value, to ensure that the final number of agents in the specie is within the population limit of that specie. If the offspring allotment value is less than 0, the agent is killed. If the offspring allotment is 1, the agent is allowed to survive to the next generation, but is not allowed to create any new offspring. If the offspring allotment is greater than one, then the function creates Normalized_MutantAlotment-1 number of offspring from this fit agent, by calling upon the create_MutantAgentCopy/1 function which returns the id of the new mutant offspring. Once all the offspring have been created, the function returns to the caller a list of ids, composed of the surviving parent agent ids, and their offspring.

```
create_MutantAgentCopy(Agent_Id)->
        AgentClone_Id = genotype:clone_Agent(Agent_Id),
        io:format("AgentClone_Id:~p~n",[AgentClone_Id]),
        genome_mutator:mutate(AgentClone_Id),
        AgentClone_Id.
```
%The create_MutantAgentCopy/1 first creates a clone of the Agent_Id, and then uses the genome_mutator:mutate/1 function to mutate that clone, returning the id of the cloned agent to the caller.

```
create_MutantAgentCopy(Agent_Id,safe)->
        A = genotype:dirty_read({agent,Agent_Id}),
        S = genotype:dirty_read({specie,A#agent.specie_id}),
        AgentClone_Id = genotype:clone_Agent(Agent_Id),
        Agent_Ids = S#specie.agent_ids,
        genotype:write(S#specie{agent_ids = [AgentClone_Id|Agent_Ids]}),
        io:format("AgentClone_Id:~p~n",[AgentClone_Id]),
        genome_mutator:mutate(AgentClone_Id),
        AgentClone_Id.
```
%The create_MutantAgentCopy/2 function is similar to arity 1 function of the same name, but it also adds the id of the cloned mutant agent to the specie record to which the parent genotype belonged. The specie with its updated agent_ids is then written to database, and the id of the mutant clone is returned to the caller.

```
top3(_Valid_AgentIds,0,Acc)->
    Acc;
top3(Valid_AgentIds,OffspringIndex,Acc)->
    Parent_AgentId = lists:nth(random:uniform(length(Valid_AgentIds)),Valid_AgentIds),
    MutantAgent_Id = create_MutantAgentCopy(Parent_AgentId),
        top3(Valid_AgentIds,OffspringIndex-1,[MutantAgent_Id|Acc]).
```
%The top3/3 function is a very simple selection algorithm, which just selects the top 3 most fit agents, and then uses the create_MutantAgentCopy/1 function to create their offspring. Each parent agent is allowed to create the same number of offspring.

```
delete_population(Population_Id)->
    P = genotype:dirty_read({population,Population_Id}),
    Specie_Ids = P#population.specie_ids,
    [delete_specie(Specie_Id) || Specie_Id <- Specie_Ids],
    mnesia:delete({population,Population_Id}).
```

%The delete_population/1 function deletes the entire population, by deleting the specie records belonging to the Population_Id, by deleting the agent records belonging to those species, and then by deleting the population record itself.

```
    delete_specie(Specie_Id)->
            S = genotype:dirty_read({specie,Specie_Id}),
            Agent_Ids = S#specie.agent_ids,
            [genotype:delete_Agent(Agent_Id) || Agent_Id <- Agent_Ids],
            mnesia:delete({specie,Specie_Id}).
```
%The delete_specie/1 function deletes the agents associated with the Specie_Id, and then deletes the specic record itself.

```
calculate_EnergyCost(Population_Id)->
    Agent_Ids = extract_AgentIds(Population_Id,all),
    TotEnergy = lists:sum([extract_AgentFitness(Agent_Id) || Agent_Id<-Agent_Ids]),
    TotNeurons = lists:sum([extract_AgentTotNeurons(Agent_Id) || Agent_Id <- Agent_Ids]),
    EnergyCost = TotEnergy/TotNeurons,
    EnergyCost.
```
%The calculate_EnergyCost/1 function calculates the average cost of each neuron, based on the fitness of each agent in the population, and the total number of neurons in the population. The value is calculated by first adding up all the fitness scores of the agents belonging to the population, then adding up the total number of neurons composing each agent in the population, and then finally by producing the EnergyCost, where EnergyCost = TotEnergy/TotNeurons. Afterwards, the function returns this value to the caller.

```
    extract_AgentTotNeurons(Agent_Id)->
            A = genotype:dirty_read({agent,Agent_Id}),
            Cx = genotype:dirty_read({cortex,A#agent.cx_id}),
            Neuron_Ids = Cx#cortex.neuron_ids,
            length(Neuron_Ids).

    extract_AgentFitness(Agent_Id)->
            A = genotype:dirty_read({agent,Agent_Id}),
            A#agent.fitness.
```
%The function extract_AgentTotNeurons simply extracts the neuron_ids list, and returns the length of that list to the caller. The length of the list is the total number of neurons belonging to the NN based system.

```
calculate_SpecieFitness({specie,S})->
    Agent_Ids = S#specie.agent_ids,
    FitnessAcc = calculate_fitness(Agent_Ids),
    Sorted_FitnessAcc=lists:sort(FitnessAcc),
    [MinFitness|_] = Sorted_FitnessAcc,
    [MaxFitness|_] = lists:reverse(Sorted_FitnessAcc),
    AvgFitness = functions:avg(FitnessAcc),
```

```
    Std = functions:std(FitnessAcc),
    {AvgFitness,Std,MaxFitness,MinFitness};
calculate_SpecieFitness(Specie_Id)->
    S = genotype:dirty_read({specie,Specie_Id}),
    calculate_SpecieFitness({specie,S}).
```
%The calculate_SpecieFitness/1 function calculates the general fitness statistic of the specie: the average, max, min, and standard deviation of the specie's fitness. The function first composes a fitness list by accessing the fitness scores of each agent belonging to it, and then calculates the above noted statistics from that list, returning the tuple with these three values, to the caller.

```
    calculate_fitness(Agent_Ids)->
        calculate_fitness(Agent_Ids,[]).
    calculate_fitness([Agent_Id|Agent_Ids],FitnessAcc)->
        A = genotype:dirty_read({agent,Agent_Id}),
        case A#agent.fitness of
            undefined ->
                    calculate_fitness(Agent_Ids,FitnessAcc);
            Fitness ->
                    calculate_fitness(Agent_Ids,[Fitness|FitnessAcc])
        end;
    calculate_fitness([],FitnessAcc)->
        FitnessAcc.
```
%The calculate_fitness/1 function composes a fitness list using the fitness values belonging to the agents in the Agent_Ids list. If the agent does not yet have a fitness score, if for example it has just been created/mutated but not yet evaluated, it is skipped. The composed fitness list is then returned to the caller.

Having now completed the population_monitor module, we move onwards and update the exoself module in the next section.

8.5.16 Updating the exoself Module

The *exoself* is a process that has a global view of the NN, and can be used to monitor the NN processes, to restore damaged neurons, to recover the NN based system from crashes, and to offer the NN system other services. It is also the program that in a sense is a phenotypical representation of the agent record. The exoself is the process that is spawned first, and which then in turn converts its NN's genotype to phenotype. It is the exoself process that tunes the NN system's neural weights, and summons the private scapes with which the NN system interfaces.

Unlike in the previous chapter, there is no trainer in the neuroevolutionary system. The population monitor will spawn exoselfs, which will then spawn the NN based systems. Previously, the exoself used an augmented stochastic hill climbing algorithm to optimize the weights. In this chapter we are creating a memetic and genetic algorithm based TWEANN system. If we evolve the agent's topology during one phase, and let the exoself optimize synaptic weights during another, the system will be a memetic algorithm based TWEANN. If we make ?MAX_ATTEMPTS equal to 0, the exoself does not optimize the weights outside the selection/mutation phase ran by the population_monitor process, weight perturbation is done during the mutation phase using the mutate_weights MO only, and thus this neuroevolutionary system begins to behave as a standard genetic algorithm based TWEANN.

Beside the switch to the mnesia database read and write functions, and the exoself's connection to the population_monitor instead of the trainer process, the main addition to the algorithm has to do with the fact that the new NN has recursive connections. Note that when we have spawned the phenotype of a NN with recurrent connections, the neurons which have these recursive output connections, cannot output any signals because they await the input signals from their presynaptic connections. Some of these presynaptic neurons cannot produce an output signal either, not until they receive their signals from the recursively connected neurons in the later layers... Thus there is a deadlock, as shown in Fig-8.14.

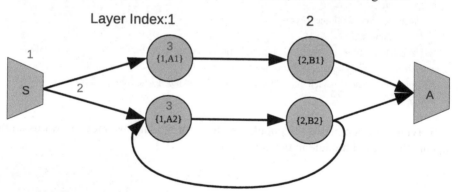

Fig. 8.14 Deadlock occurring in recurrent NN based systems.

Let us go through the steps of the above figure:

1. The sensor acquires the sensory signal, from an interaction with the environment, or by generating it internally, for example.
2. The sensor forwards the sensory signal to the two neurons it is connected to, A1 and A2.
3. Neuron A1 is only waiting for a single input signal, from S. As soon as it receives this signal, it processes it and forwards an output to B1. Neuron A2 on the other hand waits for two input signals, a signal from S, and a signal from B2. It receives the signal from S, but not from B2, because B2 is waiting for the signal from A2 before it can send a signal to A2... thus there is a deadlock.

It is for this reason that we have created the ro_ids list for each neuron. Since each neuron that has recursive connections knows about them through ro_ids. It then can, as soon as it is spawned, send a default signal: [0], to the elements in its ro_ids list. This effectively breaks the deadlock, if there was any, since any element dependent on this input signal, can now continue with processing the input signals and output a signal of its own.

But this approach also leads to a problem when our system functions as a memetic algorithm based TWEANN, and when it performs multiple evaluations of the NN system. If you look at Fig-8.15, you will note that the default recursive signals, [0], sent out by the neurons when they have just been created, ensures that when the NN has finished its evaluation and should be restarted (when for example we wish to reset or revert the neural weights and perform weight perturbation), will result in some of the neurons (those connected to from the recurrent neurons) have a populated inbox. The neurons which are connected from the recurrent neurons, will have recursive signals in their inbox. To deal with this situation and reset the neurons back to their initial, pristine conditions after the NN's evaluation has ended, we need to flush each neuron's inbox. To do this, we first ensure that all neurons are put on pause, then have their inboxes flushed, then reset all neurons (which might mean that some of the neurons will send out fresh recursive signals [0]) in the NN, and then finally reactive the cortex process, so that it can start its synchronization of sensors and actuators anew. This new flush buffering function added to the neurons, and the ability to reset/clear neurons to their initial state, is the main new functional addition to the exoself.

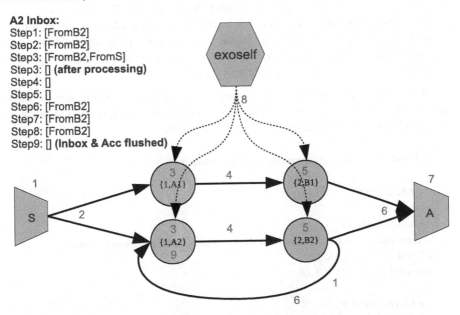

Fig. 8.15 To reset the NN based agent after its evaluation, first pause the neurons, then flush the neurons, and then reactivate all neurons. At this point each neuron which has a recurrent connection will send out a new [0] signal to all elements in its ro_ids list.

Let us quickly go through the steps of the above figure before we update the exoself module with this functionality:

1. Sensor *S* gathers sensory signals. While at the same time, neuron *B2* sends out a default *[0]* signal to elements in its *ro_ids* list, which in this case is the neuron *A2*.
2. The sensor forwards the sensory signals to *A1* and *A2*.
3. A1 and A2 process signals, and because A2 has received in step 1 the signal from B2, it is able to process the two input signals.
4. A1 and A2 forward their output signals to B1 and B2 respectively.
5. B1 and B2 process their input signals, and produce output signals.
6. B1 forwards its signal to the actuator, while B2 forwards its signal to the actuator, and to neuron A2.
7. The actuator element processes its input signals.
8. At this point the sensors could again gather the sensory signals and forward them to the neurons, but we assume here that the evaluation just finished. At this point, because in step 6 a signal was sent to A2 from B2, *the neuron A2 currently has a signal from B2 in its inbox, even though the evaluation is now over.* If we at this point restart the NN system, B2 will again send the default recurrent signal to A2, but A2 still has in its inbox the signal from the previous evaluation... For this reason the exoself first sends a pause signal to all the neurons, after which point they flush their buffers/inboxes to go back to their initial, clean states.
9. When a neuron receives a pause signal from the exoself, it first pauses, and then flushes its buffer. Afterwards it awaits the reset signal, at which point it also resets its input pids list to its initial state, to again await input signals from all the elements it is connected from. If the neuron has any ids in its ro_ids list, it outputs to those elements the default signal: [0].

Having now discussed in detail the importance of buffer flushing, and the manner in which the exoself pauses and resets neurons after each evaluation, we now update the exoself module, as shown in Listing-8.19.

Listing-8.19: The updated implementation of the exoself module.

```
-module(exoself).
-compile(export_all).
-include("records.hrl").
-record(state,{file_name,genotype,idsNpids,cx_pid,spids,npids,apids,highest_fitness,
tot_evaluations,tot_cycles}).
-define(MAX_ATTEMPTS,50).

start(Agent_Id,PM_PId)->
    spawn(exoself,prep,[Agent_Id,PM_PId]).
%The start/2 function spawns a new Agent_Id exoself process belonging to the popula-
tion_monitor process with the pid: PM_PId.
```

```erlang
prep(Agent_Id,PM_PId)->
    random:seed(now()),
    IdsNPIds = ets:new(idsNpids,[set,private]),
    A = genotype:dirty_read({agent,Agent_Id}),
    Cx = genotype:dirty_read({cortex,A#agent.cx_id}),
    SIds = Cx#cortex.sensor_ids,
    AIds = Cx#cortex.actuator_ids,
    NIds = Cx#cortex.neuron_ids,
    ScapePIds = spawn_Scapes(IdsNPIds,SIds,AIds),
    spawn_CerebralUnits(IdsNPIds,cortex,[Cx#cortex.id]),
    spawn_CerebralUnits(IdsNPIds,sensor,SIds),
    spawn_CerebralUnits(IdsNPIds,actuator,AIds),
    spawn_CerebralUnits(IdsNPIds,neuron,NIds),
    link_Sensors(SIds,IdsNPIds),
    link_Actuators(AIds,IdsNPIds),
    link_Neurons(NIds,IdsNPIds),
    {SPIds,NPIds,APIds}=link_Cortex(Cx,IdsNPIds),
    Cx_PId = ets:lookup_element(IdsNPIds,Cx#cortex.id,2),
    loop(Agent_Id,PM_PId,IdsNPIds,Cx_PId,SPIds,NPIds,APIds,ScapePIds,0,0,0,0,1).
```

%The prep/2 function prepares and sets up the exoself's state before dropping into the main loop. The function first reads the agent and cortex records belonging to the Agent_Id NN based system. The function then reads the sensor, actuator, and neuron ids, then spawns the private scapes using the spawn_Scapes/3 function, then spawns the cortex, sensor, actuator, and neuron processes, and then finally links up all these processes together using the link_.../2 functions. Once the phenotype has been generated from the genotype, the exoself drops into its main loop.

```erlang
loop(Agent_Id,PM_PId,IdsNPIds,Cx_PId,SPIds,NPIds,APIds,ScapePIds,HighestFitness,
EvalAcc,CycleAcc,TimeAcc,Attempt)->
    receive
        {Cx_PId,evaluation_completed,Fitness,Cycles,Time}->
            {U_HighestFitness,U_Attempt}=case Fitness > HighestFitness of
                true ->
                    [NPId ! {self(),weight_backup} || NPId <- NPIds],
                    {Fitness,0};
                false ->
                    Perturbed_NPIds=get(perturbed),
                    [NPId ! {self(),weight_restore} || NPId <- Perturbed_NPIds],
                    {HighestFitness,Attempt+1}
            end,
            [PId ! {self(), reset_prep} || PId <- NPIds],
            gather_acks(length(NPIds)),
            [PId ! {self(), reset} || PId <- NPIds],
            case U_Attempt >= ?MAX_ATTEMPTS of
                true -> %End training
```

```
                                    U_CycleAcc = CycleAcc+Cycles,
                                    U_TimeAcc = TimeAcc+Time,
                                    A=genotype:dirty_read({agent,Agent_Id}),
                                    genotype:write(A#agent{fitness=U_HighestFitness}),
                                    backup_genotype(IdsNPIds,NPIds),
                                    terminate_phenotype(Cx_PId,SPIds,NPIds,APIds,ScapePIds),
                                    io:format("Agent:~p terminating. Genotype has been backed
up.~n Fitness:~p~n TotEvaluations:~p~n TotCycles:~p~n TimeAcc:~p~n", [self(),
U_HighestFitness, EvalAcc,U_CycleAcc, U_TimeAcc]),
                                    gen_server:cast(PM_PId,{Agent_Id,terminated,
U_HighestFitness,EvalAcc,U_CycleAcc,U_TimeAcc});
                            false -> %Continue training
                                    Tot_Neurons = length(NPIds),
                                    MP = 1/math:sqrt(Tot_Neurons),
                                    Perturb_NPIds=[NPId || NPId <- NPIds,random:uniform()<MP],
                                    put(perturbed,Perturb_NPIds),
                                    [NPId ! {self(),weight_perturb} || NPId <- Perturb_NPIds],
                                    Cx_PId ! {self(),reactivate},
                                    loop(Agent_Id,PM_PId,IdsNPIds,Cx_PId,SPIds, NPIds, APIds,
ScapePIds,U_HighestFitness, EvalAcc+1,CycleAcc+Cycles,TimeAcc+Time,U_Attempt)
                    end
    end.
```

%The exoself process' main loop awaits from its cortex process the evoluation_completed message. Once the message is received, based on the fitness achieved, exoself decides whether to
continue tuning the weights or terminate the system. Exoself tries to improve the fitness by per-
turbing/tuning the weights of its neurons. After each tuning (synaptic weight perturbation) session, the Neural Network based system performs another evaluation by interacting with the
scape until completion (the NN solves a problem, or dies within the scape or...). The order of
events is important: When evaluation_completed message is received, the function first checks
whether the newly achieved fitness is higher than the thus far highest achieved fitness. If it is
not, the exoself sends the neurons a message to restore their weights to previous state, during
which they achieved the highest fitness, instead of their current state which yielded the current
lower fitness score. If on the other hand the new fitness is higher than the previously highest
achieved fitness, then the function tells the neurons to backup their current weights, as these
weights represent the NN's best, most fit form yet. Exoself then tells all the neurons to prepare
for a reset by sending each neuron the {self(),reset_prep} message. Since the NN can have recursive connections, it is important for each neuron to flush its buffer/inbox to be reset into an
initial fresh state, which is achieved after the neurons receive the reset_prep message. The
exoself then sends the reset message to the neurons, which returns them to their main loop.
Finally, the exoself checks whether it has already tried to improve the NN's fitness a maximum
(?MAX_ATTEMPTS) number of times. If that is the case, the exoself process backs up the updated NN (the updated, tuned weights) to database using the backup_genotype/2 function,
prints to screen that it is terminating, and sends to the population_monitor the accumulated statistics (highest fitness, evaluation count, cycle count...). On the other hand, if the exoself is not
yet done tuning the neural weights, if it has not yet reached its ending condition, it instead ran-

domly selects a set of neurons from its NPIds list, and requests that they perturb their synaptic weights, then reactivates the cortex, and then finally drops back into its main loop. Each neuron in the NPId list has a probability: 1/math(sqrt(Tot_Neurons)) of being selected for weight perturbation, a value that is proportional to the total number of neurons in the NN, and grows with the NN size.

```
spawn_CerebralUnits(IdsNPIds,CerebralUnitType,[Id|Ids])->
        PId = CerebralUnitType:gen(self(),node()),
        ets:insert(IdsNPIds,{Id,PId}),
        ets:insert(IdsNPIds,{PId,Id}),
        spawn_CerebralUnits(IdsNPIds,CerebralUnitType,Ids);
spawn_CerebralUnits(_IdsNPIds,_CerebralUnitType,[])->
        true.
```
%We spawn the process for each element based on its type: CerebralUnitType, using the gen function that belongs to the CerebralUnitType module. Then we enter the {Id,PId} tuple into our ETS table for later use, thus establishing a mapping between Ids and their PIds.

```
spawn_Scapes(IdsNPIds,Sensor_Ids,Actuator_Ids)->
        Sensor_Scapes = [(genotype:dirty_read({sensor,Id}))#sensor.scape || Id<-Sensor_Ids],
        Actuator_Scapes = [(genotype:dirty_read({actuator,Id}))#actuator.scape || Id<-
Actuator_Ids],
        Unique_Scapes = Sensor_Scapes++(Actuator_Scapes--Sensor_Scapes),
        SN_Tuples=[{scape:gen(self(),node()),ScapeName} || {private,ScapeName}<-
Unique_Scapes],
        [ets:insert(IdsNPIds,{ScapeName,PId}) || {PId,ScapeName} <- SN_Tuples],
        [ets:insert(IdsNPIds,{PId,ScapeName}) || {PId,ScapeName} <-SN_Tuples],
        [PId ! {self(),ScapeName} || {PId,ScapeName} <- SN_Tuples],
        [PId || {PId,_ScapeName} <-SN_Tuples].
```
%The spawn_Scapes/3 function first extracts all the scapes that the sensors and actuators interface with. Then it creates a filtered scape list which only holds unique scape records. Finally, from this list it selects the private scapes, and then spawns them.

```
link_Sensors([SId|Sensor_Ids],IdsNPIds) ->
        S=genotype:dirty_read({sensor,SId}),
        SPId = ets:lookup_element(IdsNPIds,SId,2),
        Cx_PId = ets:lookup_element(IdsNPIds,S#sensor.cx_id,2),
        SName = S#sensor.name,
        Fanout_Ids = S#sensor.fanout_ids,
        Fanout_PIds = [ets:lookup_element(IdsNPIds,Id,2) || Id <- Fanout_Ids],
        Scape=case S#sensor.scape of
                {private,ScapeName}->
                        ets:lookup_element(IdsNPIds,ScapeName,2)
        end,
        SPId ! {self(),{SId,Cx_PId,Scape,SName,S#sensor.vl,Fanout_PIds}},
        link_Sensors(Sensor_Ids,IdsNPIds);
```

```
    link_Sensors([],_IdsNPIds)->
        ok.
```

%The link_Sensors/2 function sends to the already spawned and waiting sensors their states, composed of the PId lists and other information which are needed by the sensors to link up and interface with other elements in the distributed phenotype.

```
    link_Actuators([AId|Actuator_Ids],IdsNPIds) ->
        A=genotype:dirty_read({actuator,AId}),
        APId = ets:lookup_element(IdsNPIds,AId,2),
        Cx_PId = ets:lookup_element(IdsNPIds,A#actuator.cx_id,2),
        AName = A#actuator.name,
        Fanin_Ids = A#actuator.fanin_ids,
        Fanin_PIds = [ets:lookup_element(IdsNPIds,Id,2) || Id <- Fanin_Ids],
        Scape=case A#actuator.scape of
                {private,ScapeName}->
                        ets:lookup_element(IdsNPIds,ScapeName,2)
        end,
        APId ! {self(),{AId,Cx_PId,Scape,AName,Fanin_PIds}},
        link_Actuators(Actuator_Ids,IdsNPIds);
    link_Actuators([],_IdsNPIds)->
        ok.
```

%The link_Actuators/2 function sends to the already spawned and waiting actuators their states, composed of the PId lists and other information which are needed by the actuators to link up and interface with other elements in the distributed phenotype.

```
    link_Neurons([NId|Neuron_Ids],IdsNPIds) ->
        N=genotype:dirty_read({neuron,NId}),
        NPId = ets:lookup_element(IdsNPIds,NId,2),
        Cx_PId = ets:lookup_element(IdsNPIds,N#neuron.cx_id,2),
        AFName = N#neuron.af,
        Input_IdPs = N#neuron.input_idps,
        Output_Ids = N#neuron.output_ids,
        RO_Ids = N#neuron.ro_ids,
        Input_PIdPs = convert_IdPs2PIdPs(IdsNPIds,Input_IdPs,[]),
        Output_PIds = [ets:lookup_element(IdsNPIds,Id,2) || Id <- Output_Ids],
        RO_PIds = [ets:lookup_element(IdsNPIds,Id,2) || Id <- RO_Ids],
        NPId ! {self(),{NId,Cx_PId,AFName,Input_PIdPs,Output_PIds,RO_PIds}},
        link_Neurons(Neuron_Ids,IdsNPIds);
    link_Neurons([],_IdsNPIds)->
        ok.
```

%The link_Neurons/2 function sends to the already spawned and waiting neurons their states, composed of the PId lists and other information needed by the neurons to link up and interface with other elements in the distributed phenotype.

```
        convert_IdPs2PIdPs(_IdsNPIds,[{bias,[Bias]}],Acc)->
```

```erlang
            lists:reverse([Bias|Acc]);
    convert_IdPs2PIdPs(IdsNPIds,[{Id,Weights}|Fanin_IdPs],Acc)->
        convert_IdPs2PIdPs(IdsNPIds,Fanin_IdPs, [{ets:lookup_element(IdsNPIds, Id,
2),Weights}|Acc]);
    convert_IdPs2PIdPs(_IdsNPIds,[],Acc)->
        lists:reverse(Acc).
```
%The convert_IdPs2PIdPs/3 converts the IdP tuples: {Id, Weights}, into tuples that use PIds instead of Ids: {PId, Weights}, such that the Neuron will know which weights are to be associated with which incoming vector signals. The last element is the bias, which is added to the list in a none-tuple form. Afterwards, the list is reversed to its proper order, and returned to the caller.

```erlang
link_Cortex(Cx,IdsNPIds) ->
    Cx_Id = Cx#cortex.id,
    Cx_PId = ets:lookup_element(IdsNPIds,Cx_Id,2),
    SIds = Cx#cortex.sensor_ids,
    AIds = Cx#cortex.actuator_ids,
    NIds = Cx#cortex.neuron_ids,
    SPIds = [ets:lookup_element(IdsNPIds,SId,2) || SId <- SIds],
    NPIds = [ets:lookup_element(IdsNPIds,NId,2) || NId <- NIds],
    APIds = [ets:lookup_element(IdsNPIds,AId,2) || AId <- AIds],
    Cx_PId ! {self(),Cx_Id,SPIds,NPIds,APIds},
    {SPIds,NPIds,APIds}.
```
%The link_Cortex/2 function sends to the already spawned and waiting cortex its state, composed of the PId lists and other information which is needed by the cortex to link up and interface with other elements in the distributed phenotype.

```erlang
backup_genotype(IdsNPIds,NPIds)->
    Neuron_IdsNWeights = get_backup(NPIds,[]),
    update_genotype(IdsNPIds,Neuron_IdsNWeights),
    io:format("Finished updating genotype~n").

get_backup([NPId|NPIds],Acc)->
        NPId ! {self(),get_backup},
        receive
            {NPId,NId,WeightTuples}->
                get_backup(NPIds,[{NId,WeightTuples}|Acc])
        end;
get_backup([],Acc)->
        Acc.
```
%The backup_genotype/2 uses get_backup/2 to contact all the neurons in the NN and request the neuron's Ids and their Input_IdPs. Once the updated Input_IdPs from all the neurons have been accumulated, they are passed through the update_genotype/2 function to produce updated neuron tuples, and are then written to database. This effectively updates the NN genotype with the now tuned neurons.

```
update_genotype(IdsNPIds,[{N_Id,PIdPs}|WeightPs])->
        N = genotype:dirty_read({neuron,N_Id}),
        Updated_InputIdPs = convert_PIdPs2IdPs(IdsNPIds,PIdPs,[]),
        U_N = N#neuron{input_idps = Updated_InputIdPs},
        genotype:write(U_N),
        update_genotype(IdsNPIds,WeightPs);
    update_genotype(_IdsNPIds,[])->
        ok.
```
%For every {N_Id,PIdPs} tuple, the update_genotype/3 function extracts the neuron with the id: N_Id, updates the neuron's input_IdPs, and writes the updated neuron to database.

```
        convert_PIdPs2IdPs(IdsNPIds,[{PId,Weights}|Input_PIdPs],Acc)->
                convert_PIdPs2IdPs(IdsNPIds,Input_PIdPs, [{ets:lookup_element(IdsNPIds,
PId,2),Weights}|Acc]);
        convert_PIdPs2IdPs(_IdsNPIds,[Bias],Acc)->
                lists:reverse([{bias,[Bias]}|Acc]);
        convert_PIdPs2IdPs(_IdsNPIds,[],Acc)->
                lists:reverse(Acc).
```
%The convert_PIdPs2IdPs/3 function performs the conversion from PIds to Ids for every {PId,Weights} tuple in the Input_PIdPs list. The updated Input_IdPs list is then returned to the caller.

```
terminate_phenotype(Cx_PId,SPIds,NPIds,APIds,ScapePIds)->
    [PId ! {self(),terminate} || PId <- SPIds],
    [PId ! {self(),terminate} || PId <- APIds],
    [PId ! {self(),terminate} || PId <- NPIds],
    [PId ! {self(),terminate} || PId <- ScapePIds],
    Cx_PId ! {self(),terminate}.
```
%The terminate_phenotype/5 function terminates sensors, actuators, neurons, all private scapes, and the cortex, making up the phenotype of the NN based system.

```
gather_acks(0)->
    done;
gather_acks(PId_Index)->
    receive
        {_From,ready}->
                gather_acks(PId_Index-1)
        after 100000 ->
                io:format("******** Not all acks received:~p~n",[PId_Index])
    end.
```
%gather_acks/1 function ensures that it receives all X number of {From, ready} messages from the neurons, before it returns the atom: done, to the caller. X is set by the caller of the function.

8.5.17 Updating the neuron Module

Though the next element in the hierarchy is the cortex element, it does not require any updates. The only remaining module that needs to be updated is the neuron module. Unlike in the previous chapter, our current neurons need to be able to support recursive connections, and all the synchronization detail that comes with it. As discussed in the previous section, the neurons which have recursive connections need to produce and forward the signal: [0], to the *ids* in the *ro_ids* list, when just being initiated. Furthermore, when the NN based system has completed interacting with a scape, and the cortex has deactivated (but not shut down), if the exoself wants to reactivate the cortex, the neurons need to flush their buffers/inboxes so that they can return to their initial, pristine form (but with updated synaptic weights). When flushing its buffer, the neuron gets rid of any recursive signals remaining in its inbox, as was shown in the previous section.

Another addition in this chapter is that the NN based systems have access to different kinds of neural activation functions. The activation function used by the neuron is randomly selected during the neuron's creation during evolution. Since in the future we will continue adding new activation functions, and in general new mathematical and geometric functions, we should create a new small module called functions.erl, which will contain all these activation and other types of functions. Thus, since the neuron record uses the element *af* which contains the name of the actual activation function, these activation function names will be the names of the actual implemented functions located in the functions.erl module. The neuron will need only call *[functions:ActivationFunction(Dot_Product)]*, to produce its output value.

With these new additions, the neuron should be able to perform the following tasks:

1. Start up in a new process, wait for the exoself to set its state, check if it has any recursive output connections, and if so, send to those elements a default signal: *{self(),forward,[0]}*, and then drop into its main loop.
2. The neuron should be able to gather all the incoming signals from the *Input_PIds* specified in its *Input_PIdPs* list, and calculate a dot product from the input signals and the weights associated with those input signals.
3. Once all the input signals correlated with the Input_PIds in its Input_PIdPs list have been received, the neuron adds the bias, if any, to the calculated dot product, and then, based on the AF (Activation Function) tag, calculates the output by executing: *[functions:ActivationFunction(Dot_Product)]*. The calculated output signal is then propagated to all the PIds in its *Output_PIds* list.
4. The neuron should be able to receive the *weight_backup* signal. When receiving this signal, the neuron should store its current synaptic weights list to memory.
5. The neuron should be able to receive the *weight_restore* signal. When receiving this signal, the neuron should restore the synaptic weights it stored in

memory, and use them instead of the weights it currently uses in association with the Input_PIds.

6. The neuron should be able to accept the *weight_perturb* message. When receiving this message, the neuron should go through all its weights, and select each synaptic weight for perturbation with probability of *1/sqrt(TotWeights)*. The perturbation intensity applied to each synaptic weight is chosen with uniform distribution to be between *-Pi* and *Pi*.

7. The neuron should be able to accept the *reset_prep* message. When the neuron receives this message, it should flush its inbox, and then wait for the *reset* message, after which it should send out the default recursive signal (if any), and drop back into its main loop. Since all the other neurons should have also flushed their inboxes (the *reset_prep* and *reset* signaling is synchronized by the exoself, to ensure that all neurons go back to initial state when needed), the neurons are ready to receive these new recursive signals. At this point, their inboxes are empty, and not containing the recursive signals from their previous cycles.

The modified neuron module updated with these features is shown in the following listing.

Listing 8.20: The updated neuron module.

```
-module(neuron).
-compile(export_all).
-include("records.hrl").
-define(DELTA_MULTIPLIER,math:pi()*2).
-define(SAT_LIMIT,math:pi()*2).
-define(RO_SIGNAL,0).

gen(ExoSelf_PId,Node)->
    spawn(Node,?MODULE,prep,[ExoSelf_PId]).

prep(ExoSelf_PId) ->
    {V1,V2,V3} = now(),
    random:seed(V1,V2,V3),
    receive
        {ExoSelf_PId,{Id,Cx_PId,AF,Input_PIdPs,Output_PIds,RO_PIds}} ->
            fanout(RO_PIds,{self(),forward,[?RO_SIGNAL]}),
            loop(Id,ExoSelf_PId,Cx_PId,AF,{Input_PIdPs,Input_PIdPs},Output_PIds,
RO_PIds,0)
    end.
%When gen/2 is executed, it spawns the neuron element and immediately begins to wait for its
initial state message from the exoself. Once the state message arrives, the neuron sends out the
default forward signals to all elements in its ro_ids list. Afterwards, prep drops into the neu-
ron's main receive loop.
```

```
loop(Id,ExoSelf_PId,Cx_PId,AF,{[{Input_PId,Weights}|Input_PIdPs],MInput_PIdPs},
Output_PIds,RO_PIds,Acc)->
   receive
          {Input_PId,forward,Input}->
                  Result = dot(Input,Weights,0),
                  loop(Id,ExoSelf_PId,Cx_PId,AF,{Input_PIdPs,MInput_PIdPs},Output_PIds,
RO_PIds,Result+Acc);
          {ExoSelf_PId,weight_backup}->
                  put(weights,MInput_PIdPS),
                  loop(Id,ExoSelf_PId,Cx_PId,AF,{[{Input_PId,Weights}|Input_PIdPs],
MInput_PIdPs}, Output_PIds,RO_PIds,Acc);
           {ExoSelf_PId,weight_restore}->
                  RInput_PIdPs = get(weights),
                  loop(Id,ExoSelf_PId,Cx_PId,AF,{RInput_PIdPs,RInput_PIdPs},Output_PIds,
RO_PIds,Acc);
          {ExoSelf_PId,weight_perturb}->
                  PInput_PIdPs=perturb_IPIdPs(MInput_PIdPs),
                  loop(Id,ExoSelf_PId,Cx_PId,AF,{[{Input_PId,Weights}|Input_PIdPs],
PInput_PIdPs},Output_PIds,RO_PIds,Acc);
          {ExoSelf,reset_prep}->
                  neuron:flush_buffer(),
                  ExoSelf ! {self(),ready},
                  receive
                      {ExoSelf, reset}->
                              fanout(RO_PIds,{self(),forward,[?RO_SIGNAL]})
                  end,
                  loop(Id,ExoSelf_PId,Cx_PId,AF,{MInput_PIdPs,MInput_PIdPs},Output_PIds,
RO_PIds,0);
          {ExoSelf_PId,get_backup}->
                  ExoSelf_PId ! {self(),Id,MInput_PIdPs},
                  loop(Id,ExoSelf_PId,Cx_PId,AF,{[{Input_PId,Weights}|Input_PIdPs],
MInput_PIdPs},Output_PIds,RO_PIds,Acc);
          {ExoSelf_PId,terminate}->
                  ok
   end;
loop(Id,ExoSelf_PId,Cx_PId,AF,{[Bias],MInput_PIdPs},Output_PIds,RO_PIds,Acc)->
   Output = functions:AF(Acc+Bias),
   [Output_PId ! {self(),forward,[Output]} || Output_PId <- Output_PIds],
   loop(Id,ExoSelf_PId,Cx_PId,AF,{MInput_PIdPs,MInput_PIdPs},Output_PIds,RO_PIds,0);
loop(Id,ExoSelf_PId,Cx_PId,AF,{[],MInput_PIdPs},Output_PIds,RO_PIds,Acc)->
   Output = functions:AF(Acc),
   [Output_PId ! {self(),forward,[Output]} || Output_PId <- Output_PIds],
   loop(Id,ExoSelf_PId,Cx_PId,AF,{MInput_PIdPs,MInput_PIdPs},Output_PIds,RO_PIds,0).
```

%The neuron process waits for vector signals from all the processes that it's connected from, taking the dot product of the input and weight vectors, and then adding it to the accumulator. Once all the signals from Input_PIds are received, the accumulator contains the dot product to which the neuron then adds the bias and executes the activation function. After fanning out the output signal, the neuron again returns to waiting for incoming signals. When the neuron receives the {ExoSelf_Pid,get_backup} message, it forwards to the exoself its full MInput_PIdPs list, and its Id. The MInput_PIdPs contains the modified, tuned and most effective version of the input_idps. The neuron process also accepts the weight_backup signal, when receiving it, the neuron saves to process dictionary the current MInput_PIdPs. When the neuron receives the weight_restore signal, it reads back from the process dictionary the stored Input_PIdPs, and switches over to using it as its active Input_PIdPs list. When the neuron receives the weight_perturb signal from the exoself, it perturbs the weights by executing the perturb_IPIdPs/1 function, which returns the updated/perturbed weight list. Finally, the neuron can also accept a reset_prep signal, which makes the neuron flush its buffer in the off chance that it has a recursively sent to it signal in its inbox. After flushing its buffer, the neuron waits for the exoself to send it the reset signal, at which point the neuron, now fully refreshed after the flush_buffer/0, outputs a default forward signal to its recursively connected elements (ro_ids), if any, and then drops back into its main receive loop.

```erlang
dot([I|Input],[W|Weights],Acc) ->
      dot(Input,Weights,I*W+Acc);
dot([],[],Acc)->
      Acc;
dot([],[Bias],Acc)->
      Acc+Bias.
```
%The dot/3 function accepts an input vector and a weight list, and computes the dot product of the two vectors.

```erlang
fanout([Pid|Pids],Msg)->
      Pid ! Msg,
      fanout(Pids,Msg);
fanout([],_Msg)->
      true.
```
%The fanout/2 function fans out the Msg to all the PIds in its list.

```erlang
flush_buffer()->
      receive
            _ ->
                  flush_buffer()
      after 0 ->
            done
end.
```
%The flush_buffer/0 empties out the element's inbox.

```erlang
perturb_IPIdPs(Input_PIdPs)->
```

```
   Tot_Weights=lists:sum([length(Weights) || {_Input_PId,Weights}<-Input_PIdPs]),
   MP = 1/math:sqrt(Tot_Weights),
   perturb_IPIdPs(MP,Input_PIdPs,[]).

perturb_IPIdPs(MP,[{Input_PId,Weights}|Input_PIdPs],Acc)->
   U_Weights = perturb_weights(MP,Weights,[]),
   perturb_IPIdPs(MP,Input_PIdPs,[{Input_PId,U_Weights}|Acc]);
perturb_IPIdPs(MP,[Bias],Acc)->
   U_Bias = case random:uniform() < MP of
          true->
                   sat((random:uniform()-0.5)*?DELTA_MULTIPLIER+Bias,-?SAT_LIMIT,
?SAT_LIMIT);
          false ->
                   Bias
   end,
   lists:reverse([U_Bias|Acc]);
perturb_IPIdPs(_MP,[],Acc)->
   lists:reverse(Acc).
```

%The perturb_IPIdPs/1 function calculates the probability with which each neuron in the In-put_PIdPs is chosen to be perturbed. The probability is based on the total number of weights in the Input_PIdPs list, with the actual mutation probability equating to the inverse of square root of the total number of weights. The perturb_IPIdPs/3 function goes through each weights block and calls the perturb_weights/3 to perturb the weights.

```
   perturb_weights(MP,[W|Weights],Acc)->
        U_W = case random:uniform() < MP of
               true->
                        sat((random:uniform()-0.5)*?DELTA_MULTIPLIER+W,-
?SAT_LIMIT, ?SAT_LIMIT);
               false ->
                        W
        end,
        perturb_weights(MP,Weights,[U_W|Acc]);
   perturb_weights(_MP,[],Acc)->
        lists:reverse(Acc).
```

%The perturb_weights/3 function is one that actually goes through each weight block, and per-turbs each weight with a probability of MP. If the weight is chosen to be perturbed, the pertur-bation intensity is chosen uniformly between -Pi and Pi.

```
        sat(Val,Min,Max)->
             if
                   Val < Min -> Min;
                   Val > Max -> Max;
                   true -> Val
             end.
```

```
%The sat/3 function simply ensures that the Val is neither less than min or greater than max.
When used with synaptic weights (or other parameters), this function makes sure that the syn-
aptic weights get saturated at the Min and Max values, rather than growing in magnitude with-
out bound.
```

As you have noticed, the neuron executes *functions:AF(DotProduct)*, since all activation functions, and other useful mathematical functions, are specified in the new *functions* module. For clarity and completeness, the functions module is shown in the following listing.

```
Listing-8.21: The implementation of the functions module.

-module(functions).
-compile(export_all).

saturation(Val)->
    case Val > 1000 of
        true -> 1000;
        false ->
                case Val < -1000 of
                    true -> -1000;
                    false -> Val
                end
    end.
%The function saturation/1 accepts a value Val, and returns the same if its magnitude is below
1000. Otherwise it returns -1000 or 1000, if it's less than or greater than -1000 or 1000 respec-
tively. Thus Val saturates at -1000 and 1000.

saturation(Val,Spread)->
    case Val > Spread of
        true -> Spread;
        false ->
                case Val < -Spread of
                    true -> -Spread;
                    false -> Val
                end
    end.
%The saturation/2 function is similar to saturation/1, but here the spread (symmetric Max and
Min values) is specified by the caller.

scale([H|T],Max,Min)->
    [scale(Val,Max,Min)||Val<-[H|T]];
scale(Val,Max,Min)-> %Nm = (Y*2 - (Max + Min))/(Max-Min)
    case Max == Min of
        true -> 0;
```

```
            false -> (Val*2 - (Max+Min))/(Max-Min)
    end.
%The scale/3 function accepts a list of values, and scales them to be between the specified Min
and Max values.

sat(Val,Max,Min)->
    case Val > Max of
            true -> Max;
            false ->
                    case Val < Min of
                            true -> Min;
                            false -> Val
                    end
    end.
%The sat/3 function is similar to saturation/2 function, but here the Max and Min can be differ-
ent, and are specified by the caller.

sat_dzone(Val,Max,Min,DZMax,DZMin)->
    case (Val < DZMax) and (Val > DZMin) of
            true -> 0;
            false -> sat(Val,Max,Min)
    end.
%The sat_DZone/5 function is similar to the sat/3 function, but here, if Val is between DZMin
and DZMax, it is zeroed.

%%%%%%%%%%%%%%%%%%% Activation Functions %%%%%%%%%%%%%%%%%%%%%%%%%%%
tanh(Val)->
    math:tanh(Val).

cos(Val)->
    math:cos(Val).

sin(Val)->
    math:sin(Val).

sgn(0)->
    0;
sgn(Val)->
    case Val > 0 of
            true -> 1;
            false -> -1
    end.

bin(Val)->
    case Val > 0 of
```

```erlang
        true -> 1;
        false -> 0
    end.
% The bin/1 function converts Val into a binary value, 1 if Val > 0, and 0 if Val =< 0.

trinary(Val)->
    if
        (Val < 0.33) and (Val > -0.33) -> 0;
        Val >= 0.33 -> 1;
        Val =< -0.33 -> -1
    end.
%The trinary/1 function converts Val into a trinary value.

multiquadric(Val)->
    math:pow(Val*Val + 0.01,0.5).

absolute(Val)->
    abs(Val).

linear(Val)->
    Val.


quadratic(Val)->
    sgn(Val)*Val*Val.

gaussian(Val)->
    gaussian(2.71828183,Val).
gaussian(Const,Val)->
    V = case Val > 10 of
        true -> 10;
        false ->
                case Val < -10 of
                    true -> -10;
                    false -> Val
                end
    end,
    math:pow(Const,-V*V).

sqrt(Val)->
    sgn(Val)*math:sqrt(abs(Val)).

log(Val)->
    case Val == 0 of
        true -> 0;
```

```
              false -> sgn(Val)*math:log(abs(Val))
    end.


sigmoid(Val)->
    V = case Val > 10 of
           true -> 10;
           false ->
                   case Val < -10 of
                          true -> -10;
                          false -> Val
                   end
    end,
    2/(1+math:pow(2.71828183,-V)) - 1.


sigmoid1(Val)->
    Val/(1+abs(Val)).


avg(List)->
    lists:sum(List)/length(List).
%The avg/1 function accepts a List for a parameter, and then returns the average of the list to
the caller.
std(List)->
    Avg = avg(List),
    std(List,Avg,[]).
    std([Val|List],Avg,Acc)->
           std(List,Avg,[math:pow(Avg-Val,2)|Acc]);
    std([],_,Avg,Acc)->
           Variance = lists:sum(Acc)/length(Acc),
           math:sqrt(Variance).
%The std/1 function accepts a List for a parameter, and then returns to the caller the standard
deviation of the list.
```

8.6 Summary

In this chapter we converted our single NN optimization system, into a fully fledged topology and weight evolving artificial neural network system. We have implemented an approach to present various problems to our NN systems, an approach utilizing the *scapes* and the *morphology* concepts. We created a *population_monitor,* a system that can spawn and monitor a population of NN based agents, select the fit, delete the unfit, and in general apply the evolutionary method to the population of agents. We also implemented the *constraint* record, through which we can specify all the various parameters which the evolving specie will be constrained by. Finally, we developed the necessary complexifying topological mutation operators, which can add/remove bias values to/from neurons, mutate their activation functions, add new neurons to the NNs, add new synaptic connections to the NNs, and add sensors and actuators to the NNs.

We have also created a new *functions* module, which will from now on contain the activation functions used by the neuron, and other mathematical functions used by our system. Through the functions module, we can fully decouple the activation functions from the neurons using them. A neuron can now use any activation function, no matter its form, as long as it returns a properly formatted value. This also means that our neuron can now function as anything, as an AND gate, as an OR gate... depending on what activation functions we give it access to. This gives our system a good starting point with regards to its flexibility, and areas in which we can apply it to.

We have now covered and created all the necessary modules of our basic neuroevolutionary system. The remaining logger and benchmark modules are non-essentials, and we will build them when we begin expanding our neuroevolutionary platform in later chapters. At this point, we are ready to move forward and perform a detailed test of the mutation operators, and then the entire neuroevolutionary system. We test our newly constructed system in the next chapter.

8.7 Reference

[1] Khepera robot: http://www.k-team.com/

Chapter 9 Testing the Neuroevolutionary System

Abstract In this chapter we test the newly created basic neuroevolutionary system, by first testing each of its mutation operators, and then by applying the whole system to the XOR mimicking problem. Though the XOR problem test will run to completion and without errors, a more detailed, manual analysis of the evolved topologies and genotypes of the fit agents will show a number of bugs to be present. The origins of the bugs is then analyzed, and the errors are fixed. Afterwards, the updated neuroevolutionary system is then successfully re-tested.

9.1 Testing the Mutation Operators

Having created the basic neuroevolutionary system, we need to test whether the mutation operators work as we intended them to. We have set up all the complexifying mutation operators to leave the system in a connected state. This means that when we apply these mutation operators, the resulting NN topology is such, that the signal can get from the sensors, all the way through the NN, and to the actuators. The pruning mutation operators: remove_inlink, remove_outlink, remove_neuron, remove_sensor, remove_actuator, may leave the NN in such a state that it is no longer able to process information, by creating a break in the connected graph, as shown in the example of Fig-9.1. We could start using the pruning mutation operators later on, after we have first created a program inside the genome_mutator module that ensures that all the resulting mutant NN systems are not disconnected after such pruning mutation operators have been applied.

G.I. Sher, *Handbook of Neuroevolution Through Erlang*,
DOI 10.1007/978-1-4614-4463-3_9, © Springer Science+Business Media New York 2013

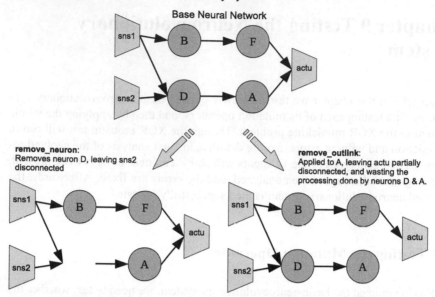

Fig. 9.1 Pruning mutation operators that leave a NN disconnected.

Let us now run a few mutation operator tests, to see if the resulting topologies after we have applied some mutation operators to the NN, are as expected. When you perform the same tests, the results may slightly differ from mine, since the elements in your NN will have different Ids, and because the mutation operators are applied randomly. The test of each mutation operator will have the following steps:

1. Generate a *test* NN, which is composed of a single neuron, connected from the sensor *xor_GetInput*, and connected to the actuator *xor_SendOutput*. This is done by simply executing *genotype:create_test()*, which creates a *xor_mimic* morphology based seed agent.
2. Apply an available mutation operator by executing: genome_mutator:test(test, Mutator).
3. Execute genotype:print(test) to print the resulting genotype to console, and then compare it to the original genotype to ensure that the resulting mutated genotype is as expected based on the mutation operator used.
4. Test the resulting NN on the simple XOR problem for which it has the sensor and actuator, by executing exoself:start(test,void). There will not exist a population_monitor process at this time, but that should not affect the results. The goal here is to ensure that the NN does not stall, that the signals can go all the way through it, from sensors to actuators, and that the NN system is functional. In this case we do not expect the NN to solve the problem, because the topology is not evolving towards any particular goal.

Let us now go through these steps for each mutation operator. For the sake of being brief, I will show the entire console printout for the first mutation operator test, but for all the other mutation operators I will only display the most significant console printout parts.

mutate_weights: This mutation operator selects a random neuron in the NN and perturbs/mutates its synaptic weights.

```
2> genotype:create_test().
{agent,test,0,undefined,test,
    {{origin,7.572689688224582e-10},cortex},
    {[{0,1}],
    [],
    [{sensor,undefined,xor_GetInput,undefined,
        {private,xor_sim},
        2,
        [{{0,7.572689688218573e-10},neuron}],
        undefined}],
    [{actuator,undefined,xor_SendOutput,undefined,
        {private,xor_sim},
        1,
        [{{0,7.572689688218573e-10},neuron}],
        undefined}]},
    {constraint,xor_mimic,[tanh,cos,gauss,abs]},
    [],undefined,0,
    [{0,[{{0,7.572689688218573e-10},neuron}]}]]}
{cortex,{{origin,7.572689688224582e-10},cortex},
    test,
    [{{0,7.572689688218573e-10},neuron}],
    [{{-1,7.572689688218636e-10},sensor}],
    [{{1,7.572689688218589e-10},actuator}]}
{sensor,{{-1,7.572689688218636e-10},sensor},
    xor_GetInput,
    {{origin,7.572689688224582e-10},cortex},
    {private,xor_sim},
    2,
    [{{0,7.572689688218573e-10},neuron}],
    undefined}
{neuron,{{0,7.572689688218573e-10},neuron},
    0,
    {{origin,7.572689688224582e-10},cortex},
    tanh,
    [{{{-1,7.572689688218636e-10},sensor},
        [-0.08541081650616245,-0.028821611144310255]}],
    [{{1,7.572689688218589e-10},actuator}],
```

```
        []}
{actuator,{{1,7.572689688218589e-10},actuator},
        xor_SendOutput,
        {{origin,7.572689688224582e-10},cortex},
        {private,xor_sim},
        1,
        [{{0,7.572689688218573e-10},neuron}],
        undefined}
{atomic,{atomic,[ok]}}
3> genome_mutator:test(test,mutate_weights).
{atomic,{atomic,ok}}
4> genotype:print(test).
{agent,test,0,undefined,test,
        {{origin,7.572689688224582e-10},cortex},
        {[{0,1}],
        [],
        [{sensor,undefined,xor_GetInput,undefined,
                {private,xor_sim},
                2,
                [{{0,7.572689688218573e-10},neuron}],
                undefined}],
        [{actuator,undefined,xor_SendOutput,undefined,
                {private,xor_sim},
                1,
                [{{0,7.572689688218573e-10},neuron}],
                undefined}]},
        {constraint,xor_mimic,[tanh,cos,gauss,abs]},
        [{mutate_weights,{{0,7.572689688218573e-10},neuron}}],
        undefined,0,
        [{0,[{{0,7.572689688218573e-10},neuron}]}]}}
{cortex,{{origin,7.572689688224582e-10},cortex},
        test,
        [{{0,7.572689688218573e-10},neuron}],
        [{{-1,7.572689688218636e-10},sensor}],
        [{{1,7.572689688218589e-10},actuator}]}
{sensor,{{-1,7.572689688218636e-10},sensor},
        xor_GetInput,
        {{origin,7.572689688224582e-10},cortex},
        {private,xor_sim},
        2,
        [{{0,7.572689688218573e-10},neuron}],
        undefined}
{neuron,{{0,7.572689688218573e-10},neuron},
        0,
        {{origin,7.572689688224582e-10},cortex},
```

```
      tanh,
      [{{{-1,7.572689688218636e-10},sensor},
       [-1.81543903255671,0.28220989176010963]}],
      [{{1,7.572689688218589e-10},actuator}],
      []}
{actuator,{{1,7.572689688218589e-10},actuator},
      xor_SendOutput,
      {{origin,7.572689688224582e-10},cortex},
      {private,xor_sim},
      1,
      [{{0,7.572689688218573e-10},neuron}],
      undefined}
{atomic,[ok]}
```

As you can see from the printout, the mutate_weights operator chose a random neuron in the NN, which in this case is just the single existing neuron, and then mutated the synaptic weights associated with the sensor that it is connected from. The synaptic weights were mutated from their original values of:

[-0.08541081650616245, -0.028821611144310255]

to:

[-1.81543903255671, 0.28220989176010963].

We now test the mutated NN system on the problem that its morphology defines it for, the XOR mimicking problem.

```
5> exoself:start(test,void).
<0.128.0>
Finished updating genotype
Terminating the phenotype:
Cx_PId:<0.131.0>
SPIds:[<0.132.0>]
NPIds:[<0.134.0>]
APIds:[<0.133.0>]
ScapePids:[<0.130.0>]
Sensor:{{-1,7.572689688218636e-10},sensor} is terminating.
Agent:<0.128.0> terminating. Genotype has been backed up.
Fitness:0.505631430344058
TotEvaluations:52
TotCycles:208
TimeAcc:7226
Cortex:{{origin,7.572689688224582e-10},cortex} is terminating.
```

It works! The exoself ran, and after having finished tuning the weights with our augmented stochastic hill-climber algorithm, it updated the genotype, terminated the phenotype by terminating all the processes associated with it (SPIds, NPIds, APIds, and ScapePids), and then printed to screen the stats of the NN system's run: the total evaluations, total cycles, and the total time the NN system was running.

To see that the genotype was indeed updated, we can print it out again, to see what the new synaptic weights are for the single neuron of this NN system:

```
7> genotype:print(test).
...
{neuron,{{0,7.572689688218573e-10},neuron},
    0,
    {{origin,7.572689688224582e-10},cortex},
    tanh,
    [{{{-1,7.572689688218636e-10},sensor},
    [-1.81543903255671,-2.4665070928720794]}}],
    [{{1,7.572689688218589e-10},actuator}],
    []}
...
```

The original synaptic weights associated with the sensor were: [-1.81543903255671, 0.28220989176010963] which have been tuned to the values: [-1.81543903255671, -2.4665070928720794]. The synaptic weight vector is of length two, and we can see that in this case only the second weight in the vector was perturbed, where as when we applied the mutation operator, it mutated only the first weight in the vector. The mutation and perturbation process is stochastic.

The system passed the test, the mutate_weights operator works, we have manually examined the resulting NN system, which has the right topology, which is the same but with a mutated synaptic weight vector. We have tested the phenotype, and have confirmed that it works. It ran for a total of 52 evaluations, so it made 52 attempts to tune the weights. We can guess that at least 50 did not work, because we know that it takes, due to the MAX_ATTEMPTS = 50 in the exoself module, 50 failing attempts before exoself gives up tuning the weights. We also know that 1 of the evaluations was the very first one, when the NN system ran with the original genotype. So we can even extrapolate that it was the second attempt, the second evaluation, during which the perturbed synaptic weights were improved in this scenario. When you perform the test, your results will most likely be different.

add_bias: This mutation operator selects a random neuron in the NN and, if the neuron's input_idps list does not already have a bias, the mutation operator adds one.

```
2> genotype:create_test().
...
{neuron,{{0,7.572678978164637e-10},neuron},
    0,
    {{origin,7.572678978164722e-10},cortex},
    gaussian,
    [{{{-1,7.572678978164681e-10},sensor},
     [0.41211176719508646,0.06709671037415732]}],
    [{{1,7.572678978164653e-10},actuator}],
    []}
...
3> genome_mutator:test(test,add_bias).
{atomic,{atomic,ok}}
4> genotype:print(test).
...
{neuron,{{0,7.572678978164637e-10},neuron},
    0,
    {{origin,7.572678978164722e-10},cortex},
    gaussian,
    [{{{-1,7.572678978164681e-10},sensor},
     [0.41211176719508646,0.06709671037415732]},
     {bias,[-0.1437300365267422]}],
    [{{1,7.572678978164653e-10},actuator}],
    []}
...
5> exoself:start(test,void).
...
```

It works! The original genotype had a neuron connected from the sensor, using a *gaussian* activation function, with the synaptic weight vector associated with the sensor: **[0.41211176719508646, 0.06709671037415732]**. After the add_bias mutation operator was executed, the neuron acquired the bias weight: **[-0.1437300365267422]**. Finally, we now test out the new NN system by converting the genotype to its phenotype by executing the exoself:start(test,void) function. As in the previous test, when I ran it with this mutated agent, there were no errors, and the system terminated normally.

mutate_af: This mutation operator selects a random neuron in the NN and changes its activation function to a new one, selected from the list available in the constraint's neural_afs list.

```
2> genotype:create_test().
...
{neuron,{{0,7.572652623199229e-10},neuron},
    0,
```

```
    {{origin,7.57265262319932e-10},cortex},
    absolute,
    [{{{-1,7.572652623199274e-10},sensor},
     [-0.16727779071660276,0.12410379914428638]}],
    [{{1,7.572652623199246e-10},actuator}],
    []}
...
3> genome_mutator:test(test,mutate_af).
{atomic,{atomic,ok}}
4> genotype:print(test).
...
{neuron,{{0,7.572652623199229e-10},neuron},
    0,
    {{origin,7.57265262319932e-10},cortex},
    cos,
    [{{{-1,7.572652623199274e-10},sensor},
     [-0.16727779071660276,0.12410379914428638]}],
    [{{1,7.572652623199246e-10},actuator}],
    []}
...
{atomic,[ok]}
25> exoself:start(test,void).
...
```

The original randomly selected activation function of the single neuron in the test agent was the *absolute* activation function. After we have applied the *mutate_af* operator to the NN system, the activation function was changed to *cos*. As before, here too converting the genotype to phenotype worked, as there were no errors when running *exoself:start(test,void)*.

add_outlink & add_inlink: The add_outlink operator chooses a random neuron and adds an output connection *from it*, to another randomly selected element in the NN system. The add_inlink operator chooses a random neuron and adds an input connection *to it*, from another randomly selected element in the NN. We will only test one of them, the add_outlink, as they both function very similarly.

```
2> genotype:create_test().
...
{sensor,{{-1,7.572648155161364e-10},sensor},
    xor_GetInput,
    {{origin,7.572648155161404e-10},cortex},
    {private,xor_sim},
    2,
    [{{0,7.572648155161313e-10},neuron}],
    undefined}
```

```
{neuron,{{0,7.572648155161313e-10},neuron},
    0,
    {{origin,7.572648155161404e-10},cortex},
    absolute,
    [{{{-1,7.572648155161364e-10},sensor},
     [-0.02132967923622686,-0.38581737041377817]}],
    [{{1,7.572648155161335e-10},actuator}],
    []}
{actuator,{{1,7.572648155161335e-10},actuator},
    xor_SendOutput,
    {{origin,7.572648155161404e-10},cortex},
    {private,xor_sim},
    1,
    [{{0,7.572648155161313e-10},neuron}],
    undefined}
{atomic,{atomic,[ok]}}
3> genome_mutator:test(test,add_outlink).
{atomic,{atomic,ok}}
4> genotype:print(test).
...
{sensor,{{-1,7.572648155161364e-10},sensor},
    xor_GetInput,
    {{origin,7.572648155161404e-10},cortex},
    {private,xor_sim},
    2,
    [{{0,7.572648155161313e-10},neuron}],
    undefined}
{neuron,{{0,7.572648155161313e-10},neuron},
    0,
    {{origin,7.572648155161404e-10},cortex},
    absolute,
    [{{{0,7.572648155161313e-10},neuron},[-0.13154644819577532]},
     {{{-1,7.572648155161364e-10},sensor},
      [-0.02132967923622686,-0.38581737041377817]}],
    [{{0,7.572648155161313e-10},neuron},
     {{1,7.572648155161335e-10},actuator}],
    [{{0,7.572648155161313e-10},neuron}]}
{actuator,{{1,7.572648155161335e-10},actuator},
    xor_SendOutput,
    {{origin,7.572648155161404e-10},cortex},
    {private,xor_sim},
    1,
    [{{0,7.572648155161313e-10},neuron}],
    undefined}
{atomic,[ok]}
```

It works! The original neuron had the form:

```
{neuron,{{0,7.572648155161313e-10},neuron},
    0,
    {{origin,7.572648155161404e-10},cortex},
    absolute,
    [{{{-1,7.572648155161364e-10},sensor},
      [-0.02132967923622686,-0.38581737041377817]}],
    [{{1,7.572648155161335e-10},actuator}],
    []}
```

It only had a single input connection which was from the sensor, and a single output connection to the actuator. After the add_outlink operator was executed, the new NN system's neuron had the following form:

```
{neuron,{{0,7.572648155161313e-10},neuron},
    0,
    {{origin,7.572648155161404e-10},cortex},
    absolute,
    [{{{0,7.572648155161313e-10},neuron},[-0.13154644819577532]},
     {{{-1,7.572648155161364e-10},sensor},
      [-0.02132967923622686,-0.38581737041377817]}],
    [{{0,7.572648155161313e-10},neuron},
     {{1,7.572648155161335e-10},actuator}],
    [{{0,7.572648155161313e-10},neuron}]}
```

In this case the neuron formed a new synaptic connection to another randomly chosen element in the NN system, in this case that other element was itself. We can see that this new connection is recursive, and we can tell this from the last element of the neuron defining tuple, which specifies *ro_ids*, a list of recurrent link ids. There is also a new synaptic weight associated with this recurrent self connection: **{{{0,7.572648155161313e-10},neuron},[-0.13154644819577532]}**. The diagram of this NN topology before and after the mutation operator was applied, is shown in Fig-9.2.

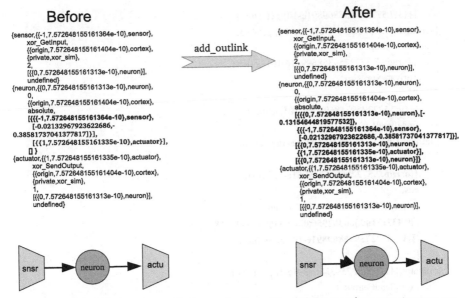

Before

```
{sensor,{{-1,7.572648155161364e-10},sensor},
    xor_GetInput,
    {{origin,7.572648155161404e-10},cortex},
    {private,xor_sim},
    2,
    [{{0,7.572648155161313e-10},neuron}],
    undefined}
{neuron,{{0,7.572648155161313e-10},neuron},
    0,
    {{origin,7.572648155161404e-10},cortex},
    absolute,
    [{{{-1,7.572648155161364e-10},sensor},
    [-0.02132967923622686,-
0.38581737041377817]}],
    [{{1,7.572648155161335e-10},actuator}],
    []}
{actuator,{{1,7.572648155161335e-10},actuator},
    xor_SendOutput,
    {{origin,7.572648155161404e-10},cortex},
    {private,xor_sim},
    1,
    [{{0,7.572648155161313e-10},neuron}],
    undefined}
```

add_outlink

After

```
{sensor,{{-1,7.572648155161364e-10},sensor},
    xor_GetInput,
    {{origin,7.572648155161404e-10},cortex},
    {private,xor_sim},
    2,
    [{{0,7.572648155161313e-10},neuron}],
    undefined}
{neuron,{{0,7.572648155161313e-10},neuron},
    0,
    {{origin,7.572648155161404e-10},cortex},
    absolute,
    [{{{0,7.572648155161313e-10},neuron},[-
0.13154644819577532]},
    {{{-1,7.572648155161364e-10},sensor},
    [-0.02132967923622686,-0.38581737041377817]}],
    [{{0,7.572648155161313e-10},neuron},
    {{1,7.572648155161335e-10},actuator}],
    [{{0,7.572648155161313e-10},neuron}]}
{actuator,{{1,7.572648155161335e-10},actuator},
    xor_SendOutput,
    {{origin,7.572648155161404e-10},cortex},
    {private,xor_sim},
    1,
    [{{0,7.572648155161313e-10},neuron}],
    undefined}
```

Fig. 9.2 The NN system topology before and after add_outlink mutation operator was applied.

We now map the genotype to phenotype, to see if the new NN system is functional:

```
5> exoself:start(test,void).
<0.101.0>
Finished updating genotype
Terminating the phenotype:
...
```

It works! Though I did not show the complete printout (which looked very similar to the first fully shown console printout), the NN system worked and terminated successfully. With this test complete, we now move to a more complex mutation operator, the addition of a new random neuron to the existing NN system.

add_neuron: This mutation operator chooses a random neural layer in the NN, and then creates a new neuron and connects it from and to, two randomly selected elements in the NN system respectively.

```
2> genotype:create_test().
...
{cortex,{{origin,7.572275935869961e-10},cortex},
    test,
    [{{0,7.572275935869875e-10},neuron}],
    [{{-1,7.57227593586992e-10},sensor}],
```

```
                    [{{1,7.572275935869891e-10},actuator}]}
{sensor,{{-1,7.57227593586992e-10},sensor},
        xor_GetInput,
        {{origin,7.572275935869961e-10},cortex},
        {private,xor_sim},
        2,
        [{{0,7.572275935869875e-10},neuron}],
        undefined}
{neuron,{{0,7.572275935869875e-10},neuron},
        0,
        {{origin,7.572275935869961e-10},cortex},
        cos,
        [{{{-1,7.57227593586992e-10},sensor},
         [0.43717109366382956,0.33904698258991184]}}],
        [{{1,7.572275935869891e-10},actuator}],
        []}
{actuator,{{1,7.572275935869891e-10},actuator},
        xor_SendOutput,
        {{origin,7.572275935869961e-10},cortex},
        {private,xor_sim},
        1,
        [{{0,7.572275935869875e-10},neuron}],
        undefined}
{atomic,{atomic,[ok]}}
3> genome_mutator:test(test,add_neuron).
{aborted,"******** ERROR:link_FromNeuronToActuator:: Actuator already fully con-
nected"}
4> genome_mutator:test(test,add_neuron).
{atomic,{atomic,ok}}
5> genotype:print(test).
...
{cortex,{{origin,7.572275935869961e-10},cortex},
        test,
        [{{0,7.572275884968449e-10},neuron},
         {{0,7.572275935869875e-10},neuron}],
        [{{-1,7.57227593586992e-10},sensor}],
        [{{1,7.572275935869891e-10},actuator}]}
{sensor,{{-1,7.57227593586992e-10},sensor},
        xor_GetInput,
        {{origin,7.572275935869961e-10},cortex},
        {private,xor_sim},
        2,
        [{{0,7.572275935869875e-10},neuron}],
        undefined}
{neuron,{{0,7.572275884968449e-10},neuron},
```

```
    0,
    {{origin,7.572275935869961e-10},cortex},
    gaussian,
    [{{{0,7.572275935869875e-10},neuron},[-0.17936473163045719]}],
    [{{0,7.572275935869875e-10},neuron}],
    [{{0,7.572275935869875e-10},neuron}]}
{neuron,{{0,7.572275935869875e-10},neuron},
    0,
    {{origin,7.572275935869961e-10},cortex},
    cos,
    [{{{0,7.572275884968449e-10},neuron},[0.2879930434277844]},
     {{{-1,7.57227593586992e-10},sensor},
     [0.43717109366382956,0.33904698258991184]}],
    [{{0,7.572275884968449e-10},neuron},
     {{1,7.572275935869891e-10},actuator}],
    [{{0,7.572275884968449e-10},neuron}]}
{actuator,{{1,7.572275935869891e-10},actuator},
    xor_SendOutput,
    {{origin,7.572275935869961e-10},cortex},
    {private,xor_sim},
    1,
    [{{0,7.572275935869875e-10},neuron}],
    undefined}
{atomic,[ok]}
```

Something very interesting happened in this test. In "**2>**" we create a new test NN system. A new NN system is fully connected to its sensors and actuators. When we try to apply the add_neuron mutation operator in "**3>**", the mutation operator must have randomly chosen to connect the new neuron to the existing actuator. But the actuator already has all the connections it needs, the vector signal it uses to execute its functionality, already has all the elements and is already connected to all the neurons it requires to function, which in this case is just a single neuron. So the mutation is rejected, as seen by the line: **{aborted,"********** ERROR:link_FromNeuronToActuator:: Actuator already fully connected"}**. During the process of neuroevolution, at this point our topology and weight evolving artificial neural network (TWEANN) system would simply try another mutation operator. Which is what I did manually in this test in "**4>**".

The new mutation worked, it created a new neuron and connected it from and to, the already existing neuron in the NN system. We can see the newly formed connection in the genotype here:

```
{neuron,{{0,7.572275884968449e-10},neuron},
    0,
    {{origin,7.572275935869961e-10},cortex},
```

gaussian,
[{{{0,7.572275935869875e-10},neuron},[-0.17936473163045719]}}],
[{{{0,7.572275935869875e-10},neuron}],
[{{{0,7.572275935869875e-10},neuron}]}
{neuron,{{0,7.572275935869875e-10},neuron},
   0,
   {{origin,7.572275935869961e-10},cortex},
   cos,
   [{{{0,7.572275884968449e-10},neuron},[0.2879930434277844]},
    {{{-1,7.57227593586992e-10},sensor},
     [0.43717109366382956,0.33904698258991184]}}],
   [{{{0,7.572275884968449e-10},neuron},
    {{1,7.572275935869891e-10},actuator}],
    [{{{0,7.572275884968449e-10},neuron}]}

The initial test NN system had a single neuron with the id: **{{0,7.572275935869875e-10},neuron}**, The newly added neuron has the id: **{{0,7.572275884968449e-10},neuron}**. We can see that after the mutation, both neurons have recurrent connections, which in our neuron record is represented by the last list in the tuple. The original neuron's recurrent connection list ro_ids is: **[{{0,7.572275884968449e-10},neuron}]**, containing the id of the new neuron. The newly added neuron's or_ids list is: **[{{{0,7.572275935869875e-10},neuron}]**, containing in it the id of the original neuron.

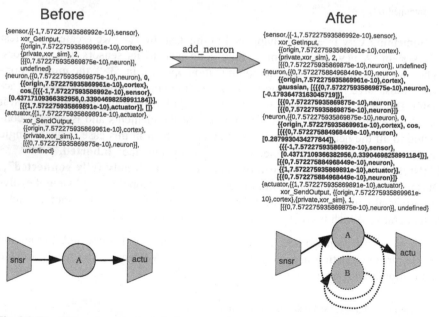

Fig. 9.3 The NN system topology before and after the add_neuron mutation operator was applied.

We can also see that the new neuron is using the gaussian activation function, and that both of the neurons formed new weights for their new synaptic connections. The above figure shows the NN system's topology before and after the add_neuron mutation operator is applied.

We now test the new topology live, by mapping the genotype to its phenotype:

```
6> exoself:start(test,void).
<0.866.0>
Finished updating genotype
Terminating the phenotype:
Cx_PId:<0.868.0>
SPIds:[<0.869.0>]
NPIds:[<0.871.0>,<0.872.0>]
APIds:[<0.870.0>]
ScapePids:[<0.867.0>]
Sensor:{{-1,7.57227593586992e-10},sensor} is terminating.
Agent:<0.866.0> terminating. Genotype has been backed up.
Fitness:1.3179457789331406
TotEvaluations:163
TotCycles:656
TimeAcc:23321
Cortex:{{origin,7.572275935869961e-10},cortex} is terminating.
```

It works! And from the highlighted NPIds, we can see the two spawned neuron PIds. The system terminated successfully, the topology we analyzed manually is correct given the mutation operator, and the phenotype works perfectly. Thus this mutation operator is functional, at least in this simple test, and we move on to the next one.

outsplice: This mutation operator selects a random neuron A in the NN, then selects the neuron's random output connection to some element B, disconnects A from B, creates a new neuron C in the layer between neuron A and element B (creating the new layer if it does not already exist, or using an existing one if A and B are one or more layers apart), and then reconnects A to B through C:

```
2> genotype:create_test().
...
{cortex,{{origin,7.57225527862836e-10},cortex},
    test,
    [{{0,7.572255278628331e-10},neuron}],
    [{{-1,7.572255278628343e-10},sensor}],
    [{{1,7.572255278628337e-10},actuator}]}
{sensor,{{-1,7.572255278628343e-10},sensor},
    xor_GetInput,
    {{origin,7.57225527862836e-10},cortex},
```

```
          {private,xor_sim},
          2,
          [{{0,7.572255278628331e-10},neuron}],
          undefined}
{neuron,{{0,7.572255278628331e-10},neuron},
      0,
      {{origin,7.57225527862836e-10},cortex},
      tanh,
      [{{{-1,7.572255278628343e-10},sensor},
       [0.4094174115111171,0.40477840576669655]}],
      [{{1,7.572255278628337e-10},actuator}],
      []}
{actuator,{{1,7.572255278628337e-10},actuator},
      xor_SendOutput,
      {{origin,7.57225527862836e-10},cortex},
      {private,xor_sim},
      1,
      [{{0,7.572255278628331e-10},neuron}],
      undefined}
{atomic,{atomic,[ok]}}
3> genome_mutator:test(test,outsplice).
{atomic,{atomic,ok}}
4> genotype:print(test).
...
{cortex,{{origin,7.57225527862836e-10},cortex},
      test,
      [{{0.5,7.572255205521553e-10},neuron},
       {{0,7.572255278628331e-10},neuron}],
      [{{-1,7.572255278628343e-10},sensor}],
      [{{1,7.572255278628337e-10},actuator}]}
{sensor,{{-1,7.572255278628343e-10},sensor},
      xor_GetInput,
      {{origin,7.57225527862836e-10},cortex},
      {private,xor_sim},
      2,
      [{{0,7.572255278628331e-10},neuron}],
      undefined}
{neuron,{{0.5,7.572255205521553e-10},neuron},
      0,
      {{origin,7.57225527862836e-10},cortex},
      absolute,
      [{{{0,7.572255278628331e-10},neuron},[0.08385901270641671]}],
      [{{1,7.572255278628337e-10},actuator}],
      []}
{neuron,{{0,7.572255278628331e-10},neuron},
```

```
0,
{{origin,7.57225527862836e-10},cortex},
tanh,
[{{{-1,7.572255278628343e-10},sensor},
 [0.4094174115111171,0.40477840576669655]}],
[{{0.5,7.572255205521553e-10},neuron}],
[]}
{actuator,{{1,7.572255278628337e-10},actuator},
    xor_SendOutput,
    {{origin,7.57225527862836e-10},cortex},
    {private,xor_sim},
    1,
    [{{0.5,7.572255205521553e-10},neuron}],
    0}
{atomic,[ok]}
```

It works! The genotype:create_test() function created the genotype of a simple test NN system, with a single neuron:

```
{neuron,{{0,7.572255278628331e-10},neuron},
    0,
    {{origin,7.57225527862836e-10},cortex},
    tanh,
    [{{{-1,7.572255278628343e-10},sensor},
     [0.4094174115111171,0.40477840576669655]}],
    [{{1,7.572255278628337e-10},actuator}],
    []}
```

Which is connected from the sensor: **{{-1,7.572255278628343e-10},sensor}** and is connected to the actuator: **{{1,7.572255278628337e-10},actuator}**. From the neuron's Id, we can see that it is in layer 0. After we executed the outsplice mutation operator, our NN system acquired a new neuron, thus the NN now had two neurons:

```
{neuron,{{0.5,7.572255205521553e-10},neuron},
    0,
    {{origin,7.57225527862836e-10},cortex},
    absolute,
    [{{{0,7.572255278628331e-10},neuron},[0.08385901270641671]}],
    [{{1,7.572255278628337e-10},actuator}],
    []}
{neuron,{{0,7.572255278628331e-10},neuron},
    0,
    {{origin,7.57225527862836e-10},cortex},
    tanh,
```

```
[{{{-1,7.572255278628343e-10},sensor},
  [0.4094174115111171,0.40477840576669655]}}],
[{{0.5,7.572255205521553e-10},neuron}],
[]}
```

Note that where as in the initial genotype the NN was composed of a single neuron: **{{0,7.572255278628331e-10}, neuron}**, which was connected from the sensor: **{{-1,7.572255278628343e-10}, sensor}**, and connected to the actuator: **{{1,7.572255278628337e-10}, actuator}**, after the mutation operator was applied, the NN acquired a new neuron, which was inserted into a new layer 0.5 (we determine that fact from its Id, which contains the layer index specification). Also note that the original neuron is no longer connected to the actuator, but instead is connected to the new neuron: **{{0.5,7.572255205521553e-10},neuron}**, which is now the one connected to the actuator. The diagram of the before and after topology of this NN system is shown in Fig-9.4.

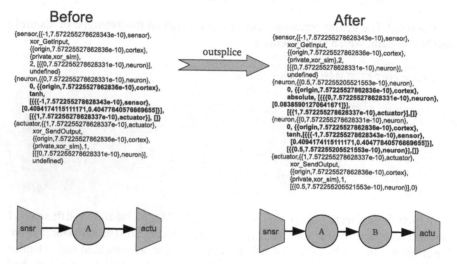

Fig. 9.4 The NN System topology before and after the outsplice mutation operator is applied to it.

Let's test this NN system by mapping its genotype to its phenotype, and applying it to the problem that its morphology defines (mimicking the XOR operator):

```
5> exoself:start(test,void).
<0.919.0>
Finished updating genotype
Terminating the phenotype:
Cx_PId:<0.921.0>
SPIds:[<0.922.0>]
NPIds:[<0.924.0>,<0.925.0>]
```

```
APIds:[<0.923.0>]
ScapePids:[<0.920.0>]
Agent:<0.919.0> terminating. Genotype has been backed up.
Fitness:0.5311848171954074
TotEvaluations:58
TotCycles:236
TimeAcc:7384
Cortex:{{origin,7.57225527862836e-10},cortex} is terminating.
Sensor:{{-1,7.572255278628343e-10},sensor} is terminating.
```

It works! And we can also see that there are two NPIds, since there are now two neurons. We have visually inspected the NN system genotype before and after the mutation operator was applied, and found the new genotype to be correct. We have also tested the phenotype, to ensure that it is functional, and confirmed that it is. We next test the two last remaining mutation operators: add_sensor and add_actuator.

add_sensor & add_actuator: The add_sensor mutation operator adds a new random sensor, still unused by the NN system. The sensor is chosen from the sensor list available to the morphology of the NN based agent. A random neuron in the NN is then chosen, and the sensor is connected to that neuron. The add_actuator mutation operator adds a new random actuator, still unused by the NN system. A random neuron in the NN is then chosen, and a link is established between this neuron and the new actuator.

```
2> genome_mutator:test(test,add_sensor).
{aborted,"********ERROR:add_sensor(Agent_Id):: NN system is already using all available sensors"}
3> genome_mutator:test(test,add_actuator).
{aborted,"********ERROR:add_actuator(Agent_Id):: NN system is already using all available actuators"}
```

This is as expected. The test NN system uses the xor_mimic morphology, and if we look in the morphology module, we see that it only has one sensor and one actuator. Thus, when we run the mutation operators for this particular test, our neuroevolutionary system does not add a new sensor, or a new actuator, because there are no new ones available. When we begin expanding the neuroevolutionary platform we're designing here, we will see the affects of a system that can incorporate new sensors and actuators into itself as it evolves. We can similarly test the mutation operators: add_sensorlink & add_actuatorlink, but just as the above two mutation operators, they have no new elements to connect to and from, respectively, when it comes to the seed NN.

We have now successfully tested most of the complexifying mutation operators on the simple, seed NN based agent. But this does not necessarily mean that there are no bugs in our system. Perhaps there are scenarios when it does fail, we just haven't come across them yet because we've only tested the operators on the most simple type of topology, the single neuron NN system topology.

Before we proceed, let's create a small program that applies X random mutation operators to the test NN system, and then converts the mutated genotype to its phenotype, to ensure that it still functions. The goal here is to ensure that the resulting NN is simply connected, and does not crash, or stall during operation. Furthermore, we can run this mutation operator test itself, a few thousand times. If at any point it gets stuck, or there is an unexpected error, we can then try to figure out what happened.

The following listing shows this simple, topological mutation testing function that we add to the genome_mutator module:

```
Listing-9.1 The long_test/1 function, which creates a seed agent, and applies
TotMutateApplications number of mutation operators to it, and tests the resulting phenotype af-
terwards.


long_test(TotMutateApplications) when (TotMutateApplications > 0) ->
     genotype:create_test(),
     short_test(TotMutateApplications).

     short_test(0)->
          exoself:start(test,void);
     short_test(Index)->
          test(),
          short_test(Index-1).
%This is a simple function that executes the test() function the number of times with which the
long_test/1 function was initially called. The test/0 function executes mutate(test), which ap-
plies a random number of mutation operators to the genotype, where that number ranges from 1
to sqrt(Tot_neurons). After all the mutation operators have been applied successfully, the func-
tion executes exoself:start(test,void), mapping the genotype to phenotype, to test whether the
resulting NN system is functional.
```

The long_test/1 function will perform the following steps:

1. Create a test genotype.
2. Execute the mutate(test) function TotMutateApplications number of times.
3. Convert the genotype to phenotype to ensure that the resulting NN system is functional.

Lets run the *long_test* function with *TotMutateApplications = 300*. For the sake of being brief, I will only present the first and last few lines of the printout to console in the following Listing-9.2.

Listing-9.2 Running the long_test function, which applies a random number of mutation operators to the original seed agent, 300 times.

```
2>genome_mutator:long_test(300).
{agent,test,0,undefined,test,
    {{origin,7.571534416338085e-10},cortex},
    {[{0,1}],
    [],
    [{sensor,undefined,xor_GetInput,undefined,
        {private,xor_sim},
        2,
        [{{0,7.571534416338051e-10},neuron}],
        undefined}],
    [{actuator,undefined,xor_SendOutput,undefined,
        {private,xor_sim},
        1,
        [{{0,7.571534416338051e-10},neuron}],
        undefined}]},
    {constraint,xor_mimic,[tanh,cos,gaussian,absolute]},
    [],undefined,0,
    [{0,[{{0,7.571534416338051e-10},neuron}]}]}}
...
Tot neurons:1 Performing Tot mutations:1 on:test
Mutation Operator:add_outlink
******** Mutation Succesful.
Tot neurons:1 Performing Tot mutations:1 on:test
Mutation Operator:add_actuator
******** Error:{aborted,"********ERROR:add_actuator(Agent_Id):: NN system is already
using all available actuators"}
Retrying with new Mutation...
Mutation Operator:outsplice
******** Mutation Succesful.
Tot neurons:2 Performing Tot mutations:1 on:test
Mutation Operator:mutate_af
******** Mutation Succesful.
...
Tot neurons:95 Performing Tot mutations:5 on:test
Mutation Operator:outsplice
Mutation Operator:add_bias
Mutation Operator:mutate_weights
Mutation Operator:add_outlink
Mutation Operator:mutate_af
******** Mutation Succesful.
<0.2460.0>
Finished updating genotype
```

```
Terminating the phenotype:
Cx_PId:<0.2463.0>
SPIds:[<0.2464.0>]
NPIds:[<0.2467.0>,<0.2468.0>,<0.2469.0>,<0.2470.0>,<0.2471.0>,<0.2472.0>,<0.2473.0>,
<0.2474.0>,<0.2475.0>,<0.2476.0>,<0.2477.0>,<0.2478.0>,<0.2479.0>,<0.2480.0>,
<0.2481.0>,<0.2482.0>,<0.2483.0>,<0.2484.0>,<0.2485.0>,<0.2486.0>,<0.2487.0>,
<0.2488.0>,<0.2489.0>,<0.2490.0>,<0.2491.0>,<0.2492.0>,<0.2493.0>,<0.2494.0>,
<0.2495.0>,<0.2496.0>,<0.2497.0>,<0.2498.0>,<0.2499.0>,<0.2500.0>,<0.2501.0>,
<0.2502.0>,<0.2503.0>,<0.2504.0>,<0.2505.0>,<0.2506.0>,<0.2507.0>,<0.2508.0>,
<0.2509.0>,<0.2510.0>,<0.2511.0>,<0.2512.0>,<0.2513.0>,<0.2514.0>,<0.2515.0>,
<0.2516.0>,<0.2517.0>,<0.2518.0>,<0.2519.0>,<0.2520.0>,<0.2521.0>,<0.2522.0>,
<0.2523.0>,<0.2524.0>,<0.2525.0>,<0.2526.0>,<0.2527.0>,<0.2528.0>,<0.2529.0>,
<0.2530.0>,<0.2531.0>,<0.2532.0>,<0.2533.0>,<0.2534.0>,<0.2535.0>,<0.2536.0>,
<0.2537.0>,<0.2538.0>,<0.2539.0>,<0.2540.0>,<0.2541.0>,<0.2542.0>,<0.2543.0>,
<0.2544.0>,<0.2545.0>,<0.2546.0>,<0.2547.0>,<0.2548.0>,<0.2549.0>,<0.2550.0>,
<0.2551.0>,<0.2553.0>,<0.2554.0>,<0.2555.0>,<0.2556.0>,<0.2557.0>,<0.2558.0>,
<0.2559.0>,<0.2560.0>,<0.2561.0>,<0.2562.0>,<0.2563.0>]
APIds:[<0.2465.0>,<0.2466.0>]
ScapePids:[<0.2461.0>,<0.2462.0>]
Sensor:{{-1,7.57153413903982e-10},sensor} is terminating.
Agent:<0.2460.0> terminating. Genotype has been backed up.
Fitness:0.5162814284277237
TotEvaluations:65
TotCycles:132
TimeAcc:21664
Cortex:{{origin,7.571534139039844e-10},cortex} is terminating.
```

From the above console printout, you can see that the first mutation operator applied was the add_outlink, which was successful. The second was add_actuator, which was not. At this stage, every time the mutate(test) gets executed, the function only applies a single mutation operator to the genotype, we know this from the line: **Tot neurons:1 Performing Tot mutations:1 on:test**. We then skip to the end, the last execution of the mutate(test). From the line: **Tot neurons:95 Performing Tot mutations:5 on:test**, we can see that at this point the NN system has 95 neurons, and the randomly chosen number of mutation operators to be applied is 5. This means that 5 mutation operators are applied in series to the NN system to produce the mutant agent, and only after the 5 mutation operators are applied, is the agent's fitness evaluated.

Once all the mutation operators have been applied, the exoself converts the genotype of the test NN system to its phenotype, applying it to the problem that its morphology designated it for. From the console printout, we see that the NN system successfully terminated, and so we can be assured that the NN topology does not have any discontinuities, and that it does produce a functional, albeit not very fit, phenotype. Also, none of the mutation operators produced any type of errors that originate from actual crashes.

Having now tested the main mutation operators and the mapping from genotype to phenotype, we can move on and see if the population_monitor is functional, by running the small XOR based benchmark, as we did in Chapter-7.

9.2 Testing the Neuroevolutionary System on the Simple XOR Benchmark

Having now tested some of the important independent functions and elements of our topology and weight evolving artificial neural network (TWEANN) system, we can move on to testing the system as a whole. Our morphology module contains various morphologies at our disposal, where a morphology is a list of sensors and actuators that a NN system can incorporate through evolution if it is of that particular morphology. Furthermore, the sensors and actuators define what the NN system can interface with, what the NN system does, and thus, what the problems the NN system is applied to. For example, if the sensor available to our NN system is one that reads values from a database, and the actuator is one that simply outputs the NN's output vector signal, and furthermore the database from which the sensor reads its data is a XOR truth table, then we could train this NN system to mimic a XOR logic operator. We could compare the NN based agent's output to what that output should be if the agent was a XOR logic operator, rewarding it if it's output is similar to the expected XOR operator output, and punishing it if not.

If the sensors were to have been programs that interfaced with a simulated world through sensors embedded in some simulated organism inhabiting a simulated world, and if the actuators were to have been programs controlling the simulated organism (avatar), then our NN system would be the evolving brain of an organism in an Artificial Life experiment. Thus, the sensors and actuators define what the NN system does, and its morphology is a set of sensors and actuators, as a package, available to the NN system during its evolution. Thus it is the morphology that defines the problem to what the NN system is applied. We choose a morphology to which the NN system belongs, and it evolves and learns how to use the sensors and actuators belonging to that morphology.

Thus far we have only created one morphology, the *xor_mimic*. The xor_mimic morphology contains a single sensor with the name *xor_GetInput*, and a single actuator with the name *xor_SendOutput*. Thus if we evolve agents of this particular morphology, they will only be able to evolve into XOR logical operator mimics. Agents cannot switch morphologies mid-evolution, but new sensors and actuators can be added to the morphology by updating the morphology module, and afterwards these new interfaces can then be incorporated into the NN system over time.

We created the population_monitor process which creates a seed population of NN systems belonging to some specified morphologies, and then evolves those NN based agents. Since the morphologies define the scapes the NN system interfaces with, and the scape computes the fitness score of the agent interfacing with it, the population_monitor process has the ability to evolve the population by having access to each agent's fitness in the population, applying a selection function to the population, and then mutating the selected agents, creating new and mutated offspring from them. We now test this process by getting the population_monitor process to spawn a seed population of agents with the xor_mimic morphology, and see how quickly our current version of the neuroevolutionary system can evolve a solution to this problem, how quickly it can evolve a XOR logic operator using neurons as the basic elements of the evolving network.

We will run the population_monitor:test() function with the following parameters:

```
%%%%%%%%%%%%%%%%% Population Monitor Options & Parameters %%%%%%%%%%%%%%%
-define(SELECTION_ALGORITHM,competition).
-define(EFF,0.2).
-define(INIT_CONSTRAINTS,[#constraint{morphology=Morphology, neu-
ral_afs=Neural_AFs}|| Morphology<-[xor_mimic],Neural_AFs<-[[tanh]]]).
-define(SURVIVAL_PERCENTAGE,0.5).
-define(SPECIE_SIZE_LIMIT,10).
-define(INIT_SPECIE_SIZE,10).
-define(INIT_POPULATION_ID,test).
-define(OP_MODE,gt).
-define(INIT_POLIS,mathema).
-define(GENERATION_LIMIT,100).
-define(EVALUATIONS_LIMIT,100000).
-define(DIVERSITY_COUNT_STEP,500).
-define(GEN_UID,genotype:generate_UniqueId()).
-define(CHAMPION_COUNT_STEP,500).
-define(FITNESS_GOAL,inf).
```

The population will thus be composed of NN systems using the xor_mimic morphology (and thus be applied to that particular problem), and whose neurons will use only the tanh activation function. The population will maintain a size close to 10. Finally, neuroevolution will continue for at most 100 generations, or at most 100000 evaluations. The fitness goal is set to inf, which means that it is not a stopping condition and the evolution will continue until one of the other terminating conditions is reached. The fitness score for each agent is calculated by the scape it is interfacing with. Having set up the parameters for our neuroeovlutionary system, we compile the population_monitor module, and execute the population_monitor:test() function, as shown next:

```
2> population_monitor:test().
Specie_Id:7.570104741922324e-10 Morphology:xor_mimic
******** Population monitor started with parameters:{gt,test,competition}
...
Selection Algorirthm:competition
Valid_AgentSummaries:[{91822.42396111514,3,{7.570065786458927e-10,agent}},
            {82128.75594984594,3,{7.570065785419657e-10,agent}},
            {66717.38827549343,3,{7.570065785184491e-10,agent}},
            {66865.26402662563,4,{7.570065786995862e-10,agent}},
            {66859.35543290272,4,{7.570065785258691e-10,agent}},
            {60974.864233884604,4,{7.570065785388116e-10,agent}}]
Invalid_AgentSummaries:[{56725.927279906005,4,{7.570065787547878e-10,agent}},
            {46423.91939090131,4,{7.570065786090063e-10,agent}},
            {34681.35604691528,3,{7.570065790439459e-10,agent}},
            {67.37546054504678,4,{7.570065785110257e-10,agent}},
            {13.178830126581289,5,{7.570065785335377e-10,agent}}]
NeuralEnergyCost:13982.434363128335
NewPopAcc:9.218546902348272
Population size normalizer:0.9218546902348272
Agent_Id:{7.570065785388116e-10,agent} Normalized_MutantAlotment:1
Agent_Id:{7.570065785258691e-10,agent} Normalized_MutantAlotment:1
Agent_Id:{7.570065786995862e-10,agent} Normalized_MutantAlotment:1
Agent_Id:{7.570065785184491e-10,agent} Normalized_MutantAlotment:2
...
******** Population_Monitor:test shut down with Reason:normal OpTag:continue, while in
OpMode:gt
******** Tot Agents:9 Population Generation:100 Eval_Acc:63960 Cycle_Acc:217798
Time_Acc:12912953
```

It works! Highlighted in green (2nd and 3rd line in the black & white printed version) are the first two lines printed to screen after population_monitor:test() is executed. It states that the population_monitor is started with selection algorithm *competition*, a population with the id *test*, and op_mode (operational mode) being gt, whose operational importance we will set in a later chapter.

Based on how we designed our population_monitor system, every generation it prints out the fitness score of the population. Highlighted in red and italicized is the 100th generation, and each agent with its fitness score. The most fit agent with its fitness score in the last generation is: {91822.42396111514, 3, {7.570065786458927e-10, agent}}. Based on how the xor_sim scape calculates fitness, this fitness score amounts to the agent having a mean squared sum error of 1/91822, and it took a total of 63960 evaluations for our neuroevolutionary system to reach it.

This is quite a bit of computational time for such a simple problem, but it is not usually the case to take the circuit to this level of accuracy. Let us change the fitness goal to 1000, make MAX_ATTEMPTS = 10 in the exoself module, and then try again.

In my experiment, I had the following results:

```
Valid_AgentSummaries:[{1000.4594763865106,2,{7.570051345044739e-10,agent}},
        {272.7339484226029,2,{7.570051345273578e-10,agent}},
        {249.64913390960575,2,{7.57005134500996e-10,agent}},
        {227.82980202627456,4,{7.570051345098297e-10,agent}},
        {193.32888692741093,2,{7.570051345440797e-10,agent}}]
Invalid_AgentSummaries:[{56.2580273824466,2,{7.570051346068126e-10,agent}},
        {18.43287953405122,2,{7.570051345575052e-10,agent}},
        {6.1532819188772505,2,{7.570051345123884e-10,agent}},
        {0.49999782678670823,3,{7.570051345394602e-10,agent}}]
...
...
...
******** Population_Monitor:test shut down with Reason:normal OpTag:continue, while in
OpMode:gt
******** Tot Agents:9 Population Generation:78 Eval_Acc:10701 Cycle_Acc:41178
Time_Acc:2259258
```

This time it took only 10701 evaluations. But there is something very interesting that happened here. Take a look at the most fit agent in the population, with the id: **{1000.4594763865106,2,{7.570051345044739e-10,agent}}**. It only has 2 neurons! That's not possible, since this particular circuit requires at least 3 neurons, if those neurons are using tanh activation function. We have the agent's Id, let's check out its topology, as shown in the following listing:

```
Listing-9.3 The console printout of the topology of the fittest agent in the population.

3> genotype:print({7.570051345044739e-10,agent}).
{agent,{7.570051345044739e-10,agent},
    15,undefined,7.570051363681182e-10,
    {{origin,7.570051345042693e-10},cortex},
    {[{0,1},{0.5,1}],
    [{add_bias,{0.5,neuron}},
     {mutate_af,{0,neuron}},
     {mutate_weights,{0.5,neuron}},
     {add_actuator,{0,neuron},{1,actuator}},
     {outsplice,{0,neuron},{0.5,neuron},{1,actuator}},
     {mutate_weights,{0,neuron}},
     {mutate_af,{0,neuron}},
```

```
{mutate_af,{0,neuron}},
{mutate_weights,{0,neuron}},
{mutate_af,{0,neuron}},
{mutate_weights,{0,neuron}},
{mutate_af,{0,neuron}},
{mutate_weights,{0,neuron}},
{add_bias,{0,neuron}},
{add_inlink,{0,neuron},{0,neuron}}],
[{sensor,undefined,xor_GetInput,undefined,
    {private,xor_sim},
    2,
    [{{0,7.570051345042682e-10},neuron}],
    undefined}],
[{actuator,undefined,xor_SendOutput,undefined,
    {private,xor_sim},
    1,
    [{{0.5,7.570051345042677e-10},neuron}],
    11},
{actuator,undefined,xor_SendOutput,undefined,
    {private,xor_sim},
    1,
    [{{0,7.570051345042682e-10},neuron}],
    undefined}]},
{constraint,xor_mimic,[tanh]},
[{add_bias,{{0.5,7.570051345042677e-10},neuron}},
{mutate_af,{{0,7.570051345439552e-10},neuron}},
{mutate_weights,{{0.5,7.570051346065783e-10},neuron}},
{add_actuator,{{0,7.57005134638638e-10},neuron},
        {{1,7.57005134636634e-10},actuator}},
{outsplice,{{0,7.57005134670089e-10},neuron},
        {{0.5,7.570051346689715e-10},neuron},
        {{1,7.570051346700879e-10},actuator}},
{mutate_weights,{{0,7.570051347808065e-10},neuron}},
{mutate_af,{{0,7.570051347949999e-10},neuron}},
{mutate_af,{{0,7.570051348731883e-10},neuron}},
{mutate_weights,{{0,7.57005134905699e-10},neuron}},
{mutate_af,{{0,7.570051352005185e-10},neuron}},
{mutate_weights,{{0,7.57005135384367e-10},neuron}},
{mutate_af,{{0,7.570051357421974e-10},neuron}},
{mutate_weights,{{0,7.570051357953169e-10},neuron}},
{add_bias,{{0,7.570051361212367e-10},neuron}},
{add_inlink,{{0,7.570051363350866e-10},neuron},
        {{0,7.570051363350866e-10},neuron}}],
1000.4594763865106,0,
[{0,[{{0,7.570051363631578e-10},neuron}]},
```

{0.5,[{{0.5,7.570051346689715e-10},neuron}]}]}
{cortex,{{origin,7.570051345042693e-10},cortex},
    {7.570051345044739e-10,agent},
    [{{0.5,7.570051345042677e-10},neuron},
     {{0,7.570051345042682e-10},neuron}],
    [{{-1,7.570051345042671e-10},sensor}],
    [{{1,7.570051345042659e-10},actuator},
     {{1,7.570051345042664e-10},actuator}]}}
{sensor,{{-1,7.570051345042671e-10},sensor},
    xor_GetInput,
    {{origin,7.570051345042693e-10},cortex},
    {private,xor_sim},
    2,
    [{{0,7.570051345042682e-10},neuron}],
    undefined}
{neuron,{{0.5,7.570051345042677e-10},neuron},
    15,
    {{origin,7.570051345042693e-10},cortex},
    tanh,
    [{{{0,7.570051345042682e-10},neuron},[-4.9581978771372395]},
     {bias,[-2.444318048832683]}]],
    [{{1,7.570051345042659e-10},actuator}],
    []}
{neuron,{{0,7.570051345042682e-10},neuron},
    14,
    {{origin,7.570051345042693e-10},cortex},
    tanh,
    [{{{0,7.570051345042682e-10},neuron},[6.283185307179586]},
     {{{-1,7.570051345042671e-10},sensor},
      [-4.3985975891263305,-2.3223009779757877]},
     {bias,[1.3462974501315348]}]],
    [{{1,7.570051345042664e-10},actuator},
     {{0.5,7.570051345042677e-10},neuron},
     {{0,7.570051345042682e-10},neuron}],
    [{{0,7.570051345042682e-10},neuron}]}
{actuator,{{1,7.570051345042659e-10},actuator},
    xor_SendOutput,
    {{origin,7.570051345042693e-10},cortex},
    {private,xor_sim},
    1,
    [{{0.5,7.570051345042677e-10},neuron}],
    11}
{actuator,{{1,7.570051345042664e-10},actuator},
    xor_SendOutput,
    {{origin,7.570051345042693e-10},cortex},

```
{private,xor_sim},
1,
[{{0,7.570051345042682e-10},neuron}],
undefined}
{atomic,[ok,ok]}
```

Though we've decided to look at the NN system's genotype to see how it was possible for our neuroevolutionary system to evolve a solution with only two neurons, instead, if you look through the genotype, you will see that we just uncovered a large number of errors in the way our system functions. Let's take a look at each part in turn, before returning to the actual evolved topology of the NN system.

Boldfaced in the console printout above are the following errors, discussed and corrected in the following sections:

1. mutate_af operator is applied to the agent multiple times, but we have opted to only use the tanh activation function, which means this mutation operator does nothing to the network, and is a waste of a mutation attempt, and thus should not be present.
2. When looking at the mutate_af, we also see that it is applied to neurons with different Ids, 5 of them, even though there are only 2 neurons in the system.
3. This NN system evolved a connection to two actuators, but this morphology supports only 1, what happened?
4. In the agent's fingerprint, the sensors and actuators contain N_Ids. This is an error, since the fingerprint must not contain any Id specific information, it must only contain the general information about the NN system, so that we can have an ability to roughly distinguish between different species of the NN systems (those with different topologies, morphologies, sensors and actuators, or those with significantly different sets of activation functions).

In the following sections, we deal with each of these errors one at a time.

9.2.1 The mutate_af Error

Looking at the agent's evo_hist list, shown in Listing-9.4, we can see that multiple mutate_afs are applied. The goal of a mutation operator is to modify the NN system, and if a mutation operator cannot be applied, due to for example the state in which the NN system is, or because it leads to a non-functional NN, then we should revert the mutation operator and try applying another one. Each NN system, when being mutated, undergoes a specific number of mutations, ranging from 1 to sqrt(Tot_Neurons), chosen randomly. Thus, every time we apply a mutation operator to the NN system, and it does nothing, that is one mutation attempt wasted. This can result in a clone which was not mutated at all, or not mutated properly.

Afterwards, this clone is sent back into the environment to be evaluated. For example assume a fit agent creates an offspring by first creating a clone of itself, and then applying to it the mutate_af operator, if mutate_af is being applied to an agent that only has tanh for its available activation functions list, the resulting offspring is exactly the same as its parent, since tanh was swapped for tanh. There is no reason to test out a clone, since we already know how such a NN system functions, because its parent has already been evaluated and tested for fitness. It is thus essential that whatever is causing this error, is fixed.

Listing-9.4 The agent's evo_hist list.

```
[{add_bias,{{0.5,7.570051345042677e-10},neuron}},
    {mutate_af,{{0,7.570051345439552e-10},neuron}},
    {mutate_weights,{{0.5,7.570051346065783e-10},neuron}},
    {add_actuator,{{0,7.57005134638638e-10},neuron},
            {{1,7.57005134636634e-10},actuator}},
    {outsplice,{{0,7.57005134670089e-10},neuron},
            {{0.5,7.570051346689715e-10},neuron},
            {{1,7.570051346700879e-10},actuator}},
    {mutate_weights,{{0,7.570051347808065e-10},neuron}},
    {mutate_af,{{0,7.570051347949999e-10},neuron}},
    {mutate_af,{{0,7.570051348731883e-10},neuron}},
    {mutate_weights,{{0,7.57005134905699e-10},neuron}},
    {mutate_af,{{0,7.570051352005185e-10},neuron}},
    {mutate_weights,{{0,7.57005135384367e-10},neuron}},
    {mutate_af,{{0,7.570051357421974e-10},neuron}},
    {mutate_weights,{{0,7.570051357953169e-10},neuron}},
    {add_bias,{{0,7.570051361212367e-10},neuron}},
    {add_inlink,{{0,7.570051363350866e-10},neuron},
            {{0,7.570051363350866e-10},neuron}}],
```

To solve this problem we need to check the *genome_mutator:mutate_af/1* function, as shown in listing-9.5.

Listing-9.5 The mutate_af/1 function.

```
mutate_af(Agent_Id)->
    A = genotype:read({agent,Agent_Id}),
    Cx_Id = A#agent.cx_id,
    Cx = genotype:read({cortex,Cx_Id}),
    N_Ids = Cx#cortex.neuron_ids,
    N_Id = lists:nth(random:uniform(length(N_Ids)),N_Ids),
    Generation = A#agent.generation,
    N = genotype:read({neuron,N_Id}),
    AF = N#neuron.af,
```

```
Activation_Functions = (A#agent.constraint)#constraint.neural_afs -- [AF],
NewAF = genotype:generate_NeuronAF(Activation_Functions),
U_N = N#neuron{af=NewAF,generation=Generation},
EvoHist = A#agent.evo_hist,
U_EvoHist = [{mutate_af,N_Id}|EvoHist],
U_A = A#agent{evo_hist=U_EvoHist},
genotype:write(U_N),
genotype:write(U_A).
```

Though: *Activation_Functions = (A#agent.constraint)#constraint.neural_afs –
[AF]*, does result in an empty list (since #constraint.neural_afs list is: [tanh]), it
does not matter because the *genotype:generate_NeuronAF(Activation_Functions)*
function itself chooses the default *tanh* activation function when executed with an
empty list parameter. This is the cause of this error. What we need to do is simply
exit the mutation operator as soon as we find that there is only one activation function, that it is already being used by the neuron, and that there is nothing to mutate. We thus modify mutate_af/1 function to be as follows:

Listing-9.6 The mutate_af function after the fix is applied.

```
mutate_af(Agent_Id)->
    A = genotype:read({agent,Agent_Id}),
    Cx_Id = A#agent.cx_id,
    Cx = genotype:read({cortex,Cx_Id}),
    N_Ids = Cx#cortex.neuron_ids,
    N_Id = lists:nth(random:uniform(length(N_Ids)),N_Ids),
    Generation = A#agent.generation,

    N = genotype:read({neuron,N_Id}),
    AF = N#neuron.af,
    case (A#agent.constraint)#constraint.neural_afs -- [AF] of
        [] ->
            exit("********ERROR:mutate_af:: There are no other activation func-
tions to use.");
        Activation_Functions ->
            NewAF = lists:nth(random:uniform(length(Activation_Functions)),
Activation_Functions),
            U_N = N#neuron{af=NewAF,generation=Generation},
            EvoHist = A#agent.evo_hist,
            U_EvoHist = [{mutate_af,N_Id}|EvoHist],
            U_A = A#agent{evo_hist=U_EvoHist},
            genotype:write(U_N),
            genotype:write(U_A)
    end.
```

The fix is shown in boldface. In this fixed function, as soon as the mutation operator determines that there are no other activation functions that it can swap the currently used one for, it simply exits with an error. The genome mutator then tries out another mutation operator.

9.2.2 Same Neuron, But Different Ids in the evo_hist List

Looking at the Listing-9.3 again, we also see that even though the NN has only 2 neurons, as was shown in the original printout to console, there were 5 mutate_af operators applied and each one was applied to a different neuron_id. But how is that possible if there are only 2 neurons and thus only 2 different neuron ids?

This error occurs because when we clone the NN, all neurons get a new id, but we never update the evo_hist list, converting those old ids into new ones. This means that the Ids within the evo_hist are not of the elements belonging to the agent in its current state, but the element ids which belong to its ancestors. Though it does not matter what the particular ids are, it is essential that they are consistent, so that we can reconstruct the evolutionary path of the NN based system, which is not possible if we don't know which mutation operator was applied to which element in the NN system being analyzed. To be able to see when, and to what particular elements of the topology the mutation operators were applied, we need a consistent set of element ids in the evo_hist, so that the evolutionary path can be reconstructed based on the actual ids used by the NN based agent.

To fix this, we need to modify the cloning process so that it does not only update all the element ids in the NN system, but also the element ids in the evo_hist, ensuring that the system is consistent. The cloning process is performed in the genotype module, through the clone_Agent/2 function. Therefore, it is this function that we need to correct. The fix is simple, we need to create a new function called map_EvoHist/2, and call it from the clone_Agent/2 function with the old evo_hist list and an ETS table containing a map from old ids to new ones. The map_EvoHist/2 function can then map the old ids to new ids in the evo_hist list. The cloned agent will then use this updated evo_hist, with its updated new ids, instead of the old ids which belonged to its parent. The updated map_EvoHist/2 function is shown in Listing-9.7.

Listing-9.7 A new function, map_EvoHist/2, which updates the element ids of the evo_hist list, mapping the ids of the original agent to the ids of the elements used by its clone.

```
map_EvoHist(TableName,EvoHist)->
    map_EvoHist(TableName,EvoHist,[]).

map_EvoHist(TableName,[{MO,E1Id,E2Id,E3Id}|EvoHist],Acc)->
```

```
    Clone_E1Id = ets:lookup_element(TableName,E1Id,2),
    Clone_E2Id = ets:lookup_element(TableName,E2Id,2),
    Clone_E3Id = ets:lookup_element(TableName,E3Id,2),
    map_EvoHist(TableName,EvoHist,[{MO,Clone_E1Id,Clone_E2Id, Clone_E3Id}| Acc]);
map_EvoHist(TableName,[{MO,E1Id,E2Id}|EvoHist],Acc)->
    Clone_E1Id = ets:lookup_element(TableName,E1Id,2),
    Clone_E2Id = ets:lookup_element(TableName,E2Id,2),
    map_EvoHist(TableName,EvoHist,[{MO,Clone_E1Id,Clone_E2Id}|Acc]);
map_EvoHist(TableName,[{MO,E1Id}|EvoHist],Acc)->
    Clone_E1Id = ets:lookup_element(TableName,E1Id,2),
    map_EvoHist(TableName,EvoHist,[{MO,Clone_E1Id}|Acc]);
map_EvoHist(_TableName,[],Acc)->
    lists:reverse(Acc).
%map_EvoHist/2 is a wrapper for map_EvoHist/3, which in turn accepts the evo_hist list con-
taining the mutation operator tuples that have been applied to the NN system. The function is
used when a clone of a NN system is created. The function updates the original Ids of the ele-
ments the mutation operators have been applied to, to the ids used by the elements of the clone,
so that the updated evo_hist can reflect the clone's topology, as if all the mutation operators
have been applied to it instead, and that it is not a clone. Once all the tuples in the evo_hist have
been updated with the clone's element ids, the list is reversed to its proper order, and the updat-
ed list is returned to the caller.
```

Having fixed this bug, we move on to the next one.

9.2.3 Multiple Actuators of the Same Type

Looking again at the Listing-9.3, we see that one of the mutation operators was *add_actuator*. Since only successful mutation operators are allowed to be in the *evo_hist* list, it must be the case that only those mutation operators that actually mutated the genotype are present in the evo_hist list, which is what allows us to use it to trace back the evolutionary path of the evolved agent. But the presence of add_actuator in evo_hist must be an error, because the xor_mimic morphology only gives the agent access to a single actuator, there are no variations of that actuator, and the agent starts with that single actuator. It should not be possible to add a new actuator to the NN system since there are no new ones available, and this tag should not exist in the evo_hist list. This mutation operator was applied in error, let's find out why.

Looking at the add_actuator/1 in the genome_mutator module, we can see that *it does* check whether all the actuators are already used. But if we look at the agent's fingerprint section of the console printout in Listing-9.3:

```
[{actuator,undefined,xor_SendOutput,undefined,
        {private,xor_sim},
        1,
        [{{0.5,7.570051345042677e-10},neuron}],
        11},
    {actuator,undefined,xor_SendOutput,undefined,
        {private,xor_sim},
        1,
        [{{0,7.570051345042682e-10},neuron}],
        undefined}]
```

We notice the problem. The last element in the record defining the actuator in the genotype is the generation element. One actuator has the generation set to *11*, the other has it set to *undefined*. In the add_actuator function, we do not reset the *generation* value, as we do with the *id* and the *cx_id*. This must be it. When we subtract the list of the actuators used by the agent from the morphology's list of available actuators, the resulting list is not empty. The reason why an actuator still remains in the list, is because we did not set the generation parameter of the agent's actuator to undefined. Since the two actuators are not exactly the same (with all their agent specific features been set to defaults), the actuator used by the agent is not removed from the list of available actuators of the morphology's actuator list.

This also raises the issue of what should we do, in a consistent manner, with the generation parameter of the actuator? Lets update the source code and treat the generation of the actuator element as we treat it in the neuron elements: Initially set it to the value of the generation when it was created, and update its value every time it has been *affected* by a mutation. We make the same modification to the sensor elements.

In the add_actuator/1 function we change the line:

```
...
case morphology:get_Actuators(Morphology)--[(genotype:read({actuator, A_Id}))#actuator{
cx_id=undefined,  id=undefined, fanin_ids=[]} || A_Id<-A_Ids] of
...
```

To:

```
...
case morphology:get_Actuators(Morphology)--[(genotype:read({actuator, A_Id}))#actuator{
cx_id=undefined, id=undefined, fanin_ids=[],generation=undefined} || A_Id<-A_Ids] of
...
```

We do the same thing to the add_sensor/1 function. And then to ensure that the actuator's generation is updated every time a mutation operator affects it, we update the function linkFromNeuronToActuator/3 from using the line:

```
genotype:write(ToA#actuator{ fanin_ids=U_Fanin_Ids})
```

To one using:

```
genotype:write(ToA#actuator{ fanin_ids = U_Fanin_Ids, generation=Generation})
```

To make sure that the sensor's generation is also updated, we modify the function *link_FromSensorTo/2* from:

```
link_FromSensor(FromS,ToId)->
    FromFanout_Ids = FromS#sensor.fanout_ids,
    case lists:member(ToId, FromFanout_Ids) of
        true ->
            exit("******** ERROR:link_FromSensor[cannot add ToId to Sensor]: ~p already a member of ~p~n",[ToId,FromS#sensor.id]);
        false ->
            FromS#sensor{
                fanout_ids = [ToId|FromFanout_Ids]
            }
    end.
```

To the function *link_FromSensorTo/3*:

```
link_FromSensor(FromS,ToId,Generation)->
    FromFanout_Ids = FromS#sensor.fanout_ids,
    case lists:member(ToId, FromFanout_Ids) of
        true ->
            exit("******** ERROR:link_FromSensor[can not add ToId to Sensor]: ~p already a member of ~p~n",[ToId,FromS#sensor.id]);
        false ->
            FromS#sensor{
                fanout_ids = [ToId|FromFanout_Ids],
                generation=Generation
            }
    end.
```

Finally, we also update the genotype module's function *construct_Cortex/3*, from using:

```
Sensors = [S#sensor{id={{-1,generate_UniqueId()},sensor},cx_id=Cx_Id}|| S<-
morphology:get_InitSensors(Morphology)],
```

```
Actuators = [A#actuator{id={{1,generate_UniqueId()},actuator},cx_id=Cx_Idn}||A<-
morphology:get_InitActuators(Morphology)],
```

To one using:

```
Sensors = [S#sensor{id={{-1,generate_UniqueId()},sensor},cx_id=Cx_Id,
generation=Generation} || S<- morphology:get_InitSensors(Morphology)],
    Actuators = [A#actuator{id={{1,generate_UniqueId()},actuator},cx_id=Cx_Id,
generation=Generation} || A<-morphology:get_InitActuators(Morphology)],
```

Which ensures that we can keep track of the generation from the very start.

9.2.4 Making Fingerprint Store Generalized Sensors & Actuators

The fingerprint of the agent is used to vaguely represent the species that the agent belongs to. For example, if we have two NN systems which are exactly the same, except for the ids of their elements and the synaptic weights their neurons use, then these two agents belong to the same species. We cannot compare them directly to each other, because they will have those differences (the ids and the synaptic weights), but we can create a more generalized fingerprint for each agent which will be exactly the same for both. Some of the general features which we might use to classify a species is the NN topology and the sensors and actuators the NN system uses.

The 4th error we noticed was that we forgot to get rid of the N_Ids in the *generalized* sensor and actuator tuples within the fingerprint. We got rid of all the Id specific parts (the element's own id, and the cx_id) of those tuples before entering them into the fingerprint tuple, but forgot to do the same for the fanin_ids and the fanout_ids in the actuator and sensor tuples respectively. The fix is very simple, in the genotype module, we modify two lines in the update_fingerprint/1 function from:

```
GeneralizedSensors= [(read({sensor,S_Id}))#sensor{id=undefined,cx_id=undefined}
|| S_Id<-Cx#cortex.sensor_ids],
    GeneralizedActuators= [(read({actuator,A_Id}))#actuator{id=undefined, cx_id=undefined}
|| A_Id<-Cx#cortex.actuator_ids],
```

To:

```
GeneralizedSensors= [(read({sensor,S_Id}))#sensor{id=undefined,cx_id=undefined,
fanout_ids =[]} || S_Id<-Cx#cortex.sensor_ids],
```

GeneralizedActuators= [(read({actuator,A_Id}))#actuator{id=undefined,cx_id =undefined, fanin_ids=[]} || A_Id<-Cx#cortex.actuator_ids],

This change fixes the 4th and final error we've noticed. With this done, we now take our attention towards the remaining noticed anomaly, the 2 neuron NN solution. How is it possible?

9.2.5 The Quizzical Topology of the Fittest NN System

The first thing we noticed, and the reason for a closer analysis of the evolved agent, was the NN's topology, the fact that it had 2 neurons instead of 3+ neurons. After our analysis though, and finding out that it also had 2 actuators, while interfacing with only a single private scape, which means that both actuators were sending signals to it... there might be all kinds of different reasons for the 2 neuron solution. Nevertheless, let us still build it to see what exactly has evolved. Fig-9.5 shows the diagram of the final evolved NN system, based on the genotype in Listing-9.3.

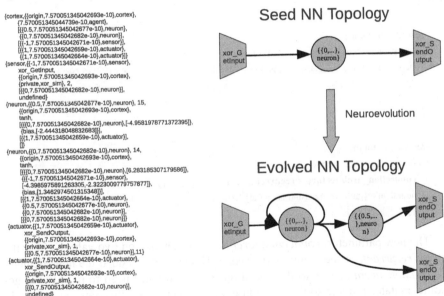

Fig. 9.5 The NN topology of the fittest agent in the population solving the XOR test, from Listing-9.3.

If we ignore the strange part about this NN system having two actuators, the reason behind which we have already solved in Section-9.2.3, we immediately spot another interesting feature. We have evolved a recurrent NN!

A recurrent NN can use memory, which means that the evolved solution, among other things, is most likely also sequence specific. This means that this solution takes into account the order in which the input data is presented. Since in the real world these types of signals would not be presented in any particular order to the XOR logic operator in question, our evolved system would not simulate the XOR operator properly anyway, even after having all the other errors fixed. A proper XOR mimicking neural network must not be sequence specific. Thus it is essential that for this problem we evolve a non recurrent NN system.

We need to be able to control and choose whether we want the evolving neural network systems to have recurrent connections or not. In the same way that we can choose what activation functions the NN system has access to (through the constraint record), we can also specify whether recurrent connections are allowed or not. To add this feature before we can retest our system, we need to: 1. Modify the records.hrl file to add the new element to the constraint tuple. And 2. Modify the genome_mutator module so that it checks whether recurrent or only feedforward connections are allowed, before choosing which elements to link together.

Modifying the records.hrl file is easy, we simply change the constraint record from:

```
-record(constraint,{
    morphology=xor_mimic, %xor_mimic
    neural_afs=[tanh,cos,gaussian,absolute] %[tanh,cos,gaussian,absolute,sin,sqrt,sigmoid]
    }).
```

To:

```
-record(constraint,{
    morphology=xor_mimic, %xor_mimic
    connection_architecture = recurrent, %recurrent|feedforward
    neural_afs=[tanh,cos,gaussian,absolute] %[tanh,cos,gaussian,absolute,sin,sqrt,sigmoid]
    }).
```

The new parameter: *connection_architecture*, can take on two values, either the atom: *recurrent*, or the atom: *feedforward*. Though we've added the new element, *connection_architecture*, to the constraint record, we still need to modify the genome_mutator module so that it actually knows how to use this new parameter. In the genome_mutator module we need to modify all the mutation_operators that add new connections, and ensure that before a new connection is created, the function takes the value of the connection_architecture parameter into consideration. The mutation operators that we need to modify for this are: *add_outlink/1*, *add_inlink/1*, and *add_neuron/1*.

The updated add_outlink/1 function first builds an output id pool, which is a list of all available ids to which the selected neuron can choose to establish a link to. The general id pool is composed by combining together the list of actuator and neuron ids. We must remove from this id list the neuron's own Output_Ids list, which leaves a list of element Ids to which the neuron is not yet connected to. We then check whether the agent allows for recurrent connections, or only feedforward. If recurrent connections are allowed, then a random Id from this list is chosen, and the neuron and the chosen element are linked together. If on the other hand only the feedforward connections are allowed, the neuron's own layer index is checked, and then the composed id pool is filtered such that the remaining id list contains only the element ids whose layer index is greater than that of the neuron. This effectively creates a list of element ids which are 1 or more neural-layers ahead of the chosen neuron, and to whom if a connection is established, would be considered feedforward. To implement this new approach, we convert the original add_outlinke/1 function from:

```erlang
add_outlink(Agent_Id)->
  A = genotype:read({agent,Agent_Id}),
  Cx_Id = A#agent.cx_id,
  Cx = genotype:read({cortex,Cx_Id}),
  N_Ids = Cx#cortex.neuron_ids,
  A_Ids = Cx#cortex.actuator_ids,
  N_Id = lists:nth(random:uniform(length(N_Ids)),N_Ids),
  N = genotype:read({neuron,N_Id}),
  Output_Ids = N#neuron.output_ids,
  case lists:append(A_Ids,N_Ids) -- Output_Ids of
      [] ->
              exit("********ERROR:add_outlink:: Neuron already connected to all ids");
      Available_Ids ->
              To_Id = lists:nth(random:uniform(length(Available_Ids)),Available_Ids),
              link_FromElementToElement(Agent_Id,N_Id,To_Id),
              EvoHist = A#agent.evo_hist,
              U_EvoHist = [{add_outlink,N_Id,To_Id}|EvoHist],
              U_A = A#agent{evo_hist=U_EvoHist},
              genotype:write(U_A)
  end.
```

To one that uses a filtered neuron id pool, *Outlink_NIdPool*, for the feedforward connections, and the entire id pool for when recurrent connections are allowed:

```erlang
add_outlink(Agent_Id)->
  A = genotype:read({agent,Agent_Id}),
  Cx_Id = A#agent.cx_id,
  Cx = genotype:read({cortex,Cx_Id}),
```

```
N_Ids = Cx#cortex.neuron_ids,
A_Ids = Cx#cortex.actuator_ids,
N_Id = lists:nth(random:uniform(length(N_Ids)),N_Ids),
N = genotype:read({neuron,N_Id}),
Output_Ids = N#neuron.output_ids,
Outlink_NIdPool = filter_OutlinkIdPool(A#agent.constraint,N_Id,N_Ids),
case lists:append(A_Ids,Outlink_NIdPool) -- Output_Ids of
    [] ->
                exit("********ERROR:add_outlink:: Neuron already connected to all ids");
    Available_Ids ->
                To_Id = lists:nth(random:uniform(length(Available_Ids)),Available_Ids),
                link_FromElementToElement(Agent_Id,N_Id,To_Id),
                EvoHist = A#agent.evo_hist,
                U_EvoHist = [{add_outlink,N_Id,To_Id}|EvoHist],
                U_A = A#agent{evo_hist=U_EvoHist},
                genotype:write(U_A)
end.
```

The *filter_OutlinkIdPool(Constraint,N_Id,N_Ids)* function has to filter the neuron ids (N_Ids) based on the specification in the constraint record. This new filter_OutlinkIdPool/3 function, is shown in the following listing:

Listing-9.8 The implementation of filter_OutlinkIdPool/3, a constraint based neuron id filtering function.

```
filter_OutlinkIdPool(C,N_Id,N_Ids,Type)->
    case C#constraint.connection_architecture of
        recurrent ->
                N_Ids;
        feedforward ->
                {{LI,_},neuron} = N_Id,
                case Type of
                    outlink ->
                                [{{Outlink_LI,Outlink_UniqueId},neuron} || {{Outlink_LI,
Outlink_UniqueId}, neuron} <- N_Ids, Outlink_LI > LI];
                    inlink ->
                                [{{Inlink_LI,Inlink_UniqueId},neuron} || {{Inlink_LI,
Inlink_UniqueId},neuron} <- N_Ids, Inlink_LI < LI]
                end
    end.
```
%The function filter_OutlinkIdPool/3 uses the connection_architecture specification in the constraint record of the agent to return a filtered neuron id pool. For the feedforward connection_architecture, the function ensures that only the neurons in the forward facing layers are allowed in the id pool.

We can modify the add_inlink/1 mutation operator in the same way. In this function though, if we are to only have feedforward connections, then the filtered neuron id pool needs to have neurons whose layer is less than that of the chosen neuron which is trying to add an inlink. The add_inlink/1 function is modified in the same manner as the add_outlink/1, only we create and use the *filter_InlinkIdPool/3* function instead, which is shown in the following listing:

Listing-9.9 The implementation of filter_InlinkIdPool/3, a constraint based neuron ids filtering function.

```
filter_InlinkIdPool(C,N_Id,N_Ids)->
        case C#constraint.connection_architecture of
            recurrent ->
                N_Ids;
            feedforward ->
                {{LI,_},neuron} = N_Id,
                [{{Inlink_LI,Inlink_UniqueId},neuron} || {{Inlink_LI,
Inlink_UniqueId},neuron} <- N_Ids, Inlink_LI < LI]
        end.
%The function filter_InlinkIdPool/3 uses the connection_architecture specification in the con-
straint record of the agent to return a filtered neuron id pool. For the feedforward connec-
tion_architecture, the function ensures that only the neurons in the previous layers are allowed
in the filtered neuron id pool.
```

Finally, we modify the add_neuron/1 mutation operator. In this operator a new neuron B is created, and is then connected *from* a randomly chosen neuron A, and *to* a randomly chosen neuron C. As in the previous two mutation operators, we compose an Id pool specified by the architecture_constraint parameter, from which the Ids of A and C are then chosen. The modified version of the add_neuron/1 function is shown in Listing-9.10.

Listing-9.10 The modified add_neuron/1 mutation operator, which now uses id pools that satisfy the connection_architecture constraint specification. The bold parts of the code are the added
and modified parts of the function.

```
add_neuron(Agent_Id)->
    A = genotype:read({agent,Agent_Id}),
    Generation = A#agent.generation,
    Pattern = A#agent.pattern,
    Cx_Id = A#agent.cx_id,
    Cx = genotype:read({cortex,Cx_Id}),
    N_Ids = Cx#cortex.neuron_ids,
    S_Ids = Cx#cortex.sensor_ids,
    A_Ids = Cx#cortex.actuator_ids,
    {TargetLayer,TargetNeuron_Ids} = lists:nth(random:uniform(length(Pattern)),Pattern),
```

```
    NewN_Id = {{TargetLayer,genotype:generate_UniqueId()},neuron},
    U_N_Ids = [NewN_Id|N_Ids],
    U_Pattern = lists:keyreplace(TargetLayer, 1, Pattern,
{TargetLayer,[NewN_Id|TargetNeuron_Ids]}),
    SpecCon = A#agent.constraint,
    genotype:construct_Neuron(Cx_Id,Generation,SpecCon,NewN_Id,[],[]),
    Inlink_NIdPool = filter_InlinkIdPool(A#agent.constraint,NewN_Id,N_Ids),
    Outlink_NIdPool = filter_OutlinkIdPool(A#agent.constraint,NewN_Id,N_Ids),
    FromElementId_Pool = Inlink_NIdPool++S_Ids,
    ToElementId_Pool = Outlink_NIdPool,
    case (Inlink_NIdPool == []) or (Outlink_NIdPool == []) of
        true ->
                exit("********ERROR::add_neuron(Agent_Id)::Can't add new neuron
here, Inlink_NIdPool or Outlink_NIdPool is empty.");
        false ->
                From_ElementId =
lists:nth(random:uniform(length(FromElementId_Pool)),FromElementId_Pool),
                To_ElementId =
lists:nth(random:uniform(length(ToElementId_Pool)),ToElementId_Pool),
    link_FromElementToElement(Agent_Id,From_ElementId,NewN_Id),
    link_FromElementToElement(Agent_Id,NewN_Id,To_ElementId),
                U_EvoHist = [{add_neuron,From_ElementId,NewN_Id, To_ElementId} |
A#agent.evo_hist],
                genotype:write(Cx#cortex{neuron_ids = U_N_Ids}),
                genotype:write(A#agent{pattern=U_Pattern,evo_hist=U_EvoHist})
    end.
```

We do not need to modify outsplice/1 mutation operator, even though it does establish new connections. The reason for this is that if the connection_architecture allows recurrent connections, then there is nothing to modify, and if it is feedforward, then all the connections are already made in the right direction, since if we add a new neuron, we either create a new layer for it, or put it in the layer located between the two spliced neurons, which allows the NN to retain the feedforward structure.

9.3 Retesting Our Neuroevolutionary System

Having now modified all the broken mutation operators, and fixed all the errors, we can compile all the modified modules, and retest our neuroevolutionary system. First, we will once again apply multiple mutation operators to our NN system, and then analyze the resulting NN architecture, manually checking if everything looks as it supposed to. We will then run multiple xor_mimic tests, each test with a slightly different parameter set. This will give us a better understanding of how our system performs.

During this test, we still let the NN evolve recurrent connections. In the following listing we first compile and load the modules by executing *polis:sync()*. We then execute *genome_mutator:long_test(10)*. And then finally, we print the resulting NN system's genotype to console, so that we can visually inspect it:

```
Listing-9.11 The long_test function applied to our now fixed neuroevolutionary system.

3> genome_mutator:long_test(10).
...
4> genotype:print(test).
{agent,test,10,undefined,test, ...
    [{mutate_weights,{{0.5,7.565644036503407e-10},neuron}},
    {add_neuron,{{0.5,7.565644036503407e-10},neuron},
            {{0.5,7.565644036354212e-10},neuron},
            {{0.5,7.565644036503407e-10},neuron}},
    {add_bias,{{0,7.565644036525425e-10},neuron}},
    {add_outlink,{{0.5,7.565644036503407e-10},neuron},
            {{0,7.565644036562396e-10},neuron}},
    {add_outlink,{{0,7.565644036562396e-10},neuron},
            {{0,7.565644036525425e-10},neuron}},
    {mutate_af,{{0,7.565644036535494e-10},neuron}},
    {mutate_af,{{0,7.565644036562396e-10},neuron}},
    {add_bias,{{0,7.565644036535494e-10},neuron}},
    {outsplice,{{0,7.565644036562396e-10},neuron},
            {{0.5,7.565644036503407e-10},neuron},
            {{1,7.565644036562401e-10},actuator}},
    {mutate_af,{{0,7.565644036535494e-10},neuron}},
    {mutate_weights,{{0,7.565644036562396e-10},neuron}},
    {add_inlink,{{0,7.565644036525425e-10},neuron},
            {{0,7.565644036525425e-10},neuron}},
    {add_neuron,{{-1,7.565644036562414e-10},sensor},
            {{0,7.565644036525425e-10},neuron},
            {{0,7.565644036562396e-10},neuron}},
    {add_neuron,{{0,7.565644036562396e-10},neuron},
            {{0,7.565644036535494e-10},neuron},
            {{0,7.565644036562396e-10},neuron}},
    {add_outlink,{{0,7.565644036562396e-10},neuron},
            {{0,7.565644036562396e-10},neuron}}],
    0.13228659163157622,0,
    [{0,
     [{{0,7.565644036525425e-10},neuron},
      {{0,7.565644036535494e-10},neuron},
```

            {{0,7.565644036562396e-10},neuron}]},
        {0.5,
         [{{0.5,7.565644036354212e-10},neuron},
          {{0.5,7.565644036503407e-10},neuron}]}]}
{cortex,{{origin,7.56564403656243e-10},cortex},
        test,
         [{{0.5,7.565644036354212e-10},neuron},
          {{0.5,7.565644036503407e-10},neuron},
          {{0,7.565644036525425e-10},neuron},
          {{0,7.565644036535494e-10},neuron},
          {{0,7.565644036562396e-10},neuron}],
         [{{-1,7.565644036562414e-10},sensor}],
         [{{1,7.565644036562401e-10},actuator}]}
{sensor,{{-1,7.565644036562414e-10},sensor},
        xor_GetInput,
         {{origin,7.56564403656243e-10},cortex},
         {private,xor_sim},
         2,
         [{{0,7.565644036525425e-10},neuron},
          {{0,7.565644036562396e-10},neuron}],
         3}
{neuron,{{0.5,7.565644036354212e-10},neuron},
        10,
         {{origin,7.56564403656243e-10},cortex},
         absolute,
         [{{{0.5,7.565644036503407e-10},neuron},[-0.07865790723708455]}],
         [{{0.5,7.565644036503407e-10},neuron}],
         [{{0.5,7.565644036503407e-10},neuron}]}
{neuron,{{0.5,7.565644036503407e-10},neuron},
        10,
         {{origin,7.56564403656243e-10},cortex},
         gaussian,
         [{{{0.5,7.565644036354212e-10},neuron},[0.028673644861684]},
          {{{0,7.565644036562396e-10},neuron},[0.344474633962796]}],
         [{{0.5,7.565644036354212e-10},neuron},
          {{0,7.565644036562396e-10},neuron},
          {{1,7.565644036562401e-10},actuator}],
         [{{0.5,7.565644036354212e-10},neuron},
          {{0,7.565644036562396e-10},neuron}]}
{neuron,{{0,7.565644036525425e-10},neuron},
        9,
         {{origin,7.56564403656243e-10},cortex},
         cos,
         [{{{0,7.565644036562396e-10},neuron},[0.22630117969617192]},
          {{{0,7.565644036525425e-10},neuron},[0.06839553053285097]},

```
    {{{-1,7.565644036562414e-10},sensor},
     [0.4907662278024556,-0.3163769342514735]},
     {bias,[-0.40416508186421978]}}],
    [{{0,7.565644036525425e-10},neuron},
     {{0,7.565644036562396e-10},neuron}],
    [{{0,7.565644036525425e-10},neuron},
     {{0,7.565644036562396e-10},neuron}]}
{neuron,{{0,7.565644036535494e-10},neuron},
    7,
    {{origin,7.56564403656243e-10},cortex},
    cos,
    [{{{0,7.565644036562396e-10},neuron},[0.30082326020002736]},
     {bias,[0.00990196169812485]}}],
    [{{0,7.565644036562396e-10},neuron}],
    [{{0,7.565644036562396e-10},neuron}]}
{neuron,{{0,7.565644036562396e-10},neuron},
    9,
    {{origin,7.56564403656243e-10},cortex},
    tanh,
    [{{{0.5,7.565644036503407e-10},neuron},[0.29044390963714084]},
     {{{0,7.565644036525425e-10},neuron},[-0.11820697604732322]},
     {{{0,7.565644036535494e-10},neuron},[2.203261827127093]},
     {{{0,7.565644036562396e-10},neuron},[0.13355748834368064]},
     {{{-1,7.565644036562414e-10},sensor},
      [-2.786539611443157,3.0562965644493305]}}],
    [{{0,7.565644036525425e-10},neuron},
     {{0.5,7.565644036503407e-10},neuron},
     {{0,7.565644036535494e-10},neuron},
     {{0,7.565644036562396e-10},neuron}],
    [{{0,7.565644036525425e-10},neuron},
     {{0,7.565644036535494e-10},neuron},
     {{0,7.565644036562396e-10},neuron}]}
{actuator,{{1,7.565644036562401e-10},actuator},
    xor_SendOutput,
    {{origin,7.56564403656243e-10},cortex},
    {private,xor_sim},
    1,
    [{{0.5,7.565644036503407e-10},neuron}],
    5}
```

It works! Figure-9.6 shows the visual representation of this NN system's topology. If we inspect the mutation operators, and the actual connections, everything is in perfect order.

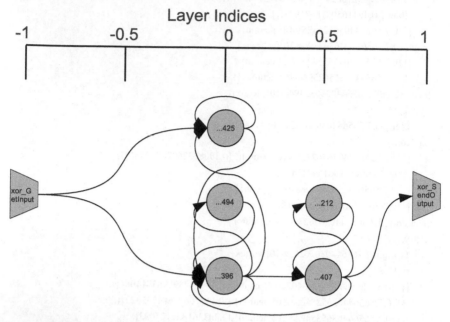

Fig. 9.6 The randomly evolved topology through the genome_mutator:long_test(10) execution.

We will now test our system on the xor_mimic problem with the following set of parameters:

1. Constraint's activation functions set to [tanh], and MAX_ATTEMPTS to 50, 10, and 1:
   This is done by changing the MAX_ATTEMPTS in the exoself module, for each separate test.
2. Activation functions are not constrained, *connection_architecture* is set to *feedforward*, and MAX_ATTEMPTS is set to 50, 10, and 1:
   This is done by changing the INIT_CONSTRAINTS in the population_monitor module from one which previously constrained the activation functions, to one that no longer does so:

```
-define(INIT_CONSTRAINTS,[#constraint{morphology=Morphology,neural_afs=
Neural_AFs, connection_architecture=CA} || Morphology<-[xor_mimic],Neural_AFs<-
[[tanh]], CA<-[feedforward]]).
```

To:

-define(INIT_CONSTRAINTS, [#constraint{morphology=Morphology, connection_architecture=CA} || Morphology<-[xor_mimic], **CA<-[feedforward]**]).

We have developed different kinds of activation functions, and created our neuroevolutionary system to give NN systems the ability to incorporate these various functions based on their need. Also, the MAX_ATTEMPTS variable specifies the duration of the tuning phases, how well each topology is tested before it is given its final fitness score. A neuroevolutionary setup using MAX_ATTEMPTS = 1 is equivalent to it using a standard genetic algorithm rather than a memetic algorithm based approach, since the tuning phase then only acts as a way to assess the NN system's fitness, and all the mutation operators (including the weight perturbation) are applied in the topological mutation phase. When the MAX_ATTEMPTS variable is set to 50, then each topology is tuned for a considerable amount of time.

To acquire the test-results of the above specified setup, we first set the parameters: INIT_CONSTRAINTS and the MAX_ATTEMPTS, to their new values, then run polis:sync() to update and load the modified modules, and then run the population_monitor:test() function to perform the actual test, the results of which are shown next:

Activation function: tanh, MAX_ATTEMPTS=50:

```
******** Population_Monitor:test shut down with Reason:normal OpTag:continue, while in
OpMode:gt
******** Tot Agents:10 Population Generation:25 Eval_Acc:14806 Cycle_Acc:59224
Time_Acc:8038997
```

With the last generation's NN systems having the number of neurons ranging from: 6-9.

Activation function: tanh, MAX_ATTEMPTS=10:

```
******** Population_Monitor:test shut down with Reason:normal OpTag:continue, while in
OpMode:gt
******** Tot Agents:10 Population Generation:33 Eval_Acc:5396 Cycle_Acc:21584
Time_Acc:2456883
```

With the last generation's NN systems having the number of neurons ranging from: 7-9.

Activation function: tanh, MAX_ATTEMPTS=1:

```
******** Population_Monitor:test shut down with Reason:normal OpTag:continue, while in
OpMode:gt
******** Tot Agents:11 Population Generation:100 Eval_Acc:2281 Cycle_Acc:9124
Time_Acc:2630457
```

In this setup, the system failed to produce a solution, with the maximum fitness reached being ~7. This is understandable, since in the standard genetic algorithm's 97% of the mutations are weight perturbation based mutations, with the remainder being topological mutation operators. In our setup though, because our system does weight tuning in a different phase, the topological mutation phase uses the weight_perturbation operator with the same probability as any other. We will change this in the future.

Activation function: tanh, cos, gaussian, absolute MAX_ATTEMPTS=50:

******** Population_Monitor:test shut down with Reason:normal OpTag:continue, while in OpMode:gt

******** Tot Agents:9 Population Generation:1 Eval_Acc:910 Cycle_Acc:3640 Time_Acc:234083

Activation function: tanh, cos, gaussian, absolute MAX_ATTEMPTS=10:

******** Population_Monitor:test shut down with Reason:normal OpTag:continue, while in OpMode:gt

******** Tot Agents:10 Population Generation:4 Eval_Acc:694 Cycle_Acc:2776 Time_Acc:209243

Activation function: tanh, cos, gaussian, absolute MAX_ATTEMPTS=1:

******** Population_Monitor:test shut down with Reason:normal OpTag:continue, while in OpMode:gt

******** Tot Agents:9 Population Generation:22 Eval_Acc:565 Cycle_Acc:2260 Time_Acc:266885

{agent,{7.565639675302518e-10,agent},
   0,undefined,7.565639675302535e-10,
   {{origin,7.565639675302501e-10},cortex},
   {{{0,1}},[],[{sensor,undefined,xor_GetInput,undefined,
{private,xor_sim},2,[],0}],
      [{actuator,undefined,xor_SendOutput,undefined,
      {private,xor_sim},1,[],0}],
      {constraint,xor_mimic,feedforward,
      [tanh,cos,gaussian,absolute]},[],4071.089031109478,0,
      [{0,[{{0,7.565639675302466e-10},neuron}]}]}}
{cortex,{{origin,7.565639675302501e-10},cortex},
   {7.565639675302518e-10,agent},
      [{{0,7.565639675302466e-10},neuron}],
      [{{-1,7.565639675302489e-10},sensor}],
      [{{1,7.565639675302477e-10},actuator}]}
{sensor,{{-1,7.565639675302489e-10},sensor},
   xor_GetInput,{{origin,7.565639675302501e-10},cortex},
   {private,xor_sim},2,
   [{{0,7.565639675302466e-10},neuron}],0}
{neuron,{{0,7.565639675302466e-10},neuron},
   0,{{origin,7.565639675302501e-10},cortex},
   cos,[{{{-1,7.565639675302489e-10},sensor},
   [-4.640518254468062,-4.789381628869486]}],
   [{{1,7.565639675302477e-10},actuator}],[]}
{actuator,{{1,7.565639675302477e-10},actuator},
   xor_SendOutput,{{origin,7.565639675302501e-10},cortex},
   {private,xor_sim},1,[{{0,7.565639675302466e-10},neuron}],0}

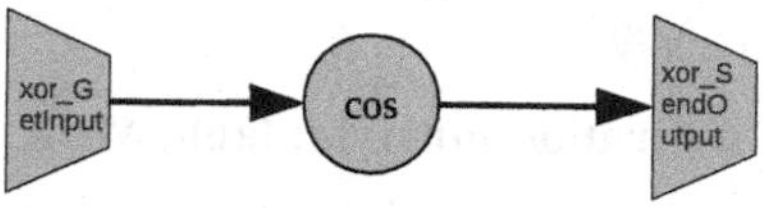

The evolved solution
W1: -4.640518
W2: -4.789381

Input: [-1,-1]
Output: cos(-4.64*-1 + -4.79*-1) = -0.9999

Input: [-1, 1]
Output: cos(-4.64*-1 + -4.79*1) = 0.9889

Input: [1,-1]
Output: cos(-4.64*1 + -4.79*-1) = 0.9889

Input: [1, 1]
Output: cos(-4.64*1 + -4.79*1) = -0.9999

Fig. 9.7 The discovered solution for the XOR problem, using only a single neuron.

The benchmark results when we allow for all activation functions to be used, are remarkably different. We've developed our neuroevolutionary system to allow the evolving NN systems to efficiently incorporate any available activation functions. In these last 3 scenarios, the evolved solutions all contained a single neuron, as shown in Fig-9.7. In all 3 tests the solutions were reached within 1000 evaluations, very rapidly. The discovered solution? It was a single neuron without a bias, using a *cos* activation function.

We have now tested our neuroevolutionary system on the basic benchmark problem. We have confirmed that it can evolve solutions, that it can evolve topologies and synaptic weights, that those solutions are correct, and that the evolved topologies are as expected. Though we've only developed a basic neuroevolutionary system thus far, it is decoupled and general enough that we can augment it, and easily improve it further, which is exactly what we will do in later chapters.

9.4 Summary

In this chapter we have thoroughly tested every mutation operator that we've added in the previous chapter. Though initially the mutation operator tests seemed successful, when testing our system on the XOR problem, and applying numerous mutation operators and then analyzing the evolved topology manually, we noticed errors to be present. We explored the origin of these detected errors, and then corrected them, re-testing our system on the XOR problem, successfully so.

The evolutionary algorithms built to evolve around problems, will also result in being able to evolve around small errors present in the algorithm itself. Thus, though it may seem that a test ran to completion, and did so successfully, as we've found out in this chapter, sometimes it is worthwhile to analyze the results, and the evolved agents, manually. It is during the thorough manual analysis that the more difficult to find errors are discovered. We have done just that in this chapter, and gained experience in the process of performing manual analysis of evolved NNs. This will give us an advantage in the future, as we continue adding more advanced features to our system, which will require debugging sooner or later.

Part III
A Case Study

In this part I will provide a case study of an already existing general topology and weight evolving artificial neural network (TWEANN) system created in Erlang. Though there are a number of neuroevolutionary systems out there, I am most familiar with the following three which have shown to be the top performers within the field: DXNN [1,2], NEAT/HyperNEAT [3,4], and EANT1/2 [5,6]. One of these TWEANNs was written in Erlang, it is the system which I created and which I called: Deus Ex Neural Network (DXNN). The case study presented in the next chapter will be of this particular TWEANN platform.

[1] Sher GI (2010) DXNN Platform: The Shedding of Biological Inefficiencies. Neuron, 1-36. Available at: http://arxiv.org/abs/1011.6022.
[2] Sher GI (2012) Evolving Chart Pattern Sensitive Neural Network Based Forex TradingAgents. Available at: http://arxiv.org/abs/1111.5892.
[3] Stanley KO, and Miikkulainen R (2002) Evolving neural Networks Through Augmenting Topologies. Evolutionary Computation 10, 99-127.
[4] Gauci J, Stanley K (2007) Generating Large-Scale Neural Networks Through Discovering Geometric Regularities. Proceedings of the 9th annual conference on Genetic and evolutionary computation GECCO 07, 997.
[5] Kassahun Y, Sommer G (2005) Efficient Reinforcement Learning Through Evolutionary Acquisition of Neural Topologies. In Proceedings of the 13th European Symposium on Artificial Neural Networks ESANN 2005 (ACM Press), pp. 259-266.
[6] Siebel NT, Sommer G (2007) Evolutionary Reinforcement Learning of Artificial Neural Networks. International Journal of Hybrid Intelligent Systems 4, 171-183.

Chapter 10 DXNN: A Case Study

Abstract This chapter presents a case study of a memetic algorithm based TWEANN system that I developed in Erlang, called DXNN. Here we will discuss how DXNN functions, how it is implemented, and the various details and implementation choices I made while building it, and why. We also discuss the various features that it has, the features which we will eventually need to add to the system we're building together. Our system has a much cleaner and decoupled implementation, and which by the time we've reached the last chapter will supersede DXNN in every way.

Deus Ex Neural Network (DXNN) platform is the original topology and weight evolving artificial neural network system that I developed in Erlang. What you and I are creating here in this book is the next generation of it. We're developing a more decoupled version, a simpler to generalize and more refined version, and one with cleaner architecture and implementation. In this chapter we'll discuss the already existing system, how it differs from what we've created so far, and what features it has that we will in later chapters need to add to the system we've developed thus far. By the time this book ends, we'll have created not just a TWEANN system, but a Topology and Parameter Evolving Universal Learning Network framework, capable of evolving neural networks, circuits, be used as a parallel distributed genetic programming framework, posses some of the most advanced features currently known, and designed in such a way that new features can easily be added to it by simply incorporating new modules (hence the importance of developing a system where almost everything is decoupled from everything else).

DXNN is a memetic algorithm based TWEANN platform. As we discussed, the most advanced approach to neuroevolution and universal learning networks in general, is through a system that uses evolutionary algorithms to optimize both, the topology and the synaptic weights/node-parameters of the graph system. The weights and topology of a NN are evolved so as to increase the NN system's fitness, based on some fitness criteria/function.

In the following sections we will cover the algorithm and the various features that make up the DXNN system.

10.1 The Reason for the Memetic Approach to Synaptic Weight Optimization

As we have discussed in the first chapters, the standard genetic algorithm performs global and local search in a single phase, while the memetic algorithm separates these two searches into separate stages. When it comes to neural networks, the global search is done through the exploration of NN topologies, and the local search is done through the optimization of synaptic weights.

Based on the benchmarks, and ALife performance of DXNN, the memetic approach has shown to be highly efficient and agile. The primary benefit of separating the two search phases is due to the importance of finding the right synaptic weights for a particular topology before deciding on the final fitness score of that topology. Standard TWEANNs typically operate using the standard genetic algorithm based mutation operator probabilities. In such systems, when creating an offspring the parent is chosen and then a single mutation operator is applied to it, with a probability of more than 97% that the mutation operator will be a synaptic weight perturbation operator. This type of operator simply selects some number of neurons and perturbs some random number of synaptic weights belonging to them The other mutation operators are the standard topology augmenting operators.

In standard TWEANNs, a system might generate an optimal topology for the problem, but because during that one innovation of the new topology the at-that-point existing synaptic weights make that topology ineffective, the new NN topology might be disregarded and removed. Also, in most TWEANNs, the synaptic weight perturbations are applied indiscriminately to all neurons of the NN, and thus if for example a NN is composed of 1 million neurons, and a new neuron is added, the synaptic weight mutations might be applied to any of the 1000001 neurons... making the probability of optimizing the new and the right neuron and its synaptic weights, very low.

As in the system we've built so far, the DXNN platform evolves new NN topologies during each generation, and then through the application of an augmented stochastic hill climbing optimizes the synaptic weights for those topologies. Thus, when the "tuning phase", which is what the local search phase is called in DXNN, has completed, the tuned NN has roughly the best set of synaptic weights for its particular topology, and thus the fitness that is given to the NN is a more accurate representation of its true performance fitness and potential.

Furthermore, the synaptic weight optimization through perturbation is not applied to all the neurons indiscriminately throughout the NN, but instead is concentrated on primarily the newly created neurons, or those neurons which have been recently affected by a mutation applied to the NN. Thus, the tuning phase optimizes the newly added neural elements so that they work and contribute positively to the NN they have been added to.

With this approach, the DXNN system is able to slowly grow and optimize the NN systems. Adding new features/elements and optimizing them to work with the already existing structures. This I believe gives DXNN a much greater ability to scale, for there is zero chance of being able to create vast neural networks when after adding a single new neuron to a 1000000 neuron NN system, we try to then perturb random synaptic weights in hopes of somehow making the whole system cohesive and functional. Building the NN slowly, complexifying it, adding new features and ensuring that they work with the existing system in a positive way, allows us to concentrate and optimize those few newly added elements, no matter how large the already existing NN system is.

Thus, during the local search phase, during the *tuning phase*, we optimize the synaptic weights of the newly added and modified elements. And during the global search, during the *topological mutation phase*, we apply enough topological mutation operators when creating an offspring, such that we are able to create innovation in the newly resulting NN system, but few enough of them such that the newly added elements to the NN can still be optimized to work with the existing much larger, already proven system.

Having discussed the *why* behind the memetic algorithm approach taken by DXNN, we now cover the two approaches this system uses when creating offspring, clarified to a much greater detail in the next two sections. These two approaches are the *generational* evolution, and the *steady_state* evolution.

The most common approach to offspring creation, and timing of selection and mutation operator application, is *generational*. Generational evolution simply means that we create a population of some size X of seed agents, apply them to some problem, wait until all agents in the population have been evaluated and given a fitness score, then select the best of the population, allow them to create offspring, and then create the next *generation* composed of the best agents of the previous generation plus their offspring, or some other appropriate combination of fit parents and newly created offspring. That is the essence of the standard generational evolution.

The *steady state* evolution tries to emulate the biological world to a slightly greater degree. In this approach there is no wait for the entire population to be evaluated before a new agent is created. Instead, as soon as one agent has finished working on a problem (has been evaluated), or has perished or gathered enough resources (in the case of an ALife simulation), a new offspring is created. The new offspring is either created by some already existing agent through the execution of a *create_offspring* actuator, or is created by the neuroevolutionary system itself, after it has calculated what genotype/s to use as the base for the offspring creation process, and whether the environment can support another agent. In this manner, the population size working on a problem, or existing in a simulated environment, is kept relatively constant. There are always organisms in the environment, when some die, new ones are created. There is a constant turnover of new agents and new genotypes and phenotypes in the population.

Before we begin discussing the general algorithm of the *generational* and *steady_state* evolution, before we begin discussing the DXNN system and its various features, it would be helpful for me to first explain the architectures of the NN systems that are evolved by it. The DXNN's genotype encoding, and the TWEANN's architecture, differs slightly from what we've been developing in the past few chapters.

10.2 The DXNN Encoding and Architecture

The genotype encoding used by DXNN is almost exactly the same as the one used by the system we are building together. It is tuple encoded, with the tuples stored in the mnesia database. The list of records composing the genotype of each NN system in the DXNN platform is as follows:

```
-record(dx,{id,cx_id,n_ids,specie_id,constraint,morphology,generation,fitness,
profile,summary, evo_hist,mode, evo_strat}).
-record(cortex,{id,sensors,actuators,cf,ct,type,plasticity,pattern,cids,su_id,
link_form,dimensions,densities, generation}).
-record(neuron,{id,ivl,i,ovl,o,lt,ro,type,dwp,su_id,generation}).
```

The *dx* record plays the role that the *agent* record does in our TWEANN. The other thing that immediately stands out is that there are no sensor or actuator elements. If you look in the DXNN's records.hrl [1] though, you will see those records, but they are not independent elements, the sensors and actuators are part of the cortex element. Indeed in the original DXNN system, the cortex element is not a synchronization element, but a gatekeeper element. The cortex element talks directly to the neurons. The connection from the cortex to the neurons is accomplished through the *ct* list (connected to), and the signals it gathers from the neurons is done through the *cf* list (connected from). The cortex also has a sensor and actuator list, which contain the names of the sensor and actuator functions, and the lists of the neurons that they are connected to and from respectively, based on the ct/cf lists. This DXNN's NN based agent architecture is shown in Fig-10.1.

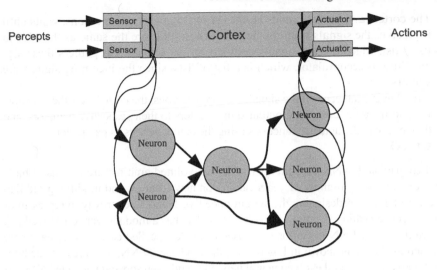

Fig. 10.1 The original DXNN based NN agent architecture.

The way a NN based system shown in Fig-10.1 functions, is as follows:

1. The genotype is first converted to the phenotype, composed of the cortex and the neurons, with the above shown architecture.
2. The cortex goes through all the sensor function names in its sensors list which has the following format: *[{Sensor1,[{N_Id1,FilterTag1}, {N_Id2, FilterTag2}...]}...]*. The cortex executes the sensor function names, and aggregates and packages the sensory signals generated through execution of the sensor functions. Because in the sensor list each sensor function comes with a list of neuron ids to which the resulting sensory signals are destined for, it is able to fanout those sensory signals to the specified neurons. Furthermore, in the above shown sensor list, the FilterTag has the following format: {single,Index}. {block,VL}, and {all,VL}. These tuples specify whether the sensor with a sensory signal of size vl, sends the entire sensory signal to the neuron, or just a single value from that vector list, a value located in the vector list at some particular Index, respectively. The third FilterTag: {all, VL}, specifies that the cortex will append the sensory signals of all the sensors, and forward that list to the neuron in question.
3. The cortex then gets the neuron ids stored in the *ct* list, and forwards sensory signals to them, by mapping from the ct neuron ids to the sensor list neuron ids and their corresponding sensory vector signals (this design made sense when I was originally building the system, primarily because it originally also supported supervised learning, which required this design).
4. The neurons in the NN then process the sensory signals until the signals are generated by the neurons in the output layer.
5. The output layer neurons send their results to the cortex.

6. The cortex, as soon as it sends all the sensory signals to the neurons, waits until it receives the signals from the neurons whose PIds are the same as the PIds in its *cf* list, which are the signals destined for the actuators. It gathers these signals into its accumulator, which is a list of lists, since the incoming signals are vectors.

7. After having gathered all the signals from the neurons, the cortex uses the actuators list and maps the composed output signal vectors to their respective actuators, and then executes the actuator functions using the output vectors as parameters.

8. GOTO 2

The original DXNN uses this particular convoluted architecture because I have developed it over a number of years, adding on new features, and modifying old features. Rather than redesigning the system once I've found a better way to represent or implement something, I simply modified it. DXNN has a modular version as well [2], where the evolved NN system is composed of modules called cores, where each core is a neural circuit, as shown in Fig-10.2. In the modular DXNN, the cores can be hopfield networks, standard evolved neural networks, and even substrate encoded NNs. At one point, long ago, DXNN even had a back-propagation learning mode, which I eventually removed as I never used it, and it was inferior to the non supervised learning algorithms I created. It is this long history of development, trial and error, testing and benchmarking, that left a lot of baggage in its architecture and implementation. Yet it is functional, and performs excellently.

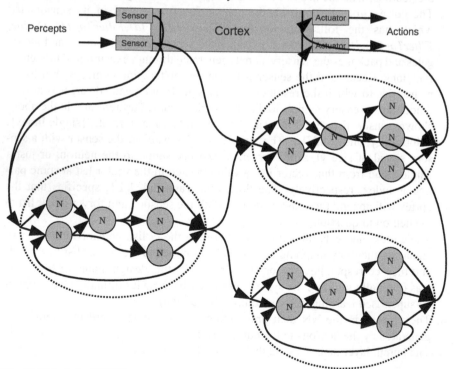

Fig. 10.2 Modular DXNN.

In some sense, the neural modules within the modular DXNN system, were meant to be used in emulation of the various brain regions. In this manner I hoped to evolve different regions independently, and then put them together into a complete system, or evolve the different modules at the same time as a single NN system, or even let the NN start of as monolithic, and then modularize through evolution. The performance though could not be established to be superior to standard homogeneous NN version at the time of experimentation, due to not yet having found a project benefiting from such an architecture. Nevertheless, the lessons learned were invaluable. The architecture of the TWEANN system we are developing in this book, is made with future use of modules in mind. Indeed, the system we are developing here will not only have more features, and will be more decoupled, but also its architecture will be cleaner, its implementation easier to understand, read, and expand, than that of DXNN. In the following sections I will explain the functionality, algorithms, and features that DXNN possesses.

10.3 Generational Evolution

I will first provide a simple list based overview of the steps taken by DXNN's general neuroevolutionary algorithm, and then elaborate on each of the more complicated sub-algorithms the DXNN system uses. When using the generational approach, DXNN uses the following set of steps:

1. **Initialization Phase:**
   Create a seed population of size K of topologically minimalistic NN genotypes.
2. **DO (Generational Neuroevolutionary loop):**
   3. Convert genotypes to phenotypes.
   4. **DO (Tuning Phase):**
      5. Test fitness of the NN system.
      6. Perturb recently added or mutation operator affected synaptic weights.
   UNTIL: NN's fitness has not increased for M times in a row.
   7. Convert the NN systems back to their genotypes, with the now updated and tuned synaptic weights.
8. **Selection Phase:**
   9. Calculate the average energy cost of each neuron using the following method:
   $TotFitnessPoints = Agent\_Fitness(1) + Agent\_Fitness(2) + ...Agent\_Fitness(K),$
   $TotPopNeurons = Agent\_TotNs(1) + Agent\_TotNs(2) + ...Agent\_TotNs(K),$
   $AvgNeuronCost = TotFitnessPoints/TotPopNeurons.$

10. With all the NNs having now been given their fitness score, sort the genotypes based on their scores.

11. Mark the top 50% of the population as valid (fit), and the bottom 50% of the population as invalid (unfit).

12. Remove the bottom 50% of the population.

13. Calculate # of offspring for each agent:

14. For every agent(i) in K, calculate:

$Agent(i)\_NeuronsAllotted=Agent\_Fitness(i)/AvgNeuronCost,$
$Agent(i)\_OffspringAlloted=$
$\qquad Agent(i)\_NeuronsAlloted/Agent(i)\_TotNs$

15. To keep the population size of the new generation the same as the previous, calculate the population normalizer, and then normalize each agent's allotted offspring value:

$TotNewOffspring = Agent(1)\_OffspringAlloted +$
$...Agent(i)\_OffspringAlloted$
$Normalizer = TotNewOffspring/(K/2)$

16. Now calculate the normalized number of offspring alloted for each agent:

$Agent(i)\_OffspringAllotedNorm =$
$\qquad round(Agent(i)\_OffspringAlloted/Normalizer)$

17. Create $Agent(i)\_OffspringAllotedNorm$ number of clones for every $Agent(i)$ that belongs to the fit subset of the agents in the population. And then send each clone through the topological mutation phase, which converts that clone into an offspring.

18. Topological mutation phase:

19. Create the offspring by first cloning the parent, and then applying to the clone, T number of mutation operators. The value T is randomly chosen with uniform distribution to be between 1 and $sqrt(Agent(i)\_TotNeurons)$, where $TotNeurons$ is the number of neurons in the parent NN. Thus, larger NNs will produce offspring which have a chance of being produced through a larger number of applied mutation operators.

20. Compose the population of the next generation by combining the genotypes of the fit parents with their newly created offspring.

UNTIL: Termination condition is reached (max # of evaluations, time, or fitness goal)

A diagram of this algorithm is shown in Fig-10.3. The steps 1 (Initialization phase), 4 (Parametric Tuning Phase), 8 & 13 (The Selection Phase & Offspring Allocation), and 18 (Topological Mutation Phase), are further elaborated on in the subsections that follow.

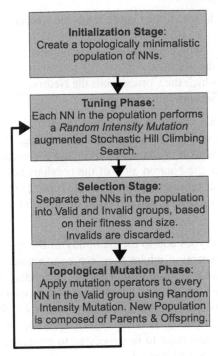

Fig. 10.3 The different stages in the DXNN's learning algorithm: Initialization Stage, Tuning Phase, Selection Stage, and Topological Mutation Phase.

10.3.1 Step-1: Initialization Phase

During the initialization, every element created has its Generation set to 0. Initially a seed population of size X is created. Each agent in the population starts with a minimal network, where the minimal starting topology depends on the total number of Sensors and Actuators the researcher decides to start the system with. If the NN is set to start with only 1 Sensor and 1 Actuator with a $vl = 1$, then the DXNN starts with a single Cortex containing a single Neuron. For example, if the output is a vector of length 1 like in the Double Pole Balancing (DPB) control problem, the NN is composed of a single Neuron. If on the other hand the agent is initiated with N number of Sensors and K number of actuators, the seed NNs will contain 2 layers of fully interconnected Neurons. The first layer contains S Neurons, and the second contains $A_1+...A_k$ Neurons. In this topology, S is the total number of Sensors, and A_i is the size of the vector that is destined for Actuator i. It is customary for the NNs to be initialized with a single Sensor and a single Actuator, letting the agents discover any other auxiliary Sensors and Actuators through topological evolution.

Furthermore, the link from a Cortex to a Neuron can be of 3 types listed below:

1. Single-type link, in which the Cortex sends the Neuron a single value from one of its Sensors.
2. Block-type link, in which the Cortex sends the Neuron an entire vector that is output by one of the Sensors.
3. All-type link, in which the Cortex sends the Neuron a concatenated list of vectors from all the Sensors in its SensorList.

All this information is kept in the Cortex, the Neuron neither knows what type nor originally from which sensor the signal is coming. Each neuron only keeps track of the list of nodes it is connected from and the vector lengths coming from those nodes. Thus, to the Neuron all 3 of the previous link-types look exactly the same in its InputList, represented by a simple tuple {From_Id, Vector_Length}. The Vector_Length variable might of course be different for each of those connections.

The different link-types add to the flexibility of the system and allow the Neurons to evolve a connection where they can concentrate on processing a single value or an entire vector coming from a Sensor, depending on the problem's need. I think this improves the general diversity of the population, allows for greater compactness to be evolved, and also improves the NN's ability to move through the fitness landscape. Since it is never known ahead of time what sensory values are needed and how they need to be processed to produce a proper output, different types of links should be allowed.

For example, a Cortex is routing to the Neurons a vector of length 100 from one of its Sensors. Assume that a solution requires that a Neuron needs to concentrate on the 53rd value in the vector and pass it through a cosine activation function. To do this, the Neuron would need to evolve weights equaling to 0 for all other 99 values in the vector. This is a difficult task since zeroing each weight will take multiple attempts, and during random weight perturbations zeroing one weight might un-zero another. On the other hand evolving a single link-type to that Sensor has a 1/100 chance of being connected to the 53rd value, a much better chance. Now assume that a solution requires for a neuron to have a connection to all of the 100 values in the vector. That is almost impossible to achieve, and would require at least 100 topological mutations if only a single link-type is used, but has a 1/3 chance of occurrence if we have *block*, *all*, and *single* type links at our disposal. Thus the use of Link-Types allows the system to more readily deal with the different and wide ranging lengths of signal vectors coming from the Sensors, and having a better chance of establishing a proper connection needed by the problem in question.

In a population, the agents themselves can also be of different types: Type = "neural", and Type = "substrate". The "neural" type agent is one that is a standard recursive Neural Network system. The "substrate" type agents use an architecture where the NNs drive a neural substrate, an encoding that was popularized by HyperNEAT [3]. In such agents the sensory vector is routed to the substrate and the output vector that comes from the substrate is parsed and routed to the actuators. The supervised NN itself is polled to produce the weights for the embedded neurodes in the substrate. The type of substrates can further differ in density, and dimensionality. A diagram of the agent architecture that utilizes a substrate encoding is shown in Fig-10.4. We will discuss the substrate encoded NN systems in greater detail in section 10.5.

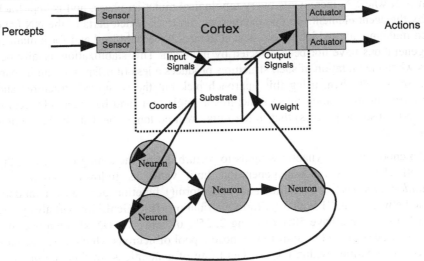

Fig. 10.4 A DXNN evolved agent that uses a substrate encoded based architecture. In this figure the cortex goes through its sensors to produce the sensory signals, which it then packages and passes to the Substrate, which produces output signals and passes those to the Cortex which then postprocesses them and executes its actuators using these output vectors as parameters. The Substrate uses the NN to set the weights of its embedded neurodes.

10.3.2 Step-4: Parametric Tuning Phase

Since the offspring is created by taking the fit parent, creating its clone, and then applying topological mutation operators to it, we can tag any neuron in the NN that has been affected by the mutation operator. What counts as been affected by the mutation operator is as follows:

1. Having been just created, for example when a new neuron has just been added to the NN.
2. Having just acquired new input or output connection, for example when a neuron has just created a new link to another element, or when another element has just created a link to the neuron in question, the neuron is counted as having been affected by the mutation operator.
3. When during the topological mutation phase, the neuron's activation function, plasticity, or another parameter (other than weights) has been mutated.

Instead of just giving to such neurons the "mutationally affected" tag, their generation parameter is reset, the same as is the case in the system we've built thus far. Thus, every element in the NN is given a generation during the initial seed population creation, and then every time the element is affected by a mutation, its generation is reset to the current generation, where the "current" generation is N where N increments every topological mutation phase, and is kept track of by the agent element. In this manner we can track which parts of the NN have been mutating, and which topological structures have stabilized and for a number of generations have not been affected by mutation. This stabilization usually occurs when the mutation of such structures produces a less fit offspring than its parent. So we can then, using this approach pick out the stabilized structures and *crystallize* them, making those structures a single unit (and be potentially represented by a single process) that in the future will no longer be disturbed by mutation.

To choose whose synaptic weights to perturb during the tuning event, first the exoself chooses a random generation limit value as follows: *GenLimit = 1/random:uniform()* where the random:uniform() function generates a random value between 0 and 1 with a uniform distribution. Thus GenLimit will always be greater than 1, and have 50% of being 2, 25% of being 4... DXNN then uses the randomly generated GenLimit to compose a pool of neurons which have been affected by mutations within the last GenLimit of generations. In this neuron pool each neuron is chosen with a probability of *1/sqrt(NeuronPoolSize)* to have its synaptic weights perturbed. The list of these chosen neurons is called the New Generation Neurons (NGN). The chosen neurons are then each sent a message by the *exoself* to have their synaptic weights perturbed. When a neuron receives such a message, it goes through its synaptic weight list and chooses each weight for perturbation with a probability of *1/sqrt(TotSynapticWeights)*. The neuron then perturbs the chosen synaptic weights with a value randomly generated with uniform distribution between -Pi and Pi.

This particular approach has the following benefits: 1. It concentrates on tuning and optimizing neurons that have only recently been added to the NN, thus ensuring that newly added neurons can contribute in a positive way to the NN. 2. There is a high variability in the number of neurons and weights that are chosen at any given time, thus there are times when a large number of neurons are all perturbed at the same time, and there are times when, by chance alone, only a few neurons and a few of their synaptic weights are chosen. Thus this approach allows the system to have a chance of doing both, tune into local optima on the fitness landscape, and also at times choose a large number of neurons and weights to perturb, and thus search far and wide in the parametric space.

After NGN is composed, a variable *MaxMistakes* is created and set to *abs(BaseMaxMistakes + sqrt(TotWeights from NGNs))* rounded to the nearest integer. The *BaseMaxMistakes* variable is set by the researcher. Finally, a variable by the name *AttemptCounter* is created and set to 1.

The reason for the creation of the NGN list is due to the weight perturbations being applied only to the these new or recently modified Neurons, a method I refer to as "*Targeted Tuning*". The reason to only apply perturbations to the NGNs is because evolution in the natural world works primarily through complexification and elaboration, there is no time to re-perturb all the neurons in the network after some minor topological or other type of addition to the system. As NNs grow in size it becomes harder and harder to set all the weights and parameters of all the Neurons at the same time to such values that produces a fit individual. A system composed of thousands of neurons might have millions of parameters in it. The odds of finding proper values for them all at the same time by randomly perturbing synaptic weights throughout the entire system after some minor topological mutation, is slim to none. The problem only becomes more intractable as the number of Neurons continues to grow. By concentrating on tuning only the newly created or newly topologically/structurally augmented Neurons and making them work with an already existing, tuned, and functional Neural Network, makes the problem much more tractable. Indeed in many respects it is how complexification and elaboration works in the biological NNs. In our organic brains the relatively recent evolutionary addition of the Neocortex was *not* done through some refurbishing of an older NN structure, but through a completely new addition of neural tissue covering and working with the more primordial parts. The Neocortex works concurrently with the older regions, contributing and when possible overwriting the signals coming from our more ancient neural structures evolved earlier in our evolutionary history.

During the Tuning Phase each NN based agent tries to solve the problem based on its morphology. Afterwards, the agents receive fitness scores based on their performance in that problem. After being scored, each NN temporarily backs up its parameters. Every neuron in the NGN list has a probability of *1/sqrt(Tot_NGNs)* of being chosen for weight perturbation. The Exoself sends these randomly chosen neurons a request to perturb some of their weights. Each chosen Neuron, after receiving such a message, chooses a set of its own synaptic weights, and perturbs them. The total number of weights to be perturbed is chosen randomly by every Neuron itself. The number of weights chosen for perturbation by each neuron is a random value between 1 and square root of total number of weights in that Neuron. The perturbation value is chosen with uniform distribution to be between -(WeightLimit/2) and (WeightLimit/2), where the WeightLimit is set to 2*Pi. By randomly selecting the total number of Neurons, the total number of weights to perturb, and using such a wide range for the perturbation intensity, we can achieve a very wide range of parametric perturbation. Sometimes the NN might have only a single weight in a single Neuron perturbed slightly, while at other times it might have multiple Neurons with multiple weights perturbed to a great degree. This allows the DXNN platform to make small intensity perturbations to fine tune the parameters, but also sometimes very large intensity (number of Neurons and weights) perturbations to allow NN based agents to jump over or out of local optima, an impossibility when using only small perturbations applied to a small number of Neurons. This high mutation variability method is referred to in the DXNN platform as the *Random Intensity Mutation* (RIM). The range of mutation intensities grows as the square root of the total number of NGNs, as it logically should since the greater the number of new or recently augmented Neurons in the NN, the greater the number of perturbations that needs to be applied to make a significant effect on the information processing capabilities of the system. At the same time, the number of neurons and weights affected during perturbation is limited only to the newly/recently added or topologically augmented elements, so that the system can try to adjust the newly added structures and those elements that are directly affected by them through new connections, to work and positively contribute to an already existing neural system.

After all the weight perturbations have been applied to the NN based agent, it attempts to solve the problem again. If the new fitness achieved by the agent is greater than the previous fitness it achieved, then the new weights overwrite the old backed up weights, the AttemptCounter is reset to 1, and a new set of weight perturbations is applied to the NN based agent. Alternatively, if the new fitness is not greater than the previous fitness, then the old weights are restored, the AttemptCounter is incremented, and another set of weight perturbations is applied to the individual.

When the agent's *AttemptCounter == MaxMistakes*, implying that a MaxMistakes number of unsuccessful RIMs have been applied in sequence without a single one producing an increase in fitness, the agent with its final best fitness and the correlated weights is backed up to the database through its conversion back to a list of tuples, its genotype, followed by the termination of the agent itself. Utilizing the AttemptCounter and MaxMistakes strategy allows us, to some degree at least, test each topology with varying weights and thus let each NN after the tuning phase to represent roughly the best fitness that its topology can achieve. In this way there is no need to forcefully and artificially speciate and protect the various topologies since each NN represents roughly the highest potential that its topology can reach in a reasonable amount of time after the tuning phase completes. This allows us to judge each NN based purely on its fitness. If one increases the *BaseMaxMistakes* parameter, then on average each NN will have more testing done on it with regards to weight perturbations, thus testing the particular topology more thoroughly before giving it its final fitness score. On the other hand the MaxMistakes parameter itself grows in proportion to the square root of the total sum of NGN weights that should be tunned, since the greater the number of new weights that need to be tuned, the more attempts it would take to properly test the various permutations of neurons and their synaptic weights.

10.3.3 Step-8 & 13: The Selection & Offspring Allocation Phase

There are many TWEANNs that implement speciation during selection. Speciation is used to promote diversity and protect unfit individuals who in the current generation do not possess enough fitness to get a chance of producing offspring or mutating and achieving better results in the future. Promoters of speciation algorithms state that new ideas need time to develop and speciation protects such innovations. Though I agree with the sentiment of giving ideas time to develop, I must point to [4] in which it was shown that such artificial and forced speciation and protection of unfit organisms can easily lead to neural bloating. DXNN platform does not implement forced speciation, instead it tests its individuals during the Tuning Phase and utilizes natural selection that also takes into account the complexity of each NN during the Selection Stage. In my system, as in the natural world, smaller organisms require less energy and material to reproduce than their larger counterparts. As an example, for the same amount of material and energy that is required for a human to produce and raise an offspring, millions of ants can produce and raise offspring. When calculating who survives and how many offspring to allocate to each survivor, the DXNN platform takes complexity into account instead of blindly and artificially defending the unfit and insufficiently tested Neural Networks. In a way, it can also be thought that every NN topology represents a specie in its own right, and the tuning phase concisely tests out the different parametric permutations of that particular specie, same topologies with different weights. I believe that speciation and niching should be done not forcefully from the outside by the researcher, but by the artificial organisms themselves within the artificial environments they inhabit, if their environments/problems allow for such a feat. When the organisms find their niches, they will automatically acquire higher fitness and secure their survival that way.

Due to the Tuning Phase, by the time Selection Stage starts, each individual presents its topology in roughly the best light it can reach within reasonable time. This is due to the consistent application of Parametric RIM to each NN during targeted tuning, and that only after a substantial number of continues failures to improve is the agent considered to be somewhere at the limits of its potential. Thus each NN can be judged purely by its fitness rather than have a need for artificial protection. When individuals are artificially protected within the population, more and more Neurons are added to the NN unnecessarily, thus producing the dreaded neural/topological bloating. This is especially the case when new neurons are added, yet the synaptic weight perturbation and mutation is applied indiscriminately to all the synaptic weights in the NN. Topological bloating dramatically and catastrophically hinders any further improvements due to a greater number of Neurons unnecessarily being in the NN and needing to have their parameters set *concurrently* to just the right values to get the whole system functional. An example of such topological bloating was demonstrated in the robot arm control experiment using NEAT and EANT2 [4]. In that experiment, NEAT continued to fail due to significant neural bloating, whereas EANT2 was successful, which like DXNN is a memetic algorithm based TWEANN. Once a NN passes some topological bloating point, it simply cannot generate enough of concurrent perturbations to fix the faulty parameters of all the new neurons it acquired. At the same time, most TWEANN algorithms allow for only a small number of perturbations to be applied at any one instance. In DXNN, through the use of *Targeted Tuning* and *RIMs* applied during the Tuning and Topological Mutation phases, we can successfully avoid bloating.

Finally, when all NNs have been given their fitness rating, we must use some method to choose those NNs that will be used for offspring creation. DXNN platform uses a selection algorithm I call "Competition", which tries to take into account not just the fitness of each NN, but also the NN's size. The *competition* selection algorithm is composed of the following steps:

1. Calculate the average energy cost of the Neuron using the following steps:
   TotEnergy = Agent(1)_Fitness + Agent(2)_Fitness...
   TotNeurons = Agent(1)_TotNeurons + Agent(2)_TotNeurons...
   AverageEnergyCost = TotEnergy/TotNeurons
2. Sort the NNs in the population based on their fitness. If 2 or more NNs have the same fitness, they are then sorted further based on size, more compact solutions are considered of higher fitness than less compact solutions.
3. Remove the bottom 50% of the population.
4. Calculate the number of alloted offspring for each Agent(i):
   AllotedNeurons = (Fitness/AverageEnergyCost),
   AllotedOffsprings(i) = round(AllotedNeurons(i)/Agent(i)_TotNeurons)
5. Calculate total number of offspring being produced for the next generation:
   TotalNewOffsprings = AllotedOffsprings(1)+...AllotedOffsprings(n).
6. Calculate PopulationNormalizer, to keep the population within a certain limit:
   PopulationNormalizer = TotalNewOffsprings/PopulationLimit
7. Calculate the normalized number of offspring alloted to each Agent:
   NormalizedAllotedOffsprings(i) =
   round(AllotedOffsprings(i)/PopulationNormalizer(i)).
8. If NormalizedAllotedOffsprings (NAO) == 1, then the Agent is allowed to survive to the next generation without offspring, if NAO > 1, then the Agent is allowed to produce (NAO -1) number of mutated copies of itself, if NAO = 0 the Agent is removed from the population and deleted.
9. The Topological Mutation Phase is initiated, and the mutator program then passes through the database creating the appropriate NAO number of mutated clones of the surviving agents.

From this algorithm it can be noted that it becomes very difficult for bloated NNs to survive when smaller systems produce better or similar results. Yet when a large NN produces significantly better results justifying its complexity, it can begin to compete and push out the smaller NNs. This selection algorithm takes into account that a NN composed of 2 Neurons is doubling the size of a 1 Neuron NN, and thus should bring with it sizable fitness gains if it wants to produce just as many offspring. On the other hand, a NN of size 101 is only slightly larger than a NN of size 100, and thus should pay only slightly more per offspring. This is exactly the principle behind the "competition" selection algorithm we implemented in the system we are developing together in this book.

10.3.4 Step-18: The Topological Mutation Phase

An offspring of an agent is produced by first creating a clone of the parent agent, then giving it a new unique Id, and then finally applying Mutation Operators to it. The *Mutation Operators* (MOs) that operate on the individual's topology are randomly chosen with uniform distribution from the following list:

1. "Add Neuron" to the NN and link it randomly to and from randomly chosen Neurons within the NN, or one of the Sensors/Actuators.
2. "Add Link" (can be recurrent) to or from a Neuron, Sensor, or Actuator.
3. "Splice Neuron" such that that two random Neurons which are connected to each other are disconnected and reconnected through a newly created Neuron.
4. "Change Activation Function" of a random Neuron.
5. "Change Learning Method" of a random Neuron.
6. "Add Bias", all neurons are initially created without bias.
7. "Remove Bias", removes a bias value in the neurons which have one.
8. "Add Sensor Tag" which connects a currently unused Sensor present in the SensorList to a random Neuron in the NN. This mutation operator is selected with a researcher defined probability of X. In this manner new connections can be made to the newly added or previously unused sensors, thus expanding the sensory system of the NN.
9. "Add Actuator Tag" which connects a currently unused Actuator present in the ActuatorList to a random Neuron in the NN. This mutation operator is selected with a researcher defined probability of Y. In this manner new connections can be made to the newly added or previously unused actuators, thus expanding the types of tools or morphological properties that are available for control by the NN.

The "Add Sensor Tag" and "Add Actuator Tag" can both allow for new links from/to the Sensor and Actuator programs not previously used by the NN to become available to it. In this manner the NN can expand its senses and control over new actuators and body parts. This feature becomes especially important when the DXNN platform is applied to the Artificial Life and Robotics experiments where new tools, sensors, and actuators might become available over time. The different sensors can also simply represent various features of a problem, and in this manner the DXNN platform naturally incorporates feature selection capabilities.

The total number of Mutation Operators (MOs) applied to each offspring of the DXNN is a value randomly chosen between 1 and square root of the total number of Neurons in the parent NN. In this way, once again a type of random intensity mutation (RIM) approach is utilized. Some mutant clones will only slightly differ from their NN parent, while others might have a very large number of MOs applied to them, and thus differ drastically. This gives the offspring a chance to jump out of large local optima that would otherwise prove impassible if a constant number of mutational operators were to have been applied every time, independent of the parent NN's complexity and size. As the complexity and size of each NN increases, each new topological mutation plays a smaller and smaller part in changing the network's behavior, thus a larger and larger number of mutations needs to be applied to produce significant differences to the processing capabilities of that individual. For example, when the size of the NN is a single neuron, adding another one has a large impact on the processing capabilities of that NN. On the other hand, when the original size is a million neurons, adding the same single neuron to the network might not produce the same amount of change in the computational capabilities of that system. Increasing the number of MOs applied based on the size of the parent NN's size, allows us to make the mutation intensity significant enough to allow the mutant offspring to continue producing innovations in its behavior when compared to its parent, and thus exploring the topological fitness landscape far and wide. At the same time, due to RIM, some offspring will only acquire a few mutations and differ topologically only slightly and thus have a chance to tune and explore the local topological areas on the topological fitness landscape.

Because the sensors and actuators are represented by simple lists of existing sensor and actuator programs, just like in the system we're developing together in this book, the DXNN platform allows for the individuals within the population to expand their affecting and sensing capabilities. Such abilities integrated naturally into the NN lets individuals gather new abilities and control over functions as they evolve. For example, originally a population of very simple individuals with only distance sensors is created. At some point a fit NN will create a mutant offspring to whom the "Add Sensor Tag" or "Add Actuator Tag" mutational operator is applied. When either of these mutational operators is randomly applied to one of the offspring of the NN, that offspring then has a chance of randomly linking from or to a new Sensor or Actuator respectively. In this manner the offspring can acquire color, sonar or other types of sensors present in the sensor list, or acquire control of a new body part/actuator, and thus further expand its own morphology. These types of expansions and experiments can be undertaken in the artificial life/robotics simulation environments like the Player/Stage/Gazebo Project [5]. Player/Stage/Gazebo in particular has a list of existing sensor and actuator types, making such experiments accessible at a very low cost.

Once all the offspring are generated, they and their parents once more enter the tuning phase to continue the cycle as was diagrammed in Fig-10.3.

10.4 Steady-State Evolution

Though the generational evolution algorithm is the most common approach, when applying neuroevolutionary systems to ALife, or even non ALife simulations and problems, steady-state evolution offered by DXNN can provide an advantage due to its content drift tracking ability, and a sub population called "Dead Pool" which can immediately be used to develop committee machines. In a steady-state evolution, the population solving the problem or existing within the simulated world (in the case of ALife for example) always maintains a constant operational population. When an organism/agent dies, or when there is more room in the environment (either due to the expansion of the food source in ALife environment, or because more computational power is added, or more exploration is wanted...) more concurrently existing agents are added to the operational phenotypes. The system does not wait for every agent in the population to finish being evaluated before generating a new agent and entering it into the population. Instead, the system computes the fitness of the just having perished agent, and then immediately generates a new genotype from a pool of previously evaluated fit genotypes. Thus the system maintains a relatively constant population size by consistently generating new offspring at the same pace that agents complete their evaluations and are removed from the live population.

In DXNN, the steady-state evolutionary algorithm uses an "Augmented Competition" (AC) selection algorithm. The AC selection algorithm keeps a list of size "PopulationSize" of dead NN genotypes, this list is called the "dead pool". The variable *PopulationSize* is specified by the researcher. When an Agent dies, its genotype and fitness is entered into this list. If after entering the new genotype into the dead pool the list's size becomes greater than PopulationSize, then the lowest scoring DXNN genotype in the dead pool is removed. In this manner the dead pool is always composed of the top performing PopulationSize number of ancestor genotypes.

In this augmented version of the selection algorithm, the AllottedOffspring variables are converted into normalized probabilities used to select a parent from the dead pool to produce a mutated offspring. Finally, there is a 10% chance that instead of creating an offspring, the parent itself will enter the environment/scape or be re-applied to the problem. Using this "re-entry" system, if the environment or the manner in which the fitness is allotted changes, the old strategies and their high fitness scores can be re-evaluated in the changed environment to see if they still deserve to stay in the dead pool, and if so, what their new fitness should be. This selection algorithm also has the side effect of having the dead pool implicitly track content drift of the problem to which the TWEANN is applied.

For example assume that the steady-state evolution with the *dead_pool* list is applied to an ALife simulation. Every time an agent in the simulated environment dies (has been evaluated), it is entered into the dead pool, and a new offspring is generated from the best in this dead pool. Once the dead pool size reaches that of

PopulationSize specified by the researcher, the DXNN system also begins to get rid of the poorly performing genotypes in the dead_pool. But what is important is that when an organism in the environment dies, there is a chance that a genotype in the dead pool has a chance of re-entering the simulated environment, instead of a new mutant offspring being generated. If it were not for this, then as the environment changes with the dynamics and fitness scoring and life expectancy all changing with it... and some organism dies, the old organisms, the genotypes from the "old world" would be used to create the offspring. If the environment is highly dynamic and malleable, after a while the whole thing might change, the useful survival instincts and capabilities that were present in the environment to which the dead_pool organisms belonged, might no longer be present in the current, evolved environment. Suddenly we would be faced with a dead_pool of agents all with high scores, which though achievable in the previously simple environment, are no longer possible in the now much more complex and unforgiving environment. Thus it is essential to re-evaluate the organisms in the dead_pool, are they still fit in the new environment, in the environment that itself has evolved and become more complex? Can the old agents compete in the new world?

The re-entry system allows us to change and update the dead_pool with the organisms that are not simply more fit, but are more fit in the current state of the environment. The environment can be either the simulated environment of the ALife system, or the new signal block in the time series of currency-pairs or stock prices for example. The patterns of the market that existed last year, might have changed completely this year, and it is essential that the new agents are judged by how they perform on this year's patterns and styles of the time series. This is the benefit of the content drift tracking dead pool. The dead pool represents the best of the population, a composition of agent genotypes that perform well in the relatively new environment, that perform well in the world of today, rather than the one of last year.

Furthermore, because the genotypes belonging to the dead_pool represent the best of the population, we can directly use the genotypes in it to compose a committee machine. The current state of the dead pool is the voting population of the committee machine, the type of system we discussed in Section-1.2.2. This type of setup is shown in Fig-10.5.

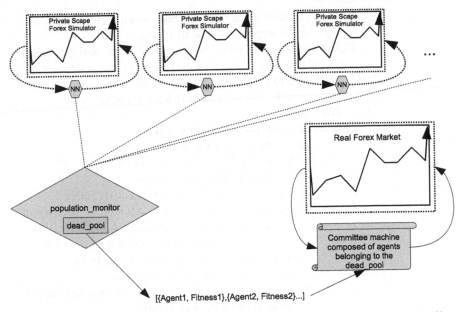

Fig. 10.5 A DXNN system using steady-state evolution used to evolve currency trading agents, and whose dead pool is used as a committee machine applied to real Forex trading.

The steps of the steady-state evolution algorithm in the DXNN platform are as follows:

1. **Initialization Phase**:
    2. Create a seed population of size K of topologically minimalistic NN genotypes.
    3. Convert genotypes to phenotypes.
4. **DO (Steady-State Neuroevolutionary loop)**:
    5. **For Each Agent, DO (Tuning Phase)**:
        6. Test fitness of the NN system
        7. Perturb the synaptic weights of recently added or mutation operator affected neurons
    UNTIL: NN's fitness has not increased for X times in a series
    8. Convert the NN system back to its genotype, with the now updated and tuned synaptic weights.
    9. Add the agent's genotype to the dead_pool list of size K.
    10. **Steady-State Selection Phase (For genotypes in the dead_pool list)**:
        11. Calculate the average energy cost of each neuron using the following method:
        TotFitnessPoints = Agent_Fitness(1) + Agent_Fitness(2) + ...Agent_Fitness(K),
        TotPopNeurons = Agent_TotNs(1) + Agent_TotNs(2) + ...Agent_TotNs(K),
        AvgNeuronCost = TotFitnessPoints/TotPopNeurons.

12. With all the NNs having now been given their fitness score, sort the genotypes based on their scores.

13. Extract the top K agents in this sorted dead_pool list, delete the others. This is done for the case when the addition of the new agent to the dead_pool, makes the size of the dead_pool larger than K. We only want to keep K agents in the dead_pool.

14. **Select a dead_pool champion agent**:

> 15. Agent(i)_NeuronsAllotted = Agent_Fitness(i)/AvgNeuronCost, Agent(i)_OffspringAllotted = Agent(i)_NeuronsAllotted/Agent(i)_TotNs
>
> 16. Convert Agent(i)_OffspringAllotted for each agent into a normalized percentage, such that a random agent from this list can be chosen with the uniform distribution probability proportional to its Agent(i)_OffspringAllotted value.
>
> 17. Choose the agent through step-16, and designate that agent as dead_pool champion.
>
> 18. Randomly choose whether to use the dead_pool champion as the parent of a new offspring agent, or whether to extract the champion from the dead_pool, convert it to its phenotype, and re-apply it to the problem. The split is 90/10, with 90% chance of using the champion's genotype to create a new offspring, and 10% chance of removing the agent from the dead_pool and re-applying (aka re-entry, re-evaluation...) the agent to the problem.

19. **IF champion selected to create offspring**:

> 20. **Topological mutation phase**:
>
> > 21. Create the offspring by first cloning the parent, and then applying to the clone T number of mutation operators, T is randomly chosen to be between 1 and sqrt(Agent(i)_TotNeurons). Where the TotNeurons is the number of neurons in the parent NN, and T is chosen with uniform distribution. Thus larger NNs will produce offspring which have a chance of being produced through a larger number of applied mutation operators to them.
>
> 22. Designate the offspring agent as **New_Agent**.

ELSE champion is chosen for re-entry:

> 23. Extract agent from the dead_pool.
>
> 24. Designate the agent as **New_Agent**.

25.Convert the agent designated as **New_Agent** to its phenotype.

UNTIL: Termination condition is reached (max # of evaluations, time, or fitness goal)

As can be noted from these steps, the algorithm is similar to the generational evolutionary approach, but in this case as soon as an agent dies (if in ALife experiment), or finishes its training or being applied to the problem, its fitness is immediately evaluated against the dead_pool agents, and a new agent is created (either through offspring creation or re-entry) and applied to the problem, or released into the simulated environment.

The tuning phase and the topological mutation phase are the same as in the generational evolutionary loop, discussed in the previous section. The steady-state selection algorithm only differs in that the allotted_offspring value is converted to a percentage of being selected for each agent in the dead_pool. The selected agent has a 90% chance of creating an offspring and 10% chance of being sent back to the problem, and being re-evaluated with regards to its fitness.

The following sections will cover a few finer points and features of DXNN. In the next section we will discuss its two types of encoding, neural and substrate. In section 10.6 we will briefly discuss the flatland simulator, a 2d ALife environment. In section 10.7 we will discuss the modular version of DXNN. Finally, in section 10.8 and 10.9 we will discuss the ongoing projects and features being integrated into the DXNN system, and the neural network research repository being worked on by the DXNN Research Group.

10.5 Direct (Neural) and Indirect (Substrate) Encoding

The DXNN platform evolves both direct and indirect encoded NN agents. The direct encoded NN systems are as discussed in the above sections, these are standard neural networks where every neuron is encoded as a tuple, and the mapping from the genotype to phenotype is direct. We simply translate the tuple containing the synaptic weights and link specifications into a process, linked to other processes and possessing the properties and synaptic weights dictated by the tuple.

The indirect encoding that the DXNN can also use is a form of substrate encoding, popularized by the HyperNEAT [3]. There are many variations of substrate encoding, and new ones are turning up every year. In a substrate encoded NN, the actual NN is not directly used to process input sensory signals and produce output signals to control the actuators. Instead, in a substrate encoded NN system the NN "paints" the synaptic weights and connectivity patterns on a multidimensional substrate of interconnected neurodes. This substrate, based on the synaptic weights determined by the NN, is then used to process the input sensory signals and produce output signals used by the actuators. The architecture of such a system is shown in the following figure.

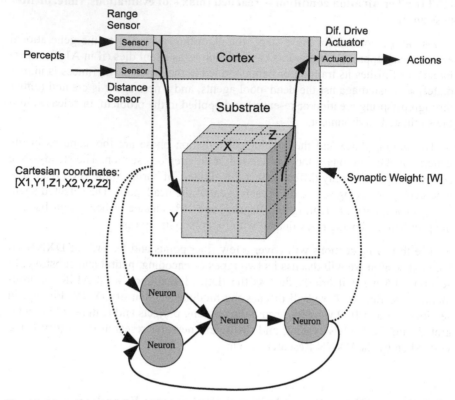

Fig. 10.6 Substrate encoded neural network system. This diagram is of a substrate encoded agent. The substrate, sensors, and actuators, are all part of the same process called Cortex. The NN is used to generate the synaptic weights between neurodes in the substrate, based on the coordinates of the presynaptic and postsynaptic neurodes. The sample agent shown is one that controls a simulated robot in an ALife experiment, a simulated robot that has a Range Sensor, a Distance Sensor, and a Differential Drive Actuator.

The neurodes in the substrate all use the sigmoid or tanh activation function, though this of course can be changed. Furthermore, the NN's output can be used for anything, and not only used as the synaptic weights for the coordinate specified neurodes. For example, the output of the NN can be used and considered as the *Delta Weight*, the change in the synaptic weight between the pre- and postsynaptic neurodes, based on the coordinates of the said neurodes fed to the NN, in addition with the pre-synaptic neurode's output, the post-synaptic neurode's output, and the current synaptic weight between the two. We will further discuss the details of substrates and their functionality in the following section, followed by a discussion of the genotype encoding DXNN uses for substrates, the phenotype representation that it uses for such substrate encoded agents, and finally the different types of "substrate_sensors" and "substrate_actuators", which further modify the substrate encoded NN systems, allowing the NN to not only use the coordinates of the two connected neurodes when computing the synaptic weight between them, but various other geometrically significant features, like distance, spherical coordinates, planner coordinates, centripetal distance...

10.5.1 Neural Substrates

A neural substrate is simply a hypercube structure whose axis run from -1 to 1 on every dimension. The substrate has neurodes embedded in it, where each neurode has a coordinate based on its location within the hypercube. The neurodes are connected to each other, either in the feed forward fashion, a fully connected fashion, or random connection based fashion. An example of a 2d substrate is shown in Fig-10.7a, and a 3d substrate in Fig-10.7b.

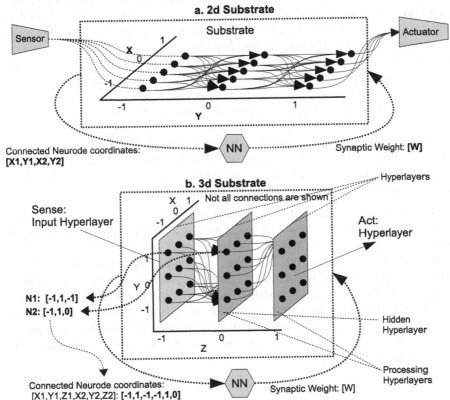

Fig. 10.7 An example of different substrates in which the neurodes are connected to each other in the feed forward fashion.

The density of the substrate refers to the number of neurons on a particular axis. For example, if the substrate is a 2d one, and the density of the substrate is 5 by 3, then this plane substrate has 5 neurons, uniformly distributed on the x axis, with 3 total of such layers, which too are uniformly distributed on the y axis, as shown in Fig-10.7a. The Fig-10.7b shows a 3d substrate with the density distribution of 3x3x3. In this substrate, there are 3 planes on the Z axis, where each plane is composed out of 3x3 neurode patterns. Each plane is connected to the plane ahead of it, hence it is a feed forward based substrate, since the signals travel from the -Z direction, towards the +Z direction. We could of course have a fully connected substrate, where every neurode is connected to every other neurode. Also, the substrate does not necessarily need to be symmetric, it can have any type of pattern, any number of neurons per layer or hyperlayer, and positioned in any pattern within that layer or hyperlayer.

From these examples you can see that the processing, input, and output hyperlayers, are one dimension lower than the entire substrate. The sensory signals travel from the negative side of the axis of the most external dimension (Y in the case of 2d, and Z in the case of 3d in the above examples), from the input hyperlayer, through the processing hyperlayers, and finally to the output hyperlayer, whose neurodes' output counts as the output of the substrate (but again, we could designate any neurode in the substrate as an output neurode, and wait until all such output neurodes produce a signal, and count that as the substrate's output). The manner in which we package the output signals of the neurodes within the output hyperlayer, and the manner in which we feed those packaged vectors to the actuators, determines what the substrate encoded NN based agent does. Finally, because the very first hyperlayer is the input to the substrate, and the very last hyperlayer is the output of the substrate, there must be at least 2 hyperlayers making up the substrate structure.

For example, assume we'd like to feed an image coming from a camera into the substrate encoded NN system. The image itself is a bitmap, let's say of resolution 10x10. This is perfect, for this type of input signal we can create a 3d substrate with a 10x10 input hyperlayer, 3x3 hidden processing hyperlayer, and a 1x5 output hyperlayer. Each hyperlayer is a 2d plane, all positioned on the 3rd dimension, thus making the substrate 3d, as shown in Fig-10.8. As can be seen, the input being the very first layer located at $Z = -1$, has its signals sent to the second layer, located at $Z = 0$, which processes it, and whose neurode outputs are sent to the 3rd layer at $Z = 1$, processed by the last 5 neurodes whose output is considered the final output of the substrate.

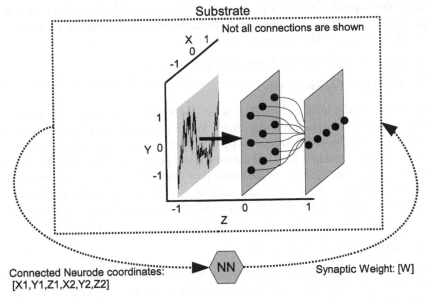

Fig. 10.8 A [{10,10},{3,3},{5,1}] substrate being fed a 2d plane image with a 10x10 ({10,10}) resolution.

You might be asking at this point "What is the advantage of using substrate encoding?" The answer is in the way we produce their weights. The weights are determined by the NN which calculates the synaptic weight between two connected neurodes based on their coordinates. The coordinates of the connected neurodes act as the input to the NN. Since the NN has the coordinates as input, it can do the following:

1. Extract geometrical patterns in the input hyperlayer, and thus it can be applied to highly complex problems where such geometrical information can be exploited.
2. Be used to generate weights for very large and very dense substrates, with the connectivity and synaptic weight patterns based on the coordinates, and thus being of almost any complexity and form.
3. Due to never seeing the actual input signals, it cannot evolve a single synaptic weight for some particular element in the input vector during training, it cannot evolve some specific set of synaptic weights to pick out a particular single small pattern. In other words, a substrate encoded NN has a much lower chance of overtraining. It paints the synaptic weights broadly on the substrate, and thus it should be able to generalize that much better.
4. Because the NN produces a smooth function, and because each neurode in the substrate has presynaptic connections from a smooth spread of neurodes, with regards to their coordinates in the previous hyperlayer, the synaptic weights produced by the NN for any particular neurode, varies smoothly. This is the reason why it is much more difficult for such synaptic weights to overtrain on

some single particular points in the input stream of signals. Hence the superior generalization. The NN paints the synaptic weights and connectivity patterns on the substrate in "broad strokes", so to speak.

Let us discuss some of the things mentioned in more detail.

Geometrical Feature Sensitivity:

As discussed, the input to the NN is a list of coordinates for the connected pre-synaptic and post-synaptic neurodes. Not only are the coordinates used as input to the NN, but also the coordinates can be first converted to spherical coordinates, polar coordinates, distance between the connected neurodes, distance to the center of the substrate... before they are fed to the NN. Because a NN is a universal function approximator, and the inputs are various geometrical elements, and because the input hyperlayer itself has coordinates, the NN gains the ability to pick out and deal with the geometrical features of the substrate, and the sensory signals.

Large Neural Network Structures:

Since the substrate neurode density is independent of the actual NN which we evolve, through substrate encoding it is possible to create very large/dense substrates, with thousands or millions of neurodes. Thinking again about the substrate analyzing the data/images coming from a camera, we can also see that the denser the substrate, the higher the resolution of images it can analyze. Also the resolution of the sensory inputs and the output of the substrate, are independent of the NN painting the connectivity and synaptic weights on it. The "curse of dimensionality" does not plague this type of system as much, since we can concentrate on a smaller number of evolving parameters and topologies (of the actual evolving NN), while controlling a vast substrate embedded NN. Finally, it is also possible to implement synaptic plasticity using *iterative, abc,* and other types of substrate learning rules [6], which we will discuss in detail and implement in later chapters.

The "Broad Stroke" property:

Because the neural network that calculates the synaptic weights for the neurodes in the substrate does not see the actual input vectors, and instead only deals with the coordinates. And because the output of the NN is a smooth function, and the input coordinates to the NN are based on the connected neurodes, and each neurode is connected from a whole spectrum of neurodes in the previous hyper-layer, with their coordinates changing smoothly from -1 to 1. The synaptic weights are painted in "Broad Strokes". Meaning, due to the inability of the NN to pick out any particular points in the incoming data, the synaptic weights it generates are smooth over the whole substrate. A change in the NN system changes the weights, the output function of the substrate, in general *and smoothly*, bringing values smoothly up or down... This means that over-training is more difficult because the weights of the neurodes do not lock up on some single particular data point in the input signals. Thus the generalization of the substrate encoded agent is superior, as was shown in papers: "Evolving a Single Scalable Controller for an Octopus Arm with a Variable Number of Segments" [7] and "Evolving Chart Pattern Sensitive Neural Network Based Forex Trading Agents" [12].

10.5.2 Genotype Representation

As we saw in Fig-10.7, the substrate is part of the cortex process. The genotypical specification for the cortex element in DXNN is:

{id,sensors,actuators,cf,ct, type,plasticity, pattern,cids,su_id, link_form,dimensions, densities, generation}

This tuple specifies the substrate dimensionsionality and its general properties through the *dimensions* and *densities* elements. Because the sensors and actuators of the substrate are independent of the actual substrate itself, the neurode densities of the substrate, the specification for the "processing hyperlayers", the "input hyperlayers", and the "output hyperlayers", are independent. Though this may at first sound somewhat convoluted, after the explanation you will notice the advantages of this setup, especially for a neural network based system that is meant to evolve and grow.

When I say "processing hyperlayer" I mean the substrate hyperlayer (2d, 3d... substrate layer of neurodes) that actually has neurodes that process signals. As was noted in the discussion on the substrate, the sensory inputs, which are sometimes multidimensional like in the case of the signals coming from a camera, are part of the substrate, located at the *-1* side of the axis defining the depth of the substrate. The output hyperlayers of the substrate are of the processing type. Because the input hyperlayers and output hyperlayers need to be tailored for the particular set of sensors and actuators used by the agent, the input hyperlayers, processing hyperlayers, and the output hyperlayers of the substrate, are all specified separately from one another.

So, to create the initial substrate for the agent, the substrate's topology is specified in 3 parts. First DXNN figures out how many dimensions the substrate will be composed of. This is done by analyzing all the sensors and actuators available to the agent. In DXNN, the sensors and actuators not only specify the vector lengths of the signals, but also the geometrical properties (if any) that the signals will exhibit. This means that they specify whether the input signals are best viewed or analyzed as a plane with a resolution of X by Y, or a cube of a resolution X by Y by Z, or if there is no geometrical data and that the vector length L of the input signal can be viewed as just a list. If the NN based agent is substrate based, then the DXNN platform will use this extra geometry specification information to create the substrate topology most appropriate for it. Thus, if the morphology of the seed population being created is composed of 2 sensors and 3 actuators as follows:

sensors:

[#sensor{name=distance_scanner,id=cell_id,format={symmetric,Dim}, tot_vl=pow(Res,Dim),
parameters=[Spread,Res,ROffset]} || Spread<-[Pi/2],Res<-[5], Roffset<-[Pi*0/2]] ++
[#sensor{name=color_scanner,id=cell_id,format={symmetric,Dim}, tot_vl=pow(Res,Dim),
parameters=[Spread,Res,ROffset]} || Spread <-[Pi/2], Res <-[4], Roffset<-[Pi*0/2], Dim=2],

actuators:

[#actuator{name=two_wheels,id=cell_id,format=no_geo,tot_vl=2,parameters=[]},
#actuator{name=create_offspring,id=cell_id,format=no_geo,tot_vl=1,parameters=[]},
#actuator{name=spear,id=cell_id,format=no_geo,tot_vl=1,parameters=[]}]

Where the *parameters* element specifies the extra information necessary for the proper use of the sensor or actuator, and the *format* element specifies the geometrical formatting of the signal. We can see that the actuators all have their formats set to *no_geo* meaning, no geometric information, so the actuators expect from the substrate single dimensional vector outputs. On the other hand, the sensors both use format= {symmetric,2}, which specifies a two dimensional sensory signal with a symmetric resolution in both dimensions: X by Y where X = Y. The parameters also specify, since these sensors are part of the simulated robot with distance and color sensors, the simulated sensor's coverage area (Spread), camera resolution (Res), and sensor's radial offset from the robot's central line (based on the actual simulation of the robot which is specified during the ALife simulation). Based on the format, the DXNN knows that the sensors will produce two symmetric 2d input signals, with a resolution of 5 and 4 respectively. Thus the first sensory input will be a 5x5 plane, and the second a 4x4 plane. The DXNN also knows that the actuators expect single dimensional output vectors, the one called *two_wheels* expects the signal sent to it be a vector of length 2, with the other two actuators expecting the signals sent to them to also be single dimensional lists, vectors, and in this case of length 1 (the length is specified by the tot_vl parameter).

Having this information, DXNN knows to expect input signals that will be at least 2d (new sensors might be added in the future, which might of course have higher, or lower dimension), and that the output signals will be 1d. The DXNN thus calculates that the input hyperlayer composed of multiple 2d inputs will be at least 3d (2d planes stacked on a 3rd dimension), and the output hyperlayer will be at least 2d (1d outputs stacked on the 2nd dimension), which means that the substrate must be at least 4d. But why 4d?

Though certainly it is possible to devise substrates whose dimension is the same as the highest dimension of the sensor or actuator used by it, I usually implement a layer to layer feedforward substrate topology which requires the substrate's dimension to be the maximum sensor or actuator dimension, *+2*. The reasoning for this is best explained through an example.

Let's say the substrate encoded NN based agent uses 2 sensors, each of which is 2d, and 2 actuators, each of which is 1d. The 2d input planes do not perform any type of processing because the processing is done in the hidden processing hyperlayers, and the output hyperlayer. So both of the 2d input planes must forward their signals to the processing hyperlayers. So we must first put these 2d planes on another dimension. Thus, to form an input hyperlayer we first put the 2d planes on the third dimension, forming a 3d input hyperlayer. But for the 3d input hyperlayer to forward its signals to another 3d processing hyperlayer, we need to put both on a 4th dimension. Thus, the final substrate is 4d. The input hyperlayer is 3d. The output hyperlayer, though really only needing to be 2d (due to the output signals being both 1d layers stacked on a 2nd dimension to form an output hyperlayer), is also 3d because all neurodes haves to have the same dimensionality.

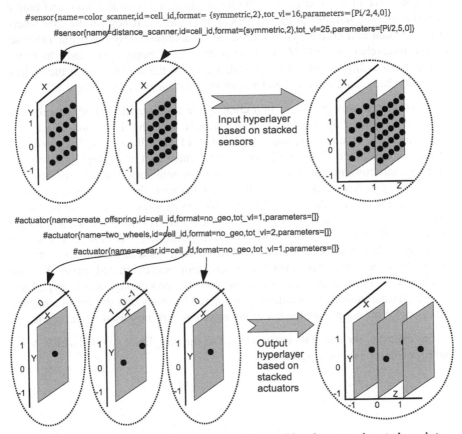

Fig. 10.9 Input and output hyperlayers composed by stacking the sensor input planes into a single multidimensional input hyperlayer, and stacking the output processing planes into a single multidimensional output hyperlayer with signals destined for actuators.

Why give an extra dimension to put the input or output planes on? Because in the future we might want to add more sensors and actuators, and have the sensors and actuators stacked on another dimension makes it easy to do so. For example we would simply add the new sensor based input plane on the same 3rd dimension, and scoot the others a bit. In this manner we can add new sensors and actuators indefinitely, without changing the substrate topology too much. Also the coordinates of the neurodes in the input planes would change only slightly due to scooting, and so the synaptic weights determined by the NN could be more easily and smoothly adjusted through synaptic weight tuning phase.

This is the gist of the idea when forming substrates dynamically, based on sensors and actuators used, and expecting to use multiple such sensors and actuators in the future. We will discuss substrate encoding in much more detail in Chapter-16.

So, now we know how to compute the dimensionality of the input and output hyperlayers. The number of the processing hyperlayers, if any (in the case where only the input and output hyperlayers exist) is determined by the depth value set by the researcher. In DXNN, the hidden processing hyperlayers, their topology and dimensionality, is set to the resolution equal to the square root of the highest resolution between the sensors and actuators of the agent's morphology.

Thus through this process, when creating the seed population of the substrate encoded NN based agents, DXNN can calculate both the dimension of the substrate to create, its topology, and the resolution of each dimension. The resolution of each hidden processing hyperlayer is set to square root of the highest resolution of the signals coming from the sensors or towards actuators. The dimensionality is set, as noted earlier, to the highest dimension between the sensors and actuators, +2. The depth, the number of total hidden processing hyperlayers, is set by the researcher, usually to 0 or 1. If it is set to 0, then there is only the input and output (which is able to process the sensory signals) hyperlayers, and 0 hidden processing hyperlayers. When set to 1, the full substrate is composed of the input hyperlayer, the hidden processing hyperlayer whose resolution was computed earlier from the resolution of the sensors and actuators, and the processing output hyperlayer whose dimensionality and topology was formed by analyzing the list of available actuators for the agent, and the list of the actuators currently used by the agent.

For example, the substrate created based on the morphology composed from the following sensors and actuators:

sensors:

[#sensor{name=internals_sensor,id=cell_id,format=no_geo,tot_vl=3,parameters=[]},

#sensor{name=color_scanner,id=cell_id,format={symmetric,2}, tot_vl=Density,

parameters=[Spread,Res,ROffset]} || Spread <-[Pi/2], Res <-[4], ROffset<-[Pi*0/2]],

actuators:

[#actuator{name=two_wheels,id=cell_id,format=no_geo,tot_vl=2,parameters=[]},

#actuator{name=create_offspring,id=cell_id,format=no_geo,tot_vl=1,parameters=[]}]

Will have the hidden processing hyperlayer resolutions set to 2, the dimensionality set to 4 = **2**+2, and the depth set by the researcher to 1. Since the input and output hyperplanes are created when the genotype is converted to phenotype, and based on the number and types of sensors involved, assuming that in this example the agent is using all the sensors and actuators, the substrate will have the following form:

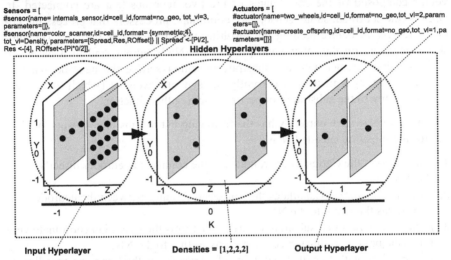

Fig. 10.10 The substrate belonging to an agent with 2 sensors and 2 actuators, with the dimensions = 4, and densities = [1,2,2,2]

Once the substrate and its properties are determined, the actual NN is then created in a fashion similar to one created when standard direct/neural encoding is used. Only in a substrate encoded NN based system, the sensors and actuators used by the NN are the substrate_sensors and substrate_actuators, because it is the substrate that is using the real sensors and actuators, while the NN gets its input (coordinates and other neurode parameters) from the substrate, and uses its output signals to execute the substrate_actuators, which set up the synaptic weights (and other parameters) between the neurodes.

In the NNs that use substrate encoding, since it is the substrate that accepts inputs from the environment and outputs signals to the outside world, and the NN is just used to set the weights for the neurodes in the substrate, the system not only has a set of sensors and actuators as in the standard NN system, but also a set of substrate_sensors and substrate_actuators. The substrate_sensors and substrate_actuators are used by the NN in the same way the standard, neural encoded NN uses sensors and actuators, and new substrate_sensors and substrate_actuators are also in the same way integrated into the NN as it evolves.

In the standard substrate encoded NN system, the NN is given an input that is a vector composed of the coordinates of the two neurodes that are connected. In DXNN, the set of substrate_sensors are coordinate processors that process the coordinate vectors before feeding the resulting vector signals to the NN. The substrate_actuators on the other hand process the NN's output, and then based on their function interact with the substrate by either setting the neurode synaptic weights, changes a neurode's currently set synaptic weights (which effectively adds plasticity to the substrate), or performs some other function.

The DXNN system currently has the following list of substrate_sensors available for the substrate encoded NNs:

1. *none:* Passes the Cartesian coordinates of the connected neurodes directly to the NN.
2. *cartesian_distance:* Calculates the Cartesian distance between the neurodes, and passes the result to the NN.
3. *polar_coordinates* (if substrate is 2d): Transforms the Cartesian coordinate vector to the polar coordinate vector, and passes that to the NN.
4. *spherical_coordinates* (if substrate is 3d): Transforms the Cartesian coordinate vector to the spherical coordinate vector, and passes that to the NN.
5. *centripetal_distance*: Transforms the Cartesian coordinate vector from the connected neurodes into a vector of length 2, composed of the distances of the two neurodes to the center of the substrate.
6. *distance_between_neurodes*: Calculates the distance between the two connected neurodes, and passes that to the NN.

This set of substrate_sensors further allows the substrate encoded NN to extract the geometrical patterns and information from its inputs, whatever dimension those input signals have. An example of an architecture of a substrate encoded NN using multiple substrate_sensors and multiple substrate_actuators, with the substrate itself using multiple sensors and actuators as well, is shown in Fig-10.11.

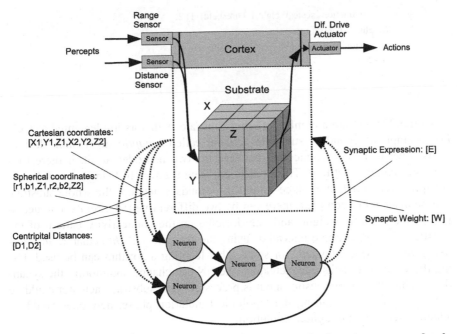

Fig. 10.11 A substrate encoded NN using different types of substrate_sensors and substrate_actuators, and standard sensors and actuators.

As can be seen from the figure, it is also possible to have different types of substrate_actuators, not just the standard *synaptic_weight* substrate_actuator which uses the NN's output to set the synaptic weight between the two neurodes based on their coordinates which were passed to the NN's substrate_sensors. The standard substrate_actuator, *synaptic_weight* setter, is one that simply uses the signal coming from the NN and converts it into a synaptic weight value using the algorithm shown in Listing-10.1. In this listing, the substrate_actuator simply takes the NN's output, and computes the synaptic weight to be 0 if the NN's output is between -0.33 and 0.33, and to be between -1 and 1 otherwise, normalizing the synaptic weight value such that there is no hole between -0.33 and 0.33 when using this below shown function:

Listing-10.1 The simple synaptic weight setting "substrate_actuator".

```
set_weight(Output)->
    [Weight] = Output,
    Threshold = 0.33,
    Processed_Weight = if
        Weight > Threshold ->
```

```
                 (functions:scale(Weight,1,Threshold)+1)/2;
        Weight < -Threshold ->
                 (functions:scale(Weight,-Threshold,-1)-1)/2;
        true ->
                 0
    end.
```

Currently there are a number of other substrate_actuators implemented as well. For example a secondary substrate_actuator called *synaptic_expression,* decides on whether there is a connection between the two neurodes at all, if there isn't then the weight is set to 0. This is different from the weight being set to 0 by the synaptic_weight actuator, since using this secondary actuator the whole substrate can be made more complex, there can be two different neural circuits, one deciding on the synaptic weight, and one deciding on the connectivity pattern of the substrate. Or for example instead of using the *synaptic_weight* actuator, an *iterative_plasticity, abc_plasticity,* or some other learning algorithm can be used. Using these plasticity substrate_actuators, the NN can change and modify the synaptic weights after every sensory input is processed. One substrate_actuator could be mutated into another during the topological mutation phase, new ones could be added or removed throughout evolution.

These substrate_actuators further allow one to experiment with different types of learning, adding more agility and robustness to the population and individual agents, providing a greater leverage to evolution to overcome various discontinuities and abstractions on the fitness landscape. Combined all together, with the various substrate specific mutation operators which increase the resolution/density of the substrate, add new sensors and actuators, add new substrate_sensors and substrate_actuators... the substrate encoding provided by the DXNN system is one of the most advanced substrate encoded neuroevolutionary approaches currently available.

The resolution and dimensionality of the substrate can be further mutated during the topological mutation stage. When the agent is substrate encoded, the platform's standard mutation operator list is further augmented to include the following substrate specific mutation operators:

1. mutate_resolution
2. mutate_dimensionality

Yes the method and representation is convoluted and could be made simpler. The problem with DXNN, as noted earlier, is that it was built up slowly, evolving through many of my various experiments and tests. And as we know, evolution does not take the cleanest path from genotype A to genotype Z, instead it is all based on the easiest and most direct path, which is based on the agent's environment, and most easily achievable niche based on the agent's genotype/phenotype at that time. Here too, the DXNN is the way it is because of the order in which I got the ideas for its various parts, and the initial, though at times mistaken, representations and implementations I used. Once a few hundred or thousand lines of code are written, the amount of motivation to recreate the system in a cleaner manner decreases. But now that we are creating a completely new TWEANN system together, and have the knowledge of my earlier experience within the field and systems like DXNN to guide us, we can create our new system with foresight, without having to go down the same dark alleys and dead ends I wondered into during my first time around.

10.5.3 Substrate Phenotype Representation

The conversion of genotype to phenotype is similar to one used by the standard direct encoded NNs in DXNN, and thus is similar to what we use in the system we've built so far. As we discussed, in DXNN the cortex process is not a synchronizer but instead is the signal gatekeeper between the NN and the sensors and actuators it itself is composed of. In the substrate encoded NNs, the cortex also takes on the role of the substrate itself. In DXNN, the entire *[substrate, cortex, sensors, actuators, substrate_sensors, substrate_actuators]* system is represented as a single element/process, because it is possible to encode the substrate in a list form and very efficiently perform calculations even when that substrate is composed of thousands of neurodes.

When the exoself generates and connects all the elements (neurons and the cortex), it does so in the same way it does with the direct encoded NN system. Since the cortex knows, based on its parameters, that it is a substrate encoded system, once it is created it builds a substrate based on dimension, densities, sensor, actuator, substrate_sensor, and substrate_actuator list specifications. The neurons and the NN that they compose neither know nor need to know that the agent is substrate encoded. In both versions, the direct encoded and the indirect encoded NN system, the input and the output layer neurons are connected to the cortex, so nothing changes for them. The cortex is the one that needs to keep track of when to use the substrate sensors/actuators, and when to use the actual sensors/actuators.

The algorithm that the substrate encoded cortex follows is specified in the following steps, with a follow-up paragraphs elaborating on the more intricate parts.

1. The cortex process is spawned by the exoself, and immediately begins to wait for its initial parameters from the same.
2. The cortex receives all its *InitState* in the form:

```
{ExoSelf_PId,Id,Sensors,Actuators,CF,CT,Max_Attempts,Smoothness,OpMode,Type,
Plasticity, Morphology,Specie_Id,TotNeurons,Dimensions,Densities}
```

3. The cortex checks the agent Type, whether it is *neural* or *substrate*. In the steps that follow we assume that the Type is *substrate*.

4. Cortex constructs the substrate:

    5. The cortex reads the number of dimensions, and the densities.

    6. The input hyperlayer is built based on the sensors the agent uses, with the neurode coordinates based on the number of dimensions (If the entire substrate has 3 dimensions, then each coordinate is [X,Y,Z], if 4d then [X,Y,Z,T]...).

    7. If *depth* > *0*, then hidden processing hyperlayers are constructed based on the densities and dimension specified, and with each neurode in the first hidden processing hyperlayer having the right number of synaptic weights to deal with the input hyperlayer.

    8. The output processing hyperlayer is constructed, and each neurode must have the right number of synaptic weights to deal with the signals coming from the hidden processing hyperlayers.

    9. The cortex combines the input, processing, and output hyperlayers into a single hypercube substrate.

10. DO Sense-Think-Act loop:

    11. DO For each neurode in the substrate:

        12. The cortex goes through the substrate_sensors, using the tuples like in the standard sensors, to forward the neurode properties (coordinates, and other parameters based on the substrate_sensor used) to the connected neurons in the NN.

        13. The output signals of the NN are then used to execute the substrate_actuators to set the synaptic weights and other parameters between the neurodes in the substrate.

    UNTIL: All neurodes have been assigned their synaptic weights and other parameters.

    14. The cortex goes through every sensor, and maps the sensory signals to the input hyperlayer of the substrate.

    15. The substrate processes the sensory signals.

    16. The output hyperlayer produces the output signals destined for the actuators. Since the output hyperlayer is created based on the actuators the agent uses, the output signals are implicitly of the right dimensionality and in the right order, such that the signals are packaged into vectors of proper lengths, and are then used as parameters to execute the actuator functions.

    17. The cortex goes through every actuator, executing the actuator function using the output signals produced by the substrate as the parameter of their respective actuators.

UNTIL: Termination condition is reached, tuning has ended, or interrupt signal is sent by the exoself.

During the tuning phase, after every evaluation of the NN, the exoself chooses which neurons should perturb their synaptic weights. After the neurons in the NN have perturbed their synaptic weights, the cortex takes the substrate through the step 11 loop, updating all the synaptic weights of the neurodes in the substrate by polling the NN for weights.

Thus the cortex first executes all the sensor functions to gather all the sensory signals, then it goes through every neurode in the substrate, until the processing output hyperlayer produces the output signals, which the cortex gathers, packages into appropriate vectors, and executes all the actuators in its actuator list with the appropriate output vector signals.

The phenotypic architecture of the substrate encoded NN based agent, composed of the Exoself, Cortex, and Neuron elements, with the Sense-Think-Act loop steps specified, is shown in Fig-10.12.

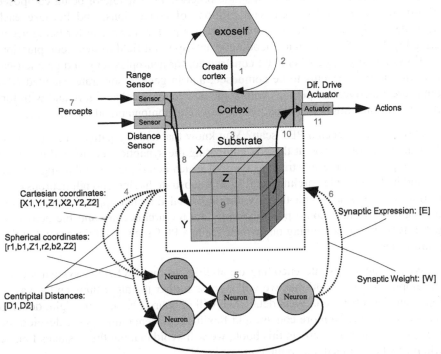

Fig. 10.12 The phenotypic architecture of the substrate encoded NN based agent, composed of the concurrent Exoself, Cortex, and Neuron processes, with the processing steps listed.

Let's quickly go over the shortened processing loop shown in the above figure.

1. The exoself creates the cortex.
2. The exoself sends the created cortex its *InitState* parameters.
3. The cortex creates the substrate based on sensors, actuators, and other specifications.
4. The cortex/substrate uses the substrate_sensors to forward to the NN the coordinates and other parameters of the connected neurodes within the substrate.
5. The NN processes the signals passed to it by its substrate_sensors.

6. The substrate_actuators and the signals produced by the NN, used as parameters for the substrate_actuators, are used to set the synaptic weights and other parameters of the embedded neurodes.
7. The cortex gathers the sensory signals from its sensors.
8. The cortex maps the sensory signals to the substrate's input hyperlayer.
9. The substrate processes the sensory signals coming from the input hyperlayer.
10. The cortex maps the output signals of the neurodes in the output hyperlayer to their appropriate actuators.
11. The cortex executes the actuators with the substrate produced output signals as their parameters.

The substrate, due to it being a single process, and capable of being composed of millions of neurodes each with millions of connections, and because each neurode simply does vector multiplication, is a perfect candidate for being accelerated with a GPU. Substrate encoding is an important field of neurocomputation, it allows for very large NNs to be constructed, for neuroplasticity and geometrical pattern sensitive systems to be composed, and in general substrate encoded NNs are more effective, and perhaps with some new topological structure and with further expansions, might be the path toward general computational intelligence.

Have you ever seen a PET scan? You know that activity pattern that it shows? It is difficult not to look at the NN computing the synaptic weights and therefore activity pattern on the substrate, as the tool which could carve out that high density, and highly complex architecture. With a substrate having enough neurons (100 billion let's say), and with the NN, the universal function approximator, having the right function, it could possibly carve out the architecture and the activation patterns similar to something one would see in a PET scan... But we are not at that point just yet.

We will add substrate encoding capabilities to the TWEANN system we are developing together, and thus we will discuss further the algorithms and a way to represent the substrate in great detail. We will of course, having foresight, develop our system to have a more concise and flexible representation. As we develop the next generation TWEANN in this book, we will avoid making the mistakes I made when I first developed the architecture of DXNN.

In the following sections we will discuss the current and ongoing projects that DXNN is being used for, and thus what the system we're developing here (which will replace DXNN, by becoming the new DXNN) will be applied to once developed. The system we're creating here is meant to supersede and replace DXNN, it is the next generation of a fully concurrent, highly general and scalable, *Topology and Parameter Evolving Universal Learning Network* (TPEULN).

10.6 DXNN Research Group & the NN Research Repository

DXNN Research group [8] is currently a small research group composed of a few mathematicians, computer scientists, and me. We are working on further expanding the DXNN platform, and finding new projects to apply it to. One of these projects is the application of DXNN to Cyberwarfare. Another deals with exchanging the neuron elements with logic gates and transistors, so that the platform can be applied towards the evolution and optimization of large scale digital circuits. The currently explored application of DXNN is towards the evolution and optimization of OpenSPARC [9], some progress has been made, but not enough to publish. The DXNN Research group is also currently working on interfacing the DXNN with the *Player/Stage/Gazebo* [5] project, allowing it to be used in 3d ALife experiments, and the evolution of robotic systems and neurocontrollers for the same. The Player/Stage/Gazebo robot simulators provide 2d and 3d simulation environments, and the drivers to interface the evolved NNs with actual hardware. The use of *Player* gives us the ability to evolve systems in artificial environments, and immediately have the ability to apply them to real hardware, and thus usable and applicable in the real world. The current main project and interest in this area is the evolution of neurocontrollers for the control of Unmanned Combat Ariel Vehicles (UCAVs). This is accomplished through the co-evolution of two, forever warring, populations of Combat UAVs in the 3d simulated environment, through Gazebo for example. Due to the use of the Player interface, we can then transfer the evolved intelligence to real UCAV systems.

The main reasons why we are trying to create a highly decoupled neuroevolutionary system is because it will allow us to easily augment it, and then provide it to the public so that crowdsourcing is used to further expand the platform, letting anyone with interest and skill to contribute various modules and computational packages to the system, further expanding and augmenting it, making it more general, and applicable to new projects, which benefits the entire community using the TWEANN system. DXNN Neural Network Research Repository [10] provides the specifications on how to add new modules to the DXNN TWEANN, where to submit them...

The goal of the Neural Network Research Repository (NNRR) is also to become the repository of neural network systems evolved through the DXNN system. NNs are by their very nature blackbox systems, different neural networks can be evolved to solve the same problem, or inhabit same environments (when NN based agents are used in ALife). NNRR provides a place where individuals can submit the NN systems they have evolved, and specify the fitness functions and other parameters they used to evolve these agents. Because everyone else on the NNRR is also using DXNN, they can then try to see what types of NN topologies they can evolve given the same fitness function and TWEANN parameters. Thus, the NNRR should over time accumulate useful NN based agents. Those who wish to simply start using these agents can do so, others can try to download the hundreds of the already evolved NN based systems for some problem, and try to data-mine their topologies, try to see what are the essential parts of these NN based systems, what are the common threads? Through this approach we can try to start building a path towards illuminating the blackbox. These types of databases also provide the data needed to figure out where the DXNN system is perhaps having difficulties when solving problems.

Finally, with the standardized interfaces between the various processes, and with the specified genotypical encoding system, the community can contribute the various activation functions, neural plasticity rules, neuron types, substrate topologies, fitness functions, selection functions... Every decoupled element is a self contained module, and thus anyone can augment the DXNN system by simply conforming to the proper interface specifications. The NNRR will propel us, and allow for the capabilities and applicability of this neuroevolutionary system to expand dramatically, making the evolved systems available globally, providing already evolved solutions to those interested, and giving a place for researchers to contribute, while at the same time giving them a place where they can gather tools and data for their own further research.

10.7 Currently Active Projects

The DXNN research group is currently actively pursuing three projects:

1. Cyberwarfare.
2. Coevolution of Unmanned Ariel Vehicle Combat Maneuvers.
3. CPU Evolution and Optimization.

When successful, the results of these 3 projects could potentially be game changing for the industrial and military sector.

10.7.1 Cyberwarfare

One of the exciting applications the DXNN platform is currently being applied toward is the evolution of offensive and defensive cyberwarfare agents. We are currently trying to evolve agents capable of using parameterized metasploit (a penetration testing program) and other tools to effectively penetrate and attack other machines, and agents capable of defending their host network against such attacks, by monitoring signals on its network for attacks being carried out against it, and then using various available tools and methods to thwart and counterattack. This is done by creating scapes, simulated network environments using network simulators like NS3, with simulated host targets, and then interfacing the NN based agents with programs like metasploit, letting them evolve the ability to combine the various attack commands to penetrate the simple hosts. With regards to the evolution of defensive agents, the NN based agents are fed signals coming from the ports, and they are required to make a decision of whether they are being actively attacked or not. If they are, they must decide on what they should do, lock the port, fully disconnect, counter-attack...

There are a number of difficulties in evolving cyberwarfare agents, because unlike in the natural environments, there are no smooth evolutionary paths from simply existing on a network, to being able to forge attack vectors using metasploit. Neither is there a smooth evolutionary path leading from mere existence, to the ability to detect more and more complex attacks being carried out against your own host. In standard ALife, there is an evolutionary path from simply running after a prey and then eating it, to trying different approaches, hiding, baiting the prey... it's all a smooth progression of intelligence. That is not the case in cyberwarfare, things are more disconnected, more arcane, requiring beforehand knowledge and experience. Nevertheless, through bootstrapping simple skills, and forging fitness functions, our preliminary results have demonstrated that the goals of this project are achievable.

10.7.2 Coevolving Unmanned Ariel Vehicle Combat Maneuvers

Another exciting application and field where evolved neurocognitive systems can provide a significant advantage is of course robotics. As with cyberwarfare, there is a significant amount of both industrial and military applications, with the successful system and implementation being potentially game changing. Due to the current increased use of unmanned aerial vehicles, particularly in combat, there is a great opportunity in evolving neural network agents specifically for controlling such systems. At the moment the UAVs are programmed to scout, or fly to particular way-points. Once the UAV gets there, a real pilot takes over. The pilot sits somewhere in the base and controls the UAV, looking at the screen which is fed by the UAV's camera. This of course provides a much lower level of situational awareness to the pilot when compared to that available when sitting in a cockpit. Also, the maneuvers available to the drone are limited by the human operator, and the time delay in the connection due to the distance of the UAV from the human operator. All of this combined, puts the Unmanned Combat Ariel Vehicle (UCAV) at a disadvantage in a standard dogfight against a piloted fighter jet. Yet a UCAV can undertake g forces and perform maneuvers that are impossible for a human piloted jet fighter. Furthermore, an evolved NN would be able to integrate the signals from many more sensors, and make the decisions faster, than any biological pilot can. Thus, it is possible for the UCAVs to have performance levels, precision levels, situational awareness, and general capabilities that far surpass those of pilots and piloted jets.

This can be mitigated by evolving NN based agents specifically for controlling UCAVs, allowing the NN systems to take full advantage of all the sensory data, and use the UCAV to its full potential with regards to maneuverability. I think that this would give the drone an advantage over standard manned aerial vehicles. To evolve such NN based agents we once again do so through an ALife coevolutionary approach. As discussed in the "Motivations and Applications" chapter, by creating a detailed simulation through a simulator like Gazebo, and creating the simulated UCAVs with high enough detail, and a set of prepro- grammed or even evolving fighter jet simulations constrained to the physical lim- its of the pilot, it is possible to coevolve UCAV controlling NN systems. To ac- complish this, we can put two populations of forever warring UCAVs into a simulated 3d environment, to coevolve the ever more intelligent digital minds within. This, as in the Predator Vs. Prey [11] simulations, will yield ever more creative NN based agents, evolving neurocontrollers with innovative combat ma- neuvers, and having the ability to use the full potential of unmanned combat air- craft, the full potential of metal that is not limited by flesh.

The preliminary testing in this project has started. At the time of this writing, the interface between the DXNN platform and the Player/Gazebo has been devel- oped, and the work is being concentrated on developing simulations of the UCAVs which are modular enough to allow for morphological evolution. Based on the performance of DXNN in ALife, there seems to be no reason why it would not evolve highly adaptive, flexible, and potent UCAV piloting agents.

10.7.3 Evolving New CPU Architectures & Optimizing Existing Ones

The third project currently being pursued by the DXNN research group, deals with the DXNN platform being applied to the evolution and optimization of digital circuits. Because the neurons in the evolving NN topologies can have any type of connections and activation functions, the DXNN platform does not in reality evolve NNs, but Universal Learning Networks, where the nodes can be anything. In this particular application, the nodes use logic operators and transistor simula- tions as activation functions, thus the evolved topologies are those of digital cir- cuits.

The OpenSPARC project provides the whole architecture and topology of the OpenSPARC T2 CPU, which our team is hoping to take advantage of. The goal of our project is composed of two parts. 1. Create the tuple encoded genotype of a system which recreates the OpenSPARC T2 architecture, and then through its mu- tation operators (complexifying and pruning), optimize the CPU, by reducing the number of gates used while retaining the functionality. 2. By specifying particular goals through the fitness function, such as increased throughput, higher core count coherency, and certain new features, evolve the existing architecture into a more advanced one.

Because OpenSPARC T2 also provides a testing suit, it is possible to mutate the existing architecture and immediately test its functionality and performance. But due to the architecture's high level of complexity, the project is still in the process of having new mutation operators being developed, the fitness functions being crafted for optimization and evolution of the CPU, and the creation of the genotype representing the OpenSPARC-T2 architecture. DXNN has been used to evolve and optimize much smaller digital circuits, which gives hope that it can successfully be applied here as well. The potential payoffs could be immense, improving and optimizing CPUs automatically, and adding new features, would revolutionize the landscape of this field. At the moment, we are only beginning to scratch the surface of this project.

10.8 Summary and Future Work

In this chapter we have discussed the DXNN Platform, a general Topology and Weight Evolving Artificial Neural Network system and framework. I briefly explored its various features, its ability to evolve complex NN topologies and its particular approach to the optimization of synaptic weights in the evolved NN topologies. We discussed how DXNN uses the size of the NN in the determination of how long to tune the new synaptic weights, which synaptic weights to tune, and which NNs should be allowed to create offspring and be considered fit. We have also discussed the substrate encoding used by the DXNN, which allows it to very effectively build substrates composed of a very large number of neurodes.

Finally, we have went into some detail discussing the DXNN Research group's current projects. The Neural Network Research Repository, the Cyberwarfare project, the Combat UAV project, and the CPU Evolution project. DXNN is the first neuroevolutionary system built purely through Erlang, and which was designed from the very beginning to be implemented only in Erlang. Without Erlang, something as complex, dynamic, and general as this neuroevolutionary platform, could not be created by a single individual so easily. There is an enormous room for growth and further improvement in this system. And it is this that you and I are working on in this book, we are building the next phase of DXNN.

10.9 References

[1] DXNN's records.hrl is available at: https://github.com/CorticalComputer/DXNN
[2] Sher GI (2010) Discover & eXplore Neural Network (DXNN) Platform, a Modular TWEANN. Available at: http://arxiv.org/abs/1008.2412

[3] Gauci J, Stanley KO (2007) Generating Large-Scale Neural Networks Through Discovering Geometric Regularities. Proceedings of the 9th annual conference on Genetic and evolutionary computation GECCO 07, 997.

[4] Siebel NT, Sommer G (2007) Evolutionary Reinforcement Learning of Artificial Neural Networks. International Journal of Hybrid Intelligent Systems 4, 171-183.

[5] Player/Stage/Gazebo: http://playerstage.sourceforge.net/

[6] Risi S, Stanley KO (2010) Indirectly Encoding Neural Plasticity as a Pattern of Local Rules. Neural Plasticity 6226, 1-11.

[7] Woolley BG, Stanley KO (2010) Evolving a Single Scalable Controller for an Octopus Arm with a Variable Number of Segments. Parallel Problem Solving from Nature PPSN XI, 270-279.

[8] DXNN Research Group: www.DXNNResearch.com

[9] OpenSPARC: http://www.opensparc.net/

[10] DXNN Neural Network Research Repository: www.DXNNResearch.com/NNRR

[11] Prdator Vs. Prey Simulation recording:
    http://www.youtube.com/watch?v=HzsDZt8EO70&feature=related

[12] Sher GI (2012) Evolving Chart Pattern Sensitive Neural Network Based Forex TradingAgents. Available at: http://http://arxiv.org/abs/1111.5892.

Part IV
Advanced Neuroevolution: Creating the Cutting Edge

The TWEANN system that we've built so far is a good start, it is clean, direct, with great potential. We have tested it on the simple XOR problem, and it does work. We have discussed that what we are building here is the new DXNN, one that is better than the original version in every way. In this part we will begin adding new advanced features to the TWEANN we've created thus far, chapter by chapter, increasing its capabilities. We will develop a TWEANN that will be the contender of the bleeding edge in this field.

In the following chapters we will first decouple our TWEANN system, in the sense that we will allow for the different features and functionalities of our platform to be held and specified through their own functions and modules. In this manner we can then put our TWEANN system online, as open source, and allow others to concentrate and add various new features and functions (selection functions, activation functions, plasticity functions, mutation operators...), without having to worry about modifying, integrating, and in general dealing with the rest of the code. In this way, contributors can just concentrate on particular aspects of the TWEANN, without digging through the rest of the source code.

Then we will modify the population_monitor module so that it can keep track of the evolutionary statistics of the population it is evolving. Afterwards we add the benchmarker module, a new process that can be used to perform experiments by performing multiple evolutionary runs of some particular problem, and then computing averages, standard deviations, max & min values of the various population parameters, and building graphable files. To actually test the performance of our system after adding these new features, we will require problems more complex than the simple XOR mimicking one, thus in Chapter-14 we add two standard, more complex problems. In Chapter-14 we implement the T-Maze navigation problem, and a few variations of the Pole Balancing problem.

Having built all the necessary tools to move forward and be able to keep track of our system and test the new features, we advance and add plasticity to the evolved neural networks. We implement everything from the standard Hebbian plasticity of various forms, to Oja's rule, and neuromodulation. Afterwards, we make a significant leap and add indirect encoding to the type of NN based agents our TWEAN can evolve. The particular indirect encoding we add is that of *substrate encoding*. Afterwards, we add substrate plasticity, all the while testing the performance and capabilities of our TWEANN on the new problems we've added earlier. By the time we add substrate plasticity, we have developed a highly advanced TWEANN platform, capable of evolving advanced NN based agents with plastic and static networks, different learning algorithms and rules, numerous activation functions, highly dynamic mutation operators, and different types of encoding.

Chapter 11 Decoupling & Modularizing Our Neuroevolutionary Platform

Abstract In this chapter we modify the implementation of our TWEANN system, making all its parts decoupled from one another. By doing so, the plasticity functions, the activation functions, the evolutionary loops, the mutation operators... become independent, each called and referenced through its own modules and function names, and thus allowing for our system to be crowd-sourced, letting anyone have the ability to modify and add new activation functions, mutation operators, and other features, without having to modify or augment any other part of the TWEANN. This effectively makes our system more scalable, and easier to augment, advance, and improve in the future.

In Chapter-10 we discussed DXNN, and the Neural Network Research Repository. I mentioned that it becomes extremely useful and necessary to decouple the TWEANN platform, because it makes it that much easier to later on expand and improve it. Our system already has a number of interesting features that make it somewhat decoupled. For example the activation functions (AFs) that the neurons use, are independent of the neurons themselves. We need only provide the name of the activation function, and if such function exists, the neuron accesses it through *functions:ActivationFunctionName(...)*. We could take this same approach with regards to other features of our TWEANN. As long as we specify a standard interfacing format with those functions, new modules and functions can then be added. Not only would it make the system more modular and upgradeable, but also make those features, where a choice in the use of a particular function is present, *mutatable and evolvable*. Anything that can be specified in the manner in which we specify activation functions, which provides us with a list of available activation functions, can be used in evolution because it gives us the ability to switch between the functionalities, between the function names available in that list.

For example neural plasticity, which we will discuss later on, is the ability of the neuron to adapt and change/learn based on the signals it is processing. This is not training or tuning, this is true learning, in the same manner that biological neurons change and develop additional receptors at a particular place on the dendrite (which is somewhat similar to increasing/decreasing the synaptic weight for some connection)... We can change the neuron to also have a place for plasticity functions. A list like we have for activation functions, can then become available. As soon as new plasticity approaches are developed and added to the *plasticity* module, the tag/name of the said plasticity function can be added to the *plasticity_functions* list. They then would become immediately available as mutatable and thus evolvable features for future and existing neurons. Then, when adding new neurons during evolution to the already existing NN, this approach could give those newly added neurons a chance to use Hebbian [1], or Oja's [2] plasticity functions, as long as the species' constraints allows for it. By adding *mutate_plasticity* mutation operator, we can also allow the already existing neurons to have a chance of mutating, and using the newly added plasticity functions from the available list of said functions.

Another thing that becomes possible when we completely decouple the various features of our TWEANN system, is allowing species to use a different selection function and a different evolutionary loop approach. In this manner the TWEANN can then be easily customizable, and use steady-state evolution, or generational evolution... on different species, depending on just the selection of that particular tag/name of the *selection* and *evolutionary loop* function. And it allows us to change between these various evolutionary strategies and approaches mid-evolution.

In the following sections we are first going to analyze which parts and which elements can have their various parameters and functionalities modularized and decoupled. Then, we will modify our existing system to use this new decoupled approach, and develop a modified genotype encoding to incorporate the new features we will implement.

11.1 What Can be Decoupled?

For the sake of convenience, Fig-11.1 shows again the visualization of our neuroevolutionary platform's architecture from Fig-8.1. The functional elements in the system we've developed so far are as follows: *[polis, scape/sim, population_monitor, agent/exoself, cortex, neuron, sensor, actuator, genome_mutator]*. The functional elements and the processes that have features which can & should be changed are numerous, and we need to figure out what they are. Let's analyze every one of these processes and parts of our neuroevolutionary system, and see what types of features it contains, and whether those features can and should be changed in some way, similar to the activation function example I keep mentioning. I will put an asterisk in front of those parts for which things could be further decoupled.

Polis: This program and system is simply the general monitoring program, in charge of the different scapes, there is nothing yet that we can modify or add to it.

Scape: Each scape, each simulation, is independent in its own right, so there is nothing to decouple here at the moment.

*population_monitor: There are numerous features that can be decoupled in the population_monitor system. *Selection_Algorithm* for example, currently we have two, competition and top3. These are chosen through the case statement, but instead we could create a new *selection_algorithm* module, put all the different types of selection algorithms there, specify the particulars and the format that the selection algorithms created in the future must abide to work with the system, and then call these selection algorithms through the use of *Mod:Fun(...)*. Another element is the *max_attempts* number, which basically specifies if the population should be evolved through a genetic algorithm, by setting the *max_attempts = 1*, or memetic algorithm, in which case we set *max_attempts > 1*. The *population_monitor* process is also the one that decides on whether to evolve the population through steady-state, or through the generational evolutionary loop.

*genome_mutator: The mutation operators are already in the list form, and new mutation operators can be added to the module to let the genome_mutator use them during the topological mutation phase. But there is another element that can be, but is not yet, decoupled: the manner in which the mutation operators are chosen and the percentage with which they are chosen. There can be different functions, different ways of choosing the mutation operators, and with different probabilities. We can have an approach that uses only complexifying mutation operators, another that uses all available mutation operators, and each of those can either choose the mutation operators with the same probability, or each mutation operator with its own probability. These parameters specify our system's evolutionary strategy, and these parameters too can be mutated, and evolved.

*Exoself: Exoself has a number of jobs that can be decoupled. For example, how do we decide what the MAX_ATTEMPTS value should be? This is the number of times we allow the exoself to fail to improve the fitness of the NN during tuning. This value should perhaps be proportional to the number of the weights in the neurons to be tuned, or perhaps it should be a static value... There are many ways that this value can be calculated, and because there are numerous ways and we do not know which is most effective, it is a good feature to decouple. This will allow people to create new *tuning_duration* functions, and test and compare them against each other. Another thing that exoself needs to derive is which neurons to choose, how to choose them, and how many of them to choose for synaptic weight perturbation. How to choose those neurons? Again, numerous approaches and functions can be viable, and so it should be made as simple as possible to create and try out different *tuning_selection_strategy* functions. Another thing that can be decoupled is the actual synaptic weight perturbation intensity. Currently this value is a constant, specified through: *-define(DELTA_MULTIPLIER, math:pi()*2,* in the neuron module. This means that the perturbation values are chosen to be between *-Pi* and *Pi*, but perhaps that is not the best way to go about it. Perhaps simulated annealing would provide a benefit. The neuron's "age", the longer neurons are untouched by mutation operators the more "stable" that we can consider them. In other words, if a NN performs better when some set of neurons is not mutated or perturbed, then it means that this set of neurons has stabilized, works well the way it is, and should continue being left alone in the future. Perhaps the *perturbation_intensity*, the range of the perturbation possible, should be dependent on the stability and age of the neuron to which it is applied. The more stable the neuron, the lower the perturbation intensity applied to it. In this manner, the new neurons will have a chance of having their synaptic weights perturbed with full strength, giving those synaptic weights a chance to jump all the way from -Pi to Pi. While at the same time, the already existing and more stable neural circuits, those that have shown to produce a stable cognitive system, or a module of a cognitive system, will have the perturbation intensity that is lower. The synaptic weight perturbations should perhaps be inversely proportional to the age of the neuron they are applied to. Finally, what about the actual local search function, should it be the augmented stochastic hill climber that we're using? Or perhaps some variant of *ant colony optimization*, or *simulated immune system*?... Again, if we decouple this feature, then others can easily form new local optimization functions, which the system can then use, and flip/mutate between.

*neuron: The neuron too has a few things that can be decoupled. The activation functions are already decoupled, the neuron uses the name of the activation function to produce an output. But perhaps the manner in which the inputs are analyzed should be decoupled. Should we use a dot product? Or something else, perhaps a diff function which calculates the difference between the previous input and the current input. Should there be plasticity? Which too can be specified by a name of the function stored in the *plasticity_function* module. What about preprocessing of the input vectors, should normalization be used? Would it add anything? What about weight saturation, should it be constant as is currently in our system, specified in the neuron module by: *-define(SAT_LIMIT,math:pi()*2)*. Or perhaps saturation limit should be dependent on the activation function? Finally, what about output and input saturation? Should that also be present and be based on some researcher specified function? All of these things could be decoupled.

cortex: Cortex is a synchronization element, and so at the moment there is nothing that can be decoupled with regards to its functionality.

*sensor: Sensors and actuators are already represented by their very own functions, belonging to their very own modules. Each sensor, based on its name, does the preprocessing. Every actuator does postprocessing of the signals sent to it. Though we could add to the sensor records a *parameter* element, which could further specify the type of pre-processing that should be done. In this manner we could have the same sensors whose functionality differs only in the way in which the data is produced, their vector lengths, the type of pre-processing that is conducted, or the format in which the data comes. Is the data simply a vector? Or is the data coming from a camera, and is arranged in a 10 by 10 grid, and is thus in possession of geometrical information. In this way, if for example the NN based agent is substrate encoded, it could then, when evolving or being seeded, use the sensor that also provides geometrical information. While a neural encoded NN based agent would request from the sensor of the same name, the data to be packaged in a simple vector form.

*actuator: As is the case with the sensor elements, the actuators too can have the *parameter* element in their records. The *parameter* could then differentiate the same actuators by the different types of post-processing they conduct, for example.

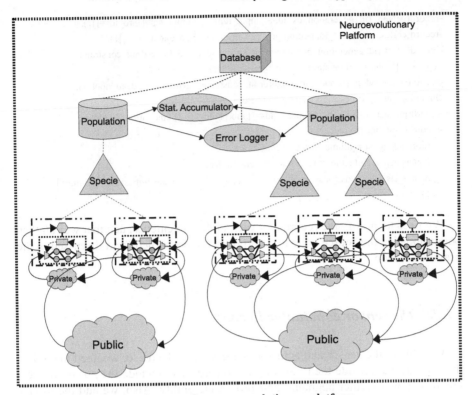

Fig. 11.1 The general architecture of our neuroevolutionary platform.

Certainly other things that should further be decoupled will turn up, as we continue developing and advancing our TWEANN. But for now, the modifications based on these observations will make our system more general, more modular, and more future proof. Though of course there is a downside to it as well, these modifications will also make our system a tiny bit slower, and a bit more complex if we are not careful in the way in which we implement them.

11.2 Updating the Genotype Representation

The elements that make up the genotype of our NN based agents are all in the records.hrl file, shown bellow for convenience:

```
-record(sensor,{id,name,cx_id,scape,vl,fanout_ids=[],generation}).
-record(actuator,{id,name,cx_id,scape,vl,fanin_ids=[],generation}).
```

```
-record(neuron, {id, generation, cx_id, af, input_idps=[], output_ids=[], ro_ids=[]}).
-record(cortex, {id, agent_id, neuron_ids=[], sensor_ids=[], actuator_ids=[]}).
-record(agent, {id, generation, population_id, specie_id, cx_id, fingerprint, constraint,
evo_hist=[], fitness, innovation_factor=0, pattern=[]}).
-record(specie, {id, population_id, fingerprint, constraint, agent_ids=[], dead_pool=[],
champion_ids=[], fitness, innovation_factor=0}).
-record(population, {id,polis_id,specie_ids=[],morphologies=[],innovation_factor}).
-record(constraint, {
    morphology=xor_mimic, %xor_mimic
    connection_architecture = recurrent, %recurrent|feedforward
    neural_afs=[tanh,cos,gaussian,absolute] %[tanh,cos,gaussian,absolute,sin,sqrt,sigmoid]
    }).
```

We need to modify the records for each of these elements such that we can then begin updating the source code to incorporate the decoupled form discussed in the previous section.

11.2.1 The sensor & actuator Records

We modify the sensor and actuator elements first. To do so, we need to modify the records that encode them, making the records also include the *parameters* element that will further augment their processing ability. Also, we add the *format* element to the record, which specifies in what format the signals are to be fed to the NN or in what format the NN should feed its output signals to the element (actuator for example). This will allow us to specify whether the input is a standard vector, or whether it is a 2d or 3d data structure, for example an image coming from a camera. This will allow the substrate encoded NN systems to take advantage of this extra information and appropriately set up the input hyperplanes (a structure used in the substrate encoded NN systems, discussed in a later chapter). Keeping an eye on the future expansions and modifications of our system, and the fact that we will at some point apply the NN based agents to ALife or robotics simulations and problems, we should also perhaps add elements that specify the representation-particulars of the sensor and actuator systems, the manner in which they are to be represented in the simulated environment. This will allow the sensors and actuators to be integrated and evolved by the artificial organisms and simulated robots, allowing the simulator to simulate the visual and physical representation of the sensors through their own physical and visual representation parameters. Thus we also add the elements: *phys_rep* and *vis_rep,* for which the specification format we can create later on, once we begin delving into that area. Finally, we add to the record the elements that the sensors and actuators can use to specify what *pre* and *post* processing functions should be used, if any. Thus the updated sensor and actuator records are as follows:

```
-record(sensor,{id,name,cx_id,scape,vl,fanout_ids=[], generation,format,parameters, phys_rep,
vis_rep, pre_f, post_f}).

-record(actuator,{id,name,cx_id,scape,vl,fanin_ids=[],generation,format, parameters, phys_rep,
vis_rep, pre_f, post_f}).
```

The following are detailed descriptions of the just added elements, and the format they should possess:

- **format**: Is a tuple, and specifies the geometrical format of the signal being generated (if in a sensor record), or expected (if in an actuator record). The format can be set to: *no_geo,* which would specify that there is no geometrical information, it is simply a vector. The specification format of this element will be: *{geo_tag,[Resolution1,Resolution2...]}.*
- **parameters**: Is a list, and can be used to specify various parameters that the sensor or actuator can use to further augment the manner in which they process the input signals, or produce output signals.
- **phys_rep**: Is a list. Specifies the physical representation, if any, of the sensor or actuator. This could be represented as a list of molecules, or hardware elements, each specifying how it is connected to the others. If for example the agent is used in Alife or robotics experiments, this element would specify the physical properties like mass, volume... of the particular sensor or actuator.
- **vis_rep**: Is a list. Specifies the visual representation, if any, of the sensor or actuator. If for example the agent is used in ALife or robotics experiments, this would specify what the sensor or actuator looks like in the simulated world.
- **pre_f**: Is an atom, a name of a function. It is the preprocessing function to be used, if any is listed. This could further separate the different types of sensors of the same type, allowing, through evolution, for our TWEANN to explore the different manners in which signal preprocessing is done for the sensor or actuator used.
- **post_f**: Is an atom, a name of a function. The postprocessing function to be used, if any. This, as the pre_f, can be used to explore the different ways to postprocess the signals for the same sensor or actuator, and thus eventually landing on a perfect combination.

11.2.2 The neuron Record

We have decided that the neuron element must also specify the plasticity function it uses, not just the activation function. We do this by adding to the record the plasticity function designating, pf element. Finally, we also add the element which will specify which aggregation function to use, should it be a simple dot product? Or perhaps the vector difference between the current input vector and the previous input vector? Or should all the input signals be multiplied? The modified neuron record is as follows:

```
-record(neuron, {id, generation, cx_id, af, pf, aggr_f, input_idps=[], output_ids=[], ro_ids=[]}).
```

The added elements and their format and detailed definitions are listed next:

- **pf**: Is an atom, the name of a plasticity function. The plasticity function accepts as input the synaptic weight list, input vector, and output vector. The output of this function is the updated version of the synaptic weights.
- **aggr_f**: Is an atom, the name of the aggregation function. Thus far we have only used the dot function, which simply aggregates the input signals, dots them with the synaptic weights, adds the bias if present, and returns the result, which is to be sent through the activation function. An alternative to the dot product might be as follows: Aggregate the input signals, save the input signals to process registry, subtract the previous input signals from the current input signals (element by element, the previous vector from the current vector), then calculate a dot product of the result and the synaptic weights.

11.2.3 The agent Record

Perhaps it would at some point be a good idea to also allow the agents to choose, or evolve whether to use simulated *annealing* during the tuning phase or not, and which of the numerous and varied *tuning selection functions* to use. Finally, we also add the element which will specify what function to use for the *tuning duration*. The modified agent record is shown below:

```
-record(agent,{id, generation, population_id, specie_id, cx_id, fingerprint, constraint,
evo_hist=[], fitness, innovation_factor=0, pattern=[], tuning_selection_f, annealing_f,
tuning_duration_f, perturbation_range, mutation_operators, mutation_selection_f}).
```

The added elements and their format and detailed definitions are as follows:

- **tuning_selection_f**: Is an atom specifying the function name. This function accepts the list of NIds as input, and then chooses which neurons should be selected for synaptic weight perturbation. There can be any number of ways to do this. We can simply select all NIds, or only those which were created or mutation effected within the last 3 generations, or we could select randomly.
- **tuning_annealing_f**: Is an atom specifying the function name. There are numerous ways to implement simulated annealing based on the various properties of the NN system, for example the neuronal or general agent age. This function should accept as input the list of the selected neuron Ids for perturbation, and then based on it and the *perturbation_range* parameter, calculate the new and

updated perturbation intensity range for each neuron, sending each neuron a signal that it should perturb its weights and the intensity range it should use.

- **tuning_duration_f**: Is a tuple composed of an atom specifying the function name, and a parameter: *{FunctionName,Parameter}*. The Max_Attempts value could also be computed in numerous ways. It could be a constant, independent of the NN's size, which is what we're using now. On the other hand, it could be proportional to the size of the NN, the number of neurons selected for perturbation. After all, the greater the number of neurons recently added to the NN, the longer it would take to get the right combination, the longer it would take to tune their synaptic weights. The input to this function should be the NN size. Though it must be ensured that all the agents which belong to the same species or population, use the same tuning_duration_f, otherwise we could end up with certain agents achieving a higher fitness merely due to having the tuning_duration_f that gives them a larger Max_Attempts. It is for this reason that this value should be set up by the population_monitor, such that all the agents are evaluated against each other based on fair grounds. We want the NN based agents that learn the fastest, that are the most dynamic and most general, given all other things are equal, including the amount of time they are given to tune in. Using different tuning_duration_f for each different agent in the same population would be the same as letting different sprint runners being given different amounts of time to run the track, and then calculating their fitness based on the proportion of time of the total allotted time that they used to run the track. Certainly the one who was given the greatest amount, even if he was a bit slower than the others, would end up wining due to having taken a smaller proportion of the allotted time. This does not make winning runner the fastest... For this reason, this element is set up by the population record, and copied to the agent records, ensuring that all agents in the same population use the same tuning duration function.

- **perturbation_range**: Is a *float()*, a multiplier of *math:pi()*, which specifies the actual perturbation range. So for example if perturbation_range is set to 2, then the actual (before annealing, if any) perturbation range is *2*math:pi()*, thus the random perturbation value is chosen by running: *math:random(2*math:pi())*. In this manner, by allowing the *constraint* record provide a list of perturbation_ranges, as it does with activation functions for example, we can have different agents using different perturbation_range parameters, which will help in experimentation and also make it easier to test this element and its affect on evolution and performance in different problems and applications.

- **mutation_operators**: Is a list of tuples: [{MO,Probability}...] composed of atoms representing the names of mutation operator functions that are available to the agent during its topological mutation phase, and floating point numbers that specify the proportional probability of that mutation operator being chosen verses another operator in the list. It might be advantageous for different agents, different species, or simply different populations, to have different sets of mutation operators. We could also, through this list, specify a particular set of mutation operators for an agent based on its encoding approach. Or we could even perturb the mutation probabilities, thus making our system have the functionality of an evolutionary strategies based evolutionary computation algorithm.

- **tot_topological_mutations_f**: Is a tuple which specifies the name of the function that produces the total number of topological mutations to be applied to the NN, and a parameter for that function. Currently, our system does this through the function: *random:uniform(round(math:pow(TotNeurons,1/2)))*. It is a clean approach and works very well, but perhaps we will later wish to try a different method, or allow different agents to use different functions, to see which work better in a single population. We could achieve this through this parameter, by letting different agents use such different functions.

11.2.4 The population Record

There are numerous things that can be decoupled in the population_monitor process, and there are a number of elements we can add to the population record, which will then independently specify some particular feature of the population. By doing this, others can then create new modules, new functions, and easily augment the general manner in which the population of agents is optimized, or controlled and evolved. We need to have an element which specifies whether the evolutionary loop is generational or steady-state, same as in DXNN. ALife would certainly work best when a variation of the steady-state evolutionary loop is used. Another element can be used to specify what function to use with regards to selection of fit against unfit agents. Should it be random? Simply top3, or the *competition* algorithm we've created? What factors should go into the computation of fitness? Just the fitness of the agent, or also its size? Should a NN based agent with 1000 neurons which has a fitness of 100 be considered more or less fit than a NN composed of 10 neurons with a fitness of 99? Thus the selection algorithm and the fitness computation algorithm can be decoupled as well. The updated record should thus be as follows:

```
-record(population,{id, polis_id, specie_ids=[], morphologies=[], innovation_factor, evo_alg_f,
fitness_f, selection_f}).
```

The added elements, their format, and detailed definitions, are discussed next:

- **evo_alg_f**: Is an atom, which specifies the name of the evolutionary loop. This could be *steady_state* or *generational*. The population_monitor process should, based on this element, choose the evolutionary loop function which will then, using the fitness_f and selection_f, deal with the population of agents, select them, mutate them, keep track of the population's progress...
- **fitness_f**: Is an atom, which specifies the name of the fitness function used to calculate the *true fitness* of the agent based on its fitness score and various

other properties. When for example using the *none* fitness function, the population_monitor accepts the fitness score of the agent as its true fitness. If on the other hand we create a function *size_proportional*, then the population monitor takes the fitness score achieved by the agent, and then scales it down proportional to the size of the NN system. The input to the *fitness f* is the agent id, since by this time the agent will have its fitness score stored in its record within the database. The output of the function is the agent's true fitness.

- **selection_f:** Is an atom, which specifies the name of the selection function. This function accepts the list of agent Ids and their true fitness, and produces a list of fit agents, and the number of offspring each is allotted. When executed within the steady-state evolutionary loop, this value (allotted number of offspring) is converted into a percentage of the agent being selected for the creation of a single offspring to replace it, and a percentage that the agent itself will be released back into the simulated world for reevaluation (If ALife application is in question), instead of producing an offspring.

11.2.5 The constraint Record

This particular record is used to initialize the population record, it specifies the *constraint* of the species to which it belongs, and the choices and functions that the population can use. It is this record that contains the initial list of the available functions for each category: activation functions, plasticity functions, selection functions... We now modify it to accommodate the new decoupled additions, as shown next, in which I also added, in comment form, the possible values from which the parameters for each constraint element can be chosen:

```
-record(constraint,{
    morphology=xor_mimic, %xor_mimic
    connection_architecture = recurrent, %recurrent|feedforward
    neural_afs=[tanh,cos,gaussian,absolute] %[tanh,cos,gaussian,absolute,sin,sqrt,sigmoid],
    neural_pfs=[none], %[none,hebbian,neuro_modulated]
    neural_agr_fs=[dot_product], %[dot_product, mult_product, diff]
    tuning_selection_fs=[all], %[all,all_random, recent,recent_random, lastgen,lastgen_random]
    tuning_duration_f={const,20}, %[{const,20},{nsize_proportional,0.5}]
    tuning_annealing_fs=[none], %[none,gen_proportional]
    perturbation_ranges= [1], %[0.5,1,2,3...]
    agent_encoding_types= [neural], %[neural,substrate]
    mutation_operators= [{mutate_weights,1},{ add_bias,1},{ mutate_af,1}, {add_outlink,1},
{add_inlink,1}, {add_neuron,1}, {outsplice,1}, {add_sensor,1}, {add_actuator,1}], %[{mu-
tate_weights,1}, {add_bias,1}, {remove_bias,1}, {mutate_af,1}, {add_outlink,1}, {re-
move_outLink,1}, {add_inlink,1}, {remove_inlink,1}, {add_sensorlink,1},
{add_actuatorlink,1}, {add_neuron,1},{remove_neuron,1}, {outsplice,1}, {insplice,1},
{add_sensor,1}, {remove_sensor,1}, {add_actuator,1}, {remove_actuator,1}]
```

```
    tot_topological_mutations_fs=[{size_power_propotional,0.5}], %[{size_power_propotional,
0.5}, {size_linear_proportional,1}]
    population_evo_alg_f=generational, %[generational, steady_state]
    population_fitness_postprocessor_f=none, %[none,size_proportional]
    population_selection_f=competition %[competition,top3]
}).
```

As can be noted, the population based parameters are not specified as lists, the way that the neural activation functions are specified for example. Instead, they are specified as single atoms. This is done for consistency. Though it is fine to give entire lists of available functions with regards to activation functions, plasticity, tuning... That is not the case when it comes to the population based functions, since when we run simulations and tests, we want those values to be specified, not chosen randomly during every different run. I've also added, as comments, lists of available functions for selection for the particular decoupled feature, some of which are not yet created, like the *tuning_duration_fs* function by the name *size_proportional* for example. We will eventually create them, as we continue to advance our neuroevolutionary system.

The added elements and their format and detailed definitions are as follows:

- **neural_pfs**: Is a list composed of plasticity function names, such as hebbian, ojas, and others that get added over time. When a neuron is created, it randomly chooses a plasticity function to use, similar to the way it chooses an activation function. In the population_monitor the researcher can choose to use a list composed of a single plasticity type, for example the *none* function, which means that the neurons of this NN will not have plasticity.
- **neural_aggr_fs**: Is a list composed of aggregation function names. The functions can be dot_product, which is the default, or some other later added function like the *diff*, or *mult* function.
- **tuning_selection_fs**: Is a list composed of tuning selection function names. The different agents can start off using different tuning selection functions (neurons chosen for tuning during evaluation), allowing the researcher to determine which of the selection functions is more advantages in a particular simulation. This is also simply a good way to specify in the population monitor, when creating a seed population using the SpeCon variable, the selection algorithm that one wishes for the agents in the population to use.
- **tuning_duration_f**: Is a tuple composed of the tuning duration function name and its parameter. All agents in the population must use the same tuning_duration_f function so that their performance is judged on equal grounds. Thus they are all given the same number of chances to improve during their tuning phase. Also, if we set it to {const,1}, then we can effectively convert our neuroevolutionary system to a genetic rather than memetic algorithm based TWEANN, since every agent will have the exoself simply perform a single evaluation to get its fitness, and then immediately terminate, waiting for the topological mutation phase.

- **tuning_annealing_fs**: Is a list composed of annealing function names, which could also be set to *none*. This is the default, and is the manner in which our current neuroevolutionary system functions. Different agents can start off with different annealing functions if the list is composed of more than one function.
- **perturbation_ranges**: This is a list of floats(), each of which specifies the multiplier of math:pi(). The actual perturbation range is: Multiplier*math:pi(). The perturbation_ranges can be composed of a single float, or a list of them if one wishes to experiment with a population composed of agents using different perturbation ranges.
- **agent_encoding_types**: This is a list of atoms, which specify the different types of encodings. At the moment we only have the *neural* encoding implemented. In later chapters we will implement a substrate encoding type, the two types used in DXNN for example. Other researchers will add other encoding approaches over time. This is what is used by the exoself when it is summoning the NN system. Based on the encoding type, it will compose the NN system differently, performing different steps for the different systems. The list can contain multiple types, thus the population could be composed of different types of agents, some neural encoded, some substrate encoded...
- **mutation_operators**: Is a list of tuples, composed of function names of the mutation operators available to a particular agent, and the probability of being used, as proportional to other operators. We would usually have a single list for the entire population, or have different populations each with a different set of mutation operator lists available, if for example we wish to test whether a mutation operator list containing both, pruning and complexifying operators, produces better results than one containing only complexifying operators.
- **tot_topological_mutations_fs**: Is a list of tuples, where each tuple is composed of a function name, and a function parameter. This allows us to have a population of agents where different agents can use different functions that determine the amount of topological mutations that is used to produce the agent's offspring.
- **population_evo_alg_f**: Is an atom specifying the evolutionary loop function, generational or steady_state for example. A population should use only a single evolutionary loop function for all its agents. A particular population_monitor must be fair to all its agents, judging them all in the same way (otherwise we cannot know whether the agent is superior due to its fitness, or due to its preferential treatment) and so only a single type of evolutionary loop type should be used for a single population. Of course one could run multiple populations, each using a different type of evolutionary loop, existing in the same scape (like in Alife simulation for example).
- **population_fitness_postprocessor_f**: Is an atom specifying the fitness postprocessor function. It could simply be none, which would imply that the fitness score achieved by the agent is what its true fitness is, or it could scale its fitness score proportional to the average complexity of the population, which would

give advantage to smaller NNs which perform similarly to larger ones, for example.

- **population_selection_f**: Is an atom specifying the name of the selection function. A single population uses a single particular selection function to separate the fit agents from the unfit.

We would specify and specialize the INIT_CONSTRAINTS tuple for each experiment we'd like to run, starting the population_monitor using the specified constraints record. We should allow our neuroevolutionary system to start with multiple populations, or a single population but multiple species, each specie could then use different constraints parameters. At this time though, we will assume that the population treats all its agents the same, and does not segregate them into particular species, each with its own specie_monitor (something that can be implemented later on).

To specify a population using some particular combination of evolutionary loop algorithms, fitness postprocessor, and selection functions, we would do as follows:

```
-define(INIT_CONSTRAINTS,
    [#constraint{morphology=Morphology, connection_architecture=CA, population_evo_alg_f
    =EvoAlg, population_fitness_postprocessor_f =FitPostProc, population_selection_f
    =Selection} || Morphology ← [xor_mimic],CA ← [feedforward], EvoAlg ← [steady_state],
    FitPostProc ← [none], Selection ← [top3]]
).
```

As you can see, the lists: [steady_state], [none], [top3], could be composed of multiple function names, in which case multiple constraints would be generated, which would then, after we implement this feature, allow our neuroevolutionary system to start with multiple species, each with its own permutation of these parameters.

11.3 Updating the records.hrl

Because the specifications, formatting, the way in which the various elements, ids, functions, parameters, of all these records are becoming more numerous and complex, we need to create a document where all this information and specifications detail can be found. We will use the records.hrl file, adding a list of comments to it which specifies the formatting, type and pattern, of every element in the various records stored. In this manner, as we continue to expand our neuroevolutionary system, we will know exactly what format and in what form, each element of the record comes. Listing-11.1 shows the new updated records.hrl.

Listing-11.1 The updated and commented records.hrl file

```
-record(sensor,{id,name,cx_id,scape,vl,fanout_ids=[],generation,format,parameters,
phys_rep,vis_rep,pre_f,post_f}).
-record(actuator,{id,name,cx_id,scape,vl,fanin_ids=[],generation,format,parameters,
phys_rep,vis_rep,pre_f,post_f}).
-record(neuron, {id, generation, cx_id, af, pf, agr_f, input_idps=[], output_ids=[], ro_ids=[]}).
-record(cortex, {id, agent_id, neuron_ids=[], sensor_ids=[], actuator_ids=[]}).
-record(agent,{id, generation, population_id, specie_id, cx_id, fingerprint, constraint,
evo_hist=[], fitness, innovation_factor=0, pattern=[], tuning_selection_f, annealing_parameter,
tuning_duration_f, perturbation_range}).
-record(specie,{id, population_id, fingerprint, constraint, agent_ids=[], dead_pool=[],
champion_ids=[], fitness, innovation_factor=0}).
-record(population,{id, polis_id, specie_ids=[], morphologies=[], innovation_factor, evo_alg_f,
fitness_f, selection_f}).
-record(constraint,{
    morphology=xor_mimic, %xor_mimic
    connection_architecture = recurrent, %recurrent|feedforward
    neural_afs=[tanh,cos,gaussian,absolute], %[tanh,cos,gaussian,absolute,sin,sqrt,sigmoid],
    neural_pfs=[none], %[none,hebbian,neuro_modulated]
    neural_agr_fs=[dot_product], %[dot_product, mult_product, diff]
    tuning_selection_fs=[all], %[all,all_random, recent,recent_random, lastgen,lastgen_random]
    tuning_duration_f={const,20}, %[{const,20},{nsize_proportional,0.5}]
    annealing_parameters=[1], %[1,0.5]
    perturbation_ranges=[1], %[1,0.5,2]
    mutation_operators= [{mutate_weights,1},{ add_bias,1}, {mutate_af,1}, {add_outlink,1},
{add_inlink,1}, {add_neuron,1}, {outsplice,1}, {add_sensor,1}, {add_actuator,1}], %[{mu-
tate_weights,1}, {add_bias,1}, {remove_bias,1}, {mutate_af,1}, {add_outlink,1}, {re-
move_outLink,1}, {add_inlink,1}, {remove_inlink,1}, {add_sensorlink,1},
{add_actuatorlink,1}, {add_neuron,1}, {remove_neuron,1}, {outsplice,1}, {insplice,1},
{add_sensor,1}, {remove_sensor,1}, {add_actuator,1}, {remove_actuator,1}]
    population_evo_alg_fs=generational_default, %[generational, steady_state]
    population_fitness_fs=size_proportional, %[none,size_proportional]
    population_selection_fs=competition %[competition,top3]
}).

%%%% sensor:
%id= {{-1::LayerCoordinate, float()::Unique_Id()}, sensor}
%name= atom()
%cx_id= cortex.id
%scape= {private|public, atom()::ScapeName}
%vl= int()
%fanout_ids= [neuron.id...]
%generation=int()
%format= {no_geo|geo,[int()::Resolution...]}
```

```
%parameters= [any()...]
%phys_rep= [any()...]
%vis_rep= [any()...]
%pre_f= atom()::FunctionName
%post_f= atom()::FunctionName

%%%actuator:
%id= {{1::LayerCoordinate,generate_UniqueId()},actuator}
%name= atom()
%cx_id= cortex.id
%scape= {private|public, atom()::ScapeName}
%vl= int()
%fanout_ids= [neuron.id...]
%generation=int()
%format= {no_geo|geo,[int()::Resolution...]}
%parameters= [any()...]
%phys_rep= [any()...]
%vis_rep= [any()...]
%pre_f= atom()::FunctionName
%post_f= atom()::FunctionName

%%%neuron:
%id= {{float()::LayerCoordinate, float()::Unique_Id},neuron}
%generation= int()
%cx_id= cortex.id
%af= atom()::FunctionName
%pf= atom()::FunctionName
%aggr_f= atom()::FunctionName
%input_idps= [{Input_Id,Weights},{neuron.id|sensor.id,[float()...]}...]
%output_ids= [neuron.id|actuator.id...]
%ro_ids= [neuron.id...]

%%%cortex:
%id= {{origin, float()::Unique_Id()},cortex}
%agent_id= agent.id
%neuron_ids= [neuron.id...]
%sensor_ids= [sensor.id...]
%actuator_ids= [actuator.id...]

%%%agent:
%id= {float()::Unique_Id(),agent}
%generation= int()
%population_id= population.id
%specie_id= specie.id
%cx_id= cortex.id
```

```
%fingerprint= fingerprint()
%constraint= constraint()
%evo_hist= [OperatorAppllied...]
% {atom()::MO_Name, ElementA.id, ElementB.id, ElementC.id}
% {atom()::MO_Name, ElementA.id, ElementB.id}
% {atom()::MO_Name, ElementA.id}
%fitness= float()
%innovation_factor= int()
%pattern= [{float()::LayerCoordinate, N_Ids}...]
%tuning_selection_f= atom()::FunctionName
%annealing_parameter= float()::FunctionName
%tuning_duration_f= {atom()::FunctionName ,any()::Parameter}
%perturbation_range= float()
%mutation_operators= [{atom()::FunctionName,float()}...]
%tot_topological_mutations_f= {atom()::FunctionName,float()}


%%%specie:
%id= atom()|{float()::Unique_Id,specie}
%population_id= population.id
%fingerprint= fingerprint()
%constraint= constraint()
%agent_ids= [agent.id...]
%dead_pool= [agent.id...]
%champion_ids= [agent.id..]
%fitness= float()
%innovation_factor= int()


%%%population:
%id= atom()|{float()::Unique_Id,population}
%polis_id= polis.id
%specie_ids= [specie.id...]
%morphologies= [atom()::Morphology_Name...]
%innovation_factor= int()
%evo_alg_f= atom()::FunctionName
%fitness_f= atom()::FunctionName
%selection_f= atom()::FunctionName


%%%fingerprint:
%generalized_sensors= [sensor()::init...]
% sensor.id = undefined
% sensor.cx_id = undefined
% sensor.fanout_ids = []
%generlized_actuators= [actuator()::init...]
% actuator.id = undefined
% actuator.cx_id = undefined
```

```
% actuator.fanin_ids = []
%generalized_pattern= [{float()::LayerCoordinate,int()::TotNeurons}...]
%generalized_evohist= [GeneralizedOperatorApplied...]
% {atom()::MO_Name,{float()::ElementA_LayerCoordinate,atom()::ElementA_Type},
{ElementB_LayerCoordinate,ElementB_Type},{ElementC_LayerCoordinate,ElementC_Type}
},
% {atom()::MO_Name,{float()::ElementA_LayerCoordinate,atom()::ElementA_Type},
{ElementB_LayerCoordinate,ElementB_Type}},
% {atom()::MO_Name,{float()::ElementA_LayerCoordinate,atom()::ElementA_Type}},
% {atom()::MO_Name},


%%%constraint:
%morphology=xor_mimic, %xor_mimic
%connection_architecture = recurrent, %recurrent|feedforward
%neural_afs=[tanh,cos,gaussian,absolute] %[tanh,cos,gaussian,absolute,sin,sqrt,sigmoid],
%neural_pfs=[none], %[none,hebbian,neuro_modulated]
%neural_aggr_fs=[dot_product], %[dot_product, mult_product, diff]
%tuning_selection_fs=[all], %[all,all_random, recent,recent_random, lastgen,lastgen_random]
%tuning_duration_f={const,20}, %[{const,20},{size_proportional,0.5}]
%annealing_parameters=[1], %[1,0.5]
%perturbation_ranges=[1], %[0.5,1,2,3...]
%agent_encoding_types= [neural], %[neural,substrate]
%mutation_operators= [{atom()::FunctionName,float()}...]
%tot_topological_mutations_fs = [{size_power_propotional,0.5}],
%[{size_power_propotional,0.5},{size_linear_proportional,1}]
%population_evo_alg_fs=generational_default, %[generational, steady_state]
%population_fitness_fs=size_proportional, %[none,size_proportional]
%population_selection_fs=competition %[competition,top3]


%%%polis
%id= atom()|float()|{float()::Unique_Id,polis}|{atom()::PolisName,polis}


%%%scape
%id= atom()|float()|{float()::Unique_Id,scape}|{atom()::ScapeName,scape}
```

Some of the defined elements, like the polis id and the scape id, we are not yet using. But we will eventually start using these elements, and so their format is defined here for convenience. Having now discussed in detail the various features and decoupled elements of our system, we will implement them in the following section.

11.4 Updating the Modules

Having discussed the additions we wish to make, and elements of the system we wish to decouple and put into their own respective modules, we are now ready to develop these functions, and update our neuroevolutionary system such that it is capable of using the modified records. We will first update the genotype module, then genome_mutator, then population_monitor, then exoself, and then finally the neuron module.

11.4.1 Updating the genotype Module

In the genotype module we need to modify the functions which set up the records for the agent and neuron elements. Also, it is in the *construct_Cortex/3* function that the actual NN genotype is created in, and the elements are linked together into a topological structure, so it is in this function that we have to set up a case that constructs the NN system based on the actual agent type (*neural* or *substrate*).

We first update the *construct_Agent/3* function to randomly select a tuning, annealing, and duration functions, and the tuning perturbation multiplier, as shown next:

```
construct_Agent(Specie_Id,Agent_Id,SpecCon)->
    random:seed(now()),
    Generation = 0,
    {Cx_Id,Pattern} = construct_Cortex(Agent_Id,Generation,SpecCon),
    Agent = #agent{
        id = Agent_Id,
        cx_id = Cx_Id,
        specie_id = Specie_Id,
        constraint = SpecCon,
        generation = Generation,
        pattern = Pattern,
        tuning_selection_f = random_element(SpecCon#constraint.tuning_selection_fs),
        annealing_parameter = random_element(SpecCon#constraint.annealing_parameters),
        tuning_duration_f = SpecCon#constraint.tuning_duration_f,
        perturbation_range = random_element(SpecCon#constraint.perturbation_ranges),
        mutation_operators = SpecCon#constraint.mutation_operators,
        tot_topological_mutations_f = random_element(SpecCon#constraint.tot_topological_
mutations_fs ),
        evo_hist = []
    },
    write(Agent),
    update_fingerprint(Agent_Id).
```

The *random_element/1* function simply accepts a list, and returns a random element from the list, chosen with uniform distribution.

We then update the *construct_Cortex/3* function, so that it uses a case to select how it builds the seed NN topology and links the elements together, based on the agent encoding type (neural or substrate):

```
construct_Cortex(Agent_Id,Generation,SpecCon)->
   Cx_Id = {{origin,generate_UniqueId()},cortex},
   Morphology = SpecCon#constraint.morphology,
   case random_element(SpecCon#constraint.agent_encoding_types) of
           neural ->
                   Sensors = [S#sensor{id={{-1,generate_UniqueId()},sensor}, cx_id=Cx_Id,
generation=Generation}|| S<- morphology:get_InitSensors(Morphology)],
                   Actuators = [A#actuator{id={{1,generate_UniqueId()},actuator},cx_id=Cx_Id,
generation=Generation}||A<-morphology:get_InitActuators(Morphology)],
                   N_Ids=construct_InitialNeuroLayer(Cx_Id,Generation,SpecCon, Sensors,
Actuators,[],[]),
                   S_Ids = [S#sensor.id || S<-Sensors],
                   A_Ids = [A#actuator.id || A<-Actuators],
                   Cortex = #cortex{
                           id = Cx_Id,
                           agent_id = Agent_Id,
                           neuron_ids = N_Ids,
                           sensor_ids = S_Ids,
                           actuator_ids = A_Ids
                   }
   end,
   write(Cortex),
   {Cx_Id,[{0,N_Ids}]}.
```

Next, a simple modification is made to the *construct_Neuron/6* function, which makes the neuron also randomly select an annealing function and an aggregation function, in addition to a randomly selected activation function:

```
construct_Neuron(Cx_Id,Generation,SpecCon,N_Id,Input_Specs,Output_Ids)->
       Input_IdPs = create_InputIdPs(Input_Specs,[]),
       Neuron=#neuron{
           id=N_Id,
           cx_id = Cx_Id,
           generation=Generation,
           af=generate_NeuronAF(SpecCon#constraint.neural_afs),
           pf=generate_NeuronPF(SpecCon#constraint.neural_pfs),
           aggr_f=generate_NeuronAggrF(SpecCon#constraint.neural_aggr_fs),
           input_idps=Input_IdPs,
```

```
                output_ids=Output_Ids,
                ro_ids = calculate_ROIds(N_Id,Output_Ids,[])
        },
        write(Neuron).
```

The *generate_NeuronPF/1* and *generate_NeuronAggrF/1* functions are analogous to the generate_NeuronAF/1:

```
        generate_NeuronAF(Activation_Functions)->
            case Activation_Functions of
                [] ->
                        tanh;
                Other ->
                        lists:nth(random:uniform(length(Other)),Other)
            end.
%The generate_NeuronAF/1 accepts a list of activation function tags, and returns a randomly
chosen one. If an empty list was passed as the parameter, the function returns the default tanh
tag.


        generate_NeuronPF(Plasticity_Functions)->
            case Plasticity_Functions of
                [] ->
                        none;
                Other ->
                        lists:nth(random:uniform(length(Other)),Other)
            end.
%The generate_NeuronPF/1 accepts a list of plasticity function tags, and returns a randomly
chosen one. If an empty list was passed as the parameter, the function returns the default none
tag.


        generate_NeuronAggrF(Aggregation_Functions)->
            case Aggregation_Functions of
                [] ->
                        dot_product;
                Other ->
                        lists:nth(random:uniform(length(Other)),Other)
            end.
%The generate_NeuronAggrF/1 accepts a list of aggregation function tags, and returns a ran-
domly chosen one. If an empty list was passed as the parameter, the function returns the default
dot_product tag.
```

With these small simple additions, this module is now fully updated, and the agents created through it in the future, will be able to include the newly added constraint parameters into their genotype.

11.4.2 Updating the genome_mutator Module

With the genotype module updated, we now have a way to create the new version of genotypes which use the updated building blocks and the updated records. We now need to update the genome_mutator module so that we can mutate such genotypes, and take advantage of the new information available in them. For the genome_mutator we want to add a method that allows different mutation operators to have different probabilities of being selected, a separate module that contains the functions that allow the genome_mutator to choose the neurons to be mutated through different algorithms, a new module that contains the functions which provide different ways of calculating how many mutation operators should be applied to the NN based agent, and finally, a new set of mutation operators that can mutate the new genotypical features (plasticity and aggregation functions for example).

The very first thing that needs to be updated in this module is the *apply_Mutators/1* function:

```
apply_Mutators(Agent_Id)->
        A = genotype:read({agent,Agent_Id}),
        Cx = genotype:read({cortex,A#agent.cx_id}),
        TotNeurons = length(Cx#cortex.neuron_ids),
        TotMutations = random:uniform(round(math:pow(TotNeurons,1/2))),
        io:format("Tot neurons:~p Performing Tot mutations:~p on:~p~n",[
TotNeurons, TotMutations,Agent_Id]),
        apply_Mutators(Agent_Id,TotMutations).
```

Because we change the very way that TotMutations is calculated, by creating a whole new function which calculates the total topological mutations value. And because *apply_Mutators/1*, after this modification, does nothing but execute the *tot_topological_mutations* function, we can delete it and move the remaining functionality to the *mutate/1* function, as shown next:

```
mutate(Agent_Id)->
    random:seed(now()),
    F = fun()->
            A = genotype:read({agent,Agent_Id}),
            {TTM_Name,Parameter} = A#agent.tot_topological_mutations_f,
            TotMutations = tot_topological_mutations:TTM_Name(Parameter,Agent_Id),
            OldGeneration = A#agent.generation,
            NewGeneration = OldGeneration+1,
            genotype:write(A#agent{generation = NewGeneration}),
            apply_Mutators(Agent_Id,TotMutations),
            genotype:update_fingerprint(Agent_Id)
    end,
    mnesia:transaction(F).
```

%The function mutate/1 first updates the generation of the agent to be mutated, then calculates the number of mutation operators to be applied to it by executing the tot_topological_mutations:TTM_Name/2 function, and then finally runs the apply_Mutators/2 function, which mutates the agent. Once the agent is mutated, the function updates its fingerprint by executing the genotype:update_finrgerprint/1 function.

As can be noted from the above implementation, we now let mutate/1 function call the apply_Mutators/2 directly. Rather than first calling apply_Mutators/1, which then called the apply_Mutators/2 function.

Since there are many ways to calculate TotMutations, we create the tot_topological_mutations module, which can store the different functions which can calculate this value. At this time, this new module will only contain 2 such functions, as shown in Listing-11.2.

Listing-11.2 The implementation of the tot_topological_mutations module, with two available functions.

```
-module(tot_topological_mutations).
-compile(export_all).
-include("records.hrl").

%ncount_exponential/2 calculates TotMutations by putting the size of the NN to some power:
Power
ncount_exponential(Power,Agent_Id)->
    A = genotype:read({agent,Agent_Id}),
    Cx = genotype:read({cortex,A#agent.cx_id}),
    TotNeurons = length(Cx#cortex.neuron_ids),
    TotMutations = random:uniform(round(math:pow(TotNeurons,Power))),
    io:format("Tot neurons:~p Performing Tot mutations:~p on:~p~n",[TotNeurons,
TotMutations, Agent_Id]),
    TotMutations.

%ncount_linear/2 calculates TotMutations by multiplying the size of the NN by the value: Multiplier.
ncount_linear(Multiplier,Agent_Id)->
    A = genotype:read({agent,Agent_Id}),
    Cx = genotype:read({cortex,A#agent.cx_id}),
    TotNeurons = length(Cx#cortex.neuron_ids),
    TotMutations = TotNeurons*Multiplier,
    io:format("Tot neurons:~p Performing Tot mutations:~p on:~p~n",[TotNeurons,
TotMutations, Agent_Id]),
    TotMutations.
```

The next thing we need to change is the way mutation operators are chosen. Instead of uniform distribution, we should, with every mutation operator, also provide a value that dictates its percentage of being chosen in comparison to other mutation operators in the list. This can be done by specifying the mutation operators in tuple form: *{MutationOperator,RelativeProbability}* for example. The probability can be a pie section, where the total is all the *RelativeProbabilities* added together. So for example if we have the following list of 4 mutation operators:

```
[{add_neuron,2},{add_sensor,1},{add_outlink,5},{mutate_weights,10}]
```

Then the total is 2+1+5+10 = 18, and we could then use *Choice = random:uniform(18)* to generate uniformly a random number between 1 and 18, and then go in order, through the mutation operators from left to right, and see where the generated value lands. It is like spinning a roulette wheel, where each mutation operator gets a slice on the wheel proportional to its RelativeProbability. Thus, if Choice = 4, then we go past the add_neuron, past the add_sensor, and land on add_outlink, since it is located between 3 and 8 inclusive, and 4 lands between those borders. This is visually demonstrated in Fig-11.2.

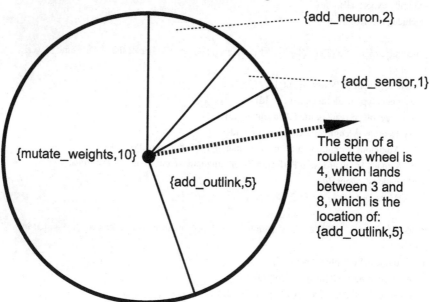

Fig. 11.2 The roulette wheel approach to mutation operator selection probability.

We can implement this approach by first modifying the way in which the *mutation_operators* are specified, changing it from a list of atoms to a list of tuples as discussed above. And then modify the function *apply_NeuralMutator/1*, which randomly picks out a mutation operator from the available list, and applies it to the NN system.

We originally stored the mutation operator function names in the *MUTATORS* macro in the genome_mutator module. Having now updated the records, all the names of the mutation operators are now listed in the constraint and the mutation_operators element of the agent's record. The mutation operators are specified in the records.hrl as follows:

```
mutation_operators= [{mutate_weights,1},{ add_bias,1},{ mutate_af,1}, {add_outlink,1},
{add_inlink,1}, {add_neuron,1}, {outsplice,1}, {add_sensor,1}, {add_actuator,1}],
```

Thus we modify the apply_NeuralMutator/1 function from its original form of:

```
apply_NeuralMutator(Agent_Id)->
  F = fun()->
        Mutators = ?MUTATORS,
        Mutator = lists:nth(random:uniform(length(Mutators)),Mutators)
        io:format("Mutation Operator:~p~n",[Mutator]),
        genome_mutator:Mutator(Agent_Id)
  end,
  mnesia:transaction(F).
```

To one that uses a function capable of extracting the mutation operators with the probability proportional to the values specified in the tuples of the mutation_operators list:

```
apply_NeuralMutator(Agent_Id)->
  F = fun()->
        A = genotype:read({agent,Agent_Id}),
        MutatorsP = A#agent.mutation_operators,
        Mutator = select_random_MO(MutatorsP)
        io:format("Mutation Operator:~p~n",[Mutator]),
        genome_mutator:Mutator(Agent_Id)
  end,
  mnesia:transaction(F).
%The apply_NeuralMutator/1 function applies the available mutation operators to the NN. Be-
cause the genotype is stored in mnesia, if the mutation operator function exits with an error, the
database made changes are retracted, and a new mutation operator can then be applied to the
agent, as if the previous unsuccessful mutation operator was never applied. The mutation opera-
tor to be applied to the agent is chosen randomly from the agent's mutation_operators list, with
the probability of each mutation chosen being proportional to its relative probability value.

select_random_MO(MutatorsP)->
  TotSize = lists:sum([SliceSize || {_MO,SliceSize} <- MutatorsP]),
```

```
Choice=random:uniform(TotSize),
select_random_MO(MutatorsP,Choice,0).


select_random_MO([{MO,SliceSize}|MOs],Choice,Range_From)->
      Range_To = Range_From+SliceSize,
      case (Choice >= Range_From) and (Choice =< Range_To) of
            true ->
                  MO;
            false ->
                        select_random_MO(MOs,Choice,Range_To)
      end;
select_random_MO([],_Choice,_Range_From)->
      exit("********ERROR:select_random_MO:: reached [] without selecting a mutation
operator.").
```
%select_random_MO/1, using the analogy of a roulette wheel, the function first calculates the entire area of the wheel by summing together all the slice sizes. The function then chooses randomly a spot on the wheel, and through select_random_MO/3 calculates where that spot is located, with regards to the mutation operator that it falls on. Since some slices are larger than others, they will have uniformly larger probabilities of being selected.

With this modification, the genome_mutator module can now function with our updated system architecture. The way we currently have the mutation operators setup and specified in the records.hrl in the constraint record, is that each one's "slice size" is 1, thus they are still all equally likely to be selected. But this new approach gives us the ability to test mutation operator lists where each operator has a different chance of being selected. In this way we can rapidly convert our memetic algorithm based neuroevolutionary system, into a genetic algorithm based one, by for example setting the max_attempts parameter to 1, and drastically increasing the probability of selecting the mutate_weights mutation operator.

Having now updated the essential parts of our mutation algorithm, we need to add the new mutation operators, ones that mutate plasticity functions, and other parameters, similar to the manner in which the mutate_af (mutate activation function) works. To be able to evolve the new decoupled features of our system, we should add the following new mutation operators:

- **mutate_pf**: Mutates the plasticity function. Checks the currently used plasticity function, and if there are other plasticity functions available in the *constraint* of the agent, then the current function is swapped for a random new one. If there are no new plasticity functions available, the operator exits with an error, thus not wasting a mutation on the non available mutation operator.
- **mutate_aggrf**: Mutates the neural aggregation function. As with plasticity and activation functions, it checks if there are other aggregation functions available. If there are, then the currently used function is mutated into another one. If there aren't, then the mutation operator exits with an error.

We add these mutate_pf and mutate_aggrf mutation operators to the genome_mutator module, as shown in Listing-11.3. Similar to the mutate_af operator, the mutate_pf mutation operator chooses a random neuron in the NN, and then changes its currently used plasticity function to another one available in the plasticity_fs list in the agent's constraint record. The same way, the mutate_aggrf operator chooses a random neuron, and then mutates its aggregation function (dot_product, diff...). In both cases, if the only available such function is the one already being used by the neuron, then it is left in place, and our neuroevolutionary system tries to use another mutation operator on the agent.

Listing-11.3 The implementation of the new mutate_pf (mutate plasticity function) and mutate_aggrf (mutate aggregation function) mutation operators.

```erlang
mutate_pf(Agent_Id)->
    A = genotype:read({agent,Agent_Id}),
    Cx_Id = A#agent.cx_id,
    Cx = genotype:read({cortex,Cx_Id}),
    N_Ids = Cx#cortex.neuron_ids,
    N_Id = lists:nth(random:uniform(length(N_Ids)),N_Ids),
    Generation = A#agent.generation,

    N = genotype:read({neuron,N_Id}),
    PF = N#neuron.pf,
    case (A#agent.constraint)#constraint.neural_pfs -- [PF] of
        [] ->
            exit("********ERROR:mutate_pf:: There are no other plasticity functions to
use.");
        Plasticity_Functions ->
            NewPF = lists:nth(random:uniform(length(Plasticity_Functions)),
Plasticity_Functions),
            U_N = N#neuron{pf=NewPF,generation=Generation},
            EvoHist = A#agent.evo_hist,
            U_EvoHist = [{mutate_pf,N_Id}|EvoHist],
            U_A = A#agent{evo_hist=U_EvoHist},
            genotype:write(U_N),
            genotype:write(U_A)
    end.
%The mutate_pf/1 function chooses a random neuron, and then changes its currently used plas-
ticity function into another one available from the neural_pfs list of the agent's constraint rec-
ord.

mutate_aggrf(Agent_Id)->
    A = genotype:read({agent,Agent_Id}),
    Cx_Id = A#agent.cx_id,
    Cx = genotype:read({cortex,Cx_Id}),
```

```
    N_Ids = Cx#cortex.neuron_ids,
    N_Id = lists:nth(random:uniform(length(N_Ids)),N_Ids),
    Generation = A#agent.generation,


    N = genotype:read({neuron,N_Id}),
    AggrF = N#neuron.aggr_f,
    case (A#agent.constraint)#constraint.neural_aggr_fs -- [AggrF] of
        [] ->
                exit("*********ERROR:mutate_aggrf:: There are no other aggregation func-
tions to use.");
        Aggregation_Functions ->
                NewAggrF = lists:nth(random:uniform(length(Aggregation_Functions)),
Aggregation_Functions),
                U_N = N#neuron{aggr_f=NewAggrF,generation=Generation},
                EvoHist = A#agent.evo_hist,
                U_EvoHist = [{mutate_aggrf,N_Id}|EvoHist],
                U_A = A#agent{evo_hist=U_EvoHist},
                genotype:write(U_N),
                genotype:write(U_A)
    end.
%The mutate_aggrf/1 function chooses a random neuron, and then changes its currently used
aggregation function into another one available from the neural_aggr_fs list of the agent's con-
straint record.
```

It is also worth adding the following mutation operators, that have nothing to do with topological mutation, but instead mutate the evolutionary strategy, the evolutionary search algorithm itself:

- **mutate_tuning_selection**: Mutates the tuning selection function used by the agent to tune the NN during training.
- **mutate_tuning_duration**: Mutates the tuning duration function used by the agent to tune the NN during training.
- **mutate_tuning_annealing**: Mutates the tuning annealing parameter used by the agent to tune the NN during training.
- **mutate_perturbation_range**: Mutates the perturbation range used by the exoself when tuning the synaptic weights of the NN.
- **mutate_tot_topological_mutations**: Mutates the function responsible for calculating the total number of topological mutations to be applied to the NN.

The evolutionary strategy mutation operators and their parameters, are unrelated to the actual topological mutation. We should apply them separately from the topological mutation operators. Not only should they be applied separately, but also the number of these evolutionary strategy mutation operators, and the probability of applying them, should be independent of the topological mutation operators. For this reason we add and define the new macro (this one is going to be a descriptive one): *?SEARCH_PARAMETERS_MUTATION_PROBABILITY*, in the genome_mutator module. We also further augment the mutate/1 function, adding the *mutate_SearchParameters/1* function to it. The mutate_SearchParameters/1 function is executed every time the agent undergoes a topological mutation phase. The new mutation probability value defines the chance that the mutate_SearchParameters/1 function performs any type of evolutionary strategy mutation.

In the case that the evolutionary strategy (ES) is mutated, the number of evolutionary strategy mutation operators applied to the agent is uniformly and randomly chosen to be between 1 and total number of ES mutation operators available. In a similar way we used to define the standard topological mutation operators at the top of the *genome_mutator* module, we now define the ES mutation operators, while having moved the topological mutation operators to the constraint record. The new ES mutation operators are defined as follows:

```
-define(ES_MUTATORS,[
    mutate_tuning_selection,
    mutate_tuning_duration,
    mutate_tuning_annealing,
    mutate_tot_topological_mutations
]).
```

Though a case could be made that we should define these ES mutation operators in the same way we are now defining the topological mutation operators, there is at this point no need for it. Since the addition of ES mutation is done primarily to allow our neuroevolutionary system to have a greater level of flexibility, and so that it can be tweaked more easily in the future with different types of search algorithms and parameters.

The updated version of the *mutate/1* function, and the *mutate_SearchParameters/1* function that it executes, is shown in Listing-11.4. As you will notice, the mutate_SearchParameters/1 function operates very similarly to the way the original function that applied topological mutation operators functioned.

Listing-11.4 The new version of the mutate/1 function, with the added mutate_SearchParamters/1 function that applies, with a probability of *?SEARCH_PARAMETERS_MUTATION_PROBABILITY*, a random number of ES mutation operators to the agent.

```
mutate(Agent_Id)->
    random:seed(now()),
    F = fun()->
        mutate_SearchParameters(Agent_Id),
        A = genotype:read({agent,Agent_Id}),
        {TTM_Name,Parameter} = A#agent.tot_topological_mutations_f,
        TotMutations = tot_topological_mutations:TTM_Name(Parameter,Agent_Id),
        OldGeneration = A#agent.generation,
```

```erlang
                NewGeneration = OldGeneration+1,
                genotype:write(A#agent{generation = NewGeneration}),
                apply_Mutators(Agent_Id,TotMutations),
                genotype:update_fingerprint(Agent_Id)
        end,
        mnesia:transaction(F).
```
%The function mutate/1 first updates the generation of the agent to be mutated, then calculates the number of mutation operators to be applied to it by executing the tot_topological_mutations:TTM_Name/2 function, and then finally runs the apply_Mutators/2 function, which mutates the agent. Once the agent is mutated, the function updates its fingerprint by executing genotype:update_finrgerprint/1.

```erlang
mutate_SearchParameters(Agent_Id)->
    case random:uniform() < ?SEARCH_PARAMTERS_MUTATION_PROBABILITY of
        true ->
                TotMutations = random:uniform(length(?ES_MUTATORS)),
                apply_ESMutators(Agent_Id,TotMutations);
        false ->
                ok
    end.
```
%The mutate_SearchParameters/1 function, mutates the search parameters of the evolutionary strategy with a probability of: ?SEARCH_PARAMETERS_MUTATION_PROBABILITY. When it does mutate the evolutionary strategy, it chooses a random number between 1 and length(?ES_MUTATORS) of evolutionary strategy mutation operators from the ?ES_MUTATORS list, and then executes them in series.

```erlang
apply_ESMutators(_Agent_Id,0)->
        done;
apply_ESMutators(Agent_Id,MutationIndex)->
        ES_Mutators = ?ES_MUTATORS,
        ES_Mutator = lists:nth(random:uniform(length(ES_Mutators)),ES_Mutators),
        io:format("Evolutionary Strategy Mutation Operator:~p~n",[ES_Mutator]),
        F = fun()->
                genome_mutator:ES_Mutator(Agent_Id)
        end,
        Result = mnesia:transaction(F),
        case Result of
                {atomic,_} ->
                        apply_ESMutators(Agent_Id,MutationIndex-1);
                Error ->
                        io:format("******** Error:~p~nRetrying with new Mutation...~n", [Error]),
                        apply_ESMutators(Agent_Id,MutationIndex-1)
        end.
```

%The apply_ESMutators/2 function chooses an evolutionary strategy mutation operator, with uniform distribution, from the ?ES_MUTATORS list of such functions. It then applies it to the agent. Whether the mutation is successful or not, the function counts down the total number of mutation operators left to apply. This is to ensure that if the researcher set for each such evolutionary strategy to be static, having only one available mutatable parameter for every agent, the system will try to mutate the strategy TotMutations number of times, and then return to the caller whether it was successful or not.

Unlike the case with the application of topological mutation operators, if the application of the ES mutation operator is not successful, we still decrement the MutationIndex value. This ensures that whether our system does or does not have multiple annealing, selection, duration, and tot_topological_mutation parameters and functions, the MutationIndex will still reach 0. Thus, even if every ES mutation operator fails, the apply_ESMutators/2 function will be able to finish and return to the caller.

As with the topological mutation operators, the ES operators also need to be implemented. For the time being we will implement these functions in the genome_mutator module, rather than their own module. These simple ES mutation operator functions are shown in Listing-11.5.

Listing-11.5 The implementation of the three new evolutionary strategy mutation operators: mutate_tuning_selection/1, mutate_tuning_duration/1, and mutate_tuning_annealing/1.

```
mutate_tuning_selection(Agent_Id)->
    A = genotype:read({agent,Agent_Id}),
    case (A#agent.constraint)#constraint.tuning_selection_fs -- [A#agent.tuning_selection_f] of
        [] ->
                exit("********ERROR:mutate_tuning_selection/1:: Nothing to mutate, only a
single function available.");
        Tuning_Selection_Functions->
                New_TSF = lists:nth(random:uniform(length(Tuning_Selection_Functions)),
Tuning_Selection_Functions),
                U_A = A#agent{tuning_selection_f = New_TSF},
                genotype:write(U_A)
    end.
```
%The mutate_tuning_selection/1 function checks if there are any other than the currently used tuning selection functions available in the agent's constraint record. If there are, then it chooses a random one from this list, and sets the agent's tuning_selection_f to it. If there are no other tuning selection functions, then it exits with an error.

```
mutate_tuning_annealing(Agent_Id)->
    A = genotype:read({agent,Agent_Id}),
    case (A#agent.constraint)#constraint.annealing_parameters --
[A#agent.annealing_parameter] of
```

```
            [] ->
                    exit("********ERROR:mutate_tuning_annealing/1:: Nothing to mutate, only
a single function available.");
            Tuning_Annealing_Parameters->
                    New_TAP= lists:nth(random:uniform(length(Tuning_Annealing_Parameters)),
Tuning_Annealing_Parameters),
                    U_A = A#agent{annealing_parameter = New_TAP},
                    genotype:write(U_A)
    end.
%The mutate_annealing_parameter/1 function checks if there are any other than the currently
used tuning annealing parameters available in the agent's constrain recordt. If there are, then it
chooses a random one from the list, and sets the agent's annealing_parameter to it. If there are
no other tuning annealing parameters, then it exits with an error.


mutate_tot_topological_mutations(Agent_Id)->
    A = genotype:read({agent,Agent_Id}),
    case (A#agent.constraint)#constraint.tuning_selection_fs -- [A#agent.tuning_selection_f] of
        [] ->
                    exit("********ERROR:mutate_tuning_selection/1:: Nothing to mutate, only a
single function available.");
            Tuning_Selection_Functions->
                    New_TSF = lists:nth(random:uniform(length(Tuning_Selection_Functions)),
Tuning_Selection_Functions),
                    U_A = A#agent{tuning_selection_f = New_TSF},
                    genotype:write(U_A)
    end.
%The mutate_tot_topological_mutations/1 function checks if there are any other than the cur-
rently used tuning tot topological mutation functions available in the agent's constraint record.
If there are, then it chooses a random one from this list, and sets the agent's
tot_topological_mutations_f to it. If there are no other functions that can calculate tot topologi-
cal mutations, then it exits with an error.
```

These new additions do of course make our source code slightly more complex, but as you've noticed, it is still very simple, and the added flexibility will pay off when we decide that we wish to test out different evolutionary strategies with different parameters. In the following sections we develop the code needed to convert this new genotype to its phenotype.

11.4.3 Updating the population_monitor Module

The population_monitor module is the one responsible for mapping the genotypes to their phenotypes. We have modified the genotype in a number of ways, and thus we must now modify the population monitor process such that it can convert the agent's elements into their corresponding process based representations. We must now also change the way population_monitor calculates the agent's true fitness, the way it uses the selection function, and the way it implements the evolutionary loop, so that it is based on whether it's steady-state or generational. Currently, the various functions and information flow in the population_monitor, has the form shown in Fig-11.3.

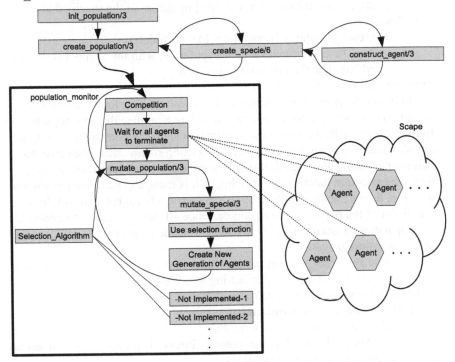

Fig. 11.3 The information flow, and function execution order, in the population_monitor process.

What we need to do is change this architecture such that the population_monitor behaves differently based on whether it is using steady-state evolution, or generational evolution. Finally, we also need to modify the init_population function such that all these parameters are specified through the constraint record, and so that the evolutionary loop function, fitness function, and the selection function is saved to the population's record, and read from the same during the population_monitor's operation. The new population monitor should operate as follows:

1. Specify the constraints, and set the INIT_CONSTRAINTS to it, then call init_population/2 with it.
2. *init_population({Population_Id,Constraints,OpMode})*
   This is the function with which we create a new population, and start the population_monitor process. We specify the id of the new population, the constraints which it should use to create species and agents within the species, and the operational mode in which it should work. We have not yet used the

OpMode parameter for anything specific, currently it is set by a constant macro to *gt*, which is just a place holder. We will finally start using this parameter when we get to Chapter-19, and hit a dilemma of having to perform generalization tests.

3. IF population with Population_Id already exists then:

4. delete_population: Delete the existing population using the same id.

5. create_population: Create a new population of the specified id.

6. Else:

7. create_population(Population_Id,Constraints)

This function creates a new population, with the agents being created based on the constraints specified.

8. Start population_monitor process.

At this point the population monitor needs to start waiting for the termination signals that are sent out by the agents when they terminate/die. The population_monitor can then act on those termination signals based on the evolutionary loop that it is using. For example, if it is using *steady_state*, then after receiving the termination signal, it should immediately generate a new agent using the selection function it's utilizing. If it is using a *generational* evolutionary loop, then it should simply count off the terminated agent, and wait for the remainder of the population to terminate. Once all the agents have terminated, the population_monitor should then use the selection algorithm to compose the next generation of agents.

9. Create the dead_pool list (empty when first created), which is to contain the genotypes of the best performing terminated agents.

10. Wait for termination signals.

11. If evo_alg_f == generational:

12. Wait for all agents to terminate.

13. Apply **fitness_f** to the agent's fitness, to produce a list of agents with their *true* fitness values.

14. Apply **selection_f** to choose the fit agents from which to compose the offspring agents.

15. Produce the offspring agents by cloning the fit organisms, and sending them through the topological mutation phase.

16. **GOTO:** Step-10

If evo_alg_f == steady_state:

17. After receiving the termination signal from an agent, enter it into the dead_pool, with its fitness updated through the application of the **fitness_f** function.

18. Using the selection function, choose an agent from the dead_pool to either create an offspring, or return/apply it to the simulation/scape.

19. Ensure that the dead_pool is of the specified size, if the dead_pool is overflowing with agents, then remove the worst performing agents in the dead_pool, until it reaches the specified size. This ensures that the dead_pool list contains the best performing agent genotypes.

20. **GOTO:** Step-10

We thus start by updating the init_population function. It originally accepted 4 parameters: Population_Id, Specie_Constraints, OpMode, and Selection_Function. The Selection_Function is now specified in the constraint record, so we can remove it from the parameter list. The init_population checks if there already exists a population with the Population_Id that it was executed with. If that is the case, the function first deletes the already existing population, and then creates a new population. If there is no such population already in existence, then it creates a new population by executing the create_population function. The modification to the init_population function is in boldface, shown in Listing-11.6.

Listing-11.6 The modified init_population function, where the selection function is specified through the constraint tuple.

```
init_population({Population_Id,Specie_Constraints,OpMode})->
    random:seed(now()),
    F = fun()->
            case genotype:read({population,Population_Id}) of
                undefined ->
                    create_Population(Population_Id,Specie_Constraints);
                _ ->
                    delete_population(Population_Id),
                    create_Population(Population_Id,Specie_Constraints)
            end
    end,
    Result = mnesia:transaction(F),
    case Result of
        {atomic,_} ->
            population_monitor:start({OpMode,Population_Id});
        Error ->
            io:format("******** ERROR in PopulationMonitor:~p~n",[Error])
    end.
```

Though the ?INIT_CONSTRAINTS contains a list of constraint records, one for each species the researcher wants the population to possess, it is nevertheless expected that the *population_evo_alg_f*, *population_fitness_f*, and *population_selection_f*, are to be the same for all these constraints. These constraint parameters are expected by the system to be global, belonging to the population to which the species belong. Thus, all the constraint tuples in the *?INIT_CONSTRAINTS* list will have these parameters equivalent. We modify the *create_population* function to accept 2 parameters, and use the parameters in the constraint record to set the population's evolutionary loop, fitness, and selection functions, as shown in Listing-11.7.

Listing-11.7 The updated create_Population/2 function, with the new elements highlighted in boldface.

```
create_Population(Population_Id,Specie_Constraints)->
        SpecieSize = ?INIT_SPECIE_SIZE,
        Specie_Ids = [create_specie(Population_Id,SpecCon,origin,SpecieSize) || SpecCon <-
Specie_Constraints],
        [C|_]=Specie_Constraints,
        Population = #population{
                id = Population_Id,
                specie_ids = Specie_Ids,
                evo_alg_f = C#constraint.population_evo_alg_f,
                fitness_f = C#constraint.population_fitness_f,
                selection_f = C#constraint.population_selection_f
        },
        genotype:write(Population).
```

As you've noticed, the init_population function, due to the selection algorithm now being stored in the population record, calls the start/1 with just the OpMode and Population_Id parameters. Thus, we must also modify the *continue/2* and *continue/3* functions from:

```
continue(OpMode,Selection_Algorithm)->
    Population_Id = test,
    population_monitor:start({OpMode,Population_Id,Selection_Algorithm}).
continue(OpMode,Selection_Algorithm,Population_Id)->
    population_monitor:start({OpMode,Population_Id,Selection_Algorithm}).
```

To ones expecting the *population record* to carry all the needed information to start the population_process:

```
continue(OpMode)->
    Population_Id = test,
    population_monitor:start({OpMode,Population_Id}).
continue(OpMode,Population_Id)->
    population_monitor:start({OpMode,Population_Id}).
```

With this done, we now modify the *init/1* function, and then the actual process's functionality by updating the call and cast handling functions of this module. The init/1 function requires that the population_monitor *state* record also keeps track of the evolutionary_algorithm (*generational* or *steady_state*), fitness_postprocessing, and selection_algorithm functions. The updated version of the state record and the init/1 function are shown in the Listing-11.8.

Listing-11.8 The updated *state* record, and the init/1 function. Modifications are shown highlighted in boldface.

```
-record(state,{op_mode,population_id,activeAgent_IdPs=[],agent_ids=[],tot_agents,
agents_left,op_tag,agent_summaries=[],pop_gen=0,eval_acc=0,cycle_acc=0,time_acc=0,
step_size,next_step,goal_status,evolutionary_algorithm,fitness_postprocessor, selec-
tion_algorithm}).
...
...
...
init(Parameters) ->
    process_flag(trap_exit,true),
    register(monitor,self()),
    io:format("******** Population monitor started with parameters:~p~n",[Parameters]),
    State = case Parameters of
            {OpMode,Population_Id}->
                    Agent_Ids = extract_AgentIds(Population_Id,all),
                    ActiveAgent_IdPs = summon_agents(OpMode,Agent_Ids),
                    P = genotype:dirty_read({population,Population_Id}),
                    #state{op_mode=OpMode,
                            population_id = Population_Id,
                            activeAgent_IdPs = ActiveAgent_IdPs,
                            tot_agents = length(Agent_Ids),
                            agents_left = length(Agent_Ids),
                            op_tag = continue,
                            evolutionary_algorithm = P#population.evo_alg_f,
                            fitness_postprocessor = P#population.fitness_f,
                            selection_algorithm = P#population.selection_f}
    end,
    {ok, State}.
```

The first cast, one which handles the terminating agents, is easily modified by updating the guard of the cast from one using a *selection_function* parameter to one using the *evolutionary_algorithm*, and by modifying the *mutate_population* function to allow it to be called with an extra parameter, the *fitness_postprocessor* function name. These modifications are shown in the following snippet of source code, showing just these modified two lines:

```
handle_cast({Agent_Id,terminated,Fitness,AgentEvalAcc,AgentCycleAcc,AgentTimeAcc},S)
when S#state.evolutionary_algorithm == generational ->
...
    mutate_population(Population_Id, ?SPECIE_SIZE_LIMIT, S#state.fitness_postprocessor,
S#state.selection_algorithm),
```

We will create the cast handling clause which implements the steady_state evolutionary loop in a later section. For now, we update the mutate_population/4 function. The updated mutate_population function, which calls the mutate_specie function for every species in the population, is shortened dramatically, because it now offloads both, the fitness postprocessing, and the actual selection of fit agents, to the specialized modules that we will create later. The updated mutate_population and mutate_specie functions are shown in Listing-11.9.

Listing-11.9 The updated mutate_population and mutate_specie functions, which utilize the specialized fitness_postprocessor and selection_algorithm modules.

```
mutate_population(Population_Id,KeepTot,Fitness_Postprocessor,Selection_Algorithm)->
    NeuralEnergyCost = calculate_EnergyCost(Population_Id),
    F = fun()->
        P = genotype:read({population,Population_Id}),
        Specie_Ids = P#population.specie_ids,
        [mutate_Specie(Specie_Id,KeepTot,NeuralEnergyCost,Fitness_Postprocessor,
Selection_Algorithm) || Specie_Id <- Specie_Ids]
    end,
    {atomic,_} = mnesia:transaction(F).
%The function mutate_population/3 mutates the agents within every specie in its specie_ids
list, maintaining each specie within the size of KeepTot. The function first calculates the aver-
age cost of each neuron, and then mutates each specie separately using the particular Fit-
ness_Postprocessor and Selection_Algorithm parameters for that specie.

mutate_Specie(Specie_Id,PopulationLimit,NeuralEnergyCost,Fitness_Postprocessor_Name,
Selection_Algorithm_Name)->
        S = genotype:dirty_read({specie,Specie_Id}),
        {AvgFitness,Std,MaxFitness,MinFitness} = calculate_SpecieFitness({specie,S}),
        Agent_Ids = S#specie.agent_ids,
        Sorted_AgentSummarie =lists:reverse(lists:sort(construct_AgentSummaries(
Agent_Ids, []))),
        io:format("Using: Fitness Postprocessor:~p Selection Algorirthm:~p~n", [
Fitness_Postprocessor_Name, Selection_Algorithm_Name]),
        ProperlySorted_AgentSummaries=
fitness_postprocessor:Fitness_Postprocessor_Name( Sorted_AgentSummaries),
        {NewGenAgent_Ids,TopAgent_Ids} =
selection_algorithm:Selection_Algorithm_Name(ProperlySorted_AgentSummaries,
NeuralEnergyCost,PopulationLimit),
        {FList,_TNList,_AgentIds}=lists:unzip3(Sorted_AgentSummaries),
        [TopFitness|_] = FList,
        {Factor,Fitness}=S#specie.innovation_factor,
        U_InnovationFactor = case TopFitness > Fitness of
            true ->
                {0,TopFitness};
            false ->
                {S#specie.innovation_factor-1,Fitness}
        end,
        genotype:write(S#specie{
```

```
            agent_ids = NewGenAgent_Ids,
            champion_ids = TopAgent_Ids,
            fitness = {AvgFitness,Std,MaxFitness,MinFitness},
            innovation_factor = U_InnovationFactor}).
```

%The function mutate_Specie/5 calls the selection algorithm function to separate the fit from the unfit organisms in the specie, and then mutates the fit organisms to produce offspring, maintaining the total species size within PopulationLimit. The function first calls the fitness_postprocessor function which sorts the agent summaries. Then, the resorted updated summaries are split into a valid (fit) and invalid (unfit) lists of agents by the selection algorithm. The invalid agents are deleted, and the valid agents are used to create offspring using the particular Selection_Algorithm_Name function. The agent ids belonging to the next generation (the valid agents and their offspring) are then produced by the selection function. Then, the innovation factor (the last time the specie's top fitness improved) is updated. And finally, the ids of the top 3 agents within the specie are noted, and the updated specie record is written to database.

```
    construct_AgentSummaries([Agent_Id|Agent_Ids],Acc)->
        A = genotype:dirty_read({agent,Agent_Id}),
            construct_AgentSummaries(Agent_Ids,[{A#agent.fitness,
length((genotype:dirty_read({cortex,A#agent.cx_id}))#cortex.neuron_ids),Agent_Id}|Acc]);
        construct_AgentSummaries([],Acc)->
            Acc.
```

%The construct_AgentSummaries/2 function reads the agents in the Agent_Ids list, and composes a list of tuples of the following format: [{AgentFitness,AgentTotNeurons,Agent_Id}...]. This list of tuples is referred to as AgentSummaries. Once the AgentSummaries list is composed, it is returned to the caller.

The population_monitor module is simplified by offloading the selection and fitness postprocessing functions to their own respective modules. The population_monitor, after this modification, primarily holds population and specie operator functions. In the following sections we build the selection and the fitness postprocessing modules.

11.4.4 Creating the selection_algorithm Module

The selection_algorithm module is a container for the selection_algorithm functions. In the original population_monitor module we had two such functions for the generational evolutionary algorithm loop. Those two functions were the *competition* selection function, and the *top3* selection function. We modified the population_monitor system in the previous section by moving the fitness postprocessing code and the selection code to their own respective modules. The following listing shows the selection_algorithm module, after the *competition* and *top3* functions were modified to be self contained within the module.

Listing-11.10 The implementation of the selection_algorithm module.

```erlang
-module(selection_algorithm).
-compile(export_all).
-include("records.hrl").
-define(SURVIVAL_PERCENTAGE,0.5).

competition(PropSorted_ASummaries,NeuralEnergyCost,PopulationLimit)->
    TotSurvivors=round(length(PropSorted_ASummaries)*?SURVIVAL_PERCENTAGE),
    Valid_AgentSummaries = lists:sublist(PropSorted_ASummaries,TotSurvivors),
    Invalid_AgentSummaries = PropSorted_ASummaries -- Valid_AgentSummaries,
    {_,_,Invalid_AgentIds} = lists:unzip3(Invalid_AgentSummaries),
    [genotype:delete_Agent(Agent_Id) || Agent_Id <- Invalid_AgentIds],
    io:format("Valid_AgentSummaries:~p~n",[Valid_AgentSummaries]),
    io:format("Invalid_AgentSummaries:~p~n",[Invalid_AgentSummaries]),
    TopAgentSummaries = lists:sublist(Valid_AgentSummaries,3),
    {_TopFitnessList,_TopTotNs,TopAgent_Ids} = lists:unzip3(TopAgentSummaries),
    io:format("NeuralEnergyCost:~p~n",[NeuralEnergyCost]),
    {AlotmentsP,NextGenSize_Estimate} = calculate_allotments(Valid_AgentSummaries,
NeuralEnergyCost,[],0),
    Normalizer = NextGenSize_Estimate/PopulationLimit,
    io:format("Population size normalizer:~p~n",[Normalizer]),
    NewGenAgent_Ids = gather_survivors(AlotmentsP,Normalizer,[]),
    {NewGenAgent_Ids,TopAgent_Ids}.
```

%The competition/3 function implements the "competition" selection algorithm. The function first sorts the agent summaries. The function then executes calculate_allotments/4 to calculate the number of offspring allotted for each agent in the Sorted_AgentSummaries list. The function then calculates the Normalizer value, which is used to normalize the allotted number of offspring for each agent, to ensure that the final specie size is within the PopulationLimit. The function then drops into the gather_survivors/3 function which, using the normalized offspring allotment values, creates the actual mutant offspring. Finally, the function returns to the caller a tuple composed of the new generation's agent ids, and the top 3 agent ids of the current generation.

```erlang
    calculate_allotments([{Fitness,TotNeurons,Agent_Id}|Sorted_AgentSummaries],
NeuralEnergyCost,Acc,NewPopAcc)->
        NeuralAlotment = Fitness/NeuralEnergyCost,
        MutantAlotment = NeuralAlotment/TotNeurons,
        U_NewPopAcc = NewPopAcc+MutantAlotment,
        calculate_allotments(Sorted_AgentSummaries,NeuralEnergyCost, [{MutantAlotment,
Fitness,TotNeurons,Agent_Id}|Acc],U_NewPopAcc);
    calculate_allotments([],_NeuralEnergyCost,Acc,NewPopAcc)->
        io:format("NewPopAcc:~p~n",[NewPopAcc]),
        {Acc,NewPopAcc}.
```

%The calculate_allotments/4 function accepts the AgentSummaries list as a parameter, and for each agent, using the NeuralEnergyCost, calculates how many offspring that agent can produce by using the agent's Fitness, TotNeurons, and NeuralEnergyCost values. The function first calculates how many neurons the agent is allotted, based on the agent's fitness and the cost of each neuron (which itself was calculated based on the average performance of the population). From the number of neurons allotted to the agent, the function then calculates how many offspring the agent should be allotted, by dividing the number of neurons it is allotted, by the agent's NN size. The function also keeps track of how many offspring will be created from all these agents in general, by adding up all the offspring allotments. The calculate_allotments/4 function does this for each tuple in the AgentSummaries, and then returns the calculated allotment list and NewPopAcc to the caller.

```
gather_survivors([{MutantAlotment,Fitness,TotNeurons,Agent_Id}|AlotmentsP],
Normalizer, Acc)->
        Normalized_MutantAlotment = round(MutantAlotment/Normalizer),
        io:format("Agent_Id:~p Normalized_MutantAlotment:~p~n", [Agent_Id,
Normalized_MutantAlotment]),
        SurvivingAgent_Ids = case Normalized_MutantAlotment >= 1 of
            true ->
                    MutantAgent_Ids = case Normalized_MutantAlotment >= 2 of
                        true ->
                                [population_monitor:create_MutantAgentCopy( Agent_Id)
|| _ <-lists:seq(1,Normalized_MutantAlotment-1)];
                        false ->
                                []
                    end,
                    [Agent_Id|MutantAgent_Ids];
            false ->
                    io:format("Deleting agent:~p~n",[Agent_Id]),
                    genotype:delete_Agent(Agent_Id),
                    []
        end,
        gather_survivors(AlotmentsP,Normalizer,lists:append(SurvivingAgent_Ids,Acc));
    gather_survivors([],_Normalizer,Acc)->
        io:format("New Population:~p PopSize:~p~n",[Acc,length(Acc)]),
        Acc.
```

%The gather_survivors/3 function accepts the list composed of the allotment tuples and a population normalizer value calculated by the competition/3 function, and from those values calculates the actual number of offspring that each agent should produce, creating those mutant offspring and accumulating the new generation agent ids. For each Agent_Id the function first calculates the normalized offspring allotment value, to ensure that the final number of agents in the specie is within the population limit of that specie. If the offspring allotment value is less than 0, the agent is killed. If the offspring allotment is 1, the parent agent is allowed to survive to the next generation, but is not allowed to create any new offspring. If the offspring allotment is greater than one, then the agent is allowed to create Normalized_MutantAlotment-1 number of offspring, by calling upon the create_MutantAgentCopy/1 function. The function create_MutantAgentCopy/1 function, creates an offspring and returns its id. Once all the offspring have been created, the function returns to the caller a list of ids, composed of the surviving parent agent ids, and their offspring, the next generation.

```
top3(ProperlySorted_AgentSummaries,NeuralEnergyCost,PopulationLimit)->
    TotSurvivors = 3,
    Valid_AgentSummaries = lists:sublist(ProperlySorted_AgentSummaries,TotSurvivors),
    Invalid_AgentSummaries = ProperlySorted_AgentSummaries -- Valid_AgentSummaries,
    {_,_,Invalid_AgentIds} = lists:unzip3(Invalid_AgentSummaries),
    {_,_,Valid_AgentIds} = lists:unzip3(Valid_AgentSummaries),
    [genotype:delete_Agent(Agent_Id) || Agent_Id <- Invalid_AgentIds],
    io:format("Valid_AgentSummaries:~p~n",[Valid_AgentSummaries]),
    io:format("Invalid_AgentSummaries:~p~n",[Invalid_AgentSummaries]),
    TopAgentSummaries = lists:sublist(Valid_AgentSummaries,3),
    {_TopFitnessList,_TopTotNs,TopAgent_Ids} = lists:unzip3(TopAgentSummaries),
    io:format("NeuralEnergyCost:~p~n",[NeuralEnergyCost]),
    NewGenAgent_Ids = random_offspring(Valid_AgentIds,PopulationLimit-TotSurvivors,[]),
    {NewGenAgent_Ids,TopAgent_Ids}.
```
%The top3/3 function is a simple selection algorithm. This function extracts the top 3 agents from the ProperlySorted_AgentSummaries list, subtracts 3 from the PopulationLimit, and then uses the function random_offspring/3 to create offspring based on these top 3 agents. Once the offspring have been created, the function returns a list of the offspring ids, and the top agent ids, back to the caller.

```
    random_offspring (_Valid_AgentIds,0,Acc)->
        Acc;
    random_offspring (Valid_AgentIds,OffspringIndex,Acc)->
        Parent_AgentId = lists:nth(random:uniform(length(Valid_AgentIds)),
Valid_AgentIds),
        MutantAgent_Id = population_monitor:create_MutantAgentCopy(Parent_AgentId),
        random_offspring (Valid_AgentIds,OffspringIndex-1,[MutantAgent_Id|Acc]).
```
%The random_offspring/3 function is part of a very simple selection algorithm, which just selects the top 3 most fit agents, and then uses the create_MutantAgentCopy/1 function to create their offspring. Each offspring is created from a randomly selected top agent.

```
competition(ProperlySorted_AgentSummaries)->
    TotEnergy = lists:sum([Fitness || {Fitness,_TotN,_Agent_Id}<-
ProperlySorted_AgentSummaries]),
    TotNeurons = lists:sum([TotN || {_Fitness,TotN,_Agent_Id} <-
ProperlySorted_AgentSummaries]),
    NeuralEnergyCost = TotEnergy/TotNeurons,
    {AlotmentsP,Normalizer} = calculate_alotments(ProperlySorted_AgentSummaries,
NeuralEnergyCost, [],0),
    Choice = random:uniform(),
```

```
{WinnerFitness,WinnerTotN,WinnerAgent_Id}=choose_CompetitionWinner(AlotmentsP,
Normalizer,Choice,0),
    {WinnerFitness,WinnerTotN,WinnerAgent_Id}.
```
%competition/1 is the competition selection algorithm for the steady_state evolutionary loop implementation. It functions similar to the competition/3 selection algorithm, but it converts the allotments to probabilities of the agent being chosen as the winner of the selection algorithm. The population monitor decides on what to do with the winner, either to create an offspring from it, re-enter it into a simulated environment, or re-apply it to some problem again.

```
    choose_CompetitionWinner([{MutantAllotment,Fitness,TotN,Agent_Id}|AllotmentsP],
Normalizer,Choice,Range_From)->
        Range_To = Range_From+MutantAllotment/Normalizer,
        case (Choice >= Range_From) and (Choice =< Range_To) of
            true ->
                    {Fitness,TotN,Agent_Id};
            false ->
                    choose_CompetitionWinner(AllotmentsP,Normalizer,Choice,Range_To)
        end;
    choose_CompetitionWinner([],_Normalizer,_Choice,_Range_From)->
        exit("********ERROR:choose_CompetitionWinner:: reached [] without selecting a
winner.").
```
%The choose_CompetitionWinner/4 function, uses the Choice value to randomly choose an agent from the AllotmentsP, with the probability of choosing the agent being proportional to the agent's MutantAllotment value.

By keeping all the selection functions in this module, it makes it easier for us to later add new ones, and then simply reference them by their name.

11.4.5 Creating the fitness_postprocessor Module

The *fitness_postprocessor* gives us an added level of flexibility when sorting and computing the fitness of the agents belonging to some species. In this manner, we can allow the scapes and various problems to concentrate on providing fitness scores to the agents based simply on their performance, rather than other properties of those agents, like size and complexity for example. The fitness_postprocessor functions modify the fitness scores of the agents, such that the updated fitness score reflects some particular property that the researcher finds important, but which is general and separate from the particular simulation or problem that the neuroevolutionary system is applied to. Listing-11.11 presents the fitness_postprocessor module which contains two simple fitness postprocessors, the *none* and the *size_proportional* functions.

Listing-11.11 The implementation of the fitness_postprocessor module.

```erlang
-module(fitness_postprocessor).
-compile(export_all).
-include("records.hrl").
-define(EFF,0.1). %Efficiency.

none(Sorted_AgentSummaries)->
    Sorted_AgentSummaries.
%The none/1 fitness postprocessor function does nothing to the agent summaries, returning the
original fitness scores to the caller.

size_proportional(Sorted_AgentSummaries)->
    SDX=lists:reverse(lists:sort([{Fitness/math:pow(TotN,?EFF),{Fitness,TotN,Agent_Id}}||{
Fitness,TotN,Agent_Id}<-Sorted_AgentSummaries])),
    ProperlySorted_AgentSummaries = [Val || {_,Val}<-SDX],
    ProperlySorted_AgentSummaries.
%The size_proportional/1 fitness postprocessor function modifies the fitness scores belonging
to the agent summaries such that they are decreased proportional to the NN size, and the ?EFF
parameter. Every fitness score is changed to: TrueFitness = Fitness/math:pow(TotN,?EFF).
Based on these true fitness scores, the agent summaries are resorted, and then returned to the
caller.
```

With this module completed, we now return back to the population_monitor function, to add the cast clause which allows our neuroevolutionary system to employ the steady-state evolutionary loop.

11.4.6 Creating the steady_state Evolutionary Loop

We need to update the population_monitor process such that when the population is set to use a steady_state evolutionary loop with its complementary selection algorithm, the population_monitor process is able to maintain a proper population size, creating a new agent for every one that terminated. The creation of new agents must be done in such a way that the average fitness goes up, that there is evolution. In Chapter-10 we discussed the manner in which the DXNN platform solves this problem, and the implementation of the dead_pool list, which allows for the neuroevolutionary system to track content drift, and allow for the selection algorithm to have a list of Ids to choose from when selecting a parent agent. We will take a similar approach with our system.

To update our population_monitor process such that it can deal with a steady_state evolutionary loop, we need to construct a cast clause that allows the population_monitor to perform the following set of steps:

1. The init_population function creates a new population of agents, with the seed population being of size X.
2. The population monitor spawns the seed population, and enters its main functional loop.
3. The population_monitor waits for termination signals from agents.
4. When the population_monitor receives the termination signal of the form: *{Agent_Id, terminated, Fitness, AgentEvalAcc, AgentCycleAcc, AgentTimeAcc}* with a the cast guard: *S#state.evolutionary_algorithm == steady_state*, it should function as follows:
    5. Update the eval_acc, cycle_acc, and time_acc parameters of the state record.
    6. If termination condition is reached (based on eval_acc, or achieved fitness), go to Step-14. Else continue to step-7.
    7. Compose and add the terminated agent's summary tuple to its species' dead_pool list.
    8. Apply the fitness_postprocessor function of the population to the dead_pool summary list.
    9. Using the newly sorted *dead_pool* summary list, use the selection function to choose an agent from the dead_pool, an agent that will either be used as a parent for the creation of an offspring, or be the agent that will be released back into the environment (if the neuroevolutionary system is applied to ALife), or reapplied to the problem. This is unlike the selection algorithm function used in the generational evolutionary loop, which returned a list of agent ids belonging to the new generation, and a list of top/champion agent ids.
    10. Randomly choose, (90/10) to either use the agent to create an offspring (in which case the agent remains in the dead pool), or apply it to the problem again (in which case the agent is extracted from the dead pool).
    11. If creating an offspring, then clone the selected agent, send the clone through the topological mutation phase, and then spawn the offspring and apply it to the problem. If the agent is selected to be re-applied to the problem, then extract it from the dead_pool, spawn it, and apply to the problem.
    12. Check if the size of the dead_pool is greater than X (population size). If the dead_pool size is greater than X, then keep the top X agents, and delete the remainder. The population size that is active is of size X, but we will also make the dead_pool of size X, thus the total number of agents stored in the population is *X*2*.
    13. **GOTO:** Step-3
14. **Termination Condition Reached:** Terminate all currently running phenotypes. This means that the population monitor must keep track of not just the inactive agents (the ones in the dead_pool), but also of the active ones.

The implemented cast clause based on this algorithm is shown in Listing-11.12

Listing-11.12 The implementation of the steady_state handle_cast clause of the population monitor.

```erlang
handle_cast({Agent_Id,terminated,Fitness,AgentEvalAcc,AgentCycleAcc,AgentTimeAcc},S)
when S#state.evolutionary_algorithm == steady_state ->
    Population_Id = S#state.population_id,
    Specie_Ids = (genotype:dirty_read({population,Population_Id}))#population.specie_ids,
    SpecFitList=[(genotype:dirty_read({specie,Specie_Id}))#specie.fitness || Specie_Id <-
Specie_Ids],
    BestFitness=lists:nth(1,lists:reverse(lists:sort([MaxFitness || {_,_,MaxFitness,_} <-
SpecFitList]))),
    U_EvalAcc = S#state.eval_acc+AgentEvalAcc,
    U_CycleAcc = S#state.cycle_acc+AgentCycleAcc,
    U_TimeAcc = S#state.time_acc+AgentTimeAcc,
    case (S#state.eval_acc >= ?EVALUATIONS_LIMIT) or (BestFitness > ?FITNESS_GOAL)
of
        true ->
                case lists:keydelete(Agent_Id,1,S#state.activeAgent_IdPs) of
                        [] ->
                                U_S=S#state{activeAgent_IdPs=[], eval_acc=U_EvalAcc, cy-
cle_acc =U_CycleAcc, time_acc=U_TimeAcc},
                                {stop,normal,U_S};
                        U_ActiveAgent_IdPs ->
                                U_S=S#state{activeAgent_IdPs=U_ActiveAgent_IdPs, eval_acc
=U_EvalAcc, cycle_acc=U_CycleAcc, time_acc=U_TimeAcc},
                                {noreply,U_S}
                end;
        false ->
                io:format("Tot Evaluations:~p~n",[S#state.eval_acc+AgentEvalAcc]),
                FitnessPostprocessorName = S#state.fitness_postprocessor,
                SelectionAlgorithmName = S#state.selection_algorithm,
                [A] = genotype:dirty_read({agent,Agent_Id}),
                Morphology= (A#agent.constraint)#constraint.morphology,
                io:format("Agent_Id:~p of morphology:~p with fitness:~p terminated.~n",
[Agent_Id, Morphology,Fitness]),
                Specie_Id = A#agent.specie_id,
                [S] = genotype:dirty_read({specie,Specie_Id}),
                Old_DeadPool_AgentSummaries = S#specie.dead_pool,
                Old_Agent_Ids = S#specie.agent_ids,
                io:format("Old_DeadPool:~p~n Old_Agent_Ids:~p~n",
[Old_DeadPool_AgentSummaries,Old_Agent_Ids]),
                [AgentSummary] = construct_AgentSummaries([Agent_Id],[]),
                DeadPool_AgentSummaries = [AgentSummary |
Old_DeadPool_AgentSummaries],
```

```
            ProperlySorted_AgentSummaries
=fitness_postprocessor:FitnessPostprocessorName(DeadPool_AgentSummaries),
            Top_AgentSummaries =lists:sublist(ProperlySorted_AgentSummaries,
round(?SPECIE_SIZE_LIMIT*?SURVIVAL_PERCENTAGE)),
            {WinnerFitness,WinnerProfile,WinnerAgent_Id}
=selection_algorithm:SelectionAlgorithmName(ProperlySorted_AgentSummaries),
            Valid_AgentSummaries = case length(ProperlySorted_AgentSummaries) >=
?SPECIE_SIZE_LIMIT of
                true ->

 [{InvalidFitness,InvalidTotN,InvalidAgent_Id}|Remaining_AgentSummaries]
=lists:reverse(ProperlySorted_AgentSummaries),
                    io:format("Informationtheoretic Death:~p::~p~n", [
InvalidAgent_Id, {InvalidFitness,InvalidTotN,InvalidAgent_Id}]),
                    genotype:delete_agent(InvalidAgent_Id,safe),
                    Remaining_AgentSummaries;
                false ->
                    ProperlySorted_AgentSummaries
            end,
            ActiveAgent_IdP = case random:uniform() < 0.1 of
                true ->
                    U_DeadPool_AgentSummaries = lists:delete({WinnerFitness,
WinnerProfile,WinnerAgent_Id},Valid_AgentSummaries),
                    {ok,WinnerAgent_PId} = exoself:start_link({S#state.op_mode,
WinnerAgent_Id,void_MaxTrials}),
                    {WinnerAgent_Id,WinnerAgent_PId};
                false ->
                    U_DeadPool_AgentSummaries = Valid_AgentSummaries,
                    AgentClone_Id = create_MutantAgentCopy(WinnerAgent_Id,
safe),
                    {ok,AgentClone_PId} = exoself:start_link({S#state.op_mode,
AgentClone_Id,void_MaxTrials}),
                    {AgentClone_Id,AgentClone_PId}
            end,
            {_,_,TopAgent_Ids} = lists:unzip3(lists:sublist(Top_AgentSummaries,3)),
            io:format("TopAgent_Ids:~p~n",[TopAgent_Ids]),
            [USpecie]=genotype:dirty_read({specie,Specie_Id}),
            genotype:dirty_write(USpecie#specie{dead_pool
=U_DeadPool_AgentSummaries, champion_ids = TopAgent_Ids}),
            ActiveAgent_IdPs = S#state.activeAgent_IdPs,
            U_ActiveAgent_IdPs = [ActiveAgent_IdP|lists:keydelete(Agent_Id,1,
ActiveAgent_IdPs)],
            U_S=S#state{activeAgent_IdPs=U_ActiveAgent_IdPs, eval_acc=U_EvalAcc,
cycle_acc=U_CycleAcc, time_acc=U_TimeAcc},
            {noreply,U_S}
```

```
    end;
%This handle_cast clause accepts a termination message from an agent. The message contains
the Id of the agent, and its reached fitness. The clause finds the species to which the agent be-
longs, processes the agent's fitness to produce the true fitness, and adds the agent to the
dead_pool. From the dead_pool the function then chooses an agent, the probability of choosing
the agent is proportional to its offspring allocation number, and thus there is a greater chance of
choosing the more fit agents. After an agent has been chosen from the dead_pool, there is 90%
that the agent will be used as a base to produce an offspring, and 10% that the agent itself will
be reapplied to the problem, for reevaluation, to ensure that it belongs in the dead_pool. This
makes sure that if the environment has changed, that if the world has advanced further than this
ancient agent can cope with, and that if it lived in an easy world compared to the current one
where fitness points are not so easily achieved... the agent is reevaluated, and its competitive-
ness is found. This allows the dead_pool to track the drift of the world, the environment... the
dead_pool is used for content drift tracking. If the offspring is produced, it is then released into
the environment or applied to the problem again. After this, because dead_pool size must stay
within a certain size X, the top X agents of the dead_pool are left in it, and the rest are deleted.
If the agent was itself chosen to be applied to the problem again, then its id is extracted from
the dead_pool, and it is applied to the problem again.
```

The population_monitor using the steady_state evolutionary loop terminates when a fitness goal has been reached, or after reaching a particular number of evaluations. When one of these termination conditions is reached, the population_monitor process stops generating new agents, and waits for all the remaining agents to terminate. Afterwards, the population_monitor itself terminates normally.

The population_monitor process utilizes the same fitness postprocessor functions in its steady_state approach as it does in its generational one. The selection algorithm though is different. In the steady_state evolutionary loop, the selection algorithm, *competition/1*, is executed with the DeadPool_AgentSummaries parameter, and it must return some fit agent. This is unlike the generational version of selection algorithms, which accept a list of summaries, neural energy cost, and population size limit, and return a tuple composed of the next generation population and a list of champion agents.

We create the necessary new selection algorithm for the steady_state evolutionary loop by modifying the original competition algorithm. We will postfix *stst* (steady-state) to the algorithm name that is used with the steady_state evolutionary loop. The new selection algorithm, *competition_stst/1*, accepts the agent summaries list as a parameter, and performs the computations similar to the original competition selection algorithm. But this selection algorithm uses the offspring allotments as probabilities, the higher the allotment the higher the chance that the agent is chosen. Based on these allotments, the algorithm then chooses one of the agents, and returns its summary back to the caller. The new competition_stst/1 selection algorithm is shown in Listing-11.13.

Listing-11.13 A new selection algorithm for the steady_state evolutionary loop.

```erlang
competition_stst(ProperlySorted_AgentSummaries)->
    TotEnergy = lists:sum([Fitness || {Fitness,_TotN,_Agent_Id}<-
ProperlySorted_AgentSummaries]),
    TotNeurons = lists:sum([TotN || {_Fitness,TotN,_Agent_Id} <-
ProperlySorted_AgentSummaries]),
    NeuralEnergyCost = TotEnergy/TotNeurons,
    {AlotmentsP,NextGenSize_Estimate}
=calculate_alotments(ProperlySorted_AgentSummaries,NeuralEnergyCost,[],0),
    {WinnerFitness,WinnerTotN,WinnerAgent_Id} =choose_CompetitionWinner(AlotmentsP,
random:uniform(round(100*NextGenSize_Estimate))/100,0),
    {WinnerFitness,WinnerTotN,WinnerAgent_Id}.

    choose_CompetitionWinner([{MutantAlotment,Fitness,TotN,Agent_Id}|AlotmentsP],
Choice,Range_From)->
        Range_To = Range_From+MutantAlotment,
        case (Choice >= Range_From) and (Choice =< Range_To) of
            true ->
                {Fitness,TotN,Agent_Id};
            false ->
                choose_CompetitionWinner(AlotmentsP,Choice,Range_To)
        end;
    choose_CompetitionWinner([],_Choice,_Range_From)->
        exit("********ERROR:choose_CompetitionWinner:: reached [] without selecting a
winner.").
```

With the modification of the population_monitor now complete, and with the addition of the new selection algorithm, we can now move forward and update the exoself module.

11.4.7 Updating the exoself Module

We now update the exoself module, primarily the prep and the loop functions of the exoself. We first add the state record:

```erlang
-record(state,{
    agent_id,
    generation,
    pm_pid,
    idsNpids,
    cx_pid,
    spids=[],
```

```
   npids=[],
   nids=[],
   apids=[], scape_pids=[],
   highest_fitness=0,
   eval_acc=0,
   cycle_acc=0,
   time_acc=0,
   max_attempts=10,
   attempt=1,
   tuning_duration_f,
   tuning_selection_f,
   annealing_parameter,
   perturbation_range
}).
```

Which will be used to keep track of all the parameters used by the exoself process. The new prep/2 function will use this state record to store all the useful information, including the perturbation parameter value, tuning selection function name, and the annealing parameter. Once the prep/2 function completes setting up the NN system, the exoself drops into its main loop. We update the loop to take advantage of the now decoupled tuning selection algorithms, and the annealing and the perturbation parameters.

The updated version of the exoself's functionality is as follows:

1. The updated exoself process' main loop awaits from its cortex process the evoluation_completed message.
2. Once the message is received, based on the fitness achieved, the exoself decides on whether to continue tuning the weights or terminate the system.
3. Exoself tries to improve the fitness by perturbing/tuning the weights of its neurons, after each tuning session, the Neural Network based system performs another evaluation by interacting with the scape until completion (the NN solves a problem, or dies within the scape, or...).

The order of events that the exoself performs is important: When evaluation_completed message is received, the function first checks whether the newly achieved fitness is higher than the highest fitness achieved thus far, which is set to 0 during the prep phase when the exoself just comes online. If the new fitness is not higher than the currently recorded highest fitness the agent achieved, then the exoself sends its neurons a message to restore their weights to their previous values, to the values which produced the highest fitness instead of their current values which yielded the current lower fitness score. If on the other hand the new fitness is higher than the previously highest achieved fitness, then the function tells the neurons to backup their current synaptic weights, as these weights represent the NN's best, most fit form yet.

The *exoself* process then tells all the neurons to prepare for a "memory reset" by sending each neuron the: *{self(), reset_prep}*, message. Since the NN can have recursive connections, it is important for each neuron to flush its buffer/inbox and be reset into its initial fresh state. Thus each neuron goes into standby mode when it receives the reset_prep signal, and begins to wait for the reset signal from the exoself. This ensures that none of the neurons are functioning or processing data when they are reset, and that all of them are synchronized. Once all the neurons go to this standby mode, by replying to the exoself that they received its reset_prep message, the exoself sends them the actual reset message, which makes them flush their buffers, and returns them into their main loop.

Finally, the exoself checks whether it has already tried to improve the NN's fitness a maximum of *S#state.max_attempts* number of times. If that is the case, the exoself process backs up the updated NN (with the updated, tuned weights) to database using the backup_genotype/2 function, prints to screen that it is terminating, and sends to the population_monitor its accumulated statistics (highest fitness, evaluation count, cycle count...). On the other hand, if the exoself process is not yet done tuning the neural weights, when it has not yet reached its termination condition, it forms a list of neuron ids and their perturbation *Spread* values, and asks them to perturb their synaptic weights.

This is the new feature that we have added, unlike before, the exoself uses the tuning selection function, the perturbation value, and the annealing value, to compose a list of tuples: *[{Nid, Spread}...]*, which dictates which neuron ids should be perturbed, and also the perturbation intensity range. The *Spread* value is the actual range of possible perturbation values. The spread is calculated through the use of perturbation range value and the annealing parameter. The NIds are chosen using the exoself's tuning selection algorithm function.

The tuning_selection_f is used to compose a list of tuples: *[{Nid,Spread}...]*, where each tuple is composed of a neuron id and the perturbation spread value. The actual tuning selection function accepts the NIds (not NPIds as in the original code), the generation value of the agent (its age), the perturbation range value, and the annealing parameter. The selection function then composes the list, and returns that list of tuples to the exoself. Once this list of tuples is composed, the exoself sends each of the selected neurons a message to perturb its synaptic weights using the *Spread* value. The message format is changed from *{self(), weight_perturb}* to *{self(), weight_perturb, Spread}*. Unlike before where we directly dealt with NPIds, since we simply chose the NPIds randomly from all the NPIds composing the NN, we now use NIds, because during the selection function, the way we compute the Spread value a neuron should use, is by analyzing that neuron's age, and its generation. Thus, once the list of selected neurons is composed, we use the IdsNPIds ets table which maps ids to pids and back, to convert the NIds to NPIds, and send each of the selected NPIds the noted message. Finally, the exoself then reactivates the cortex, and drops back into its main loop. The updated source of the prep/2 function, and the new main loop/1 function of the exoself, are shown in Listing-11.14.

Listing-11.14 The updated prep and main loop functions of the exoself module.

```
prep(Agent_Id,PM_PId)->
    random:seed(now()),
    IdsNPIds = ets:new(idsNpids,[set,private]),
    A = genotype:dirty_read({agent,Agent_Id}),
    Cx = genotype:dirty_read({cortex,A#agent.cx_id}),
    SIds = Cx#cortex.sensor_ids,
    AIds = Cx#cortex.actuator_ids,
    NIds = Cx#cortex.neuron_ids,
    ScapePIds = spawn_Scapes(IdsNPIds,SIds,AIds),
    spawn_CerebralUnits(IdsNPIds,cortex,[Cx#cortex.id]),
    spawn_CerebralUnits(IdsNPIds,sensor,SIds),
    spawn_CerebralUnits(IdsNPIds,actuator,AIds),
    spawn_CerebralUnits(IdsNPIds,neuron,NIds),
    link_Sensors(SIds,IdsNPIds),
    link_Actuators(AIds,IdsNPIds),
    link_Neurons(NIds,IdsNPIds),
    {SPIds,NPIds,APIds}=link_Cortex(Cx,IdsNPIds),
    Cx_PId = ets:lookup_element(IdsNPIds,Cx#cortex.id,2),
    {TuningDurationFunction,Parameter} = A#agent.tuning_duration_f,
    S = #state{
            agent_id=Agent_Id,
            generation=A#agent.generation,
            pm_pid=PM_PId,
            idsNpids=IdsNPIds,
            cx_pid=Cx_PId,
            spids=SPIds,
            npids=NPIds,
            nids=NIds,
            apids=APIds,
            scape_pids=ScapePIds,
            max_attempts= tuning_duration:TuningDurationFunction(Parameter, NIds,
A#agent.generation),
            tuning_selection_f=A#agent.tuning_selection_f,
            annealing_parameter=A#agent.annealing_parameter,
            tuning_duration_f=A#agent.tuning_duration_f,
            perturbation_range=A#agent.perturbation_range
    },
    loop(S).
%The prep/2 function prepares and sets up the exoself's state before dropping into the main
loop. The function first reads the agent and cortex records belonging to the Agent_Id of the NN
```

based system. The function then reads the sensor, actuator, and neuron ids, then spawns the private scapes using the spawn_Scapes/3 function, spawns the cortex, sensor, actuator, and neuron processes, and then finally links up all these processes together using the link_.../2 functions. Once the phenotype has been generated from the genotype, the exoself drops into its main loop.

```
loop(S)->
  receive
        {Cx_PId,evaluation_completed,Fitness,Cycles,Time}->
            IdsNPIds = S#state.idsNpids,
            {U_HighestFitness,U_Attempt}=case Fitness > S#state.highest_fitness of
                    true ->
                            [NPId ! {self(),weight_backup} || NPId <- S#state.npids],
                            {Fitness,0};
                    false ->
                            Perturbed_NIdPs=get(perturbed),
                            [ets:lookup_element(IdsNPIds,NId,2) ! {self(),weight_restore} ||
{NId,_Spread} <- Perturbed_NIdPs],
                            {S#state.highest_fitness,S#state.attempt+1}
                end,
            [PId ! {self(), reset_prep} || PId <- S#state.npids],
            gather_acks(length(S#state.npids)),
            [PId ! {self(), reset} || PId <- S#state.npids],
            U_CycleAcc = S#state.cycle_acc+Cycles,
            U_TimeAcc = S#state.time_acc+Time,
            U_EvalAcc = S#state.eval_acc+1,
            case U_Attempt >= S#state.max_attempts of
                    true ->%End training
                            A=genotype:dirty_read({agent,S#state.agent_id}),
                            genotype:write(A#agent{fitness=U_HighestFitness}),
                            backup_genotype(S#state.idsNpids,S#state.npids),
                            terminate_phenotype(S#state.cx_pid,S#state.spids,S#state.npids,
S#state.apids,S#state.scape_pids),
                            io:format("Agent:~p terminating. Genotype has been backed
up.~n Fitness:~p~n TotEvaluations:~p~n TotCycles:~p~n TimeAcc:~p~n",[self(),
U_HighestFitness, U_EvalAcc,U_CycleAcc,U_TimeAcc]),
                            gen_server:cast(S#state.pm_pid,{S#state.agent_id, terminated,
U_HighestFitness,U_EvalAcc,U_CycleAcc,U_TimeAcc});
                    false -> %Continue training
                            TuningSelectionFunction=S#state.tuning_selection_f,
                            PerturbationRange = S#state.perturbation_range,
                            AnnealingParameter = S#state.annealing_parameter,
                            ChosenNIdPs=tuning_selection:TuningSelectionFunction(
S#state.nids,S#state.generation,PerturbationRange,AnnealingParameter),
                            [ets:lookup_element(IdsNPIds,NId,2) ! {self(),weight_perturb,
Spread} || {NId,Spread} <- ChosenNIdPs],
```

```
                              put(perturbed,ChosenNIdPs),
                              Cx_PId ! {self(),reactivate},
                              U_S =S#state{
                                     cycle_acc=U_CycleAcc,
                                     time_acc=U_TimeAcc,
                                     eval_acc=U_EvalAcc,
                                     attempt=U_Attempt,
                                     highest_fitness=U_HighestFitness
                              },
                              loop(U_S)
              end
       end.
```

%When exoself receives the evaluation_complete message from the cortex, it first checks whether the newly achieved fitness by its NN is greater than the currently highest fitness achieved value. Before the NN based system terminates, it must fail to increase in fitness for Max_Attempts number of times. Thus, if the new fitness is not higher than highest_fitness, and the agent failed to increase in fitness more than Max_Attempts number of times, the exoself terminates its NN's phenotype, and forwards the highest achieved fitness and other statistics of its performance to the population_monitor process. If the fitness is not higher than the highest_fitness on record, but the exoself has not attempted to increase the NN's fitness more than Max_Attempts number of times, it requests that the neurons restore their previous set of synaptic weights, representing the thus far best achieved combination of weights, then it requests that they perturb their synaptic weights, and flush their inbox to get back into their initial pristine form. Finally, the exoself sends the cortex a message to reactivate, triggering it to action and its synchronization duties. The way the exoself chooses the neurons to perturb, is using the tuning_selection function. If on the other hand the newly achieved fitness is higher than the previously achieved highest_fitness, then the exoself requests that the neurons backup their current synaptic weights. The exoself then resets its attempt counter back to 0, so as to give the new synaptic weight combination another Max_Attempts number of perturbations and attempts at improvement, and then again requests that the neurons perturb their synaptic weights. Finally, the exoself then drops back into its main receive loop.

The tuning_duration module contains all the tuning duration functions, functions which calculate how long the tuning phase must run. The tuning duration function sets the max_attempts value, with the function format being as follows:

- **Input**: Neuron_Ids, AgentGeneration
- **Output**: Max_Attempts

The tuning duration function can output a constant, which is what we used thus far. It can output a value that is proportional to the number of neurons composing the NN, or it can produce a value based on the number of all neurons in the population. Listing-11.15 shows the implementation of the tuning_duration module.

Listing-11.15 The tuning_duration module which stores the various tuning duration functions.

```
const(Parameter,_N_Ids,_Generation)->
    ConstMaxAttempts = Parameter,
    ConstMaxAttempts.
%const/3 returns the preset const max_attempts value.

wsize_proportional(Parameter,N_Ids,Generation)->
    Power = Parameter,
    Active_NIds = extract_RecGenNIds(N_Ids,Generation,3,[]),
    Tot_ActiveNeuron_Weights = extract_NWeightCount(Active_NIds,0),
    20 + functions:sat(round(math:pow(Tot_ActiveNeuron_Weights,Power)),100,0).
%wsize_proportional/3 calculates the max_attempts value based on the agent's features. In this
case the max_attempts is proportional to the agent's number of weights belonging to the neu-
rons which were added or mutated within the last 3 generations.

    extract_RecGenNIds([N_Id|N_Ids],Generation,AgeLimit,Acc)->
        N = genotype:dirty_read({neuron,N_Id}),
        NeuronGen = N#neuron.generation,
        case NeuronGen >= (Generation-AgeLimit) of
            true ->
                extract_RecGenNIds(N_Ids,Generation,AgeLimit,[N_Id|Acc]);
            false ->
                extract_RecGenNIds(N_Ids,Generation,AgeLimit,Acc)
        end;
    extract_RecGenNIds([],_Generation,_AgeLimit,Acc)->
        Acc.
%extract_RecGenNIds/4 extracts the NIds of all neurons whose age is lower or equal to the
specified AgeLimit.

    extract_NWeightCount([N_Id|RecGenN_Ids],Acc)->
        N = genotype:dirty_read({neuron,N_Id}),
        Input_IdPs = N#neuron.input_idps,
        TotWeights = lists:sum([length(Weights) || {_IId,Weights} <- Input_IdPs]),
        extract_NWeightCount(RecGenN_Ids,TotWeights+Acc);
    extract_NWeightCount([],Acc)->
        Acc.
%extract_NWeightCount/2 counts the total number of weights which belong to the list of neu-
ron ids that the function was called with.

nsize_proportional(Parameter,N_Ids,Generation)->
    Power = Parameter,
    Tot_Neurons = length(extract_RecGenNIds(N_Ids,Generation,3,[])),
    20 + functions:sat(round(math:pow(Tot_Neurons,Power)),100,0).
%nsize_proportional/3 calculates the max_attempts to be proportional to the number of neurons
which were mutated or added to the NN within the last 3 generations.
```

There are many different ways in which you can calculate the max_attempts value for the tuning phase. The main thing that must be kept in mind, is that the same tuning duration function must be used by all competing agents in the population, thus ensuring that the tuning process is fair, and that no agent gets an advantage because it uses some particular tuning duration function that is not used by others. If that happens, then evolution and fitness of the competing agents becomes dependent not on true fitness of the agent but on the function it uses. The agents competing with each other, must use the same tuning duration function.

Also, when creating tuning duration functions that take into account the NN's size, we must ensure that this factor skews the fitness towards producing smaller NN systems, not larger. We do not want to reward neural bloating. For example, if we create a tuning duration function which uses the following equation: *MaxAttempts = 100*TotNeurons*, we will be giving an incentive for the NNs to bloat. Since just by adding one extra neuron, the NN has 100 extra tries to improve its fitness, and chances are that it will be a bit more fit than its better counterparts which did not get as many attempts. To avoid this, we must analyze the tuning duration functions, ensuring that they promote more concise NN systems, or that they at least do not provide the incentives which overwrite the actual fitness function. Another alternative is to use a constant MaxAttempts value. With a constant MaxAttempts value, the larger NNs will evolve such structures that leaves them general, and competitive with smaller NNs, since the larger NN systems will have the same MaxAttempts to optimize, and their architecture and topology will have to be such that they can still compete and optimize easily with the few synaptic weight permutation attempts that they are given.

The nsize_proportional and wsize_proportional functions have their *exponential power* parameters set to 0.5, and thus take the square root of the number of neurons and weights respectively. Thus, the NN systems which have a larger number of weights or neurons to optimize, will have a larger number of chances, but just barely. Hopefully this approach will not overwrite and undermine the fitness function, still push towards more concise topologies, while at the same time provide for a few more optimization attempts to the larger NN based agents, which need them due to having that many more synaptic weight permutations which can be explored. There are many different ways to create tuning duration functions, having decoupled them from the system will help us experiment with them, and perhaps find one that has the best of all worlds.

Having completed the *tuning_duration* module, we move to the *tuning_selection* module. The tuning_selection module contains all the tuning selection functions, which accept as input four parameters:

1. All NIds belonging to the NN.
2. The agent's generation, which is the number of topological mutation phases that it has undergone.
3. The perturbation range, the multiplier of math:pi(), which when used produces the *spread* value.

4. The annealing parameter, which is used to indicate how the perturbation range decays with the *age* of the neuron to which synaptic weight perturbation is applied. It makes less sense to perturb the more stable elements of the NN system, less so than those elements which have just recently been added to the NN system, and which still need to be tuned and modified to work well with the already existing larger system. The concept is that of simulated annealing [3].

We gather all these selection functions in their own module because there are many ways to select neurons which should be perturbed in local search during the tuning phase. This makes it easier for us to add new selection functions later on, and see if a new function can improve the performance. Of course it would be even better to decouple the system to such an extent that local and global searches are completely swappable, letting us have the ability to apply to the NN system anything during global search and local search phases. Being able to use particle swarm optimization, ant colony optimization... and swap between all these approaches during the parameter and topology optimization would be something interesting to explore. Eventually, that feature too shall be added. But for now, the tuning_selection module will primarily concentrate on holding the different types of local search, neuron selection algorithms.

Also, because we now wish to take advantage of the perturbation range value and the annealing parameter, the tuning selection function must not only select the neuron ids for synaptic perturbation, but also compute the perturbation intensity, the available range of the perturbation intensity, from which the neuron will then randomly generate a weight perturbation value. Thus, the selection function creates a list of tuples rather than simply a list of neuron ids. The selection function outputs a list of the following form: *[{NId,Spread}...]*, where NId is the neuron id, and Spread is the spread above and below 0, the value within which the neuron generates the actual perturbation. The Spread equals the peturbation_range value if there is no annealing, if annealing is present (annealing_parameter =< 1), then the Spread is further modified. The annealing factor must scale the Spread, proportional to the age of the neuron whose synaptic weights are to be perturbed. In our tuning selection algorithms, the spread value is calculated as follows:

Spread=PerturbationRange*math:pi()*math:pow(AnnealingParameter,NeuronAge).

When *AnnealingParameter* = *1*, there is no annealing. But when the AnnealingParameter is set to a number lower than 1, then annealing is exponentially proportional to the neuron's age.

We will create 8 such selection functions, their names and features are as follows:

1. **dynamic:** This function randomly generates a neuron age limit using math:sqrt(1/random:uniform()). The distribution of neuron age limits is thus skewed towards lower values. Once the neuron age limit is generated, all neurons in the NN of that age and lower are chosen for synaptic weight perturba-

tion. If annealing parameter is less than 1, then the Spread is calculated for every chosen neuron.

2. **dynamic_random:** This function does the same as the *dynamic* selection function, but after that pool of NIds is created, it then composes a new pool of tuples by going through the list of tuples and selecting each with a probability of 1/math:sqrt(length(TupleList)). In this manner, during every tuning evaluation, a random set of NIds is chosen for perturbation, at times a large number, and sometimes just a few. This further randomizes the intensity of tuning.

3. **active:** The active selection function chooses all neurons which were affected by mutation or created within the last 3 generations.

4. **active_random:** Performs the same function as *active*, but then creates a sublist by randomly choosing tuples from the original *active* list, each tuple is chosen with a probability of 1/math:sqrt(length(TupleList)).

5. **current:** The current selection function chooses all neurons affected during the last generation, those that were just added or affected by topological mutation.

6. **current_random:** Again, uses the tuple list created in the *current* function, but then generates a sublist with each tuple having a chance of being chosen with the probability of 1/math:sqrt(length(TupleList)).

7. **all:** The tuple list is composed of all the neurons in the NN. This would become ineffective once the NN grows in size, since it would be very difficult to find the right neuron to perturb if the size of the NN is 1000000, and during the last topological mutation phase only a single neuron has been added, for example. This tuning selection algorithm is something to compare the other tuning selection functions with. Although this function can be made effective with a proper annealing parameter. With an annealing parameter, it would then have the most recent neurons in the NN use high perturbation Spreads, while those which have stabilized, would have Spread values that were almost nonexistent. When set up in this manner, this function becomes the true annealing based tuning selection function.

8. **all_random:** The same as the *all* function, but uses the initial list to generate a new sublist by randomly choosing tuples from the *all* list, each tuple with a probability of 1/math:sqrt(length(TupleList)).

The implementation of these tuning selection functions is shown in Listing-11.16.

Listing-11.16 The implementation of the tuning_selection module.

```
-module(tuning_selection).
-compile(export_all).
-include("records.hrl").

dynamic(N_Ids,AgentGeneration,PerturbationRange,AnnealingParameter)->
    AgeLimit = math:sqrt(1/random:uniform()),
```

```
    ChosenN_IdPs = case extract_CurGenNIdPs(N_Ids,AgentGeneration,AgeLimit,
PerturbationRange, AnnealingParameter,[]) of
        [] ->
                [N_Id|_] = N_Ids,
                [{N_Id,PerturbationRange*math:pi()}];
            ExtractedN_IdPs->
                ExtractedN_IdPs
    end,
    ChosenN_IdPs.
```

%The dynamic/4 selection function randomly selects an age limit for its neuron id pool. The age limit is chosen by executing math:sqrt(1/random:uniform()), which creates a value between 1 and infinity. Using this function there is 75% that the number will be =<2, then 25% that it will be >=2, then 11% that it will be >=3... Every time this selection function is executed, the AgeLimit is generated anew, thus different executions will produce different neuron id pools for tuning.

```
    extract_CurGenNIdPs([N_Id|N_Ids],Generation,AgeLimit,PR,AP,Acc)->
        N = genotype:dirty_read({neuron,N_Id}),
        NeuronGen = N#neuron.generation,
        case NeuronGen >= (Generation-AgeLimit) of
                true ->
                        Age = Generation-NeuronGen,
                        Spread = PR*math:pi()*math:pow(AP,Age),
                        extract_CurGenNIdPs(N_Ids,Generation,AgeLimit,PR,AP, [{N_Id,
Spread}|Acc]);
                false ->
                        extract_CurGenNIdPs(N_Ids,Generation,AgeLimit,PR,AP,Acc)
        end;
    extract_CurGenNIdPs([],_Generation,_AgeLimit,_PR,_AP,Acc)->
        Acc.
```

%The extract_CurGenNIdPs/6 composes a neuron id pool from neurons who are younger than the AgeLimit parameter. This is calculated by comparing the neuron generation, which notes when it was created or affected by mutation, to the agent's generation, which increments with every topological mutation phase. Id pool accumulates not just the neurons but also the spread which will be used for the synaptic weight perturbation. The spread is calculated by multiplying the perturbation_range variable by math:pi(), and then multiplied by the annealing factor which is: math:pow(AnnealingParameter,Age). If the Annealing parameter is less than 1, then the greater the age of the neuron, the lower the Spread will be. If Annealing parameter is set to 1, then no annealing occurs.

```
dynamic_random(N_Ids,AgentGeneration,PerturbationRange,AnnealingParameter) ->
    ChosenN_IdPs = case extract_CurGenNIdPs(N_Ids,AgentGeneration,
math:sqrt(1/random:uniform()),PerturbationRange,AnnealingParameter,[]) of
        [] ->
                [N_Id|_] = N_Ids,
```

```
                        [{N_Id,PerturbationRange*math:pi()}];
            ExtractedN_IdPs->
                        ExtractedN_IdPs
    end,
    Tot_Neurons = length(ChosenN_IdPs),
    MutationP = 1/math:sqrt(Tot_Neurons),
    choose_randomNIdPs(MutationP,ChosenN_IdPs).
```
%dynamic_random/4 selection function composes the neuron id pool the same way as the dynamic/4 selection function, but after the id pool is generated, this selection function extracts ids from it randomly with a probability of 1/math:sqrt(Tot_Neurons). Thus the probability of a neuron being selected from this pool is proportional to the number of ids in that pool. If through chance no ids are selected, then the first element in the id pool is automatically selected, and given the highest spread.

```
    choose_randomNIdPs(MutationP,N_IdPs)->
            case choose_randomNIdPs(N_IdPs,MutationP,[]) of
                [] ->
                        {NId,Spread} = lists:nth(random:uniform(length(N_IdPs)),N_IdPs),
                        [{NId,Spread}];
                Acc ->
                        Acc
            end.
    choose_randomNIdPs([{NId,Spread}|N_IdPs],MutationP,Acc)->
            U_Acc = case random:uniform() < MutationP of
                true ->
                        [{NId,Spread}|Acc];
                false ->
                        Acc
            end,
            choose_randomNIdPs(N_IdPs,MutationP,U_Acc);
    choose_randomNIdPs([],_MutationP,Acc)->
            Acc.
```
% choose_randomNIdPs/2 calls choose_randomNIdPs/3 which accepts a mutation probability parameter and a list of tuples composed of neuron ids and their spreads. The function then selects randomly from this list with a probability MutationP, composes a new sublist, and returns it to the caller (choose_randomNIdPs/2). If by chance the sublist ends up being empty, the function choose_randomNIdPs/2 chooses a random tuple from the list, and returns it to the caller. Otherwise the composed sublist is returned to the caller as is.

```
active(N_Ids,AgentGeneration,PerturbationRange,AnnealingParameter)->
    extract_CurGenNIdPs(N_Ids,AgentGeneration,3,PerturbationRange,AnnealingParameter,[]).
```
%active/4 selection algorithm composes a neuron id pool from all neurons which are younger than 3 generations. I refer to the neurons as Active, if they have been affected or created within the last 3 generations, because they are still being integrated and tuned in to work with the rest of the NN based system.

```
active_random(N_Ids,AgentGeneration,PerturbationRange,AnnealingParameter)->
    ChosenN_IdPs = case extract_CurGenNIdPs(N_Ids,AgentGeneration,3,PerturbationRange,
AnnealingParameter,[]) of
        [] ->
                [N_Id|_] = N_Ids,
                [{N_Id,PerturbationRange*math:pi()}];
        ExtractedN_IdPs->
                ExtractedN_IdPs
    end,
    Tot_Neurons = length(ChosenN_IdPs),
    MutationP = 1/math:sqrt(Tot_Neurons),
    choose_randomNIdPs(MutationP,ChosenN_IdPs).
```
%active_random/4 is a selection algorithm that composes an id pool by first creating a list of all neurons who are younger than 3 generations, and then composing a sublist from it by randomly choosing elements from this list with a probability of 1/math:sqrt(Tot_Neurons).

```
current(N_Ids,AgentGeneration,PerturbationRange,AnnealingParameter)->
    case extract_CurGenNIdPs(N_Ids,AgentGeneration,0,PerturbationRange,
AnnealingParameter,[]) of
        [] ->
                [N_Id|_] = N_Ids,
                [{N_Id,PerturbationRange*math:pi()}];
        IdPs ->
                IdPs
    end.
```
%current/4 is a tuning selection algorithm that returns a list of all neurons which have been added to the NN, or affected by mutation, during the last generation.

```
current_random(N_Ids,AgentGeneration,PerturbationRange,AnnealingParameter)->
    ChosenN_IdPs = case extract_CurGenNIdPs(N_Ids,AgentGeneration,0,PerturbationRange,
AnnealingParameter,[]) of
        [] ->
                [N_Id|_] = N_Ids,
                [{N_Id,PerturbationRange*math:pi()}];
        IdPs ->
                IdPs
    end,
    Tot_Neurons = length(ChosenN_IdPs),
    MutationP = 1/math:sqrt(Tot_Neurons),
    choose_randomNIdPs(MutationP,ChosenN_IdPs).
```
%current_random/4 composes the list of tuples in the same way as current/4 does, but it then composes a sublist by randomly selecting elements from that list with a probability of 1/math:sqrt(Tot_Neurons), and returning this resulting sublist, back to the caller.

```
all(N_Ids,AgentGeneration,PerturbationRange,AnnealingParameter)->
    extract_CurGenNIdPs(N_Ids,AgentGeneration,AgentGeneration,PerturbationRange,
AnnealingParameter,[]).
%all/4 returns a list of tuples composed of all neuron ids (and their spread values) belonging to
the NN, to the caller.

all_random(N_Ids,AgentGeneration,PerturbationRange,AnnealingParameter)->
    ChosenN_IdPs = extract_CurGenNIdPs(N_Ids,AgentGeneration,AgentGeneration,
PerturbationRange,AnnealingParameter,[]),
    Tot_Neurons = length(ChosenN_IdPs),
    MutationP = 1/math:sqrt(Tot_Neurons),
    choose_randomNIdPs(MutationP,ChosenN_IdPs).
%all_random/4 first composes a list of tuples from nids and their spreads, and then creates a
sublist by choosing each element with a probability of 1/math:sqrt(Tot_neurons), returning the
result to the caller.
```

With the updated exoself module, and the newly created tuning_duration and selection_algorithm modules, the exoself decoupling is complete. We now need only update the neuron module, create the necessary plasticity and signal_accumulator modules, and we are ready to test our new, future ready, and agile, topology and weight evolving artificial neural network platform.

11.4.8 Updating the neuron Module

The neuron is the basic processing element, the basic processing node in the neural network system. The neurons in the system we've created are more general than those used by others. We created them to easily use various activation functions, and to accept and output vectors. Because we can use anything for the activation function, including logical operators, the neurons are really just processing nodes. In some sense, we have developed a system that is not a Topology and Weight Evolving Artificial Neural Network, but a Topology and Parameter Evolving Universal Learning Network (TPEULN). Nevertheless, we will continue referring to these processing elements as neurons.

At the moment, a neuron can accept vector signals from other elements. Since the inputs and outputs are standardized in their format, lists of float() values, the neuron does not need to know whether the input is from a neuron, a sensor, or from some other module capable of producing a vector signal. The problem though is that to use the aggregator functions to their full potential, to allow them full control when it comes to figuring out what to do with input signals, it would be useful to let them see the whole input vector. At this time, a neuron accepts a vector input from an element with an Id for which it has readied the appropriate synaptic weights, and then it computes the dot product. This means our neurons are looking at each input signal, one at a time, and then move on to the next. They do not see the entire input, which means they cannot look at all the input signals, and then decide how to aggregate them, what to do with them, how to process them... One of the many side effects of this, is that a neuron cannot normalize the list of input vectors, together as one.

Another way a neuron can process the input vectors is as follows: Instead of computing a dot product of every input vector with its synaptic weight list, we could have the neuron first aggregate the input signals, in the same order as its synaptic weights are, and then perform the information processing step. This is of course a bit less efficient, since it means each neuron will have to store the entire input, which might be a list of thousands of numbers. This is the way in which the DXNN neurons gather and process signals.

It is difficult to say which approach is more effective, the one we've built thus far, or the one used by DXNN, where the neuron first accumulates all the input signals from all the elements it is connected from, and then decides on what to do with them. Benchmarks show the one we have implemented here to work slightly faster, and of course each neuron takes up less memory, since each neuron does not have to store all the input signals first. At the same time, the DXNN neurons make certain things much simpler, having the entire input at your disposal when performing computations, when deciding on how plasticity affects the weights, is easy. Thus, in this second approach, what we lose in efficiency, we gain in extendibility and future readiness of the system.

To make the decision on which approach we should use, consider the implementation of the diff_aggregator: To implement the now numerously discussed *diff_aggregator* function, which instead of calculating the dot product of the input vector and the synaptic weights directly, calculates the dot product of the synaptic weights and the difference between the current input vector and the input vector the same element sent last time, the difference vector, we need to first store this previously received vector in memory. We could of course store each received input vector in process dictionary separately, but we could also aggregate the input vectors, and then store it as an ordered list of input vectors, which can then immediately be dotted with the synaptic weights list... and also be stored and then recovered if we use the diff aggregator. Also, if we wish to normalize the input vectors, though again possible with both neuron implementations, if we use the implementation where we store all input signals first, vector normalization becomes trivial.

Because the second implementation, the one used by DXNN, makes a number of these things simpler, we will use it instead. If at a later time we need to change things back, it will be easy to accomplish, and independent of the rest of the system. Thus, the new neuron implementation should use the following algorithm:

1. Neuron is spawned, and awaits in a prep state, waiting for its initialization parameters from the exoself.

2. Neuron receives its Input_PIdPs, AF, PF, AggrF, and other parameters from the exoself. Where the Input_PIdPs is a list of the form: [{Input_PId,Weights}...], in which Input_PId is that of the element that sends it a signal, and Weights are the synaptic weights associated with the vector input signal from the presynaptic element. After receiving the initialization parameters, the neuron sends out a default output signal to all the elements to which it is connected recurrently, and then drops into its main receive loop.

3. The neuron awaits signals in its main loop. It can accept signals of the following format:

   • **{Input_PId,forward,Input}**: The signal from other elements which send vector signals to it.

   • **{ExoSelf_PId,weight_backup}**: The signal from the exoself, which tells the neuron that the NN system performs best when this particular neuron is using its current synaptic weight combination, and thus it should save this synaptic weight list as *MInput_PidPs,* and that it is the best weight combination achieved thus far. This message is sent if after the weight perturbation, the NN's evaluation achieves a higher fitness than when the neurons of this NN used their previous synaptic weights.

   • **{ExoSelf_PId,weight_restore}**: This message is sent from the exoself, and it tells the neuron that it should restore its synaptic weight list to one previously used, saved as *MInput_PIdPs.* This message is usually sent if after the weight perturbation, the NN based agent's evaluation performs worse than it did with its previous synaptic weight combinations.

   • **{ExoSelf_PId,weight_perturb,Spread}**: This is a new message type, in our original version the neuron received the {ExoSelf_PId,weight_perturb} message, and used ?DELTA_MULTIPLIER macro to generate the perturbation intensities. With the new message, it will use the Spread value for the purpose of generating synaptic weight perturbations.

   • **{ExoSelf,reset_prep}**: This message is sent after a single evaluation is completed, and the exoself wishes to reset all the neurons to their original states, with empty inboxes. Once a neuron receives this message, it goes into a reset_prep state, flushes its buffer/inbox, and then awaits for the **{ExoSelf, reset}** signal. When the neuron receives the {ExoSelf,reset} message, it again sends out the default output messages to all its recurrent connections (ids stored in its ro_ids list), and then finally drops back into its main receive loop.

   • **{ExoSelf_PId,get_backup}**: When receiving this message, the neuron sends back to the exoself its last best synaptic weight combination, stored as the MInput_PIdPs list.

   • **{ExoSelf_PId,terminate}**: The neuron terminates after it receives this message.

   Except for the way the neuron processes the **{Input_PId, forward, Input}** and **{ExoSelf_PId, weight_perturb, Spread}** messages, the rest function in the same way they did in our original implementation.

4. The neuron accepts the *{Input_PId,forward,Input}* message only when the Input_PId in the message matches the Input_PId in its Input_PIdPs list. When the neuron receives the {Input_PId,forward,Input} message, unlike in the original implementation, our new neuron simply accumulates the {Input_PId,Input} message into its *IAcc* list. Once the neuron has received the Input signals from all the Input_PIds in its Input_PIdPs list, it then runs the aggregation function, synaptic plasticity function, and the activation function, to produce its final output signal. The accumulated {Input_PId, Input} messages are in the same order as the {Input_PId,Weights} tuples are in the Input_PIdPs list, since the neuron does a selective receive, forming the IAcc in the same order as the Input_PIds are in its Input_PIdPs. Because of this, once the IAcc list has been formed, taking a dot product or some function of the list, is easy. To take the dot product of the two lists, we simply dot the IAcc and the Input_PIdPs, since each is a vector composed of tuples which contain vectors.

5. When the neuron receives the *{ExoSelf_PId, weight_perturb, Spread}* message, it executes the same functions as in the original implementation, only in this implementation the *perturb_IPIdPs* function is executed with the *Spread* parameter instead of the *?DELTA_MULTIPLIER* macro.

That is essentially it. As you can see, the functionality is retained, we simply stopped computing the dot product immediately after every input message is received. Instead, we now first accumulate all the input vectors in the same order as the neuron's Input_IdPs, and then dot everything all at once. If we're using another aggregation function, we can then send the accumulated input vectors and the Input_IdPs through that function first. The implementation of this new neuron version is shown in Listing-11.17.

```
Listing-11.17 The updated neuron implementation. Only the updated parts are shown, high-
lighted in boldface.

gen(ExoSelf_PId,Node)->
    spawn(Node,?MODULE,prep,[ExoSelf_PId]).

prep(ExoSelf_PId) ->
    random:seed(now()),
    receive
            {ExoSelf_PId,{Id,Cx_PId,AF,PF,AggrF,Input_PIdPs,Output_PIds,RO_PIds}} ->
                fanout(RO_PIds,{self(),forward,[?RO_SIGNAL]}),
                IPIds = [IPId || {IPId,_W} <- Input_PIdPs],
                loop(Id,ExoSelf_PId,Cx_PId,AF,PF,AggrF,{IPIds,IPIds},[],{Input_PIdPs,
Input_PIdPs},Output_PIds,RO_PIds)
    end.
%When gen/2 is executed, it spawns the neuron element which immediately begins to wait for
its initial state message from the exoself. Once the state message arrives, the neuron sends out
```

the default forward signals to any elements in its ro_ids list, if any. Afterwards, prep/1 drops into the neuron's main receive loop.

```
loop(Id,ExoSelf_PId,Cx_PId,AF,PF,AggrF,{[Input_PId|IPIds],MIPIds},IAcc,{Input_PIdPs,
MInput_PIdPs},Output_PIds,RO_PIds)->
   receive
        {Input_PId,forward,Input}->
               loop(Id,ExoSelf_PId,Cx_PId,AF,PF,AggrF,{IPIds,MIPIds},
[{Input_PId,Input}| IAcc], {Input_PIdPs,MInput_PIdPs},Output_PIds,RO_PIds);
        {ExoSelf_PId,weight_backup}->
               loop(Id,ExoSelf_PId,Cx_PId,AF,PF,AggrF,{[Input_PId|IPIds],MIPIds},IAcc,
{Input_PIdPs,Input_PIdPs},Output_PIds,RO_PIds);
        {ExoSelf_PId,weight_restore}->
               loop(Id,ExoSelf_PId,Cx_PId,AF,PF,AggrF,{[Input_PId|IPIds],MIPIds},IAcc,
{MInput_PIdPs,MInput_PIdPs},Output_PIds,RO_PIds);
        {ExoSelf_PId,weight_perturb,Spread}->
               Perturbed_IPIdPs=perturb_IPIdPs(Spread,MInput_PIdPs),
               loop(Id,ExoSelf_PId,Cx_PId,AF,PF,AggrF,{[Input_PId|IPIds],MIPIds},IAcc,
{Perturbed_IPIdPs,MInput_PIdPs},Output_PIds,RO_PIds);
        {ExoSelf,reset_prep}->
               neuron:flush_buffer(),
               ExoSelf ! {self(),ready},
               receive
                    {ExoSelf, reset}->
                            fanout(RO_PIds,{self(),forward,[?RO_SIGNAL]})
               end,
               loop(Id,ExoSelf_PId,Cx_PId,AF,PF,AggrF,{MIPIds,MIPIds},[],{Input_PIdPs,
MInput_PIdPs}, Output_PIds,RO_PIds);
        {ExoSelf_PId,get_backup}->
               ExoSelf_PId ! {self(),Id,MInput_PIdPs},
               loop(Id,ExoSelf_PId,Cx_PId,AF,PF,AggrF,{[Input_PId|IPIds],MIPIds},IAcc,
{Input_PIdPs, MInput_PIdPs}, Output_PIds,RO_PIds);
        {ExoSelf_PId,terminate}->
               io:format("Neuron:~p has termianted.~n",[self()]),
               ok
   end;
loop(Id,ExoSelf_PId,Cx_PId,AF,PF,AggrF,{[],MIPIds},IAcc,{Input_PIdPs,MInput_PIdPs},
Output_PIds,RO_PIds)->
   Aggregation_Product = aggregation:AggrF(IAcc,Input_PIdPs),
   Output = functions:AF(Aggregation_Product),
   U_IPIdPs = plasticity:PF(IAcc,Input_PIdPs,Output),
   [Output_PId ! {self(),forward,[Output]} || Output_PId <- Output_PIds],
   loop(Id,ExoSelf_PId,Cx_PId,AF,PF,AggrF,
{MIPIds,MIPIds},[],{U_IPIdPs,MInput_PIdPs}, Output_PIds, RO_PIds).
...
```

...

...

```
perturb_IPIdPs(Spread,Input_PIdPs)->
    Tot_Weights=lists:sum([length(Weights) || {_Input_PId,Weights}<-Input_PIdPs]),
    MP = 1/math:sqrt(Tot_Weights),
    perturb_IPIdPs(Spread,MP,Input_PIdPs,[]).
perturb_IPIdPs(Spread,MP,[{Input_PId,Weights}|Input_PIdPs],Acc)->
    U_Weights = perturb_weights(Spread,MP,Weights,[]),
    perturb_IPIdPs(Spread,MP,Input_PIdPs,[{Input_PId,U_Weights}|Acc]);
perturb_IPIdPs(_Spread,_MP,[],Acc)->
    lists:reverse(Acc).
```

%The perturb_IPIdPs/1 function perturbs each synaptic weight in the Input_PIdPs list with a probability of: 1/math:sqrt(Tot_Weights). The probability is based on the total number of weights in the Input_PIdPs list, with the actual mutation probability equating to the inverse of square root of the total number of synaptic weights belonging to the neuron. The perturb_IPIdPs/3 function goes through each weights block and calls the perturb_weights/3 to perturb the weights.

```
    perturb_weights(Spread,MP,[W|Weights],Acc)->
        U_W = case random:uniform() < MP of
                true->
                        sat((random:uniform()-0.5)*2*Spread+W,-
?SAT_LIMIT,?SAT_LIMIT);
                false ->
                        W
        end,
        perturb_weights(Spread,MP,Weights,[U_W|Acc]);
    perturb_weights(_Spread,_MP,[],Acc)->
        lists:reverse(Acc).
```

%The perturb_weights/3 is the function that actually goes through each weight block (A weight block is a synaptic weight list associated with a particular input vector sent to the neuron by another element), and perturbs each weight with a probability of MP. If the weight is chosen to be perturbed, the perturbation intensity is chosen uniformly between -Spread and Spread.

I have highlighted the parts of the implementation that have been changed, added, or whose function is important for the new implementation. Once the IAcc is formed, everything hinges on the execution of:

```
Aggregation_Product = signal_aggregator:AggrF(IAcc,Input_PIdPs),
Output = functions:AF(Aggregation_Product),
U_IPIdPs = plasticity:PF(IAcc,Input_PIdPs,Output),
```

These three functions compose the Aggregation_Product (which might simply be a dot product of the input vectors and the associated synaptic weights), apply the activation function to the Aggregation_Product value to produce the final output, and then finally update the synaptic weights (Input_PIdPs) using the plasticity function (if any), respectively. The aggregation, activation, and plasticity functions are stored in their own respective modules. The activation functions are all stored in the *functions* module, the aggregation and the plasticity functions are stored in the *signal_aggregator* and *plasticity* modules respectively. In the following sections we will build these two modules.

11.4.9 Creating the signal_aggregator Module

The signal_aggregator module contains the various aggregation functions. An aggregation function is a function that in some manner gathers the input signal vectors, does something with it and the synaptic weights, and then produces a scalar value. For example, consider the dot product. The dot_product aggregation function composes the scalar value by aggregating the input vectors, and then calculating the dot product of the input vectors and the synaptic weights. Another way to calculate a scalar value from the input and weight vectors is by multiplying the corresponding input signals by their weights, but instead of *adding* the resulting multiplied values, we *multiply* them. For example consider the input vector to be: [I1,I2,I3], and the corresponding weight vector to be: [W1,W2,W3], then this *"mult_product"* is: $I1*W1 * I2*W2 * I3*W3$, compared to the dot product which is: $I1*W1 + I2*W2 + I3*W3$. Another one is the diff_product, which we can calculate if we assume that $I_{(k-1)}$ to be the input element one time step ago, and $I_{(k)}$ to be the input element in the current time step. Thus, whereas the previous time step input vector is: $[I1_{(k-1)}, I2_{(k-2)}, I3_{(k-3)}]$, the current input vector is: $[I1_{(k)}, I2_{(k)}, I3_{(k)}]$, and the synaptic weight vector is: $(W1, W2, W3)$, then the *diff_product* is: $(I1_{(k-1)} - I1_{(k)})*W1 + (I2_{(k-1)} - I2_{(k)})*W2 + (I3_{(k-1)} - I3_{(k)})*W3$. A neuron using this signal aggregation function would only see the differences in the signals, rather than the signals themselves. Thus if there is a rapid change in the signal, the neuron would see it, but if the signal were to stay the same for a long period of time, the neuron's input would be a vector of the form: [0,...].

There are certainly many other types of aggregation functions that could be created, and it is for this reason we have decoupled this functionality. Listing-11.18 shows the implementation of the signal_aggregator module, with the source code for dot_product, mult_product, and the diff_product, aggregator functions.

Listing-11.18 The signal_aggregator module containing the dot_product, mult_product, and diff_product aggregation functions.

```
--module(signal_aggregator).
-compile(export_all).
-include("records.hrl").
```

```
dot_product(IAcc,IPIdPs)->
   dot_product(IAcc,IPIdPs,0).
dot_product([{IPId,Input}|IAcc],[{IPId,Weights}|IPIdPs],Acc)->
   Dot = dot(Input,Weights,0),
   dot_product(IAcc,IPIdPs,Dot+Acc);
dot_product([],[{bias,[Bias]}],Acc)->
   Acc + Bias;
dot_product([],[],Acc)->
   Acc.


   dot([I|Input],[W|Weights],Acc) ->
        dot(Input,Weights,I*W+Acc);
   dot([],[],Acc)->
        Acc.
```
%The dot/3 function accepts an input vector and a weight list, and computes the dot product of
the two vectors.

```
diff_product(IAcc,IPIdPs)->
   case get(diff_product) of
        undefined ->
                put(diff_product,IAcc),
                dot_product(IAcc,IPIdPs,0);
        Prev_IAcc ->
                put(diff_product,IAcc),
                Diff_IAcc = input_diff(IAcc,Prev_IAcc,[]),
                dot_product(Diff_IAcc,IPIdPs,0)
   end.

   input_diff([{IPId,Input}|IAcc],[{IPId,Prev_Input}|Prev_IAcc],Acc)->
        Vector_Diff = diff(Input,Prev_Input,[]),
        input_diff(IAcc,Prev_IAcc,[{IPId,Vector_Diff}|Acc]);
   input_diff([],[],Acc)->
        lists:reverse(Acc).


        diff([A|Input],[B|Prev_Input],Acc)->
                diff(Input,Prev_Input,[A-B|Acc]);
        diff([],[],Acc)->
                lists:reverse(Acc).
```
%The diff_product/2 function accepts the IAcc and the IPIdPs tuple lists as input, and checks if
it has the previous IAcc stored in memory. If it doesn't, then the function calculates a dot product of the IAcc and PIdPs, and returns the result to the caller. If it does, then it subtracts (value
by value in the vectors) the previous IAcc from the current IAcc, then calculates a dot product
of the resulting vector and the IPIdPs, and returns the result to caller.

```
mult_product(IAcc,IPIdPs)->
    mult_product(IAcc,IPIdPs,1).
mult_product([{IPId,Input}|IAcc],[{IPId,Weights}|IPIdPs],Acc)->
    Dot = mult(Input,Weights,1),
    mult_product(IAcc,IPIdPs,Dot*Acc);
mult_product([],[{bias,[Bias]}],Acc)->
    Acc * Bias;
mult_product([],[],Acc)->
    Acc.


    mult([I|Input],[W|Weights],Acc) ->
        mult(Input,Weights,I*W*Acc);
    mult([],[],Acc)->
        Acc.
%The mult_product/2 function first multiplies the elements of the IAcc vector by their corre-
sponding weight values in the IPIdPs vector. It then multiplies the resulting values together
(whereas the dot product adds them), and finally returns the result to the caller.
```

The dot product aggregation function has already proven itself, it is used in al-most all artificial neural network implementations. The diff_product can be thought of as a neuron that looks not at the actual signal amplitudes, but the tem-poral difference in signal amplitudes. If the input signals have stabilized, then the neuron's input is calculated as a 0, if there is a sudden change in the signal, the neuron will see it. The worth of the mult_product aggregation function is certainly questionable, and should be further studied through benchmarking and testing. If there is any worth to this type of signal aggregator, evolution will find it. We can also add normalizer functions, which could normalize the input signals. The nor-malizers could be implemented as part of the aggregator functions, although it could be argued that even normalizing functions deserve their own module. Later on, we could make them a part of the aggregator functions, perhaps create two versions of each aggregation function, one which does normalize, and one which does not.

11.4.10 Creating the plasticity Module

The only remaining module left to implement is the plasticity module. True learning is not achieved when a static NN is trained on some data set through de-struction and recreation by the exoself based on its performance, but instead is the self organization of the NN, the self adaptation and changing of the NN based on the information it is processing. The learning rule, the way in which the neurons adapt independently, the way in which their synaptic weights change based on the neuron's experience, that is true learning, and that is neuroplasticity.

There are different algorithms which try to emulate biological neuroplasticity. One of such simple plasticity algorithms is the Hebbian Rule, which states that "neurons which fire together, wire together". The rule states that if a neuron A receives a positive input signal from another neuron B, and in response, after using its aggregation and activation function, neuron A produces a positive output, then A's synaptic weight for B's connection, increases in magnitude. If that synaptic weight was positive, it becomes more positive, if it was negative, it becomes more negative.

There are numerous plasticity rules, some more faithful to their biological counterparts than others, and some more efficient than their biological counterparts. We will discuss plasticity in a chapter dedicated to it. At this time, we will simply create a module, and a standardized plasticity function format, a function which accepts as input the accumulated input vector IAcc, Input_PIdPs, and Output, where IAcc is the input vector, Input_PIdPs is the associated vector of synaptic weights, and the Output value is the neuron's calculated output. In response, the plasticity function will produce an updated set of synaptic weights, the updated Input_PIdPs vector. This will simulate the adaptation and the morphing of synaptic weights due to the neuron's interaction with the world, the neuron's processing of input signals. Our neuroevolutionary system will be able to generate NN based agents with and without plasticity. At this time, the plasticity module will only contain one type of plasticity function, the none/3 function. The plasticity function none/3 does not change the neuron's synaptic weights, and thus represents the static neuron. This initial plasticity module is shown in Listing-11.19

Listing-11.19 The plasticity module containing the *none* plasticity function.

```
-module(plasticity).
-compile(export_all).
-include("records.hrl").

none(_IAcc,Input_PIdPs,_Output)->
    Input_PIdPs.
```

The none/3 plasticity function accepts the 3 parameters, and returns the same Input_PIdPs to the caller as the one it was called with. This module completes the modification to our neuroevolutionary system. Our system has now most of its important functionalities decoupled. These various functions are now exchangeable, evolvable, modifiable, making our neuroevolutionary system more dynamic, generalizable, and flexible. In the following section we will test our updated system to ensure that it works, and that all its new parts are functional.

11.5 Compiling & Testing the New System

We have made numerous modifications to the source code. Though our system is now more flexible, and we can modify the way it functions, and change its activation functions, plasticity, selection, genetic vs memetic evolution, and generational vs steady_state evolutionary loop, we have at the same time made it more complex. Our updated system has the following relation amongst the modules, processes, and functions (with regards to which are contained within which, and which are used by which):

- polis.erl
  - scape.erl

- genotype.erl
- genome_mutator.erl
- population_monitor.erl
  - evo_alg_f
  - fitness_postprocessor_f
    fitness_postprocessor.erl
  - selection_f
    selection_algorithm.erl

- **Agent:**
  - exoself.erl
    - morphology
      morphology.erl
    - tuning_duration_f
      tuning_duration.erl
    - tuning_selection_f
      tuning_selection.erl
    - annealing_parameter
    - perturbation_range
    - encoding_type
    - tot_topological_mutations_f
      tot_topological_mutations.erl
    - mutation_operators

  - cortex.erl
  - neuron.erl
    - af
      functions.erl
    - aggr_f
      signal_aggregator.erl

- ▪ pf
  plasticity.erl

- o   sensor.erl
- o   actuator.erl

The leafs of this bulleted list represent the various elements which are changeable, evolvable, and have been decoupled. For example, the population_monitor, and thus the particular population in question, behaves differently depending on the evo_alg_f (evolutionary algorithm function), the fitness_postprocessor_f (fitness postprocessor function), and the selection_f (the selection algorithm). These elements can all be set up differently for different populations, or even possibly changed/mutated during evolution. Also, because of the way we decoupled the various elements and parameters of the evolving NN based agents, each agent can have a different set of tuning_selection, tuning_duration, and tot_topological_mutations_f functions. Each agent can also evolve and use different annealing and perturbation range values. Furthermore, agents belonging to the same population can now be encoded differently, some neural, and some could employ the substrate encoding. Finally, the evolving topology can incorporate different types of neurons, each of which can have different plasticity functions, activation functions, and aggregation functions.

Because all of these now decoupled features can be identified by their tags/names, and activated by the same due to belonging to their own modules, we can evolve them. Each evolving agent can now also use the mutation operators which change, modify, and mutate these tags and values. This adds further flexibility to our neuroevolutionary system, and lets us modify its functionality by simply setting up the INIT_CONSTRAINTS macro to the set of parameters we wish to use for any particular experiment, or problem.

Though our system is now more flexible, and we can modify the way it functions, we have also made it more complex, with more movable parts, and thus more elements that can break, and hide bugs. We must now compile our new system and test its functionality. The full source code of our system thus far can be found at [4].

We have created the *polis:sync()* function to compile everything in our project folder. Thus to first test for compilation errors, all we do is execute this function:

```
1> polis:sync().
Recompile: signal_aggregator
Recompile: tot_topological_mutations
Recompile: tuning_duration
Recompile: tuning_selection
...
up_to_date
```

It works! But before we can test our new system on the XOR benchmark, due to our records having changed, we must first delete the existing mnesia database, and then create a new one. If there is no mnesia database (if you are using the provided Ch_11 work folder from [4]), then we simply create a new mnesia database by running polis:create(), and then start the polis function by running polist:start():

```
2> polis:create().
{atomic,ok}
3> polis:start().
Parameters:{[],[]}
******** Polis: ##MATHEMA## is now online.
{ok,<0.272.0>}
```

With the polis started, we will first create a test agent and test it on the xor problem independently with a few varying parameters. Once that test is complete, we will test the population_monitor, applying it to the XOR problem using the generational and steady_state evolutionary loops.

To test the exoself we must first create a test agent by executing the *genotype:create_test()* function. The *create_test/1* function creates the agent using the default *#constraint{}* record we defined in the *records.hrl* file. The default constraint record uses the following parameters:

```
-record(constraint,{
    morphology=xor_mimic, %xor_mimic
    connection_architecture = recurrent, %recurrent|feedforward
    neural_afs=[tanh,cos,gaussian,absolute], %[tanh,cos,gaussian,absolute,sin,sqrt,sigmoid],
    neural_pfs=[none], %[none,hebbian,neuro_modulated]
    neural_aggr_fs=[dot_product], %[dot_product, mult_product, diff]
    tuning_selection_fs=[all], %[all,all_random, recent,recent_random, lastgen,lastgen_random]
    tuning_duration_f={const,20}, %[{const,20},{nsize_proportional,0.5},
{nweight_proportional, 0.5}...]
    annealing_parameters=[1], %[1,0.9]
    perturbation_ranges=[1], %[0.5,1,2,3...]
    agent_encoding_types= [neural], %[neural,substrate]
    mutation_operators= [{mutate_weights,1}, {add_bias,1}, {mutate_af,1}, {add_outlink,1},
{add_inlink,1}, {add_neuron,1}, {outsplice,1}, {add_sensor,1}, {add_actuator,1}], %[
{mutate_weights,1}, {add_bias,1}, {remove_bias,1}, {mutate_af,1}, {add_outlink,1},
{remove_outLink,1}, {add_inlink,1}, {remove_inlink,1}, {add_sensorlink,1},
{add_actuatorlink,1}, {add_neuron,1}, {remove_neuron,1}, {outsplice,1}, {insplice,1},
{add_sensor,1}, {remove_sensor,1}, {add_actuator,1}, {remove_actuator,1}]
    tot_topological_mutations_fs = [{ncount_exponential,0.5}], %[{ncount_exponential,0.5},
{ncount_linear,1}]
    population_evo_alg_f=generational, %[generational, steady_state]
    population_fitness_postprocessor_f=size_proportional, %[none,nsize_proportional]
```

```
population_selection_f=competition %[competition,top3]
}).
```

With the new mnesia database created, and the polis process started, we now test the creation of a new agent using our modified genotype module, and the updated constraint record:

```
4> genotype:create_test().
{agent,test,neural,0,undefined,test,
    {{origin,7.551215163115267e-10},cortex},
    {[{0,1}]],
    [],
    [{sensor,undefined,xor_GetInput,undefined,
        {private,xor_sim},
        2,[],0,undefined,undefined,undefined,undefined,undefined,
        undefined}],
    [{actuator,undefined,xor_SendOutput,undefined,
        {private,xor_sim},
        1,[],0,undefined,undefined,undefined,undefined,undefined,
        undefined}]},
    {constraint,xor_mimic,recurrent,
        [tanh,cos,gaussian,absolute],
        [none],
        [dot_product],
        [all],
        {const,20},
        [1],
        [1],
        [neural],
        [{mutate_weights,1},
        {add_bias,1},
        {mutate_af,1},
        {add_outlink,1},
        {add_inlink,1},
        {add_neuron,1},
        {outsplice,1},
        {add_sensor,1},
        {add_actuator,1}],
        [{ncount_exponential,0.5}],
        generational,size_proportional,competition},
    [],undefined,0,
    [{0,[{{0,7.551215163115199e-10},neuron}]}],
    all,1,
    {const,20},
    1,
```

```
[{mutate_weights,1},
 {add_bias,1},
 {mutate_af,1},
 {add_outlink,1},
 {add_inlink,1},
 {add_neuron,1},
 {outsplice,1},
 {add_sensor,1},
 {add_actuator,1}],
 {ncount_exponential,0.5}}
{cortex,{{origin,7.551215163115267e-10},cortex},
 test,
 [{{0,7.551215163115199e-10},neuron}],
 [{{-1,7.551215163115238e-10},sensor}],
 [{{1,7.551215163115216e-10},actuator}]}
{sensor,{{-1,7.551215163115238e-10},sensor},
 xor_GetInput,
 {{origin,7.551215163115267e-10},cortex},
 {private,xor_sim},
 2,
 [{{0,7.551215163115199e-10},neuron}],
 0,undefined,undefined,undefined,undefined,undefined,undefined}
{neuron,{{0,7.551215163115199e-10},neuron},
 0,
 {{origin,7.551215163115267e-10},cortex},
 tanh,none,dot_product,
 [{{{-1,7.551215163115238e-10},sensor},
  [0.15548205860608455,0.17397940203921358]}],
 [{{1,7.551215163115216e-10},actuator}],
 []}
{actuator,{{1,7.551215163115216e-10},actuator},
 xor_SendOutput,
 {{origin,7.551215163115267e-10},cortex},
 {private,xor_sim},
 1,
 [{{0,7.551215163115199e-10},neuron}],
 0,undefined,undefined,undefined,undefined,undefined,undefined}
{atomic,{atomic,[ok]}}
```

It works! The genotype is printed to console, and it includes all the new features and parameters we've added. The genotype was created without any errors, and thus we can now test the agent by converting the genotype to phenotype, and applying it to the XOR mimicking problem. We do this by executing the *exoself:start(Agent_Id,void)* function, where *void* is just an atom in the place where we'd usually use a PId of the population_monitor:

```
6> exoself:start(test,void).
<0.363.0>
IPIdPs:[{<0.366.0>,[0.15548205860608455,0.17397940203921358]}]
Finished updating genotype
Terminating the phenotype:
Cx_PId:<0.365.0>
SPIds:[<0.366.0>]
NPIds:[<0.368.0>]
APIds:[<0.367.0>]
ScapePids:[<0.364.0>]
Agent:<0.363.0> terminating. Genotype has been backed up.
Fitness:0.23792642646665235
TotEvaluations:21
TotCycles:84
TimeAcc:3270
Sensor:{{-1,7.551215163115238e-10},sensor} is terminating.
Actuator:<0.367.0> is terminating.
Neuron:<0.368.0> is terminating.
Cortex:{{origin,7.551215163115267e-10},cortex} is terminating.
```

It works! The exoself converted the test genotype to its phenotype, tried to tune the NN for 21 evaluations (we know this due to the *TotEvaluations: 21* printout), and then terminated all the elements of the NN, and then itself terminated. With this test completing successfully, we can now test the whole neuroevolutionary system by creating a population of agents, applying them to the problem, evolving the population using the population_monitor, and then terminating the system once a termination condition has been reached. To do all of this, we need simply equate *#INIT_CONSTRAINTS* macro to the list of constraint tuples with the parameters we wish to use, and then execute the *population_monitor:test()* function.

We first test our neuroevolutionary system with the generational evolutionary algorithm, we do this by setting up the INIT_CONSTRAINT macro as follows:

```
-define(INIT_CONSTRAINTS,[#constraint{morphology=Morphology,connection_architecture
=CA,population_evo_alg_f=generational} || Morphology<-[xor_mimic],CA<-[feedforward]]).
```

With the constraint record set, we compile the population_monitor module, and then run it. For the sake of brevity, only a partial printout to console is shown:

```
13> c(population_monitor).
...
{ok,population_monitor}
14> population_monitor:test().
Specie_Id:7.551210273616779e-10 Morphology:xor_mimic
******** Population monitor started with parameters:{gt,test}
```

```
...
Using: Fitness Postprocessor:size_proportional Selection Algorirthm:competition
Valid_AgentSummaries:[{999529.2413070924,2,{7.551210272768589e-10,agent}},
             {1512.9118761841332,1,{7.551210272806172e-10,agent}},
             {1352.7815191404268,2,{7.551210272916421e-10,agent}},
             {302.13492581117015,1,{7.551210273600174e-10,agent}},
             {24.488124260342552,1,{7.551210273564292e-10,agent}}]
Invalid_AgentSummaries:[{10.146259718093239,2,{7.551210273018837e-10,agent}},
             {0.49999586555860426,1,{7.551210273039854e-10,agent}},
             {0.4999165758596308,1,{7.551210272834928e-10,agent}},
             {0.49062112602642133,2,{7.551210273073314e-10,agent}},
             {0.4193814651130151,1,{7.551210272863694e-10,agent}}]
...
******** Population_Monitor:test shut down with Reason:normal OpTag:continue, while in
OpMode:gt
******** Tot Agents:10 Population Generation:2 Eval_Acc:878 Cycle_Acc:3512
Time_Acc:476237
```

It works! We can execute population_monitor:test() a few more times to ensure that this was not a fluke and that it does indeed work. We next test the system using the new *steady_state* evolutionary loop. To accomplish this, all we need to do is modify the INIT_CONSTRAINTS, changing the *population_evo_alg_f* parameter from *generational* to *steady_state*:

```
-define(INIT_CONSTRAINTS,[#constraint{morphology=Morphology,connection_architecture
=CA, population_evo_alg_f=steady_state} || Morphology<-[xor_mimic], CA<-[feedforward]]).
```

With this modification, we again compile the population_monitor module, and execute population_monitor:test():

```
1> c(population_monitor).
...
{ok,population_monitor}
2> population_monitor:test().
Specie_Id:7.55120754326942e-10 Morphology:xor_mimic
******** Population monitor started with parameters:{gt,test}
...
Agent:<0.4146.0> terminating. Genotype has been backed up.
Fitness:959252.9093456662
TotEvaluations:45
TotCycles:180
TimeAcc:2621
Neuron:<0.4151.0> is terminating.
Sensor:{{-1,7.551207540548967e-10},sensor} is terminating.
Actuator:<0.4150.0> is terminating.
```

Neuron:<0.4152.0> is terminating.

Cortex:{{origin,7.551207540549013e-10},cortex} is terminating.

******** Population_Monitor:test shut down with Reason:normal OpTag:continue, while in

OpMode:gt

******** Tot Agents:10 **Population Generation:0 Eval_Acc:2338** Cycle_Acc:9352

Time_Acc:630207

It works! Note that the Population Generation is 0 in this case, because it never gets incremented. While at the same time the evaluation accumulator (Eval_Acc), is 2338. The fitness achieved is high, *Fitness: 959252*. Thus our system is functioning well, and can easily and efficiently solve the simple XOR problem. We should try the system with a few other parameters to ensure that it works. But with these tests done, we are now in a possession of an advanced, modularly designed, decoupled, scalable, and agile, neuroevolutionary platform.

11.6 Summary & Discussion

In this chapter we have modified the neuroevolutionary system we finished building by Chapter-9. We have decoupled numerous features of our system, including plasticity, signal aggregation, annealing parameters, various tuning parameters, and even the evolutionary algorithm loop type. All these decoupled elements of our neuroevolutionary system were given their own modules, and all these features can be accessed through their own function names. Due to these various elements now being specified by their names and parameters, rather than built and embedded into the functionality of the system, we can evolve them, mutate them, and change them during the evolutionary process. Thus, our system can now mutate and evolve new plasticity rules, tuning parameters, signal aggregation functions... in the same way that our original system allowed for the neurons to change and swap their activation functions.

This decoupling and modularization of the neuroevolutionary system design also makes it that much easier to add new elements, and to test out new features in the future. The new architecture of our system allows us to build new functions, new functionalities, without affecting the already tested and working elements of our TWEANN platform.

After making these modifications, we have tested the creation of a new agent using its newly modified genotypic and phenotypic elements. We have tested and found the creation of the genotype, the conversion of the genotype to phenotype, the processing ability of the exoself, and the functionality of the population_monitor with a generational and steady_state evolutionary loop, all functional and in perfect working condition. With this complete, we can now begin to add the various advanced features to our neuroevolutionary platform.

As we have found in this chapter, after adding new features, whether they simply optimize or augment the architecture, or whether they add new features to improve the evolutionary properties of the system, the resulting platform must be tested, and it must be benchmarked. For this reason, in the following chapter we will modify the population_monitor to keep track of the various evolutionary performance statistics and properties that change over time. Statistics like the average neural network size of the population, the maximum, minimum, average, and standard deviation of the population's fitness, and the numerous other evolutionary parameters that might further shine light on our system's performance.

11.7 References

[1] Paulsen O, Sejnowski TJ (2000). Natural Patterns of Activity and Long-Term Synaptic Plasticity. Current Opinion in Neurobiology 10, 172-179.

[2] Oja E (1982) A Simplified Neuron Model as a Principal Component Analyzer. Journal of Mathematical Biology 15, 267-273.

[3] Bertsimas D, Tsitsiklis J (1993) Simulated Annealing. Statistical Science 8, 10-15.

[4] Source code for each chapter can be found here: https://github.com/CorticalComputer/Book_NeuroevolutionThroughErlang

Chapter 12 Keeping Track of Important Population and Evolutionary Stats

Abstract   To be able to keep track of the performance of a neuroevolutionary system, it is essential for that system to be able to accumulate the various statistics with regards to its fitness, population dynamics, and other changing features, throughout the evolutionary run. In this chapter we add to the population_monitor of our TWEANN system the ability to compose a *trace,* which is a list of tuples, where each tuple is calculated every 500 (by default) evaluations, containing the various statistics about the population achieved during those evaluations, tracing the population's path through its evolutionary history.

As we discussed in Section-8.1, and as was presented in Fig-8.1, the architecture we're going after needs to contain, beside the *polis, population_monitor, database*, and *agent* processes, also the *stat_accumulator* and the *error_logger* concurrent processes. In some sense, we do not really need to create the error_logger, because we can use the already robust implementation offered by OTP. The stat_accumulator on the other hand is something that needs to be built, and that is the program we will develop in this chapter.

Because the goal is to continue improving and generalizing our neuroevolutionary platform, the way to test whether our neuroevolutionary system works or not is by benchmarking it. But to properly analyze the results of the benchmarks we need to gather the resulting statistics produced by the population_monitor and other processes, so that these statistics can then be graphed and perused for signs of improvements based on the new additions to the platform. In this chapter we further modify the population_monitor process, adding to it the ability to keep track of the various important population and evolutionary accumulated statistics.

The updated *population_monitor* should be able to compose useful population information, build lists of this information, and later on be able to write to file and produce data in a form that can be graphed. The population parameters that we would like to keep track of are as follows:

1. How the average NN complexity/size is changing in the population, the average NN size, the maximum NN size, the minimum NN size, and the standard deviation of the NN sizes.
2. How the fitness is changing over time with regards to evaluations. Again, we want to keep track of the average population fitness over time, maximum fitness over time, minimum fitness over time, and standard deviation of the same.
3. Population diversity is another element that is useful to keep track off, since we want to know whether our system produces diverse populations, or not at all. It

G.I. Sher, *Handbook of Neuroevolution Through Erlang,*
DOI 10.1007/978-1-4614-4463-3_12, © Springer Science+Business Media New York 2013

is essential that the TWEANN system is able to maintain a high diversity on its own, only then does it have a chance to truly be general and innovative, and have a chance of evolving solutions and NN based systems capable of solving complex and varying problems.

Without a doubt there are other interesting features that should be kept track off, and thus we should develop and implement this stat_accumulator program with an eye to the future, allowing for easy expansion of its capabilities when the time comes. In the following sections we will first discuss the new architecture and how it will work with the system we've developed so far. Then we will develop a format for how this information should be stored and accumulated. Afterwards, we will implement the actual system, making it an extension and part of the population_monitor itself, rather than an independent process. Finally, we will test our updated population_monitor on the XOR problem, demonstrating its new ability to gather data about the evolutionary path the population is taking, and the various performance statistics of the population and its species.

12.1 The Necessary Additions to the System

Whereas before each agent sent to the population monitor the total number of evaluations it had completed, the number of cycles, and the amount of time taken for tuning, we need our new system to be more precise. Since an agent can take anywhere from Max_Attempts number of evaluations per tuning attempt to hundreds or even thousands of evaluations before reporting that number to the population_monitor, we need to update the way each agent informs the population monitor when it has completed an evaluation, so that the population monitor can keep track of *every* evaluation. This will allow the population_monitor to not only stop or terminate an agent at the exact number of evaluations that is set as a limit, but also it will allow the population monitor to build statistics about its population of agents, for example every 500 evaluations. If each agent would have contacted the population monitor only at its termination, then the population_monitor would not be able to calculate the various features of the population at the specific evaluation index, and instead would be at the mercy of whenever each agent finishes all its evaluations.

To accomplish this, we simply let each agent send a signal to the population_monitor whenever it has finished an evaluation. And for its part, the population_monitor will have a new cast clause, specifically dedicated to receiving *evaluation_completed* messages from the agents.

Because we are finally at the point where we also can track the population diversity, we now have a chance to use the *fingerprint* tuple that each agent constructs. The diversity of the population loosely defines the total number of different species, or the total number of significantly different agents. This "significant" difference can be reflected in the agents having different topologies, using a different number of neurons, using a different set of activation functions, having taken a different evolutionary path (reflected by the different evo_hist lists of the compared agents), and finally by having a different set of sensors and actuators. At this point we define the specie by the particular morphology that the specie supports. Thus at this time, each specie can have many topologically different agents, but all using the same constraint and morphology, interfacing with the same type of scapes, having access to the same set of sensors and actuators, and competing with each other for fitness and offspring allotments using the same evolutionary algorithm loops. Thus for now, we will calculate the diversity not based on the number of species, but the number of significantly differing agents within the entire population.

To calculate the population diversity, we must first decide on the defining characteristics of an agent, the granularity of diversity. Though the fingerprint of the agent is a good start, let us expand it to also include not only the evolutionary path of the agent, and the sensors and actuators used, but also a few defining topological features of a NN based agent. At this time, the agent's fingerprint is defined by the tuple: *{GeneralizedPattern, GeneralizedEvoHist, GeneralizedSensors, GeneralizedActuators}*. We change this definition so that the fingerprint tuple also includes a topological summary, which is itself defined by the tuple: *{type, tot_neurons, tot_n_ils, tot_n_ols, tot_n_ros, af_distribution}* where:

- **type**: Is the NN encoding type: *neural* or *substrate*, for example.
- **tot_neurons**: Is the total number of neurons composing the NN based agent.
- **tot_n_ils**: Is the total number of neuronal input links, calculated by adding together the number of input links of every neuron in the NN based agent.
- **tot_n_ols**: Is the total number of neuronal output links, counted in the same way as input links. Though somewhat redundant, the tot_n_ils and tot_n_ols will differ from each other based on the number of sensors and actuators used by the agent.
- **tot_n_ros**: Is the total number of recurrent connections within the NN system.
- **af_distribution**: Is the count of every type of activation function used by the NN based agent. This has the format of: *{TotTanh, TotSin, TotCos, TotGaussian, TotAbsolute,TotSgn,TotLog,TotSqrt,TotLin}*, and thus agents which have the same topology, but whose neurons use different sets of activation functions, will be functionally very different, and this activation function frequency distribution tuple will to some degree summarize these differences. There could of course be numerous agents with the same topology and the same activation function frequency distribution, but which differ in the neurons which use those activation functions, and locations of those neurons within the NN topology. Nevertheless, this gives us a short and easy way to calculate a summary which could be used in addition to other fingerprint elements to distinguish between two functionally different agents. These summaries can be further considered as representing how the different agents are exploring the different areas on the topological landscape.

Thus, based on these defining characteristics, two agents with different Fingerprints (which will include their topological summaries), will warrant being considered as significantly different. The diversity is then the total number of different *fingerprints* within the population.

To allow our system to keep track of progress and the changing properties and statistics of the population, we first need to decide on the *step_size* during which these statistics will be calculated. The step size is defined as X number of evaluations, such that every X number of evaluations we measure the various evolutionary statistics and properties of the population at hand. For example, if X is defined as 500 evaluations, then every 500 evaluations we would compute the *average fitness* of the population, the *max, min*, and *std* of the fitness within the population, the *diversity* of the population, the *average size* of the NN systems in the population... And then create a format for adding the tuple with this information to a list that traces out the evolutionary path of the population. Even better, we could calculate these values for every specie composing the population, and then compose the trace from the list of tuples where each tuple was created for a particular specie (defined by a different morphology) of the population. The trace would then be a list of lists, where the inside list would be the list of Specie Stats: *[SpeciesStats1, SpeciesStats2... SpeciesStatsN]*, with the outer list then being the actual trace which traces out the various general properties of the evolving population by calculating the various decided-on properties of the species composing this population. The *SpeciesStats* is a list of tuples, where each tuple contains the general statistics and various properties (Average fitness, average NN sizes...) of a particular specie belonging to the population. Thus in the next section we will create the format and manner in which we will store and gather this information.

12.2 The Trace Format

We want the population monitor to, every X number of evaluations, calculate the general properties of each specie in the population that it is evolving. We will call the record that stores these various statistical properties of the specie: *stat*. The specie *stat* will have the following format:

```
-record(stat,{morphology,specie_id,avg_neurons,std_neurons,avg_fitness,std_fitness,
max_fitness, min_fitness,avg_diversity,evaluations,time_stamp}).
```

Where the definition of each of the elements within this record is as follows:

- **morphology**: This is the specie's morphology.
- **specie_id**: Is the id of the specie for whom the stat is calculated.
- **avg_neurons**: The size of the average NN based agent of the specie, calculated by summing up all the neurons of the specie, and dividing the number by the number of agents belonging to the specie at the time of calculation.

- **std_neurons**: The standard deviation of the avg_neurons value.
- **avg_fitness**: Is the average fitness of the agents within the population.
- **std_fitness**: Is the standard deviation of the avg_fitness value.
- **max_fitness**: The maximum fitness achieved by the agents within the specie at the time of calculation.
- **min_fitness**: The minimum fitness achieved by the agents within the specie at the time of calculation.
- **avg_diversity**: The average diversity of the specie.
- **evaluations**: The number of evaluations that the agents of this particular specie used during the given X number of evaluations. So for example if the population calculates the specie stats every 500 evaluations, and there are 2 species in the population, then one specie might have taken 300 of the evaluations if its organisms kept dying rapidly, and the other specie would then have taken the other 200 during that 500 evaluations slot. This value represents the turnover of the specie, and is dependent on numerous factors, amongst which is of course the number of the species in the population (if only one, then it will take all 500 evaluations), the general fitness of the agents (how often they die or get re-evaluated if applied to ALife for example), and the specie size.
- **time_stamp**: Finally, we also time stamp the stat record at the moment of calculation.

Thus, every X (500 by default) number of evaluations, for every specie we calculate all the properties of the *stat*, and thus form a list of stat elements: *SpeciesStats = [Specie_Stat1, Specie_Stat2,...Specie_StatN]*, where N is the number of species in the population at the time of calculating the SpeciesStats.

We then enter this list of specie stats into a list we will call the population *stats*. The *stats* list will belong to the population's element by the name *trace*. We call it a trace because when we dump the population's trace to console, we can see the general progress of the population, the number of species, and the properties of those species, as it is outlined by their stat tuples. It is a trace of the population's evolutionary history, it is the evolutionary path that the population has taken.

The trace element will be represented by the record: *-record(trace,{stats=[], tot_evaluations=0, step_size=500})*, where *stats* is the list which will contain the lists of SpeciesStats. The element tot_evaluations will keep track of the total number of evaluations, so that we can at any time pause the population_monitor, and later on continue counting the evaluations when we resume, starting from the previous stop. Finally, we specify through the *step_size* element the value which determines X, the number every how many evaluations that we will calculate the population's various general properties.

Thus the population's stats list, being a list of lists, will have the following format: *[[SpecieStat1...SpecieStatN],...[SpecieStat1...SpecieStatN]]* Allowing us to easily extract any one particular list of specie stats, a list which belongs to some particular 500 evaluations slot window.

12.3 Implementation

Having decided on the format through which we will keep track of the specie and population statistics, and the modifications that need to be added to the exoself and population_monitor, lets implement these new features. We will first modify the records.hrl file, adding the three new records: *trace*, *stat*, and *topology_summary*, needed for the new extended fingerprint tuple. Then we will implement the function that calculates the topological summary of an agent. We will then implement the function that constructs the specie stat tuples, and updates the population's trace with the accumulated specie stat list. We will then modify the population_monitor module, implementing the evaluation counting cast clause, which takes it upon itself to build and add to the population's trace every X number of evaluations, where X is specified by the step_size parameter in the trace record. Finally, we will make the small modification to the exoself module, making the agent's exoself notify the population_monitor that it has completed an evaluation after each such completion, rather than doing so at the very end when the agent is ready to terminate.

12.3.1 Updating records.hrl

This chapter's new features require us to create the new *topology_summary, stat,* and *trace,* records. We also have to update the population record, so that it has a trace parameter, and we need to update the specie record so that it can keep a list of its stat tuples. Though the population's trace parameter will keep a list of lists of the specie stat tuples (list of SpeciesStats, where SpeciesStats itself is a list), each specie will also keep a list of its own stat tuples.

The following are the three new records: *topology_summary, stat,* and *trace*:

```erlang
-record(topology_summary,{type,tot_neurons,tot_n_ils,tot_n_ols,tot_n_ros,af_distribution}).
-record(stat,{morphology,specie_id,avg_neurons,std_neurons,avg_fitness,std_fitness,
max_fitness, min_fitness, avg_diversity,evaluations,time_stamp}).
-record(trace,{stats=[],tot_evaluations=0,step_size=500}).
```

After adding these three records to the records.hrl, we now update the population and specie records. The elements in boldface, are the ones newly added:

```erlang
-record(population,{id, polis_id, specie_ids=[], morphologies=[], innovation_factor, evo_alg_f,
fitness_postprocessor_f, selection_f, trace=#trace{}}).
-record(specie,{id, population_id, fingerprint, constraint, agent_ids=[], dead_pool=[],
champion_ids=[], fitness, innovation_factor={0,0},stats=[]}).
```

With this done, we move on to building the function that constructs the topological summary.

12.3.2 Building the Topological Summary of a Neural Network

The topological summary will become part of the agent's fingerprint, cataloging the number of neurons, synaptic connections, and types of activation functions used by it. We put this new function inside the genotype module, since it will be called by the *update_fingerprint/1* function. Listing 12.1 shows the modified update_fingerprint/1 function, and the new *get_NodeSummary/1* function which calculates the activation function frequency distribution tuple (the number and types of activation functions used by the NN system), and counts the total number of links used by the NN system. The modified and added parts of the update_fingerprint/1 function are highlighted with boldface.

```
Listing-12.1 The modified update_fingerprint/1 function.

update_fingerprint(Agent_Id)->
    A = read({agent,Agent_Id}),
    Cx = read({cortex,A#agent.cx_id}),
    GeneralizedSensors = [(read({sensor,S_Id}))#sensor{id=undefined,cx_id=undefined,
fanout_ids=[]} || S_Id<-Cx#cortex.sensor_ids],
    GeneralizedActuators = [(read({actuator,A_Id}))#actuator{id=undefined, cx_id=undefined,
fanin_ids=[]} || A_Id<-Cx#cortex.actuator_ids],
    GeneralizedPattern = [{LayerIndex,length(LNIds)}||{LayerIndex,LNIds}<-A#agent.pattern],
    GeneralizedEvoHist = generalize_EvoHist(A#agent.evo_hist,[]),
    N_Ids = Cx#cortex.neuron_ids,
    {Tot_Neuron_ILs,Tot_Neuron_OLs,Tot_Neuron_ROs,AF_Distribution} =
get_NodeSummary(N_Ids),
    Type = A#agent.encoding_type,
    TopologySummary = #topology_summary{
        type = Type,
        tot_neurons = length(N_Ids),
        tot_n_ils = Tot_Neuron_ILs,
        tot_n_ols = Tot_Neuron_OLs,
        tot_n_ros = Tot_Neuron_ROs,
        af_distribution = AF_Distribution},
    Fingerprint = {GeneralizedPattern,GeneralizedEvoHist,GeneralizedSensors,
GeneralizedActuators, TopologySummary},
    write(A#agent{fingerprint=Fingerprint}).
%update_fingerprint/1 calculates the fingerprint of the agent, where the fingerprint is just a tu-
ple of the various general features of the NN based system. The genotype's fingerprint is a list
of features that play some role in distinguishing its genotype's general properties from those of
```

other NN systems. The fingerprint is composed of the generalized pattern (pattern minus the unique ids), generalized evolutionary history (evolutionary history minus the unique ids of the elements), a generalized sensor set, and a generalized actuator set.

```erlang
update_NNTopologySummary(Agent_Id)->
    A = mnesia:read({agent,Agent_Id}),
    Cx_Id = A#agent.cx_id,
    Cx = mnesia:read({cortex,Cx_Id}),
    N_Ids = Cx#cortex.neuron_ids,
    {Tot_Neuron_ILs,Tot_Neuron_OLs,Tot_Neuron_ROs,AF_Distribution} =
gct_NodcSummary(N_Ids),
    Type = A#agent.encoding_type,
    Topology_Summary = #topology_summary{
            type = Type,
            tot_neurons = length(N_Ids),
            tot_n_ils = Tot_Neuron_ILs,
            tot_n_ols = Tot_Neuron_OLs,
            tot_n_ros = Tot_Neuron_ROs,
            af_distribution = AF_Distribution},
    Topology_Summary.
%The update_NNTopologySummary/1 function calculates the total number of input links, output links, recurrent links, neurons, and uses the get_NodeSummary/5 function to compose the activation function frequency distribution tuple. It then enters all the calculated values into the topology_summary record, and returns it to the caller.


get_NodeSummary(N_Ids)->
    get_NodeSummary(N_Ids,0,0,0,{0,0,0,0,0,0,0,0,0}).
get_NodeSummary([N_Id|N_Ids],ILAcc,OLAcc,ROAcc,FunctionDistribution)->
    N = genotype:read({neuron,N_Id}),
    IL_Count = length(N#neuron.input_idps),
    OL_Count = length(N#neuron.output_ids),
    RO_Count = length(N#neuron.ro_ids),
    AF = N#neuron.af,
    {TotTanh,TotSin,TotCos,TotGaussian,TotAbsolute,TotSgn,TotLog,TotSqrt,TotLin} =
FunctionDistribution,
    U_FunctionDistribution= case AF of
            tanh ->{TotTanh+1,TotSin,TotCos,TotGaussian,TotAbsolute,TotSgn,
TotLog,TotSqrt,TotLin};
            sin ->{TotTanh,TotSin+1,TotCos,TotGaussian,TotAbsolute,TotSgn,
TotLog,TotSqrt,TotLin};
            cos ->{TotTanh,TotSin,TotCos+1,TotGaussian,TotAbsolute,TotSgn,
TotLog,TotSqrt,TotLin};
            gaussian->{TotTanh,TotSin,TotCos,TotGaussian+1,TotAbsolute,TotSgn,
TotLog,TotSqrt,TotLin};
```

```
            absolute->{TotTanh,TotSin,TotCos,TotGaussian,TotAbsolute+1,TotSgn,
TotLog,TotSqrt,TotLin};
            sgn ->{TotTanh,TotSin,TotCos,TotGaussian,TotAbsolute,TotSgn+1,
TotLog,TotSqrt,TotLin};
            log ->{TotTanh,TotSin,TotCos,TotGaussian,TotAbsolute,TotSgn, TotLog+1,
TotSqrt,TotLin};
            sqrt ->{TotTanh,TotSin,TotCos,TotGaussian,TotAbsolute,TotSgn, TotLog,
TotSqrt+1,TotLin};
            linear ->{TotTanh,TotSin,TotCos,TotGaussian,TotAbsolute,TotSgn, TotLog,
TotSqrt,TotLin+1};
            Other -> io:format("Unknown AF, please update AF_Distribution tuple with:~p~n.",
[Other])
    end,
    U_ILAcc = IL_Count+ILAcc,
    U_OLAcc = OL_Count+OLAcc,
    U_ROAcc = RO_Count+ROAcc,
    get_NodeSummary(N_Ids,U_ILAcc,U_OLAcc,U_ROAcc,U_FunctionDistribution);
get_NodeSummary([],ILAcc,OLAcc,ROAcc,FunctionDistribution)->
    {ILAcc,OLAcc,ROAcc,FunctionDistribution}.
```

As shown in the get_NodeSummary function, we create the activation function frequency distribution tuple by simply counting the different activation functions, and forming a long tuple where every activation function (thus far used by our system) has a position. Though simple, this is not the best implementation, because every time a new activation function is added, we will need to update the AF distribution tuple such that it takes the new activation function into consideration. Having now updated the update_fingerprint/1 function, we can implement in the next section the population diversity calculating function needed by the stat composing program.

12.3.3 Implementing the Trace Updating Cast Clause

Our new population_monitor no longer accepts the AgentEvalAcc, AgentCyc-leAcc, and AgentTimeAcc containing message from the agent when it terminates. The exoself no longer sends to the population_monitor the message *{Agent_Id, terminated, Fitness, AgentEvalAcc, AgentCycleAcc, AgentTimeAcc}*. This message was accepted by the cast clauses of the generational and steady_state evolutionary loops. We modify both of these cast clauses to only accept the message: *{Agent_Id,terminated,Fitness}*, because we now offload the evaluation, cycle, and time accumulation, to its own dedicated cast clause. This new cast clause will accept the message of the form: *{From,evaluations,Specie_Id,AgentEvalAcc, AgentCycleAcc,AgentTimeAcc}*, sent to it by the agent after it completes *every single* evaluation.

Because we want for the *stat* tuple to be constructed for each specie in the population, we need to keep a running evaluation counter for each specie, so that when an agent sends the {From,evaluations...} message to the population_monitor, this evaluation can be added to the evaluation counter belonging to the proper specie. We modify the init/1 function with the parts shown in boldface in the following listing.

```
Listing-12.2. The updated init/1 function.

init(Parameters) ->
    process_flag(trap_cxit,true),
    register(monitor,self()),
    io:format("******** Population monitor started with parameters:~p~n",[Parameters]),
    State = case Parameters of
         {OpMode,Population_Id}->
             Agent_Ids = extract_AgentIds(Population_Id,all),
             ActiveAgent_IdPs = summon_agents(OpMode,Agent_Ids),
             P = genotype:dirty_read({population,Population_Id}),
             [put({evaluations,Specie_Id},0) || Specie_Id<-P#population.specie_ids],
             T = P#population.trace,
             TotEvaluations=T#trace.tot_evaluations,
             io:format("Initial Tot Evaluations:~p~n",[TotEvaluations]),
             #state{op_mode=OpMode,
                 population_id = Population_Id,
                 activeAgent_IdPs = ActiveAgent_IdPs,
                 tot_agents = length(Agent_Ids),
                 agents_left = length(Agent_Ids),
                 op_tag = continue,
                 evolutionary_algorithm = P#population.evo_alg_f,
                 fitness_postprocessor = P#population.fitness_postprocessor_f,
                 selection_algorithm = P#population.selection_f,
                 best_fitness = 0,
                 step_size = T#trace.step_size,
                 tot_evaluations = TotEvaluations
                 }
    end,
    {ok, State}.
```

It is the line:

```
[put({evaluations,Specie_Id},0) || Specie_Id <-P#population.specie_ids]
```

In the above code which is the one that initializes the evaluation counters for each species in the population. This way, when an agent sends its evaluation message, we can, using the *Specie_Id* within the agent's message, execute the command: *get({evaluations,Specie_Id})*, and retrieve the proper specie's evaluations accumulator from the process registry. Also, because the population's evaluation accumulator will be held by the *#trace.tot_evaluations*, we initialize the population_monitor state's initial *tot_evaluations* value from this trace parameter. We also add to the population_monitor's *state* record the *step_size* parameter, and set it to the *step_size* specified by the population's *trace* record. The rest of the *init/1* function remains the same.

The new cast clause that will update the population's *trace*, accepts messages from the agents and keeps count of the total number of evaluations. If the number of evaluations performed by the population_monitor in question exceeds the value specified by the *step_size* parameter, the population_monitor updates the trace by composing the specie stat tuples and entering them into the trace's stats list. The implementation of this new cast clause is shown in Listing-12.3.

Listing-12.3. The population_monitor's new evaluation accumulating and trace updating cast clause.

```
handle_cast({From,evaluations,Specie_Id,AgentEvalAcc,AgentCycleAcc,AgentTimeAcc},S)->
    Eval_Acc = S#state.eval_acc,
    U_EvalAcc = S#state.eval_acc+AgentEvalAcc,
    U_CycleAcc = S#state.cycle_acc+AgentCycleAcc,
    U_TimeAcc = S#state.time_acc+AgentTimeAcc,
    U_TotEvaluations = S#state.tot_evaluations + AgentEvalAcc,
    SEval_Acc=get({evaluations,Specie_Id}),
    put({evaluations,Specie_Id},SEval_Acc+AgentEvalAcc),
    case Eval_Acc rem 50 of
        0 ->
                io:format("Evaluations/Step:~p~n",[Eval_Acc]);
        _ ->
                done
    end,
    U_S=case U_EvalAcc >= S#state.step_size of
        true ->
                gather_STATS(S#state.population_id,U_EvalAcc),
                Population_Id = S#state.population_id,
                P = genotype:dirty_read({population,Population_Id}),
                T = P#population.trace,
                TotEvaluations=T#trace.tot_evaluations,
                io:format("Tot Evaluations:~p~n",[TotEvaluations]),
                S#state{eval_acc=0, cycle_acc=0, time_acc=0,
tot_evaluations=U_TotEvaluations};
        false ->
S#state{eval_acc=U_EvalAcc,cycle_acc=U_CycleAcc,time_acc=U_TimeAcc,tot_evaluations
=U_TotEvaluations}
```

```
    end,
    {noreply,U_S};

handle_cast({_From,print_TRACE},S)->
    Population_Id = S#state.population_id,
    P = genotype:dirty_read({population,Population_Id}),
    io:format("******** TRACE ********:~n~p~n",[P#population.trace]),
    {noreply,S};
```

There is a second cast clause in the above listing: *handle_cast({_From,print_TRACE},S)*, which when receiving a *print_TRACE* request, prints to console the thus-far-composed trace. And of course the trace is also automatically printed to console every 500 evaluations by the population_monitor itself, to keep the researcher in the loop of the general evolutionary progress of the population at hand.

By default, every 500 evaluations the population_monitor executes the *gather_STATS/2* function, which is the actual function that updates all the specie stat lists and the population's trace. This function is shown in Listing-12.4. When executed, the gather_STATS/2 function executes the *update_SpecieSTAT/2* function for every specie belonging to the population. The *update_SpecieSTAT/2* function retrieves the evaluation accumulator from the process registry, so that the evaluation accumulator value can be stored in the specie's stat tuple. The function then goes through every agent and adds up the number of neurons in each, and then divides that number by the total number of agents and thus computes the average NN size and its standard deviation. In the same manner, the function then calculates the average fitness, fitness standard deviation, and the max and min fitness values reached by the agents belonging to the specie at the time of calculation. Finally, the diversity of the specie is calculated by executing the *calculate_SpecieDiversity/1* function. This function, using the agent fingerprints, calculates how many distinct fingerprints are present within the specie, which is the diversity number of that specie. With all these values computed, the function then enters this data into the *stat* record, and adds this new *stat* to the specie's *stats* list.

Listing-12.4 The implementation of the gather_STATS/2 function, which updates the population's trace.

```
gather_STATS(Population_Id,EvaluationsAcc)->
    io:format("Gathering Species STATS in progress~n"),
    TimeStamp = now(),
    F = fun() ->
        P = genotype:read({population,Population_Id}),
        T = P#population.trace,
        SpecieSTATS = [update_SpecieSTAT(Specie_Id,TimeStamp) || Specie_Id<-
P#population.specie_ids],
```

```
            PopulationSTATS = T#trace.stats,
            U_PopulationSTATS = [SpecieSTATS|PopulationSTATS],
            U_TotEvaluations = T#trace.tot_evaluations+EvaluationsAcc,
            U_Trace = T#trace{
                    stats = U_PopulationSTATS,
                    tot_evaluations=U_TotEvaluations
            },
            io:format("Population Trace:~p~n",[U_Trace]),
            mnesia:write(P#population{trace=U_Trace})
    end,
    Result=mnesia:transaction(F),
    io:format("Result:~p~n",[Result]).


    update_SpecieSTAT(Specie_Id,TimeStamp)->
            Specie_Evaluations = get({evaluations,Specie_Id}),
            put({evaluations,Specie_Id},0),
            S = genotype:read({specie,Specie_Id}),
            {Avg_Neurons,Neurons_Std} = calculate_SpecieAvgNodes({specie,S}),
            {AvgFitness,Fitness_Std,MaxFitness,MinFitness} = calculate_SpecieFitness({
specie,S}),
            SpecieDiversity = calculate_SpecieDiversity({specie,S}),
            STAT = #stat{
                    morphology = (S#specie.constraint)#constraint.morphology,
                    specie_id = Specie_Id,
                    avg_neurons=Avg_Neurons,
                    std_neurons=Neurons_Std,
                    avg_fitness=AvgFitness,
                    std_fitness=Fitness_Std,
                    max_fitness=MaxFitness,
                    min_fitness=MinFitness,
                    avg_diversity=SpecieDiversity,
                    evaluations = Specie_Evaluations,
                    time_stamp=TimeStamp
            },
            STATS = S#specie.stats,
            U_STATS = [STAT|STATS],
            mnesia:dirty_write(S#specie{stats=U_STATS}),
            STAT.

calculate_SpecieAvgNodes({specie,S})->
    Agent_Ids = S#specie.agent_ids,
    calculate_AvgNodes(Agent_Ids,[]);
calculate_SpecieAvgNodes(Specie_Id)->
    io:format("calculate_SpecieAvgNodes(Specie_Id):~p~n",[Specie_Id]),
    S = genotype:read({specie,Specie_Id}),
```

```
calculate_SpecieAvgNodes({specie,S}).

calculate_AvgNodes([Agent_Id|Agent_Ids],NAcc)->
        io:format("calculate_AvgNodes/2 Agent_Id:~p~n",[Agent_Id]),
        A = genotype:read({agent,Agent_Id}),
        Cx = genotype:read({cortex,A#agent.cx_id}),
        Tot_Neurons = length(Cx#cortex.neuron_ids),
        calculate_AvgNodes(Agent_Ids,[Tot_Neurons|NAcc]);
calculate_AvgNodes([],NAcc)->
        {functions:avg(NAcc),functions:std(NAcc)}.

calculate_SpecieDiversity({specie,S})->
    Agent_Ids = S#specie.agent_ids,
    Diversity = calculate_diversity(Agent_Ids);
calculate_SpecieDiversity(Specie_Id)->
    S = genotype:dirty_read({specie,Specie_Id}),
    calculate_SpecieDiversity({specie,S}).

calculate_diversity(Agent_Ids)->
        calculate_diversity(Agent_Ids,[]).
calculate_diversity([Agent_Id|Agent_Ids],DiversityAcc)->
        A = genotype:read({agent,Agent_Id}),
        Fingerprint = A#agent.fingerprint,
        U_DiversityAcc = (DiversityAcc -- [Fingerprint]) ++ [Fingerprint],
        calculate_diversity(Agent_Ids,U_DiversityAcc);
calculate_diversity([],DiversityAcc)->
        length(DiversityAcc).
```

Finally, because we have changed from using *eval_acc* parameter in the state record, and because we wish for the population_monitor to dump the *trace* tuple to console when it has terminated, we must also update the *terminate/2* function. The updated *terminate(Reason,S)* function is show in the following listing.

Listing-12.5 The updated terminate/2 function.

```
terminate(Reason, S) ->
   case S of
        [] ->
                io:format("******** Population_Monitor shut down with Reason:~p, with
State: []~n",[Reason]);
        _ ->
                OpMode = S#state.op_mode,
                Population_Id = S#state.population_id,
                P = genotype:dirty_read({population,Population_Id}),
                T = P#population.trace,
```

```
              TotEvaluations=T#trace.tot_evaluations,
              OpTag = S#state.op_tag,
              io:format("******** TRACE START ********~n"),
              io:format("~p~n",[T]),
              io:format("******** ^^^^ TRACE END ^^^^ ********~n"),
              io:format("******** Population_Monitor:~p shut down with Reason:~p
OpTag:~p, while in OpMode:~p~n",[Population_Id,Reason,OpTag,OpMode]),
              io:format("******** Tot Agents:~p Population Generation:~p
Tot_Evals:~p~n",[S#state.tot_agents,S#state.pop_gen,S#state.tot_evaluations])
    end.
```

With this function complete, the only remaining modification that we need to add, is one to the *exoself* module. We have modified the types of messages the population_monitor process can accept, and thus we have to update the exoself process so that it can properly send such messages to the updated population_monitor.

12.3.4 Updating the exoself Module

In our current exoself implementation, when the agent exceeds the *max_attempts* number of improvement attempts, it sends to the population_monitor its thus-far-achieved fitness and the total number of evaluations, cycles, and time taken to achieve it, by sending to the population monitor the message: *{S#state.agent_id,terminated, U_HighestFitness, U_EvalAcc, U_CycleAcc, U_TimeAcc}*. The population_monitor now accepts the evaluation, cycles, and time accumulator values separately from the agent's termination signals sent to it when the agent terminates. We modify the termination message to use the format: *{Agent_Id,terminated,U_HighestFitness}*, and make the agent execute: *gen_server:cast(S#state.pm_pid,{self(),evaluations,S#state.specie_id,1,Cycles, Time})* after every completed evaluation. With this small modification, the exoself can now send the properly formatted messages to the population_monitor. The partial source code of the exoself's main *loop/1* function, with the modified parts of the source code highlighted in bold, is as follows:

```
loop(S)->
    receive
          {Cx_PId,evaluation_completed,Fitness,Cycles,Time}->
    ...

                    true ->%End training
                           A=genotype:dirty_read({agent,S#state.agent_id}),
                           genotype:write(A#agent{fitness=U_HighestFitness}),
                           backup_genotype(S#state.idsNpids,S#state.npids),
```

```
                        terminate_phenotype(S#state.cx_pid, S#state.spids, S#state.npids,
    S#state.apids, S#state.scape_pids),
                        gen_server:cast(S#state.pm_pid,{S#state.agent_id,terminated,
    U_HighestFitness});
                    false -> %Continue training
    ...
                    loop(U_S)
            end
        after 10000 ->
                io:format("exoself:~p stuck.~n",[S#state.agent_id])
    end.
```

12.4 Compiling & Testing

With the updates to the source code complete, we now test our neuroevolutionary system using both, the generational and steady_state evolutionary loops, by applying it to the XOR problem. To do this, we must first recreate the mnesia database with the updated population record. Then compile the source, then set the population_monitor parameters appropriately, and then finally run the test.

We first execute polis:sync(), polis:reset(), and then polis:start() to recompile and load all the modules, create the mnesia database, and then start the polis process:

```
1> polis:sync().
...
...
...
up_to_date
2> polis:reset().
{atomic,ok}
3> polis:start().
Parameters:{[],[]}
******** Polis: ##MATHEMA## is now online.
{ok,<0.181.0>}
```

With this done, we go into the population_monitor module and set the INIT_CONSTRAINTS to:

```
-define(INIT_CONSTRAINTS,[#constraint{morphology=Morphology,
connection_architecture =CA, population_evo_alg_f=generational} || Morphology<-
[xor_mimic],CA<-[feedforward]]).
```

And the terminating conditions to:

```
-define(GENERATION_LIMIT,100).
-define(EVALUATIONS_LIMIT,100000).
-define(FITNESS_GOAL,inf).
```

This will allow us to first test the new features with the population_monitor running in the generational evolutionary loop, and the fitness goal set to inf, thus letting the neuroevolutionary system to run for at least 100000 evaluations or 100 generations, giving itself plenty of time to compose a long trace. With these parameters set, we compile the population_monitor module, and execute population_monitor:test(). Because the population_monitor automatically prints the trace every 500 evaluations, if you run the test to completion, and then scroll upwards on the console, you will see the trace printout. In the following listing, I run the population_monitor:test() program, and for the sake of brevity only printout the first and last stat tuples in the trace's stats list:

```
Listing-12.5 Testing the trace construction using the generational evolutionary loop.

******** TRACE START ********
{trace,[[{stat,xor_mimic,7.545734705407886e-10,2.0,0.0,899806.2187523855,
          299935.2472592368,999803.9690288296,0.4871219879281525,7,500,
          {1325,252006,807398}}],
...
    [{stat,xor_mimic,7.545734705407886e-10,1.2,0.4,165.48172889712018,
          42.53153201193604,187.42531939466735,41.051077769669675,7,500,
          {1325,251998,861970}}]],
    28000,500}
******** ^^^^ TRACE END ^^^^ ********
******** Population_Monitor:test shut down with Reason:normal OpTag:continue, while in
OpMode:gt
******** Tot Agents:10 Population Generation:100 Tot_Evals:28332
```

It works! The test ran to completion, and the trace was composed and printed to console. The trace produced by your run will differ of course, but the common features will be that the trace will represent the gradual progress from unfit agents to the more fit ones. In the above printout I've highlighted the max fitness reached during the first 500 evaluations, and during the last 500 evaluations, after **28332** evaluations in total. We can now use this trace to create a graph of *fitness vs. evaluations*, or *NN size vs. evaluations*... Also, we could run the test multiple times, gathering the traces, and then averaging them. Doing so would allow us to better understand the average and general performance of our system, how rapidly the fitness improves, and other temporally progressing features of the evolutionary runs on the particular problem we applied the system to.

In the same manner we can again modify the INIT_CONSTRAINTS, changing the *population_evo_alg_f* from *generational,* to *steady_state.* We then recompile the population_monitor module, and execute the population_monitor:test() function again, the results of which are shown in Listing-12.6.

Listing-12.6 Testing the trace construction using the steady_state evolutionary loop.

```
******** TRACE START ********
{trace,[[{stat,xor_mimic,7.545736660182336e-10,2.210526315789474,
        0.4076824574955175,684245.1500749566,464778.56244874984,
        999999.995222936,0.39673797258986543,9,500,
        {1325,251701,23562}}],
...
    [{stat,xor_mimic,7.545736660182336e-10,1.4210526315789473,
        0.4937279747182558,60098.723519683044,222254.0763078003,
        998548.771899295,0.20552720368183247,12,500,
        {1325,251655,536129}}]],
    100000,500}
******** ^^^^ TRACE END ^^^^ ********
******** Population_Monitor:test shut down with Reason:normal OpTag:continue, while in
OpMode:gt
******** Tot Agents:10 Population Generation:0 Tot_Evals:100321
```

Again only the first and last stat lists are shown, where each stat list only has a single stat tuple since there is only one specie within the population. Notice that unlike the last time, where the neuroevolutionary system stopped after 28332 evaluations, here our system continued evolving agents for 100000 evaluations, after which it stopped creating new offspring, and then waited for the remaining agents to terminate (hence the reason for **Tot_Evals:100321,** a number slightly larger than 100000). This is because in the steady_state evolutionary loop, there are no generations, hence it staying at 0. And because we set the fitness goal to *inf,* the only remaining termination condition that could be satisfied was the evaluation limit set to 100000.

We have now ran the test using both, generational and steady_state evolutionary loops, and it worked because we had modified the cast clauses for both of them. We now can be assured that the evaluation counting and other statistic counting features of the population_monitor are independent of which evolutionary loop we choose to use.

12.5 Summary & Discussion

In this chapter we have extended our neuroevolutionary system, and gave the population_monitor the ability to keep track of the population's various statistics, and an ability to generally monitor how the agents evolve and change over time. Some of those statistics are with regards to the average fitness of the species, other statistics deal with the size of the NN systems, and still other deal with the population's diversity. All of these are important to keep track of when one attempts to determine whether the system is functioning properly and is able to improve and evolve the population towards the right direction.

Every time a neuroevolutionary system is applied to a problem, or used in a simulation, we need to be able to see how the population is evolving. The temporal factors, the diversity, and everything else about the population, needs to be somehow gaged. In this chapter we created a simple extension to the population_monitor, that allows it to calculate the various statistics every X number of evaluations. The population acquired a new parameter, the *trace* tuple. The *trace* not only counts the number of evaluations performed by the population as a whole, but also keeps a list called *stats* which is a list of lists, where each list is composed of specie *stat* tuples. The stat tuple holds the statistical features of a particular specie for which it was calculated. In this manner we can keep track of specie turnover values, average neural network sizes, fitness, diversity, efficiency...

The trace constructing program and evaluation counting implementation we created in this chapter is decoupled enough from our general evolutionary system, that we can extend it in the future without worrying of also having to modify the rest of our TWEANN platform. Though at this time the *stat* tuple keeps track of simply the size, fitness, and diversity of a specie, the record can be easily modified to keep track of other statistics, such as connectedness, level of recurrence, efficiency with regards to the use of neurons, evolvability... Using the stats list, we can graph this data easily, and thus determine how our system behaves, where it lacks, what should be improved... But this only allows us to compose a trace of a single population, of a single evolutionary run. When benchmarking, an experiment is usually composed of multiple evolutionary runs and applications to a particular problem, and the resulting graphs and statistics are the averages of said evolutionary runs. In the next chapter we create another program that will assist in performing just that task.

Chapter 13 The Benchmarker

Abstract In this chapter we add the benchmarker process which can sequentially spawn population_monitors and apply them to some specified problem/simulation. We also extend the database to include the *experiment* record, which the benchmarker uses to deposit the traces of the population's evolutionary statistics, and to recover from crashes to continue with the specified experiment. The benchmarker can compose experiments by performing multiple evolutionary runs, and then produce statistical data and GNUplot ready files of the various evolutionary dynamics and averages calculated within the experiment.

Though in the previous chapter we have completed the development of the most important part of keeping track of the population's statistics and progress, we can still go a step further and add one more program, the *benchmarker*. When running a simulation or experiment, the progress of the population, the trace, represents a single evolutionary path of the population. When analyzing the functionality of our system, when we want to benchmark a new added element, we might wish to run the simulation multiple times, we might want to create multiple traces for the same problem, and then average them before starting to analyze the functionality of our TWEANN, or the results of applying it to some simulation or problem.

The *benchmarker* process we want to create here is in some sense similar to the one we implemented in Section-7.7. This program will offer us a concise and robust way in which to apply the population_monitor to some problem multiple times, and thus build a dataset by averaging the performance of our neuroevolutionary system from multiple applications to the problem, from multiple evolutionary runs. The benchmarker will be called with the following parameters:

1. The *INIT_CONSTRAINTS* parameter, which will specify the type of problem the benchmarker will create the populations for.
2. The parameter N, which will specify the number of times the benchmarker should apply the neuroevolutionary system to the problem.
3. The termination condition parameters (evaluations limit, generation limit, and fitness goal).

The benchmarker's operational scenario would be as follows: The benchmarker process would first spawn the population_monitor. Then wait for the population_monitor to reach its termination condition, send benchmarker the accumulated trace record, and then terminate. Afterwards, the benchmarker would store the trace into its trace accumulator, and spawn a new population_monitor which would try to solve the problem again. This would continue for N number of times, at which point the benchmarker would have accumulated N traces. It could then average the trace results and form a single trace average (the various averages between all the traces composing the experiment). This trace average can then be written to file in the format which can be graphed and visualized, by perhaps a program like gnuplot [1].

In the following sections we will implement this *benchmarker* process. The ability to determine and graph the performance statistics of a neuroevolutionary system allows one to advance it, to see where it might have flaws and what new features should be added, and the affect of those new features on its performance. The benchmarker program also assists in conducting research, for the results and applications of the neuroevolutionary system must be presented at one point or another, and thus a benchmark of the neuroevolutionary system's general and average performance on some task must be composed. The experiment must be run multiple times, such that the accuracy and the standard deviation of the results can bc calculated. And that is exactly what the *benchmarker* program will assist in doing.

13.1 The benchmarker Architecture

The purpose of the benchmarker process is simple, to spawn a population_monitor, wait for it to finish solving the problem or reach a termination condition and send its composed *trace* to the benchmarker process (if the benchmarker was the one that spawned the population_monitor), and then respawn another population_monitor, repeating the procedure N times. Once the benchmarker has done this N number of times, and thus has accumulated N traces, the benchmarker is to analyze the traces, build the averages of those traces, and write this data to a file, and optionally print it to console.

Because gnuplot is so prevalent in plotting data in the scientific community, we want the benchmarker to write to file the resulting benchmark data in a format that can be directly used by gnuplot. Some of the information that can be plotted is: *Fitness Vs. Evaluations, NN Size Vs. Evaluations*, and *Specie Diversity Vs. Evaluations*.

Furthermore, assume that we are running our benchmark on a single machine. We planned on applying our neuroevolutionary system to some problem 100 times, each for 100000 evaluations. And on the 90th evolutionary run there is a power outage, and we lose all 90 evolutionary run traces when we only had 10 more to go before completing the full experiment composed of 100 evolutionary runs. To prevent such situations, we must of course save the trace results which belong to the same experiment, after every evolutionary run. Thus if there is a power outage, or we wish to stop the experiment at some point, we need to ensure that whichever evolutionary runs have already been done, will have their traces backed up, and thus give us a chance to continue with the experiment when we are ready again.

To add such functionality, we will create a new mnesia table called *experiment*, which will allow for every experiment to have its own id or name, and a trace_acc list where it will accumulate the traces which belong to that particular experiment. It will be the benchmarker process that will backup the traces to their appropriate experiment entry, after every completed simulation or problem run.

To accomplish all of this, the benchmarker process needs to be able to do the following tasks:

4. Know how many evolutionary runs to perform for the experiment.
5. Know the name of the experiment, so that it can store the traces to their appropriate locations in the mnesia table.
6. Be able to specify the initial state parameters with which to start the population_monitor process, and restart it after a crash.

This means that other than adding the *experiment* record to the records.hrl file and creating a mnesia table of the same name, we must also modify how the population_monitor is started. Currently, it uses the macros defined within the module. These macros define how large the initial population size should be, the termination conditions... This makes it difficult to start the population_monitor from another module, and control the population_monitor's parameters from the same. Thus we will need to expand its *state* record to include the previously macro defined parameters, and add a new function with which to start the population_monitor, a function which can be executed with a list of parameters, the parameters that are then entered into the state tuple with which the population_monitor is started.

In the following sections we create the new records and add the new table to the mnesia database. We then make a small modification to the population_monitor module, move the previously macro defined parameters into the state record, and add a new function with which the population_monitor can be started and have its *state* record initialized. Finally, we then create the actual benchmarker module.

13.2 Adding New Records

We need to modify the population_monitor's state record, and then add two new records to the records.hrl file. The population_monitor's new state record will include all the elements that were previously defined through the macros of that module. With regards to the two new records to be added to the records.hrl, one of them will be the new mnesia table, *experiment,* and the other record, *pmp* (population monitor parameters) will be used specifically by the benchmarker to call and start the population_monitor process with a certain set of parameters, thus setting the population_monitor's initial state tuple to the proper values.

The population_monitor originally specified its state and other parameters for its operation using the macros and records at the top of the module, as shown in Listing-13.1.

Listing-13.1 The macros and records originally used by the population_monitor process.

```
-define(INIT_CONSTRAINTS,[#constraint{morphology=Morphology, connec-
tion_architecture=CA, population_evo_alg_f=steady_state} || Morphology<-[xor_mimic],CA<-
[feedforward]]).
-define(SURVIVAL_PERCENTAGE,0.5).
-define(SPECIE_SIZE_LIMIT,10).
-define(INIT_SPECIE_SIZE,10).
-define(INIT_POPULATION_ID,test).
-define(OP_MODE,gt).
-define(INIT_POLIS,mathema).
-define(GENERATION_LIMIT,100).
-define(EVALUATIONS_LIMIT,100000).
-define(GEN_UID,genotype:generate_UniqueId()).
-define(FITNESS_GOAL,1000).
-record(state,{ op_mode, population_id, activeAgent_IdPs=[], agent_ids=[], tot_agents,
agents_left, op_tag,agent_summaries=[], pop_gen=0, eval_acc=0, cycle_acc=0, time_acc=0,
step_size, next_step, goal_status,evolutionary_algorithm, fitness_postprocessor,
selection_algorithm, best_fitness }).
```

Because the population_monitor's macros are module specific, and we would like to be able to specify in which manner to start the population_monitor, what its fitness goal should be, evaluation and generation limits, and what polis it should use... we need to move all the macro defined elements into the popula-tion_monitor's state record. This way the benchmarker process can call the popu-lation_monitor and specify all these previously macro defined parameters. We al-so add one extra parameter to the state record, the *benchmarker_pid* element, which can be set to the PId of the benchmarker process, and then used by the pop-ulation_monitor to send its trace to the benchmarker process that spawned it. The population_monitor's new state record is shown in Listing-13.2, where the newly added elements are shown in boldface.

Listing-13.2 The updated *state* record of the population_monitor module.

```
-record(state,{
    op_mode = gt,
    population_id = test,
    activeAgent_IdPs = [],
    agent_ids = [],
    tot_agents,
    agents_left,
```

```
op_tag,
agent_summaries = [],
pop_gen = 0,
eval_acc = 0,
cycle_acc = 0,
time_acc = 0,
tot_evaluations = 0,
step_size,
goal_status,
evolutionary_algorithm,
fitness_postprocessor,
selection_algorithm,
best_fitness,
survival_percentage = 0.5,
specie_size_limit = 10,
init_specie_size = 10,
polis_id = mathema,
generation_limit = 100,
evaluations_limit = 100000,
fitness_goal = inf,
benchmarker_pid
}).
```

When we start the population_monitor, we want to be able to define these elements. Their default values are shown in the state record, but every-time we run an experiment, we want to be able to set these parameters to whatever we want. Thus, we add the *pmp* (population monitor parameters) record to the records.hrl, so that it can be set by the benchmarker, and read by the population_monitor. This new record is shown in Listing-13.3, and its elements are defined as follows:

1. **op_mode**: Allows the benchmarker to define the mode in which the population_monitor operates. Thus far we only used the gt, which we have not yet used to specify any particular mode of operation, but we will in a much later chapter. In the future we can define new modes, for example the *throughput* mode during which the agents are not tuned or evaluated, but simply tested for whether they are functional, whether they can gather signals through sensors and output actions through their actuators. The *throughput* op_mode could also then be used to benchmark the speed of the cycle of the NN based agent, and thus used to test which topologies can process signals faster, and which designs and architectures and implementations of neurons, sensors, actuators, and cortexes are more efficient. Or we could specify the op_mode as *standard,* which would make the population monitor function in some standard default manner. With regards to *gt,* it stands for *genetic tuning,* but due to our not yet having specified other operational modes, or taken advantage of this parameter, it is effectively the standard mode of operation until we add a new one in Chapter-19.

2. **population_id**: Allows the benchmarker to set the population's id.
3. **survival_percentage**: Allows the benchmarker to set which percentage of the population survives during the selection phase.
4. **specie_size_limit**: Allows the benchmarker to set the size limit of every specie within the population. This is an important parameter to define when starting an experiment.
5. **init_specie_size**: Allows the benchmarker to define the initial size of the specie. For example the experiment can be started where the initial specie size is set to 1000, but the specie size limit is set to 100. In this way, there would be a great amount of diversity (given the constraint is defined in such a manner that NN based agents have access to a variety of plasticity functions, activation functions...), but after a while only 100 are allowed to exist at any one time. Or things could be done in the opposite way, the initial specie size can be small, and the limit specie size large. Allowing the specie to rapidly expand in numbers and diversity, from some small initial bottleneck in the population.
6. **polis_id**: Allows the benchmarker to define in which polis the population_monitor will create the new agent population.
7. **generation_limit**: Every experiment needs a termination condition, and the benchmarker specifies the generation limit based termination condition for the population_monitor, using this parameter.
8. **evaluations_limit**: Lets the benchmarker specify the evaluations limit based termination condition.
9. **fitness_goal**: Lets the benchmarker specify the fitness based termination condition.
10. **benchmarker_pid**: This parameter is set to undefined by default. If the population_monitor has been spawned for a particular experiment by the benchmarker, then the benchmarker sets this parameter to its own PId. Using this PId, the population_monitor can, when the neuroevolutionary run has reached its termination condition, send its trace to the benchmarker process.

Listing-13.3 The new *pmp* (population monitor parameters) record added to the records.hrl

```
-record(pmp,{
    op_mode=gt,
    population_id=test,
    survival_percentage=0.5,
    specie_size_limit=10,
    init_specie_size=10,
    polis_id = mathema,
    generation_limit = 100,
    evaluations_limit = 100000,
    fitness_goal = inf,
    benchmarker_pid
}).
```

The *pmp* record does not necessarily need to be used only by the benchmarker. The researcher can of course, rather than specifying these parameters in the population_monitor module and then recompiling it, simply start the population_monitor using the pmp record and the new prep_PopState/2 function we will build in the next subsection, and in this way define all the necessary experiment parameters.

The new *experiment* table we will add to the mnesia database will hold all the general, experiment specific data, particularly the traces. This is the record that the benchmarker populates as it runs the problem or experiment multiple times to generate multiple traces. The *experiment* record is shown in Listing-13.4, and its elements are defined as follows:

1. **id**: Is the unique id or name of the experiment being conducted. Because we wish for this new mnesia table to hold numerous experiments, we need to be able to give each experiment its own particular id or name.
2. **backup_flag**: This element is present for the use by the benchmarker. When we start the benchmarker program with the experiment tuple whose backup_flag is set to false, it does not backup that particular experiment to mnesia. This might be useful when we wish to quickly run an experiment but not write the results to the database.
3. **pm_parameters**: This element will store the pmp record with which the population_monitor was started for this particular experiment. This will allow us to later on know what the experiment was for, and how the population_monitor was started (all the initial parameters) to produce the results and traces in the experiment entry. This way the experiment can be replicated later on.
4. **init_constraints**: Similarly to the pm_parameters which defines how the population_monitor runs, we also need to remember the parameters of the population itself, and the experiment to which the traces belong. This information is uniquely identified by the init_constraints list with which the population is created. Having the init_constraints will allow us to later on replicate the experiment if needed.
5. **progress_flag**: This element can be set to two values: *in_progress* and *completed*. The experiment is in progress until it has been run for *tot_runs* number of times, and thus the experiment has accumulated tot_runs number of traces in its *trace_acc* list. If for example during the experiment run there is a power outage, when we later go through all the experiments in the experiment table, we will be able to determine which of the experiments were interrupted, based on their progress_flag. Any experiment whose progress_flag is set to in_progress, but which is not currently running, must have been interrupted, and still needs to be completed. Once it is completed, the progress_flag is set to: *completed.*
6. **trace_acc**: This is a list where we store the trace tuples. If we apply our TWEANN to some particular problem 10 times, and thus perform 10 evolutionary runs, we keep pushing new trace tuples into this list until it contains

all 10 traces, which we can later use at our leisure to build graphs and/or deduce performance statistics.

7. **run_index**: We plan on running the experiment some *tot_runs* number of times. The run_index keeps track of what the current run index is. If the experiment is interrupted, using this and other parameters we can restart and continue with the experiment where we left off.

8. **tot_runs**: This element defines the total number of times that we wish to perform the evolutionary run, the total number of traces to build this particular experiment from.

9. **notes**: This can contain a data of any form; string, lists, tuple... This element simply adds an extra open element where some other data can be noted, data which does not belong to any other element in this record.

10. **started**: This element is the tuple: {date(), time()}, which specifies when the experiment was started.

11. **completed**: Complementary to the *started* element, this one stores the date() and time() of when the experiment was finally completed.

12. **interruptions**: This element is a list of tuples, whose form is: {date(), time()}. These tuples are generated every time the experiment has been restarted after an interruption. For example assume we are running an experiment, and on the 4th run, at which point the trace_acc already contains 3 trace tuples, the experiment was interrupted. Later on when we wish to continue with the experiment, we look through the mnesia database, in the experiment table, for an experiment whose progress_flag is set to *in_progress*. When we find this experiment, we know it has been interrupted, we take its pm_parameters and init_constraints and continue with the experiment, but also, we push to the *interruptions* list the tuple {date(),time()}, which ensures that this experiment notes that there was an interruption to the experiment, it was not a single continues run, and that though we do not know when that interruption occurred, we did continue with the experiment on the date: date(), and time: time().

Listing-13.4 The *experiment* record.

```
-record(experiment,{
    id,
    backup_flag = true,
    pm_parameters,
    init_constraints,
    progress_flag=in_progress,
    trace_acc=[],
    run_index=1,
    tot_runs=10,
    notes,
    started={date(),time()},
    completed,
    interruptions=[]
```

}).

With all the new records defined, we can now move forward and make the small modification to the population_monitor module, creating its new *prep_PopState/2* function, which will allow the benchmarker, and the researcher, to start the population_monitor process with its state parameters defined by the *pmp* record that the *prep_PopState/2* is executed with.

13.3 Updating the population_monitor Module

Instead of using the macros, we now store all the parameters in the population_monitor's state record. To start the population_monitor with a particular set of parameters, we now need to create a new function in which we define and set the *state* to the particular parameters we want the population_monitor to operate under. To set everything up for a population_monitor, we only need the parameters defined in the *pmp* and the *constraint* record. Thus we create the prep_PopState/2 function which is executed with the pmp record, and a list of constraint records, as its parameters. The new prep_PopState/2 function is shown in Listing-13.5.

Listing-13.5 The prep_PopState/2 function used to initialize the state parameters of the population_monitor.

```
prep_PopState(PMP,Specie_Constraints)->
    S=#state{
        op_mode=PMP#pmp.op_mode,
        population_id = PMP#pmp.population_id,
        survival_percentage=PMP#pmp.survival_percentage,
        specie_size_limit=PMP#pmp.specie_size_limit,
        init_specie_size=PMP#pmp.init_specie_size,
        polis_id=PMP#pmp.polis_id,
        generation_limit=PMP#pmp.generation_limit,
        evaluations_limit=PMP#pmp.evaluations_limit,
        fitness_goal=PMP#pmp.fitness_goal ,
        benchmarker_pid=PMP#pmp.benchmarker_pid
    },
    init_population(S,Specie_Constraints).
```

As can be seen, we now execute the init_population/2 function with the state tuple rather than the original *population_id* and the *opmode* parameters. This means that all the other functions which originally used the macros of this module, need to be slightly modified to now simply use the parameters which are now specified within the population_monitor's state record. The modifications are very small and few in number, and are thus not shown. The updated population_monitor module can be found in the 13th chapter of the available supplementary material [2].

Finally, we modify the termination clause of the population_monitor, since now at the moment of termination, the population_monitor needs to check whether it was a benchmarker that had spawned it. The population_monitor accomplishes this by checking the *benchmarker_pid* parameter. If this parameter is set to *undefined*, then the population_monitor does not need to send its trace anywhere. If the benchmarker_pid is defined, then the process forwards its trace to the specified PId. The updated *terminate/2* callback is shown in Listing-13.6.

Listing-13.6 The updated terminate/2 function, capable of sending the benchmarker the population_monitor's trace record, if the benchmarker was the one which spawned it.

```
terminate(Reason, S) ->
   case S of
        [] ->
                io:format("******** Population_Monitor shut down with Reason:~p, with
State: []~n",[Reason]);
        _ ->
                OpMode = S#state.op_mode,
                OpTag = S#state.op_tag,
                TotEvaluations=S#state.tot_evaluations,
                Population_Id = S#state.population_id,
                case TotEvaluations < 500 of
                        true ->%So that there is at least one stat in the stats list.
                                gather_STATS(Population_Id,0);
                        false ->
                                ok
                end,
                P = genotype:dirty_read({population,Population_Id}),
                T = P#population.trace,
                U_T = T#trace{tot_evaluations=TotEvaluations},
                U_P = P#population{trace=U_T},
                genotype:write(U_P),
                io:format("******** TRACE START ********~n"),
                io:format("~p~n",[U_T]),
                io:format("******** ^^^^ TRACE END ^^^^ ********~n"),
                io:format("******** Population_Monitor:~p shut down with Reason:~p
OpTag:~p, while in OpMode:~p~n",[Population_Id,Reason,OpTag,OpMode]),
                io:format("******** Tot Agents:~p Population Generation:~p
Tot_Evals:~p~n",[S#state.tot_agents,S#state.pop_gen,S#state.tot_evaluations]),
                case S#state.benchmarker_pid of
                        undefined ->
```

```
                ok;
        Pld ->
                Pld ! {S#state.population_id,completed,U_T}
    end
end.
```

With this done, and everything set up for the benchmarker to be able to spawn the population_monitor and store the experiment data if it wishes to do so, we now move forward to the next subsection and create this new benchmarker module.

13.4 Implementing the benchmarker

The benchmarker process will have three main functionalities:

1. To run the population_monitor N number of times, waiting for the population_monitor's trace after every run.
2. Create the experiment entry in the mnesia database, and keep updating its trace_acc as it itself accumulates the traces from the spawned population_monitors. The benchmarker should only do this if the backup_flag is set to true in the experiment record with which the benchmarker was started.
3. When the benchmarker has finished performing N number of evolutionary runs, and has accumulated N number of traces, it must print all the traces to console, calculate averages of the parameters between all the traces, and then finally write that data to file in the format which can be immediately graphed by GNUPlot.

In addition, because the benchmarker might be interrupted as it accumulates the traces, we want to build a function which can continue with the experiment when executed. Because each experiment will have its own unique Id, and because each experiment is stored to mnesia, this *continue* function should be executed with the *experiment id* parameter. When executed, it should read from the mnesia database all the needed information about the experiment, and then run the population_monitor the remaining number of times to complete the whole experiment.

In Listing-13.7 we implement the new benchmarker module. The comments after each function describe its functionality and purpose.

Listing-13.7 The implementation of the benchmarker module.

```
-module(benchmarker).
-compile(export_all).
-include("records.hrl").
%%% Benchmark Options %%%
-define(DIR,"benchmarks/").
```

```
-define(INIT_CONSTRAINTS,[#constraint{morphology=Morphology,
connection_architecture =CA, population_evo_alg_f=generational} || Morphology<-
[xor_mimic], CA<-[feedforward]]).
%%%%%%%%%%%%%%%%%%%%%%%%%%%%%%%%%%%%%%%%%%%%%%%%%%%%%%%%%%%%%
start(Id)->
    PMP = #pmp{
            op_mode=gt,
            population_id=Id,
            survival_percentage=0.5,
            specie_size_limit=10,
            init_specie_size=10,
            polis_id = mathema,
            generation_limit = 100,
            evaluations_limit = 10000,
            fitness_goal = inf
    },
    E=#experiment{
            id = Id,
            backup_flag = true,
            pm_parameters=PMP,
            init_constraints = ?INIT_CONSTRAINTS,
            progress_flag=in_progress,
            run_index=1,
            tot_runs=10,
            started={date(),time()},
            interruptions=[]
    },
    genotype:write(E),
    register(benchmarker,spawn(benchmarker,prep,[E])).
%start/1 is called with the experiment id or name. It first assigns all the parameters to the pmp
and experiment records, and then writes the record to database (overwriting an existing one of
the same name, if present), and then finally spawns and registers the actual benchmarker pro-
cess.

continue(Id)->
    case genotype:dirty_read({experiment,Id}) of
            undefined ->
                    io:format("Can't continue experiment:~p, not present in the database.~n",[Id]);
            E ->
                    case E#experiment.progress_flag of
                            completed ->
                                    Trace_Acc = E#experiment.trace_acc,
                                    io:format("Experiment:~p already completed:~p~n", [Id,
Trace_Acc]);
                            in_progress ->
```

```
                        Interruptions = E#experiment.interruptions,
                        U_Interruptions = [now()|Interruptions],
                        U_E = E#experiment{
                                interruptions = U_Interruptions
                        },
                        genotype:write(U_E),
                        register(benchmarker,spawn(benchmarker,prep,[U_E]))
            end
    end.
```

%The continue/1 function spawns a benchmarker to continue a previously stopped experiment. If the experiment with the name/id of the Id parameter is already present in the database, and its progress_flag is set to in_progress, which means that the experiment has not yet completed and should continue running and accumulating new traces into its trace_acc list, then this function updates the experiment's interruptions list, and then spawns the benchmarker process using the experiment tuple as its parameter. The experiment record holds all the needed information to start the population_monitor, it contains a copy of the population monitor parameters, and the initial constraints used.

```
prep(E)->
    PMP = E#experiment.pm_parameters,
    U_PMP = PMP#pmp{benchmarker_pid=self()},
    Constraints = E#experiment.init_constraints,
    Population_Id = PMP#pmp.population_id,
    population_monitor:prep_PopState(U_PMP,Constraints),
    loop(E#experiment{pm_parameters=U_PMP},Population_Id).
```

%prep/1 function is run before the benchmarker process enters its main loop. This function extracts from the experiment all the needed information to run the population_monitor:prep_PopState/2 function and to start the population_monitor process with the right set of population monitor parameters and specie constraints.

```
loop(E,P_Id)->
    receive
        {P_Id,completed,Trace}->
                U_TraceAcc = [Trace|E#experiment.trace_acc],
                U_RunIndex = E#experiment.run_index+1,
                case U_RunIndex >= E#experiment.tot_runs of
                        true ->
                                U_E = E#experiment{
                                        trace_acc = U_TraceAcc,
                                        run_index = U_RunIndex,
                                        completed = {date(),time()},
                                        progress_flag = completed
                                },
                                genotype:write(U_E),
                                report(U_E#experiment.id,"report");
```

```
                        false ->
                            U_E = E#experiment{
                                trace_acc = U_TraceAcc,
                                run_index = U_RunIndex
                            },
                            genotype:write(U_E),
                            PMP = E#experiment.pm_parameters,
                            Constraints = E#experiment.init_constraints,
                            population_monitor:prep_PopState(PMP,Constraints),
                            loop(U_E,P_Id)
                end;
            terminate ->
                ok
    end.
```

%loop/2 is the main benchmarker loop, which can only receive two types of messages, a trace from the population_monitor process, and a terminate signal. The benchmarker is set to run the experiment, and thus spawn the population_monitor process tot_runs number of times. After receiving the trace tuple from the population_monitor, it checks whether this was the last run or not. If it is not the last run, the benchmarker updates the experiment tuple, writes it to the database, and then spawns a new population_monitor by executing the population_monitor:prep_PopState/2 function. If it is the last run, then the function updates the experiment tuple, sets the progress_flag to completed, writes the updated experiment tuple to database, and runs the report function which calculates the averages and other statistical data, and produces the data for graphing, a file which can be used by the gnuplot program.

```
report(Experiment_Id,FileName)->
    E = genotype:dirty_read({experiment,Experiment_Id}),
    Traces = E#experiment.trace_acc,
    {ok, File} = file:open(?DIR++FileName++"_Trace_Acc", write),
    lists:foreach(fun(X) -> io:format(File, "~p.~n",[X]) end, Traces),
    file:close(File),
    io:format("******** Traces_Acc written to
file:~p~n",[?DIR++FileName++"_Trace_Acc"]),
    Graphs = prepare_Graphs(Traces),
    write_Graphs(Graphs,FileName++"_Graphs"),
    Eval_List = [T#trace.tot_evaluations||T<-Traces],
    io:format("Avg Evaluations:~p~n",[functions:avg(Eval_List),functions:std(Eval_List)]).
```
%report/2 is called with the id of the experiment to report upon, and the FileName to which to write the gnuplot formatted graphable data calculated from the given experiment. The function first extracts the experiment record from the database, then opens a file in the ?DIR directory to deposit the traces there, then calls the prepare_Graphs/1 function with the trace list from the experiment, and finally, with the data having now been prepared by the prepare_Graphs/1 function, the report function executes write_Graphs/2 to write the produced graphable data to the file FileName.

```
-record(graph,{morphology,avg_neurons=[],neurons_std=[],avg_fitness=[],fitness_std=[],
max_fitness=[], min_fitness=[],avg_diversity=[],diversity_std=[],evaluations=[],
evaluation_Index=[]}).
-record(avg,{avg_neurons=[],neurons_std=[],avg_fitness=[],fitness_std=[],max_fitness=[],
min_fitness=[], avg_diversity=[],diversity_std=[],evaluations=[]}).
```
%These two records contain the parameters specifically for the prepare_Graphs function. These records are used to accumulate data needed to calculate averages and other statistical data from the traces.

```
prepare_Graphs(Traces)->
    [T|_] = Traces,
    [Stats_List|_] = T#trace.stats,
    Morphologies = [S#stat.morphology || S<-Stats_List],
    Morphology_Graphs = [prep_Traces(Traces,Morphology,[])|| Morphology <-
Morphologies],
    [io:format("Graph:~p~n",[Graph])|| Graph<-Morphology_Graphs],
    Morphology_Graphs.
```
%prepare_Graphs/1 first checks a single trace in the Traces list to build a list of the morphologies present in the population (the number and types of which stays stable in our current implementation throughout the evolutionary run), since the statistical data is built for each morphology as its own specie. The function then prepares the graphable lists of data for each of the morphologies in the trace. Finally, the function prints to screen the lists of values built from averaging the traces. The data within the lists, like in the traces, is temporally sorted, composed every 500 evaluations by default.

```
prep_Traces([T|Traces],Morphology,Acc)->
    Morphology_Trace=lists:flatten([[S||S<-Stats,S#stat.morphology==Morphology]||Stats<-
T#trace.stats]),
    prep_Traces(Traces,Morphology,[Morphology_Trace|Acc]);
prep_Traces([],Morphology,Acc)->
    Graph = avg_MorphologicalTraces(lists:reverse(Acc),[],[],[]),
    Graph#graph{morphology=Morphology}.
```
%prep_Traces/3 goes through every trace, and extracts from the stats list of those traces only the stats associated with the morphology with which the function was called. Once the function goes through every trace in the Traces list, and the morphologically specific trace data has been extracted, the function calls avg_MorphologicalTraces/4 to construct a tuple similar to the trace, but whose lists are composed of the average based values of all the morphology specific traces, the average, std, max, min... of all the evolutionary runs in the experiment.

```
    avg_MorphologicalTraces([S_List|S_Lists],Acc1,Acc2,Acc3)->
        case S_List of
            [S|STail] ->
                    avg_MorphologicalTraces(S_Lists,[STail|Acc1],[S|Acc2],Acc3);
            [] ->
                    Graph = avg_statslists(Acc3,#graph{}),
```

```
                        Graph
            end;
    avg_MorphologicalTraces([],Acc1,Acc2,Acc3)->
            avg_MorphologicalTraces(lists:reverse(Acc1),[],[],[lists:reverse(Acc2)|Acc3]).
```
%avg_MorphologicalTraces/4 changes the dropped in S_lists from [Specie1_stats::[stat500, stat1000,...statN], Specie2_stats::[stat500,stat1000,...statN]...] to [[Spec1_Stat500, Spec2_Stat500... SpecN_Stat500], [Spec1_Stat1000, Spec2_Stat1000,... SpecN_Stat1000]...]. The trace accumulator contains a list of traces. A trace has a stats list, which is a list of lists of stat tuples. The stats list is a temporal list, since each stat list is taken every 500 evaluations, so the stats list traces-out the evolution of the population. Averages and other calculations need to be made for all experiments at the same temporal point, for example computing the average fitness between all experiments at the end of the first 500 evaluations, or at the end of the first 20000 evaluations... To do this, the function rebuilds the list from a list of separate temporal traces, to a list of lists where every such sublist contains the state of the specie (the stat) at that particular evaluation slot (at the end of 500, or 1000,...). Once this new list is built, the function calls avg_statslists/2, which calculates the various statistics of the list of lists.

```
    avg_statslists([S_List|S_Lists],Graph)->
            Avg = avg_stats(S_List,#avg{}),
            U_Graph = Graph#graph{
                    avg_neurons = [Avg#avg.avg_neurons|Graph#graph.avg_neurons],
                    neurons_std = [Avg#avg.neurons_std|Graph#graph.neurons_std],
                    avg_fitness = [Avg#avg.avg_fitness|Graph#graph.avg_fitness],
                    fitness_std = [Avg#avg.fitness_std|Graph#graph.fitness_std],
                    max_fitness = [Avg#avg.max_fitness|Graph#graph.max_fitness],
                    min_fitness = [Avg#avg.min_fitness|Graph#graph.min_fitness],
                    evaluations = [Avg#avg.evaluations|Graph#graph.evaluations],
                    avg_diversity = [Avg#avg.avg_diversity|Graph#graph.avg_diversity],
                    diversity_std = [Avg#avg.diversity_std|Graph#graph.diversity_std]
            },
            avg_statslists(S_Lists,U_Graph);
    avg_statslists([],Graph)->
            Graph#graph{
                    avg_neurons = lists:reverse(Graph#graph.avg_neurons),
                    neurons_std = lists:reverse(Graph#graph.neurons_std),
                    avg_fitness = lists:reverse(Graph#graph.avg_fitness),
                    fitness_std = lists:reverse(Graph#graph.fitness_std),
                    max_fitness = lists:reverse(Graph#graph.max_fitness),
                    min_fitness = lists:reverse(Graph#graph.min_fitness),
                    evaluations = lists:reverse(Graph#graph.evaluations),
                    avg_diversity = lists:reverse(Graph#graph.avg_diversity),
                    diversity_std = lists:reverse(Graph#graph.diversity_std)
            }.
```
%avg_statslists/2 calculates the averages and other statistics for every list in the S_lists, where each sublist is a list of stat tuples on which it executes the avg_stats/2 function, which returns

back a tuple with all the various parameters calculated from that list of stat tuples of that particular evaluations time slot.

```
avg_stats([S|STail],Avg)->
    U_Avg = Avg#avg{
            avg_neurons = [S#stat.avg_neurons|Avg#avg.avg_neurons],
            avg_fitness = [S#stat.avg_fitness|Avg#avg.avg_fitness],
            max_fitness = [S#stat.max_fitness|Avg#avg.max_fitness],
            min_fitness = [S#stat.min_fitness|Avg#avg.min_fitness],
            evaluations = [S#stat.evaluations|Avg#avg.evaluations],
            avg_diversity = [S#stat.avg_diversity|Avg#avg.avg_diversity]
    },
    avg_stats(STail,U_Avg);
avg_stats([],Avg)->
    Avg#avg{
            avg_neurons=functions:avg(Avg#avg.avg_neurons),
            neurons_std=functions:std(Avg#avg.avg_neurons),
            avg_fitness=functions:avg(Avg#avg.avg_fitness),
            fitness_std=functions:std(Avg#avg.avg_fitness),
            max_fitness=lists:max(Avg#avg.max_fitness),
            min_fitness=lists:min(Avg#avg.min_fitness),
            evaluations=functions:avg(Avg#avg.evaluations),
            avg_diversity=functions:avg(Avg#avg.avg_diversity),
            diversity_std=functions:std(Avg#avg.avg_diversity)
    }.
```

%avg_stats/2 function accepts a list of stat tuples as a parameter. First it extracts the various elements of that tuple. For every tuple in the list (each of the tuples belongs to a different evolutionary run) it puts the particular value of that tuple into its own list. Once all the values have been put into their own lists, the function uses the functions:avg/1 and functions:std/1 to calculate the averages and standard deviations as needed, to finally build the actual single tuple of said values (avg_neurons, neurons_std...). The case is slightly different for the max and min fitness values amongst all evolutionary runs, for which the function extracts the max amongst the maxs and the min amongst the mins, calculating the highest max and the lowest min achieved amongst all evolutionary runs. This can be further augmented to also simply calculate the avg of the max and min lists by changing the lists:min/1 and lists:max/1 to the function functions:avg/1.

```
write_Graphs([G|Graphs],Graph_Postfix)->
    Morphology = G#graph.morphology,
    U_G = G#graph{evaluation_Index=[500*Index || Index <-lists:seq(1,
length(G#graph.avg_fitness))]},
    {ok, File} = file:open(?DIR++"graph_"++atom_to_list(Morphology)++"_"
++Graph_Postfix, write),
    io:format(File,"#Avg Fitness Vs Evaluations, Morphology:~p~n",[Morphology]),
```

```
     lists:foreach(fun({X,Y,Std}) -> io:format(File, "~p ~p ~p~n",[X,Y,Std]) end,
  lists:zip3(U_G#graph.evaluation_Index,U_G#graph.avg_fitness,U_G#graph.fitness_std)),
     io:format(File,"~n~n#Avg Neurons Vs Evaluations, Morphology:~p~n",[Morphology]),
     lists:foreach(fun({X,Y,Std}) -> io:format(File, "~p ~p ~p~n",[X,Y,Std]) end,
  lists:zip3(U_G#graph.evaluation_Index,U_G#graph.avg_neurons,U_G#graph.neurons_std)),
     io:format(File,"~n~n#Avg Diversity Vs Evaluations, Morphology:~p~n",[Morphology]),
     lists:foreach(fun({X,Y,Std}) -> io:format(File, "~p ~p ~p~n",[X,Y,Std]) end,
  lists:zip3(U_G#graph.evaluation_Index,U_G#graph.avg_diversity,U_G#graph.diversity_std)),
     io:format(File,"~n~n#Avg. Max Fitness Vs Evaluations, Morphology:~p~n",[Morphology]),
     lists:foreach(fun({X,Y}) -> io:format(File, "~p ~p~n",[X,Y]) end,
  lists:zip(U_G#graph.evaluation_Index,U_G#graph.max_fitness)),
     io:format(File,"~n~n#Avg. Min Fitness Vs Evaluations, Morphology:~p~n",[Morphology]),
     lists:foreach(fun({X,Y}) -> io:format(File, "~p ~p~n",[X,Y]) end,
  lists:zip(U_G#graph.evaluation_Index,U_G#graph.min_fitness)),
     io:format(File,"~n~n#Specie-Population Turnover Vs Evaluations, Morphology:~p~n",
  [Morphology]),
     lists:foreach(fun({X,Y}) -> io:format(File, "~p ~p~n",[X,Y]) end,
  lists:zip(U_G#graph.evaluation_Index,U_G#graph.evaluations)),
     file:close(File),
     write_Graphs(Graphs,Graph_Postfix);
  write_Graphs([],_Graph_Postfix)->
     ok.
%write_Graphs/2 accepts a list of graph tuples, each of which was created for a particular spe-
cie/morphology within the experiment. Then for every graph, the function writes to file the var-
ious statistic results in the form readable by the gnuplot software. With the final result being a
file which can be immediately used by the gnuplot to produce graphs of the various properties
of the experiment.
```

With the benchmarker now implemented, we test it in the next subsection to ensure that all of its features are functional.

13.5 Compiling and Testing

Because we have created a new record, we now need to either add it to the mnesia database independently, or simply reset the whole thing (database), by executing the *polis:reset()* function. We now also need to test our new benchmarker system, and see whether it functions properly and does indeed save the data to the database, is able to continue the experiment after an interruption, and is able to produce a file which can be used by the gnuplot. Also, due to the following line in the benchmarker module: **-define(DIR,"benchmarks/")**, our benchmarker will be expecting for this folder to exist. Thus this folder must first be added, before we perform the following tests.

To test all these new features we will first recompile the code, and then reset the database. Afterwards, we will test our system in the following manner and order:

1. Set the benchmarker's *pmp* record to its current default, running the XOR mimicking experiment 10 times, to completion, using the generational evolutionary loop.
2. Examine the resulting console printout, to ensure basic structural validity, and that no crashes occurred.
3. Examine the two resulting files, the file that should have a list of traces, and the file which has data formatted in a gnuplot graphable format.
4. Plot the data in the graph based file, performing a basic sanity check on the resulting graph.
5. Again run the benchmarker, only this time, in the middle of the experiment execute: *Ctrl-C* to stop the interpreter midway, and then execute *'a'* to abort. This simulates the crashing of the machine in the middle of the experiment. We then re-enter the interpreter, and start up the polis to check whether the half finished experiment is present in the database. Once its presence is confirmed, we test *benchmarker:continue(Id)* by executing: *benchmarker:continue(test)*.
6. Finally, we examine the resulting console printout and the final experiment entry in the database, to ensure that the progress_flag is now set to: *completed*.

Because our implemented evolutionary loops (steady_state and generational) are independent of the evaluations accumulation, and thus the termination and the triggering of the benchmarker, we can simply perform these tests with the *generational* evolutionary loop, and not need to redo them with the steady_state evolutionary loop.

The default *pmp* and *experiment* records, and the ?INIT_CONSTRAINTS macro, are all set as follows:

```
-define(INIT_CONSTRAINTS,[#constraint{morphology=Morphology,connection_architecture
=CA, population_evo_alg_f=generational} || Morphology<-[xor_mimic],CA<-[feedforward]]).

#pmp{ op_mode=gt, population_id=test, survival_percentage=0.5, specie_size_limit=10,
init_specie_size=10, polis_id = mathema, generation_limit = 100, evaluations_limit = 10000,
fitness_goal = inf }

#experiment{ id = Id, backup_flag = true, pm_parameters=PMP, init_constraints
=?INIT_CONSTRAINTS, progress_flag=in_progress, run_index=1, tot_runs=10, started =
{date(),time()}, interruptions=[] }
```

Having set everything to the intended values, we now (assuming that the new source has been compiled, and the new mnesia database has been created with all the appropriate tables by executing polis:reset()) run the *benchmarker:start(test)* function, as shown in Listing-13.8.

Listing-13.8 Running the benchmarker:start(test) function to test the benchmarker functionality.

```
2> benchmarker:start(test).
...
    [{stat,xor_mimic,7.544823116774118e-10,1.0,0.0,278.5367828868784,
        235.4058314015377,979.1905253086005,112.76113310465351,4,500,
        {1325,412119,825873}}]],
    10000,500}
******** ^^^^ TRACE END ^^^^ ********
******** Population_Monitor:test shut down with Reason:normal OpTag:continue, while in
OpMode:gt
******** Tot Agents:10 Population Generation:36 Tot_Evals:10076
******** Traces_Acc written to file:"benchmarks/report_Trace_Acc"
Graph:{graph,xor_mimic,
[1.1345679012345677,1.3708193041526373,1.4792929292929293,...1.9777777777777774],
    [0.11516606301253175,0.3429379936199053,0.472713243338398,
...0.28588178511708023],
    [6376.044863498539,171964.06677104777,405553.7010466698,
...948483.9530134387],
    [13996.969949682387,305943.44537378295,421839.1376054512,
...46957.98926294873],
    [7595.914268861698,242099.32776384687,566599.7452288255,
...999402.6491394333],
[1736.703111779903,1157.4193567602842,227914.43647811364,...497519.90979294974],
    [5.111111111111111,6.444444444444445,...7.0],
    [0.7370277311900889,1.257078722109418,...2.1081851067789197],
    [500.0,500.0,500.0,500.0,500.0,444.44444444444446,...500.0],
    []}
```

It works! The console printout looks proper, a graph record, where each list is the average between all the experiments, with the averages calculated within the same evaluation frames. When we look into the *benchmark* folder, we see the presence of two files within: the *graph_xor_mimic_report_Graphs* file, and the *report_Trace_Acc* file. The report_Trace_Acc file contains a list of traces as expected, and shown in Listing-13.9.

Listing-13.9 The shortened contents of the report_Trace_Acc file.

```
{trace,[[{stat,xor_mimic,7.544235757558436e-10,2.0,0.0,999793.8069900939,
        20.85034690621442,999805.1547609345,999739.967822178,9,500,
        {1325,515312,752712}}]],...
10000,500}.
{trace,[[{stat,xor_mimic,7.544235772700672e-10,2.0,0.0,999796.4301657086,
```

3.35162014431123,999799.6097959183,999792.3483220651,8,500,
{1325,515310,43590}}],...
10000,500}.
...

So far so good, the *report_Trace_Acc* contains all 10 traces. Another file, with the name graph_**xor_mimic**_*report_Graphs,* is also present in the benchmark folder. This file contains rows of values in the format we specifically created so that we can then use gnuplot to plot the resulting data. A sample of the formatted data within the file is shown in Listing-13.10.

Listing-13.10 The format of the graph_xor_mimic_report_Graphs file.

```
#Avg Fitness Vs Evaluations, Morphology:xor_mimic
500 6376.044863498539 13996.969949682387
1000 171964.06677104777 305943.44537378295
...

#Avg Neurons Vs Evaluations, Morphology:xor_mimic
500 1.1345679012345677 0.11516606301253175
1000 1.3708193041526373 0.3429379936199053
...
```

Again, after analyzing the graph, all the data seems to be in proper order. If we wish, we can use this file to create a plot using the gnuplot program. An example of such a plot is shown in Fig-13.1. Fig-13.1a and Fig-13.1b show the plots of Fitness (Avg, Max, and Min) vs. Evaluations, and Population Diversity vs. Evaluations, respectively. In Fig-13.1a we see that the average and max fitness quickly increases, and within the first 1000 evaluations they have already reached a very good score. The Min fitness within the graph is shown to always go up and down, as is expected, since every offspring might have a mutation which might make it ineffective. But even in that plot, we see that the minimum fitness also reaches high values, primarily because the mutations that break the system in some way, are mitigated by the tuning of the synaptic weights. In Fig-13.2b we see the diversity plotted against evaluations, with vertical error bars.

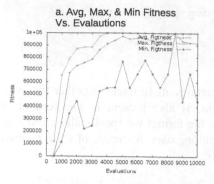
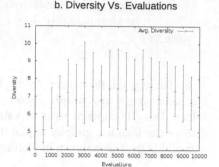

Fig. 13.1 The graphs produced with the data created by the benchmarker process, and plotted by the gnuplot program. Graph 'a' shows Fitness (Avg, Max, and Min) vs. Evaluations, and graph 'b' shows Diversity vs. Evaluations.

In the above figure we see that diversity never goes below 5 in a population of 10. A diversity of 4 is only present during the seed population, and primarily because there are only so many ways to create the minimalistic 1 neuron NN topology for this problem (through the use of different activation functions). The diversity in fact is increasing over time, not decreasing. The diversity reaches a stable value of 6-7, which means that 60%-70% of the population is different from one another, and the other 3-4 have similar topologies to those belonging to the 6-7 diverse topologies.

High population diversity is one of the important features of a memetic algorithm based TWEANN. In a system that we designed, it is simply not possible for diversity to shrink, because no matter which NN systems are fit or unfit, their offspring will have to be topologically different from them because they will pass through a topological mutation phase when created. As the size of the NN increases, so does the possible number of mutation operators applied to the clone during offspring creation, and thus the number of possible topological permutations, further increasing the number of mutants in the population, which results in an even higher diversity. As we increase the population size, again the result is greater diversity because now more agents can create offspring, and every one of those agents will produce a topological mutant, which will have a chance to be different from every other agent in the population and not just its parent.

Thus, a memetic algorithm based topology and weight evolving artificial neural network has a naturally emerging high diversity within its population, unlike the standard TWEANNs which usually converge very rapidly, and thus have a lower chance of solving the more complex problems. At the same time, the memetic TWEANN is also able to very rapidly solve problems it is applied to, and in my experience almost always faster than the standard TWEANN no matter the problem or simulation it is being used for. We will have a chance to test this bold claim when we benchmark our system against other TWEANNs in the following chapters.

With this done, we can now test the benchmarker's ability to continue a crashed or stopped experiment. You will most likely get a different result when testing on your machine, depending on when you stop the interpreter. On my machine, after having started the benchmarker, and then almost immediately stopping it by executing *Ctrl-C a*, and then re-entering the interpreter, my results were as follows when performing steps 5 and 6:

Listing-13.11 Crashing the benchmarker, and then attempting to continue by executing the benchmarker:continue(Id) function.

```
2> polis:start().
Parameters:{[],[]}
******** Polis: ##MATHEMA## is now online.
{ok,<0.35.0>}
2> benchmarker:start(test).
...
Ctrl-C
BREAK: (a)bort (c)ontinue (p)roc info (i)nfo (l)oaded
    (v)ersion (k)ill (D)b-tables (d)istribution
a
...
******** Polis: ##MATHEMA## is now online.
{ok,<0.34.0>}
2> mnesia:dirty_read({experiment,test}).
[{experiment,test,true,
        {pmp,gt,test,0.5,10,10,mathema,100,10000,inf,<0.143.0>},
        [{constraint,xor_mimic,feedforward, [tanh,cos,gaussian,absolute], [none],
[dot_product], [all],...],
        in_progress,
        [{trace,[[{stat,xor_mimic,7.544226409998199e-10,
                2.0833333333333335,0.2763853991962833,833118.8760231837,
                372581.937787711,999804.3485638215,0.34056136711788676,8,
                500,
                {1325,516955,41224}}]],
...
            10000,500}],
        2,10,undefined,
        {{2012,1,2},{7,9,12}},
        undefined,[]}]
3>benchmarker:continue(test).
...
Graph:{graph,xor_mimic,...}
4>mnesia:dirty_read({experiment,test}).
...
    completed,
```

```
   ...(TRACES)
     10,10,undefined,
start     {{2012,1,2},{7,9,12}},
end       {{2012,1,2},{7,14,51}},
          [{1325,517268,871875}]}]
```

It works! The benchmarker was first run and then abruptly stopped. After restarting the polis and checking the mnesia database, the experiment with the id *test* was present. Printing it to console showed, color coded in the above listing, that it contained the pmp record (green, and if you're reading the black & white printed version, it's the one starting with: "{pmp"), the constraints (blue, and starting with: "[{constraint"), and had a list of traces (red, and starting with: "[{trace"), 2 of which were present, out of the 10 the full experiment must contain. Finally, we also see the *in_progress* tag, which confirms that this experiment was stopped abruptly and is not yet finished. The function *benchmarker:continue(test)* was then executed, and the benchmarker ran to completion, printing the *Graph* tuple to console at the end. Finally, when rechecking the experiment entry in the database by executing *mnesia:dirty_read({experiment,test})*, we see that it contains 10 out of 10 evolutionary runs (traces), parameter *completed* is present, and we also see the start: **{{2012,1,2},{7,9,12}}** and end: **{{2012,1,2},{7,9,12}}** times respectively (which I marked with italicized "start" and "end" tags), are also present. The benchmarker works as expected, and we have completed testing it.

13.6 Summary

Every time an addition or extension is made to the neuroevolutionary system, it is important to see how it affects it as a whole. Is the neuroevolutionary system able to more effectively evolve agents? Is there high or low diversity? Does the neuroevolutionary approach taken converges too quickly, and is thus unable to inject enough diversity to overcome fitness walls present on the fitness landscape? Using a benchmarker helps us answer these questions.

We also created a new module called *benchmarker,* and a new table called *experiment,* within the database. The experiment table holds multiple complete experiment entries, each of which is composed of multiple traces, which are evolutionary runs applied to some problem. This allows for the experiment entry to be used to calculate the average performance of multiple runs of the same simulation/problem, thus giving us a general idea of how the system performs. We have created the benchmarker in such a way that it can run an experiment and save the traces to database after every successful run, such that in the case of a crash it can recover and continue with the experiment.

We are almost at the point where we can start adding new, much more advanced features. Features like plasticity, indirect encoding, crystallization... And though we can now perform benchmarks after adding such advanced features, we do not at this point have problems and simulations complex enough to test the new features on. Thus we first need to create this new set of more complex benchmarks and problems.

We need to create two types of new benchmarks. One standard neurocontroller benchmark, for which a recurrent and non recurrent solutions need to be evolved to solve it. This standard benchmark is called the pole balancing problem [3,4]. Another standard benchmark requires the NN based agent to learn as it interacts with the environment. We need such a benchmark to be able to tell whether the addition of neural plasticity to our evolved NN based systems improves them, and whether the added plasticity features work at all. The standard benchmark in this particular area is called the T-Maze navigation problem [5,6]. In the next chapter we will create both of these new problems, representing them as private scapes with which the evolving NN based agents can interact with.

13.7 References

[1] gnuplot: http://www.gnuplot.info/
[2] https://github.com/CorticalComputer/NeuroevolutionThroughErlang
[3] Gomez F, Miikkulainen R (1998). 2-D Pole Balancing with Recurrent Evolutionary Networks. In Proceedings of the International Conference on Artificial Neural Networks (Elsevier), pp. 2-7.
[4] Durr P, Mattiussi C, Floreano D (2006) Neuroevolution With Analog Genetic Encoding. Parallel Problem Solving from NaturePPSN iX, 671-680.
[5] Soltoggio A, Bullinaria JA, Mattiussi C, Durr P, Floreano D (2008) Evolutionary Advantages of Neuromodulated Plasticity in Dynamic, Reward-based Scenarios. Artificial Life 2, 569-576.
[6] Blynel J, Floreano D (2003) Exploring the T-maze: Evolving learning-like robot behaviors using CTRNNs. Applications of evolutionary computing 2611, 173-176.

Chapter 14 Creating the Two Slightly More Complex Benchmarks

Abstract To test the performance of a neuroevolutionary system after adding a new feature, or in general when trying to assess its abilities, it is important to have some standardized benchmarking problems. In this chapter we create two such benchmarking problems, the Pole Balancing Benchmarks (Single, Double, and With and Without dampening), and the T-Maze navigation benchmark, which is one of the problems used to assess the performance of recurrent and plasticity enabled neural network based systems.

Though we have created an extendible and already rather advanced TWEANN platform, how can we prove it to be so when we only have the basic XOR benchmark to test it on? As we continue to improve and advance our system, we will need to test it on more advanced benchmarks. In this chapter we develop and add two such benchmarking problems, the pole balancing benchmark, and the T-Maze navigation benchmark. Both of these benchmarks are standard within the computational intelligence field, and our neuroevolutionary system's ability to solve them is the minimum requirement to be considered functional.

To allow our TWEANN to use these benchmarks, we need to create a simulation/scape of the said problems, and create the agent morphology that contains the sensors/actuators that the NN based agents can use to interface with these new scapes. In the following sections we will first build the pole balancing simulation. Afterwards, we will develop the T-Maze simulation, a problem which can be much better solved by a NN system which can learn and adapt as it interacts with the environment, by a NN which has plasticity (a feature we will add to our neuroevolutionary system in Chapter-15).

Once these two types of new simulations are created, we will briefly test them, and then move on to the next chapter, where we will begin advancing and expanding our neuroevolutionary system.

14.1 Pole Balancing Simulation

The pole balancing benchmark consists of the NN based agent having to push a cart on a track, such that the pole standing on the cart is balanced and does not tip over and fall. Defined more specifically, the pole balancing problem is posed as follows: Given a two dimensional simulation of a cart on a 4.8 meter track, with a pole of length L on the top of a cart, attached to the cart by a hinge, and thus free to swing, the NN based controller must apply a force to the cart, pushing it back and forth on the track, such that the pole stays balanced on the cart and within 36 degrees of the cart's vertical. For sensory inputs, the NN based agent is provided with the cart's position and velocity, and the pole's angular position (from the vertical) and angular velocity. The output of the NN based agent is the force value F in newtons (N), saturated at 10N of magnitude. Positive F pushes the cart to the left, and negative pushes it to the right. Given these conditions, the problem is to balance the pole on the cart for 30 simulated minutes, or as long as possible, where the fitness is the amount of time the NN can keep the pole balanced by pushing the cart back and forth.

The temporal granularity of the simulation is 0.01 seconds, which means that every 0.01 seconds we perform all the physics based calculations, to determine the position of the cart and the pole. The Agent requests sensory signals and acts every 0.02 seconds. The simulation termination conditions are as follows: the cart must stay on the 4.8 meter track or the simulation ends, the simulation also ends if the pole falls outside the 36 degrees of the vertical.

There are multiple versions of this problem, each one differs in its difficulty:

1. The simple single pole balancing problem, as shown in Fig-14.1a. In this simulation the NN based agent pushes the cart to balance the single 1 meter pole on it. This problem is further broken down into two different versions.

    - The NN receives as a sensory signal the cart's position on the track (CPos), the cart's velocity (CVel), the pole's angular position (PAngle), and the pole's angular velocity (PVel). Sensory_Signal = [CPos, CVel, PAngle, PVel].
    - The NN receives as a sensory signal only the CPos and PAngle values. To figure out how to solve the problem, how to push the cart and in which direction, the NN will need to figure out how to calculate the CVel and PVel values on its own, which requires recurrent connections. Sensory_Signal = [Cpos,PAngle].

It is possible to very rapidly move the cart back and forth, which keeps the pole balanced. To prevent this type of a solution, the problem is sometimes further modified with the fitness of the NN based agent not only being dependent on the amount of time it has balanced the pole, but on how smoothly it has pushed the cart. One type of fitness function simply rewards the NN based on the length of time it has balanced the pole, while the other rewards the NN based on the length of time it has balanced the pole, and penalizes it for very high velocities and rapid velocity changes. The first is the standard fitness function, while the other is called the damping fitness function.

2. A more difficult version of the pole balancing problem is the double pole balancing version, as shown in Fig-14.1b. In this problem we try to balance two poles of differing lengths at the same time. The closer the lengths of the two poles are, the more difficult the problem becomes. Usually, the length of one pole is set to 0.1 meters, and the length of the second is set to 1 meter. As with the single pole balancing problem, there are two versions of this, and again for each version we can use either of the two types of fitness functions:

- The sensory signal gathered by the NN is composed of the cart's position and velocity (CPos,CVel), the first pole's angle and velocity (P1_Angle, P1_Vel), and the second pole's angle and velocity (P2_Angle, P2_Vel). Sensory_Signal = [CPos,CVel,P1_Angle,P1_Vel,P2_Angle,P2_Vel].
- The second more complex version of the problem, just as with the single pole balancing problem, only provides the NN with partial state information, the cart's position, and the first and second pole's angular position. Sensory_Signal = [CPos,P1_Angle,P2_Angle]. This requires the NN based agent to derive the velocities on its own, which can be done by evolving a recurrent NN topology.

As with the single pole balancing problem, the fitness can be based on simply the amount of time the poles have been balanced, or also on the manner in which the agent pushes the cart, using the damping fitness function.

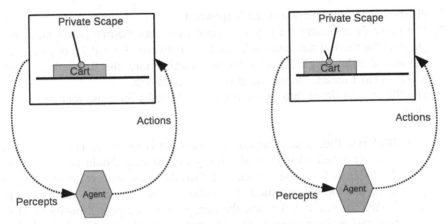

Fig. 14.1 The architecture of single (A.) and double (B.) pole balancing simulations, represented as private scapes with which the agents can interface with, to push the cart and balance the pole/s.

As with the XOR simulator, we will set the pole balancing simulation to be self contained in a private scape process, which will accept *sense* and *push* messages from the agent to whom it belongs. Since the simulation of the track/cart/pole is independent of the types of sense signals the agent wishes to use, we will only need to implement a single version of such private scape. We will implement the system using a realistic physical model of the system, and fourth order Runge-Kutta integration, as is specified and done in [1].

Because the two-pole balancing problem is simply an extension of the single pole balancing problem, and because the two poles are independent of each other, we can create a single double pole balancing simulator, which can then be used for either benchmark. It will be the *sense* and *force* messages that determine what information is sent to the sensors of the NN based agent. Furthermore, depending on the parameters sent by the actuator of the agent, the scape will calculate the fitness and decide on whether to use both poles or only a single pole with regards to the termination conditions.

Thus, the scape will always be simulating two poles. But if the agent is being applied to the single pole balancing problem, and this fact will be specified by the actuator and sensor pair used by the agent, the scape which receives the messages from the sensor and actuator of that agent, will simply not take into account the second pole. In this manner, if the second pole falls, deviates more than 36 degrees from the vertical... it will not trigger the termination condition or affect the fitness in any way. The parameter sent by the actuator will notify the scape that the agent is only concerned with the single pole being balanced.

We will set up the functionality of each such pole balancing simulation, contained and wrapped in a private scape, represented as a single process, to use the following steps:

1. PB (pole balancing) private scape is spawned.
2. The PB scape initializes the physical simulation, with the first pole's initial angle from the vertical randomly selected to be between -3.6 and 3.6 degrees, and the second pole's angle set to 0 degrees. Furthermore, the first pole's length will be set to 1 meter, and 0.1 meter for the second one.
3. The PB process drops into its main loop, and awaits for sense and push messages.
4. **DO:**
    5. **If** {From_PId, *sense*, Parameters} message is received: The Parameters value specifies what type of sensory information should be returned to the caller. If Parameters is set to 2, then the scape will return the cart position and the pole position information. If the Parameters value is set to 3, then the scape will return the cart, pole_1, and pole_2 positions. If 4, then cart position and velocity, plus pole_1 angular position and velocity, will be returned. Finally, if Parameters is set to 6, then the scape will return the cart position and velocity, and the pole_1 and pole_2 angular positions and velocities.
    6. **If** {From_PId, *push, Force,* Parameters} message is received: The PB scape applies the force specified in the message to the cart, and calculates the results of the physical simulation. The response to the push are calculated for two 0.01s time steps, taking the simulation 0.02 seconds forward, and then returning the scape back to waiting for the sense/push messages again. Furthermore, the *Parameters* value will have the form: {Damping_Flag, PB_Type}, where the Damping_Flag parameter specifies whether the fitness function will be calculated with damping features to prevent the rapid shaking of the cart, and where the PB_Type parameter specifies whether the private scape should be used as a single pole or double pole balancing simulator. If it is used as a single pole balancing

simulator, then the condition of the second pole will not affect the fitness value, and its reaching the termination condition (falling beyond 36 degrees from the vertical) will not end the simulation.

UNTIL: Termination condition is reached (goal number of time steps, or one of the boundary condition breaches).

The termination condition is considered to be any one of the following:

- The simulation has run for 30 simulated minutes, which is composed of 90000 0.02 second time steps.
- The pole has deviated 36 or more degrees from the cart's vertical.
- The cart has left the track. The track itself is 4.8 meters long, and the cart will start at the center, and thus be 2.4 meters away from either side. If it goes beyond -2.4 or 2.4 point on the axis of the track, the termination condition is reached.

Based on this architecture, we will in the following subsection create the private scape process, and its main loop which after receiving the *push* message calls the function which does the physical simulation of the track/cart/pole system. Afterwards, we will create the sensors/actuators and the new morphology specification entry in the morphology module. These will be the sensors and actuators used by the agents to interface with this type of private scape. Finally, we will then compile and run a quick test of this new problem, to see how well our system performs.

14.1.1 Implementing the Pole Balancing Scape

For the pole balancing simulation, the process will need to keep track of the position of the cart on the track, its velocity, the angular position and velocity of both poles, the time step the simulation is currently in, the goal time steps, and finally the fitness accumulated by the interfacing agent. To keep track of all these values, we will use a state record. Listing-14.1 shows the implementation of the pb_sim/2, the pole balancing simulation scape. We will add the source code of this listing to the scape module. The comments after every function in Listing-14.1 elaborate on the details of its implementation.

Listing-14.1 The complete implementation of the pole balancing simulation scape.

```
-record(pb_state,{cpos=0,cvel=0,p1_angle=3.6*(2*math:pi()/360),p1_vel=0, p2_angle=0,
p2_vel=0, time_step=0, goal_steps=90000,fitness_acc=0}).

pb_sim(ExoSelf_PId)->
    random:seed(now()),
    pb_sim(ExoSelf_PId,#pb_state{}).
```

%pb_sim/1 is executed to initialize and startup the pole balancing simulation scape. Once executed it creates initial #pb_state{}, and drops into the main simulation loop.

```
pb_sim(ExoSelf_PId,S)->
   receive
        {From_PId,sense, [Parameter]}->
              SenseSignal=case Parameter of
                      cpos -> [S#pb_state.cpos];
                      cvel -> [S#pb_state.cvel];
                      p1_angle -> [S#pb_state.p1_angle];
                      p1_vel -> [S#pb_state.p1_vel];
                      p2_angle -> [S#pb_state.p2_angle];
                      p2_vel -> [S#pb_state.p2_vel];
                      2 -> [S#pb_state.cpos,S#pb_state.p1_angle];
                      3 -> [S#pb_state.cpos,S#pb_state.p1_angle,S#pb_state.p2_angle];
                      4 -> [S#pb_state.cpos, S#pb_state.cvel, S#pb_state.p1_angle,
S#pb_state.p1_vel];
                      6 -> [S#pb_state.cpos, S#pb_state.cvel, S#pb_state.p1_angle,
S#pb_state.p1_vel, S#pb_state.p2_angle, S#pb_state.p2_vel]
              end,
              From_PId ! {self(),SenseSignal},
              pb_sim(ExoSelf_PId,S);
        {From_PId,push,[Damping_Flag,DPB_Flag], [F]}->
              AL = 2*math:pi()*(36/360),
              U_S=sm_DoublePole(F,S,2),
              TimeStep=U_S#pb_state.time_step,
              CPos=U_S#pb_state.cpos,
              CVel=U_S#pb_state.cvel,
              PAngle1=U_S#pb_state.p1_angle,
              PVel1=U_S#pb_state.p1_vel,
              case (abs(PAngle1) > AL) or (abs(U_S#pb_state.p2_angle)*DPB_Flag > AL)
or (abs(CPos) > 2.4) or (TimeStep >= U_S#pb_state.goal_steps) of
                      true ->
                              From_PId ! {self(),0,1},
                              pb_sim(ExoSelf_PId,#pb_state{});
                      false ->
                              Fitness = case Damping_Flag of
                                      without_damping ->
                                              1;
                                      with_damping ->
                                              Fitness1 = TimeStep/1000,
                                              Fitness2 = case TimeStep < 100 of
                                                      true ->
                                                              0;
                                                      false ->
```

```
                                          0.75/(abs(CPos) +abs(CVel) +
abs(PAngle1) + abs(PVel1))
                                 end,
                                 Fitness1*0.1 + Fitness2*0.9
                        end,
                        From_PId ! {self(),Fitness,0},
                        pb_sim(ExoSelf_PId, U_S#pb_state{fitness_acc
=U_S#pb_state.fitness_acc+Fitness})
                end;
        {ExoSelf_PId,terminate} ->
                ok
    end.
```

%The pole balancing simulation scape can accept 3 types of messages, *push, sense*, and *termi- nate*. When a sense message is received, the scape checks the Parameter value, and based on whether the Parameters == 2, 3,4, or 6, it returns a sensory list with an appropriate number of elements. 2 and 4 specify that the NN based agent wants a sensory signal associated with the single pole balancing problem, with partial or full system information, respectively. 4 and 6 im- plies that the NN wants the scape to send it sensory information associated with double pole balancing, with partial or full system information respectively. When the scape receives the push message, based on the message it decides on what fitness function is used (with or without damping), the actual force to be applied to the cart, and whether the termination condition should be based on the single pole balancing problem (DPB_Flag=0) or double pole balancing problem (DPB_Flag=1). When the angle of the second pole is multiplied by DPB_Flag which is set to 0, the value will always be 0, and thus it cannot trigger the termination condition of being over 36 degrees from the vertical. When it is multiplied by DPB_Flag=1, then its actual angle is used in the calculation of whether the termination condition is triggered or not. Once the mes- sage is received, the scape calculates the new position of the poles and the cart after force F is applied to it. The state of the poles/cart/track system is updated by executing the sm_DoublePole/3 function, which performs the physical simulation calculations.

```
sm_DoublePole(_F,S,0)->
    S#pb_state{time_step=S#pb_state.time_step+1};
sm_DoublePole(F,S,SimStepIndex)->
    CPos=S#pb_state.cpos,
    CVel=S#pb_state.cvel,
    PAngle1=S#pb_state.p1_angle,
    PAngle2=S#pb_state.p2_angle,
    PVel1=S#pb_state.p1_vel,
    PVel2=S#pb_state.p2_vel,
    X = CPos, %EdgePositions = [-2.4,2.4],
    PHalfLength1 = 0.5, %Half-length of pole 1
    PHalfLength2 = 0.05, %Half-length of pole 2
    M = 1, %CartMass
    PMass1 = 0.1, %Pole1 mass
    PMass2 = 0.01, %Pole2 mass
```

```
MUc = 0.0005, %Cart-Track Friction Coefficient
MUp = 0.000002, %Pole-Hinge Friction Coefficient
G = -9.81, %Gravity
Delta = 0.01, %Timestep
EM1 = PMass1*(1-(3/4)*math:pow(math:cos(PAngle1),2)),
EM2 = PMass2*(1-(3/4)*math:pow(math:cos(PAngle2),2)),
EF1 = Pmass1*PHalfLength1*math:pow(PVel1,2)*math:sin(PAngle1)+(3/4)*PMass1
*math:cos(PAngle1)*(((MUp*PVel1)/(PMass1*PHalfLength1))+G*math:sin(PAngle1)),
EF2 = Pmass2*PHalfLength2*math:pow(PVel2,2)*math:sin(PAngle2)+(3/4)*PMass2
*math:cos(PAngle2)*(((MUp*PVel2)/(PMass1*PHalfLength2))+G*math:sin(PAngle2)),
NextCAccel = (F - MUc*functions:sgn(CVel)+EF1+EF2)/(M+EM1+EM2),
NextPAccel1 = -(3/(4*PHalfLength1))*((NextCAccel*math:cos(PAngle1))
+(G*math:sin(PAngle1))+((MUp *PVel1)/(PMass1*PHalfLength1))),
NextPAccel2 = -(3/(4*PHalfLength2))*((NextCAccel*math:cos(PAngle2))
+(G*math:sin(PAngle2))+((MUp *PVel2)/(PMass2*PHalfLength2))),
NextCVel = CVel+(Delta*NextCAccel),
NextCPos = CPos+(Delta*CVel),
NextPVel1 = PVel1+(Delta*NextPAccel1),
NextPAngle1 = PAngle1+(Delta*NextPVel1),
NextPVel2 = PVel2+(Delta*NextPAccel2),
NextPAngle2 = PAngle2+(Delta*NextPVel2),
U_S=S#pb_state{
        cpos=NextCPos,
        cvel=NextCVel,
        p1_angle=NextPAngle1,
        p1_vel=NextPVel1,
        p2_angle=NextPAngle2,
        p2_vel=NextPVel2
},
sm_DoublePole(0,U_S,SimStepIndex-1).
%sm_DoublePole/3 performs the calculations needed to keep track of the two poles and the
cart, it simulates the physical properties of the track/cart/pole system. The granularity of the
physical simulation is 0.1s, and so to get a state at the end of 0.2s, the calculation of the state is
performed twice at the 0.1s granularity. During the first execution of the physical simulation we
have the force set to the appropriate force sent by the neurocontroller. But during the second,
F=0. Thus the agent actually only applies the force F for 0.1 seconds. This can be changed to
have the agent apply the force F for the entire 0.2 seconds.
```

With the simulation completed, we now need a way for our agents to spawn and interface with it. This will be done through the agent's morphology, its sensors and actuators, which we will create next.

14.1.2 Implementing the Pole Balancing morphology

Like the case with the xor_mimic morphology function, which when called returns the available sensors or actuators for that particular morphology, we will in this subsection develop the pole_balancing/1 morphology function which does the same. Unlike the xor_mimic though, here we will also populate the *parameters* element of the sensor and actuator records.

For both sensors and actuators we will again specify the scape element to be of type private: *scape = {private, pb_sim}*. For the sensor, we will set the parameters to: [2], this parameter can then be modified to 3, 4, or 6, dependent on what test we wish to apply the population of agents to. After every such *parameters value* change, the morphology module would then have to be recompiled before use. We could simply create multiple morphologies, for example: *pole_balancing2, pole_balancing3, pole_balancing4,* and *pole_balancing6,* but that would not add an advantage over changing the parameters and recompiling, since it would still require us to use our neuroevolutionary system on different problems and thus to change the constraints in either population_monitor or benchmarker modules, and then recompile them still...

Similarly, the actuator record's *parameters* element is set to: [no_damping,0]. The *no_damping* tag specifies that the fitness function used should be the simple one that does not take damping into account. The *0* element of the list specifies, based on our implementation of the *pb_sim,* that the second pole should not be taken into account when calculating the fitness and whether the termination condition is reached. This is achieved in: *(abs(U_S#pb_state.p2_angle)*DPB_Flag > AL)* , where *DPB_Flag* is either *0* or *1*. When set to 1, the second pole's condition/angle is taken into account, and when 0, it is not. This is so because *0 = 0*P2_Angle,* and 0 is never greater than *AL* which is set to 36 degrees. Listing-14.2 shows the implementation of this new addition to the morphology module.

Listing-14.2 The pole_balancing morphology; adding the new pb_GetInput sensor and pb_Push actuator to the morphology module.

```
pole_balancing(sensors)->
    [
        #sensor{name=pb_GetInput,scape={private,pb_sim},vl=2,parameters=[2]}
    ];
pole_balancing(actuators)->
    [
        #actuator{name=pb_SendOutput,scape={private,pb_sim},vl=1, parameters
=[no_damping,0]}
    ].
%Both, the pole balancing sensor and actuator, interface with the pole balancing simulation.
The type of benchmark the pole balancing simulation is used as (whether it is used as a double
```

pole or a single pole balancing benchmark) depends on the sensor and actuator parameters. The sensor's vl and parameters specify that the sensor will request the private scape for the cart's position and pole's angular position. The actuator's parameters specify that the scape should use no_damping type of fitness, and that since only a single pole is being used, that the termination condition associated with the second pole is zeroed out, by being multiplied by 0. When instead of using 0 we use 1, the private scape will use the angular position of the second pole as an element in calculating whether the termination condition has been reached or not.

Having specified the sensor and the actuator used by the pole_balancing morphology, we now need to implement them both. The pb_GetInput sensor will be similar to the xor_GetInput, only it will use its Parameters value in its message to the private scape it is associated with, as shown in Listing-14.3. We add this new sensor function to the sensor module, placing it after the xor_GetInput/3 function.

Listing-14.3 The implementation of the pb_GetInput sensor.

```
pb_GetInput(VL,Parameters,Scape)->
    Scape ! {self(),sense,Parameters},
    receive
            {Scape,percept,SensoryVector}->
                    case length(SensoryVector)==VL of
                            true ->
                                    SensoryVector;
                            false ->
                                    io:format("Error in sensor:pb_GetInput/2, VL:~p
SensoryVector:~p~n", [VL,SensoryVector]),
                                    lists:duplicate(VL,0)
                    end
    end.
```

Similarly, Listing-14.4 shows the implementation of the actuator pb_SendOutput/3 function, added to the actuator module. It too is similar to the xor_SendOutput/3 function, but unlike its neighbor, it sends its Parameters value as an element of the message that it forwards to the scape. Because we usually implement the morphologies and the scapes together, we can set up any type of interfacing, and thus be able to implement complex scapes and messaging schemes with ease.

Listing-14.4 The implementation of the pb_SendOutput actuator.

```
pb_SendOutput([Output],Parameters,Scape)->
    Scape ! {self(),push,Parameters,[10*functions:sat(Output,1,-1)]},
    receive
            {Scape,Fitness,HaltFlag}->
                    {Fitness,HaltFlag}
```

```
end.
```

Though simple to implement, this new problem allows us to test the ability of our neuroevolutionary system to evolve neurocontrollers on problems which require a greater level of complexity than the simple XOR mimicry problem. The benchmarking of our system on this problem also allows us to compare its results to those of other neuroevolutionary systems. Having implemented this new simulation, we now move forward in running a quick test on it in the next subsection.

14.1.3 Benchmark Results

In the previous chapter we have developed the benchmarking and reporting tools specifically to improve our ability to test new additions to the system. Thus all we must do now is to decide which variation of the pole balancing test to apply our system to, and then execute the benchmarker:start/1 function with the appropriate *constraint, pmp,* and *experiment* parameters.

Our benchmarker, on top of generating graphable data, also calculates the simple average number of evaluations from all the evolutionary runs within the experiment, which is exactly the number we seek because the benchmark here is how quickly a solution can be evolved on average using our system. Let us run 3 experiments, which will only entail us to execute the benchmarker:start/1 function 3 times, each time with a different sensor and actuator specification. Thus we next run three experiments, each with its own morphological setup:

1. The single pole, partial information, standard fitness function (without damping) benchmark:

```
pole_balancing(sensors)->
    [ #sensor{name=pb_GetInput,scape={private,pb_sim},vl=2,parameters=[2]} ];
pole_balancing(actuators)->
    [#actuator{name=pb_SendOutput,scape={private,pb_sim},vl=1, parameters
=[without_damping,0]}].
```

2. The double pole, partial information, standard fitness function (without damping) benchmark:

```
pole_balancing(sensors)->
    [ #sensor{name=pb_GetInput,scape={private,pb_sim},vl=3,parameters=[3]} ];
pole_balancing(actuators)->
    [#actuator{name=pb_SendOutput,scape={private,pb_sim},vl=1, parameters
=[without_damping,1]}].
```

3. The double pole, partial information, with damping fitness function benchmark:

```
pole_balancing(sensors)->
  [ #sensor{name=pb_GetInput,scape={private,pb_sim},vl=3,parameters=[3]} ];
pole_balancing(actuators)->
  [ #actuator{name=pb_SendOutput,scape={private,pb_sim},vl=1, parameters
=[with_damping,1]} ].
```

We must also set the *pmp*'s fitness goal to 90000, since with the standard, without_damping fitness function, the 90000 fitness score represents the NN based agent's ability to balance a pole for 30 minutes. But what about the *with_damping* simulation? In that event a neurocontroller will have different fitness scores for the same number of time steps that it has balanced the pole/s, since the fitness will be based on its effectiveness of balancing the poles as well. In the same manner, different number of time steps of balancing the pole/s might map to the same fitness score... This situation arises due to the fact that the more complicated problems will not have a one-to-one mapping with regards to fitness scores reached, and progress towards solving a given problem or achieving some goal. Different such simulations and problems will have different types of fitness scores, and using a termination condition based on a fitness goal value set in the population_monitor, will not work. On the other hand, each simulation/problem itself, will have all the necessary information about the agent's performance to decide whether a goal has been reached or not.

Furthermore, sometimes we wish to see just how quickly on average the neuroevolutionary system can generate a result for a problem, at those times we only care about the minimum number of evaluations needed to reach the solution. In our system no matter when the termination condition is reached, it is not until all the agents of the current generation, or all the currently active agents, have terminated, that the evolutionary run is complete. This means that the total number of evaluations keeps incrementing even after the goal has already been reached, simply because the currently-still-running agents are continuing being tuned.

To solve both problems, we can allow each scape to inform the agent that it has reached the particular goal of the problem/scape when it has done so. At this point the agent would forward that message to the population_monitor, which could then stop counting the evaluations by freezing the tot_evaluations value. In this one move we allow each scape to use the extra feature of *goal_reached* notification ability to be able to, on its own terms, use any fitness function, and at the same time be able to stop and notify the agent that it has reached the particular fitness goal, or solved the problem, and thus stop the evaluations accumulator from incrementing. This will allow us to no longer need to calculate fitness goals for every problem by pre-calculating various values (fitness goals) and setting them in the population_monitor. This method will also allow us to deal with problems where the fitness score is not directly related to the completion of the problem or to the reaching of the goal, and thus cannot be used as the termination condition in the first place. Thus, before we run the benchmarks, let's make this small program modification.

Currently when the agent has triggered the scape's stopping condition, the scape sends back to the agent the message: {Scape_PId,0,1}, where 0 means that it has received 0 fitness points for this last event, and 1 means that this particular scape has reached its termination condition. The actuator does nothing with this value but pass it to the cortex, thus if we retain the same message structure, we can piggyback it with new functionality. We will allow each scape to also have, on top of the standard termination conditions, the ability to check for its own goal reaching condition. When that goal condition is reached, instead of sending to the actuator the original message, the scape will send it: {Scape_PId,goal_reached,1}. The actuator does not have to be changed, its job is simply to forward this message to the cortex.

In the cortex we modify its *receive* clause to check whether the *Fitness* score sent to it is actually an atom *goal_reached*. The new *receive* clause is implemented as follows:

```
{APId,sync,Fitness,EndFlag} ->
    case Fitness == goal_reached of
        true ->
                put(goal_reached,true),
                loop(Id,ExoSelf_PId,SPIds,{APIds,MAPIds},NPIds,CycleAcc,FitnessAcc,
EFAcc +EndFlag, active);
        false ->
                loop(Id,ExoSelf_PId,SPIds,{APIds,MAPIds},NPIds,CycleAcc,FitnessAcc
+Fitness, EFAcc +EndFlag, active)
    end;
```

We also modify the cortex's message to the exoself when its evaluation termination condition has been triggered by the EndFlag, when the actuator sends it the message of the form: {APId, sync, Fitness, EndFlag}. The new message the cortex sends to the exoself is extended to include the note on whether *goal_reached* is set to true or not. The new message format will be: {self(), evaluation_completed, FitnessAcc, CycleAcc, TimeDif, get(goal_reached)}.

Reflectively, the exoself's receive pattern is extended to receive the *GoalReachedFlag* message, and to then forward it to the population_monitor, as shown by the boldfaced source code in the following listing:

```
Listing-14.5 The updated exoself's receive pattern.

loop(S)->
    receive
            {Cx_PId,evaluation_completed,Fitness,Cycles,Time,GoalReachedFlag}->
                case (U_Attempt >= S#state.max_attempts) or (GoalReachedFlag==true) of
                    true ->%End training
                            A=genotype:dirty_read({agent,S#state.agent_id}),
```

```
                              genotype:write(A#agent{fitness=U_HighestFitness}),
                              backup_genotype(S#state.idsNpids,S#state.npids),
                              terminate_phenotype(S#state.cx_pid,S#state.spids,S#state.npids,
S#state.apids, S#state.scape_pids),
                              io:format("Agent:~p terminating. Genotype has been backed
up.~n Fitness:~p~n TotEvaluations:~p~n TotCycles:~p~n TimeAcc:~p~n", [self(),
U_HighestFitness, U_EvalAcc,U_CycleAcc, U_TimeAcc]),
                         case GoalReachedFlag of
                             true ->
                                  gen_server:cast(S#state.pm_pid,
{S#state.agent_id, goal_reached);
                             _ ->
                                  ok
                         end,
                         gen_server:cast(S#state.pm_pid,{S#state.agent_id,terminated,
U_HighestFitness});
...
```

Next, we update the *population_monitor* by first adding to its *state* record the goal_reached element, which is set to *false* by default, and then by adding to it a new handle_cast clause:

```
handle_cast({_From,goal_reached},S)->
  U_S=S#state{goal_reached=true},
  {noreply,U_S};
```

This cast clause sets the *goal_reached* parameter to true when triggered. Finally, we add to all population_monitor's termination condition recognition cases the additional operator: "**or S#state.goal_reached**", and modify the *evaluations* message receiving handle_cast clause to:

```
handle_cast({From,evaluations,Specie_Id,AEA,AgentCycleAcc,AgentTimeAcc},S)->
  AgentEvalAcc=case S#state.goal_reached of
      true ->
           0;
      _ ->
           AEA
  end,
```

This ensures that the population_monitor stops counting evaluations when the goal_reached flag is set to true. These changes effectively modify our system, giving it the ability to use the goal_reached parameter. This entire modification is succinctly shown in Fig-14.2.

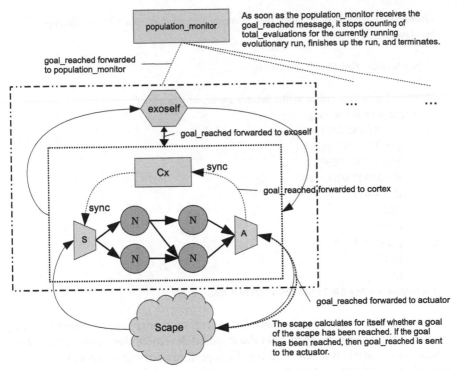

Fig. 14.2 The updated goal_reached message processing capable scape, and the goal_reached signal's travel path: scape to actuator to cortex to exoself to population_monitor.

This small change allows us to continue with our pole_balancing benchmarking test. And thus we finally set the experiment's *tot_runs* parameter to 50, which makes the benchmarker run 50 evolutionary runs in total, which means that the calculated average is based on 50 runs, which is a standard for this type of problem.

To run the first benchmark, we simply use the morphology setup listed earlier, set the fitness_goal parameter of the pmp record to 90000, the tot_runs to 50, and leave everything else as default. We then compile and reload everything by running polis:sync(), and execute the benchmarker:start(spb_without_damping) function, where *spb_without_damping* is the Id we give to this experiment, which stands for Single Pole Balancing Without Damping.

With this setup, the benchmarker will spawn the population_monitor process, wait for the evolutionary run to complete, add the resulting trace to the experiment's stats list, and then perform another evolutionary run. In total 50 evolutionary runs will comprise the benchmark. The result we are after is not the graphable data, but the report's average evaluations value (the average number of evaluations taken to reach the goal), and its standard deviation. The results of the first benchmark are shown in the following listing.

Listing-14.6 The results of the single pole balancing, partial information, without_damping, benchmark.

```
3> benchmarker:start(spb_without_damping).
...
******** Traces_Acc written to file:"benchmarks/report_Trace_Acc"
Graph:{graph,pole_balancing,
       [1.1782424242424248],
       [0.16452932686308724],
       [60910.254989899],
       [24190.827695700948],
       [75696.42],
       [32275.24],
       [6.04],
       [1.232233744059949],
       [457.72],
       []}
Tot Evaluations Avg:646.78 Std:325.8772339394086
```

It works! The results are also rather excellent, on average taking only 646 evaluations (though as can be seen from the standard deviation, there were times when it was much faster). We achieved this high performance (as compared to the results of other neuroevolutionary systems) without even having taken the time to optimize or tune our neuroevolutionary system yet. If we compare the resulting evaluations average that we received from our benchmark (your results might differ slightly), to those done by others, for example compared to the list put together in paper [1], we see that our system is the most efficient of the topology and weight evolving artificial neural network systems on this benchmark. The two faster neuroevolutionary systems ESP [2], and CoSyNE [3], do not evolve topology. The ESP and CoSyNE systems solved the problem in 589 and 127 evaluations respectively, while the CNE [4] and SANE [5] and NEAT [6] solved it in 724, 1212, and 1523 evaluations on average, respectively.

When using the non topology and weight evolving neuroevolutionary systems (ESP, CMA-ES, and CoSyNE), the researcher must first create a topology he knows works (or have the neuroevolutionary system generate random topologies, rather than evolving one from another), and then the neuroevolutionary system simply optimizes the synaptic weights to a working combination of values. But such systems cannot be applied to previously unknown problems, or problems for which we do not know the topology, nor its complexity and size, beforehand. For complex problems, topology cannot be predicted, in fact this is why we use a topology and weight evolving artificial neural network system, because we cannot predict and create the topology for *non-toy* problems on our own, we require the help of evolution.

Next we benchmark our system on the second problem, the more complex double pole balancing problem which uses a standard fitness function without damping. Listing-14.7 shows the results of the experiment.

Listing-14.7 The double pole balancing benchmark, using the *without_damping* fitness function.

```
3> benchmarker:start(spb_without_damping).
...
Graph:{graph,pole_balancing,
        [2.4315606060606063],
        [0.8808311444164436],
        [22194.480560606058],
        [15614.417335306674],
        [34476.74],
        [6285.78],
        [7.34],
        [1.4779715829473847],
        [500.0],
        []}
Tot Evaluations Avg:5184.0 Std:3595.622677645695
```

Our system was able to solve the given problem in **5184** evaluations, whereas again based on the table provided in [1], the next closest TWEANN in that table is ESP [2], which solved it in 7374 evaluations on average. But, the DXNN system we discussed earlier was able to solve the same problem in 2359 evaluations on average. As we continue advancing and improving the system we're developing together, it too will improve to such numbers.

Finally, we run the third benchmark, the double pole balancing with partial state information and with damping. Because we have added the goal_reached messaging by the scapes, we can deal with the non one-to-one mapping between the number of time steps the agent can balance the cart, and the fitness calculated for this balancing act. Thus, we modify the pmp's fitness_goal back to inf, letting the scape terminate when the goal has been reached, and thus when the evaluation run should stop (we could have done the same thing during the previous experiment, rather than using the fitness goal of 90000, which was possible due to the goal and fitness having a one-to-one mapping). The results of this experiment are shown in Listing-14.8.

Listing-14.8 The results of running the double pole balancing with damping benchmark.

```
Graph:{graph,pole_balancing,
        [3.056909090909092],
        [1.3611906067001034],
```

[67318.29389102172],
[84335.29879824212],
[102347.17542007213],
[11861.325171196118],
[7.32],
[1.5157836257197137],
[500.0],
[]}
Tot Evaluations Avg:**4792.38** Std:3834.866761127432

It works! The goal_reached feature has worked, and the average number of evaluations our neuroevolutionary system needed to produce a result is highly competitive to other state of the art systems as shown in Table-14.1 which quotes the benchmark results from [1]. The DXNN system's benchmark results are also added to the table for comparison, with the results of our system added at the bottom. Note that neither CMA-ES nor CoSyNE evolves neural topologies. These two systems only optimize the synaptic weights of the already provided NN.

Table 14.1 Benchmark results for the pole balancing problem.

Method	Single-Pole/Incomplete state Information	Double-Pole/Partial Information W/O Damping	Double-Pole W/ Damping
RWG	8557	415209	1232296
SANE	1212	262700	451612
CNE*	724	76906*	87623*
ESP	589	7374	26342
NEAT	-	-	6929
CMA-ES*	-	3521*	6061*
CoSyNE*	127*	1249*	3416*
DXNN	**Not Performed**	**2359**	**2313**
OurSystem	647	**5184**	**4792**

* These do not evolve topologies, but only optimize the synaptic weights

Having completed developing these two benchmarks, and having finished testing our TWEANN system on the pole and double pole balancing benchmark, we move forward and begin developing the more complex T-Maze problem.

14.2 T-Maze Simulation

The T-Maze problem is another standard problem that is used to test the ability of a NN based system to learn and change its strategy while existing in, and interacting with, a maze environment. In this problem an agent navigates a T shaped maze as shown in Fig-14.3. At one horizontal end of the maze is a low reward, and at another a high reward. The agent is a simulated robot which navigates the maze. Every time the robot crashes into a wall or reaches one of the maze's ends, its position is reset to the start of the maze. The whole simulation run (agent is allowed to navigate the maze until it either finds the reward and its position resets to base, or crashes into a wall and its position is reset to base) lasts X number of maze runs, which is usually set to 100. At some random time during those 100 maze runs, the high and low reward positions are swapped. The goal is for the agent to gather as many reward points as possible. Thus, if the agent has been reaching the high reward end of the maze, and suddenly there was a switch, the best strategy is for the agent when it has reached the location of where previously there was a high reward, is to realize that it now needs to change its strategy and always go to the other side of the maze, for the remainder of the simulation. To do this, the agent must remember what reward it has picked up and on what side, and change its traveling path after noticing that the rewards have been switched, which is most easily done when some of the agent's neurons are plastic.

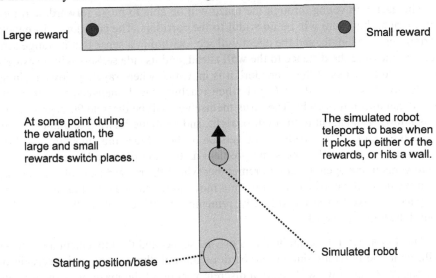

Large reward   **Small reward**

At some point during the evaluation, the large and small rewards switch places.

The simulated robot teleports to base when it picks up either of the rewards, or hits a wall.

Simulated robot

Starting position/base

Fig. 14.3 The T-Maze setup.

We will create a simplified version of the T-Maze problem. It is used widely [6,7], and it does not require us to develop an entire 2d environment and robot simulation (which we will do in Chapter-18, when we create an Artificial Life simulation). Our T-Maze will have all the important features of the problem, but will not require true navigation in 2d space. We will create a discrete version of the T-Maze, as shown in Fig-14.4.

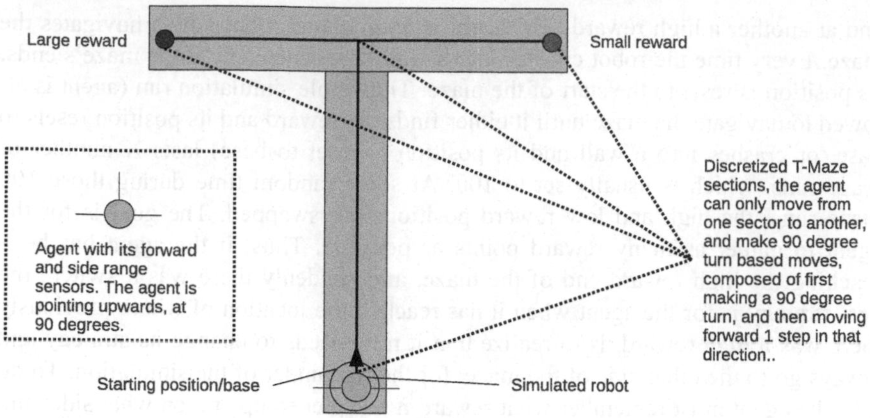

Fig. 14.4 A discrete version of the T-Maze simulation.

The agents traveling through the maze will be able to move forward, and turn left or right, but there will be no width to the corridors. The corridors will have a certain discrete length, and the agent will see forward in a sense that its range sensor will measure the distance to the wall ahead, and its side sensors will measure a distance to the sides of the "corridor" it is in, which when traveling down a single dimensional corridor will be 0, yet when reaching the T intersection, will show that it can turn left or right. The turns themselves will be discrete 90 degree turns, thus allowing the agent to turn left or right, and continue forward to gather the reward at the end of the corridor. This version of the T-Maze though simple, still requires the agent to solve the same problem as the non discrete Maze. In the discrete version, the agent must still remember where the reward is, evolve an ability to move down the corridors and turn and move in the turned direction where there is space to move forward, and finally, remember on which side of the maze it last found the highest reward.

The T-Maze will be contained in a private scape, and the movement and senses will, as in the previous simulation, be done through the sending and receiving of messages. Because we will create a discrete version of the maze, we can simulate the whole maze by simply deciding on the discrete length of each section of the corridor, and what the agent will receive as its sensory signals when in a particular section of the maze. The agent will use a combination of the following two sensors:

1. distance_sensor: A laser distance sensor pointing forward, to the left side, and to the right side, with respect to the simulated robot's direction. Since the maze is self contained and closed, the sensors will always return a distance. When traveling down the single dimensional corridor, the forward sensor will return the distance to the wall ahead, and the side distance sensors will return 0, since there is no place to move sideways. When the agent reaches an intersection, the side range sensors will return the distances to the walls on the side, thus the

agent can decide which way to turn. If the agent has reached a dead end, then both the forward facing, and the side facing range sensors will return 0, which will require the agent to turn, at which point it can start traveling in the other direction.

2. reward_consumed: The agent needs to know not only where the reward is, but how large it is, since the agent must explore the two rewards, and then for the remainder of the evaluation go towards the larger reward. To do this, the agent must have a sensory signal which tells it how large the reward it just consumed is. This sensor forwards to the NN a vector of length one: [RewardMagnitude], where RewardMagnitude is the magnitude of the actual reward.

The agent must also be able to move around this simplified, discrete labyrinth. There are different ways that we could allow the NN based agent to control the simulated robot within the maze. We could create an actuator that uses a vector of length one, where this single value is then used to decide whether the agent is to turn left (if the value is < -0.33), or turn right (if the value is > 0.33) or continue moving forward (if the value is between -0.33 and 0.33). Another type of actuator could be based on the differential drive, similar to one used by the Khepera [5] robot (a small puck shaped robot). The differential_drive actuator would have as input a vector of length 2: [Val1,Val2], where Val1 would control the rotation speed of the left wheel, and Val2 would control the rotation speed of the right wheel. In this manner if both wheels are spinning backwards (Val1 < 0, and Val2 < 0), the simulated robot moves backwards, if both spin forward with the same speed, then the robot moves forward. If they spin at different speeds, the robot either turns left or right depending on the angular velocities of the two wheels. Finally, we could create an actuator that accepts an input vector of length 2: [Val1,Val2], where Val1 maps directly to the simulated robot's velocity on the Y axis, and Val2 maps to the robot's velocity on the X axis. This would be a simple *translation_drive* actuator, and the simulated robot in this scenario would not be able to rotate. The inability to rotate could be alleviated if we add a third element to the vector, which we could than map to the angular velocity value, which would dictate the robot's rotation clockwise or counterclockwise, dependent on that value's sign. Or Val1 could dictate the robot's movement forward/backward, and Val2 could dictate whether the robot should turn left, right, or not at all. There are many ways in which we could let the NN control the movement of the simulated robot. For our discrete version of the T-Maze problem, we will use the same movement control method that was used in paper [7] which tested another NN system on the discrete T-Maze problem. This actuator accepts an input from a single neuron, and uses this accumulated vector: [Val], to then calculate whether to move forward, turn counterclockwise and move forward in that direction, or turn clockwise and then move forward in that direction. If Val is between -0.33 and 0.33, the agent moves one step forward, if it is less than -0.33, the agent turns counterclockwise and then moves one step forward, and if Val is greater than 0.33, the agent turns clockwise and moves one step forward in the new direction.

Due to this being a discrete version of the maze, it can easily be represented as a state machine, or simply as a list of discrete sections. Looking back at Fig-14.4, we can use a list to keep track of all the sensor responses for every position and orientation within the maze. In the standard discrete T-Maze implementation used in [7], there are in total 4 sectors. The agent starts at the bottom of the T-Maze located at {X=0,Y=0}, it can then move up to {0,1}, which is an intersection. At this point the agent can turn left and move a step forward to {-1,1}, or turn right and move a step forward to {1,1}.

If we are to draw the maze on a Cartesian plane, the agent can be turned to face towards the positive X axis, at 0 degrees, the positive Y axis at 90 degrees, the negative X axis at 180 degrees, and finally the negative Y axis, at 270 degrees. And if the maze is drawn on the Cartesian plane, then each sector's Id can be its coordinate on that plane. With the simulated robot in this maze being in one of the sectors (on one of the coordinates {0,0},{0,1},{1,1},or {-1,1}), and looking in one particular direction (at 0, 90, 180, or 270 degrees), we can then perfectly define what the sensory signals returned to the simulated robot should be. But before we can do that, we need a format for how to store the simulated robot's location, viewing direction, and how it should perceive whether it is looking at a wall, or at a reward located at one of the maze's ends. The superposition of the T-Maze on a Cartesian plane, with a few examples of the agent's position/orientation, and what sensory signals it receives there, is shown in Fig-14.5.

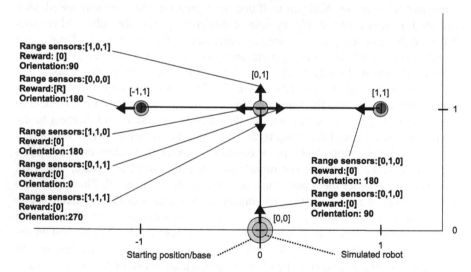

Fig. 14.5 Discrete T-Maze, and the sensory signals the simulated robot receives at various locations and orientations. The agent is shown as a gray circle, with the arrow pointing in the direction the simulated robot is looking, its orientation.

We will let each discrete sector keep track of the following:

- **id**: It's own id, its Cartesian coordinate.

- **r**: The reward the agent gets for being in that sector. There will be only two sectors that give reward, the two horizontal endings of the "*T*". This reward will be sensed by the *reward_sensor.*
- **description**: This will be the list that contains all the sensory information available when the agent is in that particular sector. In this simulation it will contain the range sensory signals. This means that each section will contain 4 sets of range sensory signals, one each for when the simulated robot is turned and is looking at 0, at 90, at 180, and at 270 degrees in that sector. Each of the range signals appropriate for the agent's particular orientation can then be extracted through a key, where the key is the agent's orientation in degrees (one of the four: 0, 90, 180, or 270). The complete form of the *description* list is as follows: *[{0, NextSector, RangeSense}, {90, NextSector, RangeSense}, {180, NextSector, RangeSense}, {270, NextSector, RangeSense}].* The *NextSector* parameter specifies what is the coordinate of the next sector that is reachable from the current sector, given that the agent will move forward while in the current orientation. Thus, if for example the agent's forward is at 90 degrees, looking toward the positive Y axis on the Cartesian coordinate, and its actuator specifies that it should move forward, then we look at the 90 degree based tuple, and move the agent to the NextSector of that tuple.

We will call the record containing all the sector information of a single sector: *dtm_sector*, which stands for *Discrete T-Maze Sector.* An example of the sector located at coordinate [0,0], and part of the maze shown in the above figure, is as follows:

```
#dtm_sector{id=[0,0],description=[{0,[],[1,0,0]},{90,[0,1],[0,1,0]},{180,[],[0,0,1]},{270,[],[0,0,0]}],r=0}
```

Let's take a closer look at this sector, located at [0,0], and on which the agent is for example turned at 90 degrees, and thus looking towards the positive Y axis. For this particular orientation when the agent requests sensory signals, they will come from the following tuple: **{90,[0,1],[0,1,0]}**, also highlighted in the above record. The first value, 90, is the orientation for which the follow-up sensory information is listed. The [0,1] is the coordinate of the sector to which the agent will move if it decides to move forward at this orientation. The vector [0,1,0] is the range sensory signal, and is fed to the agent's range sensor when requested. It states that on both sides, the agent's left and right, there are walls right next to it, and the distance to them is 0, and that straight ahead the wall does not come up for 1 sector. The value r=0 states that the current sector has no reward, and this is the value fed to the agent's reward sensor.

Thus this allows the agent to move around the discrete maze, travel from one sector to another, where each sector has all the information needed when the agent's sensors send a request for percepts. These sectors will all be contained in a single record's list, used by the private scape which represents the entire maze.

We will call the record for this private scape: *dtm_state*, and it will have the following default format:

```
-record(dtm_state,{agent_position=[0,0],agent_direction=90,sectors=[],tot_runs=60,
run_index=0, switch_event, fitness_acc=0}).
```

Let's go through each of this record's elements and discuss its meaning:

- **agent_position**: Keeps track of the agent's current position, the default is [0,0], the agent's starting position in the maze.
- **agent_direction**: Keeps track of the agent's current orientation, the default is 90 degrees, where the agent is looking down the maze, towards the positive Y axis.
- **sectors**: This is a list of all the sectors: [SectorRecord1...SectorRecordN], each of which is represented by the dtm_sector record, and a list of which will represent the entire T-Maze.
- **tot_runs**: Sets the total number of maze runs (trials) the agent performs per evaluation.
- **run_index**: This parameter keeps track of the current maze run index.
- **switch_event**: Is the run index during which the large and small reward locations are switched. This will require the agent, if it wants to continue collecting the larger reward, to first go to the large reward's original position, at which it will now find the smaller reward, figure out that the location of the large reward has changed, and during the following maze run go to the other side of the maze to collect the larger reward.
- **switched**: Since the switch of the reward locations needs to take place only once during the entire tot_runs of maze runs, we will set this parameter to *false* by default, and then to true once the switch is made, so that this parameter can then be used as a flag to ensure that no other switch is performed for the remainder of the maze runs.
- **step_index**: If we let the agents travel through the maze for as long as they want, there might be certain phenotypes that simply spin around in one place, although not possible with our current type of actuator, which requires the agent to take a step every time, either forward, to the right, or to the left. To prevent such infinite spins when we decide to use another type of actuator, we will give each agent only a limited number of steps. It takes a minimum of 2 steps to get from the base of the maze to one of the rewards, 1 step up the main vertical hall, and 1 turn/move step to the left or right. With an eye to the future, we will give the agents a maximum of 50 steps, after which the maze run ends as if the agent crashed into a wall. Though not useful in this implementation, it might become useful when you extend this maze and start exploring other actuators, sensors...

As with the pole balancing, this private scape will allow the agent to send it messages requesting sensory signals, either all signals (range sense, and the just acquired reward size sense) merged into a single vector, or one sensory signal vector at a time. And it will allow the agent to send it signals from its actuators, dictating whether it should move or rotate/move the simulated robot.

Thus, putting all of this together: The scape will keep track of the agent's position and orientation, and be able to act on the messages sent from its sensor and actuator, and based on them control the agent's avatar. The T-Maze will start with the large and small rewards at the two opposite sides of the T-Maze, and then at some random maze run to which the switch_event is set (different for each evaluation), the large and small reward locations will flip, and require for the agent to figure this out and go to the new location if it wants to continue collecting the larger of the two rewards. As per the standard T-Maze implementation, the large reward is worth 1 point, and the small reward is worth 0.2 points. If at any time the agent hits a wall, by for example turn/moving when located at the base of the maze, and thus hitting the wall, the maze run ends and the agent is penalized with -0.4 fitness points, is then re-spawned at the base of the maze, and the *run_index* is incremented. If the agent collects the reward, the maze run ends and the agent is re-spawned at the base of the maze, with the *run_index* incremented. Finally, once the agent has finished *tot_runs* number of maze runs, the evaluation of the agent's fitness ends, at which point the exoself might perturb the NN's synaptic weights, or end the tuning run... To ensure that the agents do not end up with negative fitness scores when setting the tot_runs to 100, we will start the agents off with 50 fitness points. Thus an agent that always crashes will have a minimum fitness score of 50 − 100*0.4 = 10.

Finally, though we will implement the T-Maze scenario where the agent gets to the reward at one of the maze's ends, and is then teleported back to the base of the maze for another maze-run, there are other possible implementations and scenarios. For example, as is demonstrated in Fig-14.6, we could also extend the maze to have teleportation portals located at {-2,1} and {2,1}, through which the agent has to go after gathering the food, so that it is teleported back to the base to reset the rewards. Or we could require it to have to travel all the way back to the base manually, though we would need to change the simple actuator so that it can rotate in place without crashing into walls. Finally, we could also create the T-Maze which allows for both options, teleportation and manual travel. All, the 3 extended T-Mazes, and 1 default T-Maze which we will implement, are shown in the following figure.

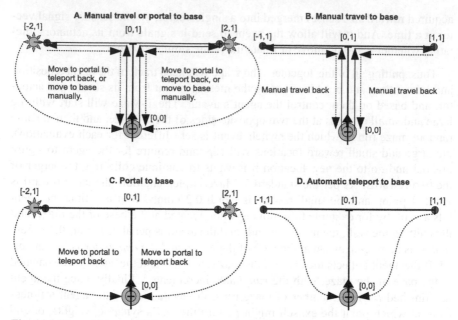

Fig. 14.6 The various possible scenarios for the T-Maze after the agent has acquired the reward.

Having decided on the architecture, and having created Fig-14.5 and Fig-14.6d to guide us in the designing and setting the T-Maze system and each of its sectors, we can now move forward to the next subsection and implement this private T-Maze scape, and the needed sensors and actuators to interface with it.

14.2.1 T-Maze Implementation

Through Fig-14.5 we can immediately map the maze's architecture to its implementation shown in Listing-14.9. For the implementation we first define the two new records needed by this new scape: the dtm_sector and dtm_state records. The function *dtm_sim/1* prepares and starts up the maze, dropping into the process's main loop. In this main loop the scape process can accept requests for sensory signals, and accept signals from the actuators and return to them a message containing the fitness points acquired. The sensors we will use will poll the private scape for an extended range sensor, which is a vector of length 4, and contains the signals from the agent's range sensor, appended with the reward value in the current maze sector: *[Reward,L,F,R]*, where Reward is the value of the actual reward, L is the range to the left wall, F is the range to the wall in front, and R is the range to the wall on the right.

Listing-14.9 The implementation of the Discrete T-Maze scape.

```erlang
-record(dtm_sector,{
   id,
   description=[],
   r
}).

-record(dtm_state,{
   agent_position=[0,0],
   agent_direction=90,
   sectors=set_tmaze_sectors(),
   tot_runs=100,
   run_index=0,
   switch_event=35+random:uniform(30),
   switched=false,
   step_index=0,
   fitness_acc=50
}).

dtm_sim(ExoSelf_PId)->
   io:format("Starting dtm_sim~n"),
   random:seed(now()),
   dtm_sim(ExoSelf_PId,#dtm_state{}).

dtm_sim(ExoSelf_PId,S) when (S#dtm_state.run_index == S#dtm_state.switch_event) and
(S#dtm_state.switched==false)->
   Sectors=S#dtm_state.sectors,
   SectorA=lists:keyfind([1,1],2,Sectors),
   SectorB=lists:keyfind([-1,1],2,Sectors),
   U_SectorA=SectorA#dtm_sector{r=SectorB#dtm_sector.r},
   U_SectorB=SectorB#dtm_sector{r=SectorA#dtm_sector.r},
   U_Sectors=lists:keyreplace([-1,1],2,lists:keyreplace([1,1],2,Sectors, U_SectorA),
U_SectorB),
   scape:dtm_sim(ExoSelf_PId,S#dtm_state{sectors=U_Sectors, switched=true});
dtm_sim(ExoSelf_PId,S)->
   receive
        {From_PId,sense,Parameters}->
              APos = S#dtm_state.agent_position,
              ADir = S#dtm_state.agent_direction,
              Sector=lists:keyfind(APos,2,S#dtm_state.sectors),
              {ADir,NextSec,RangeSense} = lists:keyfind(ADir,1, Sec-
tor#dtm_sector.description),
              SenseSignal=case Parameters of
                    [all] ->
```

```
                                        RangeSense++[Sector#dtm_sector.r];
                        [range_sense]->
                                RangeSense;
                        [reward] ->
                                [Sector#dtm_sector.r]
                end,
                From_PId ! {self(),percept,SenseSignal},
                scape:dtm_sim(ExoSelf_PId,S);
        {From_PId,move,_Parameters,[Move]}->
                APos = S#dtm_state.agent_position,
                ADir = S#dtm_state.agent_direction,
                Sector=lists:keyfind(APos,2,S#dtm_state.sectors),
                U_StepIndex = S#dtm_state.step_index+1,
                {ADir,NextSec,RangeSense} = lists:keyfind(ADir,1,
Sector#dtm_sector.description),
                if
                        (APos == [1,1]) or (APos == [-1,1]) ->
                                Updated_RunIndex=S#dtm_state.run_index+1,
                                case Updated_RunIndex >= S#dtm_state.tot_runs of
                                        true ->
                                                From_PId ! {self(), S#dtm_state.fitness_acc
+Sector#dtm_sector.r, 1},
                                                dtm_sim(ExoSelf_PId,#dtm_state{});
                                        false ->
                                                From_PId ! {self(),0,0},
                                                U_S = S#dtm_state{
                                                        agent_position=[0,0],
                                                        agent_direction=90,
                                                        run_index=Updated_RunIndex,
                                                        step_index = 0,
                                                        fitness_acc = S#dtm_state.fitness_acc
+Sector#dtm_sector.r
                                                },
                                                dtm_sim(ExoSelf_PId,U_S)
                                end;
                        Move > 0.33 -> %clockwise
                                NewDir=(S#dtm_state.agent_direction + 270) rem 360,
                                {NewDir,NewNextSec,NewRangeSense} =
lists:keyfind(NewDir, 1, Sector#dtm_sector.description),
                                U_S = move(ExoSelf_PId,From_PId,S#dtm_state{
agent_direction =NewDir},NewNextSec,U_StepIndex),
                                dtm_sim(ExoSelf_PId,U_S);
                        Move < -0.33 -> %counterclockwise
                                NewDir=(S#dtm_state.agent_direction + 90) rem 360,
```

```
                              {NewDir,NewNextSec,NewRangeSense} =
lists:keyfind(NewDir, 1, Sector#dtm_sector.description),
                         U_S = move(ExoSelf_PId,From_PId,S#dtm_state{
agent_direction=NewDir},NewNextSec,U_StepIndex),
                         dtm_sim(ExoSelf_PId,U_S);
                  true -> %forward
                         move(ExoSelf_PId,From_PId,S,NextSec,U_StepIndex)
            end;
      {ExoSelf_PId,terminate} ->
            ok
   end.
```

% The dtm_sim/2 function generates a simulated discrete T-Maze scape, with all the sensory information and the maze architecture specified through a list of sector records. The scape can receive signals from the agent's sensor, to which it then replies with the sensory information, and it can receive the messages from the agent's actuator, which it uses to move the agent's avatar around the maze.

```
   move(ExoSelf_PId,From_PId,S,NextSec,U_StepIndex)->
      case NextSec of
            [] -> %wall crash/restart_state
                  Updated_RunIndex = S#dtm_state.run_index+1,
                  case Updated_RunIndex >= S#dtm_state.tot_runs of
                        true ->
                              From_PId ! {self(),S#dtm_state.fitness_acc-0.4,1},
                              dtm_sim(ExoSelf_PId,#dtm_state{});
                        false ->
                              From_PId ! {self(),0,0},
                              U_S = S#dtm_state{
                                    agent_position=[0,0],
                                    agent_direction=90,
                                    run_index=Updated_RunIndex,
                                    step_index = 0,
                                    fitness_acc = S#dtm_state.fitness_acc-0.4
                              },
                              dtm_sim(ExoSelf_PId,U_S)
                  end;
            _ -> %move
                  From_PId ! {self(),0,0},
                  U_S = S#dtm_state{
                        agent_position=NextSec,
                        step_index = U_StepIndex
                  },
                  dtm_sim(ExoSelf_PId,U_S)
      end.
```

%The move/5 function accepts as input the State S of the scape, and the specification of where the agent wants to move its avatar next, NextSec. The function then determines whether that next sector exists, or whether the agent will hit a wall if it moves in its currently chosen direction.

```
set_tmaze_sectors()->
    Sectors = [
        #dtm_sector{id=[0,0],description=[{0,[],[1,0,0]},{90,[0,1],[0,1,0]},{180,[],[0,0,1]},
{270,[], [0,0,0]}],r=0},
        #dtm_sector{id=[0,1],description=[{0,[1,1],[0,1,1]},{90,[],[1,0,1]},{180,[-1,1],
[1,1,0]}, {270, [0,0], [1,1,1]}],r=0},
        #dtm_sector{id=[1,1],description=[{0,[],[0,0,0]},{90,[],[2,0,0]},{180,[0,1],[0,2,0]},
{270,[], [0,0,2]}],r=0.2},
        #dtm_sector{id=[-1,1],description=[{0,[0,1],[0,2,0]},{90,[],[0,0,2]},{180,[],[0,0,0]},
{270,[],[2,0,0]}],r=1}
    ].
% The set_tmaze_sectors/0 function returns to the caller a list of sectors representing the T-
Maze. In this case, there are 4 such sectors, the vertical sector, the two horizontal sectors,
and the cross section sector.
```

With the T-Maze implemented, we now need to develop the complementary sensor and the actuator. For the sensor, since the agent needs all the information appended: sensory vectors from the *range_sensor*, and the *reward* sensor, combined into a single vector, we will create a single sensor which will contain the information from both of these sensors. What sensory signal the scape sends back to the agent's sensor will be defined by the sensor's parameter message. The actuator will simply forward the NN based agent's output to the discrete T-Maze process, which will then interpret the signal as turning left and moving forward 1 step, turning right and moving forward 1 step, or just moving forward 1 step. We first create the morphology, which follows the same format as the one we created for the pole_balancing morphology. This morphology we will call *discrete_tmaze*, with its implementation shown in Listing-14.10, and which we add to the morphology module.

```
Listing-14.10 The discrete_tmaze morphology specification.

discrete_tmaze(sensors)->
    [
        #sensor{name=dtm_GetInput,scape={private,dtm_sim},vl=4,parameters=[all]}
    ];
discrete_tmaze(actuators)->
    [
        #actuator{name=dtm_SendOutput,scape={private,dtm_sim},vl=1,parameters=[]}
    ].
```

Similarly, the sensor's implementation is shown in Listing-14.11, which we add to the sensor module.

Listing-14.11 The *dtm_GetInput* sensor implementation.

```
dtm_GetInput(VL,Parameters,Scape)->
    Scape ! {self(),sense,Parameters},
    receive
            {Scape,percept,SensoryVector}->
                    case length(SensoryVector)==VL of
                            true ->
                                    SensoryVector;
                            false ->
                                    io:format("Error in sensor:dtm_GetInput/3, VL:~p
SensoryVector:~p~n", [VL,SensoryVector]),
                                    lists:duplicate(VL,0)
                    end
    end.
```

Finally, the actuator implementation is shown in Listing-14.12, which we add it to the actuator module.

Listing 14.12 The *dtm_SendOutput* actuator implementation.

```
dtm_SendOutput(Output,Parameters,Scape)->
    Scape ! {self(),move,Parameters,Output},
    receive
            {Scape,Fitness,HaltFlag}->
                    {Fitness,HaltFlag}
    end.
```

And with that we've completely developed all the parts of the discrete T-Maze benchmark. We've created the actual private scape that represents the maze and in which an agent can travel. And we created the complementary morphology, with its own sensor and actuator set, used to interface with the T-Maze scape. With this particular problem/benchmark, we will now be able to test whether our topology and weight evolving artificial neural network system is able to evolve NN based agents which can perform complex navigational tasks, evolve agents which have memory and can make choices based on it, and even learn when the neurons within the tested NN have plasticity.

14.2.2 Benchmark Results

Let's run a quick test of our system by applying it to our newly developed problem. Though I do not expect our neuroevolutionary system to evolve an agent capable of effectively solving the problem at this stage, we still need to test whether the new scape, morphology, sensor, and actuator, are functional. Before we run the benchmark, let us figure out what fitness score value represents that the problem has been solved.

An evaluation is composed of 100 total maze runs, and sometime during the midpoint, between run 35 and 65, the high and low rewards are flipped. In this implementation, we set the switch_event to occur on the run number: *35+random:uniform(30)*. It will take at least one wrong trip to the reward to figure out that its position has been changed. Also, we should expect that eventually, evolution will create NNs that always first go to the maze corner located at [1,1], which holds the high reward before it is flipped.

So then, the maximum possible score achievable in this problem, a score representing that the problem has been solved, is: 99*1 + 1*0.2 + 50 = **149.2**, which represents an agent that first always goes to the right corner, at some point it goes there and notices that the reward is now small (0.2 instead of 1), and thus starts going to the [-1,1] corner. This allows the agent to achieve 99 high rewards, and 1 low reward. A score which represents that the agent evolved to always go to {1,1}, is at most: 65*1 + 35*0.2 + 50 = **122**, which is achieved during the best case scenario, when the reward is flipped on the 65th count, thus allowing the agent to gather high reward for 65 maze runs, and low reward for the remaining 35 maze runs. The agent will perform multiple evaluations, during some evaluations the reward switch event will occur early, and every once in a while it will occur on the 65th maze run, which is the latest time possible. During that lucky evaluation, the agent can reach 122 fitness points by simply not crashing and always going to the {1,1} side. The agent can accomplish this by first having: *0.33> Output >-0.33*, which will make the avatar move forward, and during the second step have *Output > 0.33*, which will make the avatar turn right and move forward to get the reward. Finally, the smallest possible fitness is achieved when the agent always crashes into the wall: *50 – 100*0.4 = 10*.

With this out of the way, we now set the Morphology element in the benchmarker module within the *?INIT_CONSTRAINTS* macro, to *discrete_tmaze*. We then set generation limit to inf, and evaluations_limit to 5000, in the *pmp* record. Finally, we run *polis:sync()* to recompile and load everything, then start the polis, and then finally execute benchmarker:start(dtm_test), as shown in Listing-14.3.

Listing-14.3 The results of running the T-Maze benchmark.

```
Graph:{graph,discrete_tmaze,
```

```
    [1.1300000000000001,1.12,1.195,1.1816666666666666,
    1.1633333333333333,1.1561111111111111,1.2322222222222223,
    1.1400000000000001,1.1766666666666665,1.1800000000000002],
    [0.10535653752852737,0.11661903789690603,0.10234744745229357,
    0.10026354161796684,0.10214368964029706,0.08123088569087163,
    0.13765675688483067,0.11575836902790224,0.1238726945070803,
    0.092736184954957],
    [111.38000000000011,115.31900000000012,112.4590000000001,
    114.4511111111112,112.8790000000001,112.6335555555556,
    112.13066666666677,111.12500000000009,110.68722222222232,
    114.57700000000014],
    [9.305813236896594,6.245812917467183,6.864250796700242,
    8.069048898318606,8.136815662374111,9.383282426018074,
    7.888934134455533,9.98991266228088,9.41834002503416,
    8.867148978110151],
    [122.0000000000001,122.0000000000001,122.0000000000001,
    122.0000000000001,122.0000000000001,122.0000000000001,
    122.0000000000001,122.0000000000001,122.0000000000001,
    122.0000000000001],
    [10.000000000000115,10.000000000000115,10.000000000000115,
    10.000000000000115,10.000000000000115,10.000000000000115,
    10.000000000000115,10.000000000000115,10.000000000000115,
    10.000000000000115],
    [8.1,8.8,9.1,8.9,8.0,7.75,8.1,7.65,7.9,7.8],
    [0.8888194417315588,1.2884098726725124,0.8306623862918073,
    0.7681145747868607,0.8366600265340756,0.8874119674649424,
    0.9433981132056604,0.7262919523166975,1.57797338380595,
    1.3638181696985856],
    [500.0,500.0,500.0,500.0,500.0,500.0,500.0,475.0,500.0,500.0],
    []}
```

Tot Evaluations Avg:5083.75 Std:53.78835840588556

We are not interested in the "Tot Evaluations Avg" value, since the benchmark was not set up to use the goal_reached feature. But from the graph printout we do see the score **122.00**, boldfaced. I've boldfaced the list showing the highest fitness scores achieved amongst all the evolutionary runs. Though as we guessed, the system did not produce a solution (which requires plasticity as we will see in the next chapter), it has rapidly (within the first 500 evaluations), produced the score of 122, which means that agents learned to always navigate to the right corner.

It is always a good idea to at least once double check and printout all the information produced within the scape, following it in the console, and manually analyzing it to check for bugs. We will do that just this once, following a single extracted agent, and the signals its sensors acquire and its actuators produce. First, we run the function population_monitor:test() with the same parameters we started the benchmarker until a fit agent is evolved. We then add the line:

```
io:format("Position:~p SenseSignal:~p ",[Apos,SenseSignal]),
```

And lines:

```
timer:sleep(1000),
io:format("Move:~p StepIndex:~p RunIndex:~p~n", [Move,U_StepIndex,
S#dtm_state.run_index]),
```

To the receive *sense* and *move* pattern matchers, respectively. We then extract the evolved fit agent, and execute the function: *exoself:start(AgentId,void)* to observe the path the agent takes. A short console printout I saw when performing these steps is shown in Listing-14.4. The console printout shows the agent's starting moves, up to the point when the position of the rewards was switched, and a few steps afterwards.

Listing-14.4 Console printout of a champion agent's maze navigation.

```
exoself:start({7.513656492058022e-10,agent},void).

Starting dtm_sim
Position:[0,0] SenseSignal:[0,1,0,0] <0.5846.1>
Move:4.18876787545547e-15 StepIndex:1 RunIndex:0
Position:[0,1] SenseSignal:[1,0,1,0] Move:0.7692260090076106 StepIndex:2 RunIndex:0
Position:[1,1] SenseSignal:[0,0,0,1] Move:0.011886120521166272 StepIndex:3 RunIndex:0
Position:[0,0] SenseSignal:[0,1,0,0] Move:4.18876787545547e-15 StepIndex:1 RunIndex:1
Position:[0,1] SenseSignal:[1,0,1,0] Move:0.7692260090076106 StepIndex:2 RunIndex:1
Position:[1,1] SenseSignal:[0,0,0,1] Move:0.011886120521166272 StepIndex:3 RunIndex:1
Position:[0,0] SenseSignal:[0,1,0,0] Move:4.18876787545547e-15 StepIndex:1 RunIndex:2
Position:[0,1] SenseSignal:[1,0,1,0] Move:0.7692260090076106 StepIndex:2 RunIndex:2
Position:[1,1] SenseSignal:[0,0,0,1] Move:0.011886120521166272 StepIndex:3 RunIndex:2
Position:[0,0] SenseSignal:[0,1,0,0] Move:4.18876787545547e-15 StepIndex:1 RunIndex:3
...
Position:[0,0] SenseSignal:[0,1,0,0] Move:4.18876787545547e-15 StepIndex:1 RunIndex:38
Position:[0,1] SenseSignal:[1,0,1,0] Move:0.7692260090076106 StepIndex:2 RunIndex:38
Position:[1,1] SenseSignal:[0,0,0,1] Move:0.011886120521166272 StepIndex:3 RunIndex:38
Position:[0,0] SenseSignal:[0,1,0,0] Move:4.1887678754555e-15 StepIndex:1 RunIndex:39
Position:[0,1] SenseSignal:[1,0,1,0] Move:0.7692260090076106 StepIndex:2 RunIndex:39
Position:[1,1] SenseSignal:[0,0,0,0.2] Move:0.837532377697202 StepIndex:3 RunIndex:39
Position:[0,0] SenseSignal:[0,1,0,0] Move:4.1887678754555e-15 StepIndex:1 RunIndex:40
Position:[0,1] SenseSignal:[1,0,1,0] Move:0.7692260090076106 StepIndex:2 RunIndex:40
Position:[1,1] SenseSignal:[0,0,0,0.2] Move:0.837532377697202 StepIndex:3 RunIndex:40
Position:[0,0] SenseSignal:[0,1,0,0] Move:4.18876787545547e-15 StepIndex:1 RunIndex:41
Position:[0,1] SenseSignal:[1,0,1,0] Move:0.7692260090076106 StepIndex:2 RunIndex:41
Position:[1,1] SenseSignal:[0,0,0,0.2] Move:0.837532377697202 StepIndex:3 RunIndex:41
...
```

I've boldfaced the very first maze run, where we see the agent taking the steps from [0,0] to [0,1] to [1,1], and receiving the reward 1. Then we fast-forward and see that during the **RunIndex:39**, the reward has been switched. We know this because when the agent gets to [1,1] on that run, the reward is a mere 0.2 now. On the RunIndex: 40, the agent still goes to this same location, indicating it has not learned, and it has not evolved the ability to change its strategy.

14.3 Summary & Discussion

In this chapter we built two new problems to benchmark and test our neuroevolutionary system on. We built the Double Pole Balancing (DPB) simulation, and the Discrete T-Maze (DTM) simulation. We created different versions of the pole balancing problem, the single pole balancing with and without damping, and with and without full system state information, and the double pole balancing with and without damping, and with and without full system state information. The complexity of solving the pole balancing problem grows when we increase the number of poles to balance simultaneously, when we remove the velocity information and thus require the NN based agent to derive it on its own, and when we use the damping based fitness function instead of the standard one. We also created a discrete version of the T-Maze navigation problem, where an agent must navigate a T shaped maze to collect a reward located at one of the horizontal maze ends. In this maze there are two rewards, located at the opposite ends of the maze, one large and one small, and their location is switched at a random point during the 100 maze runs in total. This requires the agent to remember where the large reward was last time, explore that position, find that the reward is now small, and during the remaining maze runs navigate to the other side of the maze to continue collecting the large reward. This problem can be further expanded by changing the fitness function used, and by requiring the agent to collect the reward and then return to the base of the maze, rather than being automatically teleported back as is the case with our current implementation. Furthermore, we could expand the T-Maze into a Double T-Maze, with 4 corners where the reward can be collected, and thus requiring the agent to remember more navigational patterns and reward locations.

Based on our benchmark, the system we've built thus far has performed very well on the DPB problem, with its results being higher than those of other Topology and Weight Evolving Artificial Neural Networks (TWEANN), as was seen when the results we achieved were compared to the results of such systems referenced from paper [1]. Yet still the performance was not higher than that of DXNN, because we have yet to tune our system. When we applied our TWEANN to the T-Maze Navigation problem, it evolved NNs that were not yet able to change their strategy based on their experience. Adding plasticity in the next chapter will further expand the capabilities of the evolved NNs, giving us a chance to again apply our system to this problem, and see that the performance improves, and allows the agents to achieve perfect scores.

Having a good set of problems in our benchmark suit will allow us to add and create features that we can demonstrate to improve the system's generalization abilities and general performance. The two new problems we added in this chapter will allow us to better test our system, and the performance of new features we add to it in the future. Finally, the T-Maze problem will allow us to test the important feature that we will add in the next chapter: *neural plasticity*.

14.4 References

[1] Gomez F, Schmidhuber J, Miikkulainen R (2008) Accelerated Neural Evolution through Co-operatively Coevolved Synapses. Journal of Machine Learning Research 9, 937-965.

[2] Sher GI (2010) DXNN Platform: The Shedding of Biological Inefficiencies. Neuron, 1-36. Available at: http://arxiv.org/abs/1011.6022.

[3] Durr P, Mattiussi C, Soltoggio A, Floreano D (2008) Evolvability of Neuromodulated Learning for Robots. 2008 ECSIS Symposium on Learning and Adaptive Behaviors for Robotic Systems LABRS, 41-46.

[4] Blynel J, Floreano D (2003) Exploring the T-maze: Evolving Learning-Like Robot Behaviors using CTRNNs. Applications of evolutionary computing 2611, 173-176.

[5] Khepera robots: www.k-team.com

[6] Risi S, Stanley KO (2010) Indirectly Encoding Neural Plasticity as a Pattern of Local Rules. Neural Plasticity 6226, 1-11.

[7] Soltoggio A, Bullinaria JA, Mattiussi C, Durr P, Floreano D (2008) Evolutionary Advantages of Neuromodulated Plasticity in Dynamic, Reward-based Scenarios. Artificial Life 2, 569-576.

Chapter 15 Neural Plasticity

Abstract In this chapter we add plasticity to our direct encoded NN system. We implement numerous plasticity encoding approaches, and develop numerous plasticity learning rules, amongst which are variations of the Hebbian Learning Rule, Oja's Rule, and Neural Modulation. Once plasticity has been added, we again test our TWEANN system on the T-Maze navigation benchmark.

We have now built a truly advanced topology and weight evolving artificial neural network (TWEANN) platform. Our system allows for its various features to evolve, the NNs can evolve not only the topology and synaptic weights, but also evolutionary strategies, local and global search parameters, and the very way in which the neurons/processing-elements interact with input signals. We have implemented our system in such a way that it can easily be further expanded and extended with new activation functions (such as logical operators, or activation functions which simulate a transistor for example), mutation operators, mutation strategies, and almost every other feature of our TWEANN. We have also created two benchmarks, the double pole balancing benchmark and the T-Maze navigation benchmark, which allows us to test our system's performance.

There is something lacking at this point though, our evolved agents are but static systems. Our NN based agents do not learn during their lifetimes, they are trained by the exoself, which applies the NN based system to the problem time after time, with different parameters, until one of the parameter/synaptic-weight combinations produces a more fit agent. This is not learning. Learning is the process during which the NN changes due to its experience, due to its interaction with the environment. In biological organisms, evolution produces the combination of neural topology, plasticity parameters, and the starting synaptic weight values, which allows the NN, based on this plasticity and initial NN topology and setup, to learn how to interact with the environment, to learn and change and adapt during its lifetime. The plasticity parameters allow the NN to change as it interacts with the environment. While the initial synaptic weight values send this newborn agent in the right direction, in hope that the plasticity will change the topology and synaptic weights in the direction that will drive the agent, the organism, further in its exploration, learning, adaptation, and thus towards a higher fitness.

Of course with plasticity comes a new set of questions: What new mutation operators need to be added? How do we make the mutation operators specific to that particular set of parameters used by the plasticity learning rule? What about the tuning phase when it comes to neurons with plasticity, what is the difference between plasticity enabled NNs which are evolved through genetic algorithm approaches, and those evolved through memetic algorithm approaches? During the

G.I. Sher, *Handbook of Neuroevolution Through Erlang*,
DOI 10.1007/978-1-4614-4463-3_15, © Springer Science+Business Media New York 2013

tuning phase, what do we perturb, the synaptic weights or the plasticity parameters?...

Plasticity is that feature which allows the neuron and its parameters to change due to its interaction with input signals. In this book's neural network foundations chapters we discussed this in detail. In this chapter we will implement the various learning rules that add neural plasticity to our system. In this chapter we will create 3 types of plasticity functions, the standard Hebbian plasticity, the more advanced Oja's rule, and finally the most dynamic and flexible approach, neural plasticity through neuromodulation. We will first discuss and implement these learning rules, and then add the perturbation and mutation operators necessary to take advantage of the newly added learning mechanism.

15.1 Hebbian Rule

We discussed the Hebbian learning rule in Section-2.6.1. The principle behind the Hebbian learning rule is summarized by the quote "Neurons that fire together, wire together." If a presynaptic neuron A which is connected to a neuron B, sends it an excitatory (*SignalVal > 0*) signal, and in return B produces an excitatory output, then the synaptic weight between the two neurons increases in magnitude. If on the other hand neuron A sends an excitatory signal to B, and B's resulting output signal is inhibitory (*SignalVal < 0*), then B's synaptic weight for A's connection, decreases. In a symmetric fashion, an inhibitory signal from A that results in an inhibitory signal from B, increases the synaptic weight strength between the two, but an inhibitory signal from A resulting in an excitatory signal from B, decreases the strength of the connection.

The simplest Hebbian rule used to modify the synaptic weight after the neuron has processed some signal at time *t* is:

Delta_Weight = h * I_Val * Output,

Thus:

$W_{(t+1)} = W_{(t)} +$ Delta_Weight.

Where Delta_Weight is the change in the synaptic weight, and where the specified synaptic weight belongs to B, associated with the incoming input signal *I_Val*, coming from neuron A. The value *h* is the learning parameter, set by the researcher. The algorithm and architecture of a neuron using a simple Hebbian learning rule, repeated from Section-2.6.1 for clarity, is shown in Fig-15.1.

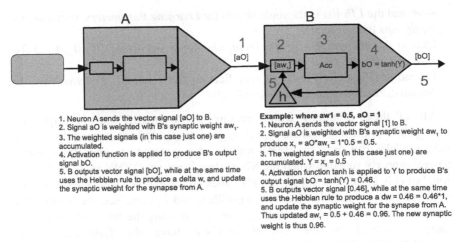

1. Neuron A sends the vector signal [aO] to B.
2. Signal aO is weighted with B's synaptic weight aw₁.
3. The weighted signals (in this case just one) are accumulated.
4. Activation function is applied to produce B's output signal bO.
5. B outputs vector signal [bO], while at the same time uses the Hebbian rule to produce a delta w, and update the synaptic weight for the synapse from A.

Example: where aw1 = 0.5, aO = 1
1. Neuron A sends the vector signal [1] to B.
2. Signal aO is weighted with B's synaptic weight aw₁ to produce $x_1 = aO*aw_1 = 1*0.5 = 0.5$.
3. The weighted signals (in this case just one) are accumulated. $Y = x_1 = 0.5$
4. Activation function tanh is applied to Y to produce B's output signal $bO = tanh(Y) = 0.46$.
5. B outputs vector signal [0.46], while at the same time uses the Hebbian rule to produce a $dw = 0.46*1$, and update the synaptic weight for the synapse from A. Thus updated $aw_1 = 0.5 + 0.46 = 0.96$. The new synaptic weight is thus 0.96.

Fig. 15.1 An architecture of a neuron using the Hebbian learning rule based plasticity.

This is the simplest Hebbian rule, but though computationally light, it is also unstable. Because the synaptic weight does not decay, if left unchecked, the Hebbian rule will keep increasing the magnitude of the synaptic weight, indefinitely, and thus eventually drown out all other synaptic weights belonging to the neuron. For example, if a neuron has 5 synaptic weights, 4 of which are between -Pi and P, and the fifth weight has climbed to 1000, this neuron is effectively useless with regards to processing since the signal weighted by 1000 will most likely overpower other signals. No matter what the other 4 synaptic weights are, no matter what pattern they have evolved to pick up, the fifth weight with magnitude 1000 will drown out everything, saturating the output. We will implement it for the sake of completeness, and also because it is so easy to implement. To deal with unchecked synaptic weight magnitudes, we will use our previously created *functions:sat/1* and *functions:sat/2* functions to ensure that the synaptic weights do not increase in magnitude unchecked, that they do not increase to infinity, and instead get saturated at some level specified by the *sat* function and the *?SAT_LIMIT* parameter specified within the neuron module.

There is though a problem with the current architecture of our neuron, which prevents it from having plasticity. That problem is that the neuron's *input_idps* list specifies only the *Input_Id* of the node that sends it an input signal, and the accompanying synaptic weight list *Weights: [{Input_Id,Weights}...]*. With the addition of plasticity, we must have the ability to also specify the various new parameters (like the learning parameter for example) of the learning rule. There are multiple ways in which we can solve this dilemma, the following are four of them:

1. Extend the input_idps from: *[{Input_Id,Weights}...]* to: *[{Input_Id, Weights, LearningParameters}...]*
2. Extend the *neuron* record to also include *input_lpps*, a list with the format: *[{Input_Id,LPs}...]*, where *input_lpps* stands for *input learning parameters*

plus, and the *LPs* list in the tuple stands for *Learning Parameters*, mirroring the *input_idps* list's format.

3. Extend the *Weights* list in the *input_idps* tuple list from: *[W₁,W₂,W₃...]* To: *[{W₁,P₁},{W₂,P₂},{W₃,P₃}...]*

4. Extend *pf* (Plasticity Function) specification from: *atom()::FunctionName* to: *{atom()::FunctionName, ParameterList}*

All of these solutions would require us to modify the *genotype, genome_mutator, exoself, neuron, signal_aggregator*, and *plasticity* modules, so that these modules can properly create, mutate, map genotype to phenotype, and in general properly function when the NN system is active. DXNN uses the 3ʳᵈ solution, but only because at one point I also allowed the evolved NN systems to use a modified back propagation learning algorithm, and P_i contained the learning parameter. There were also D_i and M_i parameters, making the *input_idps* list of the neurons evolved by the DXNN platform have the following format: *[{W₁,P₁,D₁,M₁},{W₂,P₂,D₂,M₂}...]*, where the value D contained the previous time step's change in synaptic weight, and M contained the momentum parameter used by the backprop algorithm.

Options 1-3 are appropriate for when there is a separate plasticity function, a separate synaptic weight modification and learning rule, for every synaptic weight. But in a lot of cases, the neuron has a single learning rule which is applied to all synaptic weights equally. This is the case with the Hebbian Learning Rule, where the neuron needs only a single learning parameter specifying the rate of change of the synaptic weights. For the learning rules that use a single parameter or a list of global learning parameters, rather than a separate list of learning parameters for every synaptic weight, option 4 is the most appropriate, in which we extend the plasticity function name with a parameter list used by that plasticity function.

But what if at some point in the future we decide that every weight should be accompanied not by one extra parameter, but by 2, or 3, or 4... To solve this, we could use solution-3, but have each P_i be a list. If there is only one parameter, then it is a list of length 1: [A₁], if two parameters are needed by some specific learning rule, then each P is a list of length 2: [A₁,A₂], and so on. If there is no plasticity, the list is empty.

Are there such learning rules that require so many parameters? Yes, for example some versions of neuromodulation can be set such that a single neuron simulates having 5 other modulating neurons within, each of whom analyzes the input vectors to the neuron in question, and each of whom outputs a value which specifies a particular parameter in the generalized Hebbian learning rule. This type of plasticity function could use anywhere from 2 to 5 parameters (in the version we will implement) for each synaptic weight (those 2-5 parameters are themselves synaptic weights of the *embedded* modulating neurons), and we will discuss that particular approach and neuromodulation in general in section 15.3. Whatever rule we choose, there is a price. Luckily though, due to the way we've constructed our system, it is easy to fix and modify it, no matter which of the listed approaches we decide to go with.

Let us choose the 3rd option where each P_i is a list of parameters for each weight W_i, and where that list length is dependent on the plasticity function the neuron uses. In addition, we will also implement the 4th option, which requires us to modify the *pf* parameter format. The pf parameter for every neuron will be specified as a tuple, composed of the plasticity function name and a global learning parameter list. This will, though making the implementation a bit more difficult, allow for a much greater level of flexibility in the types of plasticity rules we can implement. Using both methods, we will have access to plasticity functions which need to specify a parameter for every synaptic weight, and those which only need to specify a single or a few global parameters of the learning rule for the entire neuron.

15.1.1 Implementing the New input_idps & pf Formats

We first update the specification format for the neuron's pf parameter. This requires only a slight modification in the neuron module, changing the line:

```
U_IPIdPs =plasticity:PF(Ordered_IAcc,Input_PIdPs,Output)
```

To:

```
{PFName,PFParameters} = PF,
U_IPIdPs = plasticity:PFName(PFParameters,Ordered_IAcc,Input_PIdPs,Output),
```

And a change in the genotype module, to allow us to use the plasticity function name to generate the *PF* tuple. The way we do this is by creating a special function in the plasticity module with arity 1 and of the form: *plasticity:PFName(neural_parameters)*, which returns the necessary plasticity function specifying tuple: *{PFName, PL}*, where PL is the Parameter List. In this manner, when we develop the plasticity functions, we can at the same time create the function of arity 1 which returns the appropriate tuple defining the actual plasticity function name and its parameters. The change in the genotype module is done to the generate_NeuronPF/1 function, changing it from:

```
generate_NeuronPF(Plasticity_Functions)->
    case Plasticity_Functions of
        [] ->
            none;
        Other ->
            lists:nth(random:uniform(length(Other)),Other)
```

```
    end.
```

To:

```
generate_NeuronPF(Plasticity_Functions)->
   case Plasticity_Functions of
        [] ->
                {none,[]};
        Other ->
                PFName = lists:nth(random:uniform(length(Other)),Other),
                plasticity:PFName(neural_parameters)
    end.
```

With this modification completed, we can specify the global, neural level learning parameters. But to be able to specify synaptic weight level parameters, we have to augment the neuron's input_idps list specification format. Because our new format for input_idps stays very similar to the original, we need only convert the original list's form from: *[{Input_Id, Weights}...]* to: *[{Input_Id,WeightsP}...]*. Any function that does not directly operate on Weights, does not get affected by us changing Weights: *[W₁,W₂...]* to WeightsP: *[{W₁,PL₁},{W₂,PL₂}...]*, where PL is the plasticity function's Parameter List. The only function that does get affected by this change is the one in the genotype module which creates the *input_idps* list, *create_NeuralWeights/2*. In *genome_mutator* module, again the only affected function is the *mutate_weights* function which uses the *perturb_weights* function and thus needs to choose the weights rather than the learning parameters to mutate. Finally, the *neuron* process also perturbs its synaptic weights, and so we will need to use a modified version of the *perturb_weights* function.

The most interesting modification occurs in the *create_NeuralWeights* function. We modify it from:

```
create_NeuralWeights(0,Acc) ->
   Acc;
create_NeuralWeights(Index,Acc) ->
   W = random:uniform()-0.5,
   create_NeuralWeights(Index-1,[W|Acc]).
```

To:

```
create_NeuralWeightsP(_PFName,0,Acc) ->
   Acc;
create_NeuralWeightsP(PFName,Index,Acc) ->
   W = random:uniform()-0.5,
   create_NeuralWeightsP(PFName,Index-1,[{W,plasticity:PFName(weight_parameters)} |
Acc]).
```

The second version creates a list of tuples rather than a simple list of synaptic weights. Since each learning rule, each plasticity function, will have its own set of parameters, we defer the creation of a parameter list to its own plasticity function. To have the plasticity function create an initial synaptic level parameter list, we will call it with the atom parameter: *weight_parameters*. Thus for every plasticity function, we will create a secondary clause, which takes as input a single parameter, and through the use of this parameter it will specify whether the plasticity function will return neural level learning rule parameters, or synaptic weight level learning rule parameters. The *weight_parameters* specification will make the plasticity function return a randomized list of parameters required by that learning rule at the synaptic weight level.

We also add to the plasticity module a secondary *none* function: none/1. This none/1 function can be executed with the *neural_parameters* or the *weight_parameters* atom, and in both cases it returns an empty list, since a neuron which does not have plasticity and thus uses the *none/1* plasticity function, does not need learning parameters of any type. Thus, our plasticity module now holds two functions by the name *none:* one with arity 4, and one with arity 1:

```
none(neural_parameters)->
   [];
none(weight_parameters)->
   [].
%none/0 returns a set of learning parameters needed by the none/0 plasticity function. Since
this function specifies that the neuron has no plasticity, the parameter lists are empty.


none(_NeuralParameters,_IAcc,Input_PIdPs,_Output)->
   Input_PIdPs.
%none/3 returns the original Input_PIdPs to the caller.
```

The modification to the *perturb_weights* function (present in the neuron module, and present in the genome_mutator module in a slightly modified form) is much simpler. The updated function has the form, where the changes have been highlighted in boldface:

```
perturb_weightsP(Spread,MP,[{W,LPs}|WeightsP],Acc)->
   U_W = case random:uniform() < MP of
         true->
                 sat((random:uniform()-0.5)*2*Spread+W,-?SAT_LIMIT,?SAT_LIMIT);
         false ->
                 W
   end,
   perturb_weightsP(Spread,MP,WeightsP,[{U_W,LPs}|Acc]);
perturb_weightsP(_Spread,_MP,[],Acc)->
   lists:reverse(Acc).
```

All that has changed is the function name, and that instead of using: [W|Weights], we now use: [{W,LPs}|WeightsP], where the list LPs stands for Learning Parameters.

Finally, we must also update the synaptic weight and plasticity function specific mutation operators. These functions are located in the genome_mutator module. These are the *add_bias/1*, *mutate_pf/1*, and the *link_ToNeuron/4* functions. The add_bias/1 and link_ToNeuron/4 functions add new synaptic weights, and thus must utilize the new *plasticity:PFName(weight_parameters)* function, based on the particular plasticity function used by the neuron. The mutate_pf/1 is a mutation operator function. Due to the extra parameter added to the input_idps list, when we mutate the plasticity function, we must also update the synaptic weight parameters so that they are appropriate for the format of the new learning rule. Only the mutate_pf/1 function requires a more involved modification to the source code, with the other two only needing for the plasticity function name to be extracted and used to generate the weight parameters from the plasticity module. The updated mutate_pf/1 function is shown in Listing-15.1, with the modified parts in boldface.

Listing-15.1 The updated implementation of the mutate_pf/1 function.

```
mutate_pf(Agent_Id)->
   A = genotype:read({agent,Agent_Id}),
   Cx_Id = A#agent.cx_id,
   Cx = genotype:read({cortex,Cx_Id}),
   N_Ids = Cx#cortex.neuron_ids,
   N_Id = lists:nth(random:uniform(length(N_Ids)),N_Ids),
   Generation = A#agent.generation,
   N = genotype:read({neuron,N_Id}),
   {PFName, NLParameters} = N#neuron.pf,
   case (A#agent.constraint)#constraint.neural_pfns -- [PFName] of
        [] ->
              exit("********ERROR:mutate_pf:: There are no other plasticity functions to
use.");
        Other_PFNames ->

New_PFName=lists:nth(random:uniform(length(Other_PFNames)),Other_PFNames),
              New_NLParameters = plasticity:New_PFName(neural_parameters),
              NewPF = {New_PFName,New_NLParameters},
              InputIdPs = N#neuron.input_idps,
              U_InputIdPs = [{Input_IdP,plasticity:New_PFName(weight_parameters)}
|| {Input_IdP, OldPL} <- InputIdPs],
              U_N = N#neuron{pf=NewPF,input_idps = U_InputIdPs, generation
=Generation},
              EvoHist = A#agent.evo_hist,
```

```
        U_EvoHist = [{mutate_pf,N_Id}|EvoHist],
        U_A = A#agent{evo_hist=U_EvoHist},
        genotype:write(U_N),
        genotype:write(U_A)
  end.
```

After making these modifications, we ensure that everything is functioning as it should, by executing:

```
polis:sync().
polis:start().
population_monitor:test().
```

Which compiles the updated modules ensuring that there are no errors, then starts the polis process, and then finally runs a quick neuroevolutionary test. The function *population_monitor:test/0* can be executed a few times (each execution done after the previous one runs to completion), to ensure that everything still works. Because neuroevolutionary systems function stochastically, the genotypes and topologies evolved during one evolutionary run will be different from another, and so it is always a good idea to run it a few times, to test out the various combinations and permutations of the evolving agents.

With this update completed, we can now create plasticity functions. Using our plasticity module implementation, we allow the plasticity functions to completely isolate and decouple their functionality and setup from the rest of the system, which will allow others to add and test new plasticity functions as they please, without disturbing or having to dig through the rest of the code.

15.1.2 Implementing the Simple Hebbian Learning Rule

We need to implement a rule where every synaptic weight W_i is updated every time the neuron processes an input vector and produces an output vector. The weight W_i must be updated using the rule: *Updated_W_i= W_i + h*I_i*Output*, where I_i is the float() input value associated with the synaptic weight W_i. The Updated_W_i must be, in the same way as done during weight perturbation, saturated at the value: *?SAT_LIMIT*, so that its magnitude does not increase indefinitely.

From the above equation, it can be seen from the common h for all I_i and W_i, that the standard Hebbian learning rule is one where the neuron has a single, global, neural level learning parameter *h*, which is used to update all the synaptic weights belonging to that neuron. Because our neuron also has the ability to have a learning parameter per weight, we can also create a Hebbian learning rule where every synaptic weight uses its very own h. Though note that this approach will double the number of mutatable parameters for the neuron: a list of synaptic weights, and a list of the same size of Hebbian learning parameters. For the sake of completeness, we will implement both versions. We will call the standard Hebbian learning function which uses a single learning parameter *h* for all synaptic weights, *hebbian/4*, and one which uses a separate learning parameter h_i for every synaptic weight, *hebbian_w/4* (where *_w* stands for weights). Let us first implement the *hebbian_w* function, which uses the following weight update rule: *Updated_*$W_i = W_i + h_i * I_i * Output$, where W_i is the synaptic weight, h_i is the learning parameter for neuron W_i, and I_i is the input signal associated with synaptic weight W_i.

In the previous section we have updated our neuron to apply a learning rule to its weights through: *U_IPIdPs = plasticity:PFName(Neural_Parameters, Ordered_IAcc,Input_PIdPs,Output)*, which gives the plasticity function access to the neural parameters list, the output signal, the synaptic weights and their associated learning parameters, and the accumulated input vector. To set up the plasticity function by the name hebbian_w, we first implement the function hebbian_w/1 which returns a weight parameters list composed of a single element *[H]* when hebbian_w/1 is executed with the *weights_parameters* parameter, and an empty list when it is executed with the neural_parameters parameter. We then create the function hebbian_w/4 which implements this actual learning rule. The implementation of these two *hebbian_w* functions is shown in Listing-15.2.

Listing 15.2 The implementation of hebbian_w/1 and hebbian_w/4 functions.

```
hebbian_w(neural_parameters)->
    [];
hebbian_w(weight_parameters)->
    [(lists:random()-0.5)].
%hebbian_w/1 function produces the necessary parameter list for the hebbian_w learning rule
to operate. The weights parameter list generated by hebbian_w learning rule is a list composed
of a single parameter H: [H], for every synaptic weight of the neuron. When hebbian_w/1 is
called with the parameter neural_parameters, it returns [].

hebbian_w(_NeuralParameters,IAcc,Input_PIdPs,Output)->
    hebbian_w1(IAcc,Input_PIdPs,Output,[]).

    hebbian_w1([{IPId,Is}|IAcc],[{IPId,WPs}|Input_PIdPs],Output,Acc)->
        Updated_WPs = hebbrule_w(Is,WPs,Output,[]),
        hebbian_w1(IAcc,Input_PIdPs,Output,[{IPId,Updated_WPs}|Acc]);
    hebbian_w1([],[],_Output,Acc)->
        lists:reverse(Acc);
    hebbian_w1([],[{bias,WPs}],Output,Acc)->
        lists:reverse([{bias,WPs}|Acc]).
```

```
%hebbian_w/4 function operates on each Input_PIdP, calling the hebbian_w1/4 function which
processes each of the complementary Is and WPs lists, producing the Updated_WPs lists in re-
turn, with the now updated/adapted weights, based on the hebbian_w learning rule.

    hebbrule_w([I|Is],[{W,[H]}|WPs],Output,Acc)->
        Updated_W = functions:saturation(W + H*I*Output,?SAT_LIMIT),
        hebbrule_w(Is,WPs,Output,[{Updated_W,[H]}|Acc]);
    hebbrule_w([],[],_Output,Acc)->
        lists:reverse(Acc).
%hebbrule_w/4 applies the Hebbian learning rule to each synaptic weight by using the input
value I, the neuron's calculated Output, and each W's own distinct learning parameter H.
```

The function hebbian_w/4 calls hebbian_w1/4 with a list accumulator, which separately operates on the input vectors from each Input_PId by calling the hebbrule_w/4 function. It is the hebbrule_w/4 function that actually executes the modified Hebbian learning rule: *Updated_W = functions:saturation(W+H*I*Output, ?SAT_LIMIT)*, and updates the WeightsP list.

Note that hebbian_w/1 generates a parameter list composed of a single value with a range between -0.5 and 0.5 (This range was chosen to ensure that from the very start the learning parameter will not be too large). The Hebbian rule which uses a negative learning parameter embodies Anti-Hebbian learning. The Anti-Hebbian learning rule decreases the postsynaptic weight between neurons outputting signals of the same sign, and increases magnitude of the postsynaptic weight between those neurons that are connected and output signals of differing signs. Thus, if a neuron A sends a signal to neuron B, and the presynaptic signal is positive, while the postsynaptic neuron B's output signal is negative, and it has H < 0, and is thus using the Anti-Hebbian learning rule, then the B's synaptic weight for the link from neuron A will increase in magnitude. This means that in the hebbian_w/4 learning rule implementation, some of the synaptic weights will be using Hebbian learning, and some Anti-Hebbian. This will add some extra agility to our system that might prove useful, and allow the system to evolve more general learning networks.

With the modified Hebbian rule now implemented, let us implement the standard one. In the standard Hebbian rule, the hebbian/1 function generates an empty list when called with *weight_parameters*, and the list [H] when called with neural_parameters. Also, the hebbian/4 function that implements the actual learning rule will use a single common *H* learning parameter to update all the synaptic weights in the input_idps. Listing-15.3 shows the implementation of such standard Hebbian learning rule.

Listing-15.3 The implementation of the standard Hebbian learning rule.

```
hebbian(neural_parameters)->
    [(lists:random()-0.5)];
hebbian(weight_parameters)->
```

```
[].
%The hebbian/1 function produces the necessary parameter list for the Hebbian learning rule to
operate. The parameter list for the standard Hebbian learning rule is a list composed of a single
parameter H: [H], used by the neuron for all its synaptic weights. When hebbian/1 is called with
the parameter weight_parameters, it returns [].

hebbian([H],IAcc,Input_PIdPs,Output)->
    hebbian(H,IAcc,Input_PIdPs,Output,[]).


hebbian(H,[{IPId,Is}|IAcc],[{IPId,WPs}|Input_PIdPs],Output,Acc)->
        Updated_WPs = hebbrule(H,Is,WPs,Output,[]),
        hebbian(H,IAcc,Input_PIdPs,Output,[{IPId,Updated_WPs}|Acc]);
    hebbian(_H,[],[],_Output,Acc)->
        lists:reverse(Acc);
    hebbian(_H,[],[{bias,WPs}],Output,Acc)->
        lists:reverse([{bias,WPs}|Acc]).
%hebbian/4 function operates on each Input_PIdP, calling the hebbian/5 function which pro-
cesses each of the complementary Is and WPs lists, producing the Updated_WPs list in return,
with the updated/adapted weights based on the standard Hebbian learning rule, using the neu-
ron's single learning parameter H.

hebbrule(H,[I|Is],[{W,[]}|WPs],Output,Acc)->
        Updated_W = functions:saturation(W + H*I*Output,?SAT_LIMIT),
        hebbrule(H,Is,WPs,Output,[{Updated_W,[]}|Acc]);
    hebbrule(H,[],[],_Output,Acc)->
        lists:reverse(Acc).
%hebbrule/5 applies the Hebbian learning rule to each weight, using the input value I, the neu-
ron's calculated output Output, and the neuron's single learning parameter H.
```

The standard Hebbian learning rule has a number of flaws. One of these flaws is that without the *saturation/2* function that we're using, the synaptic weight would grow in magnitude to infinity. A more biologically faithful implementation of this auto-associative learning, is the Oja's learning rule, which we discuss and implement next.

15.2 Oja's Rule

The Oja's learning rule is a modification of the standard Hebbian learning rule that solves its stability problems through the use of multiplicative normalization, derived in [1]. This learning rule is also closer to what occurs in biological neurons. The synaptic weight update algorithm embodied by the Oja's learning rule is as follows: $Updated\_W_i = W_i + h*O*(I_i - O*W_i)$, where h is the learning parameter, O is the output of the neuron based on its processing of the input vectors using its synaptic weights, I_i is the ith input signal, and W_i is the ith synaptic weight associated with the I_i input signal.

We can compare the instability of the Hebbian rule to the stability of the Oja's rule by running this learning rule through a few iterations with a positive input signal I. Assuming our neuron only has a single synaptic weight for an input vector of length one, we test the stability of the synaptic weight updated through the Oja's rule as follows:

Initial setup: W = 0.5, h = 0.2, activation function is tanh, using a constant input I = 1:

1. O=math:tanh(W*I)=math:tanh(0.5*1)=0.46
   Updated_W = W + h*O*(I – O*W) = 0.5 + 0.2*0.46*(1 – 0.46*0.5) = 0.57
2. O=math:tanh(W*I)=math:tanh(0.57*1)=0.52
   Updated_W = W + h*O*(I – O*W) = 0.57 + 0.2*0.52(1 – 0.52*0.57) = 0.64
3. O=math:tanh(W*I)=math:tanh(0.64*1)=0.56
   Updated_W = W + h*O*(I - O*W) = 0.64 + 0.2*0.56*(1 - 0.56*0.64) = 0.71
4. ...

This continues to increase, but once the synaptic weight achieves a value higher than the input, for example when W = 1.5, the learning rule takes the weight update in the other direction:

5. O=math:tanh(W*I)=math:tanh(1.5*1)=0.90
   Updated_W = **W** + h*O*(I - O*W) = **1.5** + 0.2*0.90*(1 - 0.90*1.5) = **1.43**

Thus this learning rule is indeed self stabilizing, the synaptic weights will not continue to increase in magnitude towards infinity, as was the case with the Hebbian learning rule. Let us now implement the two functions, one which returns the needed learning parameters for this learning rule, and the other implementing the actual Oja's synaptic weight update rule.

15.2.1 Implementing the Oja's Learning Rule

Like the Hebbian learning rule, the standard Oja's rule too only uses a single parameter h to pace the learning rate of the synaptic weights. We implement ojas_w/1 in the same fashion we did the hebbian_w/1, it will be a variation of the Oja's learning rule that uses a single learning parameter per synaptic weight, rather than a single learning parameter for the entire neuron. This synaptic weight update rule is as follows:

Updated_W_i = W_i + h_i*O*(I_i – O*W_i)

We set the initial learning parameter to be randomly chosen between -0.5 and 0.5. The implementation of ojas_w/1 and ojas_w/4 is shown in Listing-15.4.

Listing-15.4 The implementation of a modified Oja's learning rule, and its initial learning parameter generating function.

```
ojas_w(neural_parameters)->
    [];
ojas_w(synaptic_parameters)->
    [(lists:random()-0.5)].
```

%oja/1 function produces the necessary parameter list for the Oja's learning rule to operate. The parameter list for Oja's learning rule is a list composed of a single parameter H: [H] per synaptic weight. If the learning parameter is positive, then the postsynaptic neuron's synaptic weight increases if the two connected neurons produce output signals of the same sign. If the learning parameter is negative, and the two connected neurons produce output signals of the same sign, then the synaptic weight of the postsynaptic neuron, decreases in magnitude.

```
ojas_w(_Neural_Parameters,IAcc,Input_PIdPs,Output)->
    ojas_w1(IAcc,Input_PIdPs,Output,[]).
ojas_w1([{IPId,Is}|IAcc],[{IPId,WPs}|Input_PIdPs],Output,Acc)->
    Updated_WPs = ojas_rule_w(Is,WPs,Output,[]),
    ojas_w1(IAcc,Input_PIdPs,Output,[{IPId,Updated_WPs}|Acc]);
ojas_w1([],[],_Output,Acc)->
    lists:reverse(Acc);
ojas_w1([],[{bias,WPs}],Output,Acc)->
    lists:reverse([{bias,WPs}|Acc]).
```

%ojas_w/4 function operates on each Input_PIdP, calling the ojas_rule_w/4 function which processes each of the complementary Is and WPs lists, producing the Updated_WPs list in return. In the returned Updated_WPs, the updated/adapted weights are based on the oja's learning rule, using each synaptic weight's distinct learning parameter.

```
ojas_rule_w([I|Is],[{W,[H]}|WPs],Output,Acc)->
    Updated_W = functions:saturation(W + H*Output*(I - Output*W),?SAT_LIMIT),
    ojas_rule_w(Is,WPs,Output,[{Updated_W,[H]}|Acc]);
ojas_rule_w([],[],_Output,Acc)->
    lists:reverse(Acc).
```

%ojas_weights/4 applies the oja's learning rule to each weight, using the input value I, the neuron's calculated output Output, and each weight's distinct learning parameter H.

The standard implementation of Oja's learning rule, which uses a single learning parameter H for all synaptic weights, is shown in Listing-15.5. The standard Oja's rule uses the following weight update algorithm: $Updated\_W_i = W_i + h*O*(I_i - O*W_i)$.

Listing-15.5 The implementation of the standard Oja's learning rule.

```
ojas(neural_parameters)->
    [(lists:random()-0.5)];
```

```
ojas(synaptic_parameters)->
    [].
%oja/1 function produces the necessary parameter list for the oja's learning rule to operate. The
parameter list for oja's learning rule is a list composed of a single parameter H: [H], used by the
neuron for all its synaptic weights. If the learning parameter is positive, and the two connected
neurons produce output signals of the same sign, then the postsynaptic neuron's synaptic
weight increases. Otherwise it decreases.

ojas([H],IAcc,Input_PIdPs,Output)->
    ojas(H,IAcc,Input_PIdPs,Output,[]).
ojas(H,[{IPId,Is}|IAcc],[{IPId,WPs}|Input_PIdPs],Output,Acc)->
    Updated_WPs = ojas_rule(H,Is,WPs,Output,[]),
    ojas(H,IAcc,Input_PIdPs,Output,[{IPId,Updated_WPs}|Acc]);
ojas(_H,[],[],_Output,Acc)->
    lists:reverse(Acc);
ojas(_H,[],[{bias,WPs}],Output,Acc)->
    lists:reverse([{bias,WPs}|Acc]).
%ojas/5 function operates on each Input_PIdP, calling the ojas_rule/5 function which processes
each of the complementary Is and WPs lists, producing the Updated_WPs list in return, with the
updated/adapted weights.

    ojas_rule(H,[I|Is],[{W,[]}|WPs],Output,Acc)->
        Updated_W = functions:saturation(W + H*Output*(I - Output*W),?SAT_LIMIT),
        ojas_rule(H,Is,WPs,Output,[{Updated_W,[H]}|Acc]);
    ojas_rule(_H,[],[],_Output,Acc)->
        lists:reverse(Acc).
%ojas_rule/5 updates every synaptic weight using the Oja's learning rule.
```

With the implementation of this learning rule complete, we now move forward and discuss neural plasticity through neuromodulation.

15.3 Neuromodulation

Thus far we have discussed and implemented the Hebbian learning, which is a homosynaptic plasticity (also known as homotropic modulation) method, where the synaptic strength changes based on its history of activation. It is a synaptic weight update rule which is a function of its post- and pre- synaptic activity, as shown in Fig-15.2. But research shows that there is another approach to synaptic plasticity which nature has discovered, a highly dynamic and effective one, plasticity through neuromodulation.

Homosynaptic Plasticity

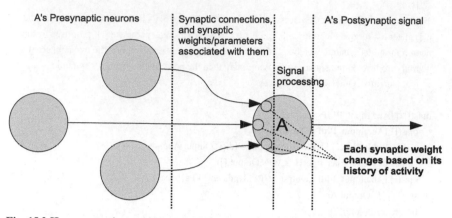

Fig. 15.2 Homosynaptic mechanism for Neuron A's synaptic weight updating, based on the pre- and post- synaptic activity of neuron A.

Neuromodulation is a form of heterosynaptic plasticity. In heterosynaptic plasticity the synaptic weights are changed due to the synaptic activity of other neurons, due to the modulating signals other neurons can produce to affect the given neuron's synaptic weights. For example, assume we have a neural circuit composed of two neurons, a presynaptic neuron N1, and a postsynaptic neuron N2. There can be other neurons N3, N4... which also connect to N2, but their neurotransmitters affect N2's plasticity, rather than being used as signals on which the N2's output signal is based on. The accumulated signals, neurotransmitters, from N3, N4..., could then dictate how rapidly and in what manner N2's connection strengths change. This type of architecture is shown in Fig-15.3.

Heterosynaptic Plasticity

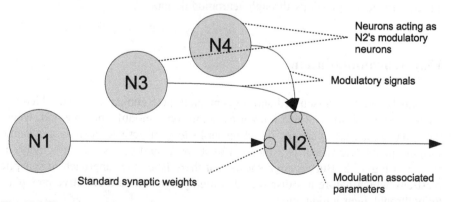

Fig. 15.3 Heterosynaptic mechanism for plasticity, where the Hebbian plasticity is modulated by a modulatory signal from neurons N3 and N4.

If we assume the use of the Generalized Hebbian learning rule for the synaptic weight update rule: Updated_W_i= W_i + h*(A*I_i*Output + B*I_i + C*Output + D), then the accumulated neuromodulatory signals from the other neurons could be used to calculate the learning parameter h, with the parameters A, B, C, and D evolved and specified within the postsynaptic neuron N2. In addition, the neuromodulatory signals from neurons N3, N4... could also be used to modulate and specify the parameters A, B, C, and D, as well.

The modulating neurons could be standard neurons, and whether their output signals are used as modulatory signals, or standard input signals, could be determined fully by the postsynaptic neuron to which they connect, as shown in Fig-15.4.

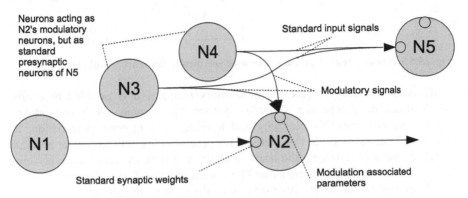

It should be noted that both, the modulatory and the standard output signals of the neurons N3 and N4, are the same neural output signals.

Fig. 15.4 Input signals used as standard signals, and as modulatory signals, dependent on how the postsynaptic neuron decides to treat the presynaptic signals.

Another possible approach is to set-up *secondary* neurons to the postsynaptic neuron N2 which we want modulated, where the secondary neurons receive exactly the same input signals as the postsynaptic neuron N2, but the output signals of these secondary neurons are used as modulatory signals of N2. This type of topological and architectural setup is shown in Fig-15.5.

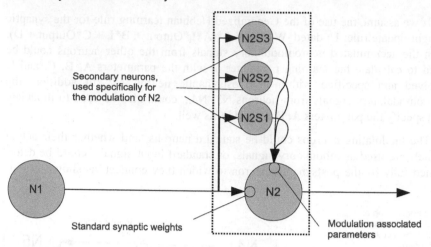

Fig. 15.5 Secondary neurons, created and used specifically for neuromodulation.

Through the use of dedicated modulatory neurons, it is possible to evolve whole modulatory networks. Complex systems whose main role is to modulate another neural network's plasticity and learning, its long-term potentiation, its ability to form memory. In this method, the generated learning parameter is signal specific, and itself changes; the learning ability and form evolves with everything else. Unlike the simple Hebbian or Oja's learning rule, these plasticity systems would depend on the actual input signals, on the sensory signals, and other regulatory and processing parts of the neural network system, which is a much more biologically faithful neural network architecture, and would allow our system to evolve even more complex behaviors.

Nature uses a combination of the architectures shown in figures 15.1 through 15.5. We have already discussed the Hebbian learning rule, and implemented the architecture of Fig-15.2. We now add the functionality to give our neuroevolutionary system the ability to evolve NN systems with architectures shown in Fig-15.4 and Fig-15.5. This will give our systems the ability to evolve self adaptation, and learning.

15.3.1 The Neuromodulatory Architecture

The architecture in Fig-15.5 could be easily developed using our already existing architecture, and it would even increase the ratio of neural computations performed by the neuron to the number of signals sent to the neuron. This is important because Erlang becomes more effective with big computations and small messages. The way we can represent this architecture is through the *weight_parameters* based approach. The weight_parameters could be thought of as synaptic weights themselves, but for the secondary neurons. These secondary neurons share the process of the neuron they are to modulate, and because the secondary neurons need to process the same input vectors that the neuron they are modulating is processing, it makes this design highly efficient. This architectural implementation is shown in Fig-15.6.

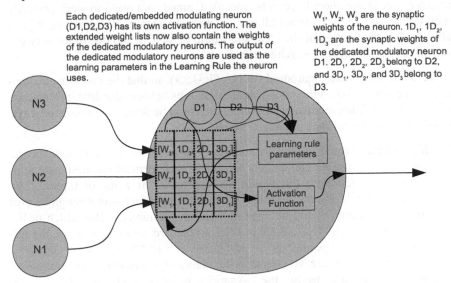

Each dedicated/embedded modulating neuron (D1,D2,D3) has its own activation function. The extended weight lists now also contain the weights of the dedicated modulatory neurons. The output of the dedicated modulatory neurons are used as the learning parameters in the Learning Rule the neuron uses.

W_1, W_2, W_3 are the synaptic weights of the neuron. $1D_1$, $1D_2$, $1D_3$ are the synaptic weights of the dedicated modulatory neuron D1. $2D_1$, $2D_2$, $2D_3$ belong to D2, and $3D_1$, $3D_2$, and $3D_3$ belong to D3.

Fig. 15.6 The architectural implementation of neuromodulation through dedicated/embedded modulating neurons.

In the above figure we see three neurons: N1, N2, and N3, connected to another neuron, which is expanded in the figure and whose architecture is shown. This neuron has a standard activation function, and a learning rule, but its *input_idps* list is extended. What we called parameters in the other learning rules, are here used as synaptic weights belonging to this neuron's embedded/dedicated modulating neurons: D_1, D_2, and D_3. Furthermore, each dedicated/embedded modulating neuron (D_1, D_2, D_3) can have its own activation function, but usually just uses the *tanh* function.

If each weight parameter list is of length 1, then there is only a single dedicated modulating neuron, and the dedicated neuron's output can be designated as the learning parameter: *h*. The learning parameters *A*, *B*, *C*, and *D*, can be specified by the *neural_parameters* list. Or we can have the weight parameters list be of size 2, and thus specify 2 dedicated modulating neurons, whose outputs would dictate the learning parameters *h* and *A*, with the other parameters specified in the *neural_parameters* list. Finally, we can have the weight parameters list be of length 5, thus representing the synaptic weights of 5 dedicated modulating neurons, whose outputs specify all the parameters (h, A, B, C, D) of the General Hebbian learning rule.

Having 5 separate dedicated modulating neurons does have its problems though, because it magnifies the number of synaptic weights/parameters our neuroevolutionary system has to tune, mutate, and set up. If our original neuron, without plasticity, had a synaptic weight list of size 10, this new modulated neuron would have 60 synaptic weight parameters for the same 10 inputs. All of these parameters would somehow have to be specified, tuned, and made to work perfectly with each other, and this would all only be a single neuron. Nevertheless, it is an efficient implementation of the idea, and would be easy to add due to the way our neuroevolutionary system's architecture is set up.

To allow for general neuromodulation (Fig-15.3), so that the postsynaptic neuron can designate some of the presynaptic signals as holding standard information, and others as holding modulatory information, could be done in a number of ways. Let us consider two of such approaches next:

1. This approach would require us adding a new element to the neuron record, akin to input_idps. We could add a secondary such element and designate it *input_idps_modulation*. It too would be represented as a list of tuples: *[{Input_Id,Weight}...]*, but the resulting computed dot product, sent through its own activation function, would be used as a learning parameter. But which of the learning parameters? H, A, B, C, or D? The standard approach is to use the following equation: *Updated_W = M_Output*H*(A*I*Output + B*Output + C*Output + D)*, where M_Output is the output signal produced by processing the input signals using the synaptic weights specified in the *input_idps_modulation list*, and where the parameters H, A, B, C, and D are simply neural_parameters, and as other parameters can be perturbed and evolved during the tuning phase and/or during the topological mutation phase.

How would the post synaptic neuron decide whether the new connection (added during the topological mutation phase) should be used as a standard signal, and thus be added to the input_idps list, or as modulatory input signal, and thus added to input_idps_modulation list? We could set up a rule so that if the neuron is designated to have general modulation based plasticity, the very first connection to the neuron is designated as standard input, and then any new connections are randomly sorted into either the input_idps or input_idps_modulation lists. To add this approach would only require adding a new list, and we would already have all the necessary functions to mutate its parameters, to clone it during neuronal cloning process, and to process input signals, because this new list would be exactly like the input_idps list. The overhead of simply adding this extra parameter, input_idps_modulation, to the neuron record, would be minuscule, and this architecture is what was represented in Fig-15.4.

2. Another way a neuron could decide on whether the presynaptic signal sent to it is standard or modulatory, is by us having neuronal types, where some neurons are type: *standard*, and others are type: *modulatory*. The signals sent by modulatory neurons are *always* used by all postsynaptic neurons for modulating the generalized Hebbian plasticity rule. The architecture of this type of system is

shown in Fig-15.7. In this figure I show a NN topology composed of standard neurons (std), and modulatory neurons (mod). They are all interconnected, each can receive signals from any other. The difference in how those signals are processed is dependent on the presynaptic neuron's type. If it is of type mod, then it is used as modulatory, if it is type std, then it is used as a standard input signal. Modulatory neurons can even modulate other modulatory neurons, while the outputs of the standard neurons can be used by both standard and modulatory neurons.

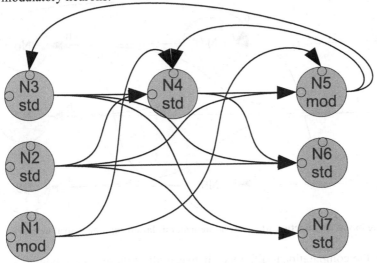

Fig. 15.7 A topology of a heterosynaptic, general, neural network system with neurons of type standard (std) and modulatory (mod).

3. But the first and second implementation does not solve the problem that the Hebbian learning rule uses multiple parameters, and we want to have the flexibility to specify 1 or more of them, based on the incoming modulatory signals. Another solution that does solve this is by tagging input signals with tags *i*, *h*, *a*, *b*, *c*, *d*, where *i* tags the standard inputs, and *h*, *a*, *b*, *c*, and *d*, tag the modulatory input signals associated with the tag named modulating learning parameter. Though this may at first glance seem like a more complex solution, we actually already have solved it, and it would require us only changing a few functions.

We are already generating weight based parameters. Thus far they have been lists, but they can also be atomic tags as follows: *[{Input_PId, [{Weight1,Tag1}, {Weight2,Tag2}...]}...]*. This is a clean solution that would allow us to designate different incoming signals to be used for different things. Mutation operators would not need to be modified significantly either, we would simply add a clause stating that if the neuron uses the *general_modulation* plasticity function, then the Tag is generated randomly from the following list: *[i, h, a, b, c, d]*. The most significant modification would have to be done to the signal_aggregation function, since we would need to sort the incoming signals based on their tags, and then calculate the different output signals based on their tags, with the i output signal being the standard one produced by the postsynaptic neuron, and the h, a, b, c, and d, output signals being used as modulatory learning parameters. But even that could be isolated to just the plasticity function, which has access to the IAcc, Input_PIdPs, and everything else necessary to compute output signals. The architecture of a neuron using this approach to general neuromodulation is shown in Fig-15.8.

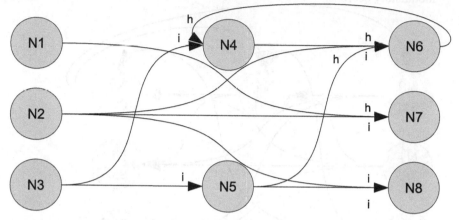

Fig. 15.8 Tag based architecture of a general neuromodulation capable neural network.

What is the computational difference between all of these neuromodulation approaches? How would the neural networks act differently when evolved with one approach rather than another? Would it even be possible to see the difference? Should we implement them all, provide all of these options to the neuroevolutionary system in hopes that it can sort things out on its own, and use the best one (throwing everything at the wall, and see what sticks)? How do we test which of these plasticity type architectures is better? How do we define "better"? Do we define it as the NN evolving faster (the neuroevolutionary system taking less number of evaluations to evolve a solution for some given problem)? Or do we define better as having the evolved NNs more dynamic, more adaptive, more general, but evolved slower due to so many different parameters for the evolutionary process to having to deal with? These are all open research questions.

We cannot test the effectiveness of plasticity enabled neural network systems on the standard double pole balancing, xor, or clustering type of benchmarks and tests. To test how well a plasticity enabled NN system functions, we need to apply our neuroevolutionary system to a problem where environment changes, where adaptation and learning over time gives an advantage. We could test plasticity by using it in the ALife simulation, T-Maze and double T-Maze navigation [2,3], or by applying it to some other robotics & complex navigation project. Though the small differences between these various modulatory approaches might require a lot of work to see, since evolution will tend to go around any small problems posed by any one implementation or architecture over another. Nevertheless, the fact that it is so easy for us to implement, test, and research these advanced learning rules and plasticity approaches, means that we **can** find out, we can determine what works better, and what approach will yield a more general, more intelligent, neural network based agent. If our system were not have been written in Erlang, adding neuroplasticity would have posed a much greater problem.

We will implement the dedicated neuromodulators (where the weight parameters represent the synaptic weights of embedded secondary neurons, whose output dictates the parameters of the general Hebbian learning rule), and the general neuromodulation plasticity through the use of the input_idps_modulation element. Our plasticity function using the first of these two approaches will be called: *self_modulation*, and the second: *general_modulation*. In the next section we will further define and implement these neuromodulatory based learning rules.

15.3.2 Implementing the self_modulation Learning Rules

We will first implement the *self_modulation* plasticity function. Given the general Hebbian learning rule for synaptic weight updating: $Updated\_W_i = W_i + H*(A*I_i*Output + B*I_i + C*Output + D)$, we can have multiple versions of this function. Version-1: where the secondary embedded neuron only outputs the H learning parameter, with the parameter A set to some predetermined constant value within the neural_parameters list, and B=C=D=0. Version-2: where A is generated randomly when generating the neural_parameters list, and B–C=D=0. Version-3: where B, C, and D are also generated randomly in the *neural_parameters* list. Version-4: where the weight_parameters generates a list of length 2, thus allowing the neuron to have 2 embedded modulatory neurons, one outputting a parameter we use for H, and another outputting the value we can use as A, with B=C=D=0. Version-5: Where B, C, and D are generated randomly by the PlasticityFunctionName(neural_parameters) function. And finally Version-6: Where the *weight_parameters* produces a list of length 5, allowing the neuron to have 5 embedded modulatory neurons, whose outputs are used for H, A, B, C, and D. All of these variations will have most of their functionality shared, and thus will be quick and easy to implement.

The *self_modulationV1*, *self_modulationV2*, and *self_modulationV3* are all very similar, mainly differing in the parameter lists returned by the *PlasticityFunctionName(neural_parameters)* function, as shown in Listing 15.6. All three of these plasticity functions use the neuromodulation/5 function which accepts the H, A, B, C, and D learning parameters, and updates the synaptic weights of the neuron using the general Hebbian rule: $Updated\_W_i = W_i + H*(A*I_i*Output + B*I_i + C*Output + D)$.

Listing-15.6 The self_modulationV1-3 functions of arity 1, generating the neural and weight parameters.

```
self_modulationV1(neural_parameters)->
    A=0.1,
    B=0,
    C=0,
    D=0,
    [A,B,C,D];
self_modulationV1(weight_parameters)->
    [(lists:random()-0.5)].

self_modulationV1([A,B,C,D],IAcc,Input_PIdPs,Output)->
    H = math:tanh(dot_productV1(IAcc,Input_PIdPs)),
    neuromodulation([H,A,B,C,D],IAcc,Input_PIdPs,Output,[]).

    dot_productV1(IAcc,IPIdPs)->
            dot_productV1(IAcc,IPIdPs,0).
    dot_productV1([{IPId,Input}|IAcc],[{IPId,WeightsP}|IPIdPs],Acc)->
            Dot = dotV1(Input,WeightsP,0),
            dot_productV1(IAcc,IPIdPs,Dot+Acc);
    dot_productV1([],[{bias,[{_Bias,[H_Bias]}]}],Acc)->
            Acc + H_Bias;
    dot_productV1([],[],Acc)->
            Acc.

        dotV1([I|Input],[{_W,[H_W]}|Weights],Acc) ->
                dotV1(Input,Weights,I*H_W+Acc);
        dotV1([],[],Acc)->
                Acc.

neuromodulation([H,A,B,C,D],[{IPId,Is}|IAcc],[{IPId,WPs}|Input_PIdPs],Output,Acc)->
    Updated_WPs = genheb_rule([H,A,B,C,D],Is,WPs,Output,[]),
    neuromodulation([H,A,B,C,D],IAcc,Input_PIdPs,Output,[{IPId,Updated_WPs}|Acc]);
neuromodulation(_NeuralParameters,[],[],_Output,Acc)->
    lists:reverse(Acc);
neuromodulation([H,A,B,C,D],[],[{bias,WPs}],Output,Acc)->
    Updated_WPs = genheb_rule([H,A,B,C,D],[1],WPs,Output,[]),
    lists:reverse([{bias,Updated_WPs}|Acc]).

    genheb_rule([H,A,B,C,D],[I|Is],[{W,Ps}|WPs],Output,Acc)->
            Updated_W = functions:saturation(W + H*(A*I*Output + B*I + C*Output + D),
?SAT_LIMIT),
            genheb_rule(H,Is,WPs,Output,[{Updated_W,Ps}|Acc]);
    genheb_rule(_H,[],[],_Output,Acc)->
```

```
            lists:reverse(Acc).

self_modulationV2(neural_parameters)->
   A=(lists:random()-0.5),
   B=0,
   C=0,
   D=0,
   [A,B,C,D];
self_modulationV2(weight_parameters)->
   [(lists:random()-0.5)].

self_modulationV2([A,B,C,D],IAcc,Input_PIdPs,Output)->
   H = math:tanh(dot_productV1(IAcc,Input_PIdPs)),
   neuromodulation([H,A,B,C,D],IAcc,Input_PIdPs,Output,[]).

self_modulationV3(neural_parameters)->
   A=(lists:random()-0.5),
   B=(lists:random()-0.5),
   C=(lists:random()-0.5),
   D=(lists:random()-0.5),
   [A,B,C,D];
self_modulationV3(weight_parameters)->
   [(lists:random()-0.5)].

self_modulationV3([A,B,C,D],IAcc,Input_PIdPs,Output)->
   H = math:tanh(dot_productV1(IAcc,Input_PIdPs)),
   neuromodulation([H,A,B,C,D],IAcc,Input_PIdPs,Output,[]).
```

The self_modulationV4 – V5 differ only in that the weight_parameters is a list of length 2, and the A parameter is no longer specified in the neural_parameters list, and is instead calculated by the second dedicated modulatory neuron. The self_modulationV6 function on the other hand specifies the neural_Parameters as an empty list, and the weight_parameters list is of length 5, a single weight for every embedded modulatory neuron. The implementation of self_modulationV6 is shown in Listing-15.7.

Listing-15.7 The implementation of the self_modulationV6 plasticity function, composed of 5 embedded modulatory neurons.

```
self_modulationV6(neural_parameters)->
   [];
self_modulationV6(weight_parameters)->
   [(lists:random()-0.5),(lists:random()-0.5),(lists:random()-0.5), (lists:random()-0.5),
(lists:random()-0.5)].
```

```
self_modulationV6(_Neural_Parameters,IAcc,Input_PIdPs,Output)->
   {AccH,AccA,AccB,AccC,AccD} = dot_productV6(IAcc,Input_PIdPs),
   H = math:tanh(AccH),
   A = math:tanh(AccA),
   B = math:tanh(AccB),
   C = math:tanh(AccC),
   D = math:tanh(AccD),
   neuromodulation([H,A,B,C,D],IAcc,Input_PIdPs,Output,[]).

   dot_productV6(IAcc,IPIdPs)->
        dot_productV6(IAcc,IPIdPs,0,0,0,0,0).
   dot_productV6([{IPId,Input}|IAcc],[{IPId,WeightsP}|IPIdPs],AccH,AccA,AccB,AccC,
AccD)->
        {DotH,DotA,DotB,DotC,DotD} = dotV6(Input,WeightsP,0,0,0,0,0),
   dot_productV6(IAcc,IPIdPs,DotH+AccH,DotA+AccA,DotB+AccB,DotC+AccC,DotD
+AccD);
   dot_productV6([],[{bias,[{_Bias,[H_Bias,A_Bias,B_Bias,C_Bias,D_Bias]}]}]],AccH,AccA,
AccB,AccC,AccD)->
        {AccH + H_Bias,AccA+A_Bias,AccB+B_Bias,AccC+C_Bias,AccD+D_Bias};
   dot_productV6([],[],AccH,AccA,AccB,AccC,AccD)->
        {AccH,AccA,AccB,AccC,AccD}.

   dotV6([I|Input],[{_W,[H_W,A_W,B_W,C_W,D_W]}|Weights],AccH,AccA,AccB,AccC,
AccD) ->
   dotV6(Input,Weights,I*H_W+AccH,I*A_W+AccA,I*B_W+AccB,I*C_W+AccC,I*D_W+
AccD);
   dotV6([],[],AccH,AccA,AccB,AccC,AccD)->
        {AccH,AccA,AccB,AccC,AccD}.
```

The architecture of the neuron using this particular plasticity function is shown in Fig-15.9. Since every synaptic weight of this neuron has a complementary parameter list of length 5, with an extra synaptic weight for every secondary, embedded modulatory neuron that analyzes the same signals as the actual neuron, but whose output signals modulate the plasticity of the neuron, each neuron thus has $x5$ number of parameters (synaptic weights) that need to be tuned. This might be a price too high to pay by amplifying the curse of dimensionality. The more parameters that one needs to tune and set up concurrently, the more difficult it is to find a good combination of such parameters. Nevertheless, the generality it provides, and the ability to use a single process to represent multiple embedded modulatory neurons, has its benefits in computational efficiency. Plus, our system does after all try to alleviate the curse of dimensionality through *Targeted Tuning*, by concentrating on the newly added and affected neurons of the NN system. And thus we might just be on the edge of this one.

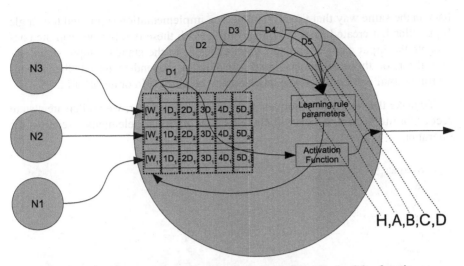

Fig. 15.9 The architecture of the neuron using self_modulationV6 plasticity function.

We noted earlier that there is another approach to neuromodulation, one that is more biologically faithful, in which a postsynaptic neuron uses some of the signals coming from the presynaptic neurons as modulatory signals, and others as standard signals. In the next section we will see what needs to be done to implement such a learning rule.

15.3.3 Implementing the input_idps_modulation Based Neuromodulated Plasticity

To implement neuromodulation using this method, we first modify the neuron's record by adding the *input_idps_modulation* element to it. The input_idps_modulation element will have the same purpose and formating as the *input_idps* element, to hold a list of tuples of the form: {Input_PId, WeightP}. The Input_PIds will be associated with the elements that send the postsynaptic neuron its modulatory signals, with the WeightP being of the same format as in the input_Idps list.

This particular implementation of neuromodulation will not require a lot of work, due to the input_idps_modulation list having a format which we already can process with the developed functions. The neuron cloning function in the genotype can be used to clone this list, the Id to PId conversion performed by the exoself to compose the Input_PIdPs list is also viable here. Even the synaptic weight perturbation can be applied to this list, due to it having such a similar format. The main changes we have to perform are to the neuron's main loop.

We must convert the neuron's main loop such that it can support 2 Input_PId lists, the SI_PIds (standard input PId list), and the MI_PIds (modulatory input PId list), in the same way that the original neuron implementation supported the single Input_PIds list created from the Input_PIdPs. With these two lists we can then aggregate the input signals, and sort them either in to the standard input signal accumulator, or the modulatory signal accumulator, dependent on whether the incoming signal was coming from an element with an SI_PId or an MI_PId.

To make the implementation and the source code cleaner, we will create a state record for the neuron, which will contain all the necessary elements it requires for operation:

```
-record(state,{
    id,
    cx_pid,
    af,
    pf,
    aggrf,
    si_pids=[],
    si_pidps_current=[],
    si_pidps_backup=[],
    mi_pids=[],
    mi_pidps_current=[],
    mi_pidps_backup=[],
    output_pids=[],
    ro_pids=[]
}).
```

With this state record, we update the prep/1 function to use it, and clean the original loop function to hide all the non-immediately used lists and data in the state record. As in the original neuron process implementation, we have to create the Input_PId list so that the incoming signals can be sorted in the same order that the Input_PIdPs are sorted. This time though, we have two such lists, designated as the SI_PIdPs (the standard one), and the MI_PIdPs (the modulatory one). Thus we create two PId lists for the loop.

The main problem here is that as the neuron accumulates its input signals, one of these PId lists will empty out first, which would require a new clause to deal with it, since our main loop uses: [SI_PId|SI_PIds],[MI_PId|MI_PIds]. We did not have such a problem when we only used a single list, because when that list emptied out, the signal accumulation was finished. To avoid having to create a new clause, we add the atom *ok* to the end of both PId lists, and put the clause: *loop(S,ExoSelf_PId,[ok],[ok],SIAcc,MIAcc)* above the main loop. Because of the *ok* atom at the end of both lists, neither goes empty, letting us keep a single clause with the final state for both lists being *[ok]*, which is achieved after the neuron has accumulated all the incoming standard and modulatory signals. The only problem with this setup is that the first clause is always pattern matched before the main loop, making the neuron process slower and less efficient. There are other ways to implement this, and we could even set up two different main process loops, one for when the neuron uses neuromodulation, and one for when it does not (and thus needing only a single PId list). But this implementation is the most concise, and cleanest. The neuron process can always be optimized later on. The modified prep/1 function, and the neuron's new main loop, are shown in Listing-15.8.

```
Listing-15.8 The updated implementation of the neuron process.

prep(ExoSelf_PId) ->
    random:seed(now()),
    receive
            {ExoSelf_PId,{Id,Cx_PId,AF,PF,AggrF,SI_PIdPs,MI_PIdPs,Output_PIds,
RO_PIds}} ->
                    fanout(RO_PIds,{self(),forward,[?RO_SIGNAL]}),
                    SI_PIds = lists:append([[IPId || {IPId,_W} <- SI_PIdPs, IPId =/= bias],[ok]),
                    MI_PIds = lists:append([[IPId || {IPId,_W} <- MI_PIdPs, IPId =/= bias],[ok]),
                    io:format("SI_PIdPs:~p ~nMI_PIdPs:~p~n",[SI_PIdPs,MI_PIdPs]),
                    S=#state{
                            id=Id,
                            cx_pid=Cx_PId,
                            af=AF,
                            pf=PF,
                            aggrf=AggrF,
                            si_pids=SI_PIds,
                            si_pidps_current=SI_PIdPs,
                            si_pidps_backup=SI_PIdPs,
                            mi_pids=MI_PIds,
                            mi_pidps_current=MI_PIdPs,
                            mi_pidps_backup=MI_PIdPs,
                            output_pids=Output_PIds,
                            ro_pids=RO_PIds
                    },
                    loop(S,ExoSelf_PId,SI_PIds,MI_PIds,[],[])
    end.
%When gen/1 is executed, it spawns the neuron element and immediately begins to wait for its
initial state message from the exoself. Once the state message arrives, the neuron sends out the
default forward signals to any elements in its ro_ids list, if any. Afterwards, the prep function
drops into the neuron's main loop.

loop(S,ExoSelf_PId,[ok],[ok],SIAcc,MIAcc)->
    PF = S#state.pf,
    AF = S#state.af,
    AggrF = S#state.aggrf,
    {PFName,PFParameters} = PF,
    Ordered_SIAcc = lists:reverse(SIAcc),
```

```
    SI_PIdPs = S#state.si_pidps_current,
    SAggregation_Product = signal_aggregator:AggrF(Ordered_SIAcc,SI_PIdPs),
    SOutput = functions:AF(SAggregation_Product),
    Output_PIds = S#state.output_pids,
    [Output_PId ! {self(),forward,[SOutput]} || Output_PId <- Output_PIds],

    Ordered_MIAcc = lists:reverse(MIAcc),
    MI_PIdPs = S#state.mi_pidps_current,
    MAggregation_Product = signal_aggregator:dot_product(Ordered_MIAcc,MI_PIdPs),
    MOutput = functions:tanh(MAggregation_Product),
    U_SI_PIdPs = plasticity:PFName([MOutput|PFParameters],Ordered_SIAcc,SI_PIdPs,
SOutput),
    U_S=S#state{
        si_pidps_current = U_SI_PIdPs
    },
    SI_PIds = S#state.si_pids,
    MI_PIds = S#state.mi_pids,
    loop(U_S,ExoSelf_PId,SI_PIds,MI_PIds,[],[]);
loop(S,ExoSelf_PId,[SI_PId|SI_PIds],[MI_PId|MI_PIds],SIAcc,MIAcc)->
    receive
        {SI_PId,forward,Input}->
            loop(S,ExoSelf_PId,SI_PIds,[MI_PId|MI_PIds],[{SI_PId,Input}|SIAcc],
MIAcc);
        {MI_PId,forward,Input}->
            loop(S,ExoSelf_PId,[SI_PId|SI_PIds],MI_PIds,SIAcc,[{MI_PId,Input}|
MIAcc]);
        {ExoSelf_PId,weight_backup}->
            U_S = S#state{
                si_pidps_backup=S#state.si_pidps_current,
                mi_pidps_backup=S#state.mi_pidps_current
            },
            loop(U_S,ExoSelf_PId,[SI_PId|SI_PIds],[MI_PId|MI_PIds],SIAcc,MIAcc);
        {ExoSelf_PId,weight_restore}->
            U_S = S#state{
                si_pidps_current=S#state.si_pidps_backup,
                mi_pidps_current=S#state.mi_pidps_backup
            },
            loop(U_S,ExoSelf_PId,[SI_PId|SI_PIds],[MI_PId|MI_PIds],SIAcc,MIAcc);
        {ExoSelf_PId,weight_perturb,Spread}->
            Perturbed_SIPIdPs=perturb_IPIdPs(Spread,S#state.si_pidps_backup),
            Perturbed_MIPIdPs=perturb_IPIdPs(Spread,S#state.mi_pidps_backup),
            U_S = S#state{
                si_pidps_current=Perturbed_SIPIdPs,
                mi_pidps_current=Perturbed_MIPIdPs
            },
```

```
                loop(U_S,ExoSelf_PId,[SI_PId|SI_PIds],[MI_PId|MI_PIds],SIAcc,MIAcc);
        {ExoSelf_PId,reset_prep}->
                neuron:flush_buffer(),
                ExoSelf_PId ! {self(),ready},
                RO_PIds = S#state.ro_pids,
                receive
                        {ExoSelf_PId, reset}->
                                fanout(RO_PIds,{self(),forward,[?RO_SIGNAL]})
                end,
                loop(S,ExoSelf_PId,S#state.si_pids,S#state.mi_pids,[],[]);
        {ExoSelf_PId,get_backup}->
                NId = S#state.id,
                ExoSelf_PId ! {self(),NId,S#state.si_pidps_backup,S#state.mi_pidps_backup},
                loop(S,ExoSelf_PId,[SI_PId|SI_PIds],[MI_PId|MI_PIds],SIAcc,MIAcc);
        {ExoSelf_PId,terminate}->
                io:format("Neuron:~p is terminating.~n",[self()])
end.
```

With the implementation of the updated neuron now complete, we need to create the neuromodulation function in the plasticity module. Since the modulatory signals will be used to compute a nonlinear value used to modulate the standard general Hebbian rule, we will not need any weight_parameters and so our plasticity function will produce an empty weight_parameters list. But we will need the general neural_parameters for the *hebbian* function, thus the neuromodulation/1 function executed with the neuronal_parameters atom will return a list with 5 randomly generated (and later tuned and evolved) parameters: *[H,A,B,C,D]*. The neuromodulation/4 function is very simple, since it is executed with a list of all the necessary parameters to call the neurmodulation/5 function that applies the general hebbian rule to all the synaptic weights. These two added functions are shown in Listing-15.9.

Listing-15.9 The implementation of the neuromodulation/1 and neuromodulation/4 functions.

```
neuromodulation(neural_parameters)->
    H = (lists:random()-0.5),
    A = (lists:random()-0.5),
    B = (lists:random()-0.5),
    C = (lists:random()-0.5),
    D = (lists:random()-0.5),
    [H,A,B,C,D];
neuromodulation(weight_parameters)->
    [].

neuromodulation([M,H,A,B,C,D],IAcc,Input_PIdPs,Output)->
    Modulator = scale_dzone(M,0.33,?SAT_LIMIT),
    neuromodulation([Modulator*H,A,B,C,D],IAcc,Input_PIdPs,Output,[]).
```

The value M is the one computed by using the synaptic weights of the input_idps_modulation, using the dot_product signal aggregator, and the hyperbolic tangent (tanh) activation function. Since H scales the plasticity in general, multiplying the *Modulator* value by H allows for the modulation signal to truly modulate synaptic plasticity based on the parameters evolved by the neuron.

The *Modulator* value is computed by executing the scale_dzone/3 function, which performs 2 tasks:

1. Zero out M if it is between -0.33 and 0.33.
2. If M is greater than 0.33 or less than -0.33, normalize and scale it to be between 0 and ?SAT_LIMIT, or 0 and -?SAT_LIMIT, respectively.

This means that M has to reach a particular magnitude for the Hebbian rule to be executed, since when the Modulator value is 0 and is multiplied by H, the weights are not updated. The scale_dzone/3 function, and its supporting function, are shown in Listing-15.10.

Listing-15.10 The implementation of scale_dzone and scale function.

```
scale_dzone(Val,Threshold,MaxMagnitude)->
    if
        Val > Threshold ->
            (functions:scale(Val,MaxMagnitude,Threshold)+1)*MaxMagnitude/2;
        Val < -Threshold ->
            (functions:scale(Val,-Threshold,-MaxMagnitude)-1)*MaxMagnitude/2;
        true ->
            0
    end.


scale(Val,Max,Min)->
    case Max == Min of
        true ->
            0;
        false ->
            (Val*2 - (Max+Min))/(Max-Min)
    end.
```

%The scale/3 function scales Val to be between -1 and 1, with the scaling dependent on the Max and Min value, using the equation: Scaled_Val = (Val*2 - (Max + Min))/(Max-Min). The function scale_dzone/3 zeroes the Val parameter if it is below the threshold, and scales it to be between Threshold and MaxMagnitude if it is above the threshold.

Though we have now successfully implemented the autoassociative learning rules, and neuromodulation, we cannot use those features until we create the necessary tuning and mutation operators, such that our neuroevolutionary system can actually tune in the various learning parameters, and add the synaptic weights needed by the neuromodulation functionality. We discuss and implement these necessary features in the next section.

15.4 Plasticity Parameter Mutation Operators

For the plasticity based learning rules to be useful, our neuroevolutionary system must be able to optimize them. For this we need to create new mutation operators. Though we could add the new mutation operators to the genome_mutator module, we will do something different instead. Since each plasticity function has its own restrictions (which learning parameters can/should be modified, and which can/should not be), and because there are so many of the different variants, and many more to be added as time goes on, it would not be effective to create these mutation operators inside the genome_mutator module. The genome_mutator should concentrate on the standard topology oriented mutation operators.

To more effectively handle this, we can offload these specialized mutation operators in the same way we offloaded the generation of the initial plasticity parameters, to the plasticity module itself. We can add a single mutation operator *mutate_plasticity,* which when executed, executes the *plasticity:PFName(Agent_Id, mutate)* function. Then the researcher which created the various plasticity function variants and types, can also create the mutation operator functions for it, whether they simply perturb neural level learning parameters, synaptic weight level parameters, or perform a more complex mutation. And of course if the plasticity function is set to none, we will have the function *plasticity:none(Agent_Id,mutate)* execute: *exit("Neuron does not support plasticity."),* which will allow our neuroevolutionary system to attempt another mutation operator, without wasting the topological mutation try.

The plasticity specializing mutation operators should perform the following general operations:

- If the neuron uses neural_parameters, randomly choose between 1 and math:sqrt(TotParameters) number of parameters, and perturb them with a value selected randomly between -Pi and Pi.
- If the neuron uses weight_parameters, randomly choose between 1 and math:sqrt(TotWeightParameters) number of parameters, and perturb them with a value selected randomly between -Pi and Pi.
- If the neuron uses both, neural_parameters and weight_parameters, randomly choose one or the other, and perturb that parameter list using one of the above approaches, depending which of the two apply.

The neuromodulation is a special case, since it does not only have the global neural_level parameters which can be mutated/perturbed using the standard method listed above, but also allows for the establishment of new modulatory connections. Because the input_idps_modulation list has the same format as the standard input_idps list, we can use the already existing synaptic connection establishing mutation operators and functions. The only modification we need to make so that some of the connections are standard, and others are modulatory, is set a case such that if the neuron to which the connection is being established has neuromodulation enabled, then the choice of whether the new connection will be standard or modulatory is 50/50, and if there is no neuromodulation enabled, then only the standard connection is allowed.

15.4.1 Implementing the Weight Parameter Mutation Operator

We first create the mutation operators which are applied to the weight_parameters. This mutation operator, executed when the plasticity function is run with the parameter: *{N_Id,mutate}*, performs similarly to the standard *perturb_IPIdPs/2* function, but instead of mutating the synaptic weights, it operates on, and mutates the, parameter values. The probability for any weight parameter to be perturbed is *1/math:sqrt(TotParameters)*. The plasticity functions that only use weight_parameters are the **hebbian_w** and **ojas_w**. Because in both of these plasticity functions the same implementation for the mutator is used, only the hebbian_w/1 version is shown (the difference for the ojas_w version is that instead of hebbian_w({N_Id,mutate}), we have ojas_w({N_Id,mutate})). This implementation is shown in Listing-15.11.

Listing-15.11 Implementation of the plasticity function based weight_parameter mutation operators.

```
hebbian_w({N_Id,mutate})->
    random:seed(now()),
    N = genotype:read({neuron,N_Id}),
    InputIdPs = N#neuron.input_idps,
    U_InputIdPs=perturb_parameters(InputIdPs,?SAT_LIMIT),
    N#neuron{input_idps = U_InputIdPs};
hebbian_w(neural_parameters)->
    [];
hebbian_w(weight_parameters)->
    [(lists:random()-0.5)].
```

%hebbian_w/1 function produces the necessary parameter list for the hebbian_w learning rule to operate. The parameter list for the simple hebbian_w learning rule is a parameter list composed of a single parameter H: [H], for every synaptic weight of the neuron. When hebbian_w/1 is called with the parameter neural_parameters, it returns []. When hebbian_w/1 is executed with the {N_Id,mutate} tuple, the function goes through every parameter in the neuron's input_idps, and perturbs the parameter value using the specified spread (?SAT_LIMIT).

```
    perturb_parameters(InputIdPs,Spread)->
```

```
        TotParameters = lists:sum([lists:sum([length(Ps) || {_W,Ps} <- WPs]) || {_Input_Id,
WPs} <- InputIdPs]),
        MutationProb = 1/math:sqrt(TotParameters),
        [{Input_Id,[{W,perturb(Ps,MutationProb,Spread,[])}|| {W,Ps} <- WPs]} || {Input_Id,
WPs} <- InputIdPs].
%The perturb_parameters/2 function goes through every tuple in the InputIdPs list, extracts the
WeightPlus blocks for each input connection, calculates the total number of weight parameters
the neuron has, and from it the probability with which those parameters will be perturbed.
The function then executes perturb/4 to perturb the said parameters.


        perturb([Val|Vals],MutationProb,Spread,Acc)->
            case random:uniform() < MutationProb of
                true ->
                    U_Val = sat((random:uniform()-0.5)*2*Spread+Val,Spread,
Spread),
                    perturb(Vals,MutationProb,Spread,[U_Val|Acc]);
                false ->
                    perturb(Vals,MutationProb,Spread,[Val|Acc])
            end;
        perturb([],_MutationProb,_Spread,Acc)->
            lists:reverse(Acc).
%The perturb/5 function is executed with a list of values and a probability with which each
value has the chance of being perturbed. The function then goes through every value and per-
turbs it with the given probability.
```

15.4.2 Implementing the Neural Parameter Mutation Operator

We next create the mutation operators which are applied to the neural_parameters, which are lists of values. To accomplish this, we just make that list pass through a function which with some probability, *1/sqrt(ListLength)*, perturbs the values within it. We add such mutation operators to the plasticity functions which only use the neural_parameters. The following plasticity functions only use the neural_parameters: **hebbian**, **ojas**, and the **neuromodulation**. Since all 3 would use exactly the same implementation, only the neuromodulation/1 implementation is shown in Listing-15.12.

```
Listing-15.12 Implementation of the neural_parameters mutation operator.

neuromodulation({N_Id,mutate})->
    random:seed(now()),
    N = genotype:read({neuron,N_Id}),
    {PFName,ParameterList} = N#neuron.pf,
    MSpread = ?SAT_LIMIT*10,
```

```
    MutationProb = 1/math:sqrt(length(ParameterList)),
    U_ParameterList = perturb(ParameterList,MutationProb,MSpread,[]),
    U_PF = {PFName,U_ParameterList},
    N#neuron{pf=U_PF};
neuromodulation(neural_parameters)->
    H = (lists:random()-0.5),
    A = (lists:random()-0.5),
    B = (lists:random()-0.5),
    C = (lists:random()-0.5),
    D = (lists:random()-0.5),
    [H,A,B,C,D];
neuromodulation(weight_parameters)->
    [].
```

%neuromodulation/1 function produces the necessary parameter list for the neuromodulation learning rule to operate. The parameter list for this learning rule is a list composed of parameters H,A,B,C,D: [H,A,B,C,D]. When the function is executed with the {NId,mutate} parameter, it calculates the perturbation probability of every parameter through the equation: 1/math:sqrt(length(ParameterList)), and then executes the perturb/5 function to perturb the actual parameters.

The above shown mutation operator, called by executing neuromodulation/1 with the parameter {N_Id,mutate}, uses the perturb/4 function from the weight_parameters based mutation operator which was shown in the previous listing, Listing-15.11.

15.4.3 Implementing the Hybrid, Weight & Neural Parameters Mutation Operator

Finally, we also have plasticity functions which have both, neural_parameters and weight_parameters. This is the case for example for the self_modulationV5, V3, and V2 learning rules. For these type of plasticity functions, we create a combination of the neural_parameters and weight_parameters mutation operators, as shown in Listing-15.13.

Listing-15.13 A hybrid of the neural_parameters and weight_parameters mutation operator, implemented here for the self_modulationV5 plasticity function.

```
self_modulationV5({N_Id,mutate})->
    random:seed(now()),
    N = genotype:read({neuron,N_Id}),
    {PFName,ParameterList} = N#neuron.pf,
    MSpread = ?SAT_LIMIT*10,
```

```
    MutationProb = 1/math:sqrt(length(ParameterList)),
    U_ParameterList = perturb(ParameterList,MutationProb,MSpread,[]),
    U_PF = {PFName,U_ParameterList},
    InputIdPs = N#neuron.input_idps,
    U_InputIdPs=perturb_parameters(InputIdPs,?SAT_LIMIT),
    N#neuron{pf=U_PF,input_idps=U_InputIdPs};
self_modulationV5(neural_parameters)->
    B=(lists:random()-0.5),
    C=(lists:random()-0.5),
    D=(lists:random()-0.5),
    [B,C,D];
self_modulationV5(weight_parameters)->
    [(lists:random()-0.5),(lists:random()-0.5)].
```

For this plasticity module, this is all that is needed, there are only these 3 variants. We now modify the genome_mutator module to include the *mutate_plasticity_parameters* mutation operator, and modify the functions which deal with linking neurons together, so that we can add the *modulatory* connection establishment functionality.

15.4.4 Updating the genome_mutator Module

Since our neuroevolutionary system can only apply to a population the mutation operators available in its constraint record, we first add the *{mutate_plasticity_parameters,1}* tag to the constraint's *mutation_operators* list. This means that the mutate_plasticity_parameter mutation operator has the same chance of being executed as any other mutation operator within the mutation_operators list. After having modified the constraint record, we add the *mutate_plasticity_parameters/1* function to the *genome_mutator* module. It is a simple mutation operator that chooses a random neuron from the NN, and through the execution of *plasticity:PFName({N_Id,mutate})* function, mutates the plasticity parameters of that neuron, if that neuron has plasticity. If the neuron does not have plasticity enabled, then the plasticity:none/1 function is executed, which exits the mutation operator, letting our neuroevolutionary system try another mutation. The implemented mutate_plasticity_parameters/1 function is shown in Listing-15.14.

Listing-15.14 The implementation of the mutate_plasticity_parameters mutation operator.

```
mutate_plasticity_parameters(Agent_Id)->
    A = genotype:read({agent,Agent_Id}),
    Cx_Id = A#agent.cx_id,
    Cx = genotype:read({cortex,Cx_Id}),
    N_Ids = Cx#cortex.neuron_ids,
```

```
N_Id = lists:nth(random:uniform(length(N_Ids)),N_Ids),
N = genotype:read({neuron,N_Id}),
{PFName,_Parameters} = N#neuron.pf,
U_N = plasticity:PFName({N_Id,mutate}),
EvoHist = A#agent.evo_hist,
U_EvoHist = [{mutate_plasticity_parameters,N_Id}|EvoHist],
U_A = A#agent{evo_hist=U_EvoHist},
genotype:write(U_N),
genotype:write(U_A).
%The mutate_plasticity_parameters/1 chooses a random neuron from the NN, and mutates the
parameters of its plasticity function, if present.
```

Having implemented the mutation operator, we now look for the connection/synaptic-link establishing functions. We need to modify these functions because we want to ensure that if the neuron uses the neuromodulation plasticity function, then some of the new connections that are added to it through evolution, are randomly chosen to be modulatory connections rather than standard ones.

The functions that need to be updated are the following four:

- add_bias/1: Because the input_idps_modulation can also use a bias weight.
- remove_bias/1: Because the input_idps_modulation should also be able to rid itself of its bias.
- link_ToNeuron/4: Which is the function that actually establishes new links, and adds the necessary tuples to the input_idps list. We should be able to randomly choose whether to add the new tuple to the standard input_idps list, or the modulatory input_idps_modulation list.
- cutlink_ToNeuron/3: Which is the function which cuts the links to the neuron, and removes the synaptic weight containing tuple from the input_idps list. We should be able to randomly choose whether to remove such a tuple from the input_idps or input_idps_modulation list.

Again, because of the way we developed, and modularized the code in the genome_mutator module, almost everything with regards to linking is contained in the link_ToNeuron and cutlink_ToNeuron, so by just modifying those, and the add_bias/remove_bias functions, we will be done with the update.

Originally the add_bias/1 function checks whether the input_idps list already has a bias, and then adds a bias if it does not, and exits if it does. We now have to check whether input_idps and input_idps_modulation lists already have biases. To do this, we randomly generate a value by executing random:uniform(2), which generates either 1 or 2. If value 2 is generated, and the input_idps_modulation does not have a bias, we add one to it. Otherwise, if the input_idps list does not have a bias, we add one to it, and thus in the absence of neuromodulation based plasticity, probability of adding the bias to input_idps does not change. The modified add_bias mutation operator is shown in Listing-15.15.

Listing-15.15 The updated add_bias mutation operator.

```
add_bias(Agent_Id)->
  A = genotype:read({agent,Agent_Id}),
  Cx_Id = A#agent.cx_id,
  Cx = genotype:read({cortex,Cx_Id}),
  N_Ids = Cx#cortex.neuron_ids,
  N_Id = lists:nth(random:uniform(length(N_Ids)),N_Ids),
  Generation = A#agent.generation,
  N = genotype:read({neuron,N_Id}),
  SI_IdPs = N#neuron.input_idps,
  MI_IdPs = N#neuron.input_idps_modulation,
  {PFName,_NLParameters} = N#neuron.pf,
  case {lists:keymember(bias,1,SI_IdPs), lists:keymember(bias,1,MI_IdPs), PFName ==
neuromodulation, random:uniform(2)} of
        {_,true,true,2} ->
              exit("********ERROR:add_bias:: This Neuron already has a modulatory bias
part.");
        {_,false,true,2} ->
              U_MI_IdPs = lists:append(MI_IdPs,[{bias,[{random:uniform()-0.5,
plasticity:PFName(weight_parameters)}]}]),
              U_N = N#neuron{
                    input_idps_modulation = U_MI_IdPs,
                    generation = Generation},
              EvoHist = A#agent.evo_hist,
              U_EvoHist = [{{add_bias,m},N_Id}|EvoHist],
              U_A = A#agent{evo_hist=U_EvoHist},
              genotype:write(U_N),
              genotype:write(U_A);
        {true,_,_,1} ->
              exit("********ERROR:add_bias:: This Neuron already has a bias in in-
put_idps.");
        {false,_,_,_} ->
              U_SI_IdPs = lists:append(SI_IdPs,[{bias,[{random:uniform()-0.5,
plasticity:PFName(weight_parameters)}]}]),
              U_N = N#neuron{
                    input_idps = U_SI_IdPs,
                    generation = Generation},
              EvoHist = A#agent.evo_hist,
              U_EvoHist = [{{add_bias,s},N_Id}|EvoHist],
              U_A = A#agent{evo_hist=U_EvoHist},
              genotype:write(U_N),
              genotype:write(U_A)
  end.
```

The remove_bias is modified in the same manner, and only a few elements of the source code are changed. Like the add_bias, we update the link_ToNeuron/4 function to randomly choose whether to make the new link modulatory or standard, and only if the chosen list (either input_idps or input_idps_modulation), does not already have a link from the specified presynaptic element. The updated function is shown in Listing-15.16.

Listing-15.16 The updated link_ToNeuron/4 function.

```
link_ToNeuron(FromId,FromOVL,ToN,Generation)->
    ToSI_IdPs = ToN#neuron.input_idps,
    ToMI_IdPs = ToN#neuron.input_idps_modulation,
    {PFName,_NLParameters}=ToN#neuron.pf,
    case {lists:keymember(FromId,1,ToSI_IdPs),lists:keymember(FromId,1,ToMI_IdPs)} of
        {false,false} ->
                case {PFName == neuromodulation, random:uniform(2)} of
                    {true,2} ->
                            U_ToMI_IdPs = [{FromId,
genotype:create_NeuralWeightsP(PFName,FromOVL,[])}|ToMI_IdPs],
                            ToN#neuron{
                                    input_idps = U_ToMI_IdPs,
                                    generation = Generation
                            };
                    _ ->
                            U_ToSI_IdPs = [{FromId,
genotype:create_NeuralWeightsP(PFName,FromOVL,[])}|ToSI_IdPs],
                            ToN#neuron{
                                    input_idps = U_ToSI_IdPs,
                                    generation = Generation
                            }
                end;
        _ ->
                exit("ERROR:add_NeuronI::[cannot add I_Id]: ~p already connected to ~p~n",
[FromId,ToN#neuron.id])
    end.
%link_ToNeuron/4 updates the record of ToN, so that it's updated to receive a connection from
the element FromId. The link emanates from element with the id FromId, whose output vector
length is FromOVL, and the connection is made to the neuron ToN. In this function, either the
ToN's input_idps_modulation or input_idps list is updated with the tuple {FromId, [{W_1,
WPs} ...{W_FromOVL,WPs}]}. Whether input_idps or input_idps_modulation is updated, is
chosen randomly. Then the neuron's generation is updated to Generation (the current, most re-
cent generation). After this, the updated ToN's record is returned to the caller. On the other
hand, if the FromId is already part of the ToN's input_idps or input_idps_modulation list (de-
pendent on which was randomly chosen), which means that the standard or modulatory link al-
ready exists between the neuron ToN and element FromId, this function exits with an error.
```

Finally, we update the cutlink_ToNeuron/3 function. In this case, since there can only be one link between two elements, we simply first check if the specified input link is specified in the input_idps, and cut it if it does. If it does not, we check the input_idps_modulation next, and cut it if this link is modulatory. If such a link does not exist in either of the two lists, we exit the mutation operator with an error, printing to console that the specified link does not exist, neither in the synaptic weights list, nor in the synaptic parameters list. The implementation of the cutlink_ToNeuron/3, is shown in Listing-15.17.

```
Listing-15.17 The cutlink_ToNeuron/3 implementation.


cutlink_ToNeuron(FromId,ToN,Generation)->
        ToSI_IdPs = ToN#neuron.input_idps,
        ToMI_IdPs = ToN#neuron.input_idps_modulation,
        Guard1 = lists:keymember(FromId, 1, ToSI_IdPs),
        Guard2 = lists:keymember(FromId, 1, ToMI_IdPs),
        if
                Guard1->
                        U_ToSI_IdPs = lists:keydelete(FromId,1,ToSI_IdPs),
                        ToN#neuron{
                                input_idps = U_ToSI_IdPs,
                                generation = Generation};
                Guard2 ->
                        U_ToMI_IdPs = lists:keydelete(FromId,1,ToMI_IdPs),
                        ToN#neuron{
                                input_idps = U_ToMI_IdPs,
                                generation = Generation};
                true ->
                        exit("ERROR[can not remove I_Id]: ~p not a member of
~p~n",[FromId,ToN#neuron.id])
        end.
%cutlink_ToNeuron/3 cuts the connection on the ToNeuron (ToN) side. The function first
checks if the FromId is a member of the ToN's input_idps list, if it's not, then the function
checks if it is a member of the input_idps_modulation list. If it is not a member of either, the
function exits with error. If FromId is a member of one of these lists, then that tuple is removed
from that list, and the updated ToN record is returned to the caller.
```

With these updates completed, the genome_mutator module is up to date. In the case that a plasticity is enabled in any neuron, the topological mutation phase will be able to mutate the plasticity function learning parameters, and add modulatory connections in the case the plasticity function is *neuromodulation*. The only remaining update we have to make is one to the tuning phase related functions.

15.5 Tuning of a NN which has Plastic Neurons

It can be argued whether both standard synaptic weights and modulatory synaptic weights should be perturbed at the same time when the neuron has plasticity enabled, or just one or the other separately during the tuning phase. For example, should we allow for the neural_parameters to be perturbed during the tuning phase, rather than only during the topological mutation phase? What percentage of tuning should be dedicated to learning parameters and what percentage to synaptic weights? This of course can be tested, and benchmarked, and in general deduced through experimentation. After it has been decided on what and when to tune with regards to learning rules, there is still a problem with regards to the parameter and synaptic weight backup during the tuning phase. The main problem of this section is with regards to this dilemma, the dilemma of the backup process of the tuned weights.

Consider a neuron that has plasticity enabled, no matter what plasticity function it's using. The following scenario occurs when the neuron is perturbed:

1. The neuron receives a perturbation request.
2. Neuron selects random synaptic weights, weight_parameters, or even neural_parameters (though we do not allow for neural_parameters perturbation during the tuning phase, yet).
3. Then the agent gets re-evaluated, and **IF:**
   4. Perturbed agent has a higher fitness: the neuron backups its *current* weights/parameters.
   5. Perturbed agent has a lower fitness: the neuron restores its previous backed up weights/parameters.

There is a problem with step 4. Because by the time it's time to backup the synaptic weights, they have already changed from what they original started with during the evaluation, since they have adapted and learned due to their plasticity function. So we would not be backing up the synaptic weights of the agent that achieved the higher fitness score, but instead we would be backing up the learned and adapted agent with its adapted synaptic weights.

The fact that the perturbed agent, or topologically mutated agent, is not simply a perturbed genotype on which its parent is based, but instead is based on the genotype which has resulted from its parent's experience (due to the parent having changed based on its learning rule, before its genotype was backed up), means that the process is now based on Lamarckian evolution, rather than the biologically correct Darwinian. The definition of Lamarckian Evolution is based on the idea that an organism can pass on to its offspring the characteristics that it has acquired and learned during its lifetime (evaluation), all its knowledge and learned skills. Since plasticity affects the agent's neural patterns, synaptic weights... all of which are defined and written back to the agent's genotype, and the offspring is a mutated version of that genotype, the offspring thus in effect will to some extent inherit the agent's adapted genotype, and not the original genotype with which the parent started when it was being evaluated.

When the agent backs up its synaptic weights after it has been evaluated for fitness, the agent uses Lamarckian evolution, because its experience, what it has learned during its evaluation (and what it has learned is reflected in how the synaptic weights changed due to the used plasticity learning rule), is written to its genome, and it is this learned agent that gets perturbed. The cleanest way to solve this problem, and have control of whether we use Lamarckian or the biologically correct Darwinian evolution, is to add a new parameter to the agent, the *darwinian/lamarckian* flag.

Darwinian vs. Lamarckian evolution, particularly in ALife simulations, could lead to interesting possibilities. When using Lamarckian evolution, and for example applying our neuroevolutionary system to an ALife problem, the agent's experience gained from interacting with the simulated environment, would be passed on to its offspring, and perturbed during the tuning phase. The perturbed organism (during the tuning phase, belonging to the same evaluation) would re-experience the interaction with the environment, and if it was even more successful, it would be backed up with its new experience (which means that the organism has now experienced and learned in the environment twice, since through plasticity the environment has affected its synaptic weights twice...). If the perturbed agent is less fit, then the previous agent, with its memories and synaptic weight combination, is reverted to, and re-perturbed. If we set the max_attempts counter to 1, then it will be genetic rather than a memetic based neuroevolutionary system. But again, when Lamarckian evolution is allowed, the memories of the parent are passed on to its offspring... A number of papers have researched the usefulness and efficiency of Darwinian Vs. Lamarkian evolution [4,5,6,7]. The results vary, and so adding a *heredity* flag to the agent will allow us to experiment and use both if we want to. We could then switch between the two heredity approaches (Darwinian or Lamarckian) easily, or perhaps even allow the hereditary flag to flip between the two during the topological mutation phase through some new topological mutation operator, letting the evolutionary process decide what suits the assigned problem best.

To implement the proper synaptic weight updating method to reflect the decided on hereditary approach during the tuning phase, we will need to add minor updates to the records.hrl file, the exoself, the neuron, and the genotype modules. In the records.hrl, we have to update the *agent* record by adding the *heredity_type* flag to it, and modifying the constraint record by adding the *heredity_types* element to it. The agent's *heredity_type* element will simply store a tag, an atom which can either be : *darwinian* or *lamarckian*. The constraint's heredity_types element will be a list of heredity_type tags. This list can either contain just a single tag, *'darwinian'* or *'lamarckian'* for example, or it could contain both. If both atoms are present in the heredity_types list, then during the creation of the seed population, some agents will use the darwinian method of passing on their hereditary information, and others will use a lamarckian approach. It would be interesting to see which of the two would have an advantage, or be able to evolve faster, and during what stages of evolution and in which problems...

After updating the 2 records in records.hrl, we have to make a small update to the genotype module. In the genotype module we update the construct_Agent/3 function, and set the agent's heredity_type to one of the available heredity types in the constraint's heredity_types list. We do this by adding the following line when setting the agent's record: *heredity_type = random_element (SpecCon#constraint.heredity_types)*. We then update the exoself module, by modifying the link_Neurons/2 function to link_Neurons/3 function, and pass to it the agent's heredity_type parameter, the parameter which is then forwarded to each spawned neuron.

With this done, we make the final and main source modification, which is all contained within the neuron module. To allow for Darwinian based heredity in the presence of learning and plastic neurons, we need to keep track of two states of the input_pidps:

1. The input_pidps that are currently effective and represent the neuron's processing dynamics, which is the input_pidps_current.
2. A second input_pidps list, which represents the state of input_pidps right after perturbation, before the synaptic weights are affected by the neuron's plasticity function.

We can call this new list the *input_pidps_bl*, where *bl* stands for Before Learning.

When a neuron is requested to perturb its synaptic weights, right after the weights are perturbed, we want to save this new input_pidps list, before plasticity gets a chance to modify the synaptic weights. Thus, whereas before we stored the Perturbed_PIdPs in input_pidps_current, we now also save it to input_pidps_bl. Afterwards, the neuron can process the input signals using its input_pidps_current, and its learning rule can affect the input_pidps_current list. But input_pidps_bl will remain unchanged.

When a neuron is sent the weight_backup message, it is here that heredity_type plays its role. When it's *darwinian*, the neuron saves the *input_pidps_bl* to input_pidps_backup, instead of the input_pidps_current which could have been modified by some learning rule by this point. On the other hand, when the heredity_type is *lamarckian*, the neuron saves the input_pidps_current to input_pidps_backup. The input_pidps_current represents the synaptic weights that could have been updated if the neuron allows for plasticity, and thus the input_pidps_backup will then contain not the initial states of the synaptic weight list with which the neuron started, but the state of the synaptic weights after the neuron has experienced, processed, and had its synaptic weights modified by its learning rule. Using this logic we add to the neuron's state the element input_pidps_bl, and update the loop/6 function, as shown in Listing-15.18.

Listing-15.18 The neuron's loop/6 function which can use both, Darwinian and Lamarckian inheritance.

```
loop(S,ExoSelf_PId,[ok],[ok],SIAcc,MIAcc)->
    PF = S#state.pf,
    AF = S#state.af,
    AggrF = S#state.aggrf,
    {PFName,PFParameters} = PF,
    Ordered_SIAcc = lists:reverse(SIAcc),
    SI_PIdPs = S#state.si_pidps_current,
    SAggregation_Product = signal_aggregator:AggrF(Ordered_SIAcc,SI_PIdPs),
    SOutput = functions:AF(SAggregation_Product),
    Output_PIds = S#state.output_pids,
    [Output_PId ! {self(),forward,[SOutput]} || Output_PId <- Output_PIds],
    Ordered_MIAcc = lists:reverse(MIAcc),
    MI_PIdPs = S#state.mi_pidps_current,
    MAggregation_Product = signal_aggregator:dot_product(Ordered_MIAcc,MI_PIdPs),
    MOutput = functions:tanh(MAggregation_Product),
    U_SI_PIdPs = plasticity:PFName([MOutput|PFParameters],Ordered_SIAcc,SI_PIdPs,
SOutput),
    U_S=S#state{
        si_pidps_current = U_SI_PIdPs
    },
    SI_PIds = S#state.si_pids,
    MI_PIds = S#state.mi_pids,
    loop(U_S,ExoSelf_PId,SI_PIds,MI_PIds,[],[]);
loop(S,ExoSelf_PId,[SI_PId|SI_PIds],[MI_PId|MI_PIds],SIAcc,MIAcc)->
    receive
        {SI_PId,forward,Input}->
            loop(S,ExoSelf_PId,SI_PIds,[MI_PId|MI_PIds],[{SI_PId,Input}|SIAcc],
MIAcc);
        {MI_PId,forward,Input}->

    loop(S,ExoSelf_PId,[SI_PId|SI_PIds],MI_PIds,SIAcc,[{MI_PId,Input}|MIAcc]);
        {ExoSelf_PId,weight_backup}->
            U_S=case S#state.heredity_type of
                darwinian ->
                    S#state{
                        si_pidps_backup=S#state.si_pidps_bl,
                        mi_pidps_backup=S#state.mi_pidps_current
                    };
                lamarckian ->
                    S#state{
                        si_pidps_backup=S#state.si_pidps_current,
                        mi_pidps_backup=S#state.mi_pidps_current
```

```
                        }
            end,
            loop(U_S,ExoSelf_PId,[SI_PId|SI_PIds],[MI_PId|MI_PIds],SIAcc,MIAcc);
    {ExoSelf_PId,weight_restore}->
            U_S = S#state{
                    si_pidps_bl=S#state.si_pidps_backup,
                    si_pidps_current=S#state.si_pidps_backup,
                    mi_pidps_current=S#state.mi_pidps_backup
            },
            loop(U_S,ExoSelf_PId,[SI_PId|SI_PIds],[MI_PId|MI_PIds],SIAcc,MIAcc);
    {ExoSelf_PId,weight_perturb,Spread}->
            Perturbed_SIPIdPs=perturb_IPIdPs(Spread,S#state.si_pidps_backup),
            Perturbed_MIPIdPs=perturb_IPIdPs(Spread,S#state.mi_pidps_backup),
            U_S=S#state{
                    si_pidps_bl=Perturbed_SIPIdPs,
                    si_pidps_current=Perturbed_SIPIdPs,
                    mi_pidps_current=Perturbed_MIPIdPs
            },
            loop(U_S,ExoSelf_PId,[SI_PId|SI_PIds],[MI_PId|MI_PIds],SIAcc,MIAcc);
    {ExoSelf_PId,reset_prep}->
            neuron:flush_buffer(),
            ExoSelf_PId ! {self(),ready},
            RO_PIds = S#state.ro_pids,
            receive
                    {ExoSelf_PId, reset}->
                            fanout(RO_PIds,{self(),forward,[?RO_SIGNAL]})
            end,
            loop(S,ExoSelf_PId,S#state.si_pids,S#state.mi_pids,[],[]);
    {ExoSelf_PId,get_backup}->
            NId = S#state.id,
            ExoSelf_PId ! {self(),NId,S#state.si_pidps_backup,S#state.mi_pidps_backup},
            loop(S,ExoSelf_PId,[SI_PId|SI_PIds],[MI_PId|MI_PIds],SIAcc,MIAcc);
    {ExoSelf_PId,terminate}->
            io:format("Neuron:~p is terminating.~n",[self()])
    after 10000 ->
            io:format("neuron:~p stuck.~n",[S#state.id])
    end.
```

With this modification, our neuroevolutionary system can be used with Darwinian and Lamarckian based heredity. If we start the population_monitor process with a constraint where the agents are allowed to have neurons with plasticity, and set the heredity_types to either [lamarckian] or [darwinian,lamarckian], then some of the agents will have plasticity and be able to use the Lamarckian inheritance.

We can next add a simple mutation operator which works similarly to the way the mutation operators of other evolutionary strategy parameters work. We simply check whether there are any other heredity types in the constraint's *heredity_types* list, if there are, we change the currently used one to a new one, randomly chosen from the list. If there are no others, then the mutation operator exits with an error, without wasting the topological mutation attempt. This simple *mutate_heredity_type* mutation operator implementation is shown in Listing-15.19.

Listing-15.19 The implementation of the genome_mutator:mutate_heredity_type/1 mutation operator.

```
mutate_heredity_type(Agent_Id)->
    A = genotype:read({agent,Agent_Id}),
    case (A#agent.constraint)#constraint.heredity_types -- [A#agent.heredity_type] of
        [] ->
                exit("********ERROR:mutate_heredity_type/1:: Nothing to mutate, only a
single function available.");
        Heredity_Type_Pool->
                New_HT = lists:nth(random:uniform(length(Heredity_Type_Pool)),
Heredity_Type_Pool),
                U_A = A#agent{heredity_type = New_HT},
                genotype:write(U_A)
    end.
```

%mutate_heredity_type/1 function checks if there are any other heredity types in the agent's constraint record. If any other than the one currently used by the agent is present, the agent exchanges the heredity type it currently uses for a random one from the remaining list. If no other heredity types are available, the mutation operator exits with an error, and the neuroevolutionary system tries another mutation operator.

Since this particular neuroevolutionary feature is part of the evolutionary strategies, we add it to the evolutionary strategy mutator list, which we created earlier:

```
-define(ES_MUTATORS,[
    mutate_tuning_selection,
    mutate_tuning_duration,
    mutate_tuning_annealing,
    mutate_tot_topological_mutations,
    mutate_heredity_type
]).
```

With this final modification, our neuroevolutionary system can now fully employ plasticity, and two types of heredity inheritance methods. We now finally compile, and test our updated system on the T-Maze Navigation problem we developed in the previous chapter.

15.6 Compiling & Testing

Our TWEANN system can now evolve NNs with plasticity, which means the evolved agents do not simply have an evolved response/reflex to sensory signals, but can also change, adapt, learn, modify their strategies as they interact with the ever changing and dynamic world. Having added this feature, and having created the T-Maze Navigation problem which requires the NN to change its strategy as it interacts with the environment, we can now test the various plasticity rules to see whether the agents will be able to achieve a fitness of 149.2, a fitness score achieved when the agent can gather the highest reward located in the right corner, and then when sensing that the reward is now not 1 but 0.2 in the right corner, start moving to the left corner to continue gathering the highest reward.

Having so significantly modified the records and the various modules, we reset the mnesia database after recompiling the modules. To do this, we first execute polis:sync(), then polis:reset(), and then finally polis:start() to startup the polis process. We have created numerous plasticity learning rules: [hebbian_w, hebbian, ojas_w, ojas, self_modulationV1, self_modulationV2, self_modulationV3, self_modulationV4, self_modulationV5, self_modulationV6, neuromodulation], too many to show the console printouts of. Here I will show you the results I achieved while benchmarking the *hebbian_w* and the *hebbian* learning rules, and I highly recommend testing the other learning rules by using the provided source code in the supplementary material.

To run the benchmarks, we first modify the ?INIT_CONSTRAINTS in the benchmarker module, setting the constraint's parameter: *neural_pfns,* to one of these plasticity rules for every benchmark. We can leave the *evaluations_limit* in the *pmp* record as 5000, but in the experiments I've performed, I set the population limit to 20 rather than 10, to allow for a greater diversity. The following are the results I achieved when running the experiments for the hebbian_w and the hebbian plasticity based benchmarks:

T-Maze Navigation with neural_pfns=[hebbian_w]:

```
Graph:{graph,discrete_tmaze,
        [1.1185328852434115,1.1619749686158354,1.1524569668377718,
        1.125571504518873,1.1289114832535887,1.1493175172780439,
        1.136998936735779,1.151456292245766,1.1340011357153639,
        1.1299993522129745],
        [0.0726690757747553,0.08603433346506212,0.07855604082593783,
        0.10142838037124464,0.07396159578145513,0.10671412852082847,
        0.07508707481514428,0.09451139923220694,0.10140517337683815,
        0.07774940615923569],
        [91.76556804891021,101.28562704890575,111.38602998360439,
        110.65857974481669,110.16398032961199,111.09056977671462,
        110.92899944938112,110.89051253132838,115.36595268212,
```

```
        111.07567142455073],
        [14.533256849468248,13.058657299854085,10.728855341054617,
        10.993110357580642,10.14374645989871,8.753610288273324,
        8.392536182954592,7.795296190771122,5.718415463002469,
        8.367092075873826],
        [122.0000000000001,122.0000000000001,148.4,149.2,149.2,149.2,
        149.2,149.2,149.2,149.2],
        [10.000000000000115,10.000000000000115,10.000000000000115,
        10.000000000000115,10.000000000000115,10.000000000000115,
        10.000000000000115,10.000000000000115,10.000000000000115,
        10.000000000000115],
        [11.45,14.3,15.3,15.8,15.3,16.15,16.15,15.55,15.95,15.7],
        [1.5321553446044565,2.451530134426253,2.1702534414210706,
        2.541653005427767,2.2825424421026654,2.7253440149823285,
        2.127792283095321,2.0118399538730714,2.246664193866097,
        2.0273134932713295],
        [500.0,500.0,500.0,500.0,500.0,500.0,500.0,500.0,500.0,500.0],
        []}
Tot Evaluations Avg:5172.95 Std:103.65301491032471
```

The boldfaced list shows the maximum achieved scores from all the evolutionary runs, and this time through plasticity, the score of 149.2 was achieved, implying our TWEANN's ability to solve the T-Maze navigation problem in under 2000 evaluationss (by the 4th of the 500th evaluations set).

T-Maze Navigation with neural_pfns=[hebbian]:

```
Graph:{graph,discrete_tmaze,
        [1.1349113313586998,1.1720830155097892,1.1280659983291563,
        1.1155462519936203,1.1394258373205741,1.1293439592742998,
        1.1421323920317727,1.1734812130593864,1.1750255550524766,
        1.2243932469319467],
        [0.07930932911768754,0.07243567080038446,0.0632406890972406,
        0.05913247338612391,0.07903341129827642,0.07030745338352402,
        0.09215871275247499,0.09666623776054033,0.1597898002580627,
        0.2447504142533042],
        [90.66616594516601,97.25899378881999,104.36751796157071,
        105.0985582137162,106.70360792131855,108.09892415530814,
        108.23839098414494,109.28814527629243,108.0643063975331,
        111.0103593241125],
        [15.044059269853784,13.919179099169385,10.613477213673535,
        13.557400867791436,13.380234103652047,12.413686820724935,
        11.936102929326337,11.580780191261242,12.636714964991167,
        12.816711475442705],
        [122.0000000000001,147.8,145.60000000000002,149.2,149.2,149.2,
```

         149.2,149.2,149.2,149.2],
          [10.000000000000115,10.000000000000115,10.000000000000115,
           10.000000000000115,10.000000000000115,10.000000000000115,
           10.000000000000115,10.000000000000115,10.000000000000115,
           10.000000000000115],
          [11.05,12.2,12.3,12.85,13.35,14.25,14.35,15.3,15.4,14.9],
          [1.6271140095272978,2.6381811916545836,2.215851980616034,
           1.7399712641305316,1.7399712641305318,2.2332711434127295,
           1.9817921182606415,2.0760539492026697,1.9078784028338913,
           2.046948949045872],
          [500.0,500.0,500.0,500.0,500.0,500.0,500.0,500.0,500.0,500.0],
          []}
Tot Evaluations Avg:5145.65 Std:91.87234349900953

In this case, our TWEANN again was able to solve the T-Maze problem. Plastic NN based agents do indeed have the ability to solve the T-Maze problem which requires the agents to change their strategy as they interact with the maze which changes midway. Our TWEANN is now able to evolve such plastic NN based agents, our TWEANN can now evolve agents that can learn new things as they interact with the environment, that can change their behavioral strategies based on their experience within the environment.

15.7 Summary & Discussion

Though we have tested only two of the numerous plasticity learning rules we've implemented, they both produced success. In both cases our TWEANN platform has been able to evolve NN based agents capable of solving the T-Maze problem, which was not solvable by our TWEANN in the previous chapter without plasticity. Thus we have successfully tested our plasticity rule implementations, and the new performance capabilities of our TWEANN. Outside this text I have tested the learning rules which were not tested above, and they are also capable of solving this problem, with varying performance levels. All of this without us having even optimized our algorithms yet.

With this benchmark complete, we have now finished developing numerous plasticity learning rules, implementing the said algorithms, and then benchmarking their performance. Our TWEANN system has finally been able to solve the T-Maze problem which requires the agents to change their strategy. Our TWEANN platform can now evolve not only complex topologies, but NN systems which can learn and adapt. Our system can now evolve thinking neural network based agents. There is nothing stopping us from producing more complex and more biologically faithful plasticity based learning rules, which would further improve the capabilities and potential of the types of neural networks our TWEANN system can evolve.

With the plasticity now added, our next step is to add a completely different NN encoding, and thus further advance our TWEANN system. In the next chapter we will allow our TWEANN platform to evolve not only the standard encoded NN based agents we've been using up to this point, but also the new indirect encoded type of NN systems, the substrate encoded NN based systems.

15.8 References

[1] Oja E (1982) A Simplified Neuron model as a Principal Component Analyzer. Journal of Mathematical Biology 15, 267-273.
[2] Soltoggio A, Bullinaria JA, Mattiussi C, Durr P, Floreano D (2008) Evolutionary Advantages of Neuromodulated Plasticity in Dynamic, Reward-based Scenarios. Artificial Life 2, 569-576.
[3] Blynel J, Floreano D (2003) Exploring the T-maze: Evolving Learning-Like Robot Behaviors using CTRNNs. Applications of evolutionary computing 2611, 173-176.
[4] Whitley LD, Gordon VS, Mathias KE (1994) Lamarckian Evolution, The Baldwin Effect and Function Optimization. In Parallel Problem Solving From Nature - PPSN III, Y. Davidor and H. P. Schwefel, eds. (Springer), pp. 6-15.
[5] Julstrom BA (1999) Comparing Darwinian, Baldwinian, and Lamarckian Search in a Genetic Algorithm For The 4-Cycle Problem. In Late Breaking Papers at the 1999 Genetic and Evolutionary Computation Conference, S. Brave and A. S. Wu, eds., pp. 134-138.
[6] Castillo PA, Arenas MG, Castellano JG, Merelo JJ, Prieto A, Rivas V, Romero G (2006) Lamarckian Evolution and the Baldwin Effect in Evolutionary Neural Networks. CoRR abs/cs/060, 5.
[7] Esparcia-Alcazar A, Sharman K (1999) Phenotype Plasticity in Genetic Programming: A Comparison of Darwinian and Lamarckian Inheritance Schemes. In Genetic Programming Proceedings of EuroGP99, R. Poli, P. Nordin, W. B. Langdon, and T. C. Fogarty, eds. (Springer-Verlag), pp. 49-64.

Chapter 16 Substrate Encoding

Abstract In this chapter we augment our TWEANN to also evolve indirect encoded NN based systems. We discuss, architect, and implement substrate encoding. Substrate encoding allows for the evolved NN based systems to become geometrical-regularity sensitive with regards to sensory signals. We extend our existing genotype encoding method and give it the ability to encode both, neural and substrate based NNs. We then extend the exoself to map the extended genotype to the extended phenotype capable of supporting substrate encoded NN systems. Finally, we modify the genome mutator module to support new, substrate NN specific mutation operators, and then test the system on our previously developed benchmarking problems.

With all the main features of a neuroevolutionary system complete, and with our TWEANN system now able to evolve learning networks, we can now move forward and add some of the more elaborate features to our platform. In this chapter we will modify our TWEANN platform to evolve substrate encoded NN systems, which we briefly discussed in Section-4.1.3, and again in Chapter-10.

In indirect encoded NN systems, the genotype and phenotype do not have a 1-to-1 mapping. *Substrate Encoding* is one of such indirect encoding methods. As we discussed in Chapter-10, and as was shown in a number of relatively recently published papers [2,3,4], it has numerous advantages, particularly when it comes to generalization, image analysis based problems, and problems with geometrical regularities. Substrate encoding allows us to build substrate modules whose embedded interconnected neurodes and their very connections and synaptic weights are defined by a directly encoded NN system. Thus by evolving a NN, we are evolving a system which accepts as input the coordinates of the substrate embedded neurodes and outputs/paints the topology, synaptic weights, connection expression patterns, and other connectivity parameters on the multidimensional substrate. In this chapter we implement the extension to our system so that it can evolve such substrate encoded NN based agents.

Though having already discussed the manner in which substrate encoding works in Chapter-10, in the next section we will cover it in a greater detail. Afterwards, we will implement this indirect encoding system, and then test it on the T-Maze problem.

G.I. Sher, *Handbook of Neuroevolution Through Erlang*,   661
DOI 10.1007/978-1-4614-4463-3_16, © Springer Science+Business Media New York 2013

16.1 A Brief Overview of Substrate Encoding

Substrate encoding was popularized by the HyperNEAT [2] neuroevolutionary system. Though simple, it is a new approach in the effort of trying to reduce the *curse of dimensionality problem* (number of variables to evolve and deal with, as the size of the NN system increases). In this encoding method, it is not the directly evolved neural network that processes the incoming signals from the sensors, and outputs signals to the actuators to interact with the world, but instead it is the neurode impregnated multidimensional substrate that interacts with the environment. A substrate is simply a hypercube with every axis ranging from -1 to 1. Within the hypercube are neurodes, as shown in Fig-16.1. The neurodes are embedded in this multidimensional space, and thus each has its own coordinate. Furthermore, the neurodes are connected to each other in some particular pattern, and thus the substrate represents a neural network. The trick here is that we do not have to evolve the neurode connectivity patterns or the synaptic weights between them, instead it is the evolved NN that sets up the synaptic weights and connectivity expression for the neurodes within the substrate. Thus, even if we have a 3d substrate containing millions of neurodes, heavily interconnected with each other, we might still only have a few dozen neurons in the NN that sets up the synaptic weights between the neurodes within the substrate. This is accomplished by feeding the NN the coordinates of the connected neurodes within the substrate, and with this NN's resulting output being used to set the synaptic weights between those connected neurodes. Thus, no matter how many millions of interconnected neurodes are within the substrate, we're still only evolving a few interconnected neurons within the direct encoded NN. Of course the greater the number of the neurons within the NN, the more complex a connection and synaptic weight pattern that it can paint on this multidimensional substrate.

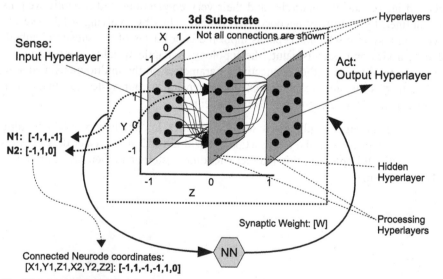

Fig. 16.1 A multidimensional substrate with embedded neurodes, connected in a feedforward, hyperlayer-to-hyperlayer fashion.

****Note****

In HyperNEAT the NN is referred to as a CPNN (Compositional Pattern Producing Network), due to the fact that the NEAT [5] neuroevolutionary system only evolves NNs which use the tanh activation function, while the CPNN evolved in HyperNEAT uses other activation functions as well. This terminology need not apply to other Neuroevolutionary systems whose neurons use various types of activation functions as a standard, and also when used with substrate encoding. Since our evolved NNs use different types of activation functions in general, we need not distinguish between the evolved NNs during direct encoding, and the evolved NNs during indirect encoding used for the purpose of painting the connectivity patterns on the substrate. This terminology would in particular be difficult to use if we were to evolve modular neural network systems, with interconnected substrate encoded modules, direct encoded modules, and other programs. Thus, because there is really no difference between the NNs used on their own and those used with substrates, we will simply refer to them as NNs. The NNs are simply being used for different purposes. In the direct encoded approach the NN is being applied to the problem directly. In the substrate encoded approach, the NN is being applied to set up the synaptic weights of the neurodes embedded in the substrate, which is applied to the problem. I will refer to the neurons embedded in the substrate, as neurodes.

****

As was shown in the above figure, we can thus feed to the NN an appended list of the coordinates of any two connected neurodes, and use the NN's output as the synaptic weight between those neurodes. In this manner we can calculate the synaptic weights between all connected neurodes in the substrate, whether there are ten or ten million neurodes, as long as we have the coordinates of those neurodes. Because the NN is now dealing with the coordinates, the length of the input vector to the NN is thus at most $2*SubstrateDimensionality$, which alleviates problems associated with extremely large NN input vectors. It is the substrate that processes the input vectors, and produces the output. Another important feature is that due to the NN dealing with coordinates, the system becomes sensitive to the geometrical regularities within the input, and allows us to set up the substrate's geometry which can further emulate the geometrical features of the problem we wish to solve. If the input to the substrate is such that there is geometrical data in it (For example an image from a camera), and it can be exploited, this type of encoding is much more suited to this data's analysis than a directly encoded NN.

The next question is of course: In what manner are the neurodes within the substrate connected; what is the substrate's topology? And how do we forward data from the sensors to the substrate, and use the output produced by the substrate to control the actuators? These two questions are related because both, the input to the substrate and the output from the substrate, are parts of the substrate's topology, as will be explained next.

The most common substrates are standard hypercubes where each hyperplane is connected to the one ahead of it. Consider a 3d substrate, a cube, as was shown in Fig-16.1. A hyperplane to hyperplane feedforward topology, where the hyperplane's dimension is one less than the dimensionality of the entire substrate, is such that all the neurodes in the hyperplane are connected in a feedforward fashion to all the neurodes in the next hyperplane, with the synaptic weights between the connected neurodes decided by the NN. Another substrate topology is where all the neurodes in the substrate are interconnected, and again the NN decides the synaptic weights between the neurodes. But we can also allow the NN to output not just the synaptic weight for the coordinates used as input to the NN, but also whether or not the neurons are at all connected. In this manner the topology is no longer set ahead of time, and instead it is the NN that decides which neurodes are connected, and with what synaptic weights (rather than just deciding on the synaptic weights between the feedforward connected neurodes). Fig-16.2a shows a hyperplane-to-hyperplane Jordan recurrent (The last plane outputs signals back to the first plane) substrate where the NN uses the coordinates between any two neurodes to output the synaptic weights between them. On the other hand, Fig-16.2b shows a substrate full of neurodes, where the NN decides both on the connectivity expression between all the neurodes, and the synaptic weights between those that are indeed connected.

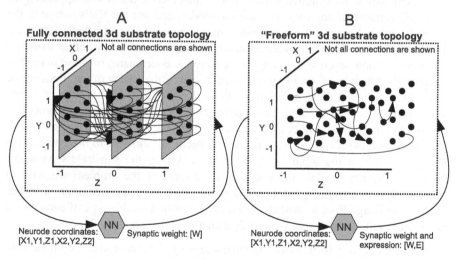

Fig. 16.2 A hyperlayer-to-hyperlayer fully connected substrate topology, and a "freeform" substrate topology. In A, the NN uses as input the coordinates of every two connected neurodes of different planes, while in B the NN outputs a vector length of 2, a synaptic weight and whether the synaptic connection is expressed, for every two neurode combination in the whole substrate.

Though usually the neurodes are equidistantly spaced within the substrate (in case of freeform), it need not be the case. For example, we can just as easily randomly pepper the hypercube with neurodes, and then use the NN to decide whether and which neurodes are connected, and what the synaptic weights between the connected neurodes is. Indeed at times it might be better to even use a mutation operator which randomly adds and subtracts neurodes to and from the substrate respectively, and thus overtime evolves a substrate with different neurode density zones, and thus different signal sensitivity and specialization zones.

****Note****

A hyperlayer is a group of neurodes all belonging to the same, most external coordinate, and thus forming a structure which is one dimension lower than the full substrate itself. If the substrate is 5d (x,y,z,a,b), then the hyperlayer is 4d, with each separate hyperlayer on its own b coordinate. If the substrate is 3d (x,y,z), then the hyperlayer is 2d, with each hyperlayer on its own z coordinate. Furthermore, I will use the term *hyperplane* to designate the planes composing the hyperlayer, forming structures one dimension lower than the hyperlayers. This will make more sense as new substrate topologies are shown. For example, multiple hyperplanes, where each designates a separate sensor, can then form a single input hyperlayer of a substrate. Similarly, multiple hyperplanes of the output hyperlayer, would each be associated with a particular actuator. This terminology will allow us to discuss the substrates, evolving substrates, and connectivity between the substrate and the sensors and actuators, much more easily.

****

Given all these substrate topologies, how do we present the sensory data to them? Since for the neurodes to have a synaptic weight for an incoming signal, the origin of that signal too must have a coordinate, the sensory signal output zone must somehow be located within the substrate. For example assume that the input is an image, and the substrate is 3d, with a standard feedforward topology, with 3 hyperlayers in total, with the hyperlayers located at $Z = -1$, $Z = 0$, and $Z = 1$, and with the hyperlayer-to-hyperlayer feedforward connections going from $Z = -1$ towards $Z = 1$. One way we can allow for the sensory image to also have coordinates, is by positioning it as the input hyperlayer at $Z = -1$. The pixels then would have coordinates, and the pixel's color can then be mapped to floating point values. In this manner the image can be used as an input to the substrate encoded NN. The NN can then produce the synaptic weights for the neurodes in the hyperlayer located at $Z = 0$ because the NN would now have the coordinates of both, the neurodes in the hyperlayer at $Z = 0$, and the sensory signal producers (the image pixels) of the hyperlayer at $Z = -1$, which is connected to the neurodes at $Z = 0$. This type of setup is shown in Fig-16.3.

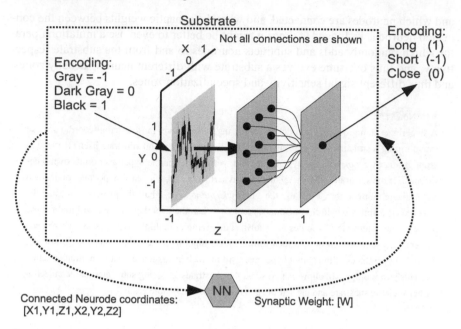

Fig. 16.3 The image being used as the input hyperlayer of the substrate.

We can also designate the neurodes in the last hyperlayer, or neurodes located at Z = -1, as the output neurodes. We would then use the output of the neurodes in the output hyperlayer, as the output signals to control the actuators. It is completely up to the researcher what combination of output neurodes is designated to control which actuators. For example in the above figure, the input hyperlayer is the image, which in this case is a financial instrument price chart, and the output hyperlayer is composed of a single neurode. And this neurode's output is then used to control some actuator. In comparison to the above figure, in Fig-16.1 the output hyperlayer had 9 neurodes. It is up to us when creating the substrate and tagging the output hyperlayer, whether all 9 neurodes are used as signals for a single actuator, or whether there are 3 actuators and each 3 neurode hyperplane within the output hyperlayer is associated with its own actuator. Fig-16.4 shows two 3d substrates, both using the same topology, but one has designated all the neurodes in the output hyperlayer to be used for a single actuator whose input vector length is 9, while in the second substrate the output hyperlayer is broken up into 3 layers, and each 3 neurode hyperplane is designated for a different actuator.

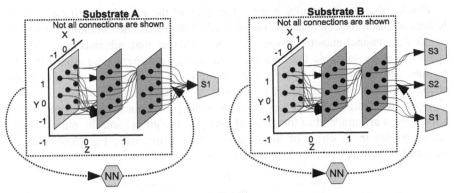

Fig. 16.4 Two 3d substrates of the same topology, using different number of actuators through some output-neurode/actuator designation method. Substrate A has designated all the neurodes in its output hyperlayer to be associated with a single actuator, while substrate B has separated the 9 neurodes into 3 groups, each group associated with its own actuator.

In the same fashion, a substrate can have multiple sensors associated with its input hyperlayer. For example we could use a four dimensional substrate, where the input hyperlayer is 3 dimensional, and is composed of 2 or more 2d hyperplanes, where each hyperplane is an image fed from a camera. Fig-16.5 shows just such an arrangement, where the 3d input hyperlayer uses sensors which produce chart images of possibly differing resolutions, and using different technical indicators.

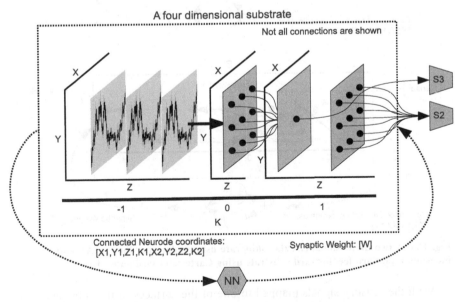

Fig. 16.5 Four dimensional substrate with multiple sensors and actuators.

Finally, the dimensionality and the topology of the substrate itself can vary. It is dependent on the problem and on the goal of the researcher whether to use 1, 5, or 20 dimensional substrate hypercube, and whether that substrate is cuboid, or spherical. If for example the data being analyzed has spherical geometrical regularities, perhaps it would be best to paint the input hyperlayer on the spherically shaped substrate, and use spherical coordinates rather than Cartesian. Fig-16.6a shows a 2d substrate of polar topology and using polar coordinates, where the sensory signals are mapped to the circumference of the circle, and the output is produced by the inner circle of the substrate. For comparison, Fig-16.6b shows a standard 2d substrate, with a layer to layer feedforward topology.

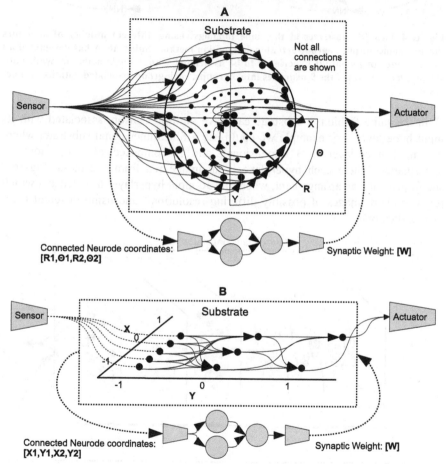

Fig. 16.6 A two dimensional circular substrate using polar coordinates (A), and a two dimensional standard feedforward substrate using Cartesian coordinates (B).

With the sensory signals mapped to one of the surfaces of the substrate, or internal structures, or geometries of the substrate, and the output signals produced by any of the neurodes within the substrate tagged for such a job, there is an enormous amount of flexibility in such an encoded system. Because NNs are universal function approximators, it is theoretically feasible to evolve any type of synaptic weight and connectivity pattern within the substrate. Indeed, consider a 3d PET (Positron Emission Tomography) scan of the brain, which outlines the metabolic activity of the same. Would it be possible for a complex enough NN to paint such an activity pattern within a 3d substrate? The sensory signals for such a substrate could be mapped to a few internal structures within it (perhaps the 3d structures similar to optical nerves...), and its output extracted from the neurodes along a 3d structure which outputs signals to be forwarded down a simulated spinal cord... But why be limited to simulating the activity patterns at the resolution of a PET scan, how about the activity patterns at an even greater detailed? Indeed, we will eventually, with a substrate dense enough and a NN complex enough, should be able to achieve producing activity patterns of the same granularity as the biological brain.

Furthermore, why be limited to 3d topologies, why not 4d, or 10d? There is certainly an enormous amount of things left to explore in direct and indirect encoded NN based systems. There is an enormous amount exploration and experimentation, still beyond the horizon, which will yield new and certainly incredible results. We start off in this direction in the next section, in which we will discuss methods of how to represent such a substrate in our TWEANN system.

16.2 The Updated Architecture of Our NN Based Systems

To implement substrate encoding we need to figure out a way to represent it within the genotype in such a way that we can then map it to phenotype in a manner that will meld well with our TWEANN system. We would also prefer that the genotype has at least the following features:

- The representation must allow us to specify any number of sensors and actuators, allow us to use mutation operators to add new sensors and actuators through evolution, and for the substrate to have any number of dimensions.
- The phenotype should be representable as a single process. Thus this entire substrate, no matter how many dimensions and how many neurodes belong to it, should have the genotype that can easily be mapped to this single process based phenotype.
- The genotype should allow us to easily represent at least the standard set of substrate topologies: hyperlayer-to-hyperlayer (HtH) feedforward, fully connected, and Jordan recurrent (HtH topology where the output hyperlayer of the substrate is used as part of its input hyperlayer).
- Finally, the encoding must be simple enough so that we can easily work with it, and extend it in the future.

These requirements were not chosen arbitrarily, they represent what is necessary for our substrate encoded system to provide all the features of the bleeding edge and beyond, of today's substrate encoded systems. What other systems do not provide, and ours will, is for our substrate to have the ability to integrate new sensors and actuators into itself through evolution. The architecture of a substrate encoded agent is diagrammed in Fig-16.7.

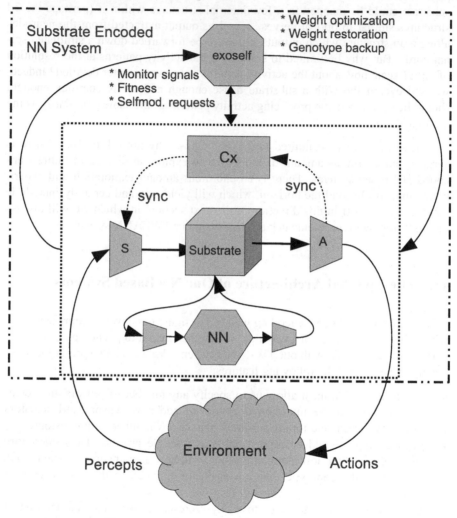

Fig. 16.7 The architecture of a substrate encoded NN based agent.

What's important to notice in this architecture is that now the sensors and actuators are used by the substrate. Whereas the NN is used for the substrate synaptic weight and connectivity pattern generation and setup. In the standard encoding, neural encoding, the NN is the one that polls the environment using its sensors, and then acts upon the environment using its actuators. But now that it is being used by the substrate, and the substrate only needs to use the NN to set or update its synaptic weights, the NN is no longer the driver behind the use of sensors and actuators. Instead, the NN is now being simply used by the substrate, being fed neurode coordinates, and producing synaptic weights and other parameters that the substrate uses.

In Chapter-10 we discussed how DXNN uses various coordinate preprocessors before they are fed to the NN, which allows the NN to use not just the Cartesian coordinates, but also evolve other preprocessors such as the: polar coordinates, spherical coordinates, neurode distance to substrate center, synaptic connection length... These coordinate preprocessors preprocess the standard Cartesian coordinates before feeding the resulting vector to the NN. Thus the NN can use combinations of these, and therefore have the ability to extract and be aware of more geometrical regularities, and produce more complex synaptic weight and connectivity patterns. But should we represent these preprocessors and postprocessors which the NN will use to feed the resulting synaptic weights and connectivity expression to the substrate, using some new set of elements like the sensors and actuators? Or should the substrate keep track of which neurons in the NN will get what signals, and which neurons should produce which outputs?

For example, we could allow the substrate to simply keep track which neurons should be fed which types of signals and through the use of which types of coordinate processors, and also from which neurons it, the substrate, should await the synaptic weight signals and connectivity expression signals. This is the way DXNN is implemented, where the substrate deals directly with the NN. Because it is the substrate that is in the driving seat, using and polling the NN, rather than the other way around, it is an effective implementation. But the system we are developing here is different enough that it would be easier for us to create a new set of elements, similar to sensors and actuators but dedicated to substrate based coordinate preprocessing and connectivity expression setting. These elements will be similar enough to sensors and actuators, such that we will be able to reuse their mutation operators for adding and integrating new such elements into a substrate encoded NN. Thus our design will follow the architecture shown in the above figure, where the substrate will poll the *substrate_cpp*/s (Substrate Coordinate Pre-Processor), and then wait for the signals from the *substrate_cep*/s (Substrate Connectivity Expression Producer) process, which will tell it what the synaptic weight is between the two neurodes with which the substrate_cpps were called with, and whether the connection between these neurodes is expressed or not. This approach should give our system an excellent amount of flexibility and scalability in the future.

So then, we will create two new process types: substrate_cpp and substrate_cep. These will be analogous to the sensors and actuators respectively, but driven and polled by the substrate when it wishes to calculate the synaptic weights and connectivity expression between its various neurodes. The substrate will forward to its one or more substrate_cpps the coordinates of the two connected neurodes in question, the called substrate_cpp will process those coordinates based on its type (If *cartesian* type for example, then simply leaving it as Cartesian coordinates and simply fanning out the vector to the neurons in the NN. If another type, then converting the coordinates to *polar, spherical,* or some other vector form first...), and forward the processed vector to the NN. The substrate will then wait for the signals from its one or more substrate_ceps, which will provide it with the various signals which the substrate will then use to set its synaptic weights, connectivity expressions, or even plasticity based synaptic weight updates (as will be discussed in the next chapter). The substrate will use its substrate_cpps and substrate_ceps for every synaptic weight/expression it wishes to set or update. Unlike the sensors and actuators, the substrate_cpps and substrate_ceps will not need to sync up with the cortex because the substrate_cpps will be triggered by the substrate, and because the signals from substrate_ceps will be awaited by the substrate, and since the substrate itself only processes signals once it has received all the sensory signals from the sensors which themselves are triggered by the cortex, the whole system will be synchronized.

Having now decided on the architecture, and representation of the substrate and its substrate_cpps and substrate_ceps as independent processes, it is time to come up with the way we will represent all of this within the genotype. We now need to create a genotype encoding.

16.3 The Genotype of the Substrate Encoded NN

We know how we want our substrate encoded NN system to function, but how do we represent a NN's genotype which is substrate encoded? If we were to give the substrate_cpp and substrate_cep their own records within the record.hrl file, they would have looked something like this:

```
-record(substrate_cpp,{id,name,substrate_id,vl,fanout_ids=[],generation,parameters, pre_f,
post_f}).
-record(substrate_cep,{id,name,substrate_id,vl,fanin_ids=[],generation,parameters, pre_f,
post_f}).
```

Let's go through each of the elements from the above records:

- **id**: This is the id of the substrate_cpp or substrate_cep.
- **name**: Similar to sensors and actuators, there will be different kinds of substrate_cpps and substrate_ceps, each with its own name.
- **substrate_id**: This element will hold the substrate's id, so that the substrate_cpp/subsrate_cep will know which process to wait for a signal from, or send its signal to respectively. This is a bit analogous to the scape id used by the sensors and actuators.

- **vl**: The vector length of the signal the process substrate_cpp/substrate_cep is certified to deal with.
- **fanout_ids**: The same as for the sensors, the list of element ids to which this substrate_cpp will forward vector signals.
- **fanin_ids**: The same as for the actuators, the list of element ids from which the substrate_cep expects to receive the signals.
- **generation**: This element keeps track of the generation during which the element was added to the NN, or last affected by a mutation.
- **parameters**: At some point it might be useful to also specify parameters to further modify how the particular substrate_cpp/substrate_cep pre or post processes the signal vectors respectively.
- **post_f**: The signal postprocessing function name, if any, used by the substrate_cpp/substrate_cep process.

Thus these two elements are basically shorter versions of the sensor and actuator elements, specializing in substrate signal pre- and post- processing. There is a large number of similarities between the sensors/actuators, and cpps/ceps respectively... And so it might be worth further consideration of whether we should give substrate_cpps and substrate_ceps their own records, or whether perhaps we should somehow modify the sensor and actuator records to allow them to be dual purpose... We will get back to this issue in just a short while; but now we finally get to the main questions of how we will represent the substrate topology.

We do not need to make our substrates hyperspheres, toroids, or possess any other type of exotic topology, because we can use substrate_cpps and substrate_ceps which will be able to convert the standard coordinates to spherical, polar, toroidal... which means we can use a standard Cartesian hypercube topology, and if the researcher or the problem requires that the input hyperplanes and output hyperplanes have spherical or toroidal or some other topology, we can position the hyperplanes within the hypercube in the preferred coordinates, and use the appropriate substrate_cpps to emulate the chosen exotic topology. Since our substrates will be hypercubes, and we will want to support at least the hyperlayer-to-hyperlayer feedforward topologies and fully connected topologies, we could implement the topology specification using a layer density list: Densities = [H...,Y,X], where the first element in the list specifies the depth of the hidden (non input or output) processing hyperlayers, shown in Fig-16.8. The rest of the elements within the Densities list specify the densities of the hidden processing hyperlayers. We can think of H as specifying the number of hyperlayers between the Input_Hyperlayer and the Output_Hyperlayer. The following figure shows 2d and 3d examples, with multiple densities. What should be further noted from the substrate diagrams is that the signals coming from the sensors are *not sent to the input hyperlayers, they **are** input hyperlayers*. In substrate encoded systems, the sensory signals acquire geometrical properties, positions, coordinates... so that the processing hyperlayers can have the synaptic weights calculated for the signals coming from those sensory coordinates. It is because we give the sensors their coordinates, which can reflect real world coordinates, (for example the actual position of the cameras on a cuboid robot, in which case the coordinates of the sensory signals would reflect the actual coordinates of where the signals are coming from on the robot's body) that this approach offers the substrate encoded NN based agent geometrical sensitivity, and allows for the system to take advantage of geometrical regularities in the sensory signals. Similar is the case for the substrate's output hyperlayers. The neurodes of the output hyperlayers can have any coordinates, and their coordinates may be geometrically significant to the way the signals are processed. For example the output hyperlayer neurodes might mimic the coordinates of the legs or wheels on some robot.

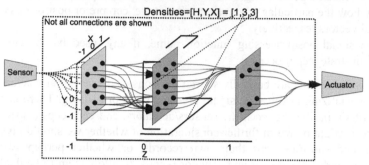

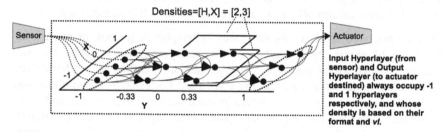

Fig. 16.8 Two examples of the substrate specification and architecture.

Now notice that this specification is Input Hyperlayer and Output_Hyperlayer blind. If for example the substrate is 3d: [Z,Y,X], then the input hyperlayer will always be located at Z = -1, and the output hyperlayer will always be located at Z = 1. The input hyperlayer represents the coordinate based plane where the sensory signals are presented to the substrate (since for neurodes to have synaptic weights, the substrate must give the sensors some kind of geometrical representation with coordinates). The output hyperlayer contains the neurodes whose output signals are gathered and used to control the actuators. The densities list specifies those in-between processing hyperlayers, and says nothing about the input or output hyperlayers.

So then, the Densities list represents the bulk of the substrate, the hidden processing hyperlayers of the substrate (though note that the output hyperlayer also processes signals, only the input hyperlayer does not, it only produces the signals). Since different sets of sensors and actuators will require different input and output hyperlayer structures, we calculate those geometrical structures and coordinates from the sensors & actuators live. We calculate how to compose the input and output hyperlayers based on the sensors/actuators, their types, their specified geometrical properties, if any, and their signal vector lengths.

As you remember, both the sensors and actuators had the element *format* within their records, we have finally reached the point where we can use it. It is this format element which will hold the geometrical information of that sensor or actuator. If for example the sensory signal is coming from a camera of resolution 500x500, we would specify this fact in the format element. If the NN is of type neural, then this has no meaning, it does not matter, and the vector fed to the NN, which in this case will be of size 500*500 = 250000, is fed directly as a single list of values. But if the NN is substrate encoded, then the input signal from this sensor is a 2d hyperplane with dimensions: 500x500. In this manner the evolved NNs can take advantage of any geometrical information, when specified.

There is a similar case when it comes to actuators. If a NN is of type *neural,* then the neurons simply forward their signals to the actuator and that is the end of that. But if the NN is of type *substrate,* and for example the output itself is an image of resolution 10x10, then we would like to have the output hyperplane destined for this actuator to be a 2d plane with dimensions 10x10, so that we can retain the geometrical properties of the actuator signal. This output signal of the output hyperplane would then be fed to the actuator. Using the *format* parameter means that the substrate will be able to take advantage of the geometrical properties associated with processing and generating images, and other geometry sensitive information, or anything that can better be handled when geometrical properties are taken into account.

So then, through the *Densities* list we can specify the general substrate properties, and the substrate specification is then completed based on the sensors and actuators used. If the sensors and actuators change, or more are added, or some are removed, it will in no way affect our system since it will be able to generate the new substrate by reading the Densities, and analyzing the new Sensor and Actuator list during the genotype to phenotype mapping. Two examples of Densities specified substrate, integrated with sensors and actuators which have their hyperlayers specified by their *format* and vl parameters, are shown in Fig-16.9.

In the below figure, the *format* element is specified through the tuple: {IHDTag, IHD}, where IHDTag stands for Input Hyperlayer Densities Tag, and IHD is Input Hyperlayer Densities. In the below figure there are two formats, the *no_geo* format (equivalent to an *undefined* format, which is simply a single dimensional vector), and the *{symmetric,IHD}* format. The *symmetric* tag specifies that the IHD uses a standard Densities format, and that the neurodes should use equidistant coordinates from each other in their respective dimensions.

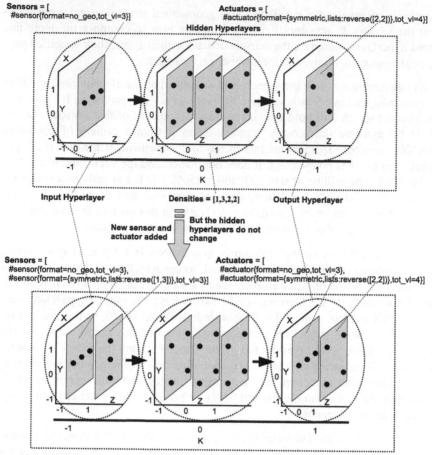

Fig. 16.9 Substrates created based on the Densities list and the sensors and actuators used by the substrate encoded NN system.

Having discussed all of this, consider now what happens when a researcher decides to use a morphology by a hypothetical name: *forex_trader*, which is a morphology of agents which trade currencies on the forex market. Some of the sensors in this morphology have a format which specify that the sensor outputs 2d images. All actuators on the other hand just accept simple unformatted signals from the output hyperlayer. There are multiple sensors in this morphology, each for its own technical indicator (a chart of closing prices, a chart for currency pair volume...). An agent which is allowed to evolve and connect to new sensors, will eventually have an input from at least two such 2d input planes (two charts). Combined, this input will be 3d, since each chart is 2d, and if we now give each one of them their own 3rd coordinate, the input hyperlayer is 3d. But if the researcher decided to have his entire substrate be 3d, which only allows 2d input hyperplanes, how can the substrate encoded NN acquire access to new sensors?

For this reason, though we will allow for the densities to be set by the research-er, the actual dimension of the substrate will be computed by the genotype con-structor function based on the morphology, and the formatting rules of its sensors and actuators. It will calculate the dimensionality of the substrate as follows:

1. Find the largest dimensionality specified in the format parameter of the sensors and actuators, and designate it as *MaxDimIOH*, which stands for Max Dimen-sionality of the Input/Output Hyperplanes. If a sensor or actuator does not spec-ify geometrical properties in its format variable, then we assume that it is single dimensional, and that the signal has a list form.
2. Because we want to allow the substrate encoded NN based system to evolve connections to multiple new sensors and actuators, it will be possible in the fu-ture for the substrate to be connected to multiple such MaxDimIOH hyperplanes. The way to put multiple such hyperplanes together, is to equidis-tantly space them out on another dimension. Thus we designate the IOHDim as MaxDimIOH+1, where IOHDim stands for Input/Output Hyperlayer Dimen-sion.
3. Finally, because the substrate must have depth as well, and the IOHDim hyperlayers should be able to connect to and be connected from the hidden pro-cessing hyperlayers (which themselves will at most be of dimensionality IOHDim), the final dimensionality of the substrate is: *SubstrateDim = IOHDim+1*, because we create a new dimension and then position the input hyperlayer at the -1, and the output hyperlayer at the 1 of this new dimension, with the hidden processing hyperlayers, if any, spaced out equidistantly be-tween -1 and 1.

The application of these 3 steps are shown in the creation of the substrate in Fig-16.10. In the below figure our *forex_trader* morphology based substrate en-coded NN has a single actuator which uses only a single dimension, since the evolved agent need only be able to produce a vector of length 1, which specifies if the agent wishes to go long, short, or hold its currently traded currency pair. The available sensors for this morphology have at most 2 dimensions. These 2d based sensors feed the substrate the image charts of various technical indicators. Thus, to allow the substrate to use multiple sensors and actuators, we need for the input and output hyperlayers to be of at least 3 dimensions. But because the substrate must have at least 2 such hyperlayers, one input and one output hyperlayer, we thus need to position these hyperlayers on another dimension. Thus the minimum di-mensionality of the entire substrate is 4. We can make the substrate have more than 4 dimensions if we believe the added dimensionality will increase the flexi-bility of the substrate, but we cannot use a substrate of a dimension less than 4 for this morphology, unless we will restrict the substrate encoded NN to use only a single sensor and a single actuator, at which point the minimum dimension would be 3, or unless we use a non hyperlayer-to-hyperlayer connection topology.

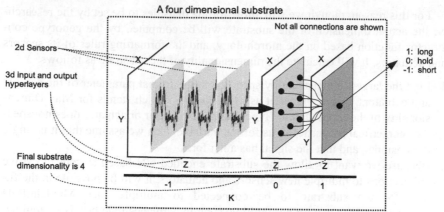

A four dimensional substrate

Not all connections are shown

2d Sensors

3d input and output
hyperlayers

Final substrate
dimensionality is 4

1: long
0: hold
-1: short

Max sensor dimensionality is 2, but using multiple sensors requires 3 dimensions.
Because there are at least 2 such hyperlayers (1 input hyperlayer, and 1 output
hyperlayer), the minimum dimensionality required by the substrate is 4.

Fig. 16.10 A four dimensional substrate composed by analyzing the morphology based sensor and actuator dimensionalities.

Certainly, we could of course encode everything on a two dimensional substrate if we wanted to. We could always try to simply aggregate all the signals together into a single vector, which would then represent a single dimensional input or output hyperplane. But then we would lose the geometrical information within those sensors and actuators. Thus the above approach is the most effective way to automatically set up hypercube substrates which will allow for the substrate encoded NNs to evolve, and have the ability to incorporate multiple sensors and actuators if needed.

So then, during the genotype creation we need only specify the Densities list for the hidden hyperlayer. The dimension of the substrate will depend on the analysis of the sensors and actuators of the NN system's morphology. We do not need to specify the weights or anything else within the genotype of the substrate encoded NN (SENN). During the mapping from genotype to phenotype, the connected sensors and actuators used by the NN system will be analyzed and the hyperlayers based on their properties will be composed, sandwiching any other hidden processing hyperlayers of the substrate, and thus producing the final substrate. Thus the way the substrate can be represented, is simply through the use of the *Densities* parameter and the Sensors and Actuators list.

But just having a way to represent the substrate is not enough. There is something beside the location of the neurodes within the substrate that we must specify. We must specify how the neurodes are interconnected. For example, we should be able to specify with a tag whether the substrate uses a hyperlayer-to-hyperlayer feedforward topology, or whether it uses a feedforward topology but where every neurode is also self recurrent, or perhaps where every hyperlayer is self recurrent... Since all of this will only matter in the phenotype, which we will discuss in the next section, in the genotype we can specify the substrate connectivity architecture using a single extra element: *linkform*. The element *linkform* should be able to take the values of: *l2l_feedforward, fully_connected, jordan_recurrent, freeform...* or any other type of architecture we decide on implementing.

To sum it all up, the new substrate encoded NN based genotype will need to keep track of the densities parameter, the list of substrate_cpps and substrate_ceps that the substrate has to communicate with, the plasticity of the substrate, the topology of the substrate (layer-to-layer, fully connected, jordan_recurrent, freeform...), with the sensors and actuators still being tracked by the cortex element. That is a lot of new parameters and lists to keep track of, which will be best done if we give the substrate its own element. Thus we add a new substrate record to the records.hrl. The new substrate element will have the following form:

```
-record(substrate, {
    id,
    agent_id,
    densities,
    linkform,
    plasticity=none,
    cpp_ids=[],
    cep_ids=[]
}).
```

Finally, because the substrate element will have its own id, we will need to add the element *substrate_id* to the agent record, so that it can keep track of this new element/process as well.

Having now discussed all the needed features to implement a substrate encoded NN based system: the new architecture, the representation of the substrate in the genotype, and the new coordinate processors and connectivity expression producers... The only thing left to decide on before we can move forward and begin the implementation of the said system, is what the substrate will look like in its phenotypic form, how will it process the signals from the input hyperlayer, and generate signals by its output hyperlayer. Thus the topic of our next section is the SENN's phenotypic representation.

16.4 The SENN Phenotype

We have the architecture, and we know how to specify the substrate topology, and even the type of substrate linkforms (l2l_feedforward, fully_connected, jordan_recurrent...), but how exactly do we represent it in its phenotypic form? How do we represent it as a single process so that it can actually process the sensory signals and produce outputs to control its actuators? How do we use the sensors, actuators, substrate_cpps, and substrate_ceps? In this section we will discuss the phenotype of our Substrate Encoded Neural Network (SENN) based system.

In the previous section we let the *format* element of the sensors and actuators have the following style: *format={Tag,HpD}*, where Tag is an atom which can further specify the formatting, and where HpD stands for Hyperplane Densities, which has a list form similar to the Densities, with the length of this list being the dimensionality of the signal.

Now let's assume that our genome constructor is creating a new SENN genotype, and is building a substrate that will from the start use 2 sensors and 2 actuators. What they do is not important and so they are simply named sensor1, sensor2, actuator1, and actuator2. These two sensors and actuators are as follows:

```
Sensors = [
    #sensor{name=sensor1,format=no_geo,tot_vl=3},
    #sensor{name=sensor2,format={symmetric,lists:reverse([2,3])},tot_vl=6}
]
Actuators = [
    #actuator{name=actuator1,format=no_geo,tot_vl=2},
    #actuator{name=actuator2,format={symmetric,lists:reverse([3,2])},tot_vl=6}
]
```

We see that the maximum dimensionality in the list of sensors and actuators is 2, and thus the substrate that will be created will be 4 dimensional. Let us also further suppose that we have specified the following substrate Densities: [1,3,2,2]. The dimensionality of the substrate is 4 as it should be. Depth is 1, so there will be one hidden processing hyperlayer, and it will be composed of three 2x2 layers. The input hyperlayer will be composed of 2 planes, the first is 1x3 associated with sensor1, and the second is 2x3, associated with sensor2. The 3d output hyperlayer will also be composed of 2 planes, the 1x2 plane of actuator1, and the 3x2 plane of actuator2. This is shown in the following figure.

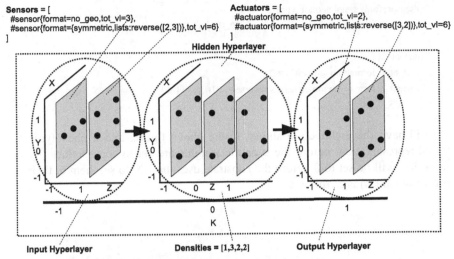

Sensors = [
#sensor{format=no_geo,tot_vl=3},
#sensor{format={symmetric,lists:reverse([2,3])}},tot_vl=6}
]

Actuators = [
#actuator{format=no_geo,tot_vl=2},
#actuator{format={symmetric,lists:reverse([3,2])}},tot_vl=6}
]

Hidden Hyperlayer

Input Hyperlayer   Densities = [1,3,2,2]   Output Hyperlayer

Fig. 16.11 Creating the phenotype based on sensors and actuators.

Note that no matter the densities, the neurodes should automatically be positioned equidistantly from each other, preferably as far from each other as possible. We do this because the further the neurodes are from each other, the more different their coordinates are from each other, and thus the NN which calculates the synaptic weights for each neurode pair will see a greater difference between every coordinate pair fed to it, allowing for a higher level of discernability between the various coordinate pairs.

Had our Densities specification had 0 for the depth, then there would only be the input and output hyperlayers present. So we now know what the phenotypes look like, for this, or for any other specified genotype. But how do we represent all these neurodes in phenotype form? And as noted, how do we effectively get them to process signals coming from the input hyperlayers?

Since all neurodes use the tanh activation function, we do not need to specify the AF for every neurode. Because in the standard l2l_feedforward substrate, every neurode in the substrate processes the signals coming from all the neurodes in the previous hyperlayer, we can represent the phenotype as a list of lists, using the following format: *[Hyperlayer1,Hyperlayer2...HyperlayerN]*, where N is the total number of hyperlayers, which is Depth+2 (total number of hidden processing hyperlayers, plus input and output hyperlayers). Each *Hyperlayer* in this list, is a list of tuples, where each tuple represents a neurode: *[{Coordinate, OutputSignal, SynapticWeights}...].*

So then, the phenotypic representation of a substrate using:

Densities=[1,3,2,2]
Sensors = [

```
    #sensor{format=no_geo,tot_vl=3},
    #sensor{format={symmetric,lists:reverse([2,3])},tot_vl=6}
]
Actuators = [
    #actuator{format=no_geo,tot_vl=2},
    #actuator{format={symmetric,lists:reverse([3,2])},tot_vl=6}
]
```

Will have the architecture shown in the above figure, and a phenotypic list based representation, before the synaptic weights are set to some values (by default they will be set to 0 before the substrate uses the NN to set them to their appropriate values) is as follows:

```
[[{[-1,-1,0,-1],0,void},
 {[-1,-1,0,0.0],0,void},
 {[-1,-1,0,1],0,void},
 {[-1,1,-1,-1],0,void},
 {[-1,1,-1,0.0],0,void},
 {[-1,1,-1,1],0,void},
 {[-1,1,1,-1],0,void},
 {[-1,1,1,0.0],0,void},
 {[-1,1,1,1],0,void}],
 [{[0,-1,-1,-1],0,[0,0,0,0,0,0,0,0,0]},
 {[0,-1,-1,1],0,[0,0,0,0,0,0,0,0,0]},
 {[0,-1,1,-1],0,[0,0,0,0,0,0,0,0,0]},
 {[0,-1,1,1],0,[0,0,0,0,0,0,0,0,0]},
 {[0,0.0,-1,-1],0,[0,0,0,0,0,0,0,0,0]},
 {[0,0.0,-1,1],0,[0,0,0,0,0,0,0,0,0]},
 {[0,0.0,1,-1],0,[0,0,0,0,0,0,0,0,0]},
 {[0,0.0,1,1],0,[0,0,0,0,0,0,0,0,0]},
 {[0,1,-1,-1],0,[0,0,0,0,0,0,0,0,0]},
 {[0,1,-1,1],0,[0,0,0,0,0,0,0,0,0]},
 {[0,1,1,-1],0,[0,0,0,0,0,0,0,0,0]},
 {[0,1,1,1],0,[0,0,0,0,0,0,0,0,0]}],
 [{[1,-1,0,-1],0,[0,0,0,0,0,0,0,0,0,0,0,0]},
 {[1,-1,0,1],0,[0,0,0,0,0,0,0,0,0,0,0,0]},
 {[1,1,-1,-1],0,[0,0,0,0,0,0,0,0,0,0,0,0]},
 {[1,1,-1,1],0,[0,0,0,0,0,0,0,0,0,0,0,0]},
 {[1,1,0.0,-1],0,[0,0,0,0,0,0,0,0,0,0,0,0]},
 {[1,1,0.0,1],0,[0,0,0,0,0,0,0,0,0,0,0,0]},
 {[1,1,1,-1],0,[0,0,0,0,0,0,0,0,0,0,0,0]},
 {[1,1,1,1],0,[0,0,0,0,0,0,0,0,0,0,0,0]}]]
```

I highlighted each hyperlayer with a different color. The hyperlayer at K = -1, the input hyperlayer, is highlighted green (if you're reading the black & white printed version, it's the first block). The hyperlayer at K = 0, the hidden processing hyperlayer, is highlighted blue (the second block). And the processing output hyperlayer at K = 1, is highlighted red (the third block). Note that the input hyperlayer has the atom void for its synaptic weights list, this is because there are no synaptic weights, since this hyperlayer represents the sensors, it only produces signals. The coordinates are inverted, rather than having the format: [X,Y,Z,K], they have the form: [K,Z,Y,X], which makes it easier to see the the separate hyperlayers. This list of lists is composed of tuples, the tuples have the following format:*{NeurodeCoordinate, OutputSignal, SynapticWeights}*. The NeurodeCoordinate is the actual coordinate of the neurode that this tuple represents. Every tuple represents a neurode, and the OutputSignal is what that neurode's output signal is. Thus, if you are looking at a l2l_feedforward substrate at any given time, the neurode's OutputSignal is actually the neurode's previous OutputSignal, because this value is calculated for it on the fly and is then immediately used as an input signal by the neurodes in the next hyperlayer. The calculation of each neurode's output is performed by our algorithm, which processes the input signals (the OutputSignals of the neurodes in the previous hyperlayer) for this neurode, and calculates this neurode's output signal by the application of the activation function tanh to the accumulated signal sum, without bias. The element: *SynapticWeights*, is a list of synaptic weights, set by querying the NN with the coordinates of this neurode, and the coordinates of all its presynaptic neurodes. Since the synaptic weights have an order in the list, and the neurode representing tuples also have a static order in the substrate, there is an implicit correlation between the synaptic weights within the SynapticWeights list, and the neurodes in the previous hyperlayer, as long as one does not change the order of either list, they will match.

Before we discuss how layer to layer feedforward processing can be efficiently implemented using this encoding once the synaptic weights are set, let's first take a closer look at each list represented hyperlayer. Starting with the input hyperlayer which was created by analyzing the sensors:

```
Sensors = [
    #sensor{format=no_geo,tot_vl=3},
    #sensor{format={symmetric,lists:reverse([2,3])},tot_vl=6}
]:

[{[-1,-1,0,-1],0,void},
 {[-1,-1,0,0.0],0,void},
 {[-1,-1,0,1],0,void},
 {[-1,1,-1,-1],0,void},
 {[-1,1,-1,0.0],0,void},
 {[-1,1,-1,1],0,void},
 {[-1,1,1,-1],0,void},
 {[-1,1,1,0.0],0,void},
 {[-1,1,1,1],0,void}]
```

The first coordinate, K, is -1 as it should be, since the input hyperlayer is always positioned at the most negative end of the substrate. There are two sensors of max dimensionality of 2, thus there should be 2 planes on the Z axis. The next coordinate in the list is Z, and there are 3 tuples which have Z = -1, and the other 6 tuples have Z = 1, as expected. The first 3 tuples represent the values originating from the first sensor, and the second 6 tuples represent the values originating from the second sensor. Also because the first sensor has no geometrical information, it is a single one dimensional vector, and so for the first 3 tuples Y = 0, with only the X taking the coordinates of -1, 0, and 1. The second sensor is 2 dimensional, and so Y takes the coordinates of -1 and 1, each Y coordinate further comes with 3 X coordinates, which take the values -1, 0, and 1. Thus indeed this tuple list does represent the input hyperlayer.

The next hyperlayer was specified using the Densities list:[1,3,2,2]:

```
[{[0,-1,-1,-1],0,[0,0,0,0,0,0,0,0,0]},
 {[0,-1,-1,1],0,[0,0,0,0,0,0,0,0,0]},
 {[0,-1,1,-1],0,[0,0,0,0,0,0,0,0,0]},
 {[0,-1,1,1],0,[0,0,0,0,0,0,0,0,0]},
 {[0,0.0,-1,-1],0,[0,0,0,0,0,0,0,0,0]},
 {[0,0.0,-1,1],0,[0,0,0,0,0,0,0,0,0]},
 {[0,0.0,1,-1],0,[0,0,0,0,0,0,0,0,0]},
 {[0,0.0,1,1],0,[0,0,0,0,0,0,0,0,0]},
 {[0,1,-1,-1],0,[0,0,0,0,0,0,0,0,0]},
 {[0,1,-1,1],0,[0,0,0,0,0,0,0,0,0]},
 {[0,1,1,-1],0,[0,0,0,0,0,0,0,0,0]},
 {[0,1,1,1],0,[0,0,0,0,0,0,0,0,0]}]
```

There is only one hidden processing hyperlayer, so it is positioned equidistantly between the input and the output hyperlayers, at K = 0. There are 3 planes in this hyperlayer, each has a 2x2 topology. Thus the next coordinate takes 3 values, Z = -1, 0, and 1. For every Z coordinate there are 4 tuples, representing the 4 neurodes, and we see that for every Z coordinate, Y takes on the values of -1 and 1, and for every Y coordinate, X takes a value of -1 and 1. Furthermore, notice that each tuple has the default *Output = 0,* and the synaptic weight list: [0,0,0,0,0,0,0,0,0]. The weight list is of length 9, which is the number of neurodes in the input hyperlayer. Thus every neurode in the hidden hyperlayer is ready to process the signals coming from every neurode of the previous hyperlayer, the input hyperlayer in this case.

Next comes the output hyperlayer, whose phenotypic representation was composed through the analysis of the actuator list that the SENN in question uses:

```
Actuators = [
  #actuator{format=no_geo,tot_vl=2},
  #actuator{format={symmetric,lists:reverse([3,2])},tot_vl=6}
```

]:

```
[{[1,-1,0,-1],0,[0,0,0,0,0,0,0,0,0,0,0,0]},
 {[1,-1,0,1],0,[0,0,0,0,0,0,0,0,0,0,0,0]},
 {[1,1,-1,-1],0,[0,0,0,0,0,0,0,0,0,0,0,0]},
 {[1,1,-1,1],0,[0,0,0,0,0,0,0,0,0,0,0,0]},
 {[1,1,0,0,-1],0,[0,0,0,0,0,0,0,0,0,0,0,0]},
 {[1,1,0,0,1],0,[0,0,0,0,0,0,0,0,0,0,0,0]},
 {[1,1,1,-1],0,[0,0,0,0,0,0,0,0,0,0,0,0]},
 {[1,1,1,1],0,[0,0,0,0,0,0,0,0,0,0,0,0]}]
```

The output hyperlayer is always located at the most positive end of the substrate. In this 4d substrate this means that it is located at K = 1. The output hyperlayer is 3d, and there are 2 planes composing it, thus Z takes on two values, -1, and 1. The signals destined for actuator1 are positioned at Z = -1. The signals destined for actuator2 are positioned at Z = 1. The output hyperlayer is a signal processing hyperlayer, and so each tuple comes with a synaptic weight list (which in this default form has not yet been set to its appropriate values through the use of the synaptic weight producing NN).

We discussed before and wondered how we would decide which neurodes should receive signals from which sensors, and which neurodes should forward their signals to which actuators. Using this representation this question can now be answered. The neurodes come in a particular pattern within their hyperlayer, and in the same order as they are listed in the sensor and actuator lists. There are *vl* number of neurodes associated with each sensor and actuator. Thus we can simply take the *vl* number of neurodes from the corresponding input or output hyperlayer and map them to their appropriate, and in the same order based, sensors and actuators respectively.

What is excellent about this substrate representation is the ease with which we can use it for signal processing. In fact it only takes a few lines in Erlang. Using the above substrate representation, the l2l_feedforward processing of signals from the input hyperlayer to the output hyperlayer, can be done using the source code shown in Listing-16.1.

Listing-16.1 Processing signals from the input hyperlayer to the output hyperlayer, in a hyperlayer-to-hyperlayer feedforward substrate.

```
calculate_output_std(Prev_Hyperlayer,[Cur_Hyperlayer|Substrate],Plasticity,Acc)->
    Updated_CurHyperlayer = [{Coord,calculate_neurode_output_noplast(Prev_Hyperlayer,
    {Coord,Prev_O, Weights}, Plasticity), Weights} || {Coord,Prev_O,Weights} <-
Cur_Hyperlayer],
    calculate_output_std(Updated_CurHyperlayer,Substrate,Plasticity, [Updated_CurHyperlayer
|Acc]);
calculate_output_std(Output_Hyperlayer,[],_Plasticity,Acc)->
```

```
    {[Output || {_Coord,Output,_Weights} <- Output_Hyperlayer],lists:reverse(Acc)}.

    calculate_neurode_output_noplast([{_I_Coord,O,_I_Weights}|I_Neurodes],
{Coord,Prev_O,[Weight|Weights]},Acc)->
            calculate_neurode_output_noplast(I_Neurodes,{Coord,Prev_O,Weights}, O*Weight
+Acc);
    calculate_neurode_output_noplast([],{Coord,Prev_O,[]},Acc)->
            functions:tanh(Acc).
```

And that is effectively it, 2 functions with 9 lines (if one does not count the lines introduced through the line breaks due to the page width of this book) of code total. Since every hyperlayer is contained in its own list, and since every neurode in the hyperlayer must process the signals from all the neurodes in the previous hyperlayer, we simply execute the *calculate_output_std/2* function with the substrate whose input hyperlayer was used as the first parameter to the function, with the remaining substrate as the second parameter. Then each neurode in the current hyperlayer is fed the signals from the neurodes in the previous hyperlayer. We calculate the output of the neurodes in the current hyperlayer, updating it in the process with the said neurodal outputs. The next iteration of the calculate_output_std recurrent function is then executed with the updated current hyperlayer as the first parameter (now it's a Prev_Hyperlayer), with the remainder of the substrate as the second parameter. Thus the current hyperlayer during the next iteration becomes the previous hyperlayer. In this manner all the hyperlayers are processed, with the end result being the updated last hyperlayer, the output hyperlayer. At this point the output hyperlayer is the only remaining updated hyperlayer, so we simply extract its Output values using list comprehension. We can then use the list of actuators and their *vl* values to extract the output lists from the output value list of the output hyperlayer.

It would even be easy to add some level of recurrence to the substrate using this encoding, which we will do within the implementation section. In this manner the substrate can contain millions of neurons, and they would be processed rather efficiently by a single process. Optimizations could be made to separate the substrate into multiple parallel hypercubes, or feed this vector based representation to a GPU, which could then process it in parallel if implemented accordingly.

The more difficult part is implementing the functions to compose these substrates from their Densities list, and their sensor and actuator lists. We will discuss just that in the substrate implementation section, but first let us finally implement the substrate_cpps and substrate_ceps.

16.5 Implementing the substrate_cpps & substrate_ceps

We have discussed how the substrate_cpps and substrate_ceps have a very similar functionality to the sensors and actuators respectively. In fact, so much so that to recreate these two functions would require copy-pasting most of the mutation operators, sensor and actuator modules, the genotype construction functions which create the seed NNs, and the sensor/actuator cloning and deleting functions. It is true that the substrate_cpps and substrate_ceps are not sensors and actuators, respectively. They are part of the NN system itself, part of the Think element in the Sense-Think-Act loop. But it also would not be effective for us to have to re-implement the same functionality we've already developed. There is an alternative though.

Since we now know what the substrate_cpps and substrate_ceps are, and that they are not sensors and actuators, we can be comfortable enough to reuse and piggyback the sensor and actuator records by extending them to include the *type* element, which will specify whether the sensor/actuator is of the standard type, or whether it is of type substrate_cpp/substrate_cep. It is a better approach at this time, because either way we will have to modify the genotype_mutator and other modules to discern between sensors/actuators and substrate_cpps/substrate_ceps. For example, if the agent is of type *substrate* rather than *neural*, the mutation operators add_sensor, add_actuator, add_sensorlink, add_actuatorlink, and the functions which perform sensor to neuron, and neuron to actuator linking, all must be modified to accommodate the fact that the addition of new sensors and actuators, and linking to them, is done very differently in a substrate encoded system. Thus, since we already have to modify these functions, we might as well use the existing sensor and actuator based functionality.

Before we continue and begin modifying the sensor and actuator records and modules, here are the similarities between the sensors & actuators, and their substrate based counterparts:

- **sensors:** The NN evolves and is able to integrate and connect to new sensors during the evolutionary process. Furthermore, the sensors are used to interface with the environment through message passing, potentially processing the data before forwarding the sensory signals to the NN.
  substrate_cpps: The NN evolves and is able to integrate and connect to new coordinate processors during the evolutionary process. Starting off with a single standard coordinate type of substrate_cpp, which simply passes the coordinates of the 2 connected neurodes to the NN, and over time integrating new substrate_cpps which convert Cartesian coordinates to polar or spherical coordinates, calculate distances between the connected neurodes, distances between the neurode and the center of the substrate... Furthermore, the substrate_cpps interact with the substrate through message passing, potentially processing the data before forwarding it to the NN.
- **actuators:** The NN evolves and is able to integrate and connect to new actuators during the evolutionary process. Furthermore, the actuator interfaces with the environment through message passing, and direct execution of its functions.
  substrate_ceps: The NN evolves and is able to integrate and connect to new substrate_ceps, which it controls and sends signals to. There can be different

types of substrate_ceps. The most basic type is one which has a vl=1, and based on the signals from the NN, it sets the synaptic weights between the two neurodes for which the substrate_cpps have acquired coordinate based data. Other types which can be integrated over time are those which deal with connectivity expression (whether there even should be a synaptic weight between the noted neurodes), synaptic weight update (a substrate_cep which is used to update synaptic weights, when one implements synaptic plasticity for example), and others which might reveal themselves and become useful in the future. Furthermore, the actuator interfaces with the substrate through message passing, and potentially by executing functions directly.

Not only is their functionality similar, where the only difference is that the sensors and actuators interface with the scape, whereas the substrate_cpps and substrate_ceps interface with the substrate, but also the mutation operators are exactly the same between the two. The NN neither knows, nor cares, whether it is getting connected to the sensors/actuators or substrate_cpps/substrate_ceps. Of course if we allow the sensors and actuators to come in two types, standard and substrate, the substrate encoded NN will need to use both types. The standard sensors/actuators will be used by the substrate itself to interface with the world/environment/scape, while the substrate sensors/actuators will be used by the substrate to drive the NN, sending it coordinate based signals and acquiring from it synaptic weight and other parameter settings. Through the use of the type element in the sensors and actuators, we can also ensure that the cortex does not sync them as it does with the standard sensors and actuators.

Having now decided that the sensors and actuators can be modified to be efficiently used in our substrate encoding implementation, let us first modify their records. The updated sensor and actuator records will have the following form:

```
-record(sensor,{id,name,type,cx_id,scape,vl,fanout_ids=[],generation,format,parameters,
phys_rep,vis_rep, pre_f, post_f}).
-record(actuator,{id,name,type,cx_id,scape,vl,fanin_ids=[],generation,format,parameters,
phys_rep,vis_rep, pre_f, post_f}).
```

Next we have to modify the morphology module, adding to it a new set of substrate type sensors and actuators, used specifically by the substrate encoded NN. We also have to modify the original sensors and actuators specified in the morphology module, setting their *type* to *standard*. We mirror the functions: *get_InitSensors/get_InitActuators* and *get_Sensors/get_Actuators*, to create *get_InitSubstrateCPPs/get_InitSubstrateCEPs* and *get_SubstrateCPPs/get_SubstrateCEPs*, as shown in Listing-16.2.

```
Listing-16.2 The implementation of the new get_InitSubstrateCPPs/get_InitSubstrateCEPs and
get_SubstrateCPPs/get_SubstrateCEPs functions.

get_InitSubstrateCPPs(Dimensions,Plasticity)->
    Substrate_CPPs = get_SubstrateCPPs(Dimensions,Plasticity),
```

```
    [lists:nth(1,Substrate_CPPs)].

get_InitSubstrateCEPs(Dimensions,Plasticity)->
    Substrate_CEPs = get_SubstrateCEPs(Dimensions,Plasticity),
    [lists:nth(1,Substrate_CEPs)].

get_SubstrateCPPs(Dimensions,Plasticity)->
    io:format("Dimensions:~p, Plasticity:~p~n",[Dimensions,Plasticity]),
    if
            (Plasticity == none) ->
                    Std=[
                            #sensor{name=cartesian,type=substrate,vl=Dimensions*2},
                            #sensor{name=centripetal_distances,type=substrate,vl=2},
                            #sensor{name=cartesian_distance,type=substrate,vl=1},
                            #sensor{name=cartesian_CoordDiffs,type=substrate,vl=Dimensions},
                            #sensor{name=cartesian_GaussedCoordDiffs,type=substrate, vl
=Dimensions}
                    ],
                    Adt=case Dimensions of
                            2 ->
                                    [#sensor{name=polar,type=substrate,vl=Dimensions*2}];
                            3 ->
                                    [#sensor{name=spherical,type=substrate,vl=Dimensions*2}];
                            _ ->
                                    []
                    end,
                    lists:append(Std,Adt)
    end.

get_SubstrateCEPs(Dimensions,Plasticity)->
    case Plasticity of
            none ->
                    [#actuator{name=set_weight,type=substrate,vl=1}]
    end.
```

In the function get_SubstrateCPP, there are two lists, the *Std* (standard), and the *Adt* (additional), of cpp (from this point on we will refer to the substrate cpp type based sensors, simply as cpp sensors or cpps, and similarly our reference to substrate ceps will be using the word: ceps) functions. The standard list contains the various cpp functions which are substrate dimension independent. While the cpps in the Adt list are dimension specific. For example the conversion of cartesian to polar coordinate requires for the substrate to be 2d, while the cpp that feeds the NN the spherical coordinates can operate only on a 3d substrate. Let us discuss each of the listed cpps next, which we will implement afterwards:

- **cartesian**: The cartesian cpp simply forwards to the NN the appended coordinates of the two connected neurodes. Because each neurode has a coordinate specified by a list of length: Dimension, the vector specifying the two appended coordinates will have vl = Dimensions*2. For example: $[X_1,Y_1,Z_1,X_2,Y_2,Z_2]$ will have a vector length of dimension: vl = 3*2 = 6.
- **centripetal_distances**: This cpp uses the Cartesian coordinates of the two neurodes to calculate the Cartesian distance of neurode_1 to the center of the substrate located at the origin, and the Cartesian distance of neurode_2 to the center of the substrate. It then fans out to the NN the vector of length 2, composed of the two distances.
- **cartesian_distance**: This cpp calculates the Cartesian distance between the two neurodes, forwarding the resulting vector of length 1 to the NN.
- **cartesian_CoordDiffs**: This cpp calculates the difference between each coordinate element of the two neurodes, and thus for this cpp, the vl = Dimensions.
- **cartesian_GaussedCoordDiffs**: Exactly the same as the above cpp, but each of the values is first sent through the Gaussian function before it is entered into the vector.
- **polar**: This cpp converts the Cartesian coordinates to polar coordinates. This can only be done if the substrate is 2d.
- **spherical**: This cpp converts the Cartesian coordinates to the spherical coordinates. This can only be done if the substrate is 3d.

In the case of the available CEPs, there is only one, by the name *weight*. This CEP is connected from a single neuron in the NN, and it sets the synaptic weight between two neurodes in the substrate. Furthermore, we will allow it to compute the synaptic weight based on the following function:

```
Threshold = 0.33,
Processed_Weight = if
   Weight > Threshold ->
         (functions:scale(Weight,1,Threshold)+1)/2;
   Weight < -Threshold ->
         (functions:scale(Weight,-Threshold,-1)-1)/2;
   true ->
         0
end
```

This function allows for the synaptic weight to either be expressed or zeroed, depending on whether the NN's output magnitude is greater than 0.33 or not. When the synaptic weight is expressed, it is then scaled to be between -1 and 1.

We could certainly add any number of other cpps and ceps, limited only by our imagination. And we could add new ones at any time, and then use our *benchmarker* to see if it improves the agility and performance of our TWEANN system on some difficult problem. But at this point, the listed cpps and ceps will be enough.

16.5.1 Implementing the substrate_cpp Module

We've established the record format for the substrate_cpp type sensors, and decided which cpp functions we will implement. Also in the previous section we have created the substrate architecture, in which the substrate triggers the cpp sensors to fanout the coordinate based information to all the neurons the cpps are connected to. To realize this architecture, we need to set up the cpps, and create their processes with the ability to receive messages from the substrate's Pid. We will have the exoself create the substrate before it links the cpps and ceps, and so by the time the exoself initializes the cpps and ceps, it will already know the substrate's Pid. We can then have the exoself tell the cpps and ceps the substrate's Pid when it initializes them. Based on this information, we can now create the cpps in their own substrate_cpp module. In Listing-16.3, we implement the cpp function in its own substrate_cpp module.

Listing-16.3 Implementation of the substrate_cpp module.

```
-module(substrate_cpp).
-compile(export_all).
-include("records.hrl").

gen(ExoSelf_PId,Node)->
    spawn(Node,?MODULE,prep,[ExoSelf_PId]).

prep(ExoSelf_PId) ->
    receive
            {ExoSelf_PId,{Id,Cx_PId,Substrate_PId,CPPName,VL,Parameters,Fanout_PIds}} ->
                    loop(Id,ExoSelf_PId,Cx_PId,Substrate_PId,CPPName,VL,Parameters,
Fanout_PIds)
    end.
%When gen/2 is executed, it spawns the substrate_cpp process which immediately begins to
wait for its initial state message.

loop(Id,ExoSelf_PId,Cx_PId,Substrate_PId,CPPName,VL,Parameters,Fanout_PIds)->
    receive
            {Substrate_PId,Presynaptic_Coords,Postsynaptic_Coords}->
                    SensoryVector = functions:CPPName(Presynaptic_Coords,
Postsynaptic_Coords),
                    [Pid ! {self(),forward,SensoryVector} || Pid <- Fanout_PIds],
```

```
loop(Id,ExoSelf_PId,Cx_PId,Substrate_PId,CPPName,VL,Parameters,Fanout_PIds);
    {ExoSelf_PId,terminate} ->
        %io:format("substrate_cpp:~p is terminating.~n",[Id]),
        ok
end.
```

Since the conversion of Cartesian coordinates to other types belongs in the mathematical function module, we implement all the coordinate operators in the *functions* module, with the substrate_cpps calling them when needed, depending on their name. The coordinate operator functions added to the *functions* module are shown in Listing-16.4

Listing-16.4 The implemented coordinate operators added to the functions module.

```
cartesian(I_Coord,Coord)->
    lists:append(I_Coord,Coord).

polar(I_Coord,Coord)->
    lists:append(cart2pol(I_Coord),cart2pol(Coord)).

spherical(I_Coord,Coord)->
    lists:append(cart2spher(I_Coord),cart2spher(Coord)).

centripital_distances(I_Coord,Coord)->
    [centripital_distance(I_Coord,0),centripital_distance(Coord,0)].

cartesian_distance(I_Coord,Coord)->
    [calculate_distance(I_Coord,Coord,0)].

cartesian_CoordDiffs(I_Coord,Coord)->%I:[X1,Y1,Z1] [X2,Y2,Z2] O:[X2-X1,Y2-Y1,Z2-Z1]
    cartesian_CoordDiffs1(I_Coord,Coord,[]).

    cartesian_CoordDiffs1([FromCoord|FromCoords],[ToCoord|ToCoords],Acc)->
        cartesian_CoordDiffs1(FromCoords,ToCoords,[ToCoord-FromCoord|Acc]);
    cartesian_CoordDiffs1([],[],Acc)->
        lists:reverse(Acc).

cartesian_GaussedCoordDiffs(FromCoords,ToCoords)->
    cartesian_GaussedCoordDiffs1(FromCoords,ToCoords,[]).

    cartesian_GaussedCoordDiffs1([FromCoord|FromCoords], [ToCoord|ToCoords],Acc)->
        cartesian_GaussedCoordDiffs1(FromCoords,ToCoords,[functions:gaussian(
ToCoord-FromCoord)|Acc]);
    cartesian_GaussedCoordDiffs1([],[],Acc)->
```

```erlang
        lists:reverse(Acc).

cart2pol([Y,X])->
        R = math:sqrt(X*X + Y*Y),
        Theta = case R == 0 of
                true ->
                        0;
                false ->
                        if
                                (X>0)  and (Y>=0) -> math:atan(Y/X);
                                (X>0)  and (Y<0)  -> math:atan(Y/X) + 2*math:pi();
                                (X<0)             -> math:atan(Y/X) + math:pi();
                                (X==0) and (Y>0)  -> math:pi()/2;
                                (X==0) and (Y<0)  -> 3*math:pi()/2
                        end
        end,
        [R,Theta].

cart2spher([Z,Y,X])->
        PreR = X*X + Y*Y,
        R = math:sqrt(PreR),
        P = math:sqrt(PreR + Z*Z),
        Theta = case R == 0 of
                true ->
                        0;
                false ->
                        if
                                (X>0)  and (Y>=0) -> math:atan(Y/X);
                                (X>0)  and (Y<0)  -> math:atan(Y/X) + 2*math:pi();
                                (X<0)             -> math:atan(Y/X) + math:pi();
                                (X==0) and (Y>0)  -> math:pi()/2;
                                (X==0) and (Y<0)  -> 3*math:pi()/2
                        end
        end,
        Phi = case P == 0 of
                false ->
                        math:acos(Z/P);
                true ->
                        0
        end,
        [P,Theta,Phi].

centripetal_distance([Val|Coord],Acc)->
        centripetal_distance(Coord,Val*Val+Acc);
centripetal_distance([],Acc)->
```

```
        math:sqrt(Acc).

calculate_distance([Val1|Coord1],[Val2|Coord2],Acc)->
        Distance = Val2 - Val1,
    calculate_distance(Coord1,Coord2,Distance*Distance+Acc);
        calculate_distance([],[],Acc)->
        math:sqrt(Acc).
```

The implementation of the new functions in the *functions* module is straight-forward. These algorithms are standard implementations of coordinate operators.

With this new substrate_cpp module, and the updated functions module, the cpps can now be called by the substrate process. When called, the cpps calculate the "sensory" vectors for the NN, and then fanout those composed vectors to the neurons that they are connected to. In the next subsection, we implement the substrate_ceps.

16.5.2 Implementing the substrate_cep Module

Similarly to the implementation of substrate_cpp module, we now implement the substrate_cep module based on the way the actuator module is setup. Similarly to the way the actuator works, the substrate_cep receives the signals from the neurons in the NN that are connected to it. The substrate_cep then processes the signals, and sends the processed message to the substrate. We only have one substrate_cep at this time, the *weight* substrate_cep, which has a single presynaptic connection to a neuron, whose signal it then processes, scales, and sends to the substrate as the synaptic weight associated with the coordinate information forwarded to the NN by its substrate_cpps. Listing-16.5 shows the implemented substrate_cep module.

```
Listing-16.5 The implementation of the substrate_cep module.

-module(substrate_cep).
-compile(export_all).
-include("records.hrl").

gen(ExoSelf_PId,Node)->
    spawn(Node,?MODULE,prep,[ExoSelf_PId]).

prep(ExoSelf_PId) ->
    receive
        {ExoSelf_PId,{Id,Cx_PId,Substrate_PId,CEPName,Parameters,Fanin_PIds}} ->
```

```
                    loop(Id,ExoSelf_PId,Cx_PId,Substrate_PId,CEPName,Parameters,
{Fanin_PIds, Fanin_PIds},[])
    end.
```
%When gen/2 is executed, it spawns the substrate_cep process which immediately begins to wait
for its initial state message.

```
loop(Id,ExoSelf_PId,Cx_PId,Substrate_PId,CEPName,Parameters,{[From_PId|Fanin_PIds],
MFanin_PIds},Acc) ->
    receive
            {From_PId,forward,Input} ->
                    loop(Id,ExoSelf_PId,Cx_PId,Substrate_PId,CEPName,Parameters,
{Fanin_PIds, MFanin_PIds},lists:append(Input,Acc));
            {ExoSelf_PId,terminate} ->
                    ok
    end;
loop(Id,ExoSelf_PId,Cx_PId,Substrate_PId,CEPName,Parameters,{[],MFanin_PIds},Acc)->
    ProperlyOrdered_Input=lists:reverse(Acc),
    substrate_cep:CEPName(ProperlyOrdered_Input,Parameters,Substrate_PId),
    loop(Id,ExoSelf_PId,Cx_PId,Substrate_PId,CEPName,Parameters,{MFanin_PIds,
MFanin_PIds},[]).
```
%The substrate_cep process gathers the control signals from the neurons, appending them to
the accumulator. The order in which the signals are accumulated into a vector is in the same order that the neuron ids are stored within NIds. Once all the signals have been gathered, the sub-
strate_cep executes its function, forwards the processed signal to the substrate, and then again
begins to wait for the neural signals from the output layer by resetting the Fanin_PIds from the
second copy of the list stored in the MFanin_PIds.

```
%%%%%%%%% Substrate_CEPs %%%%%%%%%
set_weight(Output,_Parameters,Substrate_PId)->
    [Val] = Output,
    Threshold = 0.33,
    Weight = if
            Val > Threshold ->
                    (functions:scale(Val,1,Threshold)+1)/2;
            Val < -Threshold ->
                    (functions:scale(Val,-Threshold,-1)-1)/2;
            true ->
                    0
    end,
    Substrate_PId ! {self(),set_weight,[Weight]}.
```
%The set_weight/2 function first checks whether the neural output signal has a greater magni-
tude than the Threshold value, which is set to 0.33 in this implementation. If it does not, then
the synaptic weight is zeroed out, and sent to the substrate. If the magnitude of the output is
higher, then the value is scaled between -1 and 1, and the resulting synaptic weight value is sent
to the substrate.

Mirroring the actuator, the substrate_cep gathers the signals, processes them, then sends the substrate process a message, and returns to its main process loop. Unlike the actuator, it does not need to sync up with the cortex, or receive any information from the substrate after sending it the action message.

16.6 Updating the genotype Module

Having now developed the actual substrate_cpp and substrate_cep modules, we can return to the genotype module and update it so that it is capable of creating seed SENNs. This is a very simple module update, because cpps and ceps both behave just like the sensors and actuators of the standard NN system do. In the case of the substrate encoding, we simply generate both the sensor/actuator lists and the substrate_cpp/substrate_cep lists. Afterwards, we create the seed NN topology by forwarding to it the cpps and ceps, and because there is no difference between the structure of the sensors/actuators and cpps/ceps, the seed NN topology is created.

When the encoding type is set to substrate, we create not just the substrate_cpps and substrate_ceps, but also the substrate record. It is the substrate record in which we store the cpp_ids, cep_ids, the densities, the linkform, and the plasticity of the substrate (which at this time is set to none). The updated version of the construct_Cortex/4 function within the genotype module is shown in Listing-16.6. The newly added source code is in bold text, note the significant reuse of the code when *Encoding_Type = substrate*.

Listing-16.6 The updated construct_Cortex/4 function, now capable of creating seed SENN genotypes.

```
construct_Cortex(Agent_Id,Generation,SpecCon,Encoding_Type,SPlasticity,SLinkform)->
    Cx_Id = {{origin,generate_UniqueId()},cortex},
    Morphology = SpecCon#constraint.morphology,
    case Encoding_Type of
        neural ->
                Sensors = [S#sensor{id={{-1,generate_UniqueId()},sensor},cx_id=Cx_Id,
generation =Generation}|| S<- morphology:get_InitSensors(Morphology)],
                Actuators = [A#actuator{id={{1,generate_UniqueId()},actuator},cx_id
=Cx_Id, generation=Generation}||A<-morphology:get_InitActuators(Morphology)],
                N_Ids=construct_InitialNeuroLayer(Cx_Id,Generation,SpecCon,Sensors,
Actuators,[],[]),
                S_Ids = [S#sensor.id || S<-Sensors],
                A_Ids = [A#actuator.id || A<-Actuators],
                Cortex = #cortex{
                    id = Cx_Id,
```

```
                    agent_id = Agent_Id,
                    neuron_ids = N_Ids,
                    sensor_ids = S_Ids,
                    actuator_ids = A_Ids
            },
            Substrate_Id = undefined;
        substrate ->
            Substrate_Id={{void,generate_UniqueId()},substrate},
            Sensors = [S#sensor{id={{-1,generate_UniqueId()},sensor},cx_id=Cx_Id,
generation =Generation, fanout_ids=[Substrate_Id]}|| S<- morpholo-
gy:get_InitSensors(Morphology)],
            Actuators = [A#actuator{id={{1,generate_UniqueId()},actuator},cx_id
=Cx_Id,generation=Generation,fanin_ids=[Substrate_Id]}||A<-
morphology:get_InitActuators(Morphology)],
            [write(S) || S <- Sensors],
            [write(A) || A <- Actuators],
            Dimensions=calculate_OptimalSubstrateDimension(Sensors,Actuators),
            Density = 5,
            Depth = 1,
            Densities = [Depth,1|lists:duplicate(Dimensions-2,Density)], %[X,Y,Z,T...]
            Substrate_CPPs = [CPP#sensor{id={{-1,generate_UniqueId()},sensor},
cx_id =Cx_Id,generation=Generation}|| CPP<-
morphology:get_InitSubstrateCPPs(Dimensions, SPlasticity)],
            Substrate_CEPs =
[CEP#actuator{id={{1,generate_UniqueId()},actuator},cx_id=Cx_Id,generation
=Generation}||CEP<-morphology:get_InitSubstrateCEPs(Dimensions,SPlasticity)],
            N_Ids=construct_InitialNeuroLayer(Cx_Id, Generation, SpecCon,
Substrate_CPPs,Substrate_CEPs,[],[]),
            S_Ids = [S#sensor.id || S<-Sensors],
            A_Ids = [A#actuator.id || A<-Actuators],
            CPP_Ids = [CPP#sensor.id || CPP<-Substrate_CPPs],
            CEP_Ids = [CEP#actuator.id || CEP<-Substrate_CEPs],
            Substrate = #substrate{
                id = Substrate_Id,
                agent_id = Agent_Id,
                cpp_ids = CPP_Ids,
                cep_ids = CEP_Ids,
                densities = Densities,
                plasticity=SPlasticity ,
                linkform=SLinkform
            },
            write(Substrate),
            Cortex = #cortex{
                id = Cx_Id,
                agent_id = Agent_Id,
```

```
                    neuron_ids = N_Ids,
                    sensor_ids = S_Ids,
                    actuator_ids = A_Ids
            }
    end,
    write(Cortex),
    {Cx_Id,[{0,N_Ids}],Substrate_Id}.
...
calculate_OptimalSubstrateDimension(Sensors,Actuators)->
        S_Formats = [S#sensor.format || S<-Sensors],
        A_Formats = [A#actuator.format || A<-Actuators],
        extract_maxdim(S_Formats++A_Formats,[]) + 2.
%The calculate_OptimalSubstrateDimension/2 function calculates the largest dimension be-
tween the sensors and actuators, and then returns that value + 2.


        extract_maxdim([F|Formats],Acc)->
            DS=case F of
                    {symmetric,Dims}->
                        length(Dims);
                    no_geo ->
                        1;
                    undefined ->
                        1
            end,
            extract_maxdim(Formats,[DS|Acc]);
        extract_maxdim([],Acc)->
            lists:max(Acc).
%The extract_maxdim/2 function goes through a list of formats, and returns to the caller the
largest value found, counting no_geo and undefined atoms as representing 1.
```

But this only takes care of creating the genotype of the substrate encoded NN, we also need to update the agent cloning, agent deleting, and agent genotype printing functions. Listing-16.7 shows the implementation of the noted functions, with the new source code shown in boldface.

Listing-16.7 The implementation of the updated genotype:print/1, genotype:delete_Agent/1, and genotype:clone_Agent/1 functions.

```
print(Agent_Id)->
    F = fun()->
            A = read({agent,Agent_Id}),
            Cx = read({cortex,A#agent.cx_id}),
            io:format("~p~n",[A]),
            io:format("~p~n",[Cx]),
            [io:format("~p~n",[read({sensor,Id})]) || Id <- Cx#cortex.sensor_ids],
```

```
            [io:format("~p~n",[read({neuron,Id})])]) || Id <- Cx#cortex.neuron_ids],
            [io:format("~p~n",[read({actuator,Id})])]) || Id <- Cx#cortex.actuator_ids],
        case A#agent.substrate_id of
            undefined ->
                ok;
            Substrate_Id->
                Substrate = read({substrate,Substrate_Id}),
                io:format("~p~n",[Substrate]),
                [io:format("~p~n",[read({sensor,Id})])]) || Id <-
Substrate#substrate.cpp_ids],
                [io:format("~p~n",[read({actuator,Id})])]) || Id <-
Substrate#substrate.cep_ids]
        end
    end,
    mnesia:transaction(F).
%print/1 accepts an agent's id, and prints out the complete genotype of that agent.

delete_Agent(Agent_Id)->
    A = read({agent,Agent_Id}),
    Cx = read({cortex,A#agent.cx_id}),
    [delete({neuron,Id}) || Id <- Cx#cortex.neuron_ids],
    [delete({sensor,Id}) || Id <- Cx#cortex.sensor_ids],
    [delete({actuator,Id}) || Id <- Cx#cortex.actuator_ids],
    delete({cortex,A#agent.cx_id}),
    delete({agent,Agent_Id}),
    case A#agent.substrate_id of
        undefined ->
            ok;
        Substrate_Id ->
            Substrate = read({substrate,Substrate_Id}),
            [delete({sensor,Id}) || Id <- Substrate#substrate.cpp_ids],
            [delete({actuator,Id})|| Id <- Substrate#substrate.cep_ids],
            delete({substrate,Substrate_Id})
    end.
```

%delete_Agent/1 accepts the id of an agent, and then deletes that agent's genotype. This function assumes that the id of the agent will be removed from the specie's agent_ids list, and that any other clean up procedures, will all be done by the calling function.

```
clone_Agent(Agent_Id)->
    CloneAgent_Id = {generate_UniqueId(),agent},
    clone_Agent(Agent_Id,CloneAgent_Id).
clone_Agent(Agent_Id,CloneAgent_Id)->
    F = fun()->
        A = read({agent,Agent_Id}),
        Cx = read({cortex,A#agent.cx_id}),
```

```
IdsNCloneIds = ets:new(idsNcloneids,[set,private]),
ets:insert(IdsNCloneIds,{bias,bias}),
ets:insert(IdsNCloneIds,{Agent_Id,CloneAgent_Id}),
[CloneCx_Id] = map_ids(IdsNCloneIds,[A#agent.cx_id],[]),
CloneN_Ids = map_ids(IdsNCloneIds,Cx#cortex.neuron_ids,[]),
CloneS_Ids = map_ids(IdsNCloneIds,Cx#cortex.sensor_ids,[]),
CloneA_Ids = map_ids(IdsNCloneIds,Cx#cortex.actuator_ids,[]),
case A#agent.substrate_id of
    undefined ->
        clone_neurons(IdsNCloneIds,Cx#cortex.neuron_ids),
        clone_sensors(IdsNCloneIds,Cx#cortex.sensor_ids),
        clone_actuators(IdsNCloneIds,Cx#cortex.actuator_ids),
        U_EvoHist=map_EvoHist(IdsNCloneIds,A#agent.evo_hist),
        write(Cx#cortex{
            id = CloneCx_Id,
            agent_id = CloneAgent_Id,
            sensor_ids = CloneS_Ids,
            actuator_ids = CloneA_Ids,
            neuron_ids = CloneN_Ids
        }),
        write(A#agent{
            id = CloneAgent_Id,
            cx_id = CloneCx_Id,
            evo_hist = U_EvoHist
        });
    Substrate_Id ->
        Substrate = read({substrate,A#agent.substrate_id}),
        [CloneSubstrate_Id] = map_ids(IdsNCloneIds,
[A#agent.substrate_id], []),
        CloneCPP_Ids = map_ids(IdsNCloneIds,
Substrate#substrate.cpp_ids, []),
        CloneCEP_Ids = map_ids(IdsNCloneIds,
Substrate#substrate.cep_ids,[]),
        clone_neurons(IdsNCloneIds,Cx#cortex.neuron_ids),
        clone_sensors(IdsNCloneIds,Cx#cortex.sensor_ids),
        clone_actuators(IdsNCloneIds,Cx#cortex.actuator_ids),
        Substrate = read({substrate,A#agent.substrate_id}),
        clone_sensors(IdsNCloneIds,Substrate#substrate.cpp_ids),
        clone_actuators(IdsNCloneIds,Substrate#substrate.cep_ids),
        U_EvoHist=map_EvoHist(IdsNCloneIds,A#agent.evo_hist),
        write(Substrate#substrate{
            id = CloneSubstrate_Id,
            agent_id = CloneAgent_Id,
            cpp_ids = CloneCPP_Ids,
            cep_ids = CloneCEP_Ids
```

```
       }),
       write(Cx#cortex{
              id = CloneCx_Id,
              agent_id = CloneAgent_Id,
              sensor_ids = CloneS_Ids,
              actuator_ids = CloneA_Ids,
              neuron_ids = CloneN_Ids
       }),
       write(A#agent{
              id = CloneAgent_Id,
              cx_id = CloneCx_Id,
              substrate_id = CloneSubstrate_Id,
              evo_hist = U_EvoHist
       })
   end,
   ets:delete(IdsNCloneIds)
end,
mnesia:transaction(F),
CloneAgent_Id.
```

Now that we have the ability to create the substrate encoded NN genotypes, we need to update the exoself module, so that the exoself process can properly spawn and link all the elements together when the NN is of type: *substrate*.

16.7 Updating the exoself Module

Exoself reads the genotype and produces the phenotype. When a NN based agent is substrate encoded, the exoself must behave slightly differently when spawning and linking the elements of the genotype. The exoself process must now keep track of the substrate_pid, cpp_pids and cep_pids, so that it can terminate them when the evaluation is done. Thus we update its state record by appending to it the following elements: *substrate_pid, cpp_pids=[], cep_pids=[]*.

The spawning of the substrate encoded NN and the neural encoded NN, requires us to add the new spawn and link substrate_cpps and substrate_ceps functions. We must also update the *exoself:prep/2* function so that when the agent is of type *substrate*, it can spawn and link the substrate, cpp, and the cep processes together. The updated exoself:prep/2 function is shown in Listing-16.8, with the modified and added source code shown in boldface.

Listing-16.8 The implementation of the updated exoself:prep/2 function.

```
prep(Agent_Id,PM_PId)->
```

```
random:seed(now()),
IdsNPIds = ets:new(idsNpids,[set,private]),
A = genotype:dirty_read({agent,Agent_Id}),
HeredityType = A#agent.heredity_type,
Cx = genotype:dirty_read({cortex,A#agent.cx_id}),
SIds = Cx#cortex.sensor_ids,
AIds = Cx#cortex.actuator_ids,
NIds = Cx#cortex.neuron_ids,
ScapePIds = spawn_Scapes(IdsNPIds,SIds,AIds),
spawn_CerebralUnits(IdsNPIds,cortex,[Cx#cortex.id]),
spawn_CerebralUnits(IdsNPIds,sensor,SIds),
spawn_CerebralUnits(IdsNPIds,actuator,AIds),
spawn_CerebralUnits(IdsNPIds,neuron,NIds),
case A#agent.encoding_type of
     substrate ->
               Substrate_Id=A#agent.substrate_id,
               Substrate = genotype:dirty_read({substrate,Substrate_Id}),
               CPP_Ids = Substrate#substrate.cpp_ids,
               CEP_Ids = Substrate#substrate.cep_ids,
               spawn_CerebralUnits(IdsNPIds,substrate_cpp,CPP_Ids),
               spawn_CerebralUnits(IdsNPIds,substrate_cep,CEP_Ids),
               spawn_CerebralUnits(IdsNPIds,substrate,[Substrate_Id]),
               Substrate_PId=ets:lookup_element(IdsNPIds,Substrate_Id,2),
               link_SubstrateCPPs(CPP_Ids,IdsNPIds,Substrate_PId),
               link_SubstrateCEPs(CEP_Ids,IdsNPIds,Substrate_PId),
               SDensities = Substrate#substrate.densities,
               SPlasticity = Substrate#substrate.plasticity,
               SLinkform = Substrate#substrate.linkform,
               Sensors=[genotype:dirty_read({sensor,SId})||SId <- SIds],
               Actuators=[genotype:dirty_read({actuator,AId})||AId <- AIds],
               CPP_PIds=[ets:lookup_element(IdsNPIds,Id,2)||Id<-CPP_Ids],
               CEP_PIds=[ets:lookup_element(IdsNPIds,Id,2)||Id<-CEP_Ids],
               Substrate_PId ! {self(),init,{Sensors,Actuators,
[ets:lookup_element( IdsNPIds, Id,2)||Id<-SIds], [ets:lookup_element(IdsNPIds,Id,2)||Id<-
AIds],CPP_PIds, CEP_PIds, SDensities, SPlasticity,SLinkform}};
       _ ->
               CPP_PIds=[],
               CEP_PIds=[],
               Substrate_PId = undefined
end,
link_Sensors(SIds,IdsNPIds),
link_Actuators(AIds,IdsNPIds),
link_Neurons(NIds,IdsNPIds,HeredityType),
{SPIds,NPIds,APIds}=link_Cortex(Cx,IdsNPIds),
Cx_PId = ets:lookup_element(IdsNPIds,Cx#cortex.id,2),
```

```
    {TuningDurationFunction,Parameter} = A#agent.tuning_duration_f,
    S = #state{
        agent_id=Agent_Id,
        generation=A#agent.generation,
        pm_pid=PM_PId,
        idsNpids=IdsNPIds,
        cx_pid=Cx_PId,
        specie_id=A#agent.specie_id,
        spids=SPIds,
        npids=NPIds,
        nids=NIds,
        apids=APIds,
        substrate_pid=Substrate_PId,
        cpp_pids = CPP_PIds,
        cep_pids = CEP_PIds,
        scape_pids=ScapePIds,
        max_attempts= tuning_duration:TuningDurationFunction(Parameter,NIds,
A#agent.generation),
        tuning_selection_f=A#agent.tuning_selection_f,
        annealing_parameter=A#agent.annealing_parameter,
        tuning_duration_f=A#agent.tuning_duration_f,
        perturbation_range=A#agent.perturbation_range
    },
    loop(S).
...
...

...
    link_SubstrateCPPs([CPP_Id|CPP_Ids],IdsNPIds,Substrate_PId) ->
        CPP=genotype:dirty_read({sensor,CPP_Id}),
        CPP_PId = ets:lookup_element(IdsNPIds,CPP_Id,2),
        Cx_PId = ets:lookup_element(IdsNPIds,CPP#sensor.cx_id,2),
        CPPName = CPP#sensor.name,
        Fanout_Ids = CPP#sensor.fanout_ids,
        Fanout_PIds = [ets:lookup_element(IdsNPIds,Id,2) || Id <- Fanout_Ids],
        CPP_PId ! {self(),{CPP_Id,Cx_PId,Substrate_PId,CPPName,CPP#sensor.vl,
CPP#sensor.parameters,Fanout_PIds}},
        link_SubstrateCPPs(CPP_Ids,IdsNPIds,Substrate_PId);
    link_SubstrateCPPs([],_IdsNPIds,_Substrate_PId)->
        ok.
%The link_Sensors/2 function sends to the already spawned and waiting sensors their states,
composed of the PId lists and other information which is needed by the sensors to link up and
interface with other elements in the distributed phenotype.

    link_SubstrateCEPs([CEP_Id|CEP_Ids],IdsNPIds,Substrate_PId) ->
        CEP=genotype:dirty_read({actuator,CEP_Id}),
```

```
            CEP_PId = ets:lookup_element(IdsNPIds,CEP_Id,2),
            Cx_PId = ets:lookup_element(IdsNPIds,CEP#actuator.cx_id,2),
            CEPName = CEP#actuator.name,
            Fanin_Ids = CEP#actuator.fanin_ids,
            Fanin_PIds = [ets:lookup_element(IdsNPIds,Id,2) || Id <- Fanin_Ids],
            CEP_PId ! {self(),{CEP_Id,Cx_PId,Substrate_PId,CEPName,
CEP#actuator.parameters, Fanin_PIds}},
            link_SubstrateCEPs(CEP_Ids,IdsNPIds,Substrate_PId);
    link_SubstrateCEPs([],_IdsNPIds,_Substrate_PId)->
        ok.
%The link_SubstrateCEPs/2 function sends to the already spawned and waiting substrate_ceps
their states, composed of the PId lists and other information which is needed by the sub-
strate_ceps to link up and interface with other elements in the distributed phenotype.
```

The exoself's main loop must also be updated, but not as extensively. We have to be able to tell the substrate process to reset itself when the neurons have been perturbed, or reverted. Thus after every evaluation, we let the exoself send the substrate process a message to reset itself, which makes the substrate process call all the perturbed or reverted neurons and set the synaptic weights and connectivity expression of its neurodes anew. The added code is shown in the following listing:

Listing-16.9 The extra algorithm needed to tell the substrate process to reset itself.

```
case S#state.substrate_pid of
    undefined ->
        ok;
    Substrate_PId ->
        Substrate_PId ! {self(),reset_substrate},
        receive
            {Substrate_PId,ready}->
                ok
        end
end,
```

Finally, the exoself must now also be able to terminate the substrate process, and its cpps and ceps. Thus we make a slight modification to the *terminate_phenotype* function, as shown in Listing-16.10.

Listing-16.10 The updated exoself:terminate_phenotype function.

```
terminate_phenotype(Cx_PId,SPIds,NPIds,APIds,ScapePIds,CPP_PIds, CEP_PIds,
Substrate_PId)->
    [PId ! {self(),terminate} || PId <- SPIds],
    [PId ! {self(),terminate} || PId <- APIds],
    [PId ! {self(),terminate} || PId <- NPIds],
```

```
[PId ! {self(),terminate} || PId <- ScapePIds],
case Substrate_PId == undefined of
      true ->
            ok;
      false ->
            [PId ! {self(),terminate} || PId <- CPP_PIds],
            [PId ! {self(),terminate} || PId <- CEP_PIds],
            Substrate_PId ! {self(),terminate}
end,
Cx_PId ! {self(),terminate}.
```

No other modifications are needed. With this, the exoself is ready to work with both, the direct encoded NNs, and the substrate encoded NNs. Next, we implement the most important thing, the actual substrate module.

16.8 Implementing the substrate Module

While developing the substrate_cpp and substrate_cep modules, we have also created the message format that will be used to exchange messages between the substrate process and the interfacing cpps and ceps. Now that we know the architecture of the substrate encoded NN, the manner in which cpps and ceps will process signals, and interface with the substrate, and the way we will encode the substrate, through the use of the densities list, and dynamic input and output hyperlayer creation through the analysis of sensor and actuator lists, we are ready to create the phenotypic representation of the substrate.

We now continue where we left of in section 16.4 with regards to the substrate representation and signal processing. This is going to be a bit more complex than the other things we've created. Knowing everything else about our system, the way cortex synchronizes the sensors and actuators, the way sensors then acquire, process, and fanout their sensory signals to the NN, or in this case a substrate, and the way the actuators wait for the signals from every id in their fanin_ids list, in this case just the substrate, how do we make it all work?

For the substrate to function as we planned for it in our architectural design, it must perform the following steps:

1. The substrate process is created using the gen/2 function.
2. The process then receives from the exoself a list of sensors & actuators with their pids, a list of pids for the substrate_cpps and substrate_ceps, and finally it also receives the Densities list, and the linkform. From this, it must create a proper substrate using the information from Sensors, Actuators, Densities lists, and the Linkform parameter. The substrate process must do so while keeping in

mind that every time exoself perturbs or reverts the neurons, the substrate's synaptic connection weights and expressions in general must too be updated.

3. The process must use some kind of flag, a substrate_state_flag, which will keep track of whether the substrate must be updated (as in the case when the NN has been perturbed) or can be kept for use again. The substrate process then drops into its main loop.

4. Just like other processes that accumulate incoming signals, the substrate process waits and accumulates (in the same order as the sensors are within the sensors list) the sensory signals. Once all the sensory signals have been accumulated, the substrate process drops into its processing clause.

5. The substrate process checks what the substrate_state_flag is set to. If the flag is set to *reset,* then the substrate should be recreated or reset (due to a perturbation of the NN), before being able to process the sensory signals and produce the output signals destined for the actuators. If the substrate_state_flag is set to *hold* the current substrate, then it does not need to be recreated/updated.

6. This step is executed if the substrate_state_flag was set to *reset.* The substrate process analyzes the sensors, densities, and actuators, and based on the format within the sensors and actuators, and the dimensionality and form of the Densities list, it creates a substrate in the form we have discussed in Section-16.4. At this point all the synaptic weights between this feedforward substrate (for now, we will only use the hyperlayer-to-hyperlayer feedforward substrate linkform) are set to 0. Thus they must now be set to their proper synaptic weight values.

7. For every connected set of neurodes, the substrate process forwards the coordinates of the two neurodes to the PIds of the substrate_cpps in its CPP_PIds list. And for every sent out tuple of coordinates, it waits for the signals from the PIds of the substrate_ceps in its CEP_PIds list. The signals will have some value, and the name of the function which will dictate what function to execute on the currently used synaptic weight. The function will either simply set the synaptic weight to this new value forwarded to the substrate process by the substrate_cep, or perhaps modify the existing synaptic weight in the case plasticity is implemented within the substrate... Once this is done for every connection between the neurodes, given the hyperlayer-to-hyperlayer feedforward architecture, the substrate is now considered functional and ready for use, and the substrate_state_flag is set to the value *hold.*

8. Because the input hyperlayer was created specifically based on the list of sensors that SENN uses, it will have the architecture needed for the accumulated list of sensory signals to be mapped to this input hyperlayer perfectly. The accumulated list of sensory signals is a list of vectors. Each vector has the same length as every multidimensional hyperplane within the input hyperlayer, thus we can now replace the *Output* part within the tuples *[{NeurodeCoordinate, Output, void}...]* of the input hyperplanes, by the values of the sensory signals, as shown in Fig-16.12, making these tuples into: *[{NeurodeCoordinate, RealOutput, void}...],* where RealOutput is the value taken from the accumulated sensory signals list, associated with that particular neurode coordinate.

9. Now that the Input Hyperlayer has its output values set to real output values from the sensors, the substrate can be used to process the signals. We now use the algorithm discussed in Section-16.4 to perform processing in the hyperlayer-to-hyperlayer feedforward fashion. Since the neurodes in the processing hyperlayers now have their synaptic weights, they can process all the input signals from the presynaptic neurodes of the presynaptic hyperlayer. In this manner, the substrate processes the sensory signals until the output hyperlayer's Output values are calculated.

10. The *Output* values in the tuples representing the neurodes within the output hyperlayer now contain the actual output signals of the substrate. The layers within the output hyperlayer are in the same order as the actuators within the Actuators list for which they are destined. Thus the substrate can now extract from the layers associated with each actuator the corresponding output vectors, and forward them to the PIds of their respective actuators.

11. At this point the actuators are now interacting with the environment, and the substrate drops back into its main loop, awaiting again for the signals from its sensors or the exoself.

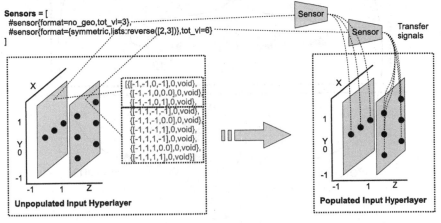

Fig. 16.12 The initial input hyperlayer with default output values, and the mapping between sensory signals produced by the sensors, to the input hyperlayer.

At any point the exoself can send the substrate process a signal to reset itself. When the substrate process receives this signal, it simply sets its substrate_state_flag to *reset*, and thus after the next time it accumulates the sensory signals, it resets. To reset, it re-queries the NN to set the synaptic weights and connectivity between its neurodes anew, before processing the new sensory signals. The diagram of the step-by-step functionality of the substrate process is shown in Fig-16.13.

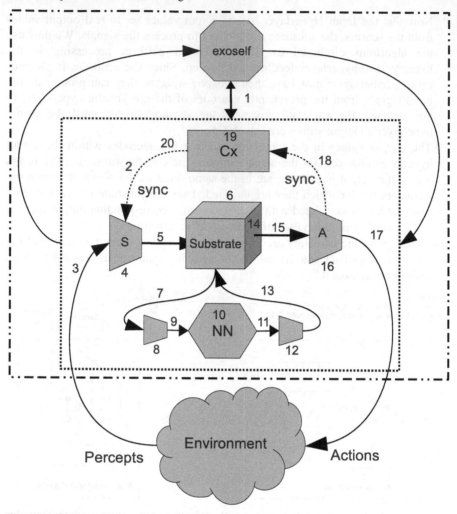

Fig. 16.13 The step-by-step functionality of the substrate process.

Lets quickly go over the steps shown in the above figure:

1. Exoself spawns neurons, sensors, actuators, substrate_cpps, substrate_ceps, substrate, and the cortex process.
2. Cortex sends the sync message to all the sensors, calling them to action.
3. Sensors poll the environment for sensory signals.
4. Sensors do postprocessing of the signals.
5. Sensors forward the processed sensory signals to the substrate.
6. Substrate process gathers all the signals from the sensors, and based on those signals, its densities, and the actuators, constructs a substrate if its substrate_state_flag is set to reset. If substrate_state_flag is set to hold, go to next step.

7. Substrate sends the coordinates of the connected neurodes to the substrate_cpps it is connected to.
8. The cpps process the coordinates, producing a new output vector.
9. The cpps forward the processed coordinate vectors to the neurons they are connected to in the NN.
10. NN processes the coordinate signals.
11. The neurons in the output layer of the NN produce output signals, which are then sent to the ceps they are connected to.
12. The ceps wait and gather the signals from all the neurons with whom they have presynaptic links. The ceps process the accumulated signals.
13. The ceps forward the vector signals to the substrate.
14. The substrate process calls the cpps for every connected neurode in the substrate. Once all the neurodes have their synaptic weights, the substrate maps the signals from the sensors to the input hyperlayer. It then processes the sensory signals, until at some later point the output hyperlayer contains the output signals.
15. Each hyperplane in the output hyperlayer is associated with its own actuator, to which the output vector is then forwarded to.
16. Actuators gather the signals sent to them from their fanin_ids list (in this case the id of the substrate process).
17. Actuators use the signals to take action and interact with the environment they are interfacing with.
18. Actuators send the sync message back to the cortex.
19. The cortex gathers all the sync messages from all its actuators.
20. The cortex calls sensors to action, for another Sense-Think-Act loop. Go to step 3.

Using all of this information, we can now create the substrate module. The implementation of the substrate module will follow the 11 step approach we discussed before the above 20 step sequence.

1. *The process is created using the gen/2 function.*

This is a simple function, similar to the one we use for every other element, as shown in the following listing.

Listing-16.11 The substrate process' state record, and the gen/2 function.

```
-module(substrate).
-compile(export_all).
-include("records.hrl").
-define(SAT_LIMIT,math:pi()).
-record(state,{
    type,
    plasticity=none,
```

```
    morphology,
    specie_id,
    sensors,
    actuators,
    spids=[],
    apids=[],
    cpp_pids=[],
    cep_pids=[],
    densities,
    substrate_state_flag,
    old_substrate,
    cur_substrate,
    link_form
}).

gen(ExoSelf_PId,Node)->
    spawn(Node,?MODULE,prep,[ExoSelf_PId]).
```

2. *The process then receives from the exoself a list of sensors & actuators with their pids, a list of pids for the substrate_cpps and substrate_ceps, and finally it also receives the Densities list, and the linkform. From this, it must create a proper substrate using the information from Sensors, Actuators, Densities lists, and the Linkform parameter. The substrate process must do so while keeping in mind that every time exoself perturbs or reverts the neurons, the substrate's synaptic connection weights and expressions in general must too be updated.*
3. *The process must use some kind of flag, a substrate_state_flag, which will keep track of whether the substrate must be updated (as in the case when the NN has been perturbed) or can be kept for use again. The substrate process then drops into its main loop.*

During this step the substrate process begins to wait for its state information from the exoself. Its implementation is shown in Listing-16.12. Because the substrate is created during the processing step based on its substrate_state_flag, the initial Substrate is set to the *init* atom. The substrate_state_flag is set to the atom *reset*. We use the atom reset because the substrate's synaptic expression and weight values have to be reset when the NN is perturbed, hence the atom *reset* is appropriate.

Listing-16.12 The implementation of the prep/1 function.

```
prep(ExoSelf)->
    random:seed(now()),
    receive
        {ExoSelf,init,InitState}->
```

```
    {Sensors,Actuators,SPIds,APIds,CPP_PIds,CEP_PIds,Densities,Plasticity, LinkForm}
=InitState,
                S = #state{
                        sensors=Sensors,
                        actuators=Actuators,
                        spids=SPIds,
                        apids=APIds,
                        cpp_pids=CPP_PIds,
                        cep_pids=CEP_PIds,
                        densities = Densities,
                        substrate_state_flag=reset,
                        old_substrate=void,
                        cur_substrate=init,
                        plasticity=Plasticity,
                        link_form = LinkForm
                },
                substrate:loop(ExoSelf,S,SPIds,[])
    end.
```

4. *Just like other processes that accumulate incoming signals, the substrate process waits and accumulates (in the same order as the sensors are within the sensors list) the sensory signals. Once all the sensory signals have been accumulated, the substrate process drops into its processing clause.*

Next we implement the main process loop, during which the substrate process gathers the sensory signals from the sensors, and receives the signal from the exoself to reset the substrate when the exoself perturbs the NN. The implementation of the main loop is shown in the next listing.

```
Listing-16.13 The implementation of the substrate process's main loop.

loop(ExoSelf,S,[SPId|SPIds],SAcc)->
    receive
        {SPId,forward,Sensory_Signal}->
                loop(ExoSelf,S,SPIds,[Sensory_Signal|SAcc]);
        {ExoSelf,reset_substrate}->
                U_S = S#state{
                        old_substrate=S#state.cur_substrate,
                        substrate_state_flag=reset
                },
                ExoSelf ! {self(),ready},
                loop(ExoSelf,U_S,[SPId|SPIds],SAcc);
        {ExoSelf,terminate}->
                ok;
    end;
```

```
loop(ExoSelf,S,[],SAcc)->%All sensory signals received
    {U_Substrate,U_SMode,OAcc} = reason(SAcc,S),
    advanced_fanout(OAcc,S#state.actuators,S#state.apids),
    U_S = S#state{
        cur_substrate=U_Substrate,
        substrate_state_flag=U_SMode
    },
    loop(ExoSelf,U_S,S#state.spids,[]).
```

As seen from the above implementation, once the sensory signals have been accumulated from all the sensors, we drop into the step where the substrate loop calls the necessary functions to create the substrate if needed, and process the sensory signals. The function which does all that is called reason/2, which is called once we drop out of the main receive loop. The function reason/2 returns the updated substrate: U_Substrate, the updated substrate_state_flag: U_SMode, and the accumulated output signal: OAcc. The function advanced_fanout/3 uses the OAcc list, breaks it up, and forwards the output signals to their respective actuators.

5. *The substrate process checks what the substrate_state_flag is set to. If the flag is set to reset, then the substrate should be recreated or reset (due to a perturbation of the NN), before being able to process the sensory signals and produce the output signals destined for the actuators. If the substrate_state_flag is set to hold the current substrate, then it does not need to be recreated/updated.*

This whole step is performed within the reason/2 function, as shown in Listing-16.14.

Listing-16.14 The implementation of the reason/2 function.

```
reason(Input,S)->
    Densities = S#state.densities,
    Substrate = S#state.cur_substrate,
    SMode = S#state.substrate_state_flag,
    case SMode of
            reset ->
                    Sensors=S#state.sensors,
                    Actuators=S#state.actuators,
                    CPP_PIds = S#state.cpp_pids,
                    CEP_PIds = S#state.cep_pids,
                    Plasticity = S#state.plasticity,
                    New_Substrate = create_substrate(Sensors,Densities,Actuators,
S#state.link_form),
                    {Output,Populated_Substrate} = calculate_ResetOutput(Densities,
New_Substrate, Input, CPP_PIds, CEP_PIds, Plasticity, S#state.link_form),
                    U_SMode=case Plasticity of
                        none ->
```

```
                        hold
            end,
            {Populated_Substrate,U_SMode,Output};
        hold ->
                {Output,U_Substrate} = calculate_HoldOutput(Densities,Substrate, Input,
S#state.link_form, S#state.plasticity),
                {U_Substrate,SMode,Output}
    end.
```

As can be seen from the above function, we are already in some sense preparing for the case where the substrate_state_flag is updated differently, when substrate plasticity is used for example. If the substrate_state_flag stored in **SMode** is set to *reset*, the function create_substrate/4 is executed to create the new substrate, and then the function calculate_ResetOutput/6 is used to perform substrate based processing. If SMode is set to *hold*, then the function processes the signals but by executing the function calculate_HoldOutput/4. The difference here is that during the *reset* state, we still need to create the substrate, where's during the *hold* state, we expect that the substrate is already created, and so we need only map the input sensory signals to the input hyperlayer.

6. *This step is executed if the substrate_state_flag was set to reset. The substrate process analyzes the sensors, densities, and actuators, and based on the format within the sensors and actuators, and the dimensionality and form of the Densities list, it creates a substrate in the form we have discussed in Section-16.4. At this point all the synaptic weights between this feedforward substrate (for now, we will only use the hyperlayer-to-hyperlayer feedforward substrate linkform) are set to 0. Thus they must now be set to their proper synaptic weight values.*

The substrate is constructed by executing the create_substrate/4 function, shown in the following listing.

Listing-16.15 The implementation of the create_substrate/4 function.

```
create_substrate(Sensors,Densities,Actuators,LinkForm)->
    [Depth|SubDensities] = Densities,
    Substrate_I = compose_ISubstrate(Sensors,length(Densities)),
    I_VL = length(Substrate_I),
    case LinkForm of
        l2l_feedforward ->
            Weight = 0,
            H = mult(SubDensities),
            IWeights = lists:duplicate(I_VL,Weight),
            HWeights = lists:duplicate(H,Weight);
        fully_interconnected ->
            Output_Neurodes = tot_ONeurodes(Actuators,0),
            Weight = 0,
```

```
                Tot_HiddenNeurodes = mult([Depth-1|SubDensities]),
                Tot_Weights = Tot_HiddenNeurodes + I_VL + Output_Neurodes,
                IWeights = lists:duplicate(Tot_Weights,Weight),
                HWeights = lists:duplicate(Tot_Weights,Weight);
        jordan_recurrent ->
                Output_Neurodes = tot_ONeurodes(Actuators,0),
                Weight = 0,
                H = mult(SubDensities),
                IWeights = lists:duplicate(I_VL+Output_Neurodes,Weight),
                HWeights = lists:duplicate(H,Weight)
end,
case Depth of
     0 ->
                Substrate_O=compose_OSubstrate(Actuators,length(Densities),IWeights),
                [Substrate_I,Substrate_O];
     1 ->
                Substrate_R = cs(SubDensities,IWeights),
                Substrate_O=compose_OSubstrate(Actuators,length(Densities),HWeights),
                [Substrate_I,extrude(0,Substrate_R),Substrate_O];
     _ ->
                Substrate_R = cs(SubDensities,IWeights),
                Substrate_H = cs(SubDensities,HWeights),
                Substrate_O=compose_OSubstrate(Actuators,length(Densities),HWeights),
                [_,RCoord|C1] = build_CoordList(Depth+1),
                [_|C2] = lists:reverse(C1),
                HCoords = lists:reverse(C2),
                ESubstrate_R = extrude(RCoord,Substrate_R),
                ESubstrates_H = [extrude(HCoord,Substrate_H) || HCoord<-HCoords],
                lists:append([[Substrate_I,ESubstrate_R],ESubstrates_H,[Substrate_O]])
end.

compose_ISubstrate(Sensors,SubstrateDimension)->
     compose_ISubstrate(Sensors,[],1,SubstrateDimension-2).
compose_ISubstrate([S|Sensors],Acc,Max_Dim,Required_Dim)->
     case S#sensor.format of
                undefined ->
                     Dim=1,
                     CoordLists = create_CoordLists([S#sensor.vl]),
                     ISubstrate_Part=[{Coord,0,void}|| Coord<-CoordLists],
                     {Dim,ISubstrate_Part};
                no_geo ->
                     Dim=1,
                     CoordLists = create_CoordLists([S#sensor.vl]),
                     ISubstrate_Part=[{Coord,0,void}|| Coord<-CoordLists],
                     {Dim,ISubstrate_Part};
```

```
            {symmetric,Resolutions}->
                    Dim = length(Resolutions),
                    Signal_Length = mult(Resolutions),
                    CoordLists = create_CoordLists(Resolutions),
                    ISubstrate_Part=[{Coord,0,void}|| Coord<-CoordLists],
                    {Dim,ISubstrate_Part}
        end,
        U_Dim = case Max_Dim > Dim of
                true ->
                        Max_Dim;
                false ->
                        Dim
        end,
        compose_ISubstrate(Sensors,[ISubstrate_Part|Acc],U_Dim,Required_Dim);
  compose_ISubstrate([],Acc,ISubstratePart_MaxDim,Required_Dim)->
        case Required_Dim >= ISubstratePart_MaxDim of
                true ->
                        ISubstrate_Depth = length(Acc),
                        ISubstrate_DepthCoords = build_CoordList(ISubstrate_Depth),
                        adv_extrude(Acc,Required_Dim, lists:reverse(ISubstrate_DepthCoords),
-1,[]);
                false ->
                        exit("Error in adv_extrude, Required_Depth <
ISubstratePart_MaxDepth ~n")
        end.

        adv_extrude([ISubstrate_Part|ISubstrate],Required_Dim, [IDepthCoord
|ISubstrate_DepthCoords], LeadCoord,Acc)->
                Extruded_ISP =
[{[LeadCoord,IDepthCoord|lists:append(lists:duplicate(Required_Dim - length(Coord),
0),Coord)], O, W} || {Coord,O,W}<-ISubstrate_Part],
                        extrude(ISubstrate_Part,Required_Dim,IDepthCoord,[]),

adv_extrude(ISubstrate,Required_Dim,ISubstrate_DepthCoords,LeadCoord,
lists:append(Extruded_ISP,Acc));
        adv_extrude([],_Required_Dim,[],_LeadCoord,Acc)->
                Acc.

                extrude([{Coord,O,W}|ISubstrate_Part],Required_Dim,DepthCoord,Acc)->
                        Dim_Dif = Required_Dim - length(Coord),
                        U_Coord= [1,DepthCoord|lists:append(lists:duplicate(Dim_Dif,0),
Coord)],
                        extrude(ISubstrate_Part,Required_Dim,DepthCoord, [{U_Coord,O,W}
|Acc]);
                extrude([],_Required_Dim,_DepthCoord,Acc)->
```

```
                                 Acc.

compose_OSubstrate(Actuators,SubstrateDimension,Weights)->
        compose_OSubstrate(Actuators,[],1,SubstrateDimension-2,Weights).
    compose_OSubstrate([A|Actuators],Acc,Max_Dim,Required_Dim,Weights)->
        case A#actuator.format of
                undefined ->%Dim=void,OSubstrate_Part=void,
                    Dim=1,
                    CoordLists = create_CoordLists([A#actuator.vl]),
                    OSubstrate_Part=[{Coord,0,Weights}|| Coord<-CoordLists],
                    {Dim,OSubstrate_Part};
                no_geo ->%Dim=void,OSubstrate_Part=void,
                    Dim=1,
                    CoordLists = create_CoordLists([A#actuator.vl]),
                    OSubstrate_Part=[{Coord,0,Weights}|| Coord<-CoordLists],
                    {Dim,OSubstrate_Part};
                {symmetric,Resolutions}->%Dim=void,OSubstrate_Part=void,
                    Dim = length(Resolutions),
                    Signal_Length = mult(Resolutions),
                    CoordLists = create_CoordLists(Resolutions),
                    OSubstrate_Part=[{Coord,0,Weights}|| Coord<-CoordLists],
                    {Dim,OSubstrate_Part}
        end,
        U_Dim = case Max_Dim > Dim of
                true ->
                    Max_Dim;
                false ->
                    Dim
        end,
        com-
pose_OSubstrate(Actuators,[OSubstrate_Part|Acc],U_Dim,Required_Dim,Weights);
    compose_OSubstrate([],Acc,OSubstratePart_MaxDim,Required_Dim,_Weights)->
        case Required_Dim >= OSubstratePart_MaxDim of
                true ->%done;
                    ISubstrate_Depth = length(Acc),
                    ISubstrate_DepthCoords = build_CoordList(ISubstrate_Depth),
                    adv_extrude(Acc,Required_Dim,lists:reverse(ISubstrate_DepthCoords),
1,[]);
                false ->
                    exit("Error in adv_extrude, Required_Depth <
OSubstratePart_MaxDepth~n")
        end.

        find_depth(Resolutions)->find_depth(Resolutions,0).
        find_depth(Resolutions,Acc)->
```

```
                    case is_list(Resolutions) of
                         true ->
                              [_Head|Tail] = Resolutions,
                              find_depth(Tail,Acc+1);
                         false ->
                              Acc
                    end.

          build_CoordList(Density)->
               case Density == 1 of
                    true ->
                         [0.0];
                    false ->
                         DensityDividers = Density - 1,
                         Resolution = 2/DensityDividers,
                         build_CoordList(Resolution,DensityDividers,1,[])
               end.

          extend(I,DI,D,Substrate)->
               void.

          mult(List)->
               mult(List,1).
          mult([Val|List],Acc)->
               mult(List,Val*Acc);
          mult([],Acc)->
               Acc.

tot_ONeurodes([A|Actuators],Acc)->
   Tot_ANeurodes=case A#actuator.format of
          undefined ->
               A#actuator.vl;
          no_geo ->
               A#actuator.vl;
          {symmetric,Resolutions}->
               mult(Resolutions)
   end,
   tot_ONeurodes(Actuators,Tot_ANeurodes+Acc);
tot_ONeurodes([],Acc)->
   Acc.

   cs(Densities,Weights)->
          RDensities = lists:reverse(Densities),
          Substrate = create_CoordLists(RDensities,[]),
          attach(Substrate,0,Weights).
```

```
        create_CoordLists(Densities)->
            create_CoordLists(Densities,[]).
        create_CoordLists([Density|RDensities],[])->
            CoordList = build_CoordList(Density),
            XtendedCoordList = [[Coord]||Coord <- CoordList],
            create_CoordLists(RDensities,XtendedCoordList);
        create_CoordLists([Density|RDensities],Acc)->
            CoordList = build_CoordList(Density),
            XtendedCoordList = [[Coord|Sub_Coord]||Coord <- CoordList,Sub_Coord <-
Acc],
            create_CoordLists(RDensities,XtendedCoordList);
        create_CoordLists([],Acc)->
            Acc.

        build_CoordList(Resolution,0,Coord,Acc)->
            [-1|Acc];
        build_CoordList(Resolution,DensityDividers,Coord,Acc)->
            build_CoordList(Resolution,DensityDividers-1,Coord-Resolution,
[Coord|Acc]).

attach(List,E1,E2)->
    attach(List,E1,E2,[]).
attach([Val|List],E1,E2,Acc)->
    attach(List,E1,E2,[{Val,E1,E2}|Acc]);
attach([],_E1,_E2,Acc)->
    lists:reverse(Acc).

extrude(NewDimension_Coord,Substrate)->
    extrude(NewDimension_Coord,Substrate,[]).
extrude(NewDimension_Coord,[{Coord,O,W}|Substrate],Acc)->
    extrude(NewDimension_Coord,Substrate,[{[NewDimension_Coord|Coord],O,W}|Acc]);
extrude(_Coord,[],Acc)->
    lists:reverse(Acc).
```

The implementation shown above can create not only the layer-to-layer feedforward substrate (l2l_feedforward), but also a jordan_recurrent, and the fully_connected substrate topology.

7. *For every connected set of neurodes, the substrate process forwards the coordinates of the two neurodes to the PIds of the substrate_cpps in its CPP_PIds list. And for every sent out tuple of coordinates, it waits for the signals from the PIds of the substrate_ceps in its CEP_PIds list. The signals will have some value, and the name of the function which will dictate what function to execute on the currently used synaptic weight. The function will either simply set the syn-*

aptic weight to this new value forwarded to the substrate process by the substrate_cep, or perhaps modify the existing synaptic weight in the case plasticity is implemented within the substrate... Once this is done for every connection between the neurodes, given the hyperlayer-to-hyperlayer feedforward architecture, the substrate is now considered functional and ready for use, and the substrate_state_flag is set to the value hold.

The function which populates all the neurodes of the processing hyperlayers with their specific synaptic weights, is called the *populate_PHyperlayers/4*. The implementation of this function is shown in the following listing.

Listing-16.16 The implementation of the populate_PHyperlayers/4 function.

```
populate_PHyperlayers_l2l(PrevHyperlayer,[{Coord,PrevO,PrevWeights}|CurHyperlayer],
Substrate,CPP_PIds, CEP_PIds, Acc1,Acc2)->
    NewWeights = get_weights(PrevHyperlayer,Coord,CPP_PIds,CEP_PIds,[]),
    populate_PHyperlayers_l2l(PrevHyperlayer,CurHyperlayer,Substrate, CPP_PIds, CEP_PIds,
[{Coord,PrevO,NewWeights}|Acc1],Acc2);
populate_PHyperlayers_l2l(_PrevHyperlayer,[],[CurHyperlayer|Substrate], CPP_PIds,
CEP_PIds, Acc1,Acc2)->
    PrevHyperlayer = lists:reverse(Acc1),
    populate_PHyperlayers_l2l(PrevHyperlayer,CurHyperlayer,Substrate, CPP_PIds,CEP_PIds,
[],[PrevHyperlayer|Acc2]);
populate_PHyperlayers_l2l(_PrevHyperlayer,[],[],CPP_PIds,CEP_PIds,Acc1,Acc2)->
    lists:reverse([lists:reverse(Acc1)|Acc2]).

populate_PHyperlayers_fi(FlatSubstrate, [{Coord,PrevO,_PrevWeights}|CurHyperlayer],
Substrate, CPP_PIds, CEP_PIds,Acc1,Acc2)->
    NewWeights = get_weights(FlatSubstrate,Coord,CPP_PIds,CEP_PIds,[]),
    populate_PHyperlayers_fi(FlatSubstrate,CurHyperlayer,Substrate,CPP_PIds,CEP_PIds,
[{Coord,PrevO,NewWeights}|Acc1],Acc2);
populate_PHyperlayers_fi(FlatSubstrate,[],[CurHyperlayer|Substrate], CPP_PIds, CEP_PIds,
Acc1,Acc2)->
    populate_PHyperlayers_fi(FlatSubstrate,CurHyperlayer,Substrate,CPP_PIds, CEP_PIds, [],
[lists:reverse(Acc1)|Acc2]);
populate_PHyperlayers_fi(_FlatSubstrate,[],[],CPP_PIds,CEP_PIds,Acc1,Acc2)->
    lists:reverse([lists:reverse(Acc1)|Acc2]).


    get_weights([{I_Coord,I,_I_Weights}|PrevHypercube],Coord,CPP_PIds,CEP_PIds,Acc)->
        static_fanout(CPP_PIds,I_Coord,Coord),
        U_W=fanin(CEP_PIds,[]),
                get_weights(PrevHypercube,Coord,CPP_PIds,CEP_PIds,
[functions:sat(U_W,3.1415,-3.1415)|Acc]);
    get_weights([],_Coord,_CPP_PIds,_CEP_PIds,Acc)->
```

```
            lists:reverse(Acc).


static_fanout([CPP_PId|CPP_PIds],I_Coord,Coord)->
    CPP_PId ! {self(),I_Coord,Coord},
    static_fanout(CPP_PIds,I_Coord,Coord);
static_fanout([],_I_Coord,_Coord)->
    done.
```

Substrates of different linkforms must have their neurode synaptic weights populated in slightly different ways. Also, substrates with different linkforms will have slightly different ways by which their processing hyperlayers are populated with the appropriate synaptic weights, and the order in which the substrate_cpps are called to action by the substrate. For this reason, for the link forms: *l2l_feedforward* and *jordan_recurrent*, we use the populate_PHyperlayers_l2l function, and for the linkform: *fully_interconnected* we use the populate_PHyperlayers_fi function.

8. *Because the input hyperlayer was created specifically based on the list of sensors SENN uses, it will have the architecture needed for the accumulated list of sensory signals to be mapped to this input hyperlayer perfectly. The accumulated list of sensory signals is a list of vectors. Each vector has the same length as every multidimensional layer within the input hyperlayer, thus we can now replace the Output part within the tuples [{NeurodeCoordinate, Output, void}...] of the input hyperlayers, by the values of the sensory signals, as shown in Fig-16.13, making these tuples into: [{NeurodeCoordiante, RealOutput, void}...], where RealOutput is the value taken from the accumulated sensory signals, associated with that particular neurode coordinate.*

There is an implicit 1:1 order of the signals accumulated from the sensors, and the order in which the neurodes are stacked in the input hyperlayer. For this reason the mapping of the accumulated sensory signals to the neurodes in the input hyperlayer is done using a very simple function shown in Listing-16.17.

Listing-16.17 The implementation of the populate_InputHyperlayer/3 function.

```
populate_InputHyperlayer([{Coord,PrevO,void}|Substrate],[I|Input],Acc)->
    populate_InputHyperlayer(Substrate,Input,[{Coord,I,void}|Acc]);
populate_InputHyperlayer([],[],Acc)->
    lists:reverse(Acc).
```

9. *Now that the Input Hyperlayer has its output values set to real output values from the sensors, the substrate can be used to process the signals. We now use the algorithm discussed in Section-16.4 to perform processing in the hyperlayer-to-hyperlayer feedforward fashion. Since the neurodes in the processing hyperlayers now have their synaptic weights, they can process all the input signals from the presynaptic neurodes of the presynaptic hyperlayer. In*

this manner, the substrate processes the sensory signals until the output hyperlayer's Output values are calculated.

As noted, we can either reset the substrate and then use it to calculate output signals, or we can hold the substrate that was composed during one of the previous cycles, and simply update the input hyperlayer neurodes with the sensory signals. We can then use the resulting substrate with the updated input hyperlayer to produce output signals. I created different functions for these two scenarios. The function dealing with the first scenario is called calculate_ResetOutput/7, and the function for the second scenario is called calculate_HoldOutput/4. Both are shown in the following listing.

Listing-16.18 The implementation of the calculate_ResetOutput/7 and calcualte_HoldOutput/4 functions.

```
calculate_HoldOutput(Densities,Substrate,Input,LinkForm,Plasticity)->
    [IHyperlayer|Populated_PHyperlayers] = Substrate,
    Populated_IHyperlayer = populate_InputHyperlayer(IHyperlayer,lists:flatten(Input),[]),
    {Output,U_PHyperlayers}=calculate_substrate_output(Populated_IHyperlayer,
Populated_PHyperlayers, LinkForm,Plasticity),
    {Output,[IHyperlayer|U_PHyperlayers]}.

calculate_ResetOutput(Densities,Substrate,Input,CPP_PIds,CEP_PIds,Plasticity,LinkForm)->
    [IHyperlayer|PHyperlayers] = Substrate,
    Populated_IHyperlayer = populate_InputHyperlayer(IHyperlayer,lists:flatten(Input),[]),
    case Plasticity of
        none ->
            Populated_PHyperlayers = populate_PHyperlayers(Substrate,CPP_PIds,
CEP_PIds, LinkForm),
            {Output,U_PHyperlayers}=calculate_substrate_output(Populated_IHyperlayer,
Populated_PHyperlayers,LinkForm,Plasticity),
            {Output,[IHyperlayer|U_PHyperlayers]}
    end.
...
calculate_substrate_output(ISubstrate,Substrate,LinkForm,Plasticity)->
    case LinkForm of
        l2l_feedforward ->
            calculate_output_std(ISubstrate,Substrate,Plasticity,[]);
        fully_interconnected ->
            calculate_output_fi(ISubstrate,Substrate,Plasticity,[]);
        jordan_recurrent ->
            [OSubstrate|_] = lists:reverse(Substrate,Plasticity),
            calculate_output_std(lists:flatten([ISubstrate|OSubstrate]),Substrate, Plasticity,
[])
    end.
```

```
calculate_output_std(Prev_Hyperlayer,[Cur_Hyperlayer|Substrate],Plasticity,Acc)->
        Updated_CurHyperlayer = [{Coord,calculate_output(Prev_Hyperlayer,{Coord,
Prev_O, Weights}, Plasticity),Weights} || {Coord,Prev_O,Weights} <- Cur_Hyperlayer],
        calculate_output_std(Updated_CurHyperlayer,Substrate,Plasticity,
[Updated_CurHyperlayer |Acc]);
    calculate_output_std(Output_Hyperlayer,[],_Plasticity,Acc)->
        {[Output || {_Coord,Output,_Weights} <- Output_Hyperlayer],lists:reverse(Acc)}.


        calculate_output(I_Neurodes,Neurode,Plasticity)->
            case Plasticity of
                none ->
                        calculate_neurode_output_noplast(I_Ncurodes,Neurode,0)
            end.


                        calculate_neurode_output_noplast([{_I_Coord,O,_I_Weights}|
I_Neurodes], {Coord,Prev_O,[Weight|Weights]},Acc)->
                        calculate_neurode_output_noplast(I_Neurodes,{Coord,Prev_O,
Weights},O*Weight+Acc);
                        calculate_neurode_output_noplast([],{Coord,Prev_O,[]},Acc)->
                        functions:tanh(Acc).

                        calculate_neurode_output_plast([{_I_Coord,O,_I_Weights}|
I_Neurodes], {Coord,Prev_O,[{W,_LF,_Parameters}|WPs]},Acc)->
                        calculate_neurode_output_plast(I_Neurodes,{Coord,Prev_O,
WPs}, O*W+Acc);
                        calculate_neurode_output_plast([],{Coord,Prev_O,[]},Acc)->
                        functions:tanh(Acc).

    calculate_output_fi(Input_Substrate,[Cur_Hypercube|Substrate],Plasticity,Acc)->
        Updated_CurHypercube = [{Coord,calculate_output(lists:flatten([Input_Substrate,
Cur_Hypercube |Substrate]),{Coord,Prev_O,Weights},Plasticity),Weights} || {Coord, Prev_O,
Weights} <- Cur_Hypercube],
        calculate_output_fi([Input_Substrate|Updated_CurHypercube], Substrate, Plasticity,
Acc);
    calculate_output_fi(Output_Hyperlayer,[],_Plasticity,Acc)->
        {[Output || {_Coord,Output,_Weights} <- Output_Hyperlayer],lists:reverse(Acc)}.
```

It can be seen from the calculate_output_std/2 function and the calculate_output_fi/2 function, the substrate processing ends with the output hyperlayer having the updated *Output* signals in the tuple encoded neurodes. Thus, all that is left to do is extract the signals from the output hyperlayer, and send them on their way to their respective actuators.

10. *The Output values in the tuples representing the neurodes within the output hyperlayer now contain the actual output signals of the substrate. The layers within the output hyperlayer are in the same order as the actuators within the Actuators list for which they are destined. Thus the substrate can now extract from the layers associated with each actuator the corresponding output vectors, and forward them to the PIds of their respective actuators.*

At this point the reason/2 function has returned the updated substrate and the output vector back to the loop function, which now calls the advanced_fanout/3 function which uses the vl values of the actuators to extract the appropriate length vectors from the substrate's output list, and forward those vectors to their respective actuators. The implementation of this function is shown in Listing-16.18.

Listing-16.18 The implementation of the advanced_fanout/3 function.

```
advanced_fanout(OAcc,[Actuator|Actuators],[APId|APIds])->
    {Output,OAccRem}=lists:split(Actuator#actuator.vl,OAcc),
    APId ! {self(),forward,Output},
    advanced_fanout(OAccRem,Actuators,APIds);
advanced_fanout([],[],[])->
    ok.
```

11. *At this point the actuators are now interacting with the environment, and the substrate drops back into its main loop, awaiting again for the signals from the sensors or the exoself.*

At this point the substrate process updates its state, and drops back into its main receive loop.

This substrate module is available with all the other source code, in the supplementary materials section [1]. It is a lengthy, and at points complicated piece of code, and definitely warrants multiple readings, and go-throughs. To play around with the create_substrate/4 function, let us also create the test_cs/0 function, which will create a test substrate and print it to console. It's a short function, but useful for debugging and testing. It is part of the substrate module, and is shown in the following listing.

Listing-16.19 The implementation of the test_cs/0 function.

```
test_cs()->
    Sensors = [
            #sensor{format=no_geo,vl=3},
            #sensor{format={symmetric,lists:reverse([2,3])},vl=6}
    ],
    Actuators = [
            #actuator{format=no_geo,vl=2},
```

```
            #actuator{format={symmetric,lists:reverse([3,2])},vl=6}
   ],
   create_substrate(Sensors,[3,2,3,2],Actuators,l2l_feedforward).
```

At this point the only thing preventing us from using the new encoding, is that genome_mutator module does not yet recognize the difference between the two encodings. We fix that in the next section.

16.9 Updating the genome_mutator Module

Before the evolutionary process can be applied to evolve the NN system used in a substrate encoded NN based agent, we need to update the genome_mutator module to be aware of the two different encodings. If it is not aware of the differences between the neural and substrate encoding, then when using the mutation operators like: add_sensor, add_actuator, add_sensorlink, and add_actuatorlink, the system will try to connect the NN to sensors and actuators instead of substrate_cpps and substrate_ceps, and try to connect the new sensors and actuators to the neurons of the NN, rather than connecting them to the substrate. Thus, we now update the noted functions, ensuring that they behave as expected.

We update the add_inlink/1 function so that when it is forming the inlink id pool, it appends either the sensor_ids or the cpp_ids to the neuron_ids, depending on whether the NN agent is neural or substrate encoded, respectively. The following listing shows the updated function, with the added and modified code in boldface.

```
Listing-16.20 The updated add_inlink/1 implementation.

add_inlink(Agent_Id)->
    A = genotype:read({agent,Agent_Id}),
    Cx_Id = A#agent.cx_id,
    Cx = genotype:read({cortex,Cx_Id}),
    N_Ids = Cx#cortex.neuron_ids,
    S_Ids = case A#agent.encoding_type of
        neural ->
                Cx#cortex.sensor_ids;
        substrate ->
                Substrate_Id=A#agent.substrate_id,
                Substrate=genotype:read({substrate,Substrate_Id}),
                Substrate#substrate.cpp_ids
    end,
    N_Id = lists:nth(random:uniform(length(N_Ids)),N_Ids),
    N = genotype:read({neuron,N_Id}),
```

```
{I_Ids,_WeightPLists} = lists:unzip(N#neuron.input_idps),
Inlink_NIdPool = filter_InlinkIdPool(A#agent.constraint,N_Id,N_Ids),
case lists:append(S_Ids,Inlink_NIdPool) -- I_Ids of
        [] ->
                exit("********ERROR:add_INLink:: Neuron already connected from all
ids");
        Available_Ids ->
                From_Id = lists:nth(random:uniform(length(Available_Ids)),Available_Ids),
                link_FromElementToElement(Agent_Id,From_Id,N_Id),
                EvoHist = A#agent.evo_hist,
                U_EvoHist = [{add_inlink,From_Id,N_Id}|EvoHist],
                genotype:write(A#agent{evo_hist=U_EvoHist})
end.
```

A similar piece of code is added to the add_neuron/1 mutation operator:

```
S_Ids = case A#agent.encoding_type of
    neural ->
            Cx#cortex.sensor_ids;
    substrate ->
            Substrate_Id=A#agent.substrate_id,
            Substrate=genotype:read({substrate,Substrate_Id}),
            Substrate#substrate.cpp_ids
end,
```

Similarly this modification is added to the add_actuatorlink/1 and add_sensorlink/1, and so their updated implementations are not shown. We next modify the add_sensor/1 and add_actuator/1 mutation operators. When adding new sensors and actuators, the functions need to know whether they are operating on the neural or substrate encoded NN. If it is a substrate encoded NN, then the sensors must be added with: *fainin_ids=[Substrate_Id]*, and the actuators must be added with: *fanout_ids=[Substrate_id]*. We make these modifications to the two mutation operators, with the add_sensor/1 function shown in Listing-16.21. The add_actuator/1 function mirrors it.

Listing-16.21 The updated implementation of the add_sensor/1 function.

```
add_sensor(Agent_Id)->
    Agent = genotype:read({agent,Agent_Id}),
    Cx_Id = Agent#agent.cx_id,
    Cx = genotype:read({cortex,Cx_Id}),
    S_Ids = Cx#cortex.sensor_ids,
    SpeCon = Agent#agent.constraint,
    Morphology = SpeCon#constraint.morphology,
```

```
        case morphology:get_Sensors(Morphology)--
[(genotype:read({sensor,S_Id}))#sensor{id=undefined,cx_id=undefined,fanout_ids=[],
generation=undefined} || S_Id<-S_Ids] of
            [] ->
                    exit("********ERROR:add_sensor(Agent_Id):: NN system is already using
all available sensors");
            Available_Sensors ->
                    NewS_Id = {{-1,genotype:generate_UniqueId()},sensor},
                    NewSensor=(lists:nth(random:uniform(length(Available_Sensors)),
Available_Sensors))#sensor{id=NewS_Id,cx_id=Cx_Id},
                    EvoHist = Agent#agent.evo_hist,
                    case Agent#agent.encoding_type of
                        neural->
                            genotype:write(NewSensor),
                            N_Ids = Cx#cortex.neuron_ids,
                            N_Id = lists:nth(random:uniform(length(N_Ids)),N_Ids),
                            link_FromElementToElement(Agent_Id,NewS_Id,N_Id),
                            U_EvoHist = [{add_sensor,NewS_Id,N_Id}|EvoHist];
                        substrate ->
                            Substrate_Id = Agent#agent.substrate_id,
                            genotype:write(NewSensor#sensor{fanout_ids
=[Substrate_Id]}),
                            U_EvoHist = [{add_sensor,NewS_Id,Substrate_Id}|EvoHist]
                    end,
                    U_Cx = Cx#cortex{sensor_ids=[NewS_Id|S_Ids]},
                    genotype:write(U_Cx),
                    genotype:write(Agent#agent{evo_hist=U_EvoHist})
    end.
```

These modifications still leave us with one problem though. There are still no mutation operators that connect the NN to the new substrate_cpps and substrate_ceps. This issue is solved in the next section.

16.10 Implementing the add_cpp and add_cep Mutation Operators

The implementation of the add_cpp and add_cep mutation operators is very similar to that of add_sensor and add_actuator operators. The largest difference here is that we first check if the NN is neural or substrate encoded. If it is neural encoded, we exit the mutation operator and try another one. If it is substrate encoded, we mimic the add_sensor/add_actuator operators, and similarly connect a new substrate_cpp and substrate_cep to the NN. The implementation of the add_cpp mutation operator is shown in Listing-16.22. The mutation operator add_cep is almost identical to add_cpp, we simply change the references from *sensor* to *actuator*, and thus its implementation is not shown.

Listing-16.22 The implementation of the add_cpp mutation operator.

```
add_cpp(Agent_Id)->
    Agent = genotype:read({agent,Agent_Id}),
    case Agent#agent.encoding_type of
        neural->
            exit("*********ERROR:add_cpp(Agent_Id):: NN is neural encoded, can not
apply mutation operator.");
        substrate->
            Cx_Id = Agent#agent.cx_id,
            Cx = genotype:read({cortex,Cx_Id}),
            Substrate_Id = Agent#agent.substrate_id,
            Substrate=genotype:read({substrate,Substrate_Id}),
            Dimensions = length(Substrate#substrate.densities),
            Plasticity = Substrate#substrate.plasticity,
            CPP_Ids = Substrate#substrate.cpp_ids,
            case morphology:get_SubstrateCPPs(Dimensions,Plasticity)--
[(genotype:read({sensor,CPP_Id}))#sensor{id=undefined,cx_id=undefined,fanout_ids=[],
generation=undefined} || CPP_Id<-CPP_Ids] of
                [] ->
                    exit("*********ERROR:add_cpp(Agent_Id):: NN system is al-
ready using all available substrate_cpps");
                Available_CPPs ->
                    NewCPP_Id = {{-1,genotype:generate_UniqueId()},sensor},
                    NewCPP=(lists:nth(random:uniform(length(Available_CPPs)),
Available_CPPs))#sensor{id=NewCPP_Id, cx_id=Cx_Id},
                    EvoHist = Agent#agent.evo_hist,
                    genotype:write(NewCPP),
                    N_Ids = Cx#cortex.neuron_ids,
                    N_Id = lists:nth(random:uniform(length(N_Ids)),N_Ids),
                    link_FromElementToElement(Agent_Id,NewCPP_Id,N_Id),
                    U_EvoHist = [{add_cpp,NewCPP_Id,N_Id}|EvoHist],
                    U_Substrate = Substrate#substrate{cpp_ids=[NewCPP_Id
|CPP_Ids]},
                    genotype:write(U_Substrate),
                    genotype:write(Agent#agent{evo_hist=U_EvoHist})
            end
    end.
%The add_cpp/1 function first checks the encoding of the NN based agent. If the encoding is
neural, it exits the function since the neural encoded NN based system does not use sub-
strate_cpps. If the agent is substrate encoded, then the function chooses randomly a still unused
```

and available substrate_cpp from the Available_CPPs list, and then links it to a randomly chosen neuron in the NN. The function then updates evo_hist list, writes the updated substrate and
agent to database, and returns to the caller.

The last remaining modification needed to make it all work, is with regards to
the *constraint* record. We modify the constraint record by adding to it the two new
elements:

```
substrate_plasticities=[none],
substrate_linkforms = [l2l_feedforward],%[l2l_feedforward,jordan_recurrent,fully_connected]
```

And by modifying the *mutation_operators* list, by appending to it the following
two tuples: *[{add_cpp,1}, {add_cep,1}]*.

With these modifications, all that's left to do is to compile the updated source
code, and to recreate the mnesia database with the newly added substrate table. We
test our updated system in the next section.

16.11 Testing the New Encoding Method

Our two benchmarking problems provide an excellent example of the differences with regards to the amount of geometrical regularities present in problems,
and how to map the said regularities to systems capable of taking advantage of
them. For example the double pole balancing problem (DPB) does not really have
any of such regularities that we can readily expose to a substrate encoded NN
based system. Whereas the T-Maze problem has more potential, but requires us to
manually expose such regularities through an appropriate set of new sensors, actuators, and the mapping of the sensory signals and the produced output signals to
the substrate from sensors and from the substrate to actuators, respectively.

We first test the new encoding on the DPB problem. To do so, we first compile
the new modules, then reset our mnesia database, and then start the polis by executing the functions: polis:sync(), polis:reset(), and polis:start(). Then we modify
the INIT_CONSTRAINTS macro in the population_monitor module to:

```
-define(INIT_CONSTRAINTS,[#constraint{morphology=Morphology,connection_architecture
=CA,population_evo_alg_f=generational,agent_encoding_types=[substrate],
substrate_plasticities =[none]}||Morphology<-[pole_balancing],CA<-[feedforward]]).
```

And finally recompile the population_monitor module, and execute the function *benchmarker:start(dpb),* as shown in the following listing:

Listing-16.23 The double pole balancing benchmark, performed with the substrate encoded
NNs.

Graph:{graph,pole_balancing,

[1.106212121212121,1.1408585858585858,1.1193686868686867,
1.161489898989899,1.143080808080808,1.0764141414141413,
1.1325252525252525,1.1934343434343437,1.1413383838383837,
1.1829797979797978],
[0.05902592904791409,0.09147103257884823,0.0803810171785662,
0.07401185164044073,0.08683375207803117,0.08533785941757911,
0.08215891142076008,0.24593906122148776,0.20476041049617125,
0.2504944656040026],
[0.0855150202020202,0.6052218588038502,1.5313114901359988,
2.599710070705357,3.797623517536588,44.833702130336846,
50.523672653857076,51.832271099817774,180.47316244780285,
158.35976811529105],
[0.010608461667327089,2.1795158240432704,6.130303687259124,
8.258297144062041,8.028234616671885,121.66517882421797,
111.40580585983162,72.48290852966396,424.3416641012721,
343.9761405284347],
**[0.1431,10.105238893248718,40.68352829762942,40.68352829762942,
77.07757425714148,887.0261903586879,887.0261903586879,
887.0261903586879,2588.3673781672096,2588.3673781672096],**
[0.0253,0.0406,0.0253,0.0253,0.0253,0.0253,0.0253,0.0171,0.0253,
0.0253],
[7.45,7.55,7.65,7.4,6.65,6.05,6.3,6.9,6.15,6.3],
[1.1608186766243898,1.116915395184434,1.5256146302392357,
1.562049935181331,1.3518505834595773,1.5321553446044565,
1.452583904633395,1.6703293088490065,1.3883443376914824,
1.4177446878757827],
[500.0,500.0,500.0,500.0,500.0,500.0,500.0,500.0,500.0,500.0],
[]}
Tot Evaluations Avg:5079.95 Std:44.72189061298728

It did not solve the problem, but that is to be expected. The most important part is that our SENN system is functional, there are no bugs, and our neuroevolutionary system did evolve more and more fit substrate encoded NN systems over time. The fact that this type of NN system does not solve the double pole balancing problem is to be expected, because the solution requires recurrent connections and topologies not available to our SENN yet. Substrate encoding of type l2l_feedforward, or jordan_recurrent, simply don't provide the right topologies. It would require us to implement the *freeform* version of the substrate, before it is able to solve this problem.

On the other hand the T-Maze problem does have geometrical regularities. For example the maze has directions, and the sensors come from the left, straight ahead, and right, and the movements based on the signals are similarly made to the left, straight ahead, or to the right. Thus the sensors and movements are geometrically correlated. But the T-Maze sensors and actuators we've created for our NN based agents do not encode the sensory information, and do not accept the output signals in the ways that take advantage of the geometrical regularities of this problem. Thus we build the new sensor and actuator which was shown to perform well in [2], which discussed the use of substrate encoded NN based systems in the T-Maze navigation based problems.

We first create two new sensors and a new actuator. The problem with our current sensor is that it mingles the reward data with the range data. The range sensory signals do have geometrical properties, the signals coming from the left, forward, and the right range sensors, hold that directional geometrical information. But the reward signal has no geometrical information, and should be in its own sensor and thus on a different input layer. Thus, we need to create two new sensors, a single dimensional range sensor that just gathers the range sensory data from the private scape, and a single dimensional reward size sensor, which forwards to the substrate a vector of length 1, containing the reward size of the reward acquired at that particular sector. But because the signals that the private scape returns to a querying sensor is based on that sensor's parameter, we have actually already implemented these two sensors. We can allow our existing *dtm_GetInput* sensor to act as the two sensors we are after by simply having one dtm_GetInput use the parameter *reward*, and the other use *range_sense*, with the vl set to 1 and 3 respectively. Thus, with regards to the sensors, we need only modify the *morphology* module, so that two sensors are produced through two different parameters, as show in Listing-16.24.

Listing-16.24 Modifying the morphology module to specify two sensors using the parameters: *reward*, and *range_sense*, rather than: *all*.

```
discrete_tmaze(sensors)->
    [#sensor{name=dtm_GetInput,type=standard,scape={private,dtm_sim},vl=VL, parameters
=[Parameter]} || {VL,Parameter} <- [{1,reward},{3,range_sense}]];
discrete_tmaze(actuators)->
    [
    %#actuator{name=dtm_SendOutput,type=standard,scape={private,dtm_sim},vl=1,
parameters=[]}
    #actuator{name=dtm_SubstrateSendOutput,type=standard,scape={private,dtm_sim},vl=3,
parameters=[]}
    ].
```

From the above listing, you will also notice that a new actuator has already been specified, the *dtm_SubstrateSendOutput* actuator, with *vl=3*. The actuator we used in the previous two chapters was a simple program which accepted a vector of length one, and based on it decided whether to send to the private scape an action that would turn the agent's avatar to the left, to the right, or move straight ahead. But now we have access to the geometry of the sensor, and thus we can use an actuator that takes advantage of that geometry. And so we make an actuator that is executed with an output vector of length 3: [L,F,R], calculates which of the elements within the vector has the highest magnitude, and based on that value performs the action. If L is the highest, then the agent turns left and moves one sector forward, if F is the highest, the agent moves forward one sector, and if R is the highest, the agent turns right and moves one sector forward. The implementation of the new actuator is shown in Listing-16.25.

Listing-16.25 The implementation of the substrate based actuator added to the actuator module.

```
dtm_SubstrateSendOutput(Output,Parameters,Scape)->
    [L,F,R] = Output,
    Action =if
            ((L > F) and (L > R)) -> [-1];
            ((R > F) and (R > L)) -> [1];
            true -> [0]
    end,
    Scape ! {self(),move,Parameters,Action},
    receive
            {Scape,Fitness,HaltFlag}->
                    {Fitness,HaltFlag}
    end.
```

Though certainly these new sensors and actuators can also be used by our standard neural encoded NNs, it is the substrate encoded NN based agent that can better take advantage of their properties. With these new sensors and actuators, we now perform the benchmark of our system on the T-Maze problem. We leave the *pmp* parameters as in the previous chapter, but we slightly change the genotype, so that the agent starts off with both of the sensors rather than just one. In this manner the agent from the very start will have access to the reward and range sensors, and access to the movement actuator (just as did our neural encoded agent). This is accomplished by us simply using the function *morphology:get_Sensors/1* instead of *morphology:get_InitSensors/1* in the *genotype* module under the encoding case type: *substrate*. We do this only for this problem, and can change it back after we're done.

To perform the benchmark, we set the benchmarker's ?INIT_CONSTRAINTS to:

```
-define(INIT_CONSTRAINTS,[#constraint{morphology=Morphology,connection_architecture
=CA, population_evo_alg_f=generational, agent_encoding_types=[substrate],
substrate_plasticities=[none]} || Morphology<-[discrete_tmaze], CA<-[feedforward]]).
```

Then execute polis:sync(), and then finally run the benchmark by executing: *benchmarker:start(substrate_dtm)*. The result of this benchmark is shown in the following listing.

Listing-16.26 The benchmark results of performing the T-Maze benchmark with a substrate encoded NN based agent.

```
Graph:{graph,discrete_tmaze,
        [1.0941666666666665,1.0963888888888889,1.1025,1.1183333333333334,
        1.0733333333333335,1.0944444444444446,1.0950000000000002,
        1.0899999999999999,1.0900000000000003,1.1072222222222222],
        [0.08648619029134716,0.09606895350299437,0.1077903056865505,
        0.09157571245210767,0.07423685817106697,0.08624541497922236,
        0.09733961166965892,0.099498743710662,0.06999999999999999,
        0.1057177117038637],
        [113.04933333333342,107.690888888889,109.23533333333341,
        110.34133333333344,112.18933333333344,117.18266666666673,
        110.90533333333342,113.21533333333343,110.77066666666674,
        111.924888888889],
        [10.895515978807254,12.527729754034578,9.791443225819389,
        9.502769093503451,9.827619673371789,6.41172966783014,
        12.66381855699315,8.934695692138094,10.400047521258944,
        8.231449225116977],
        [122.0000000000001,122.0000000000001,122.0000000000001,
        122.0000000000001,122.0000000000001,122.0000000000001,
        122.0000000000001,122.0000000000001,122.0000000000001,
        122.0000000000001],
        [10.000000000000115,10.000000000000115,10.000000000000115,
        10.000000000000115,10.000000000000115,10.000000000000115,
        10.000000000000115,10.000000000000115,10.000000000000115,
        10.000000000000115],
        [8.4,8.3,9.15,9.25,8.85,8.9,9.0,8.65,8.9,9.0],
        [1.1135528725660042,1.004987562112089,0.7262919523166976,
        0.7664854858377946,1.3883443376914821,0.8306623862918074,
        1.140175425099138,1.3518505834595775,1.1789826122551597,
        0.9486832980505138],
        [500.0,500.0,500.0,475.0,500.0,500.0,500.0,500.0,500.0,500.0],
        []}
Tot Evaluations Avg:5091.5 Std:37.78160928282436
```

As expected, and similarly to the results of the T-Maze navigation of chapter-14, our TWEANN was able to evolve agents which always go to the right corner containing the large reward before the position of the large and the small rewards are switched. And as before, we will be able to evolve agents which learn from experience after we've added plasticity in the next chapter, which will result in agents able to solve this problem and achieve the score of 149.2.

Nevertheless, the test shows that our system works, and the new actuator and sensors work. Our TWEANN system evolved a relatively competent T-Maze navigator, but the substrate still lacks plasticity, and so we cannot expect our TWEANN to evolve a perfect solution just yet. Both of these examples, double pole balancing and T-Maze navigation, demonstrate that our substrate encoded NN based systems are functional, without errors, and capable of evolving and improving, and that our TWEANN can successfully evolve such agents. We need now only to apply our substrate encoded NN based agents to a problem which offers an advantage to systems capable of extracting the problem's geometrical regularities. An example of such a problem is the analysis of financial charts. And it is this problem that we will explore in Chapter-19.

16.12 Summary and Discussion

In this chapter we have developed a substrate encoded architecture for our memetic algorithm based topology and weight evolving artificial neural network platform. We modified the implementation of our TWEANN to allow the evolution of both, neural and substrate encoded NNs. Our substrate encoded NN is able to evolve and integrate new substrate_cpps and substrate_ceps, and to also use various substrate topologies through the use of the *linkform* element in the substrate record. We have implemented and tested our new system. The tests demonstrate that our TWEANN system is able to evolve substrate encoded NNs effectively, but that the problems we have created for testing purposes are not well suited for this type of encoding.

This was not an easy chapter, the code was long, and it will require some time to analyze. Even more, our evolved SENN agents are not yet fully implemented; the substrate encoded NN based agents are still missing an important feature: *plasticity*. In the next chapter we add that feature, allowing for the substrates to not only have the evolved NNs simply set the neurode synaptic weights, but allow those same NNs to act as evolving learning rules, which update the synaptic weights of the substrate embedded neurodes, based on their location, and their pre- and post- synaptic signals.

16.13 References

[1] Supplementary material: www.DXNNResearch.com/NeuroevolutionThroughErlang
[2] Risi S, Stanley KO (2010) Indirectly Encoding Neural Plasticity as a Pattern of Local Rules. Neural Plasticity 6226, 1-11.

[3] Haasdijk E, Rusu AA, Eiben AE (2010) HyperNEAT for Locomotion Control in Modular Robots. Control 6274, 169-180.

[4] Coleman OJ (2010) Evolving Neural Networks for Visual Processing. Undergraduate Honours Thesis (Bachelor of Computer Science), University of New South Wales

[5] Stanley KO, Miikkulainen R (2002) Evolving Neural Networks Through Augmenting Topologies. Evolutionary Computation 10, 99-127.

Chapter 17 Substrate Plasticity

Abstract In this chapter we develop a method for the substrate to possess plasticity, and thus have the synaptic weights of its neurodes change through experience. We first discuss the ABC and the Iterative substrate learning rules popularized within the HyperNEAT neuroevolutionary system. Then we implement the said learning rules within our own system, through only just a few minor modifications to our existing architecture.

Our system now has a highly advanced direct encoded NN implementation with plasticity. It includes various other performance improving features. Our TWEANN platform can even evolve substrate encoded NN based agents. Yet still our TWEANN does not have all the essential elements of a bleeding edge system, one thing is missing... *substrate plasticity*.

The implementation of substrate plasticity is not as simple as turning the plasticity on in the NN itself. If we allow for the NN to have plasticity, it will *not* translate into a substrate encoded NN with plasticity because the NN will simply be changing, but simply based on the sequence of the coordinates that it is processing from the substrate embedded neurodes, as opposed to the actual sensory signals. Also, as it changes, it will have no affect on the substrate which is the one processing the sensory signals, because the NN sets the substrate's synaptic weights only at the very start of an evaluation. Thus, what we need is a method that will allow for the synaptic weights between the neurodes to update using some kind of advanced learning rule, not necessarily Hebbian. Surprisingly, this is an easy task to accomplish.

At this time the NN produces synaptic weights between the neurodes. But what if we feed the NN not just the coordinates of the connected neurodes, but also the neurode's presynaptic signal, its postsynaptic signal, its current weight for the connection, and then designate and use the NN's output not as a new synaptic weight, but as a change in that weight? And let the NN produce these changes not only at the very start of the evaluation, but continually, every cycle, every time the substrate processes its set of sensory vectors. This approach will effectively make the entire NN into a learning rule producing system. So how do we do it?

For example, if we change the substrate_cpp from feeding the NN the vector: [X1,Y1...X2,Y2...] to: [X1,Y1...X2,Y2...PreSynaptic,PostSynaptic,CurWeight], and change the standard substrate_cep currently used from outputting: [SynapticWeight] to: [Delta_SynapticWeight], and instead of setting the substrate_state_flag to hold, we set it to iterative, letting the NN produce the Delta_SynapticWeight signals after every time the substrate processes a signal, the substrate will gain a highly dynamic learning rule. After processing the sensory signals, the substrate has all its neurode weights updated from CurWeight to CurWeight+Delta_SynapticWeight. And so the substrate is changing, learning

G.I. Sher, *Handbook of Neuroevolution Through Erlang*,
DOI 10.1007/978-1-4614-4463-3_17, © Springer Science+Business Media New York 2013

through sensory experience. Of course this does mean that we have to execute the NN X number of times, every time the substrate processes the signals from its sensors, where X is the number of neurode connections. So if SENN lives for 1000 cycles, it must execute and poll the NN 1000*X number of times.

On the other hand, if we for example use a substrate_cep which outputs: [W,A,B,C,N] similarly to the substrate_cep that outputs: [W], just once during the evaluation at the beginning, then the substrate_cep outputs not just the synaptic weights between the neurodes, but the parameters the neurodes can use for the execution of a Hebbian learning rule. This too will effectively add plasticity to the substrate, since now it not only has the initial synaptic weights, but also the parameters needed to calculate the update of the synaptic weights of every neurode after it processes some signal. Not to mention, the NN is a highly complex, advanced, evolving system, and thus the learning rules, the parameters, will be coordinate and connection specific, and the learning rule itself will evolve and optimize over the generations due to the NN itself growing and evolving over time.

The two of the above rules were originally introduced in the HyperNEAT system, and tested on a discrete T-Maze problem similar to the one we built in an earlier chapter. The first method is called *iterative*, while the second method is called the *abc* update rule (aka *abcn* update rule). As you can see, we can use the NN to really produce any kind of signal, and use that NN output signal it any way we want, as a synaptic weight, as a synaptic weight update rule, as both, as none... In this chapter we implement the above two rules, and then test our new learning system on the Discrete T-Maze problem.

17.1 The Updated Architecture

We have actually already performed the brunt of the work in the previous chapter. The way we designed our substrate encoded NN system, allows us to easily use the NN on the substrate in any way we want, and it allows us to similarly repurpose the substrate to any task. To implement the *abcn* learning rule, we will need to slightly change the tuple representation of the neurodes within the substrate, such that each tuple can also keep track of the learning parameters for every synaptic weight. The case will be even simpler with regards to the *Iterative* learning rule, in which the NN can directly output a signal which simply acts as the change in the synaptic weight. The only major update to our implementation with regards to the *iterative* learning rule, is that the neurodes need to be updated after every time they process a signal, and that update has to be done by calling the NN for every synaptic weight.

The other significant update to our system will deal with creating new substrate_cpps within the morphology. As you recall, a general Hebbian learning rule requires the postsynaptic neurode's input from presynaptic neurode X, postsynaptic neurode's synaptic weight for the connection with X, and the postsynaptic neurode's output. Since our NN will now act as a learning rule by producing the change in the synaptic weight (in the case of the *iterative* implementation), or produce a set of parameters for each neurode to utilize a form of a Hebbian learning rule (in the case of the *abcn* implementation), we need to feed the NN not just the coordinates of the connected neurodes, but also these three essential values: Input, Weight, Output.

> ****Note****
>
> Although granted, we could choose to simply feed the NN just the coordinates... but that would make for a much less effective learning rule, since the NN will have that much less information about the synaptic links.
> ***********

In the next two sections we will add the necessary functions to our substrate implementation such that it can support these two types of learning rules. The best part is that these two rules encompass a whole class of other related rules, which after the implementation can easily be expanded. For example, after the *abcn* rule is implemented, we can easily change it to Oja's, or any other type of parameter based learning rule. On the other hand, after we implement the *iterative* rule, we will be able to implement any type of rule where synaptic weight or other types of parameters have to be updated after every single signal processing step (during every sense-think-act cycle).

17.2 Implementing the abcn Learning Rule

When using the abcn rule, the NN needs to be called only once every evaluation, per connection between two neurodes. The only difference between it and the standard *none* plasticity version we have implemented, is that the NN does not only set up the synaptic weight W, but also generates the parameters: A, B, C, N, for each such synaptic weight. The implementation of this learning rule will primarily concentrate on the change of the tuple representing the neurode within the substrate.

17.2.1 Updating the substrate Module

While updating the substrate module, we want to disrupt as little of it as possible. The standard neurode representing tuple has the following format: {Coordinate,Output,Weights}. The Weights list is only used for its values within the function calculate_neurode_output_std/3, which itself is executed from the function calculate_output/3, which is called for every neurode to calculate that neurode's output. This function is shown in the following listing.

Listing-17.1 The calculate_output/3 function.

```
calculate_output(I_Neurodes,Neurode,Plasticity,CPP_PIds,CEP_PIds)->
    {Coord,_Prev_O,Weights} = Neurode,
    case Plasticity of
        none ->
                Output=calculate_neurode_output_std(I_Neurodes,Neurode,0),
                {Coord,Output,Weights}
    end.
```

This is the function executed during the times when the substrate_state_flag is set to *reset* and *hold,* and it's already almost perfectly set up for use with different types of plasticities. Thus, since this is the only function that really sees the format of the Weights list, which is itself set by the *set_weight/2* function executed when the substrate_cep sends the substrate the set_weight message, we need only add a new function triggered by a substrate_cep (similar to set_weight, but which sets all the other Hebbian learning rule parameters as well), and a new calculate_neurode_output_plast/3 function, which can handle the new type of tuple representing a plastic neurode.

To allow for Oja's and Hebbian types of plasticity, we need for the neurode to store not just weights, but also the learning parameters for each weight. When the substrate uses a Hebbian type of plasticity, we need to allow for the neurodes to be represented as: {Coordinates,Output,WeightsP}, where WeightsP has the format: [{W, LearningRuleName, Parameters}...].

As we noted before, because the structure of the list representing the neurode's synaptic weights is accessed and used when those weights are being set by the *set_weight* function, and when being read to calculate the output by the *calculate_substrate_output_std* function, we need only modify those two functions to set the weights list to the new format, and create a new *calculate_substrate_output_plast* function which can read that list. Finally, we also create a new function which updates the neurode after it has calculated an output, at which point the Hebbian learning rule has the Input, Output, and the Synaptic Weights needed to calculate the weight changes.

Since we must send the substrate_cpps not just the coordinates of the two neurons, but also the neurode's Input, Output, and current synaptic Weight values, we first update the *populate_PHyperlayers_l2l, populate_PHyperlayers_fi,* and *populate_PHyperlayers_nsr* functions, from which the get_weights is called. The updated version simply checks the plasticity, and if it is of type *abcn,* it then calls the get_weights function, which calls the cpps with the three new values, as shown in the following listing.

Listing-17.2 The updated implementation of the populate_PHyperlayers_l2l function, and the new get_weights function.

```
populate_PHyperlayers_l2l(PrevHyperlayer,[{Coord,PrevO,PrevWeights}|CurHyperlayer],
Substrate, CPP_PIds, CEP_PIds, Plasticity,Acc1,Acc2)->
    NewWeights = case Plasticity of
        none ->
            get_weights(PrevHyperlayer,Coord,CPP_PIds,CEP_PIds,[]);
        _ ->
            get_weights(PrevHyperlayer,Coord,CPP_PIds,CEP_PIds,[],PrevWeights,
PrevO)
    end,
populate_PHyperlayers_l2l(PrevHyperlayer,CurHyperlayer,Substrate,CPP_PIds,CEP_PIds,
Plasticity,[{Coord,PrevO, NewWeights}|Acc1],Acc2);
    populate_PHyperlayers_l2l(_PrevHyperlayer,[],[CurHyperlayer|Substrate],CPP_PIds,
CEP_PIds, Plasticity, Acc1,Acc2)->
    PrevHyperlayer = lists:reverse(Acc1),
populate_PHyperlayers_l2l(PrevHyperlayer, CurHyperlayer,Substrate,CPP_PIds,CEP_PIds,
Plasticity,[],[PrevHyperlayer|Acc2]);
    populate_PHyperlayers_l2l(_PrvHyperlayer,[],[],CPP_PIds,CEP_PIds,Plasticity,Acc1,Acc2)->
    lists:reverse([lists:reverse(Acc1)|Acc2]).
...
    get_weights([{I_Coord,I,_I_Weights}|I_Neurodes],Coord,CPP_PIds,CEP_PIds,Acc,
[W|Weights],O)->
        plasticity_fanout(CPP_PIds,I_Coord,Coord,[I,O,W]),
        U_W=fanin(CEP_PIds,W),
        get_weights(I_Neurodes,Coord,CPP_PIds,CEP_PIds,[U_W|Acc],Weights,O);
    get_weights([],_Coord,CPP_PIds,CEP_PIds,Acc,[],_O)->
        lists:reverse(Acc).

    plasticity_fanout([CPP_PId|CPP_PIds],I_Coord,Coord,IOW)->
        CPP_PId ! {self(),I_Coord,Coord,IOW},
        plasticity_fanout(CPP_PIds,I_Coord,Coord,IOW);
    plasticity_fanout([],_I_Coord,_Coord,_IOW)->
        done.
```

The above listing only shows the populate_PHyperlayers_l2l function, with the updated source in boldface. The other two *populate_PHyperlayers_* functions are similarly updated with the new case clause. When Plasticity is not set to *none*, the new get_weights/7 function is executed, which in return calls the plasticity_fanout/4 function, which forwards the vector [I,O,W], along with the coordinates, to the NN's substrate_cpps. We will update the morphology and create the new substrate_cpps a bit later. When the NN has finished processing these signals, the NN's new *abcn* substrate_cep, sends the substrate the vector: [W,A,B,C,N], and the message to execute the set_abcn/2 function, whose implementation is shown next.

Listing-17.3 The implementation of the set_abcn function.

```
set_abcn(Signal,_WP)->
    [U_W,A,B,C,N] = Signal,
    {functions:sat(U_W,3.1415,-3.1415),abcn,[A,B,C,N]}.
```

When this function is called, it returns the tuple: {functions:sat(U_W,3.1415,-3.1415),abcn,[A,B,C,N]}, which now takes the place of the simple synaptic weight value. This is done for every synaptic weight in the weights list of every neurode.

Once all neurodes have been updated in this manner, the substrate can now start processing the sensory signals. Everything is left the same as before, the only thing that needs to be changed is the actual function which calculates the output of the neurode by processing its input and the neurode's synaptic weights. This is done in the calculate_*output* function. We thus update it to check for the *plasticity* type of the substrate, and based on it, either execute the standard calculate_neurode_output_std, or in the case of the abcn rule, the new calculate_neurode_output_plast function. Listing-17.4 shows the updated calculate_output/5 function, and the new functions which it calls.

Listing-17.4 The implementation of the updated calculate_output/5 function.

```
calculate_output(I_Neurodes,Neurode,Plasticity,CPP_PIds,CEP_PIds)->
    {Coord,_Prev_O,Weights} = Neurode,
    case Plasticity of
        none ->
                Output=calculate_neurode_output_std(I_Neurodes,Neurode,0),
                {Coord,Output,Weights};
        abcn ->
                Output=calculate_neurode_output_plast(I_Neurodes,Neurode,0),
                update_neurode(I_Neurodes,{Coord,Output,Weights},[])
    end.
...
    calculate_neurode_output_plast([{_I_Coord,O,_I_Weights}|I_Neurodes],{Coord,Prev_O,
[{W,_LF,_Parameters}|WPs]},Acc)->
        calculate_neurode_output_plast(I_Neurodes,{Coord,Prev_O,WPs},O*W+Acc);
    calculate_neurode_output_plast([],{Coord,Prev_O,[]},Acc)->
        functions:tanh(Acc).

    update_neurode([{_I_Coord,I_O,_I_Weights}|I_Neurodes],{Coord,O, [{W,LF,Parameters}
|WPs]},Acc)->
        U_W = substrate:LF(I_O,O,W,Parameters),
        update_neurode(I_Neurodes,{Coord,O,WPs},[{U_W,LF,Parameters}|Acc]);
    update_neurode([],{Coord,O,[]},Acc)->
```

```
{Coord,O,lists:reverse(Acc)}.

abcn(Input,Output,W,[A,B,C,N])->
      Delta_Weight = N*(A*Input*Output + B*Input + C*Output),
      W+Delta_Weight.
```

When plasticity is set to *abcn,* the calculate_output function first executes the calculate_substrate_output_plast function which calculates the neurode's output, and then the function update_neurode/3, which updates the neurode's synaptic weights based on the parameters stored in the tuple representing the given neurode.

What is interesting here is that the update_neurode executes the update function based on the atom within the tuple representing neurode. So if we change the learning rule specifying atom from: abcn, to for example: *ojas*, and implement the ojas/4 function, then we can easily and without any further changes, start using the Oja's learning rule.

That is effectively it with regards to updating the substrate module. We next update the morphology, and add to it the new substrate cpps and ceps needed for this learning rule.

17.2.2 Updating the Morphology Module

Our substrate can now deal with the new type of substrate_cpp and substrate_cep, yet we have neither specified nor created them yet. We do just that in this section.

When creating substrate_cpps and substrate_ceps, we have to specify the Plasticity type that the substrate will use. Thus we can modify the cpps and ceps to use different input and output vector lengths dependent on the type of plasticity. For example, since both the iterative and the abcn learning rules both require substrate_cpps to pass to the NN an extended vector with the extra three values for Input, Output, and Wieght: [I,O,W], we set the morphology in such a way that when plasticity is set to abcn or iterative, a different set of substrate_cpps is created, as shown in the following listing.

```
Listing-17.5 The implementation of the updated get_SubstrateCPPs/2 function.

get_SubstrateCPPs(Dimensions,Plasticity)->
    io:format("Dimensions:~p, Plasticity:~p~n",[Dimensions,Plasticity]),
    if
            (Plasticity == iterative) or (Plasticity == abcn) ->
                Std=[
```

```
                        #sensor{name=cartesian,type=substrate,vl=Dimensions*2+3}
                        #sensor{name=centripital_distances,type=substrate,vl=2+3},
                        #sensor{name=cartesian_distance,type=substrate,vl=1+3},
                        #sensor{name=cartesian_CoordDiffs,type=substrate,vl
=Dimensions+3},
                    #sensor{name=cartesian_GaussedCoordDiffs,type=substrate,vl
=Dimensions+3},
                        #sensor{name=iow,type=substrate,vl=3}
                    ],
                    Adt=case Dimensions of
                        2 ->
                                [#sensor{name=polar,type=substrate,vl=Dimensions*2+3}];
                        3 ->
                                [#sensor{name=spherical,type=substrate,vl
=Dimensions*2+3}];
                        _ ->
                                []
                    end,
                    lists:append(Std,Adt);
        (Plasticity == none) ->
                    Std=[
                        #sensor{name=cartesian,type=substrate,vl=Dimensions*2},
                        #sensor{name=centripital_distances,type=substrate,vl=2},
                        #sensor{name=cartesian_distance,type=substrate,vl=1},
                        #sensor{name=cartesian_CoordDiffs,type=substrate,vl=Dimensions},
                        #sensor{name=cartesian_GaussedCoordDiffs,type=substrate, vl
=Dimensions}
                    ],
                    Adt=case Dimensions of
                        2 ->
                                [#sensor{name=polar,type=substrate,vl=Dimensions*2}];
                        3 ->
                                [#sensor{name=spherical,type=substrate,vl=Dimensions*2}];
                        _ ->
                                []
                    end,
                    lists:append(Std,Adt)
    end.
```

In the above updated function, we simply add to the *vl* parameter the extra: *3,* that is required to deal with the extended vector when the plasticity is set to abcn or iterative. Listing-17.6 shows the updated get_SubstrateCEPs/2 function, with its new cep that the abcn learning rule uses.

Listing-17.6 The implementation of the updated get_SubstrateCEPs/2 function.

```
get_SubstrateCEPs(Dimensions,Plasticity)->
    case Plasticity of
        abcn ->
            [#actuator{name=set_abcn,type=substrate,vl=5}];
        none ->
            [#actuator{name=set_weight,type=substrate,vl=1}];
    end.
```

With this done, we need now only modify the substrate_cpp and substrate_cep modules.

17.2.3 Updating the substrate_cpp & substrate_cep Modules

The only remaining modification left, is one done to the substrate_cpp and sub-strate_cep modules. For the first, we simply extend the receive loop so that it can accept a message tuple of the form: {Substrate_PId, Presynaptic_Coords, Postsynaptic_Coords, **IOW**}. Which is an extended message to also accommodate the new vector **[I,O,W]** of length 3. The updated loop/8 function is shown in Listing-17.7, with the added functionality in boldface.

```
Listing-17.7 The implementation of the updated substrate_cpp:loop/6 function.

loop(Id,ExoSelf_PId,Cx_PId,Substrate_PId,CPPName,VL,Parameters,Fanout_PIds)->
    receive
        {Substrate_PId,Presynaptic_Coords,Postsynaptic_Coords}->
            SensoryVector = functions:CPPName(Presynaptic_Coords,
Postsynaptic_Coords),
            [Pid ! {self(),forward,SensoryVector} || Pid <- Fanout_PIds],
            loop(Id,ExoSelf_PId,Cx_PId,Substrate_PId,CPPName,VL,Parameters,
Fanout_PIds);
        {Substrate_PId,Presynaptic_Coords,Postsynaptic_Coords,IOW}->
            SensoryVector = functions:CPPName(Presynaptic_Coords,
Postsynaptic_Coords, IOW),
            [Pid ! {self(),forward,SensoryVector} || Pid <- Fanout_PIds],
            loop(Id,ExoSelf_PId,Cx_PId,Substrate_PId,CPPName,VL,Parameters,
Fanout_PIds);
        {ExoSelf_PId,terminate} ->
            ok
    end.
```

Since to produce the actual **SensoryVector** the cpp uses the **CPPName** function found in the *functions* module, we also add the new necessary functions to the *functions* module. The following listing shows the newly added functions which allow the substrate_cpp to process the extended vector, and produce the sensory vectors of appropriate lengths, which now will include the IOW values.

Listing-17.8 The new sensory signal processing functions in the *functions* module.

```
cartesian(I_Coord,Coord,[I,O,W])->
   [I,O,W|lists:append(I_Coord,Coord)].

polar(I_Coord,Coord,[I,O,W])->
   [I,O,W|lists:append(cart2pol(I_Coord),cart2pol(Coord))].

spherical(I_Coord,Coord,[I,O,W])->
   [I,O,W|lists:append(cart2spher(I_Coord),cart2spher(Coord))].

centripetal_distances(I_Coord,Coord,[I,O,W])->
   [I,O,W,centripetal_distance(I_Coord,0),centripetal_distance(Coord,0)].

cartesian_distance(I_Coord,Coord,[I,O,W])->
   [I,O,W,calculate_distance(I_Coord,Coord,0)].

cartesian_CoordDiffs(FromCoords,ToCoords,[I,O,W])->
   [I,O,W|cartesian_CoordDiffs(FromCoords,ToCoords)].

cartesian_GaussedCoordDiffs(FromCoords,ToCoords,[I,O,W])->
   [I,O,W|cartesian_GaussedCoordDiffs(FromCoords,ToCoords)].

iow(_I_Coord,_Coord,IOW)->
   IOW.
```

These are basically the same functions as used by the substrate plasticity of type *none*, except that they append to the resulting processed coordinates the vector IOW, as is shown above in boldface. Finally, we now add the new set_abcn/3 function to the substrate_cep module, as shown next.

Listing-17.9 A new set_abcn/3 function added to the substrate_cep module.

```
set_abcn(Output,_Parameters,Substrate_PId)->
   Substrate_PId ! {self(),set_abcn,Output}.
```

After the standard substrate_cep receive loop gathers all the signals from the presynaptic neurons, it executes the morphologically specified substrate_cep function, which is *set_abcn/3* in the case when *plasticity = abcn*. This function sends to the substrate the output vector: [W,A,B,C,N], and the message *set_abcn*, which the substrate then uses to execute the set_abcn function which we added to the substrate module earlier in this chapter.

17.2.4 Benchmarking the New Substrate Plasticity

Undramatically, these are all the modifications that were needed to allow our substrate encoded system to let the neurodes utilize the Hebbian learning rule. Now that our substrate encoded NN based system has the ability to learn, we again test it on the discrete T-Maze problem, with the results shown in Listing-17.10.

Listing-17.10 The benchmark results of the application of the substrate encoded NN based system with *abcn* plasticity, to the discrete T-Maze problem.

```
Graph:{graph,discrete_tmaze,
      [5.117069757727654,5.2276148705096075,5.256698564593302,
      5.323939393939395,5.367008430166325,5.383246753246754,
      5.340942697653223,5.335703463203464,5.310778651173387,
      5.318170426065162],
      [0.09262706161715503,0.13307346652534205,0.15643200235420435,
      0.19103627317236116,0.24840028484238094,0.3074955828617828,
      0.22050190155526622,0.2687961935948596,0.27809920403845456,
      0.2890597857666472],
      [102.30049832915634,115.57537176274028,115.82996172248811,
      119.80377705627716,117.495043745728,122.40998917748922,
      126.54832308042839,127.85407575757583,131.0029333561176,
      129.20257552973348],
      [19.387895647932833,6.436782140204616,7.641824017959771,
      9.509692909802402,11.439728974016472,8.54974974710698,
      10.520194897286766,10.492965582165443,10.152832110453105,
      10.20904378137977],
      [145.20000000000002,149.2,145.60000000000002,149.2,148.6,149.2,
      149.2,149.2,149.2,149.2],
      [0,10.000000000000115,10.000000000000115,10.000000000000115,
      10.000000000000115,10.000000000000115,10.000000000000115,
      10.000000000000115,10.000000000000115,10.000000000000115],
      [16.95,18.05,18.15,18.35,18.05,18.4,18.15,18.0,18.5,18.0],
      [1.5960889699512364,1.8834808201837359,1.3518505834595775,
      1.2757350822173077,1.8020821290940099,1.5297058540778357,
      1.3883443376914821,1.224744871391589,1.466287829861518,
      1.2649110640673518],
      [500.0,500.0,500.0,500.0,500.0,500.0,500.0,500.0,500.0,500.0],
      []}
Tot Evaluations Avg:5172.3 Std:110.92885107130606
```

As in Chapter-15, once plasticity is enabled, our TWEANN is able to evolve substrate encoded NN based agents which can effectively solve the T-Maze problem, achieving full score. As we've done once before, I will select one of the champions, and print out it's sensory and action based signals to demonstrate that indeed the agent, once it comes across the small reward occurring at [1,1] after the switch, does change its strategy and begins to move towards [-1,1], as shown next:

```
Position:[0,0] SenseSignal:[0,1,0] RewardSignal:[0] Move:0 StepIndex:1 RunIndex:0
Position:[0,1] SenseSignal: [1,0,1] RewardSignal:[0] Move:1 StepIndex:2 RunIndex:0
Position:[1,1] SenseSignal:[0,0,0] RewardSignal:[1] Move:0 StepIndex:3 RunIndex:0
Position:[0,0] SenseSignal:[0,1,0] RewardSignal:[0] Move:0 StepIndex:1 RunIndex:1
Position:[0,1] SenseSignal: [1,0,1] RewardSignal:[0] Move:1 StepIndex:2 RunIndex:1
Position:[1,1] SenseSignal:[0,0,0] RewardSignal:[1] Move:0 StepIndex:3 RunIndex:1
...

Position:[0,0] SenseSignal:[0,1,0] RewardSignal:[0] Move:0 StepIndex:1 RunIndex:55
Position:[0,1] SenseSignal:[1,0,1] RewardSignal:[0] Move:1 StepIndex:2 RunIndex:55
Position:[1,1] SenseSignal:[0,0,0] RewardSignal:[0.2] Move:0 StepIndex:3 RunIndex:55
Position:[0,0] SenseSignal:[0,1,0] RewardSignal:[0] Move:0 StepIndex:1 RunIndex:56
Position:[0,1] SenseSignal:[1,0,1] RewardSignal:[0] Move:-1 StepIndex:2 RunIndex:56
Position:[-1,1] SenseSignal:[0,0,0] RewardSignal:[1] Move:0 StepIndex:3 RunIndex:56
Position:[0,0] SenseSignal:[0,1,0] RewardSignal:[0] Move:0 StepIndex:1 RunIndex:57
Position:[0,1] SenseSignal:[1,0,1] RewardSignal:[0] Move:-1 StepIndex:2 RunIndex:57
Position:[-1,1] SenseSignal:[0,0,0] RewardSignal:[1] Move:0 StepIndex:3 RunIndex:57
```

In the above console printout, the switch event occurred on the 55th maze run, and on the 56th the agent began going to the [-1,1] corner to collect the switched, large reward. We next add the iterative learning rule, and see how it fares in this problem. Although based on the Listing-17.10, we can readily see that the substrate encoded NN based system, using the abcn learning rule, can already solve the problem within the first 1000 evaluations. There is little margin for improvement.

17.3 Implementing the iterative Learning Rule

The iterative plasticity works in a different way than the just added *abcn* learning rule. For the substrate to utilize the iterative plasticity function, it must pole the NN for every weight of every neurode after every time that neurode produces an output by processing its input signals. Whereas before the substrate used the NN to set all the synaptic weights and parameters once per evaluation, it now must call the NN for every synaptic weight every sense-think-act cycle. This requires significantly more computational power. Yet at the same time it does allow for the entire NN to act as a learning rule, and because a NN is a universal function approximator, and because it produces its output based on the coordinates, the input, the output, and the current synaptic weight between the connected neurodes, it could potentially be incredibly versatile, and allow for virtually any type of learning rule to evolve.

The implementation of this learning rule also encompasses all the learning rules in which the substrate needs to update the synaptic weights every cycle, as opposed to every evaluation as is the case with the abcn rule. Thus by implementing it here and now, we open our SENN system to all future learning rules which use this type of updating approach.

Again, surprisingly the implementation of this learning rule will require only a few minor modifications to our existing substrate module, and a small addition to the substrate_cep, and the morphology module. The first change is within the *reason* function. Though we set up and compose the new substrate as usual when the substrate_state_flag is set to reset, after the initial substrate with the default synaptic weights equaling to zero have been set, we set the substrate_state_flag to *iterative*. We do not set it to *hold* because we will need to call *get_weights* function during every cycle. Thus by setting the substrate_state_flag to *iterative*, and by creating a new case in the *reason* function, as shown in Listing-17.11, we can re-use the calculate_ResetOutput/7 function during every cycle to update the synaptic weights of the neurodes by calling the get_weights function.

```
Listing-17.11 The implementation of the updated reason/7 function.

reason(Input,S)->
    Densities = S#state.densities,
    Substrate = S#state.cur_substrate,
    SMode = S#state.substrate_state_flag,
    CPP_PIds = S#state.cpp_pids,
    CEP_PIds = S#state.cep_pids,
    Plasticity = S#state.plasticity,
    case SMode of
            reset ->
                    Sensors=S#state.sensors,
                    Actuators=S#state.actuators,
                    New_Substrate=create_substrate(Sensors,Densities,Actuators,
S#state.link_form),
                    U_SMode=case Plasticity of
                        iterative ->
                            {Output,Populated_Substrate} = calculate_ResetOutput(
Densities, New_Substrate, Input, CPP_PIds, CEP_PIds, Plasticity,S#state.link_form),
                            iterative;
                        _ ->
                            {Output,Populated_Substrate}=calculate_ResetOutput( Densities,
New_Substrate, Input,CPP_PIds,CEP_PIds,Plasticity, S#state.link_form),
                            hold
```

```
                end,
            {Populated_Substrate,U_SMode,Output};
        iterative ->
                {Output,U_Substrate} = calculate_ResetOutput(Densities,Substrate, Input,
CPP_PIds,CEP_PIds,Plasticity,S#state.link_form),
                {U_Substrate,SMode,Output};
        hold ->
                {Output,U_Substrate} = calculate_HoldOutput(Densities,Substrate, Input,
S#state.link_form, Plasticity,CPP_PIds,CEP_PIds),
                {U_Substrate,SMode,Output}
    end.
```

Since this update, shown in boldface in the above listing, ensures that the function *calculate_ResetOutput* is going to be called during every cycle, we need to update that function as shown in Listing-17.12.

Listing-17.12 The implementation of the updated calculate_ResetOutput/7 function.

```
calculate_ResetOutput(Densities,Substrate,Input,CPP_PIds,CEP_PIds,Plasticity,LinkForm)->
    [IHyperlayer|PHyperlayers] = Substrate,
    Populated_IHyperlayer = populate_InputHyperlayer(IHyperlayer,lists:flatten(Input),[]),
    case Plasticity of
        iterative ->
                {Output,U_PHyperlayers}=calculate_substrate_output(
Populated_IHyperlayer, PHyperlayers,LinkForm, Plasticity, CPP_PIds,CEP_PIds),
                {Output,[IHyperlayer|U_PHyperlayers]};
        _->
                Populated_PHyperlayers = populate_PHyperlayers(Substrate,CPP_PIds,
CEP_PIds, LinkForm, Plasticity),
                {Output,U_PHyperlayers}=calculate_substrate_output(Populated_IHyperlayer,
Populated_PHyperlayers, LinkForm,Plasticity, CPP_PIds,CEP_PIds),
                {Output,[IHyperlayer|U_PHyperlayers]}
    end.
```

As can be seen from the above listing, the difference in the functions executed when *Plasticity == iterative*, is in the fact that we no longer need to execute the populate_PHyperlayers/5, and instead we slightly modify the calculate_output/5 function called deep within the calculate_substrate_output/7 function, such that it calls the get_weights function after calculating the output of every node, and thus updating that node's synaptic weights. This updated function is shown in the following listing.

Listing-17.13 The implementation of the updated calculate_output/5 function.

```
calculate_output(I_Neurodes,Neurode,Plasticity,CPP_PIds,CEP_PIds)->
```

```
    {Coord,_Prev_O,Weights} = Neurode,
        case Plasticity of
            none ->
                    Output=calculate_neurode_output_std(I_Neurodes,Neurode,0),
                    {Coord,Output,Weights};
            iterative ->
                    Output=calculate_neurode_output_std(I_Neurodes,Neurode,0),
                    U_Weights = get_weights(I_Neurodes,Coord,CPP_PIds, CEP_PIds,
[], Weights, Output),
                    {Coord,Output,U_Weights};
            abcn ->
                    Output=calculate_neurode_output_plast(I_Neurodes,Neurode,0),
                    update_neurode(I_Neurodes,{Coord,Output,Weights},[])
        end.
```

Unlike the case when *Plasticity==none*, or *abcn*, when *Plasticity==iterative*, we call get_weights after calculating the Output value for every neurode. And it is this that allows us to update ever synaptic weight for every neurode during every cycle. This is effectively it. We now need only add, mirroring the set_abcn/2 function, the new set_iterative/2 function, as shown in Listing-17.14, and the substrate is now able to function without plasticity, with plasticity which is only set once during evaluation, and with plasticity that requires the polling of the NN during every cycle.

Listing-17.14 The implementation of the new set_iterative/2 function.

```
set_iterative(Signal,W)->
    [Delta_Weight] = Signal,
    functions:sat(W + Delta_Weight,3.1415,-3.1415).
```

We next modify the morphology module by updating the get_SubstrateCEPs/2 function, as shown in Listing-17.15. We update it by simply adding the new substrate_cep specification, which has an output vector length of 1, the value of the delta weight.

Listing-17.15 The updated get_SubstrateCEPs/2 function.

```
get_SubstrateCEPs(Dimensions,Plasticity)->
    case Plasticity of
        iterative ->
                [#actuator{name=delta_weight,type=substrate,vl=1}];
        abcn ->
                [#actuator{name=set_abcn,type=substrate,vl=5}];
        none ->
                [#actuator{name=set_weight,type=substrate,vl=1}]
```

```
end.
```

And finally we implement this new substrate_cep, updating the substrate_cep module as shown in the following listing.

Listing-17.16 The new delta_weight/3 function added to the substrate_cep module.

```
delta_weight(Output,_Parameters,Substrate_PId)->
    [Val] = Output,
    Threshold = 0.33,
    DW = if
            Val > Threshold ->
                    (functions:scale(Val,1,Threshold)+1)/2;
            Val < -Threshold ->
                    (functions:scale(Val,-Threshold,-1)-1)/2;
            true ->
                    0
    end,
    Substrate_PId ! {self(),set_iterative,[DW]}.
```

The new delta_weight/3 function is very similar to set_weight/3 function, the only difference is in the way it is used by the substrate. As we saw in Listing-17.11, the set_iterative/2 function updates the synaptic weight rather than over-writing it, which is the case with the original set_weight/2 function.

And that concludes the implementation of this learning rule. Again, completely undramatic, and accomplished very easily. In the next subsection we test this newly added plasticity learning rule on the now very familiar to use discrete T-Maze benchmark.

17.3.1 Benchmarking the New iterative Substrate Plasticity

Having now implemented the *iterative* plasticity learning rule, we test and see how it compares to the *abcn* learning rule, and the substrate which does not possess plasticity at all. The results of running the benchmark with the iterative learning rule is shown in Listing-17.17

Listing-17.17 The results of running the T-Maze benchmark with the iterative learning rule.

```
Graph:{graph,discrete_tmaze,
            [1.080697304856344,1.105477329687856,1.082608984582669,
            1.10173644338118,1.1018239026419805,1.1040638651965884,
```

1.1067042854170999,1.1083983426946815,1.0720152902017892,
1.1131932598294159],
[0.06523721492122392,0.05737539536993592,0.061080859604004445,
0.05539953173437482,0.04951815451574514,0.06096095772186648,
0.06779249262624067,0.055316036698257,0.0459640769682992,
0.0655751724549261],
[106.75590608768309,108.585491949571,114.94932017543867,
117.83561297182356,121.16001164967763,118.65738256708975,
121.01826794258375,122.92790528858384,122.86203973372172,
126.88959090909096],
[9.162803145363911,9.325149636485971,9.817899227379831,
9.10148250224565,9.783690310057073,9.788726424047805,
11.122540054241757,11.654351487379284,10.826960884668908,
10.50203798322592],
[148.4,148.4,149.2,149.2,149.2,149.2,149.2,149.2,149.2,149.2],
[11.40000000000012,10.600000000000119,10.600000000000119,
10.000000000000115,10.000000000000115,10.000000000000115,
10.600000000000119,10.600000000000119,10.000000000000115,
10.000000000000115],
[10.05,12.7,14.2,15.0,15.35,15.65,16.25,16.65,16.7,17.05],
[1.116915395184434,1.7349351572897473,1.5999999999999999,
2.32379000772445,2.1041625412500817,2.2197972880423116,
2.2107690969434146,1.7684739183827396,1.9261360284258222,
2.4181604578687494],
[500.0,500.0,500.0,500.0,500.0,500.0,500.0,500.0,500.0,500.0],
[]}
Tot Evaluations Avg:5188.85 Std:110.24122414051831

As expected, with this plasticity type, our TWEANN was again able to rapidly evolve SENNs capable of solving the T-Maze problem. Indeed, some near perfect solutions were evolved within the first 500 evaluations during a number of evolutionary runs. Unfortunately though, the iterative learning rule requires us to poll the NN for every synaptic weight of every neurode, during every sense-think-act cycle, which makes it slower than other rules, but also incredibly more versatile and powerful. Though it is possible to accelerate and optimize this system by for example transforming the evolved feedforward NNs into single functions, then embedding those functions within each neurode, and thus allowing each neurode to simply call on it as if it were a simple plasticity function... Nevertheless, the benchmark result in this subsection was a success, and we now have a fully functional, highly advanced TWEANN platform capable of effectively evolving neural and substrate encoded, static and plastic, neural network based agents.

17.4 Discussion

We have come a long way. At this point we've implemented a fully concurrent, and cutting edge, TWEANN platform. The benchmarks of both, the *abcn* and the *iterative* learning rules we've developed for our substrate encoded NNs have been a success. Both versions were rapidly (even more so than NNs with neural plasticity enabled) utilized by our TWEANN, which successfully evolved agents capable of solving the T-Maze problem. During many of the evolutionary runs composing the experiment, the solutions were evolved within the first 1000 evaluations. Yet still the iterative rule, though much more flexible, and allowing us to evolve any learning rule due to the NNs being universal function approximators, is computationally heavy. But it is possible to significantly accelerate this encoding by for example converting the feedforward NNs into single functions, which can then be utilized independently by each neurode. A feedforward NN is after all just a function of functions, which can be represented in the form of: $FF = f1(f2(f3(...)...)...)$, with the FF function then used directly by the substrate embedded neurodes. This would effectively make the entire SENN, excluding the sensors and actuators, be represented by a single process. But implementing this computational option is outside the scope of this volume, and will be covered with other advancements in the next book volume. Having now created an advanced TWEANN system, we apply it to some real world applications in the following chapters.

Part V
Applications

Our system is ready, it has direct and indirect encoding, plasticity of varying kinds, numerous activation functions, with new ones easily added, and even the ability to evolve evolutionary strategies. I noted that we will apply our system to complex, real world problems, not just benchmarks. We will do that in the next two chapters. The following two application areas are exciting, interesting, and lucrative. We will apply our system to an Artificial Life simulation, evolving the brains of 2d simulated robots, inhabiting a flatland, a 2d environment. And then we will use our system to evolve currency trading agents, an agent that reads the historical exchange rates of Euro vs. USD, and either buys or sells one against another on the Forex market, to make a profit. In fact, we will not only evolve NNs which use as sensory signals simply the lists of historical prices, but also NNs which use actual candle stick plot charts of historical prices.

Chapter 18 Artificial Life

Abstract   In this chapter we apply our neuroevolutionary system to an ALife simulation. We create new sensors and actuators for the NN based agents interfacing with their simulated environment avatars. Discuss the construction and implementation of the 2d ALife environment called Flatland. Interface our system to the said system, and then observe the resulting evolving behaviors of the simulated organisms.

We now come full circle. We started this book with a discussion on evolution of intelligent organisms, inhabiting a simulated (or real) world. In this chapter we convert that discussion into reality. We will create a flatland, a 2d world inhabited by 2d organisms, artificial life. Our neuroevolutionary system will evolve the brains of these 2d organisms, the avatars within the simulated environment controlled by our NN based agents, and through their avatars our NN based agents will explore the barren flatland, compete with other flatlanders for food, and predate on each other while trying to survive and consume the simulated food within the 2d world.

18.1 Simulated Environment and Artificial Organisms: Flatland

The goal of Alife [1,2,3] is to use evolution to evolve intelligent agents in an open ended simulated environment, using a fitness function that is at least to some degree similar to the animal world, in which the accumulation of resources and survival is correlated with achievement and therefore higher fitness and the creation of more offspring than those with a lower fitness.

Our simulation will be composed of a two dimensional environment, with food scattered throughout some region, where that food will be represented as green circles. The environment will be populated by simulated 2d herbivore robots, simulated as blue circles, and 2d predator type simulated robots, represented by red circles with small spears at one end.

Note that the circles will truly represent the morphologies of those simulated robots. The collision detection will be based on the circle's radius, and the robot's mass. The simulated environment will look something like Fig-18.1. In it you can see the world, the scattered through it food elements (small green circles), the prey (large blue circles), and the predators (smaller red circles). In honor of the book [4] "Flatland: A Romance of Many Dimensions", we will call this 2d environment simulation: *flatland*, and the evolving agents: *flatlanders*.

G.I. Sher, *Handbook of Neuroevolution Through Erlang*,
DOI 10.1007/978-1-4614-4463-3_18, © Springer Science+Business Media New York 2013

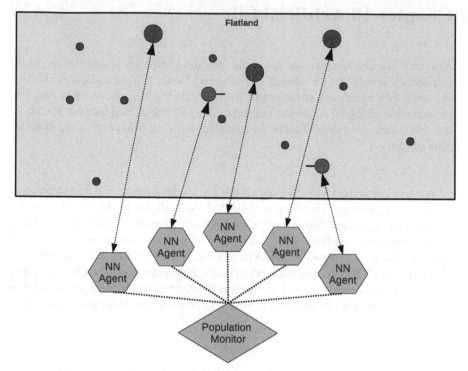

Fig. 18.1 Flatland, prey, predators, and plants.

Unlike other scapes we have developed before, flatland is a public scape. The agents when created will not spawn this scape, but join/enter it. The public scape itself must be created before any population monitor is even spawned. As we discussed in the first few chapters, it is these types of public scapes that should be spawned by the polis process, and it is these public scapes which will allow for the NN based agents to interact not just with the environment of the scape, but also with each other. The simulated robots are, in essence, avatars controlled by the NNs. We can also think of the simulated robots as the physical representations of the NN based agents, whose morphology, sensors, and actuators, dictate the physical representation of their avatars, with the NN truly then being the core of those organisms, the brains within.

18.2 The Scape and the Fitness Function

Most of the concepts we have developed when creating the XOR_Mimic, Double Pole Balancing, and particularly the T-Maze private scapes, can be reused here in the creation of the Flatland scape. The flatland will have to create a simulated representation, an avatar, for the NN that enters it. When a NN is spawned, it first sends the flatland a message that it wishes to enter the scape. At this point the scape checks the NNs morphology (specified by the message the exoself sent it), and based on that morphology creates an avatar for it. The scape also registers the NN as currently possessing an avatar within the scape, such that when the NN starts sending it action messages to control the avatar, and polls it for sensory messages based on the sensors of its avatar, the scape can move its avatar, and forward to it the sensory signals from its avatar, respectively. Thus, our system in this scenario should function as follows:

1. We create all the necessary databases to support the *polis* infrastructure by executing *polis:create()*.
2. Then the polis is started by executing *polis:start()*.
3. The polis spawns all public scapes at its disposal, which in this case is a list containing a single scape called *flatland*.
4. Once the flatland scape is created and its PId is registered with the polis, the scape creates all the basic elements within itself (all the simulated plants).
5. The researcher decides to start an ALife simulation, specifies within the constraint to use the *prey* morphology, which is a flatlander specie which the flatland scape recognizes as a type which can move around and eat plants when moving over them.
6. The researcher then compiles and executes population_monitor:test().
7. The population_monitor begins spawning agents.
8. When an agent is spawned, its exoself first determines what scapes the agent should either spawn (if private), or enter (if public).
9. The exoself thus forms a list of scape names. If private, they are spawned, and if public, the exoself sends the polis a message to request the PId of the public scape of that particular name.
10. The *polis* sends back to the exoself the PId of the particular scape. At which point the exoself sends this scape a message with its PId and morphology.
11. The scape, depending on what type of scape it is (flatland in this case), creates an avatar based on the exoself's provided morphology name, and associates the exoself's PId with that avatar.
12. The exoself spawns all the elements composing the NN based system.
13. Since sensors and actuators have the exoself's PId, when they are triggered to action they send a request for sensory signals, and action signals, to the scape. The signals contain the PId of the exoself, so that the scape can associate these messages with the right avatar.
14. When the flatland scape receives a message, it uses the PId in the message to figure out which avatar the message is associated with. And then based on the message, replies back to the caller.

15. The flatland scape keeps track of the environment, the avatars, their interactions... Performing all the physical simulation calculations, and thus having access to all the information to keep track of the fitness of every avatar.

16. Because flatland keeps track of the amount of energy every avatar has, and because it knows when two avatars collide, or interact, it will know when an avatar dies from losing all its energy, or from being eaten. As soon as an avatar dies, the scape performs the cleanup associated with that avatar's physical representation. Whether that be simply removing the avatar from the physical simulation, or leaving it there to be devoured or decay.

17. When the NN receives a message from the scape that it has just died, that is the end of that agent's evaluation, similarly to when in the T-Maze simulation the simulated robot crashes into a wall. At this point the exoself can perturb the weights, revert them to previous values, or perform other computations.

18. Afterwards, the exoself can send the scape a message requesting a new avatar... And the cycle continues.

For the simulation to be consistent, and for the world to have a constant or growing population, we will of course have to use the *steady_state* based evolution, rather than *generational*. The steady_state evolution reflects the continuous birth and death of agents within an environment, unlike generational evolution in which the entire generation must die before new agents are created, and a new generation is spawned.

The plan of attack for this application would be to first develop the actual flatland scape. This would require us to first create the Cartesian world simulation. Create the functions for collision detection between two circles, between a circle and a line, and between a line and a line. We would then have to decide on whether we want to use some kind of quad-tree to optimize the support of large number of avatars within one scape, or whether to just be content in using 20-30 avatars at any time, and allow a single process to represent the entire flatland, and thus act as a bottleneck of computing collision detections between avatars, and simulating vision and other sensors of each avatar. With regards to the scape, we would also have to decide on the schedule of when to perform collision detection, for example:

1. Do we first wait for every single agent to send an action based message to the scape, a batch form of signals from all the currently alive agents, then in one go apply the requested actions to their avatars, and then calculate the collision detections and other resulting properties of the scape after that single action step has been taken. Then, afterwards, allow the scape to again go into its receive loop, waiting for another batch of messages from all the active agents?

2. Or do we let the scape perform collision detection and other types of environment calculations (let the simulated plants grow, or spread, or create offspring, or mature and increase in the amount of energy the plant provides when eaten, or decay and turn into poison and decrease the avatar's energy reserves when eaten, or change in color over time...) after receiving every single action message from an agent?

3. Or do we run the physical simulation nonstop, updating the world's physical properties every simulated 0.01 seconds, and somehow synchronize all the agents with it...?

I believe that option-2 has an interesting advantage in that the smaller NNs will have faster "reflexes", because the smaller NNs will have lower NN topology depth, and thus go through more sense-think-act cycles for any given time than those NNs which are much deeper. For example, a 10 neuron NN with depth 1, will be able to send most likely at least 10 messages in the time frame that a 100000 neuron NN of depth 1000 can send... and thus its reflexes, and the number of actions performed per given time, will be higher than that of a more complex intelligence. This is somewhat similar to the real world, and the response times between various organisms, based on their brain structure and its complexity.

I have implemented Flatland in [5], and it uses option 2. Because the implementation of the 2d world simulation is outside the scope of this book, and because there can be so many different ways to implement it, or even use the scape as a simple wrapper for an already existing 2d robot simulator like Stage [6], we will concentrate on the discussion and implementation of features needed by our TWEANN system to interact with the provided flatland simulation (rather than building it), given that we know the interface format for it.

18.2.1 Public Scape Architectures, Polis Interface, and Scape Sectors

The general architecture of a polis, and its relation to the scapes it spawns, and the sectors into which some scapes are divided, is shown in Fig-18.2. Ideally, the polis process as we discussed, is the infrastructure, it is basically everything, it is all the things that are needed to run the actual TWEANN algorithm, and the software that synchronizes, and manages public scapes. The public scapes are the always-present environment simulations, not necessarily 3d. The scapes are a way for us to present the simulations, environments, and problems, to the agent.

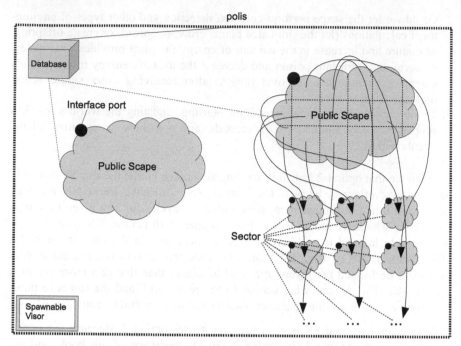

Fig. 18.2 The architecture of polis, scapes, and sectors.

Each scape can be interfaced with through messages. Each scape has a particular list of messages that it can accept, and that it expects to receive and reply to, this is the interface format for that scape. When a scape simulates an environment, that environment can be further broken up into sectors, represented by processes and running in parallel. The sectors would simply represent the small sections of the physical simulation of the environment, and thus allow for a parallelization of the collision detection, and sensory computations. Sectors allow for scapes to implement quad-trees [7], and thus improve their performance when interfacing with a lot of agents. If the scape uses sectors, it assigns the agent to a particular sector based on that agent's location within the scape. This is done by forwarding to the agent the PId of the sector, which the agent then uses as if it were a PId of the scape. Thus this is all seamless to the agent.

Finally, there is also a spawnable Visor process, which allows the researcher to poll the scape for visualizable data. The visor is independent and separate from the scape, and thus when developing a scape it is not necessary to consider how to visually represent the system. The visualization is an afterthought, and is only necessary for us to be able to actually tap into the scape and see what is occurring. It is the visor that deals with constructing a representation of the scape, based on the type of scape it was requested to poll for data.

18.2.2 The Flatland Interface

The way the scapes deal with the messages, whether there are physical representations of the agents interfacing with it or not, and whether it keeps track of particular agents or not, all depend on the scape and its purpose. The flatland scape keeps track of the agents, it requires that agents first register with it, before they are allocated their avatars. Once an agent is registered with the *flatland* scape, the scape gives it an avatar, gives that avatar physical parameters, some default amount of energy, starting coordinates within the flatland, and then allows for percept polling and action signals to be sent from the registered agent.

The flatland scape is implemented as a gen_server process. It can accept the following messages from the interfacing agents:

- {enter,Morphology,Agent_Id,Sensors,Actuators,TotNeurons}: This message is used to register and enter the flatland scape. The flatland scape uses the Sensors, Actuators, and Morphology, to generate an avatar for the agent. If the agent has the morphology of a *predator*, the avatar would be very different from one given to a *prey* type morphology. Finally, the reason for sending the scape the TotNeurons value, is because the scape might make the energy consumption and the designated size of the avatar proportional to the size of the NN itself, and for this it needs the total number of neurons composing the agent.
- {leave,Agent_Id}: The atom leave is sent by the agent that wishes to unregister, and leave the scape.
- {get_all,avatars}: Each sensor needs to perform a different set of computations to produce the sensory signal. Each sensor knows which types of computations need to be performed, thus the sensor simply requests the scape to send it the avatar list, where the avatar list is composed of the avatar records, each having all the information about the avatar's location. The avatar list includes all the avatars/objects within the scape (agent controlled avatars, static objects...). Once the needed data to calculate a sensory signal is received, the sensor performs its function, generates a sensory vector, and forwards it to the neurons in the agent's NN.
- {actuator,Agent_Id,Command,Output,Parameters}: The actuator sends to the scape a *Command* to execute with the parameter *Output*. The scape takes the Command and Output, and applies it to the avatar with which Agent_Id is associated.

Now that we know how to interface with the flatland scape, we can create the sensors and actuators to allow our agents to interface with it. But this will also require us to modify the exoself so that it can now deal with public scapes, given that all public scapes will use the request for entry and request for leaving the scape, and the messaging format specified in the above list.

18.3 Flatland's Avatar Encoding

The flatland scape keeps track of every avatar's position, pointing direction, energy reserves, morphology, set of sensors and actuators... by entering all these features into an avatar representing record when the correlated agent registers with the scape. The avatar record has the following form:

-record(avatar,{id,sector,morphology,energy=0,health=0,food=0, age=0, kills=0, loc, direction, r, mass, objects=[], state,actuators,sensors}).

The *objects* list is composed of object records, where each record has the form:

-record(object,{id,sector,type,color,loc,pivot,parameters=[]}).

In which the type can be either *circle* or *line*. It is the avatar's objects list that define what the avatar looks like, for he is composed from the objects. The collision detection too is based on the collision of the object lists of every avatar. Having all avatars being circular though, makes the collision detection calculations a lot faster and simpler.

As noted in the previous section, it is a list of these avatars that is returned to the sensor when requested, and it is the sensor which then calculates the various percepts based on this list. The scape itself can be considered to be composed of avatars, every object is an avatar. A plant is an avatar which has the morphology: *plant.* A wall section is an avatar of morphology *wall,* a rock is an avatar of morphology *rock.* The agent's sensor does not need to know the morphology of the avatar, nothing is needed by it except the objects list. Based on the objects: circles and lines, the sensor can calculate whether its line of sight (if camera, or a range sensor for example) intersects those objects. Since every object has a coordinate (loc stands for location) and a color, the sensors can then extract both the color and the range to the object.

For the agent to be able to control the avatar, the avatar must have sensors, and actuators. More precisely, the NN based agent's morphology which defines the avatar, must come with sensors and actuators, such that the agent can gather sensory signals from the avatar, and control the avatar through its actuators. In our ALife simulation we will create 2 sensors: Range Sensor and Color Sensor, and 1 actuator: Differential Drive. The range sensor works like a standard robot range sensor in which we define the resolution and the coverage angle. The resolution defines how many range rays will be cast, and the coverage area defines the angle coverage of these rays. Thus for example if the resolution is 5 rays, and the degree coverage is 90 degrees, than the avatar will cast 5 rays, each 22.5 degrees from the other. The rays cast return the distance to anything they intersect. The color sensor works similarly, but the returned values are colors encoded in some fashion. For example black = -1, green = -0.5, blue = 0, red = 0.5, and white = 1. It is simply spectrum encoding, and can be similar to frequencies of the colors of the visible spectrum, scaled to be between -1 and 1 (though not in our implementation, where I simply chose a few colors and gave them their own numbers). Finally, the actuator the avatar will be controlled through is a simulated differential drive, where the NN outputs a vector of length 2, where the first element controls the velocity of the left wheel, and the second element of the vector controls the velocity of the right wheel. The graphical representation of the avatars, sensors, and color encoding, is shown in Fig-18.3.

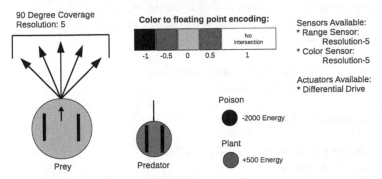

Fig. 18.3 The representation of the *prey* avatar, the *predator* avatar, the *plant* avatar, the *poison* avatar, and the available sensors and actuators for the avatars, and the color sensor encoding.

18.4 Updating the Morphology, Sensor, and Actuator Modules

Because our system is completely independent of the scapes with which the evolved NN based agents interface, we need only add the new records to the records.hrl file, then add the new sensors, one new actuator, and then finally modify the exoself module. After that, we will be able to apply our TWEANN to an ALife simulation. We add the two new records specified in the previous section to the records.hrl file. Once that is accomplished, we add two new sensors: *range_scanner* and *color_scanner*. These two new sensors are shown in the following listing.

```
Listing-18.1 The implementation of the range_scanner and the color_scanner sensors.

distance_scanner(Agent_Id,VL,[Spread,Density,RadialOffset],Scape)->
    case gen_server:call(Scape,{get_all,avatars}) of
        destroyed->
            lists:duplicate(VL,-1);
        Avatars ->
            Self = lists:keyfind(self(),2,Avatars),
            Loc = Self#avatar.loc,
```

```
                Direction = Self#avatar.direction,
                distance_scanner(silent,{1,0,0},Density,Spread,Loc, Direc-
tion,lists:keydelete(self(), 2, Avatars))
    end.
```

%The distance_scanner/4 function contacts the scape and requests for a list of all avatars within it. If for some reason the scape cannot do so, it replies with the void atom, otherwise the avatar list is returned. If the reply is void, the sensor simply composes a vector of the right length using the VL value, and returns the result. Otherwise, the function calls color_scanner/7, which performs the actual calculation to compose the color sensory vector. This is primarily done through ray casting, and seeing whether any of the cast rays intersect the objects from which the avatars in the avatar list are composed of.

```
color_scanner(Agent_Id,VL,[Spread,Density,RadialOffset],Scape)->
    case gen_server:call(Scape,{get_all,avatars}) of
        void->
                lists:duplicate(VL,-1);
        Avatars ->
                Self = lists:keyfind(self(),2,Avatars),
                Loc = Self#avatar.loc,
                Direction = Self#avatar.direction,
                color_scanner(silent,{1,0,0},Density,Spread,Loc,Direction,
lists:keydelete(self(), 2, Avatars))
    end.
```

%Functions similar to the distance_scanner/4, but returns a list of encoded colors rather than ranges. Whatever objects the cast rays intersect, their color is returned.

Due to most of the functions dealing with ray casting and collision detection, only the wrappers are shown, with the comments explaining their functionality. Because each agent keeps track of its position and the direction in which it is looking, we can easily calculate what the range sensor and color sensor should return. Besides the two sensors, the NN based agent also needs an actuator with which to move its avatar, the implementation of which is shown in Listing-18.2.

Listing-18.2 The implementation of the differential_drive actuator.

```
differential_drive(Agent_Id,Output,Parameters,Scape)->
    {Fitness,HaltFlag}=gen_server:call(Scape,{actuator,Agent_Id,differential_drive,Output,
Parameters}).
```

%The differential_drive/4 function calls the Scape with the command: differential_drive, its output and parameters. The flatland scape will use the differential_drive to simulate the said actuator for the avatar, executing the function with the Output and Parameters.

What can be noted from the three above functions, is that the parameters with which they are called, now have been extended to include the Agent_Id, which uniquely identifies the NN based agent, and can thus be used in public scapes as the unique identifier of the avatar. This means that we also have to modify sensor:prep/1 and actuator:prep/1 to accept the Agent_Id value in the initial state sent to these processes by the exoself.

To be used by the agent, the sensors and the actuator must also be added to the morphology module. Because we want to have two different species/morphologies, one for prey and one for the predator, each of which will have a different set of privileges and avatars within the flatland, yet both use the same set of sensors and actuators, we must create two morphological specifications that are identical to each other in everything but the morphology name. The two new morphological types added to the morphology.erl are shown in Listing-18.3.

Listing-18.3 The new *prey* and *predator* morphological specifications.

```
predator(actuators)->
    prey(actuators);
% The predator morphology uses the same set of actuators as the prey, thus it simply calls the
prey function to get the list of actuators available.


predator(sensors)->
    prey(sensors).
% The predator morphology uses the same set of sensors as the prey, thus it simply calls the
prey function to get the list of sensors available.


prey(actuators)->
    Movement = [#actuator{name=differential_drive,type=standard,scape={public,flatland},
vl=2, parameters=[2]}],
    Movement;
prey(sensors)->
    Pi = math:pi(),
    Color_Scanners = [#sensor{name=color_scanner,type=standard,scape={public,flatland},
vl=Density, parameters=[Spread,Density,ROffset]} || Spread <-[Pi/2], Density <-[5], ROffset<-
[Pi*0/2]],
    Range_Scanners = [#sensor{name=range_scanner,type=standard,scape={public,flatland},
vl=Density, parameters=[Spread,Density,ROffset]} || Spread <-[Pi/2], Density <-[5], ROffset<-
[Pi*0/2]],
    Color_Scanners++Range_Scanners.
```
%The prey morphology has access to two types of sensors at this time, the color and the range scanner. The density and the radial offset parameters (in which direction the mounted simulated scanner is pointing) can be modified. Thus instead of simply 2 sensors, the Resolution list can be set to: [5,10,20,50,10], and we would have 10 sensors in total, each one differing in the resolution of the sensor. The radial offsets could further be modified in a similar fashion.

Due to the predator and prey morphologies using the same set of sensors and actuators, and differing only in their avatar representations and the privileges allotted to their avatars, we can let the predator morphology simply call the prey function with the parameter *sensor* and *actuator*, to retrieve the provided sensors and actuators available. We can generate multiple sensors by changing the resolution list to contain more than a single value. In this manner we would allow evolution to decide what is the most optimal and efficient resolution for the sensors within the environment.

With the sensors, actuators, and the morphology modules updated, we now make a small update to the exoself module in the next section.

18.5 Updating the exoself Module

We've now constructed the necessary tools with which the agent can interface with the public scape, but we still need a way for the agent to actually register with the public scape in question. In the function spawn_Scapes/4 the exoself extracts unique scape names, and then from this list of unique scape names, the exoself extracts a list of private scapes. The private scapes are then spawned for the agent. We now also need to extract the public scapes from the unique list of scape names, and then for each such public scape contact the polis process to request its PId, and then finally register with that public scape. To accomplish this, we modify the spawn_Scapes/4 function, as shown in the following listing with the new functionality highlighted in boldface.

Listing-18.4 The updated spawn_Scapes/4 function.

```
spawn_Scapes(IdsNPIds,Sensor_Ids,Actuator_Ids,Agent_Id)->
    Sensor_Scapes = [(genotype:dirty_read({sensor,Id}))#sensor.scape || Id<-Sensor_Ids],
    Actuator_Scapes = [(genotype:dirty_read({actuator,Id}))#actuator.scape || Id<-
Actuator_Ids],
    Unique_Scapes = Sensor_Scapes++(Actuator_Scapes--Sensor_Scapes),
    Private_SN_Tuples=[{scape:gen(self(),node()),ScapeName} || {private,ScapeName}<-
Unique_Scapes],
    [ets:insert(IdsNPIds,{ScapeName,PId}) || {PId,ScapeName} <- Private_SN_Tuples],
    [ets:insert(IdsNPIds,{PId,ScapeName}) || {PId,ScapeName} <-Private_SN_Tuples],
    [PId ! {self(),ScapeName} || {PId,ScapeName} <- Private_SN_Tuples],
    enter_PublicScape(IdsNPIds,Sensor_Ids,Actuator_Ids,Agent_Id),
    [PId || {PId,_ScapeName} <-Private_SN_Tuples].


enter_PublicScape(IdsNPIds,Sensor_Ids,Actuator_Ids,Agent_Id)->
        A = genotype:dirty_read({agent,Agent_Id}),
        Sensors = [genotype:dirty_read({sensor,Id}) || Id<-Sensor_Ids],
        Actuators = [genotype:dirty_read({actuator,Id}) || Id<-Actuator_Ids],
```

```
        TotNeurons = length((genotype:dirty_read({cortex,
A#agent.cx_id}))#cortex.neuron_ids),
        Morphology = (A#agent.constraint)#constraint.morphology,
        Sensor_Scapes = [Sensor#sensor.scape || Sensor<-Sensors],
        Actuator_Scapes = [Actuator#actuator.scape || Actuator<-Actuators],
        Unique_Scapes = Sensor_Scapes++(Actuator_Scapes--Sensor_Scapes),
        Public_SN_Tuples=[{gen_server:call(polis,{get_scape,ScapeName}),ScapeName}
|| {public,ScapeName}<-Unique_Scapes],
        [gen_server:call(PId,{enter,Morphology,Agent_Id,Sensors,Actuators,TotNeurons}) ||
{PId,ScapeName} <- Public_SN_Tuples].
```

The modification in the above listing allows the exoself to extract not only the private scapes but also the public scapes, and then enter them. Of course the agent will get booted from the public scape every time its avatar perishes, and every time the agent's evaluation ends, the exoself receives the message: *{Cx_PId,evaluation_completed,Fitness,Cycles,Time,GoalReachedFlag}*,   after which the exoself decides whether to continue or end training. If the exoself decides to continue training, and thus perform another evaluation, we can choose to re-enter the public scape by executing the function:

```
enter_PublicScape(S#state.idsNpids,[genotype:dirty_read({sensor,Id})||Id<-S#state.spids],
[genotype:dirty_read({actuator,Id})||Id<-S#state.apids], S#state.agent_id),
```

Though elaborate, it allows us to modify nothing else within the exoself at this time. By executing this function, the exoself again finds the PId of the needed public scapes, and re-requests an entry. There is no need to re-join the private scapes, since those are spawned by the exoself, and the sensors and actuators always have access to them, until the agent terminates at which point the exoself terminates all the processes, including the private scapes.

With this modification, our system is now ready to interface with the public scapes, and be applied to the ALife simulations. We could further modify the exoself module, and add to the exoself's *state* record the elements: *sensors, actuators, morphology,* and *public_scapes,* which would allow us to then create a specialized function for re-entering public scapes by executing a reenter_PublicScape/4 function as follows:

```
reenter_PublicScape(S#state.public_scapes,S#state.sensors,S#state.actuators, S#state.agent_id,
S#state.morphology,length(S#state.nids)),
```

This function could then have a much more streamlined implementation, as shown next:

```
reenter_PublicScape([PS_PId|PS_PIds],Sensors,Actuators,Agent_Id,Morphology,
TotNeurons)->
```

```
gen_server:call(PS_PId,{enter,Morphology,Agent_Id,Sensors,Actuators,TotNeurons}),
reenter_PublicScape(PS_PIds,Sensors,Actuators,Agent_Id,Morphology,TotNeurons);
reenter_PublicScape([],_Sensors,_Actuators,_Agent_Id,_Morphology,_TotNeurons)->
ok.
```

18.6 The Simulation and Results

The updated implementation of our neuroevolutionary system with the flatland integrated and implemented as discussed above, can be found in the supplementary material [8] for Chapter-18. Now that we are to run the ALife simulation, the briefly discussed *visor* module which allows us to visualize the scape and the moving avatars within, is finally of vital use. When running the simulation without the visor, we would only see the fitness of the agents, and a few other printouts to console as the agents consumed each other (predator consuming prey), and the plants (prey consuming the plants). A sample of such a printout is shown in Listing-18.5.

Listing-18.5 A sample console printout of the Predator Vs. Prey simulation.

```
Tot_Evaluations:150
Avatar:<0.827.0> destroyed.
Avatar:<0.827.0> destroyed.
Avatar:<0.851.0> died at age:5082
Avatar:<0.835.0> died at age:3254
Avatar:<0.708.0> died at age:3058
Creating Flatlander
Avatar:<0.811.0> destroyed.
Avatar:<0.801.0> died at age:4511
Avatar:<0.819.0> destroyed.
Avatar:<0.859.0> died at age:3088
Avatar:<0.700.0> died at age:3819
Creating Flatlander
Avatar:<0.757.0> died at age:3000
Creating Flatlander
Avatar:<0.827.0> destroyed.
Avatar:<0.767.0> died at age:3903
Creating Flatlander
Avatar:<0.819.0> destroyed.
Avatar:<0.716.0> died at age:2779
Creating Flatlander
Avatar:<0.784.0> died at age:3079
Creating Flatlander
Avatar:<0.851.0> destroyed.
Avatar:<0.843.0> died at age:2468
```

But when we execute the *population_monitor:start()* function to create the population of prey or predators, or both, and then execute: *visor:start(flatland),* we will be able to observe the 2d world from above, in the same way that the *sphere* was able to observe the flatland from its third dimension in the book *Flatland.*

For the next part where we test our TWEANN system on the ALife simulation, I will assume that you have downloaded the source code for Chapter-18, with the new scape/flatland/world/visor libraries, with which you will be able to execute the same commands I will use in the following subsections to test our TWEANN's performance in this advanced application.

18.6.1 Simple Food Gathering Simulation

There are different types of ALife simulations that we could run at this time. We could run the simple *Food Gathering Simulation,* in which we set up the flatland scape to only spawn the plants, and then we set the population_monitor process to only spawn the prey. This would result in a scape with renewable food source, plants, populated by prey agents learning to navigate through it and eat the plants as quickly as they can.

Assuming you have the newly added modules (*flatland* and *world*) present in the supplementary material, and you have opened the world.erl module, we first must ensure that only the plants are spawned in the flatland simulation. Thus in the init/3 function, with the World_Type == flatland, we set the case clause as follows:

```
init(World_Type,Physics,Metabolics)->
    XMin = -5000,
    XMax = 5000,
    YMin = -5000,
    YMax = 5000,
    WorldPivot = {(XMin+XMax)/2,(YMin+YMax)/2},
    World_Border = [{XMin,XMax},{YMin,YMax}],
    case World_Type of
            flatland ->
                    Plants=[scape:create_avatar(plant,plant,gen_id(),{undefined,
scape:return_valid(Rocks++FirePits)},respawn,Metabolics)|| _ <-lists:duplicate(10,1)],
                    Poisons=[scape:create_avatar(poison,poison,gen_id(),{undefined,
scape:return_valid(Rocks++FirePits)},respawn,Metabolics)|| _ <-lists:duplicate(10,1)],
                    Plants
    end.
```

Which ensures that polis spawns the flatland scape with only the plants present. We next define INIT_CONSTRAINTS within the population_monitor module as follows:

```
-define(INIT_CONSTRAINTS,[#constraint{morphology=Morphology,
connection_architecture =CA, population_evo_alg_f=steady_state,agent_encoding_types
=[neural]} || Morphology<-[flatland],CA<-[recurrent]]).
```

We also set in the *flatland* module to allow for the agents to live for a maximum age of 20000 cycles, retain at most 10000 energy, and for the fitness function to be: *0.001*CyclesAlive + PlantsEaten*. This ensures that the fitness guides the evolution towards longevity, but also for the agents to be able to navigate the world as effectively as possible, and eat as many plants as they can. Furthermore, we set the plants to provide the agent 500 energy points when eaten, and poison to subtract 2000 energy points when eaten.

With this set, we execute polis:sync() to compile the two modified modules, and then execute population_monitor:start() function to run the ALife simulation. Finally, to observe the simulation, we also execute visor:start(). A video of one of the evolutionary runs of this simulation is available at [9,10].

We can set the termination condition for 25000 evaluations in the population monitor, and compose a trace that we could later graph to see how the fitness, NN sizes of the evolving agents, and their diversity, change over time. In fact, using our benchmarker module, we could even perform multiple evolutionary runs to compose a graph of Fitness Vs. Evaluations, NN Size Vs. Evaluations, and Population Diversity Vs. Evaluations. The following figures show the results of multiple benchmarks, where the populations were started with different constraints. I set up the constraints for the 4 performed benchmarks as follows:

1. A simulation where the population size was set to 10, and the seed agents were started with 2 sensors from the very start, each agent started with the range and the color sensors.
2. A simulation where the population size was set to 10, but the seed agents started with only the range sensor, and had to evolve the connection to the color sensor over time.
3. A simulation where the population size was set to 20, and the seed agents were started with both, color and range sensors.
4. A simulation where the population size was set to 20, but the seed agents started with only the range sensor.

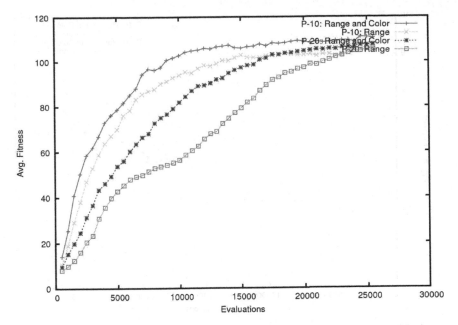

Fig. 18.4 Fitness Vs. Evaluations.

We can see from Fig-18.4 that in all scenarios the agents increased in fitness, it did not matter whether the seed population was started with just the range sensor, or both, the range and the color sensor. Our system was successfully able to evolve connections to the color sensor for the agents which did not already have such a morphological feature. Also as expected, the two simulations where the population limit was set to 10, were able to achieve a slightly higher fitness faster. This occurred because the agents in the population of 10 had less competition for food than those in a population of 20. And of course when the agents started with both, range and color sensors, they achieved higher fitness faster than those which just started with the range sensor, since those starting with just the range sensor had to take time to evolve color vision.

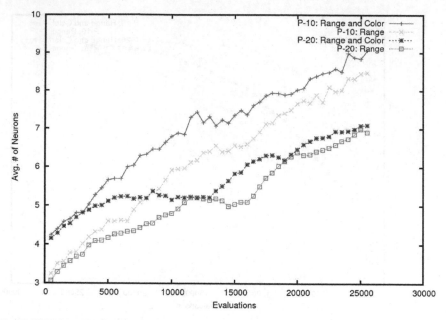

Fig. 18.5 NN Size Vs. Evaluations.

The above figure shows how the size of the NNs increased during the evolutionary runs. More complex NNs were evolved over time, as the NNs evolved better navigational capabilities. What is interesting to note is that the NNs evolved in the populations where the population size was set to 20, were able to achieve the same fitness but with smaller NNs. I think that this is the case because with a larger population, more exploration of the various genotypes can be performed, and thus more efficient NNs can be evolved.

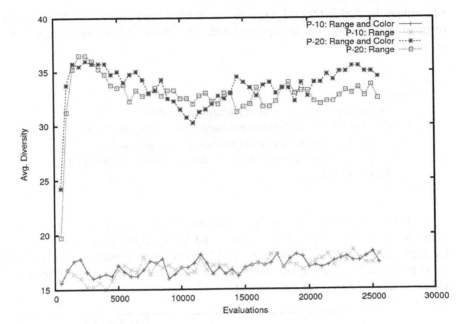

Fig. 18.6 Population Diversity Vs. Evaluations.

Finally, the above Fig-18.6 presents the diversity of the population plotted against evaluations. It is remarkable just how diverse the populations were. Diversity is calculated for the active population and the agents in the dead_pool, hence the ranges being between 0-20 and 0-40, rather than 0-10 and 0-20 agents. On every occasion, nearly 75% of the population was composed of agents which were all different from one another. We can also see that the diversity never dropped, yet as we saw from the fitness plot, the fitness did rapidly increase. This is just one of the great features of using the memetic approach to neuroevolution.

18.6.2 Dangerous Food Gathering Simulation

We can also set up the flatland scape to have not only the plants, but also the poison representing avatars. The poison avatars are just like plants, but when they are consumed, they decrease the *prey's* energy instead of increasing it, they decrease the agent's energy by 2000 rather than increasing it by 500. When the avatar's energy reaches 0, it dies. This type of simulation, if we were to execute with just the prey population, would result in the *Dangerous Food Gathering Simulation*, because the agents must now move around the 2d world, gather the plants and avoid the poison.

To perform the Dangerous Food Gathering Simulation, we can leave the population_monitor module alone, or increase the termination condition to 50000 evaluations, as I've done during my experiments, and then modify the *world.erl* file, setting the *flatland* World_Type to use 10 Plants and 10 Poisons, all of which respawn immediately after being consumed. The source code for this setup, looks as follows:

```
case World_Type of
    flatland ->
            Plants=[scape:create_avatar(plant,plant,gen_id(),{undefined,
scape:return_valid(Rocks++FirePits)},respawn,Metabolics)|| _ <-lists:duplicate(10,1)],
            Poisons=[scape:create_avatar(poison,poison,gen_id(),{undefined,
scape:return_valid(Rocks++FirePits)},respawn,Metabolics)|| _ <-lists:duplicate(10,1)],
        Plants ++ Poisons
    end.
```

As in the *Simple Food Gathering Simulation,* 4 benchmarks were performed with the previously specified constraints, and the resulting plots of Fitness Vs. Evaluations, NN Size Vs. Evaluations, and Diversity Vs. Evaluations. The plots of these benchmark scenarios, are shown in the following figures, and the recorded videos of the simulation can be found at [11,12].

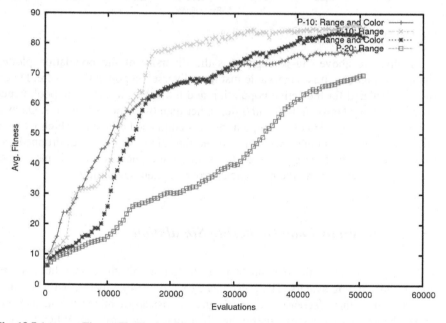

Fig. 18.7 Average Fitness Vs. Evaluations.

Similarly to the *Simple Food Gathering Simulation (SFGS)*, the above figure shows the plots of average fitness for the 4 constraints scenarios. In this simulation color plays a much more important role, because inability to differentiate between color results in one not being to tell the difference between plants and poison. On top of this, because the agents can push each other in the 2d environment, when we set the population limit to 20, there is enough of them that they will inadvert-

ently push each other on top of poison locations. Thus we can see that the benchmark in which we set the population size to 20 and started the seed agents with
just the range sensors, results in the lowest performance. While interestingly
enough the benchmark of the seed population which started with only the range
sensor, but whose population size limit was set to 10, performed the best. But in
general, in all benchmarks the agents learned how to navigate through the 2d
world, eat plants, and avoid poison. In all scenarios, though initially the agents
started off wondering aimlessly, over time the agents first learned to move towards the plants and poisons, then mostly towards the plants only, and finally in
the case of the champions of the population, swiftly navigate through the poison
ridden landscape while eating plants.

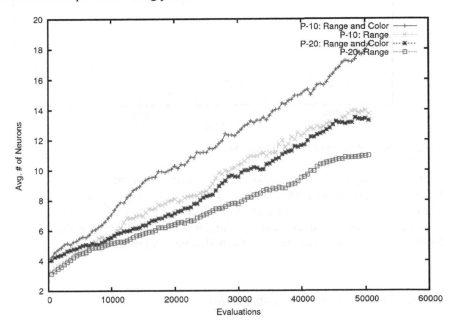

Fig. 18.8 NN Size Vs. Evaluations.

Similarly to the SFGS, the NN size grows as the NNs evolve more complex
behaviors, and adapt to the environment. The environment in this simulation is
more complex, and thus unlike in the previous simulation, the agents themselves
are more complex, reaching the size of 19 neurons. Also as in the SFGS, benchmarks conducted when the population size limit was set to 20, produce more concise NN based agents, composed of fewer neurons.

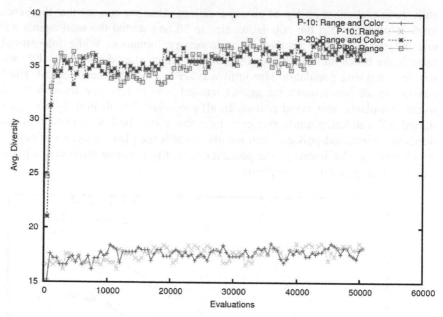

Fig. 18.9 Population Diversity Vs. Evaluations.

The diversity plot in Dangerous Food Gathering Simulation (DFGS) is similar to the one in SFGS, in both cases nearly 75% of the population is composed of agents different from one another. The diversity is maintained throughout the benchmark, there is no decline, only a sharp increases in diversity at the very start, followed by a stable maintenance of the high diversity profile.

18.6.3 Predator Vs. Prey Simulation

Finally, we can again start the polis with a flatland which initially spawns only the plants within itself, but this time when starting the population monitor, we set the constraints to start with two morphologies, *prey* and *predator*. Because the prey can only consume plants for sustenance, and the predators can only consume the prey for sustenance, absorbing the energy of the prey into themselves, this results in the Predator Vs. Prey Simulation (PPS). Furthermore, we set the simulation such that the predators can push the plants around when their energy reserve is above 1000.

In this simulation the prey agents learn how to navigate the 2d world, and eat the plants while avoiding the predators. At the same time, the predators learn to navigate the 2d world, and hunt the prey. Thus the two species co-evolve, learn how to evade and hunt, improve their strategies over time, and learn some very clever trapping and baiting methods (in the case of the predators), as will be discussed and shown next.

Because the evolutionary paths of the two species were so dependent on which of the species learned to navigate, evade, and hunt first, the averages of the evolutionary runs were meaningless. This is due to the fact that when the prey learned to navigate through the flatland and eat the plants before the predators learned how to hunt them efficiently, the prey were able to achieve high fitness scores, while the predators did not do as well. On the other hand, during the evolutionary runs in which the predator specie was able to evolve agents which could navigate and hunt, before the prey evolved agents which could evade the predators, the predators achieved high fitness, and the prey did not do as well. Thus, instead of creating the averages, I chose to plot the results of a single such evolutionary run.

Because the flatland will now be populated by a population of size 10 of prey, and a population of size 10 of predators, we will be able to see in the plots the interaction and correlations between the two competing species. The next 4 plots are of Fitness Vs. Evaluations, NN Size Vs. Evaluations, Diversity Vs. Evaluations, and the agent Turnover (death rate) Vs. Evaluations. Because we calculate the specie statistics every 500 evaluations, the Turnover Vs. Evaluations shows the death rate of the particular specie with relation to another for those 500 evaluations. Thus for example if both species survive for an equal amount of time, both will have a turnover of 250. On the other hand if it's an open hunting season on prey, and the predators are just running around eating the prey, the prey will have a very high turnover, while the predators will live for a much longer number of cycles, and thus have a much lower turnover. The recorded videos of the evolutionary run are shown in [13,14].

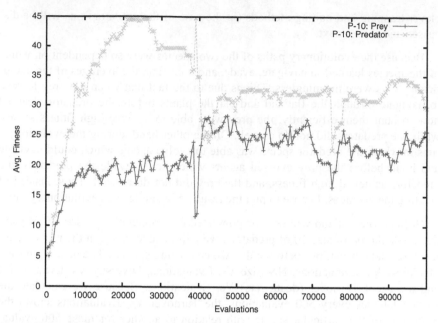

Fig. 18.10 Average Fitness Vs. Evaluations.

The average fitness for the prey drops dramatically with predators around. Almost during every simulation, eventually the predators learned to navigate effectively, and attack the prey that passed nearby. Because the prey had a slightly higher maximum speed than the predators, the predators eventually evolved to only briefly chase the prey. If the prey moved away too quickly, the predators would move back, closer towards the plants. This was too a very interesting, and highly organic adaptation. The predators would horde around the plants, because the prey at some point or another would have to go towards the plants to survive. Finally, the most interesting and complex behavior was trapping, as shown in [13]. In this evolved behavior, the agents push the plants around, and seem to be hiding behind them. Because the ray casting based sensors used by the prey only see the plants, the prey would go towards the plants, and as soon as they would consume the plant, the predators behind that plant would eat the prey, and thus consume its energy, and the energy it just gained from eating the plant. This was a very clever ambushing behavior, and one of the most complex I've seen evolved in any ALife simulation. I cannot see a more complex behavior that is possible to evolve in such a simple and barren 2d environment.

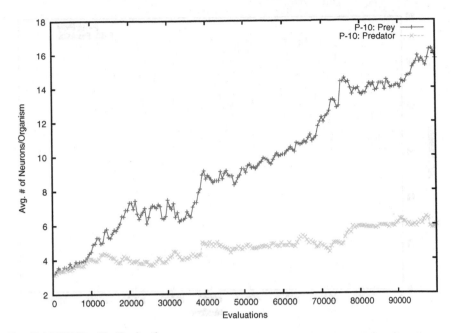

Fig. 18.11 NN Size Vs. Evaluations.

As seen in the Fig-18.11, the predators, though possessing complex behaviors, ended up with much smaller neural networks than the prey. I suspect that this occurred because of the high Turnover of the prey, and their need to deal with moving and dynamic predators. Then again, the behaviors evolved by the predators would make one think that they would require more neurons to execute such maneuvers. The evolution within this environment must have found an efficient way to encode such a behavior. The prey most likely increased in their NN size because they were getting killed too quickly, and so evolution had difficult time optimizing their topologies, due to not having enough time to work with it. Thus the selection pressure was most likely compromised, and so the prey specie's NN size increased at a higher rate than is optimal.

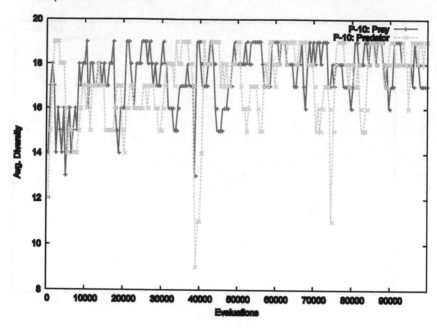

Fig. 18.12 Population Diversity Vs. Evaluations.

Figure-18.12 shows that as in the previous simulations, the population diversity within the Predator Vs. Prey Simulation, is similarly high. Almost every agent was different from every other agent in each species.

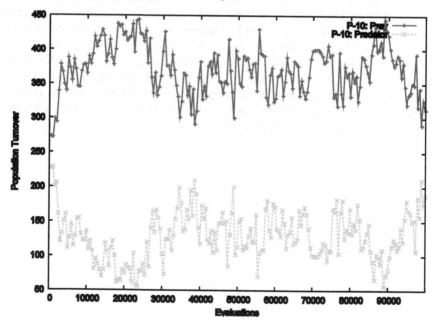

Fig. 18.13 Population Turnover Vs. Evaluations.

As expected from a simulation where one specie completely dominates another, and being able to hunt and kill it while surviving on the energy gained from consuming it, the turnover of the predators is much lower than that of the prey. As seen in Fig-18.13, though both species start off equally, the predators quickly learn to hunt the prey, and thus the prey's turnover increases while that of the predator's decreases. After 30000 evaluations the turnover for both species reaches an equilibrium. The predators maintain a turnover of about 150 evaluations per 500 evaluations. Complementary, the prey stay within a turnover average of 350 evaluations per every 500 evaluations.

18.7 Discussion

In all three simulations we have seen the agents evolve in complexity, their behavior, and fitness. In the Simple Food Gathering Simulation (SFGS), the agents learned to navigate the 2d flatland and gather the plants. In the more complex version, the Dangerous Food Gathering Simulation (DFGS), the agents learned to navigate the flatland, eat the plants, and avoid poison. Finally, in the Predator Vs. Prey Simulation (PPS), we evolved two species, that of prey and predator. The prey evolved to navigate the 2d world, gather food, and avoid being eaten by the predators. The predators evolved to navigate the 2d world and hunt the prey. All the simulations were successful, and the videos of the simulations are available online for viewing [9-14].

The most impressive results of our ALife experiment was with regards to the evolved ambushing behavior of the predator species. This behavior, shown in [13], has a very organic nature to it. It is difficult to come up with a more clever approach to hunting prey in the barren flatland. Amongst all the other ALife simulations I've had come across, the behavior evolved in Flatland and by the TWEANN system we developed here, seems as one of the more complex. Thus, we have shown that our TWEANN can indeed produce advanced behavior, and evolve complex NN structures.

But even the 9 (4 variations of SFGS, 4 variations of DFGS, and 1 type of PPS) different ALife experiments performed in this chapter do not even begin to scratch the surface within this field. The flatland could be further advanced, and we could allow the plants to grow, increase in energy, decay, produce seeds... Make the environment more dynamic and natural for the inhabiting prey and predators. We could allow for the prey and predators to evolve new and other sensors and actuators, perhaps projectile weapon actuators, and new kind of sensors, for example a simulation of a chemical sensor, a sense of smell, which could simply gage the proximity of the prey or predator, but not the direction. Numerous other sensors and actuators can be built, including those used for communication. It would be interesting to see what other behaviors would evolve, given the environment is complex enough to support them.

Even better, we could interface our TWEANN system to a 3d robot simulator like Gazebo [15], and evolve agents in a much more complex and dynamic world. The higher the granularity at which the simulated environment approximates the natural world, the more complex the organisms that we can evolve in it, and the more intelligent the agents evolved will be, due to the need to deal with the more dynamic environment, which can be modified by the agents, and require them to be modified in order to deal with the modified environment...

Though in this chapter we did not get the chance to perform the same experiments but with substrate encoded NNs, on my own I did perform such evolutionary runs, and they were just as successful. The only interesting difference I've noticed was that at the very beginning, the substrate encoded NN based agents tended to go in straight lines and turn at sharp angles, unlike the standard, direct encoded NNs, which from the very start wondered through flatland in a fluent manner. Truly there are an infinite amount things to try and experiments to run, when it comes to Artificial Life. And based on the types of behaviors evolved in our simulations, perhaps the *Artificial* part can be removed, after all, *intelligence is intelligence is intelligence*. It does not matter whether sentience and intelligence is based on the computations performed within the chemical computer of the soft and always decaying flesh, or within the analog and digital computer of the immaculate and perfect circuits of the non biological substrate.

18.8 Summary

In this chapter we extended our TWEANN system and constructed a public scape by the name *flatland*. The flatland scape provides avatars and an artificial environment to the interfacing NN based agents, and allows us to evolve 2d organisms which learn to navigate and live in the simulated 2d environment. We performed 3 ALife experiments, the *Simple Food Gathering Simulation,* the *Dangerous Food Gathering Simulation,* and the *Predator Vs. Prey Simulation.* In all three experiments our NN based agents evolved to navigate the flatland, gather food, avoid poison, and hunt and kill each other. The PPS simulation stood out in particular. In it, the predators evolved the behavior to ambush the prey, pushing the plants in front of themselves until the prey came near to eat the plant, at which point the predator ate the prey, consuming it and the energy it had gained from eating the plant.

Yet still there is much to explore when it comes to ALife. The flatland module can be much further extended. Due to the amount of non Neuroevolutionary background that was used in the creation of the 2d simulation, we did not go over every single line of code as we did in the previous chapters while developing our bleeding edge TWEANN. But the source code for the presented system is available as supplementary material in [8], and thus everything shown and presented can be replicated by using the Chapter-18 source code. Finally, the recorded videos of the simulations can be found in [9-14].

18.9 References

[1] Bedau, M. (2003). Artificial Life: Organization, Adaptation and Complexity From The Bottom Up. Trends in Cognitive Sciences 7, 505-512.

[2] Danaher PJ, Conroy DM, McColl-Kennedy JR (2007) Artificial Life Models in Software . Andrew Adamatzky and Maciej Komosinski (Eds.). (2005, Springer-Verlag.) Hardcover, 69.95, 344 pages, 189 illustrations. Journal of Service Research 13, 43-62, ISBN 9781848822849.

[3] Adamatzky (2009). Artificial Life Models in Hardware. Media, 280, ISBN 9781848825291.

[4] Abbott, E. A. (2008). Flatland: A Romance of Many Dimensions (Oxford University Press).

[5] Flatland 2d robot and environment simulator:
www.DXNNResearch.com/NeuroevolutionThroughErlang/Flatland

[6] Stage, a 2d environment and robot simulator:
http://playerstage.sourceforge.net/index.php?src=stage

[7] De BM, Van KM, Overmars M, Schwarzkopf O (2000) Computational Geometry. Springer-Verlag. ISBN 3540656200. Chapter 14: Quadtrees: pp. 291-306.

[8] Chapter-18 Supplementary material:
www.DXNNResearch.com/NeuroevolutionThroughErlang/Chapter18

[9] Simple Food Gathering Simulation 1:
http://www.youtube.com/watch?v=i0nCHMd5Oc8&feature=related

[10] Simple Food Gathering Simulation 2:
http://www.youtube.com/watch?v=i0nCHMd5Oc8&feature=related

[11] Dangerous Food Gathering Simulation 1:
http://www.youtube.com/watch?v=mZPCXZUEog8&feature=related

[12] Dangerous Food Gathering Simulation 2:
http://www.youtube.com/watch?v=yOTEMhXbow&feature=related

[13] Predator Vs. Prey Simulation 1:
http://www.youtube.com/watch?v=HzsDZt8EO70&feature=related

[14] Predator Vs. Prey Simulation 2:
http://www.youtube.com/watch?v=s0_ghNq1hwQ&feature=related

Chapter 19 Evolving Currency Trading Agents

Abstract The application of Neural Networks to financial analysis in general, and currency trading in particular, has been explored for a number of years. The most commonly [2,3,4,5] used NN training algorithm in this application is the backpropagation. The application of TWEANN systems to the same field is only now starting to emerge, and is showing a significant amount of potential. In this chapter we create a Forex simulator, and then use our neuroevolutionary system to evolve automated currency trading agents. For this application we will utilize not only the standard sliding window approach when feeding the sensory signals to the neural encoded agents, but also the sliding chart window, where we feed the evolved substrate encoded agents the actual candle-stick price charts, and then compare the performance of the two approaches. As of this writing, the use of geometrical pattern sensitive NN based agents in the analysis of financial instrument charts has not yet been explored in any other paper, to this author's knowledge. Thus in this chapter we pioneer this approach, and explore its performance and properties.

This particular chapter is based on a paper which I have recently submitted for publication, in which I present this new approach, and compare the interesting results achieved. Thus, in this chapter we are indeed pioneering the approach of performing geometrical analysis of the actual charts of the financial instruments through substrate encoded NN based agents.

Because of this chapter's similarity to the noted paper, quite a few sections will be very similar to it, and some of the sections and paragraphs quoted from it. This will be primarily the case with the results, encoding method, and the introduction to the forex sections whose content is quoted to a significant extent from the paper. But unlike the readers of the above mentioned paper, you have an intricate understanding of how our system works, and why the results are the way they are, and how exactly the simulation and interfacing are performed and the manner in which the used agents were evolved, because you and I have built this new version of DXNN together.

Foreign exchange (also known as Forex, or FX) is a global and decentralized financial market for currency trading. It is the largest financial market, with a daily turnover of 4 trillion US dollars. The spot market, specializing in the immediate exchange of currencies, comprises almost 40% of all FX transactions, 1.5 trillion dollars daily. Because the foreign exchange market is open 24 hours a day, closing only for the weekend, and because of the enormous daily volume, there are no

G.I. Sher, *Handbook of Neuroevolution Through Erlang*,
DOI 10.1007/978-1-4614-4463-3_19, © Springer Science+Business Media New York 2013

sudden interday price changes, and there are no lags in the market, unlike in the stock market. In this chapter we discuss and implement the first of its kind (to my knowledge) of a topology and weight evolving artificial neural network (TWEANN) algorithm which evolves geometry-pattern sensitive trading agents that use the actual technical indicator charts (the actual graphs) as input. Once we have discussed and developed the said application, we will compare the SENN based traders which use *Price Chart Input (PCI)*, to the standard, direct encoded NN based trading agents which use *Price List Input (PLI)*, in which the time series of closing prices is encoded as a list of said prices and/or other technical indicators. Our goal in this chapter is to implement and test the utility of using graphical input of the time series, the use of candle-stick style chart as direct input to the geometry sensitive NN systems evolved using our TWEANN, and then to benchmark the performance. To accomplish this, we will build the forex simulator, the new interfaces (sensors/actuators), and all the needed new features to make our TWEANN work within this field, and in general be used in time series analysis problems not related to finance (such as earthquake data analysis, or frequency analysis...).

One of the two ways to use machine learning in financial market is as follows: we can use the agents to predict the future price of a financial instrument, and then based on the prediction trade the said instrument ourselves, or we can have the agent trade the financial instrument autonomously, without us in the loop. We will implement and test the second approach. Neural networks have shown time and time again [7,8,9,10,11,12,13,14] that due to their highly robust nature, and universal function approximation qualities, that they fit well in the application to financial market analysis. In published literature though [15,17,18,19,20], the most commonly used neural network learning algorithm is backpropagation. Backpropagation, being a local optimization algorithm, can and does at times get stuck in local optima. Furthermore, it is usually necessary for the researcher to set up the NN topology beforehand, and since the knowledge of what type of NN topology works best for which dataset and market is very difficult, or even impossible to deduce, one usually has to randomly create NN topologies and then try them out before settling down on some particular system. TWEANN systems are relatively new, and they have not yet been tested thoroughly in financial markets. But because it is exactly these types of systems that can evolve not only synaptic weights, but also the NN topologies, and thus perform a robust global search, the use of such a TWEANN system in evolving NN based traders is exactly the concern of this chapter.

19.1 Introduction to Forex

The foreign exchange market, or Forex, is a global, fully distributed, currency trading financial market. Unlike the stock market where a single buyer or seller with enough capital can dramatically change the price of the stock, the forex market is much too vast and distributed for any currency pair to be so easily affected by a single trader. Furthermore, the fact that currencies can be traded nonstop, 24 hours a day, 5 days a week, there are a lot fewer spaces in the data stream where news might be aggregating but no technical data is available. Because of these factors, there is a greater chance that the pricing data does indeed represent the incorporated news and fundamental factors, which might thus allow for prediction and trend finding through the use of machine learning approaches to be made.

The question of predicting future market prices of a stock, or currency pairs as is the case here, has been a controversial one in general, and especially so when using machine learning to do so. There are two main market hypotheses which state that such predictions should be impossible. These two market hypotheses are the Efficient Market Hypothesis (EMH), and the Random Walk Theory (RWT).

The EMH states that the prices fully reflect all the available information, and that all new information is instantly absorbed into the price, thus it is impossible to make profits in the market since the prices already reflect the true price of the traded financial instrument. The RWT on the other hand states that historical data has no affect on pricing, and that the future price of a financial instrument is completely random, independent of the past, and thus it cannot be predicted from it. Yet we know that profit is made by the financial institutions and independent traders in the existing markets, and that not every individual and institution participating in the trading of a financial instrument has all the available information immediately at his disposal when making those trades. Thus it cannot be true that EMH and RWT fully apply in a non ideal system representing the real world markets. Therefore, with a smart enough system, some level of prediction above a mere coin toss, is possible.

There are two general approaches to market speculation, the technical and the fundamental. Technical analysis is based on the hypothesis that all reactions of the market to all the news, is contained within the price of the financial instrument. Thus past prices can be studied for trends, and used to make predictions of future prices due to the price data containing all the needed information about the market and the news that drive it. The fundamental analysis group on the other hand concentrates on news and events. The fundamental analyst peruses the news which cause the prices, he analyzes supply & demand, and other factors, with the general goal of acting on this information before others do, and before the news is incorporated into the price. In general of course, almost every trader uses a combination of both, with the best results being achieved when both of these analysis approaches are combined. Nevertheless, in this paper our NN systems will primarily concentrate on the raw closing price data. Though in the future, the use of neuroevolution for news mining is a definite possibility, and research in this area is already in the works.

19.2 Trading and the Objective

If you were to decide on trading currency, you'd first need to find a financial service provider. Just like with the stock market, the financial institution you'd choose would provide you with the access to the financial data, where the delay between the true current trading price and the one you see, would depend on the account you have. More pricier accounts with pricier brokers could provide lower lags and more accurate data. Whichever institution is chosen, and whatever account you may have decided to get with the broker, your broker would then provide you with different ways of trading currencies through them. They could simply provide you with the IP address of their servers, your password, login, and an API, the format with which to request the financial data and send to the server commands to trade the currency pairs. Or they could provide you with a web based interface, where you'd be able to see your balance, the plotted charts, have the ability to close, open and hold long and short positions, and use various plotting tools and technical indicators to try and extract or recognize various geometrical and financial patterns within the data. But web based interfaces are usually a bit slower than many like, and so many traders opt for a software they can install on their desktop. Among such trading interface programs is one that is offered by a lot of brokers, it is called MetaTrader4 (MT4), and more recently the MetaTrader5 (MT5). Both are very similar, they differ mostly in the script language offered. The MT5 offers a slightly more updated version of the embedded scripting language which resembles C/C++. For our current conversation it does not matter whether the broker offers MT4 or MT5, and so for the sake of argument we simply assume it is MT5. Fig-19.1 shows an example of the MetaTrader interface

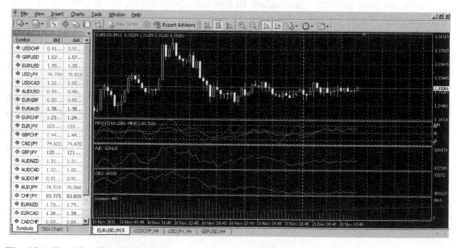

Fig. 19.1 The MetaTrader Interface.

The broker provides you with your login and password, and the IP of their server. At this point you'd install their trading platform, and then immediately be able to see the current currency pair exchange rates for various pairs. You would also have access to historical financial data. Finally, the trading platform would also usually offer even an incorporated news service from one of the news providers, it would provide plotting tools, various technical indicators, built in technical analysis graphs, and different ways to represent the currency pair plots. One of the most popular charts is the candlesticks chart, an example of which is shown in Fig-19.2. This type of plot presents the current price, the highest price achieved, and the lowest price achieved, during the chosen time intervals/steps/ticks, all in one chart. In the below figure, the candlesticks style plot uses 15 minute ticks (the change in pricing is calculated for 15 minute intervals)

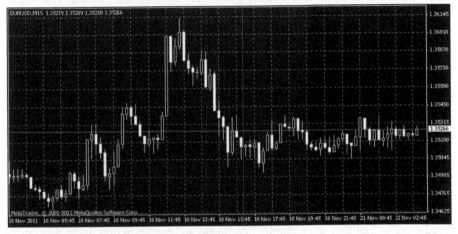

Fig. 19.2 Candlesticks chart using 15min ticks.

Though at any given time you are given the exchange rate of the two currencies you wish to exchange against each other, the broker must also make some profit. To do this, unlike in the stock market where fee is charged, in the FX market the price is given with a spread (the difference between the bidding price and the asking price) which incorporates the broker's fee. When you open a long position, buying USD against EUR, you do so at a slightly higher price than the true market exchange rate. When you go short, by for example selling USD against EUR, you do so at a slightly lower price than is the true market value. So, if immediately after you make a trade, you try to trade back, you will sustain at least a loss associated with the spread. Thus, the lower the spread that is offered by the financial service provider, the greater profit you can reach, and the more precise currency exchange price that you are observing.

Given this data, these tools, and financial instrument charts, the goal of a forex trader is to opportunistically exchange two currencies, such that when he trades them back to close the position, he is left with a profit. The technical analyst believes there are patterns and trends in the financial market and therefore in the charts observed, and that you can at least to some degree exploit these patterns and trends to make a profit. On the other hand, the fundamental analyst does not care about the patterns, he pays attention to the news, and tries to act on them before everyone else does, he tries to figure out and project what the news might mean with regards to the global economic situation and how it will affect the worth of currencies.

At this point it might seem as if the fundamental analyst is on the right track, and that there is a much lower level of predictive power that you can extract from prices alone. But consider the situation where a significant amount of institutions and individuals exist that believe in technical analysis, and therefore a lot of them trade by the rules and techniques prescribed by the technical analysis. Thus, if some particular chart pattern predicts that the price should rise, a lot of individuals and organizations will buy... and the price will rise. If another pattern predicts the price will fall, then those who believe in such patterns, will sell one currency against another, and the price will fall. We have seen what such panic and group think leads to, as we sustained a number of market crashes during the last decade. Technical analysis might or might not provide a significant advantage. But the fact that so many people believe in it, and trade based on its rules, means that they will contribute to these self fulfilling prophecies. So, because they believe in these patterns, because they trade based on these patterns, there will be, at least to some degree, such patterns in the signal, and so we can exploit it if our system can see the patterns and act on them faster and better than the other traders. If only our system too could extract such geometrical regularities from the charts.

Neural Networks have seen a lot of use and success in the financial market. One of the main strengths of NN systems, which makes them so popular as market predictors, is that they are naturally non linear, and can learn non linear data correlation and mapping. Artificial neural networks are also data driven, can be on-line-trained, are adaptive and can be easily retrained when the markets shift, and finally, they deal well with data that has some errors; neural networks are robust.

When traders look at the financial data plots, they do not usually look just at raw price lists, when a trader performs a time series analysis he instead looks at the chart patterns. This is especially the case when dealing with a trader prescribing to the technical analysis approach. The technical analyst uses the various technical indicators to look for patterns and emerging trends in these charts. There are many recurring patterns within the charts, some of which have even been given names due to their common appearance, like for example the "head and shoulders" pattern in which the time series has 3 hills, resembling head and shoulders. Other such patterns are the "cup and handle", the "double tops and bottoms", the "triangles"... Each of these geometrical patterns has a meaning to a trader, and is used by the trader to make predictions about the market. Whether these patterns really do have a meaning or not, is under debate. It is possible that the fact that so many traders do use these techniques, results in a self fulfilling prophecy, where a large number of the traders act similarly when encountering similar geometrical chart patterns, thus making the patterns and their consequences a reality. This also means that if we can evolve an agent which can respond to such patterns faster than the other traders, then we will be able to exploit this type of market behavior.

The standard neural networks used for price prediction, trend prediction, or automated trading, primarily use the sliding window approach, as shown in Fig-19.3, where the data is fed as a vector, a price list, to the NN. This vector, whether it holds only the historical price data, or also various other technical indicators, does not show these existing geometrical chart patterns which are used by the traders. If the NN does not have a direct access to the geometrical patterns used by human traders, it is at a disadvantage because it does not have all the information on which the other traders base their decisions on.

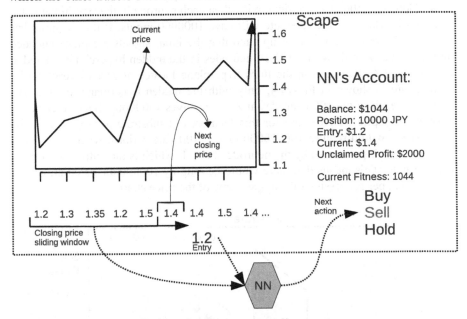

Fig. 19.3 A standard price list input based currency trading agent.

But how do we allow the NN to have access to this geometrical pattern within the data, and give it the ability to actually use it? We *cannot* simply convert these charts to bitmaps and feed them to the NN, because the bitmap encoded chart will still be just a long vector, and the NN will not only have to deal with an input with high dimensionality (dependent on the resolution of the bitmap), but also there would really be no connection between this input vector and the actual geometrical properties of the chart that could be exploited.

The solution comes in the substrate encoding we implemented in the earlier chapters. The substrate encoding approach has been actively used in computer vision, and as we discussed in the previous chapters, it has a natural property of taking geometrical properties of the sensory signals into consideration, and it can through its own geometrical topological structures, further extract and reveal the geometrical regularities within the data, and it is these geometric regularities that technical analysis tries to find and exploit.

With this type of indirect encoded neural network we can analyze the price charts directly, making use of the geometrical patterns, and trends within. Because each neurode in the substrate receives a connection from every neurode or input element in the preceding hyperlayer, the chart that is fed to the substrate must first be reconstructed to the resolution that still retains the important geometrical information, and yet is computationally viable as input. For example, if the sliding chart that is fed to the substrate is 1000x1000, which represents 1000 historical points (horizontal axis), with the resolution of the price data being (MaxPlotPrice − MinPlotPrice)/1000 (the vertical axis), then each neurode in the first hidden processing hyperlayer of the substrate will have 1000000 inputs. If the substrate has three dimensions, and we set it up such that the input signals are plane encoded and located at Z = -1, with a 10X10 neurodes in the hidden hyperplane located at Z = 0, and 1X1 neurodes in the third hyperplane located at Z=1 (a very similar architecture is shown in Fig-19.4, only with the hidden hyperplane being a 3x3 one), then each of the 100 neurodes at Z = 0 receives 1000000 inputs, so each has 1000000 synaptic weights, and for this feedforward substrate to process a single input signal would require 100*1000000 + 1*100 calculations, where the 1*100 calculations are performed by the neurode at Z = 1, which is the output neurode of the substrate. This means that there would be roughly 100000000 calculations per single input, per processing of a single frame of the price chart.

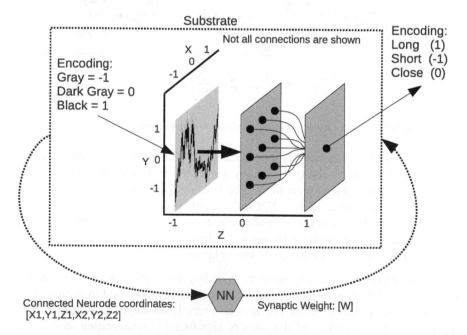

Fig. 19.4 A hyperlayer-to-hyperlayer feedforward substrate processing a 2d chart input.

Thus it is important to determine and test what resolution provides enough geometrical detail to allow for prediction to be made, yet not overwhelm the NN itself and the processing power available to the researcher. Once the number of the historical prices (horizontal axis on the price chart) and the resolution of the prices (vertical axis on the price chart) are agreed upon, the chart can then be generated for the sliding window of the currency pair exchange rates, producing the sliding chart. For example, Fig-19.5A shows a single frame of the chart whose horizontal and vertical resolution is 100 and 20 respectively, for the EUR/USD closing prices taken at 15 minute time-frames (pricing intervals). This means that the chart is able to capture 100 historical prices, from N to N-99, where N is the current price, and N-99 is the price (99*15) min ago. Thus, if for example this chart's highest price was $3.00 and the lowest price was $2.50, and we use a vertical resolution of 20, the minimum discernible price difference (the vertical of the pixel) is (3-2.5)/20 = $0.025. For comparison, Fig-19.5B shows a 10x10 chart resolution of a recreated candlesticks chart.

A. The recreated closing price chart with an 100x20 resolution.

B. The recreated closing price chart with a 10x10 resolution for comparison.

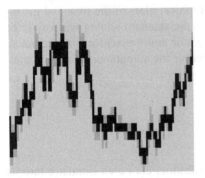
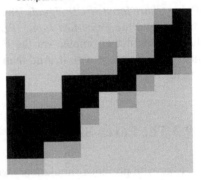

Fig. 19.5 A. and B. show a 100x20 and 10x10 resolution based charts respectively, using the candlesticks charting style.

Similar to Fig-19.4, in Fig-19.5 the pixels of the background gray are given a value of -1, the dark gray have a value of 0, and the black a value of 1. These candlestick charts, though of low resolution, can be seen to retain most of the geometrical regularities and high/low pricing info of the original higher resolution plot, with the fidelity increasing with the recreated chart's resolution. It is this type of chart that we can use as input plane that is fed to the substrate.

To accomplish this objective we need to use our TWEANN to evolve such agents, agents which instead of simply predicting the next tick's currency exchange rate, can directly interface with the financial service provider, gather currency exchange pricing data, and make the actual trades. To do so we can connect our TWEANN system through its sensors and actuators to an *electronic trading platform* like the mentioned MT4 or MT5, and then use the demo account as the simulator as we evolve the trading agents, letting the MetaTrader itself keep track of the agent's balance and therefore its implicit fitness score. But that will take too long, and we cannot very easily use thousands of MT instances, one private instance for every agent being evaluated.

Instead, we can get historical financial data from one of the brokers, and build our own Forex simulator in Erlang, simulated as a private scape. If we take that route, we could then easily spawn such private scapes for every agent in the population, allowing the agent to interface with it through its sensors and actuators. As long as we build the FX simulator accurately enough, such that it emulates the fees and the prices associated with one of the real broker offered services, and uses real world data, the historical data for example, we will be able to evolve currency trading agents which could be, after having been evolved and tested, applied to real markets and used to autonomously interface with the financial service providers and make autonomous trades.

In the next chapter we will discuss the architecture of the Forex simulator, and the sensors and actuators used to interface with it. We will discuss how to create the sensors and actuators so that we can feed our evolved NN based agents the *Price Chart Input (PCI) signals* (the actual graphical plots of the financial instruments), and the *Price List Input (PLI)* signals (the standard sliding window price list). We will then implement the Forex simulator and the sensors and actuators needed to interface with it. And then finally evolve the autonomous currency trading agents.

19.3 The Forex Simulator

Like with previous simulations, we need to abstract the Forex simulator into its own private scape. The private scape will simply simulate the forex market for a particular currency pair based on real historical data that we can download from one of the existing financial service providers.

Once we download the historical data for one of the currency pairs, let's say EUR/USD, which is the most popularly traded currency pair, we can enter it into a list, an *ets* or *dets* table, or *mnesia*, which can then be used by the simulator. In our case, we will use ets, although a simple list would have worked just as well, if not even better and faster in a scenario when the currency based properties have to be fed in a series to an interfacing trading agent. Although the list representation would not be as flexible as an ets one, and it is for that reason we are not using it.

We will then create a Forex market simulator where each interfacing NN will be given a $300 starting balance. Each agent will interface with its own private scape for which it will produce an output which will be converted by its actuator to − **1 if it's less than -0.5, 0 if between -0.5 and 0.5, and 1 if greater than 0.5**. When interacting with the Forex simulator, -1 means go short, 0 means close position (or do nothing if no position is open), and 1 means go long (if you currently have a short position opened, then first close the position, and then go long). The Forex simulator will simulate the market using 1000 real EUR/USD currency pair closing prices, stretching from 2009-11-5-22:15 to 2009-11-20-10:15, using 15 min ticks. The simulator will use a price spread of $0.00015, which is about average for a standard account from a financial service provider like OANDA or Alpari.

Because we will want to test the generalization of our evolved agents, their ability to be applied to previously unseen financial price data and successfully use it to make trades, we take the mentioned 1000 point dataset and further split it into training and generalization subsets. We will make the training set out of the first 800 time ticks, ranging from: 2009-11-5-22:15 to 2009:11-18-8:15, and the testing/generalization data we will set to the immediately following 200 time steps from 2009-11-18-8:15 to 2009-11-20-10:15. Finally, when the agent is opening a position, it is always done with $100 leveraged by x50 to $5000. Thus the losses and gains are based on the $5000 opened order. The leverage of x50 is a standard one provided by most brokers, since the change in currency pair prices is very low, profit is made by trading high volumes of the same.

The private scape simulation will interface with the agent through the agent's actuator and sensor interfacing messages. The Forex simulating private scape will accept the following list of messages from the agent:

1. **{From,sense,TableName,Feature,Parameters,Start,Finish}**: Is a request to the Forex simulator sent from the agent's sensor to acquire a list or a chart of historical financial data. The element *TableName* specifies from which table/database to read the financial data, essentially it specifies the currency pair. The element *Parameters* specifies which set of technical indicators, and the vector length the simulator should compose and send to this sensor. It could for example simply be [Hres,list_sensor], which would prompt the scape to send the sensor a PLI based signal. On the other hand if the *Parameters* element was set to [HRes,VRes,graph_sensor], the scape would first compose an input plane with a horizontal and vertical resolution of HRes and VRes respectively, and then forward that signal to the sensor. Finally, the *Start* and *Finish* parameters are used by the private scape at the very start to dictate the starting and ending indexes for this particular evaluation.

2. **{From,sense,internals,Parameters}**: This is another type of sensory signal request that a sensor could poll the scape with. This sensory signal requests information with regards to the agent's account internals, the information pertaining to the agent's account with the financial service provider. Information of things like the current balance, whether the agent is currently holding a long, short, or no position. And the percentage change of the position the agent is holding, if any.

3. **{From,trade,TableName,TradeSignal}**: This is the signal sent by the agent's actuator. It specifies the *TableName* parameter, which is effectively the currency

pair which is to be traded (though in this scape we will only use a single currency pair, in future implementations we could evolve multiple sensors and actuators that trade multiple currency pairs all at the same time using these TableName specifications). The *TradeSignal* parameter is a list of length 1, with a value set to either -1, 0, or 1, which specifies whether to short, hold, or go long on the currency pair. For example, if TradeSignal is set to -1, and the agent is already shorting a position, then it maintains its short position, if the agent holds no position, it opens a short position on the currency pair, and finally if the agent currently has a long position open, it first closes it, and then opens a short position. It acts symmetrically if the signal is 1. If it sends the signal of 0, then whatever the position is open, gets closed.

The scape will of course have to keep track of the agent's positions, fitness score (net worth), and other parameters to keep track what time it is currently simulating, and what signals it should feed the agent. To allow the scape to keep track of it all, the technical information about the currency pair, the agent's state, its position, its open and closed orders... we will need to create 4 new records, as shown next:

```
-record(state,{table_name,feature,index_start,index_end,index,price_list=[]}).
-record(account,{leverage=50,lot=10000,spread=0.000150,margin=0,balance=300,
net_asset_value=300, realized_PL=0,unrealized_PL=0,order}).
-record(order,{pair,position,entry,current,units,change,percentage_change,profit}).
-record(technical,{
    id,%Format: {Year,Month,Day,Hour,Minute,Second,Sampling_Rate}
    open,
    high,
    low,
    close,
    volume
}).
```

The *state* record keeps track of the general state, the index_start and index_end values, specified by the sensor. The current price list, which is particular to the implementation, and which makes things a bit more efficient by keeping the most recently sent signal in the list, so that the next time we need only poll the database for a single value, which is appended to the list, with the oldest value removed from it. The *account* record keeps track of the agent's standard account information. Its leverage, the currency pair lot size it trades in, the spread, margin if any, agent's current balance, its net_asset_value which is effectively the agent's fitness, and finally the realized and unrealized profit/loss. The last element in the list is the order, which is set to undefined when the agent has no order open with the simulated broker, and is set to the record *order*, when an order is opened. The record *order* specifies everything about the currently opened order. It specifies the current position (long or short), the entry price, the number of units traded, the dollar change in the position, the percentage_change of the position, and the profit (or loss) in dollars of the order. Finally, the record *technical* is used by the scape to store the actual historical financial data in its *ets* table. This table can be populated by for example first having MetaTrader5 dump a text file with historical data to the desktop, and then read the open, high, low, close, and volume parameters from the text file to ets.

Now that we've decided on the Forex simulator interfacing format and the data types this new private scape will use, we can implement it.

19.4 Implementing the Forex Simulator

We know what elements need to be implemented, and from having implemented a number of private scapes, and one public scape, we know the general architecture and structure that we need to construct. But this time we will slightly deviate from our standard approach, and instead of implementing the forex simulator inside the scape module, we will implement it in its own module, and only use the scape module to call it. As more and more scapes are added, using a single module is simply not enough, especially when the more complex scapes will require hundreds or thousands of lines of code. Thus we create the *fx.erl* module in which we will implement the private scape of the forex simulator.

We first give the private scape acting as a forex simulator a name: *fx_sim*. With that, we will be able to specify it in the sensors and actuators we will create in the next section. We then add to the scape module the function fx_sim/1, which is executed by the scape:prep/2 function when a private scape is spawned. It is the fx_sim/1 function that will be called to execute the actual private scape located in the fx module. The following shows the simple implementation of the fx_sim/1 function added to the scape module.

```
fx_sim(Exoself_PId)->
    fx:sim(Exoself_PId).
```

It is the sim/1 program and the fx module that contains all the needed functions that read from the text file, populate the ets table with financial information, and the functions that compose the PLI and PCI sensory vectors for the agent. The reading of the text file generated by MT5, and the writing of the ets table with the said data is out of scope for this text. Thus we will concentrate only on the implementation of the actual forex simulator, whose architecture and operational steps are shown in Fig-19.6, and whose implementation is shown and elaborated on, in Listing-19.1.

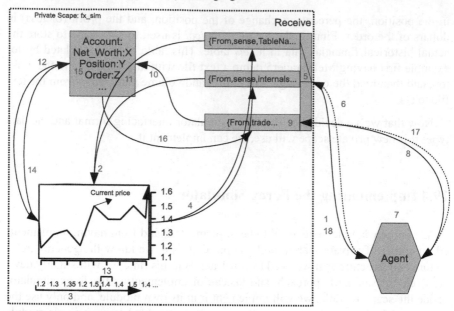

Fig. 19.6 The fx:sim/1 architecture diagram.

Let's go through the above shown steps before implementing the architecture:

1. The sensors of the agent poll the fx_sim for sensory data.
2. The scape checks what type of sensory signals are being asked for: account internals, PCI encoded signals, or PLI encoded signals.
3. The scape looks inside its database for the currency exchange rates, and based on the resolution/length of the historical currency exchange rate, builds a price list of that resolution.
4. The calling function in the receive clause is returned the price list.
5. Based on the receive clause, whether it is PCI or PLI, it encodes the returned price list accordingly, either as a simple price list, or as a price chart using trinary (-1,0,1) encoding.
6. The sensory signal (PCI or PLI, and the Internals) are forwarded to the agent's sensors.
7. The agent processes the sensory signals.
8. Based on the sensory signals and the agent's reasoning about them, the agent produces an output, and with its actuator forwards it to the fx_sim to make a trade.
9. The receive clause forwards the trading account made by the agent to the order handling function of fx_sim.
10. The signal is forwarded to the account processing function.
11. The private scape accesses the agent's account.
12. fx_sim queries the database for the current currency pair exchange rate.
13. The database checks the current currency pair exchange rate.

14. The database returns the current currency pair exchange rate, but at the same time moves the index of the "current" timestep, to the next time step, advancing one tick forward in the simulated market.

15. The private scape executes the agent's order. But also, knowing the exchange rate of the next tick, calculates the profit/loss/change within the agent's net worth.

16. Based on whether the simulation has ended, which occurs when the index used in the exchange rate database has reached '$end_of_table', or the agent's net worth has dipped below $100, the function returns to the calling receive clause a response message to be sent back to the actuator.

17. The private scape returns back to the actuator the tuple: {Fitness,HaltFlag}, where the Fitness is set to 0 when the HaltFlag is set to 0, and it is set to the agent's net worth when the HaltFlag is set to 1 (when a termination condition has been reached).

18. At this point the loop repeats and we go to step 1 if termination condition has not been reached.

Now that we know the step by step actions and interactions with the private scape, and its architecture, we can move forward and implement it. When reading the following implementation, it is essential to go through the comments, as they discuss and explain the functionality of every function they follow. Finally, the entire implementation of the forex simulator that we create in this chapter is available in the supplementary material at [1].

```
Listing-19.1 The implementation of the fx:sim/1 function.

sim(ExoSelf)->
    put(prev_PC,0),
    S = #state{},
    A = #account{},
    sim(ExoSelf,S,A).

sim(ExoSelf,S,A)->
    receive
            {From,sense,TableName,Feature,Parameters,Start,Finish}->
                {Result,U_S}=case S#state.table_name of
                    undefined ->
                        sense(init_state(S,TableName,Feature,Start,Finish),Parameters);
                    TableName ->
                        sense(S,Parameters)
                end,
                From ! {self(),Result},
                case ?SENSE_CA_TAG of
                    true ->
                        timer:sleep(10000),
```

```
                        IndexT = U_S#state.index,
                        NextIndexT = fx:next(TableName,IndexT),
                        RowT = fx:lookup(TableName,IndexT),
                        NextRowT = fx:lookup(TableName,NextIndexT),
                        QuoteT = RowT#technical.close,
                        NextQuoteT = NextRowT#technical.close;
                false ->
                        ok
        end,
        fx:sim(ExoSelf,U_S,A);
{From,sense,internals,Parameters}->
        Result = case A#account.order of
                undefined ->
                        [0,0,0];
                O ->
                        Position = O#order.position,
                        Entry = O#order.entry,
                        Percentage_Change = O#order.percentage_change,
                        [Position,Entry,get(prev_PC)]
        end,
        From ! {self(),Result},
        fx:sim(ExoSelf,S,A);
{From,trade,TableName,TradeSignal}->
        U_A = make_trade(S,A,TradeSignal),
        Total_Profit = A#account.balance + A#account.unrealized_PL,
        case ?ACTUATOR_CA_TAG of
                true ->
                        timer:sleep(10000),
                        IndexT = S#state.index,
                        NextIndexT = fx:next(TableName,IndexT),
                        RowT = fx:lookup(TableName,IndexT),
                        NextRowT = fx:lookup(TableName,NextIndexT),
                        QuoteT = RowT#technical.close,
                        NextQuoteT = NextRowT#technical.close;
                false ->
                        ok
        end,
        case (U_A#account.balance + U_A#account.unrealized_PL) =< 100 of
                true ->
                        Result = {1,0},
                        From ! {self(),Result},
                        io:format("Lost all money~n"),
                        put(prev_PC,0),
                        fx:sim(ExoSelf,#state{},#account{});
                false ->
```

```
                              case update_state(S) of
                                   sim_over ->
                                         Total_Profit = A#account.balance +
A#account.unrealized_PL,
                                              Result = {1,Total_Profit},
                                              From ! {self(),Result},
                                              put(prev_PC,0),
                                              fx:sim(ExoSelf,#state{},#account{});
                                   U_S ->
                                              Result = {0,0},
                                              From ! {self(),Result},
                                              U_A2 = update_account(U_S,U_A),
                                              fx:sim(ExoSelf,U_S,U_A2)
                              end
                    end;
          restart ->
                    fx:sim(ExoSelf,#state{},#account{});
          terminate ->
                    ok
          after 10000 ->
                    fx:sim(ExoSelf,S,A)
    end.
```

% The sim/1 function is the main receive loop of the forex simulator. It accepts messages from the agent, messages which either request for sensory signals (internal account data, or currency exchange rates), or messages from the agent requesting that the simulator opens a position for the agent. The simulator also monitors if the market has reached the end, or if the agent's net-worth dipped below 100, in which case the evaluation ends.

```
init_state(S,TableName,Feature,StartBL,EndBL)->
    Index_End = case EndBL of
          last ->
                    ets:last(TableName);
          _ ->
                    prev(TableName,ets:last(TableName),prev,EndBL)
    end,
    Index_Start = prev(TableName,ets:last(TableName),prev,StartBL),
    S#state{
          table_name = TableName,
          feature = Feature,
          index_start = Index_Start,
          index_end = Index_End,
          index = Index_Start
    }.
```

%init_state/5 function generates a default state of the simulator, based on the parameters specified by the agent's messages during the initial contact.

```
update_state(S)->
    NextIndex = fx:next(S#state.table_name,S#state.index),
    case NextIndex == S#state.index_end of
            true ->
                    sim_over;
            false ->
                    S#state{index=NextIndex}
    end.
```

%The function update_state/1 accepts the state as the parameter, and updates it by moving the historical pricing forward. During the move of the historical prices forward, the state is updated by updating the agent's account.

```
update_account(S,A)->
    case A#account.order of
            undefined ->
                    nothing_to_update,
                    A;
            O ->
                    TableName = S#state.table_name,
                    Index = S#state.index,
                    Row = fx:lookup(TableName,Index),
                    Close = Row#technical.close,
                    Balance = A#account.balance,
                    Position = O#order.position,
                    Entry = O#order.entry,
                    Units = O#order.units,
                    Change = Close - Entry,
                    Percentage_Change = (Change/Entry)*100,
                    Profit = Position*Change*Units,
                    Unrealized_PL = Profit,
                    Net_Asset_Value = Balance + Unrealized_PL,
                    U_O = O#order{current=Close,change=Change, percentage_change
=Percentage_Change, profit=Profit},
                    U_A = A#account{unrealized_PL=Unrealized_PL, net_asset_value
=Net_Asset_Value, order=U_O},
                    put(prev_PC,O#order.percentage_change),
                    U_A
    end.
```

%The update_account/2 function accepts the state and the account as parameters, and updates the account and the order, based on the state's specified current temporal position within the simulated market.

```
determine_profit(A)->
```

U_Realized_PL = A#account.realized_PL + A#account.unrealized_PL.
%The function determine_profit/1 calculates the agent's realized profit by adding to the agent's
current realized profit, the yet unrealized profit in the account.

```
make_trade(S,A,Action)->
    case A#account.order of
        undefined ->
            case Action == 0 of
                true ->%Do nothing
                    A;
                false ->%Open new position
                    open_order(S,A,Action)
            end;
        O ->
            case Action == 0 of
                true ->%Close Order
                    close_order(S,A);
                false ->%Modify Order
                    Current_Position = O#order.position,
                    case Current_Position == Action of
                        true ->
                            A;
                        false ->
                            U_A=close_order(S,A),
                            open_order(S,U_A,Action)
                    end
            end
    end.
```

%The make_trade/3 function opens an order (or keeps one open) for the agent, based on the
Action the agent specifies. If the agent holds a long position and Action specifies a short position, then the long position is closed, and a short is opened. Reflectively, other Actions are dealt
with in the same manner.

```
open_order(S,A,Action)->
    BuyMoney = 100,
    Spread=A#account.spread,
    Leverage = A#account.leverage,
    Balance = A#account.balance,
    TableName = S#state.table_name,
    Index = S#state.index,
    Row = fx:lookup(TableName,Index),
    Quote = Row#technical.close,
    Entry = Quote + Spread*Action,
    Units = round((BuyMoney*Leverage)/Entry),
    Change= Quote-Entry,
```

```
    PChange = (Change/Entry)*100,
    Profit=Action*Change*Units,
    Unrealized_PL = Profit,
    New_Order = #order{pair=TableName,position=Action,entry=Entry,current=Quote,
units=Units,change=Change,percentage_change=PChange,profit=Profit},
    A#account{unrealized_PL = Unrealized_PL,order=New_Order}.
```
%The open_order/3 function opens a position using the default leverage and buy in value
(100$), making the order short or long dependent on the value of the Action parameter.

```
close_order(S,A)->
    U_Balance = A#account.balance + A#account.unrealizcd_PL,
    U_Realized_PL = A#account.realized_PL + A#account.unrealized_PL,
    A#account{
    balance=U_Balance,
    realized_PL=U_Realized_PL,
    unrealized_PL = 0,
    order=undefined
}.
```
%The close_order/2 function, closes any currently opened position, updating the agent's
account in the process.

%%%% FX SENSORY SIGNAL FUNCTIONS %%%%
```
sense(S,Parameters)->
    case Parameters of
        [HRes,VRes,graph_sensor]->
                {Result,U_S}=plane_encoded(HRes,VRes,S);
        [HRes,list_sensor]->
                {Result,U_S}=list_encoded(HRes,S)
    end.

list_encoded(HRes,S)->
    Index = S#state.index,
    CurrencyPair = S#state.table_name,
    PriceListPs = S#state.price_list,
    case lists:keyfind(HRes, 2,PriceListPs) of
        false ->
                Trailing_Index = prev(CurrencyPair,Index,prev,HRes-1),
                U_PList = fx_GetPriceList(CurrencyPair,Trailing_Index,HRes,[]),
                U_PriceListPs = [{U_PList,HRes}|PriceListPs];
        {PList,HRes} ->
                R = fx:lookup(CurrencyPair,Index),
                U_PList = [{R#technical.open,R#technical.close,R#technical.high,
R#technical.low}|lists:sublist(PList,HRes-1)],
                U_PriceListPs = lists:keyreplace(HRes, 2, PriceListPs, {U_PList,HRes})
    end,
```

```
    U_S=S#state{price_list=U_PriceListPs},
    {[Close||{_Open,Close,_High,_Low}<-U_PList],U_S}.
% The function list_encoded/2 returns to the caller a price list of length HRes.


plane_encoded(HRes,VRes,S)->
    Index = S#state.index,
    CurrencyPair = S#state.table_name,
    PriceListPs = S#state.price_list,
    case lists:keyfind(HRes, 2,PriceListPs) of
            false ->
                    Trailing_Index = prev(CurrencyPair,Index,prev,HRes-1),
                    U_PList = fx_GetPriceList(CurrencyPair,Trailing_Index,HRes,[]),
                    U_PriceListPs = [{U_PList,HRes}|PriceListPs];
            {PList,HRes} ->
                    R = fx:lookup(CurrencyPair,Index),
                    U_PList = [{R#technical.open,R#technical.close,R#technical.high,
R#technical.low}|lists:sublist(PList,HRes-1)],
                    U_PriceListPs = lists:keyreplace(HRes, 2, PriceListPs, {U_PList,HRes})
    end,
    LVMax1 = lists:max([High||{_Open,_Close,High,_Low}<-U_PList]),
    LVMin1 = lists:min([Low||{_Open,_Close,_High,Low}<-U_PList]),
    LVMax =LVMax1+abs(LVMax1-LVMin1)/20,
    LVMin =LVMin1-abs(LVMax1-LVMin1)/20,
    VStep = (LVMax-LVMin)/VRes,
    V_StartPos = LVMin + VStep/2,
    U_S=S#state{price_list=U_PriceListPs},
    {l2fx(HRes*VRes,{U_PList,U_PList},V_StartPos,VStep,[]),U_S}.
%The function plane_encoded/3, returns to the caller a chart with a resolution of HResXVRes.

l2fx(Index,{[{Open,Close,High,Low}|VList],MemList},VPos,VStep,Acc)->
            {BHigh,BLow} = case Open > Close of
                    true ->
                            {Open,Close};
                    false ->
                            {Close,Open}
            end,
            O = case (VPos+VStep/2 > BLow) and (VPos-VStep/2 =< BHigh) of
                    true ->
                            1;
                    false ->
                            case (VPos+VStep/2 > Low) and (VPos-VStep/2 =< High) of
                                    true ->
                                            0;
                                    false ->
                                            -1
```

```
                        end
            end,
                l2fx(Index-1,{VList,MemList},VPos,VStep,[O|Acc]);
        l2fx(0,{[],_MemList},_VPos,_VStep,Acc)->
            Acc;
        l2fx(Index,{[],MemList},VPos,VStep,Acc)->
                l2fx(Index,{MemList,MemList},VPos+VStep,VStep,Acc).
%The l2fx/5 function is the one that actually composes the candle stick chart, based on the
price list, and the HRes and VRes values.


        fx_GetPriceList(_Table,EndKey,0,Acc)->
            Acc;
        fx_GetPriceList(_Table,'end_of_table',_Index,Acc)->
            exit("fx_GetPriceList, reached end_of_table");
        fx_GetPriceList(Table,Key,Index,Acc) ->
            R = fx:lookup(Table,Key),
                fx_GetPriceList(Table,fx:next(Table,Key),Index-1, [{R#technical.open,
R#technical.close, R#technical.high, R#technical.low}|Acc]).
%The fx_GetPriceList/4 function, accesses the table: Table, and returns to the caller a list of
tuples composed of the open, close, high, low exchange rate values, running from the initial
Key index, to the EndKey index within the table.
```

Having now implemented the actual simulator, we have to construct the sensors and actuators which the agent will use to interface with it. We do so in the next section.

19.5 Implementing the New Sensors and Actuators

With the private scape implemented, we now update the *sensor* and *actuator* modules to include the two new sensors that poll the scape for PLI and PCI signals, and send to the scape messages to execute trades. As with the other sensors and actuators, these are very simple due to the fact that the scape does most of the heavy lifting. Listing-19.2 shows the implementation of the three new sensor functions added to the sensor module. There are two sensors which request financial signals from the private scape, one in the standard linear sliding window format, and the other requests for that vector to be in the form appropriate for a substrate encoded NN based agent, and for that vector to represent the sensory signal using an appropriate and sensor specified resolution. The third sensor requests information with regards to the agent's account, encoded always in the linear form, as a vector of length 3.

Listing-19.2 The implementation of *fx_PCI/4, fx_PLI/4,* and *fx_Internals/4*, sensor functions.

```
fx_PCI(Exoself_Id,VL,Parameters,Scape)->
  [HRes,VRes] = Parameters,
  case get(opmode) of
        standard    ->
              Scape
!{self(),sense,'EURUSD15',close,[HRes,VRes,graph_sensor],1000,200};
        gentest ->
              Scape ! {self(),sense,'EURUSD15',close,[HRes,VRes,graph_sensor],200,last}
  end,
  receive
        {_From,Result}->
              Result
  end.


fx_PLI(Exoself_Id,VL,Parameters,Scape)->
  [HRes,Type] = Parameters,%Type=open|close|high|low
  case get(opmode) of
        standard    ->
              Scape ! {self(),sense,'EURUSD15',close,[HRes,list_sensor],1000,200};
        gentest ->
              Scape ! {self(),sense,'EURUSD15',close,[HRes,list_sensor],200,last}
  end,
  receive
        {_From,Result}->
              normalize(Result)
  end.


normalize(Vector)->
        Normalizer=math:sqrt(lists:sum([Val*Val||Val<-Vector])),
        [Val/Normalizer || Val <- Vector].


fx_Internals(Exoself_Id,VL,Parameters,Scape)->
  Scape ! {self(),sense,internals,Parameters},
  receive
        {PId,Result}->
              Result
  end.
```

The only thing that is different about these implementations is their use of the get(opmode) function, because the generalization testing and training, are performed on different subsets of the financial data. We will get back to that in the next section.

Similarly to the new sensors, we now implement the new actuator, and add it to the actuator module. The implementation of the fx_Trade/4 function is shown in the following listing. This actuator simply contacts the scape and requests to make a trade for a specified currency pair.

```
Listing-19.3 The implementation of the fx_Trade actuator.

fx_Trade(ExoSelf,Output,Parameters,Scape)->
    [TradeSignal] = Output,
    Scape ! {self(),trade,'EURUSD15',functions:trinary(TradeSignal)},
    receive
            {Scape,Fitness,HaltFlag}->
                    {Fitness,HaltFlag}
    end.
```

And finally we add the new *fx* morphological specification to the *morphology* module, as shown in the next listing.

```
Listing-19.4 The fx morphological specification.

forex_trader(actuators)->[
    #actuator{name=fx_Trade,type=standard,scape={private,fx_sim},format=no_geo, vl =1,
parameters=[]}
    ];

forex_trader(sensors)->
    PLI_Sensors=[#sensor{name=fx_PLI,type=standard,scape={private,fx_sim}, format
=no_geo, vl=HRes, parameters=[HRes,close]} || HRes<-[10]],
    PCI_Sensors = [#sensor{name=fx_PCI,type=standard,scape={private_fx_sim}, format
={symmetric,[HRes,VRes]},vl=HRes*VRes,parameters=[HRes,VRes]} || HRes <-[50], VRes
<-[20]],
    Internal_Sensors = [#sensor{name=fx_Internals,type=standard,scape={private_fx_sim},
format=no_geo,vl=3,parameters=[3]}],
    PCI_Sensors++Internal_Sensors.
```

Within this morphological specification we can choose which of the sensors to use, the one for substrate encoded NN based agents, or the one for neural encoded. We can also choose to use different sensors at the same time, sensors which gather data for different currency pairs, resolutions... It might be useful in the future to allow the agent to evolve connections and use different types of sensors which provide it with not only different signals, and different currency pair information, but also with differently encoded signals, which might allow the agent to more effectively extract and blend the information it acquires.

Having now implemented the sensors, actuators, and the new morphology, we now return to the discussion of the training and generalization testing, and what changes it entails for our TWEANN.

19.6 Generalization Testing

When we evolve a neural network to solve some problem, there is always a chance that instead of learning the concept behind the given problem, the neural network will simply memorize the associations between some specific sensory signals and actions that have to be taken, especially if the sensory signals come from some static list of data. In applications and simulations of ALife, the sensory signals and the environment itself is so dynamic, that simple memorization is not feasible, and would lead to death of the organism. Ability to deal with dynamic environments requires a greater amount of learning, and generalization is already part of the environment and what it requires from an agent if it wishes to survive. But when we deal with something like financial analysis, and the NN is trained on a some particular *static* dataset, there is a chance that it will simply memorize how to profitably trade that memorized section of the financial dataset, and when we move it to new data in the real world, it will be unable to generalize or make profitable trades with the new input signals.

The process of simple memorization rather than learning the concept, is referred to as overtraining/fitting. To prevent overtraining, stopping the evolutionary process right before the population begins to memorize rather than learn, is customarily done by dividing the given training dataset into two sections: Training and Generalization Testing. We first apply the population to the training dataset, evolving the solution. But after every generation, or every X number of evaluations, we take the champion of the population and apply it to the Generalization Testing dataset which it has not yet seen before. If at some point the agents begin to do worse and worse on the generalization datasets while continuing to improve on the training dataset, then the population is beginning to memorize, and is becoming overtrained. Thus at this point we would stop the training process, as it has shown to not be able to generalize and improve on new data any further.

Our system does not yet support such a feature. In general, the DXNN system and particularly the system we've built here, has in the problems I've applied it to, proven itself to generalize rather well even without the use of data splitting. To actually demonstrate this, to demonstrate the fact that our TWEANN system does not suffer significantly from over-training and poor generalization, we will slightly modify the population monitor such that every time a *stat* of a specie is calculated, the population monitor also takes the champion of that specie and applies it to a generalization test. This is done through a slight modification to the *population_monitor* module, the *exoself* module, and the *sensor/actuator* modules.

The amount of modification we will need to make is very little. Let us first discuss what the new behavior of an agent should be when it has been spawned only for the purpose of generalization testing. When we want to simply test a champion agent on how well it generalizes, we do not want to mutate or tune it in any way. We merely want to spawn the exoself, and apply it to a problem once, with its at-that-time topology and synaptic weight and connectivity pattern. Once the agent finishes its single evaluation, that score should then be returned to the population monitor. The population monitor should perform (if at all), the generalization test when it is building a *stat* record. Whether the agent is applied to a new problem or set of sensory signals during its generalization test is dependent on the problem. So then, we need only modify the exoself so that it can act in its standard way, but also when being generalization tested, to work in a very simple manner of just spawning and linking the NN system, waiting for the fitness score from the *cortex* element, and then forwarding that to the population monitor. The population monitor needs to be modified very little as well, it should simply, if set to do so, perform a generalization test by summoning the champion agent with the *generalization_test* operational mode, wait for its reply, and enter that score into the modified *stat* record. We will need to add to the stat record the new *gentest_fitness* element. Finally, the sensors and actuators could be modified at their core, by us changing their records to have two sets of parameters. One standard parameter element, and one *gentest_parameter*. This gentest_parameter could then specify a set of parameters that would dictate how the sensor/actuator should behave when generalization testing is performed... But we will take a simpler approach. We will not modify anything so significant with regards to sensors and actuators, and simply set the fx_PCI, fx_PLI, fx_Internals, and fx_Trade functions to check their operational mode, sent to them by the exoself, and then based on that, request signals from the private scape differently. This way we will not have to change anything. All that we would need to modify, is allow the exoself to specify the agent's operational mode when linking the sensors and actuators. The sensors and actuators would store to the process registry this operation mode, and those sensors and actuators that behave differently during standard evaluation and generalization testing, would simply use the command *get(opmode)*, to decide how to function. Thus, the sensor and actuator based modified prep/1 functions are as follows, with the small modification in boldface:

```
prep(ExoSelf_PId) ->
    receive
            {ExoSelf_PId,{Id,Cx_PId,Scape,SensorName,VL,Parameters,Fanout_PIds,
OpMode}} ->
                put(opmode,OpMode),
                loop(Id,ExoSelf_PId,Cx_PId,Scape,SensorName,VL,Parameters,Fanout_PIds)
    end.
prep(ExoSelf_PId) ->
    receive
    {ExoSelf_PId,{Id,Cx_PId,Scape,ActuatorName,Parameters,Fanin_PIds,OpMode}} ->
        put(opmode,OpMode),
        loop(Id,ExoSelf_ PId,Cx_PId,Scape,ActuatorName,Parameters, {Fanin_PIds,
Fanin_PIds}, [])
    end.
```

The first prep/1 belongs to the modified sensor module, while the second prep/1 belongs to the modified actuator module. And it is this simple modification that allows the sensor and actuator functions in Listing-19.2 to work.

Before we make the small changes to the *benchmarker, population_monitor,* and the *exoself* modules, let's go through the steps of our TWEANN when set to perform generalization testing when evolving a population of agents:

1. Because we now use the *pmp* record to set all the parameters of the population_monitor, we can use this record's op_mode element, and either set it to *gentest_off,* or *gentest_on* value. When set to gentest_off, it will function normally, without performing any kind of generalization tests every X number of evaluations. But when we set op_mode to *gentest_on*, the population_monitor will perform a generalization test. So then, we do not need to modify the benchmarker module in any way other than now having to also specify the op_mode parameter. Let us then set it in this example to: *gentest_on.*

2. The benchmarker starts the population_monitor. The population_monitor module's *state* record also has an op_mode element. And in the prep_PopState/2 function that the benchmarker uses to spawn the population_monitor with the parameters specified by the *pmp* record, the pmp record's op_mode is mapped to that of the population_monitor's state record's op_mode. It is only when we summon agents with the function summon_Agents/3 that we might wish to specify the operational mode with which the exoself should operate. But even here, we can simply create an extra exoself:start/3 function in which OpMode is specified. Thus, if the agent is started with the exoself:start/2 function (which is what we usually use), then it starts in standard mode. The only change in the population_monitor occurs in the gather_STATS/2 function. We modify it to gather_STATS/3 function, calling it with the OpMode parameter, so that when it executes: *update_SpecieSTAT(Specie_Id,TimeStamp,OpMode)* for every specie, it does so with the OpMode value. It's this function: *update_SpecieSTAT/3,* that we need to update to add this new generalization_testing functionality to our TWEANN.

3. We modify the *stat* record in the records.hrl file to also include the element gentest_fitness. The function update_SpecieSTAT, when composing the *stat* record, executes the following: *gentest_fitness = run_GenTest(S,OpMode).* The run_GenTest/2 function, based on the OpMode, either simply returns *0,* if the OpMode is set to gentest_off, or spawns the *Specie's* champion agent with the operational mode gentest. Thus for the population_monitor module, we need only update a few functions (gather_STATS/2 and update_SpecieSTAT/3) so that they can be called with the OpMode parameter. And we also need to build this new run_GenTest/2 function, which spawns the agent in the *benchmark* mode, waits for it to return its generalization score, and then returns that score to the caller, and thus setting the gentest_fitness parameter to that score.

4. The run_GenTest/2 function checks the Specie's *S#specie.champion_ids,* to get the agent id of the champion, and then spawn it in gentest mode by executing: *exoself:start(ChampionAgent_Id, self(), gentest).*

5. For step-4 to work, our exoself should be spawnable with the OpMode parameter, and we need to further update its *state* record to include the *opmode* element in it. Finally, we also need to allow the exoself to operate the *loop/1* function in two ways, the standard way, and the gentest way where it simply spawns the NN, waits for the fitness score, and then sends that fitness score as a message to the run_GenTest/2 function which spawned it, and then terminates the phenotype and itself. This can easily be done by modifying the loop/1 into loop/2: *exoself:loop(State,OpMode)*. In this way, we do not modify the standard code, instead we simply add a secondary loop clause which performs the required functionality and terminates. This will also require us to allow for the exoself to send the sensors and actuators the OpMode when linking them, but that is a simple modification, we just extend the InitState tuple that the exoself sends the sensors and actuators, such that the extended tuple also includes the OpMode as the last element.

Thus, to make it all work we now first modify the gather_STATS/3, as shown in the following listing, with the new source code in boldface:

Listing-19.3 The implementation of the updated gather_STATS/3, update_SpecieSTAT/3, and the new function run_GentTest/2. The modified and new code is shown in boldface.

```
gather_STATS(Population_Id,EvaluationsAcc,OpMode)->
    io:format("Gathering Species STATS in progress~n"),
    TimeStamp = now(),
    F = fun() ->
            P = genotype:read({population,Population_Id}),
            T = P#population.trace,
            SpecieSTATS = [update_SpecieSTAT(Specie_Id,TimeStamp,OpMode) || Specie_Id
<-P#population.specie_ids],
            PopulationSTATS = T#trace.stats,
            U_PopulationSTATS = [SpecieSTATS|PopulationSTATS],
            U_TotEvaluations = T#trace.tot_evaluations+EvaluationsAcc,
            U_Trace = T#trace{
                    stats = U_PopulationSTATS,
                    tot_evaluations=U_TotEvaluations
            },
            io:format("Population Trace:~p~n",[U_Trace]),
            mnesia:write(P#population{trace=U_Trace})
    end,
    Result=mnesia:transaction(F),
    io:format("Result:~p~n",[Result]).

update_SpecieSTAT(Specie_Id,TimeStamp,OpMode)->
        Specie_Evaluations = get({evaluations,Specie_Id}),
        put({evaluations,Specie_Id},0),
```

```
        S = genotype:read({specie,Specie_Id}),
        {Avg_Neurons,Neurons_Std} = calculate_SpecieAvgNodes({specie,S}),
        {AvgFitness,Fitness_Std,MaxFitness,MinFitness} = calculate_SpecieFitness({
specie,S}),
        SpecieDiversity = calculate_SpecieDiversity({specie,S}),
        STAT = #stat{
            morphology = (S#specie.constraint)#constraint.morphology,
            specie_id = Specie_Id,
            avg_neurons=Avg_Neurons,
            std_neurons=Neurons_Std,
            avg_fitness=AvgFitness,
            std_fitness=Fitness_Std,
            max_fitness=MaxFitness,
            min_fitness=MinFitness,
            avg_diversity=SpecieDiversity,
            evaluations = Specie_Evaluations,
            time_stamp=TimeStamp,
            gentest_fitness = run_GenTest(S,OpMode)
        },
        STATS = S#specie.stats,
        U_STATS = [STAT|STATS],
        mnesia:dirty_write(S#specie{stats=U_STATS}),
        STAT.

  run_GenTest(S,gentest)->
      TopAgent_Id = case S#specie.champion_ids of
            [Id] ->
                  Id;
            [Id|_] ->
                  Id;
            []->
                  void
      end,
      case TopAgent_Id of
            void ->
                  0;
            _ ->
                  Agent_PId=exoself:start(TopAgent_Id,self(),gentest),
                  receive
                        {Agent_PId,gentest_complete,Specie_Id,Fitness, Cycles,
Time}->
                              genotype:print(TopAgent_Id),
                              Fitness;
                        Msg ->
                              io:format("Msg:~p~n",[Msg])
```

```
                    end
        end;
    run_GenTest(_S,_)->
        0.
```

Now we modify the exoself module by allowing the exoself to be executed in 3 ways, so that it now also supports being executed with the OpMode parameter. And we also add the new loop/2 clause. This is shown in the following listing.

```
Listing-19.4 The 3 new exoself:start/1/2/3 functions, and the new loop/2 clause.

start(Agent_Id)->
    case whereis(monitor) of
        undefined ->
                io:format("start(Agent_Id):: 'monitor' is not registered~n");
        PId ->
                start(Agent_Id,PId,standard)
    end.

start(Agent_Id,PM_PId)->
    start(Agent_Id,PM_PId,standard).

start(Agent_Id,PM_PId,OpMode)->
    spawn(exoself,prep,[Agent_Id,PM_PId,OpMode]).
...
...
...
loop(S,standard)->
    receive

            ...
            ...
            ...
    end;
loop(S,gentest)->
    receive
            {Cx_PId,evaluation_completed,Fitness,Cycles,Time,GoalReachedFlag}->
                    terminate_phenotype(S#state.cx_pid,S#state.spids,S#state.npids, S#state.apids,
S#state.scape_pids,S#state.cpp_pids,S#state.cep_pids,S#state.substrate_pid),
                    io:format("GenTest complete, agent:~p terminating. Fitness:~p~n
TotCycles:~p~n TimeAcc:~p Goal:~p~n",[self(),Fitness,Cycles,Time,GoalReachedFlag]),
                    S#state.pm_pid !
{self(),benchmark_complete,S#state.specie_id,Fitness,Cycles,Time}
    end.
```

From this we can see that when exoself is started with either exoself:start/1 or exoself:start/2, it starts with an *OpMode = standard,* which is just normal operational mode in which it performs tuning. But we can also start it using exoself:start/3, specifying the OpMode directly. If that OpMode is *gentest,* after prepping and mapping the genotype to phenotype, the exoself will drop into the loop(S,gentest) clause, wait for the fitness score, and then immediately forward that fitness score to the population_monitor, and then terminate. With this, our system can now be started either in the standard mode, or in the gentest mode, in which it will perform generalization testing every X number of evaluations.

Finally, to actually build a graph of generalization test fitness scores, we also have to modify the benchmarker module, particularly the prepare_Graphs/2 function, so that it also dumps the gentest_fitness values to the file. With that done, composed of a few very simple modifications not shown here, we can now compile the modified modules, and move forward to perform the benchmarks.

19.7 Benchmark & Results

With our TWEANN now also being able to perform generalization tests when specified to do so, and store the results in the database, we can now apply our TWEANN system to the Forex simulator we've developed, and test the evolved agent's ability to generalize. Our goal now is to perform the benchmarks using Price List Input for neural encoded agents, and Price Chart Input for substrate encoded agents capable of extracting the geometrical patterns within the charts.

In the following benchmarks a single evaluation of a NN is counted when the NN based agent has went through all the 800 training data points, or if its balance dips below $100. The fitness of the NN is its net worth at the end of its evaluation. Each evolutionary run will last for 25000 evaluations, and each experiment is composed of 10 such evolutionary runs. In each experiment the population size was set to 10. Finally, in every experiment we will allow the NNs to use and integrate through evolution the following set of activation functions: *[tanh, gaussian, sin, absolute, sgn, linear, log, sqrt].*

In the experiments we will perform, we will set the NNs to use price sliding window vectors for direct encoded NNs, and price charts for substrate encoded NNs. We will also connect each agent not only to the sensors providing them with closing prices, but also the fx_sensor which produces the vector composed of: [Position, Entry, PercentageChange], where *Position* takes the value of either -1 (currently shorting the held order), 0 (no position), or 1 (currently going long on the held order), Entry is the price at which the position was entered (or set to 0 if no position is held), and PercentageChange is the percentage change in the position since entry, and finally the substrate's own output, a vector of length 1, will be fed back to the substrate's input hyperlayer. This will, due to feeding the substrate its own output, make the substrate Jordan Recurrent, an architecture of which is shown in Fig-19.7. Because we have already implemented the *jordan_recurrent* topology in Chapter-16, the use of this architecture will entail nothing more than allowing the seed agents to start with two sensors, the *fx_internals* and *fx_PCI*, and using: *substrate_linkforms = [jordan_recurrent]* in the ?INIT_CONSTRAINTS of the population to which the agent belongs.

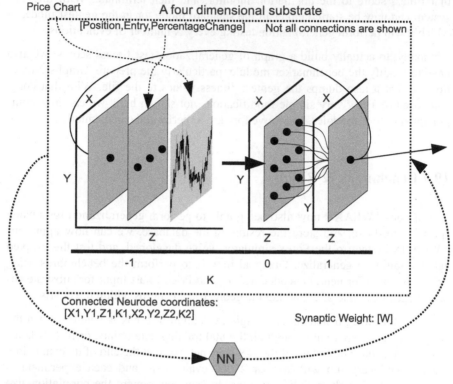

Fig. 19.7 The topology of the Jordan Recurrent substrate of the PCI using agent.

We will perform 14 benchmarks/experiments in total, each experiment is composed of 10 evolutionary runs from which the experiment's average/max/min is calculated for both the training and the generalization testing. Through the experiments we will compare the performance of PCI based NNs and the PLI based NNs. Finally, the sliding window and chart resolution that we will implement, will be comparable for both the neural and substrate encoded NN based agents. We will perform the following experiments:

- 5 PLI experiments:
  Experiments 1-5 will be performed using the PLI using NNs. Each experiment will differ in the resolution of the sliding window input the NNs use. Each NN will start with the sliding window sensor, and the fx_internals sensor. These 5 experiments are:

1. [SlidingWindow5] 2. [SlidingWindow10] 3. [SlidingWindow20]
4. [SlidingWindow50] 5. [SlidingWindow100]
Their names are based on the resolutions used by the agent's sensors.

- 9 PCI experiments:
We will perform experiments 6-14 with the PCI based NNs. In these experiments each PCI based NN will use a 4 dimensional substrate. The input hyperlayer to the substrate will be composed of the fx_PCI, fx_internals sensors, and the Jordan recurrent connection. For the PCI based NNs, we will create a 4 dimensional substrate with an input hyperlayer composed of the noted 3 hyperplanes and located at K = -1, all of which will be connected to the 5X5 hyperlayer positioned at K = 0, which then is further connected to the 1X1 output hyperlayer (composed of a single neurode in this case) located at K = 1, which outputs the short/hold/long signal, and which is also used for the recurrent connection back to the input hyperlayer. Each of the 9 experiments will use a sensor of a different resolution:

1. [ChartPlane5X10], 2. [ChartPlane5X20] 3. [ChartPlane10X10]
4. [ChartPlane10X20] 5. [ChartPlane20X10] 6. [ChartPlane20X20]
7. [ChartPlane50X10] 8. [ChartPlane50X20] 9. [ChartPlane100x10]

We will set the benchmarker to test generalization abilities of the evolved NN based agents every 500 evaluations, applying the best NN in the population at that time to the 200 data point generalization test. Performing the generalization tests consistently throughout the evolution of the population will not only allow us to test the generalization ability of the best NNs in the population, but it will also allow us to build a plot of the general generalization capabilities of that particular encoding and sensor type, and the generalization abilities of our TWEANN in general. Finally, doing this will allow us to get a better idea of whether generalization drops off as the PCI and PLI NNs are trained, whether it improves, or whether it stays the same throughout the training process.

19.7.1 Running the Benchmark

Having set everything up, we execute the benchmark for every noted experimental setup, and run it to completion. To do this, we simply modify the constraints used in our benchmarker module, and then execute benchmarker:start(Experiment_Name), for every of our experimental setups. Due to the number of the experiments, and the amount of time that the PCI based experiments take, particularly the ChartPlane100x10 and ChartPlane50x20 experiments, the benchmarking process will take up to a week even on a rather powerful quad core sandy bridge CPU. A problem which can be alleviated by interfacing Erlang with a GPU, and leveraging the vector multiplication performed by the substrate, but that is a story which will be covered in the next tome of this series...

A week later (which of course could be much less if using a much more power-ful server, or running all the experiments in parallel on different machines), we fi-nally have all the benchmarking results, similar to the results shown in Table-1. The following table presents the training average, training best, testing worst, test-ing average, testing standard deviation, and testing best fitness score results of every experiment. At the very bottom of the table, I list the Buy & Hold strategy, and the Maximum Possible profit results for comparison. The Buy & Hold profits are calculated by trading the currencies at the very start of the training or testing run respectively, and then trading back at the end. The best possible profit is cal-culated by looking ahead and trading the currencies only if the profit gained be-fore the trend changes will be greater than the spread covering cost.

Table 1 Benchmark/Experiment Results.

TrnAvg	TrnBst	TstWrst	TstAvg	TstStd	TstBst	Price Vector Sensor Type
540	550	225	298	13	356	[SlidWindow5]
523	548	245	293	16	331	[SlidWindow10]
537	538	235	293	15	353	[SlidWindow20]
525	526	266	300	9	353	[SlidWindow50]
548	558	284	304	14	367	[SlidWindow100]
462	481	214	284	32	346	[ChartPlane5X10]
454	466	232	297	38	355	[ChartPlane5X20]
517	527	180	238	32	300	[ChartPlane10X10]
505	514	180	230	26	292	[ChartPlane10X20]
546	559	189	254	29	315	[ChartPlane20X10]
545	557	212	272	36	328	[ChartPlane20X20]
532	541	235	279	23	323	[ChartPlane50X10]
558	567	231	270	20	354	[ChartPlane50X20]
538	545	256	310	37	388	[ChartPlane100x10]
311	N/A	N/A	300	N/A	N/A	Buy & Hold
N/A	704	N/A	N/A	N/A	428	Max Possible

From the above results we can note that the generalization results for both, the PCI based NNs and PLI based NNs, show profit. Indeed, the acquired profits seem rather significant as well, for example the highest profit reached during generaliza-tion, $88 (single occurrence ending with net worth of $388) out of the $128 possi-ble when the agent started with 300$. This shows that the agent was able to extract 68% of the available profit, a considerable amount. This is substantial, but we must keep in mind that even though the agents were used on real world data, they were still only trading in a simulated market, and we have chosen the best per-formers from the entire experiment..., thus it is only after we test these champions on another set of previously unseen data, would it be possible to say with some certainty that these generalization abilities carry over, and for how many time-steps before the agents require re-training (In our experiment the agents are trained on 800 time steps, and tested on the immediately followed 200 time steps).

By only analyzing the information provided in the above table, the first thing we notice is that the PCI NN generalization's worst performers are significantly worse than those of the PLI based NNs. The PCI based NNs either generalized well during an evolutionary run, or lost significantly. The PLI based NNs mostly kept close to 300 during generalization test phase when not making profit. Also, on *average* the best of PCI are lower than those produced by the best of PLI during generalization. On the other hand the training fitness scores are comparable for both the PCI and PLI NNs. Another observation we can make is that on average the higher price (vertical) resolution (X20 Vs. X10) correlates with higher achieved profits by the PCI NNs during generalization testing. And finally, we also see that for both PLI and PCI, generalization achieved by 5 and 100 based price window resolutions is highest.

We have discussed time and again that substrate encoding could potentially offer a greater level of generalization to NN based agents due to the NNs operating on coordinates, never seeing the actual input sensory signals, and thus being unable to pick out particular patterns for memorization. *NNs paint the synaptic weights and connectivity patterns on the substrate in broad strokes*. But based on Table-1, at the face of it, it would almost seem as if we are wrong. This changes if we perform further analysis of the results of our experiments, and plot the benchmarker produced GNUplot ready files. The plots produced are quiet interesting, as shown in Fig-19.8.

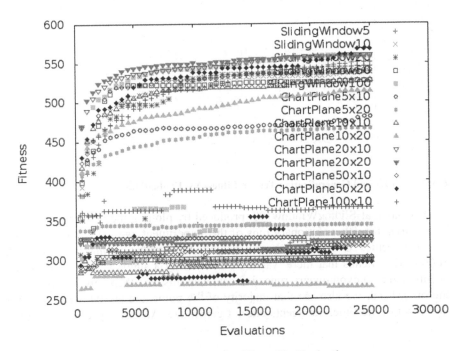

Fig. 19.8 PLI & PCI based Training and Testing Fitness Vs. Evaluations.

Though somewhat difficult to see, we can make out that though yes the PLI NNs did achieve those generalization fitness scores, they were simply tiny and very short lived blips during the experiment, occurring a few times, and then disappearing, diving back under 300. On the other hand though, the PCI NNs produced lower profits on average when generalization was tested, **but** they produced those profits consistently, they generalized more frequently. When a PCI NN system generalized, it maintained that generalization ability for most of the entire evolutionary run. This is easier to see if we analyze the graph of PLI Generalization Fitness Vs. Evaluations, shown in Fig-19.9, and the PCI Generalization Fitness Vs. Evaluations, shown in Fig-19.10.

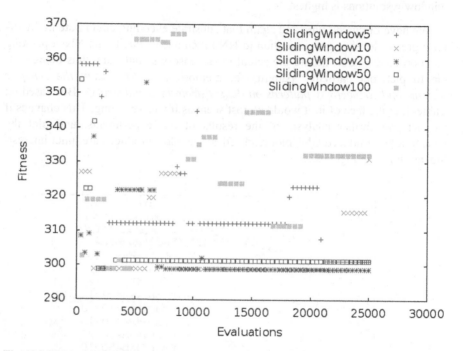

Fig. 19.9 PLI based Generalization Testing Fitness Vs. Evaluations.

If we look at SlidingWindow100, produced by plotting the best generalization scores from the 10 evolutionary runs of that experiment, we see that the score of 367 was achieved briefly, between roughly the evaluation number 5000 and 10000. This means that there was most likely only a single agent out of all the agents in the 10 evolutionary runs, that achieved this, and then only briefly so. On the other hand, we also see that majority of the points are at 300, which implies that most of the time, the agents did not generalize. And as expected, during the very beginning, evaluations 0 to about 3000, there is a lot more profit producing activity amongst all sliding window resolutions, which is rather typical of over trained NNs, whose generalization score decreases while training score increases over time. The most stable generalization and thus profitability was shown by SlidingWindow5 and SlidingWindow100, and we know this because in those experiments, there were a lot more fitness scores above 300, consistently. From this, we can extract the fact that when it comes to PLI based NNs, during all the experiments, there are only a few agents that generalize well, and do so only briefly.

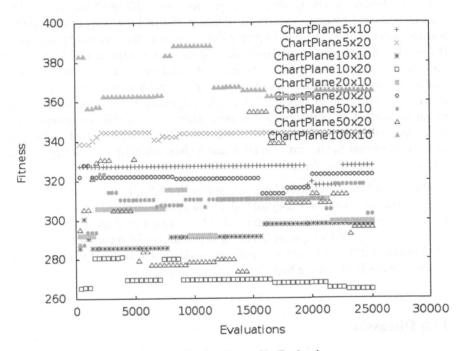

Fig. 19.10 PCI based Generalization Testing Fitness Vs. Evaluations.

Let us now analyze Fig-19.10, the generalization results for just the PCI based NN systems. The story here is very different. Not only there are more consistently higher than 300 generalization fitness scores in this graph, but they also last throughout the entire 25000 evaluations. This means that there are **more** generalizing agents which stayed within the population without being replaced due to over-fitting, or simply those few that did generalize, performed superior to those with poorer generalization, and thus stayed within the population for **longer** periods of time. Which gives hope that the generalization ability of these PCI NN based systems will carry over to real world trading.

When going through raw data, it was usually the case that for every PLI NN based experiment, only about 1-2 in 10 evolutionary runs had a few agents which generalized for a brief while to scores above 320, before being replaced by over-fitted, poorly generalizing agents. On the other hand when going through the PCI NN based experiments, 3-6 out of 10 evolutionary runs had agents generalizing, and remaining within the population for the entire evolutionary run, with scores above 320.

Analyzing the generalization plots further, we can also note that the low resolution substrates produce at times better results, and do so more often, than their high resolution counterparts... except for the *SlidingWindow100*, and *ChartPlane100x10* based experiments, which performed the best. I think that the low resolution based experiments performed well due to the fact that by increasing the number of neurodes in one layer, the neurodes in the postsynaptic layer would now have so many inputs that they become saturated, becoming unable to function effectively, although scaling and normalizing the presynaptic vectors for every neurode did not seem to improve this problem significantly, leaving this anomaly to future work. Contradictory to this assumption is of course the exceptionally well performing *SlidingWindow100*, and *ChartPlane100x10* based agents. So then, it seems that the lowest resolution and highest resolution based experiments performed the best, but the question of why is still under analysis.

With regards to the evolved high performing PLI NNs, it was clear that they all had one feature in common, they all had a substantial number of recurrent connections. I think that the high performing PLI NNs which used the sliding window vectors of size 5, did so due to having a large number of recurrent connections, which made it difficult to evolve simple memorization, and thus forcing generalization. But this is also just a hypothesis at the moment.

19.8 Discussion

We have seen that TWEANN systems can successfully be applied to financial analysis. We have also been able to compare a geometrical pattern sensitive substrate encoded NN based agent which uses price chart input, vs. standard neural encoded agent using price list input. As we hoped, the geometrically sensitive agents were able to produce profit when applied to this problem, and were the superior of the two approaches when it came to generalization. This implies that PCI agents were able to extract the geometrical patterns within the financial data just as we hoped.

These results also imply that the geometrical pattern sensitive NNs have potential in time series analysis applications. This means, anything from earthquake data analysis, to frequency and audio/voice analysis based applications, could potentially be leveraged by these types of systems. The generalization is particularly impressive, and the substrate encoded system's ability to use and improve with the resolution at which the time series analysis is sampled, implies enormous application based potential.

Though our systems have produced profits when applied to Forex trading in simulations, we still need to apply the resulting evolved agents to the real market, by connecting the evolved agent to a trading platform. Application of these types of systems to voice analysis, is now also an area of interest with regards to future applications.

19.9 Summary

In this chapter we applied our TWEANN system to evolve currency trading agents. We extended our TWEANN by adding to it the generalization testing features, allowing the benchmarker to extract the champions of the population and separately apply them to the given problem, or a separate problem, to see if the evolved agents can generalize and perform effectively on a related problem, but one not yet explored directly during evolution. We implemented the translation of the pricing data into price chart based on the candle stick style, and evolved substrate encoded geometrical pattern sensitive agents which could use these price chart inputs, and based on the geometrical patterns within those charts, trade currency. We also evolved the standard sliding window, price list input based neural networks. These types of agents simply read historical data, and then made currency pair trading decisions.

From the performed benchmarks and experiments, we have confirmed that substrate encoding does indeed provide for excellent generalization capabilities. We also confirmed that geometrical sensitivity with regards to technical analysis can give the NN an ability to trade currency. Indeed the PCI based agents performed much better, with regards to generalization, than PLI based agents. But more importantly, through experiments that we have performed, we determined that TWEANNs can indeed evolve geometry sensitive agents that are successful in this very complex and chaotic time series analysis application, thus there is hope for its application to other time series analysis problems.

19.10 References

[1] Chapter-19 Supplementary material: www.DXNNResearch.com/NeuroevolutionThrough Erlang/Chapter19

[2] Halliday R (2004) Equity Trend Prediction With Neural Networks. Res. Lett. Inf. Math. Sci., Vol. 6, pp 15-29.

[3] Mendelsohn L (1993) Using Neural Networks For Financial Forecasting. Stocks & Commodities. Volume 11:12, October. p.518-521.

[4] Min Qi, Peter GZ (2008) Trend Time-Series Modeling and Forecasting With Neural Networks. IEEE Transactions on neural networks, Vol. 19, no. 5.

[5] Lowe David (1994) Novel Exploitation of Neural Network Methods in Financial Markets. Proceedings of the 3rd IEE International Conference on Artificial Neural Networks, IEE Publications, Aston, United Kingdom.

[6] Jung H, Jia Y, et al (2010) Stock Market Trend Prediction Using ARIMA-Based Neural Networks. 2008 Proceedings of 17th International Conference on Computer Communications and Networks 4, 1-5.

[7] Versace M, Bhatt R, Hinds O, Shiffer M (2004) Predicting The Exchange Traded Fund DIA With a Combination of Genetic Algorithms and Neural Networks. Expert Systems with Applications 27, 417-425.

[8] Yao J, Poh HL (1995) Forecasting the KLSE Index Using Neural Networks. IEEE International Conference on Artificial neural networks.

[9] Kimoto T, Asakawa K, Yoda M, Takeoka M (1990) Stock Market Prediction System With Modular Neural Networks. International Joint Conference on Neural Networks 1, 1-6.

[10] Hutchinson JM, Lo AW, Poggio T (1994) A Nonparametric Approach to Pricing and Hedging Derivative Securities Via Learning Networks. Journal of Finance 49, 851-889.

[11] Refenes AN, Bentz Y, Bunn DW, Burgess AN, Zapranis AD (1997) Financial Time Series Modelling With Discounted Least Squares Backpropagation. Science 14, 123- 138.

[12] Li Y, Ma W (2010) Applications of Artificial Neural Networks in Financial Economics: A Survey. 2010 International Symposium on Computational Intelligence and Design, 211-214.

[13] Rong L, Zhi X (2005) Prediction Stock Market With Fuzzy Neural Networks. Proceedings of the Fourth International Conference on Machine Learning and Cybernetics, Guangzhou, 18-21.

[14] Maridziuk J, Jaruszewicz M (2007) Neuro-Evolutionary Approach to Stock Market Prediction. 2007 International Joint Conference on Neural Networks, 2515-2520.

[15] Soni S (2005) Applications of ANNs in Stock Market Prediction: A Survey. ijcsetcom 2, 71-83.

[16] White H, Diego S (1988) Economic Prediction Using Neural Networks: The Case of IBM Daily Stock Returns. Neural Networks 1988 IEEE International Conference on, 451-458.

[17] Dogac S (2008) Prediction of stock price direction by artificial neural network approach. Master thesis, Bogazici University.

[18] Yamashita T, Hirasawa K, Hu J (2005) Application of Multi-Branch Neural Networks to Stock Market Prediction. English, 2544-2548.

[19] Quiyong Z, Xiaoyu Z, Fu D (2009) Prediction Model of Stock Prices Based on Correlative Analysis and Neural Networks. Second International Conference on Information and Computing Science, pp: 189-192 , IEEE.

[20] Risi S, Stanley KO (2010) Indirectly Encoding Neural Plasticity as a Pattern of Local Rules. Neural Plasticity 6226, 1-11.

Part VI
Promises Kept

Promises kept. We have created a decoupled, dynamic, flexible, memetic and genetic algorithm based, topology and parameter evolving universal learning network, where a node can act as any type of function. The neurons, if they can even be called that at this point, since they are not limited to the use of *tanh* activation function, can be anything. In some sense, we can instead use the term *node* rather than *neuron*, and allow the nodes to be, amongst other things, NNs themselves, and thus transforming our system into a modular NN. Each node could potentially represent a standard neural encoded NN, or a substrate encoded NN. The encoding of our system is flexible enough to scale further, to be further molded and expanded. Our system supports both, direct encoding, and indirect encoding. It supports static neural networks, and neural networks with plasticity, where the plasticity functions can be changed and modified, and new ones added without much difficulty, they are self contained and decoupled. This extends to indirect encoding, which also supports plasticity. Furthermore, we have made even the evolutionary parameters able to evolve:

```
-define(ES_MUTATORS,[
    mutate_tuning_selection,
    mutate_tuning_duration,
    mutate_tuning_annealing,
    mutate_tot_topological_mutations,
    mutate_heredity_type
]).
```

Our system supports the mutation of various evolutionary strategy parameters. We also made the probabilities of any one mutation operator have itself a mutatable percentage value, and hence the mutation operators use the format: *{MutationOperatorName,RelativeProbability}*. Our system supports both, Darwinian and Lamarckian evolution. Our system is fully concurrent, with the processes like Cortex and Exoself, ready to act as monitors, and allow for self-healing networks to emerge, with further monitors in the hierarchy possibly being the new specie process, the already existing population_monitor process, and finally the *polis* itself. And yet there is so much more that can easily be added. And as you've seen in the previous chapters, due to the way we constructed our neuroevolutionary platform, adding new features has become trivial.

If our neurons use the activation function *tanh*, then what we have created is an advanced Topology and Weight Evolving Artificial Neural Network. If we create the activation functions AND, NOT, and OR, then our system becomes a digital circuit evolutionary system, which we can apply to the optimization of already existing digital circuits, or to the creation of new ones. If we use any activation function, then our system acts as a Topology and Parameter Evolving Universal Learning Network (TPEULN) system. If we set some of the activation functions to act as programs, our system is a genetic programming system. If we allow for the above listed evolutionary strategy mutation operators to be active, by setting the *?SEARCH_PARAMTERS_MUTATION_PROBABILITY* in the genome_mutator module to anything above 0, our system becomes an evolutionary strategy system. If we set the activation functions to be state machines, our system will act as an evolutionary programming system. If we use indirect encoding, the substrate encoding we developed in Chapter-16 & 17, our system uses evolutionary embryology. Why even call our "neurons" neurons? Why not just nodes, since our *neurons* can be anything, including NNs themselves, or substrate encoded NNs, and thus making our system into a modular universal learning network. But we do not need to force our system to use just one particular approach, we can set it in the constraints to use all available functions, all the available features, and it will evolve it all. We can increase the population size, allow our system to use everything, and it will evolve and settle on the parameters and features that gives the evolving NN based agents an advantage in the environment in which they evolve. Our system truly is a *Topology and Parameter Evolving Universal Learning Network. It encompass all the modern learning systems, and yet there is still infinite room to expand, explore, and advance.*

In the Applications part of the book, I showed how easy it was to apply our system to two completely different problems, the Artificial Life (and thus robotics, and anything related) simulation, and the Financial Analysis (and thus any other predictive, or classification problem). Because of the way we created our system to use easily modifiable and changeable sensor and actuator modules, our system is so flexible that its application to any problem needs only for the said problem specific sensor and actuator functions to be created. The ALife experiment showed that we can just as easily use our system with something like Player/Gazebo sensor/actuator driver provider and 3d robot and environment simulator, respectively. We can continue and evolve not just predators and prey, but evolve robot morphologies, allow them to learn not to just hunt each other and find food in 2d space, but to learn how to use physics to their advantage, to use their 3d bodies, to evolve new sensors and actuators, to evolve new morphologies, to evolve... We can similarly evolve NNs which control combat UAVs, in exactly the same manner, and I hope after reading this book you see that such a feat is indeed simple to accomplish, and not just words. For we have done it already, just in a 2d environment rather than 3d. The sensors and actuators would define from what systems the UAV acquires its signals, cameras, range sensors, sonars... and through actuators we can evolve and let the NN control the various morphological systems, propellers, fins, guns... Our system can also be applied to medicine, we can let the NN learn correlations between genetics and pathology, or symptoms and diseases, evolving a diagnostician. We can apply our system to bioinformatics, using the substrate encoded NN system to explore and create new drugs... Truly, the application areas in biology are enormous [1,2,3,4,5,6,7,8,9,10,11,12,13].

I noted that there is still an infinite amount of things to explore, and more advancements to be included. There are thousands more pages to fill, and so further extensions to the system will be explored in the next volume. In the last remaining chapter I will discuss some of the more pertinent things we will explore in the next book. A glimps of things to come. Though I have a feeling that by the time we get to the next book, you will already have created many of those improvements on your own, and those improvements and advancements that I have not even considered. You already have the knowledge of the system and the theory to continue and explore what I have not, all on your own, pushing beyond the horizon.

[1] Moreira A (2003) Genetic Algorithms for the Imitation of Genomic Styles in Protein Backtranslation. Theoretical Computer Science 322, 17.

[2] Terfloth L, Gasteiger J (2001) Neural Networks and Genetic Algorithms in Drug Design. Drug Discovery Today 6, 102-108.

[3] Huesken D, Lange J, Mickanin C, Weiler J, Asselbergs F, Warner J, Meloon B, Engel S, Rosenberg A, Cohen D, et al (2005) Design of a Genome-Wide siRNA Library Using an Artificial Neural Network. Nature Biotechnology 23, 995-1001.

[4] Vladimir BB, et al (2002) Artificial Neural Networks Based Systems for Recognition of Genomic Signals and Regions: A Review. Informatica 26 389-400 389

[5] Yoshihara I, Kamimai Y, Yasunaga M (2001) Feature Extraction from Genome Sequence Using Multi-Modal Network. Genome Informatics 12, 420-422.

[6] Gutteridge A, Bartlett GJ, Thornton JM (2003) Using a Neural Network and Spatial Clustering to Predict the Location of Active Sites in Enzymes. Journal of Molecular Biology 330, 719-734.

[7] Emmanuel A, Frank AI (2011) Ensembling of EGFR Mutations - based Artificial Neural Networks for Improved Diagnosis of Non-Small Cell Lung Cancer. International Journal of Computer Applications (0975 - 8887) Volume 20 - No.7.

[8] Herrero J, Valencia A, Dopazo J (2001) A Hierarchical Unsupervised Growing Neural Network for Clustering Gene Expression Patterns. Bioinformatics 17, 126-136.

[9] Wang DH, Lee NK, Dillon TS (2003) Extraction and Optimization of Fuzzy Protein Sequence Classification Rules Using GRBF Neural Networks. Neural Information Processing Letters and Reviews, 1(1): 53-59.

[10] Chan CK, Hsu AL, Tang SL, Halgamuge SK (2008) Using Growing Self-Organising Maps to Improve the Binning Process in Environmental Whole-Genome Shotgun Sequencing. Journal of Biomedicine and Biotechnology 2008, 513701.

[11] Reinhardt A, Hubbard T (1998) Using Neural Networks for Prediction of the Subcellular Location of Proteins. Nucleic Acids Research 26, 2230-2236.

[12] Oliveira M, Mendes DQ, Ferrari LI, Vasconcelos A (2004) Ribosome Binding Site Recognition Using Neural Networks. Genetics and Molecular Biology 27, 644-650.

[13] Azuaje F (2002) Discovering Genome Expression Patterns With Self-Organizing Neural Networks., in Understanding and Using Microarray Analysis Techniques: A Practical Guide. London: Springer Verlag.

Chapter 20 Conclusion

Abstract Last words, future work, and motivation for future research within this field.

We have developed a state of the art topology and weight evolving artificial neural network system. The system is developed to be scalable, concurrent, and the architecture of our system is highly modular and flexible, allowing for future extensions and modifications to the system. We have tested our system on a few standard benchmarking problems, the XOR problem, the Single and Double Pole Balancing problem, and the T-Maze navigation problem. Our system performed superbly in all scenarios without us even having tuned it or optimized it yet.

There is still an enormous amount of features we can add to our system, and due to the way we have developed it and due to it being written in Erlang, it will be easy to do so. We can make our NNs modular, add Kohonen Map, Competitive NN, Hopfield Network, and other types of self organizing network based modules. We can add and test out new mutation operators, for example the use of pruning, the use of splitting in which we would take sections of the NN and make copies of them, slightly perturb them, and reconnect the perturbed copies to the original NN. Or allow for multiple substrates to work together, where one substrate could even modulate the other. We can create committee machines using *dead_pools*. We can add new forms of neuromodulation, plasticity... There are also new fitness functions we can create, those that take into account the Cartesian distance of the connections between the neurodes within the substrate for example, which would allow us to push for closely connected neural clusters. We could also add a "crystallization" feature, where neural circuits which have been topologically stable during the NN's evolution are crystallized into a single function, a single process represented module. We could add new types of signal normalization preprocessors... Even in applications, we can spend hundreds more pages on the integration of Player/Stage/Gazebo with the TWEANN system we have created here, allowing our neuroevolutionary system to evolve the brains in simulated robots inhabiting 3d environments. We can evolve neural networks to control simulated Unmanned Combat Aerial Vehicles inside Gazebo, evolving new aerial dog fighting tactics... There is so much more to explore and create, all of it possible and simple due to the use of Erlang. These mentioned features we will develop and design in the next book, advancing this already bleeding edge TWEANN (Or is it Topology and Parameter Evolving Universal Learning Network, TPEULN?) system to the next level.

You now have the information, the tools, and the experience to continue developing this system, or a completely new one on your own. The next advancements in this field will be done by you. We've built this system together, so you are as

G.I. Sher, *Handbook of Neuroevolution Through Erlang*,
DOI 10.1007/978-1-4614-4463-3_20, © Springer Science+Business Media New York 2013

familiar with it as I am. The source code is available on GitHub [1], join the group and contribute to the source code, its modular enough that you can add hundreds of features, and those that work well will get taken up by the community working on this project [2]. Or fork the project, and create and advance a parallel version. This field is open-ended, you get to decide where it goes next, how fast it gets there, and what role you will play in it all.

******** Last Note ********

I almost forgot, we never really gave a name to the system we've developed here. If you've looked over the published papers on DXNN, then you probably know that we've basically been developing the next generation of the DXNN Platform. I do not wish to give the system we've developed together a new name, let it take on the name DXNN, it is a good name, and appropriate for such grandiose goals. I began developing DXNN many years ago, and in a sense have been growing it over time, retrofitting the system with new features. This also means that while developing it, I did not take the best path possible, due to not knowing of what else would be added and what problems I would face in the future. This is not the case with the system you and I have developed here. The system we developed in this book was done with all the foresight of having previously already developed a system of similar purpose and form. The system we have developed here is cleaner, better, more agile, modular in its implementation, and in general more flexible than DXNN. I hope you can apply it to useful problems, and that if you use it in your research, it is of help.

I sincerely hope you enjoyed reading this book, and developing this system along with me. As I mentioned at the beginning of this book, I believe that we have stumbled upon the perfect neural network programming language, and that Erlang is it. I cannot see myself using anything else in the future, and I have experimented with dozens of different languages for this research. I also think that it adds the flexibility, and the direct mapping from programming language architecture to problem space in such a way that we can now think clearly when developing distributed computational intelligence systems, which will allow us to create systems with features and capabilities previously not possible. Evolution will generate the complexity, we just need to give our system enough tools, flexibility, and the space in which it can carve out the evolutionary path towards new heights.

-Gene I. Sher

20.1 References

[1] GitHub Account with the source code: https://github.com/CorticalComputer/DXNN2
[2] Research site: www.dxnnresearch.com
[3] Supplementary Material: www.DXNNResearch.com/NeuroevolutionThroughErlang

Abbreviations

AF – Activation Function
ALife – Artificial Life
AC – Augmented Competition Selection Algorithm
BMU – Best Matching Unit
BP – Backpropagation
CI – Computational Intelligence
CL – Competitive Learning
CO – Concurrency Oriented
UCAV – Unmanned Combat Aerial Vehicle
DFGS – Dangerous Food Gathering Simulation
DXNN – Dues Ex Neural Network
EANT – Evolutionary Acquisition of Neural Topologies
EMH – Efficient Market Hypothesis
EPNet – Evolutionary Programming Network
ES – Evolutionary Strategy
FX – Foreign Exchange
GHA – Generalized Hebbian Algorithm
GSOM – Growing Self Organizing Map
GTM – General Topographic Map
HtH – Hyperlayer-to-Hyperlayer
IHD – Input Hyperlayer Densities
IHDTag – Input Hyperlayer Densities Tag
NAO – Normalized Allotted Offspring
NEAT – Neuroevolution of Augmenting Topologies
NN – Neural Network
MO – Mutation Operator
PCI – Price Chart Input
PLI – Price List Input
PPS – Predator vs. Prey Simulation
RIM – Random Intensity Mutation
RR-SHC – Random Restart Stochastic Hill Climber
RWT – Random Walk Theory
SENN – Substrate Encoded Neural Network
SHC – Stochastic Hill Climbing
SFGS – Simple Food Gathering Simulation
SOM – Self Organizing Map
TPEULN – Topology and Parameter Evolving Universal Learning Network
TWEANN – Topology and Weight Evolving Artificial Neural Network
UAV – Unmanned Aerial Vehicle

G.I. Sher, *Handbook of Neuroevolution Through Erlang*,
DOI 10.1007/978-1-4614-4463-3, © Springer Science+Business Media New York 2013

Printed in the United States
By Bookmasters